Law of Chemical Regulation and Hazardous Waste

(Release #1, 5/87) filed

Law of Chemical Regulation and Hazardous Waste

by Donald W. Stever

Clark Boardman Company, Ltd.
New York, New York   1987

(Release #1, 5/87)

For June Lily Stever
1919–1985
and
To Margo and the children

Library of Congress Cataloging-in-Publication Data

Stever, Donald W., 1944–
    Law of chemical regulation and hazardous waste.

    (Environmental law series)
    Includes index.
    1. Chemicals—Law and legislation—United States.
    2. Hazardous wastes—Law and legislation—United States.
    3. Hazardous substances—Law and legislation—United
    States. 4. Liability for hazardous substances
    pollution damages—United States. I. Title.
    II. Series.
    KE3958.S74 1986   344.73'04622   86-2249
    ISBM 0-87632-495-2   347.3044622

About the Author

Donald W. Stever is Professor of Law at Pace University School of Law, and serves as co-director of the Center for Environmental Legal Studies, a component of that law school's concentration in environmental law. He is also special counsel to the law firm Day, Berry and Howard of Hartford, Connecticut. Prior to assuming his academic position in 1982, Professor Stever practiced environmental, health and safety law at the state and federal levels for twelve years. Between 1979 and 1982, he headed first the Pollution Control Section and then the Environmental Defense Section in the U.S. Department of Justice. He also spent five years as chief of the environmental division in the New Hampshire attorney general's office. He is the author of a widely praised book on nuclear regulation, *Seabrook and the Nuclear Regulatory Commission* (University Press of New England, 1980), as well as numerous articles on various environmental law topics, and frequently lectures on health, safety, and environmental regulatory issues.

Preface

This volume on chemical regulatory law and practice fills an important gap in the literature on the subject, which has heretofore been either fragmented or overly general in nature.

There are a number of reasons for a treatise on "chemical regulation." Chief among them are that the regulatory programs addressed in the treatise all affect a single industry, which accounts for a significant part of the U.S. economy, and that the kinds of issues addressed in all of the subjects covered are related and sometimes identical. Thus, whether one works in the affected industry or for the government, or is interested in or concerned about the nature of the risks chemicals present and how those risks are managed, this book should prove useful.

My approach has been to present a reasoned analysis of the covered regulatory programs as a whole. Rather than simply discuss statutory provisions and the case law, to which many others limit themselves, the treatise also deals with the agency rules and interpretive policies that implement what are sometimes only generalized statutory directives.

The treatise is intended to provide a broader and deeper understanding of a number of regulatory programs, each of which has traditionally been the province of a specialized subgroup of the bar, and for which no analytical overview has ever seriously been attempted. Hopefully, the user, whether lawyer or manager, will be able to gain a quick understanding of the nature of any issue that might arise, and find within this one reference either a resolution of the issue or a path to follow toward resolution. I have written the treatise in a way that seeks to avoid overuse of regulatory jargon, and have taken pains to explain the statutory and regulatory material in a way that demystifies it. The basic underlying mission is to elucidate rather than simply serve as a compendium of references.

Change in the law, often dramatic, is endemic to the field, as would be expected in any field that is interrelated with technology to the extent the chemical field is. This fact affects the approach to treatise writing. Most learned treatises on more stable subjects set forth what is essentially "settled law" on the subject and thereafter ruminate on often subtle philosophical problems posed by it. Subsequent editions deal with microcosmic alterations of or exceptions to the settled principles. There are few such principles in the field of chemical law.

By contrast, I have, in this treatise, attempted to explain the origins of current law and regulations, and to discuss, where appropriate, the directions in which the law might be expected to go, given the state of science and the political pressures present in the society. I have also tried to indicate those issues that are likely to remain unsettled for a long period of time. If the reader seems frustrated with the apparent "un-neatness" of the law, that frustration is well founded and consistent with the overall thrust of the book.

I should say a word about the scope of coverage of the various subjects in the treatise. A desire to keep the work within a single volume necessitated that decisions be made as to which material to treat in greater depth and breadth, and which to treat more briefly. An attempt to provide equal space to each of the covered topics would result in inadequate treatment of all of them; thus, I decided to cover the more active regulatory programs—which have not been dealt with in any detail in other, less generalized works—in the greatest detail.

There are a number of people I would like to thank, whose hard work and patience contributed significantly to this book. Virginia Gaburo did much early research while a student at Pace University School of Law. Long hours of labor on the project were spent by my research assistants, Peter Sacripanti, Lawrence Falkin, Terrence Sullivan, Jud Siebert, and Susan Murray. Melanie Brown and Theresa Ciarcia typed portions of the manuscript and Celeste Elion provided yeoman's service doing word processing in her spare time. I should also plug my Compaq computer, which produced a significant amount of the manuscript. My colleagues, Nicholas Robinson and Richard Ottinger, provided helpful comments and encouragement, and special thanks is due to Steve Ramsey, Lloyd Guerci and David Buente, who have kept me abreast of the latest happenings in the world of waste. Fredric Strom, my editor, and Lyn Grossman, my manuscript editor, at Clark Boardman Company, deserve special thanks for their care and patience. Finally, a thanks to my family who saw less of me than they would otherwise have.

Donald W. Stever
North Tarrytown, New York

Summary of Contents

SUMMARY OF CONTENTS

Table of Contents

TABLE OF CONTENTS

CHAPTER 4
Chemicals in Consumer Products

CHAPTER 5

Regulation of the Generation, Transportation, Storage, and Disposal of Hazardous Waste

TABLE OF CONTENTS

CHAPTER 7
**Regulation of Toxic and Hazardous Air Emissions,
Wastewater Effluents, and Groundwater Pollution**

TABLE OF CONTENTS

Appendixes

TABLE OF CONTENTS

CHAPTER 1

Introduction and Organization

§1.01   Introduction and Organization

[1]   Overview

The contents of this treatise have been chosen around a central theme—health, safety, and environmental regulatory programs that affect the chemical industry and people exposed to its products and by-products. Although the industry is pervasively regulated, most of the literature on the subject has tended to be fragmented. Chemical industry waste regulation, pesticide regulation, and toxic substances regulation have traditionally been treated as environmental law subjects, the province of the environmental bar. Occupational safety and health regulation, food additive regulation, and consumer product regulation have been treated, if at all, only as subsets of larger programs.

This fragmented treatment began to change in the early 1980s, when, presumably because of an emerging recognition that the risks managed under these seemingly disparate regulatory programs were often similar, and in some cases identical, the legal education establishment began to develop continuing education programs that cut across the established boundaries. The presence of those boundaries in the first place can best be explained as a product of the combined forces of the inherent tendency of lawyers in the private bar to specialize and Congress's penchant for creating new regulatory programs to deal with newly recognized public demands with little or no thought about their relationship to existing programs.

The pattern of legislative fragmentation has borne little relation to rational factoring. For example, there are a number of good reasons for placing food additive regulation and drinking water regulation under the same regulatory umbrella—both involve human exposure via the ingestion pathway to foreign substances intentionally or unintentionally present in matter consumed by the organism, both involve unconscious, involuntary exposure, and so on. Yet, although Congress could have created a single program to regulate food and water additives, it did not do so, largely because of historical bureaucratic and law practice entrenchment.[1]

What is even more difficult to rationalize is Congress's failure to provide equivalent regulatory standards to manage similar risks. To use the same example, it would seem that when Congress, in the mid-1970s, began to put together a program for regulating drinking water, it might have looked around for another program in which similar risks were addressed, and attempted to provide at least uniformity of standard setting. It did nothing of the sort, but instead produced a set of criteria for establishing allowable contaminant levels in drinking water entirely different from that utilized for establishing safe levels of contaminants in food for human consumption.[2]

A product manager or environmental vice president may be responsible for complying with several different regulatory requirements that

---

[1] Food additive regulation had been around a long time when Congress enacted the Safe Drinking Water Act. The food and drug law bar was comfortable in its established practice with the FDA, but had not ever had to deal with water pollution problems. The water pollution bureaucracy, on the other hand, was heavily dominated by engineers. Drinking water regulation ended up in the Environmental Protection Agency, which had inherited the engineer-dominated water pollution control bureaucracy from the Federal Water Pollution Control Administration, which was abolished as a unit of the Department of the Interior by President Nixon's Reorganization Plan Number 3 in 1970.

[2] Even within the food regulatory scheme, Congress established different standards for limiting the amount of pesticide residue on foods from those applied to other chemicals. In addition, although it had originally provided for regulation of all food additives by one agency, the Food and Drug Administration, it split pesticide additives away in 1971, giving pesticide regulation to EPA, which had inherited general pesticide regulatory authority from the Agriculture Department.

The pesticide-nonpesticide food additive dichotomy can nevertheless actually be viewed as approaching rationality of choice. It reflects a decision to regulate the pesticide *industry* in a more or less uniform manner, as opposed to regulating food additive *risks* uniformly. The scheme is also rational because, though EPA inherited the bureaucratic turf, Congress left the procedures and standards pretty much as they were previously.

are applicable to a single product or active ingredient. The case of ethylene dibromide (EDB), which occupied a great deal of news media space during 1983 and early 1984, is illustrative.

EDB has a number of uses. Like most chemicals, it is produced by reacting several active ingredients. Its primary uses are as a pesticide sprayed on fruits and grains after packaging for shipment to market, as a soil fumigant, and in the petroleum industry as an additive in unleaded gasoline. The Occupational Safety and Health Administration (OSHA) has jurisdiction over workplace exposures to the chemical and its active ingredient, both in the chemical manufacturing sector and in those industries using the finished product.

The Environmental Protection Agency (EPA) has jurisdiction over the chemical in a number of ways. To the extent that it is manufactured for nonpesticidal uses, EPA possesses authority to regulate it under the Toxic Substances Control Act (TSCA). EPA's authority extends into the workplace and overlaps OSHA's jurisdiction.[3] EPA also regulates the chemical under the Federal Insecticide, Fungicide and Rodenticide Act (FIFRA) and, as to its use on raw food products, under Section 408 of the Federal Food, Drug and Cosmetic Act (FFDCA). As in the case of TSCA regulation, EPA's authority under FIFRA extends into the workplace. Finally, to the extent that EDB ends up as waste or the manufacturing facilities emit air or water pollutants, EPA asserts regulatory authority under one of the environmental protection statutes.

EDB is also subject to varying degrees of state regulation, depending on the degree of state interest or the extent of federal preemption. The significance of state regulation became apparent when the perceived hazards of EDB residues on cereal products gave rise to public agitation for regulatory action in late 1983. OSHA had refused to act. EPA had moved cautiously under FIFRA and the FFDCA, suspending some uses and lowering the allowable food residue tolerances. State health departments, however, which in many states retained control of public health

---

[3] EPA has occasionally asserted its authority over workplace exposures intentionally. Its proposed formaldehyde regulation under TSCA was aimed principally at workers, and the agency responded to arguments that workers were OSHA's territory by stating that TSCA provided an easier means to assert the needed controls. See 49 Fed. Reg. 24663 (1984).

–related food regulation,[4] imposed quarantines or more stringent tolerances, ultimately forcing EPA effectively to ban the use of EDB on grain and vegetables.[5]

The criteria for assessing risks and the procedural and substantive requirements for the imposition of standards or prohibitions differ, sometimes startlingly, between programs. There is much duplication of reporting and recordkeeping, and widely differing philosophies of enforcement.

Although in recent years there has been discussion within the government and the chemical industry about unifying risk management regulation, Congress has not demonstrated a great degree of enthusiasm for the idea. Short of such action, it is important for practitioners and scholars to understand the differences and similarities in the various regulatory programs that involve chemical hazards. Thus, this treatise outlines, in a logical fashion, the major regulatory programs affecting the chemical industry and the relevant exposed populations.

[2] Choice of Contents and Organization

The subjects included in this volume can be categorized into several subgroups: (1) programs regulating manufacturing, sale, and use of chemicals (toxic substances control and pesticide regulation); (2) programs regulating human exposure to chemicals contained in consumer products (food additive, drinking water, and consumer product safety regulation); and (3) programs regulating environmental hazards posed by chemical manufacturing, use, and disposal (worker protection, water and air pollution, and solid waste management programs).

The organization of chapters generally reflects this overall grouping, although obviously there are some overlaps and misfits, which are un-

---

4 State health department authority over residue tolerances results from the fact that originally, at the federal level, the FDA, a subunit of the Department of Health, Education and Welfare (now Health and Human Services) exerted pesticide tolerance authority, and encouraged state programs in the analogous agencies at the state level.

5 Though public concern over EDB was substantial and politically potent, the real risk posed by the chemical outside of the petroleum industry was, and remains, a subject of controversy within the scientific community. The highest risk population, based on exposure patterns and animal bioassay data, appears to be petroleum and chemical industry workers, who are exposed both to EDB and another chemical commonly present along with it. The synergistic effect of the double exposure, like that of asbestos fibers and tobacco smoke, significantly increases the statistical probability of contracting cancer as compared to the single-exposure probability. Interestingly, while EPA was moving toward emergency action, OSHA refused to do the same.

avoidable in any effort to deal with these programs. Each chapter works its way through its subject by first defining who and what are subject to regulation, then describing the substantive regulatory criteria, and finally discussing the procedural and enforcement structures employed. The numerous subdivisions are designed to facilitate comparative analysis.

The general approach to the subject is to explain, and critically examine, a group of somewhat related regulatory programs whose governing statutes and regulations are complex, and sometimes even arcane. Every lawyer, and many technicians with regulatory responsibilities, knows that reading and understanding a hundred-page statute can be an elusive, frustrating venture fraught with pitfalls. This treatise attempts to explain, restructure, and thereby simplify and enhance the understanding of exceedingly complex material.

Several of the chapters contain appendix material to which reference is made in the main text. Unlike some "treatises" that are in fact little more than general statutory outlines followed by reams of reproduced statutes, regulations, and government-issued forms, this treatise is primarily analytical text, with the key statutory or regulatory text contained in footnotes. It is assumed that serious readers will have access to federal statutes and the Code of Federal Regulations or one or more of the proprietary looseleaf services.[6] The appendix material in the treatise contains such things as forms, lists of regulated chemicals, excerpted Federal Register material, and foreign law material that is not generally available to American lawyers.

It is important to understand what is *not* covered in this treatise. Hazardous material transportation is discussed in introductory fashion in Chapter 5, but is not covered extensively, primarily because of limitations of space. Nuclear fuel cycle regulation is not included because it is a narrow subject, about which much has already been written, and because the industry segment that is regulated is small, highly concentrated, and specialized. Economic regulation, such as antitrust law and trade regulation, involves broad topics that are not unique to the chemi-

---

[6] These include the Environment Reporter (Bureau of National Affairs), Environmental Law Reporter (Environmental Law Institute), Chemical Regulation Reporter (BNA), Occupational Safety and Health Reporter (BNA), Food and Drug Law Reporter (several publishers), and Hazardous Waste and Radiation Litigation Reporter (Cohen).

cal industry.[7] Similarly, securities regulation, though it clearly affects a large segment of the chemical industry, is not unique to the industry, and is treated only in passing.

Certain of the chapters are longer and more detailed than others. The very long chapters, such as Chapter 6, which involves emergency and remedial responses to chemical spills and disposal site problems, could have been broken into three chapters or more. The single chapter organization, however, keeps connected material grouped, and the main subdivisions serve the same function as would chapter divisions.

Most of this volume is devoted to regulatory programs whose primary or sole function is to regulate all or a portion of the chemical industry. Complex regulatory programs, such as the OSHA one, are considered only in relation to their specific impact on the chemical industry. Thus, in the case of the Occupational Safety and Health Act (OSH Act) the statute as a whole is generally described, but detailed treatment is limited to the law and application of Section 6(b)(5), which is specifically aimed at toxic substance exposure in the workplace.[8]

§1.02　Philosophy

This work is the product of a belief that "chemical regulation" is becoming a separate legal discipline, with its own quirks, conventions, and history. It also rests on the premise that the elements that chemical regulatory programs have in common, and that serve to set them apart from other regulatory schemes, will tend to increase, or draw closer together over time, and that it is accordingly important for lawyers and regulatory managers to view the field as an integral whole rather than from the balkanized perspectives that have characterized it in the past.

The treatise does not have a bias other than the author's belief that government regulatory programs should make straightforward sense. It has been structured carefully to avoid any sort of subjective bias in favor of or against regulation of the areas covered. The only purposes are to describe, explicate, explain, and analyze statutory, regulatory, and judi-

---

[7] Specialized areas of economic regulation, such as data compensation under the Federal Insecticide, Fungicide and Rodenticide Act, are discussed at length, however.

[8] Most OSHA law and regulations relate to workplace safety, including such mundane topics as guards on machines, railings around stair openings, and the like, which are well beyond the scope of this treatise.

cial material objectively, and to make what are often obscure materials accessible and less obscure (where possible).

§1.03 Risk Assessment and Management

[1] In General

Perhaps the most significant element all chemical regulatory programs share is the necessity for someone to assess the level of risk or degree of hazard presented by a particular chemical or chemical-related activity and to determine whether the risk, as perceived, is an acceptable one. It has often been said that determining the nature of a given risk is a scientific, or at least inherently nonpolitical, act, while determining the acceptability of the risk is essentially a political judgment.

One of the most interesting, and for many, frustrating, things about the American law of chemical regulation is the absence of uniformity in these areas among the various programs, even when the risks required to be managed are quite similar.[9] The differences lie in the management, rather than in the assessement of risks.

Some laws, such as FFDCA, are very conservative, giving little or no latitude to the administering agency to make judgments about some kinds of risks. Others, such as FIFRA, not only give a great deal of judgmental latitude to the agency, but specifically require judgments about the acceptability of a given risk to include consideration of the economic benefits of the regulated activity, which are permitted to override the risk.

Some of these differences may be accounted for by differences in the population or other entities sought to be protected, and by the exposure pathway and duration inherent in the regulated activity. However, many, indeed, most, of the differences in legislative approach are not explainable in those terms.

Another phenomenon common to these programs is the propensity of the regulatory agencies in their practice to avoid rigorous adherence to the statutory standard, whatever it is, and the practice of the courts

---

[9] There is currently one element of reasonable uniformity. In May 1984, the Office of Science and Technology issued a set of guidelines that are binding on all federal agencies, setting forth standard assumptions and protocols for undertaking and evaluating toxicological and epidemiological studies involving carcinogenic and mutagenic risks. 49 Fed. Reg. 21875 (5-23-84).

to look aside when called upon to question the agency's practice. This phenomenon of agency reinterpretation of statutory standards and judicial deference appears to be more apparent in areas of high technology or scientific uncertainty, both earmarks of chemical regulatory practice. To a degree, agency practice has in some cases narrowed the regulatory gap between programs a bit, although even the most egregious agency legislating will not create a consistent pattern of regulation.

[2] Dealing with Uncertainty

All of the programs discussed in this work suffer from a chronic, incurably inadequate data base on which to predicate many of the required decisions. Both statutes and regulations in these programs have tended to be reactive to political concerns raised around recently perceived risks, both real and imagined.

The most widely discussed form of uncertainty affecting chemical regulation involves long latency period risks, such as those involving carcinogens. The tools of risk determination for such risks, applied toxicology and epidemiology, are imprecise and prone to error and legitimate disputes of interpretation. Animal species and microorganisms are not in all cases accurate predictors of the effects of exposure to humans. In epidemiology, long-term prospective studies are reasonably predictive, but these are impractical for regulatory programs whose purpose is to screen entry of new products into the market.

Further uncertainties stem from the time and money costs and disincentives of regulation, as well as an imperfect understanding of the costs society would incur without regulation, or with a different level of regulation. The "benefits" of regulation are elusive, both to society as a whole and to the regulated industry.

Finally, the chemical industry, second only perhaps to the nuclear energy industry, suffers under the burden of having to manage very low-probability but high-consequence risks. Unlike the nuclear power industry, however, the chemical industry also has a large share of high-probability risks, of all consequence levels, both known and unknown. Because of the nature of the risks posed, chemicals have become almost anathema to a large segment of American society. The high level of public scrutiny accorded the industry since 1975, when public anxiety forced the enactment of the Toxic Substances Control Act, places the chemical industry in the 1980s in a position not dissimilar to that occupied by the atomic energy industry a decade earlier.

CHAPTER 2

Health and Safety Regulation of Chemicals Under The Toxic Substances Control Act

The author is grateful for research done on the subject of recombinant DNA by Louis Sorell, a student at Pace University School of Law.

§2.01 In General—Substances Regulated Under Act

The basic strategem of the Toxic Substances Control Act (TSCA)[1] is to require the testing of potentially toxic chemicals to a degree sufficient to determine their capability to produce adverse health effects in humans, and to empower a regulatory agency, the Environmental Protection Agency (EPA), to prohibit or condition the manufacture, distribution, and use of such chemicals based on that information. The statute attempts to address two problems—(1) the synthesis and production of new substances after its enactment, and (2) analysis of the hazard potential of the many thousands of chemicals produced and placed into commerce (that is, the environment) prior to the statute's enactment in late 1976.

The statute regulates "chemical substances and mixtures," as defined in Sections 3(s) and 3(m) and in EPA's regulations. Specifically *not* covered are pesticides (regulated by EPA under the Federal Insecticide, Fungicide and Rodenticide Act (FIFRA)), tobacco or tobacco products and firearms (regulated by the Department of Commerce, Bureau of Alcohol, Tobacco and Firearms), source material, special nuclear material or by-product material (regulated by the Nuclear Regulatory Commission), and food, food additives, drugs, cosmetics, or devices (regulated by the Food and Drug Administration (FDA) and the Federal Food, Drug and Cosmetic Act (FFDCA)). The term "chemical

---

[1] 15 USC §2601 *et seq.*, Public Law 94-469 (Oct. 11, 1976), Stat. 2027.
For table of session law-to-U.S. Code conversion, see Appendix 2A *infra.*
For glossary of TSCA-related terms and acronyms, see Appendix 2B, *infra.*
For summaries of recent regulatory activities as to specific chemicals and chemical groups under TSCA, see Appendix 2J, *infra.*

substance" is defined very broadly, to include "any organic or inorganic substance of a particular molecular identity, including any combination of such substances ocurring in whole or in part as a result of a chemical reaction or occurring in nature, and any chemical element or uncombined radical."[1.1] "Mixtures" are combinations of two or more chemical substances that (1) do not occur in nature and (2) do not result from a chemical reaction, except that hydrates are included along with mixtures resulting from a chemical reaction if they could have been produced initially without one.[1.2] Such substances are regulated only if manufactured "for commercial purposes," although that phrase has been interpreted broadly.[1.3] Intermediate products and by-products, for example, are covered.[1.4] Chemicals that are imported are treated as if manufactured.[2]

The pesticide and food/food additive exemptions are complicated somewhat because certain raw materials, intermediates, inert ingredients, and catalysts used in the production of pesticides or food additives fall within the broad definition of chemical "substances" or "mixtures." EPA takes the position that raw materials, intermediates, and inert ingredients used or produced in the pesticide manufacture or formulation processes are subject to TSCA unless they are themselves "intended" for uses as a pesticide independently.[3] Intermediates and catalysts intended solely for use in the production of a food, food additive, drug, cosmetic, or device, however, are *not* subject to TSCA regulation, because the FDA considers such substances to be components of the ultimate food, additive, or other ultimate product, and thus subject to regulation under the FFDCA.[4]

§2.02　The Basic Regulatory Scheme

Sections 4, 5, 6, and 7 of TSCA construct the TSCA regulatory program. Section 4 establishes the framework for testing chemicals. Sec-

---

[1.1] 40 CFR §710.2(h).

[1.2] *See* 40 CFR §710(q).

[1.3] Chemicals produced solely for *intra*state commerce are not regulated, 15 USC §2602(3). Thus, the TSCA regulatory reach is somewhat shorter than that of FIFRA.

[1.4] *See* 40 CFR §§710(q) and 710(p).

[2] 40 CFR §710(o).

[3] 43 Fed Reg. 11110 (3-16-78) (Response to Comment 32). *See also* 40 CFR §162.4 (FIFRA regulations).

[4] See 43 Fed. Reg. 11110 (3-16-78) (Response to Comment 33).

tion 5 creates a screening mechanism for the production of new chemicals and new uses of existing chemicals. Section 6 prescribes EPA's range of actions to control manufacturing, use, and disposal once information developed under Sections 4 and 5 points to the need for action. Section 7 confers on EPA extraordinary authority to deal with imminent hazards. A glossary of terms and definitions may be found in Appendix 2B, *infra.*

[1] Study of New and Existing Chemical Substances and Mixtures Under Section 4—Development of Testing Rules

Section 4(e) of TSCA (15 USC §2603) established an Interagency Testing Committee (ITC), whose members are drawn from the principal federal agencies having statutory obligations with respect to chemical health risks, The National Institute of Health, The National Cancer Institute, and the National Science Foundation. The mission of that body is to screen chemicals for potential "significant risk of serious and widespread harm" and to recommend to EPA each year a list of chemicals that the ITC believes should be tested further. This list, the ITC priority list, has grown over the years and currently includes over forty chemicals.[5]

Section 4 imposes on EPA a mandatory duty, within 180 days of an ITC listing, either to issue testing rules and methods (requiring regulated entities to undertake testing) for chemicals included on a priority list generated by the ITC or to publish reasons why testing is not necessary under Section 4(e) of the statute. For a number of years, however, EPA simply did not act on the ITC recommendations. That inaction resulted in significant congressional criticism of the Agency[6] and a 1980 court order, in *National Resources Defense Council, Inc. v. Costle,* [7] placing EPA on a court-imposed schedule to respond to a backlog of ITC reports.[8] EPA's consideration of the priority list chemicals and other

---

[5] A table showing the status of the ITC list as of 1984 is included as Appendix 2C, *infra.*

[6] *See e.g.,* H.R. Rep. No. 97-86 (1981).

[7] No. 79 Civ.2411 (S.D.N.Y. 1980).

[8] EPA and the ITC have somewhat different views of the precise nature of the studies to be undertaken by the ITC. Since the ITC's principal function is to survey the tens of thousands of existing, potentially harmful, chemicals, its approach has been to survey available research literature and make recommendations based on inferences drawn from frequently sparse data. EPA's TSCA staff, on the other hand, have tended to be preoccupied with filling in gaps in the data before proposing a testing rule. EPA established an Administrator's Toxic Substances Advisory Committee (ATSAC) in 1979 to

chemicals for test rules is governed by the criteria set out in Section 4(a).[8.1]

A testing rule must be issued upon a finding by EPA *either* that—

(1) The manufacture, distribution, processing, use, or disposal, or any combination thereof "may present an unreasonable risk of injury to health or the environment,"

(2) There are insufficient existing data and experience on which to base an assessment of the risk, and

(3) Testing is needed to produce the requisite data;

or

(1) The chemical substance or mixture is produced in substantial quantities and enters or is reasonably anticipated to enter the environment, or otherwise will or may result in significant or substantial human exposure,

(2) There are insufficient existing data and experience on which to base an assessment of the risk, and

(3) Testing is needed to produce the requisite data.

If the substance is a mixture, EPA is required to determine whether testing the components would be adequate. Section 4(a)(2). Testing rules are aimed at manufacturers and/or processors of the suspect chemicals, and can include the following types of tests:

— health effects tests (normally short- or long-term bioassays; may include retrospective epidemiology);

— environmental effects tests; and

— chemical fate tests.

Especially in the case of existing chemicals, EPA's relatively scarce resources make the choice of which chemicals to test a difficult one. Chemical "A" may be highly toxic via a limited exposure route that is applicable to relatively few organisms, while chemical "B" may be considerably less toxic but involve a wide array of exposures and large numbers of people coming into contact with it. The statute provides no

---

provide recommendations for eliminating its politically embarassing inability to move the testing program along. The ATSAC has sometimes been critical of the Agency's conservation. *See* H.R. Rep. No. 97-86 (1981). In 1982, EPA and the ITC began to develop a new screening model, which the Agency presented to the public for initial comment in 1983.

[8.1] 15 USC §2603(a).

clear guidance as to how to choose between such chemicals where resource limitations dictate that a choice be made.

[a] Negotiated Testing Agreements

EPA has historically rarely imposed a testing rule. As the table in Appendix 2C, *infra*, demonstrates, the Agency has more often found reasons for declining to follow the ITC's testing recommendation. In addition, EPA has followed an administrative practice of entering into Negotiated Testing Agreements (NTAs) with industries and industry trade associations in lieu of issuing test rules, whenever possible.[8.2]

EPA's reliance on NTAs as an alternative to issuing test rules may present the agency with enforcement and data disclosure problems. Section 5(b)(1) of TSCA, for example, imposes restrictions on premanufacture notice (PMN) submitters who propose to manufacture a chemical as to which there is an outstanding test rule "promulgated under Section 2603 (Section 4 of TSCA) . . . ." Strictly speaking, NTAs are not promulgated testing rules. Thus, it may be argued the EPA may not invoke the Section 5(b)(1) restrictions with respect to NTA chemicals. In addition, Section 14(b) of TSCA authorizes EPA to disclose health and safety study data for "any chemical . . . for which testing is required under Section 2603 . . . ."[9] It might be argued that since NTAs are informal agreements, data resulting from them are not disclosable under this section. The NTA is neither fish nor fowl. It is not promulgated pursuant to the Section 4 procedures, and yet EPA's practice historically has been not to publish proposed NTAs in The Federal Register.

EPA's Negotiated Testing Program was struck down by a federal district court in *Natural Resources Defense Council, Inc. et. al. v. U.S. Environmental Protection Agency, Inc.*, as an unlawful attempt to avoid the test rule provisions of TSCA.[10]

[b] Test Rule Requirements

Although EPA has promulgated few test rules, it has issued a large number of guidelines establishing accepted testing methodologies.

[8.2] *See* 47 Fed. Reg. 335 (1-5-82). *See also* 48 Fed. Reg. 39979 (9-2-83).
[9] 15 USC §2613(b)(1)(A)(2).
[10] 595 F. Supp. 1255 (S.D.N.Y. 1984).

[i] Laboratory Practices

EPA adopted TSCA "Good Laboratory Practice Standards" in 1983.[11] After the effective date of the regulation, data generated by laboratories in conformity with the standards are deemed acceptable for Section 4(a) purposes. Data from noncomplying facilities must be accompanied by evidence demonstrating reliability and adequacy.[12] Although EPA receives data pursuant to a number of TSCA sections other than Section 4, the laboratory standards are only applicable to data generated pursuant to a test rule "promulgated" by EPA under Section 4.[13]

The standards are rather general, and reflect the basic good laboratory practice standards in use in the chemical industry. EPA does, however, specifically make a condition of data acceptability a right of entry by EPA inspectors "at reasonable times and in a reasonable manner."[14] A facility that refuses EPA inspectors entry will have its data deemed unreliable.[15]

[ii] Environmental Effects Testing Guidelines

EPA initially took the position that it need not codify its various test rule guidelines, and so did not include them as a part of its TSCA regulations. It reversed that position in 1985, and codified its guidelines in 50 Fed. Reg. 39253 (September 27, 1985). The environmental effects test guidelines are codified at 40 CFR Part.797. Appendix 2D, *infra,* provides an index of EPA's environmental effects test guidelines issued to date. The Agency also maintains technical support documents for most of the guidelines.

One difficulty with the guidelines is the presence of two sets of guidelines for doing Daphnid Chronic Toxicity testing,[16] Algal Acute Toxicity testing,[17] Fish Acute Toxicity testing,[18] and Fish Bioaccumulation testing.[19] In each case there are differences in methodology. The later-numbered guidelines (EG-8-EG-2) are EPA's version of protocols adopted by the Organization for Economic Cooperation and Develop-

---

11 40 CFR §792, 48 Fed. Reg. 53922 (11-29-83).
12 40 CFR §792.1(c).
13 40 CFR §792.17.
14 40 CFR §792.15(a).
15 40 CFR §792.15(b).
16 EG-2 and EG-18; 40 CFR §§797.1330, 797.1350.
17 EG-8 and EG-19; 40 CFR §§797.1050, 797.1060.
18 EG-9 and EG-20; 40 CFR §§797.1400, 797.1440.
19 EG-10 and EG-21; 40 CFR §§797.1520, 797.1560.

ment (OECD) and in general use in Europe. It is not clear to what extent use of the later-issued OECD protocols are intended to replace the original EPA protocols, but it appears that EPA will accept data generated under both to satisfy TSCA.

[iii] Chemical Fate Testing Guidelines

See Appendix 2E, *infra*, for an index to EPA's Chemical Fate Testing Guidelines. These guidelines are compatible with both OECD and American Standard Testing Methods (ASTM) methodologies. The chemical fate guidelines are codified at 40 CFR Part 796. EPA specifically promulgated the OECD chemical fate guidelines, which are Sections 796.1050, 796.1220, 796.1370, and 796.1520 of the chemical fate test guidelines.

[iv] Health Effects Testing Guidelines

See Appendix 2F, *infra*, for an index to EPA's Guidelines for Health Effects Testing. The health effects testing guidelines generally follow World Health Organization protocols. The health effects guidelines are codified at 40 CFR Part 798.

[c] Exemptions and Data Compensation

Section 4(c) authorizes EPA to exempt substances from the requirements of any test rule issued under Section 4(a) on application by the requestor showing that (1) the chemical or mixture is molecularly equivalent to another substance as to which data have or will be submitted and (2) if the requestor were required to conduct tests and submit data, its efforts would be duplicative of data either currently in EPA's possession or soon to be submitted to EPA by another entity.[20] This exemption is intended to prevent duplication of testing, and the statute contains a provision for compensation to be paid by the applicant to the data submitter.

Once an exemption is granted, the applicant must pay its proportional share of the data costs to the person whose data it has relied upon. The statute contemplates a voluntary compensation plan to be agreed upon between the parties involved.

If the parties, after a good faith attempt at resolution, are unable to agree upon the amount of compensation due, the statute requires the administrator to set the rate of compensation to be paid. EPA's proce-

---

[20] 15 USC §2603(c).

dures for awarding compensation are set forth in 40 CFR §791. Processors are not generally required to pay compensation, on the ground that they have indirectly fulfilled their reimbursement responsibilities through the higher prices passed on to them by the manufacturers, who are directly responsible for reimbursement. There are, however, three circumstances under which processors will be required to pay compensation:

(1) when the administrator determines that the circumstances warrant compensation;

(2) when two or more manufacturers demonstrate that it would be fair and equitable to have the processors pay; or

(3) when any one processor agrees to pay compensation, but such agreement will be binding on that processor only.

As between manufacturers, 40 CFR §791 requires the disputing parties to submit their claims to the American Arbitration Association for resolution.[21] The regulations set forth a formula for arriving at the rate of compensation to be paid, although the arbitrator is not bound by this formula and may use any other formula or take into account any additional facts that would modify the formula.[22]

---

[21] An identical requirement is contained in Section 3(c)(1)(D) of the Federal Insecticide Fungicide and Rodenticide Act.

[22] The formula can be stated algebraically as follows:

$$Rx = C \times \frac{Vx}{Vt}$$

Where Rx = The reimbursement share of Company X.

C = The total cost of the testing required by the Test Rule.

Vx = The volume of the Test Chemical in bulk produced or imported by Company X over the period that begins one year before the publication of the Test Rule in the Federal Register and continuing to the latest date available before the hearing.

Vt = The total volume in bulk of the Test Chemical produced over the period that begins one year before the publication of the Test Rule in the Federal Register and continuing to the latest date available before the hearing.

The workings of the formula are illustrated by the following hypothetical. Assume that on October 31, 1977, a Test Rule was published for Chemical Z, which is manufactured by Company A, and from October 31, 1976, to December 31, 1980, 75,000 barrels of Chemical Z were produced by Company A. Company B, which applied for and was granted an exemption, produced Chemical Z from June of 1978 to October of 1980, in the amount of 25,000 barrels. Company A incurred $1 million in costs in complying with the Test Rule. On January 2, 1981, Companies A and B go to arbitration over amount of compensation to be paid by Company B. The formula would be applied as follows:

$$\frac{25,000}{100,000} \times 1,000,000 = \$250,000.$$

[d] Special Rules for Carcinogens, Mutagens, and Teratogens

Section 4 contains a special provision relating to carcinogens, Section 4(f), the text of which states, in pertinent part:

> Upon the receipt of—
> (1) any test data required to be submitted under this chapter, or
> (2) any other information available to the Administrator,
> which indicates to the Administrator that there may be a reasonable basis to conclude that a chemical substance or mixture presents or will present a significant risk of serious or widespread harm to human beings from cancer, gene mutations, or birth defects, the Administrator shall, within the 180-day period beginning on the date of the receipt of such data or information, initiate appropriate action under section 2604, 2605, or 2606 of this title to prevent or reduce to a sufficient extent such risk or publish in the Federal Register a finding that such risk is not unreasonable. . .

In contrast to the Delaney clause of the FFDCA (discussed in detail in Chapter 8, *infra*), this provision does not contain a presumption that a given quantum of bioassay evidence will *per se* support a conclusion that the substance is carcinogenic in humans and that, therefore, human exposure should be reduced to zero. Instead, the Administrator is required to decide, when presented with evidence that "indicates" that there "may be" a "reasonable basis" to conclude that the substance "presents or will present a significant risk of serious *or* widespread harm to human beings from cancer, gene mutations and birth defects . . ." whether to take regulatory action to reduce the risk or to publish a finding that "such risk is not unreasonable."

In a rulemaking decision involving the chemical formaldehyde, EPA, in 1984, articulated the view that Section 4(f) presents a dual standard— significant risk of serious harm or significant risk of widespread harm. Under this interpretation a chemical that poses a relatively slight individual risk might still qualify for Section 4(f) action if the exposed population is very large.[22.1]

The statute's inherent circularity is problematic, particularly in view of the requirement that the decision be made in 180 days. If the Administrator has concluded on the basis of "available" information that a particular chemical "may" present a significant risk, it is hard to

---

[22.1] *See generally* 49 Fed. Reg. 21881, post and ante.

imagine what sort of studies could be completed in 180 days that would be sufficient to negate the initial conclusion. It is, accordingly, likely that the decision to act or not act to regulate the chemical will depend upon the Administrator's perception of the importance of such things as the social utility of the chemical, the economic consequences of restricting its manufacture and use, etc., to the phrase "not unreasonable."

EPA has not availed itself of many opportunities to apply Section 4(f), and has not formally articulated its interpretation of the standard for action contained in the section. The frequency with which Section 4(f) is used will turn on how narrowly or broadly the Agency views the terms "significant," "widespread," and "serious," as well as how it applies the "not unreasonable" proviso. In the absence of a clearly articulated official policy, there have been varying staff interpretations of Section 4(f), which would lead to radically different levels of protection.

The Office of Toxic Substances (OTS) career staff has consistently argued that a Section 4(f) determination "is based exclusively on risk and thus is a function only of a chemical's carcinogenicity, teratogenicity, or mutagenicity, and exposure to that chemical."[23] This interpretation appears to ignore totally the "not reasonable" finding requirements as a prerequisite to according priority testing status to a chemical under Section 4(f).

OTS has argued that "significant risk of serious harm" and "significant risk of widespread harm" cover different types of risk. The former describes candidates that "appear to pose particularly high risks to at least a small number of people," while the latter covers "lesser risks to a large number of people." [24] OTS personnel have also argued that potential exposure rather than evidence of actual exposure is the relevant exposure criterion under Section 4(f).[25]

An appointed agency official in 1982 put forth a more narrow interpretation of Section 4(f), arguing that "significant" should be construed in a relative sense—that no carcinogen risk should be considered significant in the absence of evidence that the chemical in fact induces cancer

---

[23] Quotation from draft OTS Federal Register Notice OPTS 40007 proposing Section 4(f) action for formaldehyde. See also 49 Fed. Reg. 21875 (1984).

[24] OPTS 4007 at 4.

[25] Id. at 5.

in humans.[26] It has also been argued that Section 4(f) requires a threshold evidentiary determination of actual exposure, and that a "serious" risk is not presented in a case where the exposed population is small.[27]

While this last-mentioned interpretation was apparently never adopted by an EPA administration, and has been severely criticized,[28] it serves nicely to illustrate the different policy positions that are, at least arguably, supported by the language of the statute. Most opponents of the narrow view have criticized it as being out of step with current scientific views of the nature of carcinogens.[29] Such arguments unfortunately ignore the fact that Section 4(f) is a statute that appears to give the political decisionmaker a great deal of latitude to take a broad, conservative approach or a narrow approach to risk assessment.

At bottom, it is not clear from the language of the statute what Congress had in mind.[30] EPA has not through repeated and consistent action established more precise meanings for the statutory terms. The ambiguities and questions inherent in Section 4(f) remain to be clarified and answered.

[2] Introduction of New Chemicals into Commerce Under Section 5

The Section 5[30.1] regulatory program actually begins with Section 8 of TSCA.[30.2] Section 8(b) requires EPA to maintain a current list of all chemical substances manufactured or processed in the United States. The initial list was compiled from reports submitted by manufacturers pursuant to Section 8(a).[30.3]

After publication of the initial Section 8(b) list, a person who proposes to manufacture or import a "new chemical substance" (that is, one not on the list), or a person who proposes to import, manufacture, *or* process

---

[26] Memorandum, 2-10-82, John A. Todhunter, Ph.D. to Ann Gorsuch Administration, titled Review of Data Available to the Administration Concerning Formaldehyde and . . . (DHEP).

[27] *Id.* at 2, 16.

[28] *See* Review of the Scientific Basis of the Environmental Protection Agency's Carcinogenic Risk Assessment of Formaldehyde, H.R. Rep. No. 98-216 (Committee on Science and Technology)(1983).

[29] *See, e.g.,* H.R. Rep. No. 98-216 at 25-52, 91-107.

[30] The legislative history of this section, like most of TSCA, is unenlightening.

[30.1] 15 USC §2604.

[30.2] 15 USC §2607.

[30.3] *See* Section 2.03, *infra.*

an existing chemical substance for a "significant new use" must give EPA notice at least ninety days[31] prior to the manufacture date. These notices, required by Section 5(a)(1), are called by EPA "premanufacture notices" or "PMNs." A determination that a chemical substance is "new" is simply a matter of comparing the molecular structure of the chemical with that of similar Section 8(b) chemicals. Whether a new *use* is "significant," however, is a more complex regulatory matter, discussed in more detail below.

The intent of Section 5, as expressed in the Conference Report on the TSCA,[31.1] underscores its preventive nature:

> The provisions of the section reflect the conferees' recognition that the most desirable time to determine the health and environmental effects of a substance, and to take action to protect against any potential adverse effects occurs before commercial production begins. Not only is human and environmental harm avoided or alleviated, but the cost of any regulatory action in terms of loss of jobs and capital investment is minimized.

[a] Premanufacture Notice (PMN) Requirements Generally

TSCA does not specify what tests must be performed by PMN submitters. As a result, EPA has been motivated by its resource scarcity to minimize the quantity of data required for new chemicals for which PMNs are unavoidable.[32]

EPA promulgated interim Section 5 PMN requirements in 1979[32.1] and revised the interim requirements in 1980.[32.2] On January 27, 1981, the Agency published a nonbinding policy guideline regarding the data content of future PMNs[32.3] pertaining to health and environmental effects.

It promulgated PMN final regulations on May 13, 1983,[32.4] which were to go into effect on July 12, 1983. On July 11, 1983, EPA post-

---

[31] The period may be extended to 180 days. Section 5(c), 15 USC §2604(c).

[31.1] H. Rep. No. 94-1679.

[32] Only 33 percent of PMNs submitted as of December 31, 1980, contained any health and/or environmental data whatsoever. This fact caused members of Congress to question the quality of PMN review generally. *See* H.R. Rep. No. 87-86 (1981).

[32.1] 44 Fed. Reg. 28564.

[32.2] 45 Fed. Reg. 74378.

[32.3] 46 FR 8985.

[32.4] 48 Fed. Reg. 21722.

poned the effective date of the rule for sixty days[32.5] while it considered objections raised by the Chemical Manufacturers Association and the Society of the Plastics Industry. On September 13, 1983,[32.6] the Agency placed the bulk of the rule into effect as of October 26, 1983, but "stayed" the effectiveness of several provisions, pending further evaluation of the industry complaints.[33]

The most important aspect of the PMN rules is, of course, the nature and extent of the information required from the PMN submitter. EPA developed a PMN notice form, No. 7710-25, which it requires all PMN submitters to use. The form requires several types of information to be submitted, but specifiically does *not* require any such information "which relates solely to exposure of human or ecological populations outside of the United States."[34] Information required generally falls into the following categories, by 40 CFR §720.50:

(a) *What is it?*
   — detailed description of the physical structure of the substance, the process by which it is formed, and information about components and reactants used;
   — description of impurities anticipated to be present;
   — synonyms or trade names;
   — description of by-products resulting;
   — amounts to be produced during the first three production years; and
   — intended uses and amount devoted to each type of use.

(b) *How is it to be produced?*
   — where facilities are;
   — number of workers and type of exposure;
   — detailed description of the physical manufacturing process; and
   — environmental release information;

(c) *What are its effects?*
   — health, safety, and environmental fate test data in submitter's possession or control;
   — citations to existing literatures; and

[32.5] 48 Fed. Reg. 31641.
[32.6] 48 Fed. Reg. 41132.
[33] The regulations are published at 40 CFR Part 720.
[34] 40 CFR §720.45. Exporters are subject to the regulatory requirements of the importing State.

—   data known to exist elsewhere.

The regulations do not require the submission of efficacy data or data already possessed by EPA as to which no confidentiality claim has been asserted. A controversial provision, Section 720.50(c), stayed at 48 Fed. Reg. 41132, required PMN submitters to submit all of the above data relative to impurities, by-products, degradation products, unintended reaction products, and "other chemical substances or mixtures related to the manufacture, processing, distribution . . ., use or disposal" of the substance. The chemical industry complains that the requirement is too onerous in view of the limited value of the information.[34.1]

It is not clear that EPA has statutory authority to compel submission of "related chemical" data, although, on balance, the better view would be to retain the requirement.

Section 5(d)(1)(B) authorizes EPA to require test data that are "related to the effect of any manufacture . . . use, or disposal of . . . *such* substance" (meaning the target chemical, and articles containing such substance). Section 5(d)(1)(C) allows EPA to compel submission of any *"other data"* with respect to the effects of "such substance."

The related chemicals requirement is arguably needed to permit EPA to look into potential synergistic effects produced by the target chemical and other chemicals to which the exposed population (be it workers, consumers, or others) is also likely to be exposed. Thus characterized, the related chemicals requirement should fit under the "other data" language of Section 5(d)(1)(C).

EPA utilizes its Significant New Use Rule (SNUR) authority as a device to enable it to leverage negotiated regulations without having to follow the onerous procedures required by Section 6 or Section 4. One example of this device is the agency's action with respect to 8-Acetyl-3-Dodecyl-7,7,9,9-Tetramethyl-1,3,8-Triaza-spiro[4,5] Decane-2,4-dione.[35]

The chemical was not on EPA's list of existing chemicals, and the Agency received a PMN notice from a prospective importer early in 1983. The Agency determined on the basis of limited data submitted by the PMN submitter that the data had raised a sufficient concern that some action was required, but that the data were insufficient to make the "unreasonable risk" determination required by Section 6(a). EPA

[34.1] *See* 48 Fed. Reg. 41139.
[35] 49 Fed. Reg. 1753 (1-13-84)(Proposed Rule).

and the PMN submitter then entered into a Section 5(e) consent order, in which the PMN submitter agreed to certain protective measures for workers and agreed not to produce the chemical domestically. At that point, the chemical became an existing chemical, and was no longer subject to the Section 5(a)(1)(A) PMN requirement.

At the point the substance became an existing chemical, EPA had three choices for further action to prevent others from commencing manufacture *without* regulations:

(1) It could issue a Section 8(a) reporting rule, requiring anyone intending to manufacture or import the substance without restrictions identical to those in the negotiated Section 5(e) order to report to EPA. However, before it could impose any requirements on the reporting entity, EPA would have to issue a Section 4 testing rule, amass data, and then issue a Section 6(a) rule, all of which would take time and consume resources.

(2) If it could make the requisite findings, the Agency could move to act under Section 4(f), the "unreasonable risk" emergency provision.

(3) It could issue a SNUR defining as a significant new use any manufacturing or processing without the Section 5(e) negotiated restrictions. Then any entity subject to the SNUR would have to submit a PMN, and EPA could use the Section 5(e) interim regulation device to impose restrictions on the use until sufficient data are generated.

EPA's preference for the SNUR device in such circumstances is clearly understandable, and it demonstrates a clear desire on the Agency's part for simpler regulatory procedures than TSCA gives it. Obviously the Agency hopes that it will never have to use Section 6.[36]

EPA has also proposed to use Section 5(a)(2) to impose recordkeeping requirements as a means of getting around the small manufacturer exemptions of Section 8(a).[37]

PMN submitters must submit the PMN notice within thirty days of the date of first manufacturing or importing the substance.[37.1]

---

[36] Similar reasoning is evident in SNURs published at 48 Fed. Reg. 39245 (1983), and at 49 Fed. Reg. 82, 91, and 99 (1984).

[37] *See* 49 Fed. Reg. at 93 (1984).

[37.1] 40 CFR §720.102(b)(1).

[b] Significant New Use Rules (SNURs)

EPA has authority to require the submission of testing data prior to putting an existing chemical to a significant new use. Whether a new use is "significant" must be determined by EPA "by rule" in light of the factors set out in Section 5(a)(2). They include (1) the volume produced; (2) the extent to which the new use changes the exposure of humans or the environment, in terms of either the type or form of exposure or its magnitude or duration; and (3) the manufacturing, processing, distribution, and disposal methods contemplated. Once a SNUR is issued, then a PMN is required. Submission of a PMN triggers a range of duties and authority set out in Section 5(b)-(h) of the statute. As in the case of much of the Section 4 program, EPA has adopted no implementing regulations. It does, however, publish notice of receipt of PMNs and issuance of SNURs, rules, and exemptions under Section 5 in the Federal Register and inserts its SNURs in 40 CFR Part 721.

EPA did not begin issuing SNURs until 1982, but has rapidly accelerated its use of the SNUR device, and is now issuing SNURs with substantial frequency. Consistent with this, EPA adopted new SNUR procedures, published at 40 CFR Part 721, late in 1984.[37.2]

[c] Data Submission Obligations Placed on the PMN Submitter

The obligations placed upon the PMN submitter depend a great deal on the status of other actions taken or pending under other sections of TSCA. The range of consequences is as follows:

(1)   If there is an outstanding test rule pursuant to Section 4(a) with respect to the substance proposed for manufacture, and the substance does not appear on a separate list of chemicals EPA has already determined under Section 5(b)(4) may present an unreasonable risk,[38] then the PMN submitter, if not possessing a test rule exemption issued under Section 4(c), is required to submit all required Section 4(a) data with the PMN.[38.1]

(2)   If the PMN submitter possesses a Section 4(c) test data exemption and the chemical is not on the Section 5(b)(4) "suspect" list, the PMN submitter is not required to submit the required data

---

[37.2] *See* 49 Fed. Reg. 35011.
[38] *See* 40 CFR Part 716.
[38.1] Section 5(b)(1)(A).

with the PMN, but is prohibited from manufacturing or process-ing the chemical until ninety days after the required Section 4(a) data are submitted to EPA by the person required to submit it.[38.2]

(3) If the subject chemical is on the EPA Section 5(b)(4) "suspect" list, and the PMN submitter is not already subject to a Section 4(a) test rule (either because one has not been issued or because the PMN submitter is exempt under Section 4(c)), Section 5(b)(2) requires that there be submitted with the PMN data that the submitter "believes" show that the new chemical or new use will not present an "unreasonable risk of injury to health or the environment."

Section 5(b)(3) deems all Section 5 data to be available to the public, and Section 5(b)(4) prescribes hybrid, quasi-formal rulemaking proce-dures in connection with compiling the "suspect" list. PMN submitters must at least submit all information possessed by the submitter relative to the physical properties, chemical fate, exposure patterns, and health/environmental effects, along with any test data in the submitter's possession and a description of health/environmental effects data not possessed by the submitter but known to exist.[38.3] The substance of the notice is published by EPA in the Federal Register.[39]

Once a PMN is received by EPA, the Agency may pursue one of several courses of action, depending upon how it views the information submitted.

If the information "available" to EPA is determined to be insufficient to permit a "reasoned evaluation" of the health/environmental effects, and either in the absence of more information the production, use, or disposal of the chemical "may present an unreasonable risk" or the chemical will be produced and may enter the environment in "substan-tial quantities" (or there is otherwise a "significant potential" for "sub-stantial human exposure"), EPA may, following certain required

---

[38.2] Section 5(b)(1)(B).

[38.3] Section 5(d)(1). EPA's initial nonbinding policy incorporated several elements of the international testing harmonization efforts of the Organization for Economic Cooper-ation and Development (OECD), which recommends a minimum premarket data set for new chemicals, as well as specific test protocols for developing the data. These OECD recommendations have been formally adopted by the European Economic Community (EEC). As discussed above, EPA's testing protocols are currently consistent with OECD guidelines.

[39] Section 5(d)(2).

procedures, prohibit or limit the manufacturing, processing, distribution, or disposal. At the point such an order is proposed, the statute allows the affected manufacturers or processors to specify an objection, which has the effect of preventing the order from taking effect. Then, unless EPA secures an injunction from a federal district court, the statute allows the manufacturers or processors to go ahead and produce the substance.[39.1] The statute, somewhat unusual in this regard, specifies what the federal judge must consider, and how, in the event EPA seeks an injunction, and stipulates the way any such injunction must be dissolved once sufficient information is available. EPA has historically not made any use of its Section 5(e) authority.

If the information "available leads EPA to find that there is "unreasonable basis" to conclude that the activity "presents or will present" "an unreasonable risk" before EPA can promulgate a "rule" under the cumbersome procedures required by Section 6 of TSCA,[39.2] EPA may pursue one of several courses of action, "to the extent necessary to protect against such risk." Section 5(f)(1). It may issue a "proposed" Section 6(a) rule, which is immediately effective upon publication in the Federal Register, limiting the amount of the substance manufactured, processed, or distributed; prohibit or limit the uses to be made of it; impose labeling requirements; establish recordkeeping or similar requirements; prohibit or regulate disposal; or require public disclosure of the risks.[39.3] Alternatively, the agency may issue a proposed order prohibiting the activity, which becomes effective at the end of the PMN notification period unless a Section 5(e)(1)(c) objection is made with respect to it. In the event such an objection is made, or in lieu of issuing an administrative order in the first place, EPA may seek a judicial order enjoining the activity.[39.4]

Finally, EPA may determine that the "available" data demonstrate that there is *no* "unreasonable risk," and in such case usually will informally tell the PMN submitter to go ahead prior to publishing its notice, a procedure sanctioned by the statute.[39.5]

[39.1] Sections 5(e)(1) and 5(e)(2).
[39.2] 15 USC §2605.
[39.3] Sections 5(f)(1) and 6(a)(1)-(7).
[39.4] Sections 5(f)(2) and 5(f)(3).
[39.5] Section 5(g).

[d] EPA's PMN Requirements

The regulations by which EPA formalized PMN notification requirements and procedures are codified at 40 CFR Part 720.[40] The chemical must be identified; the form of identification depends upon the nature of the chemical, that is, whether it can be represented by a structural diagram or not (Class 1 or Class 2) or whether it is a polymer.[41] The chemical's impurities and by-products must be described; its uses must be described; the location and nature of manufacturing sites must be described; and worker and environmental exposure potential must be set forth[42]

The regulations also specify what types of test data are required and for what forms of the chemical, and what data are not required.[43]

Once a PMN notice is received, EPA, after making an initial determination as to the applicability of TSCA, publishes a brief description of the contents in the Federal Register. EPA must act, if it wishes to prohibit or regulate manufacturing, within ninety days of date EPA deems the PMN complete,[44] unless the agency avails itself of the one-time ninety-day extension provided under Section 5(c). Section 720.75(e) sets forth four examples of situations in which EPA will elect to extend the review period, which it deems satisfy the good cause requirement of Section 5(c):

(1) EPA thinks it will regulate the chemical under Section 5(e) or 5(f) but does not have time to do so within ninety days.

(2) EPA thinks it needs more information.

(3) EPA received information during the notice period that it needs to evaluate.

(4) The PMN submitter has failed to correct an error in the notice.[45]

Although EPA claims that its list of good cause examples is not exclu-

---

[40] 48 Fed. Reg. 21772, 48 Fed. Reg. 31641, 48 Fed. Reg. 33872, 48 Fed. Reg. 41132. On Sept. 13, 1983, EPA stayed indefinitely the following subsections, a fact not noted in the CFR: 720.3(y), 720.36, 720.50(c), and 720.78(b).

[41] 40 CFR §720.45(a).

[42] 40 CFR §§720.45(b)-(h).

[43] Required data are set forth in 40 CFR §§720.50(a),(b). Nonrequired data are set forth in 40 CFR §720.50(d). PMN submitters need not provide nonconfidential data already in EPA's hands, efficacy data and non-United States exposure data.

[44] Section 5(a).

[45] 40 CFR §720.75(e)(4).

sive, just how much broader latitude EPA has to extend the ninety-day period involuntarily is not clear. Since EPA's implementation of TSCA has been slow, there have been no challenges to EPA extensions or refusals to extend.[46]

EPA relies heavily on voluntary "suspension" of the notice review period, a device the Agency created administratively and codified as 40 CFR §720.75(b). The voluntary suspension is important to EPA, since it is not limited in time, and in general if EPA is unable to complete a PMN review in ninety days because it suspects that it needs to regulate the chemical, it will in most cases not be able to act in an additional ninety-day period, either. Only a data submitter may request a suspension of the notice review period, and in most cases the indefinitely suspended period is used to negotiate an agreed Section 5(e) regulatory plan that is tailored to the PMN submitter's situation.

Although Section 5 does not contain a recordkeeping requirement, EPA's PMN regulations, relying on Section 8 authority, require PMN submitters to keep production data for three years and "health and environmental effects data not generated by Section 5 tests, for a period of five years."[47]

Finally, the PMN regulations set forth EPA's procedures for determining confidentiality and releasing confidential data and require PMN submitters to notify EPA of the commencement date of import or manufacture within thirty days of the event.[48]

[e]   Exemptions from PMN-Related Requirements

A manufacturer or processor may apply for an exemption from either the PMN requirements or the data-submitting requirements of Section 5 to permit manufacture or processing for test-marketing purposes.[48.1] One may also seek exemption from the data submission requirements of Section 5(b)(2) on the ground that the substance is "equivalent" to another chemical substance with respect to which ade-

---

[46] An environmental organization might wish to have EPA extend the PMN period to evaluate information it proffers.

[47] 40 CFR §720.78(a).

[48] Confidentiality procedures are set forth in 40 CFR §§720.80, .85, .87, .90, .95. The notification requirement is set forth in 40 CFR §720.102.

[48.1] Section 5(h)(1).

quate data have already been given to EPA.[48.2] In such event, Section 5 contains compensation provisions similar to those in Section 4(c).

The following chemical substances/mixtures are exempt from the PMN requirements under 40 CFR §720.30:

— small quantity substances manufactured/imported solely for research pursuant to a research exemption allowed under 40 CFR §720.36 (stayed on 9-13-83);

— substances manufactured/imported solely for use pursuant to a "test-marketing" exemption granted under 40 CFR §720.38;

— substances manufactured solely for export;

— by-products used only as fuel, or disposed of or used as a soil enricher, or used as feedstock for extraction of other chemical substances; and

— impurities and other substances formed ancillary to a chemical reaction or production process that are not in and of themselves intended for commercial use.

[3] Regulatory Powers and Options Once an Unreasonable Risk Is Concluded to Be Presented

Section 6 of TSCA[48.3] governs EPA's actions in response to a finding by the Administrator that there exists a "reasonable basis" to conclude that a particular chemical substance or mixture or a family of chemical substances or mixtures "presents or will present an unreasonable risk of injury to health or to the environment." Section 6(c) erects a formidable procedural gauntlet through which EPA must pass before issuing a Section 6(a) rule, which may explain the relative paucity of Section 6(a) rules promulgated by the Agency.[49] EPA's substantive authority is,

---

[48.2] Section 5(h)(2).

[48.3] 15 USC §2605.

[49] As of late 1985, EPA has regulated halogenated chlorofluoroalkanes (40 CFR Part 762) and partially regulated asbestos in the schools (40 CFR Part 763 Subpart F) under Section 6. EPA's lackluster performance under Section 6 has been the subject of periodic congressional oversight hearings. *See, e.g.,* Committee on Interstate and Foreign Commerce, Subcommittee on Oversight and Investigations, H.R. Rep. No. 96-134. The causes of EPA's failure to act under Section 6 with greater vigor, revealed in the testimony proffered at those hearings are several: priority within the Agency was given to the PMN review program; economic considerations have in many instances outweighed the Act's purpose of protecting health and the environment; the emerging relationship between TSCA and other federal statutes has caused deferral and delays on the part of EPA. In addition, the inadequate development of the testing and information-gathering provisions of the Act have failed to provide a base for the existing chemicals.

however, sweeping. It may prohibit or limit manufacturing, processing, or distribution. In addition, it may—

— prohibit or limit uses;
— impose labeling requirements;
— establish recordkeeping and similar requirements;
— prohibit or limit commercial use;
— regulate disposal; and
— require public disclosure or risk.[49.1]

EPA may also take action with respect to specific manufacturers or processors whose quality control procedures or manufacturing process causes the substance to present an unreasonable risk. Such action must, however, follow an adjudicatory proceeding need under Section 554 of the Administrative Procedures Act.[49.2] Such action can include, *inter alia,* new quality control measures, requirement that batches of product be repurchased from distributors and consumers, etc.[49.3]

Generally, however, Section 6(a) rules are subject to informal rule-making procedures specified by Section 6(c), which modifies the basic APA Section 553 notice and comment scheme by requiring an "informal hearing," at which oral testimony is permitted as of right, and other adjudicatory trappings, such as cross-examination, are available subject to EPA's discretion or hearing procedures.[49.4] EPA's Section 6 rulemaking procedures are published at 40 CPR Part 750. Section 6(c) also specifies the factors EPA must formally consider in determining whether to issue, and the scope of, a Section 6(a) rule. Those factors are—

(1) the magnitude of human exposure and the human health effects;

(2) the magnitude of environmental exposure and the environmental effects;

(3) the "benefits" of the product and the availability of substitutes; and

(4) the "reasonably ascertainable economic consequences of the rule, after consideration of the effect on the national economy,

---

[49.1] Section 6(a)(1)-(7).
[49.2] 5 USC §554.
[49.3] Section 6(b).
[49.4] Section 6(c)(2) and 6(c)(3).

small business, technological innovation, the environment, and public health."[49.5]

EPA also must consider the availability of a regulatory remedy under another federal law, and whether action taken thereunder would reduce the risk to a level of nonsignificance. Section 9(a)(1) requires EPA to report to any federal agency EPA determines has jurisdiction over the risk, requesting it to determine whether it may prevent or reduce the risk by its own regulatory action, and if so, to issue an order declaring whether or not the activities described in EPA's report present the risk it has described. Until the other agency responds to EPA's report, which EPA publishes in the Federal Register,[50] EPA is prohibited by Section 9(a)(2) from acting under either Section 6 or Section 7 with respect to the precise risk that is the subject of the report.[51]

Under extraordinary circumstances, EPA may issue a proposed rule, without prior hearing, immediately effective.[51.1] However, if it does so, it must expeditiously hold a hearing thearfter. Such an action is not judicially reviewable.[51.2]

Section 6(c) involves a cost-benefit exercise, in which EPA has ordinarily weighed the cost of regulation against its benefits (expressed in terms of reduction of risk). Obviously, the particular cost-benefit methodology employed by EPA will have a great impact on the result of any Section 6(c) analysis.

[4] Imminent Hazards Under Section 7

EPA's authority to act under Section 7 of TSCA (15 USC §2606) hinges upon the existence in commerce of an "imminently hazardous chemical substance or mixture," that is, a chemical substance or mixture that presents "an imminent and unreasonable risk of serious or widespread injury to health or the environment." Section 7(f) defines

---

[49.5] Section 6(c)(1)(A)-(D).

[50] *See, e.g.*, 50 Fed. Reg. 41393 (10-10-85) (transmitting report to Occupational Safety and Health Administration regarding finding of unreasonable risk to workers in rubber industry posed by 1,3-Butadiene).

[51] EPA may, of course, regulate other aspects of the risk. Thus, for example, although EPA would be obligated to report to OSHA regarding a workplace hazard it has identified posed by a regualted substance, it is free to regulate nonworkplace exposures without waiting for OSHA to respond. *See* 50 Fed. Reg. 41395 (10-10-85).

[51.1] Section 6(d).

[51.2] Section 6(d)(2).

the term "imminent risk" in terms of injury "likely to result . . . before a final rule under Section 6 . . . can protect against such risk."

Once EPA identifies such a hazard, Section 7(a) confers on it authority to commence a civil action in federal district court for the following relief:

(1) seizure of the substance (an *in rem* proceeding); and/or

(2) a temporary or permanent injunction requiring the manufacturer, processor, and/or distributor to—

    (a) notify purchasers of the risk,

    (b) issue a public notice of the risk,

    (c) recall the substance, and/or

    (d) replace or repurchase the substance.

EPA's authority is discretionary in the event it has already issued a rule under Section 4, 5, or 6 or an order under Section 5. However, the language of Section 7(a)(2) appears to impose on EPA a mandatory duty to bring an action with respect to an imminently hazardous substance in the event the agency has not issued an immediately effective rule against it under Section 6(a) and (d)(2)(A)(i).

§2.03 Data Acquisition Requirements Under Section 8

Section 8(a) of TSCA[51.3] requires EPA to promulgate recordkeeping requirements for most manufacturers and processors.[52] Section 8(b)

[51.3] 15 USC §2607.

[52] Small manufacturers and processors are exempt from the basic recordkeeping requirements. 15 USC §2607(a)(1)(A). They could be compelled by EPA to submit information for the purpose of compiling the inventory required by Section 8(b), however, and may be required to maintain records and submit reports with respect to chemicals as to which EPA has initiated action under 15 USC §§2603, 2604(b)(4), 2605, 2604(e), or 2606, provided in either case that EPA has imposed the requirement "by rule." (§2607(a)(3)(A)-(ii)). The entities subject to the small manufacturer or processor exemption are determined by EPA in consultation with the Small Business Administration (§2607(a)(3)(B)). EPA's initial inventory-reporting regulations accorded "small" status to entities whose "total annual sales" are less than $5 million, except that any such entity that manufactured at one site more than 100,000 pounds of any chemical during the 1977 calendar year would be disqualified. The $5 million "total annual sales" requirement was applied to all related corporations in an affiliated group. 40 CRF §710.2(x).

Subsequent reporting regulations exempted a different class of "small" entities from reporting requirements for all but high priority chemicals (indicated by an asterisk on the 8(a) list). *See* 40 CFR §712.25(b). "Small," for Section 712 purposes, requires total annual sales of all affiliated companies less than $30 million and total annual production of the

requires EPA to compile an inventory of chemical substances manufactured or processed for commercial purposes. Section 8(c) requires manufacturers, processors, and distributors of chemical substances or mixtures to keep records of "significant adverse reactions to health or the environment." Section 8(d) requires EPA to compile lists of health and safety studies applicable to chemical substances and mixtures. Section 8(e) requires manufacturers, processors, and distributors to pass along to EPA risk information obtained by such persons. EPA's regulations governing these matters are set forth in 40 CFR Part 710.

[1] Recordkeeping and Reporting—Generally

Section 8(a) imposes on manufacturers and processors (including importers) a requirement that records be maintained and reports be submitted to EPA "as the Administration may reasonably require."[52.1] However, as to mixtures, EPA must first conclude that the information is "necessary for the effective enforcement" of TSCA.[52.2]

EPA quickly issued regulations setting forth criteria for reporting inventories, to be used for the purpose of compiling the Section 8(b) master inventory of existing chemicals.[53] EPA's approach was to compile an initial Section 8(b) inventory based on 1977 submissions limited to manufactured and imported mixtures in existence from January 1, 1975.[54] The inventory compiled therefrom contains detailed information on about 60,000 chemicals, and consists of six volumes, with yearly updates as the data base is expanded with the introduction of new chemicals into the stream of commerce. Excluded from the list are chemical substances that are impurities; by-products that have no commercial purpose; substances created incidental to exposure of a chemical substance, mixture, or article to environmental factors; chemical substances resulting from a chemical reaction incidental to storage of

---

chemical below 45,400 kg., for the reporting period. 40 CFR §712.25(c). For the purpose of computing these numbers, all entities that are "owned or controlled" by a "parent company" must be included. The term "owned or controlled" is defined as ownership or control of "50 percent or more" of the subsidiary's "voting stock or other equity rights," or the power to "control the management and policies of the other company." 40 CFR §712.5(k). The latter test obviously involves a factual determination on a case-by-case basis.

[52.1] 15 USC §2607(1)(a).
[52.2] 15 USC §2607(a)(1)(B).
[53] 42 Fed. Reg. 64572 (1977); 40 CFR Part 710.
[54] 40 CFR §710.1 (1978).

another chemical substance or mixture; and a number of other chemicals, principally those created by reactions in manufacturing plastics, household products, oxidizers, emulsifiers, and similar products.[55]

EPA substantially increased its recordkeeping and reporting requirements in 1982, when it issued Part 712 of the TSCA regulations, titled Chemical Information Rules.[56] These regulations elicit production, use and exposure-related information on chemicals that EPA places from time to time on a special list [hereafter "8(a) list"], on what is called a "Preliminary Assessment" form.

EPA's approach in Part 712 is clearly aimed at gaining production and exposure information about the 8(a) list chemicals. Each manufacturer or importer[57] must submit information within the scope of EPA Form No. 7710-35 for each plant site. The instructions seek information about production processes, quantities, worker activities, and worker numbers. Although EPA could require detailed file and record searches, it requires only "information that is readily obtainable by management and aupervisory employees responsible for manufacturing, processing, distributing, technical services and marketing."[57.1]

In addition to small manufacturers and importers, research facilities (even if used for the development of products) and small plant sites (less than 500 kg. manufactured or imported at a single site) are exempted from the reporting requirements.[57.2] Unsold or environmentally generated by-products, impurities, or nonisolated intermediates need not be reported.[57.3]

Reports are required on a fiscal year basis.[57.4] The first report was due on November 19, 1982.

---

[55] 40 CFR §710.5. Further elaboration is unwarranted since the Section 8(b) inventory criteria are of historical interest only. The Section 8(b) inventory is available at federal depositories, and from EPA's Office of Toxic Substances (telephone 800-424-9065).

[56] 47 Fed. Reg. 26998 (6-22-82).

In 1985, EPA broadened the list of chemicals as to which reports must be submitted. Originally, reports were required only for chemicals designated by the ITC for testing within twelve months. The Agency amended 40 CFR §§712.1 and 712.30 in 50 Fed. Reg. 34805 to encompass all chemical substances and mixtures recommended by the ITC for testing.

[57] Processors are to be subject to separate requirements, designated as Subpart C, which EPA has not yet issued as of late 1985.

[57.1] 40 CFR §712.7.

[57.2] 40 CFR §§712.25(a) and 712.25(b).

[57.3] 40 CFR §712.25(d).

[57.4] 40 CFR §712.30(a).

[2] **Recordkeeping and Reporting—Significant Adverse Reactions Under Section 8(c)**

[a] **Requirements**

Section 8(c) imposes on manufacturers, processors, and distributors an obligation to "maintain records of significant adverse reactions to health or to environment, as determined by the Administrator by rule, alleged to have been caused by the substance or mixture" manufactured, processed, or distributed by the reporting entity. These records must be kept for "30 years from the date such reactions were first reported to or known by" the entity. Essentially, the statute requires the entity to make a record of such reactions regardless of how remote or apparently unreliable the source of the information coming to the regulated entity is, provided the information is "submitted to" the entity. The statute does not require the entity actively to seek out information, but it must faithfully record the information that comes to it.

[b] **What Sorts of Information Are Significant?**

Such information as is required by Section 8(c) is of obvious utility to potential plaintiffs as well as to EPA. As of September 1983, seventeen states had enacted worker or general public "toxic right to know" statutes. Arguably, under some of those statutes, information contained in Section 8(c) records is required to be disclosed, although Section 8(c) itself seems to require only disclosure to EPA.

Obviously, the scope of the recordkeeping requirement is very dependent upon EPA's regulatory definition of some of the key terms, particularly "significant adverse reactions." Moreover, since the Section 8(c) duty to keep records and the Section 8(e) duty to report observed risks to EPA are not identical, EPA's regulatory refinement of these respective obligations is doubly important. It took EPA seven years to issue Section 8(c) regulations, which were published in 48 Fed. Reg. 38187 (8-22-83). They are codified at 40 CFR Part 717.

EPA's regulations substantially refine and complicate, and to some extent dilute, this rather straightforward requirement. The term "significant adverse reaction" is defined as "reactions that may indicate a substantial impairment of normal activities, or long-lasting or irreversible damage to health or environment."[57.5] The regulations further define the term to include, without an intention to limit the scope, more specifically delineated health and environmental effects. The following types of health effects are delineated in 40 CFR §717.12(a) as significant:

(1) long-lasting or irreversible damage, such as cancer or birth defects;

(2) partial or complete impairment of bodily functions, such as reproductive disorders, neurological disorders, or blood disorders;

(3) an impairment of normal activities experienced by all or most of the persons exposed at one time; and

(4) an impairment of normal activities that is experienced each time an individual is exposed.

An important exception created by the regulations is that "reports of known human health effects" need not be recorded.[58] EPA's definition of this term is not entirely satisfactory and may lead to unfortunate gaps in the data base. Regulated entities need not report a "commonly recognized human health effect" of the substance "as described" in either scientific articles or publications "abstracted in standard reference sources or in the firm's product labeling or material safety data sheets."[59] Such an effect is not, however, "known," under the regulation if it is (1) a "significantly more severe toxic effect than previously described," (2) involves a "significantly shorter exposure period or lower exposure levels than described," or (3) involves a different exposure route.[60] Thus, in many cases whether or not a reported effect must be recorded will entail an exercise of discretion on the part of individuals employed by a regulated entity. Since the regulations require only retention of information that the regulated entity believes meets the requirements of the regulation and do not require retention of reports deemed outside of the obligation, EPA possesses no useful means of enforcement.

Environmental reactions that must be recorded are set forth in a more straightforward manner in the regulations. The following must be

---

57.5 40 CFR §717.4(i).
58 40 CFR §717.12(b).
59 40 CFR §717.3(c)(1)(ii).
60 40 CFR §717.3(c)(2)(i)-(iii).

recorded even if observations are limited to a single plant or disposal site:

(1) gradual or sudden changes in the composition of animal life or plant life, including fungal or microbial organisms, in an area;

(2) abnormal number of deaths of organisms (for example, fish kills);

(3) reduction of the reproductive success or the vigor of a species;

(4) reduction in agricultural productivity, whether crops or livestock;

(5) alterations in the behavior or distribution of a species;

(6) long-lasting or irreversible contamination of components of the physical environment, especially in the case of groundwater and surface water and soil resources that have limited self-cleansing capability.[61]

Curiously, however, EPA exempts from the recordkeeping requirement significant adverse reactions the "alleged cause" of which is an accidental spill or discharge, emission exceeding permit limits, or "other incident of environmental contamination that has been reported to the Federal Government under any applicable authority."[62] Since the obvious purpose of Section 8(c) is to produce a data base that will be useful epidemiologically, it seems nonsensical to exclude from the data base otherwise useful information simply because it is derived from a pollution incident, indeed, from an *accidental* pollution incident. As worded, the regulation appears to require recording of effects observed following an intentional spill, but not those following an accidental spill. While it may be intended that the catchall "other incident . . . reported to the Federal Government . . ." is intended to modify or explain the remaining language of the section, it does little to explain its usefulness. The federal government houses tons of data, spread among hundreds of agencies, which rarely communicate with each other. Even within EPA, data possessed by the air program may not be easily accessible to the Office of Toxic Substances, let alone an epidemiological contractor in OTS's employ. Moreover, the clause would arguably exempt the maintenance of records of occupational health effects related to incidents for which reports were filed with the Occupational Safety and Health Administration. Section 8(c), however, specifically identifies "reports of occupational disease or injury" as falling within its purview.

---

[61] 40 CFR §717.3(c).

[62] 40 CFR §717.3(d).

EPA has also limited the entities required to maintain records to manufacturers other than mining entities[63] and to processors engaged in petroleum refining and chemical processing as described in the Standard Industrial Classification (SIC) Major Groups Codes 2911 and 28.[64] Distributors (those that are not also manufacturers) and retailers are exempt from Section 8(c) recordkeeping. While the exemptions may be understandable from the standpoint of avoiding potential duplication, they undoubtedly in some cases make it more difficult for allegations to be made in cases such as adverse consumer reactions to a product whose active ingredient is distributed packaged with inert ingredients under the distributor's brand name, without listing the name of the manufacturer on the container.

This problem is magnified somewhat by EPA's insistence that the allegations of significant adverse effects be made formally, in a writing signed by the alleger, which specifically names the effluent, emission, or discharge from which the reaction is thought to result.[65]

The requirement that recordkeeping encompass waste emissions, effluents and discharges, and process activities as well as the chemical products[66] goes beyond the literal requirements of Section 8(c). So, too, does the suggestion of Section 717.10(d) (not a *requirement*, however) that firms respond to allegers, informing them of the disposition of their allegations.

The recordkeeping, inspection, and reporting requirements of Part 717 are presented in Appendix 2G, *infra*.

[3] Notice to EPA of Substantial Risks Under Section 8(e)

[a] In General

Section 8(e) of TSCA,[67] self-executing as of its effective date,[68] re-

---

63 40 CFR §§717.5(a), 717.7(a).

64 SIC codes applicable to this Part are published in the Standard Industrial Classification Manual—1972 and the 1977 Supplement. This manual and supplement may be obtained from the U.S. Government Printing Office, Washington, D.C. 20402, stock number 4101-0006 and stock number 003-005-0170-0, respectively. EPA occasionally defines a term in a way that is inconsistent with the SIC codes, however. Thus, care must be taken in using the codes and EPA regulations to verify consistency.

65 40 CFR §717.10. This requirement heightens the importance of the "whistle blower" employee protection provisions of Section 23(b) of TSCA.

66 *See* 40 CFR §717.5(a)(2)(ii) and (iii), and 40 CFR §717.5(b)(2)(ii) and (iii).

67 15 USC §2607(e).

68 January 1, 1977.

quires manufacturers, processors, and distributors to report to EPA any information received by the entity "which reasonably supports the conclusion" that a substance or mixture of the entity "presents a substantial risk of injury to health or the environment." The sole exception to this obligation is information the entity has "actual knowledge" EPA has been "adequately informed" of.

EPA has, however, adopted an enforcement policy statement, which it published as an interpretive rule,[69] that lays a gloss on the statutory language. In that statement, EPA enunciated the obligations it deems Section 8(e) to impose on regulated entities and corporate officers and employees, with an apparent view toward future punitive action. Appendix 2H, *infra,* reproduces the reporting mechanics and other material from the policy.

[b] Who Must Report?

The EPA enforcement policy seeks to impose separate, though related, reporting obligations on regulated business entities and their officers and certain employees. The entity's president, chief executive officer, and any other executive "having authority for the organization's execution of its Section 8(e) obligations" are required to establish procedures to ensure that relevant information reaching the entity finds its way to EPA within fifteen days of receipt, and the Policy Statement indicates that those persons are individually liable under TSCA's civil and criminal penalty provision for the entity's noncompliance with its Section 8(e) obligation.[70] An entity is deemed to have obtained any information "which any officer or employee capable of appreciating the significance of that information has obtained."[71] Such employees also have an individual obligation to report, but may be relieved of the obligation if the entity establishes a set of procedures following guidelines set forth in the Policy Statement.[72]

---

[69] 43 Fed. Reg. 11110 (3-16-78).

[70] Policy Statement, paragraphs II, XI.

[71] *Id.*

[72] These procedures, at a minimum, must (1) specify the information that officers and employees must submit; (2) indicate how such submissions are to be prepared and the company official to whom they are to be submitted; (3) note the federal penalties for failing to report; and (4) provide a mechanism for promptly advising officers and employees in writing of the company's disposition of the report, including whether or not the report was submitted to EPA (and, if not, informing employees of their right to report to EPA, as protected by TSCA Section 23). *Id.*

EPA's authority to hold individual officers and employees responsible for Section 8(e) reporting, and liable for penalties in the event of noncompliance, is far from clear. TSCA does not define "person" specifically to include officers and employees of corporate entities. Indeed, the context in which the phrase appears throughout TSCA implies that it is simply synonymous with the regulated entity. Moreover, language found in other environmental statutes expressly making "responsible corporate officer(s)" liable for corporate violations of regulatory requirements[73] is absent from the penal provisions of TSCA.[74]

The policy statement does not elaborate significantly on the phrase "capable of appreciating pertinent information." In response to a comment, EPA said that the term means "officers and employees who have a responsibility to be alert to and report substantial-risk information."[75] This implies that a chain-of-command directive designating a single individual as the Section 8(e) person (investing that person with responsibility to "be alert") would narrow the class of persons whose possession of information would be deemed to impose a reporting obligation on the entity. EPA's published response to a comment, however, does not serve to modify language that is clearly broader.

The phrase "capable of appreciating pertinent information," in its plain English meaning, implies the ability of the recipient (1) to understand what the information says, (2) to interpret its significance in terms of public health or environmental impact, and (3) to formulate a judgment as to its relevance to the employer's regulatory responsibility under TSCA. Phrased this way, it appears clear that the obligation is imposed at least on such employees as research scientists and other professionals with relevant technical expertise (including lawyers) who receive health, safety, and environmental information in the ordinary course of their activities. Arguably, a person with the requisite technical capability who would not normally be in the information stream, and thus not likely to have been made aware of the Section 8(e) obligation,

---

73 *See, e.g.,* Section 309(c)(3), Clean Water Act, 33 USC §1319(c)(3).

74 Section 16, 15 USC §2615.

75 43 Fed. Reg. 11110, Response to Comment 3. The Agency then reiterated that an internal procedure for moving information up the corporate hierarchy would insulate low-level employees from an individual reporting obligation, and went on to say that independent contractors and consultants (such as laboratories) are not responsible for reporting information to EPA. Their clients are responsible, said EPA, although it seems to have stopped short of deeming clients to possess information known only to contractors.

would not be sufficiently capable of "appreciating" the information to be a Section 8(e) obligant. Nevertheless, since the ultimate reach of the phrase is not precisely delineated by EPA, it would be prudent for regulated entities to establish clear, rigid internal procedures to control the flow of potential Section 8(e) information along a well-defined path.[76]

[c] What Must Be Reported

The Policy Statement also seeks, with limited success, to define what sort of information falls within the "substantial risk" category. The statute sheds no light on the meaning of the term, or on how it differs from the phrase "significant risk," used in Section 4 and elsewhere, or the phrase "unreasonable risk," used in Section 5. "Significant risk" seems to embody notions of the seriousness of effects and the probability of their occurrence.[77] "Unreasonable risk" seems to employ the same basic factors.[78] In defining "substantial risk" for Section 8(e) purposes, EPA lists the same two factors as the relevant ones.[79] What must be looked at are effects and exposure potential. EPA's guideline elevates effects over exposure data where human health is implicated, and considers exposure more significant in environmental contamination scenarios.[80]

EPA defines the risks covered by placing them in three categories— human health effects (single instances or patterns), environmental effects, and emergency incidents of environmental contamination. An important uncertainty exists as to the quantum of evidence that is sufficient to implicate a given chemical or chemicals with an observed effect.

The Policy Statement provides, for example, that information must be reported that "reasonably supports"[81] a conclusion that a chemical

---

[76] The Policy Statement also makes it clear, however, that negligence or intentional *avoidance* of potential 8(e) information will not serve to nullify the 8(e) obligation. Policy Statement, Paragraph III, Response to Comment 7.

[77] *See* Section 4(e), 15 USC §2603(e).

[78] *See* Section 5(b)(4)(A)(ii), 15 USC §2604(b)(4)(A)(ii).

[79] Policy Statement, Paragraph V.

[80] *Id.*

[81] Policy Statement, Paragraph VI.

is "strongly implicated" in an "instance of cancer. . . ."[82] It is equivocal, however, on the question of the point at which an enlarging body of test results ripens into "reasonable support" for the action-forcing conclusion. Evidence can come from a number of sources identified in the Statement and well known to chemists and toxicologists. They include designated controlled studies[83] and reports concerning uncontrolled, unanticipated, and undesigned events (such as retrospective epidemiological studies of accidents involving the release of chemicals into the environment). On the one hand, EPA asserts that regulated entities are not required to initiate "searches for information" or undertake "extraordinary efforts to acquire information."[84] However, the Agency also states that a person "is not to delay reporting until he obtains conclusive information"[85] . . . and that "preliminary results from incomplete studies" may be required to be reported "where appropriate."[86] Coupled with EPA's assertion that the client is responsible for reporting what a consulting laboratory knows, this requirement poses potentially difficult choices for regulated entities.

Private laboratories, particularly academic laboratories, are often resistent to release of preliminary animal bioassay study results. In *Dow Chemical Company v. Dr. James Allen, et al.,*[87] which arose out of a FIFRA cancellation proceeding, the Seventh Circuit upheld a United States district judge's refusal to enforce a subpoena issued by an EPA hearing officer, which sought preliminary bioassay results from an academic laboratory. The court agreed that such a study has no significant probative value, and thus did not satisfy the prerequisite in the applicable EPA subpoena regulation. In an important dictum, moreover, the court expressed serious concern about the intrusion on academic freedom that could result if such data were subject to compulsory administrative process.[88] The tests in question had been essentially completed, but the data had not been analyzed and subjected to scientific peer review. If such information has no significant "probative value" as evi-

---

82 *Id.,* Paragraph V(a).

83 (1) *In vivo* experiments and tests (that is, animal bioassays); (2) *in vitro* experiments and tests (that is, gene tests and other similar cell growth tests); (3) epidemiological studies; and (4) environmental monitoring studies.

84 43 Fed. Reg. 11110, Response to Comment 7.

85 Policy Statement, Paragraph VI.

86 *Id.,* Paragraph VI (1).

87 672 F.2d 1262 (7th Cir. 1982).

88 *Id.*

dence in a relevant proceeding solely because of its preliminary status, then one might reasonably argue that it also cannot "reasonably support" a causal connection between the subject chemical and the perceived health effects.

The strongest argument against submitting preliminary data is the risk that false negatives or false positives will find their way into the government's data bank, creating a murky morass of ultimately conflicting or confusing information, which lessens the usefulness of Section 8(e) reports. EPA offers no useful guidance as to when preliminary data reporting is "appropriate," and thus compelled to be reported under the Policy Statement. Are all positives "appropriate"? Are all negatives inappropriate? Is the judgment to be based upon some confidence factor? If so, what degree of confidence is required?[89]

EPA's desire to know as much as soon as possible cannot be quarrelled with. However, the Agency's Policy Statement threatens civil and criminal sanctions against both corporate entities and individuals for noncompliance with standards that require often difficult judgment calls.[90] Since astute regulated entities should create internal policies that force error on the side of overreporting, the result could well be frequent reporting of marginal or risky information.

Regulated entities need not report information that is required to be submitted to EPA in writing under other EPA-administered regulatory statutes or information that has been "published in the scientific literature *and* referenced by" a number of listed abstract services.[91]

[d] Confidentiality

EPA applies its usual TSCA confidentiality requirements (40 CFR Part 2) to Section 8(e) reports.

[e] Spills, Leaks, and Accidents

In responding to a comment on its Section 8(e) policy, EPA stated that it did not intend to "compel searches for information or extraordi-

---

[89] The same problems arise in connection with other types of experimental data as well. *In vitro* experiments involve another judgment call: whether corroborative information is "necessary" to reasonably support the conclusions drawn from the tests. Many would argue that the nature of *in vitro* testing requires corroboration all of the time.

[90] Policy Statement, Paragraph XI.

[91] Policy Statement, Paragraph VII.

nary efforts to acquire information."[92] It also stated, however, that one must not negligently or intentionally *avoid* information.[93]

The Agency requires reporting health and environmental effects following "uncontrolled circumstances" of exposure[94] where the effects occur in a pattern where a significant common feature is exposure to the subject chemical. The types of reports EPA looks for are "medical and health surveys," "clinical studies," and other documentary reports.[95]

One question presented by these requirements is whether an entity faced with an accidental release and exposure scenario is either negligent or guilty of intentional avoidance if it does not design and conduct organized medical or other relevant studies to capture and preserve information to be gleaned from the experiences. One could certainly argue for that result, although to reach it would render EPA's assertion that Section 8(e) looks only to passively acquired knowledge somewhat meaningless.

[4] Requirements for Submission of Health and Safety Studies Under Section 8(d)

Section 8(d) gives EPA very broad authority to promulgate rules requiring both regulated entities and others to submit health and safety studies in their possession.

Regulated entities may be required to submit, at least as to substances they manufacture, process, or distribute or *propose* to manufacture, process, or distribute, lists of health and safety studies—

— conducted or initiated by or for the entity;
— known to the entity; or
— "reasonably ascertainable" by the entity.[96]

Nonregulated persons may be required to submit copies of studies indentified by a regulated entity.[97]

---

92 Response to Comment 7.
93 *Id.*
94 Policy Statement, Paragraph VI (2).
95 *Id.*
96 15 USC §2607(d)(1).
97 15 USC §2607(d)(2). EPA issued in 1978, and then withdrew, regulations that required regulated entities to submit studies on chemicals they neither manufactured, processed, nor distributed. *See* discussion *infra.*

In 1978, EPA promulgated, and later withdrew, regulations limiting the obligations of Section 8(d) to manufacturers, processors, and distributors of substances selected for priority testing consideration under Section 4(a).[98] It reserved the right to request studies from nonregulated entities.[99] Studies published in the usual sources and abstracted, or otherwise available to EPA, were exempted from mandatory submission, but could nevertheless be required to be submitted, in EPA's discretion.[100]

EPA included within the scope of the term "health and safety studies" studies of carcinogenicity; mutagenicity; teratogenicity; behavioral disorders; cumulative or synergistic effects; and acute, subacute, and chronic effects.

EPA's use of Section 8(e) in its 1978 regulations was aimed at providing the Agency with sufficient background data on which to base a decision about the scope of its testing rules.[101] The rule expressly *included* within its grasp entities whose manufacture of the substance is solely for research or development, for use as an intermediate, or for test marketing purposes[102] and required regulated entities to submit studies relative to substances they did not manufacture, process, or distribute—the submittal requirement was triggered simply by possession of the study.[103]

In an opinion often cited for its procedural holding, the Third Circuit, in *Dow Chemical Company v. EPA*,[104] upheld EPA's by-then-withdrawn regulation against strong arguments by Dow that EPA's application of the rule to research manufacturing made a nullity of the statute's definitional limitation to activities for commercial purposes. The court also rejected Dow's argument that the statute limited the submission of study reports to those relative to the submitter's products. The court's reasoning on the first point is significant, since it would appear to apply as well to Section 5 of TSCA.

---

[98] 40 CFR §730.2(a), 43 Fed. Reg. 30984 and 43 Fed. Reg. 41206.
[99] 40 CFR §730.7.
[100] 40 CFR §730.5(b).
[101] *See* 43 Fed. Reg. 4074.
[102] 40 CFR §730.1(a).
[103] 40 CFR §730.5(a)(2).
[104] 605 F.2d 673 (3d Cir. 1979). The procedural rule established was that an agency's voluntary withdrawal of a regulation after a petition to review it has been filed under circumstances demonstrating that the agency adheres to the substantive legal position that is the subject of the lawsuit bars the agency's reliance on the mootness doctrine as a basis for avoiding litigation of the issue.

Essentially, the court concluded that any in-house research activity conducted by a manufacturer, producer, or distributor of products in commerce is for a commercial purpose because it is aimed at ultimate profit. Thus, research activities conducted by independent laboratories are exempt from the requirements of the regulation, while identical activities conducted by manufacturers are not, under the *Dow* rule.[105]

One of the arguments raised by Dow was that by being required to submit early research data to EPA, an entity could lose its competitive edge in developing a product, since its research thrust could be revealed to competitors. The court dismissed this argument by relying on Section 14's confidentiality and disclosure provisions, concluding that disclosure to EPA is not necessarily disclosure to competitors.[106]

The Third Circuit's *Dow* rulings represent the only extant judicial construction of Section 8(d). Since the court's opinion involved an already-withdrawn regulation, its precedential value is questionable.

EPA's current Section 8(d) regulations are codified in 40 CFR Part 716,[107] and contain the previously disputed provision.

§2.04 Disclosure of Information—Confidentiality Protection

EPA has attempted to standardize, insofar as possible, its disclosure and business confidentiality procedures and standards. However, because all of EPA's statutes are not identical in their treatment of release and protection of confidential business information, the general procedures and guidelines of 40 CFR Part 2 are modified by special rules applicable to substances subject to specific statutory provisions. Section 14 of TSCA[108] is one such provision, and EPA's special TSCA rules are found at 40 CFR §2.306.[109]

---

105 The court's reasoning on the second issue focused on TSCA's legislative history and the "otherwise known" language of Section 8(d).

106 *See* Section 2.04 and Chapter 3, *infra,* for a further discussion of the data confidentiality issues.

107 47 Fed. Reg. 38780 (1982); 47 Fed. Reg. 54624 (1982); 48 Fed. Reg. 13178 (1983); 48 Fed. Reg. 24366 (1983); 48 Fed. Reg. 55686 (1983); 49 Fed. Reg. 1696 (1984).

108 14 USC §2613.

109 43 Fed. Reg. 40003.

[1] Protected Information and Unprotected Information

Only information submitted to EPA and as to which a person has formally asserted a claim of confidentiality is subject to protection. Information is deemed "submitted" to EPA if it could have been obtained by EPA under TSCA's authority, and whether it was submitted by the claimant or by a third party.[110]

Health, safety, and environmental effects information is protected only to a limited extent. EPA may, without any procedural requirements, release and disseminate "health and safety studies which are applicable to a chemical substance or mixture subject to a Section 4 test rule" or for which a Section 5 PMN notice is required.[111] Although the statute does not clearly authorize it to do so, EPA also includes all chemicals on the Section 8(b) inventory list within this category.[112] EPA is also free to release, without restraint, such information that is applicable to *any* regulated substance once the substance has been "offered for commercial distribution."[113] EPA's regulations treat substances "offered" for test-marketing purposes or "offered" for use in research and development (that is, chemicals sold to laboratories or to other regulated entities for research purposes, presumably) as being offered for commercial distribution.[114] Such data may not be claimed to be confidential. The statute also authorizes the release of any "data" reported to EPA or obtained from a health and safety study.

The only restriction on EPA's release of health and safety data is a prohibition against release of health and safety data that discloses processes used in the manufacturing or processing of a chemical substance or mixture or discloses the portion of a mixture constituted by any of the chemical substances in it.[115]

Obviously the breadth of the phrase "health and safety study" is of critical importance to regulated entities seeking the greatest possible confidentiality protection. Section 14(b) uses that term instead of a broader, generic phrase, such as "health and safety data." The term is

---

[110] 40 CFR §2.306(b).

[111] 15 USC §2613(b)(1); 40 CFR §§2.306(a)(3) and 2.306(g).

[112] 40 CFR §2.306(a)(3)(i). *See also* 44 Fed. Reg. 17674.

[113] 15 USC §2613(b)(1)(i).

[114] 40 CFR §2.306(a)(3)(i).

[115] 15 USC §2613(b)(1). The statute states that if the information is not confidential, as defined, the confidentiality exception of the Freedom of Information Act (5 USC §552(b)(4)) may not be asserted to bar release. 15 USC §2613(b)(2).

undefined. In the narrowest sense, it could be defined simply to refer to studies produced under Section 8(d). If the term were so defined, then arguably the "data" encompassed by Section 14(b) could be limited to PMN and test rule data and Section 8(d) study-derived data.

EPA's regulations take a somewhat broader approach. The Agency includes within Section 14(b) *any* studies of any effect of a chemical substance or mixture on the environment, on health, or on both, including underlying data, occupational exposure studies, and epidemiological, toxicological, chemical, and ecological studies, wherever and whenever done.[116]

[2] Asserting Confidentiality Claims

TSCA incorporates the substantive standards for business confidentiality developed under Section (b)(4) of the Freedom of Information Act.[117] EPA's general confidentiality regulations are published at 40 CFR Part 2. 40 CFR §§2.201-2.208 of the general regulations apply to TSCA confidentiality claims, with exceptions set forth in a little more 40 CFR §§2.306(c)-(g). TSCA confidentiality determinations are made by the EPA General Counsel.

Any request or demand for information submitted to a regulated entity must contain a statement as to the availability of confidential treatment.[118] If the EPA document contains such a statement, then the submitter must, upon submitting the requested information, clearly state on the cover sheet that confidential information is contained within, and highlight the specific material claimed to be confidential.[119] Failure to do so waives any confidentiality claim.[120]

Once a confidentiality request has been made, EPA must follow a detailed set of procedures designed primarily to (1) ascertain the legitimacy of the request and (2) provide notice and opportunity for comment by other affected persons, including persons requesting disclosure of the information.[121]

A decision either granting or denying a business confidentiality claim

---

116 40 CFR §2.306(a)(3)(i)(A).
117 5 USC §552(b)(4).
118 40 CFR §2.203(a).
119 40 CFR §2.203(b).
120 40 CFR §2.203(c).
121 40 CFR §§2.204-2.207.

is subject to judicial review under Section 20(a) of TSCA.[122]

[3] Substantive Confidentiality Standards

A particular business may receive confidentiality treatment for information that satisfies the following criteria:

(a)   The business has otherwise taken measures to protect the confidentiality of the information;

(b)   The information is not obtainable by nongovernmental entities with the business's consent (other than through judicial discovery);

(c)   No statute specifically requires disclosure; and

(d)   Disclosure of the information is likely to cause substantial harm to the business's competitive position.[123]

[4] Disclosure of Confidential Data

Determination by EPA that confidential status should be accorded to a piece of TSCA information does not ensure that the data will never be disclosed to others. Sections 14(a), 14(c), and 14(e) permit EPA to disclose confidential data under certain circumstances.

[a] Disclosure to Congress

Confidential data may be disclosed to Congress or to the Comptroller General, when requested.[124] EPA affords notice to the affected entity prior to such transfer, and will inform the recipient of the confidentiality claim (if still unresolved) or determination. Because of the way Section 14 is structured, it is not entirely clear that the criminal sanctions for wrongful disclosure by government employees contained in Section 14(d) apply for members of Congress.[125]

---

[122] 15 USC §2619(a). Jurisdiction lies in the U.S. District Courts, and if the plaintiff is the person seeking confidentiality, a preliminary injunction against disclosure must be sought.

[123] 40 CFR §2.208, as modified by 40 CFR §2.306(g).

[124] 15 USC §2613(e); 40 CFR §2.209(b).

[125] This is because Section 14(e) begins with the phrase "notwithstanding any limitation contained in this section or any other provision of law. . . ." EPA's regulations provide that, upon transfer to an agency, a statement must be made that further disclosure will violate 18 USC §1905 and will subject the agency's employees to penalties under Section 14(d). 40 CFR §§2.209(c)(4), 2.306(b). No such statement is required on transfer to Congress or the Comptroller General. Agencies must agree not to disclose the information

[b] Disclosure to Other Federal Agencies

Section 14(a) specifically authorizes EPA to disclose confidential information to federal employees "under any law for the protection of health or the environment,"[126] or "for specific law enforcement purposes."[127] EPA's regulations require a written request containing a statement showing how the foregoing limitations are satisfied, provide for notice to the confidentiality claimant,[128] and require the recipient to agree to nondisclosure or set forth the specific authority and terms of further disclosure.[129]

[c] Disclosure of Information Relevant in a TSCA Administrative Proceeding

In addition to the generally applicable congressional, other federal agency, and court-ordered disclosures, Section 14 authorizes disclosures in a number of additional, specifically delineated, circumstances. The first of these is disclosure "when relevant in any proceeding under this chapter."[130]

Both the statute and EPA's regulations state that in the event disclosure in a "proceeding"[131] is necessary, the Agency will do so in a manner that preserves confidentiality "to the extent practicable."[132] There are somewhat different procedural rules applicable to disclosure to parties and to nonparties in adjudications and to the public in connection with rulemaking proceedings.[133]

Prior to disclosure in rulemaking proceedings, EPA affords affected businesses notice and an opportunity to comment. Following receipt of

---

further, except under specified circumstances. 40 CFR §2.209(c)(5). No such agreement is required of Congress or the Comptroller General.

126 15 USC §2613(a)(1).

127 Notice is not required prior to transfer to the Department of Justice or to another agency to perform a function on EPA's behalf.

128 40 CFR §2.209(c); 40 CFR §2.306(h).

129 A court may, of course, order disclosure of confidential information in connection with a judicial proceeding. EPA's regulations recognize that fact. 40 CFR §2.209(d). If it becomes aware of a pending order of disclosure, an affected business entity may seek to intervene for the purpose of seeking a protective order relative to the material. A form motion and order are included in the Forms section. *See* Forms, 3.

130 15 USC §2613(a)(4).

131 EPA defines the term "proceeding" broadly to encompass any "rulemaking, adjudication or licensing" (other than a confidentiality proceeding). 40 CFR §2.306(a)(6).

132 40 CFR §2.306(i).

133 40 CFR §§2.306(i)(2)-(4) (and material incorporated therein by reference).

comments, the General Counsel must determine (1) that the information is relevant to the subject of the proceeding[134] and (2) that the public interest will be served by making the information available to the public. The business entity is given a minimum of five days' advance notice of disclosure to seek a court order under Section 20 of TSCA.

Public disclosure of information in a TSCA adjudicatory proceeding (such as an administrative enforcement hearing) is subject to the same basic notice and opportunity for comment requirements. However, the presiding officer,[135] rather than the General Counsel, is the decision-maker. The presiding officer must find that (1) for reasons "directly associated with the conduct of the proceeding," disclosure would serve the public interest, and (2) the information is "relevant to a matter in controversy in the proceeding."[136] To the extent such public disclosure results in the information going to a "party of record," the presiding officer may issue a protective order. As in the case of rulemakings, five days' advance notice is required.

A third standard applies to disclosure to a "party of record" where further public disclosure is not sought. The usual notice and opportunity for comment rules apply, and the presiding officer must find that (1) the party has shown that with respect to a "significant matter" in controversy, the party's "ability to participate effectively" will be "significantly impaired" absent disclosure, and (2) any harm to the business entity from disclosure is "outweighed by the benefit to the proceeding and to the public interest" flowing from disclosure.[137] Protective orders may be issued, and the usual five days' notice is required.

EPA's adoption of a less onerous standard for full public disclosure (relevance and public interest) than for disclosure simply to a party in a proceeding (significant impairment and balancing benefit and harm) is difficult to rationalize. The protective order device arguably can ensure that confidentiality is maintained in the disclosure-to-a-party-only situation. The order can prohibit further disclosure, seal agency transcripts or exhibits containing confidential information, and require the recipient to destroy any record of the information after the proceeding is over. Since such devices are not useful where general public

---

[134] EPA does not define "relevant." Presumably the standard applied under The Federal Rules of Evidence applies.

[135] Normally the presiding officer will be an administrative law judge.

[136] 40 CFR §2.306(i)(3).

[137] 40 CFR §2.306(i)(4).

discosure is involved, it would appear that EPA has the burdens reversed.

As a practical matter, however, it is likely that most requests for information disclosure in the context of an adjudication originate with a party, and thus the Section 2.306(i)(3) scheme probably is rarely used. Nevertheless, it remains the case that the burden for disclosure to the world in a rulemaking proceeding is less than that for disclosure to a party in an adjudication—and that makes no sense.

[d]   Disclosure of Information to Contractors

EPA is specifically authorized to disclose confidential business information to TSCA contractors and their employees.[138]

The basic criterion for such transfer is that disclosure is "necessary for satisfactory performance" of the contract (or subcontract).[139] EPA's regulations require advance notice and opportunity for comment by the business entity, require retention of records of transfers, and set forth specific requirements to be inserted in the subject contracts in the case of a confidential data transfer.[140] EPA publishes notice of confidential data transfers to contractors in the Federal Register.

[e]   Disclosure When Necessary to Protect Health or the Environment Against an Unreasonable Risk of Injury

While most of the previous instances of permitted disclosure also appear in one or more of the other EPA-administered statutes, Section 14(a)(3)'s authorization of disclosure of confidential information upon finding such disclosure necessary to protect health or the environment against an unreasonable risk of injury is unique to TSCA.

EPA has administratively promised to execute any such disclosure in a way that preserves as much of the confidentiality as possible.[141] The program office of EPA seeking disclosure must disclose the facts and its intention to the General Counsel, in writing if possible and orally if

---

138 15 USC §2613(a)(2). The qualifying activity is *TSCA work*, not work for EPA. Thus, ITC or other agency contractors could qualify.

139 40 CFR §2.306(j)(1).

140 40 CFR §§2.306(j)(2)-(j)(4) (and material incorporated therein by reference).

141 *See* 40 CFR §2.306(K)(1).

not,[142] and the General Counsel then must determine whether release is necessary and provide at least oral advance notice to the affected business entity, and fifteen days' advance written notice when possible.[143]

It is difficult to postulate many circumstances under which EPA would find cause to use this authority. The provision appears to be most useful to enable EPA to avoid the self-imposed release limitations in connection with rulemakings, such as in imminent hazard actions under Section 7. The provison is an example of the legislative overdrafting that typifies TSCA.

§2.05 Imports and Exports

[1] Imports

Importers are encompassed within the definition of "manufacturer" in TSCA. For many years EPA did little to enforce TSCA against importers. The United States Customs Service, a bureau of the Department of the Treasury, exercises virtually exclusive jurisdiction over goods entering the United States from abroad. TSCA preserves the historical role of the Customs Service by requiring EPA to turn to the Service for enforcement of TSCA against importers.[144]

The Customs Service definition of "importer" is engrafted onto Section 3(7) of TSCA. On August 1, 1983, the Service promulgated regulations under Section 13 of TSCA implementing the importer program.[145] The regulations are codified at 19 CFR §§12.118 to 12.127 and 19 CFR §127.28.

The Service includes the following entities within the term "importer": (a) consignee, (b) importer of record, (c) actual owner of the merchandise if an actual owner's declaration and superseding bond has been filed under the applicable Customs Law, and (d) the transferee of the merchandise if the right to withdraw it in a bonded warehouse has been transferred to that person.[146] The primary remedy available in the event that chemical substances, mixtures, or articles in violation of

---

[142] 40 CFR §2.306(K)(2).

[143] 40 CFR §2.306(K)(3).

[144] 15 USC §2612(a).

[145] 48 Fed. Reg. 34734.

[146] 19 CFR §12.1118.

TSCA are found in the hands of an importer is confiscation and forfeiture.[147]

The Service's regulations require an importer to provide the Customs Service with a written certification that all chemical substances[148] in the shipment comply with "all applicable rules and orders under TSCA," and that the importer is not "offering any chemical substances for entry" in violation of TSCA or any applicable rule or order under it, or that all of the chemical substances in the shipment are not subject to TSCA.[149] EPA does not enforce this policy against by-products, co-products, impurities, or other toxic substances that are not "intentionally present" in the import, and the requirements apply to articles only when EPA promulgates a specific rule for a specific article.[150]

EPA's regulations also require the "principal importer" of a *new* chemical[151] to comply with the PMN requirements, although not necessarily with the degree of specificity required of other regulated entities.[152] Importers use the same PMN form as other entities.[153]

[2] Exports

TSCA's export philosophy as reflected in Section 12 is essentially "to protect the health and environment of persons in the United States and provide information to foreign governments regarding chemical substances and mixtures, so that such foreign governments can protect

---

147 15 USC §2612(a)(2). Procedures are set forth at 19 CFR §12.122 *et seq.*

148 It is important to emphasize that the importing requirements apply to chemical substances "in bulk or as part of a mixture" *and* to *articles* "containing a substance or mixture," 19 CFR §12.118. The term "article" is defined as a "manufactured item which is formed to a specific shape or design during manufacture, has end use functions dependent in whole or in part on its shape or design," and has either no change of chemical composition during its end use or "only those changes in compostion which have no commercial purpose separate from that of the article" and that result from changes in composition at end use (such as paints, adhesives, solvents, fuel additives, etc.) *See* 19 CFR §12.12. *See also* 40 CFR §704.3(b). Fluids and particles are not considered articles. *Id.*

149 19 CFR §12.121.

150 48 Fed. Reg. 34734.

151 EPA expressly refused to impose PMN requirements on importers of "articles" on the theory that to do otherwise would be too onerous. EPA used automobiles as an example of such articles. 48 Fed. Reg. 21726 (5-13-83).

152 40 CFR §720.22(b); 40 CFR §720.57; 48 Fed. Reg. 21730. Importers are, however, held to the same standard as to completeness of the notice for Section 5(e) purposes as are other entities.

153 40 CFR §720.22(b)(1).

their own citizens."[154] This philosophy is not unique to TSCA, and appears to reflect the long-dominant view of the Department of State that direct regulation of exports both interferes with free international trade and amounts to impermissible regulation of the domestic affairs of sovereign nations. These rationales can be stated, somewhat less kindly, as furthering the notion that if other nations wish to poison their populace and/or environment, that is their business and the government of the United States should permit American business to profit thereby.

In all events, Section 12[155] exempts from all of TSCA *except Section 8* chemical substances, mixtures, or articles manufactured, processed, or distributed solely for export and stamped or labeled as such while in commerce within the United States.[156]

Section 12(a)(2), however, allows EPA to require Section 4 testing of chemicals including articles that are otherwise exempt in order to determine whether the chemicals will "present an unreasonable risk of injury to health within the United States or to the environment of the United States."[157] Since the statute is phrased in a way that limits EPA's inquiry to effects within U.S. borders, the exemption is quite narrow, focusing the inquiry on effects that could occur during production and domestic transshipment, and possibly global environmental effects that have a spillover on the United States. The wording of Section 12 prevents EPA from banning export or manufacture for export of a chemical whose use in a foreign country may have posed unreasonable risk to American citizens residing in the foreign country.

The major obligation imposed by Section 12 is a reporting obligation.[158] Exporters of chemical substances and mixtures must notify EPA of their export or intended export of any substances[159] as to which, if any, of the following regulatory requirements are in effect:

(1) Data are required under Section 4 or Section 5(b);
(2) An order has been issued under Section 5;

---

154 H.R. Rep. No. 94-1679, 94th Cong., 2d Sess. p. 88.
155 15 USC §2611.
156 15 USC §2611(a)(1).
157 15 USC §2611(a)(2).
158 Section 12(b), 15 USC §2611(b).
159 Section 12(b) does not mention "articles." EPA's regulations require exporters of "PCB Articles" to file notices, and reserve the right to require notice as to other articles on a case-by-case basis. 40 CFR §707.60(b).

(3) A rule has been proposed or promulgated under Section 5 or Section 6;

(4) An action is pending or relief has been granted under Section 5 or Section 7;[160] and

(5) The substance is a PCB or PCB article.[161]

Notice must be given to EPA[162] postmarked "within seven days of forming the intent to export or on the date of export, whichever is earlier."[163] EPA defines "intent to export" as being evidenced by a contractual obligation or intracompany agreement, that is, an obligation to undertake the act.[164] Sections 707.67 and 707.70 of EPA's regulations set forth the content of export notices and stipulate what EPA will do with them. Confidentiality claims are made in the ordinary Part 2 manner.

§2.06 Specialized Reporting Requirements for Individual Chemicals Other Than PCBs

[1] Asbestos

EPA issued specific, one-time requirements under Section 8(a) for reporting commercial and industrial uses of asbestos.[165] The following entities are required to file an EPA form:

(a) Miners, primary processors, or importers of bulk asbestos as of 1981 must file Form 7710-36 for each site or activity.

(b) Secondary processors (those who process an asbestos mixture) as of 1981 must file Form 7710-37, Parts I and II, for each site activity.

(c) Importers in 1981 of asbestos mixtures or articles containing asbestos components must file Form 7710-37, Parts I and III.

(d) Some secondary processors and importers might be required to

---

160 40 CFR §707.60(a).

161 40 CFR §707.60(c).

162 Document Control Officer, Office of Pesticides and Toxic Substances (TS-793), Environmental Protection Agency, Rm E-447, 401 M Street, S.W., Washington, D.C. 20460. The notice must be clearly marked "Section 12(b) notice."

163 40 CFR §707.65(a).

164 Id.

165 40 CFR §763, Subpart D. 47 Fed. Reg. 37198. Early in 1986, EPA proposed to ban most commercial asbestos uses. 51 Fed. Reg. —.

file a full form 7710-36 if selected under EPA's random sampling methodology.[166]

Secondary processors who simply use an asbestos mixture or repackage it without modifying it and "small manufacturers, processors or importers" are exempt.[167]

EPA has also issued rules relating to asbestos under Section 6. See 40 CFR Part 763 (Regulations for Identifying Asbestos-Containing Materials in Schools (subpart F) and Regulations for Asbestos Abatement Projects (subpart G)).

[2] Polybrominated Biphenyls (PBBs)

EPA imposes on manufacturers and importers, until May 1, 1985 (unless repromulgated), an ongoing obligation to report specific manufacturing and use information with respect to PBBs.[168] Small entities (defined in terms of annual sales and quantity of manufacture[169] are exempt, as are those who manufacture or import solely for research and development, or manufacture or import the substance as a by-product or impurity, or import the substance as part of an article.[170]

[3] Tris (2,3-dibromopropyl) phosphate (DBPP, TBPP, and TRIS-BP)

Essentially the same requirements as those imposed with respect to PBBs are applicable to Tris.[171]

§2.07 Enforcement

[1] Inspection and Forcible Entry

EPA has broad authority to inspect regulated entities and subpoena records. Section II(a) allows "the Administrator, and any duly designated representative of the Administrator" to enter upon and inspect

---

166 40 CFR §763.65(d); 40 CFR §763.71.
167 40 CFR §763.65(f). "Small" entities for Part 763 purposes are those who "employed no more than 10 full-time employees at any one time in 1981."
168 40 CFR §705.195.
169 40 CFR §704.195(c)(2).
170 40 CFR §§704.195(c)(1), 704.5.
171 40 CFR §704.205.

regulated facilities (subject to the Constitutional requirement that a warrant be issued for a forced search).[172] Whether the statute permitted EPA contractors, in addition to employees, to execute forced entries was litigated in *Alcoa v. EPA,* No. C80-1178V (W.D. Wash. 1981), with the district court concluding that the statute embraced contractors.

Since EPA has never built up much of an in-house investigative capability, to the extent it has used its Section 11(a) authority it has employed consulting contractors. The Agency has also relied upon inspections by state environmental personnel at times, particularly with respect to PCB inspections, even though the states have little or no residual authority to regulate manufacturing and use of toxic substances.[173] The principal concern regulated entities have with EPA's use of contractors is that, since EPA contractors often are also employed by private entities, some of which might be in competition with the regulated entity, the opportunity for intentional or inadvertent harmful disclosure of trade secrets is heightened. This concern is muted somewhat by virtue of the fact that Section 14(d) specifically treats EPA contractors as employees for the purpose of imposing criminal liability on them for knowing disclosure of confidential information.[174] State employees, however, do not appear to be covered by Section 14(d).[175]

Sections 11(a)(1) and 11(a)(2) require EPA to be specific in any inspection requests involving financial and other potentially confidential or sensitive data[176] and provide limited constraints on the conduct of compulsory searches.

EPA's subpoena power is broad, but little used by the Agency. Section 11(c) authorizes EPA to issue subpoenas for the purpose of "carry-

---

172 *See* Barlows, Inc. v. Marshall, 436 U.S. 307 (1978), requiring that such warrants be premised upon either a neutral enforcement scheme or an administrative probable cause (a probable cause standard similar to but somewhat less onerous than that required by the Fourth Amendment for criminal investigations).

173 *See* 15 USC §2617; and Warren County, et al. v. State of North Carolina, 528 F. Supp. 276 (E.D. N.C. 1981). *But cf.,* S.E.D., Inc. v. City of Dayton, 519 F. Supp. 979 (S.D. Ohio W.D. 1981).

174 15 USC §2613(d)(2).

175 Such persons are also not subject to the similar criminal sanctions contained in 18 USC §1905.

176 Sales data other than shipment data, pricing data, personnel data, and research data not subject to TSCA requirements.

ing out this chapter."[177] Failure to respond to a TSCA subpoena is substantive violation of the Act.[178]

[2] Enforcement by the Government

[a] Judicial Enforcement

TSCA contains an uncommonly elaborate and specific set of enforcement provisions. Section 15 spells out what acts are "unlawful" under TSCA.[179] A Section 15 action may result in the levy of an administrative civil penalty under Section 16 (see *infra*, Section 5.10[2][b]). "Knowingly or willfully" committing a Section 15 act may in addition subject the violator to criminal penalties of up to $25,000 per day for each day of violation or up to one year's imprisonment, or both.[180]

One of the many curiosities of TSCA is the question of whether the degree of knowledge sufficient for a simple violation of Section 15(2) is any less than that needed to satisfy the "knowingly or willfully" criterion of Section 16(b) of TSCA. All of the other provisions of Section 15 involve simply failure or refusal to comply with some regulatory provision of TSCA. As to those violations, the "knowingly or willfully" requirement of Section 16(b) appears to add at least some degree of scienter not required for a civil violation. Section 15(2), however, makes it a violation to use a chemical where the user "knew or had reason to know" the chemical violated TSCA. Thus, the basic violation involves a degree of scienter already. Since few criminal actions have been brought under this provision of TSCA, the drafting problem has not been examined in the light of its real-world consequences.[181]

---

[177] 15 USC §2610(c).

[178] 15 USC §2614(3).

[179] The following acts are unlawful under 15 USC §2614: (1) failure or refusal to comply with any rule promulgated or order issued under Section 4; (2) failure or refusal to comply with any "requirement prescribed by" Section 5 or Section 6; (3) failure or refusal to comply with any rule promulgated or order issued under Section 5 or Section 6; (4) use for a commercial purpose of a chemical substance or mixture the user "knew or had reason to know was manufactured, processed or distributed in commerce in violation of Section 5 or 6, or an order issued under Section 5 or 6, or an order issued in an action brought under Section 5 or 7"; (5) failure or refusal to establish or maintain records, submit reports, notices, or other information, or permit access to or copying of records "as required" by TSCA or any rule promulgated pursuant to TSCA; and (6) failure or refusal to permit entry or inspection demanded under Section 11.

[180] 15 USC §2615(b).

[181] *See generally*, United States v. Pacific Hide & Fur Depot, Inc., 768 F.2d 1096 (9th Cir. 1985). This was a TSCA criminal case involving disposal of PCBs. Defendants claimed that they did not know that the material they disposed of contained unlawful concentra-

Section 17(a)[182] of TSCA spells out various forms of injunctive relief that are available to EPA. In setting forth different types of relief, the statute apparently attempts to guide the federal district judges in exercising their equitable jurisdiction. It would have been sufficient for Congress simply to invest the judiciary with the power to enjoin acts in violation of TSCA. Instead, Section 17(a)(1)(D) specifically states that the district courts shall "have the jurisdiction" to require any "manufacturer or processor" of a chemical in violation of Section 5 or 6, or a rule issued under either, to give notice of the fact to distributors and "other persons in possession of" the chemical or exposed to it, to give "public notice" of the risk of injury, and "either to replace or repurchase" the chemical. All of those remedies, of course, lie within the courts' inherent powers. The provision *limits* relief, however, to manufacturers and processors, thus targeting those classes of regulated entities where Section 5 or 6 violations are concerned, leaving distributors as the potential beneficiaries of relief.

This is, of course, somewhat odd in view of the fact that Section 15 makes knowing use by a distributor (or anyone else) of a chemical a violation of TSCA. Thus, a culpable distributor is nevertheless insulated from the sort of relief provided by Section 17(a)(1)(D), but would not be so insulated if the statute did not narrowly describe, and thus proscribe, the nature of equitable relief to be afforded.

[b] Seizure

EPA has authority under Section 17(b) of TSCA[183] to seek a judicial order to seize any chemical substance or mixture manufactured, processed, or distributed in violation of TSCA or a TSCA rule or any article containing such a substance or mixture. Any such action is against the substance, "by process of libel, for the seizure and condemnation of such substance." Section 17(b), curiously, also states that the judicial proceedings "shall conform as nearly as possible to proceedings *in rem* in admiralty."

What Congress meant by the phrase "as nearly as possible to pro-

---

tions of PCBs. The government asserted that the defendants deliberately avoided learning the facts. The court held that it produced insufficient evidence to support the claim.

182 15 USC §2616(a). Section 17(a)(2) also establishes straightforward venue rules for injunctive actions. For Section 15 violations, venue lies where the transaction constituting a violation occurred, or where the defendant is found or transacts business. For other actions, venue lies where the defendant is found or transacts business.

183 15 USC §2616(b).

ceedings *in rem* in admiralty" is not explained in the legislative history of TSCA. Just which aspects of the law of admiralty are consistent with TSCA *in rem* actions and which are inconsistent necessarily must await applications of Section 17(b) to specific factual situations, which have not yet occurred.[184]

[c] Administrative Penalties

[i] In General

What little TSCA enforcement EPA has undertaken has primarily been administrative, under Section 16(a),[185] which authorizes EPA to levy monetary penalties for violations of Section 15, of up to $25,000 per violation. Each day of a continuing violation is a separate violation under Section 16(a). EPA is required to afford penalty respondents opportunity for an adjudicatory hearing,[186] and is required to take into account, in determining the amount of the penalty levied, (1) the nature, extent, circumstances, and gravity of the violation, (2) the respondent's ability to pay, (3) the effect of the penalty on the respondent's ability to continue to do business, (4) any history of prior violations, (5) the degree of culpability, and (6) "such other matters as justice may require."[187]

A respondent who fails to request a hearing within fifteen days of receipt of an order assessing a TSCA penalty may not thereafter, either by means of judicial review of the order or as a defense to a collection action initiated by the Attorney General, challenge the validity or amount of the penalty.[188]

To commence a TSCA penalty assessment the EPA office having jurisdiction prepares a penalty assessment order and an administrative complaint, which the Agency[189] serves on the respondent. The proceedings are thereafter governed by EPA's Consolidated Rules of Prac-

---

[184] For a general overview of admiralty law, *see* Gilmore, The Law of Admiralty; Knauth's Benedict on Admiralty (1981); and Canfield, The Law of the Sea (1983).

[185] 15 USC §2615(a).

[186] 15 USC §2615(a)(2).

[187] 15 USC §2615(a)(2)(B).

[188] 15 USC §§2615(a)(2)(A), 2615(a)(3), 2615(a)(4).

[189] Generally, use-related violations are processed by EPA regional offices, and other types of violations are handled by TSCA enforcement personnel at EPA's headquarters, in Washington, D.C.

tice Governing Administrative Assessment of Penalties and Revocation or Suspension of Permits.[190]

TSCA adminstrative hearings are conducted by EPA administrative law judges, and do not differ significantly from adjudicatory hearings conducted by other federal agencies. Since EPA has subpoena power under TSCA, that device is available upon request to the presiding officer, both to EPA and to the respondent.[191]

The most striking feature of EPA's TSCA enforcement is the Agency's rigid penalty policy,[192] to which the initial penalty assessment must adhere, and which the presiding officer must "consider."[193] There are actually two penalty policies, one for general violations and one for PCBs, and the two policies differ in the approach taken to calculating penalties. It is important to understand these policies, since any negotiations aimed at settling a penalty assessment case will involve attempts to adjust the penalty within the framework of the policy.

The penalty policy represents EPA's attempt to normalize application of the Section 16(a)(2)(B) factors. Although couched in complex matrixes and formulas, the penalty policy nevertheless retains sufficient flexibility to permit the assessment of widely differing penalties for similar violations, depending upon the subjective judgment of the EPA official making the initial penalty assessment (which is not the subject of prior negotiation or discussion with the respondent).

[ii] **Mechanics of the Basic TSCA Penalty Policy**

EPA initially calculates a "gravity-based penalty" (GBP), which is adjusted downward or upward by factors, such as culpability, other than the nature, circumstances, extent, and significance to health or the environment of the violation.[194] The GBP is calculated by reference to a matrix that generates penalties from $25,000 down to $200 on the basis of two factors: probability of damage (called "circumstances") and the extent of potential damage.

Thus, for violations of chemical control requirements, for example, the highest penalty would be assessed under circumstances in which (1) the violation actually caused damage or is "likely" to cause damage and (2) the nature of the damage is "serious" in terms of human health or "major in terms of the human environment."

---

190 40 CFR Part 22. 45 Fed. Reg. 24360 (1980).

191 40 CFR §22.32.

192 45 Fed. Reg. 59770.

193 40 CFR §22.27(b).

194 EPA's entire TSCA penalty policy is set forth in Appendix 2I, *infra*.

Calculating penalties for violations of TSCA's data-gathering and hazard assessment requirements is much less straightforward. The policy requires consideration of the impact on the Agency's ability to monitor or evaluate chemicals, the amounts of chemicals involved in the reporting, and the "type of harm" a given requirement is "designed to prevent." The policy as thus articulated invites protracted administrative discovery in data-gathering cases aimed at ascertaining what EPA already knew, or was about to get, from other sources.

The adjustment factors employed by EPA are—

(1) the degree of culpability (which EPA defines to involve (a) knowledge of the regulatory requirement violated and (b) control over the act or condition);

(2) history of prior TSCA violations that resulted in a final order;[195]

(3) whether the government expended public funds for cleanup costs that should be reimbursed and that EPA does not intend to seek to recover in a civil action under Section 7 or 17;

(4) ability to pay (measured against a bottom line benchmark of 4 percent of gross sales as a "not more than" figure at which it is assumed that even a company with negative net income can pay and survive);

(5) attempts to mitigate or clean up;

(6) national defense;

(7) conflicts with other statutory requirements; and

(8) gains to the violator resulting from noncompliance.[196]

Although EPA promised to issue more specific penalty guidance,

---

[195] EPA contends, in 45 Fed. Reg. 59773, that, on its face, Section 16(a)(2)(B) would allow EPA to adjust a penalty upward on evidence of violation of another statute under which the substance is regulated, such as the Occupational Safety and Health (OSH) Act or the Consumer Product Safety Act. This interpretation is clearly debatable, and EPA has not sought to engraft it onto its TSCA penalty policy.

[196] The theory behind this adjustment is to rob the violator of financial gains resulting from its refusal to comply, for example, by depriving it of the value of money not spent on equipment. This concept was derived from EPA's 1978 Civil Penalty Policy, which employed an elaborate computer program and a "penalty panel" in an attempt to place all civil penalties on an economics foundation. The civil penalty policy failed, and was abandoned by EPA in 1981. Thus, though it remains in the TSCA policy, this factor is presently a nonfactor. The same reasoning may apply to EPA's statement in its penalty policy that it will consider credits against penalty amounts for "environmentally beneficial" expenditures not required by any regulatory law. Under this philosophy, EPA allowed some major violaters of the Clean Air and Clean Water Acts to avoid paying multimillion dollar civil penalties, on the basis of very questionable expenditures.

addressing specific types of violation, it has not yet done so, except for PCBs.

[iii] Special Considerations for PCBs

EPA applies special rules for determining the gravity-based penalty for PCB violations. The extent of damage is calculated by determining the total weight of the PCB material[197] and then reducing that number by specified percentages based upon the concentration of PCBs in the material expressed as parts per million (PPM).[198] The resultant net weight of material involved determines whether the "extent" category is major (5000 kg. or more), significant (1000 kg. – 5000 kg.), or minor (less than 100 kg.).[199]

Damage probability is determined by reference to the type of violation involved. Thus, improper disposal and improper use of PCBs are considered high probability of damage violations, and minor record-keeping violations are considered to be of low damage probability. The highest GBP would thus be applied to a disposal violation involving 5000 or more kg. of PCBs.

The extent of harm criteria are empirically derived and relatively free from subjective judgment. The probability criteria, however, are subject to wide case-by-case differences in subjective interpretation. For example, the policy considers "major recordkeeping violations, use and storage facilities," to be "medium range, Level 4" violations, carrying penalties of from $1000 to $10,000, depending upon the quantities of PCBs involved. "Minor" recordkeeping, "Level 6" violations carry penalties of between $200 and $2000. In its descriptions of these two categories, EPA defines them by example. Where there are no records, or "absence of data on PCB transformers," the violation is Level 4. Where there are "small errors in the numbers" of large capacitors or containers, the violation is Level 6. Whether a one-inspection gap in the quarterly inspection records of PCB transformers at an industrial facility is an "absence of records" or a "minor" violation is not clearly answered by EPA's policy. In practice, in the few PCB penalty proceedings it has initiated, the Agency has tended to lead off with penalty assessments skewed toward the high scale and then play with

---

197 Dielectric fluid, consisting of an oil and PCB mixture, is a "PCB" material.

198 The policy specifies certain categories of violations and substances as to which concentration reductions do not apply.

199 Criteria other than weight, such as areas of contamination, number of barrels, number of transformers, etc., may be employed in appropriate circumstances.

the probability factors to arrive at a mutually agreed-to settlement amount.

[3]   Citizen Enforcement

[a]   Citizen Suits

Citizen enforcement under TSCA is permitted by, and delineated by, Section 20 of the statute.[200] In most respects this provision is similar to citizen suit provisions contained in a number of other federal statutes.[201] If the procedural requirements of Section 20 are satisfied, any person may bring an action against any other person (including the United States) to "restrain"[202] any violation of TSCA or violation of a rule issued under Section 4, 5, or 6 or order issued under Section 5. Suit may be brought against EPA to compel the performance of "any act or duty" under TSCA "which is not discretionary."[203]

Primarily because of EPA's slowness in implementing TSCA, and perhaps because of the highly technical nature of the obligations imposed on regulated entities, no citizen suits have been brought against regulated entities under Section 20(a)(1). Such litigation as has occurred has been brought against EPA by public interest groups seeking to compel EPA to act under TSCA. These suits have usually presented an issue as to whether the action sought to be compelled is discretionary or not discretionary.[204] Whether Section 20(a)(2) is the exclusive remedy provided against EPA is, however, unclear. On its face, Section 17(a)(1)(C)[205] would appear to authorize an action against EPA to compel it to take "action required by" TSCA.

The statute requires that the plaintiff provide sixty days' advance notice of any proposed suit to the intended defendant and to EPA as

---

[200] 15 USC §2619.

[201] *See generally* Stever, *Litigating Against the Government for Fun and Profit,* 1 Pace Environmental Law Review 12 for a discussion of such provisions.

[202] No monetary penalties may be sought, but Section 20(c)(2) authorizes the award of "reasonable" attorneys' and expert witnesses' fees, as well as costs.

[203] 15 USC §2619(a)(2).

[204] *See, e.g.,* NRDC v. Costle, 14 ERC 1858 (S.D.N.Y. 1980), holding that EPA has a nondiscretionary duty to provide detailed, written reasons for a decision not to initiate testing in response to ITC recommendations within twelve months. In an unreported order, U.S. District Judge Gerhard Gesell ruled in NRDC v. Ruckelshaus (D.D.C. 1983) that EPA's obligation to act under Section 4(f) of TSCA could be the subject of a Section 20(a)(2) lawsuit.

[205] 15 USC §2616(a)(1)(C).

a jurisdictional prerequisite to suit[206] and ten days' advance notice prior to suit seeking relief against an imminent hazard.

EPA's procedural regulations for citizen suits[207] specify how notices are to be served and what they must contain. Since Section 20(b) expressly provides for EPA's notice rules, they must be strictly followed.

Citizen actions are barred where (1) EPA is "diligently prosecuting a proceeding" for issuance of a Section 16(a)(2) order or (2) where the "Attorney General[208] has commenced and is diligently prosecuting" a civil action to require compliance.[209] In such a case, however, the citizen has a right to intervene in "such proceeding."[210] The right to intervene in an EPA Section 16 penalty proceeding is unique among citizen suit provisions. It is not clear whether intervening citizens who are unhappy with EPA proposals to settle a penalty case or EPA assessment following a hearing have a right to seek judicial review. Section 19,[211] the general judicial review section, does not provide for review of Section 16 penalty assessments. Section 16(a)(3) provides for such review, but limits access to the courts to a person who "in accordance with [Section 16(a)(2)(A)]" requested a hearing and who is "aggrieved" by a penalty assessment, a limitation that seems to make review available only to the regulated entity against whom the penalty is assessed. Thus, TSCA appears to bar a citizen suit in which injunctive relief is being sought where EPA is redressing the violation administratively. As a consolation prize, the citizen may intervene in EPA's proceeding, but without much leverage to affect the outcome, being without an apparent ability to challenge the outcome.[212]

The court may award costs and "reasonable" fees for attorneys and expert witnesses upon finding that such an award would be "appropri-

---

206 15 USC §2619(b).

207 40 CFR §§702.60-702.62.

208 15 USC §2619(b)(1)(B). The specific reference to the "Attorney General" is curious, since it would appear to exempt from the ban litigation undertaken directly by EPA under Section 7 of TSCA, which gives EPA a limited right to represent itself in court in imminent hazard cases. See 15 USC §2606(e). The omission of the phrase "or the administrator" following "Attorney General" was no doubt the product of legislative oversight.

209 Proof of lack of diligence is quite difficult, and an attempt to avoid a bar on that ground will probably fail in all but the most egregious circumstances.

210 15 USC §2619(b)(1)(B).

211 15 USC §2618.

212 EPA may intervene as a matter of right in any citizen suit. 15 USC §2619(c).

ate."[213] Although similar language in the Clean Air Act has been held by the Supreme Court to require the fee claimant to prevail on at least one major issue,[214] an opinion of the D.C. Circuit, in *Environmental Defense Fund v. EPA,* resting on specific TSCA legislative history, states that under TSCA even a nonprevailing plaintiff might be awarded fees.[215]

[b]   Citizen Petitions

Similar in this respect to the FFDCA, Section 21 of TSCA[216] permits members of the public to petition EPA to initiate action under Section 4, 5(e), 6, or 8. Once such a petition is filed, EPA is required to act on it within ninety days. If EPA fails to act within ninety days or denies the petition, the petitioner has a right to a *de novo* hearing in a U.S. district court in an action commenced within sixty days to compel EPA to take the action requested. In such an action the petitioner must demonstrate "by a preponderance of the evidence" that—

(1)   with respect to a petition for action under Section 4 or 5(e)—
   (a)   the information available to EPA is insufficient to permit a reasoned evaluation of the subject chemical's effects, and
   (b)   in the absence of such information, the chemical "may present an unreasonable risk" or "will be produced in substantial quantities and it enters or may reasonably be anticipated to enter the environment in substantial quantities or there is or may be significant or substantial human exposure to it"; or

(2)   with respect to a petition for action under Section 6 or 8 there is a "reasonable basis to conclude" that the action requested is "necessary to protect health or the environment against an unreasonable risk of injury."[217]

The statute, finally, allows EPA to persuade the judge that the risks

---

[213] Identical language appears in Section 19(d), 15 USC §2618(d), providing similar relief for persons seeking judicial review of EPA rules and orders.

[214] Sierra Club v. Gorsuch, 463 U.S. 680 (1983).

[215] 672 F.2d 42 (D.C. Cir. 1982). The *Environmental Defense Fund* petitioner prevailed on nearly all of the issues. The court awarded fees for time spent on issues on which *Environmental Defense Fund* did not prevail, however. The government did not seek Supreme Court review of this case.

[216] 15 USC §2620.

[217] 15 USC §2620(b)(4)(B)(i).

posed by the subject chemical are of a lesser magnitude than those posed by other chemicals that are currently consuming all of EPA's resources, and requires the judge to postpone any order issued in the case in accordance with such priorities.[218] Presumably the judge is free to accept or reject EPA's assertions as to the relative risks.

§2.08 Miscellaneous Provisions

[1] Employee Protection

[a] Whistle Blower Protection

TSCA contains an "employee protection" provision, Section 23,[219] similar to that contained in a number of other federal environmental statutes. This provision is intended to protect workers who notify federal authorities of alleged violations of TSCA from retaliatory firing or other retaliatory action by their employers. The one reported decision applying Section 23(b) is *School District of the City of Allentown v. Marshall, Secretary of Labor.*[220]

The subject was a schoolteacher and union activist who had publicly criticized the school district for its failure to remove asbestos materials from the district's school buildings. The district barred him from access to buildings other than the one in which he worked and took other allegedly retaliatory action against him. At the time of the alleged retaliatory acts by the school district, EPA had not taken any action under TSCA with respect to asbestos.[221]

The employee, after a protracted period of confusion caused by the government's failure to adopt procedural rules under the section that carried the employees beyond the thirty-day limitation period within which complaints must be filed, lodged a complaint under Section 23 with the Secretary of Labor. The court of appeals held the complaint to have been time barred. It concluded that, although Section 23(b)(1)'s

---

218 15 USC §2620(b)(4)(B)(ii).

219 15 USC §2622.

220 657 F.2d 16 (3d Cir. 1981). Section 23(c) provides that review of determinations of the Secretary shall be on the record by the court of appeals for the circuit where the violation occurred.

221 On September 1, 1982, EPA promulgated, pursuant to Section 6, 40 CFR 763, Subpart F, which imposes inspection, sampling, warning and notice, and recordkeeping requirements on local school districts relative to friable asbestos. In 1984, EPA proposed rules requiring removal of asbestos materials from schools.

thirty-day limitation period is not jurisdictional, the complainant had not provided sufficient equitable reasons to support a waiver of the requirement.

The school district raised two other issues, which the Secretary of Labor decided in the complainant's favor, but which were not reached by the Third Circuit on appeal. First, the school district argued that it was not an "employer" within the meaning of that term intended under TSCA. The Secretary's rejection of this position appears to be correct. The argument must rest on the premise that "employer" in Section 23 is synonymous with, or limited by, "manufacturer," "processor," or "distributor," which are defined in Section 3. TSCA, in several of its provisions, also regulates "use"[222] and regulates "persons" other than manufacturers, processors, and distributors.[223] This argument no doubt lost any viability it might have had with publication of Subpart F of 40 CFR Part 463, regulating asbestos in schools.

The other issue raised, but not resolved by the court, in the *Allentown* case was the school district's claim that the employee's actions were not protected under Section 23(a). In order to secure the protection of the statute, the employee must be able to show that a discharge, or discrimination with respect to compensation, terms, conditions, or privileges of employment, resulted from actions undertaken by the employee or persons representing him/her (1) in initiating or intending to initiate or cause the initiation of a proceeding under TSCA or (2) testifying in such a proceeding or where the employee has "assisted or participated, or is about to participate in any manner in such a proceeding or in any other action to carry out the purpose of" TSCA.[224] Since at the time of the alleged retaliatory activity there were no TSCA regulations governing asbestos, the school district argued, the employee simply didn't fall within any of the three protected categories.[225] The Secretary of Labor rejected this argument, reasoning that EPA's programmatic consideration of possible action under TSCA had predated the alleged retaliatory action, and since action with respect to asbestos in school buildings was within EPA's TSCA authority, the employee's actions were arguably carrying out the purpose of TSCA.

---

[222] *E.g.*, Section 6, 15 USC §2605; Section 15(2), 15 USC §2614(2).

[223] *E.g.*, Section 8(d), 15 USC §2607(d).

[224] 15 USC §2622(a)(3).

[225] EPA first adopted asbestos regulations, applicable to commercial and industrial users, on June 30, 1982. 40 CFR Part 463, Subpart D (47 Fed. Reg. 33198).

The trouble with the Secretary's reasoning is that EPA might never have acted to regulate asbestos. Taken to its logical extreme, the action taken by Secretary Marshall in *Allentown* would serve to insulate an insubordinate employee whose actions relate to any chemical on any TSCA study list, even if the chemical is not ever likely to be found by EPA to require regulation. Section 23's emphasis on proceedings seems clearly to bespeak an intent on the part of Congress to encourage free participation in EPA's activities. The *Allentown* administrative decision seems to take Section 23 a step beyond.

[b] Layoffs and Plant Closings

Section 24 of TSCA[226] requires EPA to "evaluate on a continuing basis" potential effects on employment of actions taken under Sections 4, 5, and 6, and requires EPA to investigate employee or union allegations of layoffs, discharges or threats thereof, or other adverse employment consequences allegedly resulting from such actions. The statute does not require EPA to do anything with any such investigative findings, other than perhaps to publish them in the Federal Register.[227]

The obligation could, however, be viewed by the regulatory agency as an expression of Congress's intention that EPA consider employment effects as a factor in taking Section 4, 5, or 6 actions, although EPA has apparently not articulated such a position to date.

[2] Polychlorinated Biphenyls (PCBs)

[a] Background

Section 6(e) of TSCA[228] contains an express ban on the manufacture, processing, distribution, and use of polychlorinated biphenyls (PCBs) or mixtures containing PCBs or PCB articles. EPA has been slow to implement Congress's ban, which culminated nearly a decade of public pressure, predicated on the allegedly carcinogenic potential of PCBs, and their apparent ubiquity in the environment.[229] Eventually, all of EPA's PCB regulations will be codified in the various subparts of 40 CFR Part

---

226 15 USC §2623.
227 15 USC §2623(b)(3).
228 15 USC §2605(e).
229 *See, e.g.*, Cong. Record, Mar. 26, 1976, Senate pp. 4397 *et seq.* (Senate Debate of S.3149).

761. EPA began issuing PCB regulations in 1978[230] and continues to issue the regulations piecemeal.[231] The statute contemplates eventual removal of PCBs from the environment, although limited exemptions from the prohibitions are permitted by Sections 6(e)(3)(B)[232] and 6(e)(2).[233]

PCBs were used widely from the 1950s until the late 1970s for a variety of purposes where heat-resistant lubrication or electrical conductive fluids were needed. Primarily as a result of the disposal of PCB-containing oils and other materials, large amounts of PCBs have accumulated in the environment throughout the industrialized areas of the planet.

PCBs are a group of related chlorinated hydrocarbon chemicals useful in several industrial processes and toxic to a wide variety of organisms, including humans. PCBs fall into two chemical categories: PCBs with a low chlorine content (less chlorinated PCBs) and PCBs with a high chlorine content (more chlorinated PCBs). The more chlorinated PCBs have been manufactured and used since 1929. For decades, they served in a variety of industrial uses, such as ink solvents, plasticizers, adhesives, and textile coatings, but their principal use was in electrical

---

[230] 43 Fed. Reg. 715 (2-17-78).

[231] *See* 43 Fed. Reg. 33918 (8-2-78); 44 Fed. Reg. 31514 (5-31-79) (remanded in part). *See* Environmental Defense Fund v. EPA, No. 79-1580, 636 F.2d 1267 (D.C. Cir. 1980); 44 Fed. Reg. 54296 (9-19-79); 45 Fed. Reg. 20473 (3-28-80); 47 Fed. Reg. 19526 (5-6-82); 45 Fed. Reg. 20473 (3-28-80); 47 Fed. Reg. 37342 (8-25-82); 47 Fed. Reg. 55436 (12-3-82); 48 Fed. Reg. 124 (1-3-83); 48 Fed. Reg. 4497 (2-1-83); 48 Fed. Reg. 5729 (2-8-83); 48 Fed. Reg. 13181 (3-30-83); 48 Fed. Reg. 15125 (4-7-83).

The Agency has also issued various policy statements and "guidance" proclamations dealing with its postjudgment rulemaking following *Environmental Defense Fund. See* 46 Fed. Reg. 16090 (5-11-81) (Rule-Related Court Order and Enforcement Notice on Interim Measures for Inspecting Equipment Containing Polychlorinated Diphenyls); 46 Fed. Reg. 27615 (5-20-81) (Rule-Related Court Order and Notice of PCBs in Concentration Below Fifty Parts Per Million); 46 Fed. Reg. 27614 (5-20-81) (Clarifications on PCB Transformer Interim Self-Inspection Measures); 48 Fed. Reg. 7172 (2-18-83) (Policy on PCB Use in Electrical Equipment, TSCA Compliance Program Policy No. 6-PCB-1 (unpublished—issued 1982)).

[232] Section 6(e)(3)(B) exemptions are generally called manufacturing, processing, and distribution exemptions. The entity seeking an exemption (limited to one year at a time) must petition EPA and satisfy two conditions: (1) The exemption, if granted, will not present an unreasonable risk of injury to health or the environment; and (2) good faith efforts have been made to find a PCB substitute that does not present an unreasonable risk of injury.

[233] Section 6(e)(2) allows EPA to exempt "totally enclosed uses" of PCBs, and to allow continuation of non–totally enclosed uses if they will not present an unreasonable risk of injury.

equipment. PCBs are nonflammable liquids that are highly resistant to electrical current. Therefore, they were widely used to fill electrical devices, such as capacitors and transformers, aiding in the storage of electrical charge without creating the fire hazard that would occur if a flammable filler were used.

Awareness of the danger from PCBs to the environment and to human health was slow to develop. Although large quantities of PCBs were manufactured and leaked into the environment, the PCBs detected in the environment were long mistaken for pesticide residues, which they resemble chemically. It was not until the mid-1960s that the presence of PCBs in the environment and the harm they inflict were recognized and distinguished from the pesticide problem. It became apparent from scientific studies that the more chlorinated PCBs built up to dangerous levels in the sediments of waterways, in the water, in fish, and ultimately in humans, creating a serious risk of death for aquatic organisms and disease (particularly cancer) in humans.

In 1971, in response to public and government pressure, PCB manufacturers and users took initial steps to reduce the PCB danger. Manufacture was shifted from the more chlorinated PCBs to the less chlorinated PCBs, because it was hoped that less chlorinated PCBs were less dangerous. PCB use was limited to closed electrical equipment, where the need was greatest and the leakage was least. Some effort was made to control discharge of PCBs into waterways.

However, in 1972, seventy-four manufacturers were curtailing their efforts to find acceptable substitutes for PCBs, and manufacture of less chlorinated PCBs continued at high volumes, for example, 40 million pounds in 1974.[234]

Developments in the early and mid-1970s heightened the public concern about PCBs and resulted in new regulatory efforts in late 1975 and early 1976. Monitoring of residues in fish revealed that industrial discharges of PCBs were rendering fish in many waterways unhealthy for human consumption. This monitoring culminated in a state proceeding, *General Electric Co.*,[235] in which New York's Department of Environmental Conservation found that discharges of PCBs by General Electric, a major manufacturer of electrical equipment containing PCBs, had rendered most upper Hudson River fish dangerous to eat.

---

[234] 42 Fed. Reg. 6533 (1977).
[235] See 6 Envir. L. Rep. (Env. L. Inst.) 30007 (1976).

Similar situations threatened the fishing industry in the Great Lakes and elsewhere.

While the *General Electric* case was pending, a national conference on PCB hazards was held in November 1975. The conference resulted in greater awareness of the nationwide threat posed by PCBs and contributed to the renewed EPA effort to regulate and control PCB discharges then under existing statutory authority under the Clean Water Act.

Following the 1975 renewal of EPA's regulatory effort, further information accumulated with respect to the health hazards posed by PCBs. Moreover, substitutes for PCBs were developed in this country and in Japan that would serve adequately in electrical equipment without creating a fire hazard. Congress became impatient and wrote Section 6(e) in 1976.

Section 6(e) looks toward elimination of the manufacturing and use of PCBs and to regulation of the disposal of PCB materials. The ubiquity of PCB articles in commerce and in the environment, particularly their use in electrical transformers and capacitors, led EPA initially to exempt from the Section 6(e) ban substances containing less than 50 ppm PCBs, to define virtually all electrical transformers and capacitors as "totally enclosed" uses of PCBs, which it permitted to continue,[236] and to authorize a number of non–totally enclosed uses as not presenting an unreasonable risk. The 50-ppm and totally enclosed use exemptions were set aside in *Environmental Defense Fund v. EPA*,[237] primarily for lack of support in the rulemaking record.

Following remand of the PCB regulations, EPA, the environmental group petitioners, and industry intervenors reached an agreement that resulted in an order of the D.C. Circuit keeping the 1979 regulations intact and establishing a schedule for interim and permanent curative rulemaking. Pursuant to that agreement, EPA issued interim electrical equipment inspection requirements effective May 11, 1983,[238] which it clarified on May 20, 1981.[239] EPA published final regulations on the

---

[236] 44 Fed. Reg. 31444 (1979) (50 PPM); and 44 Fed. Reg. 31514 (1979) (totally enclosed).

[237] 636 F.2d 1267 (D.C. Cir. 1980).

[238] 46 Fed. Reg. 16090.

[239] 46 Fed. Reg. 27614.

use of PCBs in electrical equipment on August 25, 1982,[240] and published a "policy statement" interpreting the regulations as they apply to exposure to food or animal feed on February 18, 1983.[241] In general, the regulations (which EPA calls its Electrical Equipment Rule) permit the use of small PCB capacitors,[242] permit large PCB capacitors to be used until 1988, or until the end of their useful lives under certain conditions, and permit the use of PCB transformers or PCB-contaminated transformers (those once containing PCB fluid, but not currently containing it) under specified conditions.[243]

A second outgrowth of the *Environmental Defense Fund* remand was a Closed and Controlled Waste Manufacturing Processes Rule, [244] issued on October 21, 1982. This regulation replaces one aspect of EPA's broad exemption for all PCB uses of less than 50 ppm PCB concentration, which the court struck down in *Environmental Defense Fund,* and permits the manufacture, processing, and distribution in commerce of PCBs in closed manufacturing processes or controlled waste manufacturing processes (that is, those in which PCBs are in the waste stream, which is controlled) where (1) the PCBs are released only in concentration below the practical limits of quantification, in waste emissions or products, and (2) where the wastes are controlled or disposed of in accordance with methods specified in the rule. Such entities need not apply for an exemption under EPA's Manufacturing Exemp-

---

240 47 Fed. Reg. 37342.

241 48 Fed. Reg. 7172.

242 40 CFR §761.30(i).

243 40 CFR §761.30(a) *et seq.* Among other things, the rule authorizes for the remainder of their useful lives: (1) PCB Transformers not posing an exposure risk to food or feed; (2) large PCB capacitors located in restricted-access electrical substations; (3) large PCB capacitors located in contained and restricted-access indoor installations; and (4) all PCB-containing, mineral oil-filled electrical equipment. The use of PCB transformers that pose an exposure risk to food or feed is prohibited after October 1, 1985. The use of large PCB capacitors that are not located in restricted-access areas is prohibited after October 1, 1988. The rule requires weekly, quarterly, or annual inspection of authorized electrical equipment (other than mineral oil equipment) for leaks of dielectric fluid, depending on the location of the equipment and other factors. On March 23, 1984, EPA issued an advanced notice of proposed rulemaking (49 Fed. Reg. 11070), in which it sought comments on the question of whether it should amend the PCB transformer rules to cut back continued use of such devices in light of building contamination by PCBs resulting from electrical fires in Binghamton, New York, San Francisco, California, and Chicago, Illinois, over the period 1981–1983.

244 47 Fed. Reg. 46980.

tion Rules.[245] While EPA abandoned the "closed and controlled" definition in favor of a more general term, "excluded manufacturing pro-

---

[245] EPA's Interim Procedural Rules for PCB Manufacturing Exemptions, 40 CFR §750.10 *et seq.*, were published on November 1, 1978 (43 FR 50905). These rules describe the required content of manufacturing exemption petitions and the procedures EPA will follow in rulemaking on these petitions.

On January 2, 1979 (44 FR 108), EPA announced that petitioners who had previously filed manufacturing exemption petitions could continue the manufacturing or importation activity for which they sought exemption until EPA acted on their petitions.

EPA's Interim Procedural Rules for PCB Processing and Distribution in Commerce Exemptions, 40 CFR §750.30 *et. seq.*, were published May 31, 1979 (44 FR 31558). These rules describe the required content of processing and distribution in commerce exemption petitions and the procedure EPA will follow in rulemaking on these petitions. EPA proposed regulations for manufacturing exemptions, which addressed the exemption petitions received at that time, on May 31, 1979 (44 FR 41564).

On March 5, 1980 (45 FR 14247), EPA clarified its previously announced policy for acceptance of late PCB exemption petitions published in the Federal Register of January 2, 1979 (44 FR 108) and May 31, 1979 (44 FR 31514). In that notice, EPA stated that it would require filers of late exemption petitions to show "good cause" why the petition was being submitted after the filing deadlines of December 1, 1978 (for manufacturing exemptions) or July 1979 (for processing and distribution in commerce exemptions). If a petitioner shows "good cause," EPA permits it to continue the activities for which it seeks exemption until EPA acts on the exemption petition, provided the activities were under way before January 1, 1979 (for manufacturing) or July 1, 1979 (for processing and distribution in commerce.)

In the Federal Register of May 1, 1980 (45 FR 29115), EPA reiterated the policy stated in 40 CFR §761.20(b) by closing the border to the export and import of PCBs for disposal after that date. In addition, EPA affirmed that exports of PCBs for use would be permitted only if EPA granted an exemption to do so pursuant to Section 6(e)(3)(B) of TSCA. EPA set forth criteria it would consider in reviewing a petition for exemption to export PCBs. A petitioner must show that the nation to which export is destined has proper PCB disposal facilities and that the PCBs will be used for a use that is authorized in the United States. EPA also explained that, in the context of exports, the requirement to show good faith efforts to find a substitute puts the burden on the petitioner to show that there is no substitute for the PCBs, produced either by the petitioner or a competitor, and to prove that it has expended substantial amounts of time and money searching for a substitute.

As EPA acted to comply with the *Environmental Defense Fund* rulemaking, it became necessary to resolve a number of issues involving the outstanding exemption petitions. In June 1982, EPA sent a letter to each of approximately 400 petitioners who had previously requested an exemption to manufacture, process, or distribute in commerce PCBs. Since the information in many of the petitions was old, EPA asked these petitioners to renew their petitions, if necessary, by submitting updated information. EPA received and accepted 172 exemption petitions (including 164 reviewed and 8 newly filed petitions), which EPA evaluated according to the requirements of TSCA and the Interim Procedural Rules for PCB Exemptions. The remainder of the petitions were not renewed or were dismissed by EPA because the activities for which exemption was requested did not require an exemption. EPA proposed on November 1, 1983 (48 Fed. Reg. 50486) to grant 49 of these petitions and deny 73; it deferred 50, which involved

cess," in a later modification of the regulations,[246] looking at the closed and controlled process separately is helpful in developing an understanding of the PCB problem.

The Closed and Controlled Waste Manufacturing Process Rule provides an exclusion from the general ban on the manufacture, processing, and distribution in commerce of PCBs for closed and controlled waste manufacturing processes. Closed manufacturing processes are processes that generate PCBs but release PCBs in concentrations below the practical limits of quantification for PCBs in specific media. These limits are 10 micrograms per cubic meter (roughly 0.01 ppm) per resolvable gas chromatographic peak in air emissions, 100 micrograms per liter (roughly 0.1 ppm) per resolvable gas chromatographic peak in water effluent, and 2 micrograms per gram (2 ppm) per resolvable gas chromatographic peak in products and water streams. Controlled waste manufacturing processes are processes that are defined using the above limits, but the waste stream may contain greater than 2 ppm PCBs as long as these wastes are disposed of properly. According to the rule, wastes with a concentration of 50 ppm or greater PCBs must be disposed of in accordance with the PCB disposal regulations in 40 CFR 761.60. Wastes with a PCB concentration of less than 50 ppm may be disposed of either according to 40 CFR Part 761 or at facilities approved under the provisions of Section 3005(c) of the Resource Conservation and Recovery Act (RCRA).[246.1]

In the rule, concentration limits are established for products, air emissions, water effluents, and wastes. The limits set for products, emissions and effluents is the "limit of quantification" (LOQ). The LOQ appears to be higher than the limit of detection, but significantly less than the 50 ppm limit established by the initial, remanded, rule. Regulated entities are permitted to conduct theoretical estimates in lieu of actual monitoring for the purpose of determining eligibility for exemption under the rule.

The third prong of the post–*Environmental Defense Fund* rulemaking involved PCBs generated or released in less than 50 ppm concentrations from other than closed or controlled waste processes. Such

---

inadvertent contamination, until such time as the Agency took final action on that aspect of the 50 ppm definition struck down in *Environmental Defense Fund* but kept alive by the negotiated stay of the court's mandate.

246 *See* 48 Fed. Reg. 55080.

246.1 43 USC §6925(c).

releases are considered either "uncontrolled PCBs" or "inadvertently generated PCBs." The agreed *Environmental Defense Fund* post-remand court order allowed EPA's original 50 ppm broad exemption to remain in effect until EPA took further action to modify the rule.[247]

Following protracted negotiations, EPA issued rules covering inadvertently generated PCBs and "recycled PCBs"[248] in 1984.[249] EPA applies the same basic approach used for the closed and controlled category in regulating products, effluents, emissions, and wastes. However, the Agency's approach to assessing the risks posed by this class of PCBs and establishing exemption criteria were imaginative. Although rejecting the alternative of prohibiting all such PCBs, subject to individual Section 6(e)(3)(B) or Section 6(e)(2)(B) exemptions, on the ground that either approach is too resource intensive to be practical, the Agency nevertheless felt that it should apply the "unreasonable risk of injury" test contained in those sections to the class of inadvertently manufactured and recycled PCBs. EPA had two methodological choices. It could undertake a chemical-by-chemical risk analysis and set concentration levels for each inadvertent or recycled PCB-producing process, or it could attempt to deal with the risk assessment generically. It chose to do the latter.[250] It proceeded with a regulatory strategy based on a small number of hypothetical worst-case exposure scenarios that were developed to represent a whole group or class of similar exposure situations. These scenarios, which assess the exposure to a group of exposure situations, rather than individual situations, are referred to as generic exposure assessments. The risks of cancer and reproductive/developmental effects were estimated from these generic exposure assessments. These estimates of risk were then used in developing generic exclusions based on a determination that particular classes of processes generating PCBs at low levels would not present unreasonable risks.

This creative approach is arguably justified by virtue of the fact that Congress seems not to have dealt with inadvertently generated PCBs in Section 6(e), and accordingly some administrative leeway should be permitted.

---

[247] Order dated April 13, 1981. *See* 46 Fed. Reg. 27615 (5-20-81).

[248] Recycled PCBs occur in industries, such as the paper manufacturing industry, where recycled materials contain traces of PCBs left over from earlier manufacturing processes, when PCBs were used in inks or in carbonless copy paper.

[249] *See* 48 Fed. Reg. 55076 (Proposal); and 49 Fed. Reg. 28172 (Final Rule).

[250] 48 Fed. Reg. 55079.

The criteria for exemption developed under this methodology are as follows:

(1) PCB concentrations in the components of certain consumer products with a high potential for exposure are limited to less than 5 ppm. These consumer products are deodorant bars and soaps, and plastic building materials and products.

(2) PCB concentrations present in all products not named in item (1) above are limited to an annual average of 25 ppm with a 50 ppm maximum.

(3) PCB concentrations at the point where such PCBs are manufactured or processed and are vented to the ambient air are limited to less than 10 ppm.

(4) PCB concentrations discharged from manufacturing or processing sites to water are limited to less than 0.1 ppm for any resolvable gas chromatographic peak.

(5) All process wastes containing PCBs at 50 ppm or greater are to be disposed of in accordance with the PCB disposal requirements of 40 CFR 761.60.

(6) Quantifation of PCBs to meet the criteria in items (1) through (5) is to be calculated after discounting the concentration of monochlorinated biphenyls by a factor of 50 and dichlorinated biphenyls by a factor of 5.

(7) The certification, reporting, and record maintenance requirements are met.

These criteria are similar to criteria suggested jointly by the industry and environmental group litigants in a "consensus proposal."[251] For recycled PCBs, EPA does not permit the use of discounting factors for MCBs and DCBs.[252] Finally, EPA allows old PCB hydraulic and heat transfer fluid systems that contain less than 50 ppm PCBs to be used for the remainder of their useful lives.[253]

---

[251] 48 Fed. Reg. 55079.

[252] Another example of regulatory "flexibility" is EPA's allowance of discounting for PCBs that are monoclorobiphenyls or dichlorobiphenyls. MCBs are discounted by a factor of 50, and DCBs by a factor of 5. For example, soap with a PCB content of 510 ppm will be considered to contain only 10 ppm if the PCBs are all of the single chlorine atom (MCB) type. EPA apparently accepted arguments by MCB manufacturers that less chlorinated types pose a lower health risk. *See* 42 Fed. Reg. 55086.

[253] 49 Fed. Reg. 28173.

[b] PCB Regulatory Requirements

Those PCB uses allowed to continue are all regulated under 40 CFR Part 761. The requirements imposed all relate to determining and reporting information sufficient to permit a determination that the PCBs are totally enclosed, not leaking, or in concentrations that bring them within one of the non–totally enclosed exemptions. Thus, the rules impose—

(1) regular inspection and inspection-recordkeeping requirements upon entities possessing PCBs[254] (in most cases quarterly visual inspections are required);

(2) marking requirements (PCB caution labels) on all PCB articles and storage areas;[255]

(3) detailed disposal and storage requirements for PCBs no longer in service;[256]

(4) sampling, monitoring, and analytical requirements for inadvertently generated or recycled PCBs and for closed and controlled waste manufacturing processes ("excluded PCBs");[257] and

(5) reporting requirements for excluded manufacturing processes[258] (inadvertently generated PCBs in domestic or imported products).

[c] Other Statutory Regulation of PCBs

[i] Food Additives and Pesticides

FIFRA[259] and FFDCA[260] both affect chemicals that may contain inadvertently generated PCBs. If the manufacture, processing, distri-

---

[254] 40 CFR §761.30(d) and §761.30(e). *See* 40 CFR §761.30(a) (transformers other than railroad transformers); 40 CFR §761.30(b) (railroad transformers); 40 CFR §761.30(d) (heat transfer systems); 40 CFR §761.30(e) (hydraulic systems); 40 CFR §761.30(h) (electromagnets, switches, and voltage regulators); 40 CFR §761.30(l) (capacitors).

[255] 40 CFR §761.40.

[256] 40 CFR §761.60, 761.65, 761.70, 761.75, 761.79 (storage and disposal practices); 40 CFR §761.180 (recordkeeping and monitoring).

[257] 40 CFR §§761.185 and 761.193.

[258] 40 CFR §761.187. Regulated entities must report (1) the total quantity leaving the manufacturing site where such quantity exceeds 0.0025 percent of the site's rated capacity as of the date of the regulation or, for importers, such quantity exceeds 0.0025 percent of the average total quantity of such product containing PCBs for the years 1978-1982, and (2) the quantity of air and water releases over 10 pounds, in any calendar year.

[259] 7 USC §136 *et seq. See* Chapter 3.

[260] 21 USC §321 *et seq. See* Chapter 8.

bution in commerce, or use of a substance is regulated under either FIFRA or FFDCA, the substance is not subject to regulation under TSCA insofar as the substance is manufactured, processed, or distributed in commerce for use as a pesticide, food, food additive, drug, cosmetic, or device. If a substance has multiple uses, only some of which are regulated under FIFRA or FFDCA, the manufacture, processing, distribution in commerce, and use of the substance for the remaining uses come within the jurisdiction of TSCA.

EPA takes the position that raw materials, intermediates, and inert ingredients produced or used in the manufacture of pesticides are substances or mixtures that may be regulated under TSCA.[261] Furthermore, while a chemical manufactured for use as a pesticide is regulated under FIFRA, a chemical that is manufactured for undetermined purposes is regulated under TSCA. This has particular significance to 40 CFR §761.1(f). That section refers to PCBs generated as unintentional impurities in excluded manufacturing processes, as defined in Section 761.3(kk), at the time they are first manufactured until they are identified as part of a pesticide product.

Since the FDA considers intermediates or catalysts to be components of a food, food additive, drug, cosmetic, or device regulated under FFDCA, chemicals used as intermediates or catalysts for these purposes are not regulated by EPA under TSCA. As soon as the FDA regulates a product, its manufacture, processing, or distribution in commerce solely for an FDA-regulated use is excluded from the jurisdiction of TSCA.

[ii] Water Pollutant Effluents

Under Section 307(a) of the Clean Water Act, 33 USC §1317, EPA promulgated in 1977 final effluent standards for the discharge of PCBs into navigable water. These effluent standards apply to manufacturers of intentionally produced PCB fluid (that is, Aroclor products) and manufacturers of electrical transformers, and establish an ambient water quality standard for PCBs in navigable water of 0.001 ug/1.[262]

As applied to the manufacturing processes specified in 40 CFR §129.105 (EPA's effluent guidelines), these effluent standards prohibit the discharge of Aroclor PCBs as process wastes.

EPA's effluent standard for inadvertently generated PCBs, estab-

---

[261] See 48 Fed. Reg. 55093.
[262] 40 CFR §129.104 (42 Fed. Reg. 6532).

lished under TSCA in 40 CFR §761.3(kk)(4), is 0.1 ppm PCBs for resolvable gas chromatographic peak per liter of water discharged, and apparently does not affect the Clean Water Act standards for intentionally produced PCBs. EPA has never explained why it has chosen to regulate water pollution discharge of PCBs under one statute if they are intentionally produced and under another if they are unintentionally produced.[263]

EPA also proposed new source performance standards applicable to PCB-containing wastes discharged from fine paper and tissue paper mills in the deink subcategory.[264] Those standards relate to paper produced from waste paper contaminated by Aroclor 1242.[265] EPA asserts that these activities are regulated solely under the CWA and chose not to address them under TSCA.[266]

Section 405 of the Clean Water Act[267] requires EPA to issue regulations that will identify uses for sewage sludge, specify factors to be considered in determining measures and practices applicable to such uses, and identify concentrations of pollutants that interfere with such uses. One set of regulations has been issued by EPA under the authority of Section 405, the land disposal criteria for solid waste facilities, which were promulgated in 1979 under the dual authority of the Clean Water Act and RCRA.[268]

A wide range of concentrations of chemical constituents, including recycled PCBs, may be present in municipal sludges. A variety of factors influence the composition of sludges generated from publicly owned treatment works, and in some communities they have been processed as fertilizer and other soil nutrient products.

Although there are no specific standards under 40 CFR Part 761 for the use of PCB-contaminated sludge in soil nutrient products, 40 CFR

---

[263] *See* 48 Fed. Reg. 55094.

[264] EPA's authority to continue to regulate PCBs under the Clean Water Act was affirmed in Environmental Defense Fund et al. v. EPA, 598 F.2d 62 (D.C. Cir. 1968).

[265] 47 Fed. Reg. 52066 (Nov. 18, 1982).

[266] The proposed standards for effluent limitations of Aroclor 1242 based on BAT for this industrial subcategory are (1) 0.00014 kilograms per thousand kilograms (kg/kkg) and 1.4 ug/l for production of fine paper; and (2) 0.00018 kg/kkg and 1.8 ug/l for the production of tissue paper. The proposed new source performance standards for Aroclor 1242 for this industrial subcategory are (1) 0.00011 kg/kkg and 1.6 ug/l for the production of fine papers; and (2) 0.00014 kg/kkg and 1.8 ug/l for the production of tissue paper. These standards are based on maximum discarge limits for one day.

[267] 33 USC §1345.

[268] 40 CFR Part 257.

§761.60(a)(5) presents disposal requirements for dredged materials and municipal sewage treatment sludges. Sludge with concentrations of 50 ppm or greater PCBs must be disposed of in an incinerator that complies with 40 CFR §761.70, in a chemical waste landfill that complies with 40 CFR §761.75, or in an alternate method approved by the Regional Administrator.[269] Solid wastes containing PCBs in concentrations of less than 50 ppm may be subject to 40 CFR §257.3-5(b) when they are applied to land used for producing animal feed. EPA has expressed some uncertainty as to under what authority it should regulate PCBs in sludge, and the present pattern is confusing at best.

[d] Remedial Problems—Cleaning Up Old PCB Deposits and Disposing of "Found" PCBs

The plight of the Outboard Marine Corporation illustrates some of the difficulties posed by the ubiquitous use of PCBs. OMC used PCB machine oil, which it purchased from Monsanto Chemical Company, for many years at its outboard motor manufacturing facility in Waukegan, Illinois.

Much of the oil, and the PCBs, ended up in a tributary of Lake Michigan, and high concentrations of PCBs accumulated in Waukegan harbor. In 1978 the United States commenced a civil action against OMC, seeking removal of the PCBs from the bottom sediments. The government later added Monsanto as a defendant. The State of Illinois began a separate action seeking the same relief. Since most of the dumping predated TSCA and the Clean Water Act, these lawsuits were primarily premised on the Refuse Act, 33 USC §403, and the "federal common law," which the Supreme Court declared to have been eclipsed by the Clean Water Act for discharges occurring subsequent to 1972.[270] Illinois added state common law claims. Settlement of the lawsuits was hampered by difficulties in disposing of the PCBs once they were dredged from the harbor.[271]

---

269 40 CFR §761.60(a)(5).

270 *See* Milwaukee v. Illinois, 451 U.S. 304 (1981); and Middlesex County Sewerage Authority v. National Sea Clammers Association, 453 U.S. 1 (1981).

271 *See* Outboard Marine Corp. v. Illinois, 453 U.S. 917 (1981); People of the State of Illinois v. Outboard Marine Corp., 680 F.2d 473 (7th Cir. 1982); People of the State of Illinois v. Outboard Marine Corp., 619 F.2d 623 (7th Cir. 1980), *vacated and remanded,* July 2, 1981; United States of America v. Outboard Marine Corp., 549 F. Supp. 1036 (N.D. Ill. E.D. 1982); United States of America v. Outboard Marine Corp., 556 F. Supp. 54 (N.D. Ill. E.D. 1982); United States of America v. Outboard Marine Corp., 549 F. Supp. 1032

In *Chappell v. SCA Services, Inc.*,[272] one of a series of lawsuits involving the so-called Wilsonville disposal site, the plaintiffs brought an action for damages under the state common law nuisance doctrine. The site had been used for the disposal of PCBs and other chemicals. An issue in *Chappell* was whether TSCA created an implied *federal* private right of action for damages. The court held that it did not.[273]

§2.09 State Toxic Substances Control Programs

Section 28 of TSCA[274] authorized EPA to make grants to encourage state TSC programs covering risks and chemicals "with respect to which the Administrator is unable or is not likely to take action" under TSCA. Section 18,[275] on the other hand, expressly preempts state toxic substance control activities to the following degree:

— A state or other political subdivision may not, unless exempted from preemption under Section 18(b),[276] impose any testing requirements for any chemical for which EPA has imposed testing requirements by a rule promulgated under Section 2603.

— A state or other political subdivision may not, unless exempted, impose any regulatory requirements upon a chemical as to which EPA has prescribed "a rule or order under Section 2604 or 2605" (except Section 2605(a)(6)) if the EPA rule "is designed to protect against a risk of injury to health or the environment . . .," *unless* the state requirement—

  — is identical to the EPA requirement; or

  — is adopted under the Clean Air Act or other federal legal authority; or

---

(N.D. Ill. E.D. 1982); Outboard Marine Corp. v. Costle, No. 78 C 751, slip opinion (N.D. Ill. E.D. 1980); People of the State of Illinois v. Outboard Marine Corp., No. 78 C 3187, slip opinion (N.D. Ill. E.D. 1979).

[272] 540 F. Supp. 1087 (C.D. Ill. 1982).

[273] *Id.* at 1099-1100. *Accord*, Robert E. Johnson et al. v. Koppers Company, Inc., et al., 524 F. Supp. 1182 (N.D. Ohio E.D. 1981).

[274] 15 USC §2627.

[275] 15 USC §2617.

[276] In order to grant a Section 18(b) exemption, EPA must find that the state's activity will not cause a violation of an applicable TSCA requirement and that the state's regulation is significantly more protective than EPA's and does not "through difficulties in marketing" or distribution, etc., unduly burden interstate commerce. Similar language is found in the Occupational Safety and Health Act.

— prohibits the end use of the substance in the jurisdiction.

Although there has not been a groundswell of state interest in regulatory toxic chemical manufacturing, enhanced public concern in the 1980s could rekindle state legislative initiatives in this area. In such event, these provisions, now of relatively minor significance, could become important.

These provisions, and EPA's practices, particularly its test rule practices, raise a number of potentially difficult issues. Are EPA industry-negotiated testing agreements "test rules" within the meaning of Section 18(a)(2)(A)? The argument that they are not is based upon the reasoning that since such agreements are a fait accompli at the point they are placed in the Federal Register, they cannot be considered to have been "promulgated," a requirement of the statute. The statutory exclusion from preemption of outright prohibitions[277] is curious. There appears to be no sound reason to prohibit regulation of chemicals but allow their outright ban, under any theory of federal preemption.

A further complication of the TSCA preemption problem is Section 6(a)(6)(B),[278] which provides that in issuing a disposal requirement under Section 6, EPA "may not require any person to take any action which would be in violation of any law or requirement of, or in effect for, a state or political subdivision. . . ."

In *Warren County, et al. v. State of North Carolina, et al.,*[279] the plaintiff county adopted a local law that prohibited the disposal of PCBs or PCB-contaminated soils within the county.[280] The county then sought to enjoin the disposal of PCBs by the state and the issuance of a PCB landfill license by EPA on the ground (among others) that the acts would violate the county ordinance. The county relied upon Sections 6(a)(6)(B) and 18(a)(2)(B) in arguing that at least insofar as disposal requirements are concerned, TSCA does not preempt more stringent state or local requirements. On its face the statute appears so to provide.

The district court, however, ignored the parenthetical in Section

---

277 15 USC §2617(a)(2)(B)(iii).

278 15 USC §2606(a)(6)(B).

279 528 F. Supp. 276 (E.D.N.C. 1981).

280 The county's action was intended to prevent the state from placing PCB-contaminated dirt in a landfill EPA had approved for that purpose. The subject PCBs were deposited by two individual "midnight dumpers," who had previously been convicted of TSCA-based criminal charges. *See* Robert Earl Ward v. United States, 676 F.2d 94 (4th Cir. 1982) (upholding conviction).

18(a)(2)(B), and reasoned that, regardless of what the language stated, the statute should not be construed to permit state or local action that would be "an obstacle to the accomplishment and execution of" the purposes of TSCA, relying primarily upon *Ray v. Atlantic Richfield Co.*[281] On the facts, the court concluded that the Warren County ordinance would frustrate EPA's national PCB policy, and refused enforcement, striking the ordinance down.[282]

A much more thoroughly reasoned, though hardly more satisfactory, analysis of the complex TSCA preemption provision is contained in *SED, Inc. v. City of Dayton.*[283] The plaintiff in *SED* challenged a city ordinance that strictly regulated the storage of PCB-containing materials and articles, claiming that the city's ordinance was preempted by TSCA. The city raised two defenses. First, like Warren County, it argued that its ordinance was exempted from preemption by Sections 18(a)(2)(B) and 6(a)(6). Second, the city rested, in the alternative, on Section 18(a)(2)(B)(ii), claiming that its ordinance was grounded on the Clean Water Act, a source of other federal authority, and therefore exempt from preemption.

After expressing some difficulty with EPA's published position as being equivocal[284] and without adequate statutory support, the court concluded that the city's ordinance was not exempted from preemption

---

[281] 435 U.S. 151, 158 (1978). The court also placed reliance upon the district court opinion in Pacific Legal Foundation v. State Energy Resources Conservation and Development Commission. 472 F. Supp. 191 (S.D. Cal. 1979), which concluded that a California statute providing that no nuclear power plant shall be certified until a state commission finds that the authorized U.S. agency has approved technology for disposal of high-level nuclear waste was unconstitutional as impliedly preempted by the Atomic Energy Act. Subsequently, however, the Ninth Circuit reviewed the district court, and the appeals court's judgment was affirmed by the U.S. Supreme Court in Pacific Gas and Electric Co. v. State Energy Resources Conservation and Development Commission, 491 U.S. 190, 103 S. Ct. 1713 (1983).

[282] *See also* Rollins Environmental Services v. Parish of St. James, 775 F.2d 627 (5th Cir. 1985); and Chemical Waste Management, Inc. v. Broadwater, CA No. 84-G-1208-W (N.D. Ala. 1984), *appeal dismissed,* 758 F.2d 1538 (11th Cir. 1985). A contrary position is argued in Druly & Ordway, *The Toxic Substances Control Act* (monograph binder), 24 Environmental Reporter 31 (BNA 1977); *cf.* Andreen, *Diffusing the "Not in My Back Yard" Syndrome: An Approach to Federal Preemption of State and Local Impediments to the Siting of PCB Disposal Facilities,* 63 North Carolina L. Rev. 811 (1985) (arguing for preemption except where there are compelling local safety requirements justifying action, presumably arguing for a judicially created scheme similar to that which obtains legislatively under FIFRA and the OSH Act.

[283] 519 F. Supp. 979 (S.D. Ohio 1981).

[284] *See* 43 Fed. Reg. at 7153-7154 (1978); and 44 Fed. Reg. 31528 (1979).

by Section 18(a)(2)(B)'s local disposal provision. The court first concluded that the parenthetical reference in Section 18(a)(2)(B) to Section 6(a)(6)(B) was not dependent upon the enactment of nonpreemptive EPA regulations under Section 6(a)(6). It then parsed Section 18(a)(2)(B) as having three distinct components:

(1) a "triggering" provision setting forth the kind of federal action that gives rise to preemption (that is, issuance of a rule or order under Section 5 or 6 other than a requirement "described" in Section 6(a)(6));

(2) a description of the scope of preemption once it is triggered (that is, complete, as to the regulated substance]; and

(3) three specific exceptions to preemption (including the "other federal authority" exception).

The court then reasoned that if EPA adopts *any* regulations respecting a chemical *other than* regulations respecting disposal, even if they are in addition to disposal regulation, preemption of *all* local regulation of the substance springs up, subject only to the specific exemptions contained in Section 18(a)(2)(B)(i)-(iii). In other words, once EPA does more than simply regulate disposal of a substance, any and all local regulation, including regulation of disposal, is preempted.[285]

Having construed the disposal provision of Section 18(a)(2)(B) exceedingly narrowly, the court proceeded to accord an expansive interpretation to Section 18(a)(2)(B)(ii), the "local regulation based on other federal authority" exception. The city, in an argument that can only be described as concocted out of the whole cloth by an inventive lawyer as a last-ditch effort, brazenly argued that its ordinance, which regulated the storage of PCBs *inside of warehouses,* was adopted under authority of the Clean Water Act.[286]

The court latched onto this theory and concluded that since the storage of PCBs might in unforeseen circumstances lead to a discharge of PCBs into a water body, the city's regulation of PCBs fell generally

---

[285] In Chappell v. SCA Services, Inc., 540 F. Supp. 1087, 1098 (1982), the court apparently adopted EPA's administrative position, contrary to SED, that TSCA does not preempt local disposal requirements.

[286] 33 USC §1251 *et seq.*

under the Clean Water Act. Under this reasoning, there simply is no meaningful TSCA preemption.[287]

The final decision on the preemption issue, *Chappell v. SCA Services, Inc.*,[288] relying primarily on the saving clause contained in Section 20(c)(3) of TSCA,[289] held that TSCA does not preempt state common law nuisance actions for damage arising out of the disposal of TSCA-regulated wastes.

The statutory provisions and the decided cases leave the issue of preemption under TSCA rather murky. It may well be that, except for state regulations of disposal practices, the states are ill equiped to undertake direct regulation of the manufacture, distribution, and use of TSCA-regulated chemicals and therefore the issue will never assume significant stature. Public pressure has driven the state to pursue more active roles in other chemical regulatory programs in recent years, however, and the possibility of increased state activity warrants more attention to the preemption issue.

The very nature of TSCA regulations compels serious consideration of clearly enunciated broad preemption and argues against delegation of the basic risk assessment/review functions of Sections 4, 5, and 6 to the states. For premarket regulation to be both effective and fair, it must be sophisticated, centralized, and uniform. While some states have developed sophisticated pesticide regulatory schemes and hazardous waste programs, others have not done so and are not likely to do so, given their size and budgetary limitations.

§2.10 Foreign Regulation of Toxic Substances

A number of foreign governments regulate the marketing and use of toxic substances. These programs all differ from the TSCA scheme to varying extents. Some countries define the substances regulated more narrowly or more broadly than TSCA, some require premarket screening rather than premanufacture screening, and some require greater and some lesser percentages of chemicals produced to be tested.

---

[287] The court's reasoning on this issue leaves much to be desired. It acknowledges that the city's ordinance did not purport to regulate the discharge of pollutants, and acknowledged that under its reasoning almost any environmental regulation could be tucked under the Clean Water Act or other environmental authority.

[288] 540 F. Supp. 1087 (C.D. Ill. 1982).

[289] 15 USC §2619(c)(3).

The European countries that are members of the European Economic Community (EEC) and those countries that generally adhere to the OECD guidelines[290] all have some sort of toxic-substances regulatory scheme.

It is important to underscore that most European countries do not require testing prior to manufacture, but only require testing of those chemicals actually proposed for introduction into the market, and that often *all* new chemicals (even existing chemicals produced by new manufacturers) must be tested regardless of their known or suspected potential for health or environmental harm. While the foreign testing protocols and EPA's TSCA protocols are generally substantially similar, the particular testing required varies from country to country. EPA has codified the OECD chemical fate testing protocols as TSCA guidelines in Part 796 of its regulations.

§2.11 Recombinant DNA Products[291]

Although EPA has asserted FIFRA jurisdiction over genetically engi-

---

290 OECD member countries are Australia, Austria, Belgium, Canada, Denmark, Finland, France, West Germany, Greece, Iceland, Ireland, Italy, Japan, Luxembourg, The Netherlands, New Zealand, Norway, Portugal, Spain, Sweden, Switzerland, Turkey, the United Kingdom, and the United States. The current (as of late 1985) OECD premarket data requirements are set forth in Annex VII to the Council of European Communities Directive on Classification, Packaging, and Labelling of Dangerous Substances. Authority for premarket testing is contained in Amendment 6 of the Directive (Amendment 6 of Directive 67/548/EEC).

291 DNA (deoxyribonucleic acid) is the genetic material found in all living organisms and contains the genetic code responsible for all inherited characteristics of such organisms. Recombinant DNA technology is used to produce hybrid DNA molecules composed of DNA from different sources. These hybrid, or recombinant, DNA molecules may be used for purely scientific purposes, such as genetic research, or for commercial purposes, such as the production of a specific product. *See generally,* U.S. Congress, Office of Technology Assessment, Commercial Biotechnology: An International Analysis 3, 589 (1984) [hereinafter 1984 OTA Report]; U.S. Congress, Office of Technology Assessment, Impacts of Applied Genetics: Microorganisms, Plants and Animals 4 (1981) [hereinafter 1981 OTA Report]. Major chemical companies have begun to move into commercial DNA production, on a limited scale. The risks presented by DNA activities are of the "low probability–high consequential hazard" variety. House Subcommittee on Investigations and Oversight of House Committee on Science and Technology, 98th Cong., 2d Sess., Staff Report on the Environmental Implications of Genetic Engineering at II (Comm. Print 1984) [hereinafter House Committee Staff Report].

neered microbial pest control agents[292] its regulatory activity under FIFRA is limited and narrow. TSCA would provide a far more comprehensive basis for government regulation of DNA products.[293]

EPA's authority to regulate microorganisms pursuant to TSCA hinges upon whether such microorganisms fall within the TSCA definitions of "mixture" or "chemical substance." EPA's position has been that microorganisms and other life forms are not TSCA mixtures.[294] EPA employs two arguments to support this position. First, no *naturally* occurring life form can be a TSCA mixture.[295] Second, although a combination of chemical substances occurring as a result of a chemical reaction may be classified as a mixture if all the chemical substances involved appear on the TSCA Section 8(b) chemical inventory list and the combination could have been manufactured for commercial purposes without a chemical reaction, EPA does not believe that life forms fit within this category of the TSCA mixture definition because all the chemical substances in any life form are not likely to be on the inventory and it is unlikely that one could produce a life form by combining the component chemical substances without using chemical reactions. Thus, even an *artificially* produced life form cannot be a mixture.[296]

EPA initially claimed that genetically engineered organisms were also not "chemical substances" under TSCA. Although apparently admitting that recombinant DNA molecules fit the statutory definition, EPA argued that the host organism containing the altered DNA did not clearly fit within the definitional structure.[297] However, the Agency reversed its position almost immediately, and included manufactured life forms in its inventory-reporting regulations.[298]

The argument in favor of regulation of recombinant DNA products

---

[292] FIFRA clearly authorizes such jurisdiction. *See* 7 U.S.C. §§136(a) and (u). EPA's jurisdictional assertion can be found at 47 Fed. Reg. 53192 at 53203 (1982) and at 49 Fed. Reg. 40659, 40660 (1984).

[293] Other agencies have considered regulating these materials. *See, e.g., OSHA Regulation of Industrial Applications of Recombinant DNA Technology,* 50 U. Cinn. L. Rev. 284 (1981); Korwek, *FDA Regulation of Biotechnology as a New Method of Manufacture,* 37 Food Drug and Cosmetic L.J. 289 (1982).

[294] House Committee Staff Report at 144 n.2.

[295] Its argument is premised on the Section 3(8) definition.

[296] House Committee Staff Report at 144 n.2.

[297] Letter from Douglas M. Costle, Administrator, EPA, *reprinted in* House Subcommittee on Science, Technology, and Space, Oversight Report: Recombinant DNA and Its Applications, 95th Cong. 2d Sess. 88 (1978).

[298] *See* 42 Fed. Reg. 64572, 64585 (1977).

as chemical substances rests on the premise that any DNA molecule is an "organic . . . substance of a particular molecular identity" or a "combination of such substances occurring in whole or in part as a result of a chemical reaction or occurring in nature."[299] The counterargument rests on the premise that DNA molecules are not clearly identifiable as to their structure.[300]

EPA's position is supported somewhat by the Supreme Court's decision in *Diamond v. Chakrabarty*,[301] which treated genetically engineered microorganisms as functionally equivalent to nonliving chemicals for patent law purposes, looking primarily at how they are used rather than at their characteristic of being alive.[302]

TSCA's legislative history neither clearly supports nor prohibits regulation of recombinant DNA.[303]

The larger questions really involve EPA's capabilities in the area. The TSCA program does not stand out as a shining example of EPA's regulatory prowess, and EPA has historically not had much experience with biotechnology. Furthermore, many of the TSCA terms of regulatory art simply do not fit living "chemicals" very well.

EPA would undoubtedly have to restructure its PMN requirements to reflect relevant kinds of data, and it might have difficulty doing that

---

[299] Quotations are from Section 3(2)(A) of TSCA. It is also arguable that some recombinant DNA products meet the statutory definition because they are combinations of DNA molecules and other TSCA substances.

[300] EPA's view can be viewed as leading to an absurd result—that higher life forms, such as humans, are regulable under TSCA. *See, e.g.*, McGarrity & Bayer, *Federal Regulation of Emergency Genetic Technologies*, 36 Vand. L. Rev. 461, 538 (1983). The obvious response to such arguments is that EPA has sufficient regulatory latitude to exclude from TSCA chemical substances (that is, DNA) that *per se* have no use aside from the life form of which they are a part. Moreover, the limitation of TSCA jurisdiction to substances "distributed in commerce" provides a further limit on the perceived overbreadth.

[301] 447 U.S. 303 (1980). *See also* In Re Bergy, 596 F.2d. 952 (C.C.P.A. 1979). *Chackrabarty* dealt only with artificially created organisms.

[302] In *Bergy*, the Court of Customs and Patent Appeals stated that there is "no legally significant difference between active chemicals which are classified as 'dead' and organisms used for their chemical reactions which take place because they are alive." 596 F. 2d. at 975.

[303] On EPA's side, the statute is remedial in nature, and the legislative history seems to support giving an inclusive reading to its definitional provisions. *See* H.R. Rep. No. 1341, 94th Cong., 2d. Sess. (1976); S. Rep. No. 698, 94th Cong., 2d. Sess. 5-15 (1976); H.R. Rep. No. 1679, 94th Cong., 2d. Sess. 56 (1976) (naturally occurring substances). On the other hand, the legislative history contains no references to life forms, and it is unlikely that in 1976 Congress had even the slightest notion of the existence of recombinant DNA products, although the National Institutes of Health had begun DNA research regulation by 1976. *See* 41 Fed. Reg. 27911 (1976).

without amending the statute.[304] EPA's current PMN practice does not, for example, require the PMN submitter to submit toxicological data unless a structure activity anaylsis makes the chemical suspect. Structure activity analyses are not useful for evaluating the toxic or chronic potential of a living organism. Nevertheless EPA has proceeded to apply its PMN requirements to bioengineered organisms.[305]

---

[304] *See* 1984 OTA report at 372, and House Staff report at 137.
[305] *See* 49 Fed. Reg. 46006 (1984) (polymers).

CHAPTER 3

Pesticides

§3.01 Introduction

Pesticides, most of which are chemicals, have been subject to governmental regulation since 1947, when Congress adopted the original Federal Insecticide, Fungicide and Rodenticide Act (FIFRA). Since at the time of its enactment FIFRA was essentially economic legislation, aimed at equalizing the relationship between the primary pesticide users, farmers, and the emerging pesticide industry, jurisdiction to administer the legislation was vested in the U.S. Department of Agriculture (USDA).[1] Since the original FIFRA was not preemptive of state

---

[1] Congressional jurisdiction was (and still is) also vested in the committees in the House and Senate having jurisdiction over agricultural matters.

law, a number of states developed pesticide regulatory programs patterned on the federal model. In general, state pesticide programs, like the federal program, were administered by the state agriculture departments.

The 1947 FIFRA downplayed the federal role in regulating pesticide use, leaving that role essentially to the states. The USDA's primary mission was to register "economic poisons," as pesticides were then called, in accordance with the general criteria set forth in the statute.

Between 1947 and 1972, when Congress amended the statute to substantially its present form,[2] thousands of pesticides were registered with relatively little attention paid to the health and environmental risks posed by the chemicals. The 1972 Act placed somewhat greater emphasis on environmental risk analysis, and formalized President Nixon's transfer of authority by executive order from the USDA to the newly created U.S. Environmental Protection Agency (EPA), giving the Agency statutory status, ensuring its longevity. At the same time, Section 408 of the Federal Food, Drug and Cosmetic Act (FFDCA) was amended to transfer authority for establishing pesticide food residue tolerances from the Food and Drug Administration (FDA) to EPA.

A number of states followed Congress's lead and also modernized their pesticide regulatory programs. Others did not, and today the pattern of state pesticide regulatory laws is far from uniform. Some states retain the old agriculture department scheme, while others have placed pesticide regulation in an environmental protection department, an independent board, or the state health department. Some states duplicate federal regulation of pesticide residues on food, and most of those that do so place regulatory jurisdiction in the state health department.

Although portions of FIFRA—and, indeed, it is fair to say the statute's basic regulatory structure—date back to the original text, the FIFRA program as it affects the pesticide industry today is, for all practical intents and purposes, the creation of EPA's Office of Pesticide Programs, and it is still evolving. At present, American pesticide manufacturers, formulators, distributors, and users are regulated under FIFRA only in their domestic activities. Foreign production and use,

---

2 Federal Environmental Pesticide Control Act of 1972, PL 92-516, 92d Congress (H.R. 10729), October 21, 1972.

See Appendix 3A, *infra*, for table cross-referencing the session law sections to Title 7 U.S. Code sections.

and to some extent production in the United States solely for export, are not regulated.[3]

FIFRA, like the Toxic Substances Control Act (TSCA), is primarily a product-licensing statute. It establishes general criteria that the regulatory agency must follow in determining whether, in FIFRA's terminology, the pesticide can be registered. It also authorizes regulation of manufacturers and of pesticide use, although EPA has done little with the first and has traditionally left the latter to the states.

§3.02 The FIFRA Regulatory Scheme

[1] What Is Regulated?

FIFRA regulates primarily "pesticides" and secondarily, to a degree that is not clear on the face of the statute, "devices" that have the same sort of intended use as pesticides.

With specified exceptions, a pesticide is any "substance or mixture of substances" that is either "intended for preventing, destroying, repelling, or mitigating any pest" or "intended for use as a plant regulator, defoliant, or desiccant.[4] A "pest" is any insect, rodent, nematode, fungus, weed, or any "other form of terrestrial or aquatic plant or animal life or virus, bacteria or other micro-organism" (excluding viruses, bacteria, or other microorganisms "on or in man or other living animals"), "which the Administrator deems to be a pest."

The triggering concepts for FIFRA jurisdiction are action and intent. Although EPA's interpretive position has not always been consistent, the Agency's regulations look to the following factors in determining pesticidal intent, the presence of any one of which is sufficient to trigger jurisdiction:

— manufacturer's representations either on the label or in collateral advertising;

---

[3] The death of several thousand people in Bhopal, India, in late 1984 resulting from the release of a toxic intermediate product at a Union Carbide subsidiary's facility producing the pesticide Sevin could spur legislation altering this situation.

[4] Section 2(u). The exceptions are "new animal drugs" regulated under Section 201(w) of the FFDCA, or otherwise regulated under that provision, or an animal feed within the meaning of Section 201(x) of the FFDCA.

— verbal or written claims made by manufacturers, representatives, shippers, or distributors.[5]

A product intended for use as a pesticide after repackaging or reformulation (mixture with other, usually inert, ingredients) is a pesticide, as is a product that claims both pesticidal and nonpesticidal uses.[6]

EPA takes the position that a product is a pesticide if a "reasonable consumer"—given the label, accompanying circulars, and advertising representations and the collectivity of the circumstances—would use it as a pesticide.[7] Whether the claimed or implied pesticidal activity is actually effective is not relevant under EPA's interpretation of its jurisdiction.

FIFRA's breadth, along with EPA's generally expansive interpretation of it, would potentially sweep into the FIFRA regulatory web a large number of substances that EPA, for one reason or another, does not wish to regulate extensively. As a result, the FIFRA regulations contain a number of specific limited or general exemptions from the registration requirements or specifically excluding classes of products from the definition.

Definitionally excluded products include deodorants, bleaches, cleaning agents, fungicide-treated paints and other coatings, pesticide-treated building materials and fabrics, fertilizers, and intermediates used in the pesticide production process.[8] Among the products deemed pesticides but exempt from registration are pesticides being transferred between registered establishments, used under experimental use per-

---

5 EPA's regulation, 40 CFR §162.4, specifically mentions these entities, and thus by implication appears to exclude claims made by retailers not connected with any of the listed entities.

6 40 CFR §1162.4(b). EPA places all pesticides in one of a number of classes; for regulatory purposes, these classes are amphibian/reptile poisons and repellents; antimicrobial agents; attractants (including pheromones); bird poisons and repellents; defoliants; desiccants; fish poisons and repellents; fungicides; herbicides; insecticides; invertebrate poisons and repellents; mammal poisons and repellents; nematicides; plant regulators; rodenticides; and slimicides. 40 CFR §162.3(ff).

7 Although this position is not spelled out in EPA's regulations it has been consistently applied by the Agency since 1976, and was upheld as consistent with the statute in N. Jonas & Company, Inc., v. U.S. Environmental Protection Agency, 666 F.2d 829 (3d Cir. 1981). But see Gulf Oil Corporation v. EPA, 548 F.2d 1228 (5th Cir. 1977) (holding that the mere presence of oil of citronella on patio torchlight fuel is insufficient to support a conclusion that pesticidal claims are made for the product).

8 40 CFR §162.4(c). Any of these products for which pesticidal claims are made are, however, treated as pesticides.

mits or pursuant to emergency exemptions,[9] transferred for disposal, and intended solely for export to a foreign country, when prepared or packed according to the specifications of the foreign purchaser.[10]

"Biological control agents," which include the products of the recombinant DNA industry, are generally exempted from FIFRA regulation on the premise that they are adequately regulated by other federal agencies and thus meet the requirements for a Section 25(b)(1) exemption.[11] EPA has, however, left itself with the ability to regulate such substances on a case-by-case basis.[12]

Pesticides intended solely for human use that are regulated as new drugs or articles by the FDA under the Federal Food, Drug and Cosmetic Act and pheromones or similar compounds are also exempted by regulation.[13]

[2] Who Is Subject to Regulation?

[a] In General

To one degree or another, the following entities are subject to regulation under FIFRA:

— manufacturers of active ingredients;
— manufacturers of end use products;
— formulators of end use products;
— distributors;
— retailers;
— commercial applicators;
— a limited class of private applicators;
— laboratories doing pesticide-related analyses; and
— importers.

---

[9] These pesticides are regulated under other FIFRA provisions. The establishment transfer and experimental use exemptions are expressly authorized by FIFRA Section 3(b).

[10] 40 CFR §162.5(b). The labeling requirements are applicable to pesticides being transferred between establishment or for disposal.

[11] 40 CFR §162.5(c). See also 47 Fed. Reg. 53192 and 53203 (1982).

[12] 40 CFR §§162.5(c)(3) and 162.5(c)(4).

[13] 40 CFR §162.5(d).

[b]   Producers

[i]   Types of Producers Regulated

A producer is any person who manufactures, prepares, compounds, propagates, or processes any pesticide or device or any active ingredient used in manufacturing a pesticide[14] and essentially includes all entities that manufacture or formulate chemical pesticides.[15]

The pesticide industry is made up of two types of producing entities: active ingredient manufacturers and pesticide formulators. Many active ingredient ("manufacturing use product") manufacturers are also pesticide ("end use product") formulators, and the formulator group far outnumbers the manufacturer group. Formulators typically buy technical grade active ingredients from a manufacturer, add their own inert ingredients, and package the product for marketing. It is not uncommon for an independent formulator to compete for sales of end use products with the entity from which the active ingredient was purchased.

FIFRA regulates producers in two ways. Their products must be registered under Section 3, and their "establishments" must also be registered, under Section 7 of the statute. Pesticide registration is discussed *infra* at Section 3.03. Other sections of FIFRA impose ancillary regulatory burdens on producers. Section 8 provides EPA with authority to impose recordkeeping requirements and to inspect records, subject to certain restrictions. Section 9 authorizes inspection of establishments for enforcement purposes. These sections are also discussed in subsequent parts of this chapter.

[ii]   Production Establishments Regulated

All establishments producing devices, active ingredients, or pesticides must be registered and must maintain a valid registration num-

---

14 Section 2(w). End users who simply dilute a product prior to use are specifically defined out of the class. EPA's regulations, at 40 CFR §167.1(c), specifically include producers acting pursuant to Section 5 experimental use permits as producers.

15 EPA has not actively regulated the manufacture of most pesticidal devices, some of which claim a nonexistent efficacy. Pest control devices, which include among their number common backyard bug zappers and "ultrasonic" rodent repellers, tend to be of greater concern for the potential consumer fraud in their marketing than as a health and safety matter, and though the Agency has occasionally stepped forward to protect the consumer from frauds, it has historically not viewed such activity as central to its regulatory mission. Devices are not covered further here.

ber.[16] Establishment registration under FIFRA is not required for the purpose of federal regulation of the safety of the plant, or environmental protection at the site.[17] Section 7(c) of FIFRA prescribes the areas of regulatory concern, which are not broad.

The producer is required to provide EPA with information relative to the identities and amounts of pesticides and/or active ingredients currently being produced that were produced during the previous year and sold or distributed during the previous calendar year.[18] An annual report is required to be filed with EPA's Office of Pesticide Programs setting forth this information.

Section 7 deems all information submitted to EPA, except information relative to the names of the products, confidential, subject to the provisions of Section 10, which provides certain limitations on confidentiality.

Acting under its general regulatory authority, provided in Section 25, EPA requires establishments producing products solely for export and foreign establishments producing products for import into the United States to comply with the registration requirements.[19] The Agency has also required that each product of a registered entity bear on its label the registration number of the final establishment at which the product was produced.[20]

[c] **Laboratories**

Except for those laboratories operating under contract to EPA or under an EPA research grant, laboratories are not regulated directly under FIFRA, and for many years EPA was criticized for the absence of any required good laboratory practice standards in the FIFRA regulatory scheme. EPA answered this criticism by adopting 40 CFR Part 160 in 1983.[21]

EPA exerts indirect control over laboratories engaged in FIFRA-related toxicological and other relevant analytical work by means of its

---

[16] Sections 7(a) and (b).

[17] Safety at the plant is under the jurisdiction of the Occupational Safety and Health Administration (OSHA). Emissions of pollutants are regulated under the Clean Air Act, the Clean Water Act, the Solid Waste Disposal Act, and relevant state laws.

[18] 40 CFR §§167.1(g) and 167.2.

[19] 40 CFR §§167.1(b) and 167.5.

[20] 40 CFR §167.4. The regulation specifies how and where the number must be affixed.

[21] See 48 Fed. Reg. 53963 (11-29-83).

control over registrants and its control over persons seeking pesticide residue tolerances on foods pursuant to Sections 408 and 409 of the FFDCA. For any data to be considered in support of an application for a registration, exemption, or tolerance (EPA lumps all of the various types of applications into the phrase "research or marketing permits"), the applicant must provide, along with its other supporting materials, a written statement signed not only by the applicant but also by the "sponsor"[22] of the study relied upon and the study director. The statement must either certify that the study was conducted in accordance with Part 160, or describe how it differed from the Part 160 requirements, or state that the person was not a sponsor of the study, did not conduct the study, and does not know whether the study was conducted in accordance with Part 160.[23] The latter statement is necessary when the studies relied upon are old or came into the possession of the applicant from independent sources.

The good laboratory practice standards are what one would expect, generally corresponding to those employed by other federal agencies with health-related regulatory programs.[24] Section 160.15, however, gives EPA and the FDA the right to inspect testing facilities that generate data submitted to the Agency and to inspect their records. The Agency purports to enforce this requirement by refusing to deem reliable any test data submitted from a facility that has refused inspection.[25]

[d] Applicators and Dealers

[i] In General

Read together, Sections 11 and 25 provide EPA with authority to regulate pesticide applicators and dealers. The broad grant of essentially legislative rulemaking authority of Section 25 is somewhat limited by two specific restrictions contained in Section 11, which prohibits EPA

---

[22] The term "sponsor" connotes the person who initiated or supported the study, the applicant who submitted it to EPA, or the testing facility itself if it both initiated and conducted the study. 40 CFR §160.3(1).

[23] 40 CFR §160.12.

[24] Subpart B addresses organization and personnel; subpart C addresses animal care and supply, testing, and other facilities; subpart D addresses equipment practices; subpart E addresses testing facilities operation; subpart F addresses test and control substance handling and characterization; subpart G addresses study protocols; and subpart J addresses report generation and record retention.

[25] 40 CFR §160.15(b).

from imposing recordkeeping or reporting requirements on private applicators and requires the establishment of separate standards for commercial and private applicators.[26]

EPA imposes regulatory requirements only on commercial and private applicators who employ "restricted use" pesticides.[27] The Agency has established standards for certification of such applicators, which are published at Part 171 of 40 CFR. EPA directly licenses applicators only in states that have failed to submit a certification program that EPA has approved under 40 CFR §171.7 and on Indian reservations at which the tribe has not submitted a program.[28]

[ii] Commercial Applicators

A commercial applicator must receive a separate certification for each category of restricted-use pesticide application in which he intends to do business. EPA divides the universe of applications into ten mandatory categories, for which separate examinations are required.[29]

EPA requires all commercial applicators to pass a written examination that covers general pest control practices, label comprehension, environmental consequences of pesticide misuse, pest recognition, physiology and biological development, basic pesticide chemistry and toxicology, equipment, application techniques, and general understanding of the federal and relevant state pesticide laws and regulations.[30] Separate series of questions are required to be answered, in addition, relating to each category or subcategory for which certification is required.[31]

Since all restricted-use pesticides must be applied commercially ei-

---

[26] The states are permitted to regulate pesticide use without any federal preemption. Section 24(a).

[27] Restricted-use pesticides are those that contain an active ingredient that has been classified by EPA for restricted use. These ingredients are listed in a table at 40 CFR §162.31.

[28] As of January 1986, only Nebraska and Colorado did not have approved applicator certification programs.

[29] 40 CFR §171.3. The categories are agricultural pest control (plant or animal), forest pest control, ornamental and turf pest control, seed treatment, aquatic pest control, right-of-way pest control, industrial, institutional, structural, and health-related pest control, public health pest control, regulatory pest control (relating to public employees who use restricted use pesticides), and demonstration and research. States are free to add additional categories, or subcategories, but must employ at least these in order to obtain program approval and avoid direct EPA licensing of their applicators.

[30] 40 CFR §171.4.

[31] 40 CFR §171.4(c). Researchers, medical doctors, and veterinarians are not required to be examined. 40 CFR §171.4(e).

ther by a certified applicator or under the supervision of a certified applicator, additional requirements, including additional qualifying examination questions, are imposed on people who act as supervisors.[32] Among the most important issues facing commercial applicators and EPA—and one for which the Agency has provided little general guidance—is the problem of what situations demand the physical presence of a certified applicator. Pest control is a business, and, as in any other business, costs are important, and certified applicators command higher wages than do uncertified laborers. Yet most field misuse of pesticides is probably attributable to relatively unsupervised commercial or large private applicator personnel.[33]

Commercial applicator certification is valid for three years, after which certification must be renewed.[34] Certification may be denied or revoked for any number of causes, which are generally identical to FIFRA's list of prohibited acts set forth in Section 12 of the Act, although opportunity for an adjudicatory hearing must be provided.[35] Certified applicators or firms employing them are required to create and keep a limited number of records and to make them available to EPA on request.[36]

Some states levy license fees, and some require an individual permit authorizing each application of a restricted-use pesticide, or license specific types of applications, such as aerial spraying.

[iii] Private Applicators

FIFRA requires regulation only of private applicators (those who use restricted-use pesticides on their own or their employer's property, or on another's property but not for hire) who are farmers.[37] Mandatory

---

[32] 40 CFR §171.6.

[33] Some states require examinations and licensing of all applicator personnel. The practice is, however, not common.

[34] 40 CFR §171.11.

[35] 40 CFR §171.11(f)(2)(ii).

[36] 40 CFR §171.11(c)(7). Recordkeeping is also required of any person who contracts with a commercial applicator to apply restricted-use pesticides on the property of a third person. The records must reflect the name and address of each customer, where the pesticide was applied, the target pests, the crop or site of application, the date and time of application, the trade name and EPA registration number of the product used, the amount applied and the percentage of active ingredient per unit of pesticide used, and the method, date, and location of disposal of pesticides by type.

[37] Section 2(e)(2) and 40 CFR §171.2(a)(20). Some states regulate private applicators more extensively and require certification not only of farmers but also of nurserymen, foresters, golf course maintenance personnel, and other entities who use large amounts of pesticides. No state regulates homeowners.

certification requirements for private applicators are much less onerous than those applied to commercial applicators. The examination may be either written or oral, the categories of testing are narrower, and the depth of knowledge required is much less. EPA even permits certification of private applicators who cannot read.[38]

Supervisory private applicators are required to meet essentially the same supervisory requirements as are imposed upon supervisory commercial applicators.[39]

Private applicator certificates are good for four years, and the same standards for revocation, denial, and suspension that are applied to commercial applicators apply.

[iv] Dealers

In those few states in which EPA directly regulates applicators, it imposes recordkeeping and reporting obligations on retail dealers of restricted-use pesticides.[40] The Agency does not, however, make such regulation mandatory as a condition of approving a state plan.[41]

[v] State Regulation of Applicators and Dealers

Sections 24 and 26 of FIFRA point strongly to maximum deference by EPA to state regulation of pesticide use. EPA's state program approval regulations reflect its adherence to this intent by setting forth only general criteria for state program approval.[42] As a result, there is a rather wide diversity in state regulation of applicators and dealers, although EPA has managed to maintain a reasonably consistent minimum set of certification criteria for commercial applicators.

A substantial number of states impose more rigorous regulation on these people than FIFRA requires. A number of states require a broader class of private applicators to be certified. Some require distributors and retail dealers of restricted-use pesticides to be licensed. Some require special permits for certain types of application, and a number of states impose more extensive recordkeeping and reporting obligations.

No matter how closely regulated the applicators are, if the state

---

[38] *See* 40 CFR §171.5.

[39] 40 CFR §171.6.

[40] 40 CFR §171.11(g). The requirements are similar to those imposed by the FDA on pharmacists dispensing controlled substances. A record of each transaction must be kept, and the pesticides may not be sold to uncertified persons who do not produce documentation that the pesticides will be used by or under the supervision of a certified applicator.

[41] *See* 40 CFR §171.7.

[42] 40 CFR §171.7(b).

possesses inadequate capacity to provide effective field enforcement there is little assurance that widespread pesticide misuse will not occur. Because pesticide use enforcement involves nonfixed points of concern, it more closely resembles police work than most of the other environmental, health, and safety regulatory laws. That fact makes enforcement more difficult, as well as more expensive. Although EPA's regulations require "satisfactory assurances" from the states that they possess adequate personnel resources to manage the applicator regulatory program effectively,[43] EPA has historically usually just taken the state's word, and not looked behind the numbers presented to it.

EPA has the authority to initiate its own enforcement action to redress "significant violations" of the use provisions of FIFRA in a state possessing primary enforcement authority, but it must give the state thirty days in which to take action itself,[44] unless the Agency deems an emergency to exist.[45]

EPA also possesses authority to revoke state primary use enforcement authority if it determines that the state is not carrying out its responsibility.[46] The Agency promulgated regulations in 1981 establishing an elaborate set of procedures to be followed prior to state program recision,[47] which include a statement that the state may seek judicial review of program recision in the federal courts under Section 16. It is not altogether certain that EPA's attempt to provide the states with access to the federal courts in this situation will be successful, however, since Section 16 confers jurisdiction on the federal courts to hear controversies brought by "persons," and FIFRA's definition of "person" does not appear broad enough to encompass state governments in such a situation.[48]

---

[43] 40 CFR §171.7(b)(2).

[44] Section 27(a).

[45] Section 27(c).

[46] Section 27(b).

[47] 40 CFR Part 173. See 46 Fed Reg 26059 (1983); see also 48 Fed Reg 404 (1983), which interprets the regulation. For a decision concluding that FIFRA does not preempt a local ordinance that stringently regulates pesticide use by commercial applicators and public building owners and operators, see Pesticide Public Policy Foundation v. Village of Wauconda, Illinois, No. 84 C 8110 (N.D.Ill E. Div. 8-19-85).

[48] Section 2(s) defines "person" as "any individual, partnership, association, corporation, or any organized group of persons whether . . . they incorporated or not." Cf. United States v. City of New York, 14 ERC 1410 (S.D. N.Y. 1979) (construing slightly different language in Section 311(a)(7) of the Clean Water Act to include a municipality, but relying on the prefix "including," which does not appear in the FIFRA definition, and a more favorable statutory context).

§3.03 Pesticide Registration Under FIFRA: In General

[1] Historical Development and Overview

[a] In General

The original, 1947, FIFRA[49] provided for a simple and straightforward registration process. An applicant seeking to register his pesticide —or "economic poison," as it was then called—was required to file with the Secretary of Agriculture his name and address, the name of the pesticide, a complete copy of the labeling, a statement of all claims made for it, including directions for use, and, if requested by the Secretary, a full description of the tests made and the results thereof upon which the claims were based.[50] If he or she deemed it necessary for the effective administration of the Act, the Secretary could require the applicant to submit the complete formula of the pesticide.

The statute made it unlawful for any person to reveal or use to his own advantage information relative to product formulas acquired by authority of the Act, and it provided penalties for violations.[51]

The Secretary registered the pesticide if it appeared that its composition was such as to warrant the proposed claims made for it and if the pesticide, its labeling, and other submitted materials compiled with the Act.[52] If the Secretary was dissatisfied with an application, he would notify the applicant of the manner in which the application failed to comply with the Act and permit the applicant to make the necessary corrections.[53] A registration could be cancelled after it had been registered for five years, unless the registrant requested that it be continued in effect, or on motion of the Secretary in order to protect the public.

The post-1972 FIFRA[54] provided for a more complete registration process and stronger enforcement measures, and heralded a policy of thorough scientific analysis of pesticide chemicals before making them available to the public. Under Section 3(c)(5), an applicant for registration must show that his pesticide composition is such as to warrant the proposed claims for it and that its labeling and other submitted materials comply with the Act. EPA must also determine that the pesticide

---

[49] 61 Stat. 163 (1947).
[50] 61 Stat. 167 (1947).
[51] 61 Stat 167, 170.
[52] 61 Stat 167-168.
[53] *Id.*
[54] Federal Environmental Pesticide Control Act of 1972, P.L. 92-516, 85 Stat 973.

will perform its intended function without "unreasonable adverse effects on the environment" and that, when "used in accordance with widespread and commonly regognized practice," it will not "generally cause unreasonable adverse effects on the environment."[55]

Under Section 3(c)(3), EPA must review the data submitted with an application and, "as expeditiously as possible," either register the pesticide or notify the applicant that his application does not comply with FIFRA.[56]

Congress, realizing that the pesticides registered under the 1947 FIFRA had not been subjected to the same level of review required of the new products under the 1972 Act, required EPA to reregister these older pesticides under the stricter standards of the 1972 amendments within four years after the enactment of the 1972 amendments.[57]

Problems soon developed with the registration scheme. One problem was that many data submitters took advantage of FIFRA's trade secret provisions and marked their data on file with EPA as trade secrets pursuant to Section 10(a), thereby relying on Sections 10(b) and 3(c)(1)(D) to preclude EPA's use of those data to support anyone else's application without the submitter's permission. Such claims of trade secret protection thus operated to limit the amount of data available for the EPA to use in considering applications for registration and to thwart the compensation provision of Section 3(c)(1)(D).

A second problem was that many applications for new pesticides were being denied because they had insufficient data to meet the stan-

---

[55] Section 3(c)(5)(A)-(D). The statute prohibits denial of registration wholly or partially based on evidence that the pesticide is nonessential and prohibits preference for one product over another. EPA may either waive the requirements as to efficacy or rely on statute assertions as to efficacy. *Id.*

The one decision interpreting the statute's grant of authority to EPA to base its decision on product effectiveness held that the statute contains no authority for the Agency to deny a registration solely on findings that the product is ineffective, absent a finding that the degree of effectiveness is materially different from the claims made by the producer. S.L. Cowley & Sons Mfg. Co. v. Environmental Protection Agency, 615 F.2d 1312 (10th Cir. 1980). Thus, EPA's regulatory authority over a pesticide's effectiveness is limited to its control over labeling and advertising statements. *Cf.* Stearns Electric Paste Co. v. EPA, 461 F.2d 293 (7th Cir. 1972).

[56] An integral component of the registration process has been an elaborate, changing, and heavily litigated data compensation scheme, which allows an applicant to rely on data previously submitted by another applicant, and provides for compensation in such a case. The data compensation issues are touched on below, but are dealt with in some detail in Section 3.05, *infra.*

[57] 86 Stat 999. The deadline was extended to 1977 by P.L. 94-140. 89 Stat. 752.

dards of the 1972 amendments necessary for a Section 2(c)(5) finding of no "unreasonable adverse effects on the environment," while similar products registered under the 1947 Act and awaiting reregistration remained on the market. This created a double standard in registration.

Third, upon reviewing its files in undertaking separate reregistration of the previously registered pesticides, EPA discovered that the data it had were incomplete and unreliable. It realized it could not reregister any registered pesticides until it determined in what respects the data were incomplete. That EPA would have to acquire more data, plus the fact that some 40,000 products had to be reregistered, impressed upon EPA that it would have to adopt a new registration system if it were to execute FIFRA's mandate.

Congress attempted to remedy this problem by amending FIFRA again in 1978, making extensive changes to Section 3(c)(1)(D).[58] Registration applicants must file, if requested by EPA, "a full description of the tests made and the results thereof upon which the claims are based, or alternatively, a citation to data that appear in the public literature or that previously had been submitted to the Administrator. . . ."[59] Congress also removed the reregistration deadline altogether, replacing it with an "expeditious as practicable" requirement.[60]

EPA also began to streamline its registration process administratively after 1978. Prior to 1978, EPA reviewed applications one at a time, conducting full data reviews for each pesticide end use product. The duplication of effort involved where many products employed the same active ingredient, when viewed in light of EPA's obligation to reregister about 40,000 products, necessitated streamlining the registration process.

EPA changed its focus from end use products to active ingredients and began the development of a generic standard for each active ingredient. It thus conducts a review of all data pertinent to a particular active ingredient and publishes a standard detailing its findings and summarizing its position relative to the active ingredient.

Each standard is intended to set out the conditions that products containing that active ingredient must meet if they are to be registered.

---

[58] 89 Stat 819.

[59] As noted above, the citation to other's data carries with it a potential obligation to pay compensation.

[60] Section 3(g).

It will take ten years or more to develop standards for all of the active ingredients.

EPA proposed its administrative reforms prior to the 1978 amendments, and Congress provided some legitimation to the Agency's practice in amendments to Section 3(c)(2). Section 3(c)(2)(C), for example, requires EPA to publish regulations implementing simplified registration procedures. One such procedure is prescribed by Section 3(c)(2)(D), which exempts applicants who have purchased a registered pesticide from another producer and propose to formulate it into an end use product from submitting or citing safety data relevant to the purchased product and from offering to pay compensation otherwise required by Section 3(c)(1)(D) for their use of such data. This is known as the "formulator's exemption."

Finally, Congress sought to resolve the anomalous situation resulting from applicants being denied registrations for their pesticides because their data were insufficient to satisfy the standards of the 1972 amendments allowing them to remain on the market. Section 3(c)(7) was enacted to allow EPA to register pesticides *conditionally,* upon a showing that allowing each product on the market will not significantly increase the risk of unreasonable adverse effects on the environment presented by pesticides already on the market. Although such a registrant must normally submit additional data to fulfill the conditions imposed on his registration,[61] at least he is able to sell the product. Conditional registrants are required to submit the required additional data at the time EPA requires the manufacturer of the existing products to submit it, in the registration process.[62]

---

[61] See Section 3(c)(2)(B), which authorizes EPA to compel additional data. The statute details the procedures applicable when additional data are requested. Once additional data are requested, registrants must provide evidence within ninety days that they are securing the data. Two or more registrants may agree to develop the additional data jointly, and if they cannot agree on the terms of a data development arrangement, any registrants may initiate binding arbitration. As with Section 3(c)(1)(D), the findings and determination of the arbitrator are not subject to review except for fraud, misrepresentation, or misconduct. By failing to take steps to secure the additional data, cooperate with a joint development arrangement, or abide by an arbitration decision, a registrant may have his registration suspended.

[62] 40 CFR §162.167(c).

[b] Data Compensation Prior to 1978

Under the 1972 amendments, data submitters for the first time were given proprietary rights in their data. Section 10(a) permitted them to mark any portions of their data which they considered to be trade secrets or commercial or financial information, and Section 10(b) prohibited the EPA from disclosing those portions.

The amendments affected data submitters' rights in another way. As under the 1947 Act, applicants still had to submit full descriptions of the tests made and the results thereof upon which their claims were based if they were requested to do so by EPA. But Congress added the following, to what was now Section 3(c)(1)(D):

> [D]ata submitted in support of an application shall not, without permission of the applicant, be considered by the Administrator in support of any other application for registration unless such other applicant shall have first offered to pay reasonable compensation for producing the test data to be relied upon and such data is not protected from disclosure by section 10(b).[63]

The 1975 amendments limited this protection, however, to data submitted on or after January 1, 1970.[64] If the parties could not agree on the amount and method of payment, the EPA could make this determination, with the owner of the data having a right of appeal to a federal district court. But in no event was registration to be delayed pending the determination of reasonable compensation.

[c] The 1978 Data Compensation Approach

The 1978 amendments diminished the rights of the original data submitters substantially. Congress removed from Section 3(c)(1)(D) the ability of a data submitter to invoke Section 10(b) trade secret protection over his data, and substituted new procedures.

Data submitted in support of pesticides initially registered after September 30, 1978, or to support a new use for the pesticide may not be relied upon by another applicant and may not be considered by EPA

---

[63] Federal Environmental Pesticide Control Act of 1972, PL 92-516, Section 2, 86 Stat. 930. Applications processed between 1972 and 1975 were unaffected by the 1975 amendments, discussed below. *See* Amchem Products v. GAF Corporation, 422 F.Supp. 390 (N.D.Ga. 1976).

[64] Act of November 28, 1975, PL 94-140, Section 12, 89 Stat 755.

to support another person's registration without the written permission of the data submitter for a period of ten years following EPA's initial registration of the product.[65]

Data that is submitted after December 31, 1969, and is not entitled to exclusive use may be considered by EPA to support subsequent registrations without the permission of the original data submitter for fifteen years following the original submission date only if the subsequent applicants offer to compensate the original data submitter and provide evidence of such offer to EPA.[66] The statute further provides that if the interested private parties are unable to agree on the amount of compensation to be paid within ninety days of the tender of the offer, either party may initiate binding arbitration, and also provides that resolution of a compensation dispute will not delay registration. The arbitrator's award may not be set aside by federal officials or the courts except for fraud, misrepresentation, or other misconduct.[67]

After the periods of statutory exclusive use, EPA may consider the data to support any other person's application without either permission from the original data submitter or an offer of compensation.[68]

---

[65] Section 3(c)(1)(D)(i).

[66] Section 3(c)(1)(D)(ii).

[67] *Id.* The binding arbitration provision was upheld against arguments that it deprived registrants of the right to neutral judicial review in violation of Article III of the Constitution in Thomas v. Union Carbide Agricultural Products, — U.S. —, 105 S.Ct. 3325, 87 L.Ed.2d 409 (1985). *See also* Eli Lilly and Co. v. EPA, 615 F.Supp. 811, 819 (D.Ind. 1985).

[68] Section 3(c)(1)(D)(iii). In Ruckelshaus v. Monsanto Co., 104 S.Ct. 2862 (1984), the Supreme Court resolved the much-litigated claim that Section 3(c)(1)(D) constituted an unconstitutional taking of property under the Fifth Amendment essentially in the government's favor. The Court held that in no case could the statute confiscate any property rights in data submitted after 1978 or between 1969 and 1972. Data submitted between 1972 and 1978 might, however, be constitutionally protected if state law recognized a property right in trade secrets, since the 1972 amendments conveyed certain proprietary expectations not existing under the prior act or after 1978. The Court further held, however, that the exclusive remedy for any such claim is an action for damages under the Tucker Act, which must be adjudicated in the claims court. Thus, no injunction against registration of subsequent products is available.

See also Monsanto Co. v. Acting Administrator, 564 F.Supp 552 (W.D. Mo. 1983) (reversed by the Court). *Contra,* Petrolite Corp v. United States EPA, 519 F.Supp 966 (D. DC 1981); Mobay Chemical Corp. v. Costle, 517 F.Supp 252, 254 (W.D. Pa. 1981), *aff'd sub nom.* Mobay Chemical Co. v. Gorsuch, 682 F.2d 419 (3d Cir.), *cert. denied,* 459 U.S. 988 (1982); and Chevron Chemical Co. v. Costle, 499 F.Supp 732 (D. Del 1980), *aff'd* 641 F.2d 104 (3d Cir.), *cert. denied,* 452 U.S. 961 (1981). For a post-*Monsanto* decision, *see* Eli Lilly and Co. v. EPA, 615 F.Supp. 811 (D.Ind. 1985) (concluding that complaint makes out a valid due process–based Fifth Amendment takings claim with respect to EPA's use of data to support "me-too" registrations between 1972 and 1978, and holding that there

EPA interpreted the 1978 amendments to require applicants to cite in support of their applications all data in EPA's possession pertinent to the product or any of its ingredients. It accordingly published interim final regulations embodying the "cite all" concept in 1979.[69] The regulations contained a requirement that applicants include a general offer to compensate all affected data submitters in accordance with the Section 3(c)(1)(D) requirements.

The generalized compensation requirement was viewed by much of the industry as unreasonably onerous, since it required potentially massive amounts of compensation to pay for a data base that was often full of gaps. Applicants were required to follow the "cite all" procedure even if they submitted their own data in support of their applications, unless they qualified either for the Section 3(c)(2)(D) "formulators exemption" or the "alternate method of support" allowed under EPA's regulations.

Section 3(c)(2)(D) provides that an applicant who purchases a registered pesticide product from another producer and uses it to formulate an "end use" product need not submit, or offer to pay for, data on the safety of the purchased product. This "formulator's exemption" is premised on the assumption that the product vendor can recoup his data development costs in the price of the ingredient, and to require the formulator to pay compensation would constitute a double payment, impeding competition in the industry.

The "alternate method" permitted qualifying registrants to submit their own data in lieu of "cite all." This exception was limited to end use product applications, and was premised on EPA's assumption that data on end use products would normally apply only to the product for which the data were developed, or closely similar products. Thus, data submitted on other products containing the same active ingredients would not normally be useful.

In 1983 EPA's interpretation of Section 3(c)(1)(D) as essentially mandating the "cite all" scheme was rejected by a court, and the Agency was enjoined from enforcing the mandatory "cite all" scheme.[70] In

---

is no statute of limitations defense to the claim because the "me-too" registrations are continuing).

[69] 44 Fed. Reg. 27932 (1979). The regulations were codified as 40 CFR §§162.9-1 through 162.9-8.

[70] National Agricultural Chemicals Association v. United States Environmental Protection Agency, 554 F.Supp. 1209 (D. D.C. 1983).

response, EPA abandoned mandatory "cite all" and allowed applicants to follow the procedure voluntarily while it worked on revised regulations.[71] The Agency issued final registration procedure/data compensation regulations on August 1, 1984.[72]

[2] The Current Registration Scheme

[a] Substantive Requirements

[i] In General

Distribution, sale, offer for sale, holding for sale, shipping, delivering for shipment, and receipt and subsequent delivery or offer for delivery of a pesticide are unlawful unless the pesticide has first been registered by EPA.[73] An applicant for registration is required to submit, on EPA forms, an application containing, in general, the name and address of the applicant as it will appear on the label, the name of the pesticide, a complete copy of the label, including claims made about the product and directions for use, health and safety testing data, the complete formula, and a request that the pesticide be classified for general use or restricted use or both.[74]

The substantive criteria for registration are that the data support a conclusion that the pesticide, as classified and in consideration of any applicable classification restrictions—

— is composed so as to warrant the proposed claims;[75]

— bears labeling that is adequate to describe the product, how to use it, its risks, etc., and otherwise conforms to EPA's label format, and is not misleading;

— will perform its intended function "without unreasonable adverse effects on the environment"; and

— when used in accordance "with widespread and commonly

---

71 See 48 Fed. Reg. 13196 (1983).

72 See 49 Fed. Reg. 30887 (1984).

73 Section 3(a).

74 Sections 3(c)(1)(A)-(F). The reference to "test data" should be understood to implicate the complex data submission and compensation requirements discussed above and below.

75 To the extent the claims relate to efficacy, both the general tone of Section 3(c)(5) and EPA practice downplay the significance of this requirement.

recognized practice . . . will not generally cause unreasonable adverse effects on the environment."[76]

The contents of an application are dictated by EPA's Guidelines for Registering Pesticides, 40 CFR §§162.41-162.60, as well as the provisions of new Part 158.

The critical criteria are, of course, the "unreasonable adverse effect" criteria. Section 2(bb) defines the relevant phrase to mean "any unreasonable risk to man or the environment, taking into account the economic, social, and environmental costs and benefits of the use of the pesticide." The FIFRA risk-benefit standard allows registration of a product that possesses a potential for adverse human health effects if it is sufficiently beneficial and without available, less risky, substitutes.[77]

The range of options available to EPA at the time of registration is wide. Essentially, FIFRA gives EPA broad discretion to impose conditions on registration, including limitations on the pesticide's use or labeling, or to deny registration. EPA has rarely denied registration outright, however, because the FIFRA standard is geared to registration with controls rather than nonregistration, and because Section 3(c)(7) imposes a procedural barrier that must be crossed before an application for registration can be denied outright. EPA's original implementing regulation, 40 CFR §162.11, created the so-called Rebuttable Presumption Against Registration (RPAR) procedure.[78] In November 1985 the regulation was replaced and procedure revised by 40 CFR §154.7, which created the Special Review procedure.[78.1]

EPA's fundamental regulatory decision, which is premised on the available data relevant to the product for which registration has been sought, is whether to proceed to develop registration standards for the product or to review the data with an eye toward an RPAR.

Traditionally, most pesticide registration standards were developed jointly by the pesticide industry and EPA, working together in a rather informal negotiating process. Industry-assisted registration standards became the usual means of doing business in the Office of Pesticide

---

[76] Sections 3(c)(5)(A)-(D). EPA's interpretative data sufficiency regulations are published at 40 CFR Part 158 and Part 162.6 to 162.8.

[77] Chemical Specialties Manufacturers Association, et al. v. United States Environmental Protection Agency, 484 F.Supp 513 (D. D.C. 1980). *See* Environmental Defense Fund v. Environmental Protection Agency, 510 F.2d 1292 (D.C. Cir. 1975); and Environmental Defense Fund v. Environmental Protection Agency, 548 F.2d 998 (D.C. Cir. 1976).

[78] The procedure is also applied to postregistration review under Section 6 of FIFRA.
[78.1] *See* Section 3.03[2][a][ii], *infra*.

Programs, and thus pesticide registration never took on the adversarial characteristics so common in environmental regulation that developed in the 1970s. However, the Special Review process and other procedural reforms may be expected to change all that.[78.2]

[ii] The RPAR Process ("Special Review")

Under EPA's "Special Review" regulation, 40 CFR Part 154, if, on the basis of evidence developed by EPA or pursuant to a petition filed by a third party,[78.3] the pesticide's ingredients, metabolites, or degradation products meet or exceed specified "risk criteria,"[79] a presumption against registration arises, and EPA shifts the burden to the applicant to provide evidence rebutting its conclusion.[80] Of the six "risk criteria" utilized by EPA, the criterion of chronic toxicity, originally 40 CFR §162.11(a)(3), refined somewhat in the current regulation, has been the most troublesome, in the sense that it has produced most of the litigation involving the registration and cancellation process. The courts have been highly deferential to EPA, and have allowed the Agency to act on the basis of only limited test data suggesting tumor formation in two species of rat at very low doses.[81]

The RPAR process under EPA's original regulations tended to be a forum for negotiation between EPA and applicants, and historically was carried out pretty much outside of public scrutiny, as was the pesticide

---

78.2 *See* Sections, 3.03[2][a][ii] and [iii], *infra.*

78.3 40 CFR §154.10.

79 40 CFR §154.7 (11-27-85) (replacing prior §162.11). The risk criteria are evidence based on tests or other evidence that the pesticide (1) may be acutely toxic; (2) may be oncogenic, mutagenic, fetotoxic, or teratogenic, or chronically or delayed acutely toxic; (3) may result in residues on nontarget organisms that may be acutely or chronically toxic; (4) may pose a risk to the continued existence of an endangered or threatened species protected under the Endangered Species Act; (5) may result in the destruction or other adverse modification of a critical habitat designated under the Endangered Species Act; or (6) may pose some other risk to humans or the environment sufficient to merit a rebalancing of the costs and benefits.

80 40 CFR §154.1(a) states: "[I]ssuance of a Notice of Special Review means that the Agency has determined that one or more uses of a pesticide may pose significant risks and that . . . the Agency expects to initiate formal proceedings seeking to cancel, deny, reclassify, or require modifications to the registration . . . unless it has been shown during Special Review that the Agency's initial determination was erroneous, that the risks can be reduced to acceptable levels without the need for formal proceedings, or that the benefits . . . outweigh the risks." Section 154.5 makes it clear that the burden of proof at all times remains with the registrant.

81 Environmental Defense Fund v. EPA, 510 F.2d 1292 (D.C. Cir. 1975); Environmental Defense Fund v. EPA, 548 F.2d 998 (D.C. Cir. 1976) (involving EPA's cancellation of aldrin/dieldrin and chlordane/heptachlor uses, respectively).

standard-setting and registration process generally. If EPA's staff, or its consultants, raised questions about the nature and degree of risk presented, the Agency would undertake what is called "pre-RPAR review," an essentially *ex parte* negotiation with the interested company or industry group, aimed at more thoroughly evaluating the data and resolving the risk problem by agreement. For example, the applicant might agree to modify the application to eliminate some uses, or specify that applicators wear protective clothing, and the like.

As the result of a consent decree in late 1984 between EPA and several environmental and labor organizations, who had sued EPA claiming that the Agency's procedures unlawfully deprived the public of participation in the Agency's regulatory proceedings, *NRDC et. al v. EPA et al.*,[82] EPA opened up its Special Review Process in late 1985.[82.1]

Under EPA's new "Special Review" regulations, a second look at a pesticide can be initiated by third parties as well as by EPA's staff.[82.2] The Agency establishes a docket and makes a public announcement once Special Review has been initiated[82.3] and conducts notice and comment rulemaking, which may include an informal public meeting or an informal hearing,[82.4] before making its final determination whether or not to initiate cancellation proceedings or refuse registration.[82.5] The agency also publishes decisions not to initiate a Special Review.[82.6]

[iii] **Procedural Reforms**

In settling the *NRDC* litigation, EPA agreed to set up a new docketing system for each pesticide undergoing Special Review or registration standard development. Memoranda of all correspondence and meetings[82.7] and copies of all documents received from outside to govern-

---

[82] Natural Resources Defense Council, Inc., et al. v. United States Environmental Protection Agency, et al, Civil Action No. 83-1509 (D. DC.), filed October 10, 1984. EPA's registration standards implementing this agreement, 40 CFR Part 155 subpart B, were published on November 27, 1985. 50 Fed. Reg. 48998.

[82.1] *See* 50 Fed. Reg. 49003 (11-27-85).

[82.2] 40 CFR §154.10 (11-27-85).

[82.3] 40 CFR §§154.15, 154.25 (11-27-85).

[82.4] 40 CFR §§154.26, 125.27 (meeting) and §125.29 (hearing) (11-27-85).

[82.5] 40 CFR §§154.31, 154.33, 154.35 (11-27-85).

[82.6] 40 CFR §§154.23, 154.25 (11-27-85). Whether, and in what forum, such decisions are reviewable are interesting questions. They appear to be reviewable in the United States District Courts under Section 16(a) of FIFRA.

[82.7] *See* 40 CFR §155.30(d) (11-27-85).

ment are placed promptly in the public file in the docket room,[82.8] and EPA maintains an index to the docket.[82.9] Restrictions are placed on *ex parte* meetings with registrants and their representatives,[82.10] including a requirement that a written memorandum summarizing the meeting be made and placed in the public docket.[82.11] EPA maintains a mailing list of interested persons and organizations to which it will mail on a quarterly basis registration standards material and docket index entries,[82.12] and the Agency will also publish the docket index in the Federal Register on a regular basis.[82.13]

EPA also agreed to establish procedures for involving public comment in its pre-RPAR deliberations, which had traditionally been totally closed, and agreed to provide increased Federal Register publication and opportunity for public comment prior to concluding an RPAR and before referring the RPAR to EPA's Scientific Advisory Panel and the U.S. Department of Agriculture for comment.[82.14]

In a very significant change of direction, EPA agreed to abandon its practice of industry assistance in the development of registration standards, and agreed to make public its draft data evaluation reviews and registration standards by placing them in the public docket.[82.15] The Agency also agreed to solicit comment in the Federal Register on proposed registration standards for pesticides for which the data base was adequate and provide somewhat more opportunity for comment on new active ingredients or pesticides as to whose active ingredients additional data on chronic health effects were required.[82.16]

Finally, in what is essentially a symbolic gesture, EPA agreed to follow its 1976 cancer guidelines in making cancer risk assessments.[83]

[82.8] *See* 40 CFR §155.32 (11-27-85).

[82.9] *See* 40 CFR §155.32(c) (11-27-85).

[82.10] *See* 40 CFR §155.30(b) (11-27-85).

[82.11] *See* 40 CFR §155.30(d). An agreement that advance notice of any meetings be given to the public, and attendance be open, was not adopted by EPA. Such a requirement would further slow down an already slow process.

[82.12] *See* 40 CFR §§155.32(c), 155.32(d) (11-27-85).

[82.13] *See* 40 CFR §155.25 (11-27-85).

[82.14] *See generally* 50 Fed. Reg. 49003 (11-27-85), changing "RPAR" to "Special Review," and adding Part 154, and amending Parts 162 and 172 to provide public participation.

[82.15] *See* 40 CFR §155.27 (11-27-85).

[82.16] *See* 40 CFR §155.34 (11-27-85).

[83] *See* 41 Fed. Reg. 21402 (5-25-76). I say symbolic because, except for a brief period

[b] Generic Registration

The focus of EPA's efforts is the establishment of a generic standard for each active ingredient. EPA begins the generic standard process for a particular chemical with a systematic and comprehensive review of all the data EPA currently possesses for that chemical as well as all other published data and data obtained from other agencies. Next, EPA reviews these data to identify any "data gaps" and to determine (on the basis of these data) what uses and formulations of pesticides can be registered. EPA then publishes a generic standard, which summarizes its review of the data, states the data gaps it has identified, and sets forth the uses and formulations of the active ingredient that can be registered. After a generic standard is published for a particular active ingredient, EPA uses that generic standard to decide which currently registered products containing that active ingredient can be registered, and on what terms. EPA also uses the generic standard in deciding whether to issue registrations in the future for new products containing that active ingredient or for amendments to existing registrations for products containing that active ingredient.[84] As of late 1985, EPA had established generic standards for about thirty products and expected to complete the entire generic standards–setting process in ten to fifteen years.

Most of these standards contain data gaps. Thus, although the standards are fully effective for reregistration and registration purposes, they are in a sense "interim" standards, because when those data gaps are filled the standards may have to be amended.

[c] Conditional Registration and Reregistration

In addition to pressing forward with the generic standards–setting process, on May 11, 1979, EPA published regulations to implement its

---

during the first Reagan Administration when a maverick Assistant Administrator ran the EPA pesticide program, the Agency has pretty much followed the 1976 cancer principles, which are virtually identical to those followed by OSHA and a number of other agencies, and which were formally adopted by the President's Office of Technology Assessment on May 22, 1984, and published in the Federal Register. A significant aspect of the cancer principles is that they state unequivocally that evidence of oncogenicity or mutagenicity derived from multispecies animal studies may be extrapolated to humans for risk assessment purposes without consideration of species-related differences.

[84] *See* 44 Fed. Reg. 76311 (1979).

conditional registration authority and to define the compensation obligations of applicants.[85] The conditional registration regulations establish requirements governing the issuance of conditional registrations (40 CFR §§162.160 *et seq.*) and also contain several modifications to the 1975 registration regulations designed to remove the so-called "double standard" and to ensure that the generic standards program is not impeded by the issuance of registrations. Section 162.7 sets forth EPA's policy of issuing only conditional registrations for products (except for products containing new active ingredients) until generic standards are prepared for the active ingredients contained in those products. Section 162.7(d)(1) provides that EPA will generally conduct complete data reviews only as part of the generic standards program or when acting on applications for products containing new active ingredients. Section 162.7(d)(2) provides that EPA will not issue unconditional registration under Section 3(c)(5) unless EPA first has conducted a comprehensive data review; in such cases, EPA will issue only a conditional registration pursuant to Section 3(c)(7).

A conditional registrant need not submit a complete data base to EPA before a registration can be issued.

[d]   Data Compensation Today

[i]   In General
On August 1, 1984, EPA abandoned a fundamental premise of its post-1978 position on Section 3(c)(1)(D)—that "cite all" was mandatory.[86] EPA's 1984 position is that, while Sections 3(c)(5) and 3(c)(7) allow EPA to consider all relevant data, from whatever source derived, in reviewing the sufficiency of a pesticide registration application, Section 3(c)(1)(D) imposes a separate and distinct level of data review, premised on a concern for protecting the economic interests of data submitters. Thus, while "cite all" is an authorized scheme, it is not the exclusive means by which data may be considered under FIFRA.

Under the new regulations,[87] some data requirements, such as product composition, efficacy, and certain acute toxicity-related data, will ordinarily have to be supplied by the applicant, since they are essentially product dependent. All other data requirements must be satisfied by

---

[85] 44 Fed. Reg. 27932 *et. seq.;* and 44 Fed. Reg. 27945 *et. seq.*

[86] *Compare* 47 Fed. Reg. 57638 *with* 49 Fed. Reg. 30884 *et seq.*

[87] The data compensations are codified at 40 CFR Part 152.

choosing a data base and a method for demonstrating compliance with the Section 3(c)(1)(D) requirements.

The applicant is given two data base choices: "cite all" and selective identification of one or more studies that the applicant believes are sufficient to satisfy each data requirement. Once the choice of data base is made in each case, the applicant must decide how to compensate the data submitter. Where "cite all" is chosen, the applicant must either tender a generalized offer to pay all data submitters or obtain permission to cite the data.[88] Only data submitters possessing exclusive use rights under Section 3(c)(1)(D) need to be compensated, of course.

An applicant who chooses the selective method is required to identify the specific data requirements applicable to his product by reference either to an existing registration standard for the active ingredient(s) or, if none exists, to the Agency's data requirements set forth in 40 CFR Part 158. The applicant must then satisfy the data *submission* requirements in one of the following ways:

— requesting and obtaining a waiver of the data requirements;[89]
— submitting a new valid study;[90]
— citing (not submitting) a valid previously submitted study or studies;[91]

---

[88] The "cite all" rules are codified at 40 CFR §152.86, which is in all material respects identical to EPA's former "cite all" regulation, 40 CFR §§162.9-4 and 162.9-5, which the Agency repealed. EPA maintains a list called Pesticide Data Submitters by Chemical, which the Office of Pesticide Programs will provide to interested persons. EPA is not required to disclose the identity of the applicant or the active ingredient of a pesticide product while it is under review by the Agency and its Scientific Advisory Panel. *See* Monsanto Company v. Ruckelshaus, 753 F.2d 649 (8th Cir. 1985).

[89] 40 CFR §152.91. Even a "cite all" applicant can request a waiver of data requirements, upon a showing that requiring data on the particular risk-benefit issue would not be useful. A selective method applicant may, in addition, satisfy a data requirement by showing a relevant waiver has been granted in the past. The sources of waiver information are published lists of waivers and individual product Registration Standards. There are few lists, and EPA requires applicants to employ Freedom of Information Act procedures to secure whatever is available. 40 CFR §185.45 contains the requirements for making an individual waiver showing.

[90] 40 CFR §152.92. A "new" study is one that has not previously been submitted to EPA. Any claim to trade secret status under Section 10 must be stated in the study, along with the Good Laboratory Practice certification. If the study is not in English, a translation must be provided.

[91] 40 CFR §152.93. If the study falls into the exclusive use category and is owned by someone other than the submitter, or is otherwise compensable, a specific offer to pay the affected submitter must accompany the study. A general offer to pay is not required.

— citing data appearing in "the public literature";[92]
— "cite all";[93] or
— demonstrating the existence of a data gap.[94]

A significant disadvantage of the "cite all" method is that it fails if one data submitter possessing exclusive use data refuses to grant permission to the applicant to use the data. Moreover, EPA notifies all affected exclusive use data submitters prior to taking final action to register a product, affording them the opportunity to object to registration of the product on the ground that the applicant improperly relied on the data without getting permission or supported the application in a manner that improperly avoided citing the data.[95]

[ii] **Applicability of Data Compensation Requirements**

A literal reading of Section 3(c) would require all applications for registration, by anyone, to meet the data compensation requirements. EPA has never read the statute so broadly, however, having carved out the formulator's exemption following the 1978 amendments. EPA has, nevertheless, also not gone to the other extreme of attempting to narrow the scope of Section 3(c)(1)(D) to only situations in which an appli-

---

92 40 CFR §152.94. Such studies include those published in journals and studies paid for by public funds. EPA relies on language in the Senate Report on the 1978 amendments for this (Sen. Rep. No. 95-1188, 95th Cong., 2d Sess. 29). *See* 49 Fed. Reg. 30896 (1984). Its theory is that publication or public funding is inconsistent with any claim to "ownership" within the contemplation of Section 3(c)(1)(D). In responding to complaints that its position will stifle publication of the results of proprietary studies, EPA claims that in most cases the published material will not be of sufficient detail to allow the Agency to evaluate the study, and thus it will have to be purchased anyway. 49 Fed. Reg. at 33896.

93 40 CFR §152.95. Identical to the general "cite all" provision. The applicant must write to and offer to compensate every relevant data submitter on the list. Unfortunately, EPA's data submitter list does not identify persons who have submitted specific studies, only persons who have submitted data on a specific chemical. Thus, the "cite all" method has a tendency to foster gratuitous overcompensation. EPA is working on a study-specific list, called the Pesticide Document Management System, or PDMS.

94 40 CFR §152.96. If no data are available to satisfy a particular requirement and the absence of the data does not bear on the "incremental risk," EPA can conditionally register the pesticide pursuant to Section 3(c)(7). Ascertaining the existence of qualifying data gaps can be tedious if there is not a registration standard for the product's active ingredient in existence that already identifies the gap. EPA will take care of finding and notifying the applicant of data that have filled such a previously identified gap, but if no relevant standard has been issued, the applicant must make many inquiries of data submitters, who are required to respond within sixty days, or lose their proprietary rights to the data. The limitations of Section 3(c)(7), in particular its bar to constitutional registration of a new use, limit the usefulness of this option.

95 49 Fed. Reg. 30891.

cant is seeking to enter a new market or expand his market share or where the action might otherwise alter the extant competitive situation, a reading of the statute that is arguably consistent with the underlying legislative intent.[96]

[iii] The Formulator's Exemption

Section 3(c)(2)(D) provides that any applicant who purchases a registered pesticide product from another producer and uses it to formulate an end use product need not submit, nor offer to pay for, data on the safety of the purchased product.[97] This so-called formulator's exemption is premised on the assumption that whatever data development costs the vendor registrant incurred will be passed on to the vendee as a part of the cost of the product and that FIFRA-mandated compensation thus would constitute double payment.

EPA has broadened the formulator's exemption by regulation. Section 152.85 applies the formulator's exemption not only to end use products, but also to what EPA terms "formulation intermediates" or "technical concentrates," which have previously been registered by others and are purchased by formulators as technical grade active ingredients and reformulated into less concentrated intermediates, which are in turn sold for ultimate reformulation into end use products.

EPA relies for support of this regulation on language pulled from the House Committee on Agriculture report on the bill that became the 1978 Amendments to FIFRA.[98] Although the House Report language explains the formulator's exemption in general terms, it is not evident that the Committee was thinking in as sophisticated a sense as EPA's interpretation requires one to assume. The plain language of the statute speaks only in terms of end use products.

Even if narrowed to end use products only, since most registration

---

[96] EPA is thinking about this. *See* 49 Fed. Reg. 30891 (8-1-84).

[97] Data on the end use product must, of course, be submitted.

[98] The language EPA relies upon, from page 19 of H.R. Rep. No. 95-663, 95th Cong., 1st Sess., is:

[The House Bill] would obviate the need for formulators to furnish certain registration data by providing authority for "generic" registration. Under the "generic" registration plan, detailed submissions and evaluations of the basic chemical need not be repeated with each formulation . . . and formulators [will be] relieved of the need to offer to pay for the registration data except in the purchase price of the basic chemical.

EPA's position was adopted by a federal district court, which refused to set aside the standard, in PBI-Gordon Corporation v. Thomas, 609 F.Supp. 135 (W.D. Mo. 1985).

applications are for reformulation of widely used active ingredients in end use products, the formulator's exemption cuts down significantly the amount of data compensation and evaluation that must go on.

The workings of the formulator's exemption under "cite all" are, however, cumbersome. The exemption only affects the applicant's duty to offer to pay compensation under Section 3(c)(1)(D). The "cite all" rules still require the applicant to communicate with all data submitters on the Data Submitters List in order to determine which of them need not be paid. This problem does not affect applicants who choose the selective method.

Section 152.85 of EPA's regulations spells out the procedures for securing the formulator's exemption. EPA supplies forms to be used by the applicant.

[e] Nature of Data Required

Part 158 of EPA's FIFRA regulations consists of a series of tables and explanatory material that are designed to serve as a guide to applicants in their satisfaction of the Section 3(c)(5) and Section 3(c)(7) data requirements. The requirements include such categories as chemistry, residue chemistry, environmental fate, toxicology, fish and wildlife effects, effects on nontarget plants or insects, reentry protection, and efficacy data. Biochemical and microbial pesticide products are covered by separate data tables.

Data submitters are required to designate elements of data as either "required" or "conditionally required," as indicated in the tables themselves. The latter data are of the type that will vary in their significance to a risk-benefit analysis, depending on such variables as use patterns and formulated composition, while the former are significant to the same degree regardless of such variables. The regulation is structured in such a way that it strongly encourages maximum use of the "required" designation.

[f] Pesticide Classification

A mandatory component of pesticide registration or reregistration is designation of the product as for general use or for restricted use.[99] The designation of one or the other depends on whether EPA determines

---

[99] Section 3(d). The statute allows some uses to be "general use" uses while others are "restricted use" uses, provided the labeling clearly delineates the differences.

that the product "will not" or "may" "generally cause unreasonable adverse effects on the environment," including applicator injury, when used in accordance with the directions for use, or in accordance with widespread and commonly recognized practices.[100]

If EPA decides that the pesticide fails the "generally unreasonable adverse effects" test because of acute dermal or inhalation toxicity only, the only restriction that may be imposed is that the pesticide be applied by or under the supervision of a certified applicator.[101] This action does not appear to be reviewable. If the product fails the test for any other reason, then not only must the product be applied only by or under the supervision of a certified applicator, but EPA is also empowered to impose any other use restrictions "by regulation." Such other restrictions are made specifically subject to judicial review by a U.S. court of appeals on a petition filed within sixty days by a person "adversely affected."[102]

If, after a pesticide has been registered, EPA decides to change the classification from "general use" to "restricted use" in whole or in part, it must notify the registrant forty-five days in advance of its action. The registrant "or other interested person with the concurrence of the registrant" then may request an adjudicatory hearing under Section 6(b) and seek judicial review under Section 16(b) thereafter.[103]

A registrant may at any time file a petition to remove one or more uses of his pesticide from the "restricted use" list, upon a showing that the criteria requiring restricted use status are not satisfied. EPA is required to act on such a petition within sixty days, and the registrant has a right to judicial review, apparently in a U.S. district court, of a denial.[104]

---

[100] Sections 3(d)(1)(B)-(C). *See also* 40 CFR §162.11(c), EPA's regulatory criteria for new classification for new registrations.

[101] Section 3(d)(1)(C)(i).

[102] Section 3(d)(1)(C)(ii). The applicants may be the only people who may appeal. *Cf.*, Environmental Defense Fund, Inc., et al. v. Costle, 631 F.2d 922 (D.C. Cir. 1980) (holding, on labyrinthine logic, that only registrants have a right to a hearing and subsequent access directly to the courts of appeal following partial cancellation of a registration under Section 6 of FIFRA).

[103] Section 3(d)(2).

[104] Section 3(d)(3). Review is arguably in the district courts, because the statute simply says that review may be had "under section 16 of this Act." Section 16 contains two relevant subsections, 16(a) and 16(b). The former vests jurisdiction in the district courts for, *inter alia*, "refusals . . . to change classifications not following a hearing. . . ." Since Section 3(d)(3) says nothing about a hearing, this provision is applicable.

EPA maintains a list of restricted-use pesticides and the restrictions, which is published at 40 CFR §162.31. EPA also classifies certain pesticides as a group, under 40 CFR §162.30.

Certification of applicators of restricted-use pesticides is accomplished pursuant to Section 4 of FIFRA, either by EPA or by a state whose certification program has been approved by EPA.[105]

[g] Labeling

The critical nexus between whatever use restrictions EPA imposes on a pesticide product and the safety of the product's use, once the product has been registered, or, putting it another way, translation of conditions contained in a registration standard to the field, is the label and the instructions placed on or in the package. Accordingly, a significant component of the registration process is the content and form of the label. Once registered, the pesticide may not be placed in the stream of commerce without the approved label.

[h] Miscellaneous Issues

[i] Referral to Other Agencies

Every regulation, including proposed registration standards and notices of intent to cancel registrations, must be referred to EPA's Science Advisory Board and to the Secretary of Agriculture.[106] The Science Advisory Board provides comments to the Administrator on the health and safety issues only. The Secretary provides comments on those issues, as well as on the risks-benefits calculus and has special expertise in connection with the requirement of Section 25(a)(2)(B) that EPA take into account the effect of its regulations on agricultural production and prices, retail food prices, and other agricultural economic impacts.

[ii] Label or Formulation Changes

Each change in the label or formulation of a registered pesticide necessitates an amendment to the registration.

[iii] Legal Effect of Registration

Registration constitutes a license from the federal government to market and use the product in accordance with its registration standard

---

[105] *See* Section 3.02[2][d], *supra.*
[106] Sections 25(a), 25(d), and 6(b).

and any other applicable regulatory restrictions. Attempts to claim that registration is proof of safety as a defense to tort liability have not met with success.

Although it has generally been held that EPA is not required to comply with the National Environmental Policy Act[106.1] in connection with its FIFRA registration activities,[106.2] the fact that a pesticide has been registered under FIFRA does not necessarily insulate a user of the pesticide from NEPA compliance.[106.3]

[iv] Packaging Regulation

Section 25(c)(3) of FIFRA, added by the 1975 amendments, authorizes EPA to establish standards for pesticide packages, containers, and wrappings "in order to protect children and adults from serious injury or illness resulting from accidental ingestion or contact with pesticides or devices regulated by [FIFRA]." A parenthetical phrase within the provision states that any such regulations "shall be consistent with those established under the authority of the Poison Prevention Packaging Act" (PPPA),[107] which is administered by the Consumer Product Safety Commission (CPSC).

EPA's packaging regulations are codified at 40 CFR §162.16. They require that pesticides be marketed in child-resistant packages if they meet specified acute toxicity numerical thresholds[108] or, "based on human toxicological data, use history, accident data, or such other evidence as is available," they present a "serious hazard of accidental

---

106.1 42 USC §§4321 *et seq.*

106.2 *See* Wyoming v. Hathaway, 525 F.2d 66 (10th Cir. 1975), *cert. denied,* 426 U.S. 906 (1976); EDF v. EPA, 489 F.2d 1247 (D.C. Cir. 1973); EDF v. Blum, 485 F. Supp. 650 (D.D.C. 1978); and Merrill v. Thomas, 608 F. Supp. 644 (D. Or. 1985).

106.3 *See* Save Our Ecosystems v. Clark, 747 F.2d 1240 (9th Cir. 1984). This decision opined that the mere fact that EPA's registration standard does not account for a given effect is not a shield from a NEPA-based obligation to consider the effect, pointing out that under EPA's conditional registration scheme, a product can be registered and used in the absence of a complete set of data, and suggested that "widespread fraud in the tests performed by independent testing laboratories" cast doubt on the validity of the conclusions reached in support of registration. *Id.* at 1246-48 and fns. 9 and 12. The court even went so far as to suggest that NEPA authorized or compelled a federal agency using pesticides to require the chemical vendors to do additional research to fill in data gaps. *Id.* at 1247. *See also* Southern Oregon Citizens Against Toxic Sprays v. Clark, 720 F. 2d 1475 (9th Cir. 1983); Oregon Environmental Council v. Kunzman, 714 F.2d 901 (9th Cir. 1983); and Citizens Against Toxic Sprays v. Bergland, 428 F. Supp. 908 (D.Or. 1977).

107 P.L. 91-601, 15 U.S.C. §§1471 *et seq.*

108 *See* 40 CFR §162.16(b)(1)(i)-(v).

injury or illness which child-resistant packaging could reduce,"[109] and the pesticide is either expressly marketed for residential use or such use can be inferred from the label, and the pesticide is not restricted to certified applicators.[110] EPA's regulation does not require evidence of actual accident history as an element of proof to support a restriction.[111]

There are two bases for exemption from an otherwise applicable child-resistant packaging requirement. The first is if the registrant is able to convince EPA that the per se toxicity data are not indicative of human risk. The second, based on Section 1(a)(2) of the PPPA,[112] requires a showing that such packaging is not technically feasible for the registrant, and involves consideration of several listed factors that seek to determine the extent of the problem.[113]

[3] Disclosure of Proprietary Data

Section 10 of FIFRA provides the rules under which data submitted to EPA may be claimed to constitute a trade secret and prescribes the circumstances and conditions under which data subject to a trade secret claim may be disclosed by EPA to the public or otherwise.

Section 10(d) authorizes public disclosure of all information concerning the objectives, methodology, results, or significance of any test performed on or with a pesticide and of any residue, environmental chemistry, safety, toxicology, metabolism, and fish and wildlife data.

Information that discloses manufacturing or quality control processes, discloses the details of any methods of testing, directing, or measuring the quantity of deliberately added inert ingredients, or discloses the identity or percentage quantity of any deliberately added inert ingredients may not be disclosed to anyone, unless EPA determines that disclosure is necessary to protect against an unreasonable risk of injury to health or the environment. Similarly, information con-

---

109 40 CFR §162.16(b)(1)(vi).

110 Sections 162.16(b)(2) and (3). In some cases even restricted-use pesticides may be required to have child-resistant packaging. Section 162.16(d).

111 A challenge to EPA's *per se* toxicity criteria as inconsistent with the PPPA was rejected in the one case interpreting this FIFRA provision, GPS Industries, et al. v. Environmental Protection Agency, C.A. No. 80-1163 (D.D.C. 1981) (unpublished opinion by United States District Judge Charles R. Richey).

112 15 USC §1472(a)(2).

113 *See* 40 CFR §162.16(f). The lack of toxicity criterion is not satisfied by evidence of lack of exposure. GPS Industries, Inc., *supra* note 111. Financial hardship will not satisfy the technical infeasibility criteria. *Id.*

cerning production, distribution, sale, or inventories is nondisclosable except in connection with public proceedings to determine whether the pesticide or any ingredient causes unreasonable adverse effects on the environment and EPA deems disclosure to be in the public interest. Before disclosing any such data, however, EPA is required to notify the data submitter, and Section 10 contains a procedure for contesting EPA's decision.[114]

Disclosures to foreign or multinational pesticide producers without the data submitter's consent are prohibited, and anyone seeking information must affirm that he or she is not a representative of such an entity and will not disclose the information to such an entity.[115]

EPA may disclose confidential information to its contractors or their employees if the Agency determines that such disclosure is necessary for the satisfactory performance of the contractor's work under FIFRA. The contractor is required to provide evidence of adequate internal security to preserve confidentiality.[116]

Unauthorized disclosure is punishable as a criminal offense under Section 10(f).

Finally, Section 3(c)(2)(A) contains a separate data disclosure provision requiring EPA to make data contained in a registration statement public within thirty days of the registration action, along with any other scientific information EPA deems relevant to its decision, unless disclosure is prohibited by Section 10.[117]

[4] Residue Tolerances on Agricultural Commodities

[a] In General

EPA has the responsibility for determining tolerances for pesticide residues on "raw agricultural commodities" under Section 408 of the

---

[114] Section 10(d). The statute gives the data submitter time to hurry into federal district court and seek an injunction against disclosure. An injunction can be granted only if the plaintiff convinces the judge that EPA's determinations leading to disclosure were erroneous.

[115] Section 10(g). Disclosure to such entities in the context of a public proceeding of information relevant to an unreasonable adverse effects determination (for example, a cancellation or suspension hearing under Section 6) is not prohibited.

[116] Section 10(e).

[117] The constitutionality of Section 10 was established in Ruckelshaus v. Monsanto Company, — U.S. —, 104 S.Ct. 2862 (1984).

Federal Food, Drug and Cosmetic Act.[118] Under the FFDCA, a raw agricultural product is deemed "unsafe" if it contains a pesticide residue, unless the residue is within the limits of a "tolerance" established by EPA or is exempt from the requirement of a tolerance.[119]

Processed foods are not directly regulated, in that tolerances are set only for the "raw" products. However, Section 406 of the FFDCA deems a preserved or processed product unsafe unless the raw product from which it is made is either exempt from the requirement of a tolerance or in compliance with a tolerance, the raw product's residues have "been removed to the extent possible in good manufacturing practice,"[120] and the concentrations of the pesticide in the food when it is ready to eat do not exceed the tolerance permitted on the raw commodity.

Tolerances and exemptions may come about in one of three ways. The most common is by a petition filed by a proponent of the action, typically a pesticide manufacturer, or in some cases an agricultural producer.[121] Tolerances or exemptions may also be established by EPA on its own motion, or on petition by an interested person, who may be seeking either a more stringent or a more lenient tolerance.[122]

Although the FFDCA and FIFRA are in general not integrated, there is a link between the two statutes that affects Section 408(d) petitioners and Section 3 registrants, who are usually the same people. EPA takes the position that a pesticide whose uses include application to raw agricultural commodities may not be registered under FIFRA until the requisite tolerance or exemption has been secured. Its reasoning is that a decision on the labeling cannot be made until the allowed

---

[118] 21 USC §346a. This authority was transferred to EPA as a part of Reorganization Plan No. 3 (1970), which created the Agency by executive order. Prior to 1970, the statute was administered by the FDA. Section 408 dates from the 1958 amendments to the FFDCA (P.L. 83-518). EPA's regulations were first promulgated in 1971, at 36 Fed. Reg. 22533. The residue tolerance program is administered by the Pesticide Registration Division within EPA's Office of Pesticide Programs.

[119] The term "raw agricultural commodity," defined by Section 401q of the FFDCA, includes such things as fresh fruits in their unpeeled form, regardless of coloring or other treatment, vegetables in their raw or natural state, whether or not their outer leaves have been stripped or they have been waxed, raisins, nuts, meat, raw milk, eggs, grains, and similar agricultural produce. It does not encompass foods that have been processed, fabricated, or manufactured by freezing, cooking, dehydrating, or milling. 40 CFR §180.1(e).

[120] Section 406; 40 CFR §180.1(f).

[121] See 40 CFR §§180.7 et seq.

[122] See 40 CFR §180.29; and Section 408(e), FFDCA.

residue levels have been established.[123] Thus, a registrant's first stop on the road to regulatory clearance for a pesticide intended for agricultural use is to get a tolerance or exemption established.

[b] Certificate of Usefulness

Section 408(d) requires as a prerequisite to establishing a tolerance or exemption that EPA must determine that the pesticide is useful for the purpose for which the tolerance is sought.[124] A determination of usefulness involves a determination by EPA, upon evidence submitted by the petitioner, that the pesticide is useful on the basis of its practical pesticidal, or biological, effectiveness. The statute, and EPA's implementing regulations, 40 CFR Part 163, require a demonstration of the product's pest reduction ability on target crops, or yield increases, and other indicia that the product will possess economic utility in the agricultural industry. If EPA proposes to deny the usefulness of a proferred pesticide, it is required to afford the petitioner a hearing.[125]

The second preliminary decision EPA makes as a prerequisite to considering the petition for a tolerance or exemption is whether the tolerance proposed by the petitioner "reasonably reflects the amount of residue likely to result" when the pesticide is used in the manner proposed.[126] EPA does not consider a petition for a tolerance or exemption ripe for consideration until both of the Part 163 determinations have been made, and thus the time period established by Section 408 within which EPA is required to act on a tolerance petition does not begin to run until both determinations are made.[127]

[c] Establishment of a Tolerance or Exemption

[i] Substantive Criteria

Unless "generally recognized as safe" ("GRAS" in FFDCA parlance) by qualified experts, a pesticide that will be used on raw agricultural products must either be granted a tolerance under Section 408 or be

---

[123] *See* 40 CFR §163.11.

[124] Curiously, a tolerance established by EPA on its own motion, or on petition by an interested party, under Section 408(e), does not require a certificate of usefulness. *See* 40 CFR §180.29(a).

[125] *See* 40 CFR §163.9.

[126] 400 CFR §163.12.

[127] *See* 40 CFR §180.4. The statute (Section 408(d)(2)) and 40 CFR §180.7(g) require action within ninety days.

declared exempt from the requirement that it have a tolerance by EPA.[128]

The FFDCA does not provide precise criteria on which EPA bases its decision to either grant an exemption, set a numerical tolerance of "negligible,"[129] or of "zero." The sole statutory criterion, set forth in Section 408(b), is that a tolerance may be established if the "scientific evidence" supports a conclusion that the residue level is sufficient to "protect the public health." The statute requires a zero tolerance if the "scientific data before the Administrator does (*sic*) not justify the establishment of a greater tolerance."

EPA's regulations provide somewhat more specific criteria for making decisions about pesticide residues. Section 180.1001 provides that an exemption is appropriate "when it appears that the total quantity of the pesticide in or on all raw agricultural commodities for which it is useful under conditions of use currently prevailing or proposed will involve no hazard to the public health."[130]

Zero tolerances, which apply at the point of shipment of the commodity, are authorized by 40 CFR §180.5 in any of the following four circumstances, "among other reasons":[131]

— where a "safe level" in the diet of two warm-blooded animals has not been "reliably determined";
— if the chemical is carcinogenic in, "or has other alarming physiological effects upon one or more species of test animals used, when fed in the diet of such animals";
— if, though toxic, the chemical is not normally employed at times that fruit, vegetables, or other raw commodities would bear or contain it; and
— if all residue is normally removed through good agricultural

---

128 Very few pesticides have been deemed GRAS. Those that are are listed by EPA at 40 CFR §180.2.

129 A "negligible" residue is defined by 40 CFR §180.2(1) as an amount remaining on a raw product that "would result in a daily intake regarded as toxicologically insignificant on the basis of scientific judgment of adequate safety data," usually interpreted numerically as 1/2000 of the amount demonstrated to have "no effect" on the most sensitive laboratory species tested.

130 EPA's specific exemption grants, published in subpart D of Part 180, reveal that the kinds of situations warranting an exemption include the following: where normal practice would remove a water-soluble pesticide whose residue is only on the exterior of the commodity, where the properties of the pesticide demonstrate an inevitable breakdown into harmless components prior to human ingestion, and the like.

131 It has never been made clear just what "other reasons" might apply.

practice (such as washing), weathering, or changes in the chemical itself prior to introduction of the commodity into interstate commerce.[132]

Those pesticides for which tolerances have been adopted, together with the tolerances, are published in subpart C of Part 180. EPA also maintains a computer-generated alphabetical list of commodities and their tolerances, called the Pesticide Tolerance Commodity Index, which is available from the Office of Pesticides and Toxic Substances, and is published yearly as an addendum to the volume of the Code of Federal Regulations containing 40 CFR Part 180. EPA expresses tolerances in parts of pesticide by weight per million parts of raw agricultural commodity by weight. Determination of compliance with tolerances in the field is required to be accomplished by following the methodology set forth in the FDA publication *Pesticide Analytical Manual.*[133]

Subpart A of the regulations contains a number of interpretive regulations, setting forth such matters as how EPA treats related families of pesticides and how it treats animal feeds.[134]

There is no data compensation available under Section 408, even though once a tolerance has been established for a product, the tolerance is automatically applicable for that use to all other products containing the same active ingredient. There is simply no data compensation requirement in the FFDCA.

---

[132] 40 CFR §§180.5(a)-(d). The first two criteria differ significantly in their nature from the second pair. On the one hand, zero tolerances are appropriate effectively to ban a product from use on agricultural products because any human exposure to it, no matter how small, is deemed unacceptable. Section 180.5(a) appears to be premised on the last sentence of Section 408(b), while Section 180.5(b) is derived from the so-called Delaney provision of the FFDCA, which, though not contained within Section 408, has been held to bear on EPA's decisionmaking under that provision. *See* Environmental Defense Fund v. U.S. Dept. of Health, Ed. and Welfare, 428 F.2d 1083 (D.C. Cir. 1970).

On the other hand, the latter two subsections of the regulation are desinged to allow a product's use but ensure that the practices that keep the residues at a zero level are maintained. The final subsection appears duplicative of EPA's exemption criterion.

[133] 40 CFR §101(c). The manual is available from the FDA.

[134] Animals that ingest plant material containing pesticide residues may retain the pesticide in their liver or fat, or metabolize it, secrete it, or even concentrate it. Thus, EPA must establish tolerances, where it can, both for the animal products that are consumed by humans and for the plant material consumed by the animals that humans eat. Some animal pesticide residues also come from pesticides applied directly to the animals to control animal pests.

[ii] **Procedural Requirements**

The residue tolerance and exemption program is not a part of FI-FRA, and thus exists as a self-contained entity within EPA's pesticide regulatory scheme. Judicial review is governed by the FFDCA, as are the administrative procedures, which are set forth in subpart B of Part 180 and differ significantly from the FIFRA-based procedures.

A Section 408(d) applicant (the product proponent) is required to petition EPA, using a form set out in 40 CFR §180.7(b), and include with the petition a check in the amount of the requisite filing fee.[135] EPA's staff will publish notice of the petition in the Federal Register and begin reviewing the proferred data once the Agency has issued the Section 408(l) certificate of usefulness. If the staff believes that the requested tolerance satisfies the statutory criterion, and no "adversely affected" person has requested a hearing pursuant to Section 408(d)(5) and 40 CFR §180.13, the Agency will propose to adopt the tolerance and publish it in the Federal Register.

If EPA proposes to deny the tolerance, the applicant may choose to withdraw the petition and negotiate with EPA or request referral of the petition to an Advisory Committee. EPA is required to set up an Advisory Committee if it receives such a request. Section 408(g) specifies the composition of the committee, which is essentially controlled by the National Academy of Sciences.[136] An Advisory Committee report, which is supposed to contain an independent evaluation of the evidence, is not binding on EPA, but would no doubt carry great weight in a subsequent judicial review proceeding.[137]

A dissatisfied Section 408(d) petitioner, as an alternative remedy, and any other "adversely affected" person, as his sole administrative remedy, may submit objections to EPA within thirty days of publication of

---

[135] Section 408(o) authorizes the imposition of filing fees sufficient to cover the administrative costs of regulating the product. EPA has set the fee at $10,000 plus an additional $1000 for each additional tolerance or exemption requested beyond nine. *See* 40 CFR §180.33. Different fee scales are provided for temporary tolerances and other regulatory actions.

[136] Advisory Committee proceedings are governed generally by Section 408(d)(3), and specifically by 40 CFR §§180.10-180.12. EPA may also refer a petition to an Advisory Committee on its own motion. *See* Section 408(d)(2). Referral to an Advisory Committee usually results in the imposition of a surcharge on the petitioner to cover the additional administrative costs, although EPA's regulations encourage grouping referrals so that the costs can be spread around.

[137] The statute and regulations contain time limitations within which the various levels of review are theoretically required to take place.

a tolerance or exemption, whether or not the action followed an Advisory Committee referral.[138] A proper statement of objections[139] triggers an adjudicatory hearing.[140]

Section 408(e) provides an alternative basis for establishing a tolerance. Under its authority, EPA, either on its own motion or on a request filed by an "interested person," may establish a tolerance or exemption. This authority is most often invoked to take a second look at an existing tolerance in light of newly developed evidence relating to the safety of the pesticide.

An "interested person" is required to submit "reasonable grounds" for the action requested, and EPA's regulations include within the purview of that phrase a demonstration of the nature of the person's interest and all supporting Section 408(d)(1)(A)-(F) data.[141] EPA is required to publish any Section 408(e) proposal. Within thirty days of publication, either the original petitioner, or the registrant of the pesticide for which the tolerance was established or is proposed, if the two are different, may request referral to Advisory Committee, which, within a specified time period is to render a recommendation to EPA. There is no right to a hearing under Section 408(e), and where the contemplated action involves amending an existing tolerance to zero, or to some other more stringent level, it has been held that the burden of proof remains on the original petitioner to demonstrate the continued viability of the old tolerance, provided the Section 408(e) proponent has made out a *prima facie* case for the change.[142]

[iii] **Judicial Review**

Judicial review of tolerance and exemption decisions resides in the U.S. court of appeals for the circuit where the petitioner "resides or has

---

138 Section 408(d)(5). If the objector is someone other than the petitioner, the objection statement must be served on the petitioner, who has fourteen days within which to file a written response.

139 *See* 40 CFR §180.13 for the content of an objection statement.

140 The hearing proceedings are governed by 40 CFR §§180.14-180.28. The hearings are of the hybrid adjudication type, which allows some, but not all, of the trappings of judicial trial. One interesting requirement of Section 408(d)(5) is that if there has been a referral to an Advisory Committee, the National Academy of Sciences must designate one of the members to testify at a subsequent hearing.

141 40 CFR §180.29(a). *See also* 40 CFR §180.32, which specifically deals with amendments to existing tolerances. There is a filing fee of $1000, plus an additional $1000 for each affected commodity, if the request is to lower an existing tolerance. 40 CFR §180.33(c).

142 Environmental Defense Fund v. U.S. Dept. HEW, 428 F.2d 1083 (D.C. Cir. 1970).

his principal place of business"[143] or in the District of Columbia Circuit.[144]

Judicial review of action on a Section 408(d) petition is not available until an order has been issued following a hearing. Thus, requesting an administrative hearing is a remedy that must be exhausted. Since no hearing is available in connection with Section 408(l) certification or a Section 408(e) action, judicial review is ripe following EPA's action under either. The statute contains a special provision for a limited remand by the court, while it retains jurisdiction, for the purpose of allowing EPA to adduce additional evidence, if the court believes the record is deficient.

EPA's regulations define the scope of the administrative record and stipulate how petitions for review must be served on the Agency.[145]

[d] Temporary Tolerances

Section 408(j) authorizes the issuance of temporary tolerances for agricultural uses of pesticides allowed to be used pursuant to an experimental use permit issued under Section 5 of FIFRA. EPA's regulations set forth the procedures required to be followed, establish filing fees, and delimit the scope of temporary tolerances.[146]

§3.04 Special Types of Registration Under FIFRA

[1] Experimental Use Permits

[a] In General

Pesticides may be approved for experimental uses under Section 5 of FIFRA for the purpose of accumulating data necessary to register the

---

143 Section 408(i)(1).

144 28 USC §2112(a) is available to determine the court of jurisdiction in the event of a "tie" following a race to the courthouse by competing petitioners.

145 See 40 CFR §§180.23-26 and 180.30.

146 See generally 40 CFR §180.31. Section 180.31(e) specifies several mandatory condition categories. These are a limitation on the amount of the chemical to be used on designated crops; a requirement that the experimental design be demonstrated, and that only qualified personnel use the product; a requirement that the permittee immediately inform EPA of any "reports on findings" from the experimental use that have a bearing on safety; and a requirement that records of the use be generated and kept for at least two years, and be made available to EPA on request.

pesticide under Section 3.[147] Experimental Use Permits (EUPs) are available to develop test data for previously unregistered pesticides or for unregistered uses for registered pesticides.[148] If the experimental uses contemplated may reasonably be expected to leave a residue on any food or feed, a temporary tolerance under Section 408 of the FFDCA must first be obtained.[149]

It should be understood that EPA, despite the breadth of Section 5, does *not* require an EUP for tests—including land application, aquatic uses, and animal treatments—that are designed solely to yield data for the purpose of satisfying the Section 3 registration requirements. Only experimental uses that are expected to produce pest control or economic benefit to the person conducting the test require an EUP.[150] Section 5(f) provides for delegation of EUP-issuance authority to the states, and the delegation criteria are published as 40 CFR Part 172 subpart B.[151]

EPA will refuse issuance of an EUP if it believes that the permit is "not justified" or that issuance of the permit would cause unreasonable adverse impacts on the environment or for any other reason the Agency thinks is supportable.[152]

EUPs normally have a one-year term, but are renewable.[153] The EUP regulations contain requirements for the content of EUP applications,[154] required labeling,[155] and data gathering, recordkeeping, and reporting.[156] An EUP holder may import technical materials without

---

[147] Section 5(a).

[148] 40 CFR §172.2(a).

[149] Section 5(b); 40 CFR §172.4(b)(2).

[150] *See* 40 CFR §172.3(a). The regulation imposes certain *per se* limitations on the type of testing that does not require a permit, however. For example, if experimental land use involves more than ten acres of crops, the use is deemed to require a permit. *See* 40 CFR §172.3(a)(1). Small-scale field testers of microbial pesticides are required to notify EPA prior to the testing. *See* 49 Fed. Reg. 40659 (1984) (interim policy on small-scale field testing of microbial pesticides).

[151] *See generally* 44 Fed. Reg. 41787 (1979).

[152] 40 CFR §172.10(a). This seems premised in part on Section 5(e) of FIFRA, which states the bases for revocation of an EUP.

[153] 40 CFR §§172.5(b) and 172.9.

[154] 40 CFR §172.4.

[155] 40 CFR §172.6. The labeling requirements mandate, among other things, a statement that the chemical is for experimental use only, and is not for sale.

[156] 40 CFR §§172.5, 172.8.

registering them, if he has indicated in the EUP application that he will be doing so.[157]

[b] Data

It has been a matter of EPA policy, not reflected in the text of Part 172, to allow EUP registrants to cite all data existing in EPA's files relative to the product's ingredients. EPA apparently finds sufficient transferable authority in Section 3 to authorize the practice, but does not apply Section 3(c)'s data compensation provisions to EUPs. EPA's practice was upheld in *Rohm and Haas Co. v. EPA and Mobil Oil Corporation*,[158] in which a federal district court deferred to EPA's statutory interpretation, holding that Section 5 does not prohibit an EUP from being based on data that have not been submitted by the applicant, and that the data compensation restrictions of Section 3(c)(1)(D) are inapplicable to EUP applications governed by Section 5.

[c] Procedures

EUP applicants are required to submit their applications in the form and containing the contents dictated by 40 CFR §172.4. EPA will publish notice of receipt of the application in the Federal Register and solicit public comment only if it deems that the EUP "may be of regional or national significance."[159] It will schedule a legislative-type public hearing on the application if comments received in response to a Federal Register notice require it or if it determines that a public hearing would otherwise be in the public interest.[160] EPA does, however, publish notice of its issuance of all EUPs, in which it lists the active ingredients, the use patterns, the quantity of pesticide involved, the total acreage involved, the location of the application, and a statement indicating where the permit may be examined.[161]

In the event EPA decides to deny or revoke an EUP, it affords the applicant/holder an "opportunity to confer," which is something less

---

[157] 40 CFR §172.7.

[158] 651 F.2d 176 (3d Cir. 1981), *aff'g* 525 F. Supp. 921. Rohm & Haas, manufacturer of a herbicide called "Tackle," challenged an EUP issued for Mobil's "Blazer," which had the same active ingredient, acifluorfen. These multinational companies also litigated patent infringement claims. *See* Rohm & Haas Co. v. Mobil, C.A. No. 78-384 (D.Del.); and Mobil v. Rohm & Haas Co., C.A. No. 79-397 (D.Del.).

[159] 40 CFR §172.11(a).

[160] 40 CFR §172.11(b).

[161] 40 CFR §172.11(c).

than a hearing in the sense that term is ordinarily understood.[162]

[d] Miscellaneous Issues

EUPs may be issued to public or private agricultural research agencies and educational institutions "notwithstanding" the provisions of Section 5.[163] EPA has not treated these entities differently from other EUP seekers.

[2] "Special Local Needs" Registration

[a] In General

Section 24 of FIFRA allows states to provide registration for additional uses of EPA-registered pesticides to meet "special local needs." Such registration is prohibited, however, if registration for the proposed use has previously been denied, disapproved, or canceled by EPA, and the Agency is given power to veto state registrations.[164]

EPA adopted interpretive regulations in 1981,[165] although EPA required state registrations to be consistent with more general requirements as early as 1975.[166] State registrations prior to 1975 are essentially exempt from the Section 24(c) requirements by virtue of a grandfathering provision in 40 CFR §162.150(b).

EPA's regulations define "special local need" as "an existing or imminent pest problem within a State for which the State lead agency, based on satisfactory supporting information, has determined that an appropriate federally registered pesticide is not sufficiently available."[167] The regulations also include voluntary cancellation following issuance of a notice of intent to cancel by EPA on health and safety grounds as prohibiting local registration of the product for that use.[168]

The regulations substantially refine the scope of allowable state regulations under Section 24(c). A state may register any new use of a

---

[162] 40 CFR §172.10(c).

[163] Section 5(g).

[164] Sections 24(c)(1) and (c)(2). EPA may not, however, veto a state registration because of a lack of essentiality or, unless EPA finds that the use is inconsistent with the FFDCA or constitutes an imminent hazard, for any other reason if the pesticide is similar in its composition and use patterns to a federally registered pesticide. *Id.*

[165] 46 Fed. Reg. 2014 (1981); 40 CFR §§162.150-156 (subpart D).

[166] *See* 40 CFR §162.17.

[167] 40 CFR §151(h).

[168] *See* 40 CFR §162.152(a).

federally registered pesticide, and any use of a federally registered pesticide as to which some other uses have been denied, disapproved, suspended, or canceled, the latter only after consultation with EPA.[169] The regulations prohibit states from registering amendments for federally registered manufacturing-use products.[170]

In an apparent expansion of the statutory authorization, EPA's regulations allow state registration of new pesticides in addition to new uses of existing pesticides. Thus, states may register (1) new end use products that are identical in composition to a federally registered product but formulated by a different entity and packaged differently, (2) new products that contain the same inert and active ingredients as a federally registered product but in different percentages, and (3) new products that are formulated from combinations of inert and active ingredients not federally registered in those combinations if each of the active ingredients is present because of the use of one or more federally registered products and each of the inert ingredients is contained in a federally registered product (not necessarily the same products).[171] Notwithstanding such authority, states may not register manufacturing-use products.

EPA also embellished the canceled-products prohibition somewhat. It allows states to register new formulations or uses of products that have been canceled, denied, etc., provided the formulations or uses were not involved, but requires EPA consultation prior to registration of a formulation or use of a canceled or denied product if that formulation or use was not "considered" by EPA in the prior action and allowed to remain registered.[172]

State registrations that are not vetoed by EPA are considered FIFRA registrations, and are therefore subject to all of the Section 3 and Sec-

_____

169 40 CFR §§162.152(b)(i)-(iii). EPA requires a hearing prior to allowing any such use. *See* 40 CFR §§164.130 *et seq.*, and 40 Fed. Reg. 12265 (1975), for procedures governing such hearings.

170 40 CFR §162.152(b)(iv).

171 40 CFR §§162.152(b)(2)(A)-(C).

172 40 CFR §162.152(b)(2)(iv). A voluntary cancellation taken before EPA has issued a notice of intent to cancel on environmental or safety grounds does not prohibit a state registration. *Id.* This provision raises the specter of registrant's voluntary cancellation prior to formal initiation of cancellation proceedings for a chemical that is suspect and subsequent state registration.

tion 6 requirements and other FIFRA provisions.[173]

[b] Procedural Requirements

EPA's 1981 regulations establish minimum procedural requirements the states must follow in registering special local needs uses and products. Although there may be some question about the statutory authority for these requirements, EPA hangs its regulatory hat on Section 24(a), which conditions state registration on a proviso that it "does not permit any sale or use prohibited by" FIFRA, which includes EPA's power to veto state registrations and EPA's power to suspend state registration authority.

The regulations specify what supporting material must accompany a special local needs regulation and require the state agency to make a special local needs determination and an efficacy determination.[174] They require further that the state make a formal determination prior to registration that use of the product will not result in an unreasonable adverse impact, subject to three exceptions, all related to uses identical or similar to federally registered uses.[175] There are, finally, labeling and packaging standards and a classification requirement.[176]

EPA also requires states to submit to the Agency, within ten days of action on a registration, formula and labeling information and subsequently submit a copy of the final label.[177] This means that EPA does not routinely oversee state efficacy and effects determinations. Such information, including underlying test data, is only required when requested by EPA.[178]

EPA publishes a summary of state registrations periodically in the Federal Register.

[c] Disapproval Criteria

EPA has created two categories of disapproval: general disapproval and special disapproval. The primary difference, other than the grounds, lies in the fact that a general disapproval must occur, if at all,

---

[173] *See* 40 CFR §§162.152(c) and 162.156.
[174] 40 CFR §§162.153(a), (b), and (d).
[175] 40 CFR §162.151(c).
[176] 40 CFR §§162.151(e) and (f).
[177] 40 CFR §162.151(h).
[178] 40 CFR §162.151(h)(4).

within ninety days of the state action, while special disapproval may occur at any time.[179]

A general disapproval is limited to state registrations that involve a product and use pattern that are dissimilar to any that are federally registered and for which EPA finds "reasonable grounds" for disapproval. "Reasonable grounds" include refusal by the state to submit required information under 40 CFR §162.153(h), failure of submitted information to support registration, and "probable creation of unreasonable adverse effects on man or the environment."[180] A special disapproval requires a "determination" by EPA that use of the product under the state registration would constitute an "imminent hazard" or would result in a residue on a raw agricultural product not covered by an FFDCA tolerance or exemption.[181]

The state bears the burden of notifying registrants of an EPA disapproval.[182]

[d] Suspension of State Registration Authority

Section 24(c)(4) of FIFRA authorizes EPA to suspend state special local needs registration authority on the basis of criteria developed by EPA to implement the statutory criterion of failure to develop or exercise adequate controls to ensure consistency with the federal statute. EPA is required to notify the state of the reasons for the action and the state must be provided an "opportunity to respond."

EPA has elaborated on the grounds for suspension in 40 CFR §162.155, by defining the term "adequate control" to include such things as access to technical personnel for the purpose of evaluating the adequacy of claims and data, sufficient procedures, adequate records, and adequate legal authority to do what the subpart D regulations require and to provide adequate enforcement.[183]

Although Section 24(c) only provides for an "opportunity to respond" to a notice of intent to suspend, EPA has generated a veritable phalanx of procedural rights in 40 CFR §162.155(c), which virtually ensure that not many suspensions will occur. First, EPA is required to give rather

---

179 40 CFR §162.154(c).

180 40 CFR §162.154(a)(1). Subsequent subsections give the state a right to "confer" with EPA. EPA also can rescind a disapproved registration. 40 CFR §162.154(e).

181 40 CFR §162.154(b)(1).

182 40 CFR §162.154(f).

183 40 CFR §§162.155(a) and (b).

detailed advance notice of its intention. This notice does not become final until thirty days has expired and the state agency has not requested an opportunity for an informal conference.[184] If EPA does not relent, it must publish the notice of intent to suspend in the Federal Register, and the state is given the right, within ten days of the publication date, to demand a hearing, which the regulations structure as an adjudication.[185] An appeal to the Administrator is available following the hearing, and a right to seek judicial review at any time following issuance of a final order of suspension is purported to be available.[186]

[3] Exemptions

[a] In General

Section 18 of FIFRA authorizes the EPA, in its discretion, to exempt from any provision of FIFRA any state or federal agency if the Administrator determines that "emergency conditions" exist that "require such exemption." An "emergency exemption" covers state or federal agency use of a pesticide only.[187]

EPA's government exemption regulations, 40 CFR Part 166, significantly elaborate on the above statutory authority. EPA deems an "emergency" to exist when (1) a pest outbreak has or is about to occur and no pesticide registered for that particular use and no alternate method of control is available to control the pest, (2) significant economic or health problems will occur without the use of the pesticide, and (3) the time available from discovery or prediction of the pest outbreak is insufficient for a pesticide to be registered for that use.[188] However, these criteria are not the exclusive means for determining the existence

---

[184] *See* 40 CFR §§162.155(c)(1) and (2).

[185] 40 CFR §162.155(c)(3).

[186] 40 CFR §162.155(e). Although the wording is unclear, EPA apparently intends to limit judicial review to states that have run the entire administrative procedural gauntlet the whole way up to the Administrator, following a hearing. *See* 40 CFR §§162.155(c)(4)-(7). Thus, judicial review, if actually available, would fall under Section 16(b), in the courts of appeals. I hedge the prior sentence because it is arguable that the specific provisions of Section 24(c) say nothing about either a hearing or judicial review, and Section 16 seems clearly aimed at private parties.

[187] A state or federal entity may, of course, contract with private applicators and still be covered by this provision.

[188] 40 CFR §166.1.

of an emergency.[189] EPA is also required to conclude that the proposed emergency use "will not endanger man or adversely affect the environment" prior to allowing any exemption.[190] There are three distinct categories of emergency exemption, each of which is subject to separate criteria, limitations, and procedures:

(1)   specific exemption is available where there is an "outbreak of a pest in the United States" in a "specific situation."[191] Such exemptions are limited in duration to one year and are subject to such conditions and limitations "as the Administrator may prescribe." The exemption is available only on application to EPA; the application must describe the specific situation for which control is sought.[192]

(2)   A quarantine–public health exemption, which also requires a prior permit from EPA, is available in connection with a program "concerned with preventing the introduction or spread of a foreign pest into or throughout the United States."[193] These exemptions are also for a year's duration, but are renewable,[194] and may involve broad geographic areas and multiple infestations. Unlike specific exemptions, pesticides whose registration has been suspended may not be the subject of a quarantine–public health exemption.[195] The application requirements are substantially equivalent to those for a specific exemption.[196]

(3)   A crisis exemption does not require prior approval by EPA, but is limited to "situations involving the unpredictable outbreak of pests in the United States, where the responsible official in au-

---

189 *See* Environmental Defense Fund v. Blum, 458 F. Supp. 650 (D.D.C. 1978) (upholding EPA's interpretation of Section 166.1 as not establishing exclusive criteria, relying in part on EPA's 1973 preamble to the regulations. 38 Fed. Reg. 33304).

190 *Id.*, relying on the legislative history contained in H.R. Rep. No. 92-511, 92d Cong., 1st Sess. 21 (1971), and S. Rep. No. 92-970, 92d Cong., 2d Sess. 42 (1972).

191 40 CFR §166.2(a).

192 *See* 40 CFR §166.3, which details the contents of the application.

193 40 CFR §166.2(b). The regulation further defines foreign pest as one that is "not known to occur" or not previously known to be established in the United States and has become newly established or threatens to become established in the United States.

194 The permittee must seek to register the pesticide, however, if renewals are anticipated. 40 CFR §166.2(b).

195 Although the reading makes no sense, if Section 166.2(b) is read *in pari materia* with Section 166.2(c), it can be argued that pesticides that have previously been canceled, as opposed to suspended, are available.

196 *See* 40 CFR §166.4.

thority determines" that there is no readily available pesticide registered for the use required and that there is insufficient time within which to secure a specific exemption. The exemption is not available for a use of a pesticide that has been suspended or finally canceled or where EPA has specifically withdrawn the exemption from either the product or the agency involved.[197]

Except in the case of the quarantine–public health exemption, EPA does not limit exemption authority to new pest infestations.[198] EPA may specify the labeling required in the case of the permitted exemptions. Since both suspended and canceled products are available for use under a specific exemption, and, at least arguably, canceled products are available for a quarantine–public health exemption, EPA has provided an escape from the FIFRA penalty provisions for manufacturers and applicators of such products under exemption circumstances.[199]

EPA publishes notices of the grant of exemption permits and notices of crisis exemption occurrences in the Federal Register, and in some cases publishes notice of an application for a permitted exemption prior to issuance.[200]

[b] Environmental Impact Assessment

Federal agency pesticide applications and state applications that involve significant federal funding or other federal government participation must comply with the National Environmental Policy Act (NEPA) of 1969.[201] EPA requires applicants for permitted exemptions to submit a copy of the Environmental Impact Statement (EIS) pre-

---

[197] 40 CFR §166.2(c). The regulations require, however, that the agency notify EPA within thirty-six hours of the crisis determination and file a written report within ten days containing a showing that the criteria for the exemption have been satisfied and a description of the products and activities undertaken. Further, if the activity is expected to last more than fifteen days, the report must contain an application for a specific exemption. 40 CFR §166.8.

If a previously canceled or suspended pesticide is intended to be used, EPA requires a hearing to be held prior to considering such use. See 40 CFR Part 164 subpart D.

[198] EPA's position, apparently contrary to the legislative history, was upheld in Environmental Defense Fund v. Blum, supra.

[199] 40 CFR §166.11.

[200] See 40 CFR §166.10.

[201] 42 USC §§4321 et seq. See, e.g., Oregon Environmental Council v. Kunzman, 714 F.2d 901 (9th Cir. 1983). For a case involving state use of pesticides, see National Organization for the Reform of Marijuana Laws v. U.S. Drug Enforcement Administration, 545 F.Supp. 981 (D.D.C. 1982).

pared for the activity along with the permit application, although EPA does not require that the EIS, if one is required, precede its action.[202] EPA's own actions, while not statutorily exempt from NEPA, have been held to be exempt from the statute's procedural requirements, although EPA is required to address the "core issues" required to be examined under NEPA.[203]

[c] Judicial Review and Administrative Procedures

EPA at one point argued that since Section 18 vested EPA with "discretion" on the matter of exemptions, its grant of an exemption was not reviewable under Section 16, and that it should not be held to the notice and comment rulemaking requirements of Section 4 of the Administrative Procedure Act. The Agency's regulations, discussed above, reflect the latter position.

EPA's position was rejected by Judge Gesell in *Environmental Defense Fund v. Blum*,[204] who ruled that at least the permitted exemptions were reviewable and had to employ public notice and comment procedures.[205]

Historically, the Agency has in fact employed informal notice and comment procedures in connection with its Section 18 decisions, thereby enabling judicial review of its actions in the federal district courts under Section 16(a).[206]

---

[202] *See* 40 CFR §§166.3(a)(7) and 166.4(a)(5).

[203] Environmental Defense Fund, Inc. v. Blum, 458 F.Supp. 650, 661 (D. D.C. 1978).

[204] 458 F. Supp. 650 (D. D.C. 1978).

[205] As for crisis exemptions, Judge Gesell, in dictum, stated, "It may well be that some section 18 crisis exemptions by the EPA need not meet all of the requirements of section 4 of the APA." Judge Gesell's view was adopted subsequently by another federal district court judge, Harold Greene, in National Audubon Society v. Todhunter, CA No. 82-2552 (D. D.C. 1982). Virtually all of the law on emergency exemptions has involved Mississippi's efforts to use Mirex or its derivative Ferriamicide to control fire ants.

[206] There is limited authority for the proposition that if EPA chose to hold a hearing voluntarily, review would be in the court of appeals under Section 16(b). *See* State of Louisiana v. Train, 392 F. Supp. 594 (W.D. La. 1975).

§3.05 Change, Suspension, and Cancellation of Pesticide Registration Under FIFRA

[1] In General

EPA has four postregistration options available to it in the event it determines that the registration as initially approved no longer meets the statutory criteria. (1) It can require a change in the mandatory labeling requirements, under Section 3. (2) Under Sections 3(d)(2) and 6(b), it can change the use classification. (3) It may cancel the registration. (4) It may suspend the registration.

Section 6 of FIFRA sets forth an elaborate set of procedures and criteria for suspending temporarily or canceling permanently the registration of a pesticide. The labyrinthine cancellation procedures are indicative of FIFRA's bias toward relative ease of entry of new products into the market and difficulty of removal from commerce.

There are four general types of activity governed by Section 6: (1) automatic cancellation five years after registration in the absence of a request by the registrant that the registration be continued,[207] (2) cancellation of a conditional registration for failure to make progress toward satisfying a condition,[208] (3) cancellation for cause,[209] and (4) suspension.[210]

Most cancellations are of the first type, or voluntary on the part of the registrant or other interested entities. Primarily because of the combined effects of EPA's employment of the RPAR procedures[211] and the usually lengthy and expensive adjudicatory hearings required by Section 6(b), comparatively few cancellations for cause have been effected.

[2] Information Reporting

Section 6(a)(2) imposes on all registrants an ongoing obligation to submit to EPA any "factual information regarding unreasonable ad-

---

207 Section 6(a)(1).
208 Section 6(e).
209 Section 6(b).
210 Section 6(c).
211 These procedures have recently been substantially revised, and restyled "Special Review." See Section 3.03 [2] [a] [ii], supra, for a general discussion of the RPAR ("Special Review") regulations. See Section 3.05[5][b], infra, for discussion of the new regulations' effect on cancellation for cause.

verse effects on the environment" the registrant "has." This provision is important because EPA has an ongoing obligation under FIFRA to be assured that its initial determination that the pesticide and use do not present an unreasonable adverse effect remains correct.

EPA promulgated a regulation in 1975 in which it eliminated the words "factual" and "unreasonable" from the Section 6(a)(2) language, but it abandoned the regulation in 1978, replacing it with an interpretive memorandum. EPA took the position that the Section 6(a)(2) obligation encompassed any information, including factual data and expert opinion, in the registrant's possession that bears on the risk-benefit analysis required to support a registration under Section 3. That position was partly upheld and partly rejected by a district court in *Chemical Specialties Manufacturers Association et al. v. EPA.*[212]

In *Chemical Specialties*, the court agreed with EPA that EPA, and not the registrant, should decide whether factual data are accurate and reliable and relevant to the "unreasonable risk" issue, thus upholding EPA's requirement that registrants submit all data arguably bearing on the risk issue to EPA, along with any information they wish to submit bearing on the credibility of the data. The court rejected EPA's requirement that *benefits* data also be submitted, and its demand for expert opinion data, both as being outside the scope of Section 6(a)(2).

[3] Cancellation After Five Years

A pesticide registration has a five-year life. Section 6(a)(1) of FIFRA requires the registrant or another "interested person with the concurrence of the registrant" to apply to EPA for renewal of the registration at the end of each five-year cycle. EPA is required to publish a list of pesticides up for automatic cancellation in the Federal Register at least thirty days prior to the expiration of the five-year period for those products.

Despite the apparent clarity of the Section 6(a)(1) requirement, EPA, in a bold exercise of regulatory discretion, has, as of late 1985, issued no regulations governing renewal registration and suspended the applicability of the five-year renewal requirement until it had completed the reregistration process required by Section 3(g).[213]

Section 6(a) authorizes sale and use of existing stocks of pesticides

---

212 484 F. Supp. 513 (D. D.C. 1980).
213 *See* 40 CFR §162.43(f)(3); and 40 CFR §162.43(c).

canceled after five years, on whatever conditions EPA imposes, provided EPA "determines that such sale or use is not inconsistent with the purposes of" FIFRA, and "will not have unreasonable adverse effects on the environment."

[4] Cancellation of Conditionally Registered Pesticides

Acting under authority of Section 6(e), EPA may cancel a conditional registration upon a finding that the registrant has "failed to initiate and pursue appropriate action toward fulfilling any condition imposed" or, at the end of the period set for satisfying the condition, that the condition had not been met.[214] The registrant must be notified, and is given thirty days in which to request a hearing under Section 6(d).[215] Conditional cancellation hearings are required by Section 6(e)(2) to be completed within seventy-five days after receipt of a request, and are limited in scope to the statutory criteria set forth in Section 6(e)(1) and the reasonableness of any determination by EPA relative to existing stocks.

The most usual condition imposed by EPA on a conditional registrant is to supply data to fill in data gaps.[216] EPA's conditional registration rule provides that notice of intent to cancel will be provided to the registrant by certified mail, and to the public in the Federal Register, and reaffirm the expedited hearing requirements of the statute.[217]

[5] Cancellation for Cause

[a] In General

There are only two grounds upon which EPA may cancel, or change the classification of, a finally registered pesticide for cause. EPA may act if (1) it finds that the labeling or "other material submitted" does not comply with the provisions of FIFRA, or (2) it finds that "when used in accordance with widespread and commonly recognized practice" the

---

214 Sections 6(e)(1)(A) and (B). Sale or use of existing stocks is permitted on the same basis as in a Section 6(a) cancellation.
215 Section 6(e)(2).
216 See 40 CFR §162.167(c).
217 40 CFR §162.177.

pesticide "generally causes unreasonable adverse effects on the environment."[218]

Once EPA makes a preliminary determination that the statutory criteria for cancellation have been met, it may either issue a notice of intent to take the desired action, which gives rise to the registrant's right to a hearing, or EPA may schedule a hearing on its own.[219]

As a practical matter, most cancellations are negotiated between EPA and the registrant and are limited to individual uses of the product. EPA handles most problems by amending the registration standard. Although one can read Section 6(b) as affecting only entire product cancellation, it has never been read that way by EPA, which handles involuntary cancellation of individual uses of registered pesticides under Section 6(b).

A product of the dominance of the congressional agriculture committees over FIFRA, the statute requires EPA to submit, prior to formal notification of the registrant and the public, proposals for cancellation to the Secretary of Agriculture, and requires EPA to publish Agriculture's comments in the Federal Register along with the Notice of Intent to Cancel.[220] The Agriculture comments ordinarily address EPA's obligation to consider "the impact of the action proposed . . . on production and prices of agricultural commodities, retail food prices, and otherwise on the agricultural economy."[221]

Sections 25(d) and/or (e) of FIFRA also require EPA to refer all cancellation proposals to the FIFRA Scientific Advisory Panel, or some other scientific peer review group although the terms of the subsections are such that there are no binding timing constraints and EPA is not required to await a peer review report prior to acting.[222]

---

[218] Section 6(b).

[219] Sections 6(b)(1) and (2).

[220] EPA must notify Agriculture at least sixty days prior to its planned notice date. Agriculture must respond within thirty days if it wishes to have its comments published with the Notice of Intent to Cancel.

[221] Section 6(b).

[222] *See generally* Dow Chemical Company v. Ruckelshaus, 477 F.2d 1317 (8th Cir. 1973)(establishing the principle that the registrant has a continuing burden of proof to establish that its product is entitled to registration). The Scientific Advisory Panel (SAP) legislative authority ended on September 30, 1981. In 1980, Congress added Section 25(e) of FIFRA, imposing on EPA a generalized peer review obligation in connection with any "complex scientific" decisions under FIFRA. EPA may use the SAP or any other "independent" peer review group either "within or outside" EPA. P.L. 96-539. EPA's peer review obligation, however, was deferred by Section 2(b) of the session law until EPA published peer review procedures in the Federal Register.

[b] RPAR ("Special Review")

EPA's Special Review procedures, discussed generally in Section 3.03[2][a][ii], *supra*, significantly alter at least the time within which it takes EPA to cancel a registration.

If EPA's regulatory staff determines that sufficient evidence exists to establish a *prima facie* case for cancellation, the Agency will initiate Special Review proceedings under Part 154, listing all of the data on which the presumption is based, and articulating the reasons for its conclusion. EPA's new Special Review procedures are outlined in Section 3.03[2][a][ii], *infra*. Under EPA's pre-1985 RPAR regulations, 40 CFR §162.11(a) and (b), a rather lengthy series of private "pre-RPAR" negotiations would usually occur between the registrant and friendly third parties and the FIFRA product management and "special pesticide review" staffs. In most cases, the "pre-RPAR" negotiations resolved a number of the outstanding issues, leaving public airing of the RPAR, if any occurred, only for those matters on which the parties could not agree.[223]

The Special Review is a burden-shifting device. Once notice of Special Review is published, the registrant and related or similarly interested entities must submit to EPA within the time period allowed written data and other evidence aimed at rebutting the presumption raised by EPA's notice. This triggers a round of meetings, and perhaps an informal hearing, with the potential involvement of commenters, whose interest may be counter to that of the registrant group. If the evidence submitted satisfies EPA, either the proceeding is terminated or the remedy proposed in the Special Review notice is modified in accordance with the new conclusions.[224] Otherwise, EPA proceeds to publish a Notice of Intent to Cancel.

[c] Regulatory Criteria for Notice of Intent to Cancel

EPA's regulatory criteria for issuing a cancellation notice are different from the facial requirements of Section 6(b)(1). EPA will issue a notice when it concludes, on the basis of a validated test or "other significant evidence," that the use of the pesticide may—

---

[223] As discussed above, in its 1984 settlement of litigation that claimed the entire RPAR and pre-RPAR process was illegal, EPA agreed to open up the pre-RPAR proceedings to the public, and its new Part 154 procedures implement that agreement.

[224] *See generally* 40 CFR Part 154 for timetables and procedures.

— pose a risk of "serious acute injury" to humans or domestic animals or a risk of inducing *"in humans* an oncogenic, heritable genetic, teratogenic, fetotoxic, reproductive effect, or delayed toxic effect, which risk is of concern in terms of either the degree of risk to individual humans or the number of humans at some risk";

— result in unacceptably high residues on nontarget organisms, or pose a risk to the continued existence of any endangered or threatened species, or destroy the habitat of an endangered or threatened species; or

— otherwise pose a risk that will alter the cost-benefit balance.[225]

These EPA regulatory criteria must, if they are based on FIFRA at all, be based on an Agency interpretation of the statute springing from its broad intent rather than from the specific language of Section 6(b).[226]

[d]   Regulatory Criteria for Final Cancellation

Once a cancellation notice is issued, the burden lies with the registrant and similarly interested entities to request a hearing under Section 6(d) and to demonstrate either that the risks identified in the notice do not exist or that the benefits of continued registration outweigh the risks identified.

Following receipt of comments, EPA must make a "preliminary determination" on the question of cancellation. It first must decide whether the risk criteria are met, and then decide whether the packaging and/or labeling changes would reduce the risk to below the threshold. Finally, the Agency must take another look at the social, economic, and environmental costs and benefits, to determine whether the identified adverse effects are unreasonable.[227]

EPA's prior regulations drew a distinction between acute and latent

---

225 40 CFR §§154.7 and 154.31.

226 *See generally* 50 Fed. Reg. 48998. For discussion of the prior RPAR regulations, *see* 40 Fed. Reg. 28268 (1975); 40 Fed. Reg. 32329 (1975); and 40 Fed. Reg. 42746 (1975) for EPA's contemporaneous explanation of the RPAR regulations.

227 40 CFR §154.31(a).

harm and provided a detailed set of separate cancellation criteria for them.[228]

In the case of an oncogen, of course, the cancer principles followed by EPA assume that there is no threshold of exposure below which no effects are present; thus, in practical terms, in order to overcome the risk presumption predicated on laboratory studies demonstrating carcinogenicity, the registrant will have to show essentially that there will be no human exposure.

Regardless of the nature of the risk, however, a final cancellation can be averted if the registrant is able to convince EPA that the risks are outweighed by the economic, social, and environmental benefits of use of the pesticide.[229]

Once a Notice of Intent to Cancel is issued, it will not be withdrawn unless, following a hearing, EPA decides that the proponents have sustained the burden of proof or, prior to holding a hearing, EPA decides that there is insufficient public interest in the issue to warrant a hearing.[230]

EPA's previous regulations specifically provided for shifting the burden of proof in cancellation cases.[231] Part 154 does not contain such language, but there is no evidence that the Agency has abandoned its view that the applicant always has the burden of proof.

[6] **Cancellation Hearings**

[a] **Who May Initiate**

A hearing may be requested by a person "adversely affected" by a notice of intent to cancel.[232] The registrant, registrants of similar products, the manufacturer or formulator, if not the registrant, users, and similar persons who have an economic interest in the product are clearly "adversely affected" within the meaning of Section 6(b).

An interesting question, however, is presented when EPA's Special Review procedures are terminated with a notice of cancellation of some, but not all, of the subject pesticide's uses. Participants who believe that more, or all, of the uses should be canceled, have been held

---

[228] 40 CFR §§162.11(b)(1)(B) and (b)(ii)(B)(2) and §§162.11(b)(1)(A) and (b)(ii)(B)(1) (repealed 11-27-85).

[229] 40 CFR §154.31(a)(3).

[230] 40 CFR §154.33. Section 154.34 provides for expedited proceedings and action without the need for going through Special Review.

[231] 40 CFR §162.11(b)(2).

[232] Section 6(b).

not to have the right to request a hearing.[233] Although such persons would appear to be "adversely affected" by the permissive aspects of a partial or conditional cancellation, the District of Columbia Circuit in *Environmental Defense Fund v. Costle*[234] held simply that a refusal to cancel following an RPAR, the functional equivalent of Special Review under EPA's prior regulatory scheme, is not an action giving rise to a hearing right.[235]

A hearing must be requested within thirty days of receipt of the cancellation notice by the registrant or the date it is published, whichever is later. The applicant must, at the same time, file a statement of objections to the proposed EPA action.[236] The statement of objections is important, since under EPA's procedural regulations the statement of objections will ordinarily define the scope of the hearing.

[b] **Nature and Scope**

Cancellation hearings are governed by Section 6(d), which states that the purpose of the hearings is to receive "evidence relevant and material to the issues raised by the objections filed by the applicant or other interested parties," or, if the hearing is set on EPA's own motion, on issues defined by EPA. The hearings are hybrid adjudications, which are usually presided over by a panel consisting of an EPA administrative law judge and several scientists. EPA's rules of practice are published at 40 CFR Part 164.

Very often, environmental or labor organizations whose interests are inimical to those of the registrant and allied entities have intervened in cancellation hearings. EPA's regulations are permissive on the matter of intervention,[237] although there is some Agency "case law" of uncertain weight to the effect that an intervenor may not raise contentions in a cancellation hearing that the cancellation does not go far

---

[233] Environmental Defense Fund, Inc., et al. v. Costle, 631 F.2d 922 (D.C. Cir. 1980).
[234] *Id.*
[235] The court in the *Environmental Defense Fund* case opined, however, that a decision to retain registration could be challenged in a U. S. district court pursuant to Section 16(a) of FIFRA. *See also* Environmental Defense Fund v. Ruckleshaus, 439 F.2d 584 (D.C. Cir. 1971).
[236] *See* 40 CFR §164.20(b).
[237] *See* 40 CFR §164.31.

enough.[238] In general, nevertheless, the primary litigants in these cases are the registrant group, which might be quite large where a number of hearing requests have been consolidated, and EPA's staff scientists and lawyers from the Agency's Office of General Counsel.

Section 6(d) contains an unusual provision authorizing the EPA hearing examiner, upon the request of "any party," to refer "relevant questions of scientific fact" to a "Committee of the National Academy of Sciences" (NAS).[239] If such a referral is made, the NAS Committee is to render a report within sixty days, and the report "shall be made public and shall be made part of the hearing record."

Although the statute and EPA's regulations quite clearly contemplate trial-type hearings, there is no indication in either the statute or the regulations that the authors of NAS Committee reports may be subject to cross-examination, discovery, or other normal incidents of adjudicatory proceedings.

As for evidence other than NAS Committee reports, the EPA regulations provide a full range of pretrial discovery and other trappings of a typical judicial proceeding, in accordance with the Section 6(d) requirement that the proceedings be conducted in accordance with the Federal Rules of Civil Procedure, including provision for compulsory process for witnesses and documentary evidence.[240]

A subpoena issued by a FIFRA hearing examiner is enforceable in the U.S. district courts, although the federal judge retains discretion to decide whether the subpoena is proper under the circumstances.[241] The statutory standard for either compulsory discovery or compulsory process is that the information sought be relevant and of reasonable scope, and a subpoena may issue on motion of a party or on the hearing examiner's own motion.[242]

---

[238] In re Shell Oil Co., FIFRA Docket (April 9, 1979). This decision was subsequently disavowed by EPA's lawyers in the *Environmental Defense Fund* litigation and criticized by the D.C. Circuit in that case.

[239] EPA's regulations set forth procedures for such referrals at 40 CFR §164.50(e).

[240] *See* 40 CFR §§164.50-164.123.

[241] The Dow Chemical Company v. Dr. James R. Allen, et al., 672 F.2d. 1262 (7th Cir. 1982).

[242] EPA's regulations muddy the water somewhat. 40 CFR §164.51, which governs pretrial discovery, requires a showing of "significant probative value" in order to support a subpoena. For compelling documents or testimony at trial, however, Section 164.70(a) only requires a showing that the evidence is "relevant and material." A subpoena issued by the Hearing Examiner for discovery purposes in In Re Dow Chemical Company, et al., FIFRA Docket Nos. 415 *et seq.*, was quashed by a federal district judge because it

EPA provides for appeal to the Administrator as a matter of right from the initial decision of the hearing officer or panel or from an accelerated decision.[243] Interlocutory appeals require certification by the hearing officer, much as is the case in federal civil practice. EPA's regulations contain a series of time limitations for perfecting administrative appeals and other rights.[244]

[c]　Judicial Review

Judicial review of a final order of cancellation following a hearing lies in the U.S. courts of appeals under Section 16(b).[244.1] The standard of review is whether the decision was based on "substantial evidence of record of hearing," and was supported by adequate "detailed findings of fact."

Despite the relatively onerous standard of review, the courts have usually been highly deferential to EPA, relying both on the Agency's presumed expertise where the evidence is thin and on the inherent conservatism ascribed to FIFRA where health and safety are concerned. Attempts by registrants to overturn EPA's cancellation and suspension decisions on evidentiary grounds have usually failed.[245] At-

---

sought to compel production of results of incomplete primate toxicological experiments at the University of Wisconsin that had not been subjected to peer review. The judge concluded that such studies could not have significant probative value. *See* The Dow Chemical Company v. Dr. James R. Allen, et al., 494 F. Supp. 107 (W.D. Wis. 1980).

In affirming the district court ruling, the Seventh Circuit, in dictum, further complicated the process of compelling university research to be explored in FIFRA proceedings by opining that such compulsory process might violate academic freedom and therefore be unenforceable as a matter of public policy. 672 F.2d 1262, 1274-1276 (7th Cir. 1982).

243 40 CFR §164.100. Accelerated decisions are governed by 40 CFR 164.91.

244 *See* 40 CFR §164.101.

244.1 In Environmental Defense Fund v. Costle, 631 F.2d 922 (D.C. Cir. 1980), the court appears to opine that the court of appeals has jurisdiction to review an Agency action taken at the conclusion of an RPAR review, where no formal hearing had been held, at least where the issue raised was whether a nonregistrant has a right to a hearing with respect to the Agency's refusal to cancel certain uses of a pesticide subject to the RPAR (it held no such right exists). A contrary view of court of appeals jurisdiction was espoused by the Ninth Circuit in Amvac Chemical Corporation v. U.S. EPA, 653 F.2d 1260 (9th Cir. 1980).

245 The leading cases are Environmental Defense Fund, Inc. v. Environmental Protection Agency [Shell Chemical Company, et al.], 510 F.2d 1292 (D.C. Cir. 1975)(aldrin/dieldrin); and Environmental Defense Fund, Inc. v. Environmental Protection Agency [Velsicol Chemical Co., et al.], 548 F.2d 998 (D.C. Cir. 1976)(chlordane/heptachlor).

tacks on the Agency's procedures or statutory construction have been somewhat more successful.[246]

[7] Suspension of Registration

[a] In General

Section 6(c) of FIFRA authorizes EPA to suspend the registration of a pesticide immediately upon a finding that such action is necessary to prevent an imminent hazard during the time required for cancellation or change in classification. The statute requires that EPA issue a notice of intent to cancel or change the classification at the same time a suspension order is issued.[247] Unless EPA determines that an "emergency" exists, the suspension order must be accompanied by a set of findings pertaining to the imminent hazard conclusion. It must be served on the registrant prior to its issuance, and the registrant has the opportunity to request an expedited hearing, which has the effect of staying the action.[248] In contrast to cancellation hearings, only the registrant has a right to request a hearing on a proposed suspension. If EPA determines that an emergency exists, the registrant still has a right to a hearing, but the hearing request does not stay the effectiveness of the order.[249] Failure to request a hearing within five days of receipt of the notice results in the registrant's loss of his right to judicial review of the suspension order.[250]

FIFRA defines "imminent hazard" as "a situation which exists when the continued use of a pesticide during the time required for cancellation would be likely to result in unreasonable adverse effects on the environment or will involve unreasonable hazard to the survival of a species declared endangered" under the Endangered Species Act.

The statute does not, however, define the term "emergency." The sole judicial prouncement on the term is by Judge Harvey in *The Dow Chemical Company, et al. v. Blum, Acting Administrator,*[251] who defined the term as "a substantial likelihood that serious harm will be

---

[246] *See, e.g.,* Environmental Defense Fund, Inc. v. Ruckelshaus, 439 F.2d 584 at 596 (D.C. Cir. 1971).

[247] Section 6(c)(1).

[248] *See* Section 6(c)(2).

[249] Section 6(c)(3).

[250] The registrant and sympathetic parties have thirty days within which to request a hearing on the simultaneously issued notice of intent to cancel, however, under Section 6(b).

[251] 469 F.Supp. 892 (E.D. Mich. 1979).

experienced during the [time that will elapse] . . . in any realistic projection of the administrative suspension process."[252]

[b] Suspension Hearings

Suspension hearings are required to be "expedited," in that they must commence within five days of receipt of the hearing request, and the presiding officer and the Administrator are bound by stiff time limitations on getting a decision out at the conclusion of the proceedings, unless the registrant waives the statutory requirements. Hearings, other than those following an "emergency suspension," are otherwise similar in structure to cancellation hearings, except that the presiding officer is not required to be an administrative law judge. The only difference between "emergency" and other suspension hearings is that hearings following an "emergency" suspension may not have intervenors. Persons who are "adversely affected" are limited to filing briefs in emergency suspension hearings, although if they do so they are considered to be "parties" for the purpose of subsequent judicial review.[253]

In the few situations in which EPA has actually invoked Section 6(c), registrant groups have usually chosen to waive the suspension hearing, and instead pursued immediate cancellation hearings.[254] In such circumstances, EPA has usually been willing to provide a degree of expedition to move the cancellation hearings along. The reason for this choice is obvious. Although a suspension hearing is mandated to be expedited at its beginning and end, the evidentiary proceedings for a suspension hearing could well take the same amount of time as those for the cancellation hearing. This is because the issue of a suspension hearing, whether or not an imminent hazard exists, subsumes the core issue of

---

[252] Harvey then applied a variant of the normal preliminary injunction factors to the facts. These factors include the seriousness of the "threatened harm," its immediacy, the probability that the threatened harm would result, the benefits to the public if the pesticides continue to be used during the period of time involved, and "the nature and extent of the information before the administrator at the time he made his decision."

Ironically, Harvey estimated the time involved in the *Dow* case to be three and a half to four months. In actuality, the registrant group subsequently waived their right to a suspension hearing and proceeded directly to cancellation hearings, which dragged on for more than three years before Dow unilaterally quit the action.

[253] See Section 6(c)(3). EPA's regulations do not define the term "adversely affected." *See* discussion of Environmental Defense Fund v. Costle, *supra*, for confusion surrounding the term.

[254] EPA's rules of practice for suspension hearings are published at 40 CFR Part 164 subpart C (§§164.120-123).

the cancellation hearing, that is, whether an unreasonable adverse effect is presented by the product and use involved, albeit during a more limited time period. Thus, both require the same test data and exposure data to be aired and examined.

Moreover, since a request for either a cancellation hearing or a suspension hearing stays the effectiveness of the order, the registrant can easily continue to market its product while taking its time to litigate the EPA proposal administratively and in the courts by filing a suspension hearing request within five days of issuance of the joint notice, waiving the time constraints, filing a timely cancellation hearing request, and then moving to consolidate the proceedings.

If EPA has issued an emergency suspension, of course, since the suspension is effective unless stayed by action of a federal district court, employment of the expedited procedures by the registrant is in the registrant's interest.

[c] Judicial Review

[i] Suspension Following a Hearing

A final order of suspension following a hearing is reviewable by the courts of appeals under Section 16(b), notwithstanding the fact that related cancellation proceedings have not yet been completed.[255] Presumably the reason for this is that the issue in a suspension proceeding is supposedly different from that presented in the cancellation proceeding, a presumption made apparent in the statute's seeming requirement that the effect of any judicial action adverse to EPA is to stay the effectiveness of the suspension order until a final cancellation decision is issued.

There is, however, a possibility of inconsistent judicial pronouncements on the same issue under this statutory scheme, arising from the possible conjunction of overlapping elements of proof and divergent appellate venue (although the general unattractiveness of the suspension hearing to registrants makes such an occurrence only a remote possibility). The issue in a suspension hearing, as indicated above, may involve the same elements of proof as those in the cancellation proceeding. Thus, for example, a court of appeals reviewing a suspension order could be presented squarely with the question of whether the evidence supports the conclusion that unreasonable adverse effects will result.

---

[255] *See* Section 6(c)(4).

The same question, on essentially the same quantum of evidence, could be presented to the court of appeals reviewing the final order of cancellation.[256] This would not present a problem if review in each case were confined to the same court. But Section 16(b) does not confine judicial review to a single court. Review is in the circuit wherein the person "adversely affected" resides. In a case where there are intervenors, the court having venue over all appeals will be the one in which the first petition to review the action is filed.[257] It is not hard to imagine a situation in which the registrant wins the race to the courthouse in an appeal of the suspension order, and an intervenor opposed to the registrant wins the race following cancellation, in a different court.

The standard of review of a suspension order, as in the case of a cancellation order, is the "substantial evidence in the record" standard.

[ii]   Emergency Suspension

Judicial review of an emergency suspension order may be sought immediately by the registrant, or by any other interested person "with the concurrence of the registrant," in federal district court.[258] If the registrant involved has not sought a hearing within the stipulated five-day period, district court review is barred even if a complaint was filed prior to the fifth day.[259] It would appear, however, that requesting a hearing does not foreclose the registrant or interested persons with the registrant's concurrence from proceeding with a district court action simultaneously with pursuing the administrative remedy.

The standard of review by the district court is deferential. The order will be upheld unless the court concludes that it is "arbitrary, capricious or an abuse of discretion" or "not issued in accordance with the procedures established by law." Although Section 6(c)(4) is silent on the issue the legislative history of the provision indicates that the district court is to hold a limited trial *de novo* on the issues permitted to be examined.[260]

District court review of an emergency suspension order involves

---

256 Of course, the evidence may differ. The issues presented in the suspension appeal may relate to a narrower time frame or a more limited record of evidence.

257 *See* 28 USC §§2112(a) and (b).

258 Section 6(c)(4).

259 This is an important consideration for users or other interested parties who have a right to seek judicial review but are not permitted to request a hearing under Section 6(c)(3).

260 The Dow Chemical Company, et al. v. Barbara Blum, et al., 469 F.Supp. 892 (E.D. Mich. 1979).

substantial deference to EPA, which is given great latitude to act, even on a rather thin body of evidence. The deference is twofold, stemming both from the arbitrary and capricious standard of review and from the legislative history of FIFRA, which has been interpreted as requiring the judge to apply the substantive law "in the spirit of avoiding delay and recognition of the broad powers on the part of EPA in regulating pesticides."[261] The presence of "minimal evidence in the record to support EPA's decision" will be enough to sustain an emergency order.[262]

[8] Consequences of Cancellation

[a] Disposal of Canceled Pesticides

Section 19(c) of FIFRA requires that a cancellation notice include "specific provisions for the disposal of unused quantities of such pesticide." This requirement, added by the 1978 amendments, reflects EPA's general authority under Section 19(a) over the disposal of pesticide wastes.[263]

Pesticides "cancelled under section 6(c)" are entitled to special treatment.[264] EPA is required by Section 19(a) to "accept at convenient locations for safe disposal" any canceled product "if requested by the owner of the pesticide."[265] EPA's regulations setting forth the Agency's

---

261 *Id.*, citing Ethyl Corp. v. EPA, 541 F.2d 1 (D.C. Cir. 1976).

262 *Id.*

263 EPA's regulations under the Resource, Conservation and Recovery Act exempt certain FIFRA-regulated pesticide disposal practices from regulation under the hazardous waste law. *See* Chapter 5, *infra.*

264 EPA interprets this provision to obligate it to accept only pesticides that have been canceled after having been suspended as presenting an imminent hazard. While that reading is favorable to EPA, it is not rational. The Section 6(c) language relates only to temporary suspension; it contains no authority for cancellation. If the purpose of the disposal provision is to require the most dangerous pesticides to be disposed of by EPA, there is no guarantee that the universe of such products will be subject to Section 6(c) proceedings, which are often dependent upon specific exposure patterns occurring during a single season, risks totally different from those posed by improper disposal.

265 This provision predates the hazardous waste and "Superfund" laws as well as the public outcry over hazardous waste disposal that produced these laws. It places EPA in the unenviable position today of being the generator and disposer of pesticides it deems too dangerous for use. In the few instances in which EPA has invoked Section 6(b) in the absence of the consent of the registrants, it has disposed of the pesticides at commercial hazardous waste disposal facilities, some of which have or may show up on a list of dangerous sites, requiring remedial action under other laws EPA administers. The Agency therefore faces the prospect of being both the protector of the public at such sites and

requirements for acceptance of suspended and cancelled pesticides are published at 40 CFR Part 165 subpart C.[266]

EPA's general pesticide disposal requirements are published at 40 CFR Part 165 subparts C and D. The regulations are remarkable in that they are written more as informal guidelines than as firm requirements or prohibitions.[267] The usefulness of the regulations seems, therefore, limited to tort plaintiffs, who may be able to claim that the defendant's disposal practices at variance with the provisions were negligent. They do not appear to be enforceable by EPA.

[b]   Indemnities

[i]   In General

FIFRA's proregistrant bent is nowhere better reflected than in Section 15, which requires the government to reimburse the owners of pesticides suspended or canceled as imminent hazards under Section 6 for any losses encountered with respect to quantities owned immediately prior to EPA's issuance of the notice to the registrant. The potential cost to the government of such payments where the affected product is widely used and disbursed in the stream of commerce is no doubt the reason behind EPA's liberal use of Section 15(b)(2), which permits the Agency to fashion its cancellation order in such a way that existing stocks may be used up subsequent to the cancellation date without a violation of FIFRA resulting.

In order to qualify for indemnification, the claimant must be able to prove how much of the product he owned on the day the registrant received the notice and to prove he suffered a loss as a result of the EPA action. As a practical matter, unless the market for the pesticide dries up immediately, or the owner refuses to sell or use the product out of a legitimate fear of subsequent liability to third parties exposed to it, not many losses will occur in the case of a cancellation or ordinary suspension where a hearing has been requested. However, in the case of an

---

one of the parties the applicable regulatory statute deems financially responsible for the cleanup costs.

266 *See* 39 Fed. Reg. 15236 (1974).

267 Section 165.7 ("Procedures not recommended"); Section 165.8 ("Recommended procedures for disposal of pesticides"); Section 165.9 ("Recommended procedures for the disposal of pesticide containers and residues"); Section 165.10 ("Recommended procedures and criteria for storage of pesticides and containers"); and Section 165.11 ("Procedures for disposal and storage of pesticide-related waste").

emergency suspension or a cancellation or ordinary suspension that becomes final because no hearing has been requested, losses will usually be incurred throughout the stream of commerce.

EPA may attempt to avoid paying a producer claimant by showing under Section 15(a)(3) that he knew of facts that "in themselves, would have shown that such pesticide did not meet the requirements of section 3(c)(5)" and "continued thereafter to produce such pesticide without giving timely notice of such facts" to EPA.[268]

The class of potential claimants is, however, much broader than the registrant group. They include virtually everyone who might have purchased the pesticide after manufacture, from formulators who purchased a canceled technical grade product to distributors and retailers and even end users who had the product on hand just prior to cancellation or suspension. Since the registrants are in the best position to know who might hold their products, and thus be potential claimants, EPA has suggested that registrants aggregate the claims of persons up the stream of commerce from them in order to simplify the negotiating process that results in fixing the value of the claim under Section 15(b).[269]

EPA has taken the position that no indemnification is available for raw materials rendered useless by cancellation of the product into which they were destined to be made.

[ii] Calculation of Indemnity and Source of Payment

Qualifying indemnification claimants are entitled to be reimbursed in an amount equal to the cost of the pesticide to the claimant immediately prior to receipt by the registrant of the notice of cancellation, but in no event more than the market value of the pesticide at that time.[270] The market value ceiling appears to be aimed primarily at preventing the registrant and distributors from intentionally inflating the price of a pesticide they know to be under review. However, EPA's Special Review process could have a tendency to depress the market

---

[268] Sections 15(a)(3)(i) and (ii). Procedurally, EPA would deny liability on such basis, leaving the claimant to his remedy. The remedy appears to be an action brought against the United States under the Tucker Act in the claims court, which would review the facts *de novo*.

[269] Since such aggregation usually involves an assignment of Section 15 claims to the registrant-producer, attorneys for the affected parties must be aware of the Anti-assignment Act, 31 USC §203, which imposes conditions and limitations on the assignment of claims against the United States.

[270] Section 15(b)(i).

for the subject pesticide artificially, particularly if safety concerns raised by the Special Review become known generally to users.

The legislative history of Section 15 fairly clearly points to EPA's pesticide program budget as the source of indemnity payments. As one might suspect, Congress has never appropriated a budget line of any significant size to cover Section 15 payments; consequently, claimants who negotiate in good faith with EPA and arrive at an agreed indemnification amount have been told in the end that EPA has no funds from which to provide satisfaction and that a request for a special appropriation to cover the claims would be met with little enthusiasm either at the Office of Management and the Budget or on the hill.[271]

If EPA fails to pay the indemnity claims, a cause of action against the United States arises under the Tucker Act. The claimants then must file an action in the claims court and seek the amounts owed under the unsatisfied claims and judgments fund. This action is *de novo*, and the Department of Justice has taken the position that agreements made by EPA as to amounts owed, qualifying claimants, and so forth, are not binding on the United States in the claims court action.[272]

Although the tendency might be to attempt to shortcut the matter, and proceed initially in the claims court, such an action would probably fail. Section 15 quite clearly requires the claim to be made aginst EPA, and proceeding directly under the Tucker Act on the simple premise that EPA's budget has no line for indemnification would be subject to attack either on ripeness grounds or because no debt cognizable under the Tucker Act arises until EPA has admitted liability, definitively reduced the claim to a sum certain, and refused payment.

EPA has avoided the Section 15 dilemma on occasion by allowing existing stocks of canceled pesticides to be used up. It may defer the

---

[271] Determining the amount of pesticide product qualifying for indemnification and its cost as of the indemnity date can be costly for the registrant group, particularly if, as a matter of customer relations, the registrants have agreed to aggregate the claims of persons in their marketing chain.

The registrants of the herbicide Silvex, canceled along with its sister product, 2,4,5-T, in 1979, spent hundreds of thousands of dollars ascertaining the cost of $20 million or so worth of aggregated indemnity claims, which included a great deal of lawyers' time negotiating a cost formula with EPA. When informed the EPA had no funds with which to pay the claims, they were forced to proceed in the court of claims, where EPA's agreements were not binding on the government.

[272] The Silvex claimants were forced to submit to a new audit by the FBI before the government would agree to settle their claims, even though EPA had done its own audit previously.

effective date of the cancellation of most uses for a period of time calculated to be sufficient to permit existing stocks to be used up, while prohibiting manufacture immediately. Or it may cancel certain high-risk uses immediately, but allow lower-risk uses to continue for a period of time sufficient for reformulation and use of remaining stocks of the pesticide.

§3.06 Imports and Exports Under FIFRA

[1] Imports

Pesticides manufactured outside of the United States and imported into the country are required to be registered prior to redelivery by the consignee who first "received" the pesticides at a U. S. port of entry.[273] This requirement is enforced by Section 17(b) of FIFRA, which invests the U. S. Customs Service with an obligation to notify EPA of the arrival of any pesticides and to provide samples of any imported pesticide or device to EPA at its request. Whenever a pesticide is received at a point of entry and, following notification, EPA requests samples, the consignee is required to be notified of EPA's action and has a right to "appear before the Administrator and . . . to introduce testimony."[274] If EPA determines that the pesticides are adulterated, misbranded, or otherwise violate FIFRA, or are "otherwise injurious to health or the environment," the pesticides must be denied entry, seized, and destroyed. Section 17(c) uses the phrase "the Secretary . . . shall refuse delivery to the consignee and shall cause the destruction . . ." of the pesticide. This language, when read in conjunction with the first proviso of the subsection, presumes that upon initial determination by EPA that the pesticide is somehow suspect, the Customs Service must impound the shipment.

A proviso to Section 17(c) allows the consignee to avoid preliminary impoundment by posting a bond, which is forfeited if EPA determines the pesticides to be excludable and upon request by Customs they are not turned over. The statute appears to prohibit export as an alternative to seizure and destruction.

Storage, cartage, and related costs incurred by the Customs Service

---

[273] *See* Sections 3(a) and 12(a)(1).

[274] Regulations have been adopted by the Treasury Department under Section 17(e). EPA has not adopted rules of practice governing the hearings provided for.

are payable by the consignee. These costs become a lien against future imports in the event the consignee defaults.[275]

[2] Exports

Pesticides and active ingredients intended "solely for export" to a foreign country are exempt from the registration, and most other requirements of FIFRA, but the manufacturing establishment must be licensed under Section 7 and is subject to the recordkeeping requirements of Section 8.[276]

The 1978 amendments added two limitations on the exemption.[277] The labeling requirements under Section 2(p), the misbranding provisions of Section 2(q) other than those relating to registration, and a specific requirement that the label and package indicate that product is not registered for use in the United States are imposed.[278] The pesticide must be "prepared and packaged according to the specifications or directions of the foreign purchaser" (provided those do not conflict with the FIFRA requirements described above). Exporters of unregistered pesticides and pesticides whose domestic registration has lapsed but which may be sold pursuant to Section 6(a)(1) are required to secure, prior to export, a statement from the purchaser stating that the purchaser understands that the pesticide is not registered in the United States and cannot be sold in the United States. A copy of the statement is required to be "transmitted to an appropriate official of the government of the importing country."[279]

Section 17(b) requires EPA to provide the State Department with notification of cancellation or suspension of a registration, and requires the State Department to convey the information to foreign governments and international organizations.[280] The background data and

---

275 The lien attaches to future imports of the consignee or the owner.

276 Section 17(a).

277 Section 17, P.L.95-396.

278 Section 17(a)(1). The applicable requirements are Sections 2(p), 2(q)(1)(A), (C),(D),(E),(G), and (H), 2(q)(2)(A),(B),(C)(i) and (iii), and (D), and Sections 7 and 8.

279 Section 17(a)(2). The statute does not specify who has the obligation of transmitting the statement, but implicitly requires the producer to be able to produce evidence at a Section 8 inspection that such a transmittal occurred. There is no provision for EPA or the Department of State to determine who the "appropriate official" is in various countries. This is a potentially significant loophole.

280 The United Nations Environment Programme maintains a reasonably up to date list of such activities.

analyses are not routinely provided in these notices, but must be provided if requested, along with information about registered substitutes.

§3.07 Prohibitions and Enforcement Under FIFRA

[1] Prohibitions

[a] In General

FIFRA contains what is easily one of the most detailed sets of statutory prohibitions in the federal statutes. The drafters seem to have attempted to divine as many possible theories of violating the statute as they could and list them in Section 12(a).

In broad terms, FIFRA prohibitions fall into four general categories: registration-related prohibitions,[281] misbranding[282] and other labeling violations,[283] use violations,[284] and miscellaneous violations related to FIFRA's administration.[285]

[b] Registration-Related Prohibitions

The registration-related prohibitions of Section 12(a)(1) make it unlawful for any person "in any State to distribute, sell, offer for sale, hold for sale, ship, deliver for shipment or receive and (having so received) deliver or offer to deliver," to any other person pesticides that violate the various categories of prohibition.[285.1] These include unregistered pesticides not legitimized by Section 6(a)(1), registered pesticides sold under claims that differ from those forming the basis of the registration statement, or registered pesticides whose composition differs from that described in the registration statement, and pesticides not colored for consumer safety reasons in violation of a Section 25(c)(5) requirement to that effect.

---

[281] Sections 12(a)(1)(A)-(D); and Sections 12(a)(2)(C),(E),(L), and (M).

[282] Sections 12(a)(1)(E) and (F).

[283] Section 12(a)(2)(A).

[284] Sections 12(a)(2)(F),(G),(H),(J),(K),(O), and (P).

[285] Sections 12(a)(2)(B),(D),(I),(M), and (N).

[285.1] *See* N.Jonas & Co., Inc. v. U.S. EPA, 666 F.2d 829 (3d Cir. 1981)(upholding penalty predicated upon failure to register sodium hypochlorite used as a swimming pool algicide). *Compare* Gulf Oil Corporation v. EPA, 548 F.2d 1228 (5th Cir. 1977)(overturning administrative penalty upon opinion that the presence of oil of citronella on the label of patio light fuel was not substantial evidence of a pesticidal claim thereby warranting registration).

FIFRA attempts to reduce the regulatory burden on pesticide users and retailers well up the chain of distribution by allowing them to avoid potential liability for violations of the registration and misbranding provisions by permitting them to rely on a "guaranty" by their vendor to the effect that at the time of sale or distribution the product was registered and that it complies with FIFRA-imposed requirements.[286] Section 12(a)(2)(C) concurrently makes the giving of a false guaranty a separate violation of the statute.

Advertising a pesticide without giving its classification is also a specific violation of the statute, as is offering an "adulterated" pesticide.[287]

[c] Misbranding

Misbranding is elaborately defined by Section 2(q) of FIFRA to encompass a wide range of labeling and packaging prohibitions that serve to establish benchmark labeling and packaging standards that are applicable even in the absence of regulations. Most of the misbranding prohibitions involve inadequate labeling, such as false statements, failure to include the registration number, failure to provide the ingredient statement in the proper manner, failure to include the skull and crossbones insignia on acutely toxic chemicals, and the like.[287.1] Failure to comply with a child protective packaging requirement imposed by EPA under Section 25(c)(3) is also misbranding, as is offering an imitation of a registered pesticide or offering a pesticide under the name of another registered pesticide.

[d] Misuse of Pesticides

The prohibitions against misuse of pesticides are in many respects the most significant of the enforcement-related provisions; yet pesticide uses are not closely regulated by EPA. The Agency has essentially

---

[286] See Section 12(b)(1).

[287] Section 2(q) defines an "adulterated" pesticide as one whose strength or purity is less than expressed on its label, or which has had any of its ingredients replaced with a substitute, or from which "any valuable constituent . . . has been wholly or in part abstracted."

[287.1] The earliest reported FIFRA case is a misbranding case. See Victrylite Candle Company v. Brannan, Secretary, 201 F.2d 206 (D.C. Cir. 1952). Mislabling cases are rarely reported, since EPA handles mislabling violations administratively in most cases. Occasionally an administrative levy is appealed. See, e.g., Aero-Master, Inc. v. U.S. EPA, 765 F.2d 746 (8th Cir. 1985).

left all enforcement of pesticide use requirements to the states, which are by and large not adequately staffed to provide much field enforcement.

Section 12(a)(2) prohibits the use of a restricted-use pesticide other than in accordance with the classification and the registration statement, the use of a pesticide in a manner inconsistent with its labeling,[288] violation of an experimental use permit, use in contravention of a cancellation or suspension order,[289] and violation of a stop-sale order issued under Section 13.

Section 12(a)(2)(P) is a curious prohibition, which, though no doubt laudable in its purpose, seems to bear no relationship to the purposes of FIFRA. The section makes it unlawful to test pesticides on human subjects unless the subjects are fully informed of the nature of the tests and "any physical and mental health consequences which are reasonably forseeable therefrom" and having been so advised "freely volunteer to participate in the tests."[290]

[e] Miscellaneous Prohibitions

Among the other specific prohibitions in Section 12 are recordkeeping refusals, making false statements on applications,[291] and disclosing information treated as confidential under Section 10.

[2] Exemptions

Certain persons and situations are exempt from the Section 12(a)(1) prohibitions.

A receeipient of a guaranty signed by the registrant or the U. S.

---

[288] The provision was upheld against a vagueness attack in United States v. Corbin Farm Service, et al., 444 F. Supp. 510 (E.D.Cal. 1978). Probably the most significant number of undetected violations fall into this category. Discovery of such violations requires field detective work, a type of police work that is labor intensive and not part of the normal routine of most environmental enforcement personnel.

[289] EPA has occasionally prosecuted violators of cancellation orders, although the availability of compensation under Section 15 would seem to remove a major incentive to use up stocks on hand when the cancellation became effective.

[290] No such rights are accorded the nonhuman mammals, including scores of monkeys, sacrificed in order to provide evidence to satisfy FIFRA's test data requirements.

[291] These types of violations, which generally fall into the category of "lying to EPA," may also constitute violations of one or more sections of the federal criminal code. For example, making a false statement to a government agency might violate 18 USC §1001, and using the mail to transmit a misbranded pesticide might constitute mail fraud. The Title 18 crimes carry generally more severe penalties than does FIFRA.

vendor who transferred the pesticide in the original unopened package will not be held liable for any violation of Section 12(a)(1) if the guaranty provides that the pesticide was lawfully registered at the time of the sale or delivery and that it complied with the other requirements of FIFRA. In such cases, the guarantor will be liable.[292]

A carrier "lawfully shipping" pesticides or devices that are in violation of the registration prohibitions is immune from liability unless it refuses to permit a "duly designated" "officer or employee" of EPA to copy "all of its records concerning such pesticide or device."[293]

A public official "while engaged in the performance of . . . official duties" is exempt.[294] It is not at all clear what the import of this provision is, although since Section 12(a)(1) is limited to distribution and delivery rather than production and use, it would appear that the exemption is a rather insignificant one, insulating public officials from prosecution if they receive and redeliver unlawful pesticides.

An EUP holder is exempt, as is any person who "ships a substance or mixture of substances being put through tests in which the purpose is only to determine its properties and from which the user does not expect to receive any benefit in pest control from its use."[295]

[3] Enforcement

[a] In General

The FIFRA scheme assumes that EPA will maintain primary responsibility for enforcing the registration program and related requirements and that the states will be primarily responsible for enforcing pesticide use restrictions, although EPA is empowered to enforce use restrictions. The state role is spelled out in Sections 23 and 26 of FIFRA. Section 23 allows EPA to delegate its own enforcement responsibilities to the states and provides for EPA assistance in state enforcement training. Section 26 explicitly says that states possessing adequate authority and resources and making adequate enforcement reports to EPA will have the primary enforcement responsibility over use violations.[296]

---

[292] Section 12(b)(1).

[293] Section 12(b)(2).

[294] Section 12(b)(3).

[295] Section 12(b)(4) (EUP holders); and Section 12(b)(5).

[296] Section 26(a). EPA has never been very strict about the requisite commitment of resources.

A state that does not qualify for enforcement primacy under Section 26(a) will nevertheless be afforded enforcement primacy if it has entered into a Section 23 cooperative agreement with EPA.[297] As a practical matter, Section 26 effectively guarantees a minimal federal presence, if any at all, when it comes to pesticide users.[298]

FIFRA's enforcement remedies fall into three categories: (1) stop sale, use, removal, and seizure authority, (2) administrative penalty authority, and (3) criminal penalties. EPA's enforcement strategy has historically relied most heavily on the second.

[b] Injunctive-Type Remedies and Seizure

EPA is empowered to issue a "stop-sale" or "removal" order without a prior hearing when, "on the basis of inspection or tests," the Agency concludes that there is "reason to believe" that a pesticide or device is in violation of any FIFRA provision, is being or has been sold or distributed in violation of any FIFRA provision, or has been finally cancelled or suspended. Such an order is effective as to anyone possessing the pesticides and may specify precisely what the persons to whom it is directed are to do.

Enforcement of a stop-sale or removal order may be by administrative penalty or by referral of the matter to the Department of Justice for criminal prosecution under Section 14(b). Although FIFRA does not specifically provide for judicial injunctive relief, the federal courts nevertheless would have jurisdiction to enforce EPA orders under their general federal question jurisdiction.[299]

Seizure, a remedy that also occurs in the Federal Food, Drug and Cosmetic Act, and under the customs and narcotics laws, is provided for by subsections 13(b)-(d). Under FIFRA, seizure must follow a court order of "condemnation," which the government secures by means of an *in rem* action against the offending products in a U. S. district court.

The seizure remedy may be employed against misbranded pesticides

---

[297] Section 26(b).

[298] Section 27(a), moreover, requires EPA to refer use violations that come to its attention to the state, and prohibits federal enforcement until thirty days have elapsed.

[299] 28 USC §1331. Attempts by registrants and others to secure preenforcement review of EPA enforcement decisions have not been successful. *See e.g.*, CIBA-GEIGY Corporation v. U.S. EPA, 607 F. Supp. 1467 (D.D.C. 1985)(holding that mailgram from EPA informing registrants that shipment of products after a specified date without modification of label would constitute misbranding and subject shipper to enforcement action not a final Agency action giving rise to a right of judicial review).

or devices, adulterated pesticides, unregistered pesticides, improperly labeled pesticides, pesticides not colored as required, and pesticides for which claims are made that "differ in substance from the representations made in connection with its registration."[300] EPA may also seek a condemnation order with respect to a pesticide or device if "when used in accordance with the requirements imposed under this Act and as directed by the labeling, it nevertheless causes unreasonable adverse effects on the environment."[301] This is a curious provision, because it is not clear whether Congress intended it simply to be an enforcement option following a final order of cancellation or a suspension order or whether EPA may take such action even before such an order has been issued. Obviously the former interpretation is more consistent with the statute's overall scheme. It is odd, however, that Congress did not employ the same language it used in Section 13(a), which leaves no room for doubt.[302] The fact that it did not could lead to an argument that it intended something different in Section 13(b), and the only credible "difference" would be condemnation before cancellation.

The district judge may order condemned pesticides destroyed or sold, provided such action is not in violation of FIFRA; any sale proceeds go first to cover court costs, and thence to the Treasury.[303] The condemnation proceedings are required to conform, "as near as may be," to admiralty proceedings, although a jury trial may be requested by the owner.

[c] **Administrative Penalties**

Section 14 authorizes EPA to impose civil penalties, following a hearing, on all regulated entities other than private applicators in an amount up to $5000 for each offense. Private applicators may be penalized only

---

300 Section 13(B)(1)(A)-(E) and 13(b)(2).

301 Section 13(b)(3). There is an amusing proviso, obviously the work of an overly cautious herbicide lobbyist, that makes it clear that physiological effects on plants or plant parts shall not be deemed to be injury when those effects are the intended effects of the product.

302 Section 13(a) allows EPA to issue a stop-sale or removal order against, *inter alia*, a pesticide whose registration "has been canceled by a final order or has been suspended."

303 Section 13(c). The owner is permitted to pay the court costs and post a bond and then request the judge to return the products to him during the pendency of the proceedings or following an order of condemnation. The bond must ensure that the pesticides will not be sold or otherwise disposed of in violation of FIFRA or relevant state law.

up to $1000, and then only if they have previously received a written warning, or "citation," and repeated the offense.[304]

Section 14 hearings are required to be in the "county, parish, or incorporated city of residence of the person charged."[305] Although nothing in Section 14 compels a conclusion that penalty hearings be adjudicatory in nature, a penalty is the sort of action that has historically required adjudicatory proceedings in federal administrative practice; accordingly, EPA includes FIFRA penalty hearings among those governed by its rules of practice for trial-type hearings, 40 CFR Part 2.

The way a penalty is calculated is affected by Section 14(a)(4), which requires that EPA consider the "appropriateness of such penalty to the size of the business of the person charged, the effect on the person's ability to continue in business and the gravity of the violation." Similar language appears in the administrative penalty provision of Title II of the Clean Air Act, under which EPA has authority to levy penalties for violation of the act's fuel additive provisions. There is authority under that provision allowing EPA to peer behind a small one-facility corporation, and view the economic size and strength of a group of affiliated entities in order to determine the size of the respondent and its ability to pay. The modest ceiling of FIFRA penalties, however, renders this authority somewhat meaningless.

Failure of a penalty recipient either to pay the penalty or to appeal the levy in a timely fashion under Section 16(b) will result in an action for debt collection, in which the validity of the levy may not be challenged. The sixty-day period allowed for perfecting an appeal "after

---

[304] Section 14(a). The statute contains a curious proviso, added in 1978, which reads as follows:

Provided, that any applicator not included under paragraph 1 [presumably referring to commercial applicators] . . . who holds or applies registered pesticides or uses dilutions of registered pesticides, only to provide a service of controlling pests without delivering any unapplied pesticides to any person so served, and who violates any provision of this act may be assessed a civil penalty of not more than $500 for the first offense nor more than $1000 for each subsequent offense.

This provision may serve to insulate private, not commercially licensed applicators who unlawfully apply restricted-use pesticides or who misapply pesticides from larger penalties, or may be intended to remove the prior warning requirement from "for hire" private applicators, although if the latter is the intent the statute arguably does not succeed in doing so. The civil penalty authority was upheld against a constitutional attack in Continental Research Corporation v. Train, 713 F. Supp. 713 (E.D.Mo. 1976).

[305] Section 14(a)(3). This is a *sui generis* requirement insofar as EPA's programs are concerned. The Agency is used to holding hearings at its headquarters or in its regional offices.

entry of such order" is strictly construed, and the time runs from the date the order is entered, not from date of receipt by the regulated entity.[306]

[d]   Criminal Penalties

Criminal responsibility under FIFRA applies to knowing violations of the law, and for revealing, "with intent to defraud," information "relative to formulas of products acquired under the authority of section 3." Registrants and others in the marketing chain face $25,000 fines and up to one year's imprisonment for knowing violations. Private applicators may be fined only up to $1000 and imprisoned for not more than thirty days. The information disclosers, who it seems would be most likely to be EPA employees or contractors, face up to *three* years in jail and fines of up to $10,000, yet another example of FIFRA's priorities.[307]

Acts of agents or employees are imputed to the employer as well as providing a basis for liability for the actor, and liability can attach to more than one category of defendant involved in a single event.[308]

There have been relatively few federal FIFRA prosecutions, and a modest number of state law criminal actions, the latter centering on applicator violations, and a range of regulatory violations that are often *per se* offenses.[309] One explanation for the relative paucity of FIFRA criminal prosecutions is the likelihood that most criminal activity will occur in field use of pesticides, an area essentially left to the states. A second, or perhaps related, reason is the historical lack of criminal investigative resources at EPA, in conjunction with the FBI's relative lack of interest in FIFRA cases since the offenses are only classified as misdemeanors.

---

[306] Selco Supply Co. v. EPA, 632 F.2d 863 (10th Cir. 1980).

[307] *Compare* subsections 14(b)(1), (b)(2), *and* (b)(3). More recent environmental statutes have established significantly higher penalties for offenses that place people in danger of bodily harm. *Compare* Sections 3008(d) *and* (e) of the Solid Waste Act, 42 USC §§6901 *et seq.*

[308] Section 14(d). *See also* United States v. Corbin Farm Services, 444 F. Supp. 510 (E.D. Cal. 1978) (one who is personally involved in recommending the use of a pesticide that is the subject of an alleged violation and one who supervises its use may be held liable along with the applicator).

[309] A typical state prosecution of the latter type might involve fining a dealer for continuing to do business after his license, which requires yearly renewal and a monetary payment, had expired.

[4] Private Enforcement and Tort Remedies

FIFRA does not contain a citizen suit provision, and it has been held that a private right of action for enforcement or damages may not be inferred from the statutory scheme,[310] although one court has allowed a private action in which the plaintiffs sought to enjoin a federal agency from violating FIFRA, predicating jurisdiction over the subject matter of the defendant agency's actions on the Administrative Procedure Act.[311]

Tort plaintiffs, grounding their claims on state law, have fared reasonably well. Nuisance, ultrahazardous activity,[312] and negligence[313] claims involving pesticides are increasing in frequency, and, though there are substantial proof problems in cases involving latent conditions, such as malignancies, this appears to be a growing area of tort litigation.[314]

---

[310] In re "Agent Orange" Product Liability Litigation, 506 F.Supp. 737 (E.D.N.Y. 1979). *See also,* Almond Hill School, et al. v. U.S. Dept. of Agriculture, 768 F.2d 1030 (9th Cir. 1985)(holding no cause of action under Section 1983 of the Civil Rights Act exists in light of FIFRA's pervasive regulatory scheme).

[311] Oregon Environmental Council v. Kunzman, 714 F.2d 901 (9th Cir. 1983). This lawsuit more closely resembles those predicated on the National Environmental Policy Act of 1969. In both cases the defendant must be a federal agency. EPA maintains that its regulatory actions are not subject to NEPA, a position that has generally been sustained. *See* Wyoming v. Hathaway, 525 F.2d 66 (10th Cir. 1975); and EDF v. Blum, 458 F. Supp. 650, 651 (D.D.C. 1978). *See also* Eli Lilly and Co. v. EPA, 615 F. Supp. 811 D. Ind. 1985)(holding that an implied private right of action may be brought by a *registrant* seeking redress of violation of a right alleged to be provided under FIFRA, applying the Cort v. Ash, 422 U.S. 66 (1975), factors.

[312] *See, e.g.,* Langan v. Valicopters, Inc., 10 ERC 1614 (Wash. 1977) (pesticide drift causing damage to organic farmer's business).

[313] *See e.g.,* Ferrebee v. Chevron, Inc., et al., 736 F.2d. 1529 (D.C. Cir. 1984). This holding reversed a lower court's dismissal of a negligence action against a pesticide manufacturer by a government employee barred by statute from suing the United States. The case involved workplace exposure to the chemical and subsequent death from a condition linked to the chemical by animal test data. The defendant registrant unsuccessfully argued that registration of the product foreclosed the court's inquiry into its safety.

[314] *See e.g.,* Three Thousand Residents of Triana, Alabama, et al. v. Olin Corporation, et al., (D. Ala. 1983)(settled prior to trial, with defendants, who were alleged to have disposed of DDT residues while operating the Redstone Arsenal under a lease from the Defense Department, paying in excess of $25 million in damages and special programs); the *Agent Orange* litigation was settled prior to trial for $180 million to be put into a trust fund by the defendants, who manufactured the phenoxy herbicides at issue; and, finally, there is no doubt that the multitude of lawsuits filed following a catastrophic accident at a pesticide-manufacturing facility in Bhopal, India, will add to the literature on the subject.

§3.08 State Pesticide Regulation

[1] In General

A number of references and discussions throughout the preceding subsections of this chapter deal with state pesticide regulation, many of which address the primary role that Congress envisioned for the states, regulation of pesticide use. In recent years, increasing number of states have become more active in regulating other aspects of the pesticide industry, most often dealers, and some states have begun to require separate state registration and labeling, which in some cases is more stringent than EPA's regulation under FIFRA.[315]

[2] Federal Preemption

Increasing state interest in aggressive pesticide regulation has produced inevitable conflicts between the desires of state regulators in some of the more active states and FIFRA registrants, who understandably desire uniform, or at least reasonably uniform, regulation. Congress was not unaware of this concern; accordingly Section 24, in addition to providing for "special local needs" registration by states,[316] contains two preemption provisions, Sections 24(a) and 24(b).[317] The first, similar to provisions in other federal environmental laws, prohibits states from imposing less stringent regulatory requirements on the "sale or use of any federally registered pesticide . . . " than are required by or under FIFRA. It does not, however, specifically allow more stringent state regulation or, as in the case of the Occupational Safety and Health Act, limit the states to federally equivalent standards.

The second preemption provision prohibits the states from imposing labeling or packaging requirements different from those required by FIFRA. The tension between these two provisions is no better illustrat-

---

315 *E.g.*, The New York Department of Environmental Conservation adopted a statewide regulation imposing significantly more stringent use limitations on chlordane, ubiquitously used for subterranean termite control, than EPA's registration standard for the pesticide required.

316 *See supra* Section §3.04[2].

317 These sections state:

(a) A State may regulate the sale or use of any federally registered pesticide or device in the States, but only if, and to the extent the regulation does not permit any sale or use prohibited by this Act.

(b) Such State shall not impose or continue in effect any requirement for labeling or packaging in addition to or different from those required under this Act.

ed than by the regulatory issues that gave rise to *National Agricultural Chemicals Associations, et al. v. Rominger.*[318]

Acting under the California Food and Agriculture Code,[319] the California Department of Food and Agriculture adopted pesticide regulations that required, for pesticides classified as "restricted use" pesticides under FIFRA, substantially more information than EPA requires.[320] Moreover, the department's regulations arguably authorized the imposition of use restrictions above and beyond those required by EPA and, the plaintiffs argued, required those restrictions to appear on the pesticide label.

The plaintiffs in *Rominger* argued that FIFRA preempted separate state registration, and argued alternatively that the additional data requirements imposed by California imposed an impermissible burden on interstate commerce. The court rejected both arguments, and, on the preemption issue, clearly the more difficult of the two, held that FIFRA neither expressly nor by implication preempted state pesticide registration that is more stringent than EPA's. The road to this conclusion was not easy, however. Although the statute is essentially silent on the point, the legislative history, primarily from oversight hearings and from the 1978 amendments, is mixed.

Both the Senate report on the 1978 amendments and testimony by then-EPA Administrator Douglas Costle state that, except for special local needs registration, FIFRA occupies the field, including intrastate pesticide registration.[321] An earlier House Report, however, unequivocally states that in the case of restricted-use pesticides "the States are left free to impose whatever restrictions they wish (other than labeling and packaging). The States could also completely prohibit the use of . . . restricted use pesticides within their jurisdictions."[322] The 1972 Senate Report is of similar import.[323] Although apparently not recognized by the court, the *contemporaneous* legislative history clearly supported California's position. It is only postenactment legislative history

---

[318] 500 F.Supp. 445 (E.D. Cal. 1980).

[319] Cal. Food and Agric. Code Sections 12811 *et seq.*

[320] *See* 3 Cal. Admin. Code, Ch. 4, sub. 1, group 2.

[321] *See* S. Rep. No. 95-334, at 29 (1977). Costle's testimony is curious in that it contradicts a published Agency position appearing as early as 1976, to the effect that the 1972 FIFRA permitted state registration. *See* 41 Fed. Reg. 13986 (1976).

[322] H.R. Rep. No. 92-511, at 16 (1972).

[323] Sen. Rep. No. 92-838, at 30 (1972).

that is inconsistent, and such statements are usually accorded less weight.

The court in *Rominger* concluded that there was no irreconcilable difference between the California legislation and FIFRA, that the FIFRA legislative history does not clearly mandate preemption, and that the overall structure of FIFRA when viewed against the long-standing local interest in food-related pesticide regulation cut strongly against preemption by implication.

The court in *Rominger* had before it but did not address the substantive merits of two additional difficult issues. The first was a claim that the California registration requirements ran afoul of FIFRA's labeling preemption, which the court dismissed as not ripe. The second, dismissed both as not ripe and under the primary jurisdiction doctrine because the issue was pending in state court, was a claim that the California statute and regulations allowed the state to establish more stringent pesticide tolerances, preempted by the Federal Food, Drug and Cosmetic Act.

Whatever the outcome of these issues, the result of *Rominger*, that the states may maintain their own more stringent registration programs, places both the states and the industry in a difficult position, in view of the clear and seemingly unambiguous prohibition against separate state labels for federally registered pesticides. Since the label and packaging inserts are the primary means by which applicators learn of the registration restrictions, a state that seeks to impose more stringent limitations than are contained in the FIFRA registration standards is forced to find another means of informing the applicator in the field what the new requirements are. In short, the result is an enforcement nightmare.[324]

[3] Local Bans and Other Regulatory Options

Both the result in *NACA v. Rominger, supra,* and the 1972 legislative history of FIFRA point to authority on the part of state and local govern-

---

[324] States that have permit requirements for restricted use applications may insert the additional restrictions as permit conditions. States that require annual examinations for commercial applicators and supervisory personnel can use the license renewal opportunity to "get the word out." These options are not open to states not employing these regulatory devices, or where a pesticide registered for general use by EPA is restricted or prohibited by the state, particularly since pesticide purchases are often made in a state other than the one in which the application occurs.

ments to ban outright the sale, distribution, or use of federally registered pesticides within their jurisdictions.[325]

Rigorous pesticide application permit requirements, clearly allowed the states under Sections 24 and 27, provide another, although expensive, means employed by states to exert greater control over pesticides than is provided under FIFRA. By providing opponents of pesticide use an opportunity for a hearing, such statutes often serve to *de facto* prohibit pesticide use or severely restrict it in the absence of a state registration scheme, or in addition to such a scheme.[326] Although EPA does not comply with the procedural requirements of the National Environmental Policy Act, some state law analogs apply to pesticide permit decisions.[327]

§3.09 Future Directions

Recent events may shape changes in pesticide regulation in years to come, although this, like any other essentially political prognostication, is inherently risky. One change, increased public participation in the FIFRA registration process, is under way. Another area of legislative revision long sought by citizen groups is a citizen enforcement provision similar to that found in other environmental laws.[328]

Pressure for increased regulation of pesticide manufacturing facilities began to mount in late 1984 following a catastrophic leak of methylisocyanate at a chemical plant in Bhopal, India, and revelations that a similar plant in the United States had experienced a large number of smaller leaks of the same chemical over a three-year period. Such authority exists already under TSCA, and the basic air and water pollution laws, although EPA has never fully utilized it. Since manufacturing sector hazards are not peculiar to pesticide plants, TSCA is arguably the more logical place to put any such enhanced regulatory authority.

---

[325] In some communities this action has been accomplished by popular referendum or "initiative" votes. *See, e.g.,* 62 Op. Cal. Atty. Gen. 90 (3-2-79).

[326] *See, e.g.,* Cal. Food and Agr. Code, Section 14009.

[327] *See* California Environmental Quality Act, Cal Pub. R. Code Sections 21000 *et seq; cf.* State Environmental Quality Review Act, N.Y. Env. Cons. Law, Sections 8-0101 to 8-0117 (New York does not issue application permits, however).

[328] I question the viability of such a provision, however, since most of the enforcement "problems" are doubtless misuse of pesticides in the field, and field enforcement requires training and information-gathering tools that will simply never be available to citizen groups.

Toxic substance exposure-related tort litigation and the problems of causation posed by long latency effects have spawned a number of legislative efforts, at both the state and national levels, to develop standardized victim compensation schemes. Some movement in this area will undoubtedly have an effect on pesticide regulation.

Finally, the long-term environmental fate of agricultural and other pesticides, neglected by EPA for many years, has begun to attract attention.[329]

---

[329] The environmental fate of pesticide *wastes* is dealt with under separate legislation, the Comprehensive Environmental Response, Compensation and Liability Act, 42 USC §§9601 *et seq.*, and, to a lesser extent, under the Resource Conservation and Recovery Act, 42 USC §§6901 *et seq.*

CHAPTER 4

Chemicals in Consumer Products

§4.01 The Consumer Product Safety Act

[1] In General

The Consumer Product Safety Act (CPSA) regulates "consumer products," which are defined in the Act as "any article, or component part thereof, produced or distributed (i) for sale to a consumer for use in or around a permanent or temporary household or residence, a school, in recreation, or otherwise, or, (ii) for the personal use, consumption, or enjoyment of a consumer in or around a permanent or temporary household or residence, a school, in recreation, or otherwise. . . ."[1] This

---

[1] 15 USC §2052.

definition is to be liberally construed to effect Congress's purpose of protecting consumers from hazardous products.[2]

The courts have constructed a four-part test to determine whether an item is a consumer product. First, is it an article or component part thereof? This test is satisfied if the item is a distinct article of commerce or is a component is such a distinct article.[3] Components of a house or school are also "articles or component parts thereof."[4] Second, is it produced or distributed? An item is distributed if it reaches a significant number of consumers.[5] Third, is it sold to or used by consumers? This test attempts to distinguish industrial products from consumer products. An item satisfies this test, even if it is primarily industrial, if it is customarily sold or otherwise distributed to consumers.[6] Fourth, is it used around a household, residence, or school, or in recreation, or otherwise? A broad interpretation of this requirement is used to effect the legislative purpose.

The statute specifically exempts from the definition of "consumer product" industrial products, tobacco and tobacco products, motor vehicles and motor vehicle equipment, pesticides, firearms, aircraft and related parts, boats and related parts, drugs and cosmetics, and food and beverages (including alcohol).

[2] Regulatory Authority

The Consumer Product Safety Act created the Consumer Product Safety Commission as an independent regulatory body[7] charged with the functions of carrying out not only the CPSA but also the Hazardous Substances Control Act and the Poison Prevention Packaging Act.[8] The Commission is composed of five members appointed by the President

---

[2] CPSC v. Chance Mfg. Co., 441 F. Supp. 228 (D. D.C 1977).

[3] CPSC v. Anoconda Co., 593 F.2d 1314 (D. D.C. 1979).

[4] Kaiser Aluminum Corp. v. CPSC, 439 U.S. 881 (1978)(holding that aluminum branch wiring is an article or component and a consumer product).

[5] United States v. One Hazardous Product Consisting of a Refuse Bin, 487 F. Supp. 228 (D. N.J. 1980).

[6] United States v. Anaconda, 445 F. Supp. 486 (D. D.C. 1977).

[7] Section 2053(a).

[8] Section 2079(b). The U.S. Environmental Protection Agency also has jurisdiction over the Poison Prevention Packaging Act, where the poisons are pesticides. *See* Chapter 3, *supra*.

with the advice and consent of the Senate.[9] The Commission has full control over the hiring of its staff, independent of any executive branch review.[10] To carry out its functions, the Commission is empowered to conduct hearings,[11] subpoena witnesses, compel the production of reports and documents, administer oaths, take depositions, litigate both civil and criminal actions and appeals,[12] purchase consumer products,[13] enter into contracts,[14] maintain a research and testing facility,[15] etc.

[3] Regulatory Strategies

The CPSA provides several alternative ways in which consumers can be protected from hazardous consumer products.

The Commission is directed by Section 2054 of the CPSA to maintain an Injury Information Clearinghouse, which collects information associated with consumer products. This information is disseminated to the public and to public or private bodies interested in developing safety standards and test methods. The goal of this provision, in part, is to make it possible for consumers to contrast safety records of various products.[16] The release of information to consumers is subject to restrictions and detailed procedures when a manufacturer claims the information is confidential or a trade secret,[17] or when the disclosure would be misleading to consumers or not aid consumers in determining product safety.[18]

The Commission may promulgate Consumer Product Safety Standards (CPSSs) to impose performance requirements or packaging and labeling requirements on consumer products. These standards may be established only when "reasonably necessary" to prevent or reduce an "unreasonable risk" of injury.[19] An unreasonable risk may exist where there is only a very remote possibility of inflicting an extremely severe

---

9 Section 2053(b)(1).
10 Section 2053(g)(4).
11 Section 2076(a).
12 Section 2076(B).
13 Section 2076(F).
14 Section 2076(G).
15 Section 2076(H).
16 GTE Sylvania v. Consumer Product Safety Commission, 404 F. Supp. 352 (D. Del. 1975).
17 Section 2055.
18 GTE Sylvania v. CPSC, 404 F. Supp. 352 (D. Del. 1975).
19 Section 2056(a).

injury. It is not necessary for even one such accident to have actually occurred.[20] On the other hand, the mere presence of actual injuries may not show an unreasonable risk if the causation and severity are slight or inadequately documented.[21]

In assessing unreasonable risk, the Commission may consider foreseeable misuse.[22] A standard is reasonably necessary if the Commission has substantial evidence leading to the conclusion that the benefits of the standard outweigh its cost to consumers and manufacturers.[23] This does not require an elaborate cost-benefit analysis but does require at least a rough balancing of the costs and benefits. For a standard to be reasonably necessary, every portion of the standard must be reasonably necessary or the whole standard fails. It is the Commission's burden to show that the standard will actually reduce the risk of injury to consumers.[24] Severe economic impact on an industry or segment of an industry is a material factor in the balance of costs and benefits, but does not in and of itself render a standard unreasonable.[25]

The Commission must rely on voluntary standards, rather than mandatory ones, if compliance with the voluntary standard would adequately reduce the risk of injury and if it is likely that there will be substantial compliance with such voluntary standards.[26] This requirement reflects a congressional intent to impose the least burdensome requirement that will adequately protect consumers from risk of injury, disease, or death.[27]

If the Commission finds that a product poses an unreasonable risk of injury and that no feasible CPSS would adequately protect the public, then the Commission may declare the product to be a "banned hazardous product"[28] and remove it from the stream of commerce.

---

20 Southland Mower Co. v. CPSC, 619 F.2d 499, (5th Cir. 1980).

21 D.D. Bean & Sons v. CPSC, 574 F.2d 643 (1st Cir. 1978).

22 Aqua Slide N Dive Corp. v. CPSC, 569 F.2d 831 (5th Cir. 1978); Gulf South Insulation, et al. v. CPSC, 701 F.2d 1137 (5th Cir. 1983).

23 Id.

24 Id.

25 ASG Industries v. CPSC, 593 F.2d 1323 (D.C. Cir. 1979).

26 Section 2056(b).

27 Section 2058(f)(3)(F).

28 Section 2057.

[4] Procedures and Judicial Review

Adoption of a voluntary standard, a CPSS, or a product ban must be carried out according to the procedures set forth in Section 2058. The procedures of Section 2058 begin with an "advance notice of proposed rulemaking," which must be published in the Federal Register. The advance notice must identify the product and the risks being addressed; summarize alternatives; refer to any existing standards relevant to the proceeding; invite any person to submit comments, proposed voluntary standards, or proposed CPSSs;[29] and provide a thirty-day comment period.

If the risk being addressed is cancer, birth defects, or genetic mutations, the Commission may not publish an advance notice unless it has first established a chronic hazard advisory panel and received from it a report. The chronic hazard advisory panel is composed of seven scientists appointed by the Commission. Its function is to review the scientific literature and issue a report on the risks of cancer, birth defects, or genetic mutations from a given product. This report must be considered by the Commission, included with the advance notice, and incorporated into the preliminary regulatory analysis and final regulatory analysis.[30]

If a voluntary standard is submitted, and the Commission determines that compliance with the voluntary standard will adequately reduce the risk of injury and that substantial compliance with the voluntary standard is likely, it must terminate rulemaking procedures and publish its decision to rely on the voluntary standard.[31]

If proposed standards are submitted, and the Commission determines that any of them, in whole, in part, or in combination, would adequately reduce the risk of injury, it may publish those standards as proposed Consumer Product Safety Rules (CPSRs).[32] The proposed rule must be accompanied by a preliminary regulatory analysis that describes the costs and benefits of the proposed rule, explains why any proposed voluntary standard or CPSS submitted to the Commission was

---

[29] Sections 2058(g)(1-6).
[30] Sections 2080(b) and (c).
[31] Section 2058(b)(2).
[32] Section 2058(b)(1).

published as the proposed rule, and describes any reasonable alternatives and their costs and benefits.[33]

After publication of the proposed rule, written and oral comments are taken. Within sixty days after publication (unless extended), the Commission must either withdraw its notice of proposed rulemaking or promulgate the rule together with a final regulatory analysis and set of findings.[34] The required contents of the regulatory analysis and findings are spelled out in Sections 2058(f)(1-4) of the Act. The Commission may not promulgate a rule unless it finds, *inter alia*, that the rule is reasonably necessary to prevent an unreasonable risk of injury, that the rule is in the public interest, that a voluntary standard would not serve the purpose, and, if the rule declares a product a banned hazardous subject, that no CPSS could serve the purpose. The Commission is also required to consider the impact of the promulgated rule on elderly and handicapped persons and to adopt the rule that imposes the least burdensome requirements while still adequately reducing the risk of injury.

The effective date of a rule is set by the Commission not earlier than thirty days or later than one hundred eighty days after promulgation, unless it finds, for good cause, that the date should be earlier or later. In no case may a rule become effective before it is promulgated. A rule applies only to goods manufactured after the effective date of the rule, but a manufacturer may not significantly increase production rate between the date of promulgation and the effective date.[35]

A rule may be amended or revoked by the Commission at any time, but if a material change is being made, the Commission must follow the same procedures and meet the same substantive requirements as for a new rule.[36]

Any person adversely affected by a rule promulgated by the Commission may, within sixty days, file a petition for review by the court of appeals.[37] If a petition is filed, the Commission must assemble and file with the court a record consisting of the rule, any notices or proposals published relating to the rule, all written comments and transcripts of oral comments submitted by interested parties, and any other informa-

---

[33] Section 2058(c).
[34] Section 2058(d).
[35] Section 2058(g).
[36] Section 2058(h).
[37] Section 2060(a). *See generally* State Fair of Texas v. CPSC, 650 F.2d 1324 (5th Cir. 1981). The sixty-day filing deadline is absolute, and will not be waived even if a petition for reconsideration is pending. *See* Laminators Safety Glass Ass'n v. CPSC, 578 F.2d 406 (D.C. Cir. 1978).

tion considered relevant by the Commission. The court may receive additional testimony and materials only if it determines that there were reasonable grounds for the petitioner's failure to introduce such evidence in the Commission's proceedings. The court will uphold the rule if it is based on substantial evidence on the record taken as a whole.[38]

[5] Enforcement

Every product subject to a CPSS must be accompanied by a certificate from the manufacturer stating the name of the manufacturer, the date and place of production, and that the product complies with all applicable CPSSs. The certificate must be based on a reasonable testing program. The Commission may by rule prescribe a reasonable testing program.[39]

A "substantial product hazard" is a failure to comply with a CPSS that creates a substantial risk of injury to the public or a product defect that creates a substantial risk of injury to the public.[40] All manufacturers, distributors, and retailers must immediately inform the Commission of information indicating the existence of a substantial product hazard.[41]

If the Commission determines that a substantial product hazard exists and that its action is in the public interest, it may (after opportunity for a hearing) require any manufacturer, distributor, or retailer to notify the public, other manufacturers, distributors, and retailers, and any purchasers of the product that the hazard exists. It may also require that the product be recalled and (at the option of the person receiving the order) repaired, replaced, or the purchase price refunded.[42] After the Commission has commenced proceedings against a substantial product hazard, it may apply to the U. S. district court having jurisdiction for a preliminary injunction to prevent the distribution of the product while the administrative proceeding is pending.[43]

For the purpose of carrying out its functions, the Commission has the authority to enter and inspect any factory, warehouse, or conveyance

---

[38] Section 2060(c).
[39] Section 2063.
[40] Section 2064(a).
[41] Section 2064(b).
[42] Sections 2064(c-f).
[43] Section 2064(g).

in which consumer products are manufactured, held, or transported.[44] The statute requires only that the inspector present proper credentials and a notice from the Commission, but constitutional restraints will at times add the requirement of an administrative search warrant.[45] In those cases, Section 2065 provides the statutory authority to conduct an investigation, which is one of the prerequisites for an administrative search warrant.[46]

The Commission is also given the authority to impose recordkeeping and reporting requirements by rule on manufacturers and distributors of consumer products.[47]

[6] Emergency Powers

Special procedures exist for taking action against "imminently hazardous consumer products." An imminently hazardous consumer product is a consumer product that presents an imminent and unreasonable risk of death, serious illness, or severe personal injury.[48] The unreasonable risk standard is probably the same for an imminent hazard as it is in the CPSS section. The precise meaning of the term "imminent" is not provided in the statute, nor has it been judicially tested. A reasonable definition would allow an imminent hazard action when reliance on slower rulemaking procedures would not adequately reduce the risk of injury.

When the Commission believes that an imminent hazard exists, it may bring suit in the district court against any manufacturer, distributor, or retailer, or against the product itself.[49] The court may declare the product to be an imminently hazardous consumer product and, if it does so, may grant relief of several types. The court may seize and condemn the product, require that notification of the hazard be given to purchasers or the public at large, or require that the product be recalled for repair, replacement, or refund.[50]

---

[44] Section 2065(a).
[45] Normal search and seizure constraints apply.
[46] State Fair of Texas v. CPSC, 650 F.2d 1324 (5th Cir. 1981).
[47] Section 2065(b).
[48] Section 2061(a).
[49] Section 2061(a).
[50] Section 2061(b).

[7] Imports and Exports

A product can be refused admission into the United States if it falls within one of five categories listed in Section 2066(a). Generally, a foreign product that could be proceeded against by the Commission if it were domestic can be refused entry. The Commission is entitled to receive at no charge samples of any products being offered for import. The product's owner or consignee is entitled to a hearing before the product is refused entry.[51] If a product is found to be unacceptable for import, the owner or consignee may either modify the product to make it acceptable or export the product from the United States. If neither is done within a reasonable time, the Treasury Department may destroy the product.[52]

Products manufactured for export are generally exempt from the CPSA if they are labeled as for export, are actually exported, and pose no unreasonable risk to consumers within the United States.[53] If a person plans to export a consumer product that is a banned hazardous product or is not in conformity with a CPSS, that person must notify the Commission, which must notify the government of the receiving country.[54]

[8] Penalties

Any knowing violation of the CPSA makes the violator subject to civil penalties of up to $2000 per violation, not to exceed $500,000 for any related series of violations. Each consumer product not in compliance or each day that required information or reports are not provided will constitute a separate violation if the person being charged is a manufacturer or distributor who either has actual knowledge that he is in violation or has received notice from the Commission that he is in violation.[55] A series of factors are provided in Section 2069(b) to be considered by the Commission in determining the size of the penalty to be sought.

Any person who knowingly and willfully violates the CPSA is subject

---

[51] Section 2066(b).
[52] Sections 2066(c) and (e).
[53] Section 2067(a).
[54] Section 2067(b).
[55] Section 2069(a).

to criminal penalties not to exceed $50,000 or one year's imprisonment or both.

[9] Citizen Suits

The CPSA contains citizen suit provisions. Section 2072 allows any person injured by a knowing violation of the act to recover damages plus the costs of the suit in the district court. This private right of action arises only if the Commission has taken regulatory action with regard to the hazard that caused the injury.[56] Section 2073 allows any interested person to bring an action to enforce a CPSR or an order issued in response to a substantial product hazard. The term "interested person" in this section is broad, but it does not permit a suit by one manufacturer against another where the purpose is to obtain a competitive advantage and not to protect consumers.[57]

[10] State Standards

States are permitted to have consumer product regulations that are identical to or more stringent than the federal requirements.[58] If a state has a more stringent standard, the product involved may be exempted from the federal standard.[59]

§4.02 Hazardous Substances in Consumer Goods

[1] In General: Hazardous Substances Act

The Hazardous Substances Act[60] regulates any item that meets the statutory definition of "hazardous substances." This definition has two main parts. First, a substance that is toxic, corrosive, and irritant, is a strong sanitizer, is flammable or combustable, or generates pressure and that may cause substantial personal injury or illness when handled or used in a customary or reasonably foreseeable manner is a hazardous

---

56 Riegel Textile Corp. v. Celanese Corp., 493 F. Supp. 511 (S.D. N.Y. 1980), *aff'd*, 649 F.2d 894 (2d Cir. 1981).

57 Plaskolite, Inc. v. Baxt Industries, Inc., 486 F. Supp. 213 (N.D. Ga. 1980).

58 Sections 2075 (a) and (b). *See* Borden, Inc. v. Commissioner of Public Health, 338 Mass. 707 (Mass. Sup. Jud. Ct. 1983)(upholding state ban on ureaformaldehyde foam insulation after CPSC ban struck down).

59 Section 2075(c).

60 15 USC §§1261 *et seq.*

substance.[61] Second, the CPSC may by regulation declare a substance to be a hazardous substance. The Commission may take such action when, in its judgment, the purposes of the act will be furthered by avoiding or resolving uncertainty. In issuing a regulation of this type, the Commission must follow the procedures set forth in the Federal Food, Drug and Cosmetic Act (FFDCA).[62]

The Hazardous Substances Act does not cover any item that is subject to the Federal Insecticide, Fungicide and Rodenticide Act (FIFRA), FFDCA, or the Atomic Energy Act, and it does not apply to tobacco, tobacco products, or fuel for household heating, cooking, or refrigeration.[63] The Hazardous Substances Act provides additional categories of hazardous substances, which are of little relevance to chemical regulation.[64]

As a procedural matter, the CPSC must determine that an item is a "hazardous substance" before it can proceed to any regulation of the item under the Hazardous Substances Act.[65]

[2] Regulatory Scheme

[a] Labeling Requirements

All hazardous substances are subject to labeling requirements. The labeling requirements are set out in 15 USC §1261(p). The requirements include the manufacturer's name and address; the name(s) of the product's hazardous component(s); the nature of the hazard; precautionary measures to be followed or avoided; appropriate first-aid instructions; signal words when appropriate, such as "Danger," "Poison," or "Caution"; and the statement "Keep out of reach of children." These elements must be present in conspicuous and legible type in the English language.

The Commission may, by regulation, require additional labeling or

---

[61] 15 USC §1261(f)(1)(A). For an example of the application of this standard, see United States v. Chalaire, 316 F. Supp. 543, (D. La., 1970).
[62] 15 USC §§1262(a)(1) and (2).
[63] 15 USC §1261(f)(2).
[64] 15 USC §§1261 (f)(1)(C) and (D).
[65] Spring Mills, Inc. v. CPSC, 434 F. Supp. 416 (D. S.C. 1977).

waive the required labeling when appropriate to the hazards of a specific product and the practical limitations of its package size.[66]

[b] Product Bans

The Commission may, by regulation, declare a hazardous substance that is a toy or other article intended for children, or that is intended or packaged in a form suitable for use in the household to be a "banned hazardous substance." A banned hazardous substance may not be introduced into or travel in interstate commerce. To ban a hazardous substance, the Commission must show either that the objective of protecting the public health and safety cannot be adequately served by cautionary labeling and can be served only by banning the substance[67] or that the substance is a hazardous substance intended for use by children or susceptible to access by a child.[68] One court, applying this standard, found that a specific item was a hazardous substance intended for use by children, and hence banned, but that if it had borne a specified warning and not been sold in toy stores or toy departments, it would not be intended for children and hence not banned.[69]

[3] Procedures

A regulation banning a hazardous substance must be promulgated in accordance with the procedures of 15 USC §§1262(f-i). This procedure starts with the publication in the Federal Register of an advance notice of proposed rulemaking. This notice must (1) identify the article or substance to be regulated and the nature of the risks involved; (2) summarize each available alternative; (3) give information about existing standards and reasons why they are inadequate; (4) invite comments

---

[66] 15 USC §§1262(b) and (c).

[67] 15 USC §1261(9)(1)(B).

[68] 15 USC §1261(9)(1)(A).

[69] R.B. Jarts, Inc. v. Richardson, 438 F.2d 846 (2d Cir. 1971). Because of the limitations on the types of substances that can be banned, and the fact that regulation under the procedurally less onerous Consumer Product Safety Act is possible only if regulation under the Hazardous Substances Act is inappropriate, the Commission can find itself in a dilemma. In the case of ureaformaldehyde foam insulation, the Commission elected to ban the product under the CPSA, on the ground that both residences and schools were affected; since nonresidential uses are not covered by the Hazardous Substances Act, it reasoned, the risks could not overall be adequately dealt with under it. The Commission's rationale was rejected by the Fifth Circuit Court of Appeals in Gulf South Insulation, et al. v. CPSC, 701 F.2d 1137 (5th Cir. 1983), primarily on the basis of the absence of any risk data in the record on exposures to formaldehyde in structures other than residences.

from interested persons; (5) invite any person to submit existing standards as proposed regulations; and (6) invite any person to modify or develop a voluntary standard.[70]

If the Commission determines that a standard submitted in response to its notice, if adequately complied with, would adequately reduce the identified risks and that it is likely that there will be substantial compliance with that standard, the Commission must terminate proceedings and publish a notice announcing that the Commission will rely on voluntary standards to reduce the risk.

Following the notice and comment period, and absent a decision to rely on voluntary standards, the Commission may publish a proposed rule. This proposed rule may be composed in whole or in part of standards submitted to the Commission during the comment period.

The proposed rule must be accompanied by a preliminary regulatory analysis, which must contain (1) a description of the proposed regulation's costs and benefits and an identification of who will bear the costs and receive the benefits; (2) the reasons for rejecting any submitted standard not contained in the proposed regulation; (3) the reasons for believing that a voluntary standard could not be developed in a reasonable period of time; and (4) a description of reasonable alternatives, together with their potential costs and benefits and the reasons they were not adopted.

The Commission may promulgate a regulation only if it also makes and publishes findings and prepares and publishes a final regulatory analysis. The required findings are that (1) the benefits of the action bear a reasonable relationship to its costs; (2) the regulation imposes the least burdensome requirement that adequately reduces the risk; and (3) if a voluntary standard has been implemented, either the voluntary standard will not adequately reduce the risk or substantial compliance is unlikely.

The final regulatory analysis must contain a discussion of the costs and benefits, along with who will bear the costs and receive the benefits; a description of alternatives considered by the Commission; the costs and benefits of those alternatives, and the reasons for not adopting them; and a summary of significant issues raised during public comment and an assessment of those issues.

The procedures for promulgating a regulation banning a hazardous

---

[70] 15 USC §1262(f).

substance, if followed, satisfy the requirements of due process.[71] The Commission may not ban a substance without following the required procedures,[72] but if a validly enacted regulation covers a broad category of substances, the applicability of that regulation to a specific substance can be established in an informal hearing.[73] Any challenge to the procedure used by the CPSC must be made at the time the regulation is promulgated.[74]

[4] Enforcement

The Hazardous Substances Act prohibits misbranded hazardous substances and banned hazardous substances from being introduced into interstate commerce.[75] It also bans several related acts, which, if permitted, would circumvent the original prohibition. For example, tampering with the label of a hazardous substance, giving a false guarantee that a hazardous substance is not misbranded or banned, and packaging a hazardous substance in a reused food, drug, or cosmetic container are all prohibited acts.[76]

The Commission has authority to conduct investigations and inspections when necessary to enforce the Hazardous Substances Act. Such investigations may be done by Commission personnel or by officers or employees of any state or subdivision thereof when authorized by the Commission. The investigator may, at reasonable times, enter any factory, warehouse, vehicle, etc., being used for hazardous substances, inspect the same, and obtain and remove samples of products, packaging, and labels. Investigators may also inspect and copy records showing shipment or receipt of goods into or from interstate commerce.[77]

Several enforcement options are available under the Hazardous Substances Act. The Commission may proceed against the goods directly in an *in rem* action. Following admiralty procedures, the goods can be seized, held, and eventually destroyed or returned to the owner under

---

[71] Toy Mfrs. of America v. CPSC, 630 F.2d 70 (2d Cir. 1980).

[72] Pactra Industries v. CPSC, 555 F.2d 677 (9th Cir. 1977); and Spring Mills, Inc. v. CPSC, 434 F. Supp 416 (D. S.C. 1977).

[73] Toy Mfrs. of America v. CPSC, 630 F.2d. 70 (2d Cir. 1980).

[74] United States v. An Article Consisting of Boxes of Clacker Balls, 413 F. Supp. 1281 (D. Wis. 1976).

[75] 15 USC §1263(a).

[76] 15 USC §§1263 (b), (d), and (f).

[77] 15 USC §§1270, 1271.

bond for repairs.[78] This procedure is designed to permit the Commission to respond rapidly to the presence of supplies of banned or misbranded hazardous substances that have not yet reached the consumer.[79] This procedure has been challenged on due process grounds because warrants of seizure and condemnation are not scrutinized by a judicial officer. The decisions are not unanimous, but the stronger precedent upholds the procedure.[80] This view relies on a post-seizure hearing to determine the merits of the owner's claim that goods are not banned or misbranded.

The Commission may also act prospectively to block future violations of the Hazardous Substances Act by obtaining injunctions.[81] Such injunctions have been interpreted broadly and flexibly to accomplish the protection of consumers from hazards, not merely to require literal compliance with the wording of the injunction.[82]

If a banned hazardous substance has been sold in commerce, and the Commission finds that notification must be given to warn the public, any manufacturer or distributor can be required to give public notice, mail notices to all other manufacturers, distributors, and dealers of the substance, and to send notices to all known purchasers of the substance. The form of the notice can be specified by the Commission.[83]

Moreover, the Commission can order the manufacturer, distributor, or dealer of a banned hazardous substance to "repair, replace, or refund" for the benefit of consumers when it finds such action to be in the public interest. A party receiving such an order has three options. The substance may be repaired if repair will result in its no longer being a banned hazardous substance; the substance may be replaced with a like substance that is not a banned hazardous substance; or the purchase price of the substance can be refunded, sometimes with an allowance for wear and use.

Finally, the CPSC can require a person under a repair, replace, or refund order to submit a plan detailing how the order will be complied with. Consumers who avail themselves of an offered repair, replacement, or refund may not be charged for the service and must be com-

---

[78] 15 USC §1265.

[79] *See* United States v. Articles of Hazardous Substance, 588 F.2d 39 (5th Cir. 1978).

[80] *Compare* United States v. Articles of Hazardous Substance, *id., with* United States v. Articles of Hazardous Substance, 444 F. Supp. 1260 (D. N.C. 1978).

[81] 15 USC §1267.

[82] United States v. Christie Industries, 465 F.2d 1002 (1972).

[83] 15 USC §1274(a).

pensated for reasonable expenses involved in availing themselves of the remedy.[84]

[5] Emergency Powers

The Hazardous Substances Act contains two provisions dealing with imminent hazards to the public health. The first allows the CPSC to declare a hazardous substance to be a banned hazardous substance merely by publishing notice in the Federal Register. This provision requires that the Commission first "find" an imminent hazard to public health, and allows the notice to remain in effect only so long as ordinary rulemaking procedures to ban the substance are pending.[85] The second allows the Commission to disseminate to the public information regarding an imminent danger to health.[86]

[6] Imports and Exports

The Commission may obtain from the U.S. Customs Service samples of any hazardous substance proposed to be imported. If such substance is misbranded or banned, it may not be imported, and must be exported or destroyed, except that the owner may post a bond and modify or relabel the substance so that it will no longer be banned or misbranded. In that case, a final determination by the CPSC will be deferred until the modified substance can be inspected.[87]

[7] Penalties

The penalties under the Hazardous Substances Act do not represent a significant attempt at deterrence. A first violation of the Act is a misdemeanor punishable by a $500 fine or ninety days' imprisonment or both. Subsequent violations and violations committed with intent to defraud or mislead carry penalties of $3000 or one year's imprisonment or both.[88]

---

[84] 15 USC §§1274 (b) and (c).
[85] 15 USC §1261(9)(2).
[86] 15 USC §1272.
[87] 15 USC §1273.
[88] 15 USC §1264.

CHAPTER 5

Regulation of the Generation, Transportation, Storage, and Disposal of Hazardous Waste

§5.01 Introduction

Hazardous waste law has developed two distinct components: (1) laws and programs regulating the ongoing generation, transportation, storage, and disposal of hazardous wastes and (2) laws and programs dealing with hazardous waste emergencies and cleanup of old, inactive hazardous waste disposal sites. This chapter deals with the first category of regulation.

A federal statute, officially named the Solid Waste Disposal Act,[1] but more commonly known as the Resource Conservation and Recovery Act (RCRA) is the dominant hazardous waste regulatory force in the

---

1 42 USC §§6901 *et seq.*

United States. The statute was first enacted in 1965 as a grant-in-aid program to assist the states in their dealing with the problem of open, burning dumps.[2] The statute grew by yearly amendments, although its focus did not significantly shift until 1976, when it was essentially rewritten by PL 94-580, the Resource Conservation and Recovery Act of 1976. The 1976 amendments transformed the grant-in-aid statute into a full federal regulatory program aimed primarily at hazardous waste disposal practices rather than at burning dumps. It was further amended again in 1978,[3] 1980,[4] and 1984.[5]

The original focus on municipal solid waste disposal is preserved, and expanded, in Subtitle D of RCRA, which requires, *inter alia,* the promulgation of federal guidance for sanitary landfills.[6]

Whatever concern there was among the members of the public and the scientific community about chemical waste disposal before 1976, it was not until the enactment of the RCRA amendments in that year that any serious regulatory attention was paid to the problem. Most state legislation dealing specifically with hazardous waste also dates from this point as well.

Prior to the RCRA-spawned deluge of state hazardous waste legislation, state regulatory efforts were generally aimed at controlling nuisance conditions and obvious surface runoff at open dumps and landfills. Some states attempted to license solid waste disposal facilities, and by that means attempted to exercise control over the type of material disposed of in them. However, mere licensing of disposal facilities generally proved ineffective to prevent the disposal of chemical wastes in a manner that we now understand to have contributed significantly to contamination of wide areas of groundwater in some regions.

The states have responded in varying ways to Congress's lead in RCRA. Some have enacted legislation that parallels the RCRA regulatory scheme to one degree or another and contemplate receiving delegation of the federal program as provided in Section 3006 of RCRA; others have attempted to control more carefully the siting of hazardous waste disposal facilities without constructing a broader hazardous waste regulatory program.

---

[2] *Id.*
[3] P.L. 95-609.
[4] P.L. 96-482, 96-510. *See generally* 1980 U.S. Cong. & Admin. News, at 509.
[5] P.L. 98-616 (11-8-84).
[6] Sections 4001-4009.

The Environmental Protection Agency (EPA) administers RCRA, and its Solid Waste Act implementing regulations are codified at 40 CFR Subchapter I Parts 240-271. Those of concern from the chemical waste standpoint, and discussed herein, are contained in Parts 260-271.

RCRA is designed to accomplish three basic objectives: provide a system for tracking and preserving a record of the movement of hazardous waste from its origin to its ultimate disposal (euphemistically from "cradle to grave"); ensure that disposal of hazardous waste is accomplished by means that prevent escape of the wastes into the environment; and provide an enforcement mechanism to ensure compliance with the first two objectives.

§5.02 What Substances Are Regulated?

[1] Overview

RCRA imposes its regulatory obligations on three classes of entities (generators, transporters, and operators of treatment, storage and disposal facilities) to the extent they involve themselves with "hazardous wastes" as that term is defined in Section 1004 of RCRA.[7] A solid, liquid, or contained gaseous waste or combination of wastes is "hazardous" for RCRA purposes and, unless covered by one of the exemptions, is regulated if, because of its quantity, concentration, or physical, chemical, or infectious characteristics, it "may cause or contribute to an increase in mortality or an increase in serious irreversible or incapacitating reversible illness" or may "pose a substantial present or potential hazard to human health or the environment when improperly treated, stored, transported or disposed of or otherwise managed."[8]

[2] Hazardous Waste

[a] In General

Eschewing simplicity, Congress defined "hazardous waste" as a subset of "solid waste," which it defined to include liquid and contained gaseous waste as well as solid waste in the normally understood sense

---

[7] 42 USC §6903. Future footnote references to the U.S. Code citations will be omitted, since use of the session law numbers has become almost universal in practice. Appendix 5-A is a cross-reference table matching session law numbers with the corresponding U.S. Code citations.

[8] Section 1004(5).

of the term and included a modifier that appears to limit the applicability of the statute to such of these items as are "discarded."[9] "Discarded," however, is undefined. The ordinary meaning of this term assumes an element of intent to throw away.[10] Since environmental hazards can arise from chemicals stored or transported for purposes other than disposal, such as stockpiles of raw materials, whether or not environmental releases from such chemicals can be addressed under RCRA is an important issue in defining the statute's jurisdictional reach, particularly in light of the fact that EPA possesses broad authority to seek injunctive relief to abate emergencies under Section 7003.

EPA has attempted to achieve a broad interpretation of RCRA's reach in its regulations. The Agency defined "discarded" to include material that is "abandoned" or "disposed of"[11] and defined "disposed of" to include material that is "spilled or leaked,"[12] apparently relying on RCRA's definition of "disposal,"[13] which includes "spilling" and "leaking," both of which are passive terms, connoting activity that can occur in the absence of an actor's intent. While the Agency does not attempt to regulate stored raw materials while they are stored or being transported, it does claim jurisdiction if the material "exits the unit"[14] or if the storage tanks remain on the site for more than ninety days "after the unit ceases to be operated for manufacturing, or for storage or transportation of product or of raw material," and the material is not immediately recovered for the purpose of reuse or recycling. Thus, whether or not chemical products that leak into the environment are subject to RCRA depends upon the owner's intent to recapture them and his successful recapture of them.

EPA's reasoning that deems waste to fall under RCRA where it is spilled or leaked into the environment and not reclaimed appears to be sound.[15] The act of abandonment appears to satisfy the statutory requirement that the material have been "discarded."

---

9 Section 1004(27).

10 *See, e.g.*, Webster's Third New International Dictionary at 644 (1976 ed.).

11 40 CFR §261.2(c)(1)(1984). The definitions have been changed. See discussion below.

12 40 CFR §261.2(d)(1984). See discussion below for 1985 changes.

13 Section 1004(3).

14 40 CFR §261.4(c).

15 *But cf.* United States v. Waste Industries, Inc., 556 F. Supp. 1301 (E.D.N.C. 1982), *rev'd*, 734 F.2d 159 (4th Cir. 1984), in which the district court opined that RCRA was intended to apply only to "active, affirmative conduct."

EPA's inclusion of stored product or raw material remaining at a discontinued manufacturing site for more than ninety days[16] after the site has ceased to be operated as RCRA-regulated waste seems to stand on less firm footing. This requirement appears to rest, without saying so, on an assumption that such materials are *de facto* abandoned, and have therefore been discarded. Such a conclusion, however, properly requires a case-by-case analysis to determine the actual intention of the owner. RCRA does not regulate stored chemicals. It regulates stored wastes, and whether a stored product has in fact been discarded requires proof of intent. While EPA's regulation has the advantage of administrative workability, it lacks a firm statutory underpinning.[17]

EPA's regulatory definition of "solid waste" for subpart C purposes is quite broad. Solid waste is defined to include any "discarded material that is not excluded by §261.4(a) or that is not excluded by variance granted under §§262.30 and 232.31."[18]

A material is "discarded" if it is "abandoned," as defined, recycled, as defined, or "considered inherently waste-like."[19] A material is "abandoned" if it is "disposed of," "burned or incinerated," or "accumulated, stored, or treated (but not recycled) before or in lieu of disposal, burning or incineration."[20]

The definition of "recycled"[21] is complex. Materials are considered solid wastes if recycled or accumulated or treated prior to recycling if they are included on Table 1 to Section 261.2 and are indicated on that table to be considered solid wastes on the basis of their use "in a manner constituting disposal," or if they are burned for energy recovery, are

---

16 40 CFR §261.4(c).

17 *But see* United States Brewer's Association, Inc. v. EPA, 600 F.2d 974 (D.C. Cir. 1979), upholding EPA's solid waste management guidelines, issued under Section 1008(a)(1), requiring that beverages be sold in returnable containers.

18 40 CFR §261.2(a), as amended by 50 Fed. Reg. 614 (1-4-85). The exclusions are discussed *infra*. The variances relate to certain types of recycled wastes and boiler wastes that had previously not been considered solid wastes, but are now specifically included within the definition.

19 40 CFR §261.2(a)(2).

20 40 CFR §261.2(b). The 1985 definition does not define the term "disposed of." The prior regulation, 40 CFR §261.2(d) (1984), provided that a material is "disposed of" if it "is discharged, deposited, injected, dumped, spilled, leaked or placed into or on any land or water so that such material or any constituent thereof may enter the environment or be emitted into the air or discharged into ground or surface waters."

21 40 CFR §§261.2(c), 261.2(e).

reclaimed, or are "accumulated speculatively."[22] Each of these terms is also defined either in Section 261.2 or in Section 261.1.

Certain materials are deemed by Section 261.2(e) *not* to be solid wastes when recycled. These include materials used as ingredients in an industrial process, used or reused "as effective substitutes for commercial products," or returned to the original process without being reclaimed.[23]

"Inherently waste-like materials" are also considered solid wastes, unless they are specifically stated in Section 261.2(e) not to be solid wastes, when recycled.[24] These include five chlorinated dioxins and other wastes that EPA adds from time to time on the basis of how they are ordinarily managed, whether they contain any toxic constituents listed in Appendix VII to Part 261, and whether they pose a substantial hazard to human health if recycled.[25]

EPA's elaborate restructuring of Section 261.2 to incorporate recycled materials (which the regulations refer to as "secondary materials") was motivated in part by criticism that it had left a large loophole in the RCRA program by not regulating those materials and in part by general dissatisfaction with its prior rule, which attempted to finesse the recycled material issue by including within the definition of solid waste materials of nominal commercial value that are sometimes sold and "sometimes discarded."[26]

---

[22] 40 CFR §261.2(c). The materials listed, spent materials, listed sludges and sludges exhibiting the characteristics of hazardous waste, listed by-products and by-products exhibiting the characteristics of hazardous waste, listed commercial chemical products, and scrap metal, are defined in the listing regulations under Part 261 if listed, and otherwise in the general definitions of Section 261.1. Listed "commercial chemical products" burned as fuel are not solid wastes if they are themselves fuel, Section 261.2(c)(2)(ii), nor are they considered used in a manner constituting disposal if they are applied on land and that is their ordinary manner of use.

[23] 40 CFR §261.2(e)(1). Used, reused, or returned materials will nevertheless be deemed solid waste if they are used in a manner constituting disposal, are burned for energy recovery, are used to produce fuel or are contained in fuels, are accumulated speculatively, or are one of several specified listed wastes. Section 261.2(e)(2).

[24] 40 CFR Section 261.2(d).

[25] *Id.*, at (d)(2).

[26] *See* 40 CFR §261.2(b)(2)(1984); and 40 CFR §261.2(b)(3)(1984). *Also see* United States v. A & F Materials, Inc., et al., Civil No. 83-3123 Memorandum and Order March 30, 1984 at 4. The generator in *A & F Materials* was a sewer district, which produced spent caustic soda as a by-product of its sewage treatment activities. It sold whatever of the soda it could to anyone who would buy it, and sold the material at issue to a TSD operator for 7 cents per gallon. The district court found that the material had been "discarded" for RCRA purposes. A significant problem with the "sometimes discarded"

RCRA does not clearly include recycled materials within the statutory definition of solid wastes. EPA's inclusion of such materials finds support in the postenactment legislative history of the original RCRA,[27] and the 1984 amendments, which include an amendment to Section 3001(d) requiring EPA to promulgate "standards applicable to the legitimate use, reuse, recycling and reclamation of [hazardous] wastes" appear to settle the question. EPA did not, however, go as far as conceivably possible in regulating these wastes, believing that its authority is limited to practices that are not vey similar to normal production processes and those as to which the perceived harm is only potential.[28]

[b]   Criteria for Identifying Regulated Wastes

EPA's regulations refine the general definition of "hazardous waste" in two ways. The Agency developed a number of lists of wastes the Agency deems hazardous, which are codified at 40 CFR §261, Part D. EPA views these wastes as "criteria" or "characteristic" wastes that are subject to RCRA by virtue of listing, as exhibiting one or more of the specific waste characteristics EPA applies in implementing Section 1004(5),[29] or that otherwise fall under the statutory definition of hazardous waste. (Appendix 5-B, *infra*, contains EPA's hazardous waste lists.) Wastes that are not listed are also considered subject to RCRA if they exhibit the characteristics of listed waste.[30]

Wastes are listed (or delisted[31]) on the basis of specific statutory listing requirements[32] or pursuant to EPA's published listing criteria, 40 CFR §261.11. A waste must be listed if it meets any of the following criteria:

---

standard was that it applied to all materials of a given type, say, spent mateials, and thus charged generators with knowledge of what other generators do with the same material.

[27] *See* H.R. Rep. No. 98-198, 98th Cong., 1st Sess. at 46.

[28] *See* 50 Fed. Reg. at 616 and 637-639.

[29] 40 CFR Part 261 Appendix II.

[30] The criteria are set forth in detail at 40 CFR §§261.20-24.

[31] EPA allows individual requests, by petition, for delisting specific wastes. *See* 40 CFR §§260.20, 260.22. Congress overruled a fundamental premise of EPA's initial delisting regulation in 1984. EPA had permitted delisting on the basis of only the original listing factors. Section 3001(f)(1984) requires EPA to consider other factors that might cut against delisting, and requires EPA to delist by rulemaking rather than by private proceedings.

[32] Section 3001(e), added in 1984, requires EPA to specifically consider listing chlorinated dioxins and a number of other compounds by the end of 1985. EPA acted on dioxins on January 14, 1985. 50 Fed. Reg. 1978.

(1)   It is ignitable, that is, its flash point is below 140 degrees F.

(2)   It is corrosive, that is, it has a pH less than or equal to 2.0, or greater than or equal to 12.5.

(3)   It is reactive.

(4)   It is chemically unstable and can change violently without detonation, will detonate if heated, reacts violently with water, or produces toxic emissions when mixed with water or when exposed to noncorrosive-pH substances.

(5)   It exhibits "EP toxicity" that is, when tested according to EPA's "extraction procedure" or equivalent, the extract contains one or more of fourteen indicator toxins listed in 40 CFR §261.24, Table 1 at concentration at or above those set forth in the table.[33] The indicator chemicals are all heavy metals and chlorinated pesticides. EPA developed the EP test to simulate the physical processes that would occur in an actual landfill.[34] The test employs an acetic acid leaching medium with a pH of 5.0 (under the assumption that acid compounds will normally be prevalent in landfills). The solid component of the waste is mixed with the medium for twenty-four hours, and then a dilution factor of 100 is applied to the resultant constituents of the test extract in order to approximate natural dilution between leachate formation and human ingestion.[35]

(6)   It has been found to be fatal to humans in low doses or has an LD-50 or LC-50 (lowest dose or concentration at which half of the tested laboratory animals exhibit effects) below levels set forth in 40 CFR §261.11 (is "Acutely Hazardous Waste").

(7)   It contains any of the toxic constituents listed in Appendix VIII to Part 261, unless EPA concludes that the material does not pose a hazard threat, on the basis of a chemical fate, environmental fate, and health effects analysis. Appendix VIII lists substances that "have been shown in scientific studies" to have a

---

[33] Section 3001(g)(1984) requires EPA to reconsider its extraction procedure by the end of 1986.

[34] 45 Fed. Reg. 33111.

[35] The acidic medium, the use of a dilution factor, and the extraction period have all been criticized by environmental groups as underpredictive. *See, e.g.,* Hearings, Report of the Subcommittee on Resource Protection of the Committee on Environmental and Public Works, United States Senate, Serial No. 96-H6, at 152-153 and 180 *et seq.* EPA had originally proposed a dilution factor of 10. *See* 45 Fed. Reg. 33111. The requirement of Section 3001(g)(1984) that EPA reconsider the test is a product of these criticisms.

"toxic, carcinogenic, mutagenic or teratogenic" effect on "humans or other life forms" (these are called Toxic Wastes).[36]

(8) It is a waste that EPA has listed generically by industrial classification.[37]

Although Section 1004(5) specifically identifies "infectious" waste as subject to RCRA regulation, EPA has neither formally defined that term nor included such wastes in the federal RCRA program. While the Agency initially proposed to regulate infectious wastes, its final Part 261 regulations dropped the classification.[38] In 1982 the Agency made available to the states and the public a draft manual providing informal advice for regulating infectious wastes,[39] and a number of state hazardous waste management programs include infectious wastes within their jurisdiction.[40]

[c] Mixtures

EPA's mixture rule embraces mixtures of hazardous and nonhazardous waste. A mixture of a "solid waste" and a "hazardous waste" is itself a "hazardous waste" if the hazardous component is listed solely because it exhibits one of the subpart C characteristics,[41] unless the resulting mixture "no longer exhibits any characteristic of hazardous waste identified in subpart C." A mixture of solid waste and one or more hazardous wastes listed for reasons other than exhibiting the subpart C characteristics, for example, acutely hazardous, is considered a hazardous waste.[42] Such mixtures are regulated as hazardous wastes even if the mixture is not hazardous.

Noncriteria mixtures that are deemed hazardous by the mixture rule

---

[36] 40 CFR §261.11(a)(3).

[37] Section 3004(h)(1984) and §222(b) of P.L. 98-616 require EPA to promulgate additional listing criteria by the end of 1986, including "measures and indicators of toxicity," and to cooperate with the Centers for Disease Control to develop criteria for identifying and listing carcinogens, mutagens, and teratogens.

[38] 45 Fed. Reg. 33119 (5-19-80).

[39] Draft Manual for Infectious Waste Managment (U.S. Gov. Printing Office Stock No. 055-000-00273-1).

[40] EPA has apparently decided to explore regulating recombinant DNA products under the Toxic Substances Control Act, although the waste products of such activity may fit one or more of the RCRA criteria for hazardous waste.

[41] 40 CFR §361.3(a)(2)(iii) (criteria mixtures—ignitability corrosivity, reactivity, EP toxicity).

[42] 40 CFR §261.3(a)(2)(iv) (noncriteria mixtures).

or that are not themselves hazardous under Section 261.3(a)(2)(i) or (ii) are not regulated if they are wastewater subject to regulation under Section 402 or 307(b) of the Clean Water Act[43] and fit the specific categories of wastewater set out in Section 261.3(a)(iv)(A)-(E).[44]

[d] Excluded Wastes

Certain wastes, though clearly "hazardous," are excluded from most regulation under RCRA.[45]

[i] Sewage and Industrial Discharges to Water Bodies

Section 1004(27) of RCRA excludes from the definition of solid waste "solid or dissolved material in domestic sewage" and "industrial discharges which are point sources subject to permits under Section 402 of the Federal Water Pollution Control Act . . . " (FWPCA).

EPA has refined and arguably expanded this exclusion somewhat in 40 CFR §261.4. "Domestic sewage" is defined by EPA to mean "untreated sanitary wastes that pass through a sewer system."[46] The difference between "sanitary sewage" and "industrial waste" is well established in the water pollution control field, and presents no interpretative difficulty. EPA's rule, however, excludes "any mixture of and other wastes that passes through a sewer system to a publicly owned treatment works for treatment."[47]

EPA's "mixture" exemption is at the same time broader and narrower than the statutory exclusion. It is broader because the term "mixture" is broader than the statutory term, "solid or dissolved materials." EPA's rule exempts from RCRA liquid waste that is dumped into a sewer system and mixes with the sewage in it, while such waste is neither "solid" nor "dissolved." EPA's exemption is narrower in that it limits the exclusion to mixtures passing through a sewer system "to a

---

[43] *See* Chapter 7, *infra.*

[44] The categories, generally are the following: (A) carbon tetrachloride, tetrachloroethylene, and trichloroethylene wastewaters meeting certain concentration limits (Section 261.3); (B) methylene chloride and several other similar solvent wastewaters meeting certain concentrations (Section 261.31); (C) heat exchanger bundle cleaning sludge from petroleum refining (Section 261.32); and (D) laboratory discharges containing toxic wastes, subject to certain concentration limits (*id.*)

[45] Excluded wastes may nevertheless be subject to regulation under Subtitle D of RCRA if land disposed.

[46] 40 CFR §261.4(a)(1)(ii).

[47] *Id.*

publicly owned treatment works for treatment."[48] The statute contains no such modifier. EPA's language arguably limits the exclusion to wastes introduced into sewers that are intended to be treated by a publicly owned treatment works (POTW) and that the POTW is capable of treating. There is no evidence, however, in the preamble to EPA's regulation that the Agency intended the exemption to be so limited. Similarly, the language of the rule appears to make the exclusion unavailable in municipalities where the sewers are not connected to a POTW or are connected to a nonfunctioning POTW. The exclusion rule bears the earmarks of a hastily drawn provision into which the Agency put very little thought.

The exclusion for industrial point source discharges, like the sewage exclusion is intended to prevent overlapping regulation under RCRA and the Clean Water Act. The regulations again vary the statutory exclusion. Section 1004(27) excludes industrial discharges "which are point sources subject to permits under Section 402 of the" FWPCA. EPA's rule, however, excludes discharges "that are point source discharges subject to regulation under Section 402."[49] The language difference is not intended to be significant, and both statute and regulation exempt from RCRA the discharge of wastewater that is subject to regulation under the Clean Water Act. EPA's regulation makes it clear, however, that on-site wastewater treatment or storage facilities and sludge produced by such facilities are subject to RCRA.[50]

From an enforcement standpoint, these exclusions are significant. Violations of RCRA are felonies. Violations of the Clean Water Act are largely misdemeanors. RCRA contains a "knowing endangerment" offense. The Clean Water Act has none.[51]

Congress addressed the sewage exclusion in the 1984 RCRA amendments, inserting a special provision, Section 3018,[52] which requires EPA to report to Congres show much hazardous waste escapes regulation via the exclusion and requires the adoption of regulations under RCRA or Section 307 of the Clean Water Act to "assure that substances identified or listed . . . which pass through a sewer system to a publicly

---

[48] EPA also construes the mixture exemption to apply to wastes at the point they enter a sewer system "that will mix it with sanitary wastes prior to storage or treatment" by a sewage treatment plant. 45 Fed. Reg. 33097 (5-19-80).

[49] 40 CFR §261.4(a)(2).

[50] 40 CFR §261.4(a)(2) Comment.

[51] *See* Section 5.09[6][c], *infra;* and *compare with* 33 USC §1319.

[52] P.L. 96-616, Section 246(a).

owned treatment works are adequately controlled to protect human health and the environment." The 1984 provision also requires the dischargers to POTWs to report to EPA under Section 3010, and makes the information-gathering provisions of Section 3007 specifically applicable to such dischargers.[53]

Section 3018 represents not only congressional skepticism about EPA's sewage mixture exclusion, but also a statement that Congress does not believe that EPA's pretreatment program under Section 307(b) of the Clean Water Act has been successful.

[ii]   Waste in Irrigation Return Flows

Section 1004(27) excludes "solid or dissolved materials in irrigation return flows" from the definition of solid waste. Interestingly, irrigation return flows are also not regulated by the Clean Water Act.[54] While EPA could have attempted to refine this exclusion by rule to limit it to the normal components of such flows, it did not do so.[55]

[iii]   Radioactive Wastes

Also excluded from the definition of solid waste is "source, special nuclear, or byproduct material," which is regulated by the Nuclear Regulatory Commission (NRC) under the Atomic Energy Act.[56] This exclusion follows Congress's practice of leaving regulation of radioactive substances to the NRC.[57]

The scope of the NRC exclusion is made difficult by virtue of the fact that the NRC exercises pervasive licensing control over entities that utilize source, by-product, and special nuclear material. It has sometimes been asserted that any regulation of such entities by regulatory agencies other than the NRC is inconsistent with the Atomic Energy Act. Since radioactive wastes at NRC-regulated facilities are often commingled with nonradioactive chemical wastes, a question arises as to EPA's ability to impose requirements on the commingled waste. EPA's requirements for disposing of the nonradioactive components may in some instances be inconsistent with NRC requirements for the radioactive components, or vice versa. EPA has adopted a case-by-case analyti-

---

[53] Section 3018 also requires EPA to undertake a study of wastewater lagoons to determine their impact on groundwater quality.

[54] Section 502(14), 33 USC §1352(14).

[55] *See* 40 CFR §261.4(a)(3).

[56] *See* 10 CFR Parts 30-35, 40, and 70.

[57] *See* Train v. Colorado PIRG, 426 U.S. 1 (1976).

cal approach to determining where its regulation of such mixed wastes is inconsistent with the Atomic Energy Act.[58]

[iv] Mining and Mineral Processing Wastes

Section 1004(27) specifically includes waste from "mining" within the definition of solid waste. However, Sections 1006(c) and 3005(f) of RCRA, added as a part of the 1980 amendments,[59] require EPA to defer to the Interior Department with respect to "coal mining wastes or overburden" where such wastes are regulated by Interior under the Surface Mining Control and Reclamation Act of 1977.[60]

Regulation of mining wastes other than coal mining wastes is specifically precluded by Section 3001(b)(3)(A)(ii) until EPA has completed a study of the impacts of regulation of mining wastes, overburden, and at least some processing wastes under Sections 8002(f) and (p), which require EPA to study the environmental and health effects of surface and underground mine wastes and solid wastes "from the extraction, beneficiation, and processing of ores and minerals including phosphate rock and overburden from uranium mining." These studies are supposed to encompass as well an analysis of regulatory alternatives and the impacts of regulation.

On the basis of this deferral of regulation, EPA has exempted the following materials from regulation under RCRA:

— materials subjected to in-site mining techniques that are not removed from the ground as part of the extraction process;[61]
— mining overburden returned to the mine site;[62] and
— "solid waste from the extraction, beneficiation and processing of ores and minerals (including coal), including phosphate rock and overburden from the mining of uranium ore."[63]

Toxic and acid wastes are currently regulated by the Interior Department's Office of Surface Mining (OSM) under the Surface Mining Con-

---

[58] *See* BNA Environmental Reporter, Current Developments 8-19-83, at 657-58.

[59] P.L. 96-482. Section 3005(f) exempts facilities regulated by the Department of the Interior from RCRA subtitle C permit requirements.

[60] 30 USC §§1201 *et seq.*

[61] 40 CFR §261.4(a)(5). These are not "solid waste."

[62] 40 CFR §261.4(b)(3). These are not "hazardous waste."

[63] 40 CFR §261.4(b)(7). These are not "hazardous waste."

trol and Reclamation Act,[64] although the OSM regulations are not as detailed or as stringent as EPA's subtitle C land disposal regulations.

[v] Other Excluded Wastes

[A] **Wastes Under Study.** Section 8002 of RCRA requires EPA to study a number of additional types of solid waste. As in the case of mining wastes, EPA's approach has been to exclude these wastes from current regulation under RCRA by defining them as nonhazardous. Section 8002 study wastes thus exempted from regulation are—

(1) waste products of coal and other fossil fuel combustion, including fly ash waste, bottom ash waste, and flue gas emission control waste;[65]

(2) drilling fluids, produced waters, and other wastes associated with the exploration, development, or production of crude oil, natural gas or geothermal energy;[66] and

(3) cement kiln dust waste.[67]

Sections 3001(b)(2) and (b)(3) support EPA's deferral of regulation, although it would seem more straightforward for EPA to have simply said it could not regulate these wastes until it had completed its study, rather than excluding them from the "hazardous" category.

Section 3004(x)[68] provides that if and when EPA gets around to regulating these materials, it should consider special performance criteria that recognize the "practical difficulties" and "special characteristics" related to the wastes and the waste disposal sites. This provision is generally read to encourage EPA to impose less stringent disposal requirements on them.

[B] **Sludges.** Sludges are a by-product of wastewater treatment and some industrial processes. Wastewater treatment sludge consists of settled-out solid matter with which chemicals also contained in the wastewater are often mixed or bound. Industrial sludges are typically either fully or partially dewatered production residues or reaction products that may contain high concentrations of chemical substances.

Section 1004(27) of RCRA defines sludge to include within the stat-

---

64 *See* 30 CFR §§715.17(g) and (h) and 717.17(g) and (h).

65 Section 8002(m); 40 CFR §261.4(b)(5).

66 Section 8002(o); 40 CFR §261.4(b)(8).

67 Section 8002(n); 40 CFR §261.4(b)(4).

68 P.L. 98-615, Section 209.

ute's grasp sludge from "a municipal, commercial or industrial wastewater treatment plants, water supply treatment plant or air pollution control facility, or any other such waste having similar characteristics and effects."

EPA's regulatory definition of sludge, however, deletes the "any other such waste . . . " language contained in the statute.[69] Thus, process sludges are treated by EPA as ordinary hazardous wastes if they meet the listing criteria.[70]

Section 1006(b) requires EPA to "integrate" the RCRA program with other statutes under which sludge is regulated "to the extent that it can be done in a manner consistent with" the goals and policies of RCRA and the other acts.

Wastewater treatment plant sludge is also subject to regulation under the Clean Water Act. Section 405 of the Clean Water Act authorizes EPA to regulate the land disposal of sludge in areas where runoff might reach surface waters.[71] Discharge of sludge to surface waters via a point source requires a National Pollutant Discharge Elimination Program (NPDEP) permit under Section 402 of the Clean Water Act.[72] Dumping sludge in the ocean is regulated by the Marine Protection, Research and Sanctuaries Act (MPRSA)[73] and to some extent by the London Dumping Convention. Sludge incinerators are subject to regulation under the Clean Air Act.[74] Arguably, some sludge-related products may also be regulated under the Toxic Substances Control Act (TSCA) or the Consumer Product Safety Act.

EPA excluded from RCRA regulation most sludges produced by wastewater treatment.[75] Also excluded are industrial sludges that do not fail the EP toxicity test, sludges from the leather tanning industry,[76] titanium oxide pigment sludges containing trivalent chromium,[77] and certain recycled sludges.[78]

---

[69] 40 CFR §260.10.

[70] 40 CFR §261.2 (Table 1). *See* 50 Fed. Reg. 661 (1-4-85). *See also* 40 CFR §261.3(a); and 45 Fed. Reg. 33101-33102 (1979).

[71] 33 USC §1325(a).

[72] 33 USC §1325(b).

[73] 33 USC §§1401-1444.

[74] 42 USC §§7401 *et seq.*

[75] 40 CFR §261.4(b)(6).

[76] 40 CFR §§261.4(b)(6)(i)(A)-(G).

[77] 40 CFR §261.4(b)(6)(i)(H).

[78] *See generally* 40 CFR Part 266.

One type of sludge, lime stabilized waste pickle liquor sludge generated from the iron and steel industry, is partially excluded. Rather than add this sludge to the Section 261.4 list, EPA chose to generically delist the sludge from the presumptively hazardous list, while leaving open the possibility of regulating specific sludges of this type that happen to exhibit any of the characteristics of hazardous waste.[79]

Section 8001(g) requires EPA to study such questions as what should be included within the definition of sludge, what its health and environmental effects are, and what alternative disposal options are available.

[C] **Household Wastes.** Although Sections 1004(5) and (27) arguably encompass domestic-type wastes, EPA broadly excluded household, hotel, and motel waste and household septic tank pumpings from subtitle C (hazardous waste) regulation.[80] EPA based this exclusion on language in the Senate Report on the 1976 Act evidencing an intention not to regulate the disposal "of substances used in households or to extend control over general municipal wastes based on the presence of such substances."[81]

EPA's exclusion of such wastes, which can admittedly be hazardous, rests on a slender reed in the absence of language in RCRA implementing the Senate's alleged intention. However, Congress's failure to overturn the exclusion in the 1980 amendments to RCRA and in subsequent reauthorizations indicates sufficient acquiescence to legitimize the exclusion.

Congress "clarified" the household waste exclusion in 1984. It added a new section, 3001(j), which essentially provides that resource recovery (that is, "garbage to energy") facilities will not be deemed Treatment; Storage, and Disposal (TSD) facilities if they accept only "household waste" (defined as waste from residences and motels and the like) or nonhazardous waste from commercial and industrial sources and have "established contractual requirements or other appropriate notification or inspection procedures to assure that hazardous wastes are not received or burned at such facilities." EPA amended Section 261.4 of its regulations in 1985, implementing these prohibitions.

Mixtures of household waste and hazardous waste are deemed hazardous wastes,[82] although mixtures of household waste and hazardous

---

[79] 45 Fed. Reg. 33102 (1979); 49 Fed. Reg. 23284 (1984); 40 CFR §261.3(c)(2)(ii).
[80] 40 CFR §261.4(b)(1).
[81] S. Rep. No. 94-988, 94th Cong., 2d Sess. at 16.
[82] *See* 40 CFR §261.3(a)(2)(ii).

wastes produced by small-quantity generators are not regulated as hazardous wastes,[83] unless the hazardous wastes are acutely hazardous and are of the amounts and compositions set forth in 40 CFR §261.5(e).[84]

[D] Agricultural Wastes. Wastes generated by crop or animal agricultural operations "which are returned to the soils as fertilizers" are excluded from subtitle C by EPA.[85] The Agency bases this exclusion not on the language of RCRA or on a factual determination that such wastes are not hazardous, but instead on passages of RCRA's legislative history[86] in the House.[87] The exclusion apparently permits the stockpiling of large amounts of waste material, some of which may be heavily contaminated with pesticides, prior to field spreading.

Farmers are also subject to only minimal RCRA interference in their disposal of waste pesticides. Farmers are exempt from subtitle C regulation in relation to such activities,[88] and are required only to triple-rinse pesticide containers prior to disposal and to dispose of pesticide residues on their own land[89] in accordance with the directions set forth on the pesticide package label.[90]

[E] Miscellaneous. Samples of waste collected for testing purposes are exempt from subtitle C regulation, subject to a number of specific constraints spelled out in 40 CFR §261.4(d). Wastes generated in a product or raw material storage tank, transport vehicle or vessel, pipeline, or manufacturing unit are also exluded, until the waste exits the unit or after ninety days following cessation of its use.[91] Surface impoundment units are not excluded.[92]

Reclaimed and reused black pickle liquor in the Kraft pulp industry is excluded unless accumulated speculatively, and spent sulfuric acid

---

[83] 45 Fed. Reg. 33099.

[84] Basically, these are the acutely hazardous wastes listed in 40 CFR §261.33(e). *See* Appendix 5-B, *infra.*

[85] 40 CFR §261.4(b)(2).

[86] 45 Fed. Reg. 33099.

[87] *See* H.R. Rep. No. 94-1491, 94th Cong., 2d. Sess. at 2 (1976).

[88] 40 CFR §§264.1(g)(4), 265.1(c)(8), 270.1(c)(2)(ii).

[89] 40 CFR §262.51.

[90] Label instructions are specified by EPA under FIFRA, and by some state pesticide regulatory entities under state law.

[91] 40 CFR §261.4(c).

[92] *Id.*

used to make new acid is also excluded unless accumulated speculatively.[93]

There are, finally, variance procedures for case-by-case exclusion of wastes burned in boilers and certain recycling wastes.[94]

[e] Other Unregulated or Minimally Regulated Wastes

[i] Wastes Produced by Small-Quantity Generators

Except for acutely hazardous waste and accumulated hazardous waste, the hazardous wastes generated by "small-quantity generators" are not included in the subtitle C regulatory program,[95] although EPA requires the generators of such wastes to meet certain minimal handling and disposal criteria.[96] Small-quantity generators are defined as those generating no more than 1000 kg./mo. (legislatively reduced to 100 kg./mo. as of not later than March 31, 1986, by Section 3001(d)(1984)) of hazardous waste.

The small-quantity generator exemption is based on EPA's concern that if it were required to regulate the waste produced by an estimated 695,000 generators of less than 1000 kg./mo. of hazardous waste, the regulatory burden "would far outstrip the limited Agency resources necessary to achieve effective implementation."[97]

The extent to which an agency may carve out an exemption from regulation based upon administrative practicability has been the subject of litigation from time to time.[98] In general, categorical exemptions from clear statutory commands are not favored.[99] However, impossibility and lack of resources have been held a sufficient basis for limiting the scope of regulation, particularly where the legislative command is broad and general.[100]

The quantity of such waste generated nationally is not insig-

---

[93] 40 CFR §§261.4(a)(6) and 261.4(a)(7).

[94] 40 CFR §§260.31-260.41.

[95] 40 CFR §261.5.

[96] 40 CFR §261.5(g).

[97] 45 Fed. Reg. 33103 (5-19-80).

[98] *See, e.g.,* FPC v. Texaco, Inc., 417 U.S. 380 (1974); Permian Basin Area Rate Cases, 390 U.S. 747 (1968); Morton v. Ruiz, 415 U.S. 199 (1973); E.I. DuPont de Nemours & Co. v. Train, 430 U.S. 112 (1977); and Alabama Power Co., et al. v. Costle, 606 F.2d 1068 (D.C. Cir. 1979) (Leventhal opinion).

[99] FPC v. Texaco, Inc., 417 U.S. 380, 400 (1974).

[100] Morton v. Ruiz, 415 U.S. 199, 230-31. *Cf.* NRDC v. Train, 510 F.2d 692, 712 (D.C. Cir. 1974).

nificant.[101] In addition to mandating reduction of the threshold to 100 kg./mo. by 1986, Congress, in the 1984 amendments, required EPA to subject generators of 100-1000 kg./mo. of hazardous waste to compliance with the manifest system by August 1985[102] and required that they dispose of the waste only in a licensed TSD facility or at a state-regulated solid waste disposal facility.[103]

The small-quantity generator exemption involves two distinct steps: (1) determining whether the facility fits the exemption, and (2) complying with the applicable criteria. In determining the amount of waste generated in a calendar month, a facility excludes wastes that are recycled and excluded from regulation,[104] and does not count waste produced by on-site hazardous waste treatment or waste removal from the site following storage.[105]

While the general exemption is for 1000 kg./mo. of hazardous waste, only 1 kg./mo. of acutely hazardous wastes, or 100 kg./mo. of residue, soil water, or debris contaminated with acutely hazardous waste is exempt from regulation.[106]

Small-quantity generator waste may not be accumulated in amounts greater than the monthly limits for small-quantity generator status.[107]

Small-quantity generators must test their waste, or otherwise deter-

---

[101] EPA estimated in 1980 that 1 percent, or about 600,000 tons, of hazardous waste per year comes out of 100 kg./mo. or less generators.

[102] Only basic information is required to be provided, however. *See* Section 3001(d)(3)(1984).

[103] EPA is permitted to vary the stringency of regulation in its 1986 regulations from that required of large-quantity generators. Small-quantity generators are allowed to accumulate waste on site for 180 days, rather than 90 as for others. EPA must require disposal after 1986 at a permitted or interim status facility. If EPA fails to issue regulations within the statutory time period, small-quantity generators are, as a matter of law, treated largely like others. Sections 3001(d)(3)-(9). EPA's initial SQG regulations, amending Section 261.5, were published at 50 Fed. Reg. 28743 (7-15-85).

[104] *See* 40 CFR §261.5(c) (excluding from computation specified recycled materials).

[105] 40 CFR §§261.5(c) and (d).

[106] 40 CFR §261.5(e). If more than the qualifying monthly amount is generated, all such wastes are regulated under subtitle C. Note that the monthly limits apply to the hazardous component of the waste only. If the hazardous wastes are mixed with nonhazardous materials, the overall bulk does not affect applicability of the exemption. *See* 40 CFR §§216.5(h) and (i).

[107] 40 CFR §261.4(f). If a generator accumulates on his site more than the monthly qualifying amount of waste (100 kg. hazardous waste, 1 kg. acutely hazardous waste, 100 kg. material contaminated by acutely hazardous waste), the amounts in excess of the minimum permitted accumulation are regulated under subtitle C. This prohibition was modified, effective June 20, 1985, to permit accumulation indefinitely in satellite areas of the generator site up to 5 gallons (that is, 1 barrel) of hazardous waste or 1 quart of acutely hazardous waste. *See* 49 Fed. Reg. 49568.

mine whether it is a regulated waste, to the same extent as required for other generators.[108] They are required to dispose of the waste on-site, at an EPA-authorized state or federally permitted TSD facility (or one holding interim status), or at a state-licensed municipal or industrial solid waste facility.[109]

The primary benefit of small-quantity generator status to the generator is exemption from the manifest system established under Section 3002 of RCRA. This benefit may be somewhat illusory, however, since in a comment to its later-issued permanent TSD standards, EPA suggests that TSD facilities require a "certificate" from small-quantity generators certifying their compliance with the small-quantity generator rule.

By mandating a rollback of the exemption to 100 kg., and requiring generators over the threshold to comply with the manifest system, Congress has swept vastly increased numbers of generators within the regulatory loop.[110]

[ii]   Used, Reused, Recycled, or Reclaimed Materials

It was initially argued by recyclers and others that wastes destined for recycling, reuse, or reclamation were not "discarded," and therefore did not fall within the RCRA definition of solid waste. These entities also argued that regulation of such activity under RCRA would have a chilling effect on the relatively young recycling industry. Those arguments were rejected by the D.C. Circuit in *United States Brewers' Association, Inc. v. EPA*,[111] in which guidelines issued under Section 1008(a)(1) for recycling beverage containers were challenged.

EPA's regulatory definition of solid waste in the subtitle C regulations clearly encompasses such materials, and industry proponents continued to press the *Brewers' Association* arguments in post-promulgation challenges to the May 19, 1980, regulations, which were mooted by the 1984 amendments to RCRA.

EPA's approach to such materials is to regulate them unless they are of a group that EPA has decided to exempt.[112]

Under 40 CFR §261.6, recycled hazardous wastes are required to be

---

108 40 CFR §261.5(g)(1).

109 40 CFR §261.5(g)(3).

110 Congress also suggested in Section 3001(d) that EPA consider eliminating the exemption entirely.

111 600 F.2d 974 (D.C. Cir. 1979).

112 50 Fed. Reg. 614 (1-4-85).

regulated under the provisions regulating generators, transporters, and TSD facilities, unless they fall within one of the categories of wastes specifically designated as not requiring regulation.[113] Exempt materials include reclaimed ethyl alcohol, used batteries held for regeneration, used oil that exhibits hazardous waste characteristics, and scrap metal.[114]

The primary vehicle for regulating recycled waste is Part 266, the relevant provisions of which were added early in 1985.[115] Part 266 governs recyclable materials used in a manner constituting disposal,[116] hazardous waste burned for energy recovery,[117] recyclable materials used for precious metal recovery,[118] and spent lead-acid batteries being reclaimed.[119]

EPA's initial approach had been not to regulate recycling at all, unless it was not "legitimate" and "beneficial." The primary focus of criticism of that approach had been the practice, enabled by the regulation, of blending combustible hazardous wastes with fuel oil for "energy recovery." EPA had chosen to address the issue on a case-by-case enforcement basis, and administratively deemed water with a BTU content of less than 5000-8000 to have insufficient energy content to be "legitimately" reused or recycled when blended with fuel oil.[120]

[iii] Polychlorinated Biphenyls (PCBs)

PCBs are regulated exclusively under TSCA and are accordingly outside RCRA's jurisdiction. EPA'S PCB disposal and storage regulations under TSCA must be consulted for guidance.[121]

---

[113] 40 CFR §§261.6(a)(1) and 261.6(a)(2).

[114] 40 CFR §261.6(a)(3). The used-oil exemption is short lived. Section 241 of P.L. 98-616 rewrote Section 3014, mandating a regulatory program for used oil. EPA began regulating the burning of used oil in 1985.

[115] 50 Fed. Reg. 666 (1-4-85).

[116] Subpart C.

[117] Subpart D. It does not include used oil. That is regulated under subpart E, reserved by EPA at the time of writing.

[118] Subpart F.

[119] Subpart G.

[120] RCRA Enforcement Guidance: Burning Low Energy Hazardous Wastes Ostensibly for Energy Recovery Purposes, 48 Fed. Reg. 11157 (1983). Most chlorinated solvents failed EPA's threshold energy test.

[121] See Chapter 2, supra.

[iv]   **Residues in Empty Containers**

Containers that once contained material that would be an identified or listed waste will nevertheless not be treated as hazardous waste if the generator has followed the cleaning criteria set forth in 40 CFR §261.7. Lined containers are also "empty" if the liner prevented contact between the product and the container and has been removed.[122]

The empty container exemption is intended primarily to benefit industrial facilities and other entities that either consume products whose residues become hazardous wastes when left in their containers or transfer wastes from small containers into large ones. Its primary benefit to such entities is that it prevents them from becoming TSD facilities under the ninety-day rule if they do not remove their empty containers within that time period.

Although EPA has resisted utilizing a "degree of hazard" approach to excluding wastes from regulation generally,[123] its different treatment of technical grade wastes and other hazardous wastes in Section 261.7 reflects at least limited use of a degree of hazard approach.

[f]   **Exclusion by Petition ("Delisting")**

One may petition EPA to exclude a waste "at a particular generating facility."[124] Under EPA's 1980 regulations, the applicant had to demonstrate that the waste produced by the facility does not meet "any of the criteria" under which it was listed (and, if it is listed as an acutely toxic waste, that it does not meet the Section 261.11(a)(3) criterion).[125]

Similarly, a waste that is regulated under the mixture rule could also be delisted upon petition. The applicant must make the requisite showing with respect to the constituents.[126]

Even though delisted, a waste may still be considered hazardous if it exhibits one of the hazardous criteria set forth in Sections 261.20-261.24. Criteria hazardous wastes may be delisted if the applicant dem-

---

122 40 CFR §261.7(a)(1).

123 *See, e.g.,* 45 Fed. Reg. 33103-33104 (1980).

124 40 CFR §260.22(a). In addition, anyone may petition EPA under Section 260.20 to amend Parts 260 through 265.

125 40 CFR §260.22.

126 40 CFR §260.22(b).

onstrates that the waste does not exhibit the relevant characteristics.[127]

Applicants must follow the procedures set forth in 40 CFR §260.22(i). Such exclusions apply only to the specific facility that is the subject of the petition.[128] EPA may grant a temporary exclusion prior to completing review of the evidence in reasonably straightforward cases.[129]

It had been argued that many wastes may in fact possess hazardous characteristics other than those upon which EPA based its listing. For example, a waste listed because it is ignitable may also possess some other hazardous characteristic, such as acute toxicity, which was not considered at the time the waste was listed.

In 1984, Congress mandated EPA to amend the delisting regulations to require consideration of factors other than those that formed the basis of the listing if such factors "could cause the waste to be hazardous" and to provide opportunity for notice and comment on the additional factors before acting on a delisting petition.[130]

Congress also imposed notice and comment procedures on temporary delistings granted by EPA prior to November 8, 1984, and provided that the temporary delisting would expire on November 8, 1986, unless EPA had taken final action.[131]

Although delisting is a facility-specific action, EPA does not permit delisting applicants to base their case on site-specific hydrogeologic characteristics or site-specific management and disposal operations. Instead, applicants must employ "reasonable worst case" scenarios in environmental fate modeling.[132]

[g] **Addition by Petition**

States and individuals may petition EPA to add wastes to the Part 261 lists.[133]

---

[127] 40 CFR §§260.22(c)-(g).

[128] 40 CFR §260.22(k).

[129] 40 CFR §260.22(m).

[130] Section 3001(f)(1984). EPA's implementing amendment to 40 CFR §260.22 was published on July 15, 1985. 50 Fed. Reg. 28742.

[131] Id.

[132] See, e.g., 49 Fed. Reg. 88962fn 1, 88966 (1984); and Union Carbide Corporation Petition for Exclusion, 49 Fed. Reg. 8964.

[133] State requests are authorized by Section 3001(c) of RCRA. Citizen petitions are authorized by 40 CFR §260.20.

§5.03 Regulation of Generators of Hazardous Waste

[1] Regulated Generators

A generator is "any person, by site, whose act or process produces hazardous waste identified or listed in Part 261 [of 40 CFR] or whose act first causes a hazardous waste to become subject to regulation."[134] Section 3002 of RCRA requires EPA to regulate generators' record-keeping and labeling practices, specify the nature of containers used for hazardous waste containment, require generators to inform transporters and TSD facilities of the nature of the waste they receive, and require the submission of reports to EPA and the states as to the quantities of hazardous waste generated and how it is disposed of. The most important requirement, however, is that generators employ the manifest system and "any other reasonable means necessary"[135] to ensure that the waste they generate arrives at a permitted TSD facility. The manifest system is the means by which hazardous waste is tracked from the "cradle to the grave," and is intended to provide a paper trail of all regulated hazardous waste.

EPA's generator requirements are published in 40 CFR Part 262, and those requirements generally apply to all generators except small-quantity generators,[136] generators who do not ship their waste off site,[137] and farmers who generate pesticide wastes.[138]

---

134 40 CFR §260.10. *See* 45 Fed. Reg. 72028 (1981). The definition is EPA's, there being no statutory definition of the term. Importers are considered generators. 40 CFR §262.10(c).

135 A TSD owner or operator becomes a generator if he initiates a shipment of hazardous waste out of his facility. 40 CFR §262.10(e). Each site is a separate generator, even if owned by the same entity that owns other sites.

136 *See* Section 5.02, *supra*. Most small-quantity generators exempt from EPA's initial manifest regulations were required to comply, although not fully, with the manifest system by section 3001(d)(1984). In accordance with a requirement of the Solid and Hazardous Waste Amendments of 1984, EPA proposed on August 1, 1985, a set of regulatory requirements affecting generators of between 100 kilograms per month and 1000 kilograms per month. *See* 50 Fed. Reg. 31278.

137 Such generators are treated as TSD facilities and must comply with Parts 264, 265, 266, and 270 of EPA's regulations. They are also required to comply with certain of the identification and recordkeeping provisions of Part 262 (Sections 262.11, 262.12, 262.34, 262.40(c) and (d), 262.43, 262.51).

138 Farmers are required only to triple-rinse pesticide containers or otherwise follow the instructions on the packaging label. 40 CFR §262.51.

[2] Identification of Waste

Generators are responsible for determining whether the waste they generate is a hazardous waste—either listed in Part 261 or, if not listed, meeting the criteria of Part C (by testing or other means)—or is excluded under Section 261.4.[139] A generator may, of course, seek delisting of his waste if he believes it meets the delisting criteria of §260.22.

[3] Generator Identification Number

Every generator, that is, every site where hazardous waste is generated must have an EPA identification number.[140] Offering waste for transportation, treatment, storage, or disposal prior to acquiring an identification is a violation of RCRA.[141]

[4] Manifest Requirements

A manifest is the shipping document[142] that must be prepared by all generators for waste leaving the site, according to EPA's uniform manifest system,[143] which was developed jointly by EPA and the U.S. Department of Transportation (DOT), which regulates transporters under the Hazardous Materials Transportation Act (HMTA).[144]

EPA first established manifest rules in 1980,[145] but did not at that time attempt to impose uniform manifest requirements. EPA hoped that its manifest would in most circumstances be able to serve as the

---

[139] 40 CFR §262.11. Generators are also required to analyze representative batches of waste destined for off-site disposal, treatment, or storage.

[140] 40 CFR §262.12. Some states require their own identification numbers, although most accept the EPA number.

[141] EPA's regional offices have authority to issue provisional (temporary) identification numbers over the telephone in emergency or in unusual circumstances. A completed Form 8700-12 (*see* Appendix 5-C, *infra*) must be sent to EPA within ten days of receipt of a provisional identification number. 45 Fed. Reg. 85022.

[142] EPA Forms 8700-22 and 8700-22A. *See* Appendix 5-D, *infra*. The manifest rules for generators are 40 CFR §§262.22-23 and 262.50(b)(3), (b)(4), (d), and (e). A 1984 amendment, effective September 1, 1985, requires the manifest to contain a certification by the generator that he has a "waste minimization program" in conformity with Section 3005 in effect, and that the TSD method being utilized is the "practicable . . . available [one which] minimizes the present and future threat to human health and the environment." Sections 3002(a)(5)(1)-(3). *See* 50 Fed. Reg. 28746 (7-15-85).

[143] *See generally* 49 Fed. Reg. 10490.

[144] 49 USC §1801 *et seq.*

[145] 45 Fed. Reg. 12722.

DOT shipping paper required by its HMTA rules.[146] By 1984, almost half of the states had developed their own manifest forms, which created a number of problems for regulated entities, the most important of which was a requirement that a transporter passing through a number of states en route to a TSD site had to possess a manifest for each state. Generators were forced to prepare a number of duplicate manifests for each shipment, and the wide range of manifests in use made law enforcement, such as searches, complex. The uniform manifest system was implemented to solve these problems and standardize the industry.

Under the uniform system, both EPA and DOT require use of the uniform manifest form. The DOT regulations are nationwide, apply to all transporters, and are totally preemptive as of September 20, 1984. EPA phased in its generator requirements to accommodate states seeking delegation of RCRA permitting authority,[147] and designed the manifest form to accommodate some state-required information.

Only under limited circumstances may states impose their own manifest information or management requirements. EPA's authority to allow or restrict such additional state requirements in authorized states (states to which RCRA permit and enforcement authority has been delegated) involves the coordination of two statutory provisions: Section 3006, which requires approved state programs to be "consistent" with the federal program, and Section 3009, which reserves to states the latitude to be more stringent. In balancing these two provisions, EPA allows a state to impose more stringent requirements, except in those cases where the Agency has determined that consistency requires that state programs conform precisely to the federal requirement.

---

[146] 49 CFR §§171.3-171.8.

[147] In unauthorized states (those to which RCRA permitting authority has not been delegated), all generators and transporters were required to employ the uniform manifest form as of September 20, 1984. Authorized states and states seeking final authorization are required to employ the uniform manifest form by revising their programs to specify it in accordance with the timetables established in 40 CFR §271.21 (generally one year after September 20, 1984). States with only interim RCRA authorization were not required by EPA rules to employ the uniform manifest unless and until final authorization was sought, but shipper generators and transporters in such states were required to employ the uniform manifest anyway by DOT's regulations until either the state sought final authorization and adopted the uniform manifest or interim authorization expired by operation of law, giving rise to EPA control of generators and transporters in the state. 49 Fed. Reg. 10492 (1984). It is not clear why the DOT regulations would not act similarly in states with final authorization or seeking final authorization as of September 20, 1984, in the intervening period until the states revised their own forms. EPA implies that they would not. 49 Fed. Reg. 10491.

Consequently, EPA's regulations do not prohibit authorized states from imposing requirements that provide more rigorous or comprehensive control of hazardous waste activities than do EPA's regulations, such as requirements that handlers of hazardous waste send copies of completed manifests to state agencies for tracking purposes. On the basis of the need for consistency, however, states with final authorization are required to use the uniform manifest form and may not require any additional information to accompany the waste shipment other than what is permitted on the uniform manifest.

EPA's regulations do not prohibit states without final authorization (either states with interim authorization or unauthorized states) from imposing more stringent manifest requirements. However, under the authority of Section 112 of HMTA,[148] DOT's regulations prohibit such states from requiring separate state manifests or other information to accompany waste shipments. Section 112 of HMTA expressly preempts any state or local requirement inconsistent with that Act or HMTA regulations,[149] and DOT's regulations deem different state manifests or additional state shipping papers to be inconsistent with its hazardous materials regulations.

The uniform manifest accommodates limited "optional" state-required information from the generator state and the TSD state.[150] Intermediate states may not require any additional information on the form. States are prohibited from applying enforcement sanctions on the transporter during the transportation of hazardous waste for any failure of the form to show optional state information entries. States may hold transporters responsible only for ensuring that the information included in the federally required portion of the uniform manifest form accompanies the shipment. However, states could hold the generator responsible for failure to comply with the manifest information requirements.

EPA and DOT also allow states to require generators (or TSD facilities) to send other information related to the shipment under separate cover (for example, by mail), as long as this does not interfere with the actual movement of the waste. Such requirements would not be "incon-

---

[148] 49 USC §1811(a).

[149] The preemptive effect is premised on the Commerce Clause, Art. I Section 8 of the U.S. Constitution.

[150] Some states, for example, regulate more wastes than EPA regulates. Those states have to accommodate their information needs as to such wastes within the confines of the EPA-DOT form.

sistent" for purposes of HMTA, if they (a) did not conflict with federal requirements or otherwise unduly burden commerce and (b) were not so numerous that their cumulative effect was to burden commerce. Just how much of an additional burden the Constitution and HMTA will permit must, of course, be adjudicated case by case as states seek to require additional generator acts.[151]

The underlying theory of the uniform manifest is that generators and transporters should have to produce only one piece of paper for RCRA compliance.[152] EPA is apparently willing, however, to permit states to require the filing of additional copies of that piece of paper. For example, a number of states require, for enforcement purposes, out-of-state generators to file copies of the completed manifests that relate to wastes disposed of within their borders. EPA has stated that such requirements are not inconsistent with the uniform manifest system,[153] and in fact requires generators to use uniform manifest forms printed by the consignment state that contain in the "optional state information" section a recitation that a copy of the original manifest must be filed with that state, if the consignment state imposes such a requirement.[154]

Consignment (disposal) state jurisdiction over generators whose only contact with the state is disposal of waste is governed by the principles enunciated in *International Shoe Co. v. Washington*,[155] and the scope of the disposal state's long-arm statute.

---

[151] P.L. 98-616 (1984) added a sentence to Section 3009 that allows states to demand a separate copy of each manifest relating to waste either generated in the state or transported into it.

[152] At one time the Interstate Commerce Commission (ICC) required a bill of lading to accompany interstate commercial shipments of all hazardous waste. However, in 1982 the ICC ruled that "hazardous waste of no economic value destined for disposal (other than nuclear or radioactive waste) does not constitute 'property' within the meaning of 49 USC §10521. Accordingly, the Commission does not have jurisdiction over the for-hire transportation by motor carriers of such wastes." 4 FR 29403, July 6, 1982. To the extent RCRA regulates nuclear or radioactive wastes, a bill of lading will be required in addition to a manifest.

[153] 49 Fed. Reg. 10496.

[154] 40 CFR §262.21. Generators must use such forms if they are available. If not, generators must use manifest forms supplied by the generator's state. If that state does not print such forms, the generator can acquire the form anywhere. Imports and exports are similarly treated.

[155] 326 U.S. 310 (1945).

[5] Use of the Manifest and Special Manifest Rules for Bulk Shipments

Normally the generator is required to produce two copies of the manifest for himself, each transporter in the chain of transportation, and the TSD owner-operator;[156] the initial transporter is given all but the generator's copy.[157] However, where the shipments are to be in bulk, within the United States, and solely by water, the generator is required to send three copies of the signed manifest directly to the TSD facility to which the wastes are destined or to the last water transporter. In such event, copies are not required for intermediate transporters.[158]

Where rail shipments that originate on a rail spur at the generator's site are involved, the generator is required to send three copies of the manifest to the next nonrail transporter if there is one, to the TSD facility if the transport is solely by rail within the United States, or to the last rail transporter to handle the waste prior to export.[159]

[6] Packaging, Labeling, Marking, and Placarding

Generators are responsible for packaging their waste, labeling the packages, marking them with the required warning, and offering to provide the transporter with DOT-required placards. The substantive criteria are the DOT requirements set forth in 49 CFR Parts 172, 173, 178, and 179.

[7] Recordkeeping and Reporting

[a] Recordkeeping

Generators are the primary custodians of the paper produced by the manifest system. The TSD facility that receives the waste is required to send a copy of the completed, signed manifest to the generator, who must retain the record for three years from the date the waste was accepted by the initial transporter.[160]

In addition to copies of manifests, generator must retain the following records:

---

[156] 40 CFR §262.22.
[157] 40 CFR §262.23(b).
[158] 40 CFR §262.23(c).
[159] 40 CFR §262.23(d).
[160] 40 CFR §262.40(a) (time period extendable if an enforcement action is pending).

— test results, waste analyses, quantity measurements, and other descriptive information required to be on the manifest, for three years from the date the waste was "last sent to on-site or off-site treatment, storage, or disposal";[161] and

— copies of biennial reports and exception reports, for three years from the "due date of the report."[162]

[b] Reporting

Generators are responsible for producing three types of reports, and may from time to time be required to render special reports.[163]

Exception reports are required when a completed, signed manifest is not returned to the generator within forty-five days of the date the waste was accepted by the initial transporter.[164] A prerequisite to filing an exception report with the EPA regional office for the generator's region is an attempt by the generator to contact the TSD facility to which the waste was consigned if the manifest has not been returned within thirty-five days of the date the waste was accepted by the initial transporter.[165]

Biennial reports, which also should be filed with the regional EPA office, are required to be filed by March 1 of even-numbered years[166] on the EPA form for such reports.[167] These reports, though biennial, are required to cover the generator's activities for the previous calendar year[168] (that is the odd-numbered calendar years). The biennial report must essentially present a complete picture of the generator's hazardous waste output for the covered year.[169]

A new provision, Section 3002(a)(6), requires a report detailing the previous year's efforts to reduce waste volume and toxicity, showing comparative changes over the prior year.[170]

---

161 40 CFR §262.40(c) (same extension as above).
162 40 CFR §262.40(b) (same extension as above).
163 40 CFR §262.41.
164 40 CFR §262.42.
165 40 CFR §262.42(a).
166 40 CFR §262.41(a).
167 Id.
168 Id.
169 Id. Also see 48 Fed. Reg. 14293 (1983).
170 Section 3002(b), inserted by P.L. 98-616, Section 224 (1984). See also 40 CFR §§262.41(a)(6)-(a)(8) (1985).

Generators who treat, store, or dispose of waste on-site are also required to file TSD facility reports.[171]

[8] Exporters and Importers

Importers and exporters of hazardous waste are subject to a number of special requirements, which in some cases differ from the requirements imposed on other generators.

[a] Exporters

Exporters are subject to the same packaging, labeling, marking, and placarding requirements as are other generators, and must secure a generator identification number.[172] They must also employ the uniform manifest, but are not required to employ uniform manifest forms printed by foreign consignee governments.

Exporters were originally required to file preexport notices with EPA's Office of International Affairs, showing the hazardous waste identification number, the DOT shipping description, and the name and address of the foreign consignee.[173] A 1984 provision, Section 3017, requires either a treaty allowing export or express consent of the receiving State, and requires the exporter to notify EPA, which in turn notifies the State Department, which communicates the facts to the foreign government. Under the revised scheme, the consent must be appended to the manifest.

Exporting generators must confirm receipt of the waste by the consignee and, in executing the manifest, must identify the point of departure of the waste from the United States.[174] The exporter is required to receive confirmation of departure from the transporter within forty-five days of the date the waste was accepted by the initial transporter, and to file an exception report if such confirmation is not received. Written confirmation of receipt by the consignee must be received within ninety days from the date of receipt by the initial transporter to avoid an exception report obligation.[175]

---

[171] 40 CFR §262.41(b).

[172] 40 CFR §262.50(a).

[173] 40 CFR §262.50(b).

[174] 40 CFR §262.50(b)(3)(ii).

[175] 40 CFR §262.50(c). EPA also requires exporters to file a yearly summary of export activities. 40 CFR §262.50(d).

[b] Importers

A U.S. importer is required to execute a manifest that conforms to 40 CFR §262.21, and must sign the certification statement on the form that is normally signed by the generator.[176] The manifest must also include both the name and address of the foreign generator and the name, address, and EPA identification number of the importer.[177]

[9] Limitation on Generator Status

A generator who accumulates hazardous waste on-site for more than ninety days becomes an "operator" of a "storage facility," and thereby subject to Parts 264, 265, and/or 270, which regulate TSD facilities.[178] Each container of hazardous waste must bear on its label the date it was placed in the container and accumulation began.[179] The only basis for extension of the accumulation period is the occurrence of "unforeseen, temporary and uncontrollable circumstances," in which case the EPA regional office may grant up to a thirty-day extension.

Generators accumulating waste for less than ninety days are required to meet the following standards:[180]

(1) The waste containers must comply with 40 CFR Part 265 subparts I and J (except §265.193).

(2) The containers must bear the accumulation date and be labeled or marked "Hazardous Waste."

(3) The site operator must comply with the emergency preparedness and contingency planning requirements of 40 CFR Part 265 subparts C and D.

(4) Personnel must be trained to handle emergencies in accordance with the 40 CFR §265.16 criteria.

---

176 40 CFR §262.50(d); 40 CFR §262.10(c).

177 Id.

178 40 CFR §262.34(a). EPA added a new subsection (C) in 1985, which allows a generator to accumulate indefinitely in satellite areas of the generator's facility up to 55 gallons of hazardous waste or 1 quart of *acutely* hazardous waste. *See* 49 Fed. Reg. 49568.

179 Id.

180 40 CFR §262.34(b).

[10] Generator Liability for Improperly Disposed Waste or for Imminent Hazards

Generators are held liable, without proof of fault, for cleanup costs and natural resource damage at TSD sites at which the generator's wastes have been treated, stored, or disposed.[181]

§5.04 Regulation of Transporters of Hazardous Waste

[1] In General

Transporters of hazardous waste are subject to only minimal regulation under RCRA, primarily because they are regulated extensively by the U.S. Department of Transportation under the Hazardous Materials Transportation Act.[182]

Section 3003 of RCRA requires EPA only to regulate transporters' recordkeeping and compliance with the manifest system[183] and to require transporters to ensure that the wastes they transport are properly labeled.[184] EPA's discretionary rulemaking authority is, however, quite broad. The Agency may promulgate "such standards . . . as may be necessary to protect human health and the environment."[185] Nevertheless, Section 3003(b) makes it clear that, to the extent EPA's regulations enter the area covered by HMTA, EPA's role is subsidiary to that of DOT. EPA has in fact not sought to regulate outside of the four areas required by Section 3003(a), although it claims authority to enforce DOT's regulations.[186]

EPA regulates only off-site transportation of hazardous waste. Thus, on-site transportation of waste by generators or by TSD owner/operators is not regulated.[187]

---

181 *See generally* Chapter 6, *infra.*

182 49 USC §§1801 *et seq.;* 49 CFR subchapter C. The HMTA governs a wide range of hazardous materials other than hazardous waste.

183 Sections 3003(a)(1), (3), and (4).

184 Section 3003(a)(2).

185 Section 3003(a).

186 40 CFR §263.10(a) (note).

187 40 CFR §263.10(b).

[2] Transporters as Generators

A transporter who transports hazardous waste into the United States from abroad is treated as a generator, and must comply with Part 262 at the point of entry.[188] A transporter who mixes hazardous wastes "of different DOT shipping descriptions" by placing them in a single container is also treated as a generator.[189]

[3] Transporter Identification Numbers

Transporters are prohibited from transporting hazardous wastes without securing an EPA identification number.[190] The procedures for acquiring these numbers are discussed in Section 5.03, *supra.*

[4] Transporters as Treatment, Storage, and Disposal (TSD) Facilities

In EPA's original transporter regulations, the Agency maintained that any transporter who stored hazardous waste had to comply with the TSD regulations and obtain a permit as a storage facility.[191] This requirement presented a potentially serious problem to a number of transporters, particularly railroads, which unavoidably "stored" containers on tank cars for short periods of time at transfer stations or rail yards in the normal course of their transportation activities.

EPA subsequently amended the provisions to allow a transporter to store manifested shipments of hazardous waste in containers "meeting the requirements of §262.30" at a transfer facility for a period of ten days or less, without becoming a TSD facility.[192]

The wording of this provision is such that it applies to both wastes in small containers and bulk wastes in tank cars.[193]

The term "transfer station" is defined in Part 260 as "any transportation related facility including loading docks, parking areas, storage areas and other similar areas where shipments of hazardous waste are

---

188 40 CFR §263.10(c)(1).

189 40 CFR §263.10(c)(2).

190 40 CFR §263.11.

191 45 Fed. Reg. 33151 (1980).

192 40 CFR §262.12; 45 Fed. Reg. 86968 (12-31-80).

193 Section 262.30 simply adopts DOT's container standards set forth in 49 CFR Parts 173, 178, and 179. Part 179 regulates rail tank cars.

held during the normal course of transportation."[194] EPA's intention, as expressed in the 1980 preamble, was to exempt waste "held for short periods . . . as part of the routine transportation of the waste. . . ."[195] Depending on how broadly the term is construed, it could encompass truck depots, railroad yards, train make-up sidings, shipping wharves, and any other place or structure used in the ordinary course of transportation activity to transfer cargo from one vehicle to another, to transfer trailers from one tractor to another or onto rail cars, to transfer rail cars from one train to another, and so forth, and, in addition to such entities, holding, resting, or stopover areas.

EPA's definition is not very helpful. It defines "transfer facility" by reference to exemplary transportational storing or staging areas ("docks," "parking areas"), and then qualifies the term by the phrase "where shipments . . . are held during the normal course of transportation." Under this definition a railroad parking car of hazardous waste on sidings often used for that purpose does not become a "storer," but if the car is parked on a siding normally not used for that purpose the railroad must acquire a permit.

EPA construes Section 263.12 to allow up to ten days' storage at each transfer facility along the transportation route. Therefore, a transporter or a series of transporters could arguably hold onto the waste for a very long period of time by tiering transfer facility storage periods.[196] Since EPA views each transfer facility as a separate, potentially permittable entity, it appears that the person required to secure the permit for waste stored more than ten days would be the owner of that facility.

Once the ten days have expired, the storer must issue a new manifest to continue the transportation, and return the generator manifest to the generator.

The definition of "transfer facility" is obviously of crucial significance to the potential for multiple ten-day storage periods stretching out the transportation period. The broader the definition of the term, the greater the number of sites at which manifested waste can be stored for up to ten days. It is, therefore, all the more suprising that EPA has not defined the term more precisely.

A number of states avoid this problem simply by deeming all trans-

---

[194] 40 CFR §260.10(a).

[195] 45 Fed. Reg. 86968.

[196] If the maximum transportation time exceeds 45 days, however, the TSD consignee is required to file an exception report.

porters who store manifested wastes for any period of time, or who possess the capacity to store waste, to be owner/operators of a storage facility, requiring a permit.[197]

[5] Manifest Requirements

[a] In General

A transporter is prohibited from accepting hazardous waste from a generator unless the waste is accompanied by a properly executed uniform manifest.[198] The transporter is required to sign the manifest and date it prior to commencing transportation of the waste, leaving one signed copy with the generator.[199]

[b] Motor Vehicle, Air, and Containerized Water Transport

The manifest must accompany the waste throughout its journey, and each new transporter must sign and date the manifest, leaving a copy with the previous transporter,[200] who must retain the record for at least three years[201] from the date the generator turned the waste over to the initial transporter. The final transporter must secure the signature of the TSD facility owner or operator and retain his copy for a like period.

[c] Bulk Water Transport

If the entire journey of the waste from the generator's site to the TSD site is over water in bulk shipment, the transporter is not required to convey the manifest, but instead must carry a shipping paper that contains all of the information on the manifest except the EPA identification number, generator certification, and signature.[202] Upon delivery to the TSD facility, the final transporter must secure the signature and date of delivery from the TSD owner/operator, either on the manifest (which the generator will have mailed to the TSD facility) or on the

---

197 See, e.g., §25-54cc(c)-12(b), Connecticut Code of Admin. Regulations.

198 40 CFR §263.20(a).

199 40 CFR §263.20(b).

200 40 CFR §263.20(c) and (d).

201 40 CFR §263.22(a). The retention period is lengthened automatically during the pendency of enforcement proceedings regarding the activity. 40 CFR §263.22(e).

202 40 CFR §263.20(e).

shipping paper.[203] The shipping paper must be retained for three years from the date of initial acceptance.[204] Interim shippers are required to sign and date the shipping paper, and the previous shipper must keep its copy for the three-year period.

If waste is transported by truck and transferred to a bulk water carrier, or if it is delivered directly by the generator to a bulk water carrier, the delivery entity must secure the bulk carrier's dated signature on the manifest and send the manifest to the TSD facility.[205]

[d] Railroads

The manifest regulations for railroads are written so as to ensure that intermediate rail transporters are not required to sign either a manifest or shipping paper. The initial rail transporter is required to sign and date the manifest, give a copy to the entity who turned over the waste to it, retain a copy, and give at least three copies to the next nonrail transporter, if any, to the TSD facility if no subsequent nonrail transporters are involved, or to the last rail transporter designated to handle waste destined for export.[206]

All rail transporters, including intermediate transporters, are required to carry a shipping paper containing all of the manifest information except the EPA identification number, generator certification and signature.[207] If the TSD facility has not received the manifest by the time the rail transporter delivers his cargo, the transporter must obtain the dated signature of the TSD facility on the shipping paper.[208] Copy retention requirements are as for other transporters, except that intermediate rail transporters are not required to keep copies of the shipping documents.[209]

[e] Exports

The transporter who removes hazardous waste from the United

---

203 *Id.*

204 40 CFR §263.22(b). The period is extended if an enforcement action is pending. 40 CFR §262.22(e).

205 40 CFR §263.20(e)(4).

206 40 CFR §263.20(f)(1).

207 40 CFR §263.20(f)(2).

208 40 CFR §263.20(f)(3).

209 40 CFR §263.22(c).

States must sign and date the manifest as of the exit date, retain a copy for the usual period, and return a signed copy to the generator.[210]

[f] State Requirements

The EPA uniform manifest rule appears to allow states to license or otherwise regulate transporters,[211] and a number of states impose permit requirements on all hazardous waste transporters who travel in or through the state.[212]

[6] Delivery of Waste for Treatment, Storage, or Disposal

A transporter is obligated to deliver all of the waste accepted from the generator to the designated TSD facility, to the alternate designated TSD facility if an "emergency" prevents delivery to the primary facility,[213] or to the next designated transporter or extraterritorial delivery point designated by the generator.[214]

If delivery in accordance with the manifest is not possible, the transporter must contact the generator for instructions on how to proceed, and revise the manifest to reflect those instructions.[215] This requirement is important to preserving the paper-tracking system in the event of difficulties occurring in the field.

[7] Transportation-Related Spills and Discharges

The Part 263 regulations impose the following obligations on transporters who experience an accident or other release of hazardous waste:

— They must take "appropriate immediate action to protect human health and the environment."[216]

— They are required to comply with orders from federal, state, or

---

210 40 CFR §263.20(g).

211 49 Fed. Reg. 10498.

212 *See, e.g.,* Section 25-54cc(c)-11 of Connecticut's Code of Administrative Regulations. States may also demand a copy of the manifest accompanying waste being carted through or into the state. *See* Section 3009 (last sentence) (1984).

213 40 CFR §§263.21(a)(1) and (a)(2).

214 40 CFR §§263.21(a)(3) and (a)(4).

215 40 CFR §263.21(b).

216 40 CFR §263.30(a).

local officials acting within the scope of official responsibilities to remove discharged waste.[217]

— Air, rail, highway, or containerized water transporters are required immediately to notify EPA's National Response Center,[218] and must report the incident in writing to the Director, Office of Hazardous Materials Regulations, Hazardous Materials Transportation Bureau, U.S. Department of Transportation.[219]

— Bulk water transporters are required to notify EPA or the Coast Guard pursuant to Section 311 of the Clean Water Act.[220]

Essentially, the regulations require transporters to clean up any hazardous waste that escapes into the environment.[221] They are, in addition, required to take any other action either ordered or approved by federal, state, or local officials to eliminate any existing hazard.[222]

The obligations, deceptively simple on their face, present a number of potentially thorny issues for transporters. The response of public officials to transportation accidents involving hazardous materials can be chaotic.[223] As a practical matter, local fire or police officials will frequently direct response actions.[224]

The uniform manifest does not require the shipper to describe the nature of the hazard posed by the cargo in any greater detail than placing the DOT hazard codes on the form, and they are not required to indicate on the forms any special precautions that must be taken by cleanup personnel.[225] The DOT placards and labels also provide a generalized description of the nature of the hazard posed.[226] Chemicals with widely different toxicological characteristics, or significantly different explosion characteristics, will bear the same label or placard. The

---

217 40 CFR §263.30(b). In such event, neither an identification number nor a manifest is required of transporters employed to remove the waste.

218 Telephone numbers 800-424-8802, 202-426-2675. *See also* Chapter 6, *infra*, for materials relating to EPA's National Contingency Plan and the Comprehensive Environmental Response, Compensation and Liability Act.

219 Washington, D.C. 20590.

220 33 USC §1321; 33 CFR §153.203; 40 CFR §263.30(d).

221 40 CFR §263.31.

222 *Id.*

223 *See* Cushman, Hazardous Materials Emergencies: Response and Control at 15-36 (Technomic Publishing Co. 1983).

224 *Id.*

225 Line 32 of the manifest makes such information discretionary.

226 *See generally* 49 CFR §§172.500 through 172.558 (placards); and 49 CFR §§172.400 through 172.448.

manifest may not tell a nonexpert emergency official the characteristics of the waste.

If the numbers on the manifest are not sufficient to allow complete chemical identification of the waste, there are at least three ways the transporter's personnel can learn more about the waste by making a telephone call, although the manifest form does not contain the telephone numbers. The Chemical Manufacturers' Association System (CHEMTREE)[227] maintains a toll-free telephone number[228] at which information about most industrial chemicals can be obtained. EPA participates in a proprietary data base called OHMTADS, which contains 126 fields of data on over a thousand substances. One must, however, possess a modem and a computer, and pay a yearly subscription fee and hourly connect fee for this service.[229]

While EPA's regulations require the transporter to call the National Response Center in the event of a release,[230] that entity functions primarily as a clearinghouse and may not provide complete information about the substances involved.

The sorts of legal problems that can arise in the context of a transportation spill are illustrated by the facts in *Lowe, et al. v. Norfolk and Western Railway Company, et al.*[231] Following a derailment, a tank car owned by another entity spilled its contents. The incident was reported to the National Response Center, and for some reason the contents of the tank car were reported to be carbolic acid. Operating on that information, EPA officials apparently ordered or acquiesced in cleanup activities by railroad employees and contractors not dressed in protective clothing. The tank car contents were actually crude orthochlorophenol, which contained trace amounts of dioxin, which is highly toxic and a suspected carcinogen. The result was a tangled web of lawsuits brought by the unprotected workers, and third party claims brought by

---

227 Chemical Transportation Emergency Center, 2501 M. Street, N.W., Washington, D.C.

228 Telephone numbers 800-424-9300, marine and extraterritorial calls 202-483-7616 (collect).

229 OHMTADS, Information Sciences Corporation, 2135 Wisconsin Ave., N.W., Washington, D.C., Telephone numbers 800-424-2722 (toll-free), 202-298-6200. Appendix 7 lists other data bases.

230 40 CFR §263.30(e). The telephone number is printed in the regulation, but not on the manifest form.

231 529 F. Supp. 491 (S.D. Ill. 1982) (opinion on motions to sever and to dismiss third party claims).

the primary defendants, including the railroad and the generator,[232] against EPA and others.[233]

Both the transporter and on-scene emergency personnel must rely on the veracity and completeness of the manifest in the event of a transportation-related release of the substance. The potential for generator liability to injured transporter or response personnel, and the uncertain legal status of recovery against EPA for negligent regulation,[234] should be a powerful incentive for case in preparation of the manifest.

§5.05 Overview of Regulation of TSD Facilities

[1] In General

Although RCRA is generally viewed as establishing a "cradle to grave" regulatory program for hazardous waste, the clear emphasis of the subtitle C program is on the "grave." Sections 3004 and 3005 erect a permit program under which all owners and operators of treatment, storage, or disposal facilities must ultimately possess a permit as a prerequisite to doing business and require EPA to adopt standards and other regulatory restrictions for such entities.

Congress correctly foresaw that EPA would experience a relatively long start-up period and consequently provided for phasing in the TSD facility regulatory program.[235] Facilities in existence on November 19, 1980, were required either to qualify for "interim status" or to go out of business.[236] Acquiring interim status was not difficult for most TSDs. EPA was required to develop interim standards for such facilities, and then develop permanent standards, after which permits would be is-

---

[232] This incident took place in 1979, before the manifest system was in place.

[233] Suit against EPA must be brought in federal district court under the Federal Tort Claims Act.

[234] Damages for negligent exercise of regulatory authority have rarely been awarded.

[235] Section 3005(e).

[236] As originally written, Section 3005(e) spoke as of the effective date of RCRA. The section was amended in 1980 to insert the November 19, 1980, date, which was the effective date of EPA's intitial set of RCRA regulations, including Part 265. Section 3005(e)(3)(1984) created a new interim status category, facilities "in existence on the effective date of statutory or regulatory changes . . . that render the facility subject to the requirement to have a permit . . . ." For land disposal facilities, this interim status expires within twelve months if a permit is not issued, unless the owner/operator has filed a complete Part B permit application and certified compliance with the applicable groundwater-monitoring and financial responsibility requirements imposed as a consequence of other provisions of RCRA added in 1984 by P.L. 98-616.

sued to interim status facilities case-by-case, affording "permanent" or "permitted" status.

Section 3004 of RCRA requires EPA to set different standards, "where appropriate," for new and existing facilities, as of the date facility standards are issued. EPA adopted "interim" new facility standards in 1981 for landfills, surface impoundments, land treatment, and underground hazardous waste injection facilities,[237] which were effective for facilities coming into existence between August 13, 1981, and February 13, 1983.[238] These Part 267 permits became obsolete in 1983 with EPA's promulgation of permanent Part 264 land disposal facility standards[239] and final adoption of underground injection control (UIC) regulations for underground injection.[240]

It took EPA an exceedingly long time to put together its permanent program for regulating TSD facilities; permanent land disposal standards were not issued until 1983, following a series of mandamus orders.[241] Permitting began in early 1983 and will take several years to complete. The time lag between interim status and permitting for some facilities could be as long as ten years, and allows for the accumulation of substantial amounts of waste that is subject to the relatively weak standards of Part 265. This fact, coupled with EPA's refusal to prohibit landfilling of hazardous waste, probably ensures a continuing scenario of "imminent hazards," primarily groundwater contamination, well into the twenty-first century.[242]

[2]　Who Is Regulated?

[a]　In General

In order to be subject to regulation under the RCRA permit pro-

---

237 40 CFR Part 267; 46 Fed. Reg. 12429 (2-13-81). Authority to regulate injection wells is also contained in the Safe Drinking Water Act, 33 USC §§1421-1431.

238 40 CFR §267.3(a).

239 See generally 47 Fed. Reg. 32349 (6-26-82); 40 CFR Part 264, subparts K, M, N.

240 See 48 Fed. Reg. 14293 (4-1-83); 40 CFR §144.14.

241 See Illinois, et al. v. Gorsuch, 530 F. Supp. 340 (D. D.C. 1981), aff'd, 684 F.2d 1032 (D.C. Cir. 1982); and 47 Fed. Reg. 32274 (6-26-82).

242 In P.L. 98-616, Congress imposed a number of statutory standards, and imposed other sanctions intended to speed up the permitting process. These are discussed generally below and in the next section.

gram, a person must be an "owner" or "operator"[243] of a "facility" at which hazardous wastes are "treated," "stored," or "disposed." Although both Section 3004 and Section 3005 use the phrase "owners and operators of facilities for the treatment, storage and disposal of hazardous waste,"[244] RCRA's definitional provision, Section 1004, does not define all of the terms. "Storage," "treatment," and "disposal" are defined. "Facility," "owner," and "operator" are not defined. Section 1004(29) defines a term that does not appear in subtitle C, "solid waste management facility," to include, *inter alia,* "any facility for the collection, source separation, storage, transportation, transfer, processing, treatment or disposal of solid wastes, including hazardous wastes, whether such facility is associated with generating such wastes or otherwise."

EPA has defined "facility" by rule to mean "all contiguous land, and structures, other appurtenances, and improvements on the land, used for treating, storing, or disposing of hazardous waste."[245] A "facility" may comprise one or more "units," such as landfills, incinerators, surface impoundments, and the like.[246]

[b] Storage Facilities

"Storage" is defined both by what is storage, in definitions contained in RCRA[247] and in EPA regulations,[248] and by what is not storage, such as EPA's exemption for short-term transporter storage at transfer facilities.[249] The statutory definition of the term is essentially containment in a manner that does not constitute disposal, whether the containment is "temporary" or "for a period of years."[250]

EPA defines the term somewhat differently. Storage means "the holding of hazardous waste for a temporary period at the end of which

---

[243] These terms are defined in a straightforward manner in 40 CFR §260.10(a).

[244] The quoted language is from Section 3004. Section 3005 differs slightly, but not significantly.

[245] 40 CFR §260.10(a). Intention to operate a facility is not relevant. *See* Fishel v. Westinghouse Electric Corp., — F. Supp. —, No. 85-0216 (M.D. Pa. 1985).

[246] *Id.*

[247] Section 1004(33).

[248] 40 CFR §260.10(a). *See also* 40 CFR §270.2.

[249] 40 CFR §263.2.

[250] 40 CFR §260.10(a).

the hazardous waste is treated, disposed of, or stored elsewhere."[251] Since the statutory definition uses the term "temporary" as well, but disjunctively with "for a period of years," EPA's regulatory definition is arguably narrower. In addition, EPA's definition attempts to make definite the indefiniteness of the statutory definition by requiring that something must in fact follow the "storage" to make it storage.

Although many of the Part 264, Part 265, and Part 270 standards are equally applicable to all facilities, some requirements, such as closure and postclosure requirements,[252] are not applicable, or only partially applicable, to storers. Since the overall regulatory burden imposed on disposers is greater than that imposed on storers, to the extent the statute and regulations permit a gray area to exist between storage and disposal, disputes will arise in the implementation of the program.

Since EPA has not refined the term "temporary," one may anticipate an argument that it must encompass the statutory phrase "period of years" and accordingly "storage" should be permitted for a potentially very long time. At some point, of course, "permanent" storage becomes disposal, at least in the ordinary sense of that term.

Conceptually, moreover, almost any conceivable form of storage constitutes "disposal" as that term is defined by Section 1004(3) of RCRA, encompassing the "placing of . . . hazardous wastes into or on any land . . . so that such . . . waste or any constituent thereof may enter the environment . . . ." EPA defines "disposal" using the statutory definition, but also defines the term "disposal facility" as one "at which hazardous waste is intentionally placed into or on any land or water, and at which waste will remain after closure."[253] The EPA approach would clearly turn a closed storage facility into a disposal facility if any waste remained on the site. It does not, however, provide much help in determining at what point long-term storage at an ongoing site becomes *de facto* disposal.[254]

It would not do violence to the statutory definitions for EPA to construct a regulatory definition of overlong storage as *per se* disposal by limiting the period of storage and arbitrarily deeming storers who

---

251 *Id.*

252 40 CFR Part 264 subpart G.

253 40 CFR §§260.10(a) and 270.2.

254 Since the purpose of the closure and postclosure provisions from which storage facilities are exempt is to ensure financial responsibility for long-term maintenance of the site, it is in EPA's interest to identify potential "disposers" from among the storage facilities at some point prior to cessation of the entity's business.

hold waste longer than that period to be subject to the disposer requirements.

Depending on the nature of the physical facilities employed, storers are subject to many of the same substantive standards that are applied to treaters, disposers, or both. Appendix 5-G, *infra*, contains a chart delineating the applicability of Part 264 regulations and standards to storers, treaters, and disposers.

[c] Treatment Facilities

"Treatment" is defined generally both by Section 1004(34) of RCRA and in 40 CFR §260.10(a).[255] The statutory and regulatory definitions differ in only a few respects, the most significant of which is EPA's addition of treatment processes to enable energy recovery. The statutory definition is "any method, technique, or process, including neutralization, designed to change the physical, chemical, or biological character or composition of any hazardous waste so as to neutralize such waste or so as to render such waste nonhazardous, safer for transport, amenable for recovery, amenable for storage, or reduced in volume." Such term includes any activity or processing designed to change the physical form or chemical composition of hazardous waste so as to render it nonhazardous.

EPA also breaks the universe of treaters down definitionally by providing separate definitions for "thermal treatment," "land treatment facility," "totally enclosed treatment," "wastewater treatment unit," "chemical, physical, and biological treatment facility, and "elementary neutralization unit."[256]

Of these, only thermal treatment and land treatment facilities are regulated to any significant extent under RCRA.[257] Thermal treatment facilities are those at which treatment involves "a device which uses elevated temperatures as the primary means to change the chemical,

---

[255] The definition also appears in 40 CFR §270.2.

[256] 40 CFR §§261.10(a), 270.2.

[257] The other three types of treatment are largely exempt from RCRA regulation. Wastewater treatment facilities are regulated primarily under the Clean Water Act, 42 USC §§1201 *et seq.* and only minimally under RCRA. *See* 40 CFR §264.1(e). Elementary neutralization units are simply tanks in which corrosive materials are neutralized in site. Totally enclosed treatment facilities are those that are connected to production streams and do not pose a threat of release of the waste prior to neutralization, such as pipes in which acid is neutralized. Both are exempt from regulation. *See* 40 CFR §§264.1(g)(5)-(g)(6); and 45 Fed. Reg. 76075.

physical or biological character or composition of the waste." EPA gives as examples of such processes "incineration, molten salt, pyrolysis, calcination, wet air oxidation and microwave discharge."

Land treatment facilities are those at which hazardous waste is "applied onto or incorporated into the soil surface," although such facilities become disposal facilities "if the wastes will remain after closure."[258] Such facilities operate on the principle of biological or chemical degradation, transformation, or immobilization. Since land treatment facilities involve application of the waste to the ground, and accordingly pose a greater risk or environmental (primarily groundwater) contamination, they are regulated basically as if they were land disposal facilities.[259]

Most treaters are also storage facilities by virtue of EPA's definition of storage to include holding of waste prior to treatment. Treaters whose treatment of the waste does not neutralize it or otherwise render it nonhazardous become disposal facilities if they do not remove the waste to a disposal or storage facility after treatment, since EPA defines "disposal facility" as "any facility or part of a facility at which hazardous waste is intentionally placed into or on any land or water, and at which waste will remain after closure."

Depending on the nature of the physical facilities employed, treaters are subject to many of the same substantive standards that are applied to disposers and storers. Appendix 9 contains a chart delineating the applicability of Part 264 standards to treaters, storers, and disposers.

[d] Disposal Facilities

To a great extent, problems at disposal facilities lie behind the enactment of RCRA and the regulation of disposal facilities in EPA's RCRA program. As discussed above, the RCRA definition of "disposal" is very broad, encompassing both intentional and unintentional placement of solid or hazardous waste "into or on any land or water" so that the waste "or any constituent thereof may enter the environment or be emitted into the air or discharged into any waters, including ground waters."[260]

EPA's regulations define "disposal facility" somewhat more narrowly than "disposal," to encompass a facility or a part of a facility "at which

---

258 40 CFR §260.10(a); 40 CFR §270.2.
259 *See* 40 CFR §§264.270-282.
260 Section 1004(3).

hazardous waste is intentionally placed into or on any land or water and at which waste will remain after closure."[261] EPA employs this phrase in a number of its substantive regulations.[262] However, in its Part 270 permit regulations and in Section 264 subpart N, EPA refers to "facilities that dispose of" hazardous waste in landfills as requiring a landfill permit.[263]

EPA has not articulated whether it intends the two phrases to be construed differently. On their face, and in light of EPA's adoption of the statutory definition of "disposal" in Section 260.10, the phrases are different. Regulations applicable to "disposal facilities," apply only to facilities intentionally disposing of waste. Regulations applicable to "facilities that dispose of" hazardous waste are arguably applicable to facilities at which disposal is unintentional as well. (Appendix 5-G, *infra*, sets forth in tabular or matrix form the substantive requirements of Part 264 for various types of disposal and other types of TSD facilities. That appendix should be consulted for general technical facts about the regulations.)

Disposers are subclassified by EPA regulations as to the type of activity involved. Large disposers may include among their operations one or more of the subclassifications. For example, a landfill facility may also contain a surface impoundment, a waste pile, or both.

Some types of disposal facilities are generally not regulated under RCRA, because they are subject to regulation under other statutes, but may be regulated to the extent the other scheme has not completely covered their activities. Facilities disposing of hazardous waste by dumping it in the ocean are only minimally regulated under RCRA, but must receive permits from EPA pursuant to MPRSA.[264] Disposers employing deep well injection, similarly, are principally regulated under a statute other than RCRA, the Safe Drinking Water Act.[265] If the

---

261 40 CFR §260.10.

262 *See e.g.*, 40 CFR Part 264 subpart G (§264.110(b)(1)).

263 40 CFR §270.21; and 40 CFR §264.300.

264 33 USC §§1420 *et seq. See* Appendix 5-G, *infra*. Disposal of toxic substances is also subject to an international convention, the 1972 Convention on the Prevention of Marine Pollution by Dumping of Wastes and Other Matter, known generally as the London Dumping Convention, which the MPRSA was amended to execute by the United States. The London Dumping Convention has been signed by thirty-seven nations.

265 *See generally* Chapter 7, *infra*.

facility at which waste is disposed is a POTW, it is subject to regulation, primarily under the Clean Water Act.[266]

For RCRA purposes, disposer subcategories include tanks,[267] surface impoundments,[268] waste piles,[269] land treatment facilities,[270] landfills,[271] and incinerators.[272]

(3) Notification Requirements

Section 3010 of RCRA required all generators, transporters, and TSD facilities to notify EPA,[273] within ninety days of promulgation of the Part 261 identification and listing regulations, if they generate, transport, treat, store, or dispose of any waste identified or listed, specifying the location and describing the activity associated with the waste. Transporting, treating, or disposing of a waste after it is identified or listed under Part 261 prior to submission of the notification is expressly prohibited.[274]

In the event EPA adds additional identifying characteristics to 40 CFR §261.10, or when it lists additional substances under Part 261, the Agency has discretion to require notification as to the newly regulated substances or not to require it.

§5.06   TSD Facility Standards

[1]   In General

Unlike generators and transporters, whose activities must comply with certain RCRA requirements but may be carried out as a matter of right, TSD facilities are required to operate pursuant either to the limited rights afforded by interim status or to a permit issued by either

---

[266] 33 USC §§1201 *et seq. See* Appendix 5-G, *infra*, for RCRA applicability.
[267] 40 CFR §264 subpart J.
[268] *Id.*, subpart K.
[269] *Id.*, subpart L.
[270] *Id.*, subpart M.
[271] *Id.*, subpart N.
[272] *Id.*, subpart O.
[273] Or states authorized to run the RCRA program under Section 3006 as of that date.
[274] Only one notification per waste type is required. For example, a facility disposing of trichloroethylene must have reported that fact to EPA following the listing of that substance under Part 261, but it is not required to tell EPA each time it receives a new batch of the waste for disposal.

EPA or an authorized state.[275] The permits are the principal enforcement mechanism for the substantive standards designed to govern TSD facilities.[276]

[2] Interim Status

[a] Significance of Interim Status

Congress anticipated that it would take EPA some time to develop substantive TSD standards, put together a federal permit program, and delegate the permit program to willing states. In the 1976 RCRA amendments, Section 3005(e) established "interim status," a kind of preliminary level of regulation without permits that was to be applicable to facilities "in existence on the date of enactment" of RCRA.

Unfortunately, EPA was somewhat slower in implementing RCRA than Congress apparently anticipated, so in the 1980 amendments to RCRA[277] Congress rolled back the date interim status began to November 19, 1980, the effective date of EPA's initial identification and listing, permit, interim status, and new facility regulations.[278] This amendment had the effect of leaving TSD facilities totally unregulated under RCRA between the effective date of the 1976 amendments and November 19, 1980. It also allowed persons contemplating entry into the developing TSD market, who but for the amendment would not have been grandfathered as existing facilities, to scramble about to take advantage of interim status. Section 3005(e)(1)(A) was amended in 1984 to also grant interim status to facilities in existence at the time new regulatory requirements come into being that require the facility to have a permit.[279]

[b] Who Qualifies for Interim Status?

The statute accords interim status to any person who—

(1) owns or operates a TSD facility "in existence on November 19,

---

[275] Sections 3005(a)-(d).

[276] *See generally,* Section 5.08, *infra.*

[277] P.L. 96-482.

[278] *See* 45 Fed. Reg. No. 98 (5-19-80), where the initial RCRA regulations were published.

[279] P.L. 98-616, Section 213(a)(11-8-84). This amendment also renumbered Section 3005. Old Sections 3005(e)(1)-(3) were renumbered 3005(e)(1)(A)-(C), and a number of new subsections were added.

1980" or at the time a RCRA permit obligation comes into being through a change of law or regulations;[280]

(2) has not previously been denied a RCRA permit or had interim status terminated;[281]

(3) has complied with the Section 3010(a) notification requirements;[282] and

(4) has "made application for a permit" under Section 3005(a)-(b).[283]

Entities with interim status are treated as if they had been issued a permit "until such time as final administrative disposition" of the application has been made[284] or "unless the Administrator or other plaintiff proves that final administrative disposition . . . has not been made because of failure of the application reasonably required or requested in order to process the application."[285] Interim status facilities in existence on November 8, 1984, if land disposal facilities, lose it twelve months thereafter unless they have by that time filed a complete Part B permit application and have certified that the facility is in compliance with new, statutory groundwater protection requirements and financial responsibility requirements.[286] Facilities entering interim status thereafter face the same termination requirement, calculated from the date they acquired interim status.[287]

EPA refined the "in existence on November 19, 1980" requirement by adopting a two-part test for defining "existing hazardous waste management facility."[288] Under EPA's definition a facility was "existing" on November 19, 1980, if on or before that date it was "in operation" or "construction commenced" on it. A nonoperational facility qualifies if the owner or operator has as of November 19, 1980, secured "all necessary Federal, State and local approvals required" prior to construction

---

[280] Section 3005(e)(1)(A).
[281] Section 3005(e)(1)(C).
[282] Section 3005(e)(1)(B); and see Section 5.05 (3), supra.
[283] Section 3005(e)(1)(C).
[284] Id.
[285] Id.
[286] Section 3005(e)(2)(1985).
[287] Section 3005(e)(3)(1985).
[288] See 45 Fed. Reg. 33074; and 46 Fed. Reg. 2348.

under "hazardous waste control statutes, regulations or ordinances"[289] and as to which either a continuous on-site physical construction had begun as of that date or contractual obligations were entered into as of that date that (1) were not cancellable or modifiable without substantial loss and (2) provided for physical construction of the facility to be completed within a "reasonable time."

Although November 19, 1980, is the interim status date for most facilities, it is possible that facilities not at that time subject to RCRA may subsequently become subject to the regulatory program by virtue of EPA's later amendment of Parts 261, 264, and 265 to bring more facilities under the scope of regulation.[290] In such event, EPA requires newly regulated entities to file a Part A permit application within six months of the publication date of the regulations to bring the facilities under the RCRA program or within thirty days of the date they first become subject to the standards, whichever occurs first.[291]

Although interim status provided a rather substantial benefit to a facility,[292] there was surprisingly little litigation over individual claims to interim status or lack thereof after the interim status deadline passed.

In *Ada-Cascade Watch Co., Inc. v. Cascade Resource Recovery, Inc.*,[293] the Sixth Circuit refused to sanction federal court jurisdiction over a suit in which the plaintiff claimed that state-issued permits for the defendant's facility were ineffective to grant interim status because a new state law enacted in early 1980 preempted the statute under which the permits were issued and that law required the facility to obtain additional permits it did not possess.[294] The facility owner relied

---

[289] 46 Fed. Reg. 2348 (1-9-81). By narrowing the requirement that the facility possess applicable regulatory approvals to hazardous waste control approvals, EPA made it considerably easier for many facilities to obtain interim status. Relatively few state and local hazardous waste control siting requirements were in place as of November 19, 1980, but there are a great many zoning and other land use requirements and state or local water and air pollution permit requirements that could have served to narrow the field significantly.

[290] 40 CFR §270.10(e) and note following.

[291] EPA's regulation appears to make sense when applied to facilities covered by Section 3005(e)(1)(A)'s 1984 amendment, which was apparently enacted to legitimize EPA's preexisting regulation, although Section 3005(e)(1)(C), if read literally, would require the facility to have had to anticipate regulatory changes and file a Part A application prior to the date the permit obligation ripens.

[292] *See* Section 5.06(2)(C), *infra.*

[293] 720 F.2d 897 (6th Cir. 1983).

[294] In parallel state court litigation the local government sought to enjoin construction of the facility on the basis of its failure to secure local land use and environmental permits. The court refused to grant the requested relief and dismissed the action, finding that the Michigan Hazardous Waste Management Act (1979 Mich. Pub. Acts 64, Mich. Comp.

upon a state Department of Natural Resources rule that effectively grandfathered facilities licensed under the prior, less stringent statute, a rule that the plaintiff contended was unlawful. The court applied the abstention doctrine of *Burford v. Sun Oil Company*,[295] concluding that since the issues raised were solely matters of state law, they were matters that the state courts should decide.

EPA also refined the statutory requirement that a facility owner/operator have applied for a permit in order to qualify for interim status. EPA developed a two-part permit application process.[296] In order to qualify for interim status, a facility must have filed with EPA a completed Part A permit application.[297]

A Part A application is "complete" if all of the information required by 40 CFR §270.13 is included in the application.[298] EPA's regulations provide that if the Agency determines that an applicant's Part A is deficient, it will notify the applicant of that fact in writing, giving rise to an obligation on the part of the applicant to submit the necessary supplemental information within thirty days.[299] If the information is not provided, EPA's regulation states that the Agency "may take" enforcement action.[300] The application is "complete" when all needed information is received.[301]

EPA believes that it has the administrative latitude to extend the deadline for submitting a complete Part A application, by means of a compliance order issued under Section 3008.[302] As a consequence of that position, failure to complete a Part A application before the deadline does not automatically disqualify an existing source from interim status. While EPA's position appears justified in the case of sources brought into the program by rule changes after November 19, 1980, it

---

Laws Ann. §§299.501 *et seq.*) preempted all local regulation of hazardous waste facilities. Township of Cascade v. Cascade Resource Recovery, Inc., 118 Mich. App. 580, 325 N.W.2d 500 (1982).

295 319 U.S. 315, 63 S. Ct. 1098, 87 L. Ed. 1424 (1943).

296 *See generally* 40 CFR Part 370, subpart B.

297 40 CFR §270.70(a)(2).

298 The required information is set forth in Appendix 10.

299 40 CFR §270.70(b).

300 *Id.*

301 40 CFR §270.10(c).

302 *See* 49 Fed. Reg. 17716 at fn.1 (4-24-84).

seems to be inconsistent with Section 3005(e)(1)(A) for sources required to comply as of that date.[303]

An interesting issue has arisen regarding the reviewability of EPA's denial of interim status by letter, as provided for in Section 270.70, or of a formal opinion in a contested case concluding that a facility has interim status.

In the latter situation, the Eighth Circuit, in *Hempstead County, et al. v. EPA*,[304] concluded that a formal opinion by an EPA Regional Administrator that a facility met the requirements for interim status was not the issuance of a "permit" giving rise to a right to appeal the action under Section 7006(b) of RCRA directly to a court of appeals.[305] However, the court transferred the action, pursuant to 28 USC §1631, to the local U.S. district court, which the court of appeals felt had jurisdiction under the citizen suit provision of RCRA, Section 7002.[306]

The plaintiffs in *Hempstead* sought to challenge a decision concluding that the applicant had interim status. But what if an applicant is denied interim status by EPA? May it seek review of EPA's action, and, if so, in what forum? *Hempstead's* reasoning would seem clearly to foreclose direct review by a court of appeals, since the court there concluded that interim status "is not a permit action." A disappointed permit applicant's access to the district courts is problematic. The *Hempstead* opinion relied upon Section 7002(a)(1) in preserving a remedy for the plaintiff in that case.[307] The nature of that Section 7002(a)(1) action is a suit against the offending facility to enjoin it from operating without a Part 264 new facility permit. The language of Section 7002(a)(1) appears to preclude that section's use by an unsuccessful interim status seeker. The inescapable conclusion seems to be that an entity whose bid for interim status has been rejected by EPA may be forced to wait until EPA initiates an enforcement action to raise

---

[303] This is not a mere academic problem, for as of mid-1984 EPA had still not completed its review of the original set of Part A applications it received. *See* 49 Fed. Reg. 17717 (4-24-84).

[304] 700 F.2d 459 (8th Cir. 1983).

[305] *Id.* Section 7006(b) authorizes direct appeals from actions "issuing, denying, modifying or revoking any permit under Section 3005" and from actions affecting state RCRA program approvals.

[306] Section 7002 authorizes suits against EPA to compel it to perform a nondiscretionary act, and against any person alleged to be in violation of "any permit, standard, regulation, condition, requirement or order which has become effective . . . ."

[307] Section 7002(a)(2) provides a *mandamus* remedy against EPA, which would clearly be unavailable, at least in a case where EPA's denial of interim status was premised on its judgment that the applicant's Part A was deficient, clearly a discretionary act.

objections to EPA's action. The uncertainty of the entity's status in the interim could have serious financing and other operational consequences.[308]

[c] Interim Status Requirements

Interim status lasts from, at the earliest, November 19, 1980, until EPA or an authorized state acts on the TSD facility's Part B permit application and issues a permit[309] or until interim status is terminated for failure to file a Part B application or information requested by EPA in connection with the Part B application[310] or for failure to certify compliance with applicable groundwater protection and financial responsibility requirements.[311] Simply closing the facility will not terminate interim status.[312]

Interim status facility activities are governed by the substantive requirements of EPA's Part 265 regulations[313] and are limited by Sections 270.71 and 270.72.[314]

An interim status facility is limited to the specific wastes, processes, and design capacities set out in its Part A application, and it may not accept different wastes or employ different processes without advance approval by the EPA Regional Administrator or the state RCRA Program Director, as the case may be. New hazardous wastes not previously identified or listed by EPA as hazardous may be accepted as of right,

---

308 EPA's view is that an EPA pronouncement that a facility has met the statutory prerequisites for interim status is a decision not to initiate a discretionary enforcement action. Although EPA sends a letter to interim status applicants in which the parameters of allowable interim status operations are spelled out, EPA's position is that the letters simply repeat information contained in the Part A, and confer no rights on the recipient.

309 *See generally* 40 CFR §270.73. (Or between the date the facility was made subject to the RCRA program and action on the Part B application. *See* 40 CFR §270.10(e)(5).)

310 EPA had proposed to terminate interim status for failure to pursue the permit application. In 1984 amendments to Section 3005(c), Congress imposed strict time deadlines on EPA's completion of permitting for the various TSD categories, and provided that interim status terminates on the deadline (four years for land disposers, five years for incinerators, eight years for all others) for all then-unpermitted facilities. *See* Section 3005(c)(2)(1985).

311 Sections 3005(e)(2) and (e)(3).

312 "Closure" is a term of art, requiring postclosure permit unless the facility is exempt. Exemptions are limited, *see, e.g.,* 40 CFR §295.258, and unavailable in a number of states.

313 *See* Section 5.06[2][d], *infra.*

314 These sections were previously codified as 40 CFR §§122.23(b) and 122.23(c). They were recodified in 1983, when EPA "deconsolidated" its consolidated permit regulations.

provided the facility submits a revised Part A application prior to accepting such waste.[315]

A change in design capacity requires a revised Part A application and approval by EPA or the state regulatory authority based on a finding that there is "a lack of available treatment, storage, or disposal capacity at other hazardous waste management facilities."[316] The TSD facility owner or operator must justify the increase in design capacity. Obviously it would be in an interim status facility's best interest to indicate as large a capacity as possible on its initial Part A application. EPA's regulation does not specify how a "lack" of available capacity can be shown. Specifically, it does not answer the question of what geographic area is relevant to the question of "availability," and for whom such capacity is available.

Congress addressed the expansion issue in Section 243(a) of P.L. 98-616. Section 3015 of RCRA requires that new units, replacement units, and lateral expansion of existing units of waste piles, landfills, or surface impoundments at interim status facilities may not commence receipt of waste after May 8, 1984, unless they are able to meet the liner and leachate collection requirements statutorily imposed by Section 3004(o)(11-8-84).[317] Landfills and surface impoundments are protected from the imposition of more stringent requirements for complying units when the facility is permitted.[318]

A change in the treatment, storage, or disposal process also requires prior approval of a revised Part A application, and the owner or operator is required to demonstrate that the change is necessary either to "prevent a threat to human health or the environment because of an

---

[315] 40 CFR §270.72(a). This provision has been controversial. A number of states have elected to freeze interim status strictly to the original Part A disclosures, and several bills submitted to the Congress would achieve a similar result. *See, e.g.*, H.R. 2867, 98th Cong., 1st Sess. §7(A)(1983).

[316] 40 CRR §270.72(b).

[317] Waste piles are required to comply with respect to expansions "within the waste management area identified in the permit application . . ." (presumably the Part A), and must meet EPA's regulatory requirements for new facilities promulgated prior to October 1, 1982, as revised pursuant to §3004(o). Section 3015(a). Landfills and surface impoundments must also notify EPA (or the state if the state runs the program) prior to receipt of waste at a new unit (Section 3015(b)(2) and must file a Part B application within six months thereafter "for each facility submitting such notice" (*id.*). Although somewhat ambiguous, this provision appears to establish a permitting priority of sorts, putting active, expanding facilities at the front of the line.

[318] Section 3015(b)(3)(1985). *See also* §3005(i).

emergency situation" or to comply with Part 265 or with applicable "State or local laws."[319]

TSD facilities holding interim status may be sold or otherwise changed in either their ownership or operational control without approval by EPA, but the regulations require that a revised Part A application be filed by the new owner or operator, as the case may be, at least ninety days prior to the transfer.[320] However, EPA requires the old owner or operator to maintain financial responsibility for the facility[321] until EPA (or the state authority) is satisfied that the new entity has satisfied the interim status financial responsibility requirements.

Finally, if the capital investment in changes to an interim status facility exceeds "fifty percent of the capital cost of a comparable entirely new HWM facility,"[322] EPA considers it a new facility, and as such it may not operate without a permit.

[d]   Interim Status Standards

[i]   Sources of Standards

[A]   **Part 265.** EPA's interim status standards[323] are structured to mirror the permanent standards. For each subpart of the permanent standards there is an equivalent subpart of the same alphabetical delineation in the interim status standards, except that the interim status regulations contain three subparts not yet promulgated in permanent form.[324] In general, however, the substantive requirements for interim status facilities were intially promulgated as less onerous than those imposed on permitted facilities.[325] For example, while both in-

---

319 40 CFR §270.72(c). Although the meaning is probably implicit, it is curious that EPA did not specify that the only applicable state and local laws requiring compliance are hazardous waste ones. *Compare* 40 CFR §270.2 (definition of "Federal, State and local approvals or permits necessary to begin physical construction"). As written, this requirement would appear to be satisfied if the change in process were required by, say, a zoning ordinance.

320 40 CFR §270.72(d).

321 *See* 40 CFR Part 265 subpart H.

322 40 CFR §270.72(e).

323 40 CFR Part 265, as amended. *See, e.g.,* 50 Fed. Reg. 16044 and 50 Fed. Reg. 28749 (amending landfill and surface impoundment regulations to consistency with the 1984 amendments).

324 These are Subpart P (Thermal Treatment), Subpart Q (Chemical, Physical and Biological Treatment), and Subpart R (Underground Injection). *See generally* Appendix 5-G, *infra.*

325 The closure, post-closure and financial responsibility (insurance) requirements and

terim status and permitted facilities were required to maintain a groundwater-monitoring program, the rigor of the monitoring required and the obligations imposed on the TSD facility in the event groundwater migration of contaminants is detected varies significantly between the two sets of requirements. Thus, while Parts 264 and 265 both contained a subpart F dealing with groundwater monitoring, Part 265's subpart F required only modest monitoring, while Part 264 labeled its subpart F "Groundwater Protection" and imposed extensive monitoring, analysis, and response obligations on regulated entities.

[B] **Effect of 1984 Amendments.** Congress radically altered the world of interim status for land disposal facilities in 1984, imposing on them (as well as on permitted facilities) onerous limitations, primarily aimed at preventing migration of leachate into groundwater.

Section 3005(i) requires that all waste piles, landfills, surface impoundments, and land treatment units operating under interim status and receiving waste after July 26, 1982, meet the same groundwater monitoring, unsaturated zone monitoring, and corrective action standards applicable to new units under Section 3004.[326]

Section 3008 was also amended to allow EPA to issue administrative orders requiring corrective action for releases of hazardous waste into the environment from interim status facilities, and provided for judicial enforcement of the orders.[327]

Interim status surface impoundments are dealt with by Section 3005(j), which subjects them to the liner and leachate control requirements imposed on new surface impoundments by Section 3004(o) (or

---

the general requirements, set forth in subparts A-H, tend to be more similar than the performance or operating requirements of subparts I *et seq.*

[326] Section 3005(i)(11-8-85). The groundwater-monitoring and unsaturated zone-monitoring requirements are those imposed in Part 264 under the specific provisions of Section 3004 applicable to the facility class and Section 3004(p). They are applicable whether or not the facility is located above the seasonal high-water table, has two liners and a leachate collection system, or is capable of liner inspection, unless a Section 3004(p) exemption is granted to EPA for a particularly sophisticated system. The corrective action requirements referred to are those mandated by Section 3004(v)(1984), which are to be promulgated by EPA to address what actions will be required of TSDs (and what financial responsibility needed to ensure compliance) where off-site migration of waste constituents requires response action to protect the public health or the environment. Whether Section 3004(u) corrective action is also implicated is unclear. If it is, the effect is draconian, since that provision requires cleanup of past pollution, whatever the time of its occurrence. EPA's revised Sections 265, 254 (waste piles), 265, 301 (landfills), and 265.221 (surface impoundments) were published on July 15, 1985. 50 Fed. Reg. 28749-28750.

[327] Section 3008(h). *See* discussion *infra.*

to more stringent requirements promulgated by EPA) and requires that the controls be in place by not later than November 8, 1989, in order for the facility to continue thereafter to accept waste.[328] Facilities that install the double liners and leachate collection requirements imposed by Section 3004(o) are protected against the imposition of more stringent requirements as conditions to their initial permit.[329]

Interim status corrective action orders are apparently the product of Congress's desire to give EPA the authority to begin cleanup operations at existing facilities prior to permitting and outside of the Comprehensive Environmental Response, Compensation and Liability Act (CERCLA) program.[330] The statute appears broad enough to cover environmental problems resultant from activities not covered by interim status, such as exempt units and units closed prior to November 19, 1980. The orders may include suspension of operation, and could arguably be a vehicle to impose Section 3004 standards prior to permitting. Although the statute does not mention a right to a hearing, the nature of interim status corrective action orders appears consistent with a right to a prior hearing.

EPA, in guidance interpreting Section 3008(h), sent to its regional offices and to states on December 16, 1985, stated that it believes a hearing is required prior to the issuance of a corrective action order, and that, although the Agency already has existing hearing procedures (40 CFR Part 22), new procedures would have to be developed for Section 3008(h).

EPA's interpretive guidance is interesting in other respects as well. It relies upon the Conference Report and a 1983 Senate Report in stating that a Section 3008(h) order may address releases of hazardous *constituents* (those substances listed in Appendix VIII to Part 261) as well as hazardous waste identified or listed under subtitle C, except for

---

[328] There are three limited exceptions, spelled out in detail in §§3005(j)(2)-(4) and subsequent subsections, which are available only upon petition filed within a specified time period. The exceptions involve unleaking limed impoundments, "aggressive biological treatment facilities" permitted under the Clean Water Act, and facilities found to have no potential for migration of waste to groundwater at any time. EPA's regulatory incorporation of those standards is found at 50 Fed. Reg. 28749 (amending 40 CFR §§265.1, 265.18, 265.221.

[329] Section 3005(j)(8). There are a number of other requirements in Section 3005(j), relative to response to leaks in exempt facilities, definitional provisions, provisions dealing with special problem wastes, and other provisions, which result in the section's being cumbersome and complex.

[330] *See* H.R. Rep. No. 1133, 98th Cong., 2d. Sess. at 111 (1984)(Conference Report). CERCLA is discussed in Chapter 6, *infra.*

releases from underground storage tanks, which are subject to Section 3008(h) only as to subtitle C wastes. This interpretation reflects EPA's correct reading of Congress's intent to ensure that all environmental problems are addressed before a TSD facility is permitted.

Similarly, EPA also reads the statute as giving it authority to address releases from *solid* waste management units as well as *hazardous* waste cells at facilities handling both hazardous and other solid waste, relying on language in House Report No. 98-1133 critical of EPA's prior regulatory approach, which limited corrective action obligations to "regulated units" (that is, those subject to subtitle C). Finally, the Agency makes it clear that it intends to apply Section 3008(h) to illegal interim status facilities, that is, to facilities that failed to meet the criteria for interim status but were allowed to operate by EPA pursuant to enforcement agreements and to facilities that had previously lost interim status. These interpretations, though not compelled by the language of Section 3008(h), are reasonable in view of its purpose, and appear to fall within the decisional latitude accorded to the Agency by the courts in recent years.

Section 3008(h) orders issued by EPA appear to be subject to judicial review under Section 7006(b), by the United States Court of Appeals for the recipient's area.

The interim status substantive requirements existing as of late 1985 are set out clearly in the regulations, and need no elaboration. The following discussion deals with selected issues, and contains a general overview.

[ii] General Requirements

In general, facilites must have a variety of written plans pursuant to which they are operated; these include waste analysis plans,[331] facility inspection plans,[332] personnel training plans,[333] and emergency contingency plans.[334] Waste inventories, inspection logs, and similar records must be maintained. Facility security systems must be maintained.[335] Emergency equipment must be maintained and tested.[336]

Facilities must comply with the manifest system, by signing the

---

[331] 40 CFR §265.13.
[332] 40 CFR §265.15.
[333] 40 CFR §265.16.
[334] 40 CFR §265.51-.52.
[335] 40 CFR §265.14.
[336] 40 CFR §265.33.

manifest and mailing a copy to the generator, noting discrepancies and filing discrepancy reports and unmanifested waste reports, and so forth.[337] While the facility must perform a waste analysis on each shipment to determine that the waste conforms to the manifest description, the analysis need not precede signing the manifest.[338]

Facilities with hazardous waste surface impoundments, landfills, or land treatment operations must install and maintain groundwater-monitoring systems to determine whether or not any wastes are leaking into an aquifer. The original requirements are minimal, and, as discussed above, for the classes of facilities most affected, they have been displaced by statutory requirements. Essentially, background levels of pollutants for which drinking water standards have been established, seven specific commonly occurring substances, and four pollution "indicators" must be determined in upgradient wells, and compared against subsequent samples[339] taken periodically downgradient of the facility.[340]

The groundwater-monitoring provisions establish the procedures and standards required for well maintenance and placement, sampling and analysis, and reporting to EPA.[341] The TSD is required to undertake more sophisticated analysis, to search for specific hazardous waste constituents migrating from the facility to the groundwater only if the analysis of the four indicators demonstrates possible contamination.[342]

[iii]   Closure, Postclosure, and Insurance Requirements

[A]   **Closure.** All interim status facilities must have written closure and postclosure plans, describing how the facility will be closed when its use is terminated and any contemplated decontamination procedures.

---

337 40 CFR §§265.71-77.

338 40 CFR §265.71(a)(2)(Comment).

339 40 CFR §265.92, §265.93, Appendixes III and IV.

340 Quarterly measurements of the "indicator pollutants," pH, specific conductance, Total Organic Carbon, and Total Organic Halogen must be taken during the first year of interim status operation and semiannually thereafter. 40 CFR §265.92(c)(2). Yearly analysis of the groundwater for cholorides, iron, manganese, phenols, sodium, and sulfates is required. 40 CFR §265.92(c)(3).

341 EPA also publishes several guidance manuals. *See, e.g.,* Procedures Manual for Ground-Water Monitoring at Solid Waste Disposal Facilities, EPA-530/SW-611 (August 1977); and Methods for Chemical Analysis of Water and Wastes, EPA-600/4-79-020 (March 1979).

342 40 CFR §265.93(d).

The closure regulations are intended to provide, early in the regulated life of the facility, consideration by the TSD owner or operator of what kinds of wastes will be stored or treated at any one time during the operating life, what steps are proposed for decontaminating equipment and structures at the end of the facility's operating life, and, in general, how the owner/operator will go about closing the facility in a manner that comports with the closure performance standard contained in 40 CFR §265.11.

The closure performance standard (identical to that contained in Part 264) involves two considerations: (1) minimization of the need for long-term maintenance after closure and (2) minimization of postclosure escape of hazardous substances or contaminated rainfall from the site to groundwater, surface water, or the atmosphere and of other health or environmental hazards.[343]

Six months prior to closure, or within fifteen days of termination of interim status without a permit or a judicial or administrative enforcement order to shut down, the owner/operator must submit the closure plan to EPA, which will evaluate the plan, notify the public, and possibly hold an informal public hearing.[344] EPA has a right to modify the plan and impose its modified plan on the TSD facility.[345] Unless an extension is granted by the regulatory authority, closure activities must be completed within 180 days of receipt of the last waste shipment or approval of the closure plan, whichever occurs later. Both the owner/operator and an "independent professional engineer" must certify that closure has been in accordance with the plan.

[B] **Postclosure.** By far the most significant policy issue facing EPA in developing its interim status regulations was how long after closure the Agency should require the owner/operator to maintain some degree of control over the site, particularly with respect to landfills. Since interim status landfills were by and large unlined or only minimally lined, and since many had enjoyed years of unregulated activity, the Agency could not be confidant that operational design would, to any useful degree, limit future environmental contamination from hazardous constituents buried at the site. On the other hand, the Agency had

---

[343] 40 CFR §§265.11(a) and (b).
[344] 40 CFR §§265.112(c) and (d).
[345] 40 CFR §265.112(d).

to come to grips with economic reality—perpetual care by TSD owner/ operators would be a pipe dream.

EPA settled on a thirty-year postclosure monitoring, surveillance, and security requirement[346] and a qualified permanent prohibition against site disturbance for facilities where waste remains, the latter secured by a requirement that a notation of the prohibition be recorded with the deed or other instrument of title and a plat showing the restricted area and bearing a recitation of the restrictions be prepared and filed in the local land records.[347] The regulations specify the content of the required notice and what must be shown on the plat.

What must be noted on the deed[348] is a recitation of the specific site disturbance prohibitions required for the site pursuant to Section 265.117(c), which will usually include a prohibition against disturbing the integrity of the cover, liner(s), containment systems, and monitoring systems. The facts that the owner/operator or some other person funded by the postclosure trust fund or insurance proceeds is obliged to operate the monitoring system and may be required to maintain active security for thirty years are not required to be noted and recorded.

Postclosure plans are required to be prepared and, prior to closure, approved by EPA in the same manner as are closure plans.[349]

[C]   **Financial Requirements—Closure and Postclosure.** Subpart H[350] requires owner/operators of all TSD facilities to provide a means of assurance that the costs of closure in accordance with the closure plan will be able to be met.[351] Disposal facilities are required to provide similar assurance for postclosure costs.[352] These requirements are discussed in more detail in connection with the Part 264 permanent standards. There are several ways the TSD owner/operator can satisfy these

---

[346] 40 CFR §265.117(a).

[347] 40 CFR §§265.117(c), 265.119, 265.120.

[348] In most jurisdictions, recording a notation on the owner/operator's existing recorded deed will not be possible. Thus, the recording of a separate declaration of restrictions, and indexing on the grantor index, in the manner of a declaration of convenants and restrictions, or a lien, will be the means employed.

[349] *See generally* 40 CFR §265.118. State and federal entities are excluded from this requirement.

[350] 40 CFR §§265.142, 265.143. State and federal entities are excluded.

[351] 40 CFR §§265.140(b) and 265.144-146.

[352] 40 CFR §265.146 allows a disposal facility to utilize one method to handle both closure and postclosure costs.

requirements. They are (a) by establishment of a trust fund,[353] the *res* of which is produced by cash input over time, (b) by obtaining a surety bond from a surety company listed as acceptable in U.S. Treasury Circular 570,[354] by obtaining an irrevocable standby letter of credit from a state or federally "regulated and examined" institution,[355] by purchasing insurance from an insurance company licensed as either an insurance company or a surplus lines company in one or more states,[356] or by being a large enough or solvent enough entity to meet EPA's "financial test."[357]

An entity may use one or more of the above mechanisms for meeting its closure and postclosure obligations. EPA specifies wording required in the financial assurance documents.[358]

[D] Liability Insurance Requirements. Unless granted a variance under Section 265.147(c), or unless eligible for self-insurance under Section 265.147(f), all TSD owners or operators must maintain liability insurance covering "sudden accidental occurrences" of at least $1 million per occurrence and $2 million annual aggregate exclusive of legal defense costs and covering "non-sudden accidental occurrences" of at least $3 million per occurrence and with an amount aggregate of at least $6 million exclusive of legal defense costs.[359]

---

[353] 40 CFR §§265.143(a), 265.145(a).

[354] 40 CFR §§265.143(b), 265.145(b). The owner/operator must, however, also establish a standby trust fund.

[355] 40 CFR §§265.143(c), 265.145(c). In plain words, a bank. A standby trust fund is also required.

[356] 40 CFR §§265.143(d), 265.145(d).

[357] 40 CFR §§265.143(e), 265.145(e).

[358] *See* 40 CFR §264.151 (which is applicable both to interim status and permitted facilities).

[359] The terms are intended to be used in the ordinary sense they are used in the insurance industry. 40 CFR §265.141(g). EPA does, however, define several of the applicable terms:

"Accidental occurrence" means an accident, including continuous or repeated exposure to conditions, which results in bodily injury or property damage neither expected nor intended from the standpoint of the insured. "Legal defense costs" means any expenses that an insurer incurs in defending against claims of third parties brought under the terms and conditions of an insurance policy. "Nonsudden accidental occurrence" means an occurrence which takes place over time and involves continuous or repeated exposure. "Sudden accidental occurrence" means an occurrence which is not continuous or repeated in nature.

The liability insurance requirement came under review during 1985 because of insurance industry reluctance to offer the product. *See* discussion at Section 5.06[3][e][ii], *infra*.

The insurance requirements are discussed in detail *infra,* at Section 5.06[3][e][ii], in connection with the Part 264 standards.

[E] **Miscellaneous Financial Considerations.** A TSD owner or operator facing bankruptcy, and the entity's guarantor, must notify EPA of the pending bankruptcy.[360]

Bankruptcy of a trust fund trustee, surety, letter of credit issuer, or insuror triggers a sixty-day timetable for the TSD to establish a replacement financial assurance mechanism.[361]

Sections 3004(a) and (t)(1984) authorized EPA to increase financial responsibility requirements to cover the cost of corrective action required under Section 3004(v) and to look to any guarantor of a TSD owner or operator who is either in bankruptcy proceedings or otherwise beyond EPA's or a court's jurisdiction.

A state may establish its own financial assurance requirements, which will supplant the EPA requirements if they are "at least equivalent" to them.[362] A state may also relieve TSD facilities within its borders of the financial assurance obligations by undertaking the entity's closure, postclosure, and/or liability obligations as a guarantor if the EPA Regional Administrator approves the arrangement.[363]

[iv] **Substantive Standards**

EPA has developed substantive requirements for containers (Sections 265.17-265.177), tanks (Sections 265.19-265.199), suraface impoundments (Sections 265.22-265.230), waste piles (Sections 265.25-265.257), land treatment facilities (Sections 265.27-265.282), landfills (Sections 265.30-265.315), incinerators (Sections 265.34-265.351), thermal treatment facilities (Sections 265.37-265.382), and chemical, physical, and biological treatment facilities (Sections 265.40-265.406).

Technical appendixes to Part 265 include recordkeeping instructions, primary drinking water standards, significance tests, and examples of potentially incompatible waste.

---

360 40 CFR §265.148(a).
361 40 CFR §265.148(b).
362 40 CFR §265.149(a).
363 40 CFR §265.150.

[3]   Permanent Permitted Status

[a]   Transition from Interim Status

Interim status continues in effect, unless terminated prematurely, for a TSD facility "until final administrative disposition" of the facility's permit application is made, either pursuant to EPA's RCRA permit regulations[364] or by an authorized state regulatory entity. EPA's implementation of the two-step permit program contemplated the "calling in" of Part B of the permit applications of existing facilities following the promulgation of substantive standards in Part 264 for each class of facility.[365]

---

[364] 40 CFR §264.3. The permit regulations, Part 270, are analyzed *infra. But see* at this point 40 CFR §270.73, which, as amended by 50 Fed. Reg. 28753 (7-15-85), incorporates the termination requirements of the 1984 amendments. It is estimated that over one-half of the interim status landfills in the United States would close by November 8, 1985. EPA's enforcement policy affecting facilities failing to qualify by November 8, 1985, is published at 50 Fed. Reg. 38946. EPA proposed an elaborate program for implementing the 1984 amendments' land disposal restrictions at 51 Fed. Reg. 1802 (1-14-86).

[365] "New facilities" are subject to a number of special requirements, which are described below:

(1) Facilities that commence operation or on which physical construction commences after the effective date of Part 264 standards for the class of facility to which the facility belongs must, before such physical construction or operation (whichever is earlier) have submitted both a Part A and Part B and have "received a finally effective RCRA permit." 40 CFR §270.10(f). A 1984 amendment to Section 3005(a) makes the preconstruction permit requirement a clear statutory requirement.

(2) Facilities other than landfills, injection wells, land treatment facilities, or surface impoundments were permitted to commence physical construction between November 19, 1980, and the effective date of relevant Part 264 standards upon submission of a Part A and evidence that all necessary permits had been acquired, and upon representation that physical construction would be completed within a "reasonable time." Construction could continue, even though the applicable Part 264 standard became effective before construction was completed, although operation could not commence until a finally effective permit was issued on a Part B submission. 40 CFR §270.10(f)(3).

(3) Landfills, surface impoundments, land treatment facilities, and Class I underground injection wells (that is, hazardous waste injection wells other than radioactive waste injection wells) as to which operation or physical construction commenced between November 19, 1980, and the effective dates of Part 264 subparts N, K, M, and R or, for underground injections, the effective date of a UIC permit issued by a state with a UIC program approved under Section 1422 of the Safe Drinking Water Act were/are subject to interim new facility standards, published at 40 CFR Part 267.

With the promulgation in 1983 of Part 264 standards for all of the above facilities except injection wells, Part 267 has become largely moot. However, the Part 267 requirements were less stringent in a number of significant respects than the Part 264 standards, and the Part 264 standards are only applied prospectively to unused portions of the facilities. Thus, facilities operated under Part 267 were given a regulatory benefit that

EPA's processing of Part B applications began in mid-1983, and the Agency proceeded to process permits rather slowly thereafter.[366]

EPA effectively grandfathered in perpetuity the existing portions of interim status facilities, such as landfills and waste piles, that would be physically impossible to retrofit with protective requirements, such as synthetic liners, required by the Part 264 regulations.[367] As a consequence, facilities low on EPA's call-in list could indulge in only minimally regulated activity for a substantial period of time.[368]

As discussed above and below, the 1984 amendments contained in P.L. 98-616 radically altered this state of affairs, imposing the equivalent of permanent standards, sometimes more stringent than the permanent standards EPA had in effect immediately preceding the effective date of the amendments, on interim status land disposal facilities, and placing a limit on the amount of time EPA had to complete permitting, after which point interim status ends as a matter of law for unpermitted facilities unless they have complied with the permanent standards.

As in the case of the interim status standards, the permanent standards are designed as "minimum national standards which define the acceptable management of hazardous waste."[369]

The 1984 amendments also required fundamental changes in many of EPA's permanent TSD standards. The severe restrictions placed on land disposal facilities, particularly landfills, raise serious questions about the continued viability of that segment of the hazardous waste disposal industry. The cost of doing business under RCRA arguably may make unlawful disposal more attractive, and thus the effectiveness of the enforcement mechanisms available to EPA and state governments, discussed below, may become a critical issue.

The amendments also address, or require EPA to address, a number of hazardous waste problems not addressed at all under the original statute. These include underground storage tanks, used oil, and fuel made from hazardous waste or blended with hazardous waste.

---

for some facilities was, in economic terms, significant.

366 *See* 49 Fed. Reg. 17717(4-24-84); and 47 Fed. Reg. 32038(7-23-82).

367 *See, e.g.,* 40 CFR §270.21; 48 Fed. Reg. 14151 (4-1-83).

368 40 CFR §264.1(a).

369 The minimal interim status standards applied until "final administrative disposition" of the permit is made. Following call-in, the permit application could be the subject of potentially lengthy hearings prior to resolution. *See* 40 CFR §124.12; and 49 Fed. Reg. 17717-17718.

[b] Applicability of Part 264 Standards[370]

The permanent standards are applicable to all TSD facilities except those as to which categorical subpart I and following standards have not yet been promulgated, exempt or "permit by rule" facilities,[371] and entities "engaged in treatment or containment activities during immediate response" to a discharge or threat of a discharge of hazardous waste or material that becomes hazardous upon discharge.[372]

[c] Standards Applicable to All TSDs

[i] Identification Number
All TSDs must have an EPA identification number.[373]

[ii] Notice Requirements
If a TSD receives waste from an off-site nonforeign source, the TSD owner/operator must notify the generator in writing that he possesses permits for, and will accept, the waste, and must keep a copy of the notification in his operating records.[374] Recipients of foreign-generated hazardous waste must notify EPA's regional office at least four weeks in advance of the expected date of receipt of the initial shipment of such waste.[375]

An owner/operator contemplating transferring ownership or operation of the facility to a third party must notify the transferee of the Part 264 and Part 270 requirements applicable to the facility.[376]

[iii] Waste Analysis
Each time a new waste or waste from a new generator is accepted, or if the TSD facility has reason to believe that an existing generator's process or operation has changed, the TSD facility must perform a

---

[370] It should be noted that the 1984 amendments to RCRA, P.L. 98-616, will cause significant changes in the standards governing TSD facilities, particularly land disposal facilities, and may well make such facilities economically or technologically unviable. As of late 1985, the rulemaking changes required by the 1984 amendments had not been accomplished. This book indicates the parameters of anticipated changes, and future editions will address them as they are made by EPA. *See, e.g.*, 51 Fed. Reg. 1602 (proposed system for implementing land disposal restrictions).

[371] *See* Section 5.03, *supra.*

[372] 40 CFR §264.1(8); 48 Fed. Reg. 2511.

[373] 40 CFR §264.11.

[374] 40 CFR §264.12(b).

[375] 40 CFR §264.12(a).

[376] 40 CFR §264.12(c).

"detailed chemical and physical analysis" of a "representative sample" of the waste.[377] The sampling and analytical criteria are those set forth in Part 261 of EPA's regulations. The activity must be carried out in accordance with a "waste analysis plan," which must be spelled out in the facility's Part B application.[378]

The waste analysis obligation may be shifted to the generator, if the generator accepts the responsibility. It may be satisfied by existing analytical data either developed under Part 261 by generators or others, during interim status or developed from "existing published data on the hazardous waste or on hazardous waste generated from similar processes."[379]

In addition, each "movement of hazardous waste received" at a TSD facility accompanied by a manifest must be sampled to a degree sufficient to determine that the waste received is the same as the waste described on the manifest.[380]

[iv]   Security

TSD facilities must either be designed so that potential injurious contact with the waste, structures, or equipment at the facility by people or livestock cannot occur or have entry controls or barriers sufficient to prevent entry into the active area.[381]

[v]   Inspection

A pattern of inspections of operating and structural equipment, monitoring and emergency equipment, and security devices must be maintained pursuant to a schedule contained in the Part B application, and inspection records must be kept for three years.[382]

[vi]   Personnel Training

All personnel must be put through a training program, identified in

---

[377] 40 CFR §§264.13(a)(1) and (a)(3). EPA added a specific requirement in 1985 that a specified "paint filter test" be used to detect the presence of three liquids in containerized or bulk hazardous waste. See 50 Fed. Reg. 18370 and EPA Pub. SW-846.

[378] 40 CFR §§264.13(b), 264.13(c), 270.14.

[379] 40 CFR §264.13(a)(2).

[380] 40 CFR §264.13(c). Most TSD facilities contract with consulting analytical laboratories to perform their waste analysis.

[381] 40 CFR §264.14.

[382] 40 CFR §264.15.

the Part B application, involving various operating, safety, and emergency parameters.[383]

[vii] Ignitable, Reactive, or Incompatible Waste

Ignitable or reactive waste must be handled, stored, and disposed of in a manner that will not expose it to conditions that will foster reaction or ignition, and that will prevent the waste, if it does ignite, from igniting other waste.[384] Special precautions are also required for incompatible wastes to prevent chemical reactions among incompatible wastes or between incompatible wastes and other materials.[385]

[viii] Seismic and Floodplain Location Standards

In areas EPA has identified as high seismic risk areas,[386] TSD facilities must demonstrate, as part of the Part B submission, compliance with a requirement that "portions of new facilities" not be located "within 61 meters (200 feet) of a fault which has had displacement in Holocene time."[387]

Facilities covered by subparts I through O that are located in a 100-year floodplain[388] must either be designed, constructed, and maintained to prevent a washout (that is, movement of hazardous waste from the active portion) by a 100-year flood[389] or be able to demonstrate to EPA either that the waste can be removed prior to flooding or that, in the case of existing waste piles, land treatment units, surface impoundments, and landfills, if washout occurs, no "adverse effects on human health or the environment will result."[390] Since in the case of most existing landfills and other land TSDs, such a demonstration probably is impossible, diking should probably be required in most cases.

Significant omissions from EPA's initial siting requirements were prohibition of siting land disposal facilities over water supply aquifers

---

383 40 CFR §264.16.

384 40 CFR §264.17(a). There are special buffer zone requirements for container storers and tanks. *See* 40 CFR §§264.176 and 264.198. The buffer zone requirements are also discussed *infra*, at Section 5.06[3][g][iii].

385 40 CFR §264.17(b). *See also* Appendix V to Part 264 (reproduced in Appendix 5-H, *infra*).

386 40 CFR §270.14(b)(11).

387 40 CFR §264.18(a). "Fault," "displacement," and "Holocene time" are defined in the section.

388 The 100-year floodplains in coastal areas or along inland flowing water bodies are generally mapped by state and federal agencies charged with that responsibility.

389 40 CFR §264.18(b). The relevant terms are defined in the regulation.

390 40 CFR §264.18(b)(ii). EPA prohibited siting in salt dome formations, and underground mines and caves, as of 1985. *See* 40 CFR §264.18 (added 50 Fed. Reg. 28746).

and other standards, such as required access to emergency services, minimum distances from inhabited areas, and the like. Section 3004(o)(7), added as part of the 1984 amendments, required EPA to establish siting criteria for both new and existing TSD facilities within eighteen months of November 8, 1984, and, in addition, to identify areas of vulnerable ecology.

[ix] Preparedness for and Prevention of Emergencies

As part of the Part B demonstration, an owner or operator must demonstrate that the facility is designed, constructed, maintained, and operated so as to minimize the possibility of fire, explosion, or unplanned release of hazardous waste;[391] that it possesses certain required alarm, communication, and fire suppression equipment;[392] and, if aisle space is not maintained, that the operation does not require aisle space for emergency purposes.[393] Equipment must be tested periodically;[394] there must be access to specified communications equipment unless EPA's regional office waives the requirement;[395] and the owner or operator must "attempt to make" emergency preparedness cooperative arrangements and agreements with local emergency authorities.[396] Finally, each facility, as part of its Part B submittal, must demonstrate that it has developed a contingency plan adequate to minimize damage from fire, explosion, or unplanned release.[397]

[x] Manifest System Requirements

Upon receipt of a shipment of waste, the owner/operator is required to sign and date the manifest, note any significant discrepancies in the manifest on each copy of it,[398] and give the transporter one copy of the signed manifest.[399]

The generator's copy must be mailed within thirty days, and the

---

391 40 CFR §264.31.
392 40 CFR §264.32.
393 40 CFR §264.35.
394 40 CFR §264.33.
395 40 CFR §264.34.
396 40 CFR §264.37.
397 40 CFR §§270.14(b), 264.50-56.
398 For bulk water, or rail shipments, the same requirements apply to the shipping paper that accompanies the waste in the event the generator-mailed manifest was not received prior to receipt of the waste. *See* 40 CFR §264.71(b).
399 40 CFR §264.71(a).

facility must retain its copy for a minimum of three years from the date of delivery.[400]

Manifest discrepancies are differences in either the quantity of the waste in the shipment or the type of waste actually received.[401] A discrepancy in quantity is deemed "significant" if a bulk shipment has a 10 percent weight discrepancy or a batch shipment has "any variation in piece count."[402]

In many cases, a variation in the type of waste will not be determined until the waste has been analyzed. EPA does not, however, require on-the-spot waste analysis prior to manifest signing,[403] but requires any such discrepancy to be reported separately to the generator and the transporter and, if not reconciled within fifteen days of receipt of the waste, reported by letter to EPA.[404] This effectively requires that the TSD facility's sampling and analysis be completed within ten days or so of receipt of the waste.

Activity reports must be filed biennially by March 1 of even-numbered years (covering the odd-numbered years' activities) on EPA Form 8700-13B. All receipts of unmanifested waste must be reported on the same form, within fifteen days of receipt of the waste.[405] The only exception from this requirement is waste received from small-quantity generators, which need not be reported if the generator has provided the TSD facility with a certification that the waste qualifies for exclusion.[406]

The 1984 amendments added a statutory notice requirement that generators report each year their efforts of the previous year to reduce the volume and toxicity of their waste output and to provide a comparative analysis of any changes in those parameters.[407] This requirement was added as an enforcement mechanism for the corresponding substantive obligation imposed by an amendment to Section 3005.[408]

The 1984 amendments also imposed on the generators an obligation to certify on the uniform manifest form (1) that the generator has in

---

[400] 40 CFR §264.71(a)(5). The three-year retention period may be extended by EPA, and is automatically extended "during the course of any unresolved enforcement action regarding the facility." 40 CFR §264.74(b).

[401] 40 CFR §264.72(a).

[402] Id.

[403] See 40 CFR §264.71(a)(2)(Comment).

[404] 40 CFR §264.72(b).

[405] See Form 8700-13B (reproduced in Appendix 5-I, infra); 40 CFR §264.75.

[406] 40 CFR §264.76 (Comment).

[407] Section 3002(a)(6). See also 40 CFR §264.73 (1985).

[408] Section 3005(h) (effective for permits after September 1985).

effect a waste minimization program and (2) that the treatment, storage, or disposal method chosen is the "practicable" method "available" that "minimizes the present and future threat to human health and the environment."[409]

Releases, fires and explosions, and closures must be reported.[410]

[d] Groundwater Protection

Surface impoundment, waste pile, land treatment, and landfill TSD facilities are required to comply with subpart F's groundwater protection requirements for wastes contained in any "waste management unit" that "receives hazardous waste" after January 26, 1983.[411] Inactive units, originally not required to upgrade their interim status groundwater-monitoring programs to meet the more stringent Part 264 subpart F requirements, were required to do so by a 1984 amendment to Section 3005, which legislatively overruled EPA's regulatory policy.[412]

Certain types of the regulated classes of entities were initially exempt from the subpart F requirements.[413] These included surface impoundment, waste pile, and landfill units that had chosen to employ double liners.[414] Totally covered waste piles producing no runoff or leachate and single-lined waste piles located above the seasonal high water table and meeting certain performance standards were also exempt, as were land treatment facilities whose treatment zone had been shown not to contain hazardous constituent levels above background levels to a statistically significant degree.[415] Finally, if, using conservative assumptions about the maximum rate of liquid migration, the TSD could demonstrate that there was no potential for migration to the "uppermost aquifer" during useful life and postclosure period, EPA

---

[409] Section 3002(a)(6) (effective 9-1-85).

[410] See 40 CFR §§264.77, 264.56(j), and 264.115.

[411] 40 CFR §264.90(a).

[412] See Sections 3005(e) and (i). Part 264-exempt entities are, of course, not required to comply with this or any other provision of Part 264. See 40 CFR §264.90(b)(1).

[413] 40 CFR §264.90(b)(2) (1983); and see 40 CFR §264.222 (double-liner requirement for surface impoundments), 264.252 (double-liner requirement for waste piles), and 264.302 (double-liner requirement for landfills).

[414] Id. See 40 CFR §§264.250(c) and 264.253.

[415] 40 CFR §264.90(b)(3).

could waive the subpart F requirements.[416]

Congress nullified most of these blanket exemptions in 1984 by amending Section 3004 to add a new subsection (p), which prohibits EPA's blanket exemption of facilities not located above the seasonal high water table, double-lined facilities, and facilities employing liner inspection. Subsequent to 1984, EPA is allowed to exempt specific evidentiary findings of no impact.

Facilities subject to subpart F must maintain their groundwater protection system at least during the active life of the unit. Facilities that have been required to undertake "detection monitoring"[417] must do so throughout the postclosure period (usually thirty years), and those required to do "compliance monitoring"[418] or undertake "corrective action"[419] must continue for a "compliance period," which can range from the number of years of active life (including prepermitted active years and the closure period) to an indefinite period until the applicable "groundwater protection standard" has not been exceeded for three consecutive years.[420]

The permits of facilities at which the groundwater has been contaminated by any hazardous constituents attributable to a regulated unit will also contain (1) the location where monitoring samples must be taken and at which the "groundwater protection standard" (if any) applicable to the facility applies,[421] (2) the hazardous constituents for which the facility must monitor,[422] (3) the "concentration limits" applicable to the hazardous constituents for which the facility must monitor,[423] and (4) other groundwater protection requirements. Normally the "concentration limits" will be background levels determined by prepermit upgradient well sampling and analysis, although EPA has

---

[416] 40 CFR §264.90(b)(4).

[417] *See infra*, this subsection.

[418] *Id.*

[419] *Id.*

[420] *See* 40 CFR §§264.90(c) and 264.96. EPA amended 40 CFR §§90(a) and (b) on July 15, 1985, implementing the 1984 amendments' prohibitions. 50 Fed. Reg. 28746-28747.

[421] This location is established at a vertical surface at the hydraulically downgradient limit of the area that extends into the uppermost aquifer underlying the regulated units. 40 CFR §264.95(a).

[422] 40 CFR §264.93(a). These can range from a few substances to the entire Part 261 Appendix VIII list, depending upon (a) what constituents have been identified in the aquifer above background in prepermit sampling and (b) what constituents are being disposed of that are considered by EPA likely to find their way into the groundwater. For criteria used to exclude constituents from monitoring, *see* 40 CFR §§264.93(b) and (c).

[423] 40 CFR §264.94. Concentration limits are usually expressed in milligrams per liter.

established specific "maximum concentration" limits for a list of fourteen heavy metals and pesticides, which will apply in lieu of a lesser background concentration.[424] EPA's (or the state's) permit writer may also set "alternate concentration limits" (ACLs), based on a set of published criteria, that are greater than background levels but do not "pose a substantial present or potential hazard to human health or the environment."[425]

One of the criteria upon which alternative concentration limits may be based is the "quantity of ground water and the direction of ground water flow."[426] It thus appears that dilution is a consideration relevant to groundwater contamination under RCRA, although it has largely been prohibited by Congress from being considered in connection with surface water pollution standard setting.[427]

Facilities at which hazardous constituents have not been found in the uppermost aquifer are required only to perform "detection monitoring,"[428] which involves sampling for a simple group of "indicator parameters"[429] and a selected list of constituents that the permit writer selects as providing a "reliable indication of the presence of hazardous constituents in the groundwater."[430] At all times EPA's general groundwater monitoring requirements must be followed.[431] If at any point a statistically significant increase in any of the parameters or constituents over background level is found, the entity is required immediately to sample all groundwater-monitoring wells for the presence of any of the

---

424 40 CFR §264.94(a)(2).

425 40 CFR §§264.94(a)(3) and 264.94(b)-(c). The regulated community is, understandably, seeking to make the ACL criteria as liberal as possible. The environmental protection community does not like the concept.

426 40 CFR §264.94(b)(1)(iii).

427 *See* Weyerhaeuser Co. v. Costle, 590 F.2d 1011, 1041-1044 (D.C. Cir. 1979); and Section 301(h), Clean Water Act, 33 USC §1311(h) (limited exemption for dilution by ocean waters applicable to municipal discharges).

428 40 CFR §264.91(a)(4).

429 40 CFR §264.98. The indicator parameters include specific conductance, total organic carbon, and total organic halogens.

430 40 CFR §264.98(a). Subsequent paragraphs of the regulation establish the ground rules for taking samples and determining the statistical significance of variations from background, and for notifying EPA and taking further action if a statistically significant increase in the indicator parameters or constituents is found.

431 These are set out in 40 CFR §264.98(h).

entire list of hazardous constituents listed in Appendix VIII of Part 261.[432]

Once hazardous constituents are detected in the groundwater, a facility that had previously been required only to do detection monitoring will, by permit amendment, be required to escalate to the next stage. "compliance monitoring."[433] The critical factors in compliance monitoring are (1) the point of compliance, (2) the hazardous constituents that must be monitored for, and (3) the "ground water protection standard," which is one of the trigger levels of concentration that initiates the facility's obligation to undertake the next stage, "corrective action."[434]

A compliance monitoring program generally involves the drilling of a number of monitoring wells at and downgradient of the active portion of the facility and sampling for exceeding of the "ground water protection standard" established for the hazardous constituents for which monitoring is required.[435]

Once the corrective action trigger levels are found, a corrective action program will inevitably be imposed on the facility, unless it can be shown that the levels are a result of erroneous "sampling, analysis or evaluation," or are caused by "a source other than a regulated unit."[436]

Under EPA's pre-1984 regulations a corrective action program would be inserted in the facility's permit if either the compliance monitoring revealed an exceeding of the groundwater protection standard established for the facility[437] or any of the relevant hazardous constituents were found at levels exceeding the concentration limits that form the bases of the groundwater protection standard at any point between

---

[432] This is an expensive requirement. In 1984 dollars, the average cost of a laboratory analysis is $1000 per constituent.

[433] 40 CFR §264.98(h)(4); 40 CFR §264.91(a)(1); 40 CFR §264.99.

[434] 40 CFR §264.91(a)(2); 40 CFR §264.100.

[435] 40 CFR §§264.99(a)-(b). The "ground water protection standard" is somewhat ambiguously defined in 40 CFR §264.92 as "conditions . . . designed to ensure that hazardous constituents . . . entering the ground water . . . do not exceed the concentration limits in the uppermost aquifer underlying the area beyond the point of compliance." The term used in Section 99, however, appears to mean the concentration limits that must not be exceeded at the point of compliance, and other limits and monitoring points designed to detect migration of contaminated groundwater.

[436] 40 CFR §§264.99(i), 264.99(j).

[437] 40 CFR §264.91(a)(2).

the compliance point and the "downgradient facility property boundary."[438]

If corrective action is indicated either at the point of permit issuance or later, EPA might set a more stringent groundwater protection standard than the compliance monitoring one.[439] That is because what may be required to "ensure that hazardous constituents . . . entering the ground water do not exceed the concentration limits . . ." will vary depending upon the state of extant contamination.

The permit (or, as the case may be, modified permit) is intended to specify the corrective actions required to be taken.[440] In general, corrective actions may include excavation of contaminated soils from which constituents are leaching, collection of leachate or runoff, pumping out, treatment and return of polluted groundwater, or measures to retard off-site groundwater migration.

EPA's pre-1984 regulations state that corrective action will be required for a "reasonable period of time considering the extent of contamination,"[441] but the aim of such a program is to reduce the concentration of hazardous constituents "to levels below their respective concentration limits."[442] Therefore, although the permit could establish a fixed "compliance period,"[443] it is likely that in most cases the period will be indefinite—"to the extent necessary" to achieve the result.[444] The regulations contemplate this possibility, and the possibility that corrective action may well extend beyond the active life of the unit.[445] Termination of corrective action may occur only upon a showing that the groundwater protection standard has not been exceeded for three successive years[446] or if EPA (or the state) modifies the facility's permit upon an application by the owner or operator claiming that "the corrective action program no longer satisfies the requirements" of Section 264.100.[447]

---

438 40 CFR §264.91(a)(3).

439 A groundwater protection standard is required to be inserted in the facility's permit by both 40 CFR §§264.99(a) and 40 CFR 264.100(a).

440 40 CFR §264.100(e).

441 40 CFR §264.100(e)(1).

442 40 CFR §264.100(e)(2).

443 40 CFR §§264.100(a)(4), 264.96.

444 40 CFR §264.100(f).

445 *Id.* Insurance is also required to ensure that the program will continue even if the owner/operator defaults. See 47 Fed. Reg. 33274 *et seq.*

446 *Id.*

447 40 CFR §264.100(g). It is not at all clear what sort of showing would be required to satisfy the burden of this provision. The owner/operator could perhaps seek less

Since EPA has chosen to enforce the groundwater-monitoring program by permit condition, there arises a distinct probability that lengthy permit modification proceedings, including contentious hearings, will, for some facilities, occur more than once. Citizen activists will claim rights to participate in such proceedings,[448] and litigious owners or operators might delay the effectiveness of groundwater protection requirements by taking maximum advantage of their hearing rights[449] and their right to judicial review of any permit modification.[450]

Arguably, EPA could have treated groundwater protection as an enforcement matter. It could have established general groundwater protection standards for classes of the Part 261 hazardous constituents, and enforced compliance by means of orders under Section 3008 of RCRA.[451] Such an approach would avoid the potential for protracted and costly hearings, but would have required EPA to establish groundwater purity standards by rule; EPA is required to set such standards under the Safe Drinking Water Act, but has been unwilling or unable to do so for a number of years.[452]

In the 1984 amendments, Congress required EPA to develop corrective action standards by rule not only for currently active units but also for portions of facilities closed before permitting.[453] In addition, the 1984 amendments require the new standards to ensure financial responsiblity, and also address corrective action beyond the site boundary of permitted TSD facilities *and* interim status landfills, surface impoundments, and waste piles active after January 26, 1982, unless the off-site landowner refuses entry.[454] Until EPA issues its corrective action regulations, it will continue to act on a case-by-case basis.

The requirements of Section 3004(u) that permittees undertake cor-

---

stringent concentration limits, or claim that he has evidence that his facility is not producing the concentrations detected.

[448] *See* RCRA §7004(b).

[449] *See* 40 CFR Parts 122, 124.

[450] *See* RCRA §7006(b).

[451] *See infra,* this chapter.

[452] 42 USC §§300g to g-5. *See* Council on Environmental Quality, Eleventh Annual Report at 87 (1980). The Safe Drinking Water Act may provide an independent legal means for emergency groundwater cleanup. *See* United States v. Price, 523 F. Supp. 1055 (D.N.J.1981), *aff'd on other grounds,* 688 F.2d 204 (3d Cir. 1982). *But see* City of Evansville v. Kentucky Liquid Recycling, 604 F.2d 1008 (7th Cir. 1979).

[453] Section 3004(u)(1984); *see also* Section 3008(h). EPA's implementing regulation is 40 CFR §264.101(7-15-85). *See* 50 Fed. Reg. 28747.

[454] Section 3004(v) (1984).

rective action relative to past environmental problems associated with the site are potentially draconian in their impact. Any sort of RCRA permit will invoke the remedial requirements, even for contamination resulting from quite different activity. Thus, a permit for a storage tank could require corrective action over a broad area where the contamination stemmed from other kinds of RCRA-related activities, long ago ceased. This is clearly an attempt by Congress to provide a privately financed alternative to the superfund program.[455]

A TSD may not escape the corrective action requirements simply by closing the facility prior to permitting, since Section 3008(h) provides EPA with essentially the same remedy over interim status facilities in the guise of the "interim status corrective action order."[456]

The Section 3004(u) requirements are immediately effective as to all federal and state permits issued after November 8, 1984. The combination of Sections 3004(u) and 3008(h) seems clearly designed to require private industry remediation of releases occurring at active sites as an alternative to CERCLA.

[e] Financial Responsibility

[i] In General

Section 3004(a)(6) of RCRA specifically requires that EPA develop standards governing "the maintenance and operation of . . . TSD facilities, requiring such additional qualifications as to ownership, continuity of operation . . . and financial responsibility as may be necessary or

---

[455] See H.R. Rep. No. 198 (Pt.1), 98th Cong., 1st Sess. 61 (1983).

[456] P.L. 98-616, Section 233 (11-8-84). There are some differences in the text of the two provisions, although EPA initially read them to provide identical authority, even allowing the Agency to insert Section 3004 standards into interim status corrective action orders. For example, Section 3004(u) applies to releases of hazardous "constituents," which has traditionally been construed broadly by EPA to include breakdown or reaction products of identified or listed hazardous *wastes. See* S. Rep. No. 284, 98th Cong., 1st Sess. 32 (1983). Section 3008(h) applies only when there has been a release of "hazardous waste." In some cases the two terms could embrace very different degrees of liability, but EPA's initial interpretive guidelines on the 1984 amendments treated the jurisdictional reach as coextensive. *See* discussion of Section 3008(h) at Section 5.06[2][d][i], *supra.* Subsequently, the Agency has modified its position somewhat. In an interpretive memorandum dated December 16, 1985, the Agency argued that, although Section 3004(u)'s authority is limited to releases from "solid waste management units at a facility," Section 3008(h) is broader. *See* discussion *supra.*

desirable . . . ."[457] EPA's implementation of this requirement requires owner/operators to provide one of three mechanisms for insuring liabilities during the facility's active life and to provide one or more of six mechanisms to ensure that the cost of compliance with the closure and postclosure requirements[458] will be met throughout the regulated death of the entity.

Liability coverage must be ensured by means of liability insurance,[459] self-insurance,[460] or state assumption of liability.[461] Coverage of closure and postclosure costs must be ensured by means of a trust fund,[462] surety bond, [463] bank letter of credit,[464] insurance,[465] self-insurance,[466] state cost assumption,[467] or a combination of the above.[468] States may, and often do, require different mechanisms. The regulatory requirement is that alternative state mechanisms be "at least equivalent" to the subpart H requirements."[469] State mechanisms may be employed even in states in which EPA administers the RCRA program, when authorized by the Regional Administrator.[470]

Finally, there are notification and other requirements respecting transfer of ownership or operation, and incapacity of either the owner or operator or the financial guarantor.[471]

An amendment in 1984 inserted a special requirement that the financial responsibility demonstration include financial responsibility to carry out corrective action orders relating to off-site groundwater con-

---

[457] Section 3004 is qualified by a provision stating: "No private entity shall be precluded by reason of criteria established under paragraph (6) from the ownership or operation of facilities . . . where such entity can provide assurances of financial responsibility and continuity of operation consistent with the . . . risks . . . ." This provision, unenlightened by the legislative history, appears to preclude EPA from conditioning TSD facility ownership or operation on such factors as absence of criminal record or general moral acceptability.

[458] See Section 5.06[3][f], infra.

[459] 40 CFR §§264.147(a) and (b).

[460] 40 CFR §264.147(f).

[461] 40 CFR §264.150.

[462] 40 CFR §§264.143(a)(closure), 264.145(a)(postclosure).

[463] 40 CFR §§264.143(c)(closure), 264.145(c)(postclosure).

[464] 40 CFR §§264.143(d)(closure), 264.145(d)(postclosure).

[465] 40 CFR §§264.143(e)(closure), 264.145(e)(postclosure).

[466] 40 CFR §§264.143(f)(closure), 264.145(f)(postclosure).

[467] 40 CFR §264.150.

[468] 40 CFR §§264.143(g)(closure), 264.145(g)(postclosure).

[469] 40 CFR §264.149.

[470] Id.

[471] 40 CFR §264.148.

tamination. These orders were an innovation of Section 3004(v), added in 1984.

[ii] Liability Insurance Requirements

RCRA did not initially clearly mandate a requirement that TSD facilities be insured against third-party bodily injury and property damage claims, although EPA believed that Section 3004(6) (renumbered 3004(a)(6) by Section 201 of P.L. 98-616) provided sufficient authority for the Agency to impose such a requirement by rule.[472] EPA's requirement, contained in Section 264.147, that facilities too small to qualify as self-insurers or unable to shift liability to the state[473] must purchase insurance in specified amounts to cover both "sudden" and "nonsudden" accidental occurrences is unique as a regulatory device, and controversial.[474] A brief historical discussion is necessary to put these requirements into perspective.

The insurance industry is a state-regulated industry. While there is vigorous competition among insurers, the regulated nature of the industry and the need to cooperate in reinsurance pools to cover very large risks have resulted in a certain amount of standardization of liability and other casualty insurance contracts. Thus, while individual insurers tailor their contracts to fit their own marketing needs, the variations tend not to affect the fundamental legal undertaking by the insurer and the language by which that undertaking is expressed.

Prior to 1966 most industrial liability insurance policies covered bodily injury or property damage caused "by accident." That language was construed by a number of courts to provide coverage for claims based on the cumulative effect of prolonged exposure to a hazardous condition or substance. In 1966 the comprehensive general liability (CGL) policy used by American insurers was modified to reflect these decisions; in the revised policies, coverage was premised on an "occurrence," which was defined to include continuous repeated exposure to conditions resulting in bodily injury or property damage.

About 1970 the "pollution exclusion" began to appear in CGL policies. This provision excluded from coverage bodily injury or property

---

[472] *See* 46 Fed. Reg. 2847 *et seq.*; and 47 Fed. Reg. 16554.

[473] *See* 40 CFR §264.150.

[474] *See, e.g.*, Cheek, *Risk-Spreaders or Risk Eliminators? An Insurer's Perspective on the Liability and Financial Responsibility Provisions of RCRA and CERCLA,* 2 Va. J. Nat. Resources L. 131 (1982); and M. Meyer, *Compensating Hazardous Waste Victims: RCRA Insurance Regulations and a Not So "Super" Fund,* 11 Envtl. L. 689 (1981).

damage resulting from the discharge, dispersal, escape, or release of pollutants into the environment, unless the event was "sudden and accidental." Beginning around 1980, insureds began to litigate the applicability of the pollution exclusion clause to damage arising from the slow leaking of hazardous constituents from landfills and other areas where hazardous wastes are present. The pattern of decisions is not uniform, although in a majority of the cases the courts have either found the "sudden and accidental" language to be ambiguous and construed the coverage liberally in favor of the insured or limited the language to situations in which the damage either was intended by the insured or could reasonably have been expected to result from the insured's acts.[475]

As a result of these decisions, the insurance industry argues that insurers are being forced to defend and indemnify on risks they did not knowingly assume when the policies were issued. These arguments have led some courts to construe the pollution exclusion in the insurers' favor.[476]

The industry began to rewrite the CGL policies in 1984 to provide greater exclusion for pollution events. The standard CGL policies were rewritten by the Insurance Services Office (ISO) to exclude all pollution coverage from the basic coverage and provide coverage for sudden and accidental pollution events only for an additional premium. Pending acceptance of the new forms by state insurance regulators, a number of insurers began inserting restrictive endorsements on CGL policies excluding all coverage of pollution-related damages. Others have dramatically increased the premiums for the standard CGL coverage, or simply refused to write the coverage. Finally, some companies are seeking regulatory clearance to issue "claims-made" CGL policies.[477]

EPA defined the term "sudden accidental occurrence," for subpart

---

[475] *See, e.g.,* Jackson Twp. Mun. Utilities Auth. v. Hartford Accident & Indemnity Co., 186 N.J. Super. 156, 159, 457 A.2d 990, 994 (1982); Keene Corp. v. INA, 667 F.2d 1034 (D.C. Cir. 1981); Farm Family Mutual Insurance Co. v. Bagley, 64 App. Div. 2d 1014, 409 N.Y.S.2d 294 (4th Dept. 1978).

[476] *See* Barmet of Indiana v. Security Insurance Group, 425 N.E.2d 201 (Ind. App. 1981); National Standard Insurance Company v. Continental Insurance Company, CA-3-81-1015-1 (N.D. Tex. 1983); Great Lakes Container Corp. v. National Union Fire Insurance Co., 727 F.2d 30 (1st Cir. 1984); and American States Insurance Co. v. Maryland Casualty Co., Civ. No. 82-70353 (E.D. Mich. 1984).

[477] Under a claims-made policy, the coverage is triggered only when claims are made during the policy period, or any extension bought by the insured for an additional premium. The claims-made policy was developed to reduce the exposure from claims brought long after the occurrences on which they are based, and to make losses more predictable.

H purposes, as "an occurrence which is not continuous or repeated in nature."[478] A "nonsudden accidental occurrence" is one that "takes place over time and involves continuous or repeated exposure."[479]

An occurrence is "accidental" if it "results in bodily injury or property damage neither expected nor intended by the insured."[480] By specifically requiring coverage for both sudden and nonsudden occurrences, as defined, EPA prospectively avoids the problem presented by the CGL policy's pollution exclusion provision.[481]

By defining "nonsudden occurrence" as it does, EPA's nonbinding definition seems to attempt to address, albeit unsuccessfully, the problem of at what point (for example, exposure, manifestation of symptoms, or other) the "occurrence" happens. Much recent insurance coverage litigation has involved the issue of which policy covers a claim of injury premised on latent disease. CGL policies are typically one-year contracts, and a facility may contract with a number of different insurers over time. In either the latent disease following chemical exposure scenario or a situation in which a drinking water source is contaminated by leachate that escaped from an upgradient landfill years earlier, which policy covers the claim will depend upon how the phrase "damages . . . caused by an occurrence" is construed.

The typical CGL policy defines "occurrence" as an "accident, including injurious exposure to conditions, which results, during the policy period, in bodily injury or property damage neither expected nor intended from the standpoint of the insured."[482] As in the judicial literature construing the application of statutes of limitation to latent diseases,[483] courts construing the CGL policy in cases of latent disease following chemical exposure have divergently interpreted the time of occurrence of and consequent liability for the disease. Some courts have placed liability on the insurer covering the risk at the time of exposure

---

[478] 40 CFR §264.140(g).

[479] Id.

[480] Id.

[481] It does not eliminate the problem, however, for older facilities previously covered by the 1970 version of the CGL policy. "Occurrences" traceable to those policy years will still be subject to the problem of interpretation outlined above. EPA also disclaims any binding effect for its definitions, stating that they are "not intended to limit their meanings in a way that conflicts with general insurance industry usage." 40 CFR §264.140(g).

[482] EPA's nonbinding definition inserts the words "continuous or repeated" before "exposure," and deletes the phrase "during the policy period."

[483] See, e.g., Harig v. Johns-Manville Products Corp., 284 Md. 70, 394 A.2d 299 (1978)(discussing the evolution of the discovery rule).

(the "exposure rule").[484] Others have fixed liability at the point the symptoms became manifest, the point the diagnosis was made, or the date of death if the decedent died undiagnosed.[485] Still others have swept into the coverage net both all the policies on the risk from the point exposure began until it ended (or, in the case of an employee injury, until employment at the site(s) of exposure ended) and the policies in effect at the time of manifestation, on a sort of enterprise liability theory.[486] There are other theories as well, including several holdings that the relevant occurrence happens at the point the exposure actually produces diseased tissue, whether or not the disease is diagnosable at that time.[487]

EPA's nonbinding definition seems intended to fix the insurer liability to the entity on the risk at the time the exposure or release occurs. Nevertheless, the CGL policies are not required to follow EPA's language, and even if they were to do so, there is no guarantee that the courts would construe EPA's language uniformly.[488]

EPA apparently felt that it was on insufficient statutory footing to go the next step—and mandate a wholesale revision of environmental risk insurance coverage.

Between 1970 and 1980, the insurance industry began to offer a new type of claims-made coverage tailored to environmental damage risks, environmental impairment liability [EIL] insurance. Initially, this coverage was only available for sudden releases of pollutants. EPA's regulations produced a demand for EIL policies that provided coverage for nonsudden releases, and by 1981 the few excess or surplus lines compa-

---

[484] Insurance Company of North America v. Forty-Eight Insulations, Inc., 633 F.2d 1212 (6th Cir. 1980), *clarified and aff'd on rehearing*, 657 F.2d 814 (6th Cir. 1981), *cert. denied*, 454 U.S. 1109 (1981). *Accord*, Porter v. American Optical Corp., 641 F.2d 1128 (5th Cir. 1980), *cert denied*, 454 U.S. 1109 (1981).

[485] Eagle-Pitcher Industries, Inc. v. Liberty Mutual Insurance Co., 523 F. Supp. 110 (D. Mass. 1981), *aff'd as modified*, 682 F.2d 12 (1st Cir. 1982).

[486] *See* Keene Corp. v. Ins. Co. of North America, 667 F.2d 1034 (D.C. Cir. 1981), *cert. denied*, 455 U.S. 1007 (1982).

[487] American Home Products Corp. v. Liberty Mutual Ins. Co., 565 F. Supp. 1485 (S.D.N.Y. 1983); Sandoz, Inc. v. Employer's Liability Assurance Corp., 554 F. Supp. 257 (D.N.J. 1982).

[488] Insurance policy provisions are normally a matter of state law, since the insurance industry is state regulated. Federal courts construing policy language do so in diversity cases, applying state law.

nies[489] writing such policies were joined by a number of the larger insurers and a reinsurance pool, the Pollution Liability Insurance Association, was formed.

The premiums for nonsudden occurrence EIL policies did not stabilize, however, and by 1985 several companies previously offering the coverage ceased offering it, and premiums rose dramatically. The industry's explanation for this is its concern about the potential ramifications of the Bhopal, India, gas leak, the high litigation costs of hazardous waste cleanup cases, and its concern that the pattern of court decision construing the CGL policy to cover risks they had not anticipated will repeat itself with the EIL policies.

Because of the tightening of the insurance market, EPA has begun to explore alternatives. As of late 1985, the Agency had solicited comment from the affected public on the conditions facing the industry and options for liability coverage.[490]

Unless a variance is obtained[491] from the EPA Regional Administrator, the liability limits required of TSD facility insurance are $1 million per occurrence and $2 million annual aggregate for sudden occurrences and $3 million per occurrence and $6 million annual aggregate for nonsudden occurrences.[492] An appendix sets forth mandated certificates and endorsements.

A sufficiently large and solvent entity is permitted to be a self-insurer. It must satisfy the "financial test for liability coverage,"[493] which is substantially equivalent to the "financial test" for closure and postclosure financial assurance.[494] A combination of insurance coverage and self-insurance is also permitted.

EPA's prescribed liability insurance provisions were challenged as lacking statutory authority, but before the matter was adjudicated, Congress amended Section 3004, adding subsection 3004(t). The new provision specifically authorizes EPA to adopt methods of establishing

---

489 Excess and surplus lines are a designation that state insurance regulators give to insurance companies that provide insurance that is not readily available from companies licensed ("admitted") to transact insurance business in the state.

490 50 Fed. Reg. 33902 (8-21-85).

491 40 CFR §§264.147(c)-(d).

492 40 CFR §§264.147(a)-(b). EPA phased in the nonsudden occurrence liability insurance requirements, requiring larger facilities to have insurance in effect in 1982, and the smallest group by 1984. See 40 CFR §264.147(b)(4).

493 40 CFR §264.147(e).

494 See Section 5.06[3][e][iv], infra, and Appendix 17 in the regulations. Several states require a more onerous test for self-insurance than the EPA one.

financial responsibility by rule, and states unequivocally that EPA may "specify policy requirements or other contractual terms, conditions or defenses. . . ." It thus puts EPA squarely in the insurance regulatory business. Nonetheless, the insurance method has not developed as rapidly as EPA had hoped, and remains a relatively rare form of TSD financial responsibility, both because of the reluctance of individual insurers to move aggresively into hazardous waste disposal, and because the premiums charged by those that have are high.

[iii] State and Federal TSD Facilities

Neither the liability nor the other financial responsibility requirements of Part 264 apply to state or federal facilities (which are natural self-insurers and are presumed, because of the ability to raise revenue by taxation, to be solvent). In addition, EPA allows state governments to assume the financial obligations of private TSD facilities,[495] including their liability insurance requirements, by acting as guarantors. It is unlikely that there will ever be many takers of the guarantor offer.

[iv] Closure and Postclosure Financial Responsibility[496]

Since EPA requires up to thirty years of maintenance after a facility is closed, it had to develop a mechanism for ensuring that money would be available during that period, while the owner/operator will not be generating income, at least not from the closed portion.

In order to satisfy this need, the Agency developed a pay-during-active life mechanism, the closure or postclosure trust fund,[497] and provides a number of lump sum options for guaranteeing the estimated cost of sealing up the facility or removing waste at closure and the monitoring and maintenence costs estimated for the postclosure period.[498] The alternatives are surety bonds, letters of credit, insurance, self-insurance, and state guarantees.

[v] Bankrupt or Absent Owner/Operators

A serious problem in hazardous waste regulation is the bankrupt TSD owner or operator, or the one who for some other reason is outside the

---

[495] 40 CFR §264.150.

[496] These requirements apply to facilities that must comply with the closure and postclosure regulations—essentially disposal facilities and, most significantly, landfills.

[497] 40 CFR §264.145(a). References will be to the postclosure requirements. The closure requirements are substantially identical.

[498] Cost estimates must be made in accordance with guidelines set forth in 40 CFR §264.144.

Agency's jurisdictional reach at the time the site turns sour, and the financial responsibility chit has to be called.

A theoretical problem arose as to whether EPA could proceed directly against a third party guarantor or insuror when the owner or operator was insolvent and under the protection of the Federal Bankruptcy Code, or solvent but outside of the jurisdictional reach of the federal or state courts. Congress addressed this problem by adding Sections 3004(t)(2) *et seq.* to the statute in 1984, giving the Agency such authority.

A more complete discussion of bankruptcy-related issues may be found in Section 5.10[8], *infra.*

[f] Substantive Closure and Postclosure Requirements

All disposal facilities and, to a lesser extent, waste piles and surface impoundments from which wastes are intended to be removed upon closure, must comply with the closure and postclosure requirements. Subpart G contains a general closure performance standard.[499] It also includes more specific closure and postclosure requirements applicable to all classes of TSD facilities.[500] Still more specific requirements appear in the TSD performance standards for individual classes of facility.[501] The closure and postclosure provisions involve a public proceeding, and the application of long-term maintenance and security obligations.[502]

The duration of the postclosure period established by EPA is thirty years following completion of closure,[503] although the period may be either reduced or extended by EPA on the basis of the Agency's perception of the degree of hazard posed by the unit.[504] The thirty-year benchmark is more or less arbitrary, since experience, particularly with landfills, has demonstrated that the possibility of release of waste may

---

[499] 40 CFR §264.111. The standard is minimization of the need for further maintenance and minimization of future threats to health or the environment resulting from release of wastes.

[500] These are (1) the adoption and approval by EPA of closure and postclosure plans (§§264.112, 264.118), (2) specification of a closure timetable (§264.113), (3) preparation and filing of a survey plat with the local zoning or land use authority setting forth the postclosure restrictions on use of the property (§264.119) and (4) recording of an instrument of title setting forth the use restrictions (§264.120).

[501] Containers—§264.178; surface impoundments—§264.228; waste piles—§264.258; land treatment—§264.280; landfills—§264.310; incinerators—§264.351.

[502] 40 CFR §264.117.

[503] 40 CFR §264.117(a)(1).

[504] 40 CFR §264.117(a)(2).

exist for a long time beyond that point. EPA's adoption of the thirty-year period was a compromise, albeit a controversial one.[505]

[g] Specific TSD Facility Performance Standards

[i] In General

Performance standards, inspection, management, operating, and monitoring requirements are published at Part 264 subparts I *et seq.*[506] The initial standards, for tanks and containers, were promulgated in 1981. Standards for the various land disposal methods were issued in 1982, effective in 1983. These are national minimum standards, and a number of states have adopted more stringent requirements for some or all TSD facility types.

[ii] Land Disposal

The most controversial of EPA's 1983 standards is subpart N, governing landfills. The regulation was controversial primarily because a substantial body of political and scientific opinion holds that hazardous waste should not under any circumtances be disposed of in landfills.[507] The basic thrust of EPA's 1983 landfill requirements is to (1) limit the placement of liquids in landfills,[508] (2) require a single, synthetic liner and leachate collection system, and (3) require extensive groundwater monitoring.[509] A facility is relieved of the monitoring requirements if double liners are employed.[510] The EPA scheme was criticized because of concern about the impacts of disposal of corrosive liquids and solvents, which in a sort of symbiotic relationship can destroy a liner and carry contaminants quickly downgradient into the water table.

In a study of twenty-two large landfills released in 1984, EPA revealed evidence that substantial groundwater contamination had invariably occurred downgradient of landfills and storage trenches

---

[505] *See* 47 Fed. Reg. 32349 (1982).

[506] Subparts I (containers), J (tanks), K (surface impoundments), L (waste piles), M (land treatment), N (landfills), and O (incinerators). The permit specifies the particular requirements.

[507] Some of this opinion is discussed by EPA in 47 Fed. Reg. 32349 (7-26-82). As discussed in the text below, Congress legislatively overruled many of EPA's standards in 1984, and required EPA to undertake further rulemaking as to others. A number of states prohibit landfills.

[508] 40 CFR §264.314.

[509] 40 CFR §264.302.

[510] *Id.* There are special requirements for some dioxins. 40 CFR §264.317.

employing single liners and monitoring groundwater in accordance with the interim status monitoring requirements.

A substantial thrust of the Hazardous and Solid Waste Amendments of 1984 was the legislative modification of EPA's land disposal regulations. Congress substantially expanded Section 3004, imposing for the first time statutory performance standards in a number of areas, which become effective on the expiration of a deadline imposed on EPA for promulgating regulations covering the subject. EPA is usually given somewhat broader authority to fashion regulations, which arguably are permitted to be less onerous than the "default" standards. This technique, new to environmental legislation, is guillotinelike, in that the default standards crash down on a date certain if EPA fails to meet its deadline. The scheme was no doubt motivated in part by frustration at the failure of the judicial *mandamus* remedy to force federal agencies to respect congressional rulemaking deadlines.

Section 3004(c) (1984) prohibits, after May 1985, disposal of noncontainerized hazardous waste or "free liquids contained in hazardous waste," in landfills, and only allows containerized liquid waste disposal to resume if EPA adopts regulations permitting the activity.[511] Beginning twelve months from the effective date, disposal of nonhazardous liquids in a landfill is prohibited unless EPA finds that such disposal is the best alternative and poses "no present risk of contamination of any underground source of drinking water."[512]

Another 1984 rejection of prior EPA regulations is found in Section 3004(d). This provision prohibits "land disposal"[513] of cyanide-contain-

---

[511] EPA is required to issue regulations fifteen months from the effective date minimizing the disposal of containerized hazardous waste in landfills and minimizing the presence of free liquids in containerized hazardous waste to be disposed of in landfills. The regulations are "to prohibit landfilling of liquids that have been absorbed in materials that biodegrade or that release liquids when compressed. . . ." H.R. Rep. No. 98-1133 (10-3-84), at 84.

[512] The "no present risk" test is arguably a weak one, requiring the Agency to focus only on present conditions and presently used sources of drinking water.

Liquids are also the subject of Section 3004(b), which prohibits placement of noncontainerized or bulk liquid hazardous waste in a salt dome, salt bed formation, underground mine, or cave until EPA has held an adjudicatory hearing and thereafter determined that such activity is "protective of human health and the environment," promulgated performance standards and permitting standards, and issued a permit.

[513] "Land disposal" is defined by Section 3004(k) to include landfills, surface impoundments, waste piles, injection wells, land treatment facilities, salt dome and salt bed formations, underground mines, and caves.

ing wastes, waste containing eight listed heavy metals,[514] strong acids, liquid wastes containing PCBs in less than 50 ppm,[515] and halogenated organics in concentrations greater than 1000 mg/kg. The ban is effective thirty-two months after the effective date of the 1984 amendments, but allows EPA to make specific exceptions in accordance with specified criteria, and exempts contaminated soil and debris resulting from a CERCLA action for eighteen months after the commencement of the ban.[516]

Solvents and dioxins are treated similarly, although the time frame for the ban on land disposal is twenty-four months.[517] The remainder of the universe of identified or listed hazardous wastes must be studied by EPA over a sixty-six-month period, on a schedule setting priorities on a one-third by one-third basis, which EPA must provide to Congress within twenty-four months. EPA is required to consider, for each chemical on the list, whether land disposal should be prohibited. If EPA fails to adhere to the schedule, land disposal is prohibited for all the chemicals due to be studied by the missed deadline, except in new TSD facilities complying with stringent statutory performance standards, and then only if the generator certifies that there is no available means of treatment.[518] EPA is given limited authority to grant variances from the time requirements of Sections 3004(d),(e),(f), and (g).[519]

Finally, Congress flatly rejected EPA's landfill and surface impoundment performance standards. Section 3004(o) requires the Agency to promulgate by the end of 1986 regulations requiring that land disposal

---

514 Arsenic, cadmium, hexavalent chromium, lead, mercury, selenium, thallium, and their compounds. These are primarily of interest to California.

515 50 ppm is the regulatory cutoff for regulation of a number of PCB articles under EPA's PCB regulations adopted under Section 6(e) of the Toxic Substances Control Act. Including less than 50 ppm PCBs in a land disposal ban constitutes a legislative disapproval of EPA's TSCA decision.

516 A related provision, Section 3004(f), requires EPA to rethink its position allowing these wastes to be disposed of by deep well injection. EPA is given forty-five months to apply the Section 3004(d) criteria and announce a decision. If EPA does not act within the time period, the activity is automatically prohibited. An identical scheme is provided for dioxins and solvents.

517 Section 3004(e) (1984).

518 Section 3004(g) (1984). The minimum technological performance requirements are set out in Section 3004(o). Any automatic ban ends when EPA takes action with respect to the chemical. Any chemical that EPA decides may not be land disposed must be given mandatory treatment standards. Section 3004(m).

519 Section 3004(h). As of early 1986, EPA had not finalized its regulatory program implementing the Section 3004 land disposal restrictions. Its proposed program is published at 51 Fed. Reg. 1604(1-14-86).

and storage TSDs employ a leak detection system. The statute also requires that new landfills and surface impoundments, or new units or cells of existing such facilities, or lateral expansions, permitted after the effective date of the 1984 amendments, be constructed with double liners (landfills), double leachate control systems, and groundwater monitoring capability.[520]

[iii] **Ignitable and Reactive Waste Stored in Containers or Tanks**

EPA's original buffer zone requirements for ignitable or reactive waste in containers or tanks were also controversial.[521] The requirements were adapted from the Flammable and Combustible Liquids Code[522] of the National Fire Prevention Association (NFPA) and applied by EPA to both liquid and nonliquid ignitables and reactants. For containers, EPA adopted a flat 15-meter buffer, and for tanks, it incorporated requirements by reference. The primary objection to the container requirement was that it was too rigid.[523] In 1984 EPA amended the container requirements to provide a flexible buffer, varying with the physical characteristics of the facility, imposed a buffer zone for underground tanks,[524] and inserted new requirements, based generally on Section 43A of the NFPA code,[525] for nonliquid oxidizers.

---

[520] The double liner/leachate collection requirements are waivable, however, on satisfaction of a number of statutory criteria at the permit-issuing stage, and monofills may be exempted upon meeting a set of statutory criteria. In order to qualify for a variance, the owner/operator must essentially show that the design and operation of the facility prevents waste migration as effectively as a double liner would. A curious provision does not allow any variances for facilities in Alabama, possibly a retributive act punishing the state for withdrawing from the federal RCRA program during 1984. Section 3004(o)(5)(B) actually establishes detailed interim specifications for the double liner/leachate systems, which are required to be inserted into all permits until EPA has adopted implementing regulations. EPA issued revised design and operating requirements for landfills and surface impoundments on July 15, 1985. 40 CFR §§264.221(a), 264.221(c), and removing former Sections 222, 252, and 253. *See* 50 Fed. Reg. 28747-28748; 40 CFR §§264.301(a), 264.301(c), and removing Section 302. The Agency also prohibited the placement of bulk or noncontainerized waste in landfills whether or not absorbents have been added, and tightened the requirements for containers. 40 CFR §§264.314(b) and (c). *See also* 51 Fed. Reg. 1602 (1986).

[521] *See* 45 Fed. Reg. 33066; and 46 Fed. Reg. 2802. The existing requirements are published at 40 CFR §§265.176 and 265.198(b).

[522] NFPA 30(1977).

[523] *See* 49 Fed. Reg. 23291 (6-5-84).

[524] The lack of such a requirement was an apparent oversight of the 1981 regulations.

[525] Code for Storage of Liquid and Solid Oxidizing Materials, NFPA.

[iv] Incinerators

Incineration of hazardous waste is viewed by many as a far superior method of disposal than land disposal, and Congress's 1984 amendments indirectly urge incineration on the industry for those wastes, such as solvents, dioxins, and PCBs, that have essentially been banned from land disposal. Incineration is not, however, without problems. High-temperature incinerators tend to be temperamental and difficult to monitor, and EPA's initial incinerator performance standards were the subject of significant pulling and tugging over the questions of what destruction and removal efficiency was economically or technologically feasible.

EPA's initial incinerator performance standards, issued in the waning days of the Carter administration, were stringent, requiring 99.99 percent destruction and removal efficiency. The Agency repealed the initial standards on June 25, 1982, replacing them with less stringent standards. EPA argued at the time that relaxation was needed to shore up the incinerator industry, but EPA's lax land disposal regulations, issued at about the same time, eliminated whatever incentive the relaxed incinerator standards created.

Congress legislatively overruled EPA's 1982 regulation in 1984. Section 3004(o)(1)(B) establishes as statutory incinerator performance standards the EPA regulations "in effect on June 24, 1982." The statutory standards are effective for all incinerators permitted after the effective date of the 1984 amendments.

[v] Miscellaneous Section 3004 Requirements

Congress adopted several additional statutory prohibitions or rule-making requirements in 1984. Section 3004(l) imposes a ban on the use of waste oil or used oil containing dioxins or other identified or listed hazardous waste, except for purely ignitable waste, for suppression of dust. This provision appears to be a reaction to the Times Beach Missouri dioxin contamination episode, and adds little to RCRA other than making such activity a *per se* violation of the statute.

Section 3004(n) requires EPA to develop a program for monitoring and controlling air emissions at TSD facilities. This provision is aimed primarily at volatile compounds and fugitive dust emissions. These types of air pollution have not been dealt with successfully by EPA under the Clean Air Act, and there is no reason to believe that the Agency will be any more successful simply because Congress has told it to do the job again, this time under RCRA.

[vi] **Chemfuel**

Sections 3004(q), (r), and (s), and an amendment to Section 3010, all inserted in 1984, seek to get a regulatory handle on curtailing hazardous waste and fuel oil. Originally, hazardous waste blended with fuel for the purpose of energy use was exempt from RCRA. The exemption proved a disaster when it became apparent that substantial human exposure to hazardous wastes was occurring from exposure to blended fuel and its combustion by-products, and that as much as 10 million metric tons of hazardous waste escaped regulation each year as a result of the exemption.

The 1984 provisions establish a subsidiary regulatory program that affects the heating fuel industry. Section 3010, as amended, requires producers, users, distributors, and marketers of fuel consisting of a blend of petroleum and an identified or listed hazardous waste to notify EPA of their identity and the particulars of their activities, within fifteen months of the effective date of the provision.

Section 3004 imposes essentially an immediately effective labeling requirement, which prohibits the distribution or marketing of fuel that is made from or contains hazardous waste without a warning label containing the information required by Section 3004(r)(1).[526] EPA is required to promulgate regulations by the end of 1986 regulating chemfuel producers, users, marketers, and distributors of fuel that contains hazardous waste[527] and to develop regulations establishing record-keeping requirements for regulated entities.[528]

EPA subsequently decided to commence regulation of the burning of fuel mixed with hazardous waste and of used oil in boilers and indus-

---

[526] The invoice or bill of sale is required to contain the following statement: WARNING: THIS FUEL CONTAINS HAZARDOUS WASTES. In addition, the document is required to list the wastes contained in it. There are specific exemptions for certain petroleum-refining wastes. *See* Sections 3004(r)(2)-(3).

[527] Section 3004(q). EPA has all of the regulatory options contained in Section 3004(a). Petroleum refinery wastes containing oil that are converted into petroleum coke at the same facility at which the wastes were generated are exempt unless the coke itself is a hazardous waste. Section 3004(q)(2)(A). EPA is allowed to exempt generators who burn *de minimus* amounts of hazardous waste for energy recovery purposes at the facility where the wastes are produced, if the fuel burning is designed and operated to EPA's satisfaction. Section 3004(q)(2)(B). A subsection, apparently aimed at a particular facility, prohibits cement kilns located in areas of 500,000 or more population from burning fuel containing hazardous waste, until EPA's regulations are issued, unless the facility meets the incinerator performance standards. Section 3004(q)(2)(C). Finally, Section 3003 was amended to require EPA to develop specific standards for transporters of chemfuel.

[528] Section 3004(s).

trial furnaces, adding new subparts D and E to 40 CFR part 266.[529]

EPA's general approach in regulating chemfuel is to prohibit the burning of hazardous waste for energy recovery; prohibit the use of used oil containing in excess of specified percentages of arsenic, cadmium, chromium, lead, or halogens or having a flash point below 100 degrees Fahrenheit ("off-specification" used oil), in residential, commercial, and institutional furnaces and boilers; and regulate industrial furnaces and industrial or utility boilers (and, in the case of used oil, generator-operated space heaters). The authorized combustion is subject to notification, storage, and recordkeeping requirements imposed on burners and marketers (used oil marketers are subject to an additional invoicing requirement, and used oil burners are required to do waste analyses to prove that their oil is not off-specification and thus subject to regulation). Generators of either type of chemfuel who are not marketers or on-premises burners are required to comply with the manifest system, and transporters of hazardous waste fuel that is subject to subpart D are regulated under Part 263.

In explaining the regulations, EPA argued at 50 FR 49191 that the prohibitions are aimed at apartment-building and commercial burning that pose a greater threat to public health than does industrial burning. Its reasons are not compelling, however, and it is more likely that the Agency's inability to administer a regulatory program involving small boilers operated by persons not used to close regulation was behind the decision. Enforcement of the prohibition against nonindustrial burning will inevitably fall on the state and local governments.

[vii] Underground Storage Tanks

EPA's initial Part 264 standards basically avoided underground storage tanks that could not be entered for inspection. This removed from federal regulation most underground storage tanks, although experience with underground gasoline and fuel oil tanks clearly demonstrated that such tanks can and do leak, causing groundwater contamination.

A number of states unilaterally began moving toward developing

---

[529] 40 CFR §§266.30-266.44. *See* 50 Fed. Reg. 49164 (1985). Subpart D contains prohibitions and regulation of hazardous waste energy recovery activities. Subpart E contains prohibitions and regulation of used oil activities. The regulation prohibits the burning of chemfuel and off-specification used oil (that is, used oil that fails a test for specified levels of toxic constituents or flash point) in nonindustrial boilers; imposes regulatory standards on industrial boilers; and imposes notification, manifest, or invoice requirements and recordkeeping requirements on marketers and burners.

performance standards for underground tanks shortly after 1980. In 1984, Congress joined the movement, ordering EPA to promulgate permitting standards for such tanks by March 1, 1985,[530] and inserting an entire new subtitle into RCRA, subtitle I.

Subtitle I (Sections 9001-9010) establishes a subsidiary regulatory program within the overall RCRA framework aimed at identifying and regulating underground storage tanks that contain either hazardous waste or petroleum. Tanks that are more than 10 percent below ground level are subject to regulation. The statute establishes interim performance and other standards that are applicable to tanks installed between March 1985 and the effective date of EPA's implementing regulations,[531] and provides for limited preemption and delegation of the federal regulatory program to the states.[532] The subtitle contains its own enforcement provisions[533] and exemptions.[534]

[h] Hazardous Waste Facility Siting

Other than the minimal seismic and floodplain restrictions of 40 CFR §264.18, nothing originally in RCRA or EPA's regulations directly controlled the siting of TSD facilities.[535] Many states do regulate siting, however, and it is in connection with regulatory decisions on new TSD facility siting that the fiercest citizen opposition is likely to be asserted.

---

530 Section 3004(w) (1984). EPA issued interim standards, which are general, requiring cathodic corrosion protection, soil compatibility, and structural integrity, on July 15, 1985. 40 CFR Part 280 (new), 50 Fed. Reg. 28755.

531 The regulatory program, referred to by EPA as the Leaking Underground Storage Tank (LUST) program, essentially revolves around testing for tank integrity, leak detection systems, recordkeeping and reporting requirements, corrective action requirements, and financial responsibility requirements. *See* Section 9003(c). The standards are aimed at groundwater, soil, and surface water contamination. The interim provisions, contained in Section 9003(g), require new tanks to be constructed so as not to corrode or leak as a result of structural failure for the operational life; to be cathodically protected against corrosion, constructed of noncorrosive material, or clad with a noncorrosive material; and to be lined with material that is compatible with the substances to be stored. External corrosion protection may be avoided for tanks located in soils exhibiting 12000 ohm/cm or higher resistivity. Sections 9003(g)(1)(A)-(C), (2).

532 Section 9004.

533 Sections 9005 and 9006.

534 Section 9001. Exempt are farm or residential gasoline or diesel fuel tanks of less than 1100-gallon capacity, on-premises heating oil tanks, septic tanks, certain pipeline and petroleum production facilites, and tanks in cellars, tunnels, mineshafts, and the like.

535 Obviously the performance standards themselves affect siting decisions indirectly. A landfill located in a high groundwater table area will be more expensive to manage than one located where the groundwater is at great depth, for example.

By avoiding the direct licensing of sites,[536] EPA appears to have chosen the path of regulatory expediency, leaving the hard choices to the states, without guidance.

EPA's long-standing preference for engineering controls over siting regulation, which pervades virtually all of the Agency's regulatory programs, may be explainable in part by the historical dominance of engineers in its water programs, from the time of EPA's predecessor, the Federal Water Pollution Control Administration. More important today, however, may be the Agency's recognition of the fact that Congress has traditionally been reluctant to authorize federal agency intrusion into land use regulation, long recognized as a special province of state and local governments.[537]

Congress, however, did a turnabout in 1984, requiring EPA to adopt criteria for siting "new and existing" TSD facilities "as necessary to protect human health and the environment" and to publish within eighteen months "guidance criteria" identifying areas of "vulnerable hydrology."[538]

§5.07 TSD Facility Permit Requirements and Procedures

[1] Overview of the Permit Regulations

Section 3005(a) provides that, after the effective date of EPA permit regulations, the treatment, storage, or disposal of RCRA-regulated hazardous waste is prohibited. EPA's initial RCRA permit regulations were promulgated effective November 19, 1980, as a component of the Agency's "consolidated permit regulations."[539] In 1983, EPA revised its

---

[536] Sections 3004 and 3005 appear originally to have been broad enough to authorize EPA to license siting. They did not, however, compel such action.

[537] Even in the pervasively federally controlled nuclear power arena, Congress has left siting decisions almost exclusively to the states. See Stever, Seabrook and the Nuclear Regulatory Commission: The Licensing of a Nuclear Power Plant (Univ. Press of New England 1980).

[538] Section 3004(o)(7). EPA issued its initial siting guidance to permit writers on February 7, 1985, and asked for comment on the development of further guidelines. The initial guideline is titled Permit Writers' Guidance Manual for Location of Hazardous Waste Land Storage Facilities—Phase I: Criteria for Location Acceptability and Existing Applicable Regulations. See 50 Fed. Reg. 5268 (1985).

[539] 45 Fed. Reg. 33290 (5-19-80). EPA consolidated into a single regulation the permit requirements of its Clean Water Act, Clean Air Act, Safe Drinking Water Act (SDWA) Underground Injection Control, and RCRA programs (40 CFR Part 122), and similarly consolidated the permit procedures for the programs (40 CFR Part 124).

permit regulations, and reissued its RCRA permit requirements in a new provision, Part 270.[540]

General requirements for permit applications, what information must be submitted, who must sign the permit application, rules for establishing permit conditions and permit modification, and other general information are contained in Part 270. Procedural requirements, such as hearing procedures, are contained in Part 125.

[2] Who Must Have a Permit?

Owners and operators of new noninterim status TSD facilities, called "hazardous waste management" (HWM) facilities in Part 270,[541] and those interim status facilities whose Part B permit applications are due are required to hold permits during their active life, closure period, postclosure period, or longer compliance period.[542]

Excepted from this requirement are hazardous waste injection wells regulated by states with delegated underground injection control programs under the Safe Drinking Water Act, publicly owned waste water treatment works regulated under the Clean Water Act, and barges and vessels dumping in the ocean under the jurisdiction of the Marine Protection, Research and Sanctuaries Act. These entities are said to be excluded "by rule."[543] Though not required to hold RCRA permits, they are subject to some of the substantive requirements.[544]

Also excluded are PCB incinerators to the extent they burn only PCB

---

[540] The consolidated permit regulations, conceived as an effort to simplify EPA's octopuslike regulatory universe, proved to be both cumbersome and controversial. The experiment lasted three years. On April 1, 1983, EPA "deconsolidated" the permit regulations, and Part 270 of the RCRA regulations was born. 48 Fed. Reg. 14151 (4-1-83).

[541] Originally Section 3005(a) did not clearly require that new facilities have a permit before construction commences. Some other environmental permits, such as NPDES permits issued under Section 402 of the Clean Water Act, need only be acquired prior to operation. Congress amended Section 3005(a) in 1984 to require unequivocally that a permit must be acquired prior to construction. P.L. 98-616, Section 211. See 40 CFR §270.10(f) (amended 50 Fed. Reg. 28751). In 1985 EPA also developed criteria for the issuance of permits for research and demonstration facilities. 40 CFR §270.65 (1985).

[542] Facilities that closed prior to January 26, 1983 (the effective date of the closure and postclosure substantive requirements of Part 264) are not required to hold a permit after closure. 40 CFR §270.1(c). The "compliance period" is derived from EPA's groundwater protection regulation, 40 CFR §264.96, and refers to facilities required to take action as a result of the detection of groundwater contamination.

[543] 40 CFR §270.1(c)(1).

[544] See Appendix 5-G.

wastes,[545] the entities generally exempted from subtitle C regulation,[546] and entities engaged in treatment or containment activities in "immediate response" to a discharge or an imminent and substantial threat of a discharge of hazardous waste or a discharge "of a material which when discharged becomes a hazardous waste" [that is, "product"].[547] This latter exclusion terminates "after the immediate response is over."

EPA may issue a permit for classes of facilities, issue a permit for an entire facility, or issue separate permits for individual units within a facility.[548] The "unit permit" approach is employed where different units represent separate processes, or where each unit is an independently managed, self-contained entity. Where one person owns a facility that is operated by another person, both are required to sign the permit application, and the permit is issued in both names.[549]

[3] Permit Application Requirements

[a] RCRA-Based Requirements

New facilities are required to submit both a Part A application form and the information required for Part B purposes by 40 CFR §270.14 and whichever of §§270.15 or 270.21 is applicable to the facility type involved prior to beginning physical construction. No form is available for Part B information, which is provided as narrative. Interim status facilities have already submitted their Part A applications. They are required to submit an updated Part A form along with the relevant Part

---

[545] Section 3005(a), as amended by Section 211, P.L. 96-616 (11-8-84).

[546] See supra, this chapter. These are (1) generators who accumulate hazardous waste on site for less than ninety days, (2) farmers who dispose of waste pesticides from their own use in accordance with the product instructions, (3) TSD facilities that handle only waste excluded under Section 261.4 or waste produced by "small generators" pursuant to Section 261.5 (to the limited extent such exemption survived the 1984 amendments), (4) totally enclosed treatment facilities, (5) elementary neutralization units, (6) privately owned waste water treatment units that do not discharge their waste to the environment, (7) transporters storing manifested waste in containers at transfer facilities for less than ten days, and (8) entities adding absorbent material to waste in a container or adding waste to absorbent material in a container.

[547] 40 CFR §270.1(c)(3).

[548] 40 CFR §270.1(c)(4).

[549] 40 CFR §270.10(b).

B information.[550] For existing facilities, once EPA or the state requests the submission of Part B, the facility has "at least" six months to supply the necessary information.[551]

Any information for which a claim of confidentiality is wished to be asserted must be designated as such upon submission.[552] For a discussion of EPA's confidentiality requirements, see Chapter 2, *supra.*

All permit applications (and all reports required to be submitted to the permitting authority) must be signed.[553] EPA's requirements for who must sign the permit application were modified significantly in 1983 as a result of the provisions of settlement of a lawsuit challenging the consolidated permit regulations.[554] EPA originally required corporate applications to be signed by "a principal executive officer of at least the level of vice-president."[555] Partnership or sole proprietorship applications were to be signed by "a general partner or the proprietor."[556] Government entity applications were required to be signed by "either a principal executive officer or ranking elected official."[557]

EPA's primary reasons for requiring the corporate signatory to be a "principal executive officer" were to impress upon corporate management the significance of the permits, and to prevent the scapegoating of low-level corporate officials in the event an application contained false or misleading statements, giving rise to criminal responsibility under Section 3008(d)(3).[558]

Most opposition to the corporate signatory requirement came from large corporations, which argued that their vice presidents were too busy to become sufficiently familiar with the contents of a permit application to make a meaningful judgment sufficient to justify the certification of accuracy required by what is now Section 270.11(d).

Ultimately, the corporations were able to convince EPA to modify the requirement to allow such people as large facility managers, envi-

---

550 40 CFR §§270.10(g), 270.72.

551 40 CFR §270.10(e)(4). *See generally* revisions to 40 CFR §270.10 made at 50 Fed. Reg. 28751 (7-15-85), incorporating requirements of 1984 amendments.

552 40 CFR §270.12. *See* 40 CFR Part 2.

553 40 CFR §§270.11(a)-(b).

554 48 Fed. Reg. 39619 (9-1-83), implementing settlement of NRDC, et al. v. Gorsuch, Nos. 80 et seq. (D.C. Cir.).

555 45 Fed. Reg. 33425 (5-19-80), former 40 CFR §122.6(a)(1).

556 *Id.*, former 40 CFR §122.6(a)(2). This requirement was not changed by the NRDC settlement.

557 *Id.*, former 40 CFR §122.6(a)(3).

558 EPA was at the time also thinking of its other permit programs.

ronment vice-presidents, and subsidiary vice-presidents to sign permit applications.[559] At the same time, EPA gratuitously amended the governmental signatory requirement to allow "senior executive" federal officers "having responsibility for the overall operations of a principal geographic unit of the agency" to sign.[560] EPA does not define the term "principal geographic unit" other than by example, listing its own Regional Administrators. For agencies broken down into regions (such as the General Services Administration or the Army Corps of Engineers), this provision poses no ambiguity. But the military branches of the Defense Department, which are large disposers of hazardous waste, are not so neatly organized. Logic would dictate that a base commander would be the appropriate signatory. The services however, have layers of command that are often premised on geographic regions (for example, Atlantic Fleet), within which there are a number of individual bases.

All regulated entities are permitted to delegate signature authority on reports to officials such as plant managers.[561]

[b] Requirements of Other Laws

While not specifically required by EPA's Part B information requirements, applicants must (or at least should, in their own interests) provide information in the application relevant to the five federal statutes that EPA must consider in connection with its licensing activities.

Section 7 of the Wild and Scenic Rivers Act[562] prohibits the issuance of a permit "that would have a direct, adverse effect on the values for which a national wild and scenic river was established."

---

[559] Corporate applications must be signed by a "responsible corporate officer," which includes "president, secretary, treasurer, or vice-president of the corporation in charge of a principal business function, or any other person who performs similar policy or decisionmaking function," or "the manager of one or more manufacturing, production or operating facilities employing more than 250 persons or having gross annual sales or expenditures exceeding $25 million (in second quarter 1980 dollars), if authority to sign documents has been delegated." 40 CFR §270.11(a)(1). The signatory does not need to prove delegation; EPA presumes it. See Note following 40 CFR §261.11(a)(1).

[560] 40 CFR §270.11(a)(3).

[561] 40 CFR §270.11(b).

[562] 16 USC §1273 et seq. This statute is administered by the U.S. Department of the Interior. A list of designated rivers, and other regulations is published in Volume 16, CFR. State issued permits may be further affected by state-designated scenic rivers that are not part of the federal program.

Section 7 of the Endangered Species Act[563] requires a federal permitting agency to "consult" with the Secretaries of Interior and Commerce with respect to any action that might jeopardize the continued existence of any endangered or threatened species of animal or plant, or adversely affect its critical habitat. EPA must act in a manner that will ensure that the adverse effect will not occur.[564]

Section 106 of the National Historic Preservation Act[565] requires EPA to adopt, when feasible, measures to mitigate potential adverse effects of a licensed activity on properties listed or eligible for listing in the National Register of Historic Places.

The above three statutes require, at a minimum, that a careful site environs inventory be made to demonstrate the absence of any of the conditions protected by them. In most cases that is all the owner/operator will have to do. If a protected condition is identified, then, depending upon which statute is implicated, either absence of impact or sufficient mitigation of impact will have to be demonstrated.

The Fish and Wildlife Coordination Act[566] may be implicated by facilities that impound, divert, control, or modify any body of water.[567] The statute requires consultation by the federal permit issuer with the state wildlife agency (usually the state fish and game agency or the state environmental protection or natural resources agency and, in certain circumstances, the U.S. Fish and Wildlife Service or the National Marine Fisheries Service). The consultation is intended to result in conservation of fish and wildlife resources, and usually is satisfied by the permit applicant's offer to undertake mitigation measures or to provide

---

[563] 16 USC §1531 *et. seq.* Regulations published at 50 CFR Part 402.

[564] In TVA v. Hill, 437 U.S. 153 (1978), the Supreme Court held that the prohibition contained in this statute is absolute. Once a project's potential threat to a listed endangered or threatened species is identified, the project may not go forward. Some states have state endangered-species programs.

[565] 16 USC §470 *et seq.* Regulations published at 36 CFR Part 800. Normally either the state Historic Preservation Officer, the Advisory Council on Historic Preservation, or both, will become involved in the decisionmaking process. *See generally* Robinson, Environmental Regulation of Real Property (Law Journal-Seminars Press).

[566] 16 USC §§661 *et seq.*

[567] Activities that involve placing fill in wetlands and other water bodies, whether navigable or not, require a separate permit either from the Department of Army, Corps of Engineers, under Section 404 of the Clean Water Act, 33 USC §1344, and Corps Regulations (33 CFR §320 *et seq.*), a state wetland protection authority under state law, or both. Activities that involve dredging, filling, or altering traditionally "navigable" waters require authorization by the Secretary of the Army under Section 9 or Section 10 of the Rivers and Harbors Act of 1899, 33 USC §§403, 404.

replacement habitat for that consumer by the facility.

The statute that will affect more facilities than any of the foregoing is the Coastal Zone Management Act.[568] Section 307(c) of this statute prohibits EPA, as a federal licensing entity (state analogs contain identical prohibitions on state licensing entities), from issuing a permit for an activity affecting land or water use in the "coastal zone" of a state, as established under state law, until the applicant certifies that the activity complies with the applicable State Coastal Zone Management Program, and the state concurs in the certification.[569] In a number of states the coastal zone extends quite far inland, and the restrictions on industrial activities in the coastal zone are severe.

One significant environmental statute that EPA believes is not applicable to its RCRA permitting activities is the National Environmental Policy Act of 1969 (NEPA).[570] This statute normally applies to federal licensing agencies, requiring an environmental impact statement (EIS) to be produced for all major federal actions significantly affecting the human environment. EPA's RCRA permit regulations do not require compliance with NEPA, because EPA contends that its environmental protective mission makes its normal permit review process the "functional equivalent" of a NEPA review and that it therefore is exempt from compliance with the statute.

EPA's position has been accepted by courts dealing with some of its other regulatory programs, and is supported by a certain logic, but it should be noted that Congress has in the past seen fit specifically to exempt some EPA activities from NEPA[571] and that EPA is specifically required to produce an EIS prior to issuing a permit for a new source of water pollution.[572] RCRA is silent on NEPA, and the absence of an express NEPA exemption in RCRA does not help EPA's position. Moreover, at least one other federal licensing agency acting under an environmental protection mandate, the Corps of Engineers, complies with NEPA.[573]

---

[568] 16 USC §§1451 et seq. Department of Commerce regulations published at 15 CFR Part 930.

[569] The Secretary of Commerce has the power to override a state nonconcurrence, but in all but the most compelling cases of national interest will not do so.

[570] 42 USC §§4321 et seq.

[571] See Section 504, Clean Water Act, 33 USC §1354.

[572] Id.

[573] The Corps' Section 404 activities admittedly arise under the Clean Water Act, 33

Once EPA has delegated RCRA permitting to a state, the NEPA issue becomes moot, since NEPA does not apply to state licensing activities. A number of states have state laws patterned on NEPA that clearly apply to state environmental licensing activities,[574] however, and in some of these states an additional permit-related requirement of producing an EIS will be imposed on the applicant.

[c] Information Requirements

In addition to the basic regulatory information requirements imposed by EPA, Section 3019, added by P.L. 98-616, requires that all Part Bs contain information "reasonably ascertainable" by the owner/operator on the potential for public exposure, including foreseeable releases from normal operation, accidents, and transportation spills, the potential pathways for human exposure, and the potential magnitude of human exposure.[575]

EPA also must inquire about the history of the site's use and its releases as part of its duties under Section 3004(u).

[4] Procedures Governing the Issuance, Modification, and Revocation of RCRA Permits

[a] Issuance, Modification,[576] and Revocation Followed by Reissuance

Once EPA's regional permits branch personnel[577] have determined that the Part A and Part B are complete and have made a preliminary

---

USC §1344, but they are arguably not covered by the express inclusionary language of Section 504. In any event, the Corps also complies with NEPA in issuing Rivers and Harbors Act permits.

[574] California, New York, and a number of other states have such laws.

[575] Already permitted facilities must submit the information as well. EPA, or the state, as the case may be, must send the information to the Agency of Toxic Substances Disease Registry, set up under Section 104(i) of CERCLA, and may request the agency to do a "health assessment" if EPA or the state feels the initial information evidences a "substantial potential risk to human health." The agency is to do such an assessment if "funds are provided." The statute specifies the topics of health assessments, which fall short of full-scale epidemiological and medical evaluations, and provides that if exposure is found, the costs of the assessment are recoverable under Section 107 of CERCLA.

[576] Minor, ministerial permit modifications do not require compliance with permitting procedures. *See* 40 CFR §270.42.

[577] In approved states, the state hazardous waste permitting official.

determination that a permit should be issued,[578] a draft permit[579] along with a statement of basis for issuing the permit[580] and, for large facilities, a "fact sheet"[581] are prepared. The formal administrative record is established, and public notice establishing a written comment period is issued.[582] Interested persons are required to raise all matters they wish to contest during the comment period, including requests for a hearing.[583]

EPA takes the position that, since Section 3005 says nothing about a hearing, it is not required to provide a hearing prior to issuing a RCRA permit.[584] Nevertheless, EPA's permit regulations authorize the permit issuer to hold a "public hearing" when someone requests one and on the basis of the request or requests, it appears that there is a "significant degree of public interest" in the matter.[585] The permit issuer may also elect, on his or her own motion, to hold a public hearing to "clarify one or more issues involved in the permit decision."[586]

Ordinarily RCRA hearings will be informal, legislative-type hearings. The permit issuer has discretion, however, to provide a hybrid "nonadversary panel hearing,[587] at which an opportunity for very limited cross-examination of witnesses may be allowed.[588] Such a hearing may be requested by any participant for new facilities, but EPA allows only the permit applicant to request a hybrid hearing for interim status facilities, modified permit proceedings, or renewed permits.[589]

Following the closing of the comment period, or a closing of any hearing, the permit issuer is required to make the final permit decision

---

[578] EPA left itself very little substantive latitude for denying RCRA permits.

[579] 40 CFR §124.6.

[580] 40 CFR §124.7.

[581] 40 CFR §124.8. The purpose of the fact sheet is to provide a more detailed explanation of the facts and analysis supporting the permit issuance than is provided in the statement of basis. The document is intended to inform the public.

[582] 40 CFR §124.10. Notice in the Federal Register is limited to "major" facility permits.

[583] 40 CFR §§124.11, 124.13.

[584] See 45 Fed. Reg. 33409-33411.

[585] 40 CFR §124.12(a).

[586] Id.

[587] 40 CFR §124.12(e).

[588] Nonadversarial panel procedures are set forth at 40 CFR §§124.111 et seq.

[589] 40 CFR §124.12(e). See 49 Fed. Reg. 17718. There may be some cases in which, because of a close linkage between RCRA permit conditions and NPDES permit conditions, the RCRA issues will be consolidated into the fully evidentiary hearings held on the NPDES permit that are required upon request. See 40 CFR §124.71(b).

and provide notice of the decision, along with a response to comments submitted,[590] to interested parties.[591]

Appeal of the permit issuer's decision, where EPA is the decision-maker,[592] is to the Administrator, and the appeal must be perfected within thirty days of issuance of the final permit decision.[593] Appeals to the Administrator are based on the administrative record, and are decided on the record and briefs submitted by the parties. Contested permit conditions are stayed during the pendency of an administrative appeal, and new facilities are without a permit until the appeal is concluded.[594]

Judicial review may not be sought unless the contesting party has first exhausted an appeal to the Administrator.[595] Only issues raised during the comment period or during a public hearing may be the subject of an appeal,[596] although it is not required that the issues have been raised by the commenter.[597]

Permits normally become effective, unless stayed by judicial action, thirty days following issuance of the permit decision.[598]

[b]   Suspension and Revocation

EPA affords the permit holder an opportunity for a full evidentiary hearing prior to "termination" of a RCRA permit and prior to "termination of interim status for failure to furnish information needed to make a final decision."[599] This is premised on EPA's interpretation of Sections 3008(b) and (c), which make "suspension or revocation" of a permit part of an "order," which must be preceded by a "public hearing," if one is requested by the persons named in the order. The federal Administrative Procedure Act requires that formal, evidentiary hearings precede issuance of an "order."[600]

---

590 40 CFR §§124.15.

591 The regulations do not provide for publication of the final decision.

592 State programs are not required to provide for administrative appeals. Some do.

593 Appeals are governed strictly by 40 CFR §124.19.

594 40 CFR §124.16(a). Interim status facilities seeking a permit remain in interim status as to conditions on appeal.

595 40 CFR §124.19(e).

596 40 CFR §124.19(a).

597 Id.

598 40 CFR §124.15.

599 40 CFR §124.71.

600 5 USC §§551(6), 554, 556. See discussions at 43 Fed. Reg. 34730 (8-4-78); and 45

In affording unsuccessful interim status Part B submitters opportunity for a public hearing, EPA appears to have gone well beyond the statutory mandate, and, indeed, contradicted its own regulatory position that interim status is not a permit. It is also curious that EPA affords an opportunity for an evidentiary hearing prior to denial of a permit for an existing facility while denying the opportunity to a new facility applicant. Evidentiary proceedings can be lengthy, and by invoking this right an interim status TSD might extend its interim status life for several years.

Congress attempted to deal with this problem in the 1984 amendments by amending Section 3005(e) so that interim status is terminated for a land disposal facility unless the facility has applied for a final permit determination within twelve months of November 8, 1984, and has certified compliance with the applicable groundwater and financial responsibility requirements,[601] and requiring EPA action within a specified number of years.[602]

Detailed procedures for EPA evidentiary hearings and administrative appeals from evidentiary hearings are set forth in subpart E of Part 124.[603] They provide for trial-type hearings, and are straightforward. EPA also has published rules of practice, which govern its evidentiary proceedings.[604]

[5] Permit Contents

The RCRA permit is the device for enforcement of the RCRA standards on TSD facilities. RCRA permits contain a series of general, boilerplate conditions inserted verbatim in all permits;[605] monitoring,

---

Fed. Reg. 33410 (5-19-80). EPA's position was initially premised upon the pre-1980 version of Section 3008(b), which did not clearly embrace "suspension or revocation of a permit" within the term "order." In 1980, Congress amended Sections 3008(b) and (c) to clearly legitimize EPA's earlier administrative interpretation.

[601] P.L. 98-616, Section 213(a) (inserting Section 3005(e)(2)).

[602] *See* Section 3005(c)(2) (1984).

[603] 40 CFR §§124.71-124.91. Certain of those procedures, which relate to procedures for granting or denying discretionary requests for evidentiary hearings in connection with other EPA programs, are inapplicable to the RCRA permits.

[604] 40 CFR Part 20.

[605] 40 CFR §270.30.

recording, and reporting requirements;[606] conditions required by Part 264[607] or RCRA, which take effect prior to permit issuance;[608] and such enforcement-related conditions as the permit duration,[609] compliance schedules for corrective action,[610] and any special requirements imposed as a result of the impact of other federal or state law.[611]

[6] Permit Duration, Transfer, and Effect

[a] Duration

EPA's original permit regulations provided for a ten-year term. As part of its settlement of litigation challenging the regulations, EPA agreed in 1984 that it had no authority to limit the term of RCRA permits, and revised its regulations to provide that the permit licensed the facility for its lifetime. Congress reversed this in the 1984 amendments, inserting Section 3005(c)(3), which establishes a fixed term "not to exceed 10 years" for land disposal facilities, storage facilities, incinerators "or other treatment facility."

The 1984 provision also requires mandatory review of land disposal facility permits every five years, at which time EPA is required to modify the permit to insert currently applicable Section 3004 requirements.[612]

Although issued for periods of ten years, EPA may modify, revoke, or reissue a permit prior to its expiration date "for cause."[613]

[b] Modification[614]

The "causes" for modification are (1) material and substantial alterations to the facility not contemplated by the permit; (2) receipt by EPA or the state of information not available at the time of permit issuance

---

606 40 CFR §270.31.

607 State-issued permits include state regulatory conditions.

608 40 CFR §§270.32(b), 270.32(c).

609 40 CFR §270.50. RCRA permits are normally issued for ten years.

610 40 CFR §§270.33(a) and (b).

611 40 CFR §§270.32(a), 270.3; see Section 5.07[3][b], supra.

612 See generally P.L.98-616, Section 212, and H.R. Rep. No. 98-1133, 98th Cong., 2d Sess. at 94-95; and 40 CFR §270.50(d) (7-15-85).

613 70 CFR §270.41(b).

614 The EPA regulations discussed below predate the 1984 amendments, which Amended Section 3005, clearly giving EPA authority to reopen permits to insert new regulatory requirements. Nothing in Section 3005(c)(3), however, requires the Agency to amend the preexisting reopening criteria, except as noted below.

that would have justified the imposition of different permit conditions; (3) for modification of a compliance schedule, circumstances over which the permittee had little or not control; (4) to insert adjustments into the permit relative to the closure and postclosure, financial responsibility, and groundwater protection programs of Part 264, to add units to permit coverage or add conditions to cover added units, and to remedy an unsuccessful land treatment unit;[615] and (5) to effectuate transfer of the facility to a new owner or operator where the transfer is not deemed sufficiently innocuous to constitute a "minor modification."[616]

EPA also allows a pretermination permit modification if "the standards or regulations on which the permit was based have been changed by promulgation of amended standards or regulations or by judicial decision after the permit was issued." EPA initially allowed such modifications only upon "request by the permittee" within ninety days of the regulatory change.[617] This effectively ensured that only backsliding changes would occur, since it is unlikely that a permittee would request EPA to insert a new requirement based on a more stringent standard. This provision appears to have been vitiated, at least partly, by Section 3005(c)(3).[618]

EPA may either modify the permit or choose to terminate and reissue the permit in two instances: (1) where cause to terminate exists but, in its exercise of enforcement discretion, EPA decides to allow the facility to continue to operate, but on new conditions,[619] and (2) to effect permit transfer.[620]

A curious provision of the regulations stipulates that suitability of a facility's location will not be considered at the time of modification or termination/reissuance "unless new information or standards indicate

---

[615] 40 CFR §§270.41(a)(1), (2), (4), and (5). Minor modifications to make certain "corrections or allowances for changes in permitted activity," such as to correct typographical errors, change interim compliance schedules, permit noncontroversial changes in ownership, etc., may be made without formal proceedings. 40 CFR §270.42.

[616] 40 CFR §270.40 (1984).

[617] 40 CFR §270.41(a)(3) (1984).

[618] The amendment states: ". . . Nothing in this subsection shall preclude the Administrator from reviewing and modifying a permit at any time." For land disposal, storage facilities, incinerators, and other treatment facilities, the mandatory five-year upgrading overrules the regulation. Otherwise, it appears that EPA is required to consider inserting more stringent requirements at renewal.

[619] 40 CFR §§270.41(a)(3)(i)(C) (EPA actions) and 270.41(a)(3)(ii) (judicial actions).

[620] 40 CFR §270.41(b). In neither modification nor termination/reissuance are evidentiary hearing procedures available. *See* Section 5.07[4][a], *supra.*

that a threat to human health or the environment exists which was unknown at the time of permit issuance."[621] This provision predates the Part 264 regulations, and thus appears to have anticipated a greater EPA role in site selection than the initial Part 264 regulations permitted. Congress's amendment of RCRA in 1984 to require a more active EPA role in siting, and to require siting considerations in permitting existing facilities, makes this provision meaningful.

[c] Termination

A permit may be terminated (or renewal denied) (1) for noncompliance with any condition of the permit; (2) for failure to disclose in the permit application or during the permit issuance process "fully all relevant facts," or misrepresentation of relevant facts "at any time" (including in reports made to EPA or in response to enforcement inquiring); or (3) on the basis of a determination that the activity "endangers human health or the environment" and can only be regulated to acceptable levels by permit modification or termination.[622]

[d] Expiration and Reissuance

Ten years is the maximum period of life for a RCRA permit, and this term may not be extended by modification.[623] The permit does, however, continue in force during new permit proceedings by action of 5 USC §558(c), provided a complete new application has been submitted at least six months prior to the expiration date and EPA's failure to issue the new permit prior to expiration was not the fault of the applicant.[624] An EPA-issued permit will, on like terms, remain in effect while an authorized state agency processes the new permit.[625]

---

621 40 CFR §270.41(c); *see* 45 Fed. Reg. 33316.

622 40 CFR §270.43. Permittees have a right to an evidentiary hearing prior to premature termination. *See* Section 5.07[4][b], *supra.*

623 40 CFR §270.50. New owners or operators who assume ownership or operation of a facility prior to the expiration of its term, and who desire a full ten years' permit protection, will request EPA to follow the revocation-reissuance procedure provided by §270.41(b)(2).

624 *See* 40 CFR §270.51(a).

625 40 CFR §270.51(d).

Refusal of a new permit may be predicated upon noncompliance with conditions of the prior permit.[626]

[e] Effect

Possession of a RCRA permit is *prima facie* evidence of compliance with the RCRA regulations, or delegee state regulations, as the case may be. The permit does not, however, convey a property right or exclusive privilege, and is not preemptive of state or local nuisance, zoning, environment, and similar laws or regulations.[627]

EPA asserts that possession of a RCRA permit is not a defense to an "imminent hazard" abatement action brought under Section 7003 of RCRA, or to actions for abatement or cost recovery brought under Section 106 or 107 of CERCLA. If a facility can demonstrate that it operated at all times in strict compliance with the requirements of its RCRA permit, and still created a condition of imminent hazard, that fact would doubtless weigh heavily on the degree of relief awarded the government were it to bring such an action.

[7] Permits by Rule, Emergency Permits, and Underground Injection Control (UIC) Well Permits

Ocean disposers, publicly owned treatment works, and state-regulated hazardous waste injection wells are not required to apply for and hold a separate RCRA permit. These facilities are simply required to comply with their own permits and meet a list of specified Part 264 requirements.[628] They are said to have permits "by rule." Regular Part 270 permits are issued for UIC wells in states that do not possess UIC authority under the Safe Drinking Water Act, but such permits terminate automatically on state UIC program approval.[629]

Unpermitted TSD facilities and permitted facilities not licensed to take certain wastes may be authorized to accept wastes for which they do not have a permit on a "temporary emergency" basis when acting

---

[626] 40 CFR §270.51(c).

[627] *See* 40 CFR §270.4.

[628] 40 CFR §270.60.

[629] 40 CFR §270.64. For UIC permits issued after November 8, 1984, the facility is required to comply with 40 CFR §264.101.

in response to an "imminent and substantial endangerment" to human health or the environment.[630]

[8] Incinerators and Land Treatment Facilities

Both incinerators and land treatment facilities are governed by a special set of permit requirements, which essentially provide, in the case of incinerators, for trial burns and other air pollution–related preoperational testing and monitoring[631] and, for land treatment facilities, field testing requirements.[632]

[9] Surface Impoundments

Among the many significant changes in RCRA produced by P.L. 98-616 (1984) is an elaborate set of specific requirements for surface impoundments, which are designed to dovetail with the double liner and leachate collection standards imposed by Section 3004(o).[633] Interim status for surface impoundments not complying with the double liner and monitoring requirements of Section 3004(o) is terminated, subject to limited exceptions,[634] on November 8, 1988. EPA is prohibited from imposing *more* stringent liner requirements than the statutory Section 3004(o) requirements unless leakage is demonstrated, and must require decontamination of clay liners as a condition of closure.

Similarly, impoundments containing wastes that are found to be incompatible with land disposal must meet the new facility liner requirements, unless exempt because of distance from groundwater or other circumstances that make migration to groundwater impossible.

Finally, the corrective action, groundwater-monitoring, and un-

---

630 40 CFR §270.61. Such permits may last for ninety days and may be issued without following the Part 124 procedures.

631 *See* 40 CFR §270.62.

632 40 CFR §270.63.

633 Sections 3005(j) and (i). *See* H.R. Rep. No. 98-1133, 98th Cong., 2d Sess., at 96.

634 Exempt from the requirement are single-lined impoundments shown not to be leaking, specified wastewater treatment impoundments (facilities waived by EPA on the basis of a showing of no possible migration to groundwater that have made application for waiver within two years of November 8, 1984), and, finally, impoundments EPA waives because they hold only mining waste, certain flue gas and other fossil fuel–related wastes, cement kiln dust, and certain ore and mineral production wastes, if EPA has begun to regulate those wastes. Section 3005(j)(3). The statute also establishes criteria for loss of exempt status. *See* Section 3005(j)(5). Impoundments receiving waste pursuant to a consent decree may enjoy modified requirements, provided they are equivalent to the Section 3004(o) requirements.

saturated zone–monitoring requirements of Section 3004(c) are applicable to surface impoundments that received waste after July 26, 1982.

[10] Research and Development Activities

Section 3005(g), added by the 1984 amendments, allows EPA to issue permits for experimental facilities prior to the development of substantive standards covering such facilities or classes of facilities. The permits are for one year, and are renewable three times. EPA is allowed to expedite issuance or renewal by not strictly complying with its general permit process requirements, except for those relating to public participation and insurance. The Agency's regulations are published at 40 CFR §270.65 (7-15-85).

[11] Permit Deadlines, Interim Status Termination, and Permit Denials

In 1984 Congress imposed deadlines on EPA and the TSD industry that were intended to speed up the lagging permit program. Interim status for land disposal facilities holding that status on November 8, 1984, terminated twelve months later unless the owner/operator had submitted a completed Part B and had certified compliance with the applicable groundwater-monitoring and financial responsibility requirements. Land disposal facilities that gain interim status subsequent to the 1984 date[635] have twelve months from the date they became interim status facilities to file the Part B and certification.

EPA is required to complete its permitting for land disposal facilities possessing interim status prior to November 8, 1984, within four years of that date, and there is language in the conference report indicating that EPA should place highest priority on facilities with a history of groundwater contamination.[636] Permitting of incinerators must be completed within five years, and all other permitting within eight years.

Incinerator and TSDs other than land disposal facilities lose interim status at the expiration of the four- and eight-year permitting deadlines,

---

[635] A previously unregulated facility might become an interim status facility if, for example, the waste it disposed of was listed by EPA as a hazardous waste for the first time, and it had previously not disposed of any listed waste. *See* Sections 3005(e)(2) and 3005(e)(3); *also see* Section 3005(e)(1)(A)(ii).

[636] *See* H.R. Rep. No. 98-1133, 98th Cong., 2d Sess., at 95. *And see* EPA's regulation, 40 CFR §270.73.

unless they had filed their Part Bs by November 8, 1986, and November 8, 1988, respectively.[637]

Finally, an ambiguity in the prior law was eliminated when Section 3005(e) was amended in 1984 to state clearly that a facility that has been denied a permit, or whose authority to operate has been terminated otherwise, no longer has interim status.

5.08   State Program Delegation

[1]   Delegation

Like many other government regulatory programs, RCRA permit and enforcement authority is delegable to qualifying states. Section 3006 establishes the delegation parameters, which, unlike those found in some other statutes, most notably the Clean Water Act, are quite general. Delegation is in two steps: interim authorization[638] and final authorization.[639]

States with existing hazardous waste management programs as of ninty days following promulgation of all subtitle C regulations could be granted interim authorization if their programs were deemed "substantially equivalent" on EPA's. Interim authorization was initially to last only two years thereafter, and, calculating from the point EPA met its own rulemaking obligation, all interim authorizations were to have expired on January 31, 1985. Congress extended that deadline until January 31, 1986 in order to accomodate changes required by the 1984 amendments.[640]

Final authorization must be based on "guidelines" issued by EPA.[641] The delegation standards for final authorization inexplicably differ from those for interim authorization. Authorization may be denied if the state's program is "not equivalent" to EPA's,[642] is "not consistent"[643] with the federal or other state programs, or does not provide "adequate enforcement."[644]

---

[637] Section 3005(c)(2).
[638] Section 3006(c).
[639] Section 3006(b).
[640] P.L. 98-616, Section 227.
[641] Section 3006(a). EPA's guidelines are published at 40 CFR Part 271.
[642] Section 3006(b)(1).
[643] Section 3006(b)(2).
[644] Section 3006(b)(3).

The statute accordingly gives EPA a degree of latitude in determining by regulation what sorts of state programs are acceptable. Many issues can be raised in connection with delegation decisions, both by states and by interested members of the public. For example, since "equivalent" does not mean "identical," is EPA within its authority if it requires the states to adopt its penalty policy, clearly an extrastatutory provision?

The delegation provisions were modified by the 1984 amendments. Essentially, Congress made a number of its new substantive requirements immediately effective as to regulated entities regardless of the status of federal delegation in the state wherein the entity resides. In such a case, the state must seek interim authorization to administer the new requirements, and EPA issues or modifies permits until the state's program has been modified to conform to the new requirements.[645]

EPA may withdraw authorization after a public hearing upon determining that the state is not administering and enforcing its program in accordance with the Section 3006 requirements, after a period for correction.[646] EPA's regulations retain a right to veto state permit conditions by inserting federal conditions. No such authority appears in Section 3005 or Section 3006.

State program requirements for the fifty states are listed in Appendix 5-L, *infra.*

[2] **Local Action Affecting Hazardous Waste Disposal**

Increasing numbers of municipalities have begun to attempt to address the problem of hazardous waste disposal on their own. Section 3009 of RCRA clearly authorizes state programs that are more stringent than the federal program, but, except for the general savings clause contained in that section, the statute does not address local programs.

Municipalities have frequently grounded local regulatory programs, as well as outright prohibition of the disposal of hazardous waste within their borders, on public nuisance. The usual attack on such ordinances

---

[645] Sections 3006(b), (c), (f), and (g) (1984). EPA revised its Part 271 regulations to bring them into compliance with Section 3006 on July 15, 1985. *See* 50 Fed. Reg. 28753. For the Agency's explanation of its approach to implementing delegation under the 1984 amendments, *see* 50 Fed. Reg. 496 and 50 Fed. Reg. 24362.

[646] Section 3006(e).

is that they are inconsistent with either the state or federal programs and are accordingly preempted. These attacks have almost uniformly been rejected as a matter of federal preemption,[646.1] and several courts have found local bans to be preempted by state law.[646.2]

§5.09 Enforcement

[1] Overview

Early RCRA enforcement efforts began in 1979, with a few actions brought under the imminent hazard provision, Section 7003.[647] RCRA enforcement continued to be dominated by Section 7003 actions until EPA got its regulatory program in place in 1983, and began to issue permits. Even then, regulatory enforcement was slow to develop. Section 7003 became of less significance following the passage of CERCLA[648] in 1980, after which Sections 106 and 107 of that statute became the primary tools used by the government to address hazards emanating from abandoned TSD facility sites, and major hazardous waste release to the environment.

The enforcement provisions of RCRA include Sections 3007 and 3013, which are intended to provide EPA with information about regulated entities that has not been provided voluntarily; Section 3008, which sets forth the basic administrative and judicial remedies available to the government; Section 7002, the citizen suit provision; and Section 7003, which authorizes the government to bring lawsuits to abate imminent and substantial endangerments to health or the environment.

Unless Congress eliminates CERCLA, it is likely that, over time, Section 7003 will develop as a backup remedy for the RCRA regulatory program, similar to Section 505 of the Clean Water Act,[649] on which it is based. With CERCLA providing the primary means of addressing

---

646.1 *See* Sharon Steel Corp. v. City of Fairmont, 334 S.E.2d 616 (W.Va. Sup. Ct. App. 1985); Neal v. Darby, 318 S.E.2d 18 (S.C. App. 1984); EDF v. Lamphier, 714 F.2d 331 (4th Cir. 1983); State v. Schenectady Chemicals, Inc., 103 A.2d 33, 479 N.Y.S.2d 867 (1984); State v. Monarch Chemicals, Inc., 90 A.2d 907, 456 N.Y.S.2d 867 (1982). *Contra*, Rollins Environmental Services of Louisiana, Inc. v. Iberville Parish Policy Jury, 371 So.2d 1127 (La. 1979).

646.2 *See, e.g.*, Stablex Corp. v. Town of Hooksett, 122 N.H. 1091, 456 A.2d 94 (N.H. 1982); *compare* Sharon Steel Corp. v. City of Fairmont, 334 S.E.2d 616 (W.Va. 1985).

647 The Section 7003 cases are discussed in Chapter 6, *infra*.

648 42 USC §§9601 *et seq*.

649 33 USC §1364.

hazards stemming from pre-RCRA dumps, Section 7003 logically should be utilized solely to deal with hazards caused by regulated facilities that cannot wait for ordinary remedial measures.

RCRA's criminal provisions are potentially its most significant enforcement aspect. It is unique to federal environmental laws in having penalties that fall into the felony category. Its knowing endangerment provision[650] is complex and confusing, and, if utilized by the government to any degree, will generate interesting case law.

EPA's enforcement efforts under the more mature Clean Air Act and Clean Water Act programs have been plagued by lack of clearly defined enforcement policies and priorities. The Agency has been unable or unwilling to "target" enforcement rationally, or to differentiate consistently between serious and nonserious violators in its case referrals to the Department of Justice. As EPA develops its RCRA enforcement program, these traditional failures in its other programs will undoubtedly emerge as issues to be reckoned with.

[2] Information Gathering

Government regulatory agencies need information about their regulatory targets, both to establish standards and permit conditions and to marshal sufficient factual information to determine whether established requirements are being violated or whether a regulated entity's activities are endangering the public. There are generally five means by which a government agency gains information: (1) voluntary submission by regulated entities, (2) response to a formal demand for information where failure to respond is a statutory violation, (3) permissive entry onto a regulated entity's property, (4) forced entry under a search warrant, and (5) external surveillance.

Under RCRA, voluntary information is produced by self-monitoring and other reporting requirements established under Part 264 and in TSD facility permits, and through manifest system reporting requirements imposed on generators and transporters. In theory, if the regulated entities adhere faithfully to those reporting requirements, and freely provide EPA with access to their records, the enforcement-related information-gathering tools provided in Sections 3007 and 3013 become unnecessary.

Although EPA possesses formal information enforcement authority

---

[650] Section 3008(e).

under most of its older statutes, the Agency has not used such authority widely in the past, and when it has attempted to use the authority it has often not used it well or effectively.[651]

[a] Enforceable Demands for Information, Site Access, and Records Access

Section 3007(a)[652] is the primary information enforcement tool provided by RCRA. It provides the authority for EPA to (1) make formal, written demands for information relating to a regulated entity's hazardous waste activity, (2) gain access to and copy records, and (3) enter sites for inspection and sampling purposes. Although broad in its grant of authority, the statute's language does contain limiting language that could be the subject of dispute between enforcement targets and EPA.

[i] What Use Can Be Made of Section 3007 Information?

Section 3007 may be used only for the purpose of developing regulations or enforcing "the provisions of this title." EPA's initial hazardous waste enforcement efforts have centered on imminent hazardous waste TSD sites, and EPA's approach to these sites has been to utilize all of

---

651 *See, e.g.,* Bradley Pieper v. EPA, 606 F.2d 1131 (8th Cir. 1979).

652 Section 3007(a) reads as follows:

Sec. 3007(a) Access Entry. For purposes of developing or assisting in the development of any regulation or enforcing the provisions of this chapter, any person who generates, stores, treats, transports, disposes of, or otherwise handles or has handled hazardous wastes shall, upon request of any officer, employee or representative of the Environmental Protection Agency, duly designated by the Administrator, or upon request of any duly designated officer, employee or representative of a State having an authorized hazardous waste program, furnish information relating to such wastes and permit such person at all reasonable times to have access to, and to copy all records relating to such wastes. For the purposes of developing or assisting in the development of any regulation or enforcing the provisions of this chapter, such officers, employees or representatives are authorized—

(1) to enter at reasonable times any establishment or other place where hazardous wastes are or have been generated, stored, treated, disposed of, or transported from;

(2) to inspect and obtain samples from any person of any such wastes and samples of any containers or labeling for such wastes. Each such inspection shall be commenced and completed with reasonable promptness. If the officer, employee or representative obtains any samples, prior to leaving the premises, he shall give to the owner, operator, or agent in charge a receipt describing the sample obtained and if requested a portion of each such sample equal in volume or weight to the portion retained. If any analysis is made of such samples, a copy of the results of such analysis shall be furnished promptly to the owner, operator or agent in charge.

its available statutory reminders in combination, most frequently combining Section 3007 of RCRA, Section 104, 106, or 107 of CERCLA, and Section 504 of the Clean Water Act in a single site-related enforcement action.

CERCLA's information-gathering authority is not as broad as and less readily enforceable than Section 3007; consequently, EPA has tended to use Section 3007 to gain information from past and present site owners, generators, or transporters that may ultimately be used primarily to support a CERCLA-based cleanup and cost recovery action. While such a use of Section 3007 may be justified as incidental, so long as Section 7003 of RCRA covers the same subject matter, there may be cases in which either the subject matter or information targets are subject only to CERCLA jurisdiction.[653] In such a case, EPA's use of Section 3007 to gain information would arguably be inappropriate.

The use of Section 3007 information to support a criminal prosecution is, despite the breadth of the first clause of the section, circumscribed by Fourth, Fifth, and Sixth Amendment constitutional restrictions. At the point an enforcement investigation becomes a criminal enforcement investigation, Section 3007 becomes largely moot, except where EPA is pursuing parallel civil proceedings, which it must do with the utmost of care.

[ii] To Whom Does Section 3007 Apply?

In addition to the RCRA-regulated active entities,[654] Section 3007 demands may be addressed to any person who "has handled" hazardous wastes. This addition, inserted by the 1980 RCRA amendments, was apparently intended to allow EPA to extract information from persons who, though not themselves subject to RCRA regulation, may have handled, and thus gained information relating to, a particular waste. Such persons would clearly include individuals, such as laborers, who are themselves not licensed or otherwise subject to direct regulation and testing laboratories that analyze waste but, because of the definitional structure of RCRA, might not be considered generators or TSD facilities. The phrase also seems broad enough to encompass past gener-

---

[653] A substantial body of case law, discussed in Chapter 6, *infra*, held that Section 7003 was not applicable to acts that were completed prior to RCRA's enactment in 1976. Congress amended Section 7003 in 1984, overruling that line of cases.

[654] The present tense phraseology of the statute arguably precludes its use as to past generators, transporters, or TSD owner/operators who no longer perform such activity.

ators, transporters, and TSD owner/operators who ceased their activities prior to the advent of RCRA regulation.

Section 3007 does not appear to authorize EPA to extract information from the owner of an inactive TSD site who did not actively manage the wastes at the site or from a past owner of a currently active site. Such a person, since no longer owning the site, is not one who "stores, treats, or ... disposes" of hazardous waste.[655] As a passive former owner, the entity did not "handle" waste, within the usual and customary meaning of the term.[656]

[iii]   What Persons Are Authorized to Request Information or Enter a Site, and on What Terms?

Section 3007 authority is conferred upon any "officer, employee or representative"[657] of EPA and any "duly designated officer, employee or representative of a State having an authorized hazardous waste program." EPA-generated information requests are always produced by EPA employees, in letter form. Confidentiality of data submitted in response to a Section 3007 request may be asserted under Section 3007(b) and EPA's confidentiality provisions. Knowing and willful disclosure of confidential information to persons other than EPA, the Department of Justice, or a "duly authorized committee of the Congress"[658] by federal employees is prohibited by 18 USC §1905, and such disclosure by persons other than federal employees is prohibited by Section 3007(b)(2) of RCRA.[659] Data for which confidential treatment is sought must be specifically designated as such or given to EPA separately from nonconfidential data.[660]

While the language of subsections 3007(a)(1) and (a)(2) appears to authorize site inspections without a warrant, the Supreme Court has

---

[655] *Compare* Section 3013(b), which contains a specific reference to "previous owners and operators ... who could reasonably be expected to have ... actual knowledge ...."

[656] Congress did not define the term in RCRA.

[657] The phrase "or representative" was added by the 1980 amendments at EPA's request. It had been unclear whether the previous language, "officer or employee," was sufficiently broad to encompass private entities acting under contract to EPA. *See* Stauffer Chemical Co. v. EPA, 647 F.2d 1075 (10th Cir. 1981).

[658] Section 3007(b)(4). Congressional requests must be made to the Administrator of EPA, in writing.

[659] The offense is punishable by a fine of not more than $5,000 and imprisonment of up to one year (federal misdemeanor).

[660] Section 3007(b)(3).

ruled, in *Marshall v. Barlows, Inc.*,[661] that nonconsensual entries must be authorized by a judicially issued search warrant issued on the basis of an affidavit demonstrating either (1) that there is probable cause to believe that there is evidence of a statutory violation on the site or (2) that the inspection is part of a neutral enforcement scheme.[662] Such warrants are issued exparte by U. S. Magistrates.[663]

Site inspections may be made at either presently active sites or sites where hazardous wastes "have been generated, stored, treated, or disposed of, or transported from."[664] This arguably allows inspection of an unregulated site whether or not it is or was in the past owned or operated by a regulated entity. Inspections must occur at "reasonable times" and must be "commenced and completed with reasonable promptness."[665]

Section 3007 also contains separate authority for EPA or state personnel or representatives "to inspect and obtain samples from any person" of any RCRA listed or identified hazardous wastes "and samples of any containers or labeling for such wastes."[666] This, too, arguably allows entry to unregulated sites (for example, the printer of labels or a barrel vendor). If samples are taken, a receipt describing the sample must be left, and "if requested," split samples must be provided to the site owner or operator or agent in charge. Copies of analytical results are required to be provided to the entity "promptly," even if not requested."[667]

[iv] What Remedies Are Available to EPA in the Event a Section 3007 Demand Is Not Complied With?

EPA has available all of the Sections 3008(a)-(d) remedies to redress Section 3007 noncompliance. In addition, there are a number of general federal criminal statutes that relate to government information receipt. For example, 18 USC §1001 makes it a crime to submit false

---

[661] 436 U.S. 307 (1978).

[662] That is, the site was picked on the basis of a neutral selection process that is a normal component of the agency's regulatory enforcement program.

[663] *See* In Re Order Pursuant to Section 3013(d) RCRA, etc., 550 F. Supp. 1361, 1364 (W.D. Wash. 1982). *See also* Bunker Hill v. EPA, 658 F.2d 1280 (9th Cir. 1981).

[664] Section 3007(a)(1).

[665] *Id.*

[666] Section 3007(a)(2).

[667] *Id.*

information to a federal agency pursuant to a duty to provide the information.[668]

EPA's typical response to a nonresponse to a Section 3007 demand is first to threaten an administratively levied penalty, and then, if no response is forthcoming, to issue an administrative complaint and penalty assessment under Sections 3008(a)(1) and (c).

Enforcement authority for information gathering is useful only to the extent it is employed by the regulatory agency. Congress attempted to take a stick to EPA in 1984 by amending Section 3007 to add a new subsection (e), which requires mandatory inspection of TSD facilities required to have RCRA permits at least once every two years.[669]

[b]　Monitoring and Other Site Activity Orders—Section 3013

[i]　Monitoring, Analysis, and Testing Orders

Congress inserted Section 3013 into RCRA in 1980,[670] as part of a package of amendments intended to address the problems EPA was having in applying Section 7003 to inactive disposal sites. It was no doubt also motivated in part by a desire on EPA and Congress's part to minimize the amount of federal resources expended on site and groundwater contamination studies of suspect sites.

Section 3013 provides authority for EPA,[671] after making the required findings, to order the "owner or operator" of a "facility or site,"[672] or, where the present owner of a nonoperational site was not involved with it during the operational period, "the most recent previous owner or operator who could reasonably be expected to have" relevant knowledge, to undertake "monitoring, testing, analysis and reporting" as EPA "deems reasonable to ascertain the nature and extent" of the "hazard" posed at the site.[673]

A Section 3013(a) order, unlike a Section 3007 order, results immedi-

---

[668] If material false information is mailed to EPA, a mail fraud offense might be charged. See 18 USC §1341.

[669] EPA was also required to promulgate regulations establishing inspection frequency for classes of TSD facilities, and to study the use of nongovernmental personnel to supplement Agency employees in inspecting regulated facilities. See P.L. 98-616, Section 231.

[670] P.L. 96-482.

[671] Although Section 3007 specifically refers to EPA or state authorities, Section 3013 does not mention state authorities, except for Section 3013(d), which provides that EPA may authorize a state to undertake monitoring in individual cases.

[672] Section 3013(a).

[673] Section 3013(b).

ately in the recipient's expenditure of potentially large amounts of money.[674] The prerequisite to a Section 3013(a) order is a "determination" by EPA that the presence or release of hazardous waste from a "facility or site may present a substantial hazard to human health or the environment."[675]

The "determination" and order required by Section 3013(a) arguably constitute a "final agency action" within the meaning of that term as it is used in Section 704 of the Administrative Procedure Act.[676] Since the order imposes obligations on the recipient the violation of which can result in penal action, it is more than a "mere prerequisite to suit"[677] or to further administrative action for which a suit to recover costs is the sole remedy.[678] Since there is no provision in the statute for a prior or postorder administrative hearing, a strong argument can be made that a Section 3013(a) order is reviewable by a U. S. district court.[679]

Another interesting question presented by Section 3013(a) is what factual predicate must underlie EPA's determination that conditions at the site "may present a substantial hazard to human health or the environment." A fair amount of recent case law has fleshed out the meaning of "may present an imminent and substantial endangerment," the prerequisite to a Section 7003 lawsuit,[680] and, although the phraseology is somewhat different, it is likely that Congress intended the same general factors to apply to Section 3013. Essentially, those include (1) whether it is likely that there is hazardous waste at the site and (2) whether conditions are such that the waste might escape into

---

[674] A simple, nonbedrock monitoring well, for example, costs, in 1984 dollars, about $3000 to install in Connecticut, a representative jurisdiction. A modest groundwater monitoring and testing program will cost several hundred thousand dollars.

[675] The overall syntax of Section 3013 seems to limit its use to TSD facilities. Unfortunately, Congress did not employ in Section 3013 the terminology that is used elsewhere in subtitle C, so the jurisdictional reach of the section is far from clear.

[676] E.I. DuPont de Nemours & Co. v. Daggett, 610 F. Supp. 260 (W.D.N.Y. 1985). *See generally* FTC v. Standard Oil Co., 449 U.S. 232, 240 (1980).

[677] Ewing v. Mytinger & Casselberry, Inc., 339 U.S. 594, 600 (1950).

[678] *Compare* Sections 104(a), 106, and 107 of CERCLA, (discussed in Chapter 6, *infra*).

[679] Review of an enforcement order does not fall within any of the categories of action made reviewable by courts of appeals by Section 7006.

[680] Identical language also appears in Section 106 of CERCLA.

the environment, or that people might otherwise come into contact with it.[681]

The final limitation on the use of Section 3013 is that a Section 3013 monitoring and testing order may be issued only in order "to ascertain the nature and extent of . . . hazard" at the site. This means that monitoring and testing may be required to the extent necessary to determine (1) the identity and properties of the contaminants on the site, (2) their distribution within the site or in the groundwater, (3) the proximity, direction of flow, and rate of flow of groundwater, and (4) other environmental fate information. Monitoring and testing for the purpose of formulating a cleanup plan, or to apportion liability among potentially responsible parties, or to ascertain whose waste is at the site appears to lie outside Section 3013's scope.

[ii] **Section 3013 Responses and Remedies**

A recipient of a Section 3013 order desiring to comply with it must submit a monitoring, testing, and analysis proposal to EPA for its approval within thirty days of issuance of the order.[682] Since most recipients will have to enter into a contract with an environmental consultant, who will need to become familiar with the site before putting the proposal together, the thirty-day period is somewhat unrealistic. EPA's regional offices have ordinarily not required rigorous adherence to such deadlines where the regulated entity is cooperating.

If a recipient fails or refuses to comply with a Section 3013(a) or (b) order, or does an inadequate job in response to the order, EPA may either bring a civil action seeking enforcement of the order and a penalty,[683] or arrange to do the required monitoring, etc. itself, or have the state or local authorities or "other person" (such as cooperative generators?) do it and then order the site owner or operator to reimburse the cost.[684]

Section 3013(d)(3) allows EPA, a state or local authority, or an "other person" authorized to undertake a monitoring or testing program

---

[681] *See* United States v. Price, 688 F.2d 204 (3d Cir. 1982)(statute should be construed broadly in favor of an expeditious remedy); United States v. Vertac Chemical Corp., 489 F. Supp. 870 (E.D. Ark. 1980).

[682] Section 3013(c).

[683] Section 3013(e). Because Section 3013 contains its own remedy, the Section 3008 remedies are arguably unavailable, notwithstanding the breadth of Section 3008(a).

[684] Section 3013(d)(1). EPA may not, however, do merely confirmatory studies at the site owner/operator's expense. Section 3013(d)(2). Section 3013(c)'s judicial remedy is also available to be used in the recovery of Section 3013(d) reimbursements. The maximum civil penalty is $5000 for "each day during which such failure or refusal occurs."

under Section 3013(d)(1) to "exercise the authorities set forth in Section 3007." Since Congress failed to limit the term "other person" to, say, EPA contractors, there arises a distinct possibility that Section 3013(d) monitoring could be undertaken by a generator or a group of generators of waste at the subject site, who would prefer to do the work themselves rather than let EPA do it at Davis-Bacon Act prices, and end up later having to reimburse EPA at its high cost in a CERCLA or Section 7003 action. In such event, Section 3013(d)(3) appears to allow private parties, who might ultimately be litigation adversaries of the owner/operator, exercise the significant discovery powers of Section 3007 to learn about the owner/operator's activities, thus putting what amounts to a quasi-subpoena power in the hands of nongovernmental entities. Because of the potential for abuse of Section 3007, EPA must be judicious in authorizing nongovernmental entities to act under Section 3013(d).

[3] Administrative and Civil Enforcement by the Government

Section 3008(a) allows EPA to enforce violation of subtitle C either by issuing a compliance order, which may include an administratively issued civil penalty and/or suspension or revocation of a permit,[685] or by seeking injunctive relief or a civil penalty, or both, in the U.S. district court having jurisdiction and venue.[686] Failure to comply with a compliance order within the time limits specified in it may result in a further civil penalty and is a separate ground for revocation or suspension of a permit.[687]

If EPA issues a compliance order, it must afford the recipient a

---

[685] Sections 3008(a), (c). The amount of the penalty is that which EPA deems "reasonable taking into account the seriousness of the violation and any good faith efforts to comply. . . ." Arguably, the penalty may not exceed $25,000 for each violation, which is the maximum civil penalty a court may impose. See Section 3008(g). Section 3008(g) does not require, as a prerequisite to EPA's issuance of a penalty, violation by the respondent of a formal compliance order or administrative subpoena, and willfulness is not an element necessary to be shown as a prerequisite to levy of an administrative penalty. United States v. Liviola, 605 F. Supp. 96 (N.D. Ohio E.D. 1985).

[686] Sections 3008(a), (g). The maximum civil penalty is $25,000 for "each violation," with each day of a violation considered a separate violation.

[687] Section 3008(a)(3). The maximum penalty is $25,000 "for each day of continued noncompliance." This appears to require EPA to go to court to seek the penalty assessment. The subsection uses language ("shall be liable for a civil penalty") that is more consistent with a judicial levy than with an administrative levy. Compare Section 3008(c), which states, "Any order . . . may . . . assess a penalty. . . ."

"public hearing" if one is requested within thirty days of service of the order.[688] Both the language of Section 3008(b) and EPA's regulations[689] require that the compliance hearing be adjudicatory. A hearing request stays the effectiveness of the order, and thus the matter is not ripe for judicial review until the hearing procedure is exhausted.

If EPA proceeds, either directly or after issuing an order, to the district court, it must refer its case to the appropriate unit of the Justice Department.[690] Primarily because it retains control of the matter if it proceeds administratively, EPA relies heavily on its administrative penalty authority as the primary RCRA enforcement tool.

[a] RCRA Penalty Policy

On May 8, 1984, EPA issued a formal, internal "RCRA Civil Penalty Policy," which is binding on the regional offices in their assessment of administrative penalties authorized by Section 3008(c).[691] The policy does not affect judicial enforcement.[692]

The statute requires EPA to take into account two factors in assessing

---

[688] Section 3008(b).

[689] Section 3008 administrative proceedings occur at the regional office level. The branch chief will authorize the regional counsel to draft an administrative complaint and a proposed order, which is then presented to the Regional Administrator for signature. The complaint and order are then served on the named respondents. If the respondents request a hearing, a hearing clerk is appointed in the regional office, who establishes a hearing file for the proceeding, and makes a written request to the chief EPA Administrative Law Judge (ALJ) in Washington, D.C., for the appointment of an ALJ to the case. Once appointed, the ALJ is in control of the case, and will establish the schedule for the proceedings, hear the evidence, rule on motions, and, ultimately, issue a decision. Appeal from an ALJ's decision is to the Regional Administrator, and from there to the appropriate U. S. court of appeals.

[690] The current entity with jurisdiction to initiate EPA enforcement suits is the Environmental Enforcement Section of the Land and Natural Resources Division. Some EPA cases are handled by attorneys assigned to this unit; some are sent to the field to be handled by U.S. Attorneys' staffs; and some are teamed. All EPA enforcement cases include an EPA lawyer as part of the litigation group, usually from the initiating regional office.

[691] This document is one of a series of enforcement policy guidance documents that are considered internal Agency action and hence not subject to rulemaking procedures.

[692] EPA does, however, suggest that the policy might be employed by EPA and Justice Department lawyers in litigation on a voluntary basis. Although EPA penalty policies under its other regulatory statutes were on occasion urged on judges, prosecutors generally abandon them for settlement purposes. EPA's staff traditionally has been unwilling to abandon the policies in settlement, insisting on trying to fit any settlement into one of the niches of the policy. The Agency's Administrative Law Judges, though arguably not bound by the policy, tend to follow it.

administrative penalties—the seriousness of the violation and any "good faith efforts" by the respondent to comply with the "applicable" requirements. EPA's policy, like its analogous TSCA penalty policy attempts to translate the first of the statutory factors into a formula, and refines the "seriousness" criterion into what EPA terms a "gravity-based" component consisting of the potential for harm resulting from the violation and the "extent of deviation" from the applicable requirement. The universe of violations is categorized into "major," "moderate," and "minor," and EPA's enforcement personnel are required to determine into which "harm" and which "deviation" category the violation fits, and then calculate the penalty using a simple matrix.[693]

EPA considers two types of "harm": potential for exposure of the public to hazardous waste, and adverse effects on "the statutory or regulatory purposes or procedures for implementing the RCRA program." The first is empirically determinable; the second is not. A violation is "major," "moderate," or "minor" if the effects or deviations are, respectively, "substantial," "significant," or neither.

Once the "gravity-based penalty" is calculated, it may be either increased or decreased by the application of two other criteria: (1) the "economic benefit of noncompliance" and (2) equitable factors, such as good faith efforts to comply, degree of willfulness or negligence, the source's compliance history, ability to pay (a downward adjustment only), or other factors unique to the situation.

The "economic benefit of noncompliance" criterion is a holdover from EPA's pre-1980 general civil enforcement policy and statutory factors engrafted onto Section 120 of the Clean Air Act. The underlying theory presumes that if an industry does not spend money today to abate its pollution, it benefits by employing that money for income-producing purposes. This theoretical gain, which may be partially offset in an inflationary period by higher compliance costs later, is viewed as ill gotten, and one that should be recouped by the government, as the

---

[693] This matrix is as follows:

Potential for Harm	Extent of Deviation from Requirement		
	Major	Moderate	Minor
Major	$25,000 to 20,000	19,999 to 15,000	14,999 to 11,000
Moderate	10,999 to 8,000	7,999 to 5,000	4,999 to 3,000
Minor	2,999 to 1,500	1,499 to 500	499 to 100

representative of the public, who "paid" for the increased period of noncompliance by suffering the effects of the defendant's pollution longer than the law permitted.

In its simplest guise, this theory is applied by the use of a formula, which EPA has adopted for its RCRA policy.[694] In the past, the Agency employed a complex computer model, but the method produced outrageously high penalties, which the Agency could not collect. EPA then constructed the artifice of the "credit," by which the Agency allows defendants to offset penalties by taking credit for some environmentally beneficial expenditure not required by any law or regulation.

In spite of its facial rationality, EPA's penalty policy has never yielded consistent results.

[4] State Enforcement

Sections 3006 and 3009 require that state enforcement remedies be at least as stringent as EPA's. State enforcement procedures, however, can differ significantly from EPA's, and therefore can not be presented here in a generalized format. See Appendix 5-L, *infra,* for specific state substantive requirements.

Although it will rarely do so, EPA is empowered to enforce state program requirements against regulated entities in authorized states.[695]

[5] Citizen Enforcement

[a] Issues Related to the Language of the Citizen Suit Provision (Section 7002)

Section 7002 is the RCRA "Citizen Suit" provision. "Any person" may commence a civil action on his own behalf against "any person," including the United States or any other governmental entity, to the extent permitted by the Eleventh Amendment, alleged to be in viola-

---

694 Economic Benefit = Avoided Costs $(1 - T) +$ (Delayed Costs $\times$ Int.R), where T = the source's marginal tax rate, or 46 percent if the actual rate is unknown. Interest rates are those used by the IRS: 2-1-80 through 1-31-82—12 percent; 2-1-82 through 12-31-82— 20 percent; 1-1-83 through 6-30-83—16 percent; 7-1-83 through 6-30-84—11 percent; etc.

695 EPA's RCRA Program Quality Criteria Document defines what EPA believes constitutes "timely and appropriate enforcement action."

tion of any requirement or prohibition[696] under the act and against the Administrator for failure to perform nondiscretionary functions. District courts have jurisdiction. There is a sixty-day prior notice requirement for enforcement of subtitle C requirements, and a ninety-day notice requirement for citizen imminent hazard actions, although the latter is waived if the suit alleges subtitle C violations as well.[697]

The 1976 RCRA granted a statutory right of intervention to citizens if EPA or the state had brought action in a U.S. or state court. Citizen suits were otherwise barred if EPA or the state was diligently pursuing an enforcement action. The 1984 amendments, while strengthening citizen enforcement to an extent, eliminated the intervention right, but left the bar in place.[698]

Section 7002(e) provides that a court may award payment of "costs of litigation," including reasonable attorneys' and expert witnesses' fees, to "prevailing or substantially prevailing parties."[699]

Section 7002(a) provides that the district court shall have jurisdiction "to enforce such regulation or order, or to order the Administrator to perform such act or duty." Clearly, the public may obtain injunctive relief. RCRA did not expressly provide for payment of civil penalties in citizen suits, even though the term "enforce" might have been construed broadly enough to encompass such payments. Section 7002(a)(2) was amended in 1984 to remedy this omission, and the current RCRA specifically authorizes award of civil penalties under Sections 3008(a) and (g).[700]

---

[696] Inclusion of "prohibition" among the types of RCRA provisions enforceable by citizens was among the amendments made by Section 401 of P.L. 98-616 (1984). Prior to that time, citizens were not able to address outright prohibitions, including the imminent and substantial endangerment prohibition of Section 7003.

[697] See generally Section 7002(b) (1985). The notice requirement has been held to be jurisdictional. See Garcia v. Cecos International, 761 F.2d 76 (1st Cir. 1985); and Walls v. Waste Resources Corp., 761 F.2d 311 (6th Cir. 1985).

[698] As a sort of consolation prize, Congress amended Section 7003, adding a new subsection (d), which requires EPA to hold a "public meeting" and provide opportunity for public comment on proposed Section 7003 settlements. No right of judicial review is provided, however; in fact the provision expressly negates judicial review.

[699] The present language was inserted by Section 401(e) of P.L. 98-616 (1984), amending Section 3007(e). The 1984 language modifies the basic substantive requirement, that the award be "appropriate," and is a codification of the Supreme Court's holding in Sierra Club v. Ruckelshaus, 103 S. Ct. 3274 (1983).

[700] P.L. 96-616, Section 401(b)(2).

[i]   Limitations and Prohibitions Derived from the 1984 Amendments

Although the 1984 amendments on balance augmented the citizen suit remedy, they imposed some serious limitations on the right. Most of the limitations are on the newly created right to bring Section 7003 actions. There are two substantial limits on exercising citizen suit authority under subtitle C, however. Citizens may not seek to enjoin the siting of a new TSD facility or to enjoin the issuance of a permit under Section 3005.[701]

Limitations on citizen imminent hazard suits are legion. Such actions are barred if EPA has commenced and is diligently prosecuting a Section 7003 or a CERCLA Section 106 action, is engaging in a CERCLA removal action, has begun a Remedial Investigation/Feasibility Study (RI/FS) under Section 104 of CERCLA, has begun remedial action at the site, or has issued a CERCLA Section 106(a) administrative order under which responsible parties are conducting a RI/FS or are undertaking remedial action.[702]

Citizen suits must be served both on the Attorney General and on EPA.

[ii]   Intervention

EPA has a right to intervene in any citizen suit. Any "person" may intervene in a subtitle C citizen suit or a mandamus suit in federal court, but intervention as of right in citizen imminent hazard suits (including those brought in federal court by a state) is limited to persons who allege an interest "relating to the subject of the action" and who are "so situated that the disposition of the action may, as a practical matter,

---

701 Section 7002(b)(2)(D). The bar against enjoining issuance of a permit appears to be significant only in the case of state-issued permits, since Section 7006(b) provides for judicial review of EPA-issued permits in the courts of appeals, which have the power to issue injunctive stays. There is also a special bar against suing railroads in the absence of negligence attributed to them. Section 7002(g).

702 Section 7002(b)(2)(B). Slightly different bars apply where a state rather then EPA is the actor. Section 7002(b)(2)(C) bars a citizen imminent hazard suit when the state has commenced and is diligently prosecuting its own citizen suit in federal court, when it is actually engaging in a removal action, and when it has incurred costs to initiate a RI/FS and is proceeding with remedial action under CERCLA. The one court called upon to interpret this provision has held that a citizen suit raising regulatory issues that are additive to the issues pending in a preexisting Section 106 action is not barred. Fishel v. Westinghouse Electric Corporation, No. 85-0216 (M.D. Pa. 1985).

impair or impede [their] ability to protect that interest."[703] As a practical matter, only site owners, generators, or the like will satisfy the intervention test in a Section 7003 citizen suit.[704]

Intervention by citizens in federal government enforcement actions appears to have been eliminated by the 1984 amendments. The prior statute contained a proviso in old Section 7002(b)(2) stating that in any "such" action (syntactically meaning any federal or state enforcement action) in a federal court, "any person may intervene as a matter of right." The revised subsection, renumbered Section 7002(b)(1)(B), contains the bar against instituting a citizen suit in the face of a pending federal or state enforcement action, but contains no "provided" clause. Instead, immediately following the text of the bar is the language "In any action under subsection (a)(1)(A) in a court of the United States, any person may intervene as a matter of right." All this language does is provide a general right to intervene in other citizen suits and in state enforcement actions that happen to have been brought in federal court under Section 7002(a).[705]

[b] Considerations Bearing on the Feasibility and Expense of Citizen Enforcement Under RCRA

[i] Enforcement of TSD Facility Standards

Except in certain very limited circumstances, the paper trails established in accord with RCRA do not establish *prima facie* cases of violation.[706] Therefore, most RCRA enforcement requires at least some ability to ascertain facts not necessarily provable from documents in EPA or state files.

RCRA establishes one monitoring system that requires the automatic filing of reports for groundwater quality. Only facilities with surface

---

[703] Section 7002(b)(2)(E). Even if an applicant makes this showing, the state or EPA can defeat intervention by showing to the satisfaction of the trial judge that the interest alleged is adequately represented by existing parties. The burden of that showing, however, rests squarely on the governments.

[704] The usual theories of intervention as of right and permissive intervention under the federal rules may or may not be available. At least as to intervention as of right, it might be argued that Section 7002 is the exclusive remedy.

[705] EPA enforcement actions are not brought "under subsection (a)(1)(A)." They are brought under Section 3008, or directly under Section 7003.

[706] By contrast, the Clean Water Act NPDES permit program, under which citizen enforcement has been reasonably successful, requires all permitted discharges to file "discharge monitoring reports" with EPA and the state. These reports are *prima facie* evidence of the amounts of pollutants discharged each month.

impoundments, waste piles, landfills, and land treatments are covered. Monitoring occurs on a quarterly or semiannual basis. The facility must report any finding of a statistically significant change in specified parameters to the authorized state, or to EPA if the state is not authorized. The finding of significant change is not a violation. Instead, the finding gives rise to several responsibilities, reporting, and ultimately possible corrective action. Failure to report or take corrective actions is an enforceable violation, but such failures are not readily apparent on the face of documents filed with the agencies.

A visit to an EPA or state office will ordinarily reveal only those facilities that have filed significant change reports and those that have been required to provide additional data by EPA enforcement personnel (to the extent the enforcement files are willingly shared). If EPA or the state has followed up the report and required further action by the facility, a record of those requests will exist, and should be available unless the Agency claims an enforcement privilege as to it. Similarly, internal Agency memoranda and copies of facility responses to follow-up requests would also exist in the Agency files. Proving an action against a facility requires more than these documents, however. The actual status of facility compliance or noncompliance must be discovered and proven, either by testimony of EPA personnel or through evidence gathered at the site. Since citizens possess no prelitigation compulsory evidence-gathering authority, the latter form of evidence will seldom, if ever, be available.[707]

Other types of TSD facilities, such as storage facilities, incinerators, and the like, are required to undertake some monitoring, but are not required to report the monitoring results to EPA unless specifically requested to do so.[708] Thus, unless the state were to require more extensive reporting, knowledge of monitored violations of TSD permit requirements will ordinarily not be acquired by looking at facility reports at EPA or state offices. Failure to monitor will effectively be undiscoverable. A similar analysis is applicable to landfill and similar TSDs with respect to good management practice and other permit requirements (other than groundwater-monitoring data).

---

[707] A very few authorized states, like New Jersey, require more extensive reporting, and, to the extent state law permits full public access to state files, citizen researchers can in those states learn much more about the compliance status of regulated facilities.

[708] *See, e.g.,* Section 264.347.

[ii]   Citizen Enforcement of Manifest System Requirements

RCRA establishes two other reporting procedures. A generator must file an "exception" report with EPA or the authorized state if it does not receive confirmation of delivery of its wastes to the designated site.[709] Conversely, a facility must file a "discrepancy" report with EPA or the authorized state if it receives (and accepts) wastes that are not accompanied by a manifest, are accompanied by an incorrect manifest, or are not in conformity with the manifest. Filing of either an exception or a discrepancy report triggers an investigation by the responsible agency. The investigation is designed to determine whether a paper error or actual violation accounts for the disparity. In neither case does the report itself establish a *prima facie* violation. Instead, at a minimum, the manifest must be obtained for comparison. Manifests are public documents, which must be retained by the facility, the generator, and, in most cases, the transporter for three years.

A manifest may be obtained under the Freedom of Information Act (FOIA)[710] only if it is in the possession of a government entity. One might argue that the private entity holding the manifest does so as the government's agent, and that a FOIA request aimed at EPA and the TSD facility or generator jointly should be enforceable. The theory is untried.

In a few states, the reporting process is more efficient. In New York, for example, the actual manifests are all submitted to a central computer system, which automatically checks for discrepancies. Because this system does not rely on generator or facility reports, it is more likely to produce a more accurate list of discrepancies or paper violations. Access to such a system would facilitate citizen suits because it would pinpoint those facilities, transporters, or generators with persistent or numerous discrepancies and because the manifests themselves would be readily available from the agency.

In many cases even acquisition of the manifest will not yield sufficient information to make a *prima facie* case. If the discrepancy report states that the wastes received were at variance from the manifest description (say, eighty drums arrived, while the manifest states that ninety drums were shipped), some empirical evidence of the truth of the discrepancy report is required, since the discrepancy report is not

---

[709] *See* 40 CFR §262.42.
[710] 5 USC §551.

an admission of the apparent violator (in this case either the generator or a transporter or both).

Except as discussed above, the RCRA reporting system is neither systemized nor centralized. Where there is an authorized state, EPA does not even necessarily receive courtesy copies of reports. Therefore, in most states, citizens must go directly to the state to obtain reports. It is not clear to what extent states without centralized computer systems will compile or cross-reference reports received.

[6]   Criminal Enforcement

[a]   In General

RCRA contains both a general criminal liability provision governing "knowing" violations of the act or regulations, and a special provision, added in 1980, that imposes severe sanctions for a relatively new criminal responsibility concept, "knowing endangerment," for which Congress established a complex set of special definitions and presumptions relating to the *scienter* requirement, primarily to allay the fears of the corporate business community.

[b]   RCRA Crimes

One commits a criminal violation of RCRA if one *knowingly* transports or causes transportation of RCRA-regulated waste to a TSD facility not possessing interim status or a permit for that waste;[711] treats, stores, or disposes of any RCRA-regulated waste without a permit or in "knowing violation of" any material condition of a permit or interim status regulation or standard;[712] or dumps any RCRA-regulated waste into the ocean without a permit issued under the Marine Protection, Research and Sanctuaries Act.[713]

It is also a criminal offense *knowingly* to make a false material state-

---

[711] Section 3008(d)(1). Causing language added effective 11-8-84. P.L. 98-616, Section 232.

[712] Sections 3008(d)(2)(A), (B), and (C). Subsection C added effective 11-8-84, P.L. 96-616, Section 232. Section 3008(d)(2)(A) was construed in United States v. Johnson & Towers, Inc., 741 F.2d. 662, 21 ERC 1435 (3d Cir. 1984), wherein the court held that TSD employees as well as the owner and operator may by liable under the provision. In addition, the court construed the "knowingly" requirement, which is discussed *infra*.

[713] The MPRSA provides a separate basis for liability.

ment or representation or to omit material information[714] in documents filed, maintained, or used for the purpose of complying with EPA or state RCRA regulations;[715] to destroy, alter, conceal, or fail to file[716] any document or record required under the EPA or a state RCRA program,[717] to transport or cause the transportation of hazardous waste without a manifest;[718] or to export hazardous waste to a foreign country without consent of the recipient government or in the absence of a treaty allowing export.[719]

The nature of the *scienter* requirement imposed by the "knowing" term in Section 3008(d) has been addressed by one appellate court. In *United States v. Johnson & Towers, Inc,*[720] the Third Circuit addressed the questions of just what an individual defendant is required to "know" in order to be culpable under Section 3008(d)(2)(A) and what the government's burden of proof is on the knowledge issue.

The government had indicted both the corporate waste handler and two individuals employed in nonmanagerial positions under Section 3008(d)(2)(A), on evidence that the defendants had stored and disposed of hazardous waste without a permit. The individual defendants moved to dismiss the indictments, claiming that they did not allege an adequate degree of knowledge as to either the hazardous nature of the chemicals at issue or the regulatory requirements on the part of the defendants.

The government argued that all it needed to allege was that the defendants knew they were disposing of waste and that the waste was in fact hazardous, and thus that it did not need to show that the defendants actually knew that the waste was hazardous or that the facility needed, and did not have, a permit. The court rejected the govern-

---

[714] Section 3008(d)(3), as amended by P.L. 98-616, Section 232. The 1984 amendment added the omission offense. The statute lists as examples of covered documents applications, labels, manifests, records, reports, and permits.

[715] *Id.*

[716] Section 3008(d)(4), as amended by P.L. 98-616, Section 232. The 1984 amendment added the failure to file offense. In general this provision applies only to generators, TSD facilities, and transporters (and employees of all), and any other person who "otherwise handles" hazardous waste, although it encompasses all persons who conducted such activity whether it occurred before or after the date of enactment (in 1976).

[717] *Id.*

[718] Section 3008(d)(5), added by P.L. 98-616, Section 232 (11-8-84). The amendment closed a loophole in the original scheme.

[719] Section 3008(d)(6), added by P.L. 98-616, Section 245.

[720] 741 F.2d. 662, 21 ERC 1435 (3d Cir. 1984).

ment's argument, holding that each of the "knowing" requirements had to be shown. Thus, in a Section 3008(d)(2)(A) prosecution, the government must allege and prove that the defendant knew that the waste was hazardous and that the facility did not have a permit.

In response to a strong argument made by the government that it could never meet the burden of the knowledge requirement, the court held that in appropriate circumstances, the requisite knowledge may be imputed to the defendant.[721] Thus, the court opined, individuals employed in the waste industry for a reasonable period of time may be assumed to have knowledge of the properties of the waste they handle and the status of permit compliance.

The *Johnson & Towers* rule will not be easy to apply. First, there will arise questions as to how long and in what position an individual defendant must be employed in order for knowledge to be imputed. In addition, disposal or storage without a permit, the issue in *Johnson & Towers*, in many respects presents the easy case. A Section 3008(d)(2)(B) or (C) violation, for example, where violation of specific permit terms or conditions, or the requirements of interim status standards, is at issue, presents a more difficult case for imputing knowledge of the regulatory requirements to relatively low-level employees.

The other, more common, circumstances for imputing knowledge involves corporate managers who may be deemed to have knowledge possessed by their subordinates. Since Section 3008(d) includes a number of paper violations, this sort of knowledge imputation is of significance to potential white-collar defendants whose job it is to oversee the creation and filing of reports. This class of potential RCRA defendants is also exposed to potential criminal liability for the same acts under one or more of the white-collar provisions of Title 18.[722]

[i] **Penalties**

The maximum penalties for RCRA criminal violations were upgraded in 1984. Section 3008(d)(1) and (d)(2) violations carry a fine of not more than $50,000 per day of violation and imprisonment of not more than five years, or both, for the first offense. Other violations carry the same fine, with a maximum of two years' incarceration, or both. In each

---

[721] The court relied on United States v. International Minerals & Chemical Corp., 402 U.S. at 563, for this proposition.

[722] These include obstruction of justice (18 USC §§1501 *et seq.*), mail fraud (18 USC §1001), interfering with government operations (18 USC §1001), conspiracy, fraud, and racketeering (*see, e.g.,* 18 USC §§1961 *et seq.*).

case, the sanctions are doubled on the second offense.[723]

[c] Knowing Endangerment

The very complexity of the knowing endangerment provision will deter all but the most zealous white-collar prosecutors from seeking indictments under it, particularly since it is much easier to prove a simple Section 3008(d) offense and the penalties available under Section 3008(d) are within the felony range.

The knowing endangerment offense, stated as simply as possible, arises when a transporter or TSD facility owner commits a substantive Section 3008(d) offense and "knows" at the time he commits the offense "that he thereby places another peson in imminent danger of death or serious bodily injury."[724]

Section 3008(f)(1) states that a person "knows" an existing circumstance if "he is aware or believes that the circumstance exists,"[725] and "knows" that a result will follow his conduct if "he is aware or believes that his conduct is substantially certain to cause danger of death or serious bodily injury."[726] Knowledge may be imputed to an organization, as defined, but not to a natural person,[727] although circumstantial evidence, including steps to shield oneself from relevant information, may be employed to prove the requisite knowledge.[728]

Under this provision, if X, an individual, knew that a substance was lethal if ingested and knowingly disposed of it in a manner he knew or believed would cause it to find its way to a private drinking water well in concentrations sufficient to be lethal, X would be guilty of knowing

---

[723] The prior penalties, applicable to offenses committed prior to the November 8, 1984, effective date of P.L. 98-616, were, for subsection (1) and (2) offenses, $50,000 per day fine and imprisonment not to exceed two years or both and, for other offenses, $25,000 and imprisonment not to exceed one year or both, with a doubling only of the lesser offenses on a second offense.

[724] Section 3008(e) was amended by Section 232(b) of P.L. 98-616, which eliminated what was previously designated Section 3008(e)(2). That subsection added an additional qualifier to the offense, requiring that the actor's conduct "in the circumstances manifests an unjustified and inexcusable disregard for human life, or . . . extreme indifference to human life." It would have been virtually impossible to construct a meaningful linguistic distinction between these two states of mind, and in all probability impossible for the government to carry its burden of proof as to either, given their subjectivity.

[725] Section 3008(f)(1)(B). Section 3008(f) establishes a number of definitions, presumptions, and qualifiers that bear on the proof needed to prove a Section 3008(e) offense.

[726] Section 3008(f)(1)(C).

[727] Section 3008(f)(2).

[728] *Id.* ("provided" clause).

endangerment. But if X was mistaken about the properties of the chemical, and instead the chemical, by means unknown to him, volatized in the well and exploded, killing the homeowner and family, all of the necessary elements of the offense are not present.

If X were an "organization," however, and one employee possessed knowledge of the properties of the chemical and another knew that the chemical, as disposed, would find its way to the well, X may well be found to have committed a knowing endangerment, unless it were established that for imputation of knowledge to occur, the individuals possessing the knowledge must each be in the chain of decisionmaking that resulted in the action at issue.

There are two statutory affirmative defenses to a knowing endangerment charge.[729] Both involve situations in which the person endangered consented to the "conduct charged."[730] If the harm was a "reasonably foreseeable hazard" of the endangered person's occupation or business or of medical treatment or medical or scientific experimentation "conducted by professionally approved methods" and the endangered person had been made aware of the risks, the defense is absolute.

Clearly, the most uncertain aspect of the knowing endangerment offense is the tiered *scienter* requirement, and the resulting significance placed on the defendant's state of mind. Arguments by opponents of the RCRA knowing endangerment provision that it imposes draconian criminal liability on what are usually, at worst, acts of gross negligence are unpersuasive. The multiple *scienter* requirement probably rules out use of the provision against all but the most egregious and callous actors.

This point can be illustrated if we consider Sections 3008(e) and (f) in relation to the acts of an individual convicted of willfully dumping toxic pollutants in Louisville, prior to the 1980 RCRA amendments. The facts resulting in the defendant's conviction for knowing and willful violation of the Clean Water Act, distilled from papers filed in *United States v. Distler*,[731] follow. Distler owned a facility at which he hoped to blend hazardous wastes and petroleum products to produce industrial grade fuel. His operation never quite got off the ground, although he

---

[729] Normal defenses to criminal charges are also available. *See* Section 3008(f)(4).

[730] Section 3008(f)(3).

[731] 671 F.2d 954 (6th Cir. 1980), *cert. denied*, 454 U.S. 827 (1981), *rehearing denied*, 454 U.S. 1069 (1981). Interestingly, because of the sewer exemption, Distler's activities, as described, would probably be exempt from RCRA. For the purpose of this exercise, however, we assume that the sewer exemption did not exist.

was steadily accumulating waste, primarily spent solvents, which he stored in tanks located on his premises. Apparently the inflow of waste[732] exceeded Distler's combined fuel production and storage capacity, and Distler began to dump waste by the tank truck load into a sewer manhole located on his property. The manhole was part of the Louisville storm/sanitary sewer system, which was connected to a sewage treatment plant. On the day of the offense for which Distler ultimately was convicted and sent to jail, a solvent[733] he dumped into the sewer system volatilized in the treatment plant, seriously injuring several employees at the facility,[734] and temporarily destroying the plant's ability to treat sewage, until a bypass valve was activated shunting all of the sewage inflow into the Ohio River, untreated.

Would Distler's actions satisfy the elements of Section 3008(e)? It is doubtful that they would. Distler clearly knew that he was dumping waste into a manhole, and it could be inferred from that fact that Distler knew he was dumping waste into a Louisville storm sewer. If Distler actually knew that in Louisville the storm sewers were combined with the sanitary sewers, then circumstantial evidence would probably be able to show that Distler knew that the waste would enter the plant and that people worked in the plant. However, it is not at all certain that Distler's actual knowledge that the storm sewers were combined with the sanitary sewers could be proved.[735]

If Distler did not know that the sewer systems were combined, then he would have reasonably believed that his waste would combine with storm water, and go directly to the Ohio River, possibly injuring fish, but not people.[736]

It is also not at all certain that it could be shown that Distler knew what it was he was dumping into the manhole, and even less likely that it could be proved that he knew what it was likely to do if it got into the treatment plant. Apparently all that Distler was concerned about

---

[732] The sources of Distler's waste were uncertain. Apparently he got some of the waste from individuals in Ohio, who were in a similar line of work. At least some of the waste originated at generator facilities whose owners or operators were unaware that it had ended up in Louisville. All of the actions predated the RCRA manifest requirements.

[733] Hexachlorocyclopentadiene.

[734] The symptoms described in trial testimony were similar to those associated with mustard gas poisoning.

[735] Combined storm and sanitary sewers have been prohibited by EPA for a number of years. Only older portions of municipal systems are combined.

[736] Distler's waste would quickly be diluted to the point of nondetection, given the volume of water in the Ohio at Louisville.

in acquiring waste was its potential to yield BTUs. Thus, unless it could be shown that any lack of knowledge on Distler's part was based on "affirmative steps to shield himself" from knowledge,[737] a tricky exercise at best, he might successfully claim that since he did not know the stuff would volatize and poison someone, he did not knowingly endanger anyone.

[d] Other Crimes Potentially Arising from Hazardous Waste Activity

Obstruction of justice,[738] mail fraud,[739] and interfering with government operations[740] are all possible offenses that could stem from false or misleading statements made in connection with RCRA's manifest system, permit program, or reporting requirements.[741] The Justice Department has tended to charge one or more of these statements made to EPA to connection with its other environmental programs.

As yet little used but potentially significant hazardous waste criminal enforcement devices are the federal and state racketeering (RICO) statutes.[742] These are essentially criminal conspiracy statutes that make it a crime to undertake a pattern of conduct that might result in the commission of a crime.[743]

§5.10 Miscellaneous RCRA Provisions Relating to Hazardous Waste

[1] Imminent Hazards

Section 7003 authorizes the United States to bring lawsuits and authorizes EPA to issue orders seeking abatement of hazardous waste-related conditions that "may present an imminent and substantial endangerment to health or the environment." The rather substantial body of case law that has developed under this provision is discussed in

---

[737] Section 3008(f)(2).

[738] 18 USC §§1501 et seq.

[739] 18 USC §1341.

[740] 18 USC §1001.

[741] False or misleading statements to EPA are also punishable under Section 3008(d)(3) of RCRA.

[742] See, e.g., 18 USC §§1961 et seq.; and 18 Pa.C.S. 911.

[743] See generally Blakey & Gettings, Racketeer Influenced and Corrupt Organizations (RICO): Basic Concepts—Criminal and Civil Remedies, 53 Temple L.Q. 1009 (1980); and Blakey, The RICO Civil Fraud Action in Context: Reflections on Bennett v. Berg, 58 Notre Dame L.Rev. 237 (1982).

Chapter 6, *infra*, which is devoted to emergency and remedial response.

[2] Judicial Review of EPA Actions

[a] Actions of General Applicability

Promulgation, amendment, or repeal of any "regulation, or requirement," or denial of a citizen petition under Section 7004 seeking promulgation, amendment, or repeal of a regulation, is reviewable only by the U.S. Court of Appeals for the District of Columbia Circuit.[744] A petition seeking review[745] must be filed within ninety days of the promulgation date, unless it can be shown that filing later than that date is based "solely on grounds arising after such ninetieth day."[746]

Challenges to such actions in defense to a civil or criminal enforcement action are barred.[747]

[b] Permit Actions and State Program Authorizations

Decisions relative to individual permits, and granting, denying, or withdrawing authorization or interim authorization may be reviewed only in the U.S. court of appeals for the judicial district where the permittee or state resides or transacts business. The same ninety-day filing limitation applies.

Ordinarily appeals are on the administrative record closed as of the date the administrative proceedings are terminated. Nevertheless, if a petitioner challenging one of EPA's decisions following an evidentiary hearing is able to demonstrate a need for further evidence that is material to the EPA determination and "reasonable grounds for the failure to address such evidence" in the prior administrative proceedings, a partial remand for the limited purpose of presenting that evidence is possible.[748]

---

[744] Section 7006(a).

[745] *See generally* Federal Rules of Appellate Procedure, Rules 15-20.

[746] Section 7006(a)(1).

[747] *Id. But see* Adamo Wrecking Co. v. United States, 434 U.S. 275 (1978), holding that an identical provision of the Clean Air Act did not preclude a criminal defendant from claiming that the regulation on which the offense charged was based was adopted without statutory authority, and thus null and void.

[748] Section 7006(a)(2).

[c]   State Program Decisions

Each state has its own set of procedures for challenging state agency decisions. Permit decisions made by authorized state agencies must be challenged within the state's judicial system. State actions are not reviewable by the federal courts.

[d]   Other Actions

Federal enforcement actions, citizen enforcement and *mandamus* actions, and any reviewable actions of EPA not covered by Section 7006[749] lie within the jurisdiction of the U. S. district courts, wherever venue is proper.

[3]   Public Participation

RCRA "encourages" public participation in EPA actions implementing the statute.[750] The statute, in addition, specifically allows citizens to petition EPA for the promulgation, amendment, or repeal of any regulation, and requires EPA to publish its written response in the Federal Register within a "reasonable time."[751]

There are also specific public notice and public hearing requirements relative to permit decisions made by either EPA or authorized states.[752]

[4]   Employee Protection

[a]   Whistle Blowers

RCRA contains a provision virtually identical to the one contained in TSCA[753] and several other enviromental statutes prohibiting employers from taking discriminatory job action against employees or union officials who institute any "proceeding" under RCRA or testify

---

[749] Certain EPA enforcement actions, such as Section 3013 orders, may be reviewable. In the absence of special RCRA judicial review procedures, those actions would be reviewable by the district courts under the procedures of 5 USC §§701-706.

[750] Section 7004(b)(1).

[751] Section 7004(a). Similar provisions exist in the Toxic Substances Control Act (*see* Chapter 2, *supra*).

[752] Section 7004(b)(2).

[753] *See* Chapter 2, *supra.* The RCRA provision appears to have been taken verbatim from the Clean Air Act.

or agree to testify in any "proceeding" "resulting from the administration or enforcement" of the statute or regulations.

An employee's remedy in the case of alledged discrimination lies with the Secretary of Labor.[754]

[b] Employment Security and Workplace Safety

EPA is empowered to hold adjudicatory hearings to study allegations of employment loss resulting from the RCRA program.[755] It has no authority to act following such an investigation.

EPA is required to provide certain information to the Department of Labor that is relevant to the Department's Occupational Safety and Health Act responsibilities.[756]

[5] Used Oil

The original RCRA, and various RCRA-related session laws addressed the problem of used oil in various, and sometimes conflicting ways, a consequence of Congress's schizophrenic attitude toward that particular waste.[757]

On the one hand, recycling of used oil was encouraged,[758] but there was a recognition that used oil is, or can be, a hazardous waste.[759] EPA was originally required to issue performance standards and other regulations for recycled oil, after analyzing the economic impact of RCRA regulation on the oil-recycling industry.[760]

EPA had not attempted to regulate recycled oil as of late 1984, although some states had begun to regulate the product. Congress then took another whack at used oil. After renumbering the ambiguous "recycled oil" provision from 3012 to 3014,[761] it rewrote the provision to install a tentative subregulatory program within the overall RCRA umbrella.[762]

---

[754] Sections 7001(b)-(d).

[755] Section 7001(e).

[756] Section 7001(f).

[757] See Sections 2(1), 2(2), 4(c), and 9 of P.L. 96-463.

[758] See Sections 2(3) and 8 of P.L. 96-463; and RCRA Sections 2005 and 3012 ("Restriction on Recycled Oil") (all 1983).

[759] Section 3012 (1983).

[760] Section 4003(c).

[761] P.L. 98-616, Section 502.

[762] P.L. 98-616, Section 241. Under this program EPA is required within two years

Interestingly, EPA swept used oil into its regulatory scheme for regulating the burning of fuel containing hazardous waste, under its mandate contained in Section 3004(q). The EPA program, designated 40 CFR Part 266, was adopted late in 1985.[763]

[6] Federal Facilities

The federal government is a large generator, storer, transporter, and disposer of hazardous waste. The military branches account for the greatest volume of hazardous waste attributable to the federal establishment.

Section 6001, like its counterparts in other environmental statutes, requires federal facilities to comply with both the substantive and the procedural requirements of RCRA, EPA, and state hazardous waste programs "in the same manner, and to the same extent, as any person is subject to such requirements," including sanctions for violations, and "service charges."

The President may exempt a facility for up to one year "if he determines it to be in the paramount interest of the United States to do so,"[764] but a lack of funds necessary for compliance may not form the basis for exemption.

Section 6001 appears to allow federal entities to be sued in state courts, without providing them with the right to remove such actions to a federal court.[765] Whether a federal entity may invoke the federal courts in challenging state permit actions is an interesting issue. There are arguments that they can, and the Navy successfully challenged a state NPDES permit veto in federal court, in spite of a provision in the Clean Water Act similar in its language to Section 6001.[766]

---

to decide whether to identify or list used automobile and truck crankcase oil, and to decide whether to regulate generators and transporters of recycled oil, although the statute provides a number of escape hatches for generators who ship waste oil to recyclers. *See* Section 3014(b)(2)(B). Recyclers are exempt from the subtitle C requirements unless EPA determines that they need a permit. *See* Section 3014(d).

[763] 50 Fed. Reg. 49164 (1985) (final rule); and 50 Fed. Reg. 1684 (proposed rule). *See* discussion at Section 5.06[3][g][vi], *supra.*

[764] This authority has only been invoked once. In 1980, President Carter exempted a proposed detention center for Cuban and Haitian refugees, located in Juana Diaz, Puerto Rico, from all RCRA-related requirements.

[765] *Compare* Section 118 of the Clean Air Act, 42 USC §7418, which provides for removal as of right.

[766] United States v. Puerto Rico, 721 F.2d 832 (1st Cir. 1983).

The atomic energy establishment resisted compliance with RCRA, arguing that the entire nuclear establishment was subject to exclusive regulation under the Atomic Energy Act. In *Legal Environmental Assistance Foundation v. Hodel*,[767] a federal district court held that RCRA applies to atomic energy facilities only to the extent that its application is not inconsistent with the Atomic Energy Act. The court concluded that only wastes expressly regulated by the Atomic Energy Act are precluded from RCRA regulation, thus leaving the door open for regulation under RCRA of wastes that are not nuclear or radioactive materials generated, stored, treated or disposed of, or transported from federally owned or licensed atomic energy facilities.

As a part of the 1984 amendments package, Congress required EPA, and urged authorized states, to inspect federally owned or operated TSD facilities at least annually, and provided that the inspection records are public documents.[768]

The government often finds itself on both sides of a hazardous waste dispute involving a federal facility, and is constantly prone to allegations that it does not deal as harshly with itself as it does with the private sector. Such charges, though rarely supportable if one looks solely at the staff level of EPA, have some validity when interagency disputes over compliance end up in the Office of the President or the Office of Management and the Budget. Federal facilities are thus a prime target of citizens' groups, who do not trust the government's zeal in such cases.[769]

Obviously unsatisfied with the state of knowledge about federal waste disposal, Congress added in 1984 a requirement that federal agencies inventory their hazardous waste sites every two years, and authorized EPA to undertake the inventory for defaulting agencies.[770] Finally, Congress specifically mandated federal facility compliance with the new subtitle I requirements for underground storage tanks.[771]

---

[767] 586 F. Supp. 1163 (E.D. Tenn. 1984).

[768] Section 3007(c), as amended by P.L. 98-616. EPA is required to inspect state or locally owned TSDs that are required to have permits under Section 3005 annually. *Id.*

[769] The Justice Department, which represents EPA in its litigation under RCRA, also represents federal defendants. That position—one of apparent conflict of interest—has on occasion logically required the Department to deny representation to one or the other of the parties. It has not always chosen to do so, however.

[770] Section 3016. There is no authorization for expenditures by EPA for this purpose.

[771] Section 9007(a). There is an exemption for national security purposes similar to the RCRA one. Section 9007(b).

[7] Exports

Although there is no evidence that exporting hazardous waste to unwary foreign countries is a popular, or even minor, method of disposal, Congress took steps in 1984 to eliminate the possibility. Section 3017 prohibits export of hazardous waste to a country not having an agreement with the United States relative to such matters, unless the foreign government has been notified and has consented.[772]

[8] Bankruptcy

Because of the business uncertainties and regulatory burdens inherent in the hazardous waste disposal field, the interrelation between the federal Bankruptcy Code[773] and the regulatory obligations imposed by RCRA and its state law equivalents is important. Although the consequences of the bankruptcy of a regulated treatment, storage, or disposal facility owner or operator are generally potentially more significant in a CERCLA context,[774]

The key issues are whether and to what extent the filing of a bankruptcy petition may serve to relieve the debtor of ordinary regulatory obligations, or remedial action obligations, or penalty payment obligations. In addition, there are questions about whether a trustee stands in a different position with respect to any of the above issues than does a debtor in possession.

The filing of a bankruptcy petition, either for liquidation under Chapter 7 or for reorganization under Chapter 11, vests the bankruptcy court[775] with jurisdiction over the property of the debtor. Thereafter, any expenditure of assets by the debtor in possession or the trustee or

---

772 The statute specifies the contents of the requisite notification, which must be transmitted to the state department and relayed to the government involved. A copy of the consent must be attached to the manifest, and the shipment must conform to the terms of the consent. EPA is to address the matter with regulations under Sections 3002 and 3003 by the end of 1985.

773 11 USC §§1 et seq. The Bankruptcy Code was substantially amended in 1984 by the Bankruptcy Amendments and Federal Judgeship Act of 1984, P.L. 98-353, 98 Stat. 333.

774 See Chapter 6, infra.

775 Bankruptcy courts have exclusive jurisdiction over all cases arising under the Bankruptcy Code. Bankruptcy court opinions are published in the West Bankruptcy Reporter.

creditors' committee is within the jurisdiction of the bankruptcy judge. Ordinarily, expenditures that are in the nature of asset accumulation or preservation are permitted by a blanket order, but extraordinary expenditures or nonproductive expenditures require a special order of the court. In most cases, significant hazardous waste regulatory costs will be viewed as expenditures requiring such approval.

The filing of a bankruptcy petition operates as an automatic stay of the commencement or continuation of actions or proceedings against the debtor that were or could have been commenced prior to the filing date, and also of actions to cover claims that arose prior to the filing date.[776] This "automatic stay" is expressly not applicable to actions or proceedings "by a governmental unit to enforce . . . police or regulatory power."[777] This language, plus legislative history pointing to environmental enforcement as its intent, has been relied upon by several courts, which have refused to allow the automatic stay provision to affect hazardous waste regulatory requirements, even when they have required a significant commitment of the debtor's assets.[778]

Federal district judges and bankruptcy judges also have the power to issue discretionary stay orders aginst preexisting claims, actions, and proceedings.[779] The cases are not uniform on the question of the extent of the courts' authority to stay existing hazardous waste enforcement actions.[780] Bankruptcy does not, however, affect criminal actions pending or commenced against the debtor.[781]

Although many pending actions against a debtor are subject to removal from state to the federal court following the filing of a bankrupt-

---

[776] Section 362(a), 11 USC §362(a).

[777] Section 362(b)(4), 11 USC §362(b)(4).

[778] *See, e.g.,* In re Commonwealth Oil Refining Company, Inc., No. 5-84-01153E (Chapter 11) (Bkrtcy, W.D.Tx, San Ant. Div. 5-16-85); In re Bayonne Barrel & Drum Co., Inc., No. 82-0474 (D.N.J. 7-17-84); Matter of Canarico Quarries, Inc., 466 F. Supp. 1333,-1339 (D.P.R. 1979); In re Pester Corporation, No. 85-338-C (Bkrtcy, S.D. Iowa, 1985). *Cf.* Penn Terra Ltd. v. Pennsylvania Department of Natural Resources, 733 F.2d 267 (3d Cir. 1984) (state CERCLA-type action).

[779] Section 105, 11 USC §105. The legislative history indicates that the grounds for such an order are essentially the same as those for issuing an injunction. *See* S.Rep. No. 989, 95th Cong., 2d Sess. 51, *reprinted in* 1978 U.S. Code Cong. & Admin. News 5837; and H.R. Rep. 595, 95th Cong., 2d Sess. 342, *reprinted in* 1978 U.S. Code Cong. & Admin. News 6298.

[780] *Compare* In re Thomas Solvent Company, 44 B.R. 83 (Bkrtcy., W.D. Mich., 1984) *with* In re Commonwealth Oil Refining Company, Inc., No. 5-84-01153E (Chapter 11) (Bkrtcy, W.D. Tx, S.Ant. Div., 5-16-85).

[781] Section 362(b)(1), 11 USC §362(b)(1).

cy petition, state regulatory actions are not subject to removal.[782]

Assessment and collection of regulatory penalties are subject to the automatic stay provisions, but penalties assessed against the debtor prior to the filing of the bankruptcy petition are not collectable except as claims against the estate,[783] unless relief is granted by the bankruptcy court.[784] However, penalties assessed against the debtor in possession or the trustee in bankruptcy for regulatory transgressions that postdate the filing of the petition have been held to be outside of the automatic stay provision, and classified as administrative expenses.[785]

Corrective action orders, which can require site cleanup activities similar to those undertaken under CERCLA, could effectively deplete all of the assets of a debtor's estate. Trustees and debtors in possession have raised a number of issues under CERCLA that have direct relevance to RCRA corrective action orders.

The most draconian act of avoidance available to a bankruptcy trustee is abandonment of unproductive assets under Section 554(a) of the Bankruptcy Code[786] The polluted site of a failing treatment, storage, or disposal business is clearly unproductive; accordingly a number of trustees have sought to avoid compliance with remedial orders issued under CERCLA and RCRA by abandoning such a site. The Third Circuit denied such an attempt in *In re Quanta Resources*[787] in a decision affirmed by the Supreme Court in a 5-4 decision.[788]

---

[782] 28 USC §1452. A similar provision existed in the prior bankruptcy law, 11 USC §1478 (1977).

[783] Section 362(a), 11 USC §362(a).

[784] *See* Section 362(d), 11 USC §362(d).

[785] *See* United States Department of Interior v. James W. Elliott, Jr., 761 F.2d 168 (4th Cir. 1985).

[786] 11 USC §554(a).

[787] 739 F.2d 912 (3d Cir. 1984), *affirmed sub nom.* O'Neill v. New York, 53 L.W. — (1986); and Midatlantic Nat'l Bank v. New Jersey, No. 84-801, — U.S. — (1986).

[788] The key issue raised by *Quanta Resources* is whether the judge-made exceptions to the judge-made abandonment power under the old bankruptcy act survived the 1978 Code's codification of the abandonment concept. *See, e.g.*, Ottenheimer v. Whitaker, 198 F.2d 289 (4th Cir. 1952). The court in *Quanta Resources* concluded that they did, and applied one of those exceptions, the "public policy exception" to prohibit the trustee in that case from abandoning a pile of leaking hazardous waste drums. The Supreme Court majority in *O'Neill* found the exception implicit in the legislative history but limited it to state health and safety regulations "reasonably calculated to protect the public health or safety from imminent and identifiable harm." The dissenting justices were concerned that the majority failed to address the extent of the trustee's cleanup obligation, that is, whether it was only necessary to eliminate the immediate hazard or the obligation extended to complete site remediation.

A bankruptcy court, agreeing with the *Quanta Resources* holding, provided another basis for reaching essentially the same result, in *In Re T.P. Long Chemical, Inc.*,[789] reasoning that even if the law allowed the trustee to abandon the property, which contained leaking drums of chemical waste, that act was insufficient to eliminate liability under Section 107 of CERCLA. The act of abandonment, the court reasoned, simply transfers ownership of the property from the debtor's estate, which is in the hands of the trustee, to the debtor. That transfer of title, however, is insufficient to eliminate liability for regulatory remediation. Liability attaches at the instant the estate accedes to ownership of the property, and since the trustee has the duty to comply with the requirements of regulatory laws, the estate's liability survives transfer of the assets giving rise to the liability.[790]

The critical question that follows either result, however, is to what extent the remedial costs must be borne by the trustee at the expense of the creditors. The court in *T.P. Long* answered this question first by concluding that remedial expenses fall into the category of expenses of administering the debtor's estate, and are thus entitled to administrative expense priority, to the extent that they are "reasonable and necessary."[791] If there are insufficient unencumbered assets available to satisfy the regulatory obligation, however, the trustee (or the government standing in the shoes of the trustee if it has undertaken remedial activities under a remedial fund) may use assets subject to the interests of secured creditors, subject to the constraints imposed by Section 506(c) of the Bankruptcy Code.[792]

---

[789] 45 B.R. 278 (Bkrtcy, N.D. Ohio, 1985).

[790] 45 B.R. at 284-285, relying on Ottenheimer v. Whitaker, 198 F.2d 289 (4th Cir. 1952), and In re Chicago Rapid Transit Co., 129 F.2d 1 (7th Cir. 1942). Although *T.P. Long* is a CERCLA case, its reasoning would appear to apply with equal force to RCRA remedial orders.

[791] 45 B.R. at 286. An interesting issue that that was not raised in *T.P. Long* is whether the bankruptcy court has the power to second-guess EPA or a state agency on the reasonableness of its CERCLA expenditures or its remedial plan.

[792] This may not be much of a threat to secured creditors, since it will be the rare case in which a hazardous waste remedial action will sufficiently "benefit" the secured creditors to satisfy the statutory criteria. Moreover, the court took pains to rule that a secured creditor is not an "owner/operator" for CERCLA purposes and thus is not directly liable for remedial costs. 45 B.R. at 287-290.

CHAPTER 6

Emergency and Remedial Response to Chemical Hazard Situations

§6.01 Introduction

Chemical emergencies arise when significant amounts of a toxic or otherwise hazardous chemical are released into the environment in an uncontrolled manner, or when hazardous waste constituents enter the environment following disposal. This chapter deals with the three most significant federal statutes that address chemical emergencies specifically: Section 311 of the Clean Water Act,[1] Section 7003 of the Resource, Conservation and Recovery Act (RCRA), and the Comprehensive Environmental Response, Compensation and Liability Act of 1980 (CERCLA), as amended by the Superfund Amendments and Reauthorization Act of 1986 (SARA). Also discussed is the federal Rivers and Harbors Appropriation Act of 1899, which is occasionally used in surface water contamination cases.

There are a number of state emergency and remedial response programs, which differ significantly from the federal program in certain respects, and also a number of other federal statutes that contain emergency response provisions.[2] These statutes may be discussed briefly in

---

[1] In this chapter, references are to session law numbers, which is the common practice in the industry. Appendix 6-A, *infra*, matches session law numbers with U. S. Code numbers.

[2] Virtually all states have oil spill legislation. State statutes addressing remedial response and emergency situations in a hazardous waste context include 82 Ark. Stat. Ann. §4208; Ark. Act 479, Laws of 1985; Tit. 20 Cal. Health and Safety Provisions, Ch. 6.8; Tit. 25 Col. Rev. Stat. Art. 16; Tit. 7 Del. Code §6308; Tit. 27 Fla. Stat. Ann. §403.726; Tit. 39 Idaho Code §39-4417; Ill. Env. Prot. Act., Title V, Secs. 20 *et seq.*; Tit. 13 Indiana Code Art. 7, Ch. 8.7; Tit. XVII Iowa Code Ann. Ch. 455B, Pt. 4; 65 Kansas Stat. Ann. §65-3443; Kansas Laws of 1984, Ch. 219; Tit. 30 La. Rev. Stat. Ch. 2 §1143; Ch. 299, Mich. Comp.

the text, but are not treated separately, given their lesser significance.

Many still unsettled issues have been raised in connection with the federal emergency and remedial response program, particularly under CERCLA. Congress and state legislatures are also likely to continue to tinker with the legal mechanisms they have created, as they have done in virtually every legislative session since enactment of the basic statutory provisions. In 1986, Congress enacted, and The President signed into law, sweeping changes to CERCLA.[2.1] In this chapter, potential issues are also raised, and an attempt is made to predict the future course of the laws, where it is possible to do so.

§6.02 Oil Spills—Section 311, Clean Water Act

[1] In General

Section 311 was created with the Federal Water Pollution Control Act Amendments of 1972.[3] It was a congressional response to the disastrous Santa Barbara oil well blowouts and the Torrey Canyon spill, which occurred during the 1960s. The development of Section 311 paralleled attempts to establish an international regime for addressing oil spills on the high seas. Much of the considerable complexity of Section 311 is a result of Congress's efforts to engraft onto it many of the established doctrines of maritime law, to appease the international maritime establishment and insurance carriers, while not applying those provisions to nonmaritime spillers.

The premise on which Section 311 rests is that the custodian of the oil at the time it escapes into the environment is in the best position to

---

L. Ann.; Vol. 9 Minn. Stat. Ann. Ch. 115B; Mo. Rev. Stat. §260.230; Mo. Rev. Stat. §260.391, §260.420; Tit. 75 Mont. Code Ann. Ch. 10, §§601 *et seq.* and §§7.01 *et seq.*; Tit. 40 Nev. Rev. Stat. §§444.752, 444.754; N.H. Rev. Stat. Ann. Ch. 147-B; Title 13 N.J. Stat. Ann. Ch. 1K; Tit. 13 N.J. Stat. Ann. Ch. 1E; Tit. 74 N.M. Stat. Art. 4 Secs. 7 and 8; NY Env. Cons. Law §27-0916; N.Y. Env. Cons. Law §§27-1301 *et seq.*; Tit. 23 N.D. Code §23-20.3-08; Tit. 37 Ohio Rev. Code Ch. 34, §§3734.20-3734.99; Tit. 63 Ok. Stat. Ann. Art. 20, §§1.2015-1.2021; Or. Rev. Stat. §459.680; Tit. 35 Pa. Stat. Art. VII; Tit. 23 R.I. Gen. Laws §19.1-16, §§19.1-23 *et seq.*; Code Laws of S.C. §§44-56-160 *et seq.*; Tit. 68 Tenn. Code. Ch. 46 Part 2; Tit. 26 Utah Code Ann. Ch. 14, §§19-20; Tit. 10 Vt. Stat. Ann. §6610; Tit. 10 Vt. Stat. Ann. Ch. 237; W.Va. Code Ch. 20 Art. 5G; Tit. XV Wisc. Stat Ann. §§144.442 *et seq.* and §144.76-144.77. Federal statutes include the Clean Water Act, Section 505; Safe Drinking Water Act, Section 1431(a); and Toxic Substances Control Act, Section 7.

[2.1] P.L. 99-499 (10-17-86).

[3] P.L. 92-500.

clean up the spill, and should be obligated to do so without regard to who was actually at fault in the accident. In the event the custodian fails to undertake this obligation, a fund of federal money is made available to accomplish the task. In addition, it assumes that the private sector should ultimately be responsible financially for oil spill cleanup, and accordingly the government should have a right of action to recover public monies spent on oil spills from the defaulting custodian. Finally, since there may be cases in which the custodian is in no sense at fault, there should be a mechanism for shifting the financial responsibility to the person who is at fault. All these concepts are contained within Section 311.

Congress amended Section 311 in 1978,[4] adding a provision authorizing the government to recover, in addition to cleanup costs, the value of lost or damaged natural resources.[5] It also substantially broadened Section 311's coverage, originally limited to petroleum products, to include a wide range of toxic and hazardous chemicals.[6]

Between 1978 and 1981, when the CERCLA program came into being, Section 311(z) contained the sole authority for government-financed cleanup of hazardous waste sites posing a threat to human health or the environment. During that period, the Environmental Protection Agency (EPA) expended millions of dollars from the Section 311 revolving fund on hazardous waste sites. Not all of these sites posed a threat to surface waters. Since Section 311 is part of the Clean Water Act, its jurisdiction is coterminous with the Act. As a result, Section 311 arguably only authorized the expenditure of funds on hazardous waste

(*Text continued on page 6-7*)

---

4 P.L. 95-576.

5 *See* United States v. M.V. Zoe Colcatroni, 602 F.2d 12 (1st Cir. 1979), for a general discussion of this provision.

6 EPA subsequently promulgated a list of hazardous substances subject to the authority of Section 311(b)(2)(A). *See* 40 CFR §116.4.

sites that posed a threat to "waters of the United States,"[7] which encompass only surface waters. Accordingly, a strong argument can be made that a number of EPA's post-1978 Section 311 hazardous waste expenditures were unauthorized, since they addressed sites at which only *groundwater* pollution was implicated.

Section 311's usefulness as a mechanism to address hazardous waste problems ceased with the enactment of CERCLA,[8] although as will become apparent, CERCLA owes its essence to the Section 311 scheme. Since Congress chose to exempt "petroleum, including crude oil or any fraction thereof . . ."[9] from its definitions of "hazardous substance" and "pollutant or contaminant," Section 311 remains the primary source of federal authority to address petroleum product spills.[10] It is unclear to just what extent CERCLA applies to petroleum derivatives[11] and whether both CERCLA and Section 311 are applicable when CERCLA does apply to a petroleum derivative.

The centerpiece of the Section 311 program was, and continues to be, the National Oil and Hazardous Substances Contingency Plan (NCP).[12] This regulation was initially developed by the Council on Environmental Quality under Section 311(c)(2).[13] Following enactment of CERCLA, President Reagan delegated authority to revise the NCP, as mandated by Section 105 of CERCLA, to EPA. The revised NCP addresses both oil and hazardous substance response, but preserves the

---

[7] *See* Sections 502(7 and 12), Clean Water Act.

[8] Section 304(b) of CERCLA transferred one-half of the unobligated balance of the Section 311(k) oil pollution cleanup fund to the CERCLA Hazardous Substance Response Trust Fund. Section 340(c) of CERCLA provides that in the event of a conflict between Section 311 and CERCLA, the latter applies. In the event the Section 311 fund runs out of money, the CERCLA trust fund can be tapped for oil spills.

[9] CERCLA Sections 101(4) ("hazardous substance") and 104(a)(2) ("pollutant").

[10] The Trans Alaska Pipeline Authorization Act, 43 USC §§1651-1655, contains its own oil spill provision, which is similar to but in some respects more stringent than Section 311. *See* Alyeska Pipeline Service Co. v. U.S., 649 F.2d 831 (Ct. Cl. 1981). Limited oil spill cost recovery is also provided for under the Deepwater Ports Act, 33 USC §1517(c), and the Outer Continental Shelf Lands Act, 43 USC §1313(b).

[11] Section 101(14) removes from the petroleum exemption "any fraction . . . otherwise specifically listed or designated as a hazardous substance under subparagraphs (A) through (F) of this paragraph. . . ." Subparagraphs (A) through (F) incorporate by reference to RCRA Part 261 list and other hazardous waste lists compiled by EPA under its various statutes. Thus, when benzene is a petroleum fraction, since it appears on the RCRA Part 261 list, it is subject to CERCLA.

[12] 40 CFR Part 300. The NCP was significantly amended, primarily as it pertains to hazardous substances, on Nov. 20, 1985. 50 Fed. Reg. 47912.

[13] The NCP was previously codified at 40 CFR §1510.

basic intergovernmental coordination scheme originally put together for oil spill response.

[2] Administration

Oil spill response involves the shared jurisdictional responsibility of a number of federal and state agencies, with EPA at the top of the jurisdiction pyramid. The same structure is used for CERCLA purposes, although some of the substantive directives differ for oil and hazardous substances.

[a] Policy and Coordination

Overall national response policy is set by the National Response Team (NRT), a federal agency task force chaired by an EPA official and vice-chaired by a U.S. Coast Guard official.[14] The NRT maintains a National Response Center (NRC), which serves as a clearinghouse for spill notifications, maintains statistics, and provides advice on cleanup activities to federal on-scene personnel, state officials, and private entities performing cleanup activities.[15]

EPA and the Coast Guard jointly assign an "on scene coordinator" (OSC) for each area, whose functions are to maintain a local response plan, oversee private cleanup activities, and direct or coordinate federally funded cleanups.[16] Ordinarily, the OSC for marine, coastal, and Great Lakes spills is a Coast Guard employee. Inland water spills are generally handled by EPA employees.

The NCP also establishes Regional Response Teams (RRTs), which are responsible for providing regional oil spill contingency plans[17] and for regional oversight of response actions. These terms are made up of field personnel of NRT member agencies and state personnel from

---

14 40 CFR §300.32. The U.S. Coast Guard is a uniformed branch of the U.S. Department of Transportation, at present. NRT agencies are, in addition, the Departments of Agriculture, Commerce, Defense, Energy, Health and Human Services, Interior, Justice, Labor, State, and Transportation and the Federal Emergency Management Agency (REMA).

15 The NRT is located at Headquarters, U.S. Coast Guard, Washington, D.C., telephone number 800-424-8802.

16 40 CFR §300.33(a). Cooperating states may supply assistance as well.

17 See generally 40 CFR §300.32.

cooperating states.[18] The RRTs have no real authority. They are planning and recommending entities, which are expected to provide input to the NRT and the OSCs.

The regional contingency plans[19] are essentially notification and mobilization schemes, whose function is to ensure that adequate resources are available when needed.

[b] Response Activities—Cost Documentation

Once the NRT, or the local EPA[20] or Coast Guard office receives a report that a spill has occurred, the OSC for the affected areas is notified, and at that point the OSC has virtually plenary authority over activities that occur on the scene. Subpart E of the NCP[21] sets forth the general and specific guidelines the OSC must follow. The Coast Guard maintains Strike Teams in the Atlantic, Pacific, and Gulf coastal areas, which the OSC can call upon if necessary.[22] There is also a Scientific Support Coordinator (SSC), who may be made available by the NRT to provide assistance to the OSC.[23]

EPA maintains an Environmental Response Team (ERT), primarily to provide biological, chemical, hydrological, geological, and engineering expertise in connection with its CERCLA-based response activities.[24] The OSC may call upon ERT support in oil spill cases as well.[25]

Although the OSC's primary functions are to secure prompt cleanup of the released petroleum and to minimize environmental damage, an important subsidiary responsibility is carefully to document the expenditures of public funds on each removal action.[26] The Coast Guard Marine Safety Manual[27] and the Depart of Transportation Regula-

---

[18] 40 CFR §300.24. *See also* 40 CFR Part 109, which specifies the contents of such plans. Statutory authority is 33 USC §1161(j)(1)(B).

[19] States have statewide contingency plans, which are dovetailed into the regional plans. *See generally* 40 CFR §§300.41-300.43.

[20] 40 CFR §300.51. EPA's ten regional offices (Boston, New York, Philadelphia, Atlanta, Chicago, Kansas City, Dallas, Denver, Seattle, and San Francisco) supply the OSCs for EPA. The Coast Guard district offices supply Coast Guard OSCs.

[21] CFR §§300.51-58.

[22] 40 CFR §300.34.

[23] 40 CFR §300.34(d).

[24] 40 CFR §300.34(c).

[25] *Id.*, §§300.34(c)(3), (C)(4).

[26] 40 CFR §300.54.

[27] Commandant Instruction M16000.3.

tions[28] specify the evidentiary and cost documentation procedures and requirements that must be followed in the case of federal removal actions.

Cost documentation is important because Section 311(h) authorizes the United States to recover from the owner or operator the "actual costs of removal."[29] The OSC's cost-related responsibilities in the case of owner/operator removal actions involve observing what is done carefully enough so that, in the event the owner/operator seeks reimbursement from the oil pollution revolving fund,[30] a determination can be made that the expenditures were "reasonable."[31]

Documentation of the fact, extent, and value of natural resource damage is the responsibility of the governmental entity that has been designated by subpart G of the NCP as the "trustee" of the resource.[32]

[3] What Is Prohibited?

Section 311(b) prohibits the discharge by any person of "oil" in "harmful quantities" into or upon the "waters of the United States, adjoining shorelines or into or upon the waters of the contiguous zone." "Oil" is defined to include oil "of any kind or in any form, including, but not limited to, petroleum, fuel oil, sludge, oil refuse, and oil mixed with other wastes other than dredged spoil."[33]

A "harmful quantity" of oil is enough either to violate a state water quality standard approved by EPA under Section 303 of the Clean Water Act or to "cause a film or sheen upon or discloration of the surface of the water or adjoining shorelines or cause a sludge or emul-

---

28 33 CFR Part 153.

29 *See* Section 6.02[7][c][i], *infra.*

30 *See* 40 CFR §300.58. Reimbursement is possible only where the owner/operator can demonstrate that the release was caused *solely* by an act of God, act of war, or act of a third party.

31 Section 311(i)(1). The limitation to "reasonable costs," while the government may recover "actual costs," is not explained in the legislative history. Perhaps Congress assumed that EPA and the Coast Guard would not overspend and that private entities might. There is no empirical basis for such an assumption.

32 40 CFR §300.52(d). *See* 40 CFR §§311(f)(4) and f(5). Guidelines for assessing natural resource damages are codified at 43 CFR Part II. *See* 50 Fed. Reg. 52126 (12-20-85).

33 40 CFR §110.1(a). "Dredged spoil" is regulated pursuant to Section 404 of the Clean Water Act, 33 USC §1344, under a program managed cooperatively by EPA and the Department of the Army, Corps of Engineers. *See generally* 33 CFR §§320 *et seq.*

sion to be deposited beneath the surface of the water or upon adjoining shorelines."[34]

This general prohibition applies to any "person," defined to include "individual, firm, corporation, association and a partnership."[35] Municipal entities are also covered.[36] Discharges from a "property function vessel engine" are exempt from the prohibition.[37]

The use of dispersants or emulsifiers prior to discharge of oil is also prohibited.[38]

[4] Who Are the Regulated Entities?

Although Section 311's prohibition, and its basic affirmative cleanup obligation apply to all persons, three classes of potential discharges receive special treatment. These are vessels, onshore facilities, and offshore facilities.

[a] Vessels

Vessels[39] are accorded special treatment because of their potential to spill large quantities of oil, and because Congress acceded to industry demands to limit vessel liability to the limits contained in the international conventions,[40] except in cases in which the discharge "was the result of willful negligence or willful misconduct within the priority and knowledge of the owner."[41]

Most oil-carrying vessels are owned by a shell corporation whose only asset is the vessel. Since the "willful negligence or willful misconduct"

---

[34] 40 CFR §110.3. A "sheen" is an "iridescent appearance" on the surface of the water.

[35] 40 CFR §110.1(g).

[36] U.S. v. City of New York, 481 F. Supp. 4, aff'd, 614 F.2d 1292 (1979), cert. denied, 446 U.S. 936 (1980).

[37] 40 CFR §110.6. Bilge discharges are, however, prohibited.

[38] 40 CFR §110.7.

[39] "Vessel" is defined as "every description of water craft or other artificial contrivance used, or capable of being used, as a means of transportation on water other than a public vessed." 40 CFR §110.1(C). A "public vessel" is one "owned or bareboat chartered" or operated by a sovereign nation, except when "engaged in Commerce." 40 CFR §110.1(d).

[40] The limitations are, for an inland oil barge, $125 per gross ton of the barge, or $125,000, whichever is greater, and, for other vessels, $150 per gross ton, or, for oil-carrying vessels, $150 per gross ton or $250,000, whichever is greater. The CERCLA limits for hazardous waste are higher.

[41] Section 311(f)(1). The statute misstates somewhat the standard maritime insurance ("privity or knowledge"), although Congress's intention was to engraft onto Section 34 the industry standard, around which much case law has developed.

exception is difficult to prove, most vessel spills are effectively insulated from significant removal liability. This fact, coupled with the U.S. government's reluctance to limit access to U.S. water to double-hulled oil tankers,[42] leaves the maritime industry reasonably immune from oil spill–related costs.

The technology employed to explore the continental shelf for oil deposits has occasionally produced situations in which it is unclear whether a piece of equipment is a vessel. Semisubmersible mobile drilling rigs, for example, float and can move from one location to another. They are clearly "capable of being used as a means of transportation," and are, therefore, arguably "vessels," in the broadest sense of the term. While drilling, however, these platforms are jacked up onto legs that are anchored to the bottom. In the drilling mode, they do not float, and cannot be moved. What, then, are they for Section 311 purposes? Since only vessels enjoy the statutory liability limits,[43] the classification of such a device is of obvious significance both to its owner and to the government.

Courts that have addressed the issue of "fixed" vessels have tended to do so in the context of maritime law. In the one case in which a semisubmersible mobile drilling rig was addressed in a Section 311 context, the judge opined that the thing was probably a vessel.[44] EPA and the Coast Guard claim that such devices, when in a fixed position, are "non-transportation-related offshore facilities."[45]

[b] Onshore and Offshore Facilities

The two other entities receiving particular Section 311 treatment are "onshore facilities" and "offshore facilities." An "onshore facility" is "any facility (including but not limited to motor vehicles and rolling stock) of any kind located in, on, or under, any land within the United States other than submerged land."[46] An "offshore facility" is a facility "located in, on, or under any of the navigable waters of the United

---

[42] *See* Ray v. Atlantic Richfield Co., 435 U.S. 151 (1978), discussing the government's implementation of the Ports and Waterways Safety Act, 33 USC §1221-1232, and 46 USC §391a.

[43] Small onshore facilities enjoy some limits on liability not relevant to this discussion. *See* Section 311(f)(2), and 40 CFR Part 113.

[44] In re Complaint of Sedco, Inc., 543 F. Supp. 561 (S.D. Tex. 1982).

[45] 40 CFR Part 112 (Appendix).

[46] 40 CFR §110.1(h).

States other than a vessel or public vessel."[47]

The primary distinction attributable to facilities is an obligation to have a Spill Prevention Control and Countermeasure (SPCC) Plan, mandated by Section 311(j) of the Clean Water Act.[48] The term "facility" has been interpreted broadly, to effect the remedial purpose of Section 311.[49]

[c] "Owner or Operator"

It is the "owner or operator" of a vessel or of an onshore or offshore facility who bears the actual Section 311 responsibilities. Very often, particularly in the case of vessels and tank trucks, the owner and operator will be different entities. The operator is the "person in charge" of the facility at the time of the spill.[50] Since owner and operator liability is joint and several, there never arises under Section 311 an issue as to which person of the two is primarily responsible. Private insurance and contractual risk-shifting schemes sort out such liabilities among the private entities.

It is the owner or operator of the facility *from which oil is discharged* who is initially responsible for removing the oil from the environment. Thus, the responsible owner/operator is defined in large part by the scope of the definitions of "facility" and "vessel," for Section 311 purposes. Arguments by barge owners that they are insulated from liability where the spill was caused by a tug not owned by the defendant and arguments by tug owners or operators that they should not be liable for cleaning up oil spilled from a barge in tow but owned by someone else have been rejected.[51] While innovative arguments are occasionally

---

[47] 40 CFR §110.1(i).

[48] *See* 40 CFR Part 112.

[49] Union Petroleum Corporation v. United States, 651 F.2d 734 (Ct. Cl. 1981). In *Union Petroleum,* the spill at issue emanated from a tank car located on a siding just beyond Union's gate. The OSC ordered Union to clean up the spill, and it did so. When Union sued the government for reimbursement, alleging that vandals caused the spill, the government claimed that since the tank car was not part of Union's "facility," Union's removal activity was voluntary. The court rejected this position, and ruled that the statute should be construed to effect maximum private cleanup.

[50] Section 311(a)(6). In the case of a vessel, the owner or operator is the person "owning, operating, or chartering by demise" the vessel. *Id. See also* CERCLA, Section 101(20), which defines the terms in somewhat greater detail.

[51] *See, e.g.,* United States v. LeBeouf Brothers Towing Co., 621 F.2d 787 (5th Cir. 1980), *cert. denied,* 452 U.S. 906 (1981); United States v. M/V BIG SAM, et al., 454 F. Supp. 1144 (E.D.La. 1978); *but see* Tug Ocean Prince, Inc. v. United States, 436 F. Supp. 907,

raised in unusual contexts,[52] the courts have generally read the owner or operator language in a commonsense way, in accordance with the obvious congressional intent to impose the initial cleanup responsibility on the person closest to the event.

[5] Exclusive Federal Remedy

It is now settled that Section 311 is the federal government's exclusive remedy for oil spill cleanup costs, and, arguably, for recovering damages for natural resource harms from the owner or operator of a discharging vessel or facility.[53] The government had attempted to raise maritime tort claims and Rivers and Harbors Act claims[54] in vessel discharge cases where the facts supported such claims, as a means of avoiding the Section 311 liability limitations.

Interestingly, the case law that developed around these assertions, while barring the government from raising the alternate claims against *discharging* vessels, permitted the government to raise them against third party causers of oil spills under Section 311(g).[55] Thus, if an oil barge discharges its cargo as a result of the actions of its owner or operator, the government can recover its costs only up to the limits of liability under Section 311(f). But if the barge's discharge was solely caused by the negligent acts of another vessel that itself did not spill oil, the United States is free to seek full reimbursement from the third party vessel.

The absence of a federal "common law" remedy for private parties (for exampler, private property or personal injury damages) is now virtually certain.[56]

[6] State Law Remedies

It is generally assumed that the state law savings clause of the Clean

---

923-24 (S.D.N.Y. 1977), *aff'd in part and rev'd in part on other grounds*, 584 F.2d 1151 (2d Cir. 1978).

52 *See* United States v. LeBeouf Brothers Towing Co., *supra* note 51.

53 United States v. Dixie Carriers, Inc., 627 F.2d 736 (5th Cir. 1980).

54 33 USC §§407, 411, 412.

55 *See* United States v. M/V BIG SAM, 681 F.2d 432 (5th Cir. 1982), *rehearing denied*, 693 F.2d 451 (5th Cir., 1982), *cert. denied*, 103 S. Ct. 3112 (1983); and U.S. v. T/B ARCADIAN 95, 714 F.2d 470 (5th Cir. 1983).

56 Middlesex County v. National Sea Clammers Ass'n, 453 U.S. 1 (1981).

Water Act[57] preserves both state oil spill remedies and state common law remedies available to injured third parties. State oil spill cleanup laws were held in *Askew v. American Waterways Operators, Inc,*[58] not to have been preempted by Section 311.

A number of states have oil spill programs patterned on Section 311, and some of these contain treble damages provisions, thus providing potentially much greater liability than exists under Section 311.

[7] Affirmative Obligation

[a] Duty to Report Spills

The "person in charge" of a vessel or an onshore or offshore facility has an affirmative duty to report the discharge of a "harmful quantity" of oil, as defined by EPA. Reports may be made either to the NRT, via its toll-free number, or to the local EPA or Coast Guard office.[59]

Failure to report will subject the person having the duty to civil and criminal penalties.[60] Even though the information contained in such a report may form the basis of a subsequent civil penalty levied by either EPA or the Coast Guard,[61] the reporting requirement does not violate the constitutional right against self-incrimination.[62]

[b] Spill Prevention Control and Countermeasure (SPCC) Plans

Owners or operators of "non-related onshore and offshore facilities"[63] are required to have a SPCC plan if they are engaged in "drilling, producing, gathering, storing, processing, refining, transferring, distributing, or consuming" oil or oil products and "due to their location could reasonably be expected to discharge oil in harmful quantities" into a water body.[64]

---

57 33 USC §510.

58 411 U.S. 325 (1973).

59 *See generally,* Section 311(b); 40 CFR §110.9; and 33 CFR Part 153, Subpart B.

60 Section 311(j).

61 *Id.*

62 Ward v. Coleman, 598 F.2d. 1187 (10th Cir. 1979).

63 This term is defined in a memorandum of understanding between EPA and the Department of Transportation set forth in an Appendix to 40 CFR Part 112.

64 40 CFR §§112.1(a)-(b). The Coast Guard has similar requirements for transportation-related facilities. There are exceptions for small aboveground and underground storage facilities. *See* 40 CFR §112(d)(2). The exceptions seem to be aimed primarily at retail gasoline stations.

SPCC plans overlap state and local fire prevention plans, which have historically been applicable to tank farms and other petroleum-related facilities. Most states adopt the federal SPCC plan requirements, or simply do not impose their own SPCC requirements.

Failure to maintain an adequate and up-to-date plan for a facility that requires one has been held to constitute an act of contributory negligence sufficient to defeat an otherwise meritorious "third party cause" claim for reimbursement.[65]

The requirements for SPCC plans are prescribed at 40 CFR §§112.3 and 112.7[66] EPA does not either approve or receive a copy of a facility's SPCC plan. It requires instead that the plan, which must be reviewed every three years and be revised periodically to account for site and process alterations and spill experience, must be reviewed "and certified" by a registered professional engineer.[67] Since there is a wide variation in facilities' and engineers' skill, level of commitment, and objectivity, this procedure virtually ensures a wide variation in both the cost and effectiveness of SPCC plans. The regulations, in their open-ended revision requirement, appear to allow EPA or the Coast Guard to reexamine the SPCC plan at the time a spill occurs, and to declare the plan deficient at the point.

Failure to have an SPCC plan, implement the plan, amend the plan, submit information to EPA following a spill,[68] review the plan every three years, or have the plan certified can result in the imposition of a civil penalty, levied by the EPA Regional Administrator or the Coast Guard.[69]

---

65 Anglo Fabrics, Inc. v. United States (unpublished) (Ct. Cl. 1980).

66 Essentially, onshore facilities must design and install such things as dikes, berms, weirs, retention ponds, etc., and maintain an inventory of accessible cleanup equipment. Offshore facilities are required to develop a number of fail-safe and quality control mechanisms.

67 40 CFR §112.3(d).

68 See 40 CFR §112.4.

69 Section 311(j). The maximum penalty is $5000 for each day of a continuing violation. EPA provides opportunity for a hybrid, quasi-adjudicatory hearing, and appeal to the Administration. See 40 CFR Part 114. The Coast Guard provides similar procedures for transportation-related entities.

[c] Cleanup of Spilled Oil

[i] Private Discharger Obligations

Regardless of the cause, the owner or operator of a facility or vessel from which harmful quantities of oil are discharged either into surface water or on land from which the oil is likely to reach surface water is primarily liable to arrange for removal of the oil.[70] Ordinarily, this means, in the case of a large spill, that the discharging facility will engage the services of a specialized oil spill cleanup contractor, who will act under the general direction of the federal on-scene coordinator, who will have arrived at the scene in response to the discharger's report of the spill.

Section 311 is structured in such a way that the discharging entity has a legal obligation to clean up its oil even though it is clear that the discharger will ultimately be able to demonstrate that it was not at fault in the event one of the statutory defenses is alleged.[71] The discharger is expected to expend its own resources to remedy the situation, and then seek reimbursement either from the government[72] or from the person at fault.

Failure to carry out the cleanup obligation will result in removal, where possible, being accomplished by the government, ordinarily using a contractor. Where cleanup has become impossible as a result of the discharger's failure to act, imposition of a civil penalty is likely.[73] The government will ordinarily seek from the discharger the "actual costs of removal" it incurred.[74] A discharger who believes that a third party was the sole cause of the spill, and who reimburses the govern-

---

[70] Section 311(c).

[71] *See* Section 6.02[8], *infra,* for a discussion of available defenses and procedures for asserting the defenses.

[72] Section 311(i). In the event a defense is proved, "reasonable costs" may be reimbursed. The statutory language appears to preclude governmental reimbursement of a "Good Samaritan," such as the owner of a facility adjacent to a spill from an unrelated vessel. Such a person is limited to a direct action against the discharger or other responsible party.

[73] Section 311(j). The Coast Guard will often impose a penalty even if the discharger does clean up the spill, but will mitigate the amount to reflect the discharger's good faith.

[74] Vessels enjoy liability limits. Section 311(f). Onshore fixed storage facilities with a capacity of less than 1000 barrels also enjoy limited liability. Section 311(f)(2); 40 CFR Part 113.

ment, is subrogated to the government's right to recover from the third party.[75]

The government has the right to seek cost reimbursement directly from a nondischarging third party who actually caused a spill,[76] and it occasionally does so, when it is in the government's interest to do so, for example, when the third party is not subject to the limitation on liability enjoyed by the discharger.[77] In the majority of cases, however, the government will seek reimbursement from the discharger, who is liable without proof of fault.

If the responsible private entity does not voluntarily reimburse the government, the government's remedy is to bring a collection action in the appropriate U.S. district court.[78]

[ii] Government-Funded Removals—Reimbursement Issues and Defenses

Three of the statutory liability exclusions, act of God, act of war, and negligence on the part of the U.S. government, may be raised by the discharger as defenses to bar the government's cost recovery action.[79] The fourth statutory exclusion, spills caused solely by the actions of a third party,[80] is not a defense to an action to recover cleanup costs.[81] In such event the discharger's remedy, if he cannot convince the government to look elsewhere, is to pursue the third party as the subrogee of the government's rights.[82] This provision was obviously inserted to simplify the government's litigation burden. The government need prove only (1) that a discharge of a "harmful quantity" occurred (the notice filed by the discharger makes a *prima facie* case), (2) that the discharge emanated from the defendant's facility or vessel, and (3) the amount of the costs incurred.

Defendants in Section 311 reimbursement actions have occasionally been able to avoid liability by successfully claiming that the government's action is barred by the three-year general statute of limitation on instituting contract actions. Congress did not insert a separate stat-

---

[75] Section 311(g).

[76] *See* Section 311(h).

[77] *See, e.g.,* United States v. M/V BIG SAM, 681 F.2d 432 (5th Cir. 1982); and United States v. T/B ARCADIAN 95, et al., 714 F.2d 470 (5th Cir. 1983).

[78] Section 311(f)(3).

[79] Section 311(f)(1).

[80] *See* Section 6.02[8], *infra*.

[81] Section 311(g).

[82] *Id.*

ute of limitation for Section 311[82.1] claims, and the government, which had frequently been unable to get itself to the courthouse within three years of its expenditure, has argued that the applicable statute of limitation is the five-year statute applicable to tort actions or the six-year statute for restitution.[82.2]

In fairness to the government's position, it cannot clearly be said that the Section 311 obligation is any more contractual than it is tort based. The best that can be said about the obligation is that it is neither. In the absence of congressional action fixing a time limitation, those courts that have opted for the shorter time bar, forcing the Coast Guard and EPA to assert their claims more quickly, seem to be taking a reasonable approach.

It is difficult for a defendant to challenge the government's computation of its "actual costs of removal," where the OSC has done a decent job of documenting the expenditures. Had Congress limited the government to recovering "reasonable" removal costs, of course, the nature of the defense would be quite different. It does not do so, however, and thus the defendants are left with only limited arguments for mitigating the government's claims.

One might argue that a particular expenditure was not a "cost of removal." If, for example, the Coast Guard made an extra helicopter run over the sight to show the oil slick to the local congressperson, that helicopter time would arguably not be a cost *of removal*. In the end, however, such arguments will usually involve only small amounts of the overall bill.

[iii]   Natural Resource Damages

Sections 311(f)(4) and (f)(5) allow the government to recover for injury to, destruction of, or loss of natural resources. Unlike cleanup costs, both the amount and the valuation of resource damage are contestable and, for the government, can present enormous problems of proof.

82.1 28 USC §2415(b). *See* United States v. T/B 7026, C.A. No. 82-0192 (W.D. W. Va. 1983); and United States v. P/B STCO 213, C.A. No. G-82-464 [19 ERC 2205] (S.D. Tex. 1983).

82.2 *See* United States v. Healy Tibbits Construction Co., 607 F. Supp. 540 (N.D. Cal. 1985) (holding 28 USC §2415(a), the six-year statute for restitution actions, applicable); United States v. T/B STCO 225, C.A. No. B–82–946 (E.D. Tex. 1984); United States v. C. & R. Trucking Co., 537 F. Supp. 1080 (N.D. W. Va. 1982); and United States v. Poughkeepsie Housing Authority, CH. No. 80-1998 (S.D.N.Y. 1981).

These issues are discussed in more detail in connection with Section 107(a)(4)(C) of CERCLA, *infra*.

[8] Statutory Exclusion

[a] In General

A discharger is relieved of his financial responsibility if the discharge was caused "solely by an act of God, act of war, negligence on the part of the United States Government, or an act or omission of a third party without regard to whether such any act or omission was or was not negligent," or a combination of these.[83]

The act of war exclusion has, obviously, never been asserted. The act of God and federal government negligence exclusions have rarely been asserted.[84] The latter could, however, be applied in a number of possible situations—wrongly placed, defective, or nonoperational navigation aids maintained by the Coast Guard is one obvious possibility—that might arise. Most often, however, dischargers have raised the third party causation exclusion as a basis for actions against the United States for reimbursement from the oil spill fund. The defense most frequently asserted by the government to such claims is that the action of the third party was not the sole cause of the discharge.

[b] Caused Solely by a Third Party

The most frequently asserted third party causation claims involve allegations that the discharge was caused by acts of vandals.[85] Marine spills and tank truck spills often involve collisions, where the discharger

---

[83] Section 311(f)(1).

[84] Some general rules have emerged from the few act of God cases that have been litigated. Soil settlement below a pipeline or tank, causing it to rupture, has been held not to constitute an act of God, since such an occurrence was foreseeable at the time of construction. Sabine Towing & Transportation Co. v. United States, 229 Ct. Cl. 265, 269-70 (1981). That a risk is foreseeable, and the discharger did nothing to alter its activities in light of the facts known or reasonably knowable, has defeated many reimbursement claims. *See* Atlantic Richfield Co. v. United States, 1 Cl. Ct. 261, 263-64 (1982) (owner should have foreseen risk of parking tank truck where containment measures were inadequate); and Shell Pipeline Corp. v. United States, 11 ERC 1389 (BNA) (Ct. Cl.) (pipeline owner should have been aware of facts indicating potential rupture).

[85] *See, e.g.*, Union Petroleum Corporation v. United States, 651 F.2d 734 (Ct. Cl. 1981) (vandals broke seal on railroad tank car; contents leaked onto ground and entered water body).

claims that the other vessel or vehicle was the sole cause of discharge.[86] The remaining third party causation cases do not fall into identifiable categories. The causation theories run from the most straightforward and mundane to the bizarre.[87]

The government has been adept at advancing arguments that some

(*Text continued on page 6-21*)

---

[86] *See, e.g.,* United States v. LeBeouf Brothers Towing Company, 621 F.2d 787 (5th Cir. 1980), *cert. denied,* 425 U.S. 906 (1981).

[87] In one unreported case, the discharger operated a gasoline tank truck, which was stolen by a vandal, who jacknifed the rig on a city street. The local fire department hosed down the area, forcing the gasoline, which otherwise apparently would have gone nowhere, into a catch basin, from which it ultimately found its way to a water body. The discharger claimed that the fire department caused the "discharge" of gasoline.

aspect of the discharger's conduct actually contributed to the event causing the discharge and that, therefore, the third party's acts or omissions were not the sole cause of the discharge.

In the vandal cases, inadequate security (locks, lighting, fences, guard stations) to prevent vandalism is a frequently asserted defense.[88] Failure to maintain an adequate SPCC plan or to be aware of conditions on the property that could permit oil to escape into a water body are also often claimed as reasons to defeat an otherwise meritorious third party causation claim.[89]

In accident cases, contributory negligence is always a potential issue. Since *any* degree of discharger contribution will defeat the discharger's claim,[90] seemingly insignificant faults may serve to defeat a claim. Failure to act promptly, where prompt action could have stopped the oil from reaching the water, will defeat a third party or act of God claim. A vessel with a burned-out running light or inadequately marked subsurface pipeline might provide the basis for rejecting a claim, as will defective equipment, such as emergency shutoff valves and alarm bells.[91]

If the person alleged to have caused the discharge is contractually related to the discharger, the third party causation exclusion does not apply.[92] Thus, a discharger may not point to a negligent structural engineer or contractor he engaged, the preparer of a faulty SPCC plan, or a tug operator under contract to the barge owner as a "third party."[93]

---

[88] Union Petroleum Corporation v. United States, 651 F.2d 734 (Ct. Cl., 1981).

[89] Anglo Fabrics, Inc. v. United States, *supra* note 65.

[90] Reliance Insurance Co. v. United States, 677 F.2d 844, 848-49 (Ct. Cl. 1982). Unlike the comparative negligence and contributory negligence doctrines, which require a substantial degree of fault to defeat the plaintiff's cause of action against a negligent defendant, Section 311's requirement that someone other than the discharger be the *sole* cause of the discharge allows the government to defeat a claim with a relatively insubstantial evidentiary showing. United States v. Bear Marine Services, 509 F. Supp. 710, 715 (E.D. La. 1980) ("discharger must be totally free of fault").

[91] Anglo Fabrics v. United States, *supra* note 65.

[92] St. Paul Fire & Marine Insurance Co. v. United States, 4 Cl. Ct. 762, No. 264-82L (Cl. Ct. 1984).

[93] *Id. See also* United States v. LeBeouf Brothers Towing Co., 621 F.2d 787, 789-90 (5th Cir. 1980), *cert. denied,* 452 U.S. 906 (1981); Burgess v. M/V TAMANO, 564 F.2d 964, 982 (1st Cir. 1977), *cert. denied,* 435 U.S. 941 (1978).

[c] Procedures

Reimbursement claims must be asserted in accordance with procedures prescribed in the regulations of the Coast Guard, which is the administrator of the oil pollution fund.[94] Since only "reasonable" removal costs may be reimbursed, justification for all expenditures is important.

If the government refuses reimbursement, the discharger must bring an action against the United States under Section 311(i) in the U.S. Claims Court.[95] The proper party to bring the action is the person paying the remedial costs. Thus, if the discharger's insurance carrier handled the cleanup, it must seek reimbursement in its own name.[96] Unless all parties agree otherwise, the claims court judge assigned to the case will normally conduct the evidentiary proceeding in the federal courthouse nearest the sites of the spills, primarily for the convenience of the witnesses. Papers are filed at the Claims Court headquarters in Washington, D.C.

If the plaintiff is alleging that the sole cause of the discharge was an act or omission of a third party, either the plaintiff or the United States may serve notice of that claim on the third party named in the complaint. The third party may thereafter intervene in the claims court proceeding. Third parties may not, however, be forcibly brought into claims court proceedings, and the claims court has jurisdiction only to make awards against the United States. Accordingly, litigation of a third party's liability under Section 311 must occur in a separate proceeding in the U.S. district court.

If a third party enters the Claims Court proceeding, however, and the claims court makes findings of fact and rulings of law with respect to the third party causation claim, those findings and rulings will in all likelihood be binding on the parties in a later action.[97]

A more troublesome issue arises when the merits of a third party causation claim are litigated in the Claims Court between the government and the discharger and the noticed third party does not partici-

---

[94] 33 CFR Part 153.

[95] Under the United States Claims Court Rules, claims court judges utilize a standard Order Governing Proceedings Before Trial (OGPBT), which schedules discovery and other pretrial activities.

[96] Wellen Oil Co. v. United States, 1 Cl. Ct. 98 (1982).

[97] If not *res judicata*, the third party's participation is clearly sufficient to bar relitigation of the issues under the collateral estoppel doctrine.

pate. Clearly if the third party causation claim is rejected by the claims court, the discharger should be collaterally estopped from making the same claim in subsequent lawsuits against the third party. If the assertion is upheld by the Claims Court, however, then the question becomes whether the mere fact that the third party received notice of the assertion is sufficient to estop that person from relitigating the issue in another forum. It probably is not.

A nonmeritorious reimbursement claimant who filed an action in the claims court without at least a debatable position could find himself ordered to pay the government's attorneys' fees.[98]

Appeals from Claims Court decisions are to the United States Court of Appeals for the Federal Circuit.[99]

§6.03 Imminent Hazard Actions Under the Resource Conservation and Recovery Act (RCRA)

[1] Background and Overview

Section 7003 of RCRA[100] authorizes lawsuits and, subsequent to the 1980 amendments,[101] the issuance of abatement orders[102] where evidence in EPA's possession indicates that the handling, storage, treatment, transportation, or disposal of "any solid waste or hazardous waste may present an imminent and substantial endangerment to health or the environment."

In 1980 the words "may present" were inserted in Section 7003 to replace the previous antecedent, "is presently." The prior language was identical to the operative language of Section 505 of the Clean Water

---

[98] *See* St. Paul Fire & Marine Ins. Co. v. United States, 4 Cl. Ct. 762, No. 264-82L (1984)(awarding attorneys' fees under the "bad faith" provision of the Equal Access to Justice Act, 28 USC §2412(b).

[99] In 1982, the United States Court of Claims, which had trial and appellate divisions, and the United States Court of Customs and Patent Appeals were abolished, and in their place the United States Claims Court and the United States Court of Appeals for the Federal Circuit were set up. Prior to 1982, Court of Claims trial division decisions were published in the Court of Claims Reports (cited "00 Cl. Ct. 00"). The Federal Circuit decisions continue to be published in West's Federal Reporter.

[100] There is virtually no contemporaneous legislative history. The only reference to Section 7003 is found in H.R. Rep. No. 1491, 94th Cong., 2d Sess. 73, *reprinted in* 1976 U.S. Code Cong. & Adm. News at 6312.

[101] P.L. 96-482.

[102] Section 7003(b) is a penalty provision for willful violation of a Section 7003 order. That is arguably the exclusive remedy for refusal to carry out such an order.

Act[103] and Section 1341(a) of the Safe Drinking Water Act (SDWA).[104] Because of a dictum in *Reserve Mining Co. v. EPA*[105] that the "is presenting" language evidenced an intention to require more than a *potential* for harm,[106] defendants in early Section 7003 cases made arguments that in order to secure relief under Section 7003, the government must prove that hazardous waste has actually migrated off the site or will inevitably do so and thereby pose an empirically cognizable hazard to someone.[107] Replacement of the earlier language with "may present" was obviously intended by Congress to make it absolutely clear that EPA could gain relief in situations where it could prove the existence of hazardous wastes at a site, but only infer conditions that could, at some future time, cause these wastes to enter the environment or come into contact with people, thus allowing it to address risks rather than proven hazards.

Although Section 7003 was contained in RCRA when the statute was enacted in substantially its present form in 1976, the government did not begin to utilize the provision until almost three years later, when the Justice Department relied on it in bringing lawsuits against the Hooker Chemical Company and others to force cleanup of several inactive disposal sites in Niagara Falls, New York.[108]

At least one reason for the slow start of Section 7003 litigation was EPA's initial view of the statute as being applicable only to active,

---

103 33 USC §1364.

104 42 USC §300.

105 514 F.2d 492 (8th Cir. 1975)(en banc). The Clean Water Act analogs may also be limited to cases where a violation of an applicable federal standard is alleged. *See* United States v. Hooker Chemicals and Plastics Corp., 540 F. Supp. 1067 (W.D.N.Y. 1982). Section 7003 is not so limited. *See* United States v. Waste Industries, Inc., 734 F.2d 159 (4th Cir. 1984)(rejecting argument that Section 7003 is not self-executing in the absence of subtitle C regulations).

106 *Id.*

107 *See, e.g.,* United States v. Vertac Chemical Corp., 489 F. Supp. 870 (E.D. Ark. 1980)(similar arguments rejected after lengthy analysis). The 1976 legislative history of RCRA contains no useful discussion of Section 7003. The legislative history of the Safe Drinking Water Act analog was, however, helpful to the government's position. The House Report on the SDWA contains language evidencing an intention to address risks. *See* H.R. Rep. No. 93-1185, 93d Cong., 2 Sess. at 35-36 (1974), *reprinted in* 1974 U.S. Code Cong. & Admin. News 6454, 6488.

108 *See* United States v. Hooker Chemicals & Plastics Corp., 540 F. Supp. 1067 (W.D.N.Y. 1982)(approving consent decrees and discussing objectives thereto—Hyde Park site); United States v. Hooker Chemicals and Plastic Corp., Nos. 97-987 (102d St. Site), 79-988 ("S" Area site), and 79-990 (Love Canal site)(W.D.N.Y.).

regulated facilities.[109] Since EPA did not get around to implementing the RCRA subtitle C regulatory program until 1980, prior to that time no sites qualified for Section 7003 action, in EPA's view. The government's position changed between 1978 and early 1980, primarily as a result of public pressure to do something about abandoned hazardous waste sites.[110] EPA reversed its position publicly on May 19, 1980,[111] although it did so without attempting to reconcile its new position with its contrary earlier one.

By the end of 1980, the Justice Department had filed about thirty Section 7003 cases. Congress enacted CERCLA[112] during a lame duck session of Congress late in 1980. CERCLA contains its own imminent hazard provision, Section 106, and, following the enactment of CERCLA, the government began adding Section 106 claims to its existing Section 7003 cases, and filed new actions either solely under CERCLA or with dual claims. The issues raised in these cases have frequently involved the question of to what extent Section 7003 and CERCLA are jurisdictionally coterminous, or different. These issues and others are discussed in the following sections.

Section 7003 has largely been relegated to a supporting role in the government's hazardous waste emergency response program. Its long-term significance may ultimately lie exactly where EPA thought it did in 1978, as an adjunct to the subtitle C regulatory program, an extraordinary remedy to use when regulation has failed to prevent the occurrence of a potentially serious problem.

[2] Section 7003–Related Issues[113]

[a] Jurisdiction

[i] Waste Types

Section 7003 is available only to address hazards posed by "solid waste or hazardous waste." Only substances regulated under RCRA are

---

[109] *See* 43 Fed. Reg. 58984 (12-18-78).

[110] *See, e.g.,* H.R. Rep. No. 96-191, 96th Cong., 1st Sess. at 5 (1979).

[111] 45 Fed. Reg. 33170.

[112] 42 U.S.C. §§9601 *et seq.*

[113] Discussed herein are only issues that are peculiar to past, present, or future Section 7003 lawsuits and orders. Issues that are common to Section 7003 and CERCLA are discussed in Sections 6.04 *et seq., infra.*

within Section 7003 jurisdiction;[114] essentially the "wastes" on the 40 CFR Part 261 list constitute the majority of wastes addressable under Section 7003. The provision is broader than the more limited Clean Water Act and Safe Drinking Water Act emergency provisions, which are limited to wastes for which specific regulatory standards have been set,[115] but somewhat narrower than Section 106 of CERCLA.[116]

Section 1006 of RCRA further limits Section 7003's jurisdictional reach, although it is not clear just how much. Section 1006(a) states that "nothing in this Act shall be construed to apply to . . . any activity or substance which is subject to . . . [the Clean Water Act, SDWA, Marine Protection, Research and Sanctuaries Act (MPRSA), or Atomic Energy Act] except to the extent that such application is not inconsistent with the requirements of such Acts." Section 1006(b) requires EPA to "intergrate" RCRA with the Clean Air Act, Clean Water Act, Federal Insecticide, Fungicide and Rodenticide Act (FIFRA), SDWA, MPRSA, and other EPA-administered statutes, and Section 1006(c) requires EPA to defer to the Interior Department in the regulation of mining wastes where the latter's regulations are adequate for RCRA purpose.

Section 7003 begins, however, with the phrase "Notwithstanding any other provision of this Act." If that phrase is read to super sede the "Nothing in this Act" language of Section 1006(a), then the government may utilize Section 7003 to address hazards also regulated under other authority, such as hazards caused by the discharge of a hazardous pollutant into a water body. The contrary view would limit Section 7003's applicability to Clean Water Act–regulated pollutants to groundwater contamination, which is not within Clean Water Act jurisdiction.[117]

The issue is of potential significance both to the government and to dischargers, in light of the linguistic differences in the emergency provisions of the Clean Water Act and SDWA[118] and the absence of any similar provision in several of the other EPA-administered statutes. Competing policy considerations are involved. Section 1006, on the one hand, aims at minimizing regulatory duplication. On the other hand, a persuasive argument can be made that the government should have

---

114 *See generally* Chapter 5, *supra.*

115 United States v. Hooker Chemicals and Plastics Corp., 540 F. Supp. 1067 (W.D.N.Y. 1982).

116 *Compare* Section 101(14) of CERCLA (defining "hazardous substance") and Section 104(a)(2) of CERCLA (defining "pollutant or contaminant").

117 *Cf.* United States v. Burns, 512 F. Supp. 916 (W.D. Pa. 1981).

118 *See* Section 6.03[1], *supra.*

available as much legal authority as possible to deal with true emergencies.[119] The force of this latter policy argument was blunted significantly with the enactment of CERCLA in 1980, which provides a much more varied set of authorities expressly covering a significantly wider set of materials.

[ii] Activities, Sites, and Persons Liable

[A] **Inactive and Abandoned Sites.** Unquestionably the most frequently litigated jurisdictional issue in the early Section 7003 actions was whether the government may rely on Section 7003 to address hazards presented at sites that were abandoned or otherwise became inactive prior to the filing of the action. Although sometimes inaccurately phrased as whether Section 7003 is retroactive, the issue boils down to a question of legislative intent—whether Congress intended Section 7003 to be used to recover remedial costs in situations where there is no longer any active conduct to restrain.

On its face, Section 7003 appeared to limit the government to lawsuits seeking to restrain ongoing active conduct.[120] This fact plus the absence of contemporaneous legislative history and statements made by members of Congress in connection with the need for enactment of CERCLA, which was enacted principally to deal with the abandoned-site problem, led at least one district judge to conclude that the provision is inapplicable to abandoned and inactive sites.[121]

---

[119] The argument for broader applicability of Section 7003 than the RCRA regulatory program is aided somewhat by the location of Section 7003 in subtitle G of RCRA, albeit without supporting legislative history explaining the significance of placing the provison outside of subtitle C. Several courts have been persuaded that, by standing alone, Section 7003 is unencumbered by subtitle C. *See, e.g.,* United States v. Waste Industries, Inc., 734 F.2d 159 (4th Cir. 1984)(". . . Section 7003 stands apart from the other sections of the Act defining the EPA regulatory authority . . ., it is designed to deal with situations in which the [hazardous waste and solid waste] schemes break down or have been circumvented"). This reasoning must be regarded as suspect, however, since, taken to its logical extreme, it would authorize EPA to redefine "hazardous waste," for Section 7003 purposes, to a degree clearly not envisioned by Congress.

[120] The section contains the phrase "Upon receipt of evidence that the handling, storage, treatment, transportation or disposal of. . . ."

[121] United States v. Waste Industries, Inc., 556 F. Supp. 1301 (E.D.N.C. 1982), *rev'd,* 734 F.2d 159 (4th Cir. 1984)(stating that the section regulates endangerments, not conduct, and relying on the definition of disposal to include "leaking"); United States v. A & F Materials, Inc., 578 F.2d 1249, 20 ERC 1353 (1984); *cf.* United States v. Northeastern Pharmaceutical & Chemical Co., 579 F. Supp. 823, 20 ERC 1401 (W.D. Mo. 1984) (refusing to decide issue by analyzing statute and postpromulgation legislative history in a manner consistent with district court in *Waste Industries,* stating, ". . . Congress, knowl-

The government, and the courts adopting its position, seized on the definition of "disposal" in Section 1004(3), which encompasses "leaking," and argued that since Section 7003 is a remedial provision, it should be construed liberally.[122]

An inactive disposal site on which there is no "leaking" of contaminated leachate may not be the subject of the Section 7003 action simply because the government fears it might someday leak.[123] The postenactment legislative history, stemming from 1979 congressional oversight hearings[124] and the 1980 amendments to RCRA,[125] in connection with the enactment in 1980 of CERCLA,[126] is inconsistent and contradictory, and has been relied upon in support of both positions on the issue.[127]

By the time the 1984 amendments to RCRA were adopted, the government, in an almost classic case of having its cake and eating it too, seemed to have managed to convince Congress in 1979 that Section 7003 was both jurisdictionally and remedially insufficient, in order to

---

edgeable of the existence of hazardous waste problems, chose to principally direct RCRA's provision toward the regulation of the source and not the results of hazardous waste disposal").

122 See United States v. Waste Industries, Inc., 734 F.2d 159 (4th Cir. 1984), rev'g 556 F. Supp. 1301; United States v. Price, 688 F.2d 204 (3d. Cir. 1982); United States v. Reilly Tar and Chemical Corp., 546 F. Supp. 1100 (D. Minn. 1982); United States v. Hardage, 18 ERC 1685, No. Civ. 80-1031-W (W.D. Okla. 1982); United States v. Diamond Shamrock Corp., 17 ERC 1329 (N.D. Ohio 1981). The government's reliance on Section 1004 seems to be at odds with its position that jurisdictional constraints in subtitle C are inapplicable to Section 7003. Compare arguments made with respect to Section 1006 in United States v. Burns, 512 F. Supp. 916, 918 (W.D. Pa. 1981).

123 United States v. Price, 523 F. Supp. at 1071 (D. N.J. 1981); United States v. A & F Materials, Inc., 578 F Supp. 1249, 20 ERC 1353 (S.D. Ill. 1984).

124 Report on Hazardous Waste Disposal by the Subcommittee on Oversight and Investigations of the House Committee on Interstate and Foreign Commerce, 96th Cong., 1st Sess. Parts 1-4, esp. at 3, 7, 31, 43 (Committee Print, 1979) (called the Eckhardt Report).

125 S. Rep. No. 172, 96th Cong., 2d Sess. 5, reprinted in 1980 U.S. Code Cong. & Adm. News 5019, 5023.

126 See H.R. Rep. No. 1016, Part I, 96th Cong., 2d Sess. 22, reprinted in 1980 U.S. Code Cong. & Adm. News 6119, 6125; H.R. Rep. No. 1016, Part II, 96th Cong., 2d Sess. 4, reprinted in 1980 U.S. Code Cong. & Adm. News 6151, 6153.

127 Compare analysis in United States v. Waste Industries, Inc., supra, 556 F. Supp. 1311 et seq. (rejecting postenactment statements as unreliable, and relying more on CERCLA-related statements that Section 7003 does not cover inactive sites), with United States v. Waste Industries, Inc., 734 F.2d 159 (1984) (relying on one portion of the Eckhardt report, which the district court had rejected as internally inconsistent at 556 F. Supp. at 1312).

secure the passage of CERCLA,[128] and then later convince a number of courts[129] that the statute wasn't quite so narrow as previously claimed. Congress amended Section 7003 in 1984, inserting language legislatively overruling those court decisions that had held Section 7003 inapplicable to sites where the hazardous conditions resulted from completed past acts of disposal.

Several of the earlier cases in which the inactive site issue was presented contain extensive discussion of the issue as involving the question of whether Section 7003 is merely a jurisdictional statute, and thus must be viewed in light of common law limitations, or whether it creates a substantive cause of action.[130] While this approach to Section 7003 may well have relevance to the issue of what persons may be liable and what remedies may be imposed,[131] the real issue in the case of site and activity jurisdiction is congressional intent as embodied in the language of the statute and the legislative history.

In all events, the clear weight of authority now holds that RCRA and CERCLA provide a sufficiently pervasive regulatory scheme that "federal common law" has been preempted, on the reasoning of *Milwaukee v. Illinois,*[132] although, as discussed *infra* in connection with CERCLA, certain common law concepts may well have been intended to be borrowed in fashioning relief.

[B] **Generators and Transporters.** The government recognized early that if meaningful relief is to be obtained in hazardous waste disposal site cases, a liable deep pocket must be found. It also recog-

---

128 *See, e.g., Hazardous and Toxic Waste Disposal: Joint Hearings on 5.1341 and 5.1480 Before the Subcommittees on Environmental Pollution and Resource Protection of the Senate Committee on Environmental and Public Works* (Part 4), 96th Cong., 1st Sess. 7, 43 (1979)(statement of Thomas C. Jorling, Assistant Administrator, Water and Waste Mangement, EPA).

129 United States v. Price, 688 F.2d 204 (3d Cir. 1982); United States v. Waste Industries, Inc., 734 F.2d 159 (4th Cir. 1984); United States v. Conservation Chemical Co., 628 F. Supp. 391 (W.D. Mo. 1985).

130 *See, e.g.,* United States v. Solvents Recovery Service, 496 F. Supp. 1127 (D. Conn. 1980); United States v. Midwest Solvent Recovery, Inc., 484 F. Supp. 138 (N.D. Ind. 1980).

131 *See, e.g.,* United States v. Waste Industries, Inc., 734 F.2d 159 (4th Cir. 1984).

132 451 U.S. 304 (1981); United States v. NEPACCO, 579 F. Supp. 823, 20 ERC 1413 (W.D. Mo. 1984); United States v. Waste Industries, Inc., 556 F. Supp. 1314 (E.D.N.C. 1983), *rev'd on other grounds,* 734 F.2d 159 (4th Cir. 1984); United States v. Outboard Marine Corporation, 556 F. Supp. 54 (N.D. Ill. 1984); City of Philadelphia v. Stepan Chemical Corp., 544 F. Supp. 55 (N.D. Ill. 1983); City of Philadelphia v. Stepan Chemical Corp., 544 F. Supp. 1135 (E.D. Pa. 1982); United States v. Price, 523 F. Supp. 1055 (D.N.J. 1981).

nized that it would be unlikely, particularly in abandoned site cases, that persons from the "treater, storer and disposer" ranks would have sufficient resources to fund a substantial cleanup.[133] Generators and, to a lesser extent, transporters[134] accordingly became the primary targets of Section 7003 actions.

Since Section 7003 provides relief only against "any person contributing to" the "handling, storage, treatment, transportation, or disposal" of waste that is posing an imminent and substantial endangerment, generators and transporters who sent waste to a now inactive TSD facility argue that they are not "contributing to" any covered activity.

This defense has fared reasonably well, although two strands of authority developed, one broader than the other. Nonnegligent past off-site generators[135] have generally been held not liable under Section 7003.[136] The basis for this is gloss on the language "contributing to," whose origin is a statement contained in 1980 Senate oversight hearings to the effect that a company that generated hazardous waste might be a person "contributing to" an endangerment at a disposal site if it knew the disposal was improper at the time or failed to exercise due care in selecting the disposer and overseeing the disposal.[137] While such post-enactment legislative history is generally considered suspect, deserving little weight, the courts accepting the nonnegligent past generator defense have seized upon this language as indicating Congress's intent.

A subordinate, perhaps more defensible, basis for the rule is that so

---

[133] Problems of proof relevant to Section 7003 are discussed in Section 6.03[2][c], *infra*, and in connection with Sections 106 and 107 of CERCLA, *infra*. With more than 30,000 potentially dangerous sites identified by EPA, it is not unreasonable to assume that many owner/operators will be judgment proof.

[134] Congress inserted language in Section 7003 in the 1984 amendments essentially barring Section 7003 liability for transporters who only carried waste from a generator's site to a TSD facility selected by the generator.

[135] That is, generators who had no connection with the TSD facility, who only sent waste to it prior to the initiation of government response action, and who neither had knowledge of "illicit" disposal of the waste nor "failed to exercise due care in selecting or instructing the entity actually conducting the disposal." S. Rep. No. 172, 96th Cong., 2d Sess. 5, *reprinted in* 1980 U.S. Code Cong. & Adm. News 5019, 5023.

[136] *See* United States v. Northeastern Pharmaceutical and Chemical Co. 579 F. Supp. 823, 20 ERC 1401, 1413 (W.D. Mo. 1984); United States v. Waste Industries, Inc., 546 F. Supp. 785, 790 (E.D. Pa. 1982); United States v. A & F Materials, Inc., 579 F. Supp. 1249, 20 ERC 1353 (S.D. Ill. 1984). *Cf. United States v. Price*, 577 F. Supp. 1103 (D.N.J. 7-28-83). *Contra*, United States v. Ottati and Goss, Inc., 630 F. Supp. 1361 (D.N.H. 1985); and Jones v. Inmont Corp., 584 F. Supp. 1425 (S.D. Ohio 1984).

[137] S. Rep. No. 172, *supra*.

broad an interpretation of "contributing to" as would sweep nonnegligent past generators into the liability net, should demand a clear expression of legislative intent, which is not apparent either on the face of the statute or in its legislative history.[138]

Most generators, prior to 1980, simply arranged with a transporter to take their waste away, often being totally unaware of its final destination. Few generators who knew where their waste was disposed had any detailed knowledge of the site or the disposal practices of the owner/operator. They had no reason to need to know such information, because there were no regulatory requirements to that effect, and state common law nuisance doctrine did not attach liability to generators for nuisance conditions at disposal sites. It is therefore unlikely that many past generators would ever have been forced to contribute to inactive site cleanup under Section 7003.

Transporter liability may be easier for the government to prove, if the transporters are held to possess knowledge of site conditions observed by their employee drivers.[139] Nevertheless, the nature of the waste transportation business has historically been such that assetless transporters are almost as large a problem for the government as assetless TSD owner/operators.

[C] **Owners and Operators of TSD Facilities.** Several classes of owner/operators have emerged in the Section 7003 cases. Some of these have "no negligence" arguments nearly as strong as those advanced by past generators in the inactive site cases, but, unlike the generators, they have generally not managed to escape liability.

The classes of potentially liable owners include the present owner/operator who has always been such, past owners who were and who were not operators of the site, intermediate owners, and present owners who had nothing to do with the site at the time waste was disposed on it.

Clearly present owner/operators are persons "contributing to" disposal. Past owner/operators are "contributing to" a present "leaking" at an imminent hazard site, on the theory that their acts placed chemi-

---

[138] United States v. Northeastern Pharmaceutical & Chemical Corp., 579 F. Supp. 823, 20 ERC at 1412 (W.D. Mo. 1984).

[139] One court refused to afford transporters a defense, limiting the "nonnegligent past conduct" defense to generators. United States v. Wade, 546 F. Supp. 785, 788-92 (E.D. Pa. 1982). The distinction does not appear to be rational, and was legislatively overruled by an amendment to Section 7003 in 1984.

cals at the site that are presently leaking into the environment, a "contribution" similar to that of one who creates conditions at one point in time that inexorably create a nuisance.[140]

A prior owner who did not operate the site may nevertheless be liable for conditions created during his ownership, although liability may turn on the degree of control over the site he retained or exercised.[141]

A subsequent owner is also liable, even though he was never actively engaged in any disposal activities, just as the present owner of a property on which a nuisance is occurring is liable for abatement of the nuisance.[142]

[D] Governmental Entities. State and local governmental entities are not shielded from Section 7003 liability by the Tenth Amendment.[143]

Section 6001 of RCRA makes federal facilities subject to all RCRA requirements; thus, federal generators, transporters, and treatment, storage, and disposal (TSD) facilities are potentially subject to liability under Section 7003. Since it has been a long-standing policy of the federal government not to sue itself, however, federal agency involvement in a Section 7003 action ordinarily must be instigated by another defendant.[144] As discussed in Chapter 5, *supra*, the sovereign immunity

---

140 United States v. Reilly Tar & Chemical Corp., 546 F. Supp. 1100 (D. Minn. 1982); United States v. Price, 523 F. Supp. 1055, 1072-74 (D.N.J. 1981); United States v. Conservation Chemical Co. 619 F. Supp. 162 (W.D. Mo. 1985). Theories for shifting liability among former and present site owners are discussed *infra*.

141 United States v. Ottati and Goss, Civ. No. C80-225-L(D.N.H. 1980)(landowner retaining a right of access to the site and other control held liable). Although such owners might argue for a negligence standard, in at least one case liability was held to attach without consideration of fault. United States v. Hardage, 18 ERC 1685 (No. CCU-80-10310W)(W.D. Okla. 1982).

142 United States v. Vertac Chemical Corp., 489 F. Supp. 870, 877 (E.D. Ark. 1980); United States v. Price, 523 F. Supp. 1055, 1073 (D.N.J. 1981)(dictum). *See infra*, for a discussion of exculpatory clauses and similar devices employed to shift liability among prior and subsequent owners.

143 United States v. Duracell, et al., 510 F. Supp. 154, 156 (M.D. Tenn. 1981).

144 Section 7003 was initially not available to citizen groups as plaintiffs. *See* United States v. Stringfellow, 20 ERC 1659 (No. CV-83-250L-MML) (C.D. Cal. 2-17-84). *But see* United States v. Olin Corp., No. CV80-PT-5300 NE (N.D. Ala. 1982)(unreported decision, not carefully reasoned). In 1984 Congress rewrote the citizen suit provision, Section 7002, adding Section 7002(a)(1)(B), which specifically authorizes citizen suits to remedy imminent and substantial endangerments, although a citizen action is barred if EPA has commenced and is diligently prosecuting its own action, either under Section 7003 or under Section 106 of CERCLA, or is engaging in Section 104 CERCLA removal or

waiver of Section 6001 may, nevertheless, not be sufficient to allow all such lawsuits.[144.1]

[b] Procedural Issues

[i] Indispensable or Necessary Parties

Attempts by defendants to compel joinder of other alleged tortfeasors[145] and attempts to secure dismissal based on the government's failure to name all potentially liable parties in its complaint[146] have not met with success.

The government has sometimes sought to join adjacent landowners in Section 7003 actions solely for the purpose of securing access to the target site through their property, or for the purpose of monitoring groundwater. Usually adjacent landowners are more than happy to cooperate with the government, since their property stands to gain from remedial action at their neighbor's site. The one reported decision involving refusal of adjacent property owners to consent to joinder refused to order it.[147]

[ii] Intervention by Private Plaintiffs and Others

Occasionally, prior to the 1984 RCRA amendments, the state, a local municipality, neighboring landowners, or environmental groups sought to intervene in a pending Section 7003 action, to raise ancillary or pendent claims,[148] to affect the course of settlement negotiations, or to oppose a settlement.[149]

Although it was frequently asserted as a basis for intervention in the government's action as of right, Section 7002(b)(2), the RCRA citizen suit provision, was almost uniformly held not to provide a jurisdictional

---

remedial actions. Similar, though somewhat less extensive, bars exist as to state actions. A ninety-day prior notice to the government and affected parties is imposed, although the notice requirement is waived if the complaint also alleges a subtitle C violation.

[144.1] *See* Florida Dept. of Environmental Regulation v. Silvex Corp., 606 F. Supp 159 (M.D. Fla. 1985).

[145] United States v. Price, 523 F. Supp. 1055, 1075 (D.N.J. 1981).

[146] United States v. A & F Materials, 578 F. Supp. 1249, 20 ERC 1353 (S.D. Ill. 1-20-84); United States v. Conservation Chemical Co., 589 F. Supp. 59, 20 ERC 1427, 1431 (1984) (discussing Fed. R. Civ. P. 19).

[147] United States v. Conservation Chemical Corp., 523 F. Supp. 127 (W.D. Mo. 1981).

[148] Individuals might seek damages under state common law theories; states might raise state statutory claims; municipalities might raise local ordinances or common law claims.

[149] *See* United States v. Hooker Chemicals and Plastics Corporation, 540 F. Supp. 1067 (W.D.N.Y. 1982).

basis for intervention in a Section 7003 action.[150]

Intervention as of right under Fed. R. Civ. P. 24(a)(2) has sometimes been allowed and sometimes denied, on the basis of the applicant's showing of interest according to the prevailing law on Rule 24(a)(2) in the circuit.[151]

Unsuccessful applicants for intervention as of right were sometimes allowed to intervene permissively, under Rule 24(b). A court has the power under Rule 24(b), however, to restrict the intervenor's activities,[152] and may prevent the intervenor from raising new issues, particularly issues that could slow down the proceedings.[153]

The 1984 RCRA amendments amended the citizen suit provision, expressly providing authority for the bringing of citizen suits to abate imminent hazards.[154] In so doing, Congress rewrote Section 7002(b), dividing it into a complex set of limitations. The amended statute eliminated the general right of "any person" to intervene in government subtitle C enforcement actions.[155] No right to intervene in government enforcement actions brought under Section 7003 was provided,[156] although generators and other persons whose interests may be adversely affected by the outcome of an imminent hazard citizen suit are accorded intervention as a matter of right, provided they can make a facial

---

[150] United States v. J.D. Stringfellow, 20 ERC 1659, 1662 (C.D. Calif. 1984); United States v. Hooker Chemicals & Plastics Corp., 540 F. Supp. 1067 (W.D.N.Y. 1982) (denying intervention under Section 7002, but allowing intervention under the Clean Water Act citizen suit provision). *Contra, but without analysis,* United States v. Olin Corp., No. 80-PT-530-NE (N.D. Ala. 1982)(allowing Triana, Alabama, to intervene in Clean Water Act/Section 7003 case).

[151] *See, e.g.,* United States v. J. B. Stringfellow, 20 ERC 1659, 1664-66 (C.D. Calif. 1984) (denying intervention by neighbors' group); United States v. Ottati and Goss, No. C80-225-L (D.N.H. 10-2-80)(unreported—allowing intervention); United States v. Solvents Recovery Service, No. H79-704 (D. Conn. 8-21-80)(unreported—granting intervention). *See generally* 7A Wright, Miller & Kane, Federal Practice and Procedure §1908. A defendant's insurer was found to have an insufficient interest to intervene as of right, in United States v. Northeastern Pharmaceutical and Chemical Co., No. 80-5066-CV-SW (W.D. Mo. 5-3-83)(unreported).

[152] *See* 7A Wright, Miller & Kane, Federal Practice and Procedure §1922.

[153] *See* United States v. J.B. Stringfellow, *supra,* 20 ERC at 1666 (refusing to allow intervenors to raise new claims or to participate in government claims they have not standing to raise, and limiting their conduct of discovery).

[154] P.L. 98-616, Section 401.

[155] *Compare* Section 7002(b)(2)(1983) *with* Section 7002(b)(1)(B)(1985).

[156] *See* Section 7002(b)(2).

showing of their interest.[157] Congress remedied the oversight in 1986. Section 113(i) of CERCLA provides a right of permissive intervention for interested persons in any actions brought under RCRA.[157.1]

As a sort of consolation prize, Congress amended Section 7003 in 1984, inserting Section 7003(d), requiring EPA to hold a "public meeting" and afford "reasonable opportunity for comment" on any proposed administrative or judicial settlement. The statute denies access to the courts for review of any such settlement, however.

(Text continued on page 6-35)

---

[157] *See* Section 7002(b)(2)(E).
[157.1] Section 113, P.L. 99-499.

[iii] Jury Trial

Demands by defendants for jury trials under Section 7003, understandably rare, have not met with success.[158]

[c] Proof

In general, proof of a Section 7003 case involves similar burdens to those involved under Section 106 of CERCLA, but the law on what must be proven to show that an "imminent and substantial endangerment" exists developed in the early Section 7003 cases, and is therefore worthy of separate mention here.

The elements of the government's Section 7003 cases are that (1) hazardous waste (2) that is being or has been handled, stored, treated, transported, or disposed (3) is situated such that it "may present an imminent and substantial endangerment to health or the environment" and that (4) the defendant or defendants "contributed to" the handling, storage, etc.

Proof of the first two elements is reasonably straightforward, and the courts have tended to go along with an expansive definition of "waste."[159]

The third element is, of course, the key element. The legislative histories of the analogous SDWA provision and RCRA oversight indicate a general intention to incorporate into Section 7003 "the legal theories used for centuries to assess liability for creating a public nuisance (including intentional tort, negligence, and strict liability) . . .," leaning toward such liberalization of those concepts as is necessary to achieve an adequate remedy.[160]

Most of the analytical focus has been on the meaning of "imminent,"

---

[158] United States v. Northeastern Pharmaceutical and Chemical Co., No. 80-5066-CV-SW (W.D. Mo. 9-30-83); *cf.* United States v. Wade, 577 F. Supp. 1326, 20 ERC 1853 (E.D. Pa. 1984)(RCRA and CERCLA); *and* United States v. Reilly Tar & Chemical Corp., 20 ERC 1052 (D. Minn. 1983)(ruling that government's claim for restitution under Section 107 of CERCLA is equitable rather than legal). Most lawyers for hazardous waste defendants believe either that the cases are too complex for jury presentation or that juries will tend to be too harsh on their clients.

[159] *See, e.g.,* United States v. A & F Materials, Inc., 582 F.2d 842 (S.D. Ill. 3-30-84)(material normally sold to recycler still waste since it is "sometimes discarded," therefore falling under EPA's Part 261 definition, 40 CFR §261.2(b)(2)).

[160] S. Rep. No. 172, 96th Cong., 1st Sess. 5 (1979), *reprinted in* 1980 U.S. Code Cong. & Adm. News. 5019, 5023. *See also* H.R. Doc. No. 96-1FC-31, 96th Cong., 1st Sess. 31 (Comm. Print 1979) (RCRA); H.R. Rep. No. 1185, 93d Cong., 2d Sess. 35 (1974)(SDWA legislative history).

since defendants have been wont to argue that the harm alleged to occur must be virtually certain to occur almost immediately in order for there to be an "imminent and substantial endangerment." The requirement that the endangerment[161] be "substantial," though arguably a separate element of proof, has rarely been an issue, perhaps because the chemicals involved have tended to be the more dangerous ones. There is some, limited, separate legislative history of the SDWA on the meaning of "substantial," which defines the term very much as one would define "imminent."[162]

The case law developing the meaning of "imminent" appears to have broadened the concept beyond the meaning articulated by Congress in 1973 when the phrase was inserted in the Safe Drinking Water Act. The sole reference to the term in the SDWA legislative history states:

> Imminence must be considered in light of the time it may take to prepare admistrative orders or moving papers to commence and complete litigation and to permit issuance, notification, implementation, and enforcement of administrative or court orders to protect the public health.
>
> Furthermore, while the risk of harm must be "imminent" . . . the harm itself need not be. Thus . . . the Administrator may invoke this section when there is an imminent likelihood of the introduction into drinking water of contaminants that may cause health damage after a period of latency.[163]

The judicial gloss on the statutory language is derived from decisions under Section 7003, the SDWA, the Clean Water Act, and the Clean Air Act emergency provisions. In *Environmental Defense Fund, Inc. v.*

---

161 "Endangerment" has been long held "to mean something less than actual harm." Ethyl Corp. v. EPA, 541 F.2d 1, 13 (D.C. Cir. 1976)(en banc), *cert. denied,* 426 U.S. 942 (1976)(Clean Air Act). It also "includes potential as well as actual harm." Reserve Mining Co. v. EPA, 514 F.2d 492, 529 (8th Cir. 1975)(en banc), *cert.denied,* 426 U.S. 941 (1976) (Clean Water Act).

162 H.R. Rep. No. 1185, 93d Cong., 2d Sess. 35-36, *reprinted in* 1974 U.S. Code Cong. & Adm. News 6454, 6487-88, stating, "Among those situations in which the endangerment may be regarded as "substantial" are the following: (1) a substantial likelihood that contaminants capable of causing adverse health effects will be ingested by consumers if preventive action is not taken; (2) a substantial statistical probability that disease will result from the presence of contaminants in drinking water; or (3) the threat of substantial or serious harm (such as exposure to carcinogenic agents or other hazardous contaminants.) . . ."

163 H.R. Rep. No. 1185, at 35-36.

Ruckelshaus,[164] a Clean Air Act emergency provision case, the District of Columbia Circuit stated that "a hazard may be 'imminent' even if its impact will not be apparent for many years." In *United States v. Vertac Chemical Corp.,*[165] a very early Section 7003 decision, the court stated that the two elements that must be considered are the toxicity of small concentrations of the substance involved and the likelihood that there will be human or environmental exposure to it if nothing is done. And in *United States v. Hardage,*[166] another early Section 7003 decision, the court said that the "imminency of a hazard does not depend on the proximity of the final effect but may be proven by the setting in motion of a chain of events which could cause serious injury."

Typically, the proof involves evidence on which an "assessment of the relationship between the magnitude of risk and harm arising from the presence of the hazardous waste"[167] can be made. The elements of proof, therefore, are (1) the properties of the substances at the site (that is, their toxicity, carcinogenicity, mobility, persistence, etc.), (2) the physical characteristics of the site (that is, soil characteristics, bedrock configuration, water table, etc.), and (3) the environmental fate of the substance if it exits the site (that is, do people use groundwater for drinking, will windblown particles reach inhabited areas, what will the concentrations be, etc.).

Once an "imminent and substantial endangerment" has been shown to be present, liability for all persons "contributing to" the site is strict, without requirement of proof of negligence or other fault,[168] with the possible exception of past off-site generators and transporters, as discussed above.

[d] Remedies

[i] In General

Section 7003 authorizes the imposition of injunctive relief to "restrain" any person contributing to an endangerment situation, or to require "such other action as may be necessary." This has been held to

---

[164] 439 F.2d 584, 597 (D.C. Cir. 1971).

[165] 489 F. Supp. 870 (E.D. Ark. 1980).

[166] 18 ERC 1685, 1688, No. 80-1031-W (W.D. Okla. 12-2-80).

[167] United States v. Northeastern Pharmaceutical and Chemical Co., 579 F. Supp. 823; 20 ERC 1401, 1421 (W.D. Mo. 1984).

[168] United States v. Wade, 546 F. Supp. 785, 791-92 (E.D. Pa. 1982); United States v. Hardage, 18 ERC 1685, No. CIV 80-1031-W, slip op. at 2 (W.D. Okla. 9-29-82).

provide the "traditional equitable remedies against nuisances . . . and to enhance those remedies to the extent necessary to meet an acute contemporary problem."[169] The nature of the relief authorized by the statute is broad and flexible.[170]

Defendants have been required to pay for or undertake studies of the site and remedial options,[171] to provide temporary or permanent alternate water supplies to potentially exposed persons,[172] to undertake monitoring and surveillance and surface or groundwater remedial action,[173] and/or to alter present operational practices.[174]

An unresolved issue is the degree to which cost-effectiveness may be considered in fashioning a Section 7003 remedy. The government's initial position had been that complete elimination of the hazard was required, but in at least one consent decree the government agreed to make cost-effectiveness a factor in selecting an appropriate remedial plan.[175] Since the Section 7003 remedy is predominantly premised on common law equitable considerations, cost-effectiveness and economic feasibility are clearly appropriate issues for the court to consider.[176]

Finally, the government has successfully sought restitution from Section 7003 defendants for expenses it incurred investigating the site and taking remedial action prior to bringing the action.

[ii]   Joint and Several Liability

The government has fought hard to establish that liability among all contributing defendants is joint and several. It has succeeded in estab-

---

169 United States v. J.B. Stringfellow, No. CV-83-2501-MML (C.D. Calif. 4-5-84)(citing SDWA legislative history).

170 *See* United States v. Price, 688 F.2d 204, 212 (3d Cir. 1982) (defendants may be required to pay for studies of the site; such monetary payments are different from damages).

171 *Id. See also* United States v. Ottati and Goss, No. C80-225-L (D.N.H. 1980)(unreported).

172 United States v. Price, *supra.*

173 United States v. Solvents Recovery Service, 496 F. Supp. 1127, 1142 (D. Conn. 1980); United States v. Vertac Chem. Corp., 489 F. Supp. 870, 887 (E.D. Ark. 1980)(preliminary injunction).

174 United States v. West, No. C80-1342M (W.D. Wash. 2-18-81)(unpublished).

175 *See* United States v. Vertac Chemical Corp., 588 F. Supp. 1294, 21 ERC 1458, Nos. LR-C-80 109 and 110 (E.D. Ark. W. Div. 7-18-84).

176 *See* Weinberger v. Romero-Barcelo, 456 U.S. 306 (1982)(discussing Clean Water Act); United States v. Moretti, 526 F.2d 1306 (5th Cir. 1976)(wetland restoration). *Cf.* TVA v. Hill, 437 U.S. 153 (1978)(holding Congress foreclosed use of equitable considerations in Endangered Species Act).

lishing this as the law under Section 311 of the Clean Water Act,[177] and appears to have succeeded under Section 107 of CERCLA.[178] It had had mixed results with Section 7003 and with Section 106 of CERCLA.

The argument against imposing joint and several liability under the endangerment provisions is that the remedy authorized is purely injunctive and thus equitable, and joint and several liability, if not expressly provided for by the statute, is a legal remedy associated with damages actions rather than an equitable one.[179]

Other issues relative to joint and several liability are discussed in Section 6.04, *infra*.

[iii] Bankrupt Defendants

Bankruptcy of a primary defendant could present a barrier to relief, if Section 7003 actions are not exempt from orders staying proceedings issued by a bankruptcy.

The early decisions on the issue resulted in conflicting decisions. In the one case involving the federal government as a Section 7003 plaintiff and a bankrupt defendant, *United States v. Johns-Manville Sales Corp.*,[180] the district court applied the automatic stay provision of the Bankruptcy Code[181] to stay the "police regulatory powers" exception.[182]

In *Penn Terra Ltd. v. Pennsylvania Department of Environmental Resources*,[183] however, the Third Circuit refused to bar Pennsylvania's action brought under state law seeking a mandatory injunction requiring the bankrupt defendant to undertake cleanup activities at a waste site. The court reasoned that the police power exemption applied in that case.

---

177 *See, e.g.*, United States v. M/V BIG SAM, 611 F.2d 432, 439 (5th Cir. 1982), *cert. denied*, 103 S. Ct. 3112 (1983).

178 *See* case law discussed in Sections 6.04-6.09, *infra*.

179 *See* United States v. J.B. Stringfellow, (C.D. Calif. 4-5-84)(concluding that liability for cost recovery and damages under Section 107 of CERCLA is joint and several, but rejecting joint and several liability under Section 106 of CERCLA and Section 7003). *Compare* United States v. Ottati and Goss, Inc., 630 F. Supp. 1361 (D.N.H. 1985).

180 United States v. Johns-Manville Sales Corp., 18 ERC 1177 (D.N.H. 11-15-82).

181 11 USC §362(b).

182 The federal government does not possess "police powers," as such. Its regulatory activities are grounded in the Commerce Clause.

183 733 F.2d 267 (3d Cir., 1984).

The Supreme Court's decision in *Ohio v. Kovacs*[184] seems to muddy the water further. The Court upheld a Sixth Circuit decision concerning a state court judgment that had been executed by the appointment of a receiver to seize the assets of the bankrupt waste site owner as an avoidable claim for money. Although the court appeared to approve of *Penn Terra* in a footnote, the opinion in other places seems clearly only to exempt negative injunctions from the proscriptions of the bankruptcy code. As a practical matter, if mandatory relief is unavailable in an imminent and substantial endangerment suit, the goverments are essentially without any relief at all.[185]

In *Midlantic Bank v. New Jersey Dep't of Environmental Protection*,[186] the Court again addressed the bankruptcy issue. In a closely divided opinion, the Court concluded that a bankruptcy trustee may not abandon a hazardous waste site to avoid compliance with state hazardous waste laws requiring cleanup.[187]

§6.04   Overview of Comprehensive Environmental Response, Compensation and Liability Act (CERCLA)

[1]   In General

The Comprehensive Environmental Response, Compensation and Liability Act of 1980[188] was the result of several years of congressional hearings, and much public clamor about the hazards presented by abandoned hazardous waste dumps.[189] It is a complex statute, pat-

---

[184] 469 U.S. 274, 105 S. Ct. 705 (1985).

[185] If the bankrupt defendant is a TSD facility that had earlier complied with EPA's financial responsibility requirements, Section 3004(t), added in 1984, lets EPA proceed directly against the guarantor.

[186] — U.S. —, 106 S.Ct. 755 (1986), consolidated with O'Neill v. City of New York et al. (lower court decision: In the Matter of Quanta Resources Corp., 739 F.2d 912, 21 ERC 1241 (3d Cir. 1984)).

[187] The Court did not address the question of the level of cleanup to which the site must be remediated out of the assets of the debtor's estate.

[188] 42 USC §§9601 *et seq.*; P.L. 96-510 (12-11-80) as amended by the Superfund Amendments and Reauthorization Act of 1986, P.L. 99-499 (10-17-86).

[189] *See generally,* H.R. Rep. 1016, 96th Cong., 2d Sess., *reprinted in* 1980 U.S. Code Cong. & Adm. News 6119 *et seq.* CERCLA emerged after a somewhat lengthy debate over whether to further amend Section 311 of the Clean Water Act to cover hazardous wastes more broadly. *See Hazardous and Toxic Waste Disposal: Joint Hearings on 5.1341 and 5.1480 Before the Subcommittees on Environmental Pollution and Resource Protection of the Senate Committee on Environment and Public Works, 96th Cong., 1st Sess.*

terned on Section 311 of the Clean Water Act,[190] but embodying a number of concepts borrowed from RCRA, and much that is unique.

CERCLA was pushed out by a lame duck session of the Congress. Its legislative history is riddled with uncertainty because the lawmakers drafted the bill hastily and because last minute compromises forced changes that went largely unexplained.[191]

CERCLA contains four components. Section 106(a) is an imminent and substantial endangerment provision similar to Section 7003 of RCRA. Sections 104, 105, and 107 establish government emergency response authority and provide for private sector liability for reimbursing the government's response costs and compensating for natural resource damages. Sections 111 and 112 provide a mechanism for government compensation of persons suffering property damage as a result of hazardous substance release. Title II of CERCLA levied a tax on crude oil received at the refinery and imported petroleum products, levied a sales tax on forty-two basic chemicals,[192] established a Hazardous Substance Response Trust Fund,[193] and appropriated monies for use under CERCLA during its first five years of operation.

The original taxing provisions terminated under a sunset provision that tolled in late 1985. The 1986 Superfund Amendments changed the taxing provisions significantly. The reauthorized superfund was increased from the original $1.6 billion amount to $8.5 billion, for an additional five-year period (which ends in 1991). The fund is financed by a combination of continuation of the excise tax on petroleum and feedstock chemicals,[194] a new excise tax on a group of imported chemicals,[195] and an income tax on corporations.[195.1] A final part of the CER-

---

[190] *See generally* Section 6.02, *supra.*

[191] *See* Eckhardt, *The Unfinished Business of Hazardous Waste Control,* 33 Baylor L. Rev. 253 (1981); Grad, *A Legislative History of the Comprehensive Environmental Response, Compensation and Liability Act of 1980,* 8 Colum. J. Env. L. 1 (1982); Note, *Liability for Generators of Hazardous Waste: The Failure of Existing Enforcement Mechanisms,* 69 Geo. L. J. 1047, 1056 *et seq.* (1981). *See generally Superfund: Legislative History,* Environmental Law Institute (1983)(section-by-section excerpts from legislative proceedings); and Note, 130 U. Pa. L. Rev. 1229, 1242-45 (1982).

[192] Subtitle A, 26 USC §§4611-12, 4661-62. The chemicals taxed are those commonly used as feedstock in the production of more complex chemical products.

[193] Subtitle B, 42 USC §9631-33.

[194] Sections 4611 and 4661-4662, Internal Revenue Code of 1986.

[195] Sections 4671-4672, Internal Revenue Code of 1986. Chemicals subject to taxation are listed in Section 4672(a)(3).

[195.1] Section 59A, Internal Revenue Code of 1986. How much money these taxes will

CLA tax package, a tax on motor fuels and oils, was enacted to fund a trust fund for cleanups of leaking underground storage tanks under the RCRA LUST program.[195.2]

Much debated was whether or not to provide a victim compensation provision in CERCLA allowing compensation for bodily injury as well as for property damage. Section 301(e) represents the compromise reached on that issue in 1980. It provided funding for, and directed the carrying out of, a study on the adequacy of existing common law and statutory remedies for harm following exposure to hazardous substances.[196] Section 309, added in 1986, is an outgrowth of the Section 301(e) study. It establishes a uniform federal commencement date for state statutes of limitation covering actions for personal injury or property damage arising from "exposure to hazardous substances, or pollutants or contaminants released into the environment from a facility."[196.1] Effective retroactive to December 11, 1980, the uniform commencement trigger is the date the plaintiff knew or reasonably should have known that the injury or damage was caused or contributed to by the substance.[196.2]

CERCLA, as originally enacted, could not even begin to address the whole of the abandoned-site problem. There were known to be thousands of sites, on which cleanup would cost tens of billions of dollars. Congress initially provided for raising via taxation not more than $1.38 billion for the Trust Fund.[197] That amount, in addition to funds transferred from the Section 311 and Section 504 Clean Water Act trust funds,[198] created a fund whose total was in the neighborhood of $1.5 billion. Spending authority was authorized for five years,[199] with $44

---

actually raise, and the extent to which the President will be willing to commit general revenue funds to the program, will ultimately determine the size of the superfund.

[195.2] Amendment to Section 4081, Internal Revenue Code 1986.

[196] The study was completed late in 1982.

[196.1] Section 309(a)(1).

[196.2] Section 309(b)(4). There is a tolling provision for minors and incompetents.

[197] Section 303.

[198] Section 221(b)(3).

[199] Section 221(b)(2). The taxing provision "sunsetted" after four years as well. *See* Section 303. The Reauthorized CERCLA, P.L. 99-499 (1986), funds an $8.5 billion superfund.

million available to be appropriated in each of the first four years.[200]

The relative paucity of cleanup funds provided under the 1980 CERCLA presented EPA[201] with a dilemma. The Agency could either clean up relatively few sites completely, or address a larger number of sites only partially. Congress provided some guidance in CERCLA. Section 105(8) required the compillation of a list of "at least four hundred" sites as the "top priority among known response targets."[202] Section 104(c)(4), in addition, requires that remedial actions be "practicable . . . and . . . provide for that cost-effective response which provides a balance between the need for protection of public health and welfare and the environment at the facility under consideration, and the availability of amounts from the Fund . . . to respond to other sites . . . taking into consideration the need for immediate action."

Which site gets how much money when quickly developed into a political contest among competing states. Section 105(8)(B) requires the government to "consider any priorities established by the States," and to include at least one site from each state on the list. Selection of sites for the list was accomplished by EPA's requesting each state to submit a list of candidate sites along with a numerical assessment of the degree of hazard each represented calculated by means of EPA's Hazard Ranking System (HRS).[203]

The core of the HRS is a mathematical model developed under contract to EPA by the Mitre Corporation. The model translates raw data about the site, its environs, and the type of chemicals present into a number. In theory, sites with the greatest potential for human exposure to more dangerous substances will score the highest, and thus receive earlier attention. The Mitre model was criticized by industry analysts during its development as employing overly conservative as-

---

200 Section 221(b)(2).

201 CERCLA vests administrative authority in the President, but allows delegation of the authority. Section 115. Administration of CERCLA was delegated to EPA by Executive Order 12316, 47 Fed. Reg. 42237 (8-20-81).

202 The priority list was published as a proposed rule on December 30, 1982. 47 Fed. Reg. 58476, promulgated on Sept. 8, 1983, 48 Fed. Reg. 40669, and amended on May 8, 1984, 49 Fed. Reg. 19482, on September 21, 1984, 49 Fed. Reg. 37030, on February 14, 1985, 50 Fed. Reg. 6320 (adding sites to the list), on September 16, 1985 (adding one site to the list and altering the mechanism by which new sites can be added), on March 7, 1986, 51 Fed. Reg. 7935, and on June 10, 1986, 51 Fed. Reg. 21077. As of late 1986, 703 sites had been listed. The list is Appendix B to 40 CFR Part 300.

203 40 CFR Part 300, Appendix A.

sumptions about exposure pathways and travel times. The greatest flaw in the HRS, however, is the fact that the state employees who filled out the HRS score sheets often did so with very little information about the site. In the absence of actual data, if one made "worst case" assumptions about important inputs, the site's score would be higher than if one made "realistic" inputs.

EPA's strategy was initially to coerce as much privately financed response action as possible, utilizing Section 106 of CERCLA along with Section 7003 of RCRA,[204] and to encourage state-funded cleanups. Partly as a consequence of this strategy, and partly because of the elaborate multilayered study process EPA established for evaluating sites prior to cleanup,[205] EPA had completed remedial work on less than ten sites when Congress began to consider reauthorization of the about-to-sunset CERCLA in mid-1984.

[2] Summary of Superfund Amendments and Reauthorization Act of 1986 (SARA)

The Superfund Amendments and Reauthorization Act of 1986 (SARA) imposed major modifications and reforms on CERCLA, including changes in methods of program funding, the establishment of new priorities and timetables, and modifications of affected parties' liabilities and rights in litigation. All the changes effected by the 1986 Superfund Amendments are comprehensively and integrally reflected throughout this chapter, but some of the major changes are noted here for the reader's convenience.

It took two years of congressional negotiation, and several short-term funding resolutions to keep the superfund program afloat, before a reauthorized CERCLA was finally presented to the President in early October 1986. The reauthorized CERCLA, P.L. 99-499, called the Superfund Amendments and Reauthorization Act of 1986, and generally referred to as "SARA," in addition to substantially increasing the superfund, to $8.5 billion for the authorization period ending in 1991, amended the substantive provisions of the bill in a number of significant

---

[204] *See* Guidelines for Using Imminent Hazard, Enforcement, and Emergency Response Authorities of Superfund and Other Statutes, 47 Fed. Reg. 20664 (5-13-82).

[205] See *infra.*

ways, addressing virtually all of the issues that had arisen under the superfund program in its first five years of management. Among those amendments are a requirement that EPA review the HRS model, to focus on "relative degree of risk" and to look again at water contamination pathways;[205.1] the imposition of time limits for the completion of site assessments on sites in EPA's data base of potential priority list sites;[205.2] and numerical targets for undertaking remedial action at listed sites.[205.3]

The reauthorized CERCLA also radically restructured the criteria under which remedies are selected and the procedures involved in remedy selection. The "how clean is clean" issue, which dominated the post-1980 debate over CERCLA, is addressed head-on by a new provision, Section 121. This section basically codified EPA's 1985 extent of remedy standard, which the Agency inserted in the NCP in that year, but toughened the standard, imposing a bias toward remedies that are "permanent" (that is, involving destruction of hazardous substances rather than reburying them). This change may increase the average cost of a superfund cleanup by three times the pre-1986 cost.

The SARA amendments also impose a structured settlement process on the government and potentially responsible parties, and, on a related issue, establish a separate, parallel track for deciding on remedial action for federal facilities.

A number of litigated and other issues were addressed. These included insertion of a statutory right of contribution among PRPs, clearing up the statute of limitation muddle that had plagued CERCLA from its outset, addressing the plight of innocent landowners, insertion of a general penalty provision, and a citizen suit provision. EPA's inspection and information-gathering authority was broadened significantly, EPA's power to enter sites and adjacent areas was clarified, and the right of eminent domain was clearly provided. The bar against preenforcement review, which had been found to exist by several courts under the old CERCLA, was made explicit. The SARA amendments did a number of other things, as well, which are discussed throughout this chapter *infra*.

[205.1] Section 105(c) (1986).

[205.2] Sections 116(a) and 116(b) (1986).

[205.3] Sections 116(d) and 116(e) (1986). The numerical targets (450 new Remedial Investigation/Feasibility Studies and commencement of on-site remedial action at 375 sites over five years) are optimistic, in light of the Agency's prior record.

Finally, Congress enacted a wholly new program as Title III of CER-CLA, the Emergency Planning and Community Right to Know Act of 1986.[205.4]

§6.05   Private Remedial Actions Under CERCLA Section 106

[1]   In General

Section 106(a), the CERCLA imminent and substantial endanger-ment provision, authorizes the government to sue to abate an "immi-nent and substantial endangerment to the public health or welfare or the environment" caused by "an actual or threatened release of a haz-ardous substance from a facility."

Shortly after CERCLA was signed into law, the Department of Jus-tice began amending the complaints in the pending Section 7003 ac-tions to include a separate claim for relief under Section 106(A). EPA began to issue notice letters to potentially responsible parties connect-ed with sites under investigation advising them of potential liability for reimbursement of federal response costs, and offering them an oppor-tunity to undertake remedial action on their own.[206] Actions against private parties commenced subsequent to CERCLA's enactment have generally contained both Section 106(a) and Section 7003 claims, and, where the government has or expects to spend public funds on the site, a claim for reimbursement under Section 107.

[2]   Persons Liable

Unlike Section 7003, which identifies the persons to whom it ap-plies,[207] Section 106(a) does not designate the class of defendants. It merely authorizes the Attorney General to secure relief with respect to conditions caused by actual or threatened "release" of a hazardous substance from a "facility." Section 101(9) defines "facility" broadly, to include pipelines, structures, land areas, motor vehicles, rail cars, or

---

[205.4] *See* Section §6.11, *infra.*

[206] Guidelines for Using Imminent Hazard, Enforcement, and Emergency Response Authorities of Superfund and Other Statutes, 47 Fed. Reg. 20664 (5-13-82).

[207] The language used is "person contributing to . . .."

aircraft where a "hazardous substance"[208] has "been deposited, stored, disposed of, or placed, or otherwise come to be located." "Relese" is defined by Section 101(22) as "any spilling, leaking, pumping, pouring, emiting, emptying, discharging, injecting, escaping, leaching, dumping or disposing into the environment. . . ."[209]

The applicability of Section 106 to spill emergencies is clear and unambiguous. What is not clear is the extent to which the statute applies to inactive or abandoned waste disposal sites, which are the primary targets of Sections 104 and 107, the range of defendants from whom the government may seek relief, and what sort of relief may be obtained.

[a] Inactive and Abandoned Sites

Although Sections 104 and 107(a) are clearly retroactive in their application, by both their language and the legislative history,[210] Section 106(a) on its face provides no more evidence of applicability to inactive sites than does Section 3007 of RCRA. The legislative history on the House side, where CERCLA originated, nevertheless evidences an intention that Section 106(a) provide a remedy for releases or threatened releases from abandoned sites.[211]

Primarily on the strength of the House legislative history, a majority of the courts considering the issue have concluded that Section 106(a) applies to inactive or abandoned sites.[212] In *United States* v. *Northeast-*

---

[208] "Hazardous substance" is defined by Section 101(14).

[209] There are specific exclusions for engine exhaust emissions (regulated under the Clean Air Act), releases confined to the workplace (subject to OSHA regulation), nuclear incidents (Atomic Energy Act and Uranium Mill Tailing Act), and "[t]he normal application of fertilizer." *See* Sections 101(22)(A)-(D).

[210] *See* State ex rel. Brown v. Georgeoff, 562 F. Supp. 1300, 1302-12 (N.D. Ohio 1983).

[211] *See* H. R. Rep. No. 1016, 96th Cong., 2d Sess. 27-28, *reprinted in* 1980 U.S. Code Cong. and Adm. News at 6130-31.

[212] United States v. Northeastern Pharmaceutical and Chemical Co., Inc., 579 F. Supp. 823, 20 ERC 1401, 1415 (W.D. Mo. 1984); United States v. Ottati and Goss, Inc., 630 F. Supp. 1705 (D.N.H. 1985); United States v. Outboard Marine Corp, 556 F. Supp. 54, 57-58 (N.D. Ill. 1982); United States v. Price, 577 F. Supp. 1103, No. 80-4104 (D.N.J. 7-28-83). *See also* United States v. Reilly Tar and Chemical Corp., 546 F. Supp. 1100, 1113-14 (D. Minn. 1982). *Contra*, United States v. Wade, 546 F. Supp. 785, 793 (E.D. Pa. 1982) (pointing to semantic differences between Section 7003 and Section 106 and absence of sufficient congressional intention to use Section 106(a) as a site cleanup, as opposed to a spill abatement, device). As discussed *infra*, the 1984 amendment to Section 7003 makes it clearly retrospective in scope.

ern Pharmaceutical and Chemical Co., Inc.,[213] the court concluded that Section 106(a), while "not a general cleanup provision," was available "when the normal route through Sections 104 and 107(a) proved to be too time consuming and cumbersome in the face of an imminent and substantial endangerment."[214] This reasoning is not persuasive. Sections 104 and 107(a) allow the government to spend its money quickly, and litigate for reimbursement later. Section 106(a) only creates a cause of action, requiring litigation prior to cleanup action. A direct remedy will always be quicker than a litigative one.[215]

The better argument for retroactive application of Section 106(a), at least in terms of sites, is that for CERCLA to provide a full remedial scheme, Section 106(a) must be allowed to work in tandem with Sections 104 and 107(a), particularly in view of the monetary limits of the superfund.[216] Viewed in this light, the government is provided with a menu of remedies with which to address inactive and abandoned sites that happen to present an imminent and substantial endangerment. EPA can spend such superfund monies as quickly as is necessary to stop an immediate threat, while the full remedy can await the outcome of Section 106(a) litigation.

Notwithstanding the availability of and the government's initial desire to use Section 106(a) generally as a mechanism for achieving complete site cleanup where the superfund limitations prevent the government from achieving that goal under Section 104,[217] not every site that is eligible for Section 104 expenditures will also meet the "imminent and substantial endangerment" criterion of Section 106(a). Section 104(a)(1) authorized government expenditures in all cases involving a "release" or a "substantial threat of" a relase of a hazardous

----

213 579 F. Supp. 823, 20 ERC at 1415.

214 *Id.,* at fn. 17.

215 The *Niagara Falls* cases, for example, filed initially in 1979, consumed over four years of pretrial activities before a majority of the cases were settled, and initial remedial work could begin.

216 *Cf.* Northeastern Pharmaceutical, 579 F. Supp. 823, 20 ERC at 1416 (footnote); and United States v. Ottati and Goss, Inc., *supra* note 212.

217 *See* Guidelines for Using Imminent Hazard . . . Authority, *supra* note 204; United States v. Price, 577 F. Supp. 1103 at fn.8 (D.N.J. 7-28-83). EPA, for reasons not articulated by it, virtually stopped referring Section 106 actions to the Justice Department during 1985. This use of Section 106(a) had essentially ceased by late 1984, apparently because, as a policy matter, EPA decided that it is more expeditious to spend federal money first and litigate later, or to bring prospective Section 107 cost reimbursement actions.

substance into the environment.[218] Although Sections 104(c) and 105 make it clear that only releases that pose a potential hazard to health, welfare, or the environment warrant public expenditures, the degree of hazard for Section 104 purposes is not required to rise to the "imminent and substantial endangerment" level.

Therefore, particularly as the superfund program matures, and the most urgent problem areas are taken care of, there will be some sites that can be addressed jointly under Sections 104/107 and 106, but many that qualify only for Section 104/107 treatment.[219]

[b] Acts Completed Prior to CERCLA's Enactment

Site owners and transporters whose acts at a site entirely predated CERCLA's effective date are nevertheless subject to lawsuits brought under Section 106(a).[220] In contrast to the law that developed under Section 7003 of RCRA prior to its amendment in 1984, a majority of the courts considering the issue concluded that past, nonnegligent off-site generators are appropriate defendants in Section 106(a) actions.[221] This appears to be a classic retroactive imposition of liability for conduct not unlawful at the time it occurred.[222]

---

[218] Curiously, the wording of Section 104(a) authorizes federal expenditures in the case of release or threat of release of a "pollutant or contaminant" only when it poses "an imminent and substantial danger to the public health or welfare." The term "pollutant or contaminant" is defined in Section 104(a)(2) as a substance that, if ingested, causes death, disease, or injury. *See* discussion *infra.*

[219] In United States v. Price, No. 80-4104, slip op. at 25fn.9 (D.N.J. 7-13-83), the court, in dicta, opined that Section 106(a) allows EPA "to at least have a judicial remedy against potentially responsible parties prior to spending taxpayer money." The court did not, however, address the issue raised here.

[220] United States v. Reilly Tar and Chemical Corp., 546 F. Supp. 1100, 20 ERC 1058, 1068 (D. Minn. 1983) (prior owner); United States v. Outboard Marine Corp., 556 F. Supp. 54, 58n.3 (N.D. Ill. 1982) (prior owner); State ex rel. Brown v. Georgeoff, 562 F. Supp. 1300, 1311 (N.D. Ohio 1983) (transporters).

[221] United States v. Ottati and Goss, Inc., 630 F. Supp. 1361 (D.N.H. 1985); United States v. Price, 577 F. Supp. 1103, 19 ERC 1638 (D.N.J. 1983); United States v. Conservation Chemical Co., 589 F. Supp. 59, 20 ERC 1427 (W.D. Mo. 1984); United States v. A. & F. Materials Co., Inc., 578 F. Supp. 1249, 20 ERC 1353 (S.D. Ill. 1984); United States v. Northeastern Pharmaceutical & Chemical Co., Inc., 579 F. Supp. 823, 20 ERC 1401 (W.D. Mo. 1984). *Contra,* United States v. Wade, 546 F. Supp. 784, 793 (E.D. Pa. 1982).

[222] United States v. J. B. Stringfellow, 20 ERC 1912, 1914 (C.D. Cal. 1984) (Section 107). *But see* United States v. Price, 688 F.2d 204 (3d Cir. 1982)(reasoning that since the resultant activity (leaking) is ongoing, the statute is not retroactive in its application to past completed acts that set in motion the ongoing condition); United States v. Ottati & Goss, Inc., 23 ERC 1705 (12-9-85).

Retroactive liability under Section 106 has given rise to arguments that the statute violates the due process clause of the Fifth Amendment. In the wake of the Supreme Court decision in *Usery v. Turner Elkhurn Mining Co.*,[223] requiring the plaintiff to show that Congress's action was "arbitrary and irrational,"[224] such arguments stand little likelihood of success.[225]

[c]　Relationship to Section 107

Whether the range of potential defendants under Section 106 is identical to the persons liable for reimbursement under Section 107 is an intriguing issue that could be of importance to some defendants. The issue arises because Section 107(a) delineates the range of potentially responsible persons with language that is in some respects not clear.[226] Section 107's language making transporters liable, for example, encompasses only transporters who actually selected the TSD facility to which the wastes were delivered and from which a release has occurred.[227]

The issue of parity between Sections 106(a) and 107(a) has most frequently been raised in connection with the inactive site issue, where a conclusion that jurisdiction is coextensive tends to broaden the range of potential defendants under Section 106(a). In several of such cases, the courts have opined that only persons listed as liable under Section 107(a) are liable under Section 106(a).[228]

Another reading of the statutory scheme would include all Section 107(a)–liable entities within Section 106(a)'s reach but not limit Section

---

[223] 428 U.S. 1 (1976).

[224] *Id.*, at 15.

[225] *See* United States v. Ottati and Goss, Inc., *supra;* United States v. Northeastern Pharmaceutical & Chemical Co., Inc., 579 F. Supp. 823, 20 ERC at 1416 (W.D. Mo. 1984); United States v. South Carolina Recycling and Disposal, Inc., 20 ERC 1753 (D.S.C. 2-23-84)(opining that CERCLA not "retroactive," but would not be unconstitutional even if it were)(Section 107 case); State ex rel. Brown v. Georgeoff, 562 F. Supp. 1300, 1307n.7 (N.D. Ohio 1983) (dictum); United States v. Ottati & Goss, Inc., *supra* note 222.

[226] *See* discussion at Section 6.07, *infra.*

[227] Section 107(a)(4).

[228] *See, e.g.*, Cadillac Fairview/California v. Dow Chemical Co., 20 ERC 1108, 1113 (C.D. Cal. 1984); United States v. A & F Materials, Inc., 578 F. Supp. 1249, 20 ERC 1353, 1360 (S.D. Ill. 1984); and United States v. Northwestern Pharmaceutical & Chemical Co., 579 F.Supp. at 823, 20 ERC at 1415.

106(a) relief to Section 107 entities.[229] A third view is that there is no parallelism whatever between Sections 106(a) and 107(a), and therefore that the persons potentially liable for injunctive relief are not necessarily the same as those liable for cost reimbursement under Section 107(a).[230]

[d] Miscellaneous Jurisdictional Issues

Defendants in several early Section 106(a) actions argued that the statute was merely jurisdictional, and that liability must be premised on the federal common law of nuisance, which had been held to require allegations of an interstate effect. Those arguments, also raised in several Section 7003 RCRA cases, were uniformly rejected by the courts.[231]

Section 106(a) does not expressly provide a basis for a private action for injunction relief. Further, it has been held that an *implied* private right of action may not be inferred from the CERCLA statutory scheme.[232]

Arguments in the earlier cases that Section 106(a) was inactive until the revised National Contingency Plan was adopted or until enforcement guidelines under Section 106(c) were adopted were generally rejected.[233]

[3] Trial and Remedial Issues

[a] Elements: Imminent and Substantial Endangerment . . . Because of an Actual or Threatened Release of Hazardous Substance from a Facility . . .

The elements of a Section 106(a) action that must be proved by the government are—

---

[229] *Cf.* United States v. Outboard Marine Corp., 556 F. Supp. 54, 56 (N.D. Ill. 1982)("Whatever the source of the substantive law to be applied in a 106(a) action, it is most probable that those who would be liable under Section 107 were intended to be liable in an action under 106(a) for injunctive relief.")

[230] *Cf.* United States v. J. B. Stringfellow, 20 ERC 1905, 1910 (C.D. Cal. 4-5-84)(reasoning that there is no joint and several liability under Section 106).

[231] United States v. Reilly Tar and Chemical Corp., 546 F. Supp. 110, 1113 (D. Minn. 1982); *see also* United States v. Solvents Recovery Service of New England, 496 F. Supp. 1133-39 (D. Conn. 1980)(Section 7003 RCRA).

[232] Cadillac Fairview/California Inc. v. Dow Chemical Co., 20 ERC 1108, 1116 (C.D. Cal. 1984)(applying a Cort v. Ash, 422 U.S. 66 (1975), analysis).

[233] *See* United States v. Outboard Marine Corp., 556 F. Supp. 556, (N.D. Ill. 1982).

(1)   an imminent and substantial endangerment

(2)   posed by an actual or threatened release

(3)   of a hazardous substance

(4)   from a facility.

What is required in the way of pleading and proof arguably depends upon whether Section 106(a) is a substantive statute, imposing liability either with or without fault, or is merely jurisdictional, requiring some other source of law, such as the common law, or other federal statutory provisions to define the nature of the evidence needed to support liability. Whether Section 106(a) is a substantive or a jurisdictional statute has been the subject of some controversy.[234] It does provide some substantive guidelines.

CERCLA defines two of the elements, "hazardous substance" and "facility."[235] The statute also defines "release."[236] Proof that an "actual" release has occurred involves rather straightforward gathering of physical evidence.[237] Difficulty arises, however, in determining when there is a "threatened" release and determining what constitutes an "imminent and substantial endangerment to public health or welfare or the environment" because those terms are not defined.

As one might suspect, the courts have managed to define the terms on a case-by-case basis, and have developed a sort of imminent hazard "common law." In general, the government's argument that it should not be held to a rigorous standard of proof has prevailed.

In *United States v. Northeastern Pharmaceutical and Chemical Co.*,[238] the court found that the government had met its burden of proof

---

234 *See* United States v. Reilly Tar & Chemical Corp., 546 F. Supp, 1110, 1113, 17 ERC 2110 (D. Minn. 8-20-82)(statute substantive by common law principle applicable); United States v. Outboard Marine Corp., 556 F. Supp. 54 (N.D. Ill. 1982)(statute carries some substantive requirements, common law inapplicable); United States v. A.&F. Materials, 578 F. Supp. 1249, 20 ERC 1353 (S.D. Ill. 1-20-84); United States v. Price, 577 F. Supp. 1103, 19 ERC 1638, 1647 (D.N.J. 1983) (Section 106(a) dependent on Section 107 substantive standards).

235 Sections 101 (14) and 101 (9).

236 Section 101 (22).

237 For example, if off-site groundwater migration is the "release," groundwater samples from downgradient wells can be introduced showing contamination by some of the constituents found at the facility. Unless there is another potential source of the constituents, such proof would be sufficient to satisfy the second element. Expert testimony on the local groundwater hydrology is required if there is more than one possible source of the contamination.

238 579 F.Supp. 823, 20 ERC at 1421 (W.D. Mo. 1984).

by showing that the "compounds found at the . . . site were highly toxic at low dosage levels and given the conditions of the soil and bedrock beneath the site there was a substantial likelihood of human and environmental exposure," relying heavily on the case law developed under Section 7003 of RCRA.[239] The government need not show that "a crisis has arisen or a catastrophic disaster has struck."[240]

If Section 106 is to function as an emergency provision, rather than a general cleanup provision, however, the government must be required to prove more than the presence of hazardous constituents in or on the ground. Some showing of the likelihood of escape and contamination of an important part of the environment or human exposure must be proven. In addition, there is some evidence suggestive of congressional intent that such statutes as Section 106(a) be utilized only when the ordinary administrative and judicial remedies will be too slow to achieve a salutary result.[241]

In spite of the apparent logic of the position, the government has managed to prevail in a number of cases with its argument that Section 106(a) provides an alternative remedy to Sections 104 and 107, even in situations where government expenditure and recoupment is possible.[242] The better view, however, is that Section 106(a) is available "when the normal route through Sections 104 and 107(a) proved to be "too time consuming and cumbersome" or otherwise inadequate in "the face of an imminent and substantial endangerment."[243] Section

---

[239] *E.g.*, United States v. Hardage No. 80-1031-W, slip op. at 3-4 (W.D. Okla. 12-2-80)("imminency of hazard does not depend on the proximity of the final effect but may be proven by the setting in motion of a chain of events which could cause serious injury").

[240] EDF v. Lamphier, 12 ELR 20843, 20844 (E.D. Va. 1982).

[241] The only legislative history directly addressing an imminent hazard provision is from the Safe Drinking Water Act. H.R. Rep. No. 1185, 93d Cong., 2d Sess. 35-36 (1974). Since the SDWA deals only with public health, that legislative history is of limited usefulness as far as Section 106(a) is concerned. In discussing "imminence," the House Committee stated that the term should be considered "in light of the time it may take to prepare administrative orders or moving papers to commence and complete litigation and to permit issuance, notification implementation, and enforcement of administrative or court orders to protect the public health."

[242] *See* United States v. Reilly Tar & Chemical Co., 546 F. Supp. 1100, 114 (D. Minn. 1982); United States v. Price, No. 80-4140 (D.N.J. 1983); and United States v. A. & F. Materials, Inc., 578 F. Supp. 823, 20 ERC 1353 (S.D. Ill. 1984)(mandatory injunction available).

[243] United States v. Northeastern Pharmaceutical and Chemical Company, 579 F.

106(a) is obviously the remedy of choice where what is needed is an order to cease some ongoing activity. Conceptual problems with the Section 106(a) remedy are greatest with its use to force private sector cleanup of old, leaking disposal sites.

[b]   Standard of Liability

Since Section 106(a) addresses hazards and not parties,[244] the statute provides no guidance as to whether liability on the part of persons responsible for abating the conditions is strict, or must be premised on a showing of fault, such as negligence.

In this case, resort to Section 107 is not helpful, because that provision does not clearly provide for either strict liability or a fault-based standard to be imposed for recovering cleanup costs expended by the government under Section 104. The legislative history compounds the problem because the Senate version of Section 107(a), which was not adopted, contained express language imposing strict liability on responsible persons.[245] Nevertheless, a majority of the courts considering the issue have reasoned that both Section 106(a) and Section 107(a) impose strict liability, relying on the fact that Section 101(32) of CERCLA incorporates the Clean Water Act's Section 311 strict standard of liability by reference.[246]

In *United States v. Ottati and Goss, Inc.*, [246.1] the district court concluded that the standard of liability under Section 106 was determined by reference to Section 107, and that Section 106(a) is dependent upon the substantive liability provisions of Section 107.

Supp. 823, 20 ERC at 1415n.17 (W.D. Mo. 1984). In most cases, however, the expenditure of federal funds may provide a quicker remedy than does Section 106(a) litigation.

[244] *Compare* the text of Section 7003, RCRA.

[245] S. 1480, 96th Cong., 2d Sess., *reprinted in The Environmental Emergency Response Act: Hearings Before the Senate Committee on Finance on S. 1480*, 96th Cong., 2d Sess. 5 (1980). *See also* 38 Cong. Q. Weekly Rep. 3436 (11-29-80); and 126 Cong. Rec. H. 11,787 (daily ed. 12-3-80)(remarks of Rep. Florio).

[246] United States v. Conservation Chemical Co., 628 F. Supp. 391 (W.D. Mo. 1985); United States v. Wade, 546 F. Supp. at 793fn.24 (E.D. Pa. 1982); United States v. Price, 577 F. Supp. 1103 (D.N.J. 1983); United States v. Northeastern Pharmaceutical and Chemical Co., Inc., 579 F. Supp. 823, 20 ERC 1401, 1419 (W.D. Mo. 1984).

[246.1] 630 F. Supp. 1361 (D.N.H. 1985).

[c] Joint and Several Liability

The joint and several liability issue is discussed in detail in connection with Section 107, *infra,* and that discussion is also generally applicable to Section 106(a).

The government has sought to establish that all responsible parties are jointly and severally liable to abate imminent hazard conditions at sites that are the subject of Section 106(a) lawsuits. Similarly, the government argued that it is not required in individual cases to prove that the chemicals found to be leaking or migrating from the site are actually those placed at the site by or on behalf of a particular defendant.[247] As discussed *infra,*[248] CERCLA as originally enacted was silent on the question of joint and several liability. Although most of the courts considering the issue have not focused on a distinction between Sections 106 and 107, it is arguable that such a distinction should be made, and that the question of joint and several liability may well be decided differently under the two provisions.

The argument in favor of joint and several liability under Section 106(a) is that Congress intended Sections 106(a) and 107(a) to be parallel and equivalent in their scope. The language of CERCLA, however, does not support the proposition, and the legislative history is ambiguous.

The argument against joint and several liability under Section 106 begins with the premise that the source of law for joint and several liability under Section 107(a) is the common law, since the legislative history points in that direction. Joint and several liability, the argument goes, is a legal, as opposed to an equitable, remedy, which is consistent with Section 107(a), under which the federal government seeks money from a group of defendants. Since the Section 106(a) remedy is equitable in nature, that statute should be unavailable as a surrogate for Section 107 in recovering federal cleanup costs, and thus the common law premise upon which joint and several liability rests is absent.[249]

The contrary argument, represented by the reasoning of *United*

---

[247] Such was held in United States v. South Carolina Recycling and Disposal, Inc., 20 ERC 1753 (D.S.C. 1984)(generators liable if they contributed wastes "like those . . . present at the time of clean-up").

[248] See Section 6.07[2][i], *infra.*

[249] *See* United States v. J. B. Stringfellow, 20 ERC 1905, 1910 (C.D. Cal. 1984).

States v. Ottati and Goss, Inc.,[249.1] and *United States v. Conservation Chemical Co.*, [249.2] is that Sections 106 and 107 are so closely linked in their mission that the standards under each must be identical.

Whichever line of argument will ultimately prevail may depend, in the absence of clarifying legislative action, upon the general scope of the relief available in a Section 106(a) action. If Section 106(a) is viewed as a relatively narrow, prospective statute under which only injunctive relief may be secured, imposition of joint and several liability may be disfavored. Mandatory injunctive relief normally requires the court to spell out what is required to be done and who must do it. Although it is not inconceivable that a court would order a group of defendants to undertake an action jointly and severally, the apportionment of responsibility among the defendants may in such a case be more difficult than simply apportioning a monetary judgment.[250]

[d] Scope of Relief

Prohibitive or mandatory injunctive relief is available under Section 106(a), although mandatory relief may require a more compelling evidentiary case.[251] It is doubtful that Section 106(a) can provide an alternative basis for reimbursement of money spent by the government on the site.[252]

Sections 104(c) and 105(7) both contain language that imposes cost-effectiveness limitations on government-financed response activities.[253] Thus, CERCLA implies that, in most federally financed response cases, *complete* site cleanup will not occur. It appears that Section 106(a)'s applicability to imminent and substantial endangerment pro-

---

[249.1] 630 F. Supp. 1361 (D.N.H. 1985).

[249.2] 628 F. Supp. 391 (W.D. Mo. 1985).

[250] The counterargument to this case, of course, is that even a mandatory injunctive order can be reduced to money. In most cases the defendants will not themselves clean up the site, but will retain contractors. Apportionment of those costs among the defendants would seem to be no more difficult then apportioning a money judgment. In some cases, moreover, the courts, acting under equity jurisdiction, have ordered the payment of money to be used to accomplish a stated end. *See* United States v. Price, 688 F.2d 204 (3d Cir. 1982)(holding that the payment of money is a permissible form of equitable relief).

[251] *See* United States v. A. & F. Materials, Inc., 578 F. Supp 1249, 20 ERC 1353, 1361 (S.D. Ill. 1-20-84).

[252] *See* United States v. J. B. Stringfellow 20 ERC at 1910 (C.D. Cal. 1984).

[253] *See* discussion at Section 6.06[d], *infra.*

hibits the government from tiering a Section 106(a) action on top of a Section 107(a) cost recovery action to secure a greater level of cleanup.

A more difficult question is the extent to which the cost-effectiveness limitations otherwise limit the extent of relief available under Section 106(a). The statutory standard for relief is that which "the public interest and the equities of the case require." A Section 106(a) defendant could, it would seem, reasonably argue that he ought to be responsible for a cost-effective level of abatement that is, at most, sufficient to eliminate the imminent threat. For example, in a case of off-site groundwater contamination, he could argue that he should be responsible only for stopping the movement of contaminated water but cannot be required to clean up the site. Remaining site cleanup then would have to be accomplished under the Section 104/107(a) regime, or be the subject of litigation based on some other source of law, probably state common law.

If Section 106(a) is construed to provide a general cleanup remedy, then the general litigative considerations discussed in connection with Section 107, *infra*, would also generally apply to Section 106(a) litigation.[254]

[4] Miscellaneous Issues

[a] Preenforcement Judicial Review

Section 106 provides authority for EPA to act by administrative order as an alternative to seeking judicial relief. Although the issue has not been widely litigated, such orders appear to be sufficiently "final" actions to support an action seeking judicial review brought by the recipient, although the courts considering the issue have all concluded that they are not reviewable except in defense of an enforcement suit.[255]

---

[254] As of late 1985, a number of hybrid cases are pending. These cases involve expenditives by EPA, and thus have Section 107(a) claims alongside Section 106(a) and Section 70003 (RCRA) claims. The government claims that it may secure in a Section 107(a) action reimbursement for money not yet spent; thus, the hybrid cases present a type of prospective cleanup litigation that is the functional equivalent of a "general cleanup" Section 106(a) suit.

[255] *See* Wagner Seed Co. v. Daggett, 800 F.2d 310 (2d Cir. 1986) (refusing to review

Whether EPA must provide opportunity for a hearing prior to issuance of a Section 106 order is another significant issue that has spawned litigation. The argument for a prior hearing is prompted by the fact that CERCLA imposes potentially draconian penalties on recipients who fail or refuse to comply with a Section 106 order.[255.1] The developing majority view seems to be that, though a hearing is not required for due process, a defendant may interpose a good faith defense and challenge any such order in a subsequent judicial enforcement action predicated on it.[255.2]

[b] Applicability of RCRA and Other Statutory Requirements and Limitations to Section 106 Remedies

A nagging issue in the first five years of CERCLA's administration was to what extent wastes removed from a site pursuant to a Section 106 order must be disposed of in strict conformity with RCRA requirements, and to what extent Section 106 removals or remedial actions must comply with the requirements of the National Contingency Plan applicable to Section 104 and Section 107 actions.

EPA addressed this issue in its 1985 amendments to the NCP. 40 CFR §300.68(l) and §300.71 provide that either EPA or the state lead agency must approve in advance the adequacy of response actions ordered under Section 106, although strict consistency with the NCP is not required. Section 300.65 provides specifically that the Section 104 limitations on removal actions are not applicable to Section 106 removals, and Section 300.65(f) makes it clear that Section 106 removals are not required to comply with federal, state, and local regulatory laws.

---

order and denial of act of God defense, but hearing arguments on constitutionality of the statutory scheme); *see also* United States v. Reilly Tar & Chemical Corp., 22 ERV(BNA) 1753, 1757 n.2 (D. Minn. 1985); Wagner Electric Corp. v. Thomas, 612 F. Supp. 736 (D. Kan. 1985); and Solid State Circuits, Inc. v. EPA, 23 ERC(BNA) 1758 (W.D. Mo. 1985).

255.1 Section 106(b) provides a $25,000 per day penalty for a willful violation of an order. Section 107(c)(3) provides punitive damages of up to three times the remedial costs if one fails "without sufficient cause" to take remedial action ordered under Section 106(a).

255.2 *See* Wagner Seed Co. v. Daggett, 800 F.2d 310 (2d Cir. 1986); United States v. Reilly Tar & Chemical Corp., 22 ERC(BNA) 1753 (D. Minn. 1985); Wagner Electric Corp. v. Thomas, 612 F. Supp. 736 (D. Kan. 1985); Solid State Circuits, Inc. v. EPA, 23 ERC(BNA) 1758 (W.D. Mo. 1985). *But see* Industrial Park Development Co. v. EPA, 604 F. Supp. 1136 (E.D. Pa. 1985).

EPA also issued a policy memorandum on October 2, 1985, subsequently codified in the NCP, stating its view that, while CERCLA does not require that responses comply with regulatory laws other than RCRA's subtitle C, the Agency's policy, waivable in Section 106 cases, is to adopt remedies that comply with or exceed "applicable or relevant and appropriate" federal public health and environmental statutes.

Finally, EPA adopted an interim policy for managing off-site responses under CERCLA and Section 7003 of RCRA, which it published at 50 Fed. Reg. 45933 (November 5, 1985). This policy articulated a bias in favor of treatment of exhumed wastes rather than reburial at another site.

Congress finally spoke in 1986, when, in Section 121 of P.L. 99-499, it provided identical remedial standards applicable to cleanups under Sections 104 and 106. The standards, which codify the "applicable or relevant and appropriate" criterion, and contain a strong bias toward "permanent" remedies as opposed to capping, are discussed *infra,* in the material dealing with Section 104.

[c]   State Input into Section 106(a) Settlements

Section 121(f)(2), added to the statute in 1986, requires EPA to invite the state in which a facility subject to a Section 106(a) enforcement action[255.3] is located into its settlement negotiations with the defendant if the remedy being considered would not meet or exceed applicable or relevant and appropriate standards.[255.4] The state is given an opportunity to concur in the remedy. If it affirmatively non-concurs, the state is provided a right to intervene in the litigation and attempt to convince the court not to enter the consent decree.

[d]   Recovery of Remedial Costs from the Superfund

Persons who, pursuant to a Section 106(a) order, complete remedial action at a facility may seek reimbursement from the superfund of all or a part of their remedial expenditures, plus statutory interest pursu-

---

[255.3] The statutory language clearly limits its applicability to judicial enforcement under Section 106(a).

[255.4] These terms are discussed in detail in connection with Sections 104 and 121, *infra.*

ant to authority contained in Section 106(b)(2).[255.5]

In order to recover, the claimant must be able to demonstrate by a preponderance of the evidence either that he is not a potentially responsible party under Section 107[255.6] or that the ROD he was required to implement by the order was, on the basis of its administrative record, arbitrary and capricious or was otherwise not in accordance with law.[255.7] The first class of claimant may recover only costs that are reasonable in light of the requirements of the order. The second may recover such costs only to the extent that his expenditures exceed those costs that would have been incurred under a ROD for the facility that was not arbitrary and capricious.

The statute creates a cause of action in the federal district courts for a Section 106(b)(2) claimant whose claim has been rejected by the Fund manager. Costs and fees may be sought under 28 USC §§2712(a) and (d).

§6.06   Government-Funded Cleanup Under CERCLA Sections 104 and 105

[1]   Overview

The CERCLA Section 104/107 scheme is designed to provide direct federal and state action to clean up, at least partially, a large number of sites at which hazardous waste is contaminating the environment or posing a risk to public health or poses a threat thereof. The primary limitations on the degree of federal cleanup that can occur under CERCLA are the amount of money in the Hazardous Substances Superfund (the Fund)[256] available for expenditure under Section 104, and the government's success in securing private reimbursement, under Section 107, of monies expended.

The evidence before Congress in 1980 on the scope of the problem indicated the existence of between 30,000 and 50,000 existing hazardous waste sites that could pose environmental or public health problems.[257] The initial appropriation to the Fund was $1.6 billion,[257.1] an

---

[255.5] The provision was added by Section 106 of P.L. 99-499. The interest rate, as in other CERCLA interest payments, is the same as the rate specified for investment of the superfund under Chapter 98 of the Internal Revenue Code.

[255.6] Such claimants will probably be limited, as a practical matter, to innocent good faith purchasers of the property or adjacent property owners who volunteered to clean up the site.

[255.7] Section 106(b)(2)(D).

[256] This is commonly referred to as the "Superfund."

[257] H.R. Rep. No. 96-1016, 5 U.S. Cong. & Admin. News 6119, 6120 (1980).

[257.1] P.L. 99-499 increased the superfund to $8.5 billion.

amount that would, according to most estimates, clean up only a small percentage of the problem sites.

EPA's initial CERCLA strategy was motivated by a desire to stretch the available appropriation among as many sites as possible. This strategy involved (1) placing heavy reliance on state assumption of primary responsibility for cleanup of as many sites as the states would accept, (2) targeting most sites for only partial cleanup using CERCLA funds, and (3) placing heavy emphasis on lawsuits seeking direct cleanup by private parties premised on Section 106(a) of CERCLA or Section 7003 of RCRA or brought under Section 107(a) of CERCLA seeking prospective reimbursement of future federal response costs.

The government's initial strategy was largely a failure. Its effects to apply Section 7003 to inactive sites and past generators met with little success. Its Section 106 claims, which fared better jurisdictionally, moved slowly and encountered remedial difficulties. The government's efforts to secure prospective reimbursement of Section 104 response costs met with some success, however. Defendants argued that since Section 107(a) allows recovery only of costs *incurred,* a lawsuit seeking a judgment that the defendants are liable for future response costs is premature. The courts ruling on this defense generally followed *Brown v. Georgeoff,*[258] wherein it was held that an action could be maintained once some response costs had been incurred.[259]

Congress put the issue largely to rest in 1986, when it added Section 133(g), which specifically allows EPA to bring an action under Section 107 to recover any costs already spent and in that proceeding seek a declaratory judgment on the liability issue, which would be binding in actions to recover future costs at the site.

[2] Government Cleanup of Hazardous Waste Sites and Spills—Sections 104 and 105

Sections 104 and 105 of CERCLA establish the authority and ground rules for expenditure of money from the Hazardous Substance Re-

---

[258] 562 F. Supp. 1300 (N.D. Ohio 1983).

[259] *Id.,* at 1315-16. The state of Ohio, plaintiff in that case, had incurred 10 percent of its anticipated response costs at the time it initiated its cost recovery action. *See also* United States v. Price, No.80-4104 (D.N.J. 7-28-83); and *see* United States v. A. & F. Materials, Inc., 578 F. Supp. 1249, 20 ERC 1353, 1362 (S.D. Ill. 1984); *see also* United States v. Conservation Chemical Co., 628 F. Supp. 391 (W.D. Mo. 1985).

sponse Fund. The statute contains guidance and a mechanism for identifying candidate sites, for determining how much to spend on targeted sites, how many sites are expected to be addressed over the life of the Fund, state participation, and the goals for levels of cleanup.

The CERCLA program is patterned closely on Section 311 of the Clean Water Act;[260] accordingly, a number of the Section 311 terms and concepts were engrafted onto CERCLA, including the operational centerpiece of the program, the National Oil and Hazardous Substances Pollution Contingency Plan, which Section 105 of CERCLA required to be substantially revised.

[a] Applicability

CERCLA funds may be utilized to fund a "response" to a "release" from a "facility" of a "hazardous substance" or "pollutant or contaminant." All of these terms are defined by CERCLA, and the definitions are important.

The term "hazardous substances" is defined by Section 101(14) broadly to include either substances listed under five other federal statutes or those specially designated under Section 102 of CERCLA.[261] The statute specifically *excludes* "petroleum, including crude oil or any fraction thereof" unless otherwise "specifically listed or designated as a hazardous substance." The scope and intent behind the petroleum exclusion is far from clear, particularly since many of the

---

260 *See generally* Section 6.02, *supra.*

261 Section 101 (14) provides:

"[H]azardous substance" means (A) any substance designated pursuant to section 311(b)(2)(A) of Federal Water Pollution Control Act, (B) any element, compound, mixture, solution, or substance designed pursuant to section 102 of this Act, (C) any hazardous waste having the characteristics identified under or listed pursuant to Section 3001 of the Solid Waste Disposal Act (but not including any waste the regulation of which under the Solid Waste Disposal Act has been suspended by Act of Congress), (D) any toxic pollutant listed under section 307(a) of the Federal Water Pollution Control Act, (E) any hazardous air pollutant listed under section 112 of the Clean Air Act, and (F) any imminently hazardous chemical substance or mixture with respect to which the Administrator has taken action pursuant to section 7 of the Toxic Substances Control Act. The term does not include petroleum including crude oil or any fraction thereof which is not otherwise specifically listed or designed as a hazardous substance under subparagraphs (A) through (F) of this paragraph, and the term does not include natural gas, natural gas liquids, liquefied natural gas, or synthetic gas usable for fuel (or mixture of natural gas and such synthetic gas).

CERCLA's reach is significantly broader than that of RCRA. For example, wastes suspended from regulation under RCRA by legislative or administrative action may

normal breakdown constituents of refined petroleum, such as benzene, toluene, and xylene, are separately listed as hazardous substances.[262] It appears that the petroleum exclusion bars federal action only where there is a release of a reasonably common petroleum product, before weathering has broken it up into other compounds.[263]

The petroleum exclusion was limited in significance, however, by the adoption in 1984 of the RCRA leaking underground storage tank (LUST) provisions,[263.1] which apply to petroleum tank leaks, and amendments to those provisions contained in PL 99-499, which set up a mini-superfund program for petroleum tank leaks.[263.2]

The terms "pollutant" and "contaminant" are defined in Section 101(33). Certain authorities provided with respect to "hazardous substances," such as Section 107 cost recovery and Section 106 lawsuits, are not available with respect to pollutants or contaminants. Unlike "hazardous substance," which is defined with respect to lists of specific chemicals drawn up by EPA, "pollutant or contaminant" is defined generally by reference to characteristics that describe effects on living organisms.[264] Although a large percentage of substances that will satisfy the "pollutant or contaminant" definition will also appear on one or more of the Section 101(14) lists, some will not.

---

nevertheless be hazardous for CERCLA purposes. *See* Eagle Pitcher Industries v. U.S. EPA, 759 F.2d 905 (D.C. Cir. 1985).

[262] One obvious basis for the exclusion, of course, is that petroleum is covered by Section 311 of the Clean Water Act, although that statute is jurisdictionally more limited than CERCLA.

[263] *Cf.* United States v. Union Gas Co., 586 F. Supp. 1522, 20 ERC 1001 (E.D. Pa. 1984)(holding that coal tar constituents, including nephthalene, xylene, and ethylbenzene, listed separately as hazardous substances in 40 CFR §401.15 and elsewhere were sufficient to bring the defendant's coal tar pits under CERCLA).

[263.1] 42 USC §§9001 *et seq.*

[263.2] P.L. 99-499, Sections 205 and 521.

[264] Section 101(33). "For the purpose of this section, pollutant or contaminants shall include, but not be limited to, any element, substance, compound, or mixture, including disease-causing agents, which after release into the environment and upon exposure, ingestion, inhalation, or assimilation into any organism, either directly from the environment or indirectly by ingestion through food chains, will or may reasonably be anticipated to cause death, disease, behavioral abnormalities, cancer, genetic mutation, physiological malfunctions (including malfunctions in reproduction) or physical deformations, in such organisms or their offspring. The term does not include petroleum, including crude oil and any fraction thereof which is not otherwise specifically listed or designated as hazardous substances under Section 101(14)(A) through (F) of this title, nor does it include natural gas liquefied natural gas, or synthetic gas of pipeline quality (or mixtures of natural gas and such synthetic gas)."

"Release" is broadly defined by Section 101(22) to cover just about any conceivable pathway for hazardous waste to enter the environment.[265] In derogation of the breadth of the basic definition, however, the statute specifically exempts workplace releases,[266] emissions from various transportation devices and pipeline pumping station engines,[267] high-level radioactive substance releases subject to regulation under the Atomic Energy Act and the Uranium Mill Tailings Radiation Control Act of 1976,[268] and human fertilizer application.[269]

CERCLA also contains a related term, "federally permitted release," which in rather great detail describes various "releases" that would ordinarily be legitimated by permits issued by EPA or by other federal agencies pursuant to authorities under specified federal environmental, health, and safety statutes.[270] Federally permitted releases are not required to be reported to EPA under Section 103.

---

[265] Section 101(22). " '[R]elease' means any spilling, leaking, pumping, pouring, emitting, emptying, discharging, injecting, escaping, leaching, dumping, or disposing into the environment (including the abandonment or discarding of barrels, containers and other closed receptacles containing any hazardous substance or pollutant or contaminant) [parenthetical added 1986], but excludes (A) any release which results in exposure to persons solely within a workplace, with respect to a claim which such persons may assert against the employer of such persons, (B) emissions from the engine exhaust of a motor vehicle, rolling stock, aircraft, vessel, or pipeline pumping station engine, (C) release of source, byproduct, or special nuclear material from a nuclear incident, as those terms are defined in the Atomic Energy Act of 1954, if such release is subject to requirements with respect to financial protection established by the Nuclear Regulatory Commission under section 170 of such Act, for the purposes of section 104 of this title or any other response action, any release of source byproduct, or special nuclear material from any processing site designated under section 102(a)(1) or 302(a) of the Uranium Mill Tailings Radiation Control Act of 1978, and (D) the normal application of fertilizer."

[266] Section 101(22)(A).

[267] Section 101(22)(B).

[268] Section 101(22)(C). *Cf.* Legal Environmental Assistance Foundation, Inc. v. Hodel, 586 F. Supp 1163 (E.D. Tenn. 1984) (RCRA applicable to some nonradiation wastes of AEA regulated facilities].

[269] Section 101(22)(D).

[270] Section 101(10) provides:

"[F]ederally permitted release" means (A) discharges in compliance with a permit under section 402 of the Federal Water Pollution Control Act, (B) discharges resulting from circumstances identified and reviewed and made part of the public record with respect to a permit issued or modified under section 402 of the Federal Water Pollution Control Act and subject to a condition of such permit, (C) continuous or anticipated intermitent discharges from a point source, identified in a permit or permit application under section 402 of the Federal Water Pollution Control Act, which are caused by events occurring within the scope of relevant operating or treatment systems, (D) discharges in compliance with a legally enforceable permit under section 404 of the Federal Water Pollution Contron Act,

"Facility" is defined in exceedingly broad terms, to include both fixed and transportation entities and any site or area where hazardous waste has "come to be located."[271]

Finally, CERCLA trust funds may be spent to finance a "response" activity. CERCLA defines "response" to include "remove, removal, remedy, and remedial action, and related enforcement actions."[272] Although these subordinate terms are defined with rather bulky language in CERCLA, the basic distinction between "removal" responses and "remedial" responses is that the former involve quick, emergency, and

---

(E) releases in compliance with a legally enforceable final permit issued pursuant to section 3005(a) through (d) of the Solid Waste Disposal Act from a hazardous waste treatment, storage, or disposal facility when such a permit specifically identifies the hazardous substances and makes such substances subject to a standard of practice, control procedure or bioassay limitation or condition, or other control on the hazardous substances in such releases, (F) any release in compliance with a legally enforceable permit issued under section 102 of section 103 of the Marine Protection, Research, and Sanctuaries Act of 1972, (G) any injection of fluids authorized under Federal underground injection control programs or State programs submitted for Federal approval (and not disapproved by the Administrator of the Environmental Protection Agency) pursuant to part C of the Safe Drinking Water Act, (H) any emission into the air subject to a permit or control regulation under section 111, section 112, title I part C, title I part D, or State implementation plans submitted in accordance with section 110 of the Clean Air Act (and not disapproved by the Administrator of the Environmental Protection Agency), including any schedule or waiver granted, promulgated, or approved under these sections, (I) any injection of fluids or other materials authorized under applicable State law (i) for the purpose of stimulating or treating wells for the production of crude oil, natural gas, or water, (ii) for the purpose of secondary, tertiary, or other enhanced recovery of crude oil or natural gas, or (iii) which are brought to the surface in conjunction with the production of crude oil or natural gas and which are reinjected, (J) the introduction of any pollutant into a publicly owned treatment works when such pollutant is specified in and in compliance with applicable pretreatment standards of section 307(b) or (c) of the Clean Water Act and enforceable requirements in a pretreatment program submitted by a State or municipality for Federal approval under section 402 of such Act, and (K) any release of source, special nuclear, or byproduct material, as those terms are defined in the Atomic Energy Act of 1954, in compliance with a legally enforceable license, permit, regulation, or order issued pursuant to the Atomic Energy Act of 1954.

271 Section 101(a). See State of New York v. General Electric Company, 592 F. Supp. 291, 20 ERC 1097, 1100-1101 (N.D.N.Y. 1984)(dragstrip on which waste oil sold by defendant to a third party was dumped is a "facility," and language of Section 107(a)(3) limiting liability to the generators who "arranged for disposal . . . of hazardous substances . . . at any facility . . . containing such hazardous substances" does not provide an escape route for the first-time disposal at a virgin site).

272 Section 101(25)(1986) [reference to enforcement added in 1986].

---

often temporary relief measures,[273] and the latter involve long-term, or permanent remedies.[274]

[b] Choosing Targets for Federal Expenditure of Trust Funds—Reportable Quantities

Determining where CERCLA funds should be spent necessarily requires the government to identify where the problem sites are located and which sites need addressing first. CERCLA provides a three-step process of identification and prioritization. First, Section 102(a) re-

---

[273] Section 101(24) provides:

"Remedy" or "remedial action" means those actions consistent with permanent remedy taken instead of or in addition to removal actions in the event of a release or threatened release of hazardous substances into the environment, to prevent or minimize the release of hazardous substances so that they do not migrate to cause substantial danger to present or future public health or welfare or the environment. The term includes, but is not limited to, such actions at the location of the release as storage, confinement, perimeter protection using dikes, trenches, or ditches, clay cover, neutralization, clean-up of released hazardous substances **and associated** contaminated materials, recycling or reuse, diversion, destruction, segregation of reactive wastes, dredging or excavations, repair or replacement of leaking containers, collection of leachate and runoff, onsite treatment or incineration, provision of alternative water supplies, and any monitoring reasonably required to assure that such actions protect the public health and welfare and the environment. The term includes the costs of permanent relocation of residents and businesses and community facilities where the President determines that, alone or in combination with other measures, such relocation is more cost-effective than and environmentally preferable to the transportation, storage, treatment, destruction, or secure disposition offsite of hazardous substances, or may otherwise be necessary to protect the public health or welfare. The term **includes** offsite transport **and offsite** storage, treatment, destruction, or secure disposition of hazardous substances **and associated** contaminated materials. [Language added in 1986 is boldface.]

[274] Section 101(23) provides:

"Remove" or "removal" means the cleanup or removal of released hazardous substances from the environment, such actions as may be necessary taken in the event of the threat of release of hazardous substances into the environment, such actions as may be necessary to monitor, assess, and evaluate the release or threat of release hazardous substances, the disposal of removed material, or the taking of such other actions as may be necessary to prevent, minimize, or mitigate damage to the public health or welfare or to the environment, which may otherwise result from a release or threat of release. The term includes, in addition, without being limited to, security fencing or other measures to limit access, provision of alternative water supplies, temporary evacuation and housing of threatened individuals not otherwise provided for action taken under section 104(b) of this Act, and any emergency assistance which may be provided under the Disaster Relief Act of 1974.

quired EPA to issue regulations that specify the substances it believes will present a "substantial danger" to the public health or welfare, or the environment,[275] and to establish the quantities of release sufficient to warrant government attention ("reportable quantities").[276]

EPA's reportable quantity regulation, 40 CFR Part 302,[276.1] lists those substances for which EPA has established reportable quantities.[276.2] Releases of the substances in excess of those quantities within a twenty-four-hour period must be reported to the National Response Center.[276.3]

Determining whether one must report a release of the virgin form of a substance on the list is simple, if one knows how much was released. Determining whether one has to report the release of a mixture, such as a sludge, that contains some hazardous and some nonhazardous material is more complex.

Section 302.6(b) of the regulation states that notification of releases of mixtures or solutions is required "only where a component hazardous substance . . . is released in a quantity equal to or greater than its reportable quantity." If, however, the substance released is a RCRA-regulated "solid waste" that has not been excluded from regulation as

---

[275] The Section 102(a) list has not been issued by EPA.

[276] Section 102(b) established a statutory interim reportable quantity of either 1 pound or the quantity previously set by EPA under Section 311(b)(4) of the Clean Water Act, published at 40 CFR §117.3. Early in 1985, EPA issued regulations altering the reportable quantities for several hundred substances, increasing some and decreasing others. Congress amended Section 102(a) in 1986 to establish mandatory deadlines on EPA, requiring it to issue final regulations establishing reportable quantities not later than April 30, 1988.

[276.1] See 51 Fed. Reg. 34541 (9-29-86). The tables are reprinted in Appendix 6F, *infra.*

[276.2] 40 CFR §302.4, Table 302.4. Chemicals are listed by common name, Chemical Abstracts Service Registry (CASR) number, any regulatory synonyms used for the substance, and RCRA waste number. The table also indicates for each listed chemical the statutory origin of the listing and a code letter indicating the general magnitude of the reportable quantity. The specific reportable quantities are listed in both pounds and kilograms.

[276.3] Section 302.6. The NRC's telephone numbers are (800) 424-8802 and (202) 426-2675. The twenty-four-hour period limitation is not contained in the statute, and thus would appear not to require an immediate report of discovery of reportable quantities of a substance that had accumulated over a long period of time. Section 103 appears to require reporting of such releases, but "immediate" reporting appears to have been waived by EPA.

a hazardous waste under RCRA[276.4] and it exhibits the characteristic of EP toxicity, the rules are different.

In such a case, if the waste (which might itself be a mixture or solution) contains a contaminant for which there is a reportable quantity listed in EPA's regulation, then the reportable quantity for the *waste*, regardless of the amount of the contaminant in the waste, is the quantity listed for the contaminant.[276.5] If the waste contains two toxic contaminants, or a toxic contaminant and a contaminant that exhibits another hazardous characteristic, the reportable quantity is the lower of those possible.

Section 103(a) of CERCLA then requires the owner or operator of a vessel or an offshore or an onshore facility[277] to notify the National Response Center[278] in the event of a release (other than a federally permitted release) of a hazardous substance in an amount equal to or greater than the reportable quantity.[278.1] Section 103(b) provides criminal penalties for failure to make notification or knowingly submitting a false or misleading report,[279] and a grant of limited immunity from use of the information submitted in a criminal prosecution.[280] Although this limited immunity, quasi-exclusionary rule was obviously intended to encourage complete reporting, it may in the long run have the unintended result of impeding criminal prosecution of willful acts under other environmental statutes. A willful discharge of a toxic water pollutant in amounts that grossly exceed the source's National Pollutant Discharge Elimination System (NPDES) permit, for example, is a violation of the Clean Water Act. It is also not a "federally permitted relea-

---

[276.4] *See generally* Section 5.03, *supra.*

[276.5] *See* Section 302.5(b). RCRA wastes that exhibit one of the other characteristics that make them hazardous under RCRA are deemed to have a reportable quantity of 100 pounds, but the regulation does not state that the same factors apply to them as apply to EP toxic wastes.

[277] These terms are defined by Sections 101(17),(18), (20), and (28) identically to their definition in Section 311, Clean Water Act. *See* this chapter *supra.*

[278] *See* this chapter *supra;* and 40 CFR §300.63.

[278.1] Reportable quantities are listed in 40 CFR Part 302 and cross-referenced to Part 117. *See* 50 Fed. Reg. 1374.

[279] Penalties, set forth in Section 103(d)(2), are for felonies as provided in the Federal Criminal Code; fines are those commensurate with the three- to five-year prison sentences provided.

[280] The grant of immunity does not apply to perjury or false statements.

se"[281] and is accordingly subject to reporting. If the willful discharger promptly notifies the National Response Center or EPA, pursuant to the Section 103(a) obligation, use of the evidence in a prosecution for the willful discharge under the Clean Water Act will be barred.

The third aspect of site targeting is the National Priorities List (NPL) required to be developed by EPA under Section 105(a)(8) of CERCLA. The priorities list serves two functions. Since Section 105(8)(B) requires the states to establish their own priority lists and submit them to EPA, an additional method for identifying abandoned sites is provided.[281.1] The list also forms the basis for ordering the priority of federal expenditures.

[c] The National Priorities List

[i] Criteria and Development

Section 105(a)(8)(A) requires the President[282] to develop criteria for determining priorities for taking "remedial action and, to the extent practicable taking into account the potential urgency of such action, for the purpose of taking removal action." The distinction rests on an assumption that many, if not most, removal actions will be unanticipated emergencies, and are inherently incapable of prioritization.

The criteria and priorities are to be based on a number of factors listed in the statute,[283] which are considered relevant to determining the potential degree of hazard to humans and sensitive ecosystems and the level of state commitment to financial assistance. The latter criteria reflect Congress's desire that the hazardous waste site cleanup effort be

---

[281] Federally permitted releases are limited by Section 101(10) of CERCLA to those in compliance with the applicable permit.

[281.1] This provision was amended in 1986 to limit the states to one top priority listing each.

[282] President Reagan delegated all significant CERCLA authority to EPA in Executive Order 12316. See 46 Fed. Reg. 42237.

[283] "Criteria and priorities under this paragraph shall be based upon relative risk or danger to public health or welfare or the environment, in the judgement of the President, taking into account to the extent possible the population at risk, the hazard potential of the hazardous substances at such facilities, the potential for contamination of drinking water supplies, the potential for direct human contact, the potential for destruction of sensitive ecosystems, **the damage to natural resources which may affect the human food chain and which is associated with any release or threatened release, the contamination or potential contamination of the ambient air which is associated with the release or threatened release,** State preparedness to assume State costs and responsibilities, and other appropriate factors." [Language added in 1986 is boldface.]

a joint one, with the states paying a share of the cleanup costs for sites within their borders.

EPA's implementation of the Section 105(a)(8)(A) obligation was to develop a mathematical model and associated input criteria and worksheets, which the Agency called the Hazard Ranking System.[284] The HRS is published as Appendix A to 40 CFR Part 300, and is designed to be employed primarily by state field personnel.

The HRS, as noted *supra,* produces a single risk value reflecting exposure potential and substance dangerousness. It tends to produce the highest scores when the scorer indicates that relatively toxic contaminants are in an exposure pathway that will contaminate drinking water. Unfortunately, because the 1980 version of CERCLA required the states to submit their priority candidates to EPA by December 11, 1982, in the rush to compile field scores, state employees were forced to guess at HRS inputs for a large number of sites about which very little was known either about the contents and the site or the groundwater configuration. As a consequence, the government's priority list undoubtedly assigns some high priorities to relatively undangerous sites, and some low priorities to relatively dangerous sites.

[ii] Compilation, Effect, and Challenges

EPA compiled its initial National Priorities List in 1983, and published it as a proposed Appendix B to 40 CFR Part 300. Consistent with Section 105(8)(B)'s requirement, the initial list contained just over 400 sites, with one of each of the top 100 sites from each state. Virtually the entire list was made up of sites contained on lists submitted by the states. States with aggressive hazardous waste programs managed to

---

[284] *See* 40 CFR §300.66 and Appendix A to Part 300. The HRS was actually developed by the Mitre Corporation under contract to EPA, and as a result the HRS is sometimes referred to as the Mitre model. Different ranking approaches were suggested to EPA by the Chemical Manufacturers Association (CMA), which felt that the Mitre approach was unrealistically conservative. EPA ultimately stayed with the Mitre approach, although it attempted to alter the HRS to respond to a degree to CMA's criticims. The Mitre model was upheld against industry challenges in Eagle Pitcher Industries v. U.S. EPA, 759 F.2d 905 (D.C. Cir. 1985). Congress's 1986 amendments to Section 105 required a second look at the Hazard Ranking Model, imposing a substantive performance standard (the model must "accurately assess relative risks to human health and the environment"). The Conference Report (H.R. Rep. No. 99-962) places a gloss on the statutory requirement in several ways. It, first, refers to a Senate Report (No. 96-848, 96th Cong., 2d Sess. at 60 (1980)), which purports to have expressed the original legislative intent with respect to hazard ranking, and then suggests that EPA evaluate the Department of Defense "preliminary pollutant limit value system" as a possible alternative to the Mitre model.

dominate the list, which included a number of sites on which either private parties or states had already begun remedial work, and on which little or no federal expenditure was anticipated. P.L. 99-499 eliminated the reference to 400 sites and limited states to only one "top priority" site.[284.1]

EPA's initial practice was to limit the NPL to sites that scored above 28.50 on the hazard-ranking model and sites designated by state governors as high-priority sites. The Agency backed off from this rigid approach late in 1985 when it amended 40 CFR §300.66(b), adding additional criteria upon which listing could be premised.[284.2] Under the new rule, a site can be listed if the Agency for Toxic Disease Registry has issued a health advisory recommending dissociation of individuals from a release associated with the site, EPA determines that the site poses a significant threat to public health, and EPA determines that remedial action would be more cost-effective than removal action.

Congress amended Section 105 in 1986, adding a number of new provisions affecting the NPL.

Section 105(c) mandates revision of the NPL, focusing on "relative degree of risk" and on water contamination pathways. Existing priorities based on the old Hazard Ranking Model do not have to be reconsidered, but such reconsideration is not prohibited.

Section 118(a) imposes a mandatory high priority for sites where a release has resulted in closing of a drinking water well or contaminated a principal water supply. It requires reprioritizing some sites.[284.3]

Section 105(d) requires EPA to undertake a "preliminary assessment" upon petition of persons who are "or may be" affected by a release or threatened release.[284.4] Section 105(e) requires relisting sites at which remedial action was taken in the past ("cleaned up to date" sites) and at which after January 1, 1985, a "significant release" is discovered. Section 105(g) establishes ground rules for EPA's consideration of listing sites containing certain of the "special study wastes" listed

---

[284.1] Section 105(a)(8)(B)(1986).

[284.2] *See* 50 Fed. Reg. 37624 (9-16-85).

[284.3] An amendment to Section 104(a)(1) also affects prioritization. It requires that "primary attention" be given to "those releases . . . which present a public health threat."

[284.4] A preliminary assessment, once termed a "FIT Report," is a rough determination of the risks posed by the site and a preliminary screening of potentially responsible parties. The obligation imposed by Section 105(d) does not apply to sites as to which EPA performed a preliminary assessment within the twelve months prior to receipt of the petition.

in Section 3001(b) of RCRA.[284.5] Section 125 prohibits future listing of fly ash and related fossil fuel combustion wastes until EPA has revised the HRS to better consider toxicity and concentration factors applicable to them.

No CERCLA funds may be spent for remedial work on sites not on the National Priorities List. Thus, inclusion of a site on the NPL constitutes a prerequisite to federally funded remedial action.[284.6] This conclusion grows out of the requirement of Section 104(a)(1) that federal actions be "consistent with" the National Contingency Plan, of which the NPL is a part.[285] Since expenditure of remedial funds[286] on an unlisted site would deprive a listed site, and hence one deemed to need priority treatment, of those funds, such expenditure would, almost by definition, be inconsistent with the NCP. Thus, as new problems are uncovered, EPA expands the NPL. As of late 1986, EPA had included 703 sites on the NPL.[286.1]

EPA attempted to circumvent the statutory requirement limiting remedial action to NPL sites by inventing, in its National Contingency Plan, a category of action called "planned removal."[287] CERCLA draws a distinction between "removal" and "remedial" action, the former being an immediate response to an emergency that cannot wait and is limited both in time and the amount of money that can be spent[288] and the latter involving long-term remedial action.[289]

EPA seized on language in Section 104(c)(1) to break the universe of removal actions into "immediate" removal and "planned" removal, the key difference between the two being the presence of a state funding

---

284.5 The wastes to which this provision applies are (1) drilling fluids and other petroleum extraction wastes, (2) ore and mineral extraction and processing wastes, and (3) cement kiln dust waste.

284.6 Listing is *not* a prerequisite to action under Section 106 or Section 107, however. *See* United States v. Conservation Chemical Co., 628 F.2d. 391 (W.D. Mo. 1985). In addition, EPA may undertake a remedial investigation/feasibility study prior to listing. SCA Services of Indiana v. Thomas, 634 F. Supp. 1355 (N.D. Ind. 1985).

285 Section 105.

286 Arguably removal actions are not so constrained, because of the language of Section 105(8)(A) ("to the extent practicable . . .").

286.1 40 CFR Part 300, App. B.

287 40 CFR §300.67, 47 Fed. Reg. 31180 (7-16-82).

288 *See* Section 104(C)(1).

289 Section 104(C)(2).

participation commitment as the primary prerequisite for "planned" removal. EPA continued to adhere to the monetary and time limits imposed by Section 104(c)(1) on removal actions[290] but left itself the option to extend any given planned removal action beyond these limits.[291]

As a consequence, the distinction among "planned removal," "immediate removal," and "remedial" actions blurred somewhat, and EPA was severely criticized for developing an overly complex pattern of actions, causing delay in site cleanup. Section 104(c)(1) did, however, appear to provide EPA with adequate support for the scheme.

In revisions to the NCP published on November 20, 1985,[291.1] EPA eliminated the immediate removal/planned removal dichotomy from the NCP, and replaced it with a unitary "removal" criterion, along with a list of exemplary actions that would fall within that category.[291.2]

Congress resuscitated the original approach in 1986, by amending Section 104(c) to permit EPA to exceed the monetary and time limitations imposed by Section 104(c)(1) for removal actions where further removal action is "otherwise appropriate and consistent with remedial action to be taken."[291.3] In addition, Section 104(c)(8) was added, which allows EPA to undertake "interim remedial actions" without following the procedures required in selecting a permanent remedy, up to a $2 million cap, so long as it is necessary to "recontract" to address "new sources, types or quantities not known at the time of the original contract."[291.4]

Section 104(a) was also amended to require that removal actions

---

[290] 40 CFR §300.67(e)(1980). The limits, originally $1 million and 6 months, were doubled by P.L. 99-499 (1986).

[291] *Id.*

[291.1] 50 Fed. Reg. 47912.

[291.2] 40 CFR §300.65 (11-20-84). In order to minimize its administrative burden, however, EPA also invented a new concept, the "operable unit," by which the Remedial Project Manager may divide a superfund site into "operable units," some of which are earmarked for removal action and some for remedial action. *See* 40 CFR §300.68(c); and discussion in proposed rule, 50 Fed. Reg. 5062 (2-12-85).

[291.3] Section 104(c)(1)(C) (1986).

[291.4] This appears to aim at the situation in which the original RI/FS was not sufficient to identify the scope of the problem sufficiently before design work was commenced. If the removal limits had previously been exhausted, emergency action to deal with new hazards would otherwise be unlawful.

"contribute to the efficient performance of any long term remedial action," where "practicable."[291.5]

Listing a site on the NPL also triggers the potential liability of the site owner, generators, and other responsible private parties under Section 107 for response costs or natural resource damages. Following publication of the initial NPL, several such entities sought judicial review of the EPA "action" of listing the site, in which they attempted to challenge the legality or rationality of specific employment of the HRS. In the few reported decisions, the trial judge dismissed the complaint, ruling that the NPL was a regulation and, accordingly, exclusive jurisdiction over preenforcement review lies with the District of Columbia Circuit, under Section 113(a).[292]

The NPL was attacked in a petition to review the National Contingency Plan brought in the District of Columbia Circuit by the Environmental Defense Fund and the State of New Jersey.[293] That litigation was settled early in 1984, and EPA agreed to revise the NPL in a number of respects, primarily to include federal facilities, which EPA had originally refused to include on the list.[293.1]

The initial NCP did not address the circumstances under which a site listed on the NPL could be removed from it. That omission was criticized, and was challenged in legal actions brought against the NCP by site owners who argued that improper or erroneous listing of a site caused them economic or reputation damage and that the absence of a formal mechanism for deleting a site deprived them of due process. EPA codified its informal practice in the 1985 revision, allowing dele-

---

[291.5] Section 104(a)(2) (1986) (replacing previous text, which was the definition of "pollutant or contaminant" moved to Section 101 by P.L. 99-499).

[292] S.C.A. Services of Indiana, Inc. v. Thomas, 634 F. Supp. 1355 (N.D. Ind. 1985); U.S. Ecology, Inc. v. Carlson, 21 ERC 2009 (C.D. Ill. 10-3-84); Tinkham v. Reagan, 19 ERC 1742 (D.N.H. 1983); United States v. Rodgers, 575 F. Supp. 246, 254 (D. Ill. 1983); Cotter Corp. v. EPA, No. 84-M-1443, slip op. (D. Colo. 1984). Whether the NCP is intended to be a regulation is not entirely clear. EPA did not initially promulgate the "old" NCP, issued under Section 311 of the Clean Water Act, as a regulation. The prefatory language of Section 105 does require EPA to go through what amounts to rulemaking proceedings, but if Congress clearly intended the NCP to be a regulation it could have said so more simply. The requirement that judicial review be limited to petitions to review the priorities list in the D.C. Circuit effectively foreclosed any real opportunity to challenge site-specific application of the HRS, since EPA's record on individual site selection consists of little more than the HRS score sheets and a letter from the State. The court in *S.C.A. Services* opined that review of a listing could be had in defense of a Section 107 cost recovery action.

[293] Nos. 82-2234 and 82-2238.

[293.1] Federal facilities were addressed extensively in the 1986 reauthorization. *See* discussion *infra*.

tion only when either all appropriate response action has been completed or "based on a remedial investigation, EPA has determined that the release poses no significant threat to public health or the environment."[293.2]

EPA's deletion rule only partially addresses the problem confronting site owners who believe that their sites do not warrant priority listing. An EPA determination that a site does not in fact present a hazard must follow a remedial investigation, and at the pace EPA has historically proceeded, it could be many years before it gets around to a Remedial Investigation and Feasibility Study (RI/FS) for a contested site. EPA could provide a procedure for removal by petition, placing the burden on the site owner to do sufficient studies to demonstrate the absence of hazard, and by so doing would eliminate what is at least an equitable problem with the NPL.

[d]   The National Contingency Plan

[i]   Statutory Requirements

Section 104 requires that federal response actions be "consistent with" the National Contingency Plan, and Section 107(a)(4)(A) allows the government to compel private reimbursement of removal and remedial costs "not inconsistent with" the NCP.[294] The NCP is thus the operational centerpiece of the government's hazardous waste cleanup program.

The content of the NCP is prescribed in general terms by the provisions of Section 105. The NCP must include methods for identifying and prioritizing hazardous substance problem sites (Sections 105(a)(1), 105(a)(6), and 105(a)(8)), methods for assigning responsibilities among the various levels of government or private entities involved (Sections 105(a)(4) and 105(a)(9)), and methods for procuring and maintaining equipment and supplies (Section 105(a)(5)). These elements relate to

---

[293.2] 40 CFR §300.66(c)(7) (11-20-85).

[294] Section 104(a)(1). The plan is officially called the National Oil and Hazardous Substances Pollution Contingency Plan. See 40 CFR §300.1 Initially adopted, for CERCLA purposes, in 1982, the NCP was significantly revised and fine-tuned on November 20, 1985. See 50 Fed. Reg. 5062 (2-12-85)(proposed rule) and 50 Fed. Reg. 47912 (11-20-85)(final rule). The portion of the contingency plan specifically addressing hazardous waste is called the National Hazardous Substance Response Plan. See Section 105 and 40 CFR Part 300 subpart F. In this treatise, the plan is referred to as "National Contingency Plan" or "NCP."

the mechanics of operating the program, and require the maintenance of procedures very similar to those already in place under the old Clean Water Act NCP.[295]

Section 105 also requires the development of the criteria to be employed in deciding how much money will be spent on the site, and how. Section 105(a)(2) requires the NCP to include "methods for evaluating, including analysis of relative cost, and remedying any releases or threats to releases from facilities which pose substantial danger to the public health or the environment." Section 105(a)(3) requires "methods and criteria for determining the appropriate extent of removal, remedy[296] and other measures authorized. . . ." Finally, Section 105(a)(7) requires the NCP to include "means for assuring that remedial action measures are cost-effective over the period of potential exposure to the hazardous substances or contaminated materials."[297]

These substantive criteria were predictably difficult for EPA to develop in the revised NCP,[298] and EPA's choices in implementing the Sections 105(a)(2), 105(a)(3), and 105(a)(7) criteria and methodologies became a focal point for criticism of EPA's implementation of the superfund program between 1980 and 1985.[299]

---

[295] The Clean Water Act NCP does not, of course, contain a prioritization requirement since it addressed spills rather than *in-situ* hazards. The original NCP did, however, prioritize oil spills into minor, moderate, and major categories.

[296] The probable intent was to use the word "remedial." The enacted text appears to be a drafting error.

[297] The Section 105(a)(7) cost-effectiveness requirement should not be confused with an additional requirement expressed in similar language in Section 104(c)(4), which requires that government-financed remedial actions constitute "that cost-effective response which provides a balance between the need for protection of public health and welfare and the environment at the facility under consideration, and the availability of amounts . . . to respond to other sites . . .." This requirement imposes a separate limitation on federal expenditures that is quite different from the Section 105(7) requirement. Section 105(7) requires the government to determine what level of cleanup provides the maximum degree of protection for the efficient expenditure of funds. Section 104(c)(4) then requires the government to weigh *that* expenditure against competing expenditure needs, and could result in government-funded cleanup to a lower degree of protection.

[298] EPA promulgated the revised NCP on July 16, 1982. 47 Fed. Reg. 31180. It proposed a significant revision on February 12, 1985. *See* 50 Fed. Reg. 5862. The rerevised NCP was adopted on November 20, 1985. 50 Fed. Reg. 47912.

[299] CERCLA was reauthorized in 1986, with significant amendments addressing these issues and others. The amendments are discussed below.

[ii] Evaluation and Analysis[300]

[A] **In General.** EPA's implementation of the Section 105(a)(2) requirement was the development of a rather elaborate series of studies of candidate sites that are required to be undertaken by the "lead agency." As a practical matter, the lead agency will in most cases be either EPA or the state hazardous waste regulatory entity. When EPA is the lead agency, the studies are done by EPA contractors[301] or by contractors employed by interested private parties.[302]

Initially, the Agency does a "preliminary assessment," the purpose of which is essentially to determine whether removal action is required.[303] If immediate action either is not required or may not be sufficient, a more elaborate evaluation is done, whose purpose is to "scope" the potential site of the project, and suggest the areas where further fieldwork is necessary to secure data on which an NPL listing and a remedial plan can be based. This evaluation involves some preliminary fieldwork and evaluation of available data.[304]

If, on the basis of the initial screening, remedial action is deemed necessary, EPA or the state lead agency develops a community relations plan, and the Remedial Project Manager (RPM), who is the hazardous waste response equivalent of the oil spill "on scene coordinator," begins the process of determining what remedial action is appropriate. First, the project is determined to constitute one or more "operable units," and the retained EPA CERCLA contractor is sent to commence a "Remedial Investigation" and "Feasibility Study."[305] The RI/FS establishes the approach to remedial action, assesses the risks, and is required to consider alternative approaches to remedying the condi-

---

[300] EPA's 1985 revision of the NCP and P.L. 99-499 altered some of the bases for the discussion below. Those revisions are discussed.

[301] EPA is required by federal budget constraints to select new contractors each year. This fact has led to delays in the Agency's site investigations on numerous occasions.

[302] 40 CFR §300.64.

[303] Potentially responsible parties (PRPs) may, under 40 CER §300.68(f), volunteer to undertake the investigative work. They may elect to do so for two reasons: (1) to have more input into the recommendations, and (2) to be able to do the work more cheaply, unconstrained by the Davis-Bacon Act.

[304] *See* 40 CFR §300.64 and 40 CFR §300.66.

[305] 40 CFR §§300.67, 300.68(c), and 300.68(d) (amended 50 Fed. Reg. 47912 (11-20-85)). In April 1985 EPA issued a document providing guidance for EPA contractors, titled "Guidance on Feasibility Studies Under CERCLA" and available from the Agency's Office of Emergency and Remedial Response.

tions at the site.[306] A typical RI/FS table of contents is shown in Appendix 6C, *infra.*

In the original NCP, EPA employed the "on scene coordinator" concept borrowed from the oil spill plan, and designated one of its employees to undertake that role. It did not, however, have any specific guidelines governing the authority of this individual. In its 1985 proposed revision of the NCP, the Agency created a new entity, the RPM, to replace the OSC in remedial actions.[306.1] Thus, where only petroleum is involved, or where the only action taken is removal action, an OSC will be appointed. If remedial action is contemplated, a regional response team will be activated, and the RPM will take over the responsibilities of the OSC.[306.2]

EPA's creation of the RPM recognizes the fact that remedial actions under CERCLA more closely resemble public works projects than they do emergency actions and thus the "coordinator" concept, born of the need to have someone direct and mobilize prompt response, is not relevant to them. The RPM is a field decisionmaker, deciding such things as whether to break the project into separate segments or "operable units,"[306.3] the deployment of consultant resources, and the like. That person does not make the ultimate, critical decisions on remedial choices, but makes recommendations to EPA regional and headquarters managers on these matters.

In general, there are two broad categories of remedial action contemplated under the original NCP: on-site protection against migration of contaminants, called "source control remedial actions," which essentially involve surface cleanup, and "management of migration" actions, which include such things as groundwater cleaning, soil removal, slurry wall construction, and other such activities directed at remediating off-site contamination. EPA's on-site practice tended to blur this distinction, and the NCP revision eliminated it as a formal aspect of the

---

[306] *See* 40 CFR §§300.68(g), (h).

[306.1] 40 CFR §300.68(a)(2)(50 Fed. Reg. 47973).

[306.2] *Id.* The responsibilities are spelled out in 40 CFR §300.33.

[306.3] *See* 40 CFR §300.68(d) (50 Fed. Reg. 47973). The operable unit authority is designed to allow partial site remediation where, for example, the private parties potentially responsible for the cost of the cleanup can agree on some actions but not others, and to allow removal actions on one portion of the site while reserving others for more expensive, long-term remedial action.

regulation.[307] The 1986 amendments significantly altered the approach to remedy selection. They are discussed in subsections [ii][B],[iii], and [iv], *infra.*

EPA's initial NCP approach was blamed as one reason for the Agency's slow implementation of the CERCLA program.[308] The Agency's problems were exacerbated by its frequent change of regional contractors, and the resultant lack of study continuity.

[B] **Public Participation.** The original NCP also contained no provisions for formal public comment on its remedial decisions. EPA agreed, however, in the settlement of *Environmental Defense Fund, Inc. v. EPA,*[309] to provide for public review of "Feasibility Studies" for fund-financed responses, and to "provide comparable public participation for private-party response measures undertaken pursuant to enforcement actions."[310] EPA's revised NCP dealt with this by requiring a "community relations plan" to be developed for all sites, including sites addressed under Section 106, other than those facing only short-term removal action and sites not included on the NPL.[310.1] Essentially, the regulation provided for mandatory public review of remedial plans and a mandatory comment period prior to the final decision on the response action.[310.2]

An entirely new approach was established in 1986, with the addition of Section 117 to CERCLA. It spells out in precise terms what EPA is required to do in order to apprise the public of its site selection activities, and in fact codifies much of the community relations plan adopted in the 1985 NCP.

EPA must publish notice, in a newspaper serving the area, of a proposed remedial plan prior to adoption of the plan in a Record of Decision (ROD), and state in the notice whether the plan will be implemented by the government or by private parties. It must also include

---

[307] 40 CFR §300.68(d).

[308] By mid-1985 EPA had managed to clean up less that ten sites.

[309] No. 82-2234, et al. (D.C. Cir. 1984).

[310] Joint Motion To Defer Briefing, Appendix A, page 2, paragraph 5 (1-16-84).

[310.1] This latter exemption would appear to affect only 106 direct enforcement actions.

[310.2] 40 CFR §300.67, 50 Fed. Reg. 47912(11-20-85).

in the notice an analysis of the plan and alternatives to it.[310.3] There must also be a local public document repository where key documents relating to the remedial process are kept, a local public meeting on the remedy selection must be held, and the Agency must solicit and respond to oral and written comments.[310.4]

The final remedial plan must be made available to the public, and must articulate the reasons for any changes in the remedy described in the original proposal.[310.5]

Groups of citizens who "may be affected" by a release from a site on the NPL are potentially entitled to grants of up to $50,000 for "technical assistance in interpreting information."[310.6]

[C] **Private Party Voluntary Cleanups.** Private parties, usually such Section 107 potentially responsible parties (PRPs) as site owners or groups of generators, often agree, informally or as a result of settlement of administrative or judicial actions brought by EPA or the state, to implement the remedial action. This often occurs after EPA has selected a remedy, but private parties may seek to do the RI/FS. Several issues arose under the original CERCLA that were the subject of congressional action in the 1986 reauthorization.

One such issue is the freedom with which PRP groups may conduct the RI/FS. A 1986 amendment to Section 104(a)(1) allows private RI/FSs, but mandates EPA oversight by a government contractor financed by the private parties. The statute also prohibits EPA from accepting a lesser remedial scope in exchange for the private cleanup, and requires such arrangements to be entered into pursuant to rules affecting settlement of Section 106 and Section 107 actions that are set forth in Section 122 of the statute.[310.7]

An interesting problem confronting private party cleanup studies under the original CERCLA was presented when the site owner or

---

310.3 Section 117(a).

310.4 Section 117(b). A transcript of the meeting is required.

310.5 Section 117(b). Changes in the remedy occasioned by a negotiated consent decree or administrative settlement, or by information encountered in the field during design, must also be publicly explained. Section 117(c).

310.6 Section 117(e). Grants are subject to available appropriations and EPA's regulations. The monetary limit is subject to express waiver. Grants require a 20 percent match (also waivable), and only one grant is permitted per facility, though a grant is renewable.

310.7 Section 122 is discussed in connection with litigation issues, *infra*. One requirement of that section is that where EPA agrees to a private RI/FS, it must embody the arrangement in an enforceable order. *See* Section 122(d)(3) (1986).

adjacent landowners refused entry to the site or environs by the consultants retained by a generator or group of generators. Although CERCLA and the NCP contemplate, and EPA encourages, privately financed investigative studies, statutory authorities available to EPA that enable it forcibly to enter a site or acquire information about it are not clearly available to voluntary private investigators. The government's compulsory entry and information-gathering authority is limited to government officers and employers, and to "duly designated representatives" of the government.[311] Although an EPA contractor may be considered a "duly designated representative," a more difficult question is presented as to whether EPA may designate a contractor under financial control of a private party as its "representative" *pro tem* in order to convey to him the Agency's information-gathering authority to be used against other private persons.[312] Nothing in CERCLA appears to prevent such a designation, although it might be argued that once such designation occurs the contractor becomes subject to the Davis-Bacon Act.[313]

Although Congress beefed up EPA's authority to enter areas subject to remedial action in the 1986 amendments,[313.1] it did not resolve this issue. The problem is particularly acute for generator groups where the site owner is unfriendly. The government wants to be free of remedial obligations when it makes a deal for a private site remediation. On the other hand, without the government's cooperation, the private settling parties could be forced by a recalcitrant site owner into an unfair release in exchange for site access.

Potentially responsible parties may well disagree with the govern-

---

[311] Section 104(e) provides a basis for compulsory acquisition and site entry by a "duly designated" "officer, employee or representative" of the state or EPA. The Agency has also used RCRA's information-gathering authority, Sections 3007 and 3013, in connection with CERCLA investigations. These statutes are similarly limited. EPA itself encountered difficulty in Outboard Marine Corporation v. Thomas, 773 F.2d 883 (7th Cir. 1985), in which CERCLA was found to confer no right of eminent domain to take uncontaminated private property even temporarily for use as a storage area for contaminants excavated from a superfund site. *Outboard Marine* was legislatively overruled on the point by amendments to Section 104(e) contained in P.L. 99-499.

[312] To the extent that the entities against whom the authority is directed assert confidentiality claims, such a designation appears to be covered by Section 104(e)(2)(B), which provide a penalty for wrongful disclosure of confidential information.

[313] *See* Section 104(g).

[313.1] Amendments to Section 104(e) provide for entry upon property adjacent to the site, authority not previously possessed by EPA, and provide the Agency with the eminent domain power it had previously lacked. *See* Sections 104(e)(3), 104(j).

ment's assessment of the site contents and migration rates, and may seek to raise those disagreements later in defense to the government's Section 107(a) cost recovery action.[314] Litigants in Section 106(a)/RCRA 7003 actions have tended to employ their own hydrogeological consultants either to critique the RI/FS or to do independent site evaluations. It has been held that a potentially responsible party (PRP) does not have the right to an EPA hearing on its objections to EPA's proposed remedial plan[315] and may not seek court review of EPA's "record of decision" (ROD), which authorizes the expenditure of Fund monies to implement the plan, but must await EPA's cost recovery action to raise the issue as a defense.[316]

[D] **Administrative Record.** EPA instituted formal administrative procedures prior to selecting a remedy in its 1985 NCP revision. The 1986 CERCLA amendments contain further requirements, drawing a distinction between removal actions and remedial actions.

Procedures for making removal action decisions are not mandated, and such decisions would appear to be satisfied by notice and comment rulemaking. The governing statute[316.1] requires only that EPA develop procedures that provide "for the appropriate participation of interested persons in the development of the administrative record." Since the public participation requirements of Section 117 are applicable only to "remedial actions," EPA can satisfy the statute by compiling a paper

---

314 *See* discussion *infra*, regarding limitations on Section 107(a) defenses.

315 U.S. v. Midwest Solvent Recovery, No. H-79-556 (N.D. Ind. 12-14-84) (unpublished).

316 *See* United States v. United Nuclear Corporation, 610 F. Supp. 527 (D.N.M. 1985); Wheaton Industries v. EPA, 781 F.2d 354 (3d Cir. 1986); Charter Company et al. v. Thomas — F. Supp. —, 4 H.W. Lit. Rep. 892, No. 83-974-Civ-J-12 (M.D. Fla. 1986); Jefferson County v. United States, — F. Supp. —, No. 85-935C(L) (E.D. Mo. 1986); Peters v. EPA, 767 F.2d 263 (6th Cir. 1985), *aff'g* 584 F. Supp. 1005 (N. D. Ohio 1984); Lone Pine Steering Committee v. EPA, 777 F.2d 882 (3d Cir. 1985), *aff'g* 600 F. Supp. 1487 (D.N.J. 1985). The lower court in *Peters* opined in a dictum that a cause of action might exist for a PRP who alleges, with factual backup, that EPA acted without a rational basis. The Sixth Circuit opinion appears to preclude this result. A decision with breathtaking potential for PRPs is United States v. Ward, 618 F. Supp. 884 (E.D.N.C. 1985). One of a number of judicial pronouncements stemming from widespread disposal of waste oil containing PCBs along North Carolina roadsides, this opinion by Judge Britt stated (1) that EPA's choice of remedy is entitled to great deference and (2) that any defensive challenge would be decided under an "arbitrary and capricious" standard of review. This view, which raises potential due process problems, makes active involvement in EPA's remedial administrative recordmaking mandatory for PRPs.

316.1 Section 113(k)(2)(a) (1986).

record, placing it at a depository in the area of the proposed action,[316.2] and publishing a proposed removal decision in the Federal Register.

The difficult issue for removal actions is whether EPA has authority to commence an emergency removal action prior to soliciting comment from interested parties. The thrust of the statutory language is against such a course, but the overall statutory scheme and the purpose of the dichotomy between removal and remedial actions favor latitude.

Another interesting procedural question is whether EPA may apply the same relaxed procedures to actions taken under its "recontracting" authority contained in Section 104(c)(8). That statute calls such actions "interim remedial actions," and says nothing about procedures. The "interim remedial actions" lie midway between removal and remedial actions, and are not otherwise addressed in the procedural provisions of CERCLA. Extended removal actions, authorized under Section 104(c)(1)(C) (1986), seem to be in a similar category. Although EPA could take the easy route by making a semantic distinction between the two kinds of actions, in many cases such a distinction would be without a difference.

Actions that are clearly remedial in nature not only must comply with the public participation requirements of Section 117, but are also subject to specific record development requirements contained in Section 113(k). The statute requires EPA to develop regulations ensuring notice to "potentially affected persons and the public" and a "reasonable opportunity to comment and provide information regarding the [remedial] plan, providing for a public hearing, and response to significant comments and data."[316.3] A "statement of basis and purpose" is also required.[316.4]

In general, the requirements of the reauthorized CERCLA did not significantly affect EPA's procedural management of remedial action decisionmaking. The procedures adopted in the 1985 NCP revision appear to satisfy the statute. The NCP already required a public docket and public meetings, and the ROD clearly satisfies the statement of basis and purpose requirement. The existing provisions were not, however, sufficient in the notice category.

EPA's prereauthorization procedures did not provide for rigorous

---

[316.2] Section 113(k)(1).
[316.3] Sections 113(k)(2)(B)(i)-(iv). An adjudicatory hearing is not required. Section 113(k)(2)(C).
[316.4] Section 113(k)(2)(B)(v).

efforts on the Agency's part to identify and provide notice to PRPs. Its preliminary assessment contractors are generally required to identify PRPs, but rigor and avoidance of under- or overselection have not been hallmarks of the program[316.5] Congress addressed the problem, though not satisfactorily, in the 1986 amendments, requiring only that "reasonable efforts" be made "to identify and notify" PRPs as "early as possible before selection of a response action."[316.6]

[iii] Extent of Remedy

[A] **Pre-1986 Practice.** EPA initially chose to address the obligation to develop "methods and criteria for determining the appropriate extent of removal, remedy, and other measures . . ."[317] in vague, general language in the NCP. EPA's guidance is spread throughout subpart F in such terms as "consistent with permanent remedy to prevent or mitigate . . . migration . . . into the environment"[318] and the "remedial alternative which the [land] agency determines is cost-effective (i.e. the lowest cost alternative that is technologically feasible and reliable and which effectively mitigates and minimizes damage to and provides adequate protection of public health, welfare and the environment)."[319]

This approach effectively left the extent of remedy (a/k/a "level of clean-up") decisions to field operating personnel on a case-by-case basis. It also avoided for EPA the necessity of setting acceptable levels of contaminant residue in the groundwater for all 270 or so listed hazardous substances.

Unfortunately, EPA's approach fostered significant disputes in virtually all CERCLA cases between potentially responsible parties and the government over just how clean the site had to be to satisfy CERCLA's mandate. The difference between a benchmark at the limit of detection for a given constituent and, say, 10 ppm in the groundwater covered determine whether the cleanup cost of the site is in the millions or the

---

316.5 In the preliminary assessment for the Beacon Heights Landfill site, for example, EPA's FIT contractor listed as PRPs all entities that employed any of two transporters, on the basis of scant, hearsay evidence of use of the site at one time or another by the transporters.

316.6 Section 113(k)(2)(D) (1986). The statute specifically bars a defense to subsequent cost recovery or injunctive action based on EPA's failure to carry out this requirement.

317 Section 105(a)(3).

318 40 CFR §300.68(a), 47 Fed. Reg. 31203 (1982).

319 40 CFR §300.68(j)(1982).

tens of millions of dollars, an issue of obvious concern to PRPs. Similarly, the starting point, prior to reducing the level of effort to satisfy Section 104(c), is of obvious concern to the potentially exposed public.

Litigants challenging the legal sufficiency of the NCP argued that Sections 104(3) and 104(7) required EPA to establish clear quantitative standards for hazardous constituents that establish a level of cleanup baseline applicable as a starting point for all sites. EPA ultimately agreed to amend the NCP to require that "(1) relevant quantitative health and environmental standards and criteria developed by EPA under other programs be used in determining the extent of remedy, and (2) if such standards or criteria are substantially adjusted (e.g., for risks level or exposure factors), then the lead agency must explain the basis for this adjustment."[320]

EPA's 1985 revision of the NCP replaced the previous extent of remedy provision with a new one, which required, except where the rule provided otherwise, that the remedial option selected be one that "attains or exceeds applicable or relevant and appropriate Federal public health or environmental requirements that have been identified for the specific site.[320.1]

The regulation hedged, however, in several significant ways. First, it allowed the use of federal "criteria and advisories" and state standards, where appropriate, in addition to Federal standards.[320.2] In addition, a partial remedy that does *not* meet applicable and relevant standards is nevertheless a permissible remedy in cases where the remedy required by the standards is technically impractical, would cause unacceptable

---

[320] Appendix A to Joint Motion to Defer Briefing in Environmental Defense Fund Inc. v. United States Environmental Protection Agency, Nos. 82-2234, 82-2238 (D.C. Cir. 1-16-84).

[320.1] 40 CFR §300.68(i) (50 Fed. Reg. 47975). EPA defines the phrase "relevant and appropriate" in 40 CFR §300.6 as referring to requirements that, although not legally applicable, are "designed to apply to problems sufficiently similar to those encountered at CERCLA sites that their application is appropriate." *See* 50 Fed. Reg. 47918 (11-20-85).

In a lengthy Federal Register discussion, EPA states that its intention is primarily to give the RPM enough flexibility to apply standards that meet the situation at hand. For example, the Agency states that it might use RCRA standards even though they would be inapplicable to wastes deposited before the effective date of the RCRA regulations, and, on the other hand, may choose not to apply RCRA groundwater protection standards because they are designed to address a different physical situation. Similarly, the Agency indicates that it intends to make liberal use of the "alternate concentration limits" (ACLs) established under 40 CFR §264.94(b) as an alternative to more stringent RCRA groundwater requirements where appropriate. *See* 50 Fed. Reg. 47922 (1985).

[320.2] 40 CFR §300.68(i)(4)(1985).

environmental impacts, or would consume too much of the Fund in light of competing needs and in privately financed actions under Section 106 coercion where there is a need for quick action and litigation over a more rigorous remedy would "probably" not result in the desired remedy.[320.3]

Since the most difficult and most prevalent hazardous waste cleanup situations involve groundwater contamination, the only available "other programs" to which EPA may look for relevant "standards and criteria" are the RCRA regulations and the Safe Drinking Water Act and, indirectly, the Clean Water Act.[321] EPA did not develop quantitative standards and criteria of the sort envisioned in its RCRA program.[322]

The Agency has issued few SDWA "standards," primarily because the National Academy of Sciences, which must recommend the standards, believes that for carcinogenic contaminants there is no threshold exposure level, and thus that the statutory requirement that SDWA standards (called "maximum contaminant levels") be set at the level "safe" for human consumption can never be met for suspected carcinogens and mutagens. The Agency instead has issued a large number of what it calls Health Advisories (HAs), sometimes referred to as Suggested No Adverse Response Levels (SNARLs), for toxic chemicals in drinking water. EPA has consistently disclaimed any regulatory force behind the HAs, which are not issued with any semblance of procedural regularity, and are not even announced in the Federal Register. They are intended as suggestions for use by the states, which EPA cautions to exercise independent judgment on utilization of the HAs for regulatory purposes. The HA levels are rough-cut numerical guidelines based on literature reviews, and can in no sense be viewed as "standards" or "guidelines" without careful consideration of the methodology, data, and assumptions behind them.

For CERCLA purposes, the only relevant Clean Water Act standards

---

[320.3] 40 CFR §300.68(i)(5)(1985). It should be pointed out that each of the exemptions requires a judgment call on the part of an EPA official, which would no doubt be litigable. It is unclear on what basis EPA would decide that litigation would not result in the imposition of a remedial requirement that would be consistent with federal standards. Presumably such a determination could only be made by the General Counsel after consultation with the Department of Justice.

[321] Congress limited Clean Water Act jurisdiction to point source discharges to surface water bodies; thus, any borrowing of Clean Water Act standards or criteria involves consideration of important differences in the contaminated media.

[322] See Chapter 5, supra.

or guidelines are those promulgated for toxic pollutants under Section 307 of the Act. EPA grudgingly issued Section 307 limitations for a modest list of toxic pollutants pursuant to a 1976 consent decree entered in *National Resources Defense Council v. Train*.[323] The usefulness for CERCLA purposes of even those toxic effluent limitations promulgated by EPA under Section 307 is limited, however, since Section 307(a) imposes primarily technology-based standards.[324] Alternatively, EPA may develop pollutant-limited standards to protect "affected organisms" in surface waters into which the pollutants are discharged.[325] Most of the standards EPA has adopted are premised on pollutant removal technology available to subcategories of affected discharges.

Level of cleanup disputes are common between the government and responsible parties.[326] One reason for the Environmental Defense Fund plaintiffs' insistence on quantitative criteria may have been their perception that hassling over level of cleanup issues had slowed down the CERCLA program; another may have been distrust of EPA regional personnel or state lead agencies, and the desire to lock them into some sort of standard, variations from which could be the subject of judicial review under Section 113(b).

Quite clearly the NCP as originally issued provided scant basis for a claim that a given expenditure was not "consistent."

[B] **Cleanup Standards Under Section 121 (1986).** Easily the most significant change in the CERCLA program wrought by the 1986 amendments was the adoption of Section 121, which imposes detailed remedial standards on CERCLA-funded or CERCLA-ordered remedial actions,[326.1] which are generally believed to have increased the cost of

---

[323] 8 ERC 2121 (BNA) (D.D.C. 1976). EPA unsuccessfully sought to relieve itself of much of the burden of the decree in 1981.

[324] *See* A Legislative History of the Clean Water Act of 1977, Senate Comm. on Pub. Works and Env't. at 459-460.

[325] Section 307(a)(1), Clean Water Act.

[326] *See, e.g.*, United States v. Vertac Chemical Corp., 21 ERC 1459 (E.D. Ark. 1984)(accepting defendant's proffered remedial plan and rejecting government's more expensive plan, applying as the law of the case in RCRA Section 7003 action consent decree provisions similiar in substance to the original version of 40 CFR §300.68.

[326.1] The Section 121 standards are generally applicable to remedial actions under either Section 104 or Section 106. *See* Section 121(a) (1986). Section 104(c)(4) (1986), in addition, specifically ties Fund-financed cleanups to Section 121, and Section 105(b) (1986) required EPA to amend the NCP within eight months of enactment of the 1986 amendments to incorporate the new requirements affecting selection of remedies, including the Section 121 standards.

the average remedy by at least three times. The Section 121 standards are applicable to all postenactment remedial action, regardless of EPA action to conform the NCP,[326.2] except for a narrow class of grandfathered decisions.[326.3] They represent a rejection of risk assessment–based remedial choices.[326.4]

Section 121(b) sets forth "general rules" to be followed in all CERCLA remedial actions. These include a requirement favoring remedial options that reduce volume, toxicity, or mobility (that is, treatment/incineration remedies).[326.5] Off-site transportation for disposal that does not involve treatment is not favored where "practicable treatment technologies are available."[326.6] The statute spells out the factors required to be considered in assessing alternative treatment solutions, and establishes a new general cleanup standard: the remedial action that is "protective of human health and the environment, that is cost effective, and that utilizes permanent solutions and alternative treatment technologies to the maximum extent practicable." Choice of a remedy that fails to meet this criterion requires a detailed explanation.[326.7]

EPA may select a remedy that has not yet been achieved in practice.[326.8] This authority, similar to the technology-forcing provisions of the Clean Air and Clean Water Acts, requires definition and bounds, and the statute provides none. Analogy to the pollution control statutes is imperfect.

Section 121(c) imposes mandatory review every five years of any remedial decision that leaves hazardous substances in place at the site, and requires reopening of the remedy if EPA ever decides that "human

---

326.2 *See* Section 105(b) (1986).

326.3 Section 121(b) of the Superfund Amendments and Reauthorization Act of 1986 states that the standards are not applicable to any remedial action for which a ROD was signed or for which a consent decree incorporating the standards was *lodged* with the federal court before the effective date (October 13, 1986), except that any such ROD modified or supplemented as to the remedy is covered by the Section 121 requirements. RODs and consent decrees signed or lodged within thirty days after the effective date were subject to a more limited grandfathering; EPA was required to certify that the remedy complies "to the maximum extent practicable" with Section 121.

326.4 *See, e.g.,* H.R. Rep. No. 99-962, 99th Cong., 2d Sess. at 249.

326.5 Section 121(b)(1) (1986).

326.6 *Id.*

326.7 *Id.*

326.8 Section 121(b)(2).

health or the environment" is no longer being protected.[326.9]

The general criteria set forth in Section 121(b) are significantly refined by Section 121(d). That provision requires the remedial option selected to be "relevant and appropriate" and to ensure, at a minimum, "protection of human health and the environment." For material remaining on the site, if there are "legally applicable" "standard[s], requirement[s], criteria, or limitation[s]" in force under a federal or a more stringent state "environmental or facility siting law" or "contained in a program . . . authorized or delegated" under a federal environmental statute, those standards must be met or exceeded.[326.10] If such standards are not legally applicable to the substance but are deemed "relevant and appropriate under the circumstances," then the remedial action must achieve a "level or standard of control" that "at least attains" them.[326.11]

There is an exception in Section 121(d)(4), which allows a remedy that does not meet the Section 121(d)(2) criteria if EPA formally concludes that it is a partial remedy, that full application of the requirements either would pose a greater risk or is technically impractical from an engineering perspective, and that the standard of performance achieved by the partial remedy will at least meet the general remedial standard of Section 121(d)(1).[326.12]

The use of RCRA ACLs for CERCLA remedies is substantially curtailed by Section 121, which effectively forecloses their use where there

---

[326.9] It is not clear whether Congress intended this reopener to apply to grandfathered sites. Most CERCLA consent decrees adopted subsequent to 1984 provide their own reopener provisions, which are typically triggered by imminent and substantial endangerment situations.

[326.10] Sections 121(d)(2)(A)(i) and 121(d)(2)(A)(ii). The reference to state laws and requirements is limited by a provision that they have been "identified . . . in a timely manner." EPA may also select a remedy that is not in compliance with a state standard if the standard has not been consistently applied or if the state has not at least demonstrated an intention to apply it consistently. See Section 121(d)(4)(E). State statutes that effect a statewide ban on land disposal are not favored. For further discussion of state involvement in CERCLA remedies, see Section 6.06[2][d][v], infra.

[326.11] Section 121(d)(2)(A). The statute refers specifically to standards under the Safe Drinking Water Act, water quality criteria and standards under Sections 303 and 304 of the Clean Water Act, and standards under the Marine Protection, Research and Sanctuaries Act and RCRA. If there is a SDWA "Maximum Contaminant Level" in effect for a given substance, that standard is mandatory.

[326.12] If the site is an "orphan" site (that is, one as to which there are no viable PRPs), the "applicable or relevant and appropriate" remedy may be compromised, provided that (1) the general level of cleanup required by Section 121(a) is met and (2) there are more pressing competing demands on the superfund. See Section 121(d)(4)(F).

is projected human exposure beyond the facility, except in very limited circumstances.[326.13]

Off-site transport is prohibited except to a TSD facility operating in compliance with Sections 3004 and 3005 of RCRA (or TSCA, where applicable).[326.14] Transfer to a land disposal facility is permitted, however, only if EPA determines that the unit into which the material will be put is not releasing any hazardous waste or constituent to groundwater or soil and that all releases from other units at the facility are being controlled by an approved corrective action program.[326.15]

Finally, it is made clear that no federal, state, or local permits are required in connection with on-site remedial or removal action carried out in compliance with Section 121.[326.16] This is an important provision only for those sites for which EPA has chosen to select a remedy that does not meet a particular state standard.

[iv] Cost-Effectiveness

EPA's implementation of the Section 105(a)(7) requirement that remedial actions be "cost-effective over the period of potential exposure" involves a requirement that alternative remedial scenarios be evaluated,[327] that part of the evaluation involve "cost estimation, including distribution of costs over time."[328] EPA had originally required that where two or more approaches are "adequate," in terms of the degree of protection (more precisely, fall within the range of acceptable protection levels), the "lowest cost alternative that is technologically feasible" be selected, but the Agency abandoned this requirement when it revised the NCP in 1985.[329]

In practice, what is done is a comparative analysis of the short-term

---

326.13 Section 121(d)(2)(B)(ii). The critical inquiry for ACLs is the point of human exposure. The statute arguably precludes the use of ACLs except where contaminated groundwater discharges to a river.

326.14 Section 121(d)(3). TSCA is relevant to disposal of PCBs.

326.15 *Id.*

326.16 Section 121(e)(1). *But see* Section 6.06[2][d][v], *infra*, regarding state involvement and rights.

327 40 CFR §300.68(h).

328 40 CFR §300.68(i)(2)(B).

329 *Compare* 40 CFR §300.68(j) (1982) *with* 40 CFR §300.68 (i) (11-20-85) and §300.68(q), which allow the Agency to choose among alternatives that are roughly cost-equal to select the alternative that "effectively minimizes threats to and provides adequate protection of public health and welfare and the environment, considering cost, technology, and the reliability of the remedy." *And see* discussion of cost-effectiveness at 50 Fed. Reg. 47921 (11-20-85).

front-end costs and capital costs and the long-term maintenance costs for each alternative. Predicting front-end capital costs is obviously a less uncertain exercise than projecting 30-40 year maintenance costs, and most cleanups contain elements of both.

EPA's treatment of cost-effectiveness in the NCP was subject to an interpretation that would allow the remedial decisionmaker to select the lowest-cost, minimally adequate remedial option in all cases. The Agency's 1985 revision of the NCP modifies the approach of the NCP to require the decisionmaker to examine a range of alternative remedies, and choose "a cost-effective . . . alternative which effectively mitigates and minimizes threats to and provides adequate protection of public health, welfare and the environment. . . ."[329.1] The proposed methodology requires the decisionmaker first to find a range of alternatives that provide equivalent levels of protection, measured against available standards, and then consider costs, technological feasibility, administrative convenience, and the like to guide the final choice.

The new EPA approach is more of a cost sensitivity analysis than a cost-benefit analysis in its methodology, and as such provides a more useful set of criteria than were present in the original NCP.

Section 105(a)(7) and Section 121, and the NCP, require establishment of the cost-effective *complete* remedy for each site considered. It was impossible under the original CERCLA for the government to be able to expend sufficient monies under Section 104 to accomplish a complete remedy, because of a further requirement imposed by Section 104(c)(4)(1980) that Fund expenditures at one site reflect a "balance" between the needs at that site and other demands on the Fund. The most cost-effective *complete* remedy, when limited to a partial remedy by dint of Section 104(c)(4), could lose its cost-effective edge. Neither the NCP nor any other published EPA guidelines provided adequate guidance toward resolving this tension.[330] Section 104(c)(4) was amended in 1986 to eliminate the fund-balancing language. The amended language simply cross-references Section 121. That section contains two references to cost-effectiveness.

Section 121(a) requires that all CERCLA remedies "provide for cost-effective response" and that, in evaluating cost-effectiveness, both

---

[329.1] 40 CFR §300.68(i) (50 Fed. Reg. 47975 (1985)).

[330] 40 CFR §300.68(i)(ii), a new provision added in 1985, requires that where competing demands on the Fund prohibit implementation of the chosen alternative, the lower cost alternative that "most closely approaches" the desired level of cleanup be employed.

short- and long-term costs be considered. The Conference Report claims that the revision is intended to be a "recognition of EPA's existing policy as embodied in the National Contingency Plan."[330.1]

Section 121(d)(4)(F) embodies the original Section 104(c)(4) concept of fund balancing, but limits the selection of remedies that are less than Section 121 would otherwise compel to remedies that are "solely Fund-financed."[330.2] This appears to limit the double cost-effectiveness analysis to unquestionably "orphan" sites, those with no hope of PRP involvement.

The cost of operating and maintaining a land disposal site that has been capped and had leachate collected from it for the thirty-year postclosure maintenance period required by Subtitle C of RCRA is significant. The question of O&M costs was unaddressed in the original CERCLA, and EPA sought to push O&M costs off onto states, where PRPs were not available to absorb them.

O&M costs were addressed head on in an amendment to Section 104(c) inserted by P.L. 99-499. The amended CERCLA limits the use of appropriated superfund monies for funding groundwater or surface water treatment at a CERCLA site to ten years after the remedial program for the site becomes operational.[330.3] Treatment that is required beyond that point is not considered "remedial action," but becomes "operation and maintenance." After the tenth year, maintenance by superfund-derived funds is limited to "moneys received by the . . . Superfund from amounts recovered on behalf of such fund under this Act."[330.4] Although this would allow O&M to be paid out of a separate account containing money derived from Section 107 cost recovery actions, it obviously makes more sense for EPA to secure a funding commitment for O&M at a given site from PRPs involved in it.

[v]   State and Local Standards and Participation

[A]   **Status Prior to 1986 Amendments.** Section 105(a)(4) of CERCLA envisioned a cooperative intergovernmental effort at site cleanup, and Section 104(c)(2) requires that EPA "consult" with the affected state or states "before determining any appropriate remedial action." Section

---

330.1 H.R. Rep. No. 99-962, 99th Cong., 2d Sess. at 245.

330.2 *Id.* at 249; and text of subsection.

330.3 Sections 104(c)(6) and 104(c)(7).

330.4 Section 104(c)(7).

114(a), further, preserves for the states the authority to impose "additional liability or requirements" with respect to the release of "hazardous substances"[331] within the state.

The NCP did not initially spell out a state consultative role, and did not address the question of the effect of more stringent state law requirements with respect to residual levels after remedial action, and other parameters. The NCP's treatment of the states' role is limited to spelling out the terms of state assumption of federal cleanup authority at individual sites, state financial participation, and installing states as "trustees" of certain resources.[332]

In the *Environmental Defense Fund* settlement, EPA agreed to propose several changes to the NCP affecting the state role. First, EPA agreed to propose that all Fund-financed measures contain a "community relations plan." In addition, the Agency agreed to require public review of the feasibility studies developed for all Fund-financed response measures, and to provide "comparable" public participation where response actions are taken by private parties pursuant to enforcement actions.[333]

Whether response activities must, as a matter of compliance with the NCP, be required to meet more stringent state or local environmental legal requirements was handled less straightforwardly in the *Environmental Defense Fund* settlement. EPA agreed only to "promulgate a rule addressing the issue." EPA's revised NCP simply stated, at 40 CFR §300.68(i)(4), that "pertinent . . . State standards will be considered and may be used in developing alternatives, with adjustments for site-specific circumstances."

Interweaving state or local requirements into the CERCLA process complicated EPA's task, particularly if state or local nuisance law, which envisions case-by-case application of a very general standard, were in-

---

[331] To the extent that the terms "hazardous substances" and "pollutant or contaminant" do not overlap, state authority to take separate action with respect to the latter is arguably preempted. *Cf.* Exxon Corp. v. Hunt, — U.S. —, 106 S.Ct. 1103 (1986) (construing preemption provision strictly in partially striking down New Jersey's spill compensation fund) (legislatively overruled by P.L. 99-499 (1986)).

[332] The Trustee concept is derived from Section 111(b) of CERCLA, which authorizes states to make claims for damage to natural resources "within the boundary of " the state and "belonging to, managed by, controlled by, or appertaining to the State. . . ."

[333] *EDF* settlement, *supra* note 6, at 5. EPA's community relations plan requirements were promulgated as 40 CFR §300.67, at 50 Fed. Reg. 47973 (11-20-85), and its requirements for public comment on private responses as 40 CFR §300.71(a)(2)(ii)(D), adopted at 50 Fed. Reg. 47977 (11-20-85).

volved. State and local requirements posed a problem generally for responsible parties, who are led to enter into megadollar cleanup agreements with EPA unless all governmental entities with jurisdiction sign on to the deal.

[B]   1986 Amendments. Congress dealt with the state remedy issue in the 1986 reauthorization of CERCLA. Provisions were inserted into the statute dealing both with state participation in the selection of remedies and with the extent to which more stringent state remedial options will be honored in federal remedial actions.

Section 121(f) addresses state involvement in the remedial action selection process. Some of what is required reflects extant EPA practice, but much is quite different, and is aimed at resolving problems that faced private parties whose desires to undertake voluntary remedial action were frustrated by concerns about the subsequent imposition of state requirements that would render their expenditures meaningless.

States must be provided "substantial and meaningful involvement" in the "initiation, development and selection of remedial actions" undertaken within their borders.[333.1] States must be allowed to participate in "decisions whether to perform a preliminary assessment and site inspection" and allocated "responsibility for hazard ranking system scoring."[333.2] They must be provided an opportunity for "concurrence" in the deletion of sites from the NPL, and invited to participate in the "long-term planning process for all remedial sites" within their borders.[333.3]

As for remedial decisions, states must have a "reasonable opportunity for review and comment" on the critical components of remedial decisionmaking.[333.4] They must, further, be notified of negotiations with PRPs and be provided with an opportunity to participate in them and

---

[333.1] Section 121(f). EPA regulations are required to fill in the details.

[333.2] Sections 121(f)(1)(A), 121(f)(1)(B). Both were EPA's prior practice.

[333.3] Sections 121(f)(1)(C), 121(f)(1)(C).

[333.4] Section 121(f)(1)(E). Specifically, these include the RI/FS and underlying technical documents, the remedy as proposed in the ROD, the design of the remedial work, and other "technical data and reports relating to implementation of the remedy." In practical terms, most states had essentially such opportunities previously, and often simply declined to participate because of internal resource constraints.

to become a party to any settlement.[333.5] Finally (and somewhat gratuitously), EPA must provide a separate response to state comments on the remedial alternative selected in the ROD.[333.6]

There are, nevertheless, significant restraints on a state's insistence on its own remedy for NPL-listed sites. Section 121(d)(2)(C), for example, overrides state requirements that effectively preclude land disposal within the state if the remedy of choice under Section 121 would conflict with such a prohibition.[333.7] State nonconcurrence in Section 106 settlement–based remedies will not necessarily ensure that the state's remedy will be adopted.[333.8] Similarly, a state that is dissatisfied with the interagency agreement–based remedy selected for a federal facility located within its borders is limited to suing EPA and seeking a determination that the record does not provide substantial evidence in support of the findings made by the Agency under Section 121(d)(4).[333.9]

[e] State Mandatory Cooperation

EPA is prohibited from expending Fund monies for remedial actions in states that have not entered into a "contract or cooperative agreement" with the federal government that is sufficient to satisfy the requirements of Section 104(c)(3).[334] The burden imposed on the states

---

[333.5] Section 121(f)(1)(F). As is discussed *infra*, and in connection with Section 106 issues, *supra*, however, states' rights to affect the terms of a an EPA settlement are limited. While EPA must consult, there does not appear to be a concomitant obligation to act in accordance with the state's wishes.

[333.6] Section 121(f)(1)(G). This provision arguably imposes no greater obligation on EPA than did the general public participation provisions of Section 117.

[333.7] If the state can demonstrate legitimate environmental bases for the ban, *and* agrees to pay the incremental remedial costs occasioned by the requirement, then the requirement can be imposed on the site. Exhumation and treatment of a large landfill could put a sizable dent in many a state treasury.

The lone exemption from this preemption is Section 121(d)(2)(C)(iv), which requires the state remedy to be imposed at the Picillo Pig Farm site in Rhode Island (doubtless the handiwork of Senator Chafee, a key member of the Senate Environment and Public Works Committee).

[333.8] *See* discussion in Section 6.05[4][c], *supra*.

[333.9] Section 121(f)(3).

[334] This prohibition does not apply to removal action, although Section 104(c)(1)(1986) limits the amount of money and time that can be committed to such actions to $2 million and twelve months, subject to an exception for "continued response action" that is "consistent with remedial action to be taken."

is potentially heavy. EPA's initial NCP did not significantly embellish the statutory requirements.[335]

The state must agree (1) to provide for "future maintenance of all remedial and removal actions," [336] (2) to provide at least one hazardous waste disposal facility, licensed under RCRA, to receive wastes removed from sites cleaned up under CERCLA,[337] and (3) to agree to cost-share all Fund-financed remedial actions at a level that is 50 percent or more[337.1] for state-owned and municipally owned facilities[337.2] (so owned at the time disposal occurred) and 10 percent for others.[338] For cost-sharing purposes, "facility" does not include "navigable waters

---

[335] 40 CFR §300.62 (11-20-85).

[336] Section 104(c)(3)(A).

[337] Section 104(c)(9). The requirement was originally in Section 104(c)(3)(B). It proved politically, and practically, difficult for a number of states. The original concept was to force each state to have at least one RCRA-licensed TSD facility available for disposal of wastes exhumed from superfund sites. The 1986 amendment bars the expenditure of any superfund monies for remedial action after October 17, 1989, unless the state has entered into a cooperative agreement with EPA that "reasonably assures" that the state will have, either within or outside of its borders (the latter pursuant to an interstate compact or regional agreement), sufficient RCRA-permitted TSD capacity for the "destruction, treatment, or secure disposition" of all hazardous wastes "reasonably expected to be generated within its borders" during the twenty-year period following the agreement. This is an effort to prod those states that have been slow to develop in-state TSD capacity into developing such capacity.

[337.1] The state must also agree to additional cost-sharing as the federal government "deems appropriate, taking into account the degree of responsibility of the State or political subdivision for the release." This provision effectively places the states at the mercy of EPA with respect to state-owned facilities, and creates a disincentive on the part of states to list public facilities on the NPL. While this strategy may have been successful prior to the 1986 amendments, when the states had significant control over the shape of the NPL, new provisions that allow citizen groups to trigger listings place the states at greater risk.

[337.2] A 1986 amendment makes it clear that privately owned facilities operated under contract to state or municipal entities are considered state or municipal facilities for purposes of the 50 percent cost-sharing requirement.

[338] Section 104(c)(3)(C) of the original CERCLA provided that the states could claim credit against their mandatory 10 percent or 50 percent funding contribution for priority-listed sites for out-of-pocket expenditures made for cost-eligible response actions or compensable claims arising out of the site subsequent to January 1, 1978. P.L. 99-499 moved the credit provision to Section 104(c)(5), and substantially changed it. Under the new scheme, a state can receive credit against its Section 104(c)(3) cost-sharing obligations for (1) amounts expended out-of-pocket on remedial actions at priority-listed sites pursuant to a cooperative agreement with EPA; (2) amounts expended on sites prior to listing or the effective date of the cooperative agreement, provided the event actually subsequently takes place, and provided EPA agrees that the expenditures would have been creditable if they had been made after the fact; (3) expenditures made for qualifying remedial or compensatory purposes between January 1, 1978, and the effective date of the original CERCLA (December 11, 1980); (4) expenditures made to clean up a site owned but not

or the beds underlying those waters."[338.1]

States or subdivisions may, in addition, voluntarily agree, under Section 104(d), to assume EPA's role within the state. If EPA concludes that the state is financially capable of carrying the up-front costs,[338.2] the state may assume the federal role, and be entitled to reimbursement of its response costs. Congress sought to make the contracts enforceable in federal court,[339] and to retain the federal government's right to initiate an active role even in states that have assumed federal responsibility.[340]

Section 104(d)(4) declares that the government may treat two non-contiguous facilities as one where they are "reasonably related" by "geography," "threat," or "potential threat." The language crept into S. 1480 sometime between November 19 and November 24, 1980, as part of Amendment No. 2631, the last-minute compromise that was enacted as CERCLA,[341] without a clarifying explanation. It appears to

---

operated by the state or one of its subdivisions between the effective date of the original CERCLA and the effective date of the 1986 amendments (October 17, 1986) if they were made pursuant to a then-extant cooperative agreement; and (5) expenditures made after the effective date of the 1986 amendments on a case-by-case basis, in EPA's discretion. States are permitted to bank credits, and transfer unused credits from one site to another.

[338.1] Thus, states, such as New York and Illinois, that are seeking superfund monies for the removal of hazardous substances from water bodies are not required to come up with 50 percent funding.

[338.2] The willingness of states to take on a voluntary burden was affected significantly by the Supreme Court's decision in Exxon Corporation v. Hunt, 54 L.W. 4249 (March 10, 1986). The Court concluded that state superfund taxes (most of which are levied either on chemical feedstocks or on waste) are preempted by Section 114(c) of CERCLA insofar as they generate revenues that are used to pay expenses that are eligible for federal payment under CERCLA. Such taxes are *not* preempted, however, insofar as they raise money to cover costs that are *ineligible* for payment out of the federal fund (such as the state's mandatory cost share required by Section 104; third party damage compensation; personnel, fund administration, equipment, and research costs; and costs incurred to remediate sites not on the NPL or cover remedial expenditures prohibited by the NCP. Congress legislatively overruled the decision in 1986 by repealing the original text of Section 114(c).

[339] *See* Section 104(d)(2). The federal government's power to compel a contracted state's legislature to appropriate money is not without Tenth Amendment ramifications, however. *See* National League of Cities v. Usery, 726 U.S. 833 (1976); *but see* United States v. Ohio Department of Highway Safety, 635 F.2d 1195 (6th Cir. 1980), *cert. denied*, 451 U.S. 949 (1981).

[340] Section 104(d)(3).

[341] Cong. Record, Nov. 24, 1980, S. 14948 *et seq.* House of Representatives action, adopting identical language, occurred on December 3, 1980.

have been intended to function as a device to prevent the states from fragmenting related contamination events in an effort to increase the total amount of federal funds available. If a state lists a hazardous waste dump and a downgradient contaminated well field separately, it can theoretically have two bites of the CERCLA apple. Section 104(d)(4) allows EPA to lump the two together, thereby reducing the ultimate federal exposure.

[f]   Information-Gathering Authority

The government's authority to compel the disclosure of information about a site or its contents or past disposal practices was initially limited under CERCLA. Section 104(e) imposes an obligation on TSD owner/operators, generators, and transporters and, since 1986, on certain others to respond to EPA requests for information and authorizes entry by government representatives into a suspect site.[343] Section 104(e) was originally not enforceable, and information gathering from persons other than TSDs was limited.

The statute was essentially rewritten in 1986,[343.1] to be significantly broader and tougher. Penalty provisions added to CERCLA in 1986[343.2] cured the enforceability problem that had previously compelled EPA to rely more on Section 3007 of RCRA than on Section 104(e) in seeking CERCLA-related information.[343.3]

---

[342] [Reserved.]

[343] Forcible entry requires a judicial warrant. *See* Marshall v. Barlow's, Inc., 429 U.S. 1347 (1977). In *Bunker Partnership, Ltd. v. United States,* __ F. Supp. __, 23 ERC (BNA) 2041 (1985), a case involving a challenge to a warrant issued under Section 104(e), the district court held that Section 104(e)-based warrants were more like administrative subpoenas than like criminal search warrants, and suppressed a broad warrant that authorized EPA employees to search all of the target's records and determine which ones were relevant for CERCLA purposes. The court stated that determining which records were responsive was for the recipient to decide.

[343.1] P.L. 99-499, Section 104.

[343.2] *Id.,* Section 109.

[343.3] There is some legislative history from 1980 suggestive of an intention to allow EPA to use its RCRA authority to gather information for CERCLA purposes. *See* S. Rep. No. 96-848, at 62 (1980). There are serious semantic problems with Section 3007, however, and EPA's use of that provision for CERCLA purposes prior to 1986 did not go unchallenged. *See, e.g.,* United States v. Charles George Trucking Company, 642 F. Supp. 327 (D. Mass. 8-15-86) (upholding the practice).

In general, information may be demanded and access and entry to private property secured by EPA officers or employees, and "representative[s] of the President, duly designated," and by state or local officers, employees, or representatives pursuant to a cooperative agreement with EPA. The authority, spelled out particularly in following paragraphs, is generally limited to use "for the purposes of determining the need for response, or choosing or taking any response action"[343.4] under CERCLA or of "otherwise enforcing" the statute."[343.5]

[i] Information Requests

Section 104(e)(2) specifies the broad categories of information that may be the subject of a Section 104(e) information demand. The 1986 amendment provides a much more explicit and broader scope of permissible inquiry than did the prior version.

An information request may be directed at any person who "has or may have information relevant to" the nature or quantity of materials generated, treated, stored or disposed of at a "vessel or facility," the nature or extent of an actual or threatened release, or "the ability of a person to pay for or perform a cleanup."[343.6] The last clause is aimed at insurance coverage and other financial information that PRPs consistently refused to provide under the original statute, arguing correctly that EPA had no authority to seek it under the 1980 language of Section 104(e).

Both the original statute and the 1986 version contain a trade secret protection provision.[343.7] The amended provision is the narrower, and reflects the trend of such provisions subsequent to the Third Circuit's decision narrowing the scope of a trade secret provision in the OSHA hazard communication rule.[343.8] A confidentiality claim may not be asserted unless the claimant carries the burden of proof on four points: (1) it has not released the information to anyone other than specified government officials under a confidentiality agreement; (2) the infor-

---

[343.4] Section 104(e)(1) (1986). Although the authority clearly would be applicable to EPA contractors, whether it can be extended to contractors of PRP groups, or whether EPA should be willing to designate such entities, is problematical. *See* discussion at Section 6.09[4][e], *infra*.

[343.5] *Id.* The 1980 version did not contain a reference to "choosing or taking any response action," and was thus significantly narrower.

[343.6] Section 104(e)(2)(A)-(C) (1986). This authority approaches in scope the broad subpoena power given EPA under TSCA.

[343.7] *Compare* Section 104(e)(2) (1980) *with* Section 104(e)(7) (1986).

[343.8] United Steelworkers, AFL-CIO-CLC v. Auchter, 763 F.2d 728 (3d Cir. 1985).

mation is not "required to be disclosed . . . to the public under any other Federal or State Law," (in particular TSCA, FIFRA, or OSHA); (3) if the information sought is a specific chemical identity, it is "not readily discoverable through reverse engineering"; and (4) disclosure of the information is likely to cause "substantial harm" to the claimant's "competitive position."[343.9]

[ii] Access, Entry, and Condemnation

Entry onto private property by governmental representatives is authorized, in general, if the property is one on which a hazardous substance "has been or may have been released," where a release is "threatened" within the meaning of CERCLA, or where entry is needed "to determine the need for a response or the appropriate response, or to effectuate a response action."[343.10] Entry for the purpose of taking samples is authorized, in addition, for "any location of any suspected hazardous substance or pollutant or contaminant."[343.11]

The provision for entry for sampling significantly broadens the reach of the statute. It would appear to allow the government to enter a generator's plant to sample its output or waste for the purpose of matching it with substances found at a CERCLA site.[343.12]

A final addition in 1986 was authority for the exercise of eminent domain to purchase property for CERCLA-related purposes. Section 104(j) authorizes the acquisition of real property to the extent that EPA determines that the property is "needed to conduct a remedial action."[343.13] A significant limitation on the use of this authority, however, is Section 104(j)(2), which limits property acquisition to sites as to which

---

343.9 Section 104(e)(7)(E). In addition, subsection (F) bars confidentiality protection for trade names, common names, generic classifications, physical properties, health and environmental hazard information, potential human exposure routes, "the location of disposal of any waste stream," monitoring data relating to waste disposal activity, hydrogeologic or geologic activity, and groundwater monitoring data.

343.10 Section 104(e)(3) (1968). The 1980 provision was somewhat narrower. The 1986 statute allows entry onto areas that are adjacent to the actual superfund site, for the purpose of effectuating remedial action, legislatively overruling Outboard Marine Corporation v. Thomas, 773 F.2d 883 (7th Cir. 1985).

343.11 Section 104(e)(4).

343.12 The government must provide a receipt and offer to split the samples, and provide a copy of the analytical results to the facility owner.

343.13 Section 104(j). EPA may not be compelled to take property, however, nor do governmental entities incur any liability solely by acquiring property. *Id.* Eminent domain acquisitions are governed procedurally by federal statutes relating to property acquisition.

the state or political subdivision will agree to take title following completion of the remedial action.[343.14]

[iii] Enforcement

Enforcement of information gathering is governed by specific enforcement authority contained in Section 104(e)(5). There is provision for the issuance of compliance orders and follow-up injunctive and/or penalty actions by the Department of Justice. There is no right to a formal hearing in connection with a Section 104(e)(5) order; the only right is to "consultation as is reasonably appropriate under the circumstances."[343.15]

Refusal to comply with a Section 104(e) order may subject the actor to treble damages in a later Section 107 cost recovery action, on a later Section 112(c) subrogation action.[344] This provision may be a sufficient incentive to spark compliance by Section 104(e) order recipients.

[g] Cleanup Contractor and Employee–Related Issues

[i] Contractors

CERCLA-financed response actions, whether undertaken directly by EPA contractors or indirectly by state or local entities on a reimbursable basis, must comply with the Davis-Bacon Act.[345] This statute, well known to government contractors, indexes government contract laborers' and mechanics' wages for work involving "construction, repair or alteration" to the prevailing local wage rates.

CERCLA produced a significant new, specialized market for engineering and hydrogeologist firms, as well as for heavy construction firms. Though most CERCLA-related work is "low technology" in na-

---

[343.14] In practice, many sites will be owned or managed during the postremediation period by PRP groups or individual PRP owners. Issues will arise over the relationship between EPA and PRPs if eminent domain is required in order to do remedial action at a site for which PRPs, rather than the state, will have responsibility.

[343.15] *Compare* Section 3008(a) of RCRA, which provides for adjudicatory hearings in connection with Section 3007 enforcement orders.

[344] *See* Section 107(c)(3). *But see* Aminoil, Inc. v. EPA, 599 F. Supp 69 (C.D. Cal. 9-28-84)(holding Section 106(c) and Section 107(c)(3) unconstitutional for failure to provide for a hearing or opportunity to challenge order prior to incurring daily penalties or treble damages). *Accord,* Industrial Park Dev. Co., v. EPA, 604 F. Supp. 1136 (E.D. Pa 1985). *Contra,* Wagner Electric Corp. v. Thomas, 22 ERC 2079 (D. Kan. 1985); United States v. Reilly Tar & Chem. Corp. 606 F. Supp. 412 Minn.); and Solid State Circuits, Inc. v. EPA, 23 ERC 1758 (W.D. Mo. 1985).

[345] 40 USC §276a.

ture, there are obvious hazards involved for contractor employees, and thus project management can be a complex matter.

Determining the extent of contamination and the nature of the subsurface hydrogeology for the purpose of remedial design also carries risks.[346] Finally, response action contractors were occasionally named as defendants in contribution actions, and attorneys representing engineering firms became increasingly concerned, as the CERCLA program progressed, about tort liability. Contractors, along with everyone else, found liability insurance difficult, and then impossible, to acquire. Contracts, particularly between groups of PRPs and remedial contractors, thus became increasingly difficult to negotiate, in terms of both price and indemnification agreements insisted upon by the contractors.

Section 119 was added to CERCLA in 1986, in an attempt to alleviate some of these problems. It purports to immunize "response action contractors"[347] from liability "under any other Federal law," except for the consequences of negligent or grossly negligent acts or intentional misconduct.[348] PRPs are barred from defending Section 107 cost recovery actions on the basis of raising a third party action defense under Section 107(b)(3) with respect to the acts of response action contractors.[348.1]

Section 119(a) is effective in limiting contractor exposure to contribution actions brought under CERCLA, or for natural resource damages, and other claims founded on federal law. It does not purport to insulate contractors from, or limit their liability under, state common law. Liability based on state law is addressed by Section 109(c), which allows the

---

[346] For example, at one of the Missouri NPL sites the remedy chosen involved, in part, a slurry wall, which requires excavation to bedrock. It has been reported that during construction it was discovered that what was thought to be bedrock was in fact a boulder field, and that bedrock was in fact many feet lower. That fact alone doubled the remedial costs.

[347] A "response action contractor" is one who enters into a "response action contract" with respect to a release or a threatened release at a facility, does a field demonstration project under Section 311, or is retained or hired by another response action contractor "to provide any services relating to a response action." Section 119(e)(2). A "response action contract" is defined by Section 119(e)(1) as a "written contract or agreement" entered into with EPA, a federal agency, a state that has a cooperative agreement in force, or "any potentially responsible party carrying out an agreement under section 106 or 122," to carry out a remedial or removal action at a NPL facility or to do "evaluation, planning, engineering, surveying and mapping, design, construction, equipment, or any ancillary services thereto".

[348] Section 119(a) (1986).

[348.1] Section 119(b).

government to indemnify CERCLA response action contractors (other than RCRA-regulated facilities)[348.2] from liability above a deductible amount[348.3] predicated on strict liability or simple negligence.[348.4]

The indemnification scheme is limited to amounts of potential liability in excess of that which is insurable in the market "at a fair and reasonable price" at the time the response action contract is entered into.[348.5]

[ii] **Worker Protection**

Section 104(f) of the 1980 CERCLA[348.6] required EPA, and other authorized agencies, to require their contractors to comply "with Federal health and safety standards" established under Section 301(f). That Section contemplated that EPA, the Department of Transportation (DOT), the Occupational Safety and Health Administration (OSHA), and the National Institute for Occupational Safety and Health (NIOSH) would jointly develop standards for the protection of the health and safety of employees involved in CERCLA response action. Such standards were to have been included in a modification of the NCP within two years of the effective data of CERCLA.

The government did not implement this provision within the statutory time period. Instead, EPA inserted a provision in the NCP simply requiring compliance with "applicable" OSHA requirements as "any

---

348.2 *See* Section 119(c)(5)(D). The indemnification is available to all government contractors and, subject to some preconditions, to PRP-retained contractors. Applicability to the latter group is conditioned on their being retained under a Section 122 settlement or pursuant to a Section 106–ordered action. Section 119(c)(5)(C) establishes several other limitations on PRP contractor indemnification. One that is significant is that any such indemnity is limited to the amounts beyond the amount that the PRPs are "able" to indemnify, up to the contractor's "reasonable potential liability" arising from its negligence (EPA makes the critical determinations, which are not appealable). Section 119(c)(5)(C)(ii). PRP contractors are required to exhaust their claims against their employers prior to seeking payment on the federal indemnity. *Id.*

348.3 Section 119(c)(5)(B).

348.4 These costs are passed on as cost recovery expenses to responsible parties under Section 107.

348.5 Section 119(c)(4)(A). The determination of what is a "fair and reasonable price" is EPA's to make. *See* Section 119(e)(3). Contractors have an affirmative obligation to make "diligent efforts" to secure insurance, and the obligation is a continuing one for multisite contractors.

348.6 Section 104(f) was amended in 1986, when the 1980 text was replaced with an unrelated provision.

other requirements deemed necessary by the lead agency."[349]

The 1986 amendments included a new provision, Section 126, which required the Occupational Safety and Health Administrator to promulgate standards under Section 6 of the OSH Act[349.1] covering employees engaged in "hazardous waste operations." Until such regulations are promulgated, Section 126(f) requires OSHA to impose interim standards that mirror an EPA guidance document.[349.2] The OSHA standards are applicable to federal employees and contractors and PRP contractors, but they apply to state and local employees only in states with programs approved under Section 18 of the OSH Act. Section 126 requires EPA to issue regulations applicable to state and municipal employees in states not covered by OSH Act standards.

Workers' claims arising out of exposure to hazardous chemicals during response actions can be anticipated to occur with increasing frequency. Such claims, which typically allege negligence on the part of the government as well as involved private parties, began to find their way into courts soon after EPA commenced implementation of CERCLA for hazardous substance response.[350]

[h] Impact on Private Property

Although CERCLA as originally enacted gives the government a right of entry to a site where hazardous materials are found for information-gathering purposes,[350.1] it did not clearly give the government the right to force its way onto adjacent or nearby property that does not contain such materials. The statute also failed to provide EPA with the power of eminent domain in connection with its remedial activities, although exercise of the power of eminent domain by a court acting

---

[349] 40 CFR §300.71.

[349.1] *See generally* Chapter 9, *infra.*

[349.2] *Health and Safety Requirements for Employees Engaged in Field Activities* (1981). The interim standards may be no less stringent than existing, applicable OSHA standards.

[350] *See, e.g.,* Lowe, et al. v. Norfolk and Western Railway, et al., 529 F. Supp. 491 (S.D. Ill. 1982) (action by workers engaged in cleanup of hazardous chemical spill under EPA direction, alleging negligence on the part of EPA and the waste cleanup contractor in exposing them to orthochlorophenol, erroneously believed to be carbolic acid).

[350.1] Section 104(e)(1)(1980).

pursuant to Section 106(a) may be fairly inferred from the breadth of the text of that provision.[350.2]

Amendments to Section 104(e) in 1986 expressly provide for government entry and use of adjacent properties, and provide a qualified right of eminent domain, which may be exercised only if the state or local government will take title following completion of the remedial action.

[3] Assessment of Damages to Natural Resources

[a] Statutory Requirements

Section 107(a)(4)(c) of CERCLA makes "damages for injury for destruction of, or loss of natural resources"[351] and the costs of asserting such damage recoverable by the government from responsible parties. The entities entitled to seek recovery are "the President, or the authorized representative of any State . . . on behalf of the public as trustee. . . ."[352] The federal authority to assess natural resource damages must be delegated by the President to federal agencies.[353]

Federal delegation was accomplished initially in subpart G of the

---

[350.2] *See* Outboard Marine Corp. v. Thomas, 773 F.2d 883, No. 85-1753 (7th Cir. 1985). In this case, Outboard Marine Corporation, a manufacturing facility, discharged PCB oil over a number of years into a watercourse adjacent to a manufacturing facility on a site that also contained the company's corporate headquarters. EPA's remedial plan envisioned dredging the bottom sediments and dewatering, treating, and entombing the PCB-contaminated material on OMC's site, using portions of the company's parking lot. The court overturned a warrant issued to EPA authorizing entry onto the site for the purpose of undertaking preliminary surveys, holding that EPA possessed no authority under CERCLA to condem a property interest in private land, and had no authority forcibly to enter land that did not contain a hazardous substance.

[351] "Natural resources" means "land, fish, wildlife, biota, air, water, ground water, drinking water supplies, and other such resources belonging to, managed by, held in trust by, appertaining to, or otherwise controlled by the United States (including the resources of the fishery conservation zone established by the Fishery Conservation and Management Act of 1976), any State or local government, or any foreign government." Section 101(16).

[352] Section 107(f)(1980). Claims for natural resource damage may theoretically also be asserted against the Fund, under Section 112. *See* 40 CFR §300.74(b) (November 1985). Trustees may, in addition, request EPA or the state to act under Section 106 or related state authority, request governmental removal or remedial action, or proceed directly against PRPs under Section 107. *See* 40 CFR §300.74(b)(1)-(4).

[353] Section 111(h)(1)(1980).

NCP.[354] The basic thrust of the delegation is that (1) the federal land manager with jurisdiction over the area where the damaged natural resources reside will function as the trustee for such resources; (2) as to nonfixed resources, the federal agency having jurisdiction over them[355] is trustee; (3) for most tidal water areas, the trustee is the Department of Commerce or other agency with a more specific jurisdictional claim; and (4) for Native American treaty lands, the Interior Department serves as trustee.

The NCP designated states as trustees of resources within their boundaries "belonging to, managed by, controlled by, or appertaining to such state."[356]

Congress "fine tuned" the natural resource damage assessment provisions of CERCLA in P.L. 99-499, in 1986. Section 111(h), which had previously established the basic trustee mechanism, was moved into Section 107, as Section 107(f)(2), and somewhat modified.[356.1] Under the revised approach, federal trustees are appointed in the NCP, and governors appoint state agencies to act as trustees for state resources.[356.2]

Revisions to Section 107(f)(1) clarified an uncertainty under the original version as to whether sums recovered from PRPs as damages would have to be appropriated before they could be spent; the revision stated that they do not.[356.3] Use of recovered funds is limited, however, to expenditures by the affected trustee[356.4] to "restore, replace, or acquire the equivalent of" lost or damaged resources, although the measure of

---

354 40 CFR §§300.72-300.74.

355 For example, the U. S. Department of the Interior is the trustee for fish and wildlife.

356 40 CFR §300.73.

356.1 The old text of Section 107(f) became (f)(1), and was also modified.

356.2 There is specific provision in Section 107(f)(2) for states to request federal agencies to perform damage assessments for them.

356.3 In the absence of such a provision, the federal Antideficiency Act, 31 USC §1341, probably required that recovered sums be paid over into the treasury.

356.4 The original CERCLA was silent as to which entity should actually receive the damage awards. The House Bill would have had EPA retain and expend all natural resource damage awards, but the conference committee substituted language providing explicitly that each trustee retain awards applicable to trust resources assigned to it. See H.R. Rep. 99-962, 99th Cong., 2d Sess. at 205.

damages is not limited to these amounts.[356.5] There is, however, a specific statutory prohibition against double recovery.

Damage determinations and assessments made in accordance with Section 301(c) regulations by trustees carry a "rebuttable presumption" of validity.[357]

Quite clearly, the means by which natural resource loss is assessed is of significance both to the public in general and to potentially responsible parties. Section 301(c) of the 1980 CERCLA required the government to promulgate, after study, and within two years of CERCLA's effective date, damage assessment regulations. The responsibility was delegated to the Interior Department, which failed to issue the regulations on time.[358]

The government's failure to implement Section 301(c) was raised as a defense to Section 107 damage recovery actions in several cases.[359] Several states also sought to obtain *mandamus* enforcement of the regulations[360] or predicate a challenge to EPA's denial of Fund monies under Section 111 of CERCLA. A court issued a *mandamus* order

---

[356.5] In other words, damages claims can cover such things as the costs of determining the extent of loss, and administrative costs related to developing the evidentiary basis of the claim, which can be large, particularly under the elaborate damage assessment regulations issued by the Department of the Interior under Section 301(c). This requirement was in the original CERCLA, and was not materially changed by P.L. 99-499.

[357] Section 107(f)(2)(C).

[358] Interior issued two advance notices of proposed rulemaking, 48 Fed. Reg. 1084(1-10-83) and 48 Fed. Reg. 34768(8-1-83), and proposed its procedures and criteria for coastal environments on December 20, 1985. 50 Fed. Reg. 52126. It issued final assessment regulations covering everything but simplified assessment methods on August 1, 1986. 51 Fed. Reg. 27674. The regulations are discussed below.

[359] United States v. Reilly Tar & Chemical Corp., 20 ERC 1058 (D. Minn. 1983)(defense rejected; state damages claim allowed). Other cases in which the defense has been raised but not adjudicated as of late 1985 are United States v. AVX, et al. (D. Mass.); and United States v. Shell Oil Co., et al. (D. Colo.).

[360] *E.g.*, State of New Jersey v. Ruckelshaus, No. 84-1668 (D.N.J.); and Goldberg-Secretary, et al. v. Clark, No. 84-1802 (D.D.C.)(both *mandamus* suits). An order requiring the Secretary of the Interior to issue regulations was issued in the *New Jersey* case late in 1984. New Jersey v. Ruckelshaus, CA No. 1668 (D.N.J. 12-12-84). The court also ordered EPA to prescribe forms and procedures for processing claims under Section 112(b)(1), *and* to reinstate and process New Jersey's claims. The court also ruled that preauthorization by EPA of a restoration plan is not a prerequisite for filing a damage claim under Section 112. Interior is required to issue the regulations on a schedule that sets final promulgation for some aspects in April 1986 and for others in August 1986. Interior proposed the first set at 50 Fed. Reg. 52126.

against Interior and EPA in *New Jersey v. Ruckelshaus.*[360.1]

Congress addressed the issue of the late damage assessment regulations in P.L. 99-499, mandating final damage assessment regulations to be issued within six months of enactment.[360.2]

[b] Department of the Interior Regulations

Assessment of natural resource damage presents significant certainties on a number of fronts. Particularly in the case of nonfixed resources, such as fish and wildlife, determining the scope of the loss often requires estimation based on assumptions that can not be validated empirically. Once a reasonable estimate of the extent and nature of the harm is made, a monetary value must be placed on it. That activity is fraught with uncertainty, and, in the absence of well-crafted standards, each attempt by the government to quantify the monetary losses could be the subject of fact-dependent litigation.[361]

The DOI natural resource damage assessment regulations, codified at 43 CFR Part 11,[361.1] are complex. They are very important not only to the federal government, but also to states, and, for a different reason, to PRPs, for only damage assessments done in conformity with these regulations are entitled to the statutory presumption of correctness provided by Section 107(f). These regulations also represent the first effort at development of a comprehensive methodology for quantifying and monetizing ecosystem damage.

The regulations contain a mixture of scientific methodology, policy

---

[360.1] *Supra* note 360.

[360.2] P.L. 99-499, Section 107(d)(3). The deadline was consistent with Interior's own schedule. It had already issued the detailed assessment regulations, and projected issuance of the simplified regulations (so-called Type A methods) by February 1987. The statutory deadline had the effect of modifying the court's order in *New Jersey v. Ruckelshaus,* but the Conference Report (p. 205) professes a desire that the Court retain jurisdiction.

[361] For example, let us assume that a release of a hazardous substance resulted in a fish kill. If we further assume that an accurate count of the lost population can be made, then there are a number of possible ways to value the loss. These might include (A) market value per pound of dead individual fish, (B) market value per pound of lost individual fish plus lost propagation potential, or (C) replacement cost, in terms of hatchery and rearing costs to duplicate lost population.

[361.1] *See* 51 Fed. Reg. 27674 (8-1-86) for the Secretary's contemporaneous explanation of the regulations. "Simplified" assessment methodology ("Type A" assessments) is scheduled to be issued in February 1987, and will be discussed in a later update of this treatise.

choices, and procedural requirements, and are dominated by the latter. The general damage determination and assessment procedure involves a four-stage process: preassessment,[361.2] assessment planning,[361.3] assessment,[361.4] and postassessment.[361.5]

The preassessment phase involves an initial determination as to whether injury to a natural resource has occurred, and, if so, whether the injury is attributable to a "discharge or release."[361.6] During this phase, the following actions are taken. The responsible trustee or trustees are identified and notified. Preliminary sampling is undertaken. Necessary emergency action is taken. Finally, a document called a "preassessment screen" is prepared. The purpose of the preassessment screen is to form the basis of a decision to proceed with the assessment process or not to do so.[361.7] The preassessment screen document is required to answer five questions set forth in Section 11.23(e); affirmative answers are necessary for all five before the assessment process can continue.[361.8]

Assessment planning involves creation of a second document, the "assessment plan," which is supposed to be the methodological road map that will be followed throughout the remainder of the process. It is also the decisional document for deciding whether to pursue a "simplified" Type A assessment or the elaborate "Type B" methodologies, and it is the first point at which the public, including PRPs, are provided

---

[361.2] Subpart B (Sections 11.20-11.25).

[361.3] Subpart C (Sections 11.30-11.35).

[361.4] Subpart D (simplified ("Type A") assessments—expected February 1987); and Subpart E (alternative ("Type B") assessments, Sections 11.60-11.84).

[361.5] Subpart F (Sections 11.90-11.93).

[361.6] Section 11.20(b). The reference to "discharge" relates to the fact that the damage assessment regulations apply equally to Section 311 of the Clean Water Act (33 USC §1321).

[361.7] Sections 11.23-11.25. The regulations repeatedly refer to the "authorized official" as being responsible for the various tasks. Only governmental entities may be authorized officials, and it seems clear that the intent is to allow for the development of a federal assessment group with expertise, which could be called upon by any trustee.

[361.8] The five questions are (1) whether a discharge or release has occurred, (2) whether relevant resources have been "or are likely to have been" adversely affected, (3) whether the quantity of substances discharged or released is sufficient potentially to cause injury, (4) whether sufficient data for pursuit of an assessment are either "readily available" or acquirable at a "reasonable cost," and (5) whether the response action planned for the site will not remedy the injury.

an opportunity for input into the damage assessment.[361.9] Finally, the assessment plan must confirm whether exposure of a resource to oil or a hazardous substance has in fact occurred.[361.10]

A critical component of the assessment planning phase—and one that is most likely to be the subject of dispute by PRPs or other interests —is the "economic methodology determination."[361.11] The regulation essentially embraces cost-benefit analysis as the basis for determining whether to use resource restoration or replacement costs or diminution of use values as the measure of damages.[361.12] Since this decision shapes the entire assessment process from that point on, an erroneous or flawed decision will jeopardize recovery in the end.

For Type B assessments, the "assessment phase" includes three subsidiary phases: "injury determination,"[361.13] "quantification,"[361.14] and "damage determination."[361.15] The injury determination regulations are reasonably straightforward, albeit conservative, and appear to reflect, in the main,[361.16] relatively noncontroversial scientific judgments about how one goes about determining what is harm. They inform the public of just what the government will consider injury and what it will not, and define the universe of resources that is the subject of concern.

Quantification of the extent of injury or loss, particularly where biological communities are involved, is subject to a much greater degree of inherent uncertainty. First, any quantification must be relative to a baseline, and determination of the baseline is often not possible by means of empirical evidence. Section 11.72 addresses the baseline prob-

---

361.9 *See* Section 11.32(c), which provides a notice and comment opportunity. The procedural rules are precise, and provide, *inter alia*, that significant modifications of any component of the plan must be revealed and comment solicited. *See* Section 11.32(e).

361.10 *See* Section 11.34. If exposure cannot be confirmed for at least one resource on the basis of the existing data, then a set of analytical methodologies provided in the Injury Determination regulations (Sections 11.61-11.64) may be resorted to.

361.11 Section 11.35.

361.12 *See* Section 11.35(c). The least costly damages measure is required to be selected, except where a cheaper restoration or replacement remedy is not feasible. *See* Section 11.35(b)(3).

361.13 Sections 11.61-11.64. What is considered injury for surface waters, groundwater, air, and "geologic" and biological resources is defined; pathway determination methodology is provided; and protocols for testing and sampling are spelled out.

361.14 Sections 11.70-11.73.

361.15 Sections 11.80-11.84.

361.16 The regulations are quite conservative in some areas; for example, by adopting Clean Water Act water quality criteria as a measure of injury, Section 11.62(b), DOI is, in some cases, elevating legislative judgment above chemical and biological reality. *See* discussion at 51 Fed. Reg. 27707 (1986).

lem intelligently, listing the sources of information likely to yield useful information upon which to premise an estimate.

Other quantification uncertainties involve, with biological resources, problems of predicting the extent of long-term losses, and accounting for confounding variables, and, for other dynamic systems, accounting for natural recovery. The regulations address these matters as well, leaving much latitude to the decisionmaker. The DOI approach focuses on the concept of reduction of "services" occasioned by the contamination,[361.17] but provides little clear guidance as to how the loss of services is to be determined, essentially relying on the combined and cooperative expertise of "economists and natural resource specialists."[361.18] The regulations do not, and indeed cannot, eliminate the wide uncertainties inherent in this activity. Thus, government decisions as to how much of a given resource has been damaged as a result of contamination will always be the subject of disagreement, and will be upheld in many cases solely because of the statutory presumption of validity, the burden of proof that it imposes on the challenger, and the wide deference accorded EPA and DOI by the courts.

The damage assessment methodologies, which are designed to turn the quantified losses into dollar equivalents, are also full of inherent uncertainties, particularly where the resources are not marketable. There is no way for the government to eliminate these uncertainties, and the damage assessment regulations do not attempt to do so, choosing to rely on the application of largely theoretical economic models as the "best available procedures" for carrying out the statutory requirements.[361.19]

The final phase, "postassessment," involves the rendering of a report on the assessment phase, making a demand on the PRPs, and formulating and carrying out a restoration plan.[361.20]

[4] The Fate of Removed Substances

The extent to which hazardous substances removed from a superfund site must be handled and disposed of in accordance with all of the

---

361.17 *See* 51 Fed. Reg. at 27713.

361.18 *Id.*

361.19 *See* Section 301(c)(2), and discussion at 51 Fed. Reg. 27721.

361.20 *See* Sections 11.90, 11.91, and 11.93, respectively. Section 11.92, which establishes an accounting system, and Section 11.93 are affected by the 1986 amendments to Section 107(f) of CERCLA, and their revision is expected sometime in 1987.

regulatory requirements imposed under the Resource Conservation and Recovery Act[361.21] or other law was an issue on which EPA took a great deal of time to formulate a position. The argument against RCRA applicability is strongest where the remedial action is of an emergency nature and the time it would take to secure the necessary regulatory compliance would place the public in jeopardy.

In its 1985 revisions to the NCP, EPA formalized its theretofor informal practice of requiring that where removal and remedial actions require storage, treatment, or disposal of hazardous substances at off-site locations, the off-site facilities must be in compliance with RCRA and other applicable law.[361.22] Section 121(d)(3), inserted in 1986, codifies this requirement, and requires, in addition, that the unit into which the material is placed not be releasing any hazardous waste or constituents into the soil, groundwater, or surface water.

[5] Miscellaneous Limitations on Section 104 Expenditures

Section 104(a)(3) of CERCLA, added to the statute in 1986, curtails the expenditure of superfund money to clean up hazards that are of natural origin,[361.23] hazards to building occupants caused by "products which are part of the structure of residential buildings or business or community structures,"[361.24] and hazards posed by the deterioration of the physical plant of public drinking water supplies.

Such expenditures are authorized only if EPA concludes that a public health emergency exists and no person with the authority to deal with the problem is able to do so in a timely manner.[361.25]

361.21 *See generally* Chapter 5, *supra.*

361.22 40 CFR §300.65(g) (1985); 40 CFR §300.68(a)(3)(1985).

361.23 One such hazard is radon gas, which achieved public notoriety during 1985 as a radioactive contaminant of many structures in Pennsylvania, New Jersey, and New York. Radon is also associated with uranium mill tailings; in that context, it is not a natural hazard, and is addressed by the Uranium Mill Tailings Act.

361.24 The intent of this provision seems to relate primarily to asbestos, although much asbestos used in buildings is arguably not "part of the structure."

361.25 Section 104(a)(4) (1986).

§6.07 Actions Against Responsible Parties Under CERCLA Section 107

[1] Overview

[a] In General

Section 107 is patterned to a degree on Section 311 of the Clean Water Act, in the sense that it imposes primary responsibility for bearing the cost of hazardous waste site cleanup or covered damages on the entities the statute deems responsible, and provides a defense only where the costs resulted solely from acts of God, acts of war, or acts or omissions of third parties.[362] The statute is also similar to Section 311

---

[362] Section 107(a) provides:

Notwithstanding any other provision or rule of law, and subject only to the defenses set forth in subsection (b) of this section—

(1) the owner and operator of a vessel or a facility,

(2) any person who at the time of disposal of any hazardous substances owned or operated any facility at which such hazardous substances were disposed of,

(3) any person who by contract, agreement, or otherwise arranged for disposal or treatment, or arranged with a transporter for transport for disposal or treatment, of hazardous substances owned or possessed by such person, by any other party or entity, at any facility or incineration vessel owned or operated by another party or entity and containing such hazardous substances and

(4) any person who accepts or accepted any hazardous substances for transport to disposal or treatment facilities, incineration vessels or sites selected by such persons, from which there is a release, or a threatened release which causes the incurrence of response costs, of a hazardous substance, shall be liable for—

(A) all costs of removal or remedial action incurred by the United States Government or a State not inconsistent with the national contingency plan;

(B) any other necessary costs of response incurred by any other person consistent with the national contingency plan;

(C) damages for injury to, destruction of, or loss of natural resources, including the reasonable costs of assesing such injury, destruction, or loss resulting from such a release; and

(D) the costs of any health assessment or health effects study carried out under section 104(i).

The amounts recoverable in an action under this section shall include interest on the amounts recoverable under subparagraphs (A) through (D) . . . [remaining text defining interest parameters].

Section 107(b) provides:

There shall be no liability under subsection (a) of this sectiofor a person otherwise liable who can establish by a preponderance of the evidence that the release or threat of a release of a hazardous substances and the damages resulting therefrom were caused solely by—

(1) an act of God;

(2) an act of war;

(3) an act or omission of a third party other than an employee or agent of the

---

in its inclusion of specific limitations on liability for vessels, other than incineration vessels,[362.1] although it is embellished by limitations on liability for motor vehicles, aircraft, pipelines, and other types of facilities,[363] and a provision allowing the government to overcome the limitations by showing that the release or threat was the result of willful misconduct or willful negligence within the privity or knowledge of the actor.[364] CERCLA adds to the "privity or knowledge" waiver two addi-

---

defendant, or than one whose act or omission occurs in connection with a contractual relationship, existing directly or indirectly, with the defendant (except where the sole contractual arrangement arises from a published tariff and acceptance for carriage by a common carrier by rail), if the defendant establishes by a preponderance of the evidence that (a) he exercised due care with respect to the hazardous substance concerned, taking into consideration the characteristics of such hazardous substance, in light of all relevant facts and circumstances, and (b) he took precautions against foerseeable acts or omissions of such third party and the consequences that could foreseeably result from such acts or omissions; or

(4) any combination of the foregoing paragraphs.

[362.1] Congress excluded "incineration vessels" as part of a package of amendments addressing ocean incineration of hazardous waste contained in Section 127 of P.L. 99-499 (1986). An "incineration vessel" is defined by Section 101(38)(1986) as one "which carries hazardous substances for the purpose of incineration of such substances, so long as such substances or residues of such substances are on board." Incineration vessels are treated as "facilities" rather than as vessels, and thus are stripped of the liability limits normally given to vessels. The overall approach seems to be aimed toward encouraging EPA to permit such activity, by removing the objectionable aspects argued by opponents, such as the incinerator ships' having been effectively judgment proof under maritime law and CERCLA.

[363] Section 107(c)(1) provides:

Except as provided in paragraph (2) of this subsection, the liability under this section of an owner or operator or other responsible person for each release of a hazardous substance or incident involving release of a hazardous substance shall not exceed—

(A) for any vessel, other than an incineration vessel, which carries any hazardous substance as cargo or residue, $300 per gross ton, or $5,000,000, whichever is greater;

(B) for any other vessel, other than an incineration vessel, $300 per gross ton, or $500,000, whichever is greater;

(C) for any motor vehicle, aircraft, pipeline (as defined in the Hazardous Liquid Pipeline Safety Act of 1979), or rolling stock, $50,000,000 or such lesser amount as the President shall establish by regulation, but in no event less than $5,000,000 (or, for releases of hazardous substances as defined in section 101(14)(A) of this title into the navigable waters, $8,000,000). Such regulations shall take into account the size, type, location, storage, and handling capacity and other matters relating to the likelihood of release in each such class to the economic impace of such limits on each such class; or

(D) for any incineration vessel or any facility other than those specified in subparagraph (C) of this paragraph, the total of all costs of response plus $50,000,000 for any damages under this title.

tional bases for removing the liability limitations: Releases that are within the privity or knowledge of the actor a violation of a "safety, construction or operating" standard or regulation are not covered by the liability limitations,[365] nor are releases with respect to which the actor refused to cooperate with NCP officials.

Section 107(a) makes responsible persons liable for (1) all removal and remedial costs "incurred by the United States Government or a State not inconsistent with the National Contingency Plan,"[366] (2) any other "necessary costs of response incurred by any other person consistent with the national contingency plan,"[367] (3) damages for "injury to, destruction of, or loss of natural resources," including "reasonable"

---

[364] "Section 107(c)(2) Notwithstanding the limitations in paragraph (1) of this subsection, the liability of an owner or operator or other responsible person under this section shall be the full and total costs of response and damages, if (A)(i) the release or threat of release of a hazardous substance was the result of willful misconduct or willful negligence within the privity or knowledge of such person, or (ii) the primary cause of the release was a violation (within the privity or knowledge of such person) or applicable safety, construction, or operating standards or regulations; or (B) such person fails or refuses to provide all reasonable cooperation and assistance requested by a responsible public official in connection with response activities under the national contingency plan with respect to regulated carriers subject to the provisions of title 49 of the United States Code or vessels subject to the provision of title 33 or 46 of the United States Code, subparagraph (A)(ii) of this paragraph shall be deemed to refer to Federal standards or regulations."

[365] *Id.* Section 107(c)(2) appears to contain a typographical error in that, syntactically, Section 107(c)(2)(B) should end with the word "plan." As enacted, however, the last sentence, which should begin with the word "with," runs on at the end of (B). As enacted, the merged sentences make no sense. Clarified as a separate sentence, however, the last sentence of Section 107(c)(2) emerges as a modifier of Section 107(c)(2)(A)(ii), removing the liability limitations for DOT-regulated carriers and vessels only for violations of *federal* standards. This provision implicity would appear to remove the liability limitations for other types of actors where the release or threat violated state or local laws or regulations.

[366] Section 107(a)(4)(A).

[367] Section 107(a)(4)(B). Congress did not explain whether it intended something different in the use of the two phrases "not inconsistent with" in Section 107(a)(4)(A) and "consistent with" in Section 107(a)(4)(B). In United States v. Northeastern Pharmaceutical and Chemical Co., Inc., 579 F.Supp 823 (W.D. Mo. 1984), the district court opined that by using the phrase "not inconsistent" in Section 107(a)(4)(A), Congress intended a presumption that the costs expended by the government are reasonable, placing the burden on the responsible parties to prove inconsistency. The different language in Section 107(a)(4)(B), the court reasoned, was intended to place the burden of proof on private claimants to show their actions were consistent with the NCP. The court's analysis is reasonable and consistent with CERCLA's overall structure and purpose. One court has held that the burden of proving the government's expenditures are inconsistent with the NCP rests with the PRP defendants, and that the standard against which the government's actions will be judged is whether they were arbitrary and capricious. *United States v. Ward*, 618 F. Supp. 884 (E.D.N.C. 1985). The detailed extent of remedy provisions of Section 121, added in 1986, significantly minimized the significance of this semantic problem.

assessment costs,[368] and, subsequent to October 17, 1986, (4) the costs of health assessments or health effects studies undertaken by the Agency for Toxic Substances Disease Registry pursuant to Section 104(i).[368.1]

Potentially responsible parties include (1) owners and operators of "vessels" or "facilities," as defined by CERCLA,[369] (2) persons who "at the time of disposal of any hazardous waste" owned or operated a facility at which hazardous wastes were disposed of,[370] (3) most persons

---

[368] Section 107(a)(4)(C). *See* discussion, of damage assessment at Section 6.06[3], *supra*.

[368.1] Section 107(a)(4)(D). Health assessments are epidemiological evaluations of presumably affected populations.

[369] Section 101(a) provides:

"Facility" means (A) any building, structure, installation, equipment, pipe or pipeline (including any pipe into a sewer or publicly owned treatment works), well, pit, pond, lagoon, impoundment, ditch, landfill, storage container, motor vehicle, rolling stock, or aircraft, or (B) any site or area where a hazardous substance has been deposited, stored, disposed of, or placed, or otherwise come to be located; but does not include any consumer product in consumer use or any vessel. . . .

Section 101(28) provides:

"[V]essel" means every description of watercraft or other artificial contrivance used, or capable of being used, as a means of transportation on water.

[370] Sections 107(a)(1), 107(a)(2). Section 101(20) provides that "owner or operator" means

(A)(i) in the case of a vessel, any person owning, operating, or chartering by demise, such vessel, (ii) in the case of an onshore facility or an off shore facility, any person owning or operating such facility, and (iii) in the case of any facility, title or control of which was conveyed due to bankruptcy, foreclosure, tax delinquency, abandonment, or similar means to a unit of State or local government, any person who owned, operated, or otherwise controlled activities at such facility immediately beforehand. [Text of (iii) added 1986.] Such term does not include a person, who, without participating in the management of a vessel or facility, holds indicia of ownership primarily to protect his security interest in the vessel or facility;

(B) in the case of a hazardous substance which has been accepted for transportation by a common or contract carrier and except as provided in Section 107(a) (3) or (4) of this Act, (i) the term "owner or operator" shall mean such common carrier or other bona fide for hire carrier acting as an independent contractor during such transportation, (ii) the shipper of such hazardous substance shall not be considered to have caused or contributed to any release during such transportation which resulted solely from circumstances or conditions beyond his control;

(C) in the case of a hazardous substance which has been delivered by a common or contract carrier to a disposal or treatment facility and except as provided in section 107(a)(3) or (4) (i) the term "owner or operator" shall not include such common or contract carrier, and (ii) such common or contract carrier shall not be considered to have caused or contributed to any release at such disposal or treatment facility resulting from circumstances or conditions beyond its control.

(D) the term "owner or operator" does not include a unit of State or local government which acquired ownership or control involuntarily through bankruptcy, tax delinquency, abandonment, or other circumstances in which the government involuntarily acquires title by virtue of its function as sovereign. The exclusion

who generated hazardous substances found at a facility "containing such hazardous substances,"[371] and (4) transporters who convey hazardous substances to sites chosen by them rather than by the generators.

[b] Statutory Provisions Affecting PRP Liability

Section 107 includes a number of provisions that affect the liability of potentially responsible parties. Some of these increase the exposure, others limit it, and still others impose procedural or other obligations on the government.

[i] Limitations on Liability

Vessel owner/operator liability is limited to the higher of $300 per gross ton or either $5 million or $500,000, depending on whether the vessel carried a hazardous substance as cargo or residue, or did not. These limitations are generally higher than those available under the Limitations on Liability Act,[372] which is expressly displaced by CERCLA.[373]

Other types of transportation facilities are given separate, higher limitations,[374] and, as discussed above, incinerator ships are treated as facilities rather than as vessels.

All of the limitations are subject to waiver if the government can show the requisite degree of fault on the part of the actor.[375]

---

provided under this paragraph shall not apply to any State or local government which has caused or contributed to the release or threatened release of a hazardous substance from the facility, and such a State or local government shall be subject to the provisions of this Act in the same manner and to the same extent, both procedurally and substantively, as any nongovernmental entity, including liability under section 107. [Text of subsection (D) added 1986.]

[371] Section 107(a)(3). The statutory language, reprinted *supra* note 362, is complex. Case law involving the language of this provision is discussed *infra*. A person who arranged for disposal of hazardous waste at a site owned by a third party and entrusted the waste to a transporter is liable if that type of waste is found at the arranged-for site, or if the specific waste is identified as being present at some other site, even though such disposal was not intended by the generator. A generator who arranges for transport of the material to a site owned by the generator would, however, appear not to be liable if the waste showed up at a site owned by a third party.

[372] 46 USC §183

[373] Section 107(h).

[374] *See supra* note 363.

[375] *See* discussion, *supra*.

[ii]   Punitive Damages

Liable persons who have "failed without sufficient cause to properly provide removal or remedial action upon order . . ." pursuant to Section 104 or 106, may be liable in addition for punitive damages of up to three times the "costs incurred by the Fund as a result of such failure to take proper action."[376] In the first five years of CERCLA's operation this provision was not invoked by EPA.

The statutory language is unclear as to the exact nature of the Section 104 order the disobeying of which will give rise to punitive damages, but since the only types of orders authorized by Section 104 are information-gathering orders under Section 104(e), it appears that punitive damages are CERCLA's means of enforcing such orders.

The most difficult problems with the provision are its lack of clarity as to the base cost on which the penalty rests and CERCLA's apparent failure to provide a basis for challenge, or a hearing, prior to fixing liability.[377] The phrase "costs incurred . . . as a result of such failure to take proper action" is subject to a number of possible interpretations. In the case of a Section 104(e) order, a reasonable reading would limit punitive damages to a multiple of the costs of the government's undertaking tests to gain information withheld by the target of the information request. A broadly worded Section 106 order, however, could arguably support a claim for three times the total cleanup costs.[378]

---

[376] Section 107(c)(3). Subrogation recoveries under Section 112(c) may not be counted to set off any such penalties. Order violators are also subject to civil and criminal penalties under Section 109 (1986).

[377] Since Sections 106(b), 104(e), and 109 all provide a substantial monetary penalty for violating an order, the punitive damage provision may be viewed as a secondary penalty. It is unlikely that the government would seek a double remedy.

[378] On the latter point, see Aminoil, Inc. v. EPA, 599 F. Supp 69, 21 ERC 1817 (C.D. Cal. 9-28-84)(Section 107(c)(3) and Section 106(a) both deny fundamental due process). *Contra*, United States v. Reilly Tar & Chem. Co., 606 F.2d 412 (D. Minn. 4th Div. 1985) (relying on the fact that punitive damages remedy is not mandatory and the availability of a forum to contest the penalty under §107(c)(3)); and Wagner Electric Corp. v. Thomas, 612 F. Supp. 736 (D. Kan. 1985) (reasoning that Section 107(c)(3) contains authority for a court to deny a punitive damages award against a defendant who refused to comply with an EPA order in the reasonable belief that it had a defense to the order, although hedging somewhat by saying that its conclusion was premised on two assumptions—(1) that the court was not tied to any administrative record, and (2) that the court would not have unbridled discretion to impose such a penalty once a showing of good faith belief had been made). Industrial Park Dev. Co. v. EPA, 604 F. Supp. 1136 (E.D. Pa. 1985), is in

[iii] **Shield Provision**

Private parties or federal government personnel engaged in CERCLA-directed response activities, who are not responsible parties as to the site, are shielded from liability for damages resulting from their activities, except for acts of negligence.[379] The current standard of responsibility is the product of a 1986 amendment to Section 107(d); the amendment replaced the previous shield language, which had insulated such people from any but acts of gross negligence or intentional misconduct.[379.1] The shield provision is affected, for response action contractors, by the provisions of Section 119, which provide certain indemnifications and a shield from federal statutory liability. Section 119 is discussed in Section 6.06[2][g], *supra*.

[iv] **Indemnification and Exculpatory Schemes**

Liability to the government may not be avoided by means of indemnification, hold harmless, or similar contractual devices often employed in the transfer of title to real property, or between generators and transporters and/or site owner/operators.[380] While such devices are ineffective to insulate one from the government's claims, CERCLA does not attempt to eliminate such agreements. They are only effective as between the parties.[381]

[v] **Substantive and Procedural Limitations on Natural Resource Damage Recovery**

A claim against an entity for natural resource loss or damage is barred if the resource at issue was identified as irreversibly and irretrievably committed (that is, that the resource would be destroyed or consumed) in an environmental impact statement or equivalent analysis done pursuant to the Natural Environmental Policy Act or similar state law and the activity that caused the loss has not violated the terms of its authori-

---

agreement with *Aminoil.* Solid State Circuits, Inc. v. EPA, 23 ERC 1758 (W.D. Mo. 1985), is in accord with *Reilly Tar* and *Wagner Electric.* All of the courts' reasoning is premised on Ex Parte Young, 209 U.S. 123 (1908).

[379] Section 107(d)(1).

[379.1] The gross negligence or intentional misconduct standard was retained for state and local governments responding to an "emergency created by the release or threatened release of a hazardous substance generated by or from a facility owned by another person." Section 107(d)(2) (1986). If the state or local government is a PRP with respect to the site (other than as having become an involuntary owner), there is no shield. *See* Section 107(d)(3).

[380] Section 107(e)(1).

[381] *Id.*; and Section 107(e)(2).

zation.[382] Recovery is fully barred, in addition, if both the release and the damages occurred prior to the effective date of CERCLA.[383]

The statute of limitation on pursuing natural resource damage claims against private parties is Section 113(g)(1), which fixes the limitation period at three years and contains three alternative commencement dates[383.1] and some conditions on the bringing of suits under Section 107 to collect damages.[383.2] Section 113(g)(1) was added to the statute in 1986 to resolve an ambiguity as to the limitation period that plagued the original version of CERCLA.[384]

[vi] Federal Facilities

As is the case under most of the other federal environmental protection statutes, federal facilities were, under the original statutory language, expressly subject to the provisions of CERCLA "in the same

---

[382] Section 107(f)(1). *See* discussion at Section 6.06[3], *supra.*

[383] *Id.*

[383.1] The statute commences running on the later of the date of discovery of the loss and its connection with the release or the promulgation date of Section 301(c) regulations (presumably the last promulgation date, upon which those regulations are complete), except that for NPL sites or federal facilities or any other "vessel or facility at which a remedial action under this Act is otherwise scheduled," the statute commences running on the date "remedial action (excluding operation and maintenance activities)" is completed.

The provision relating to the promulgation date of the Section 301(c) regulations is intended to revive claims that may have been time barred owing to DOI's failure to promulgate the regulations in a timely fashion. *See* H.R. Rep. No. 99-962, 99th Cong., 2d Sess. at 223.

The additional time for completion of remedial actions is obviously intended to defer the decision point until it is determined whether the remedial action took care of the problem, but the reference to operation and maintenance (O&M) activities is ambiguous. Other sections of CERCLA define O&M to be remedial action for a period of ten years and not to be such thereafter; thus, Section 104 money cannot be spent for O&M for more than ten years. It is not clear whether the reference in Section 113(g) is to *all* O&M activities, thus commencing the running of the statute at the end of the remedial action, or to *"remedial"* O&M, providing an additional period of up to ten years before the statute commences to run. Reason would dictate the former.

[383.2] The conditions are that notice be provided to the potential defendants sixty days in advance of filing suit, and that suits *may not be brought* while the government is diligently pursuing a RI/FS or before the remedial action has been decided upon (essentially until the ROD is issued). *See* Section 113(g)(1).

[384] *See* United States v. Allied Corp., 587 F.Supp 1205, No. C-83-5898-SC (N.D. Cal. 4-27-84); and United States v. Cramblit, et al., No. 84-0188-RAR (E.D. Cal. 6-20-84).

manner and the same extent, both procedural and substantively, as any nongovernmental entity. . . ."[385]

Arguments that such facilities should be barred from seeking damages or reimbursement under Section 107(a) from private parties on equitable estoppel or "unclean hands" theories because such entities are also responsible parties by virtue of Section 107(a) were usually rejected by the courts that considered them.[386]

Federal facilities liability is, however, somewhat more limited under CERCLA than under many other federal environmental statutes in that Section 107(a) did not expressly make federal facilities subject to more onerous state standards or procedures.[387]

Congress significantly altered the rules under which federal facilities are to comply with CERCLA when it amended the statute in 1986. The text of Section 107(g) was replaced by a simple cross-reference to Section 120, an entirely new subdivision of CERCLA. The general thrust of Section 120 is to remove federal facilities from the normal remedial action enforcement loop, but subject them to separate timetables and obligations that are, by and large, mandatory.[387.1]

Sections 120(a)(1) and 120(a)(2) make it clear that federal facilities are treated, for the purpose of preliminary assessments, priority listing, and remedial action *selection* just like any other facilities. Subsection (a)(3) indicates, however, that the timing of remedial compliance for federal facilities will not be determined unilaterally by EPA or be subject to negotiated Section 106 orders or judicial consent decrees. The provision also excludes insurance, bonding, and financial responsibility requirements from application to federal facilities.

In an effort to develop better information about the degree of contamination caused by federal facilities, Section 120(b) requires the list of federal agency–controlled sites where hazardous waste has been stored, treated, or disposed, compiled pursuant to RCRA Section 3016(a)(3), to be amended to include information about contamination

---

[385] Section 107(g)(1980). Originally, EPA did not include federal facilities on the National Priority List, and the initial NCP prohibited such listing. EPA withdrew the prohibition in 1985. *See* 49 Fed. Reg. 37074 (1984) (proposal), 49 Fed. Reg. 40323 (1984) (proposed), and 50 Fed. Reg. 47931 (final rule) (1985).

[386] *See, e.g.,* United States v. Cramblit, No. S-84-188-RAR (E.D. Cal. 6-20-84).

[387] *Compare* Section 6001, RCRA.

[387.1] Department of Defense facilities are subject to a wide range of additional requirements relating to munitions and old buildings, which are set forth in 10 USC Chapter 160 (Sections 2701-2707), which was added by Section 211 of the Superfund Amendments and Reauthorization Act of 1986 (P.L. 99-499).

at each listed facility if the contamination "affects contiguous or adjacent property," whether owned by the agency or by others, and to include monitoring data in the agency's possession.

The most significant changes wrought by the 1986 amendments, however, related to the procedural mechanism by which federal agency compliance with CERCLA is to be assured. EPA is to keep a federal agency compliance docket containing relevant information spelled out in Section 120(c) and make it available to the public and publish it in the Federal Register Once the docket is compiled, EPA is required to do a preliminary assessment for each site and list on the NPL the sites that qualify for NPL listing.

Agencies with NPL sites are required by Section 120(e) to begin an RI/FS within six months of listing[387.2] and are required to enter into interagency agreements with EPA for undertaking remedial action within specified time periods following EPA review of their studies.[387.3] The section also requires, at a minimum, substantial on-site construction within fifteen months of completion of the RI/FS.

Agencies are required to detail their CERCLA compliance activities and the hazards posed by the sites in their annual budget submissions,[387.4] and must make annual reports to Congress detailing their progress.[387.5]

There is express authority in Section 120 for federal agency participation in multi-PRP settlements,[387.6] which eliminates an issue of contention under the original statute. Such settlements, however, must be consistent with the time frames provided in Section 120 for federal facility cleanups.[387.7]

Section 120(h) requires federal agencies selling property to include in the purchase and sale documents, and in the relevant deeds, a notice relating to the presence of hazardous substances on the property. In deeds to entities other than another PRP with respect to the site, a covenant must be inserted warranting that the United States will com-

---

[387.2] Sites that are already listed must begin an RI/FS within one year of the enactment date (October 17, 1986).

[387.3] Section 120(e)(4) states what should be in them—essentially the same sort of information contained in a ROD.

[387.4] Section 120(e)(3).

[387.5] Section 120(e)(5).

[387.6] Settlements are governed by Section 122 (1986), which is discussed in Section 6.09[e], *infra*.

[387.7] *See* Section 120(e)(6).

plete already identified remedial actions and do any other remedial action subsequently discovered to be necessary.[387.8]

Another significant innovation of the 1986 revision is the adoption of a limited shield provision for federal facilities in relation to state and local laws.

State laws "concerning removal and remedial action, including State laws regarding enforcement" are applicable by virtue of Section 120(a)(4) only to federal facilities that are *not* included on the NPL. By specifically mentioning state laws, the statute arguably precludes the applicability of local laws.[387.9] That provision expressly prohibits states from discriminating against federal facilities in terms of the level of remedial action that they require.

For federal facility sites that are listed on the NPL, states and local governments are provided an opportunity to review and comment on the remedy selected pursuant to the interagency agreement.[387.10] States, but not local governments, are given, in addition, somewhat broader rights under Section 121(f)(3), under limited circumstances.

If EPA and the federal facility manager propose to enter into an agreement that selects a remedy that does not meet or exceed "applicable or relevant and appropriate standards," EPA must offer the state in which the facility is located an opportunity to "concur" in the remedy. If the state refuses to concur, its sole remedy is a cause of action in federal district court to seek a determination from the court that EPA's findings under Section 121(d)(4)[387.11] are not supported by "substantial

---

[387.8] Section 120(h)(3). This obligation ripens six months after EPA promulgates notice regulations, which are due, at the latest, in April 1988. The warranty provision represents a significant departure from the long-established federal property management practice of giving only quitclaim deeds.

[387.9] In other sections of the 1986 amendments, the statute expressly includes reference to local laws along with state laws, clearly indicating that Congress was selective in permitting the application of local laws under CERCLA.

[387.10] Section 120(f).

[387.11] EPA is required, by Section 121(d)(4), to make a number of findings in support of its acceptance of a remedial alternative that does not meet the basic Section 121 criteria. Those findings are that that the remedy is protective of the public health and the environment, and that (A) the action is only part of a total remedy that will, when completed, attain the standard, (B) compliance with the standard would entail greater risk to health and the environment than alternatives, (C) compliance with the standard is technically impractical, or (D) if the standard is a state standard, it has not been consistently applied.

evidence."[387.12] A state that is unsuccessful in persuading EPA to impose its more stringent remedial standards on a federal facility, and which has lost its lawsuit challenging EPA's denial, may subsequently require adherence to the more stringent requirements if it funds the excess cost thereof itself.

There is, finally, a limited exemption from CERCLA compliance for national security reasons.[387.13] The exemption is limited to Department of Defense and Department of Energy facilities, and requires an affirmative finding by the President, who must conclude that the national security interests are peculiar to the particular site or facility. Exemptions are limited to a year at a time, and they may not be granted for lack of an appropriation unless a specific request for such an appropriation has been made of the Congress and not provided.

[vii] **Pesticides**

Response costs or damages resulting from "the application of a pesticide product registered under the Federal Insecticide, Fungicide and Rodenticide Act"[388] are not recoverable under Section 107. This embargo is limited to pesticide *applications,* and does not appear to affect claims based on *disposal* of pesticides. Nevertheless, substantial groundwater contamination has been linked to agricultural pesticide application.[389]

Since many pesticides are included on the various lists that constitute the universe of hazardous substances, and since neither Section 104 nor Section 111 contains a similar embargo on the expenditure of Fund monies, it appears that environmental contamination caused by pesticide applications may be remedied by government expenditure of Fund monies. Without a right of recovery, however, it is unlikely that EPA would authorize expenditures for such a purpose.

FIFRA contains no clear authority for the government to seek remedial action in cases of groundwater contamination caused by the proper use of registered pesticides.[390] Common law and state remedies

---

387.12 The lawsuit is limited to EPA's administrative record.

387.13 Section 120(j).

388 *See generally* Chapter 3, *supra.*

389 Section 107(i).

390 Contamination caused by pesticide *misuse,* or by the use of unregistered pesticides, is a violation of FIFRA. The statute does not expressly authorize injunctive relief, however, to remedy violations.

are, however, expressly preserved by Section 107(i) of CERCLA, insofar as such remedies exist.

[viii] Federally Permitted Releases

As in the case of pesticides, costs and damages resulting from "federally permitted releases," as defined in Section 101(10)[391] are not recoverable under Section 107.[392] However, Section 107(j) of CERCLA contains a sentence that has the effect of amending Section 309(b) of the Clean Water Act[393] to permit the government to sue point source discharges to recover "costs of response" incurred by the government in connection with Clean Water Act–regulated discharges listed in Sections 101(10)(B) and (C) of CERCLA.[394]

This provision is important to the government since a significant amount of hazardous waste may reside in the sediments at the bottom of rivers and some lakes. As in the case of pesticide contamination, EPA apparently is not prohibited from spending Fund monies on such wastes. The ability to recover at least some water pollution–related Fund expenditures should encourage such expenditures.

[ix] RCRA-Permitted TSD Facilities

Section 107(k) shields owners/operators of RCRA-permitted TSD facilities from CERCLA liability or liability under "any other law" by shifting any such liability to the Post-Closure Liability Fund established

---

[391] *See supra* note 360.

[392] Section 107(j).

[393] 33 USC §1319(b)

[394] The statute describes these as "(B) discharges resulting from circumstances identified and reviewed and made part of the public record with respect to a permit issued or modified under Section 402 of the Federal Water Pollution Control Act and subject to a condition of such permit, (C) continuous or anticipated intermittent discharges from a point source, identified in a permit or permit application under Section 402 of the Federal Water Pollution Control Act, which are caused by events occurring within the scope of relevant operating or treatment systems. . . ." Releases that originated with discharges permitted under the Clean Water Act that were in compliance with the permit terms are not included. Subsection (C) discharges are those discharges of hazardous substances listed under Section 311 of the Clean Water Act that, though not prohibited were required to be identified in the NPDEP permit application. Subsection (B) discharges could include chemicals introduced into a sewer system by contributors or midnight dumpers. *See* S. Rep. No. 96-848, 96th Cong., 2d Sess. at 47-48. These provisions were adopted verbatim from the 1978 amendments to Section 311 of the Clean Water Act.

by subtitle C of the Hazardous Substance Response Act of 1980.[395]

The liability transfer is effective only as to facilities operated in compliance with all RCRA-imposed requirements that "may affect the performance of such facility after closure"[396] and closed and monitored postclosure in accordance with EPA's RCRA-based regulations and the conditions of the facility's permit.[397] The statute contains procedural requirements[398] and provides for a federal study of private insurance schemes that might do away with the Post-Closure Tax and Fund.[399]

[x]   Gasoline Service Stations and Used Oil Reclaimers

As a consequence of a 1986 amendment to Section 114 of CERCLA, legitimate gasoline service station owners and used oil recycling transporters are insulated from CERCLA liability that, once EPA begins to regulate used oil, would otherwise be incurred in the event some of their oil ended up at a NPL-listed site they do not own or operate, as of the effective date of recycled oil regulations that EPA is required to promulgate under Section 3014 of RCRA.[399.1]

The shield provision is limited to "service station dealers,"[399.2] as

---

[395] Use of the Post-Closure Liability Trust Fund was suspended by Section 107(k)(5) (1986), pending further legislative action that may be taken following a study by EPA and report to the Congress about the potential scope of liability under the provision and alternative strategies for managing RCRA-regulated TSD facilities after closure. The scope of the inquiry is set out in Section 107(k)(6).

[396] Section 107 (k)(1)(A).

[397] Section 107(k)(1)(B).

[398] Section 107(k)(2).

[399] Section 107(k)(4).

[399.1] Section 114(c) (1986). By replacing the prior text of this section with the service station provision, Congress also legislatively overruled Exxon v. Hunt, 106 S.Ct. 1103 (1986), which, in limiting the means by which states could finance their own superfunds, had relied on that text, which was a preemption provision.

[399.2] Section 101(37) (1986) defines the term as any person—

   (i) who owns or operates a motor vehicle service station, filling station, garage, or similar retail establishment engaged in the business of selling, repairing, or servicing motor vehicles, where a substantial percentage of the gross revenue of the establishment is derived from the fueling, repairing, or servicing of motor vehicles, and

   (ii) who accepts for collection, accumulation, and delivery to an oil recycling facility, recycled oil that (I) has been removed from the engine of a light duty motor vehicle or household appliances by the owner of such vehicle or appliances, and (II) is presented, by such owner, to such person for collection, accumulation, and delivery to an oil recycling facility.

Section 101(37)(A). Note: subsection (B) also includes within the definition certain government-operated recycling transporters and facilities, and refuse collectors who are required to cart used oil by state law.

defined, and is inapplicable to recycled oil that is mixed with other hazardous substances or that is not handled in compliance with the used oil provisions of RCRA.[399.3]

[2] Specific Issues

[a] Preexpenditure Review and Declaratory Relief

Ordinarily the initial formal governmental action with respect to CERCLA activity at a site is listing the site on the NPL. That action is reviewable in the District of Columbia Circuit.[400]

After initial information gathering during the preliminary assessment phase, EPA's next step is ordinarily to send notification letters to the site owner/operator and other potentially responsible parties, insofar as their identities are known to EPA, informing them of EPA's tentative findings at the site, its intention to spend CERCLA funds if the PRPs do not clean up the site, and its intention to recover any such expenditures under Section 107 and inviting them to confer with one another and EPA. The site owner or some other PRP may wish to assert defenses to liability before EPA has expended significant Fund monies. Whether a declaratory judgment is appropriate at this point was litigated in a number of cases prior to enactment of the 1986 amendments to CERCLA.

In *D'Imperio v. United States, et al.*,[401] the plaintiffs filed a complaint seeking a declaratory judgment that (1) they were not liable under Section 107(a), and (2) if they were to contribute to the cleanup cost, they qualified for reimbursement under Section 107(a)(4)(B).[402] The district court held first that neither the notice letter from EPA notifying the site owner of potential liability under Section 107 nor inclusion of the site on the NPL constituted sufficiently "final" Agency action to invest the court with jurisdiction. On the claim for a declaration that the plaintiffs were entitled to reimbursement, the court held that a

---

[399.3] Section 114(c)(1). There is a statutory presumption, contained in Section 114(c)(2), that oil that has been removed from a light-duty motor vehicle engine or a household appliance, and is presented by the owner thereof to the dealer does not contain hazardous substances.

[400] *See* Section 6.06[2][c][ii], *supra.*

[401] 575 F. Supp. 248, 20 ERC 1091 (D. N.J. 1983)

[402] They also sought to enjoin EPA from calling the subject site the "D'Imperio Tract," as it was listed on the NPL. The court, relying on Tinkham v. Reagan, 19 ERC 1942 (D.N.H. 1983), dismissed this claim for lack of subject matter jurisdiction.

cause of action does not arise until response expenditures are actually incurred.

In *J.V. Peters Co. v. Ruckelshaus*,[403] the plaintiffs sought to enjoin EPA from taking any response action at their storage facility. They alleged inconsistency with the NCP as the primary basis for their action.[404] The district court, after concluding that the plaintiffs had standing and the case presented no ripeness or finality barriers, dismissed the action nevertheless, on the premise that the delay attendant on a preexpenditure lawsuit would be inconsistent with the basic CERCLA legislative scheme. The court did, however, suggest that these might be situations that could give rise to a preemptive lawsuit, but that "in order to maintain the integrity of the CERCLA legislation," any such lawsuit would have to be premised on specific, factually supported allegations that "EPA had absolutely no rational basis for undertaking a response action, and that no preliminary assessment had been made."[405]

Less willing to consider the possibility of any review by PRPs of prospective Section 104 expenditures was Judge Debevoise in *Lone Pine Steering Committee v. EPA*.[406] The *Lone Pine* generators' group undertook their own remedial study, which they proffered to EPA as an alternative to the remedial plan developed by EPA's contractor, although the proffer did not include a commitment to do the work. EPA issued a Record of Decision[407] adopting its own plan, which the generator group sought to review. The court dismissed for lack of subject

---

[403] 584 F. Supp. 1005, 20 ERC 2222 (N.D. Ohio 1984), *aff'd*, 767 F.2d 263 (6th Cir. 1985).

[404] The plaintiffs also claimed that CERCLA denied them due process of law by its failure to provide for a hearing prior to expenditure of Fund monies on the site. The district court concluded that since the plaintiffs could raise whatever claims they had as defenses to a subsequent Section 107(a) collection action, CERCLA did not tread on the plaintiffs' due process rights.

[405] 20 ERC at 2225. *But cf.* United States v. Outboard Marine Corp., 619 F.2d 623 (7th Cir. 1980) (no preenforcement review of Section 107 notice).

[406] 600 F. Supp. 1487 (D.N.J. 1985), *aff'd*, 777 F.2d 882, 23 ERC 1568 (3d Cir. 1985). *See also* United States v. Ward, 618 F. Supp. 884 (E.D.N.C. 1985) (preenforcement challenge to EPA remedial plan unavailable, and challenge raised in defense of a Section 107(a) cost recovery action will be subject to "arbitrary and capricious" standard of review and deference to EPA).

[407] The Record of Decision (ROD) must be issued by EPA's Assistant Administrator for Solid and Hazardous Waste, or a delegee, as a prerequisite to the expenditure of CERCLA funds.

matter jurisdiction, and in doing so criticized *J. V. Peters Co.*[408] A dictum in the opinion hinted at the possibility that the result would have been different if the plaintiff bringing the action had claimed that EPA's remedial plan was inadequate to protect public health.[408.1]

Congress laid the dispute over preenforcement review essentially to rest in 1986 when it added Sections 113(h)-113(j) to CERCLA. These sections basically codify, with certain modifications, the *Peters, Lone Pine,* and 1985 *Ward* decisions.[408.2]

Section 113(h) deprives federal court jurisdiction from any action seeking to challenge a removal or remedial action decision made under Section 104 or embodied in a Section 106(a) order,[408.3] except in the context of a cost recovery, natural resource damage, or contribution action that has been instituted pursuant to Section 107(a),[408.4] a Section 106–based action to enforce an order or collect a penalty for violation of an order,[408.5] a Section 106(b)(2) action against the government for reimbursement of voluntary cleanup expenditures,[408.6] or a citizen suit brought under Section 310 of CERCLA[408.7] or in a Section 106 action to compel remedial action.[408.8]

Review of the adequacy of the remedial decision in any such action is limited to the administrative record compiled in connection with the

---

[408] *Accord,* United States v. Midwest Solvent Recovery, No. H-79-556(N.D. Ind. 12-14-84).

[408.1] *But see* Jefferson County, et al. v. U.S., __ F. Supp. __, 25 ERC(BNA) 1029 (E.D. Mo. 1986) (dismissing suit seeking to compel EPA to apply more stringent state and local standards as beyond the court's jurisdiction).

[408.2] *Peters, supra* note 316; *Lone Pine, supra* note 316; *Ward, infra* note 408.10.

[408.3] Actions that are founded on state nuisance laws or state statutory claims brought in federal court on diversity jurisdictional grounds are not barred.

[408.4] Section 113(h)(1).

[408.5] Section 113(h)(2).

[408.6] Section 113(h)(3). *See generally* Section 6.05[4][d], *supra.*

[408.7] Section 113(h)(4). *See generally* Section 6.09, *infra,* for a discussion of citizen suits. This challenge appears contextually limited to plaintiffs who are claiming that the remedy selected is inadequate, and is limited to remedial actions, unless removal is intended to be the ultimate remedy. There is interesting language in the Conference Report to the effect that citizens who seek to challenge a remedy do not necessarily have to wait until completion of all remedial action. In cases where EPA has broken the site into two or more "operable units," a challenge may be brought at the completion of remedial action as to each unit separately. *See* H.R. Rep. No. 99-962, 99th Cong., 2d Sess. at 224.

[408.8] Section 113(h)(5).

ROD, under ordinary principles of administrative law,[408.9] and the government's decision will be upheld unless found to be arbitrary and capricious.[408.10] Even if a ROD is overturned, that fact will not constitute a defense to liability, since Section 113(j)(3) provides that in such event the court is limited to reducing the amount of the government's award to the extent the remedy is found to be excessive.[408.11]

Declaratory or injunctive relief in actions brought by one PRP against others, following issuance of a Section 106 or a Section 107 notice letter, is not available.[409]

[b] Recoverable Response and Ancillary Costs

Section 107(a) imposes liability for "all costs of removal or remedial action" incurred by the federal or state governments.[410] Just what "costs" that phrase encompasses is determined by reference to the definitions of "remove," "remedy," and "respond" in Section 101 of CERCLA. Those definitions are very broad, and consequently the government has been awarded a wide range of investigative and litigation costs incurred at CERCLA sites.[411] Such costs may include costs of investigations, monitoring, and testing to identify the extent of public endangerment, or the extent of release of hazardous substances, response-related planning costs, and EPA and Justice Department staff

---

[408.9] Section 113(j)(1).

[408.10] Section 113(j)(2). This approach to reviewing the remedy in effect codifies EPA's position asserted in United States v. Ward, 618 F. Supp. 884 (E.D.N.C. 1985).

[408.11] A citizen suit could result in the imposition of a more rigorous remedy. Procedural errors may result in a disallowance of a portion of response cost recovery or natural resource damage recovery only if the procedural errors were "of such central relevance to the action" that in their absence "the action would have been significantly changed." Section 113(j)(4).

[409] Earthline Co. v. Kin-Buc, Inc., et al., C.A. No. 83-4226(D.N.J. 7-23-84).

[410] Section 107(a)(4)(A).

[411] There is a split of authority over whether expenditures incurred prior to CERCLA's enactment date are recoverable. A district court in United States v. Shell Oil Co., 605 F.Supp. 1064 (1985) held that they are. *Accord*, United States v. Ward 618 F. Supp. 884, No. 83-63-Civ-5 (E.D.N.C., Raleigh Div. 9-9-85). For cases holding that pre-CERCLA effective date or response costs are unrecoverable, *see* United States v. NEPACCO, 579 F. Supp. 823, 20 ERC 1414, 1424 (W.D. Mo. 1984); United States v. Wade, 20 ERC 1849 (E.D. Pa. 3-23-84); and U.S. v. Morton-Thiocol, Inc., No. 83-4787 (unpublished D.N.J. 7-2-84). Costs incurred prior to revision of the NCP are recoverable if not inconsistent, *Id.*

costs "associated with such actions,"[412] as well as litigation costs, including attorneys' fees.[413] Prejudgment interest has also been held consistent with CERCLA.[414] Costs related to investigation of the *defendant*, as opposed to the site, however, were held not recoverable under the 1980 CERCLA. [415] By amending the definition of "response" to include enforcement-related costs, Congress, in 1986, clarified the issue.[415.1]

[c] Timing of Cost Recovery Actions

Closely related to the issue of what costs are recoverable is the timing of Section 107 cost recovery actions. The issue was framed, in those cases in which it was raised, in two ways: whether the government's action must await the completion of its response activities,[416] and whether the government may recover future (that is, yet to be incurred) response costs.[417]

The "future costs" issue was a difficult one, and the courts reached disparate results. The language of Section 107(a) did not clearly permit institution of an action for recovery of monies not yet spent. It is written in the past tense, and those courts that allowed the government to proceed to seek such recovery did so acknowledging the linguistic difficulty.[418]

---

[412] *Id.*, at 20, ERC at 1425. *See also* State of New York v. General Electric., 592 F. Supp. 291, 21 ERC 1097 (N.D. N.Y. 6-26-84). *But see* Cadillac Fairview/California, Inc. v. Dow Chemical Co., 21 ERC 1108 (C.D. Cal. 3-5-84) (holding investigative costs not recoverable in a private cost recovery action, relying primarily on Section 107(a)(B), which the court felt provided a narrower remedy than did Section 107(a)(A)); and *see* D'Imperio v. U.S., 575 F. Supp. 248, 20 ERC 1094 (D.N.J. 1983)(opining that RI/FS and related investigative costs are "preresponse" costs, and thus not covered).

[413] 20 ERC at 1426 (relying primarily on the language of Section 101(23) and Section 104(b)). The normal measure of government attorneys' fees is the hourly salary multiplied by the hours spent. The government has, however, argued in various forums that its fee awards should be calculated either at market rates, or at the hourly rate paid by the government to compensate private practitioners it retains.

[414] 20 ERC at 1427. A 1986 amendment to Section 107(a) specifically authorizes interest awards.

[415] *See* EDF v. Lamphier. 12 ELR 20843 (E.D. Va. 1982), *affirmed on other grounds,* 714 F.2d 331 (4th Cir. 1983), 20 ERC 1780.

[415.1] *See* Section 101(25)(1986).

[416] *See* U.S. v. South Carolina Recycling & Disposal, 20 ERC 1753 (D.S.C. 2-23-84).

[417] *See, e.g.,* United States v. Wade, 577 F. Supp. 1326, 20 ERC 1283 (E.D. Pa. 1983).

[418] *See* United States v. Wade, 577 F. Supp. 1326, 20 ERC at 1283 (E.D. Pa. 12-20-83).

The majority view by mid-1986 was that, while incurring some re-sponse costs is a necessary prerequisite to instituting a Section 107(a) action,[419] once the court obtains jurisdiction, it may issue a declaratory judgment on the issue of the defendant's liability to the government for subsequently incurred response costs.[420]

None of the courts, however, have come to grips with the question of whether a defendant who has been adjudged liable for future govern-ment response costs may challenge the amount of the costs once they are incurred, and if so, in what forum. Litigation over the amount of the expenditure can involve such difficult issues as whether the particular expenditures were consistent with the NCP, or, in the case of natural resource damages, fact-bound issues involving identification and valua-tion. The logical resolution to this issue is, of course, bifurcation of the proceedings to provide for an initial determination of liability, and a later opportunity for the court to entertain arguments about the extent of the remedy.[421]

EPA's position in the prior litigation was adopted by Congress in 1986 and codified as Section 113(g)(2)(B). That provision, which also establishes a six-year statute of limitation (from the date remedial action is initiated) on cost recovery actions, provides that "the court shall enter a declaratory judgment on liability for response costs or damages that will be binding on any subsequent action or actions to recover further response costs or damages. . . ." It also provides that "subsequent action

---

[419] Otherwise the case is not ripe. *See* United States v. Price, No.80-4104 (D.N.J. 7-28-83).

[420] *See* United States v. Conservation Chemical Co., 619 F. Supp. 162 (W.D. Mo. 1985); United States v. NEPACCO, 579 F. Supp. 823, 20 ERC at 1427 (W.D. Mo. 1984); State ex rel. Brown v. Georgeoff, 562 F. Supp. 1300 at 1315 (N.D. Ohio 1983); United States v. Wade, 20 ERC 1277, 1283; United States v. A & F Materials, Inc. 578 F. Supp. 1279, 20 ERC 1353, 1362 (S.D. Ill. 1984); and *see* Jones v. Inmont Corp., 584 F. Supp. 1425, 20 ERC 2001 (S.D. Ohio 1984)(applying same rule to private Section 107 action).

[421] *See* United States v. Wade, 20 ERC 1853, 1856 (E.D. Pa. 2-21-84)(bifurcating liability and cost trials over objection of generator defendants). In some cases, however, the defendants have sought litigation of the remedy issue first. The government's attempt to obtain an open-ended liability judgment and pursue successive accountings as it ex-pended monies in the future was rebuffed by the district court in United States v. Mottolo, 605 F. Supp. 898 (D.N.H. 1985), where the court held that all of the issues must be tried in one consolidated action, opining, "[T]he Court finds no mandate in CERCLA for a rolling accounting procedure whereby the government may seek judgment for unlimited damages and return at its convenience to seek additional payments from the defendants."

or actions may be maintained at any time during the response action" (up to three years after the completion of "all" response action),[421.1] and that "an action may be commenced under section 107 for recovery of costs at any time after such costs have been incurred."[421.2]

[d] Jury Trial

CERCLA defendants have occasionally demanded a jury trial, premising their arguments on the Seventh Amendment right to a jury trial in statutory damages actions.[422] Those courts presented with a jury demand by a Section 107(a)(4)(A) cost recovery defendant have all rejected the request, insofar as the government's action was concerned, concluding that the Section 107(a)(4)(A) action is essentially one in the nature of restitution, an equitable remedy, for which there is no right to a jury trial.[423]

Claims brought under Section 107(a)(4)(C), however, could raise a more troublesome issue, which has not been dealt with satisfactorily by the courts. Although some natural resource damages claims might well be framed as restitution claims,[424] as where the state has replaced or repaired damaged resources, some natural resource damages are not subject to physical remediation, and thus a claim could well sound not as an equitable claim for restitution but rather as a legal claim for money damages.[425] Such a claim arguably would support a jury demand.

[421.1] Since ten years' worth of operation and maintenance activity is considered to be remedial action under Sections 104(c)(6) and 104(c)(7), it might be argued that the government can wait a long time before bringing its action, should it choose to do so.

[421.2] The statute thus sanctions the kind of "rolling accounting procedure" rejected by the district court in *Mottolo, infra* note 423.

[422] *See generally* Curtis v. Loether, 415 U.S. 189 (1973).

[423] *See* United States v. Mottolo, 605 F. Supp. 898 (D.N.H. 1985); Missouri v. Independent Petrochemical Corp., 22 ERC(BNA) 1735 (E.D. Mo. 1985); Mola Development Corp. v. United States, 22 ERC(BNA) 1443 (C.D. Cal. 1985); United States v. Ward, 618 F. Supp. 884 (E.D.N.C. 1985); United States v. Reilly Tar & Chemical Co., 20 ERC 1052 (D. Minn. 1983); United States v. Wade, 20 ERC 1853 (E.D. Pa. 2-21-84); United States v. Argent Corp., 21 ERC 1353 (D.N.M. 12-20-83); United States v. Mottolo, 605 F. Supp. 898 (D.N.H. 1985).

[424] *See* United States v. Wade, 20 ERC 1853 (E.D. Pa. 1984).

[425] In United States v. Wade, *id.*, the Commonwealth of Pennsylvania asserted a Section 104(a)(C)(3) claim, but limited the claim to recovery of funds it had expended in asserting the injury and rehabiliting or restoring the injured resources. The district judge reasoned that the jury trial issue rested on the nature of the remedy sought rather than on the language of the statute *per se*, and held that a jury trial was not required.

Ancillary state common law–based damages claims are also arguably jury matters. The difficulty posed by a Section 107 cost recovery action that also has attached to it a *damage*-type natural resource loss claim and one or more pendent common law claims raised by intervenors is illustrated by *United States v. Reilly Tar and Chemical Co.,*[426] where the defendants argued that a decision by the court on the government's equitable claims may have a collateral estoppel effect on the legal claims raised by the intervenors before a jury trial on those claims could be completed. That, they argued, would abridge their Seventh Amendment rights.[427] In *Reilly Tar* the court avoided the problem by consolidating both the equitable and legal issues in one hearing, in the presence of the jury that would decide the legal issue.

The *Reilly Tar* fix may not be possible in all cases, particularly those in which the government is demanding expedited relief necessitating bifurcated trials of the equitable and legal issues.

[e] Joinder of All Potentially Liable Parties

CERCLA does not require EPA to join all potentially liable persons in its Section 107 actions, and in fact the Agency has never attempted to do so. Its strategy has generally been to seek recovery only from the largest contributors of waste to the site, under its joint and several liability theory.[428]

Attempts to require joinder of all potentially liable entities have not met with success.[429] If the court adopts the government's joint and several liability theory, it is settled that compulsory joinder of alleged joint tort-feasors is unavailable.[430] Joinder may also be denied absent joint and several liability because the courts may determine each defendant's share of the liability,[431] or because Fed. R. Civ. P. 14 provides an opportunity for the defendant to implead other alleged liable parties.[432]

---

[426] 20 ERC at 1057 (6-23-83).

[427] *See* Parklane Hosiery Co. v. Shore, 439 U.S. 322 (1979); and Beacon Theatres, Inc. v. Westover, 359 U.S. (1959).

[428] *See* Section 6.04[4][b][ix], *infra.*

[429] Joinder arguments have been premised variously on the language of Section 107 and on F.R. Civ. P. 19 and 21.

[430] *See* Picard v. Wall St. Discount Corp., 526 F. Supp. 1248, 1252 (S.D. N.Y. 1981).

[431] *See* United States v. Chem Dyne Corp., 19 ERC 1953 (S.D. Ohio 1983).

[f] Persons Liable

[i] Owners and Operators

The current owner or operator of a "facility,"[433] regardless of his involvement with any hazardous substances,[433.1] and past owners and operators[433.2] during whose period of connection with the site the hazardous substances were disposed of at the site are potentially liable under Section 107.[434] In general, the statute has been given a very broad reading by those courts confronted with specific claims by defendants that they should not be considered to be "owners" or "operators" for one reason or another.[434.1]

"Innocent" owner-lessors, who leased the subject property to third parties unaware of the disposal of hazardous waste, are nevertheless "owners" for Section 107 purposes.[435] A lessee who subleases the facility to a third party operator is also an "owner" for Section 107 purposes.[436]

---

[432] See New York v. Shore Realty Corp., 21 ERC 1430 (E.D. N.Y. 6-4-84), remanded on other grounds, aff'd upon more particular findings, 759 F.2d 1032 (2d Cir. 1985).

[433] The government's broad view of "facility" as a place where hazardous substances have "come to be located" has been accepted by the courts. See, e.g., State of New York v. General Electric Company, 592 F.Supp. 291, 21 ERC 1097 (N.D. N.Y. 1984)(drag strip where PCB oil was used for dust suppression is a "facility").

[433.1] See, e.g., New York v. Shore Realty Corp., 759 F.2d 1043 (2d Cir. 1985); United States v. Franklin P. Tyson, et al., No. 84-2663 (E.D. Pa., 8-22-86) (available on Lexis and Westlaw); United States v. Maryland Bank and Trust Company, 23 ERC (BNA) 1193 (D. Md. 1986).

[433.2] See United States v. Ottati & Goss, Inc., 23 ERC (BNA) 1708 (D.N.H. 1985).

[434] Sections 107(a)(1), 107(a)(2). Owners and operators of "vessels" are also liable, although vessel liability is, as a practical matter, related only to spills. See generally Section 6.01, supra.

[434.1] Section 101(20) of CERCLA, which defines "owner or operator," was amended by Section 101 pf P.L. 99-499 (1986) to exclude any state or local governmental entities that acquired title to a facility involuntarily, for example, through bankruptcy, provided that they had no part in the activities that contributed to contamination of the site. In the event there has been such a transfer, the immediate past owner or operator or the person who "otherwise controlled" the site is considered the owner or operator.

[435] United States v. Argent, 21 ERC 1354 (D.N.M. 5-4-84). The concept of "owner" embraces innocent owner/lessors whose lessees caused the conditions, sublessors, and even innocent purchasers of already contaminated property or a debtor's estate. See, e.g., State of New York v. Shore Realty Corp, 759 F.2d 1032 (2d Cir. 1985); United States v. South Carolina Recycling and Disposal, Inc., 21 ERC(BNA) 1577 (D.S.C. 1984); United States v. Mirabile, 23 ERC(BNA) 1511, No. 84-2280 (E.D. Pa. 1985) (available on Lexis and Westlaw); and In re T.P. Long Chemical, Inc., Debtor, 45 Bank. Rept. 278 (Bky. N.D. Ohio, 1985).

[436] See United States v. South Carolina Recycling and Disposal, Inc., 21 REC 1577

Whether one is an "operator" involves a factual determination regarding the nature of the activities undertaken, and one can be an "operator" without direct involvement in activities at the site if found to be a joint venturer with one who was so engaged.[437]

As a practical matter, most Section 107 cases have involved either an innocent owner or a judgment-proof owner or operator. Inclusion of such persons as defendants is necessitated, however, by the need for access to records or access to the site for investigative or remedial purposes.

Congress chose to deal with the problem of "innocent" site owners when it reauthorized CERCLA by enabling them to settle out with the government, and secure what amounts to a full release, with a minimum of difficulty, should EPA be so inclined,[437.1] and also provided truly innocent purchasers of contaminated property with a "third party" defense to liability under Section 107(b)(3).[437.2]

So-called de minimis settlements of Section 106 or Section 107 cases are available to anyone who is "the owner of real property on or in which the facility is located" and "did not conduct or permit the generation, transportation, storage, treatment or disposal of any hazardous substances at the facility," did not "contribute to the release or threat of release . . . at the facility through any action or omission," and did not purchase the property with "actual or constructive knowledge that the property was used for the generation, transportation, storage, treat-

---

(D.S.C. 8-28-84)(relying in part on definition of "owner and operator" in Section 101(20)(A), and in part on venerable notions of property). In United States v. Mirabile, No. 84-2280 (E.D. Pa. 6-6-85) (available on Lexis and Westlaw), the court dismissed third party claims brought by the site owner against one of two banks and the Small Business Administration, holding that mere financial control of the sort possessed by secured creditors is not enough to make them "owners" for CERCLA purposes. The court refused to dismiss a third party claim against a second bank, concluding that an issue of fact was presented as to the degree of participation an officer of that bank had in the management of the facility. *See also* In re T.P. Long Chemical, Inc., Debtor, 45 Bank Rept. 278 (Bky. N.D. Ohio 1985) ("person," for CERCLA purposes, is broad enough to encompass a debtor's estate that took title to contaminated property after the waste was placed on the site).

[437] United States v. South Carolina Recycling and Disposal, Inc., *supra* note 436, at 1582-83.

[437.1] Section 122(g) (1986). Section 122 is discussed generally in Section 6.09[4][e], *infra*.

[437.2] *See* Section 101(35), discussed in Section 6.07[2][m], *infra*.

ment, or disposal of any hazardous substance."[437.3]

The third party defense, which was originally not clearly available to innocent purchasers or lessees, was made available to them in 1986 by amendment of the definition of "contractual relationships," which would otherwise bar use of the third party defense of Section 107(b)(3), to exclude from its reach persons who acquired an already contaminated facility under circumstances in which they did not know or have reason to know it was contaminated, governmental entities that acquired the property involuntarily, and acquisitions by inheritance or bequest.[437.4]

By keeping innocent "owners" and innocent "purchasers" within the general PRP category, yet providing them with escape routes that can insulate them from significant liability, the amended statute provides the government with enough of a handle over them to gain cooperation in such matters as site access, while not penalizing them for matters as to which they have no fault. To this limited degree, the 1986 amendments to CERCLA abandon the pure "no fault" concept of the original statute.

[ii] Generators

Section 107(a)(3) includes among those persons potentially liable any person who "arranged for disposal or treatment by any other person" of hazardous substances "owned or possessed" by the first person, or who "arranged with a transporter" for transport "for disposal or treatment" of such substances "by any other person" at any facility owned or operated by another person or entity *and containing such hazardous substances*" (emphasis added).

The underlined statutory language has been relied upon by a number of generator defendants to argue that they may not be held responsible for remedial costs at a facility unless the government can prove that the wastes present at the site are in fact the generator's wastes. The government has, however, argued successfully that all it need show is

---

[437.3] Section 122(g)(1)(B). The last-mentioned limitation codifies the thrust of the Second Circuit's decision in New York v. Shore Realty Corp., 759 F.2d 1032 (2d Cir. 1985).

[437.4] There is much discussion about this provision in the Conference Report. *See* H.R. Rep. No. 99-962, at 186-88. The important issue is the extent to which there is a duty to inquire into the history of the property, and the Conference Report indicates that a higher degree of care should be expected of purchasers who purchased property subsequent to 1980. *Id.* at 187. Purchasers must also satisfy the other requirements of Section 107(b)(3).

that (1) the generator arranged for disposal or transportation for disposal of hazardous substances at the facility at issue, and (2) that substances *of the same type* as those sent by the defendant are found at the site.[438]

Read literally, Section 107(a)(3) is at best ambiguous, and is at worst nonsensical. It would appear, for example, if read literally, to require at least three parties in the act to fix liability on a generator: the generator, the "any other party or entity" who disposes of the generator's waste at a facility owned or operated by "another party or entity," and the "another party" referred to. Congress clearly envisioned no such result, and the poor draftsmanship undoubtedly has aided the government in securing from the courts a commonsense approach to construction of the statute.

The hard case is where the generator arranged with a transporter to convey the wastes to disposal site A, and the transporter without the generator's knowledge instead took the waste to disposal site B. Is the generator a proper defendant in a Section 107(a) action brought with respect to site B? And what of site A if water "of the type" sent by the generator turns up there? Is it possible that the generator might be on the hook at both sites?[439] All of these scenarios appear to present a potential for generator liability. It is not clear whether the formulation of liability articulated by those courts that have construed Section

---

[438] United States v. Wade, 20 ERC 1277 (E.D. Pa. 12-20-83); United States v. South Carolina Recycling and Disposal, Inc., 21 ERC 1577 (D.S.C. 8-28-84); United States v. Ottati & Goss, 23 ERC 1705 (D.N.H. 1985). A three-part test, enunciated in United States v. South Carolina Recycling and Disposal, Inc., 20 ERC (BNA) 1753 (D.S.C. 1984), has been fairly consistently applied to generators. What must be shown is that (1) the generator's hazardous substances were, at some point in the past, shipped to a facility; (2) the generator's hazardous substances or ones like those of the generator are present at the site; and (3) there was a release or threatened release of *any* hazardous substance at the site that caused a response.

It is not a defense that the generator sold his substances to a third party, who disposed of them. United States v. Ward, 618 F. Supp. 884 (E.D.N.C. 1985). It is also not a defense that the generator shipped the wastes to a location other than the one where they ended up, or that they were transshipped from their original disposal site to the one at issue. *See* United States v. Ward, *supra;* and State of Missouri v. Independent Petrochemical Corp., 610 F. Supp. 4 (E.D. Mo. 1985). Finally, the fact that the generator sent a *de minimus* amount of a substance does not relieve him from liability. *See* United States v. Conservation Chemical Co., 619 F. Supp. 162 (W.D. Mo. 1985).

[439] The transporter appears to be liable only if the terms of his arrangement with the generator provided for selection of the disposal site by the transporter. *See* Section 107(a)(4).

107(a)(3) to date would impose liability on the generator for site A or site B.[440]

A chemical company that sells a hazardous substance to another entity for a purpose other than disposal or treatment does not become liable under Section 107(a)(3) if the purchaser disposes of the substances.

[iii] Transporters

Transporter liability is limited to transporters who were given discretion to select the disposal or treatment site by the generator.[441] The generator does not, however, cease to be liable upon transferring a hazardous substance to a transporter vested with discretion, since Section 107(a)(3) contains an independent basis for generator liability regardless of who, as between the generator and the transporter, chose the disposal or treatment site.

[g] Corporate Officers and Other Individuals

Individual corporate officers have occasionally been found to be individually liable in Section 107(a) actions, even in the absence of the usual showing required to pierce the corporate veil, on the ground that Section 107(a), read in light of the historical construction of Section 311(a)(7) of the Clean Water Act, allows the imposition of liability on a person who "owns an interest in a facility and is actively participating in its management."[442]

Whether this line of reasoning will support liability in the case of an officer who is *not* an owner, solely by reason of the individual's control over the fate of the corporation's hazardous waste stream is as yet

---

[440] On facts similar to the Site B variant, the district court in United States v. Ward, 618 F. Supp. 884 (E.D.N.C., Raleigh Div. 9-9-85), refused to dismiss a Section 107(a)(3) action brought against a generator who was unaware of the fact that the transporter with whom he contracted spread the waste across miles of roadside shoulders. In *United States v. Wade*, 21 ERC 1346(E.D. Pa, 3-8-84), the court, at one point, stated that "the government will have to show that a given defendant's waste was in fact disposed of at the waste site," and elsewhere that there must be "credible evidence" linking a generator's waste to the site.

[441] Section 107(a)(4).

[442] State of New York v. Shore Realty Corp., 759 F.2d 1032 (2d Cir. 1985)(controlling stockholder who is also officer); United States v. Northeastern Pharmaceutical & Chemical Co., et al., 579 F. Supp. 823, 20 ERC 1401 (W.D. Mo. 1-31-84) (relying on two Section 311 cases, Apex & Oil, Co. v. United States, 530 F.2d 1291 (8th Cir. 1976), and United States v. Mobil Oil Corporation, 464 F.2d 1124 (5th Cir. 1972)); United States v. Mottolo, 605 F. Supp. 898 (D.N.H. 1985); United States v. Ward, 618 F. Supp., 884 (E.D.N.C. 1985); United States v. Conservation Chemical Co., 619 F. Supp. 162 (W.D. Mo. 1985).

unanswered. Absence of the key element of ownership, however, should weigh heavily against liability of most corporate officers.

[h] Standard of Liability—Strict Liability

It is settled that Section 101(32) of CERCLA clearly adopts the strict liability standard of Section 311 of the Clean Water Act.[443]

The strict liability theory consistently prevented small generators from defending CERCLA cost recovery or injunctive actions on the grounds that their contributions were de minimis,[443.1] or that liability under the circumstances would be unfair.[443.2]

In an effort to alleviate the potential transaction cost burden on small generators, the government encouraged organized PRP groups to offer "de minimis buyouts" to such people, and "global" settlements of superfund cases began to include such provisions by 1985.[443.3]

In 1986, Congress retreated slightly from the strict liability concept by providing special treatment for small-quantity generators of low-hazard waste. Section 122(g) authorized expedited settlements, with full releases, for entities who meet a statutory de minimis criterion. The criterion is that both the amount and the toxic or hazardous effects be "minimal in comparison to other hazardous substances at the facility" and the settlement involve "only a minor portion of the response costs."[443.4]

The 1986 provision is also significant in that it marks the first congressional acceptance of the notion that the degree of hazard could be relevant in determining the extent of a responsible party's liability under CERCLA.

---

443 *See* New York v. Shore Realty Corp., 739 F.2d 1032 (2d Cir. 1985); J.V. Peters Co. v. EPA, 767 F.2d 263 (6th Cir. 1985); United States v. Tyson, CA 84-2663 (E.D. Pa. 8-21-86); United States v. Argent Corp., 21 ERC 1356 (D.N.M. 1984); United States v. Northeastern Pharmaceutical & Chemical Co., 579 F. Supp. 823 (W.D. Mo. 1984); United States v. Price, 577 F. Supp. 1103 (D.N.J. 1983); and City of Philadelphia v. Stepan Chemical Co., 544 F. Supp. 1135, 1140n.4 (E.D. Pa. 1982).

443.1 *See, e.g.*, United States v. Conservation Chemical Co., 619 F. Supp. at 233 (W.D. Mo. 1985); and United States v. Franklin P. Tyson, et al., CA #84-2663 (E.D. Pa. 8-21-86) (available on Lexis and Westlaw).

443.2 *Id.*

443.3 The subject is treated more thoroughly in Section 6.09[4][e], *infra*, in the discussion of settlements.

443.4 Section 122(g)(1)(A) (1986). *See also* discussion in Section 6.09[4][e], *infra*.

[i] Scope of Liability—Joint and Several Liability and Correlative Rights of Contribution

The courts have almost unanimously ruled that joint and several liability may be imposed in a Section 107 action.[444] Similarly, the courts have generally argued with the conclusion expressed first in the *Chem Dyne* case, that joint and several liability is not mandated by CERCLA, but rather is to be applied on a case-by-case basis where warranted by the facts.[445] This conclusion is consistent with the legislative history.[446]

The primary determiner of whether liability should be joint and several is whether the harm is divisible.[447] As a practical matter, subsurface cleanup costs will nearly always be indivisible. Surface cleanup may prevent either a divisible harm scenario or an individual harm scenario, depending on the neatness of the operation historically.

Although the trial courts were unanimous in concluding that joint and several liability is available, they have diverged in their views of from where joint and several liability is ultimately derived in these cases, and in their views on how to apply it.

The prevailing view developed that the legislative history points to a congressional desire to "have the scope of liability determined under common law principles."[448] From this point, however, there sprung

---

[444] *See* United States v. Northeastern Pharmaceutical & Chemical Co., 579 F. Supp. 823 (W.D. Mo. 1984); United States v. Chem Dyne Corp., 572 F. Supp. 802, 19 ERC 1953 (S.D. Ohio 10-11-83); United States v. A & F Materials, Co., 578 F. Supp. 1279 (S.D. Ill. 1984); United States v. Conservation Co., 589 F. Supp. 59, 20 ERC 1427 (W.D. Mo. 2-3-84); United States v. Stringfellow, 20 ERC 1905 (C.D. Cal. 4-5-84); United States v. Argent, 21 ERC 1356 (D.N.M. 1984); United States v. SCRDI, 20 RC 1753 (D.S.C. 2-23-84); New York v. Shore Realty Corp., 727 F.2d 1032 (2d Cir. 1985); United States v. Ottati & Goss, Inc., 23 ERC 1705 (D.N.H. 1985); United States v. Ward, 618 F. Supp. 884 (E.D.N.C. 1985); United States v. Shell Oil Co., 605 F. Supp. 1064, 1083 (D. Colo. 1985).

[445] Chem Dyne, *supra* note 444; *see also* United States v. Wade, 20 ERC 1277, 1285 (E.D. Pa. 12-10-83); and United States v. Ottati & Goss, 23 ERC 1705 (D.N.H. 1985).

[446] *See, e.g.,* 126 Cong. Rec. §14964 (daily ed. Nov. 24, 1980)(statement of Sen. Randolph); 126 Cong. Rec. S14969 (daily ed. Nov. 24, 1980) (statement of Sen. Stafford); 126 Cong. Rec. H11787 (daily ed. Nov. 24, 1980) (statement of Rep. Florio); *see generally* United States v. A & F Materials Co., Inc., 578 F. Supp. 1249, 20 ERC 1353 (S.D. Ill. 1984), and legislative history cited therein. *But see* 126 Cong. Rec. S15004 (daily ed. Nov. 24, 1980) (statement of Sen. Helms).

[447] United States v. Chem Dyne Corp., 572 F. Supp. 802, 19 ERC 1953 (S.D. Ohio 10-11-83).

[448] United States v. Chem Dyne Corp., 572 F. Supp. 802, 808 (S.D. Ohio 1983).

two lines of opinion, one holding that the governing body of law is *federal* common law,[449] the other looking to *state* common law.[450]

The emerging majority view by the end of 1986 appears to have been that, for reasons of uniformity of application, the development of a federal common law of joint and several liability is more consistent with the overall congressional policy behind CERCLA.[450.1]

Universal adoption of a "federal common law" basis for joint and several liability will not, however, ensure uniform application of the remedy. Some courts applied equitable factors, for example, to temper

---

449 *See* United States v. A & F Materials, Inc., 578 F. Supp. 1249 (S.D. Ill. 1984). The A & F Materials court concluded that in developing the new federal common law of hazardous waste liability, the court could be guided by policies set forth in an amendment to CERCLA that had been proferred by Congressman Gore and adopted by the House, but dropped by the Senate when it decided not to deal expressly with the joint and several liability issue in CERCLA. Under this view even where joint and several liability was appropriate, the court could apportion the damages to take account of the following:

  (i)   the ability of the parties to demonstrate that their contributions to a discharge release or disposal of a hazardous waste can be distinguished;

  (ii)   the amount of the hazardous waste involved;

  (iii) the degree of toxity of the hazardous waste involved;

  (iv) the degree of involvement by the parties in the generation, transportation, treatment, storage, or disposal of the hazardous waste;

  (v)   the degree of care exercised by the parties with respect to the hazardous waste concerned, taking into account the characteristics of such hazardous waste; and

  (vi) the degree of cooperation by the parties with federal, state, or local officials to prevent any harm to the public health or the environment.

Accord, United States v. Stringfellow, 20 ERC 1905 (C.D. Cal. 4-5-84); and *see* United States v. Wade, 577 F. Supp. 1326, 20 ERC 1277 (E.D. Pa. 12-20-83).

450 *Cf.,* United States v. Northeastern Pharmaceutical & Chemical Corp., 579 F. Supp. 823 (W.D. Mo. 1984)(applying Missouri law).

450.1 Several courts concluded that a federal right of contribution was implicit in Section 107. *See* Colorado v. ASARCO, Inc., 22 ERC (BNA) 1926 (D. Colo, 1985); Wehner v. Syntex Agribusiness, Inc., 22 ERC (BNA) 1732 (E.D. Mich. 1985); Mola Development Corp. v. United States, 22 ERC (BNA) 1443 (C.D. Cal. 1985); and Kelley v. United States, 23 ERC (BNA) 1500 (W.D. Mich. 1985). *Cf.* United States v. Conservation Chemical Co., 619 F. Supp. 162 (W.D. Mo. 1985) (holding that a right of contribution exists for recovery of response costs, but not for injunctive relief); United States v. Medley, — F. Supp. — (D.S.C. 1986). Another thread of authority argues for apportionment of response costs on the basis of comparative fault principles premised on the factors contained in an amendment to CERCLA proposed by Congressman Gore and adopted by the House but dropped from the final bill. The so-called Gore amendment factors consider such things as relative toxicity and volume, differing migratory potentials, and the effect of settlements on nonsettling parties. *See* discussion in note 449, *supra;* United States v. Conservation Chemical Co., *supra;* and the lengthy discussion in United States v. A & F Materials, Inc., 578 F. Supp. 1249, at 1256 (S.D. Ill. 1984).

what might otherwise be a harsh result of rigorous imposition of joint and several liability.[451] The equitable difficulties inherent in strict joint and several liability are illustrated by considering a hypothetical disposal site at which the groundwater analysis shows contamination by chemical of the type sent by generators of only 1 percent of the waste by volume. It is not at all clear whether Congress's initial intention was to spread the costs to the broadest possible group of generators (the other 99 percent) or whether some degree of "fault" was intended to be considered, which in this case would limit liability to the 1 percent whose wastes actually found their way into the environment. The "de minimis buyout" provision, Section 122(g), mitigates but does not completely solve this conceptual problem, since it is (1) discretionary with the government and (2) available only to generators of low-hazard waste.

A more significant addition to CERCLA in this regard is Section 113(f)(1) (1986), which creates a statutory right of contribution among persons who are "liable or potentially liable under section 107(a), during or following any civil action under section 106 or under section 107(a)."[451.1] The statute states further that the claims will be "governed by Federal law" and that the courts may use "equitable factors" in apportioning costs.[451.2]

Section 113(f) concludes the debate over whether joint and several liability and the correlative right of contribution are federally based or subject to the vagaries of state law, in favor of the uniform federal basis. It also settles the argument over what factors the courts should use in apportioning liability in contribution cases in favor of broad judicial discretion. Courts may continue to apply the "Gore factors" adopted in the *A&F Materials* decision,[451.3] or adopt a basis for apportionment from other sources.

One clear thrust of the 1986 amendments to CERCLA is the encouragement of settlement. Since Section 113(f)(2) prohibits contribution actions against parties who settle with the government, it may well be

---

[451] United States v. A & F Materials, Inc., *supra* note 449.

[451.1] The statute also provides that contribution actions are not barred in the absence of such actions.

[451.2] Contribution actions brought by nonsettling parties against parties who have entered into a settlement with the government are barred, however, "regarding matters addressed in the settlement." Section 113(f)(2).

[451.3] *See* H.R. Rep. No. 99-253, Part 3 [Judiciary Committee] at 19, wherein *A&F Materials* and *Chem Dyne* are cited approvingly.

that in most cases the inducement to settle will be so great so as to render the prospect of many contribution actions dim. One disincentive to settlement is Section 113(f)(3), which provides that parties who settle with the government in a way that leaves the government with some costs are subordinated to the government's claims for recovery of its costs in any subsequent contribution action against nonsettlers.

An interesting issue where there are potential third party defendants in the picture is the potential for the government and settling parties to prejudice the ability of the nonsettlers to raise divisibility and other defenses, by obliterating potential sources of evidence during surface cleanup. It would seem to be in the interest of the settling parties to make every effort to preserve as complete an inventory record as possible during surface cleanup, so as to avoid a later argument by the nonsettlers in contribution actions that they should not be held jointly and severally liable because of the prejudice to their case caused by the initial cleanup.

[j] Relationship of Section 107 to Section 104

If the government had not chosen to institute Section 107 cost recovery actions before completing remedial work, there would be no issue as to how the various restrictions contained in Section 104 affect the scope of recovery allowed under Section 107. The government's strategy, however, raised a difficult issue in this regard, which has not been addressed adequately by those judges to whom the issue has been presented.

Stated simply, the original text of Section 104 imposed limitations on the government's expenditure of superfund monies for remedial purposes. Those limitations included a prohibition against massive expenditures in states that had not entered into a cooperative agreement under Section 104(c)(3), in light of competing demands placed on the superfund by other priority sites. Since Section 107(a)(4)(A) allows the government to recover only costs "incurred," it would seem that a Section 107(a)(4)(A) action for "future costs"[452] should have been limited to "incurrable" costs, that is, only that amount the government would be able to spend were it to actually spend the money first and seek reimbursement later.

The government brazenly argued, with considerable success, that

---

[452] See also Section 6.07[2][c], supra.

"section 107(a) was meant to stand by itself,"[453] and that liability under it could be determined without consideration of Section 104 limitations.[454] Those courts that addressed the issue did so in connection with motions to dismiss the government's claims as premature.

Most of the courts concluded that the Section 104 limitations were not a barrier to a ruling on the defendants' *liability* in advance of response costs' actually being incurred. That is not to say, however, that the scope of the *remedy* was not limited by the restraints imposed by Section 104, a proposition that appears to have been obviously correct on the face of the statutes.

This issue all but disappeared with the 1986 amendments to CER-CLA. First, the most significant limitation of Section 104, the requirement of "fund balancing" contained in Section 104 (a)(4), was limited by the amendments to "orphan sites" (those without any PRPs). In addition, the Section 121 remedial scheme ensures that a formal, administrative decision will have been made on the selection of the remedy prior to the expenditure of significant remedial funds. Finally, Section 113(g)(2) expressly authorizes the commencement of cost recovery actions before completion of remedial action, and allows in the context of such actions liability determinations that are binding in future actions to recover further expenditures.

[k] Relationship of Section 107 to Sections 111 and 112

A less difficult issue under the original CERCLA was whether the limitations of Sections 111 and 112 on the presentation of private claims against the superfund, such as statutes of limitation[455] and notice requirements,[456] also imposed limits on the government in actions brought under Section 107. Although defendants frequently raised such claims in tandem with similar claims as to the Section 104 limits, result-

---

[453] United States v. Reilly Tar and Chemical Corp., 20 ERC 1060, 1072 (D. Minn. 1983).

[454] *See* United States v. Wade, 577 F. Supp. 1326, 20 ERC 1277, 1284 (E.D. Pa. 12-20-83).

[455] Section 111(d), Section 112(d).

[456] Section 112(a). *See* U.S. v. S.E.P.T.A., — F.2d — (E.D. Pa. 1986).

ing in judicial treatment of the issues identically,[457] they are arguably different, with the government's position on Sections 111 and 112 clearly correct.

The argument that Sections 111 and 112, which create a detailed mechanism for perfecting private superfund claims and paying out superfund monies in satisfaction thereof, are really a separate and distinct program, unrelated to Section 107 (or to Section 104 for that matter), is consistent with CERCLA's structure.[458] The issue was put to rest late in 1986, when Congress adopted separately applicable notice and limitations provisions governing actions under Sections 106 and 107.[458.1]

[l] Private Cost Recovery Actions

There are three classes of potential plaintiffs under Section 107(a)(4)(B), which authorizes the recovery from responsible parties of "any other necessary costs of response incurred by any other person consistent with the national contingency plan." These are (1) "innocent" site owners,[459] (2) implicated site owners or principal generators,[460] and (3) neighbors who incur costs of protective action.[461]

CERCLA's language and structure raise several issues that affect the

---

[457] *See* United States v. Reilly Tar, *supra* note 453.

[458] *See* State of New York v. General Electric Co., 592 F. Supp. 291, 21 ERC 1097 (N.D.N.Y. 1984); State of Colorado v. Asarco, Inc., 608 F. Supp. 1484 (D. Colo. 1985) (holding natural resource damage claim under Section 107 brought beyond the Section 111 statute of limitation not barred); and Kelley v. United States, 23 ERC (BNA) 1503 (W.D. Mich. 1985) on the natural resource damages issue. *Compare* United States v. Mottolo, 605 F. Supp. 898 (D.N.H. 1985) (holding state claim barred).

[458.1] P.L. 99-499, Section 113(b).

[459] *E.g.*, Cadillac Fairview/California Inc. v. Dow Chemical Co., et al., 21 ERC 1108 (C.D. Calif.)(plaintiff a real estate developer who bought the property not knowing that it contained hazardous substances). *See also* Levin Metals Corp. v. Parr-Richmond Terminal Co., 799 F.2d 1312 (9th Cir. 1986).

[460] *E.g.*, Bulk Distribution Centers, Inc. v. Monsanto Co., 589 F. Supp 1437, 21 ERC 1080 (S.D. Fla. 1984) (site owner); City of New York v. Exxon Co., et al., 24 ERC 1361 (S.D.N.Y. 1986) (city landfills).

[461] Walls v. Waste Resources Corp., 761 F.2d 311 (6th Cir. 1985)(affirming right of neighbors' association to seek recovery under Section 107(a)(4)(B) of costs incurred by them to clean up releases emanating from defendant's landfill); Jones v. Inmont Corp., 589 F. Supp. 1925, 20 ERC 2002 (S.D. Ohio 1983); *cf.* O'Leary v. Moyer's Landfill, Inc., 536 F. Supp. 218 (No. Civ. 80-3849)(E.D. Pa.)(downstream property owners—actions predate CERCLA); Artesian Water Co. v. New Castle County, 22 ERC (BNA) 1345 (D. Del. 1985) (polluted water wells); Jefferson County, et al. v. U.S., 25 ERC 1029 (E.D. Mo. 1986).

scope of relief available to private Section 107 plaintiffs. The first of these issues is whether a private cause of action exists under the statute with respect to a site not subject to government action, such as listing on the National Priority List. The argument for the negative, which appears to be the weaker, is premised upon a broad reading of the phrase "consistent with the national contingency plan." Since the NCP contains the NPL as one of its components, and since remedial action, at least,[462] may be taken only at NPL-listed sites, the argument holds that in order to prove "consistency" in an action to recover remedial costs, the plaintiff must plead that the site is on the NPL[463] or that the government has undertaken or ordered some removal or containment action.[464]

A second issue, and one on which the government has asserted strong negative views, is whether in order for private remedial action to be "consistent" with the NCP, the remedial plan must have been approved by EPA. Several federal courts have opined that government approval of a private remedial plan is the only practical way to ensure that the public's interests are being served, and have accordingly required such a showing as a prerequisite to Section 107(a)(4)(B) recovery.[465]

---

[462] Removal actions, which are limited in duration and the amount of the expenditure, are not so limited.

[463] *See* Cadillac Fairview/California v. Dow Chemical Co. et al, 21 ERC 1108 (C.D. Cal. 3-4-84); *contra*, Bulk Distribution Centers Inc. v. Monsanto Co., 589 F.Supp. 1437, 21 ERC 1080 at fn.18 (S.D. Fla. 1984) (relying on EPA's questionable "planned removal" provision of the original NCP, 40 CFR §300.67(a)(2), and a metaphorical reading of the meaning of the NPL as described in D'Imperio v. United States, 575 F. Supp. 248, 20 ERC 1090, 1092 (D.N.J. 1983). The Second Circuit held unequivocally in New York v. Shore Realty Corp., 759 F.2d 1032 (2d Cir. 1985) that inclusion on the NPL was not a prerequisite to a state Section 107 action, reasoning that the NPL, while a specific prerequisite to EPA action under Section 104, was not a core requirement of the NCP and thus not within the "consistency" mandate.

[464] Cadillac Fairview/California Inc. v. Dow Chemical Co., 21 ERC 1584 (C.D. Cal. 8-24-84)(clarifying the earlier opinion, *supra* note 463, and claiming that its earlier opinion had been "mischaracterized" as "requiring" the site to appear on the National Priorities List)

[465] *See, e.g.*, Bulk Distribution Centers, Inc. v. Monsanto Co. 584 F. Supp. 1437, 21 ERC 1080, 1088 (S.D. Fla. 1984); *But cf.* Jones v. Inmont Corp., 20 ERC 2001 (S.D. Ohio 1983)("Consistency . . . goes more to the recoverability of various items of damages than to the existence of a claim for relief . . ."); Artesian Water Co. v. New Castle County, 22 ERC 1345 (D.Del. 1985); Wickland Oil Terminals v. Asarco, Inc., 590 F.Supp. 72 (N.D.Cal. 1984). *Contra*, New York v. Shore Realty Corp., 759 F.2d 1032 (2d Cir. 1985)(failure of state to secure EPA preauthorization prior to expenditure of state funds for remedial action is not a bar to Section 107(a)(4)(B) cost recovery action); Pinole Point Properties,

The problem here seems to be an understandable reluctance on the part of the federal judiciary to undertake a determination that any of the plaintiff's expenditures were "necessary" and "consistent with" the NCP, which is, after all, an EPA regulation. For its part, judging by the position it has taken in those cases, EPA seems to have been uninterested in acting as umpire in what it saw as essentially private disputes. This issue may be particularly important to neighbors who take self-protective action without preparing an overall remedial plan and seeking EPA approval and later seek reimbursement for their efforts from responsible parties.

EPA addressed the issue of the extent of its involvement in the 1985 revisions to the NCP.[465.1] Its position, set forth principally in 40 CFR §300.71, is that response actions by private parties undertaken pursuant to a consent decree or administrative order under Section 106 must be approved in advance by the lead agency and any response action by a person who anticipates making a claim against the Fund must be preauthorized by EPA.[465.2]

Other private response actions do not require prior approval, and EPA makes it clear that it does not intend to "approve" Section 107 cost recovery actions that do not involve government participation in advance. Section 300.71 does, however, set forth some general criteria EPA feels are required for *any* private response to be consistent with the NCP[465.3] and provides a mechanism for "certification" of organiza-

---

Inc. v. Bethlehem Steel Corp., 596 F. Supp. 283 (N.D. Cal. 1984); and City of New York v. Exxon Corp., — F. Supp. —, 24 ERC 1361 (S.D.N.Y. 1986).

[465.1] 50 Fed. Reg. 47934-47935 (11-20-85).

[465.2] 40 CFR §300.71. *See also* 40 CFR §300.25(d).

[465.3] 40 CFR §300.71(a)(2) provides:

(2) For purposes of cost recovery under section 107 of CERCLA, except for actions taken pursuant to section 106 of CERCLA or pursuant to preauthorization under §300.25 of this Plan, a response action will be consistent with the NCP (or for a State or Federal government response, not inconsistent with the NCP), if the person taking the response action:

(i) Where the action is a removal action, acts in circumstances warranting removal and implements removal action consistent with §300.65.

(ii) Where the action is a remedial action:

(A) Provides for appropriate site investigation and analysis of remedial alternatives as required under §300.68;

(B) Complies with the provisions of paragraphs (e) through (i) of §300.68;

(C) Selects a cost-effective response; and

(D) Provides an opportunity for appropriate public comment concerning the selection of a remedial action consistent with paragraph (d) of §300.67 unless compliance with the legally applicable or relevant and appropriate State and local

tions wishing to assist or conduct site responses.[465.4]

As a practical matter, the revised remedial scheme provided in the 1986 amendments eliminates the issue with respect to claimants involved with NPL sites. Section 122(e)(6) prohibits "any potentially responsible party" from undertaking any remedial action at a facility at which EPA "or a potentially responsible party pursuant to an administrative order or consent decree" has "commenced a remedial action and feasibility study" without preauthorization.[465.5]

A third issue that has received judicial attention is whether one "responsible party" may utilize Section 107(a)(4)(B) as a vehicle to seek reimbursement of his cleanup expenditures from other similarly situated entities. This issue was raised in *City of Philadelphia v. Stepan Chemical Co., et al.*,[466] but was not resolved.

On its face Section 107(a)(4)(B) permits one culpable party to expend money to clean up the site, and then to proceed against others for contribution.[467]

Congress cured a related semantic problem with an amendment to Section 112(a) in 1986. The original language of that provision appeared, on its face, to impose a sixty-day notice requirement on persons seeking recovery under Section 107(a). The intention clearly was to require a sixty-day notice on PRPs of Fund claimants before they sought

---

requirements identified under paragraph (4) of this section provides a substantially equivalent opportunity for public involvement in the choice of remedy.

(3) For the purpose of consistency with §300.65 and §300.68 of this Plan, except for response actions taken pursuant to section 106 of CERCLA or response actions for which reimbursement from the Fund will be sought, any action to be taken by the "lead agency" in §300.65 or §300.68 may be taken by the person carrying out the response.

(4) Persons performing response actions that are neither Fund-financed nor pursuant to action under section 106 of CERCLA shall comply with all otherwise legally applicable or relevant and appropriate Federal, State, and local requirements, including permit requirements.

[465.4] 40 CFR §300.71(b)(1985) and §300.71(c)(1985). Although certification is not a prerequisite to either preauthorization for Fund claim purposes or preapproval of a Section 106–related response, EPA hints strongly that it might make the requisite approval easier to secure. *See* 40 CFR §300.71(c).

[465.5] Section 113(1) (1986) requires that EPA and the Department of Justice receive notification of the commencement of any action in federal court premised on CERCLA.

[466] 544 F. Supp. 1135 (E.D. Pa. 1982). *Cf.* City of New York v. Exxon Corp., — F. Supp. —, 24 ERC 1361 (S.D.N.Y. 1986).

[467] Section 113(f) (1986), which creates a clear statutory right of contribution, does not prohibit the commencement of such actions before, or even in the utter absence of, government response.

recovery from the superfund for their expenditures or damages. A technical amendment removed the ambiguous language, making it clear that the sixty-day notice requirement is a prerequisite only to access to Fund monies under Section 111 and Section 112, and is not a prerequisite to instituting a cost recovery action in court.

A related amendment to Section 112(a) prohibits the payment of a Fund claimant while cost recovery litigation instituted by the claimant is pending.

An interesting ancillary issue is whether private cost recovery actions may contain claims for injunctive relief premised on CERCLA.[468] Such plaintiffs, particularly state natural resource damage plaintiffs,[468.1] often seek to require monitoring and abatement action. On its face, except for the citizen suit provision added in 1986, the statute provides an injunctive remedy only to the United States,[469] and EPA has agreed with defendant arguments that no broader injunctive remedy can be inferred. The few reported cases are in accord with the government's position.[470]

The citizen suit provision, Section 310, authorizes injunctive relief. Such relief, however, is limited to enforcement of any "standard, regulation, requirement, or order which has become effective" pursuant to CERCLA.[470.1] Other than Section 106(a) orders, RODs, federal facility orders, and related remedial decisions by EPA, there are not many "standards," etc., that are available to be enforced under CERCLA.

---

[468] Such claims may, of course, be premised on state common law. *See* New York v. Shore Realty Corp., 759 F.2d 1032 (2d Cir. 1985); State of New York v. General Electric Co., 592 F. Supp. 291, 21 ERC 1105 (N.D.N.Y. 1984).

[468.1] An interesting variant on this issue was present in City of New York v. Exxon Corp., et al., — F. Supp. —, 24 ERC 1361 (S.D.N.Y. 1986). There the city raised a natural resources damages claim, as to which the defendants filed a motion to dismiss. Rejecting the motion to dismiss, but acknowledging that the city had no statutory basis for such a claim, the court stated that it was possible for the state to delegate its right to the city and remanded the issue for trial.

[469] Section 106(a).

[470] New York v. Shore Realty Corp, 759 F.2d 1032 (2d Cir. 1985) (relying on legislative history on the Senate side and statutory construction analogy from antitrust cases); Velsicol Chemical Corp. v. Reilly Tar & Chemical Corp., 21 ERC 2119, 2121 (E.D. Tenn. 8-16-84); Earthline Co., v. Kin-Buc, Inc., et al., (D.N.J. 7-23-84). A private citizen's lawsuit seeking a more stringent remedy and seeking to enjoin EPA's cleanup of a site in the absence of such a remedy was rejected in Jefferson County v. United States, — F. Supp. —, 25 ERC (BNA) 1029 (E.D. Mo. 9-10-86).

[470.1] Sections 310(a)(1), 310(b)(2).

[m] **Statutory Defenses**

An otherwise responsible party may nevertheless escape liability upon a showing that the release or threat of a release *and* the resulting damages were caused *solely* by an act of God, an act of war, or the act or omission of a third party unrelated to the defendant.[471]

Because these defenses are derived from Section 311 of the Clean Water Act, many of the terms will be construed in light of the substantial body of case law that has developed under Section 311.[472] The lengthy qualifying language following Section 107(b)(3), however, is unique to CERCLA. It serves to impose an additional burden on a defendant, not imposed under the Clean Water Act, to demonstrate not only that a third party was the sole cause of the occurrence, but also that the innocent defendant otherwise acted with due care under the circumstances.

The most likely PRPs to raise a successful third party defense[473] in the case of a leaking facility[474] are generators whose waste was disposed of illegally by thieves, or where the condition resulted solely as a result of the actions of successors in title to a TSD facility, with whom the

---

[471] The statutory text provides:

Section 107 (b) There shall be no liability under subsection (a) of this section for a person otherwise liable who can establish by a preponderance of the evidence that the release or threat of release of a hazardous substance and the damages resulting therefrom were caused solely by—

(1) an act of God;

(2) an act of war;

(3) an act or omission of a third party other than an employee or agent of the defendant, or than one whose act or omission occurs in connection with a contractual relationship, existing directly or indirectly, with the defendant (except where the sole contractual arrangement arises from a published tariff and acceptance for carriage by a common carrier by rail), if the defendant establishes by a preponderance of the evidence that (a) he exercised due care with respect to the hazardous substance concerned, taking into consideration the characteristics of such hazardous substance, in light of all relevant facts and circumstances, and (b) he took precautions against foreseeable acts or omissions of any such third party and the consequences that could foreseeably result from such acts or omissions; or

(4) any combination of the foregoing paragraphs.

[472] *See generally* this chapter *supra.*

[473] As experience under Section 311 has demonstrated, the act of God and act of war defenses will seldom, if ever, be available.

[474] Spill-related defenses will more likely than not be raised in the same types of circumstances as under Section 311.

generator had no ongoing relationship; subsequent good faith purchasers of already contaminated property; and certain passive owners whose property was used by waste disposers without permission, and not under any form of tenancy.

Out of concern that Section 107(b)(3) might be unclear as to its relationship to land purchasers, Congress added a new definition to CERCLA in 1986, defining the term "contractual relationship"[474.1] The only place this term is used in the statute is in Section 107(b)(3), which bars use of the third party defense by anyone in a "contractual relationship" with the third party alleged to be the sole cause of the release or threat.

The term is defined by the 1986 amendment to specifically *include* "land contracts, deeds, or other instruments transferring title or possession, *unless* the real property was acquired by the defendant after the disposal or placement of the hazardous substance" occurred at the facility *and* the defendant either is a governmental entity that acquired title involuntarily or by eminent domain[474.2] or is a private entity that either acquired the property by inheritance or bequest[474.3] or at the time of acquisition "did not know and had no reason to know that any hazardous substance which is the subject of the release or threatened release was disposed of in, or at the facility."[474.4]

A purchaser's duty of care is spelled out in Section 101(35)(B), which embellishes the meaning of "has reason to know." The purchaser must

---

[474.1] Section 101(35).

[474.2] Section 101(35)(A)(ii).

[474.3] Section 101(35)(A)(iii). Interestingly, Congress seems to have got its terminology wrong. It is here concerned with *real* property. Under the law of most states, the term "bequest" applies to testate distribution of *chattels*. The only sort of land interest that is a chattel is a leasehold (a "chattel real"). The proper terminology would have been "inheritance or devise."

[474.4] Section 101(35)(A)(i). This provision is interesting. It does not require the purchaser to be ignorant of *any* disposal activities at the site. He need only be able to show ignorance of the disposal of substances that are involved in the release. Thus, one could, except for the presumptions contained in Section 101(35)(B), which are discussed herein, purchase a dump, and if at the time one thought only demolition material was disposed of in it, one could escape liability under CERCLA for releases of chemicals dumped there. The language is different from that of the de minimus buyout provision, Section 122(g), which would disqualify a purchaser who knew at the time of the purchase that hazardous substances of any kind had been generated, stored, or disposed of on the property.

have undertaken "all appropriate inquiry" into the previous "ownership and uses," consistent with "good commercial or customary practice," at the time of the transfer.[474.5] In deciding whether the defendant complied with the standard, the court is to "take into account any specialized knowledge or expertise on the part of the defendant, the relationship of the purchase price to what the value of the property would be if it were uncontaminated, commonly known or reasonable information about the property, the obviousness of the presence of contamination at the property, and the ability to detect such contamination by appropriate inspection."[474.6]

The knowledge requirements do not, on the face of the statute, apply to heirs and devisees or to governmental entities.[474.7]

[n] **Superlien**

A 1986 addition to CERCLA imposes a lien in favor of the United States on all real property that "belongs to" a Section 107 responsible party and is the subject of or is "affected by" a removal or remedial

---

[474.5] There is important gloss on this provision in the Conference Report. There it is stated that defendants "shall be held to a higher standard as public awareness of the hazards associated with hazardous substances has grown, as reflected by this Act, the 1980 Act and other Federal and State statutes." The Conference Report further states that "good commercial or customary practice . . . shall mean that a reasonable inquiry must have been made in all circumstances, in light of best business and land transfer principles." H. R. Rep. No. 99-962, 99th Cong., 2d Sess. at 187.

[474.6] A defendant seeking to avail himself of the third party defense will not only have to produce evidence about his own knowledge at the time, but will need an experienced appraiser, and, in many cases, an environmental consultant, in order to satisfy this burden of proof.

[474.7] There is, however, a curious statement in the Conference Report that "those who acquire property through inheritance or bequest *without actual knowledge* may rely upon this section *if they engage in reasonable inquiry. . .*" and that the inquiry requirement would be inapplicable only to those who "acquire property by inheritance without knowing of the inheritance . . .." H.R. Rep. No. 99-962 at 187-88.

It is not clear what the Conference Committee would require of an heir or devisee who knows of the condition. A devisee can, in most jurisdictions, renounce the devise before it becomes effective, so one who is the beneficiary of a devise of a superfund site can probably avoid liability by refusing the conveyance out of the estate. An heir may not be so lucky, however, since heirs are generally held to be seized of property of the decedent as of the instant of death, and predeath renunciation of an interest in an estate may not always be effective. The "sins of the father" might, on the Conference Committee's reading, certainly be visited on the children, with a vengeance.

action.[474.8] The lien arises on the later of the date costs are first incurred "with respect to a response action" or the date notice of potential liability is given to the person.[474.9]

Perfection of the lien to establish priority as to other creditors' interests requires recording, and its priority is established according to the state's law respecting judgment liens.[474.10] Actions in rem are authorized for execution.[474.11]

Vessels, finally, are subject to a maritime lien, established under Section 107(m), with respect to releases or threatened releases.

§6.08   Claims Against the Fund—CERCLA Sections 111 and 112

[1]   Overview

Section 111(a) of CERCLA delimits the uses to which monies contained in the Hazardous Substance Response Fund may be put. In addition to underwriting the Section 104 response program,[475] Fund monies may be utilized for paying "necessary response costs" incurred by "any other person" certified by EPA as incurred "as a result of carrying out" the NCP,[476] for paying leftover damage claims asserted under Section 311 of the Clean Water Act with respect to costs incurred

---

474.8 Section 107(1) (1986). This lien is narrower than some state "superliens," which purport to cover all property of which a PRP is seized. *See, e.g.*, N.H. RSA §147-B:10 (lien "upon business revenues and all real and personal property of any person causing expenditures from the" state hazardous waste cleanup fund).

474.9 Notice is effectuated by certified or registered mail. Section 107(1)(2)(B).

474.10 Section 107(1)(3). Some state laws afford a statutory priority for their superliens. *Compare, e.g.*, N.H. RSA §147-B(10).

474.11 Section 107(1)(4).

475 Sections 111(a)(1), 111(a)(4), and 111(c). Fund monies are used by EPA not only to pay direct Section 104 response costs, but also to pay the administrative and overhead costs of the EPA superfund program and the CERCLA-related overhead of the Environmental Enforcement and Environmental Defense sections of the Justice Department, all of which EPA had deemed "reasonably necessary for and incidental to the implementation of . . ." CERCLA. The legislative history indicates both congressional intent and a promise on EPA's part, to use Fund monies only for personnel directly involved in removal and remedial actions and "associated" administrative costs, and not for overall CERCLA programmatic support. 126 Cong. Rec. H 11792 (12-3-80).

476 Section 111(a)(2). *Compare* Section 107(a)(4)(B); and *see* Section 6.07[2][l], *supra*. The phrase "other necessary response costs" is essentially defined by Sections 101(23) and (24), and is broad enough to cover an injured neighbor's protective action. It does not appear to be broad enough to cover property damage.

prior to CERCLA's effective date,[477] and for paying natural resource damage claims asserted by a federal trustee, a state, or a foreign entity.[478] Natural resource damage claims payable by the Fund (as opposed to those that can be recovered from responsible parties under Section 107) do not include claims for the cost of damage assessment,[478.1] and natural resource damage claimants are required to exhaust their administrative and judicial remedies against PRPs before any payment from the Fund can be made.[478.2]

A number of additional provisions were added to Section 111 in 1986 to conform the uses of the Fund to new programs added in P.L. 99-499.[478.3]

Provisions authorizing recovery for private economic damage and personal injury contained in early versions of the bills that were eventually merged into CERCLA were dropped prior to passage,[479] with an apparent intention to reconsider the issue during reauthorization of the statute in light of the conclusions of a study of existing remedies funded by Section 301(e).[480] The one substantive provision relating to third party injury that was retained is Section 111(g), which requires the

---

[477] Sections 111(a)(3), 111(b).

[478] *Id;* and Section 107(f).

[478.1] *See* Section 111(b)(2)(B) (1986).

[478.2] *See* Section 111(b)(2)(A) (1986).

[478.3] These include payment of the cost of epidemiological studies and health assessments undertaken under Section 104(i), costs incurred in evaluating citizen petitions that seek preliminary assessments, costs of privately conducted remedial oversight contracts, land acquisition costs, research development and demonstration project costs, reimbursements to local governments authorized under Section 123, and several other costs. *See generally* Sections 111(c)(4)-111(c)(14)(1986).

[479] *See* 126 Cong. Rec. 14721 (11-18-80); S. 1480 (11-18-80); S. 1480 (as reported out of Senate Committee on Environment and Public Works, 7-11-80).

[480] The Section 301(e) study was published in 1982, and called for the creation of a new statutory scheme for victim compensation and new rights of action. U.S. Congress Senate, Committee on Environment and Public Works, Injuries and Damages from Hazardous Wastes—Analysis and Improvement of Legal Remedies, A Report to Congress in Compliance with Section 301(e) of the Comprehensive Environmental Response, Compensation, and Liability Act of 1980 (P.L. 96-510) by the Superfund Section 301(e) Study Group, 97th Congress, 2d session, September 1982, at 21. Following that event a number of victim compensation schemes were proposed in the 98th Congress, none of which were enacted. *See, e.g.,* S. 917 (Strafford-Randolph); S. 945; S. 946 (Mitchell); H. R. 2842 (LaFalce, et al.); H.R. 2582 (Markey, et al.); H.R. 4304 (Florio, et al.); and H.R. 5640 (CERCLA reauthorization—Florio, et al.). A limited legislative response, contained in P.L. 99-499, is Section 310, which establishes a uniform commencement date for all state statutes of limitation on actions for personal injury or property damage premised on releases of hazardous substances from facilities.

government to promulgate regulations requiring notification by owners and operators of "potentially injured parties."

Section 112 creates the framework for presentation and decisions with respect to CERCLA-allowed claims, and imposes a number of limitations, which are discussed below. As a practical matter, EPA chose to obligate virtually all Fund monies to remedial actions and CERCLA administration, and thus in CERCLA's first five years Section 111 and 112 were virtually ignored. Section 111(e)(2) was amended in 1986 by the addition of language allowing the Fund manager to refuse to spend money to satisfy natural resource damage claims in any year "the President determines that all of the Fund is needed for response to threats to public health. . . ."

For a general discussion of natural resources damages claim issues, see Sections 6.06[3]-6.07[1][b][v], *supra*, and see discussion *infra*.

[2] Limitations

[a] Time Limitations

Superfund monies may not be used to pay natural resource damages claims where both the "injury, destruction, or loss" and the release from which such damage resulted "occurred wholly before" the enactment of CERCLA.[481] In the case of most groundwater contamination problems, which are generally the most expensive to address, this limitation will not bar a claim, since, it is unlikely, even in very old dumps, that the "release," as broadly defined by CERCLA, will have entirely ceased.

The more significant time bar is Section 112(d), which bars claims for response costs brought more than six years from the date of "completion of all response action." Claims for natural resource damages are barred unless they are brought before the later of three years from the date of discovery of the loss "and its connection with the release in question" or three years from the date on which final Section 301(c) damage assessment regulations are promulgated.[482]

---

[481] Section 111(d)(1).

[482] The subsection was amended in 1986. An ambiguity in the 1980 text caused a number of Section 107(a)(4)(C) defendants to raise Section 112(d) as a defense to natural resource damages claims brought directly against them as responsible parties under Section 107(a). Plaintiffs in those actions argued that Section 112(d) was limited to claims against the Fund and thus did not affect Section 107 actions. EPA, at 50 Fed. Reg. 51214 (12-13-85), stated unequivocally its belief that the Section 112(d) statute of limitation

EPA's claims procedures, which were developed under the original text of Section 112(d), define "date of discovery" for the purpose of submission of natural resource damage claims as the date the "trustee became aware of the injury,"[483] in terms of the availability of documentary evidence of the injury made available to the trustee "prepared for the trustee."[483.1] Although the 1986 revision to Section 111(d) requires changes in EPA's procedures, the critical definitions contained in the Agency's extant regulations are not inconsistent with the amended language.

[b] Specific Limitations on Natural Resource Damage Claims

As noted heretofore, natural resource damages claimants are required to have exhausted their administrative and judicial remedies under Section 107 before they may receive any reimbursement out of the superfund.

The expenditure of Fund monies to satisfy natural resource damage claims is subject to a number of substantive requirements. Claims must be asserted by federal "trustees" or states,[484] and, except in emergencies, there must be a "plan for the use of" funds that has been adopted by the "affected Federal agencies" and the "Governor or Governors" of affected states and has been subject to "adequate public notice and opportunity for hearing and consideration of all public comments."[485]

---

applied to "actions against responsible parties under section 107 as well as claims against the Fund." A separate statute of limitation for Section 107 lawsuits was enacted in Section 113 by Section 113 of P.L. 99-499 (1986). The statute also contains a proviso tolling the statute of limitation for minors under eighteen years of age and incompetents.

[483] 40 CFR §306.12(f) (effective 3-13-86).

[483.1] *Id.* This regulation defines the date of discovery as follows: ". . . the date on which the trustee became aware of the injury to natural resource: (1) For an injury that can be visually observed, this is the date on which the trustee has available, or reasonably should have available, a document or memorandum prepared for the trustee verifying the observed injury . . . the types of injury, and which suggests that the injury may be related to the release of a hazardous substance; or (2) for an injury that cannot be visually observed . . . the date on which the trustee has available, or reasonably should have available, a document or memorandum prepared for the trustee, including such sampling and laboratory analysis as is necessary, which identifies the injured resource, the types of injury, and which suggests that the injury may be related to the release of a hazardous substance."

Litigation can be anticipated over questions of when a document "reasonably should have" been available, and whether a document that contains only one or two of the three types of information specified is sufficient to start the running of the statute.

[484] Sections 111(b), 107(f).

[485] Section 111(i).

Section 107(f) gives administrative damages assessments "the force effect of a rebuttable presumption" on behalf of a claimant on subsequent litigation.[486]

Natural resource damages that are reimbursable out of the superfund do not include the cost of damage assessment, because of the limited definition of the term in Section 111(b)(2)(B). Assessment costs may be significant in amount in view of the complexities of the Department of Interior's damage assessment procedures.[486.1]

One issue originally of concern was whether EPA would have to have approved the state's plan for resource remediation as a prerequisite to filing a Section 112 claim. In *New Jersey v. Ruckelshaus*,[487] the court ruled that EPA preauthorization was not a prerequisite.

EPA's claims procedure regulations, which are effective as to claims filed as of March 13, 1986, however, require preauthorization in all but limited specified emergency situations.[487.1]

[c] Other Limitations

Section 111(d)(2) specifically prohibits the payment of any claim predicated on "long-term exposure to ambient concentrations of air pollutants from multiple diffuse sources." This provision is intended to bar "acid rain"–related claims.

Fund monies may be expended only for specified remedial activities at federal facilities, which essentially prohibits actual site cleanup costs at federal installations to be borne by the Fund.[488]

A 1986 amendment to Section 111(e)(3) qualified this prohibition, by allowing Fund monies to be used for the purpose of providing an alternative water supply where groundwater contamination outside the boundaries of a federal facility has resulted from the activities of more entities than just the facility.

EPA is prohibited from implementing a partial payment scheme where available funds are limited. Claims are required to be paid in full

---

[486] *See* Section 6.06[3], *supra*.

[486.1] For discussion of these procedures, *see* Section 6.06[3], *supra*.

[487] CA No. 84-1668 (JWB) (D.N.J. 12-12-84).

[487.1] *See* 40 CFR §306.22, 50 Fed. Reg. 51217 (12-13-85). Further protection against double recovery was provided by Section 112(f)(1986).

[488] Section 111(e)(3).

or not processed at all until funds are available.[489]

Finally, Fund monies may not be spent to remedy problems emanating from RCRA-regulated TSD facilities that have been closed in accordance with subtitle C requirements and maintained under the postclosure regulations.[490] Any such response costs must be borne by the postclosure liability fund established by Section 231 of CERCLA.

[3] State Programs

Section 111(f) authorizes delegation of authority to obligate Fund monies and settle claims to states that have entered into cooperative agreements under Section 104(d). EPA has not aggressively sought to delegate such authority.

[4] Claims Procedures

[a] Presentation

Section 112(a) of CERCLA makes presentation of a claim to the "owner or operator, or guarantor of the owner or operator of the vessel or facility from which a hazardous substance has been released, if known to the claimant," and to any other person potentially liable under Section 107 a prerequisite to making a claim against the Fund.

Sixty days following such presentation of the claim, the claimant may present the claim to the Fund for payment, which will then be considered unless the claimant is involved in a pending court action with respect to the subject matter of the claim.[491]

EPA's claims procedures, compiled at 40 CFR Part 306, require that claims be preauthorized, in terms of how the Fund monies will be spent, except that preauthorization is not required for situations requiring immediate action to avoid a substantial loss of evidence, to avoid irreversible loss of a resource, or to prevent or rescue from continuing

---

[489] Section 111(e)(1).

[490] Section 111(j). Section 201 of P.L. 99-499, however, barred the use of this fund until further action of Congress.

[491] The wording of this provision was amended in 1986 to add the last-mentioned limitation, and to eliminate an ambiguity that had been the subject of litigation. *See* State of Colorado v. Asarco, Inc., 608 F. Supp. 1484 (D. Colo. 1985).

danger to the resource.[491.1] The claims procedures are straightforward, and are set forth, along with applicable forms, in Appendix 6-E, *infra*. The claims procedures were developed under the 1980 version of Section 112. Significant amendments, discussed below, required changes.

[b] Decisionmaking Procedures

Claimants who elect to file a claim are required to use forms and follow procedures prescribed by the President,[492] which must include a sworn verification of the claim.[493]

The original CERCLA contained an elaborate compulsory negotiation and binding arbitration scheme for third party claims for remedial costs and natural resource damage claims.[494] Section 112(b) of the Superfund Amendments and Reauthorization Act of 1986 (P.L. 99-499, or SARA) eliminated those procedures and replaced them with a simple process that provides for an initial decision on eligibility and the amount of the award and an opportunity for an "administrative hearing" followed by judicial review.[495]

Under the amended claims procedures, an initial decision to accept or reject all or part of the claim is made by EPA,[496] which has no authority to accept a claim or a portion thereof as to whose costs a "judicial judgment" has been rendered.[497]

To the extent a claim is denied, the claimant may, within thirty days of receiving notice of the denial, seek an administrative hearing.[498] Section 112 hearings appear to be intended to be adjudications, before an administrative law judge.[499] The burden of proof in such hearings is on the claimant.[500]

[491.1] *See* 40 CFR §§306.22 and 306.23.

[492] EPA's forms are reproduced in Appendix 6-E, *infra*. They were issued on December 13, 1985. *See* 50 Fed. Reg. 51220.

[493] Section 112(b)(1). A specific criminal penalty is provided for knowing false statements.

[494] Sections 112(b)(1)-(b)(4) (1980).

[495] *See generally* Sections 112(b)(1)-(b)(6) (1986).

[496] It is assumed that the President will delegate claim management to EPA.

[497] Section 112(b)(2).

[498] *Id*.

[499] *See* Section 112(b)(4).

[500] Section 112(b)(3).

There are mandatory time limits imposed on the hearing process, and the claimant is given the right to seek judicial review in the federal district court for the district where the release or threat took place, though the standard of review is the highly deferential "arbitrary and capricious" standard.[501]

[c] Subrogation

Payment of a claim by the Fund results in subrogation to the United States of the claimant's rights against potentially responsible parties.[502] The government may seek interest, attorneys' fees and other "adjudicative costs" and administrative costs in any subrogation action. Presumably the government could recover its entire Section 112–related costs in addition to the amounts paid to the claimant.

[d] Statute of Limitation

Claims against the Fund were, under the original CERCLA, barred unless "presented . . . within three years from the date of discovery of the loss" or the date of CERCLA's enactment,[503] whichever was later.[504]

The statute of limitation was rewritten in 1986. The amended statute bars claims for recovery of response costs after six years following the "date of completion of all response action."[505] Natural resource damage claims must be presented within the later of three years following discovery of the loss "and its connection with the release in question"

---

[501] Section 112(b)(5). Appeals must be perfected within thirty days. The statute does not state unequivocally that appeal is on the administrative record. It does state, however, and rather laconically, that the "decision shall be considered binding and conclusive."

[502] Section 112(c)(1). Section 112(c)(2) also provides a general subrogation right to "any person . . . who pays compensation pursuant to the Act to any claimant for damages or costs resulting from a release . . ." to any rights possessed by the claimant. This provision would arguably give a generator group that paid the government a cause of action against other generators or other responsible parties.

[503] December 11, 1980.

[504] Section 112(d) 1980.

[505] Section 112(d)(1) (1986). It is unclear whether the term "response action" encompasses operation and maintenance activities, which could extend thirty years.

or the date on which final Section 310(c) regulations are promulgated.[506]

§6.09 Issues of Administration and Litigation Under CERCLA

[1] Judicial Review and General Litigation-Related Matters

[a] Judicial Review

Review of any "regulation" promulgated under CERCLA is exclusively by the District of Columbia Circuit on petitions filed within ninety days of the promulgation date.[507] Matters with respect to which review "could have been obtained" may not be raised collaterally in an enforcement action or a Section 107 cost recovery action.

The National Contingency Plan is a "regulation," as is the National Priority List, which Section 105(a)(8) requires to be a part of the NCP.

Other disputes, which are primarily enforcement actions, Section 107 cost recovery actions, and preenforcement review actions, must be filed in the U. S. district court for the district in which the "release or damages occurred" or in which the "defendant resides, may be found, or has his principal Office."[508] There is no monetary jurisdictional requirement.

[b] Contribution and Other Matters Involving Litigation

Section 113 was expanded in 1986 to address some important issues that had arisen in litigation under Sections 106 and 107, under the old CERCLA.

Section 113(e) expressly provides for nationwide service of process in any actions brought under CERCLA by the United States. This provision was necessary because a number of courts had concluded that the

---

[506] Section 112(d)(2). There is a tolling of the statute for minors and incompetents. The provision relating to the Section 301(c) regulations reopens a large number of claims barred under the old statute.

[507] Section 113(a). Disputes over the taxing provisions of Title II of CERCLA are excepted, and are governed by the procedural provisions of the Internal Revenue Code. *See* Section 113(e).

[508] Section 113(b). The Fund "resides" in Washington, D.C. *Id.*

original language of CERCLA did not support nationwide service of process.[509]

An express cause of action for contribution is provided by Section 113(f) in connection with, or following, "any civil action under section 106 or under section 107." This provision also states that the contribution claim is a "matter of federal law" and provides that the federal courts may use "equitable factors" in allocating responsibility among the parties.[510]

The 1986 amendments to Section 113 also contain a number of provisions relating to preenforcement review of remedial decisions. These amendments are discussed in Section 6.07[2][a], *supra.*

Section 113(l) requires notice of all private CERCLA-based lawsuits to be provided to the Attorney General and to EPA; both must receive a copy of the complaint.

Finally, Section 113(i) gives a right of permissive intervention to interested persons with respect to any action brought under either CERCLA or RCRA.[510.1]

[c]   Statutes of Limitation

The 1980 CERCLA produced a good deal of confusion over statutes of limitation. The statute contained no statute of limitation directly applicable to cost recovery actions instituted under Section 107. It did, however, contain a statute applicable to claims asserted for reimbursement from the superfund.

The 1986 amendments to CERCLA contain specific statutes of limitation affecting cost recovery and contribution actions, natural resource damage actions, and several other types of CERCLA-premised actions.

Natural resource damage actions must be commenced within three

---

[509] The leading case is Violet v. Picillo, 613 F. Supp. 1563 (D.R.I. 1985). The Picillo Pig Farm wins the prize for the most CERCLA amendments spawned by one site. In addition to Section 113(e), Congress inserted a special provision in Section 121, applicable only to that site, requiring adoption of a more stringent state law remedy.

[510] Section 113(f)(1). *See also,* for a more detailed treatment, the discussion in Section 6.07[2][i], *supra,* and the discussion of settlement in Section 6.09[4][e], *infra.* As discussed therein, there is no right of contribution for nonsettling parties against persons who have settled with the government.

[510.1] The reference to RCRA is a curative amendment, which took care of a drafting omission in the 1984 RCRA amendments. Permissive intervention is distinguished from intervention as a matter of right in that the person seeking to intervene must demonstrate not only that he has an interest that could be affected by the outcome of the litigation but also that the interest will not be adequately represented by any other party.

years of the date of discovery of the alleged loss and its connection with the release involved,[510.2] except that actions involving sites listed on the NPL, federal facilities, or any other "vessel or facility at which remedial action . . . is otherwise scheduled" must be brought within three years of the date of completion of all remedial action (excluding "operation and maintenance" action).[510.3] Such actions may not be brought with respect to NPL and other CERCLA-involvement sites before completion of the RI/FS and issuance of the ROD (or, for federal facilities, entry of an interagency agreement as provided for in Section 120.[510.4]

Separate limitations are provided for Section 107(a) removal and remedial cost recovery actions. The time period for removal cost recovery actions is three years, which commences on the date of completion of removal action, or, in the case of "continued response action," six years, commencing on the date a "determination" is made under Section 104(c)(4) to waive the removal limits and pursue "continued response action."[510.5] For remedial cost recovery actions, the statute commences running on the date physical on-site construction of the remedial action is *initiated*.[510.6] A remedial cost recovery action may otherwise be brought "at any time after" such costs have been incurred.

510.2 Section 113(g)(1) (1986). There is also a saving provision that allows suits otherwise barred by the general provision to be commenced within three years of the promulgation of final Section 301(c) regulations.

510.3 The statute's reference to operation and maintenance action refers to Section 104(c)(6), which separates construction from operation and maintenance activities for federal funding purposes. The interface is not clear. Section 104(c)(6) essentially defines ten years' worth of groundwater monitoring and treatment as "remedial action" and such activity beyond the tenth year as "operation and maintenance." The legislative history does not elucidate whether the parenthetical reference in Section 113(g)(1) to "operation and maintenance" is intended to defer running of the statute in landfill/groundwater remediation cases until the expiration of the ten-year Section 104(c)(6) period or the end of on-site construction activities.

510.4 This limitation is applicable only to actions filed on or before the effective date of the 1986 amendments. There is also a requirement that the trustee provide sixty days' prior notice of suit to EPA and PRPs.

510.5 Section 113(g)(2)(A). There is an exception where remedial action is commenced within three years of the completion of removal activity, in which case a timely action for recovery of the remedial costs can include claims for recovery of the removal costs, which might otherwise have been barred. Section 113(g)(2)(B).

510.6 Section 113(g)(2)(B). There is also express authority for the commencement of an initial action resulting in a determination of liability, which is binding on subsequent follow-up collection actions. *Id.* This provision, which authorizes such subsequent collection actions to be brought up to three years after the "completion of all response action," suffers from the same ambiguity as does the natural resource damages statute of limitation —whether the "completion of all response action" occurs at the completion of on-site construction, after the ten-year Section 104(c)(6) "remedial O&M" period, or after the completion of all O&M activities.

Contribution actions must be commenced within three years of the date of judgment rendered in a cost recovery or natural resource damage action, or the date of entry or judicial approval (where invoked) of an administrative order entered pursuant to Section 122 with respect to cost recovery or natural resource damages.[510.7]

There are, finally, special limitation periods for subrogation actions arising from claims paid out under Sections 111 and 112[510.8] and for actions to recover contractor indemnification payments under Section 107 pursuant to arrangements made under Section 119 with a contractor.[510.9]

There are special tolling provisions for minors and incompetents.[510.10]

[2] Financial Responsibility Requirements

CERCLA originally mimicked the financial responsibility requirements for vessels and offshore facilities created by Section 311 of the Clean Water Act. The statute was amended in 1986 to address the problems posed by incineration vessels.[511]

[510.7] Section 113(g)(3).

[510.8] Section 113(g)(4).

[510.9] Section 113(g)(5).

[510.10] Section 113(g)(6). The statute begins to run, for minors, at age 18 or on the date that a legal representative is appointed, and, for incompetents, when the incompetency ends or a legal representative is appointed.

[511] Section 108(a) provides:

(a)(1) The owner or operator of each vessel (except a non self-propelled barge that does not carry hazardous substances as cargo) over three hundred gross tons that uses any port or place in the United States or the navigable waters or any offshore facility, shall establish and maintain, in accordance with regulations promulgated by the President, evidence of financial responsibility of $300 per gross ton (or for a vessel carrying hazardous substances as cargo, or $5,000,000, whichever is greater) **to cover the liability prescribed under paragraph (1) of Section 107(a) of this Act.** Financial responsibility may be established by any one, or any combination, of the following: insurance, guarantee, surety bond, or qualification as a self-insurer. Any bond filed shall be issued by a bonding company authorized to do business in the United States. In cases where an owner or operator owns, operates, or charters more than one vessel subject to this subsection, evidence of financial responsibility need be established only to meed maximum liability applicable to the largest of such vessels.

(2) The Secretary of the Treasury shall withhold or revoke the clearance required by Section 4197 of the Revised Statutes of the United States of any vessel subject to this subsection that does not have certification furnished by the President that the financial responsibility provisions of paragraph (1) of this subsection have been complied with.

For other facilities, some are governed by the financial responsibility requirements of RCRA, and others are subject to special financial responsibility requirements that were originally to be established by the end of 1985.[512] Those requirements are to be developed for "classes of facilities" and be "consistent with the degree and duration of risk associated with the production, transportation, treatment, storage, or disposal of hazardous substances,"[513] with those classes exhibiting the highest degree of risk (in the government's opinion) addressed first.

The slow schedule, which is subject to phasing in,[514] is intended to allow development by the insurance industry of appropriate insurance coverage.

The insurance industry did not respond positively to the financial responsibility encouragement of Section 108. Section 108(b) was amended in 1986 by the addition of a list of financial responsibility devices that could be utilized[515] and the addition of language providing express authority for the specification of insurance policy or other contractual terms, "conditions, or defenses which are necessary, or which are unacceptable, in establishing . . . evidence of financial responsibility."

Congress also addressed the problem of insurance by enacting in 1986 a new subtitle of CERCLA, Title IV, which it called "Pollution

---

(3) The Secretary of Transportation, in accordance with regulations issued by him, shall (A) deny entry to any port or place in the United States or navigable waters to, and (B) detain at the port or place in the United States from which it is about to depart for any other port or place in the United States, any vessel subject to this subsection that, upon request, does not produce certification furnished by the President that the financial responsibility provisions of paragraph (1) of this subsection have been complied with.

(4) In addition to the financial responsibility provisions of paragraph (1) of this subsection, the President shall require additional evidence of financial responsibility for incineration vessels in such amounts, and to cover such liabilities recognized by law, as the President deems appropriate, taking into account the potential risks posed by incineration and transport for incineration, and any other factors deemed appropriate.

Language added in 1986 is boldface.

[512] Section 108(b)(1). Motor carriers are governed by Motor Carrier Act of 1980, P.L.96-296.

[513] *Id.* Section 109 establishes a penalty for noncompliance.

[514] Sections 108(b)(2) and (b)(3). The phase-in was amended in 1986 to "in no event more than 4 years."

[515] These include insurance, guarantees, surety bonds, letters of credit, and self-insurance.

Insurance."[515.1] These provisions seek to preempt state insurance law prohibitions against self-insurance pools by allowing the formation of "risk retention groups" formed under any single state law to operate in all states regardless of state laws or regulations prohibiting or proscribing such activity. The statute also legitimizes special insurance deals for "purchasing groups," effectively insulating self-selecting risk groups from the widely employed limitations on group insurance found in insurance regulatory laws.

Sections 108(c) and 109(d) relate to guarantors. Guarantors of financial responsibility of vessels are liable directly to a Section 107 or Section 111 claimant, subject to any defense to the underlying liability that might be available to the vessel owner or operator. In such a suit, the guarantor may not invoke against the third party claimant any technical defenses that could be raised vis-à-vis the insured, except for a defense that the incident was caused by the "willful misconduct" of the insured.[515.2]

In the case of guarantors of the financial responsibility of a facility, a direct action may be brought against such a guarantor by a Section 107 or Section 111 claimant only if the liable entity is "in bankruptcy, reorganization, or arrangement" under the federal bankruptcy code or is one over whom federal court jurisdiction cannot "with reasonable diligence" be obtained so that judgment can be entered while the entity is solvent.[515.3] In such a suit, the guarantor may raise any Section 107 defenses available to the liable entity, and may invoke "all rights and defenses that would have been available to the guarantor" if an action had been brought against him by the insured.[515.4]

The total liability of any guarantor in a direct action suit is limited, however, to the aggregate amount of the monetary limits of the instrument creating the obligation, unless some other provision of law provides for the expansion of such liability.[515.5]

Whether these provisions will help alleviate the "insurance crisis" remains to be seen. In the meantime, litigation between PRPs and insurors has been frequent and acrimonious. One notable case, which

---

[515.1] Sections 401-405 (1986).

[515.2] Section 108(c)(1).

[515.3] Section 108(b)(2).

[515.4] Id.

[515.5] Sections 108(d)(1), 108(d)(2). For example, Section 108(d)(2) suggests that bad faith in refusal to negotiate a settlement might be a basis for imposing liability above the policy limits.

exemplifies the nature of the ongoing litigation, *Maryland Casualty Co. v. Armco, Inc.*,[515.6] held that an insurer's liability for its insured's "damages" includes only damages at law (that is, for which a jury trial is available), and thus would not include coverage of CERCLA-based cleanup costs, which EPA has successfully established in other litigation to be in the nature of restitution.

[3] Bankruptcy of a PRP

The Supreme Court, in *Ohio v. William Lee Kovacs, a/k/a B&W Enterprise, et al.*,[516] addressed the question of how state hazardous waste site cleanup action is affected by the site owner/operator's bankruptcy. Ohio had obtained an injunction against Kovacs and others that required them to clean up the Chem Dyne site in Hamilton, Ohio. When Kovacs *et al.* failed to carry out the state court order, the state secured the appointment of a receiver, whose charge was to take possession of the terms of the original order. Before the receiver did very much, Kovacs filed a personal bankruptcy petition, and sought to avoid the obligation imposed by the injunction as a dischargeable debt under the Bankruptcy Code.

The Court held that, on the facts of the case, the injunction, as modified by the appointment of the receiver, was a "debt" or "liability on a claim," dischargeable under Section 727(b) of the Bankruptcy Code.[517] It became such, the Court reasoned, at the point the receiver was appointed. At that point, what had begun as an action to enforce the state's environmental laws[518] became an obligation to collect money.

The Court stated that bankruptcy will not shield the bankrupt from criminal prosecution for violating environmental laws or from criminal contempt for not performing the obligations imposed by the injunction prior to bankruptcy. In addition, the Court made it clear that bankruptcy will not nullify the obligation to pay a fine or civil penalty imposed prior to bankruptcy.

515.6 — F. Supp. —, Civil No. Y-85-1396 (D. Md. 9-8-86).

516 105 S.Ct. 705, 83 L.Ed.2d 649 (1985).

517 11 USC S727(b).

518 *See* Penn Terra Ltd. v. Dept. of Environmental Resources, 733 F.2d 267 (3d Cir. 1984) *cited approvingly by the court in Kovacs,* 105 S.Ct. 705, 83 L.Ed.2d at 658, n.11, for the proposition that the automatic stay provision of Section 362 of the Bankruptcy Code does not apply to injunctive actions brought to enforce state environmental laws.

As to the probable outcome if Kovacs had filed prior to appointment of the receiver and a trustee had been designated under Section 541 of the Bankruptcy Code, the Court suggests alternative scenarios. Either the trustee would sell the property "and the buyer would clean up the property," or, if the property were of "no value to the estate," the trustee would "abandon it to its prior owner" under Section 554(c), "who would have to comply with the state environmental law to the extent of his or her ability."[519] Unfortunately, however, the Court's neat logic sags under the stress of reality. It is unlikely that many buyers will be willing to purchase old waste sites along with liabilities of an unascertained amount.[520] As for the bankrupt, since the bottom line is ability to pay, the inquiry ends.

Finally, the Court sought to reassure the government that the environmental laws could still be enforced, although its reassurance would no doubt not warm the cockles of the hazardous waste regulators' collective hearts. The Court stated that negative injunctions are not barred or discharged. However, the opinion fairly clearly also states that a mandatory injunction that imposes an "affirmative duty to clean up the site and the duty to pay money to that end" is dischargeable. In most CERCLA cases, a negative injunction is not worth much.

The Court addressed the interface between bankruptcy and hazardous substance site remediation again in *Midlantic Nat'l Bank v. New Jersey* and *O'Neill v. City of New York*.[521] In a divided decision, it held that a bankruptcy trustee may not abandon a contaminated site and thereby avoid state superfund obligations "reasonably calculated to protect the public health or safety from imminent and identifiable harm." The Court did not address whether the trustee's obligation extended to complete site remediation or only to the extent of elimination of imminent hazards, although the latter seems implicit in the Court's opinion.[521.1]

---

[519] 105 S.Ct. 705, 83 L.Ed. 2d at 659 n.12.

[520] EPA, for example, had its own view of what should be done at the Chem Dyne site, and its view was quite different from Ohio's.

[521] Nos. 84-801 and 85-805, 54 L.W. 4138 (1-27-86). *See also* discussion at Section 5.10[8], *supra.*

[521.1] In the first follow-up case to *Midlantic Bank*, a bankruptcy judge in Minnesota permitted the trustee in In re Franklin Signal Corp, —N.R.—, 25 ERC (BNA) 1001 (Bkrptcy. D. Minn. 9-29-86) to abandon fourteen drums of hazardous waste, finding remaining assets to be insufficient. Reading *Midlantic Bank* liberally, essentially siding with Justice Rehnquist's dissenting opinion, the judge concluded that abandonment was appropriate where the trustee had given notice of his intention to the authorities, the

A related, and no less significant issue, which the Supreme Court expressly declined to address in *Midlantic Bank,* is whether CER-CLA-based response costs are entitled to any priority in bankruptcy distribution under Section 503(b) of the Bankruptcy Code.[521.2] The precise issue is whether the statutory obligation to pay for remedial or removal action is an "actual or necessary" cost or expense of "preserving the estate" of a debtor owner or operator who is a CERCLA responsible party,[521.3] giving rise to administrative expense priority over unsecured creditors. There are conflicting decisions.

The bankruptcy court in *In re T.P. Long Chemical, Inc.*[521.4] concluded that such costs, claimed by EPA, should be accorded administrative priority. It reasoned that since "the estate cannot avoid the liability imposed by CERCLA, it follows that the cost incurred by the E.P.A. in discharging this liability is an actual necessary cost of preserving the estate. . . ."[521.5]

The opposite conclusion was reached by the court in *In re Wall Tube and Metal Products Company, Debtor.*[521.6] There, both the bankruptcy court and the district court concluded that the state's claim for CERCLA-based costs was not entitled to priority, opining that *T.P. Long* was contrary to both the language and the purpose of Section 503,[521.7] and rejecting arguments made by the state that the Supreme Court's *Midlantic Bank* decision compelled a different result.[521.8]

---

trustee had taken some steps to protect the public, and the wastes were not particularly dangerous. This approach rejects a *per se* reading of *Midlantic Bank,* which would result in a prohibition of abandonment whenever the hazardous waste was present in violation of state law, in favor of a reading that would prohibit abandonment in such a case only if, in addition, the wastes were posing a threat to public health.

521.2 11 USC §503(b).

521.3 The issue is less likely to be raised with respect to a generator PRP.

521.4 45 B.R. 278 (Bkrptcy. N.D. Ohio 1985).

521.5 *Id.* at 286.

521.6 56 B.R. 918 (Bkrptcy. E.D. Tenn. 1986), *aff'd,* — F. Supp. —, No. Civ-2-86-99 (E.D. Tenn., N.E. Div. 8-12-86).

521.7 The basic difference is in the breadth of each court's view of the provision. The court in *T.P. Long* read the statute broadly to encompass regulatory obligations as falling within the scope of the debtor's "business." The courts in *Wall Tube* chose to view the "business" of the debtor more narrowly to encompass only income-seeking activities.

521.8 The state argued that *Midlantic Bank* required one to view Section 959(b) of the Bankruptcy Code as requiring a liquidating trustee to assume the same duties and responsibilities under the environmental laws as those incumbent on any property owner, and that thus State response costs are a "necessary" expense of the debtor's business. The courts rejected this argument, taking the position that Section 959(b)'s duties apply only

So far there has been no reported judicial reaction to any efforts by states that have sought to take Justice O'Connor up on her suggestion in *Ohio v. Kovacs* that they utilize state law to structure their environmental claims in a manner that would afford them priority under the Bankruptcy Code, making them secured creditors or giving them lien status.[521.9]

[4] Litigation and Settlement of CERCLA Cases

[a] Overview

Shortly after CERCLA was enacted, the Environmental Enforcement Section of the Justice Department began to add Section 106 claims to the existing docket of RCRA Section 7003 "imminent hazard" cases, and to file new actions premised primarily on Section 106, in light of problems the Department had in convincing the judiciary that Section 7003 had retroactive applicability.

The Section 107 cases did not commence until EPA started to spend Fund monies in earnest under Section 104; thus, by the CERCLA "sunset" date,[522] the universe of CERCLA litigation remained relatively small. Nevertheless, some generalizations can be drawn.

[b] Prelitigation Information Gathering

Typically EPA utilizes the information-gathering provisions of RCRA[523] as well as Section 104(e) as the basis for sending interrogatory letters to potentially responsible parties, in which the Agency requests copies of documents relating to waste shipment to the priority list site at issue. If the owner/operator is known and has records, those records are used to find the transporters, whose records are in turn used to help determine the identity of the generators whose waste went to the site. Physical examination of drums for labels or other indicia of origin also contributes to the initial information-gathering process.

---

to trustees and debtors in possession who are operating the business of the debtor, not to liquidating trustees, and refused to extend the *Midlantic Bank* analogy beyond its express facts.

[521.9] 469 U.S. —, 105 S. Ct. 705, 83 L.Ed. 2d 649, 660 (1985) (concurring opinion).

[522] September 30, 1985.

[523] Sections 3007 and 3013. *But see* E.I. DuPont de Nemours & Co. v. Daggett, 610 F. Supp. 260 (W.D.N.Y. 1985) (preenforcement review of a RCRA Section 3013 order might be appropriate where the order was not predicated on the existence of an imminent and substantial endangerment).

On the basis of the physical inspection,[524] review of the owner/ operator and transporter records, and review of the generator responses, EPA has occasionally ranked the generators according to its assessment of their respective volumes of waste contributed, although until the 1986 amendments, it had no clear authority to spend superfund money to do so.[524.1] The Agency consistently rejected suggestions that the ranking should be based in part on the degree of hazard presented by the waste, and that has remained an important unresolved issue under CERCLA.[524.2] The rankings are normally computer generated and are called "waste-in lists." In later cases EPA developed two lists, one that includes only liquid waste and one that converts solid waste and sludge into liquid waste equivalents.[525] A generator whose waste was primarily solid will obviously be ranked differently depending on which method is used.

Since many priority list sites ceased active use many years before the CERCLA investigatory process began, the waste-in lists may be based in great measure on assumptions, estimates, and guesses.[526] Though in many cases these lists will be erroneous, proof of the error may be very difficult for a contributor to make. In the more common case, EPA's preliminary assessment contractor, or RI/FS contractor, does nothing more than compile a list of potentially responsible parties on the basis

---

[524] This is usually done by EPA's contractor rather than by employees of the Agency. The inspection also involves some sampling and analysis of the contents of intact and leaking drums and contaminated soil and groundwater. EPA has occasionally issued an order under Section 106(a) demanding entry onto the site. In the one reported case in which a site owner sought to enjoin EPA from executing such an order, the court opined that EPA's action, which resulted in the removal of waste material from the site, might constitute a deprivation of the owner's property without due process in the absence of a pre- or postaction hearing, although the court denied a remedy on the facts because of the absence of a showing of harm. Industrial Park Development Co. v. EPA, 604 F. Supp. 1136 (E.D. Pa. 1985). As noted heretofore, the Section 104(e) information-gathering provisions were broadened significantly in 1986.

[524.1] *See* discussion of Section 122 (1986), *infra*, for EPA's post-1986 authority.

[524.2] Degree of toxicity was recognized for the first time as relevant, in Section 122(g), which provides for "de minimus" settlements in situations where both the volume and toxicity of a contributor's substances are minimal in comparison with other material at the site.

[525] EPA converts 1 cubic yard into a 202-gallon equivalent.

[526] Ohio State and EPA estimates of the number of drums of waste contributed to the Chem Dyne site in Hamilton, Ohio, by individual generators varied, for example, in some cases by factors of from two to ten.

of rather unreliable evidence.[526.1] Much attention thus must be paid by organized PRP groups to the development of an allocation process that uses the available evidence as fairly as possible. Allocation agreements are discussed further in Section 6.09[4][e], *infra*.

[c] Demand and Prelitigation Response

Usually no earlier than completion of the preliminary assessment, and no later than completion of the RI/FS, EPA ordinarily would send a form letter to all contributors (generators and transporters) apprising them of its activity at the site, its expenditures to date,[527] and, if it had the information, the anticipated response costs. The letter would invite the parties to confer and to propose a private response scheme. As is discussed in some of the provisions that follow, Section 122 (1986) radically altered and severely bureaucratized EPA's preliminary overtures to PRPs.

If the number of generators is large, EPA will internally divide the group into two or more subgroups, and will put the "major contributors" subgroup on a Section 107 litigation track. The cutoff between "major" generators and others will, of course, vary in terms of volume from case to case. Also when the number of generators is large, EPA requests that the contributors organize themselves into committees, in order to minimize confusion in the negotiating process.

The natural subgroupings for committee formation, based on commonality of interest, are (1) owner/operator group (if such are available), (2) major contributor group, and (3) minor contributor group.[528] The major and minor contributors will frequently meet as one group prior to the commencement of the Section 107 legal action, and form a joint steering committee to regulate with the owner/operator group and/or the government, and determine recommendations for strategic planning. A large steering committee may contain various subcommittees.

[526.1] In the case of the Beacon Heights Landfill site, for example, the PRP list was derived, as stated in the FIT report, from such evidence as hearsay recollections of state officials.

[527] Determining the veracity of EPA's expenditures usually requires entering into a confidentiality agreement with EPA, since the Agency's contractors almost uniformly claim Privacy Act (5 USC §552 (a)) protection for their bid documents.

[528] The origin of the committee organization was the early multidefendant imminent hazard litigation, which is typified by the Chem Dyne litigation, Ohio, et al. v. Rohm and Haas Company, et al., No. C-1-82-962 (S.D. Ohio).

The primary responsive activities following notification and prior to trial are (1) assembling information in possession of the government or other willing parties, (2) undertaking monitoring and analysis and/or reviewing the government's work,[529] (3) negotiating the parties' contributions to the response costs, (4) if litigation appears inevitable, selection of liaison counsel for each subgroup, and (5) negotiating all allocation formulas.

Selection of liaison counsel can be a delicate matter. Liaison counsel should, ideally, be an experienced trial lawyer in the district wherein the litigation will be situated and should not, in the absence of clear waiver of conflict of interest concerns by all parties, represent any of the defendants either in the matter or generally. While the potential for conflict of interest is much greater where the steering committee is joint, representing both major and minor contributors, at some point the interests even of the various major contributors may diverge.[529.1]

Liaison counsel's role must be carefully defined, as must be the lines of communication with the contributor group. Frequently a litigation steering subcommittee is established for the purpose of guiding liaison counsel's activities.

[d] Litigation

Few of the major Section 107 cases filed between 1981 and 1985 had been tried and decided by the "sunset" date of CERCLA.[530] As is the case with any complex multiparty litigation, the cases involved extensive pretrial motions and discovery. One interesting threshold matter involves service of process. CERCLA's original text contained no personal jurisdiction provision. This was a potential problem for private and state plaintiffs, since in the absence of an explicit provision providing for nationwide service of process, it may be impossible to secure jurisdiction over out-of-state PRPs.[531] The problem was partially addressed in the 1986 amendments to CERCLA with the addition of

---

[529] This activity essentially involves funding and selecting a consultant.

[529.1] This problem can be minimized, however, by the adoption of a carefully drafted alternative dispute resolution agreement. *See* Appendix 6I, *infra*.

[530] There have, of course, been a number of settlements.

[531] *See* Violet v. Picillo, 613 F. Supp. 1563 (D.R.I. 8-1-85) (holding that there is no such provision); and United States v. Bliss, 23 ERC 1638 (E.D. Mo. 1985) (holding that Section 106 implies authority for nationwide service of process but Section 107 does not). The case law discussed in this chapter, *supra*, is largely a product of pretrial actions.

Section 113(e), which specifically provides for nationwide service of process in actions by the United States. It thus appears that nationwide service of process is available to EPA (and to its defendants who bring third party contribution claims) in Section 107 actions brought by EPA, but is not available to state plaintiffs or to settling parties who bring independent contribution actions against nonsettling parties. The most expensive cases are those in which the government has sued only the major contributors and the site owner, and third party contribution actions have been filed against the minor contributors, who have counter- and cross-claimed.[532]

One important litigation matter is the order of presentation of the case. Virtually all hazardous waste cases present several factual issues: (1) the kinds of substances present at the site, (2) the amount of hazardous material at the site, (3) the nature of the release involved, (4) proof that each of the defendants meets the Section 107 criteria for liability,[533] (4) whether joint and several liability is appropriate, which turns on the question of whether the harm is divisible,[534] (5) the costs or damages that have been incurred by the plaintiffs, or, in the event the site has not yet been cleaned up, the sort of remedial action that will be necessary,[535] and (6) whether joint and several liability has been imposed, or, if contribution is sought by third party actions or cross-claims as part of the main action, instead of in a separate action, how liability is to be apportioned.

[i] Issues of Proof

The proof required in order to determine what wastes are present at the site is relatively straightforward, though expensive to put to-

---

[532] In the *Chem Dyne* litigation, for example, twenty-three of the major contributor defendants entered into a settlement with the government, and then brought third party actions for contribution against the remaining original defendants and several hundred minor contributors who had not been named as defendants in the underlying action.

[533] *United States* v. *Chem Dyne Corp.*, 572 F. Supp. 802 (S.D. Ohio 1983). The government has successfully argued that the divisibility issue is a defense, the burden of going forward and proof as to which is borne by each defendant. If a sufficient showing of divisibility is made, then the burden shifts to the government to prove each defendant's share of the liability. If not, each defendant is liable for the entire harm. *Id.* in the latter event, it is up to the defendants to apportion the damages among themselves.

[534] Collectively, these can be termed the "liability" issue.

[535] This can be termed the "remedy" issue.

gether.[536] Proof of the volume of the chemicals present involves use of available records, obtained through administrative process or discovery, as well as physical sampling and analysis. Obviously the accuracy of volumetric assessments lessens with the degree of leaking and off-site migration that has occurred. Proof of what has been released, or is likely to be released, is also relatively straightforward, although to the extent that the remedial option of choice must be dependent upon proof of migration routes and rates, large gaps present in hydrogeological knowledge create a significant degree of uncertainty, which is difficult for the courts to address.

"Weathering," or degradation, and other alterations in chemical structure that occur when chemical wastes are released into the environment or commingled with other, reactive chemicals can make the proof of "what" and "how much" very difficult. Although some chemcials maintain their structural integrity reasonably well in the groundwater,[537] others do not.[538] In addition, a determination of long-term risk often requires an assessment of the direction and rate of migration vis-à-vis human habitation. In areas of complex geology, such assessments are prone to uncertainty.

Although EPA, as a settlement position, has generally refused to develop cost-sharing formulas based on toxicity or other indications of hazard, some federal judges have indicated that they consider toxicity a relevant matter for a defendant to raise at trial.

The extent to which CERCLA cases that go to trial will involve a "battle of experts" over the issues of the degree of risk or the appropriate remedial level very much depends upon the degree of deference accorded to EPA's remedial plan and order of decision implementing it. The tendency among trial judges has been to give rather substantial

---

[536] This information is usually developed as part of the RI/FS. Arguably the contents of every container present should be sampled and analysed for the full spectrum of known hazardous substances, since labels, particularly those that predate the RCRA subtitle C regulatory program, are often incomplete, and might be misleading, or false. Soil and groundwater samples, though less numerous, require more sophisticated preparation prior to analysis.

[537] Chlorinated solvents, which are among the more common substances that escape from landfills, for example, are relatively easily detectable.

[538] Petroleum, for example, readily degrades into its fractions. Although in the case of petroleum, the presence of certain fractions, such as benzene, toluene and xylene in certain percentages is indicative of petroleum, each of those materials could be contributed from other sources as well.

deference to the Agency on these matters,[539] and thus the burden on the defendants to overcome EPA's plan is rather heavy. The PRPs must be able to show that EPA's action is inconsistent with the NCP,[540] and, subsequent to the 1986 amendments, arbitrary and capricious.

[ii] Order of Proceedings

Even more so than would be expected of complex litigation, the CERCLA cases have tended to move slowly. This has been attributable primarily to the large number of parties involved in most of the suits, and, in those cases EPA filed prior to completing its remedial plan, the time it has taken to do so.

Defendants have sometimes been successful in arguing bifurcation of Section 107 or Section 106/107 cases, with the issue of remedy addressed first. Although this may seem to put the proverbial cart before the horse, bifurcation in this matter accomplishes two potentially salutary functions. First, knowing the extent of remedy is almost a prerequisite to settlement.[541] Second, information required for the remedial plan can be useful for determining whether the harm is divisible, thus affecting the liability of some parties.

Other bifurcation schemes have been proposed or attempted. The liability issue might be tried first. Where surface cleanup is relatively straightforward and the chemicals at the surface are different from those that have contaminated the groundwater, bifurcation of surface and subsurface issues might make sense. In all events, such matters lie almost wholly within the trial judge's discretion.

---

[539] *See generally,* on the subject of judicial deference to EPA, Stever, *Deference to Administrative Agencies in Federal Environmental, Health and Safety Litigation— Thoughts on Varying Judicial Interpretations of the Rule,* 6 W.N.E.L.Rev. 35 (1983); and Scalia, *Responsibilities of Regulatory Agencies,* —Houston Law Review— (December, 1986).

[540] The success of such a defense, of course, also depends upon what is contained in the NCP.

[541] The *Love Canal* litigation presents a classic case of what happens when a case is "settled" before the scope of remedy is established. The parties settled one of the *Love Canal* cases (United States v. Hooker Chemicals & Plastics Corp., No. CV-79-989C) by agreeing to an elaborate mechanism for site evaluation and remedial plan development at Hooker's expense, essentially leaving for a later day the hard decisions. United States v. Hooker, 540 F. Supp, 1067 (W.D.N.Y. 1982). Three years later the parties (which included the State of New York and a local interest group) were still haggling over the remedial plan, and the district judge had been required to issue fourteen supplemental orders. In a November 28, 1984, order, the judge chided the parties for their squabbling, stating that "the delay caused by continued disagreement is harmful to the citizens of this State."

When the trial must await completion of the remedial plan, the attendant delay in the proceedings can be frustrating to the judge, particularly if the government has alleged that an imminent hazard exists. The delay factor in these cases has motivated many of the judges to attempt to impose rigid motion and discovery deadlines on the parties in an effort to either force settlement or bring the cases to trial.

[iii]   Cases Not Involving a Waste Disposal Site

The government faces somewhat more difficult problems of proof of causation where the priority list site is not a treatment, storage, or disposal site. An example of such a case might be water supply aquifer contamination by diverse off-site sources.[542]

Instead of simply having to show that the generator defendant's waste is of the type found at the site and there is a nexus between the generator and the site, in this type of case the government must be able to prove a hydrological connection between the off-site defendant's waste and the contamination. This is the sort of issue upon which reasonable experts might well disagree vigorously, and EPA may in such cases be vulnerable to charges that its RI/FS did not adequately sample the surrounding area in order to locate all potentially responsible parties.

From a defendant's standpoint, the proof problems are also difficult. First, defendants are in the position of having to prove that EPA's RI/FS is inconsistent with the NCP. Unless they have their own comprehensive remedial study, they will probably be unable to make such a showing, and many of the incentives that push waste site generators into common cost sharing are not applicable in the diverse site cases. The most obvious of these, of course, is the absence of an easy cost allocation formula, such as one based on "waste-in."[543]

By the time the contamination at a well field becomes apparent, it may have been ten or more years since the contaminants were placed in the environment at a site a mile or more away, depending upon the properties of the substance and the rate and direction of groundwater. Moreover, subsequent operators of the facility may have contributed similar, or other chemicals that are still "in the pipeline."

---

[542] *E.g.*, Kellogg-Deering Wellfield Superfund Site, Norwalk, Connecticut.

[543] Diverse source contamination cases usually result from periodic spills of hazardous substances at plant sites, over a series of years, where a given plant may have had a number of unrelated owners, some of whom used the chemicals at issue. Under such circumstances, development of a realistic allocation formula is impossible.

[e] Settlement

[i] In General—Dominant Issues and Pre-1986 Litigation

Three issues tend to dominate final resolution of most Section 107/ 106 cases: (1) what degree of cleanup is acceptable to all parties, (2) what sort of release or other protection against future claims will be provided, and (3) what will be the formula utilized to allocate shares of liability among the defendants. Inability of all of the parties to agree on one or more of these issues has been, and continues to be, an impediment to settlement of CERCLA cases.[544]

The level of cleanup problem is in part a product of EPA's initial failure to place firm standards in the NCP, although even firm standards in the NCP will not insulate state or private plaintiffs or intervenors from arguing for a strict level of cleanup.[545] This problem would not be solved by amendments to the NCP establishing clearer guidelines for determining acceptable residual levels of specific contaminants, since under CERCLA the state remains free to demand compliance with its own standards under applicable provisions of state law. Even if the state is brought into the litigation as a party, the state officials may feel it politically impossible to agree to a remedial plan that is acceptable to EPA but leaves in the environment levels of contamination that exceed state guidelines or, in the absence of such guidelines, that are detectable.

Settlement may be attractive to some parties and not to others. The government's settlement policy encourages settlements by groups of settlement-minded defendants, and, as discussed *infra*, in order to encourage such settlements the government is willing to give settling parties releases, the purpose of which is to insulate the settling group from additional liability arising out of contribution claims made by nonsettling parties later in the litigation.

These settlements, in which the settling defendants pay a fixed sum that covers a percentage of the remedial costs, leaving the government to go after the B list and nonsettling A list PRPs, present an interest-

---

[544] Most CERCLA cases have been filed prior to cleanup, and thus the parties are not simply agreeing to share costs already incurred. Indeed, since many sites require long-term groundwater pumping as a primary remedial activity, the fixed-cost CERCLA case is a rarity.

[545] One of the impediments to settlement of the *Chem Dyne* litigation is the inability of the United States to insulate the defendants from more onerous demands made later by the State of Ohio, or raised in connection with private common law actions.

ing issue of whether the settling defendants can really freeze their liability at the settlement figure, or whether they will be liable for additional sums in a subsequent cross-claim or other action for contribution brought by nonsettling parties.

Settling defendants, with the government understandably in support, argue that the consent decree represents a final adjudication of their liability, and acts to bar contribution claims against them. These parties urged the trial judges to adopt as rule of decision Section 4 of the Uniform Contribution Among Joint Tortfeasors Act (1955 Revision),[546] which provides that a covenant not to sue, given in good faith, discharges the tort-feasor to whom it is given from all liability for contribution from any other tort-feasor.[547] Under this scheme, subsequent awards against nonsettling defendants are reduced by the amount paid to the plaintiff by the settling defendant(s), and suits for contribution by the nonsettling group are barred.[548]

The concern articulated by nonsettlers about this scheme is that if the government and the settlers grossly underestimate the ultimate cost of cleanup, the nonsettlers could end up paying more than their fair share. They argued that either they should be entitled to seek contribution against the settlers for amounts awarded against the nonsettlers that are in excess of the settlement figure or, alternatively, the government should bear the excess costs.[549]

As is discussed below, Congress effectively codified The Uniform Contribution Among Joint Tortfeasors Act into CERCLA in amendments to Section 113 and the addition of Section 122 in 1986. In *United*

---

[546] This is an issuance of the National Conference of Commissioners on Uniform State Laws. *See* Wheeler v. Denton, 9 N.C. App. 167, 175 S.E.2d 769 (1970), applying the North Carolina version, N.C. Gen. Stat. sec. 1B-4, for an example of the application of this provision.

[547] *See*, for cases discussing the provision, Bishop v. Klein, 380 Mass. 285, 402 N.E.2d 1365 (1980); In re MGM Grand Hotel Litigation, 570 F. Supp. 913, 926-27 (D. Nev. 1983); Stambaugh v. Superior Court of Sonoma County, 62 Cal. App. 3d 231, 132 Cal. Rptr. 843 (1976); Mayhew v. Berrien County Road Comm., 414 Mich. 399, 326 N.W.2d 366 (1982).

[548] The most lucid discussion of this issue in a CERCLA case is contained in the report of the Special Master in United States v. Conservation Chemical Co., 628 F. Supp. 1985 (W.D. Mo.7-2-85). *See also* United States v. Wade, 14 ELR 20439 (E.D. Pa. 1983).

[549] There is support for this view in the joint and several liability scheme employed under the Securities Act of 1933. *See* Gould v. American-Hawaiian Steamship Co., 387 F. Supp. 163 (D.Del. 1974).

States v. Conservation Chemical Co.,[550] the court concluded that liability of nonsettling third parties in a contribution action is several, but not joint and several, thereby preventing the third party plaintiffs from recovering more than the defendant's equitable share of liability.[551] Section 113(f)(1) appears to embrace this conclusion.

Settlement of the surface cleanup portion of a TSD facility case may precede trial or settlement of the potentially more expensive groundwater portion,[552] although to the extent settlement is indicated to avoid litigation costs, such a settlement may be unattractive unless the government agrees to postpone the liability portion of the remainder of the case.

CERCLA settlements will ordinarily involve what are actually two separate sets of negotiations. The first is agreement between the government and the defendants collectively on their contribution to the remedial costs. The second, without which the first cannot occur, is negotiation among the defendants of a formula for allocating responsibility. There is no generally agreed-upon formula, although there is a basic issue: whether degree of toxicity should be a component of the allocation formula.

Even "simple" allocation formulas, predicated upon "waste-in" volumes, can be difficult to resolve. For example, often the wastes at the site are a mixture of liquids, solids, and semisolids. Volumetric computations obviously will vary depending upon how the solids and semisolids are measured.[553] Generators whose waste remained on the surface in solid form understandably would have no interest in contributing to groundwater cleanup costs.

One approach to the problem has been the development of elaborate "sharing agreements," an example of which may be found in Appendix 6I, *infra*. Such agreements can provide a system for developing an

---

[550] 628 F. Supp. 391 (W.D. Mo. 1985). For detailed discussion, *see* Section III of the report of the Special Master, appended thereto.

[551] Both the Uniform Contribution Among Joint Tortfeasors Act and the Uniform Comparative Fault Act, each of which has been relied upon by litigants in CERCLA cases, support this result.

[552] In *Chem Dyne* litigation, the settling defendants and the United States agreed on a surface cleanup scheme, and deferred the groundwater issue until completion of the RI/FS, leaving the settlers free to litigate against the nonsettlers and the minor generators for costs, in excess of the agreed amount, and for contribution.

[553] EPA has occasionally attempted to apply conversion factors to solids and sludges, converting solid measures into gallon equivalents.

allocation formula and dispute resolution provisions, along with a framework for managing the site through remedial action.

[ii] Government Settlement Policy Prior to the 1986 Amendments

EPA and the Department of Justice began following an "interim settlement policy" in all CERCLA and Section 7003 RCRA cases late in 1984.[554] The policy addressed how EPA will review private party cleanup proposals, develops internal negotiation guidelines, sets the ground rules for release of information in the government's possession to PRPs, establishes criteria for evaluation of settlement proposals, and sets forth the general ground rules under which the government will accept partial settlements, agree to consent decree provisions that protect settling defendants from increased liability resulting from subsequent third party contribution actions, or provide releases from liability.

Excerpts from the interim settlement guidelines are reproduced in Appendix 6-D, *infra*.

[iii] Settlement under Section 122 of the Superfund Amendments and Reauthorization Act of 1986 (SARA)

[A] **In General.** Section 122 was added to CERCLA as part of the Superfund Amendments and Reauthorization Act of 1986, partly in reaction to issues that had arisen in connection with CERCLA settlements prior to the reauthorization, and partly to institutionalize the settlement process as an administrative proceeding. The package of amendments relating to litigated issues addressed such things as mixed funding,[555] contribution actions by and against settling parties, the content of covenants not to sue contained in settlement agreements, public participation in settlements, and small-quantity generator de minimis buyout settlements.

The administrative provisions provide express authority and a framework for negotiating settlements outside of the judicial apparatus. They also provide a rigid settlement procedure applicable to all types of settlements. One very interesting element is the degree to which the Department of Justice has been inserted into EPA's administrative settlement decisions, having been given what is effectively a veto

---

[554] *See* 50 Fed. Reg. 5034 (2-5-85).

[555] Remedial actions funded in part by the government and in part by private parties.

power over settlements in excess of $500,000, even if they do not involve the judiciary.[556]

[B] Settlement Procedures. Section 122(e) establishes a structure for negotiations between the government and PRPs, which effectively provides the sole basis for private remedial activity on NPL-listed sites. Section 122(e)(6) requires preauthorization by the government for any remedial action once an RI/FS has been commenced, either by the government or by a responsible party pursuant to government order or a consent decree.

The settlement scheme of Section 122 is the mechanism by which preauthorization occurs. It begins with a requirement that PRPs be provided with a list of all the names and addresses of PRPs that EPA possesses, along with information about the volume and nature of substances contributed by each PRP and a volumetric ranking of the substances at the site, if the Agency has enough information to provide one.[557] Thereafter commences a formalistic negotiation structure that contains the following elements.

Stay of proceedings. If EPA decides to negotiate, it is prohibited from taking any action under Section 104(a) or Section 106 for a period of 120 days following issuance of a notice to PRPs of the commencement of a negotiation period, and it may not commence work on a RI/FS for 90 days after the notice date.[558] Additional parties may be added to the negotiation by EPA during the negotiating period.

PRP proposal. PRPs have sixty days following receipt of a Section 122(e) notice to make a proposal for undertaking or financing remedial actions under Section 106 or doing a RI/FS in accordance with Section

---

[556] *See* Section 122(h).

[557] Section 122(e)(1). Any information turned over to PRPs is subject to the confidentiality protection provisions of Section 104(e)(4). Often PRPs submit information that is routinely claimed to be confidential. Whether the provisions of the amended statute will deter such actions remains to be seen, but in any event any such claim must be either waived or adjudicated to be meritless by EPA prior to release of material covered by the claim.

[558] Sections 122(e)(2)(A), 122(e)(5). The Agency may, however, continue to design a remedial plan during the negotiation period, and may act to address "significant threats" to public health and the environment. *Id.* EPA's position on the stay has been that it will stretch out the 120-day period if progress is being made, but may elect to proceed to remedial design in order to focus subsequent litigation in the event settlement is not reached.

104(b), whichever is responsive to the notice.[559] The sixty-day time frame appears totally insufficient from a practical standpoint. Even a PRP group that is highly organized at the time it receives a notice is unlikely to be able to put together a viable proposal that all of its members can live with as to any but the simplest sites.

Nonbinding Allocation. EPA is required to develop "nonbinding" guidelines for the development of a cost allocation agreement for the site. The Agency is permitted, though not required, to consider "volume, toxicity, mobility, strength of evidence, ability to pay, litigative risks, public interest considerations, precedential value, and inequities and aggravating factors" in the guidelines.[560] It is given subpoena power for this purpose, presumably to compel PRPs to disgorge previously confidential settlement documents to aid it in developing a general methodology, and/or information that would be useful in making a site-specific allocation, as discussed below.

The Agency is also empowered to provide to PRPs "nonbinding preliminary allocations of responsibility" (NBARs), based on the general guidelines, in order to facilitate settlement. Such documents are not admissible as evidence in any proceeding, they are not reviewable, and the statute disclaims the documents as constituting "an apportionment or other statement of the divisibility of harm or causation."[561] Costs incurred by EPA in producing NBARs are recoverable under Section 107, and must be reimbursed if the parties enter into a settlement.[562]

Offer and response. In the event EPA is made a "substantial offer providing for response" by a PRP group, the Agency is required to respond. If the offer is rejected, a "written explanation" setting forth the reasons for rejection must be provided, although there is no opportunity for judicial review of a rejection.[563] If, following receipt of an NBAR, the PRPs fail to propose a "good faith proposal for financing action," the temporary embargo on government action ends.[564]

---

[559] Section 122(e)(2)(B). EPA places any information it receives relative to the remedy in its public file.

[560] Section 122(e)(3)(A). Subpoena authority is contained in Section 122(e)(3)(B).

[561] Section 122(e)(3)(C).

[562] Section 122(e)(3)(D). EPA is not enthusiastic about undertaking this role.

[563] Section 122(e)(3)(E).

[564] Sixty days is a very short time in CERCLA reality. It is likely that PRPs will propose partial or staged programs in an effort to control the course of the remedial activities, while buying time to organize their own relationships with one another. EPA appears to have wide discretion to accept or reject such proffers, and the issue of good faith will be litigated, if at all, in the context of subsequent cost recovery or enforcement action.

Public notice and participation. The procedures for public notice and participation vary somewhat, depending upon whether the settlement will be included in a judicially approved consent decree or is embodied in an administrative order. For consent decrees, Section 122(d)(2) codifies 28 CFR §50.7, requiring publishing of notice of a proposed settlement in the Federal Register, and solicitation of comment.[565] The Attorney General is given express authority to refuse entry of a settlement where the comment process has revealed "facts or considerations which indicate" that the settlement is "inappropriate, improper or inadequate."[566]

Administrative settlements, which may relate to either de minimis contributors or general cleanup of a site,[567] are subject to a similar Federal Register notice and comment process. The governmental entity in charge of the process for the site is able to withdraw consent on the same basis as can the Attorney General in judicial settlements.[568]

Natural resource damage claims. Federal trustees of natural resources that are implicated in a superfund release are required to be notified and encouraged to participate in settlement negotiations. Although failure to address natural resource damage claims will not bar a settlement, a covenant not to sue with respect to damages is not available unless the relevant trustee has consented in writing.[569] Such covenants, moreover, are available only in judicial consent decrees that contain an express agreement on the part of the settling PRPs that they will take appropriate actions to protect and restore resources damaged by the release.[570]

This requirement essentially codifies the practice followed immediately prior to the 1986 amendments. In most cases the Department of the Interior will be the trustee, and, in general, PRP groups have been willing to finesse the natural resource damage issue, and accept settlements without full releases rather than deal with an additional federal party in the negotiations.

---

[565] Section 50.7 was an innovation of Attorney General Griffin Bell, as part of a 1977 settlement of a dispute with EPA concerning the Department of Justice's handling of the Agency's litigation in previous years.

[566] Section 122(d)(2).

[567] Sections 113(g), 113(h). These provisions are discussed further below.

[568] Section 113(i).

[569] Section 122(j)(1).

[570] Section 122(j)(2).

[C] **Covenants Not to Sue.** The limited nature of covenants not to sue provided by the government to settling parties under the first round of CERCLA cases was a significant sore point for PRP groups. In general, settling parties would be released only to the extent of the work they did, and the government insisted on broad reopeners to cover unforeseen events. Settling parties consistently argued for broader covenants not to sue in return for the expenditure of the enormous remedial costs, based often on slim evidence of responsibility. Many of the issues raised in the early proceedings were addressed in the 1986 amendments.

Section 122(f) lays out the basic ground rules for covenants not to sue. They must, in each case, be found to be in the public interest, expedite response action, and be conditioned on full compliance with the terms of the decree and related response action approved by the government. Specific authority is provided for releases by which the government agrees to limit a party's future liability to the same proportion as that established in the original settlement agrement.[571]

In general, the factors affecting the breadth of a covenant not to sue relate to the nature of the remedy agreed to, with broader releases available to more permanent remedies.[572] A complete release is required for a total treatment remedy, or one where the government has required off-site disposal at a RCRA facility in lieu of an on-site remedy that would have been consistent with the NCP. In each case the release is effective only when the remedial action is complete.[573]

Section 122(f)(6) provides, except as to de minimis settlers, that no release may be provided to settling parties from conditions unknown

---

[571] *See* Section 122(c)(1). This principle is important for partial cleanups and mixed-funding settlements, since protection from third party contribution claims by nonsettlers is otherwise limited to matters addressed in the settlement. The statute further provides that broader protection from future liability is available for settlements adopting a more permanent remedy.

[572] *See* Section 122(f)(4). The factors are the effectiveness and reliability of the remedy in comparison to alternatives, the nature of the remaining risks, the extent to which "performance standards are included," the extent to which the remedy is a complete one, the extent to which the technology to be used is demonstrated to be effective, whether public or private funds will be looked to for any future corrective action, and what percentage of the remedial action will be carried out by the parties themselves.

[573] Section 122(f)(2).

at the time the remedy is completed.[574] In addition, the government may withhold from its release future enforcement action to deal with public health or environmental concerns.[575]

One complaint PRP groups constantly voice is EPA's inability to make quick policy decisions on issues that arise in settlement negotiations. Early in 1987, EPA established a "settlement policy committee," in hopes of improving its performance.

[D] Administrative Settlements. Departments or agencies "with authority to undertake a response action" are encouraged by the statute to settle administratively (by consent order) claims against PRPs if the aggregate of such claims exceeds $500,000.[576] Arbitration, for which the agencies are to develop regulations, is encouraged as a means to achieve such settlements.[577]

Such settlements are not subject to judicial review. In the event a settling party defaults on an administrative settlement, statutory interest can be included in the amount of the judgment in a collection action.[578]

Administrative settlers are insulated from contribution actions brought by nonsettling parties, although an amendment to Section 308 of CERCLA essentially nullifies the contribution bar for these purposes in the event a court concludes that it works a Fifth Amendment taking.[579]

[E] De Minimis Buyouts. Relief to innocent landowners and low volume/low toxicity generators is provided by Section 122(g), which

---

[574] Section 122(f)(6)(A). Subsection (B) allows this to be waived in an exercise of prosecutorial discretion.

[575] Section 122(f)(6)(C). This provision replaces a standard exception to covenants not to sue that had been included in settlements under CERCLA, which had provided a reopener if conditions posed an imminent and substantial endangerment to public health.

[576] Section 122(h)(1). Though larger administrative settlements are not prohibited, settlements in excess of this amount must be approved by the Attorney General, and it is unlikely that the Justice Department will approve many large settlements that are not directly enforceable by consent decree.

[577] Section 122(h)(2).

[578] Section 122(h)(3). Although EPA will negotiate the lion's share of these, it is possible that another agency, such as the Department of Defense or the Bureau of Land Management, could have Section 107 claims against private parties.

[579] Section 122(h)(4) is the bar provision. The amendment to Section 308 is found in Section 122(b) of P.L. 99-499. This separability provision is a hedge against the possibility that the scheme of cutting off rights by administrative order would be found unconstitutional.

authorizes expedited administrative[580] or judicial settlements and broader than usual covenants not to sue for such people. Such an arrangement, which is essentially a "cashout" for qualifying people, is, however, more limited than the small-quantity generator buyouts that had begun to be experimented with in the later preamendments CERCLA settlements among PRPs.

There are two criteria. First, the amount of money involved must be a "minor portion of the response costs at the facility,"[581] and, second, the PRP must either be a qualifying generator or landowner.

In order for a generator to qualify, both the amount of its hazardous material and its toxic or other hazardous effects must be "minimal in comparison to other hazardous substances at the facility."[582] Qualification by a current site owner requires a showing that the candidate (1) did not conduct or permit the generation, transportation, storage, treatment, or disposal of any hazardous substance at the facility;[583] (2) did not contribute to the release or threat of release through any action or omission;[584] and (3) did not purchase the property "with actual or constructive knowledge that the property was used for the generation, storage, treatment, or disposal of any hazardous substance."[585]

A covenant not to sue, which may be somewhat broader than those available to larger players at the site, is available within EPA's discre-

---

[580] The Attorney General must consent to settlements at sites where the total response costs exceed $500,000.

[581] Section 122(g)(1).

[582] Section 122(g)(1)(A). In post-SARA pronouncements, EPA officials indicated a continuing lack of interest in the toxicity criterion, and implied that they would pay it only lip service. In practice, EPA has viewed 1 percent or less of the volume as a de minimis rule of thumb for a generator. A premium (such as 2.5 times the volumetric share) is usually demanded, and in some circumstances releases are conditional, reopened if the remedy exceeds a certain threshold or if the contributor's share is found to be other than originally believed.

[583] Section 122(g)(1)(B)(ii).

[584] Section 122(g)(1)(B)(iii). Presumably actions interfering with EPA's access to the site would disqualify a claimant. Whether failure to spend money voluntarily would disqualify one would seem to be a fact-bound issue.

[585] This language differs significantly from the similar language found in Section 101(35) that would disqualify a current owner from a Section 107(b)(3) defense if he bought the property with knowledge. The latter provision is narrower, disqualifying a smaller number of landowners from the benefit. The Conference Report contains no elucidation of the difference.

tion,[586] and protection against contribution claims "regarding matters addressed in the settlement" is provided.[587]

The import of the limitation of the contribution bar to "matters addressed in the settlement," is here, as in the more general provision, Section 113(f)(2), not entirely clear. The legislative history is not as enlightening as it could be, and the language itself does not clearly bar all contribution claims against settlers. In a remedial settlement, the language has some meaning—a settlement for partial remediation will not insulate settling parties from contribution relating to remedial costs not addressed. This rationale does not, however, fit the de minimis settler, who, presumably because of significantly lower culpability, is given a cheap out.

[F]   **Mixed Funding.** EPA had, almost without waiver, steadfastly refused to accept "mixed-funded" settlements with PRPs during the first five years of CERCLA. As the Agency ran out of money toward the end of the extended initial authorization, it talked about mixed funding, but did little, even at sites where the industrial contribution was comparatively small in comparison to the amount of the volume contributed by municipalities.[588] Some had argued that mixed funding was inconsistent with CERCLA's spirit, if not its letter.

Section 122(b)(1), added in 1986, specifically allows mixed funding, but leaves the matter to the government's discretion, and insulates the decision from judicial review.[589] The Conference Report contains a statement that the government is required to seek to recover public funds committed to mixed-funded remedies from nonsettlers.[590]

---

[586] Section 122(g)(2). The Attorney General is required to consent to such arrangements if the total amount of response costs at the site exceeds $500,000, and obviously Justice Department involvement will affect the scope of such a covenant.

[587] Section 122(g)(5). The liability of nonsettlers to the government is reduced by the amount of such settlements.

[588] EPA refused to sue municipalities involved in superfund sites, even though the Agency's own studies indicated that there are significant amounts of hazardous substances in municipal waste.

[589] Section 122(b)(2). EPA has promised guidance in February or March, 1987. In general, the mere fact that a site contains orphan shares will not qualify it for mixed funding. Settling PRPs must provide a remedy as good as or better than the government's, and agree to advance the cost of the government's share, recovering it after the fact from the Fund.

[590] H.R. Rep. 99-962, at 252. In addition, Section 113(f) subordinates contribution recovery by settling parties from nonsettlers to the government.

Section 122(a) appears to make it clear that settlement remedies must be "consistent with" the NCP; and Section 122(b)(4) provides that in mixed-funding settlements the liability of the superfund is limited to the amount specified in the deal, unless further sums are required in the future to correct a failed remedy.

[G] Miscellaneous Settlement-Related Issues—Vessels; Modification; Liability; Contribution. The settlement scheme provided in Section 122 is not available to vessel-related litigation.[591]

Settlements entered into pursuant to Section 122 may be modified by federal courts applying general principles of federal law on the subject.[592] The penalties provided in Section 109 are applicable to violations of administrative consent orders or consent decrees.[593]

One ironic provision of Section 122 makes it unnecessary for EPA to recite findings that would support an imminent and substantial endangerment as a predicate for administrative or judicial settlements.[594] The Agency had insisted on such findings in preamendment settlements; and PRPs, wary of the potential for third party toxic tort suits, swallowed such boilerplate as a bitter pill. In the same vein, Section 122(d)(1)(B) states that entry of a settlement will not constitute an admission by a settling party of liability for any purpose, and that the fact that a party has participated in a settlement "shall not be admissible in any judicial or administrative proceeding," including a subsequent CERCLA proceeding, "except as otherwise provided in the Federal Rules of Evidence."[595]

---

[591] Section 122(l).

[592] Section 122(m).

[593] Section 122(l). The penalties are also applicable to violations of federal facility interagency agreements negotiated under Section 120. Of course, civil and criminal contempt is also a remedy available in the case of violation of the terms of a judicially approved consent decree.

[594] Section 122(d)(1)(A).

[595] Section 122(d)(1)(B). The reference to the F.R.E. is to Rule 408, which states:
  Evidence of (1) furnishing or offering or promising to furnish, or (2) accepting or offering or promising to accept, a valuable consideration in compromising or attempting to compromise a claim which was disputed as to either validity or amount, is not admissible to prove liability for or invalidity of the claim or its amount. Evidence of conduct or statements made in compromise negotiations is likewise not admissible. This rule does not require the exclusion of any evidence otherwise discoverable merely because it is presented in the course of compromise

As noted heretofore, settling parties are provided protection from contribution actions brought by nonsettling parties,[596] and are, along with other persons, given a statutory cause of action for contribution against nonsettlers for the amounts expended in the settlement.[597] The right of contribution is watered down, however, by a statutory subordination of the plaintiffs' claims to those of the federal or state government (as the case may be) to recover from the defendants government expenditures not recovered from settling parties.[598]

As discussed in connection with de minimis buyouts, contribution protection for settling parties is not absolute, but is limited to "matters addressed in the settlement." The meaning of this restriction, if it is indeed that, is not clear. In the House Report on the bill, from which the language was taken, it is stated that private parties "who have entered into a . . . settlement under the Act will be protected from paying any additional response costs to other responsible parties in a contribution action."[599] It is arguable that in a "global" settlement, where the PRPs agree to total site cleanup, contribution protection is, and should be, complete. In a partial settlement, where the settling parties undertake only a partial remedy, it would appear that other remedial actions would not be "addressed" in the settlement.

[5] Penalties

The original CERCLA did not contain a general penalty provision. Specific sanctions were provided for violations of Section 106(a) orders and for submitting false information under Section 103, but the absence of a more general set of sanctions was viewed by many as a serious oversight on the part of the drafters. Congress sought to remedy the omission in the SARA amendments, and did so in a most bizarre fashion. Section 109 of the statute was amended to add criminal sanctions and

---

negotiations. This rule does not require exclusion when the evidence is offered for another purpose, such as proving bias or prejudice of a witness, negativing a contention of undue delay, or proving an effort to obstruct a criminal investigation or prosecution.

596 Section 113(f)(2).

597 Section 113(f)(3)(B).

598 Section 113(f)(3)(C).

599 See H.R. Rep. No. 99-253, Part 1, 99th Cong., 1st Sess. at 80 (8-1-85). There is no more useful discussion in the Judiciary Committee's report, H.R. Rep. No. 99-253, Part 3 (10-31-85), although there is discussion of an intention not to bar indemnification claims, which are based on contract rather than on common law.

a rather elaborate set of generally applicable civil penalties. Civil penalties, which may be levied administratively or by a federal judge, are applicable to violations of the notification requirements of Sections 103(a) and (b); destruction of records in violation of Section 103(d)(2); violation of the financial responsibility requirements of Section 108 (or a regulation or order thereunder); violation of an order issued under Section 122(d)(3); and failure or refusal to carry out the terms of a settlement agreement, consent decree entered into under Section 122, or interagency agreement entered into under Section 120.[600]

There are two tiers of civil penalties, Class I and Class II, which may be levied administratively in amounts up to $25,000. Substantively, the only difference between the two classes of penalties is that Class II penalties apply to per day violations, while Class I penalties apply to per violation offenses.[601] Procedurally, however, the two classes of penalties are significantly different.

Class I penalties are subject to a requirement of "notice and opportunity for a hearing."[602] Class II penalties, however, are expressly made subject to adjudicatory hearings under 5 USC §554.[603] Subpoena power is provided in either case, but the language providing it is different. Second and subsequent offenders subject to Class II penalties are liable to a penalty multiplied by three times the statutory amount, but no such multiplier is applicable to repeat offenders who have paid a Class I penalty.[604]

Perhaps the most bizarre aspect of this penalty scheme is the judicial review scheme. Judicial review of class I penalties is in the "appropriate" U.S. district court, and is secured by filing "notice of appeal" and sending a copy of the notice by mail to the government.[605] Appeals of Class II penalties, however, must be to a U.S. court of appeals in the circuit where the appellant resides or does business, or to the D.C.

---

[600] Sections 109(a), 109(c). The penal provisions of Sections 103(b), 103(d), and 112(b) were also amended, to increase the criminal sanctions.

[601] *Compare* Section 109(b) *with* Section 109(a).

[602] Section 109(a)(2).

[603] Section 109(b).

[604] *Compare* Section 109(b) *with* Section 109(a). Section 109(c) also allows a court to apply a multiplier for per day violations.

[605] Section 109(a)(4).

Circuit, where EPA resides.[606] To anyone remotely familiar with administrative procedure, this makes absolutely no sense.

Class I penalties must be calculated pursuant to a set of factors that are reminiscent of the various EPA civil penalty policies and Section 208 of the Clean Air Act.[607] No such limit is imposed on Class II penalties.

This peculiar provision is perhaps best explained by the Conference Report, which states that the section "contains provisions from the House and Senate amendments."[608] So it does, without any attempt at reconciliation. The result is a morass.

The amended Section 109 also contains a bounty provision. Section 109(d) allows the government to pay, from the superfund, an "award" of up to $10,000 for information leading to the arrest and conviction of any person for a criminal CERCLA offense.

Finally, an important provision for the Justice Department, Section 109(e), allows it to retain expert witnesses without following the normal government contracting procedures.

[6] Citizen Suits

Citizen initiative was addressed in two ways by the 1986 SARA amendments. Section 105(d) authorizes citizen petitions seeking a preliminary assessment at a site not otherwise scheduled for response action.[609] A citizen suit provision, Section 310, authorizes a lawsuit to be brought by any person in a federal district court against any other person (other than EPA or the Agency for Toxic Substances Disease Registry) alleged to be in violation of "any standard, regulation, condition, requirement, or order which has become effective" under the statute, specifically including interagency agreements establishing remedial actions for federal facilities.[610]

The statute contains the familiar prior notice, governmental action, attorneys' fees, and intervention provisions contained in other environ-

---

[606] Section 109(b).

[607] Section 109(a)(3).

[608] *See* H.R. Rep. No. 99-962, 99th Cong., 2d Sess. at 207.

[609] Section 105(d). *See also* discussion of public participation, *supra*, which includes a discussion of the potential for grants to be awarded to local groups.

[610] Sections 310(a)(1), 310(b)(2). One issue surely to be litigated will be just what sort of activity falls within the statutory language, since CERCLA is not a regulatory statute, and thus does not impose many "standards."

mental citizen suit statutes,[611] and specifically authorizes injunctive and civil penalty relief.[612]

Actions may be brought against EPA or the Agency for Toxic Substances Disease Registry only in the District of Columbia, to compel performance of a nondiscretionary duty.[613]

[7] State Enforcement of CERCLA Requirements

States, but not municipalities, may bring lawsuits in federal courts to enforce CERCLA-imposed requirements.[614] Any settlement of such a lawsuit, however, must contain a dispute resolution provision that requires inclusion of "appropriate Federal and State agencies" in any resolution of a dispute involving the implementation of remedial action at the site.[615] Moreover, the settlement must also include stipulated penalties of up to $25,000 per day, which are specifically enforceable by EPA as well as by the state.[616]

§6.10 Other Authority

[1] Rivers and Harbors Appropriation Act of 1899

The federal government has occasionally sought to secure removal of hazardous substances from the beds or banks of streams by means of securing injunctive relief under Section 13 of the Rivers and Harbors Act of 1899.[617] This provision, popularly known as the Refuse Act, prohibits the discharge of "any refuse matter of any kind or description

---

611 Sixty days' prior notice to the offender and the government is required, and a suit is barred if EPA is diligently prosecuting a CERCLA or RCRA action that addresses the problem. Section 310(e). EPA or the state may intervene in such a suit as of right. Section 310(g). Attorneys' fees, costs, and expert witness fees are available for prevailing or substantially prevailing parties. Section 310(f). Section 113(1) requires, in addition, that a copy of the complaint be provided to EPA and to the Attorney General.

612 Section 310(c).

613 Section 310(b)(2).

614 Section 121(e)(2). A copy of the complaint must be mailed to EPA and to the Attorney General, by reason of Section 113(1).

615 Id.

616 Id.

617 33 USC §407. Although this provision initially also regulated the discharge of "refuse" into water bodies, its active regulatory functions were subsumed into the Federal Water Pollution Control Act (FWPCA) amendments of 1972. See 33 USC §1371. Congress did not, however, repeal the statute, and it remains available to address forms of water body pollution that are not covered under the FWPCA.

whatever other than that flowing from streets and sewers and passing therefrom in a liquid state" into navigable waters.[618] A series of court decisions during the 1960s defined the term "refuse" broadly to include virtually any substance that would affect water quality;[619] thus, the statute's prohibition covers a wide range of potential activities, except for discharges of pollutants regulated under the Clean Water Act, which partially preempts Section 13.

Although the Refuse Act appears on its face to provide only criminal penalties, judge-made law under the act created injunctive remedies and provided authority for the courts to order the government to enforce the act and recover its costs in a civil action.[620]

Accordingly, the government, prior to the enactment of CERCLA, filed a number of Section 13 actions in which it sought both negative and affirmative injunctions to remedy either nonpoint source discharges of hazardous pollutants from riverbank disposal areas or accumulations of sediments that were the result of discharges that occurred prior to the effective date of the 1972 Federal Water Pollution Control Act (FWPCA) amendments.[621] The enactment of CERCLA in 1980 significantly reduced the significance of the Refuse Act as a device for securing hazardous waste cleanup. Nevertheless, the government has continued to plead Refuse Act claims in CERCLA or RCRA emergency and remedial response actions as an additional theory where navigable waters are contaminated or face a threat of contamination.

The Second Circuit's decision in *United States v. Pollution Abatement Services of Oswego, Inc., et al.*[622] illustrates the continuing vitality

---

618 The jurisdiction of the statute is limited to waters that are within reach of federal jurisdiction under the navigation clause of the United States Constitution. *See* United States v. Standard Oil Company, 384 U.S. 224 (1966); and Wyandotte Transportation Company v. United States, 389 U.S. 191.

619 *See generally* Druly, *The Refuse Act of 1899*, 2 Envt. Rep. (BNA), Monograph No. 11 (1972).

620 Wyandotte Transportation Co. v. United States, 389 U.S. 191, 204 (1967); United States v. Perma Paving Co., 332 F.2d 754, 757-58 (2d Cir. 1964); In re Oswego Barge Corp., 664 F.2d 327, 335 (2d Cir. 1981).

621 *See, e.g.*, United States v. Pollution Abatement Services of Oswego, Inc., et al., 763 F.2d 133 (2d Cir. 1985) (adjacent nonpoint discharge); and United States v. Outboard Marine Corporation, 556 F.Supp 54 (N.D.Ill. 1982) (sediments—the RHA claims constitute only one of several theories in this case).

622 763 F.2d 133 (2d Cir. 1985).

of this old statute. The government sued Pollution Abatement Services, a closely held corporation, and two of its stockholder-officers, alleging that refuse from its chemical water storage facility had, over a long period of time, been discharged into a tributary of Lake Ontario. The trial court found for the government and entered a judgment against the corporation, which was essentially defunct, and the individual defendants jointly and severally. The judgment ordered the United States to clean up the site and assessed the cost of the activity against the defendants. The original order left the amount of the judgment blank, and it was later amended to reflect the actual cost of the government's cleanup.

In affirming the trial court, the court of appeals reaffirmed the availability of civil remedies under the Refuse Act, and established the principle that such liability could attach to corporate officers or owners who were "personally involved" in the activity giving rise to the discharges of refuse.[623]

The *Pollution Abatement* decision provides the government with a useful supplement to CERCLA for contamination involving or threatening traditionally navigable waters. It can in such cases secure a judgment against available responsible parties in advance of the expenditure of any public funds, thereby avoiding a drain on the federal superfund, and without the built-in uncertainty of recovery that is endemic to CERCLA actions.

The Refuse Act, however, unlike CERCLA, requires the government to prove the existence of a causal link between the offending discharge and the defendant's activities. It does not impose liability without fault.[624]

[2] **Marine Tort and Marine Regulatory Law**

A number of amendments to CERCLA in 1986 were aimed at "incin-

---

[623] The court arrived at this conclusion by analogy to Section 16, 33 USC §411, the criminal sanction provision.

[624] *See* United States v. Sexton Cove Estates, Inc., 526 F.2d 1293 (5th Cir. 1976) (decided under Section 10, but under analogous reasoning).

eration vessels."[625] As discussed heretofore, amendments to Sections 107 and 108 essentially deprive such vessels of treatment as vessels under CERCLA. The principal result of these changes is elimination of the limitations on liability contained in the statute and under maritime law.

In addition, an amendment to Section 107(h), which had made the more favorable limits of the Limitation of Liability Act[626] inapplicable with respect to cleanup costs, broadens, as to *all* vessels, the unavailability of those limitations in actions brought under "maritime tort law," and, further, authorizes maritime tort actions to be brought by persons without any damage to a proprietary interest. This provision effectively creates a cause of action for citizen suits sounding in tort against any vessel that has released a hazardous substance.

Finally, Section 106 of the Marine Protection, Research and Sanctuaries Act of 1972 was amended by Section 127 of SARA to legislatively overrule a portion of the Supreme Court's opinion in *Middlesex County Sewerage Authority v. National Sea Clammers Association,*[627] in which the court had held that the MPRSA had preempted state and any federal common law–based actions for damages. The amendment to Section 106 is an express savings provision stating that the statute does not preclude damages actions under state law, including common law, federal maritime tort law, or "other Federal law," premised on acts that are a violation of the MPRSA or a permit issued under it.

The legislative history, particularly the Conference Report on P.L. 99-499, seems to indicate that Congress's intent in enacting these provisions was actually to hasten licensing of incineration vessels.[628] EPA had been reluctant to issue MPRSA permits to incineration vessels, largely because of public outcries that the vessels were effectively judgment proof in the event of a catastrophic accident. Ironically, the 1851 Limitation on Liability Act, originally intended to further the development of maritime commerce in the United States, was seen as a barrier to the development of commerce in hazardous substances.

---

625 The term is defined by Section 101(38) as "any vessel which carries hazardous substances for the purpose of incineration of such substances, so long as such substances or residues of such substances are on board."

626 46 USC §183(f)(1851).

627 453 U.S. 1 (1981).

628 *See, in particular,* H.R. 99-962, at 259-60.

[3]   State Real Property Cleanup Laws

An interesting development under state law that parallels the implementation of CERCLA and RCRA is the enactment in a number of states of "environmental cleanup responsibility laws," the first of which, and the model for most of the subsequent provisions, was the New Jersey Environmental Cleanup Responsibility Act (generally known as ECRA).[629] These statutes require, prior to the transfer of ownership or control of property within a class of suspect types, that the state environmental protection department approve the transfer by determining either that the site is free from hazardous contaminants or that a remedial plan has been agreed to that will clean up the site.

The critical parameters of any such law are the definition of the facilities to which the obligation applies,[630] and the transactions that trigger review of the conditions of the property.[631]

---

[629] NJSA Sections 13:1K-6 et seq. See also Conn. Public Act 85-568.

[630] ECRA, for example, defines the obligation to apply to any "industrial establishment," which is defined to include—

>   any place of business engaged in operations which involve the generation, manufacture, refining, transportation, treatment, storage, handling, or disposal of hazardous substances or wastes on-site, above or below ground, having a Standard Industrial Classification number within 22-39 inclusive, 46-49 inclusive, 51 or 76. . . .

Section 13:1K-8f.

The Connecticut Statute, by comparison, defines the term "establishment" as—

>   any establishment which generates more than one hundred kilograms of hazardous waste per month or which recycles, reclaims, reuses, stores, handles, treats, transports or disposes of hazardous waste which is generated by another person or municipality.

PA 85-568, Section 2(3).

[631] It is again useful to compare the New Jersey and Connecticut statutes. ECRA triggers the obligation on "closing, terminating or transferring operations," which is defined by Section 13:1K-8b. to include—

>   the cessation of all operations which involve the generation, manufacture, refining, transportation, treatment, storage, handling or disposal of hazardous substances or wastes, or any temporary cessation for a period of not less than two years, or any other transaction or proceeding through which an industrial establishment becomes nonoperational for health and safety reasons, or *undergoes a change in ownership*, except for corporate reorganization not substantially affecting the ownership of the industrial establishment, *including but not limited to sale of stock in the form of a statutory merger or consolidation, sale of the controlling share of assets, the conveyance of the real property, dissolution of corporate identity, financial reorganization and initiation of bankruptcy proceedings.*

The Connecticut statute limits the trigger to a "transfer of establishment," which is defined to include a "transfer of operations which involve the generation, recycling, reclamation, reuse, transportation, treatment, storage, handling or disposal of hazardous

The statutes generally require the closing owner or transferor to file, within a set time period before the contemplated action, either a "negative declaration" or a "cleanup plan," together with some form of security.[632] If a cleanup plan is required, the closure or transfer cannot take place until the department approves the plan, and transactions in violation of such provisions are usually deemed to be voidable.[633] Violation of the provisions may also result in the imposition of penalties or liability for civil damages to the transferee.[634]

The Connecticut statute allows the obligations to be carried out by the transferee in lieu of the transferor, apparently recognizing that the business arrangement may provide for a shifting of such responsibility. A curious problem arises under all of these statutes, however, for tender offerors in hostile takeover situations. Such transactions are covered by virtually all of these statutes, and tender offerors cannot, in short, comply prior to the transfer of control. Since the private remedies for noncompliance run to the transferee, this would not appear to be a significant problem. Theoretically, though, the state could extract a penalty, and most surely would compel the new owner to undertake a cleanup if one were needed.

The bottom line for purchasers of industrial property is that the transaction costs will be higher, but the overall risks lower, in states adopting ECRA-type laws. Sellers in New Jersey and Connecticut, for example, retain environmental consultants to survey the property, and buyers in those states retain their own consultants to review the seller's documents.

The problem, however, lies in financial institutions and slippage in closing dates where the state has not been able to review a remedial plan before the deal is set to close. Real estate lenders, particularly in light of the breadth of CERCLA liability and the Supreme Court's handling of bankruptcies, tend to be conservative if there is the slightest potential for contamination of a property by hazardous substances. State environmental bureaucracies are notoriously understaffed and underfunded; thus prudence dictates that long executory periods be built into transactions that require approval under one of these laws.

---

waste," and a "change in ownership," which is defined in the same terms as in the New Jersey provision.

[632] See N.J.S.A. Section 13:1k-9; Conn. P.A. 85-568 Section 3.

[633] See N.J.S.A. Section 13:1K-13b.

[634] See N.J.S.A. Section 13:1K-13a, 13c; Conn. P.A. 85-568, Section 3(b), 4.

§6.11   Hazard Disclosure and Emergency Response—SARA's Community Right-to-Know Provisions

[1]   Overview

Title III of CERCLA was added by the Superfund Amendments and Reauthorization Act of 1986 (SARA).[635] It is the first significant piece of legislation whose roots are directly traceable to the Bhopal, India, disaster, in which thousands of people were killed or seriously injured when exposed to a toxic mist created by an accidental release of methylisocyanate at a fertilizer manufacturing facility.[636]

The statute, overall, does three things. It first provides a mechanism for the public to receive information about the location of amounts of "extremely hazardous" substances[637] within the community. It then requires employers required to possess material safety data sheets under the Occupational Safety and Health Act to provide copies of such sheets for "hazardous chemicals"[638] to designated local officials. Finally, it provides for the creation of multiple layers of emergency planning

---

[635] P.L. 99-499, effective October 17, 1986.

[636] A release of the same substance from a facility at Institute, West Virginia, within a few months of Bhopal, though producing no known casualties, galvanized public opinion that facilities in the United States were not immune from a Bhopal phenomenon.

[637] The term is defined by Section 329(3) simply by reference to a list to be compiled by EPA under Section 302. Section 302(a)(2) incorporates as the initial list a list of 403 chemicals published by EPA on November 15, 1985, as a part of its voluntary emergency preparedness program and amended by the Agency on November 17, 1986 (the list is reprinted in Appendix 6G, *infra*). EPA is empowered to amend the list from time to time, taking account of "the toxicity [including both short and long term effects following short-term exposure], reactivity, dispersability, combustability, or flammability of the substance." Section 302(a)(4).

[638] The term "hazardous chemical" is defined by Sections 329(5) and 311(e) to mean the same thing as the definition contained in the OSHA Hazard Communication Standard, 29 CFR §1910.1200(c), except for certain types of chemicals listed in Sections 311(e)(1)-(e)(5). The OSHA definition is "any chemical which is a physical hazard" (that is, one for which there is "scientifically valid evidence that it is a combustible liquid, a compressed gas, explosive, flammable, an organic peroxide, an oxidizer, pyrophoric, unstable (reactive), or water-reactive," as those terms are defined in the regulation), or a "health hazard" (that is, a chemical "for which there is statistically significant evidence based on at least one study conducted in accordance with established scientific principles that acute or chronic health effects may occur in exposed [persons] . . .," including "chemicals which are carcinogens, toxic or highly toxic agents, reproductive toxins, irritants, corrosives, sensitizers, hepatotoxins, nephrotoxins, neurotoxins, agents which act on the hematopoietic system, and agents which damage the lungs, skin, eyes, or mucous membranes"). 29 CFR §1910.1200(c). OSHA further refines its methodology in Appendixes A and B to the regulation, which are incorporated by reference.

and response at the state and local government levels, and creates an elaborate, enforceable scheme of notification in the event of a release of a hazardous substance or a "toxic chemical."[639]

It is far from clear that Congress had any reason to require the use of three different jurisdictional lists of chemicals. One could postulate that the Section 302 list might be intended to include chemicals likely to be acutely hazardous, while the more general reporting requirements applicable to "toxic chemicals" might apply to substances of lower acute toxicity but higher chronic injury potential. The initial lists adopted do not, however, reflect such a clear line of demarcation.

Though enacted as Title III of CERCLA, the statute is actually a self-contained regulatory program, much like the LUST program under RCRA or Section 311 of the Federal Water Pollution Control Act. It contains its own definitions, its own substantive requirements, and its own enforcement scheme. In many respects, it has more in common with the Toxic Substances Control Act than with CERCLA.

[2] Emergency Planning Requirements—Subtitle A

[a] Obligations of Facility Owners and Operators

[i] Initial Notification

Since the initial step in emergency planning involves targeting potential sources of releases, those entities having regulated substances present on their premises are required to provide information about them to the designated state authority.[640] The responsible entity is the "owner or operator" of a "facility"[641] at which a substance contained on the initial list or a subsequently amended list of "extremely hazard-

---

[639] Section 313(c). This term is defined by reference to characteristics, and initially encompasses a group of chemicals on a list compiled by the Senate Committee on Environment and Public Works, which was incorporated by reference into the statute. This list is reprinted in Appendix 6H, *infra*.

[640] The statute, Section 301(a)(1), contemplates designation of a state "emergency response commission" by executive order of the governor, within six months of the enactment date.

[641] "Facility" is defined by Section 329(4) to include a site or contiguous or adjacent sites containing buildings or not, owned by the same or affiliated persons, and includes motor vehicles, rolling stock, and aircraft. Whether federal facilities are subject to this program is an interesting question. Title III contains no federal sovereign immunity waiver, and CERCLA's waiver is rather narrow.

ous substances" is present[642] in amounts above a regulatory threshold, initially set at 2 pounds[643] unless EPA promulgated different thresholds within thirty days of enactment.[644]

The initial reporting obligation ripens on May 17, 1987. There is a continuing obligation to submit notification within sixty days of the initial presence of a regulated substance at one's facility, or of the addition of a substance already present at the facility to the list.[645]

A governor or state emergency response commission may designate for inclusion in the emergency planning program additional facilities that do not meet the federal notification criteria, following public notice and opportunity for comment.[646]

Facilities required to submit a notification, and those placed on the emergency planning list by the state, are also required to provide a "facility emergency coordinator" as the contact person for the local emergency committee. They have an ongoing obligation to inform the committee of changes at the facility, and to "promptly provide information to such committee necessary for developing and implementing" its emergency plan.[647]

[ii] **Emergency Notification in the Event of a Release**

Section 304 imposes an emergency notification obligation on owners and operators of facilities "at which a hazardous chemical is produced,

---

[642] Section 302(b), Section 302(c). The interim list is reprinted in Appendix 6G, *infra.* EPA is to required to publish the interim list, and then may, from time to time, amend it upon consideration of the hazard factors contained in Section 302(a)(4). *See supra* note 637.

[643] Section 302(a)(3)(C).

[644] As in the case of Section 103 of CERCLA, EPA is to develop chemical-specific or class- or category-specific thresholds for each substance on the Section 302(a)(2) list, based on the Section 302(a)(4) general criteria. Substances as to which EPA fails to publish interim final thresholds within thirty days of the effective date are assigned a 2-pound threshold, which will be applicable until EPA promulgates regulations establishing a different threshold. Final regulations, revising the interim final list, are to be promulgated, but not on any time schedule. EPA's initial thresholds were published in the November 17, 1986, Federal Register. It calculated the reporting thresholds on the basis of the known propensity of the substances or the class to become airborne if released, and their acute toxicity.

[645] Section 302(c).

[646] Section 302(b)(2).

[647] Sections 303(d)(2), 303(d)(3). These information obligations are subject to the trade secret protection provisions contained in Section 322, which are discussed in Section 6.11[4], *infra.*

used, or stored"[648] that have experienced a "release" of a regulated substance. The degree of detail required is specified in Section 304(b), and is generally greater than is required under Section 103(a) of CER-CLA. Since the term "hazardous chemical" is defined in terms of the exceedingly broad definition contained in the OSHA hazard communication rule,[649] the universe of persons subject to the obligation is potentially enormous.

The reporting obligation does not apply to a "release which results in exposure to persons solely within the site or sites on which" the facility is located.[650] This limitation is in many cases illusory, since it will be practically impossible for a facility manager to determine in most cases that an airborne release that is significant enough to warrant the reporting threshold will not expose someone off-site. The prudent manager will err on the side of overreporting, unless a pattern of nonenforcement develops.

The specific reporting requirements vary according to the nature of the substances released. It is important to understand that the statute does not initially impose any specific monitoring or surveillance requirements on facilities. They are required to report only releases of which they are aware.[651] Section 305, however, requires EPA to study the effectiveness of the notification program, and report to Congress about, among other things, the technological capabilities of current monitoring and detection equipment, and the effectiveness of the monitoring efforts at randomly inspected facilities, thus leaving open the possibility that regulatory monitoring requirements might be imposed in the future.[652]

[A] **Extremely Hazardous Substances.** In the event of the "release"[653] of a listed "extremely hazardous substance" in quantities that

---

[648] Section 304(a).

[649] 29 CFR §1910.1200(c). *See* discussion at *supra* note 638.

[650] Section 304(a)(4).

[651] There is no apparent bar to *state* imposition of specific monitoring and detection requirements.

[652] Section 305(b)(2)(A). In addition, the Agency is to report on the status of the public alert systems set up under Title III (Section 305(b)(2)(B)), and "the technical and economic feasibility of establishing, maintaining, and operating perimeter alert systems for detecting releases . . . into the atmosphere, surface water, or groundwater . . ." at facilities where there are "significant quantities" of extremely hazardous substances (Section 305(b)(2)(C)). The report is due in late April 1988.

[653] "Release" is defined by Section 329(8), which is similar but not identical to the first clause of Section 101(22) and does not contain the definitional exemptions contained in

are reportable under Section 103(a) of CERCLA from a facility where a "hazardous chemical" is produced, used, or stored, the owner or operator is required immediately to notify the "community emergency coordinator," designated pursuant to Section 301,[654] in the degree of detail required under Section 304(b)(2). If the release is of an extremely hazardous substance and is from such a facility, but is not subject to Section 103(a) reporting (either because it is below the Section 102 reportable quantity, or because the substance for some other reason is not subject to CERCLA Subtitle I reporting, such as a substance that falls between the cracks of the Section 101(14) definition of "hazardous substance"), then the obligation to notify applies if (1) the release is not "federally permitted,"[655] (2) it is in the amount determined by EPA to warrant notification or, in the absence of an EPA regulation, is 1 pound or more, and (3) it "occurs in a manner which would require notification under section 103(a). . . ."[656]

[B]   Other Substances. A release of a substance other than one listed as extremely hazardous is nevertheless reportable to the community emergency coordinator in Section 304(b)(2) detail if the event is report-able under Section 103(a) of CERCLA (that is, if it is not a federally permitted release and is of a substance contained on one of the CER-CLA lists) and the release is of a substance for which a reportable quantity has been established under Section 102(a) of CERCLA.

If no Section 102(a) reportable quantities have been established at the time of the release, but a report is still required under Section 103(a), then the reportable quantity is 1 pound, and complete Section 304(b)(2) reports are required only for releases occurring on or after April 30, 1988.[657] Until that time, the facility is required only to dupli-cate its Section 103(a) notice for the local committee.

---

the latter. The term is defined, for Title III purposes, as—
    . . . any spilling, leaking, pumping, pouring, emitting, emptying, discharging, injecting, escaping, leaching, dumping, or disposing into the environment (includ-ing the abandonment or discarding of barrels, containers, and other closed recepta-cles) of any hazardous chemical, extremely hazardous substance or toxic chemical.
    [654] Section 302(a)(1). *See* discussion in Section 6.11[2][b], *infra*, regarding the role of the community emergency coordinator.
    [655] As defined by Section 101(10) of CERCLA.
    [656] Section 304(a)(2).
    [657] April 30, 1988, is the date by which EPA is required under Section 102(a), as amended by Section 102 of the 1986 amendments, to publish reportable quantity thresh-olds for all substances listed under CERCLA.

The Conference Report[658] states that the Section 304 notification requirement also does not apply to "continuous or frequently recurring" releases.[659] Except for "federally permitted releases," which, either expressly or by the cross-reference to Section 103(a), are exempt from Section 304 reporting, there does not appear to be any statutory basis for the statement.[660]

[C] **Contents of Notification.** Section 304 notices from everyone except transporters[661] are required to be provided to the "community emergency coordinator" for the "local emergency planning committee" and to the "State emergency planning commission," both established under Section 301.

Rather than rely primarily on the knowledge of response authorities, which is the approach of Section 103(a) and the notice scheme of the Hazardous Materials Transportation Act,[662] Section 304(b) requires the owner or operator to provide a detailed notice with respect to the release, which covers not only the chemical's name and identity, but also information about the amounts released, time and duration, environmental fate, and information about its health effects and suggested modes of action.[663] In theory, if the community preparedness planning

---

[658] H.R. Rep. No. 99-962, 99th Cong., 2d Sess. at 285.

[659] These, if of "toxic substances," as defined, are covered under Section 313, discussed *infra.*

[660] Though the Section 101(10) definition of "federally permitted release" is lengthy, the fact is that there are many recurring releases, particularly airborne releases, that are not subject to federal permitting at all, and thus fall outside of the definition. EPA has never regulated many substances that are emitted in relatively small amounts but would at least meet the 1-pound threshold under Section 111 or Section 112 of the Clean Air Act. State air pollution implementation plans have historically not addressed small-quantity toxic emissions.

[661] Spills from transporting vehicles or storage areas "incident to" transportation can be reported by dialing 911 or, "in the absence of a 911 emergency telephone number," calling "the *operator*"(!). Section 304(b)(1). Neither the various police departments who man the 911 numbers nor the local telephone companies appear to be required by the statute to cooperate. One might ask what liabilities might flow from a call by a hapless transporter to an operator like Lily Tomlin's unforgettable "Ernestine."

Transporters are exempted by Section 327 from all other requirements of Title III.

[662] 49 USC §10921.

[663] Section 304(b)(2). The notice is to provide "to the extent known at the time of the notice . . . :"

  (A) The chemical name or identity of any substance involved in the release.
  (B) An indication of whether the substance is on the list referred to in §302(a).
  (C) An estimate of the quantity . . . that was released into the environment.
  (D) The medium or media into which the release occurred.

process has effectively employed the information provided under Section 302, much should already be known about the released substance, and thus the information provided by the owner or operator should be, at least in part, redundant.

Section 304(c) requires a follow-up notice, containing information about the response actions taken by the facility, and additional information about known or anticipated health effects and recommended medical responses.

[b] Duties of Governmental Representatives

[i] Formation and Operation of Local Emergency Planning Committees

The principal governmental players in the emergency response scheme set up under Title III are "local emergency planning committees," which are to be appointed by the governor of the state, or by a state "emergency response commission" appointed by the governor.[664] The local committees serve as the primary drafters of local emergency response plans, and are primarily responsible for reacting to emergencies covered by the plan, subject to overall supervision by the state commission.[665]

(E) Any known or anticipated acute or chronic health risks associated with the emergency and, where appropriate, advice regarding medical attention necessary for exposed individuals.

(F) Proper precautions to take as a result of the release, including evacuation (unless such information is readily available to the emergency coordinator pursuant to the emergency plan).

(G) The name and telephone number of the person or persons to be contacted for further information.

[664] Sections 301(a), 301(c). Interestingly, although the statute speaks in mandatory language regarding the obligation to establish state and local planning entities, there is no federal fallback in the event of a state's failure to do so, no federal funds are made available to induce the states to do so, and it is unlikely that, as a matter of federalism, EPA could force a foot-dragging governor to participate. Moreover, the citizen suit provision, Section 326(a)(1), is narrowly drawn, and does not authorize citizen suits to compel state officials to do more than provide a mechanism for public dissemination of Section 324(a) information (*see infra*) or respond to a request for information submitted to the state under Section 312(e)(3). *See* Sections 326(a)(1)(C) and (D).

[665] *Id.;* and Section 303. Section 301(b) authorizes the creation of regional "emergency planning districts" that are multijurisdictional or multistate (these require an interstate compact under the Constitution). Districts appear to have no function other than an organizational one, since there is no provision for district operating entities or any functions assigned to districts under the statute. A primary purpose of the "district" concept appears to be to allow the state to designate one local planning committee for several

Local emergency planning committees are required to be constituted with a broad cross-section of relevant community interests, including representatives of facilities and of environmental organizations, although the statute does not require anything remotely approaching balance among the interests.[666] An interesting provision, Section 301(d), purports to allow any "interested person" to petition the state to reconstitute the committee, but there is no provision for judicial review of denial of such a petition or inaction with respect to it. Such a right must come, if at all, out of state law.

The key individual in the scheme is the "official" designated as the "community emergency coordinator," who serves as the basic front-line decisionmaking person for virtually all local Title III activities.[667]

[ii] Emergency Response Plans

Initially, local committees receive information from facilities required to report the presence of extremely hazardous substances under Section 302.[668] Once that information is received, it forms the core of the data base required for the development of a local emergency plan, for which the statute provided a two-year development period.[669] The

---

contiguous or nearby municipalities or unincorporated places, to ensure the existence of a body that has a sufficient resource base to do the job effectively.

[666] Section 301(c). Mandatory representation is required for each of the following categories of "groups or organizations:" (1) state and local officials, (2) law enforcement, civil defense, firefighting, first aid, health, local environmental, hospital, and transportation personnel, (3) broadcast and print media, (4) community groups, and (5) facility owners and operators.

It will not be politically possible in many communities to exclude any of the category (2) representatives; thus, many local committees will be very large. It is also not clear what some of the terms mean. For example, "local environmental" groups or organizations and "community groups" are undefined, and many local police and fire departments are headed by "local officials."

[667] See Section 303(c)(3). Section 301(c) refers to appointment of a community "information coordinator," whose primary role is to manage and dispense information to the public pursuant to Section 324, discussed infra, which governs release of information to the public. There appears to be no reason why the public official designated under the plan to be the emergency coordinator could not also be the information coordinator.

[668] Copies of this information are also tendered to the state commission, which is required to turn it over to EPA, along with lists of facilities designated by the state for emergency planning purposes, which would not otherwise be included.

[669] Section 303(a). Initial plans are due on October 17, 1988. Emergency plan contents appear to be modeled loosely on the emergency planning system employed by the Nuclear Regulatory Commission and the Federal Emergency Management Agency for nuclear power plants under the Atomic Energy Act amendments adopted after the Three Mile Island reactor accident.

contents of the local emergency plans may be influenced by nonbinding guidelines required to be issued by the National Response Team, set up under the NCP.[670]

Emergency plans are supposed to identify the facilities at risk and transportation routes followed by carriers of extremely hazardous substances in and out of the facilities,[671] describe methods and procedures to be followed by facility owners and local medical and emergency personnel in the event there is a release,[672] designate the community emergency coordinator and facility coordinators for each facility,[673] develop procedures for notification by the facility and community emergency coordinators to persons with response duties,[674] develop "methods for determining the occurrence of a release and the area of population likely to be affected by such a release,"[675] provide an inventory of available emergency facilities and equipment and identify who is responsible for it,[676] describe an evacuation plan,[677] prescribe training programs for local emergency response and medical personnel,[678] and provide "methods and schedules for exercising the emergency plan."[679]

The statute provides only modest federal grant support for state and local emergency planning activities.[680] Therefore, the quality of local

---

670 *See* Section 303(f). For a general discussion of the NRT, see Section 6.06[2][d], *supra.* In addition, the local committees may seek the advice of the Regional Response Teams on the terms of their draft plans. Section 303(g).

671 Section 303(c)(1).

672 Section 303(c)(2).

673 Section 303(c)(3). Facility coordinators are provided by the facility owners or operators. *See* Section 303(d)(1).

674 Section 303(c)(4).

675 Section 303(c)(5). This is, of course, the sixty-five-dollar question. There does not appear to be authority for enforcement of any such requirements. Even if the committee has the resources sufficient to hire a consultant who figures out what sort of monitoring network should be installed at a facility to provide the sort of information necessary to protect the public, Title III does not require the facilities to install such equipment. Such a requirement could, of course, be imposed under State law.

676 Section 303(c)(6).

677 Section 303(c)(7).

678 Section 303(c)(8).

679 Section 303(c)(9). Presumably this means drills.

680 The Federal Emergency Planning Agency is provided by Section 305(a)(2) with $5 million per year for the five-year life of the program to provide grants to "support programs of State and local governments, and to support university-sponsored programs . . ." related to emergency planning and response. Any federal grants require a 20 percent local match.

plans will be in part dependent upon state or local funding sources, and, in the absence of such funding, on the willingness of local industries to provide the resources needed for local planning.[681]

Section 305(b) requires EPA to study the state of the art in on-site emergency preparedness, detection, and response, and to prepare a report to Congress with recommendations for further legislation.[682]

[3] Routine or Periodic Reporting Requirements—Subtitle B

Facility owners or operators must provide three types of reports to state and local preparedness entities: (1) copies of material safety data sheets (MSDSs), (2) emergency and hazardous chemical inventory forms, and (3) toxic chemical release forms. The MSDSs are existing forms generated under the OSHA hazard communication rule. The other two forms are unique to the community right-to-know provisions of CERCLA.

[a] Material Safety Data Sheets

Material safety data sheets are required by the OSHA hazard communication rule[683] to be prepared by chemical manufacturers for all chemicals that are "hazardous" within the elaborate definition contained in the regulation[684] and to be retained by employers covered by the rule, generally those in the chemical manufacturing sector.[685] Section 311 of CERCLA employs the MSDS as a principal source of data input for the local emergency planning committees, and requires the committees to make MSDSs in their possession available to members of the public who request them.[686]

Section 311's basic requirement is that an owner or operator turn over, subject to confidentiality claims premised on trade secret allega-

---

[681] EPA or FEMA may provide emergency training for state or local officials. Section 330 appears to authorize appropriations for such purposes.

[682] EPA will hire a contractor to undertake the subject studies, which Section 305(b)(2) delineates as to content.

[683] 29 CFR §1910.1200(g).

[684] 29 CFR §1910.1200(d). The definitions are at §1910.1200(c). *See also supra* note 640.

[685] The rule covers employers in SIC Codes 20 through 39 (Division D, Standard Industrial Classification Manual). 29 CFR §1910.1200(b).

[686] Section 311(c)(2).

tions,[687] either the MSDSs required to be kept at its facility or a list[688] of hazardous chemicals or mixtures[689] for which MSDSs are required to the local emergency planning committee, the State Commission, and the local fire department,[690] unless EPA has previously established a threshold for nonreportable quantities that the facility meets.[691] The duty is a continuing one.[692] It is important to understand that a facility is required only to disclose what it knows. Thus, if a facility purchases a mixture from a vendor and receives from the vendor an MSDS for the mixture that does not reveal the contents of the mixture, the facility need only turn over that sheet, or, if it chooses the list alternative, list the mixture. It does not have to make an effort to discover the elements or compounds that make up the mixture.

The statute essentially adopts the OSHA definition of "hazardous chemical," with two exceptions. An OSHA "hazardous chemical" is not subject to Section 311 reporting if it meets one of the following definitions: a "food, food additive, color additive, drug, or cosmetic regulated

---

687 These are governed by Section 322, which is discussed *infra*.

688 The listing alternative, permitted by Section 311(a)(2), allows the facility to submit a listing of the hazardous chemicals present at the facility, grouped according to the categories of health and physical hazards defined in the OSHA rule, or according to any alternative grouping methodology subsequently promulgated by EPA, by chemical or common name and the name of any hazardous components, if known, as they were provided on the MSDSs. EPA is empowered by Section 311(a)(2)(B) to vary the groupings according to similarity of hazard.

Section 311(c) requires facilities that have chosen the list alternative to turn over the underlying MSDSs to the local committee on request.

689 For *mixtures*, Section 311(a)(3) straightforwardly allows the facility to submit either a MSDS for or a list containing each hazardous component or the mixture itself, and does not require duplication of effort if the same hazardous element or compound is a part of more than one mixture. This provision is designed to cure a problem inherent in the OSHA hazard communication rule, whose definition of "chemical" includes compounds, elements, and mixtures, which has led to massive "double-sheeting," resulting in the creation of MSDSs for over 50,000 compounds. The Conference Report explains the working of this provision by the example of the fragrance industry, in which a producer may use twenty chemical elements, some of which may be hazardous, to produce hundreds of mixtures. Under Section 311, only the hazardous elements or compounds need be reported. H.R. Rep. No. 99-962, 99th Cong., 2d Sess. at 287.

690 Section 311(a)(1).

691 Section 311(b).

692 Section 311(d)(1) requires initial submission within twelve months of the effective date of the 1986 amendments, and within three months of a facility's first becoming subject to an OSHA MSDS requirement. There is also a continuing duty to submit revised sheets within three months of discovery of "significant new information concerning an aspect of a hazardous chemical" for which a MSDS was previously provided. Section 311(d)(2).

by the Food and Drug Administration";[693] a "solid in any manufacturing item to the extent exposure to the substance does not occur under normal conditions of use";[694] substances "used for personal, family or household purposes," or products or chemicals that are in the same form and concentration as any such substances;[695] substances present in research laboratories, hospitals, or medical facilities "under the direct supervision of a technically qualified individual";[696] and substances "to the extent . . . used in routine agricultural operations or is a fertilizer held for sale by a retailer to the ultimate consumer."[697] The second potential variance from the OSHA definitions is the authority provided to EPA by Section 311(a)(2)(B) to redefine the categories of health and physical hazards "by requiring information to be reported in terms of groups of hazardous chemicals which present similar hazards in an emergency."

State and local agencies are required to employ EPA's form, but Section 322(b) allows them to ask for information not solicited on the form by attaching additional sheets to it.

[b] Emergency and Hazardous Chemical Inventory Reporting

[i] Compilation and Contents of Reports

Section 312 provides a second level of information, premised on the Section 311 data. All facilities with Section 311 obligations are required

---

[693] Section 311(e)(1). Pesticide additives, which are regulated under Section 408 of the Federal Food, Drug and Cosmetic Act, but by EPA rather than the FDA, appear not to be covered by this exemption. An interesting question is whether drug manufacturing process intermediates are included within the term "drug." The regulatory history of the use of the term in TSCA suggests that they are. Trade secret chaos could result if they are not.

[694] Section 311(e)(2).

[695] Section 311(e)(3).

[696] Section 311(e)(4). It is difficult to justify this exemption. The presence of a technically qualified supervisor at a research or medical facility would seem no greater deterrent to a potential release or more accessible source of information in the event of a release than the presence of such a person at a manufacturing facility or other type of facility.

[697] Section 311(e)(5). This exemption appears to provide a broad loophole for agricultural pesticide warehouses and formulating facilities, though it may have been intended to protect farmers from paperwork.

to submit[698] to the same local and state entities an inventory form (which is to be designed by EPA)[699] containing so-called Tier I information (described below) on or before March 1, 1988, and annually thereafter.[700] As in the case of Section 311 data, EPA is empowered to create thresholds for reporting, and to vary the chemical classifications employed by OSHA to classifications more useful for Title III's purposes.[701]

Tier I information, which is generally available to the public, includes the facility's estimate (in ranges) of the maximum amount of chemicals in each OSHA hazard category present at the facility "at any time during the preceding calendar year" and of the average daily amount present during the previous year, along with an indication of the "general location of hazardous chemicals in each category."[702] Tier I information is accordingly of a general nature, requiring no specific inventorying of individual chemicals or locations of chemicals on the site.[703]

Tier II inventory information, which is much more detailed, is required to be compiled and provided if requested by one of the emergency entities or by the fire department.[704] Tier II information includes the chemical or common name of above-threshold chemicals as they appear on the MSDSs, an estimate (in ranges)[705] of the maximum one-time and average daily amounts of each chemical within the previous year, a brief description of the manner of storage, the precise location

---

[698] Subject to claims of trade secret confidentiality, governed by Section 322.

[699] Section 312(g). If EPA defaults on production of the form, the information must be submitted by letter. *Id.* For EPA's proposed forms, *see* 52 Fed. Reg. 2836 (1-27-87).

[700] The obligation to submit Tier I information for any given year is satisfied if the submitter has elected to submit, or has for any other reason submitted, more extensive Tier II information for that year. Section 312(a)(2).

[701] Sections 312(b), 312(d)(1)(C).

[702] Section 312(d)(1).

[703] However, Section 312(f) requires specific location information to be given to the fire department upon request.

[704] Section 312(d)(2).

[705] The limitation to ranges is explained in the Conference Report as having been intended to tread the thin line between protecting trade secrets and providing important information to the community. Perhaps envisioning a future dispute over the breadth of the ranges that would be permissible, the Conference Committee opined, "In order to protect chemical process trade secret information, the reporting ranges may need to be broad. . . . The reporting ranges should provide a reasonable accommodation between [the community's need to know and the need to protect legitimate trade secrets]. . . . EPA may want to look at ranges used to develop the 1977 inventory reporting under §8(b) of the Toxic Substances Control Act for guidance." H.R. Rep. No. 99-962, 99th Cong., 2d Sess. at 290.

of the chemicals at the facility, and a statement as to whether the submitter elects to withhold its location information from public disclosure.[706]

[ii] **Disclosure to the Public**

Tier I information is treated as public information. Tier II information is somewhat protected. It is available without restriction to the state and local emergency entities and the fire department having jurisdiction over the submitter's facility, and to any other "State or local official acting in his or her official capacity."[707] Release of "any Tier II information" to a member of the general public is subject both to conditions set forth in Section 312(e)(3), and to the rather complex trade secret protection provisions of Section 322.[708]

Citizen requests for Tier II information must be in writing and inquire about a specific facility. Citizen access to information is generally governed by Section 324, which appears to allow on-premises inspection of information at the office of the state or local emergency entity, but, apparently, not copying, although there is no express embargo against that. Nonconfidential Tier II information already in the hands of the emergency entities at the time a request is made is turned over automatically.[709] If the information is not yet in the possession of the entity, it is obligated to acquire it if the request relates to a facility that has stored the chemical that is subject to the request "in an amount in excess of 10,000 pounds . . . at any time during the previous calendar year."[710] For facilities with lesser amounts, the emergency entity is not required to demand the information unless it decides to do so upon a

---

[706] Sections 312(d)(2)(A)-(F). Election to withhold public disclosure of the location of chemicals is authorized by Section 324, and may not be overridden by the emergency authorities.

[707] §312(e)(2). A request by such an official can serve as a trigger for the emergency entity to demand that a facility provide a Tier II inventory.

[708] These provisions are discussed *infra*.

[709] The statutory response time is forty-five days. Section 312(e)(3)(D).

[710] Section 312(e)(3)(B). It is not immediately apparent on the face of the statute how the emergency entity will know the critical fact if it does not already possess the Tier II information from some other source. The statute would have been better drafted if the automatic request obligation were triggered by facilities whose *Tier I* inventory showed the presence of 10,000 pounds of chemicals *of the same hazard classification.*

citizen request that states the "general need" for the information.[711]

[c] Toxic Chemical Release Reporting

[i] In General

Section 313, unlike the previous two provisions, requires reporting about effluents and emissions of "toxic chemicals" that are contained on the list of chemicals subject to the requirement, in addition to reporting their presence at the facility. Reports, on forms to be developed by EPA pursuant to directives contained in Section 313(g), are required to be submitted each year by persons subject to reporting, beginning on July 1, 1988. Section 313(g)(2) states that the statute is not intended to require "monitoring or measurement of the quantities, concentration, or frequency of any toxic chemical released into the environment beyond that . . . required under other provisions of law or regulations," although if a facility does not possess available information on a matter as to which it has a reporting obligation it must provide "reasonable estimates of the amounts involved."[712]

Also unlike the previous two sections, Section 313 seems to have little to do with emergency preparedness. Rather, it creates a data base for which the statute contemplates two uses. Section 313(j) requires EPA to set up a computer data base, accessible by the public, containing Section 313 data, which is also available under the general public availability provision, Section 324. The usefulness of the data to interest groups, such as plaintiffs or defense lawyers, will depend on the form the data base takes, which is not prescribed. The second use is the development of initial data for a mass balance study EPA is required to perform by Section 313(1).

[ii] Who Must Report

Persons with reporting obligations are industries in Standard Industrial Classification Codes 20 through 30 that, in any relevant calendar year, "manufactured, processed or otherwise used a toxic chemical" in

---

[711] Sections 312(e)(3)(B) and (3)(C).

[712] Since Section 313(g)(1)(A) requires certification by a "senior official with management responsibility for the . . . persons completing the report, regarding the accuracy and completeness of the report," estimates could be risky.

excess of thresholds established under Section 313(f). "Manufacture"[713] and "processing"[714] are defined in the regulation. For Section 313 purposes, "toxic chemicals" are those contained on a list produced in the Senate and incorporated into Section 313 by reference (the list is reproduced in Appendix 6H, *infra*), or as subsequently modified by EPA,[715] either on its own motion or acting on a petition from a citizen or a state governor.[716]

Additions to the list are governed by Section 313(d)(2), which establishes health effects criteria that must be met prior to listing, and by Section 313(e), which imposes special rules for additions based on citizen petitions or petitions by governors. There are three categories of effects that could bring a chemical onto the list: acute toxicity,[717] long latency period or chronic human health effects,[718] and serious environmental effects.[719]

---

[713] Section 313(b)(1)(C) defines this as "to produce, prepare, import, or compound a toxic chemical."

[714] *Id.* Defined as "the preparation of a toxic chemical, after its manufacture, for distribution in commerce, (I) in the same form or physical state as, or in a different form or physical state from, that in which it was received by the person . . ., or (II) as part of an article containing the toxic chemical."

The first of the above clauses captures repackagers, distributors, warehousemen, etc.; the second captures a group of manufacturers that have historically been substantially exempted from the Toxic Substances Control Act regulatory program, although, since the term "article" is undefined, the precise scope of this provision remains to be seen.

[715] Sections 313(c), 313(d). EPA may revise the list up to December 1 of any calendar year, effective for reporting purposes in the next calendar year. Section 313(d)(4). Thus, if EPA adds a chemical to the list on November 30, 1987, facilities' reports for calendar year 1988, which are due on July 1, 1989, must include that chemical.

[716] There are different rules for adding substances, depending upon the initiating act. *See* discussion *infra.*

[717] Section 313(d)(2)(A). The standard is "sufficient evidence to establish" that the "chemical is known to cause or can reasonably be anticipated to cause significant adverse acute human health effects at concentration levels that are reasonably likely to exist beyond facility site boundaries *as a result of continuous, or frequently occurring, releases.*" *Id.* (emphasis added).

[718] Section 313(d)(2)(B). The standard is ". . . sufficient evidence to establish" that the "chemical is known to cause or can reasonably be anticipated to cause in humans (i) cancer or teratogenic effects, or (ii) serious or irreversible (I) reproductive dysfunctions, (II) neurological disorders, (III) heritable genetic mutations, or (IV) other chronic health effects." *Id.* By excluding the "continuous or frequently recurring release" qualifier that modifies the acute toxicity criterion, Congress seems implicitly to have codified the "one hit" viewpoint as to carcinogens and mutagens.

[719] Section 313(d)(2)(C). The standard is ". . . sufficient evidence to establish" that the "chemical is known to cause or can reasonably be anticipated to cause, because of its toxicity, its toxicity and persistence in the environment, or its toxicity and tendency to bioaccumulate in the environment, a significant adverse effect on the environ-

Deletions from the list are based on a finding that the listed chemical does not meet the toxicity criteria established under the statute for additions.[720]

Additions to or deletions from the list may also be triggered by "any person" or by a governor. Citizens may petition only for changes based on human toxicity.[721] Governors may seek revisions based on any of the Section 313(d) criteria.[722] EPA is required to respond to a citizen petition within 180 days, either by initiating a Section 313(d) rulemaking or by publishing an explanation of why it is denying the petition.[723] Petitions filed by governors seeking deletion are treated in the same manner, but governors' petitions for additions are automatically granted unless EPA acts within the 180-day time period.[724]

Although the statute creates a cause of action to force EPA to act on a Section 313 citizen petition,[725] there is no express provision for judicial review of denial or grant of a petition by either a citizen or a governor to list or delete a chemical.[726] Mere manufacture, processing, or use of a listed chemical does not automatically result in a reporting obligation. The activity must be above the thresholds established under Section 313(f)(1) or modified thresholds established by EPA under Section 313(f)(2). There are different thresholds for users and for manufacturers/processors, the thresholds for users being significantly lower.[727]

---

ment of sufficient seriousness, in the judgment of the Administrator, to warrant .reporting. . . ." *Id.*

The Conference Report lists six types of harm EPA is to consider, involving destruction or interference with higher organisms, and species diversity, impacts on agriculture, and long-lasting or irreversible contamination of groundwater and other resources that have limited self-cleansing capability. H.R. Rep. No. 99-962, 99th Cong., 2d Sess. at 295.

Congress wisely limited EPA's employment of this criteria so that not more than 25 percent of the list can comprise "environmental," as opposed to human, toxins.

720 Section 313(d)(3).

721 *See* Section 313(e)(1).

722 Section 313(e)(2).

723 Section 313(e)(1).

724 *See* Section 313(e)(2).

725 *See* Section 326(a)(1)(B)(ii).

726 Since Congress specifically provided for judicial review of EPA decisions to modify the frequency of reporting under Section 313, *see* Section 313(i)(6), its failure to mention judicial review in the listing context, coupled with the absence of a general judicial review provision in Title III, probably forecloses it. Section 706 of the Administrative Procedure Act does not provide jurisdiction to review statutory actions where the governing statute does not authorize it. Califano v. Sanders, 430 U.S. 99 (1977).

[iii] What Must Be Reported

Entities meeting the reporting thresholds are required to file a report annually, on or before July 1, unless the reporting frequency is modified to a lesser frequency by EPA under Section 313(i), on forms provided by EPA, if available, or otherwise by letter.[728] Reports are filed with EPA and the state agency designated by the governor to receive them.[729] They are subject to trade secret confidentiality claims, which must be made in the manner and under the limitations set forth in Section 322.[730]

Reports include general business and location information about the facility; certification by a senior management person that the report is complete; and "for each toxic chemical known to be present at the facility," information as to its relationship to the facility (that is, whether it is manufactured or used) and the categories of its use,[731] an "estimate of the maximum amount (in ranges) . . . present at any time during the preceding calendar year,"[732] "for each waste stream, the waste treatment or disposal methods employed, and an estimate of the treatment efficiency typically achieved,"[733] and "the annual quantity of the toxic chemical entering such environmental medium."[734]

EPA is empowered to modify, through rulemaking, the frequency of reporting, on a broad (geographic or by chemical or class of chemical), or a narrow (facility-by-facility) basis, under a provision that appears to be designed to provide relief if the paperwork becomes more burdensome than the information is worth.[735] Curiously, provision is made for judicial review of a frequency modification, which appears to be gratuitous and out of proportion to the significance of the action, particularly since judicial review is unavailable for other Section 313 decisions.

---

[727] The threshold for users is use of 10,000 pounds per year; for manufacturers/processers, there are descending thresholds from an initial threshold of 75,000 pounds for the July 1, 1988, report (covering calendar year 1987), 50,000 for the 1989 report, and 25,000 for the 1990 and subsequent reports.

[728] Section 313(g)(1).

[729] Section 313(a). The obvious candidate would seem to be the agency designated as the emergency response commission under Section 301.

[730] *See* Section 6.11[4], *infra.*

[731] Section 313(g)(1)(C)(i).

[732] Section 313(g)(1)(C)(ii). *See supra* note 705 for a discussion of the reason for the language "(in ranges)."

[733] Section 313(g)(1)(C)(iii).

[734] Section 313(g)(1)(C)(iv).

[735] Section 313(i).

[4] Trade Secret Protection

[a] In General

Reporting entities may, at the time the submission is due to be made, seek protection for information relating to the "specific chemical identity" of a substance, subject to a rather elaborate procedural scheme under Section 322. EPA is required to promulgate regulations that define what is meant by "specific chemical identity," and to flesh out the statutory factors that determine whether a given claim of confidentiality may be upheld.[736]

[b] Procedure for Claiming Protection

Trade secret claimants must insert in their submissions in lieu of the specific chemical identity information about the "generic class or category" of which the protected chemical is a member.[737]

They must also state in the report that the specific information is being withheld as a trade secret, and state the reasons why the withheld information satisfies the four-factor test contained in Section 322(b). Finally, the report *and the information that has been withheld* must be sent to EPA.[738]

Since Section 322(f) makes anything submitted to EPA except a specific chemical identity available to the public, a trade secret claimant must be careful in drafting the supporting arguments so as not to compromise the information inadvertently.[739]

[c] Criteria

The substantive factors upon which trade secret claims are judged are as follows: (1) The information may not have been disclosed, except

---

[736] Section 322(c).

[737] Section 322(a)(2).

[738] Sections 322(a)(2)(i)-(iii). Claimants may either include the information sought to be withheld in highlighted sections of the report or submit it on separate sheets. Most will elect the latter.

[739] The statute does provide that a claimant may be able to prevent public disclosure of the contents of its submission if EPA is convinced that disclosure would violate 18 USC §1905. That statute makes it a crime for a federal official to disclose any information "which concerns or relates to trade secrets, processes, operations, style of work, or apparatus, or to the identity, confidential statistical data amount or source of income, profits, losses or expenditures of any person . . ., except as provided by law." *See* Alcolac v. Wagoner, 610 F. Supp. 745 (E.D. Mo. 1985).

under a confidentiality agreement that has been enforced, to anyone other than "a member of a local emergency planning committee, a state, federal or local officer or employee," or the claimant's own employees.[740] (2) The information is not required to be disclosed under any other federal or state law. (3) Disclosure is "likely to cause substantial harm to the competitive position of such person." (4) The "chemical identity is not readily discoverable through reverse engineering."[741]

[d] Citizen Petition for Disclosure

Section 322(d) provides procedures for members of the public to petition EPA for disclosure of trade secret–embargoed information, and provides for judicial review of the Agency's decisions.[742] This provision and Section 326(a)(1)(B)(6), which authorizes a mandamus suit to compel a decision following nine months of EPA inaction on such a petition, are intended to replace the Freedom of Information Act as a means for the public to challenge the legitimacy of trade secret claims, for Title III purposes.[743]

Following receipt of a petition for release of trade secret data, EPA must decide (1) whether the trade secret claimant's assertions would, if supported by evidence, satisfy the Section 322(b) standard, and (2) if they would, or after the claimant supplements them they would, then whether evidence the claimant is given an opportunity to submit ("de-

---

[740] This limitation is facility specific. Thus, even though a given chemical in use at the facility has been disclosed generally by its manufacturer or other users, the claimant who asserts that knowledge of the chemical in *its* process would adversely affect its competitive position is not disqualified unless it had disclosed the information in a manner that breaches the guideline.

[741] Section 322(b). EPA is required to issue interpretive regulations. EPA regulations that relate to the reverse-engineering factor are required to be "equivalent" to OSHA's comparable requirements issued as a part of the Hazard Communication Rule, pursuant to the remand order in United Steelworkers of America, AFL-CIO-CLC v. Auchter, 763 F.2d 728 (3d Cir. 1985). *See* Section 9.04[5], *infra*, regarding the OSHA rules.

[742] EPA may also review the claim on its own motion. The Agency is unlikely to do so in many cases, however, simply because it has so many other statutory responsibilities that are not discretionary. Thus, as a practical matter, the burden of ensuring that the trade secret provision is not abused will fall primarily on the public interest organizations interested in full disclosure.

[743] *See* H.R. Rep. No. 99-962, 99th Cong., 2d Sess. at 306-07. Curiously, however, the Conference Report's assertion that these provisions "supersede" the FOIA is not reflected in the language of the statute. Section 321, the "other affected laws" provision, makes no mention of superseding FOIA. Thus, any supersession must be inferred.

tailed information") supports a determination that the assertions are true.[744]

[e] Disclosure to Health Professionals and Treating Doctors and Nurses

The confidentiality provisions do not apply in full force to medical personnel who request information.[745] There are three circumstances under which owners or operators who have withheld information related to specific chemical identities must turn the information (along with other nonprotected information) over to medical personnel.

Any "health professional"[746] must be given the information upon a written request stating that the information is needed for the purposes of diagnosis or treatment of an individual, that the individual "has been exposed to the chemical concerned, and that knowledge of the specific chemical identity will assist in the diagnosis and treatment, accompanied by a signed confidentiality agreement containing the restrictions set forth in Section 323(d).[747]

A "treating physician or nurse" may secure such information without a prior confidentiality agreement or prior statement of need, for the purpose of use in what the physician or nurse decides is a "medical emergency" where the specific chemical identity is "necessary for or will assist in emergency or first aid diagnosis or treatment" and the

---

[744] Sections 322(d)(3), 322(d)(4). The statute provides timetables for submission of information in a Section 322(d) proceeding. There is no express time period within which EPA must make a decision, except that the citizen suit section, Section 326, appears to impose a ninety-day outside limit on the action. As in the case of the original submission, any supplemental material submitted in the context of a Section 322(d) proceeding, except for the specific chemical identity, is considered public information under Section 322(f).

[745] See Section 323, which sets forth the conditions under which trade secret data must be turned over to medical personnel under various circumstances.

[746] This term is not defined. EPA may define it in regulations. Section 323(e).

[747] Section 323(a). Section 323(d) is not clear as to whether the statements contained in it are all that the owner or operator can demand. The statute states that the person seeking the information "shall be required to agree . . . that he will not use the information for any purpose other than the health needs asserted in the statement of need, except as may otherwise be authorized by the terms of the agreement or by the person providing such information," and preserves to the parties any remedies provided under the law. It is not, for example, apparent whether the submitter can require the recipient to agree to an indemnity or liquidated damages in the event of a breach of confidentiality.

patient has "been exposed to the chemical concerned."[748]

Finally, a "health professional (such as a physician, toxicologist, or epidemiologist)" employed by or under contract to a local government, may secure confidential information upon submitting a written statement of need that meets one or more of six statutory criteria,[749] and signing a confidentiality agreement.

[f]   Disclosure to Governor

EPA is required to turn over any information in its possession to a state governor who requests it.[750]

[g]   Enforcement and Confidentiality Protection

There are three areas of enforcement that relate to trade secret protection. The statute imposes civil penalties for frivolous trade secret claims, which may be levied administratively or by a federal judge,[751] and criminal responsibility for "knowingly and willfully" divulging or disclosing any information entitled to trade secret protection.[752]

Section 325(e) authorizes mandatory injunctive actions in federal district courts for "health professionals" seeking to compel information they have sought unsuccessfully under Section 323.

[5]   General Enforcement Provisions

[a]   Administrative Orders and Civil and Criminal Penalties

Section 325's enforcement scheme is unduly complex, providing a

---

[748] Section 323(b). A written request setting forth the grounds for the request and a confidentiality agreement are required to be given to the data submitter after the fact.

[749] The criteria are "(A) To assess exposure of persons living in a local community to the hazards of the chemical . . . (B) To conduct or assess sampling to determine exposure levels of various population groups. (C) To conduct periodic medical surveillance of exposed population groups. (D) To provide medical treatment to exposed individuals or population groups. (E) To conduct studies to determine the health effects of exposure. (F) To conduct studies to aid in the identification of a chemical that may reasonably be anticipated to cause an observed health effect."

[750] Section 322(g).

[751] Section 325(d)(1). The penalty is a flat $25,000 per claim. EPA must determine that the claim was made without sufficient assertion of support, or that it was not supported by the evidence, and that it was frivolous.

[752] Section 325(d)(2). The fine is up to $20,000 or one year in prison or both.

smorgasbord of penalties for various types of violations, when it would seem that a straightforward, simple provision would have sufficed.

EPA must issue an order to recalcitrant entities with respect to the information required by Sections 302(C) and 303(d)[753] before it may seek a judicial civil penalty of up to $25,000 per day.[754] There are no criminal sanctions for violating the emergency planning information requirements.

If one fails to make a required emergency notification under Section 304, one is subject to all manner of potential penalties. There are separate levels of administrative penalties for violations and continuing violations,[755] which provide for different amounts of levies and, possibly, different procedures.[756] EPA may also elect to seek a civil penalty from a federal judge.[757] Violations that are knowing *and* willful are subject to criminal sanctions.[758]

A nongovernmental entity who violates a Section 312 or Section 313 obligation is liable for an administrative penalty of up to $25,000 per violation, but one who violates Section 311 or Section 323(b), or who fails to supply information requested by EPA under Section 322(a)(2),

---

[753] Facilities required to report solely because a governor has put them on the list are not liable for federal sanctions if they fail to report. Those the state adds are the state's enforcement responsibility.

[754] Section 325(a).

[755] Section 325(b)(1), 325(b)(2).

[756] Continuing violations appear to require adjudicatory hearings, since Section 325(b)(2) requires that the penalties be "assessed and collected in the same manner and subject to the same provisions, as in the case of civil penalties assessed and collected under section 16 of the Toxic Substances Control Act," which requires Administrative Procedure Act Section 554 adjudications. (There is an interesting conflict between the language of this section, which seems to include all of Section 16, including its judicial review provision, which limits judicial review of a penalty assessment to the United States Court of Appeals for the District of Columbia Circuit, and Section 325(f), which purports to confer jurisdiction to appeal a penalty assessment to the federal district courts.)

Penalties under Section 325(b)(1) are subject to "notice and opportunity for a hearing." In practical terms, those hearings may also be adjudicatory. *See* Seacoast Anti-Pollution League v. Costle, 572 F.2d 872 (1st Cir. 1978) (construing identical language in the Federal Water Pollution Control Act). *Cf.* Buttrey v. United States, 690 F.2d 1170 (5th Cir. 1982) (coming to opposite conclusion on same language in Section 404 of FWPCA, but relying on specific legislative history).

[757] Section 325(b)(3).

[758] Section 325(b)(4). First offenses yield maximum sentences of a $25,000 fine and/or two years in prison. Subsequent offenses result in twice the maximum fine and up to five years in prison. Curiously, Congress did not seek to conform the Title III criminal penalties to the new federal criminal code, as it did the other CERCLA criminal sanctions.

is liable to be assessed an administrative penalty only up to $10,000 per violation.[759]

The procedural requirements for administrative penalty assessments are redundant, in some ways potentially inconsistent, and generally confusing.

[b] Citizen Suits and Suits by State and Local Governments

The Title III citizen suit provision is narrowly drawn. Actions against facility owners or operators are limited to compelling the submission of four types of information: Section 304(c) notices, material safety data sheets or lists, Section 312(a) inventories, and Section 313(a) release forms.[760] Mandamus actions against EPA, which may be brought only in Washington, D.C.,[761] lie only to compel it to publish a Section 312 inventory form, act on petitions under Section 313(e)(1) (within 180 days after receipt), act on petitions under Section 322 (within 9 months of receipt), publish a toxic substance release form under Section 313(g), establish a computer data base under Section 313(j), promulgate trade secret regulations,[762] or provide a mechanism for public dissemination of information as provided in Section 324,[763]

A citizen suit may be brought against a state entity to compel response to a request for Tier II information under Section 312(e)(3).[764]

EPA or the state may intervene as of right in any citizen suit.[765]

State or local governments are allowed, by Section 326(a)(2), to sue owners or operators who have not complied with the obligations imposed on them by Sections 302(c), 311(a), 311(c), and 312(a). State emergency response commissions and local emergency planning committees can sue owners or operators for failure to provide information required

---

[759] Section 325(c).

[760] Section 326(a)(1)(A). Venue is in the local federal district court. Section 326(b). There is a requirement that notice have been given at least sixty days prior to commencement of the action to the alleged violator, EPA, and the state. Section 326(c). If EPA is "diligently pursuing" administrative or judicial enforcement, a citizen action is barred, Section 326(e), and intervention by citizens in any such action is permissive, Section 326(h)(2).

[761] Section 326(b)(2). There is a sixty-day prior notice requirement, as well. Section 326(d)(2).

[762] Section 326(a)(1)(B).

[763] Section 326(a)(1)(C). Suit may also include the state entity under this provision.

[764] Section 326(a)(1)(D). The sixty-day prior notice requirement of Section 326(d)(2) applies.

[765] Section 326(h)(1).

by Sections 303(d) and 303(e)(1),[766] and states (presumably governors) may sue EPA if it refuses to turn over trade secret information pursuant to Section 322(g).[767]

The statute makes provision for costs and reasonable attorneys' and expert witnesses' fees to be awarded to the "substantially prevailing party whenever the court determines such an award is appropriate."[768] There is, finally, specific authorization for the court to require the filing of a bond in the event preliminary or temporary relief is requested,[769] which deprives citizens from arguing that the public purposes of the citizen suit would be frustrated by a bonding requirement.

---

[766] *Compare* Section 326(a)(2)(A) *with* Section 326(a)(2)(B).

[767] Section 326(a)(2)(C).

[768] Section 326(f).

[769] *Id.*

CHAPTER 7

Regulation of Toxic and Hazardous Air Emissions, Wastewater Effluents, and Groundwater Pollution

§7.01   Introduction

This chapter deals with environmental regulation of the waste emissions of industries that emit exotic, toxic or hazardous waste into the air, surface water, or groundwater in a form other than "solid waste," which is treated in Chapters 5 and 6. In essence, it discusses the relevant regulatory subparts of the Clean Air Act,[1] the Clean Water Act,[2] and the Safe Drinking Water Act (SDWA).[3]

These programs, particularly the Clean Air and Clean Water programs, affect nearly every industry in the United States, and a large amount of primary and secondary published material exists with respect to them. This discussion will not describe the programs exhaustively; to do so would consume far too many volumes and would be of only marginal utility here.

These programs are not specifically aimed at the chemical industry or chemical production and use. They affect both, sometimes profoundly, but incidentally. What follows are discussions of those aspects of each of these environmental regulatory programs that most nearly, either at present or possibly in the future, represent exclusive or at least special significance to chemical manufacturing processes and the use of chemicals in other manufacturing processes.

---

[1] 42 USC §§7401 *et seq.*
[2] 33 USC §§1201 *et seq.*
[3] 42 USC §§300f *et seq.*

§7.02 Hazardous Air Emissions

[1] Overview of the Clean Air Act

The Clean Air Act was enacted in its current basic format in 1970,[4] and substantially revised to its current text in 1977.[5] It is a complex piece of legislation, and often difficult to comprehend in its complexity.

The act's core are Sections 108, 109, and 110.[6] Section 108 requires EPA, for a small group of listed, high-volume pollutants, and authorizes it for any others, to develop criteria upon which ambient air quality standards may be based that are adequate to protect the public health (in the case of so-called "primary" ambient air quality standards) or the environment (for "secondary" standards).

The criteria established under Section 108, which are supposed to be reviewed every five years, must underlie the national ambient air quality standards (NAAQSs) the Agency develops under Section 109.[7] The NAAQSs are applicable to all "air quality control regions" within the United States, and constitute the minimum levels of air pollution deemed acceptable in the country.[8] The goal of the act was to achieve compliance with the primary, public health–based NAAQSs within three years of issuance.[9]

The method of achieving compliance with the NAAQSs was by means of the Section 110 regulatory process. Section 110 created as the principal enforcement mechanism, the state implementation plan (SIP), a set of regulations setting emission limitations for criteria pollutants issued by classes or categories of emission sources. The state regulations, which must be approved by EPA as meeting the Section 110(a) crite-

---

[4] P.L. 91-604 (12-31-70).

[5] P.L. 95-95 (8-87-77).

[6] References are to session law numbers. A table cross-referencing session law and U.S. Code numbers is given in Appendix 7-A, *infra.*

[7] The original NAAQSs, issued for six pollutants shortly after the act's passage, were based on admittedly sketchy data. EPA has had difficulty meeting its Section 108 obligations ever since.

[8] Individual states are free to adopt more stringent state ambient air quality standards. Initially some states adopted the more restrictive federal secondary standards as their primary standards, but in the end most states simply fell into lockstep with EPA.

[9] The secondary standards are to be achieved within a "reasonable time."

ria,[10] are intended to be based on calculations derived from data on emission loads, background air quality information, and meteorological data.

The original SIPs were little more than guesses as to what degree of emission control would be necessary to achieve the NAAQSs, and the combination of wrong guesses and law enforcement caused wholesale failure of the basic provisions of the act to clean up the air by 1977.

The 1977 amendments added Part D to the act, which contains an elaborate set of provisions aimed at addressing the nonattainment of the NAAQSs in wide areas of the country.[11] They also added Part C, which attempts to prevent areas not already degraded from deteriorating.[12]

In addition to the NAAQSs/SIP program, the Clean Air Act contains a separate part, Title II, devoted to regulating the emissions from automotive vehicles and, to a lesser extent, aircraft engines, and contains separate requirements for regulating emissions from new facilities[13] and for regulating the emission of hazardous air pollutants.[14]

[2] Regulation of Hazardous Air Pollutants Under Sections 108, 109, and 110

Hazardous air pollutants are defined only by Section 112(a)(1) of the Clean Air Act, in which they are defined as air pollutants "to which no ambient air quality standard is applicable, and which . . . causes or contributes to, air pollution which may reasonably be anticipated to result in an increase in mortality or an increase in serious irreversible, or incapacitating reversible, illness." That definition is sufficiently

---

10 If EPA refuses to approve a state's SIP, the initial remedy provided by the act was promulgation by EPA of a federal SIP, and direct EPA regulation of sources of air pollution in the state. The 1977 amendments added two other weapons to force state cooperation. EPA could impose a moratorium on the construction of new sources of pollutants for which the NAAQSs had not been achieved, and the Agency could require the withholding of certain federal funds. Section 110(a)(2)(I).

11 Sections 172-178; various amendments to Section 110; and an amendment to Section 107. *See also* 48 Fed. Reg. 90686 (1983); and Chevron v. NRDC, 104 S.Ct. 2778 (1983).

12 Primarily Sections 160–169; and Section 169A (which relates to visibility protection). For those with sufficient interest in the subject, Alabama Power Co. v. Costle, 606 F.2d 1068 (D.C. Cir. 1979), is required reading.

13 Section 111.

14 Section 112.

broad to cover a wide range of pollutants emitted from chemical-processing facilities.

Section 108(a)(1) allows EPA to add to its "criteria pollutant list"[15] air pollutants the emissions of which "cause or contribute to air pollution which may reasonably be anticipated to endanger public health or welfare" and "the presence of which in the ambient air results from numerous and diverse mobile or stationary sources."[16] Any pollutant that falls within the definition of "hazardous" contained in Section 112 clearly would meet the first prong of the Section 108(a)(1) test. The second, however, is sufficiently subject to varying interpretations that EPA could well determine that most hazardous pollutants are not emitted on a sufficiently wide scale to warrant triggering the cumbersome SIP process.

[a]   Particulates and Volatile Organic Compounds

Two of the original "criteria" pollutants are actually no more than terms that embrace a wide range of individual pollutants, all of which differ in their chemical compositions and, to one degree or another, in their potential for health effects.

EPA originally regulated "total suspended particulates" (TSPs), a catchall phrase for anything that was light enough to become suspended in the atmosphere long enough to move any significant distance from the source, yet was a solid particle capable of being trapped in a filter and counted. Although any physicist knows that there are particles, and then there are particles, and then . . ., air pollution monitoring technology, which was in a rather unsophisticated state when EPA began to implement the Clean Air Act, no doubt played a role in the inclusive nature of the particulate NAAQS. Some particles are hazardous because the substance of which they are made is hazardous or toxic. Some are not. Some particles are respirable. Some are not.

Although EPA moved a step toward isolating respirable particles for

---

[15] The current criteria pollutants are sulfur dioxide, particulate matter, carbon monoxide, ozone, oxides of nitrogen, and lead. *See* 40 CFR Part 50.

[16] Sections 108(a)(1)(A) and (B). Listing a pollutant triggers a mandatory obligation to develop a criteria document and issue a NAAQS for the pollutant. *See* Sections 108(a)(2) and 109(a)(2).

separate treatment in the late 1980s,[17] it has never attempted to isolate particles for separate treatment based on their individual chemical composition.[18]

Hydrocarbons, or "volatile organic compounds" (VOCs), which are the actual pollutants controlled in connection with the criteria pollutant ozone,[19] present another example of a NAAQS that lumps together a wide variety of chemical compounds of varying significance from the public health standpoint. The primary reasons for this are, as in the case of particulates, simplicity of enforcement, and also perhaps because the environmental manifestations of these compounds tend to be sufficiently similar that addressing them separately, from an overall air quality standpoint, would make no sense.

Many exotic chemicals emitted from chemical manufacturing facilities have enjoyed relative regulatory freedom for over fifteen years, since they have been lumped in with either TSPs or VOC emissions, and thus are not subject to specific regulation in the absence of listing and regulation under Section 111 (which provides emission standards for new sources based on technology-predicated performance standards) or under Section 112 (which provides for pollutant-specific emission limitations for hazardous pollutants).

[b] Lead

The one clearly hazardous air pollutant EPA developed a NAAQS for was lead. Lead was a specific target of automotive fuel regulation under Title II of the Act, and in the late 1970s EPA moved to regulate nonautomotive sources of lead, some of which, such as smelters, are large and concentrated, while others are small and diverse.

Regulating lead was not easy for the Agency. First, there was little useful epidemiological evidence available linking airborne lead concen-

---

17 *See* 49 Fed. Reg. 10408 (1984) (proposed revised NAAQS controlling only particles 10 microns or smaller).

18 The best-publicized failure in this regard involves sulfate particles, which have been implicated by a substantial body of scientific opinion, including that of the National Academy of Sciences, in the acid rain phenomenon. EPA's stock response to lawsuits brought by acid rain recipient states seeking tighter emission controls on sulfur-emitting stationary sources has been to demur on the ground that there is no sulfate NAAQS. *See, e.g.*, Connecticut Fund for the Environment, et al. v. EPA, 696 F.2d 169 (2d Cir. 1982). The Agency has not, however, moved seriously to develop a separate sulfate standard.

19 VOCs are called "ozone precursors." They react with sunlight and other atmospheric contents to form ozone in the lower atmosphere.

trations to specific observed health effects, or even to elevated blood lead levels, from which subclinical effects could be extrapolated. Second, translating air lead to blood lead concentrations on the basis of toxicological tests was not as straightforward as the Agency perhaps would have hoped.

The NAAQS picked by the Agency was attacked by the lead industry trade association as overly conservative, but was upheld in *Lead Industries Association v. EPA*.[20] The Agency's standard, and ultimately its defense of the standard, rested heavily on the language of Section 109(b)(1), which requires NAAQSs to be set at the level, "which in the judgment of the Administrator, based on . . . [Section 108] criteria *and allowing an adequate margin of safety*, are requisite to protect the public health" (emphasis added).

From the regulator's standpoint, this is a very friendly standard. It not only allows but indeed requires the Agency to err on the side of conservatism. It also leaves no room for balancing risks against benefits. Nevertheless, EPA's difficulties with the lead standard point to the inherent difficulties presented when the Agency sets about developing an ambient concentration standard for a pollutant. The less ubiquitous the pollutant, the narrower the data base—and the narrower the data base, the greater the likelihood that the standard will tend toward fiction.

In addition, the enforcement mechanism, the SIP process, is cumbersome at best; consequently, EPA would be hard pressed to move very far down the road to vastly increasing the number of NAAQSs for the purpose of regulating hazardous chemical emissions, at least for chemicals not emitted in substantial quantities in most of the states.

[3] New Source Performance Standards

In contrast to the Sections 108-109-110 scheme, under which, in most circumstances, the federal government does not directly impose emission limitations on specific sources or source categories, it has such authority as to "new sources," pursuant to Section 111 of the Clean Air Act. The act defines "new source" as any "stationary source, the construction or modification of which is commenced after the publication

---

[20] 647 F.2d 1130 (D.C. Cir. 1980).

of regulations (or, if earlier, proposed regulations)[21] prescribing a standard of performance under this section which will be applicable to such source."[22]

A source category must be regulated if EPA has included it on a list of sources to be regulated if it "causes, or contributes significantly to, air pollution which may reasonably be anticipated to endanger public health or welfare."[23]

EPA has interpreted and applied Section 111 to limit its applicability to industry categories that are reasonably geographically diverse and in which at least some new construction is going on. It also regulates only "criteria pollutants" emitted by the source categories it controls, even though the language of Section 111 does not preclude it from regulating new sources emitting noncriteria pollutants.[24]

Sources controlled under Section 111 are subject to technology-based performance standards or work practice standards designed to reduce the level of emissions.[25] For pollutants emitted by regulated

---

21 *See* United States v. City of Painesville, 644 F.2d 1186 (6th Cir. 1981), *cert. denied,* 454 U.S. 894 (6th Cir. 1981).

22 Section 111(a)(2).

23 Section 111(b)(1)(A). EPA has regulated under Section 111 the following categories of sources, which emit chemical waste products into the atmosphere (all published in 40 CFR Part 60): incinerators (subpart E), nitric acid plants (subpart G), sulfuric acid plants (subpart H), petroleum refineries (subpart J, GGG), petroleum storage vessels (subpart K), aluminum reduction plants (subpart S), various fertilizer plant types (subparts T–X), Kraft pulp mills (subpart BB), metal furniture surface coating (subpart EE), lead acid battery plants (subpart KK), automotive surface coating operations (subpart MM), printing plants (subpart QQ), various industrial surface coating operations (subparts RR–UU and WW), synthetic organic chemicals manufacturing (VOC leaks from equipment only—subpart VV), bulk gasoline terminals (subpart XX), flexible vinyl and urethane coating and printing (subpart FFF), synthetic fiber production facilities (subpart HHH), and petroleum dry cleaners (subpart JJJ).

24 Section 111(d) lends significant weight to the proposition that Section 111 could be used to regulate exotic, noncriteria pollutants. Section 111(a) requires state implementation plans aimed at regulating *existing* sources that emit—

any air pollutant (i) for which air quality criteria have not been issued or which is not included on a list published under section 108(a) [pollutants for which criteria are being developed] or 112(b)(1)(A) [EPA's list of hazardous pollutants to be regulated under Section 112] but (ii) to which a standard of performance under this section would apply if such existing source were a new source. . . .

Congress obviously contemplated that EPA would be issuing New Source Performance Standards (NSPSs) for sources that issue pollutants not regulated either under the SIP process or under Section 112.

25 *See* National Lime Association v. EPA, 627 F.2d 416 (D.C. Cir. 1980), for a thoughtful discussion of this standard.

facilities, the statute requires EPA to set numerical emission limits that reflect "the degree of emission reduction achievable through the application of the best system of continuous emission reduction which . . . has been adequately demonstrated."[26] EPA must assess the operating technology and determine which is the "best system" in terms of operating efficiency, removal efficiency, cost-effectiveness, etc., that has been "adequately demonstrated."[27]

Because the Section 111 standard is a technology standard, it does not provide EPA with authority to prohibit the emission of specific pollutants, unless there exists a removal technology that makes 100 percent removal feasible and cost-effective for the industry subcategory involved.

The statute, though aimed primarily at continuous emissions, can also be employed to deal with spikes, such as the accidental release associated with a large number of deaths at Bhopal, India, in 1984, although it has not generally been used by EPA for that purpose.[28]

(Text continued on page 7-9)

---

[26] Section 111(a)(1)(C).

[27] *Id. See also* Sierra Club v. Gorsuch, 715 F.2d 653 (D.C. Cir. 1983). EPA may promulgate a "design, work practice or operational standard" if an emission standard is not "feasible." Section 111(h). The statute also makes provision for waivers for sources experimenting with "innovative technology." Section 111(j). The statute also provides several bases for state governors to require EPA to include or temporarily exclude sources from NSPS. *See* Section 111(g).

[28] The Bhopal incident involved a massive volatilization and leak of methylisocyanate from a storage tank at a pesticide manufacturing facility. The leak apparently occurred, at least in part, as a result of a valve malfunction, where there was no automatic backup.

[4] Hazardous Emission Standards

[a] Applicability

As noted above, the definition of the term "hazardous air pollutant" contained in Section 112(a)(1) requires a "judgment" that the pollutant "causes or contributes to pollution which may reasonably be anticipated to result in an increase in mortality or an increase in serious irreversible, or incapacitating reversible, illness." This definition contrasts with the more generalized standard applicable to the listing of criteria pollutants under Section 108 and listing of sources to regulate under Section 111, which involves the question of whether the pollutant (or, in the case of Section 111, source category) may cause or contribute to air pollution that "may endanger public health. . . ."[29]

The most significant difference in the language of Section 112(a)(1) is that, instead of focusing on broad public health danger, it speaks in terms of "an increase in mortality or . . . illness." This language, in its specificity, arguably allows EPA to look at *individual* risks as well as overall population risk, and to act to regulate pollutants whose potential for harm is very localized, even limited to a single plant site.

The decision to "list" a pollutant on the hazardous pollutant list triggers a mandatory duty on EPA's part to propose emission standards for the pollutant within 180 days, hold a public hearing 30 days thereafter, and then either promulgate the standards or publish a statement explaining why information at the hearing supports a conclusion that the pollutant "clearly is not a hazardous air pollutant."[30]

EPA has listed few pollutants for regulation under Section 112. One of the few pollutants EPA has regulated, radionuclides, was actually listed legislatively.[31] EPA's reluctance to list pollutants on the Section

---

EPA has, in a few instances, set NSPSs for storage tanks. *See, e.g.,* 40 CFR Part 60 subpart K (Storage Vessels for Petroleum Liquids).

[29] *Compare* Sections 108(a)(1)(A) and 111(b)(1)(A). EPA's procedural and substantive regulations are published at 40 CFR Part 61.

[30] Section 112(b)(1)(B). *See* Sierra Club v. Gorsuch, 551 F. Supp 785 (N.D. Cal. 1984) (ordering EPA to promulgate regulations for radionuclides); and 49 Fed. Reg. 43906 (10-31-84) (articulating EPA's view of the statutory requirements).

[31] Sierra Club v. Ruckelshaus, *infra* note 38. In addition to radionuclides, EPA has promulgated hazardous emission standards for beryllium (40 CFR 61 subparts C and D), mercury (*id.,* subpart E), vinyl chloride (including ethylene dichloride plants, vinyl chloride plants, and polyvinyl chloride plants) (*id.,* subpart F), benzene (equipment leaks) (*id.,* subpart J). In New York v. Gorsuch, 554 F.Supp. 1060 (S.D.N.Y. 1983), the Agency was ordered to list arsenic, on the basis of its record demonstrating potential hazards, and its failure to act.

112(b)(1)(A) list and its slowness in acting to regulate pollutants already on this list have led to serious criticism by the public interest bar and the Congress.[32]

EPA's interpretation of the statute is that in order to support regulation following listing, a pollutant must be shown to present a "significant risk" of harm.[33] The "significant risk" threshold for regulation appears to have been borrowed from Section 3 of the Occupational Safety and Health (OSH) Act and the Supreme Court decision interpreting that provision, *Industrial Union Dept., AFL-CIO v. American Petroleum Institute*,[34] although there appears to be no statutory basis for using the OSH Act standard under Section 112.

EPA has attempted to undertake quantitative risk analyses in order to form an evidentiary basis for action or inaction under its threshold criterion. Although the plain language of Section 112(a)(1) would appear to allow EPA to regulate any pollutant found to be carcinogenic, the Agency has taken a less conservative approach, stating that population risks on the order of 0.06 fatal cancers per year from all plants emitting a pollutant and a 1 in 1000 risk of cancer to an individual residing near the most concentrated emission source are too insignificant to regulate.[35] What is important about this exercise is not the degree of risk EPA felt was significant,[36] but rather the fact that the

---

[32] *See* General Accounting Office Report, Delays in EPA's Resolution of Hazardous Air Pollutants, GAO/RCED-83-199 (8-26-83), which states: "Various policy shifts at the EPA and uncertainty over the type and amount of scientific data needed to support a regulatory action are major contributing factors to delays in developing hazardous substance listing. Delays also occurred in proposing emission standards after pollutants were listed because of the time required to develop technical and cost information and analyze public comments." For a discussion of factors EPA considers in connection with listing under Section 112, *see* 40 Fed. Reg. 52422 (12-23-85) (proposal to list trichloroethylene).

[33] *See* 48 Fed. Reg. 33116 (1983) (arsenic—proposed); 49 Fed. Reg. 23558 (benzene—proposed); 49 Fed. Reg. ____ (1984) (benzene); and 49 Fed. Reg. 4306, 50 Fed. Reg. 5191 (radionuclides).

[34] 448 U.S. 607 (1980). *See* 49 Fed. Reg. 23559 (1984). *Cf.* 50 Fed. Reg. 15388 (4-17-85) (radon) (increased risk of developing lung cancer of 1 in 100 indicates that radon-222 emissions from uranium mines "significantly affect a nearby individual's lung cancer risk").

[35] *See* 50 Fed. Reg. 5191, 5193 (2-6-85) (stating that on the basis of those risks there is no reason to regulate elemental phosphorus plants). *See also* EPA's discussion of risk assessment for nonthreshold pollutants at 48 Fed. Reg. 33115 *et seq.* (1983).

[36] The degree of risk EPA considers significant enough to support regulation will take on greater meaning as EPA becomes more active under Section 112. The Agency will begin to develop certain norms that will become the boundaries of future Agency decisions.

Agency's approach to risk analysis does not appear to differ markedly from that taken under Section 108, except perhaps for a slightly greater willingness to look at individual risks.

[b] The Section 112 Regulatory Authority

If EPA lists a pollutant as hazardous, and, after a public hearing, does not "delist" the chemical by deciding that it "clearly is not a hazardous pollutant,"[37] it must establish an emission standard for the pollutant at a level "that provides an ample margin of safety to protect the public health. . . ."[38]

Hazardous emission standards are applicable to both new and existing sources of the pollutant, although existing sources may be granted temporary waivers by EPA or the President.[39] The statute shows a decided preference for capture and control technology, but allows EPA to impose design, equipment, work practice, or operation standards if capture and control technology is "not practicable due to technological or economic limitations" or is "inconsistent with any federal, State or local law."[40]

There might well be circumstances in which Section 112 could be used by EPA to require substitution of one chemical feedstock for another, or to require backup leak protection or relief valve protection. The same type of regulatory controls can be imposed under Section 6 of the Toxic Substances Control Act (TSCA), however, arguably with a

---

[37] Section 112(b)(1)(B). Although EPA is required to *list* a pollutant that *may reasonably be anticipated to* result in mortality or illness, delisting must be based on a more strongly affirmative finding that the pollutant *clearly is not* hazardous.

[38] In the case of radionuclides, EPA found itself in a dilemma. One source category, uranium mines, clearly posed risks of sufficient magnitude that they had to be regulated. Thus, radionuclides could not be delisted as a hazardous pollutant. Several other sources of radionuclides, however, were determined by the Agency to present insufficient risks to warrant regulation. The Agency thus attempted simply not to regulate the low-risk sources. *See* 49 Fed. Reg. 43906 (10-31-84). Judge Orrick, however, disagreed with the Agency's position and ordered it to promulgate regulations even for the low-risk sources, holding that its only choice was to regulate or delist. Sierra Club v. Ruskelshaus, No. 84-0656 WHO (N.D. Cal. 12-11-84). A better tactic for EPA might have been to promulgate regulations requiring only monitoring. The problem arose because "radionuclides," listed by Congress rather than EPA, is too broad a pollutant term; because of its breadth, the Section 112 logic broke down. *See also* discussion, *supra*, of EPA's policy regarding nonthreshold pollutants.

[39] Sections 112(c)(1) and (c)(2).

[40] Section 112(e). A source may also employ "alternative means of emission limitation" provided they provide an equivalent level of emission reduction. Section 112(e)(4).

greater degree of control and flexibility; thus, EPA might be wise to look first to TSCA for regulating facilities otherwise under that statute's jurisdiction.[40.1]

§7.03   Toxic and Hazardous Wastewater Effluents

[1]   The Clean Water Act in General

The Clean Water Act in substantially its present form was enacted in 1972[41] and amended significantly in 1977.[42] The act's primary function is the establishment of a nationwide floor of technology-based effluent standards for the pollutants most commonly discharged from industrial facilities and municipal wastewater treatment plants, and a federally controlled permit program to enforce the national standards.[43] Like the Clean Air Act, the Clean Water Act contains separate regulatory requirements for new sources[44] and a somewhat different

---

[40.1] *But see* TSCA Sections 6(c)(a)(1) and 9(b), which imply that EPA should first seek to regulate under more specific regulatory authority before invoking TSCA. Spurred by public concern over the Bhopal incident and a number of domestic releases of unregulated hazardous pollutants, EPA increased the visibility of its hazardous emissions program in November 1985 by releasing a list of 409 "acutely hazardous" pollutants as an appendix to a proposed "Guidance for Developing Community Awareness and Preparedness Programs" document. N.Y. Times, Nov. 19, 1985, B9; BNA Environment Reporter Vol. 16 No. 28, p.1233. EPA's list was adopted by Congress as one of the lists of chemicals subject to disclosure requirements under the Emergency Preparedness and Community Right-to-Know provisions of Title III of the Superfund Amendments and Reauthorization Act of 1986 (SARA), P.L. 99-499 (10-17-86). *See* Section 6.11, *supra.*

Rather than attempt to regulate the emission of these chemicals, which ordinarily would occur only in the context of an industrial accident, EPA's approach seems to be one of emergency response preparedness.

[41] P.L. 92-500.

[42] P.L. 95-217. The act was also amended in 1980. P.L. 96-483.

[43] *See generally* Sections 301, 302, 304, 309, and 402. States are permitted to impose more stringent standards, which might be based on water quality criteria rather than pollutant removal technology. *See* Sections 303, 401, and 510.

[44] Section 306. This provision, quite similar in its structure to Section 307 of the Clean Air Act, provides for more stringent technology-based standards than those applied initially to existing sources under the act's two-phase standards process for existing sources. Section 306 also provides a ten-year period of protection against shifting regulatory requirements.

regulatory approach to exotic pollutants that happen to be "toxic."[45]

(*Text continued on page 7-13*)

---

[45] Section 307(a). This section also addresses industrial discharges to municipal public-ly owned wastewater treatment works (POTWs). Section 307(b). The term "toxic pollu-tants" is defined by Section 502(13) of the Clean Water Act as "those pollutants or combinations of pollutants, including disease-causing agents, which after discharge and upon exposure, ingestion, inhalation or assimilation into any organism, either directly from the environment or indirectly by ingestion through food chains, will, on the basis of information available to the administrator, cause death, disease, behavioral abnormali-ties, cancer, genetic mutations, physiological malfunctions (including malfunctions in reproduction) or physical deformations, in such organisms or their offspring."

Most facilities that produce or consume chemicals are subject to some form of regulation under the Clean Water Act, although histori- cally most facilities having the potential for or actually discharging chemical wastes were not regulated specifically with respect to the compounds discharged. The technology-based standards were devel- oped around a relatively small number of pollutant parameters that had come to be regulated by the states prior to the federalization of water pollution control in 1972. Those parameters are biochemical oxygen demand (BOD), total suspended solids (TSS), fecal coliform bacteria, pH, oil and grease, various metals, cyanide, and a catchall organic chemical pollutant, "phenols," and chemical oxygen demand (COD). Even those specialized parameters applicable to particular industries tend not to be compound specific.[46]

[2]   Section 307(a)

[a]   Historical Background

P.L. 92-500 contained the original Section 307(a), which required EPA to list toxic pollutants and establish specific technology-based ef- fluent limitations for them based on the factors of toxicity, persistence, degradability, the usual or potential presence of the affected organisms in any waters, the importance of the affected organisms, and the nature of the toxic effects.[47]

The Section 307(a) limitations were a special form of the technology- based standard, "best available technology," which was originally in- tended to be imposed, for all industry subcategories, by 1983.[48] In addition, although the statutory command was far from clear, Section 307(a)(2) arguably required EPA to set even more stringent standards for discharges of listed toxics into waters that experienced severe result- ant degradation.

EPA failed to implement the provision, preferring instead to treat all dischargers, regardless of the toxicity of their effluents, pretty much the same, subjecting them to the rather broad categories of effluent stan-

---

[46] *See, e.g.,* 40 CFR Part 455 (effluent guidelines for the pesticide chemicals manufac- turing point source category). The effluent limitations are for COD, BOD, TSS, pH, and "organic pesticide chemicals," which the regulation defines as "the sum of all organic active ingredients listed in . . . [a list of compounds provided elsewhere in the regulation] which are manufactured at . . . [the regulated facility]." 40 CFR §455.21.

[47] 86 Stat. 856.

[48] Section 301(b)(2)(A) (1972).

dards employed to meet the two-tiered base criteria: best practicable control technology (BPT) for 1977 and best available technology (BAT) for the mid-1980s.

As a consequence of this policy, EPA became the subject of a *mandamus* action, *Natural Resources Defense Council v. Train,*[49] which the Agency settled prior to trial in 1976. The so-called toxics consent decree required EPA to promulgate BAT effluent guidelines and new source performance standards for a list of sixty-five "priority" toxic pollutants, established a schedule for the Agency to follow, and stated a policy that zero discharge would be required where technologically and economically feasible.[50] It also specified a procedure (under paragraph 8, and subsequently called the "paragraph 8 procedure") for removal of substances from the initial toxics list,[51] a procedure for excluding point source categories from Section 307 requirements,[52] and a requirement that EPA conduct a water quality survey to pinpoint "toxic hot spots," for which special, more stringent toxic effluent standards under Section 307(a)(2) must be developed.[53]

[b] Current Requirements

[i] Substantive Standards

The 1977 amendments to the Clean Water Act rewrote Section 307 to insert into the statute some of the terms of the toxics consent decree. The list of sixty-five toxic pollutants[54] was incorporated into the statute

---

[49] Nos. 72-2153 etc. (D.D.C.). The consent decree is published at 8 ERC 2121 (BNA) (D.D.C. 1976).

[50] For an interesting industry challenge to the consent decree, *see* Environmental Defense Fund, Inc. v. Costle, 636 F.2d 1229 (1980).

[51] The standard for removal was (a) where existing standards are more stringent, (b) where the pollutants are naturally occurring, (c) where the pollutant is not detectable by means of state-of-the-art detection technology, (d) where detectable levels of the pollutant come exclusively from a small group of sources, (e) where the pollutant is not likely to cause effects because it is present only in trace amounts, or (f) where the pollutant cannot be removed effectively since it exists in too small a quantity in the effluent.

[52] Essentially, the decree allows nonregulation of point source subcategories only where 95 percent of the members of the source category discharge to a publicly owned treatment works that removes the toxic components.

[53] Paragraph 12. The report, which EPA unsuccessfully sought to avoid by seeking a modification of the decree in 1981, was completed in 1984.

[54] The list contained a number of generic, or chemical, family names. EPA subsequently revised to list to substitute specific chemicals for generic names, and the list grew thereby to 129. *See* A Legislative History of the Clean Water Act of 1977, Serial No. 95-14, 95th Cong., 2d Sess. at 331-334 (1977).

by reference. EPA was required to promulgate BAT effluent guidelines for the list by the middle of 1980,[55] and was authorized to add or delete substances from the list, although the statute did not incorporate the paragraph 8 criteria for delisting.[56]

The amended statute also clarified the Agency's responsibilities regarding the issuance of alternate "revised" toxic effluent standards under Section 307(a)(3), making it clear that prior to issuing any such standards, the Agency must hold an adjudicatory hearing, and establishing that judicial review of any such standard shall be under the "substantial evidence" standard of review. EPA is required to review any such standards periodically. Compliance with such standards by individual point sources is mandated within three years of promulgation.[57]

EPA subsequently issued a substantial number of BAT standards for toxics, and has issued very few "revised" standards to address specific problems.[58]

Enforcement of toxic effluent standards, like all other Clean Water Act standards, is achieved by inserting an effluent *limitation* setting numerical limits on the amount of the pollutant that may be discharged in a permit issued to an individual point source discharger.[59] A discharger is required to have specific effluent limitations established for each point source discharge (usually referred to as "outfalls") at a single facility.

Clean Water Act permits are for a five-year term, after which they must be renewed. The original (and many of the second round of) state- and EPA-issued National Pollutant Discharge Elimination System

---

[55] The target date for achieving BAT effluent limitations was slipped to July 1, 1984. Both dates move back the consent decree deadlines. *See* A Legislative History of the Clean Water Act of 1977, Serial No. 95-14, 95th Cong., 2d Sess. at 327.

[56] Section 307(a)(1)-(a)(2)(1977). Language in the House debate on the conference report, however, demonstrates unequivocal intent on the part of the proponents that EPA follow the consent decree criteria. *See* A Legislative History of the Clean Water Act of 1977, Serial No. 95-14, 95th Cong., 2d Sess. at 328 (1977).

[57] Sections 307(a)(2) and (a)(6).

[58] *See* Appendix 7-B, *infra*. Revised standards are published at 40 CFR Part 129. Toxic BAT standards are published as a component of the effluent limitations for the relevant source category.

[59] A point source under the Clean Water Act is any "discernible, confined and discrete conveyance, including but not limited to any pipe, ditch, channel, tunnel, conduit, well, discrete fissure, container, rolling stock, concentrated animal feeding operation, or vessel or other floating craft from which pollutants are or may be discharged," except for agricultural irrigation return flows. Section 502(14).

(NPDES) permits[60] did not contain any Section 307–derived effluent limitations because of the slow pace of the Agency's implementation of Section 307. Once Section 307 BAT was established, EPA and the states had to learn what facilities were discharging toxic pollutants in order to begin inserting appropriate effluent limitations in the permits.

[ii] Reporting Obligations

Most industrial dischargers, as late as 1980, did not know the identity and relative amounts of specific organic compounds contained in their wastewater. This was because they were required to sample for only the parameters contained in their permits, and those parameters, as discussed above, were most often catchall phrases for total organics.

EPA's NPDES permit regulations,[61] as amended initially in 1980 and thereafter, impose reporting requirements on the industry subcategories most likely to discharge toxic pollutants.[62] The reporting requirements, which are applicable when a new permit is issued or an existing one renewed, require quantitative data to be provided relative to the presence "in each outfall containing process wastewater" of any of a group of toxic pollutants listed in an appendix contained at the end of the regulation.[63]

Any new or renewal permit applicant is required to report "whether it knows or has reason to believe that any of the pollutants in . . . [a list of conventional and nonconventional pollutants][64] is discharged." Quantitative data are required for any such pollutant for which EPA has promulgated an effluent limitation or that is related to an "indicator" for which EPA has promulgated an effluent limitation.[65]

All applicants are also required to "indicate" whether they know or have reason to believe whether any of the listed toxic pollutants or

---

[60] These are the permits issued under authority of the Clean Water Act.

[61] 40 CFR Part 122

[62] 40 CFR §122.21(g)(7)(ii) and Appendix A to Part 122 (list of industries affected).

[63] 40 CFR §§122.21(g)(7)(ii)(A) and (B). The pollutants are those contained in Tables I and III of Appendix D.

[64] 40 CFR Part 122, Appendix D, Table IV.

[65] 40 CFR §122.21(g)(7)(iii)(A). If no limitations are applicable, then the applicant may report either quantitative data or provide an explanation of why the pollutant is expected to be discharged.

phenols[66] for which the applicant is not required to report quantitatively under the other provisions of Section 122.21(g) is discharged, and are required to provide quantitative data for every such pollutant discharged in 10 parts per billion or greater concentrations.[67]

All applicants are also required to indicate whether they know or have reason to believe that any of the "hazardous" pollutants contained in another list is discharged,[68] to describe the reasons for the discharge, and to provide any quantitative data they have.[69] Finally, applicants must report information relative to the dioxin 2,3,7,8 tetrachlorodibenzodioxin (TCDD) and various phenoxy herbicides and other phenoxy compounds generally associated with TCDD contamination,[70] list any toxic pollutant that the applicant "currently uses or manufactures as an intermediate or final product or byproduct,"[71] and identify "any biological tests which the applicant knows or has reason to believe have been made within the last three years on any of the applicant's discharges of a receiving water in relation to a discharge."[72]

In addition to the reporting requirements at the permit application stage, the NPDES regulations also impose an ongoing reporting requirement on permit holders to report planned production changes that are likely to affect the effluent characteristics,[73] and impose on most dischargers a duty to report as soon as they know or have reason to believe that any activity "has occurred or will occur which would result in the discharge on a routine or frequent basis of any toxic pollutant which is not limited in the permit . . ." if the amounts discharged

---

[66] 40 CFR Part 122, Appendix D, Tables II and III.

[67] 40 CFR §122.21(g)(7)(iii)(B). Higher threshold concentrations are applicable to four listed polymers. Applicants not meeting the threshold for quantitative reporting are required to file qualitative reports or quantitative data. "Small businesses," as qualified under 40 CFR §122.21(g)(8), are exempt from the requirements for reporting quantitative data for organic toxics under Section 122.21(g)(7)(iii)(B), the Section 122.21(g)(7)(iii)-(A) requirements, and the Section 122.21(g)(7)(ii)(A) requirements. A "small business" is generally defined as one with gross total annual sales of less than $100,000 second quarter 1980 dollars. 40 CFR §122.21(g)(8)(ii).

[68] 40 CFR Part 122, Appendix D, Table V

[69] 40 CFR §122.21(g)(7)(iv).

[70] 40 CFR §122.21(g)(7)(v).

[71] 40 CFR §122.21(g)(9).

[72] 40 CFR §122.21(g)(11).

[73] 40 CFR §122.41(l)(1). See 49 Fed. Reg. 38046 (9-26-84).

will exceed certain "notification levels" set forth in the regulation.[74]

[iii]   Toxics Permit Conditions and Limitations

The information received by EPA or a delegated NPDES state pursuant to the toxics reporting requirements serves as the basis for the permit writer to determine whether any of the extant toxic BAT guidelines or revised toxic effluent standards are applicable to the discharge,[75] or whether to reopen the permit to insert "best professional judgment" toxic effluent limitations for any of the list of sixty-five "consent decree" toxics.[76]

All permits must contain special toxics limitations, which are spelled out in 40 CFR §122.44(e); these provide essentially that effluent limitations must be developed for toxics that the permit writer believes are being discharged at levels greater than the levels that can be achieved by the "technology based treatment requirements appropriate to the permittee. . . ."[77] Toxic effluent limitations may be imposed on the pollutants themselves, or on other pollutants that will in turn provide treatment for the toxics.[78]

Toxic effluent limitations are not subject to the variance mechanisms provided by Section 301(c) and 301(g) of the Clean Water Act, which are otherwise available to individual dischargers who need relief from BAT requirements.[79]

---

[74] 40 CFR §122.48(a). *See* 49 Fed. Reg. 38046 (9-26-84).

[75] *See* 40 CFR §§122.44(a) and (b). Existing permits may be modified, or revoked and reissued to insert newly applicable more stringent toxic effluent standards.

[76] The reopener authority is limited to the industries listed in Part 122, Appendix A. The reopener provision is 40 CFR §122.44(c). A "best professional judgment" permit term must be revoked or modified to insert a more stringent limitation required by an after-promulgated toxic standard, and the permits of Appendix A industries are subject to revocation and modification to insert effluent limitations to control a toxic pollutant not previously regulated. *Id.*, section 122.44(c)(3).

[77] The technology-based requirements are determined by reference to 40 CFR §125.3

[78] *See* 40 CFR §122.44(e)(2).

[79] Toxic dischargers subject to Section 307(b) requirements for pretreatment of wastes discharged to publicly owned treatment works are apparently able to seek "fundamentally different factors" variances, similar to those available generally from the 1977 BPT requirements. *See* Chemical Manufacturers Association v. NRDC, — U.S. —, No. 83-1013 (2-27-86). Whether the reasoning of the Court will also serve to provide such variances to direct toxics dischargers remains to be determined.

[3] Discharges of Toxics to Public Sewers

Section 307(b) of the Clean Water Act requires EPA to issue regulations establishing "pretreatment standards" for pollutants that are introduced into public sewer systems and either are not susceptible to treatment by a municipal publicly owned treatment works (POTW) or would interfere with its operation. EPA was slow to implement this provision. Its approach has been to develop "categorical" pretreatment standards for the same types of source categories for which it develops technology-based effluent limitations.

Pretreatment standards may be established for toxics. Section 307(b)(1), however, contains a clause that allows "removal credits" against otherwise applicable pretreatment requirements for Section 307(a) toxics that the pretreater is able to demonstrate are removed from the sewage prior to discharge by the POTW in whole or in part to a sufficient degree that the amount of the pollutant in the POTW effluent is not greater than would be permitted for a direct discharge under the other provisions of the act.[80]

It is not, *per se*, a violation of the Clean Water Act to discharge toxics to a sewer and interfere with the operation of a downsewer POTW or endanger the lives of the workers in it. Sections 307(d) and 309(f) make it an offense to violate any pretreatment standard or prohibition promulgated by EPA. If there is no applicable standard or prohibition, or if the POTW has not imposed by ordinance a local prohibition for the pollutant involved, the discharger will not be found to be in violation.[81]

[4] Imminent and Substantial Endangerments

The Clean Water Act contains a provision, similar to Section 7003 of RCRA and Section 106 of CERCLA, authorizing EPA to bring a lawsuit to abate a water-polluting activity that is presenting an imminent and substantial endangerment to human health or to the livelihood of peo-

---

[80] Pretreaters can apparently seek variances upon a showing that the plant or process is fundamentally different from those upon which EPA based its categorical pretreatment standards. *See* Chemical Manufacturers Association v. NRDC, — U.S. —, No. 83-1013 (2-27-85).

[81] EPA's judicial remedy, if there is a violation, is to sue the POTW (that is, in most jurisdictions, a municipality, and the source jointly). *See* Section 309(f).

ple dependent on the aquatic resource.[82]

§7.04   Groundwater and Drinking Water Protection

[1]   In General

The federal Safe Drinking Water Act[83] was initially enacted in 1974[84] and was amended in 1976, 1977, 1979, 1980, 1984, and 1986.[85] The act was, in effect, amended, though not formally so, by a provision of the Hazardous and Solid Waste Amendments of 1984.[86]

The SDWA is really two separate programs. Parts B, D, and E create a regulatory scheme for setting national "maximum contaminant levels" for public drinking water supplies, and for ensuring that regulated public drinking water systems meet the minimum requirements. Part C creates a federally overlaid program for state regulation of land uses that could affect public drinking water wells or critical aquifers and the injection of waste into wells. Section 1424(e), which is functionally related to Part C, authorizes the designation of groundwater aquifers as "sole sources" of drinking water that would create a significant hazard to public health if polluted, giving rise to additional limitations on certain types of activities in the area.[87]

[2]   Water Supply Regulation

[a]   Regulatory Scheme Prior to 1986

The principal regulatory device employed by the SDWA to regulate the quality of public drinking water is the creation of maximum levels of harmful pollutants that are permitted to exist in water delivered to

---

[82] Section 504(a). This provision was construed and discussed at length in Reserve Mining Co. v. EPA, 514 F.2d 492 (8th Cir. 1975).

[83] 42 USC §§300f et seq.

[84] P.L. 93-523 (12-16-84).

[85] P.L. 94-317; P.L. 94-484; P.L. 95-190; P.L. 96-63; P.L. 96-502; P.L. 98-620; and P.L. 99-339.

[86] P.L. 98-616, Section 405(a) (11-8-84). See discussion, infra.

[87] The sole source aquifer program was amended and restructured significantly in 1986, by P.L. 99-339. For the regulatory program in place prior to the amendments, see generally 40 CFR Part 149 (EPA Regulations on Review of Projects Affecting Sole Source Aquifers); and Montgomery County v. EPA, 662 F.2d 1040 (4th Cir. 1981) (challenge to sole source aquifer designation). EPA's regulatory powers were limited to reviewing federally assisted projects (such as highways and sewers). It had no control over private or state-financed projects, even if they were federally licensed.

human populations for consumption.[88] This standard-setting exercise has become important in the hazardous waste area, since SDWA standards are looked to as a basis for making determinations as to the appropriate level of cleanup at hazardous waste disposal sites.[89]

EPA was, under the original scheme, required to promulgate national drinking water standards in three phases. The first phase led to the promulgation of "interim primary drinking water regulations."[90] The regulations set "maximum contaminant levels" (MCLs) for substances the Agency found may have an adverse effect on health. If MCLs are not feasible, "treatment techniques" may be prescribed. The interim primary standards were required to be based on consideration of a number of factors, including health effects, availability of treatment or removal technology, and costs.[91]

The second phase, under the original statutory regime, was the promulgation of "revised national primary drinking water regulations," which also set MCLs or specify treatment techniques.[92] The statutory criterion for revised primary standards was reduction of contaminant levels as nearly as feasible to levels at which "no known or anticipated adverse effects on . . . health" occur, which allows an "adequate margin of safety."[93] "Feasibility" involves consideration of the technology generally available, taking cost into consideration.[94]

EPA could not promulgate a revised primary standard, however, until it had received a report from the National Academy of Sciences (NAS) recommending "safe" maximum contaminant levels for known drinking water contaminants.[95] The NAS report, which was also re-

---

[88] Section 1412 (1984).

[89] See 50 Fed. Reg. 4719 (11-20-85) (revisions to hazardous substances National Contingency Plan), and see Section 121 of the Superfund Amendments and Reauthorization Act of 1986 (codifying in part and amending in part EPA's 1985 NCP).

[90] See 40 CFR Part 141. Standards have been issued for inorganic chemicals, organic chemicals, turbidity, microbiological contaminant levels, and certain radioactive compounds.

[91] EPA's implementing regulations are published at 40 CFR Part 142. Its interim primary standards were upheld in Environmental Defense Fund, Inc. v. Costle, 578 F.2d 337 (D.C. Cir. 1978).

[92] Section 1412(b)(1984).

[93] Section 1412(b)(1)(B)(1984).

[94] Section 1412(b)(3)(1984).

[95] Section 1412(e)(1984).

quired to be tendered to the Congress, formed the evidentiary basis for revised MCLs. The EPA had issued no revised primary standards, prior to 1986 for carcinogens or mutagens, primarily because the NAS had taken the position that the statutory standard is unworkable, at least as to nonthreshold contaminants, such as carcinogens. EPA argued that, though it had no *obligation* to issue revised MCLs in the absence of NAS recommendations, it nevertheless had the *authority* to do so.[96]

EPA proposed a number of MCLs and RMCLs in 1985, signaling new movement in its program,[96.1] motivated in part by its forced revision of the National Hazardous Substances Contingency Plan under the Comprehensive Environmental Response, Compensation and Liability Act (CERCLA) to require consideration of "applicable and relevant" standards in groundwater cleanup actions.[96.2]

The third phase, "national secondary drinking water regulations,"[97] was to be promulgated within 270 days of the SDWA's enactment, and govern such things as color, odor, and other parameters not having public health significance.[98]

The critical standards are, for public health purposes, the national revised primary standards. In order to compensate for its failure to promulgate many national interim standards, and for its total failure to issue any revised regulations, EPA began in the late 1970s to issue what it termed "health advisories" on drinking water contaminants.

The Office of Drinking Water Health Advisory Program health advisories, which are not published in the Federal Register, and as to which EPA disclaims any regulatory force, generally describe the toxicological profile of subject contaminants and usually recommend a "suggested no adverse response level" (SNARL) for the contaminant. The health advisories are provided to state water pollution agencies and health departments for whatever use they desire to make of them. In

---

[96] Brief of EPA in American Water Works Ass'n, et al. v. EPA, No. 80-1048 (D.C. Cir. 1980), at 16.

[96.1] *See* 50 Fed. Reg. 46880 (proposed MCLs for eight volatile organic compounds and monitoring requirements for fifty-one unregulated VOCs); 50 Fed. Reg. 46936 (proposed RMCLs for eleven organic chemicals, twenty-eight synthetic organic chemicals, and four microbiological contaminants); 50 Fed. Reg. 47042 (request for comment on tetrachloroethylene).

[96.2] *See* discussion in Chapter 6, *supra.*

[97] Section 1412(c)(1984).

[98] Section 1401(2). *See* 40 CFR Part 143.

some cases, states have adopted SNARLs as though they were drinking water standards.[99]

[b]   Changes in Direction Resulting from the 1986 Amendments

[i]   Standard-Setting Terminology and Schedules

[A]   **Terminology and Criteria.** Public Law 99-339[100] made a number of sweeping changes in the SDWA, most of which are aimed at forcing the development of numerical drinking water standards on an enforceable timetable. These changes were motivated in part by congressional dissatisfaction with the pace of regulation under the old act,[101] and also by the regulatory tie-in of national drinking water standards to the extent-of-remedy provisions of the amended superfund law.[102]

Section 1412(a) was amended to eliminate the old three-phase standard-setting mechanism, replacing it with a two-phase system. RMCLs are replaced by "maximum contaminant level goals."[103] National interim drinking water standards and revised primary drinking water regulations are lumped together into one entity, called "primary drinking water regulations." The National Academy of Sciences has been dropped from the standard-setting process entirely. EPA is required only to solicit the views of its own Science Advisory Board prior to proposal of an MCL goal or primary regulation, and is not bound by the Board's comments or required to await a response from it.[104]

MCL goals are required to be set at the "level at which no known or anticipated adverse effects on the health of persons occur and which

[99] In 1983 EPA issued an advance notice of proposed rulemaking in which the Agency proposed a program of issuing national revised primary drinking water regulations. 48 Fed. Reg. 45502 (1983).

[100] Effective June 19, 1986.

[101] See S. Rep. No. 99-575, 99th Cong., 2d Sess., at 29-35 (5-5-86).

[102] See P.L. 99-499, Section 121 (10-17-86) and Section 1412(b)(3)(B) (requiring standard-setting priorities to consider Section 101(14) of CERCLA).

[103] The statute converts all RMCLs published by EPA prior to the effective date into MCL goals.

[104] Section 1412(e). The SAB was set up as a Clean Air Act–related advisory body by the Environmental Research, Development and Demonstration Act of 1978 (ERDDA). It has subsequently gained statutory roles under a number of EPA-administered statutes.

allows an adequate margin of safety."[105]

Primary drinking water regulations, which must be reviewed at least every three years,[106] must be set as close to the MCL goals as is "feasible," in the sense that they must reflect the "use of the best technology, treatment techniques and other means which the Administrator finds, after examination for efficacy under field conditions and not solely under laboratory conditions, are available (taking cost into consideration)."[107] Each primary drinking water regulation that establishes a maximum contaminant level must also list the technologies, treatment techniques, and other means that EPA finds are feasible, although no specific technology or technique may be required.[108]

Treatment techniques may be employed in lieu of MCLs for a national primary drinking water regulation where EPA makes a finding that "it is not economically or technologically feasible to ascertain the level of the contaminant."[109]

[B]   Choosing Chemicals to Evaluate for MCLs and Establishment of Priorities for the Development of Standards. A second significant change in the SDWA that sprang from the 1986 amendments was a firm requirement that EPA publish MCL goals and primary drinking water regulations for a list of eighty-three chemicals pursuant to a phased-in

---

105 Section 1412(b)(4)(1986).

106 Section 1412(b)(9). More frequent review and revision may be initiated by advances in technology or techniques.

107 *Id.;* and Section 1412(b)(5). The latter subsection, embellished by language in the Conference Report, establishes granular activated carbon treatment as the technological floor for synthetic organic chemicals. The Conference Report points to the removal capability of systems designed for trichloroethylene described in 47 Fed. Reg. 9354 (1982) as representative of its intention. *See* S.Rep. No. 99-575, 99th Cong. 2d Sess. at 32 (5-5-86).

The reference to cost does not mandate a cost-benefit analysis, since identical language used in the Clean Water Act has been construed to require only sensitivity to cost concerns.

108 Section 1412(b)(6).

109 Section 1412(b)(7). In such event, EPA is required to identify treatment techniques that in its judgment would "prevent known or anticipated adverse health effects . . . to the extent feasible." Variances from treatment techniques listed under these circumstances (except for filtration, which is a statutory requirement of Section 1412(b)(7)(C), and disinfection, which is a statutory requirement of Section 1412(b)(8), for which special variance requirements are applicable) are available under Section 1415(a)(3) upon a showing that an alternative technique not listed is at least as efficient in lowering the level of the contaminant as the techniques contained in the regulation.

timetable.[110] The list, which is reprinted in Appendix 7D, *infra,* was originally generated by EPA.[111] The phased-in priorities are mandatory unless EPA decides that another contaminant is of greater significance than one listed for consideration in the list, in which case a substitution can be made.[112]

In addition, the Agency is required to appoint a technical working group to assist in the development of additions to the list of contaminants that are candidates for drinking water regulations,[113] and on January 1, 1988, and at three-year intervals thereafter, publish a list of additional contaminants that the Agency believes fit the criteria for regulations.[114] Once the list is published, there are mandatory timetables for the proposal and promulgation of MCL goals and primary drinking water regulations applicable to the listed contaminants.[115] Statutory priority for consideration by EPA and the working group is given to contaminants on the Section 101(14) lists under CERCLA and pesticides.[116]

Finally, EPA is required to issue, on a mandatory timetable, national primary drinking water regulations specifying criteria under which filtration and disinfection are required as treatment techniques for public water supplies.[117]

A related set of provisions, contained in Section 1417, prohibits the use of any solder, flux, or pipe that contains lead. This prohibition extends to public water supply systems and, via mandatory amend-

---

[110] Section 1412(b)(1).

[111] 47 Fed. Reg. 9352; and 48 Fed Reg. 45502 (*see supra* note 99).

[112] Section 1412(b)(2). The decision to substitute is not subject to judicial review. *See* Section 1412(b)(2)(D). EPA is limited to seven substitutions. The phase-in requires decisions on at least nine contaminants by June 1987, at least forty more by June 1988, and the remainder of the list by June 1989. Section 1412(b)(1). -

[113] *See* Section 1412(b)(3)(B). This group, which must include members from the National Toxicology Program and from EPA's offices of Drinking Water, Pesticides and Toxic Substances, Ground Water, Solid Waste and Emergency Response, is a replacement for the NAS, although its role, unlike that of NAS under the prior SDWA, is purely advisory.

[114] Section 1412(b)(3)(A).

[115] Sections 1412(b)(3)(C) and (D).

[116] *See* Section 1412(b)(3)(B).

[117] Sections 1412(b)(7)(C), (b)(8). Special variance provisions are provided for the disinfection regulations. Both of these programs are delegable to States.

ments to state building codes, to residential and nonresidential plumbing.[118]

[C] **Administrative Procedures and Judicial Review.** The 1986 amendments did not alter the administrative procedural scheme established under the original SDWA, which provided for notice and comment rulemaking with respect to standard-setting activities.[119] Judicial review, which is governed by Section 1448, was addressed in 1986. MCL goals and national primary drinking water regulations may be challenged only by petitions to review the rulemaking filed in the U.S. Court of Appeals for the District of Columbia Circuit.[120]

[ii] **Enforcement and Monitoring**

Since states are intended to have primary enforcement authority for the Part B program,[121] EPA's enforcement powers vis-à-vis public water supply systems are geared to failure by the state to enforce. Under the original SDWA, EPA had discretion to enforce or not enforce in the face of a violation of a SDWA regulation. Section 1414 was amended in 1986 to eliminate this discretion, and subsequently the Agency was required either to commence a civil enforcement action or to issue an administrative order[122] if a violation of its regulations in a delegated state went unaddressed for more than thirty days.[123]

Civil penalties, originally available only with respect to willful violations, were made applicable to all violations by P.L. 99-339, which also increased the maximum amount to $25,000.

A new federal civil and criminal offense, tampering with a public water supply system, was created by Section 1432. Either tampering or

---

118 The prohibition is, however, prospective, and thus does not require retrofitting existing structures. Moreover, the prohibition is not absolute. "Lead Free" is defined, for solders, to mean not more than 0.02 percent lead, and, for pipes and fittings, not more than 8 percent lead. *See* Section 1417(c).

119 Adjudicatory procedures are provided for enforcement actions. *See* Section 1414(g).

120 Section 1448(a)(i). Subsection (a)(2), which provides review of any "other action" of EPA in the circuit where the petitioner resides or transacts business, was not amended. This raises an interesting question as to whether and where additions to the list of contaminants to be regulated are reviewable.

121 Section 1413.

122 Administrative order authority, which includes authority to levy civil penalties up to $5000, was added in 1986 by Section 1414(g).

123 Section 1414(a)(1)(B). In states without delegated enforcement authority, EPA must commence enforcement action immediately upon discovering a violation. Section 1414(a)(2).

attempting or threatening to tamper is an offense.[124] "Tampering" is defined as either introducing a contaminant into a public water system with the intention of harming persons or otherwise interfering with the operation of a public water system with the intention of harming persons.[125]

New monitoring requirements were added by Section 1445(a). EPA is required to maintain a list of unregulated contaminants for which public water systems are required to monitor, and to develop regulations governing the monitoring activities, which must occur at least once every five years.[126]

In addition, Section 1414(c) was amended to increase significantly the burden of notice by a public water supply to its customers regarding its failure to monitor, its failure to meet MCL's treatment techniques or testing procedures, the fact that it has applied for a variance, or its failure to comply with the terms of a variance or exemption, although the mandatory notice requirements are far from adequate to protect the public health in the event of a true emergency.[127]

Aside from variances, which were not significantly amended in 1986, water supplies may escape enforcement sanctions for noncompliance with national regulations only by the securing of an "exemption" under Section 1416. Exemptions are limited; amendments made in 1986 require that enforceable compliance schedules designed to cure the deficiency be in place when an exemption is granted; and all exemptions are limited to three years for "compelling factors," which may include economic factors.[128]

---

[124] Sections 1432(a), 1432(b).

[125] Section 1432(d). The absence of a reckless endangerment offense is a significant omission, however. Although reckless discharge of contaminants into groundwater is probably subject to the reckless endangerment provisions of RCRA, there are no comparable provisions in the Clean Water Act (as it exists as of December 1986); thus, the reckless deposit of contaminants into a surface water that is used as the source of a public supply may not be adequately punished.

[126] States are allowed to add to the list, but only if the addition does not increase the cost.

[127] Notice is, for example, required by Section 1414(c)(2)(B) to be given with respect to a violation of an MCL or other violation that poses "a serious potential health effect" within fourteen days of the occurrence.

[128] Sections 1416(a), 1416(b)(2)(B). Systems serving 500 or fewer connections may get an additional two years if they need financial assistance that will not be available in less time. Exemptions are granted by EPA or by delegated states.

[3] Protection of Underground Waters from Contamination by Sources Other than Injection Wells

The limited sole source aquifer protection provisions of the original SDWA were replaced in 1986 by two more ambitious programs, the "sole source aquifer demonstration program"[129] and the "wellhead protection program."[130] These programs fall far short of more draconian proposals contained in competing legislation in the 99th Congress, which would have established more or less uniform groundwater quality standards across the nation and a regulatory program akin to the federal water pollution control program as it existed prior to 1972.

[a] Wellhead Protection

Under the wellhead protection program, states must submit to EPA, by June of 1989, programs to protect "wellhead protection areas"[131] from contaminants. State programs are required to designate the agency with responsibility for implementing the program, determine the geographic limits of wellhead protection areas, identify within each such area all potential "anthropogenic" sources of contamination that may pose a threat to human health, describe the program's methodologies for protecting the sources, and include contingency plans for the provision of alternate water supplies in the event of contamination.[132]

Disapproval by EPA of a proffered state program is final if it occurs within nine months of the program's submission[133] and the program is not modified to cure the defect within six months thereafter. There is, however, no significant penalty or federal primacy stemming from disallowance. One benefit of having an approved program, however, is mandatory federal agency compliance with it.[134]

---

129 Section 1427

130 Section 1428.

131 This term is defined by Section 1428(e) as "the surface and subsurface area surrounding a water well or wellfield, supplying a public water supply system, through which contaminants are reasonably likely to move toward and reach such water well or wellhead," as determined by the state. EPA is required to provide technical guidance.

132 Sections 1428(a)(1)-(6). Public participation is encouraged, though not mandated, by Section 1428(b).

133 EPA inaction deems the program approved. Section 1428(c)(1).

134 Section 1428(h). Federal facilities are subject to the states' substantive and proce-

There are special provisions relating to states with a large amount of reinjection of brines between the production and surface casings of conventional oil and gas production wells.[135]

[b] Sole Source Aquifer Demonstration

The second addition to Part C in 1986 was the sole source aquifer demonstration program, contained within Section 1447. The thrust of this program is to encourage states to identify and protect "critical aquifer protection" areas[136] by providing federal grants amounting to 50 percent of the implementation costs.[137]

Applicants, which may be states, or, with the consent of the Governor, municipalities, other local governmental entities, or intra- or interstate regional planning entities having jurisdiction over the area, must petition EPA for inclusion in the demonstration project.[138] The statutory criteria for acceptability of an applicant's planning program encompass a broad range of land use planning concepts. The basic standard, set forth in Section 1427(h), is that the demonstration program "would provide protection for ground water quality consistent with the objectives stated in [Section 1427(f)]."

The subsection (f) objectives are detailed. What is required is a "comprehensive plan" designed to "maintain the quality of the ground water in the critical protection area in a manner reasonably expected to pro-

---

dural "requirements," including "reasonable charges and fees," but not to enforcement sanctions. There is a "paramount interest of the United States" presidential exemption available, which is not available for lack of funding unless funding has been requested of the Congress and denied.

[135] Section 1428(i). This is termed "annular injection." States with more than 2500 active wells that reinject brines are required to certify to EPA that they have a program to control contamination associated with this practice.

[136] A "critical aquifer protection area" is either (1) an area within an area for which sole source aquifer designation has been sought pursuant to Section 1424(e) and which meets the criteria developed by EPA pursuant to Section 1427(d), which relate to the vulnerability of the aquifer to contamination and the consequences and entail a benefit-cost analysis, or (2) an area within an area that was, prior to the enactment date of P.L. 99-339, *designated* as a sole source aquifer, for which an "areawide ground water protection plan has been approved under section 208 of the Clean Water Act prior to such enactment."

[137] Section 1427(j). There is a limitation of $4 million for any one aquifer in any fiscal year.

[138] Section 1427(c).

tect human health, the environment and ground water resources."[139] Although not required to do so, the plan may also be designed to "maintain, to the maximum extent possible, the natural vegetative and hydrogeological conditions." Plans must contain certain elements[140] and may contain others.[141]

The statute provides for informal hearings in connection with development and approval of state demonstration plans.[142]

[4] Underground Injection Control (UIC)

Part C of the SDWA establishes a program for regulating deep well injection of wastes, called the Underground Injection Control (UIC) program.[143] The disposal of wastes, particularly petroleum extraction wastes, by injecting them into deep "dry" wells, is a relatively common practice, particularly in the Southwest. As the hazardous waste land disposal industry began to come under regulatory scrutiny in the 1970s, disposal of hazardous wastes into wells began to increase. Migration of contaminants injected into injection wells is the concern of the UIC provisions.

There is an obvious interrelationship between the thrust of the Resource Conservation and Recovery Act (RCRA) regulatory program and the UIC program. Indeed, though the two programs are administered by different subparts of the EPA, the injection of hazardous wastes has come to be considered more of a hazardous waste regulatory issue than a drinking water regulation issue.

The original language of the UIC sections clearly expressed a con-

---

[139] Section 1427(f)(1).

[140] *Id.* The plans must contain a map showing the boundaries of the area, identify existing and potential point and nonpoint sources of groundwater pollution, assess the relationship between surface activities and groundwater pollution, describe management practices proposed to protect the groundwater, identify "authority adequate to implement the plan," and include program cost estimates. Sections 1427(f)(1)(A)-(E).

[141] Optional elements that may be contained in a plan include analysis of water quality and recharge profiles; regulatory requirements imposed in the event water quality is compromised; limits on "Federal, State and local government, financially assisted activities and projects which may contribute to degradation" (thus, federal aid highway projects may be controlled); a "comprehensive statement of land use management;" actions that would avoid adverse impacts; "consideration of special techniques, which may include clustering, transfer of development rights, and other innovative measures sufficient to achieve the objectives . . .;" development of new institutions to implement the programs; and pollution abatement measures. Sections 1427(f)(2)(A)-(I).

[142] *See* Section 1427(h).

[143] Sections 1421-1424.

gressional intent to promote state regulation of injection wells to the maximum possible extent. Amendments contained in Section 201 of P.L. 99-339, however, evidence a tightening of federal oversight of state regulation of Class I wells.

EPA maintains four sets of UIC regulations: (1) general criteria and performance standards for injection wells, which form a national regulatory floor;[144] (2) standards and procedures for approval of state UIC programs;[145] (3) standards and related provisions from state UIC programs that have been approved in whole or in part by EPA;[146] and (4) procedural and substantive permit requirements for injection wells regulated directly by EPA in those states whose UIC program elements for that class of well have not been approved by EPA.[147]

EPA's Part 146 regulations divide the universe of injection wells into five categories. Class I wells are those used by hazardous waste generators or owner/operators of hazardous waste treatment, storage, and disposal facilities, as those entities are defined in the RCRA regulations,[148] and other industrial and municipal injection wells.[149] Class II

---

[144] 40 CFR Part 146. The regulations were issued on June 24, 1980, 45 Fed. Reg. 42500, and amended at 46 Fed. Reg. 43160 (1981), 47 Fed. Reg. 4998 (1982), 47 Fed. Reg. 32129 (1982), 48 Fed. Reg. 14153 (1983), and 48 Fed. Reg. 31404 (1983). A number of the later amendments stemmed from EPA's settlement of litigation challenging the original regulations.

[145] 40 CFR Part 145. *See* 48 Fed. Reg. 14153 (1983); and 48 Fed. Reg. 39619 (1983).

[146] 40 CFR Part 147. See 49 Fed. Reg. 20197 (1984). These regulations are amended frequently to reflect additions, deletions, or modifications to the state program provisions. They resemble EPA's State Implementation Plan listings under the Clean Air Act.

[147] 40 CFR Parts 144, 146, and 147. Permit procedures under 40 CFR Part 124 are also applicable. EPA's failure to promulgate federal UIC permit requirements for states not having primary enforcement authority was the subject of National Wildlife Federation v. Ruckelshaus, C.A. No. 83-JM-133 (D. Colo.). A consent decree, entered on December 22, 1983, resulted in the issuance of a number of federal UIC permit programs. *See* 49 Fed. Reg. 21038 (1984); and 49 Fed. Reg. 45292 (1984)

[148] EPA's classification regulation, 40 CFR §146.05(a), defined Class I wells to include only wells where the waste was injected "beneath the lowermost formation containing, within . . . 1/4 mile of the well bore, an underground source of drinking water." Wells injecting waste into or above such a formation are Class IV wells. EPA regulated Class I wells. Class IV wells were not regulated. Section 405(a) of the Hazardous and Solid Waste Amendments of 1984 inserted a new Section 7010 into RCRA, which legislatively overrules the Class IV inaction. The RCRA provision prohibits the disposal of *hazardous* waste by injection into or above a formation that contains "within one quarter mile of the well . . ." an underground source of drinking water. The prohibition is self-executing as of May 8, 1985, except in states with more stringent preexisting UIC requirements, and except for reinjections of treated groundwater pursuant to a response action under the Comprehensive Environmental Response, Compensation and Liability Act of 1980 (CERCLA). The provision is made specifically enforceable under the SDWA.

wells are those used by the petroleum industry in connection with conventional oil and gas extraction.[150] Class III wells are those used in the mining and power generation (including geothermal) industries. Class IV wells are hazardous waste disposal wells in which hazardous or radioactive waste is disposed of above or into a formation where there is an underground source of drinking water within 1/4 mile of the well bore.[151] Class V wells include such things as cesspools and septic systems serving multifamily or industrial structures, drainage wells, and assorted other wells.[152]

There are standards and criteria of a substantive nature applicable to Class I, II, and III wells.[153] Class IV hazardous waste injection wells are prohibited under a 1984 amendment to the federal solid waste law.[154] Class V wells are subject to a requirement that the well be identified to the applicable state program director, and a study of its contamination potential be done within three years of the date of approval of the state UIC program.[155]

Amendments to the statute adopted in 1986 imposed additional regulatory requirements on EPA, which arose out of concerns that the Agency's regulations, at least as to Class I and Class V wells, were not sufficient. EPA was required to identify, by January 1988, additional methods for groundwater monitoring at Class I wells in such a way as to provide the earliest possible detection of fluid migration into or in the direction of drinking water.[156]

For Class V wells, the Agency was required to study and report to

---

149 *Id.*

150 40 CFR §146.05(b).

151 40 CFR §146.05(d). EPA did not promulgate regulatory standards for this class of wells, although EPA's Part 144 regulations did contain a requirement that they be phased out. The disposal of hazardous waste into them was prohibited by Section 7010 of RCRA, added by Section 405 of P.L. 98-616. The RCRA "interim prohibition" is self-executing as of May 8, 1985, and is applicable in all states except those with more stringent UIC requirements. Such wells may be used to reinject treated waste extracted from the ground and treated pursuant to a CERCLA response action. RCRA Section 7010(b). The prohibition is enforceable under the SDWA. It does not appear to be applicable to radioactive waste, at least to the extent the waste is not subject to regulation under RCRA.

152 40 CFR §146.05(e).

153 40 CFR 146.09, and subparts B (Class I), C (Class II), and D (Class III).

154 *See* Chapter 5, *supra.*

155 40 CFR §146.52.

156 Section 1426(a). The statute also freezes EPA's existing definition of Class I wells. There is an exemption possible if it can be shown that there is no potential for migration from the injection zone.

Congress about the numbers of Class V wells in each subcategory and the primary contamination problems associated with them and to recommend design, installation, and siting techniques for protecting underground drinking water supplies from contamination caused by them.[157]

The substantive requirements for the regulated wells, which are enforced by permits issued by the states or by EPA, affect construction, operation, and closure of the wells. States may impose more stringent requirements. Decisions on the rate of migration of pollutants, for the purpose of permit conditions are premised in part on a complex formula set out in Section 146.06 of EPA's regulations, from which the "zone of endangering influence" is derived.

Not regulated under the UIC program are wells located in aquifers that are not now, cannot now, and will not in the future be suitable for water supply purposes and aquifers that are "mineral, hydrocarbon or geothermal energy producing, or are capable of becoming commercially mineral or hydrocarbon energy producing."[158] Petroleum extraction activities are potentially subject to special treatment by states with such activities in them. Section 1425 allow states to develop alternative programs for handling the injection of brines and other extraction fluids, and injection "for the secondary or tertiary recovery of oil or natural gas," which does not have to comply with the Section 1422(b)(1) criteria.

Although Congress has prohibited hazardous waste disposal into Class IV wells, EPA's generally permissive regulatory requirements for Class I wells appear to make them a viable hazardous waste disposal method in states that have not adopted outright prohibitions or more stringent requirements. This is particularly so in light of the fact that under RCRA such facilities are not required to have a permit, and have thus been largely outside of the RCRA regulatory loop.

Congress has, however, moved in several directions under the RCRA umbrella to eliminate at least some deep well injection of hazardous waste. As noted above, the 1984 RCRA amendments prohibit hazardous waste injection into Class IV wells. In addition, another 1984 addition to RCRA, Section 3004(f), requires EPA to reconsider allowing the injection of cyanides, heavy metals, acids, polychlorinated biphenyls

---

[157] Section 1426(b). Obviously, the largest single source of contamination is from septic tank systems, which are regulated closely by some states, and hardly at all by others.
[158] 40 CFR §146.04.

(PCBs), and halogenated organics, solvents, and dioxins, and prohibits further injection of those wastes after August 1988 unless EPA has affirmatively determined that continued injection, with whatever controls it imposes, complies with public health protection criteria set forth in the RCRA provision.

Since the UIC program is intended to be a state-enforced program, EPA is prohibited from enforcing the state's requirements directly for thirty days following notice to the state that a violation has been discovered.[159] In such event, EPA may either issue an administrative order[160] or seek civil or criminal judicial relief.[161]

---

[159] Section 1423(a)(1).

[160] *See* Section 1423(c) (added by P.L. 99-339 (1986). The maximum administrative penalty is $125,000, based on a penalty schedule of up to $10,000 per day (the daily penalty for petroleum extractors is $5000). There are elaborate adjudicatory hearing requirements, and appeal is to the U.S. District Court for the District of Columbia, which is limited to the administrative record.

[161] Section 1423(b). Injunctive relief and monetary sanctions (up to $25,000 per day) are available as civil remedies. Criminal sanctions of imprisonment of up to three years and commensurate Title 18 criminal fines are possible.

CHAPTER 8

Regulation of Chemicals in Foods

§8.01 Introduction and Overview

[1] Development of the Law

The Federal Food, Drug, and Cosmetic Act[1] (FFDCA or Act) is the principal food safety statute in the United States.[2] It establishes the framework through which chemicals in foods are regulated. The Act is a complicated and somewhat circular statute, mainly because of its piecemeal development and incorporation of divergent legislative strategies toward food safety.[3]

---

[1] 21 USC §§301-392 (1982).

[2] Other food safety statutes include the Poultry Products Inspection Act, 21 USC §§451-470 (1982); the Meat Inspection Act of 1907, 21 USC §§601-695 (1982); and the Egg Products Inspection Act, 21 USC §§1031-1056 (1982).

[3] *See* Merrill, *Regulating Carcinogens in Food: A Legislators' Guide to the Food Safety Provisions of the Federal Food, Drug, and Cosmetic Act,* 77 Mich. L. Rev. 171, 173 (1978).

In this chapter, only those portions of the FFDCA that have a significant bearing on chemicals—the food additive provisions—are dealt with in any detail. Although the pharmaceutical industry is, in the broad sense, a chemical industry, drug regulation is a complex specialty that is beyond the scope of this discussion.

The FFDCA's primary purpose is the protection of public health.[4] It rests upon the commerce power and is designed "to keep interstate channels free from deleterious, adulterated, and misbranded articles"[5] of food. To this end, courts have been generally willing to construe the provisions of the Act liberally.[6] Enforcement powers provided in the Act include seizures,[7] injunctive proceedings,[8] and criminal penalties.[9]

Chapter IV of the Act deals specifically with food.[10] It prohibits the introduction into interstate commerce of any "adulterated" food.[11] The definition of "adulterated" has changed considerably over the years.[12]

Under the forerunner of the FFDCA, the Federal Food and Drugs Act of 1906 (1906 Act),[13] food was considered adulterated if it contained "any added poisonous or other added deleterious ingredient which may render such [food] injurious to health."[14] While the 1906 Act was a historic step in food safety legislation,[15] it offered inadequate protection against unsafe substances in foods. This was true for several reasons.

---

[4] United States v. Walsh, 331 U.S. 432, 434 (1947).

[5] *Id.*

[6] *See* International Nutrition v. United States Dept. of Health and Human Services, 676 F.2d 338, 341 (8th Cir. 1982). *See also* United States v. Nova Scotia Food Products Corp., 568 F.2d 240, 246 (2d Cir. 1977).

[7] 21 USC §334 (1982).

[8] 21 USC §332 (1982).

[9] 21 USC §331 (1982). The penalty for a first offense includes a $1000 fine or imprisonment for a period of up to one year, or both. A second offense or a violation of the statute with intent to defraud carries a penalty of imprisonment for a period not exceeding three years or a $10,000 fine, or both. The statute does not permit the imposition of criminal penalties in certain situations, most notably when the violator has received and delivered in interstate commerce prohibited articles while acting in good faith.

[10] 21 USC §§341-348. "Food" is defined as "(1) articles used for food or drink for man or other animals; (2) chewing gum; and (3) articles used for components of any such article." 21 USC §321(f)(1982).

[11] 21 USC §331 (1982).

[12] Continental Chemiste Corp. v. Ruckelshaus, 461 F.2d 331, 336-37 (7th Cir. 1972).

[13] Act of June 30, 1906, ch. 3915, 34 Stat. 768 (repealed 1938).

[14] *Id.* at 770.

[15] The Federal Food and Drugs Act was the first federal statute that sought to protect the public from unsafe and impure foods. The 1906 Act created the Food and Drug Administration (FDA), as the agency charged with the administration of food safety legislation.

First, the 1906 Act was only applicable to "added" substances; it made no mention of harmful ingredients inherent in foods.[16] Second, the 1906 Act placed the burden of proving an "added" substance's harmful characteristics on the government.[17] This permitted potentially harmful foods to enter and remain on the national market until the government could establish that they contained harmful substances.[18] Third, the Supreme Court, in *United States v. Lexington Mill and Elevator Co.*,[19] held that the statute required a showing that "the food itself, rather than the added substance, was dangerous."[20] This exacerbated the burden of proof problem by requiring the government to prove not only that an added substance was itself harmful but also that its presence rendered an article of food injurious to health.

In 1938, Congress passed the Federal Food, Drug, and Cosmetic Act.[21] The Act expanded the provisions of the 1906 Act.[22] The Act redefined "adulteration" as the bearing or containing of "any poisonous or deleterious substance which may render [food] injurious to health."[23] This definition covered all ingredients in food. The Act, however, made an important distinction. The Act provided that ingredients present in food that had not been "added" to it would not adulterate the food "if the quantity of such substance does not ordinarily render [such food] injurious to health."[24] The Act further redefined "adulteration" as the bearing or containing of any added poisonous or deleterious substan-

---

[16] Merrill, *supra* note 3, at 174.

[17] *See* Turner, *The Delaney Anticancer Clause: A Model Environmental Protection Law*, 24 Vand. L. Rev. 889, 890 (1971).

[18] *Id.*

[19] 232 U.S. 399 (1914). In this case, the government sought to condemn sacks of flour that had been treated with nitrogen peroxide gas. The government contended that the treatment had added poisonous and deleterious ingredients to the flour. The Court ruled against the government, holding that the statute required a showing that the treated flour, rather than merely the nitrogen peroxide, was harmful.

[20] Continental Chemiste Corp. v. Ruckelshaus, *supra* note 12, at 337.

[21] Federal Food, Drug, and Cosmetic Act, ch. 675, 52 stat. 1040 (1938) (codified as amended at 21 USC §§301-392 (1982)).

[22] Merrill & Schewel, *FDA Regulation of Environmental Contaminants of Food*, 66 Va. L. Rev. 1357, 1360 (1980).

[23] Federal Food, Drug, and Cosmetic Act, §402(a)(1) (codified at 21 USC §342(a)(1)(1982)).

[24] *Id.* This standard remains in force today. *See* discussion *infra* at text accompanying notes 28-30. While a distinction exists between "added" and "not added" substances, the statute does not define the term "added."

ce,[25] "except where such substance is required in the production [of the food] or cannot be avoided by good manufacturing practice. . . ."[26] In the case of these "required" substances, the Act empowered the Food and Drug Administration (FDA) to set tolerances, which, if followed, permitted the use of possibly harmful substances in food.[27]

The Act thereby established three standards for harmful substances in foods.[28] The "may render injurious" standard applied to all substances found in foods.[29] The "ordinarily injurious" standard applied to substances inherent in foods.[30] Finally, the existence of a FDA-promulgated tolerance permitted the use of added harmful substances "necessary in the production of food."[31]

These definitions "modified the rule of *Lexington Mill* by focusing attention on the character of the added substance rather than the character of the food. . . ."[32] The Act, however, failed to resolve the burden of proof problem. The government was still required to affirmatively show that a particular substance was poisonous or deleterious in an enforcement action under the Act.

[2] The 1958 Act

The Food Additives Amendment of 1958[33] alleviated this problem. This amendment was the result of congressional concern over the growing use of chemicals in foods.[34] Under the Food Additives Amendment, a food is adulterated if it contains a statutorily defined type of added

---

25 *Id.* at Section 402(a)(2) (codified at 21 USC §342(1)(2)(1982)).

26 *Id.* at Section 406 (codified at 21 USC §346 (1982)).

27 *Id.*

28 Merrill, *supra* note 3, at 175.

29 *Id.*

30 *Id.*

31 *Id.*

32 Continental Chemiste Corp. v. Ruckelshaus, *supra* note 12, at 337.

33 Food Additives Amendment of 1958, 72 Stat. 1784 (codified at 21 USC §348 (1982)).

34 In the 1950s, Congress created the House Select (Delaney) Committee to Investigate the Use of Chemicals in Foods. The committee was chaired by James Delaney of New York, who spearheaded the movement to establish tighter regulation over chemicals in foods. This movement led to several amendments to the Federal Food, Drug, and Cosmetic Act including the Pesticides Residue Amendment of 1954, the Food Additives Amendment of 1958, and the Color Additives Amendment of 1960. *See* Kleinfeld, *The Delaney Proviso—Its History and Prospects*, 28 Food Drug Cosm. L. G. 556 (1973).

substance, the "food additive."[35]

A "food additive" is any substance intentionally or incidentally added to food.[36] A substance is not a food additive if it is "generally recognized as safe" among experts[37] or is used within the terms of a sanction granted by the FDA or the Department of Agriculture prior to 1958.[38]

Like the 1938 Act's tolerance provisions for "required" added substances, the Food Additives Amendment established a licensure scheme for "food additives." A "food additive" may be used if its use is in compliance with a regulation promulgated by the Secretary of Health and Human Services.[39] A regulation is promulgated upon a showing that it is safe within its intended use.[40] The amendment thereby shifts the burden of proving the safety of a food additive from the government to the proponent of its use.

Included in the 1958 Act was the oft-criticized, controversial Delaney clause,[41] an attempt to ban the use of any possible carcinogens in food.[42] It prohibits the issuance of a food additive regulation if the substance is found to induce cancer in humans or animals.[43]

The clause was included in the Color Additives Amendment of 1960.[44] Like the 1958 Food Additives Amendment, the Color Additives Amendment established a licensure scheme for substances used as coloring agents in foods.[45] The use of a "color additive"[46] is deemed to

---

[35] 21 USC §342(a)(2)(c)(1982).

[36] See 21 USC §321(s)(1982). See also S. Rep. No. 2422, 85th Cong., 2d Sess., reprinted in 1958 U.S. Code Cong. & Ad. News 5300, 5303-04. The definition of "food additive" is discussed infra.

[37] 21 USC §321(a)(1982). The definition of "generally recognized as safe" is discussed infra.

[38] Id. The definition of "prior sanctioned substance" is discussed infra.

[39] 21 USC §348(a)(1982). Under the Food Additives Amendment, the power to promulgate regulations was given to the Secretary of Health, Education, and Welfare. This Department was redesignated the Department of Health and Human Services in 1979.

[40] Id.

[41] 21 USC §348(c)(3)(A)(1982).

[42] See Kleinfeld, supra note 34, at 5.

[43] 21 USC §348(c)(3)(A)(1982).

[44] Color Additives Amendment of 1960, 74 Stat. 397 (codified at 21 USC §321(t), 376(1982)).

[45] 21 USC §376 (1982). Under the 1938 Act, when additives had been given special statutory treatment, the Act had established certification procedures for coal tar colors. Federal Food, Drug, and Cosmetic Act, ch. 675, 52 Stat. 1040, 1047 (repealed 1960). In Fleming v. Florida Citrus Exchange, 358 U.S. 153 (1958), the Supreme Court held that the FDA could withhold certification if the coal tar color, regardless of dosage, was

adulterate a food unless that use is within the terms of a regulation promulgated by the Secretary of Health and Human Services. The burden of proving its safety falls on the proponent of its use.

With each amendment, Congress has added to the confusion over the regulation of chemicals in foods. Each amendment has established new classes of substances and differing standards of safety without modifying preexisting statutory language. The result is a patchwork of overlapping provisions, each intended to deal with a particular type of substance. An analysis of a food chemical problem must begin with an examination of the nature of the substance itself. A determination of whether a substance is a "food additive," "color additive," "added," or "not added" substance is important as each will be treated separately under the statute.

§8.02   Food Additive Regulation

[1]   In General—Substantive Requirements

The definition of the term "food additive" is of key importance in the food chemicals regulatory scheme. Substances that fall into this category are subjected to very conservative regulatory assumptions under Chapter IV of the FFDCA.

The use of a food additive in the absence of a regulation issued by the FDA[47] results in the food's being deemed adulterated, and hence not permitted to be placed in the stream of commerce.[48]

The statutory standard for issuing a regulation authorizing use of the additive is that under the conditions of use prescribed by the regulation,

---

harmful, since Congress had made a determination that the substances should be deemed harmful until the industry produced affirmative evidence that they were harmless. The 1960 Color Additives Amendment was a legislative reaction to food industry pressure to establish provisions that would allow the use of colors within regulated conditions. *See* Toilet Goods v. Gardner, 278 F. Supp. 786, 789.

[46] "Color additive" is defined at 21 USC §321(f)(1982).

[47] The Food and Drug Administration, headed by an Administrator, exercises by delegation the statutory authority conferred by the FFDCA on the Secretary of Health and Human Services.

[48] 21 USC §342(a)(2)(c)(1982) states: "A food shall be deemed to be adulterated— . . . if it is, or if it bears or contains, any food additive which is unsafe within the meaning of section 348 of this title." Section 348(a), in turn, provides that a food additive will be deemed unsafe unless it and its use conform to either a statutory exemption or an FDA-promulgated regulation.

the proposed use will be "safe."[49] The statutory burden rests squarely on the proponent of the use of the additive; in order to satisfy the burden, the proponent must undertake extensive prepetition toxicological and other relevant testing. In addition, the statute provides an adjudicatory forum in which opponents of the additive can delay action on a petition for a long period of time.

The FDA possesses broad authority to establish conditions on the use of additives, and those conditions, if sufficiently stringent, can effectively render the chemical uneconomic.[50]

For all the above reasons, food manufacturers have generally sought to avoid having chemical substances associated with food labeled as food additives. The government, on the other hand, has a significant incentive to take a broadly inclusive view of the subject, since added substances that are not food additives are treated very differently by the Act. Most significantly, products containing "added substances" may be placed in the stream of commerce without prior FDA approval, and the government bears the burden of proving that the substances are deleterious.[51]

[2] The Delaney Provision

An additional conservative feature of the food additive regulatory scheme is the Delaney clause, which exists as a proviso in Section 409 of the FFDCA.[52] This provision deems any food additive to be unsafe if it "is found to induce cancer when ingested by man or animal, or if it is found, after tests which are appropriate for the evaluation of the

---

[49] 21 USC §348(c)(3)(1982).

[50] 21 USC §348(a)(2).

[51] The government must show that the substance "may render" the food to which it is an additive "injurious to health." 21 USC §342(a)(1).

[52] 21 USC §348(c)(3)(A) (*provided* clause). An identical provision applies to color additives and to animal drugs used on animals intended for human consumption. *See* 21 USC §376 (color additives); and 21 USC 360(b)(3)(d)(1)(H) (animal drugs). Animal feed additives are covered under Section 348, but are subject to special provisions. *See* Marshall Minerals, Inc v. Food and Drug Administration, 661 F.2d 409 (5th Cir. 1981). Animal drugs, though now covered by a separate subchapter of the FFDCA, were at one time regulated as food additives. *See* Bell v. Goddard, 366 F.2d 177 (7th Cir. 1966). Pesticide additives are not directly subject to a Delaney provision, although a 1971 decision of the D.C. Circuit appears to have imposed an equivalent burden on the government in establishing pesticide tolerances. *See* Environmental Defense Fund v. Ruckelshaus, 439 F.2d 584 (D.C. Cir. 1971) (relying on EDF v. U.S. Dept. HEW, 428 F.2d 1083 (D.C. Cir. 1970)).

safety of food additives to induce cancer in man or animal. . . ."[53]

This provision reflects in its terminology the limitations of science in 1958, when it was written. Whether a substance "induces" cancer is not as easy to determine as might initially be thought to be the case, and it is only by application of governmentwide carcinogen assessment principles promulgated by the Office of Science and Technology[54] that the terminology can be made reasonably workable. Those guidelines make certain assumptions about carcinogens, both initiators and pro- moters, and deem a substance that results in statistically significant tumor formation in two species of test animals or behaves as a mutagen in Ames tests and related *in vitro* tests to be a carcinogen. In the absence of such assumptions and conventions, the phrase "induce can- cer" would be difficult to apply, since the term "cancer" has come to be related to a range of diseases. To "induce cancer" means something different from "promote tumors," but in recent years the two have been applied synonomously.

The phrase also contains a significant limitation. It is only if the additive induces cancer by the ingestion exposure route that it is deemed unsafe by the statute. Thus, an additive that off-gasses and is inhaled by the food handler or one that is absorbed through the skin on contact is not subject to Delaney limitations.

The FDA's "constituent policy"[54.1] is representative of the Agency's attempt in recent years to soften the impact of the Delaney clause. Under this policy, the Agency applies the Delaney clause only where the food additive as a whole is found to induce cancer; where an addi- tive that has not itself been shown to induce cancer contains a constitu- ent or an impurity that is carcinogenic, the Agency applies the "general safety clause" of Section 409(c)(3)(A).[54.2]

---

[53] If the additive is to the feed of animals raised for food production, however, it is deemed unsafe only if "(i) . . . under the conditions of use and feeding specified in proposed labeling and reasonably certain to be followed in practice, such additive will not adversely affect the animals . . . and (ii) that no residue of the additive will be found (by methods of examination prescribed or approved by the Secretary by regulations . . .) in any edible portion of such animal after slaughter or in any food yielded by or derived from the living animal. . . ." 21 USC §321 (c)(3)(A). For some of the difficulties presented by this provision, *see* Marshall Minerals, Inc. v. FDA, 661 F.2d 409 (5th Cir. 1981).

[54] 49 Fed. Reg. 21594 (5-22-84).

[54.1] *See* 50 Fed. Reg. 49684 (12-4-85). This is also referred to as the "carcinogenic impurities policy."

[54.2] 21 USC 348(c)(3)(A). Using this methodology, the FDA has granted petitions for food additive regulations for substances containing constituents that pose a cancer risk

The FDA argues that its policy is not inconsistent with the Delaney clause, notwithstanding the fact that it is derived by means of a crabbed reading of the language of the statute. The one judicial decision on the subject to date, *Scott v. FDA*,[54.3] affirmed a color additive listing premised on the policy.[54.4]

Notwithstanding its anachronisms and limitations, the Delaney clause remains perceived as something to avoid, and has consequently spurred disputes over the inclusiveness of the food additive definition over the years.

[3] What Is a Food Additive?

The Act defines "food additive" as "any substance the intended use of which results or may reasonably be expected to result in its becoming a component or otherwise affecting the characteristics of any food . . . if such substance is not generally recognized . . . to be safe under the conditions of its intended use. . . ."[55] Expressly excluded from the scope of the definition are color additives, substances used in foods under an FDA or U.S. Department of Agriculture sanction prior to 1958[56] ("prior sanctioned substances"), pesticides,[57] and "new animal drugs."[58]

The test imposed by the statute has two parts.[59] First, the substance must become a component or affect the characteristics of the food to

---

calculated by the Agency to be as high as 1 in 10 million. *See* 48 Fed. Reg. 13018 (4-2-84) (Uniroyal Chemical Co.).

[54.3] 728 F.2d 322 (6th Cir. 1984).

[54.4] EPA, which administers the portion of the FFDCA regulating pesticide residues on raw agricultural products, has not formally adopted the constituent policy to date and is not bound by the FDA policy. If EPA does not adopt the policy, and if it survives anticipated additional legal attacks by public interest groups, an interesting situation will exist in which essentially identical risks will be managed quite differently under the same statutory scheme.

[55] 21 USC §321(s)(1982).

[56] The Department of Agriculture sanctioned food additives under the Poultry Product Inspection Act, 21 USC §§451 *et seq.*, and the Meat Inspection Act of March 4, 1907, as amended, 21 USC §§601 *et seq.*

[57] Pesticide additives are regulated pursuant to Section 408 of the FFDCA, 21 USC §346a, but since 1970 the Environmental Protection Agency rather than the FDA has administered that part of the FFDCA program. *See generally* Chapter 3, *supra.*

[58] Prior to 1968 animal drugs were regulated as food additives. In that year Congress amended the FFDCA and inserted a new subdivision, Part 360b, under which thereafter "new" animal drugs are regulated.

[59] United States v. 41 Cases, More or Less, 420 F.2d 1126, 1131 (5th Cir. 1970).

which it is added. Second, it must not be generally recognized as safe (GRAS).

[a] Is It a Component?

The universe of food additives is divided into two broad categories, "direct" additives and "indirect" additives, essentially differentiated by the mechanism by which they come into contact with food. The assertion of jurisdiction over indirect additives has historically been more difficult for the FDA, and its batting average lower, than for direct additives.

[i] Direct Additives

Direct food additives are substances that are intentionally added to food for a particular purpose. Examples are preservatives, antioxidants, nutritional supplements, and flavoring agents. A substance intentially placed in food becomes a component of the food almost by definition.

It is important to understand that actual "addition" of the substance to the food is not a necessary element of jurisdiction. All that is necessary is that it somehow come to reside in the food. Further, the fact that the substance is actually the principal or sole ingredient of the "food" does not necessarily render it not an additive.[60]

In certain cases, chemicals inherent in raw foodstuffs may become additives as a result of processing. Thus, in *United States v. Ewig Bros. Co.*,[61] pesticide residues found in smoked chubs were deemed food additives even though the defendants had not done anything to put them in the fish (they had accumulated in the fatty tissue of the fish).[62] Nevertheless, the court in *Ewig Bros.* concluded that the preexisting

---

[60] *See* United States v. An Article of Food, 678 F.2d 735 (7th Cir. 1982). Defendants argued that the principal ingredients of foods did not fall within the statutory definition. The court, while agreeing that in common usage something that is a principal component would not be considered "added," nevertheless held that the statutory definition was sufficiently broad to encompass such substances. *See also* National Nutritional Foods Association v. Kennedy, 572 F.2d 377 (2d Cir. 1978) (substances that qualify as "foods" under the act may also be deemed "food additives"); and *see* United States v. An Article of Food . . . Orotic Acid, 414 F.Supp. 793 (E.D.Mo. 1976) (substance processed as a dietary supplement may be deemed a food additive).

[61] 502 F.2d 715 (7th Cir. 1975), *cert. denied,* 420 U.S. 945 (1975).

[62] *Id.* Defendants had smoked fish contaminated while alive and living in the wild with DDT. They argued that "a process, such as smoking, during which nothing new is added to a food, cannot 'transmogrify' a preexisting component of a food into an additive." *Id.* at 722.

contaminants became additives upon processing of the food.[63]

Contaminants present in *raw* foods, such as mercury in fish, have been held to be "added substances" if the evidence demonstrates that "some portion" of the substance "has been introduced by man."[64]

[ii] Indirect Additives

Indirect additives are not easy to classify or define. In general, they may be distinguished from direct additives by the basic distinction that they are not intentionally added to foods, although as the *Ewig* case[65] illustrates, that distinction is not altogether satisfactory.

Indirect additives include substances that "may reasonably be expected"[66] to be introduced into foods through "use in producing, manufacturing, packing, processing, preparing, treating, packaging, transporting, or holding food."[67] Substances accidentally introduced into food are not included within this definition.[68]

This group contains substances that contact food, although not directly added to it, and as a result of the contact become components of the food. It includes a wide range of substances that are components of packaging materials and the like that one would not normally think of as food additives. Lead, for example, which was a component of the glaze used on pottery dinnerware, was found to be a food additive in *United States v. Articles of Food Consisting . . . of Pottery . . . Labeled . . . Cathy Rose.*[69] The FDA's food additive regulations encompass a

---

63 *Id.* "Although it may seem odd to place the label 'additive' on a chemical substance which was a component of the raw product and which is not changed by processing, Congress' choice of that label does not result in any 'transmogrification.' Before processing, DDT is a 'pesticide chemical' on a raw product; after processing it is an additive." *Accord,* United States v. City Smoked Fish Co., No. 33669 (E.D. Mich. 1970), *summarized in* 21 ALR Fed. 314, 337 (1974).

64 United States v. Anderson Seafoods, Inc., et al., 622 F.2d 157 (5th Cir. 1980). Thus, mercury in fish is an "added substance" if the FDA can show that some mercury likely to get into fish results from man-caused pollution of the fish's habitat.

65 *Supra* note 61.

66 21 USC §321(s).

67 *Id.* The definition includes "any source of radiation intended for any such use. . . ."

68 S.Rep. No. 2422, 85th Cong., 2d Sess. Accidental additives are treated as "added substances" under the Act. *See* United States v. Anderson Seafoods, *supra,* note 64.

69 370 F.Supp. 371 (E.D. Mich. 1974). The government argued that 1000 sets of dinnerware contained lead that was capable of migrating from the plates to the food served on them. The defendants moved for dismissal, claiming that only substances intentionally and directly added to food fell within Section 321(s). The court agreed with the government, concluding that the "legislative history leading to the Food Additives

wide range of materials associated with materials that come into contact with food incidentally,[70] including adhesives,[71] coatings,[72] adjuvants, and sanitizers.[73]

An indirect additive becomes a component of food when there is sufficient migration from the food-contacting material into the food to satisfy the regulatory threshold. The amount of migration considered sufficient to trigger the threshold has been the subject of controversy. The FDA at one time took the position that any *possibility* of migration, even in the absence of empirically measured concentrations in the food, was sufficient to trigger regulation.[74] This interpretation of the statute avoided the problems inherent in detecting minute quantities of substances in food, and the regulatory problems that arise when advances in the technology of detection permit the discovery of residues of migrant substances when only a few years earlier the state of the art could detect none.

In *Monsanto v. Kennedy*,[75] however, the District of Columbia Circuit held that "Congress did not intend that the component requirement . . . would be satisfied by a mere recitation of the diffusion principle,[76] a mere finding of any contact whatever with food."[77] The court stated that satisfaction of the "component" element of Section

---

Amendment of the Act shows a clear Congressional intent that substances which are subject to being ingested by human beings because of migration are 'food additives.' . . ." *Id.* at 373.

70 *See generally* 21 CFR §§174.5-178.3970 (1984).

71 *See, e.g.,* 21 CFR §175.105

72 *See* 21 CFR §§175.210-175.390.

73 *See, e.g.,* 21 CFR 178.1010.

74 *See* Natick Paperboard Corp v. Weinberger, 389 F. Supp 794 (D. Mass. 1974), in which the FDA successfully argued that polychlorinated biphenyls (PCBs) found in food packaging materials were food additives. The agency could not show actual migration of PCBs into the food, but convinced the court that if established principles of physics demonstrated a possibility of migration, the agency could regulate the substance.

75 613 F.2d 947 (D.C. Cir. 1979).

76 The "diffusion principle" is the second law of thermodynamics, which essentially holds that any two molecular substances coming into contact with each other will experience some molecular diffusion. The FDA had relied on this principle to assert food additive regulatory control over beverage containers manufactured of acrylonitrile. *See* 42 Fed. Reg. 48528 (1977). The FDA's position was that "[o]nce the applicability of the diffusion principle has been reasonably confirmed, projections based on the diffusion process are sufficient to satisfy the burden of proof with respect to migration, even though the amounts projected to migrate are below the level of analytical detectability." *Id.* at 48530.

77 613 F.2d 947, 955 (D.C. Cir. 1979).

321(s) required a finding, based on reliable data, that "a substance migrates into food in more than insignificant amounts."[78]

Monsanto v. Kennedy imposed on the FDA the burden of demonstrating the existence of some detectable migration of packaging and other chemicals that come into contact with food incidentally before subjecting them to food additive regulation. In addition, the decision established a *de minimus* exception, exercisable at the discretion of the FDA, where amounts detected are felt to be insignificant, although any such determination must clearly be articulated in the Federal Register notice announcing the decision not to regulate.[79]

The FDA's position with respect to indirect food additives stands in stark contrast to the less conservative approach it takes to regulating animal feed additives under the so-called DES exemption under the Delaney clause. In both cases the question is often how to deal with residues below the limit of detection for substances, such as carcinogens, that are generally held to have no dose threshold below which there are no effects.

Where animal feed additive residues are concerned, the FDA follows a modified Mantel-Bryan analysis that allows an estimation of the dose of a carcinogen that would lead to cancer below dose levels that can actually be detected.[80]

[b] Is It Generally Recognized As Safe (GRAS)?

A substance that falls into one of the definitional food additive categories will nevertheless escape regulation if it is "generally recognized, among experts qualified by scientific training and experience to evaluate its safety, as having been adequately shown through scientific procedures . . . to be safe under the conditions of its intended use."[81]

The statutory standard devolves into four issues. What is the meaning

---

[78] *Id.*

[79] *Id.* at 955-956. This amounts to a determination that the chemical, when ingested in the amounts found, is generally recognized as safe.

[80] This analysis is contained in the FDA's so-called Sensitivity of the Method (SOM) regulation, which was published at 42 Fed. Reg. 10412-10437 (1977). Historically the FDA has been willing to allow carcinogenic animal feed additives to be used until a residue has been detected. *See, e.g.,* Bell v. Goddard, 366 F.2d 177 (7th Cir. 1966). The *Monsanto* decision moves the FDA in the same direction in dealing with other types of potential indirect additives, although a statutory basis appears to be nonexistent.

[81] 21 USC §321(s). Prior sanctioned substances may be found to be GRAS on the basis of either scientific studies or knowledge founded upon "experience based on common use in food." *Id.*

of safe? What is a sufficient body of scientific opinion to constitute a general recognition of safety? What are acceptable scientific procedures, and, for prior sanctioned substances, what constitutes sufficient experience "based on common use in food"?

[i]   The Concept of "Safe"

The long history of the FFDCA has produced a statutory gloss on the word "safe"[82] that can be summarized as reasonable certainty that no harm to humans will result from the use of the additive. It is less than absolute certainty of harmlessness, but clearly does not encompass substances that present known or suspected risks.[83] The FDA's regulatory definition[84] employs three factors, which are derived from the Senate Report on the Food Additive Amendments[85]—(1) the probable consumption of the substance and of any substance formed on food because of its use, (2) the cumulative effect of the substance in the diet, taking into account any chemically or pharmacologically related substance or substances in the diet, and (3) "safety factors, which in the opinion of experts . . . are generally recognized as appropriate." The overall regulatory standard, which has been employed by the FDA since 1977,[86] is "reasonable certainty in the minds of competent scientists that the substance is not harmful under the intended conditions of use."

It is probably fair to say that the GRAS concept works best when it is applied to ordinary, often naturally occurring additives like pectin in fruit jams and salt, and that it works most poorly when it is applied to synthetic, exotic chemicals about which little health impact data are available but which have been around for a long time.

---

[82] 21 USC §321(u).

[83] *See generally,* for a detailed discussion of the legislative history, *Food Additives,* 7 Ecol. L.Q. 245, 246-56 (1978).

[84] 21 CFR §170.3(i).

[85] S.Rep. No. 2422, 95th Cong., 2d Sess., *reprinted in* 1958 U.S. Code Cong. & Admin. News 5300, at 5305.

[86] *See* 41 Fed. Reg. 14,483 (1977). The agency's regulations have not always reflected a consistent pattern of interpretation, however. At one point the agency followed a "no significant risk of harm" criterion. *See* 36 Fed. Reg. 12,093 (1971) (adopting definition codified at 21 CFR §121.1(i)(1972)). It has occasionally expressed the determination of "safe" to include a weighing of risks against benefits (*see, e.g.,* 41 Fed. Reg. 53,600 (1976)), but has at other times expressly refused to engage in a risk-benefit exercise. *See* 41 Fed. Reg. 1804, 1805-07 (1976); *but compare* 37 Fed. Reg. 23,456 (1972).

[ii] How Much Scientific Opinion Is Needed?

What is required to sustain the statutory burden is a substantial consensus among scientists trained or experienced in food safety matters.[87]

The FDA's regulations attempt to refine the nature of scientific opinion needed for a GRAS affirmation. The agency states that "general recognition . . . requires common knowledge about the substance throughout the scientific community knowledgeable about the safety of substances directly or indirectly added to food."[88] In addition, for GRAS predicated upon scientific opinion rather than prior sanctioned use, the agency requires that the demonstration be based on published toxicological studies and other empirical data.[89]

The FDA employs expert panels to evaluate or reevaluate GRAS for particular substances, and although the relevant expertise may be subject to dispute, the literature does not hold any examples of GRAS being affirmed or denied on the basis of the credentials of the scientists involved in the decisionmaking process.

A "conflicting reputation" is insufficient to support GRAS status.[90]

[iii] Prior Sanctioned Substances

The alternative GRAS requirements for substances sanctioned by the FDA or the Department of Agriculture prior to 1958 has produced a fair amount of litigation.

Two main issues have arisen repeatedly around this provision. What sort of use and during what time period constitutes "common use," and at what point do changed circumstances of use warrant termination of GRAS status for prior sanctioned substances?[91]

It appears that only uses that occurred prior to 1958 that are *present-*

---

[87] United States v. Articles of Drug Labled "Quick-o-ver," 274 F. Supp. 443 (D. Md. 1967). (Note: some of the law relating to food additives is drawn from the analogous provisions that have existed in the drug relation subchapters of the FFDCA, sometimes for significantly longer periods of time than have the food additive provisions.)

[88] 40 CFR §170.30(a).

[89] 40 CFR §170.30(b).

[90] United States v. Articles of Food and Drug, Coli-Trol 80 Med, 372 F. Supp. 915, 917 (N.D. Ga. 1974); *accord*, Weinberger v. Hynson, Westrott & Dunning, 518 F.2d 743 (5th Cir. 1975).

[91] The regulations affecting prior sanctioned ingredients are published at 21 CFR Part 181.

ly recognized as being safe qualify for GRAS status.[92] Domestic use will more readily support a prior sanctioned GRAS status than will foreign use prior to 1958, at least where there are profound social and cultural differences among the exposed populations.[93]

Both FDA regulations and the courts construe the prior sanction GRAS criterion narrowly. The FDA regulations state that "[a] prior sanction shall exist only for a specific use(s) of a substance in food, i.e., the level(s), conditions(s), product(s), etc., for which there was explicit approval . . . prior to September 6, 1958."[94] The regulations impose on the holders of GRAS exemptions a duty to disclose to the FDA changes in circumstance that might affect GRAS status.[95]

Though the courts have tended to construe the prior sanction GRAS exemption narrowly, a high degree of deference has been accorded to the FDA, even in cases where it has not exercised its discretion in a conservative manner.[96]

[iv]   Procedural Issues Involving GRAS Status

[A]   Determination or Affirmation of GRAS Status. The FFDCA establishes no procedural mechanism for determining in the first instance whether a substance is GRAS or for terminating GRAS status. In a regulatory universe that is filled with administrative processes and procedures, this absence is truly remarkable, explainable perhaps only

---

[92] *See* United States v. Naremco, Inc., 553 F.2d 1138 (8th Cir. 1977) (involving gentian violet). For other cases involving the interesting regulatory battles over this old chemical, *see* United States v. An Article of Food . . . 345/50-Pound Bags, 622 F.2d 768 (5th Cir. 1980); Southeastern Minerals, Inc. v. Harris, 622 F.2d 758 (5th Cir. 1980); and Marshall Minerals, Inc. v. FDA, 661 F.2d 409 (5th Cir. 1981).

[93] *See* Emali Herb, Inc. v. Heckler, 715 F.2d 1385 (9th Cir. 1983) ("Experience based on common use in food serves only as a means of showing safety. If the foreign experience cited by the proponent does not clearly demonstrate safety, because of doubts about cultural compatibility or the adequacy of public health data, then the substance must be deemed a food additive.").

[94] 21 CFR §181.5. *See also* United States v. Articles of Food . . . Buffalo Jerky, etc., 456 F. Supp. 207 (D. Neb. 1978) (refusing to give nitrate jerky made from buffalo meat GRAS status because the Meat Inspection Act prior to 1958 applied only to cattle, sheep, goats, pigs, and horses).

[95] *See* 21 CFR §§181.5(d) and 181.5(e); and *see generally* discussion of the issues in 31 Food, Drug & Cosmetic L.J. 264.

[96] *See, e.g.,* Public Citizen, et al. v. Foreman, 631 F.2d 969 (D.C. Cir. 1980) (case involving a Department of Agriculture determination under the Meat Inspection Act, but discussing deference to food regulatory agencies generally).

by reason of the fact that the last significant amendment occurred twenty years ago, before the society took on its current litigious posture.

The FDA maintains a list, which it amends from time to time, indicating the substances it believes are GRAS, and occasionally including limitations on GRAS uses.[97] The agency's general position has been that manufacturers should determine for themselves whether their products are GRAS,[98] but such a decision carries with it a risk that the FDA will disagree and seek to force the manufacturer to submit to food additive regulation.[99]

In 1978 the agency amended Part 170 to establish a formal procedure for reviewing and "affirming" GRAS status for the large numbers of chemicals that either were prior sanctioned or simply had been marketed by manufacturers under the assumption that they were GRAS, because that was a simpler approach than petitioning for a food additive regulation.[100]

The GRAS affirmation process is, in practical terms, little more than a review and reaffirmation or removal of substances on the preexisting GRAS list, although both the GRAS affirmation regulation and the accompanying regulation providing procedures for determining that a substance is *not* GRAS, allow any "interested person" to petition for a determination.[101]

Although citizen groups have demonstrated some interest in the GRAS *termination* procedures, product manufacturers have not been overly anxious to petition for affirmation of new ingredients, preferring to go ahead and use the substance in food on the bet that the FDA won't be interested enough to commence affirmative litigation to force a

---

[97] 21 CFR Parts 182, 184, and 186. *See* 23 Fed. Reg. at 9516 (1958), for the agency's contemporaneous explanation of these lists. The Part 184 and 186 lists contain affirmed GRAS ingredients. *See* discussion in text *infra*.

[98] *See* General Recognition of Safety and Prior Sanctions for Food Ingredients, 41 Fed. Reg. 53,600 (1976).

[99] This is not a great risk, since it is not an offense under the Act to use and market a new ingredient that is a food additive in the absence of a regulation, unless the substance had previously been determined to be a food additive by a formal FDA proceeding. The theory of the government's lawsuit is that the defendants are marketing adulterated food, and that the activity should be enjoined pending FDA rulemaking.

[100] 21 CFR §§170.30(e), 170.35, 184. The procedures provided are essentially notice and comment rulemaking on a public record into which all assembled data relevant to the ingredient are placed.

[101] 21 CFR §§170.35(a) and 170.38(a). The FDA's regulations do not provide it with authority to compel a GRAS affirmation petition from a manufacturer of an unlisted ingredient.

petition for a food additive regulation. This reasoning, from the manufacturer's point of view, is no doubt sound, at least as to products the manufacturer reasonably believes are without human health effects.

The chances are that the bureaucratic effort entailed in commencing affirmative litigation will deter the FDA from initiating lawsuits in all but those situations in which an "informally GRAS" ingredient has become the subject of public clamor resulting from publication of new toxicological evidence that the ingredient might produce an effect not previously known. Moreover, the public notice and comment proceedings associated with an affirmation proceeding take time, and invite scrutiny by the public interest food and drug groups.

The gentian violet litigation illustrates the strategies played out by the industry and FDA under the GRAS regime.

Several manufacturers had begun using gentian violet as a fungicide and bactericide in animal feed, and the FDA, contending that the substance should be treated as a food additive, sought to enjoin the use of the feed containing the substance as adulterated. Although the FDA prevailed in a number of the early cases,[102] the manufacturers simply altered the composition of the product and marketed the feed.

The FDA did not, however, always prevail, and the Fifth Circuit court of appeals became increasingly annoyed at the FDA's failure to employ a mechanism to resolve the dispute administratively. In *United States v. An Article of Food . . . 345/50-Pound Bags*,[103] the court upheld denial of summary judgment to the FDA on the strength of a single witness produced by the defendant who testified that the substance was GRAS. In *Southeastern Minerals, Inc. v. Harris*,[104] the Fifth Circuit reviewed the ongoing pattern of litigation and chastised the FDA for having made no conclusive administrative determination as to the use of the substance,[105] and suggested that had the agency done so, a lot of needless litigation would have been avoided.[106]

---

[102] *See, e.g.,* United States v. 41 Cases, More or Less, 420 F.2d 1126 (5th Cir. 1970) (high degree of deference to agency determination).

[103] 622 F.2d 768 (5th Cir. 1980).

[104] 622 F.2d 758 (5th Cir. 1980).

[105] The agency had issued an "advisory letter" to the industry stating that it believed that gentian violet was not GRAS.

[106] The court also, however, dissolved a district court injunction that had stopped the FDA and state officials from undertaking seizure actions under 21 USC §334, essentially holding that the courts are without jurisdiction to review an FDA determination that sufficient probable cause exists to initiate enforcement proceedings. 661 F.2d at 760.

[B] Termination of GRAS Status. Aside from the procedural morass illustrated by the gentian violet cases, the FDA's post-1977 regulations provide for termination of GRAS status by two related mechanisms. First, if in the course of a Section 170.35 GRAS affirmation review, the FDA determines that there is a "lack of convincing evidence that the substance is GRAS," it must publish a notice, under Section 170.38, stating that the substance is not GRAS, but a food additive.[107] The second mechanism is the direct initiation of proceedings, which may be either on the FDA's own motion or on a petition of any interested person, under Section 170.38(b).[108]

The FDA has four options once it determines that a substance is not GRAS. It may promulgate a food additive regulation,[109] require discontinuance of the use of the substance as an additive,[110] promulgate an "interim food additive regulation" governing use of the additive under Part 180,[111] or employ a combination of these authorities.[112]

The "interim food additive regulation" is a device invented by the FDA to soften the transition from GRAS status to food additive status.[113] Interim food additive regulations are available "when new information raises a substantial question about the safety or functionality of the substance but there is a reasonable certainty that the substance is not harmful and that no harm to the public health will result from the continued use of the substance for a limited period of time while the question raised is being resolved by further study."[114]

This standard is a curious one, since in its breadth it applies to substances that are suspect carcinogens, for which general scientific opinion holds there is no threshold of exposure below which effects do not occur, and for which a single exposure episode may be sufficient to

---

[107] 21 CFR §§170.35(b)(4) and 170(c)(5). These sections, when read alongside 21 CFR §170.38(a), appear to allow the FDA to make an immediately effective determination.

[108] Petitions must conform to the requirements of 21 CFR §171.130(b). The procedures followed by the FDA are notice and comment rulemaking. *Id.* There is a separate procedural requirement for prior sanctioned substances. *See* 21 CFR §170.38(d).

[109] 21 CFR §170.38(c)(1).

[110] 21 CFR §170.38(c)(3).

[111] 21 CFR §170.38(c)(2).

[112] 21 CFR §170.38(c)(4).

[113] *See Food Additives*, 7 Ecol. L.Q. 245, 260-64 (1978) (criticizing the regulation as beyond FDA's statutory authority). The regulations, codified at 21 CFR Part 180, were upheld against such a challenge in Jacobson v. Edwards, 1971 Food Drug Cos. L. Rep. (CCH) 56,059.10 (D.D.C. 1971), *aff'd*, (D.C. Cir. 1971).

[114] 21 CFR §180.1(a). *See also* 37 Fed. Reg. 6207 (1972).

produce the effect. For suspected carcinogens, then, one would think that the FDA should not apply the regulation; yet in at least one such case, saccharin, it did so.[115]

---

[115] *See* 36 Fed. Reg. 12,109 (1971) (saccharin); and 21 CFR §180.37 (1971) (saccharin—interim status).

CHAPTER 9

Government Regulation of Worker Exposure to Chemicals

§9.01　Introduction

Exposure to chemicals in the workplace constitutes the most concentrated exposure potential of all types of chemical exposure. Chemical exposure in the workplace is accordingly the subject of specific regulatory requirements.

Employers who use chemical substances in the workplace are potentially subject to regulatory control under the Occupational Safety and Health Act (OSH Act).[1] The regulated entity is the employer, rather than the manufacturer of the chemicals that are the subject of regulation.[2]

The OSH Act applies to chemicals and other potentially dangerous substances in the workplace. It also covers more mundane aspects of workplace safety, such as machinery use, temperature, and the like. Toxic chemicals and "harmful physical agents," however, are singled out for special treatment, and are given their own OSH Act provision, Section 6(b)(5), which gives them special signficance.

The OSH Act establishes rather general regulatory commands to be carried out by the Occupational Safety and Health Administration (OSHA), a subunit of the U.S. Department of Labor. The OSH Act program is enforced in a number of states by state agencies to whom authority has been delegated under the act.[3]

---

[1] 29 USC §§651 *et seq.*, 84 Stat 1593 (12-29-70). Commonly used session law numbers are referred to in the text. A U.S. Code–session law cross-reference table is provided in Appendix 9-A, *infra*.

[2] There are jurisdictional overlaps, however, among the OSH Act, the Federal Insecticide, Fungicide and Rodenticide Act (FIFRA), and the Toxic Substances Control Act (TSCA). The Environmental Protection Agency (EPA) has, for example, acted or threatened to act under both TSCA and FIFRA to impose limitations on the use of products on the basis of workplace risks.

[3] 29 USC §667. States may also regulate under state law any issue "with respect to which no standard is in effect" under the act. *Id.*

OSHA control standards are subject to the advisory jurisdiction of an independent government advisory body, the National Institute of Occupational Safety and Health (NIOSH)[4] This body of scientists advises OSHA on the scientific and medical implications of exposure to substances in the workplace. Although its role is purely advisory, NIOSH recommendations have been accorded substantial weight by the courts.[5]

The OSH Act's regulatory scheme embodies a broad "general duty" on employers to provide a workplace that is free from "recognized hazards" posing a threat of death or serious physical harm,[6] and a specific duty to comply with standards promulgated by OSHA.[7] The act contemplates three categories of standards relevant to chemical use, in the following order of stringency, the least stringent first: national consensus standards,[8] occupational safety and health standards promulgated by rule,[9] and emergency temporary standards.[10]

§9.02 The General Duty Clause

[1] In General

Section 5(a)(1) of the OSH Act, known as the "general duty clause," requires that "[e]ach employer . . . furnish to each of his employees employment and a place of employment which are free from recognized hazards which are causing or are likely to cause death or serious physical harm to his employees."

The clause was enacted as a catchall to provide protection in only those circumstances in which a specific OSHA standard does not apply. Whether a given condition constitutes a violation of the general duty clause requires a subjective case-by-case determination by OSHA en-

---

[4] 29 USC §671. NIOSH is under the Department of Health and Human Services, a separate cabinet-level agency.

[5] *See, e.g.,* United Steelworkers of America, AFL-CIO v. F. Ray Marshall, 647 F.2d 1189 (D.C. Cir. 1980).

[6] Section 5(a)(1).

[7] Section 5(a)(2).

[8] Section 6(a).

[9] Section 6(b).

[10] Section 6(c).

forcement personnel, and citations for violations of the clause will be vacated if a specific standard is applicable.[11]

[2]　Elements of the Obligation

[a]　Place of Employment

The general duty clause is applicable only to the employer's "place of employment." That phrase has been construed broadly to mean virtually any place where one of the employer's employees is or was present, including a room usually locked and unavailable to most employees,[12] the shoulder of a public highway,[13] and a truck.[14]

[b]　Recognized Hazards

Only "recognized hazards" must be eliminated. This term is defined to mean a condition that is known by the employer to be hazardous,[15] although the requisite knowledge will be imputed to a particular employer if knowledge of the hazard is common within the industry of which the employer is a part. Actual or constructive knowledge of recognized hazards includes not only those hazards detectable by the

---

[11] American Smelting and Refining Company v. Occupational Safety and Health Review Commission, 501 F.2d 504, 2 OSHC 1041 (8th Cir. 1974). The Occupational Safety and Health Review Commission (OSHRC) is the administrative hearing body to which enforcement citations are appealed. The citation to "2 OSHC 1041" is to the Bureau of National Affairs "Occupational Safety and Health Cases," a proprietary, unofficial, reporting service. Hereafter, judicial decisions will be cited to the West reporter system and administrative decisions to the OSHC. Most judicial decisions are also reported in the OSHC, but those citations will be provided only if the decision is not officially reported. See also R.L. Saunders Roofing Company, 7 OSHC 1566 (1979); and A. Prokosch & Sons Sheet Metal, Inc., 8 OSHC (1980) (both administrative decisions of the OSHRC). Occasionally a case will be cited "Brennan v. OSHRC (name of a substance)." Such a citation connotes an appeal by the Secretary of Labor from a decision of the OSHRC, a procedure allowed by Section 11(b) of the act.

[12] REA Express, Inc. v. Brennan, 495 F.2d 882 (2d Cir. 1974).

[13] Sugar Cane Growers Cooperative of Florida, 4 OSHC 1320 (1976).

[14] Clarkson Construction Co. v. OSHRC, 531 F.2d 451 (10th Cir. 1976).

[15] Cases involving the actual knowledge concept include Magma Copper Co. v. Marshall, 608 F.2d 373 (9th Cir. 1979); Empire Detroit Steel Div. v. OSHRC, 579 F.2d 378 (6th Cir. 1978); Usery v. Marquette Cement Mfg. Co., 568 F.2d 902 (2d Cir. 1977); Titanium Metal Corp v. Usery, 579 F.2d 536 (9th Cir. 1978); Brennan v. OSHRC, 494 F.2d 460 (8th Cir. 1974).

senses but also those detectable only by using sensitive monitoring instruments.[16]

In *American Smelting and Refining Co. v. OSHRC*,[17] the employer argued that hazards detectable only by monitoring devices could not be considered "recognized." The court of appeals rejected this argument, relying in part on legislative history of the OSH Act revealing that an early version of the bill containing the language "readily apparent hazards" was rejected in favor of the current phraseology.[18] The court construed the provision broadly in light of the realities of current technology and the remedial and public health purposes behind the OSH Act.

Imputed, or constructive, knowledge of the existence of a hazard requires the presence of common knowledge within the industry that the condition is hazardous.[19] The nature of the "common knowledge" requirement involves the "common knowledge of safety experts who are familiar with the circumstances of the industry or activity in question."[20]

[c] "Free" from Recognized Hazards

The tension arising from the obligation in the general duty clause that the workplace be "free" from recognized hazards involves the degree to which the clause makes the employer the equivalent of an insurer, or imposes liability without fault. Arguments that the requirement is only that the workplace be "reasonably" free from recognized hazards have been rejected.[21] However, the notion that strict liability is imposed has also been rejected, and the preferred construction seems to be that the clause imposes only a duty to eliminate preventable

---

[16] American Smelting and Refining Co. v. OSHRC, 501 F.2d 504 (8th Cir. 1974).

[17] *Id.*

[18] See 3 U.S. Code Cong. & Adm. News at 522 (1970); 2 U.S. Code Cong. & Adm. News at 5177, 5222 (1970).

[19] National Realty & Const. Co. v. OSHRC, 489 F.2d 1257 (D.C. Cir. 1973); Brennan v. OSHRC, 499 F.2d 460 (8th Cir. 1974); Getty Oil Co. v. OSHRC, 530 F.2d 1143 (5th Cir. 1976); Magma Copper Company v. Marshall, 608 F.2d 373 (9th Cir 1979).

[20] National Realty & Construction Co. v. OSHRC, 489 F.2d 1257 (D.C. Cir. 1973); General Dynamics Corporation, Quincy Shipbuilding Div. v. OSHRC, 599 F.2d 453 (1st Cir. 1979).

[21] *See* National Realty & Constr. Co. v. OSHRC, 489 F.2d 1257 (D.C. Cir. 1973).

[22] *Id. See also* Brennan v. OSHRC (Conrad Precision Industries), 502 F.2d 946 (3d Cir. 1974); Brennan v. OSHRC (Hanovia Lamp Div.), 502 F.2d 946 (3d Cir. 1974); Marshall v. L.E. Myers Company, 589 F.2d 270 (7th Cir. 1978); Atlantic & Gulf Stevedores, Inc.

hazards.[22] Hazards resulting from unpredictable reckless or demented behavior are not covered.

Whether a given hazard is preventable is determined by an inquiry as to whether a safety expert would take it into account in prescribing a safety program.[23] If a hazard is so implausible or idiosyncratic, or the means of protecting against it are so infeasible that a safety expert would disregard it, the general duty clause does not require an employer to eliminate the hazard from the place of employment.

Nevertheless, it is not a defense that a safety precaution for a known hazard is not in general use in the industry. The question is whether a precaution is recognized by safety experts as feasible, not whether the use of the precaution has become customary.[24] The presence of a standard, however, even if it is informal, is conclusive on the issue.[25]

[d] Causing or Likely to Cause Death or Serious Physical Harm

Only hazards that cause or are "likely to cause death or serious physical harm" are subject to the general duty obligation. The word "likely" modifies only the consequences of the event once it occurs, not the probability of occurrence;[26] thus a hazard must be prevented even if its occurrence is not likely.[27]

[3] Burden of Proof

[a] In General

The burden of proof, which rests on the Secretary of Labor, since the general duty clause is effectively an enforcement provision, involves three elements. OSHA must prove that (1) the employer failed to render its workplace free of a hazard that was (2) recognized and (3)

---

v. OSHRC, 534 F.2d 541 (3d Cir. 1976); Getty Oil Co. v. OSHRC, 530 F.2d 1143 (5th Cir. 1976).

[23] National Realty, *supra* note 21. *See also* General Dynamics Corp v. OSHRC, 599 F.2d 453 (1st Cir. 1979).

[24] *Id.*

[25] *See* Ensign-Bickford Co. v. OSHRC, 717 F.2d 1419 (D.C. Cir., 1983).

[26] National Realty, *supra* note 21. *See also* Pratt & Whitney Aircraft Div. of United Technologies Corp, 8 OSHC 1332 (1980); Illinois Power Company v. OSHRC, 632 F.2d 25 (7th Cir. 1980); and Allis Chalmers Corp v. OSHRC, 542 F.2d 27 (7th Cir. 1976).

[27] *Id.;* and *see* Babcox and Wilcox Co. v. OSHRC, 622 F.2d 1160 (3d Cir. 1980); Usery v. Marquette Cement Mfg. Co., 568 F.2d 902 (2d Cir. 1977); Usery v. Hermitage Concrete Pipe Co., 584 F.2d 127 (6th Cir. 1978); Shaw Const. Co. v. OSHRC, 534 F.2d 1183 (5th Cir. 1976); Marshall v. L.E. Myers Co., 589 F.2d 270 (7th Cir. 1978); Storey Electric Co. v. OSHRC, 553 F.2d 357 (4th Cir. 1975).

causing or likely to cause death or serious physical harm.[28] It is not required that the government prove that an accident actually occurred, but proof of the occurrence of an accident is not in and of itself sufficient to support an allegation of violation of the clause. There is, therefore, a fourth element in the government's case. It must show that demonstrably feasible measures would have materially reduced the likelihood that such an event would have occurred.[29]

The statutory burden of proof requires that the government's case be supported by substantial evidence in the record considered as a whole.[30]

[b] Specific Elements

[i] Proof of Recognized Hazard

To prove that a hazard is recognized requires the government to establish that the employer had actual or constructive knowledge that the hazardous condition exists or existed. Where actual knowledge is shown, OSHA must demonstrate that the safety experts in the industry would have thought the employer's precautions to be inadequate or unacceptable.[31] This requires proof that a reasonably prudent employer would have protected against the hazard by means other than those chosen by the respondent.[32] The standard that OSHA alleges should have been followed must be one sanctioned by reasonably prudent safety experts familiar with the industry.[33]

In order to prove constructive knowledge of a hazard, OSHA must be able to establish the custom and practice of the industry. Custom and practice may be proven by means of testimony by knowledgeable safety experts,[34] manufacturers' warnings, or other documentary evidence, or by reference to national consensus or other standards.[35]

---

[28] National Realty & Const. Co. v. OSHRC, 489 F.2d 1257 (7th Cir. 1973)

[29] *Id.*

[30] Section 6(f).

[31] Magma Copper Co. v. Marshall, 608 F.2d 373 (9th Cir. 1979).

[32] Bristol Iron & Steel Works v. Marshall, 601 F.2d 717 (4th Cir. 1979).

[33] General Dynamics Corp. v. OSHRC, 599 F.2d 453 (1st Cir. 1979).

[34] *See, e.g.,* Getty Oil Co. v. OSHRC, 530 F.2d 1143 (5th Cir. 1976); Shcriber Sheet Metal & Roofers, Inc. v. OSHRC, 597 F.2d 78 (6th Cir. 1979); and Continental Oil Co. v. OSHRC, 630 F.2d 446 (6th Cir. 1980).

[35] *See, e.g.,* Titanium Metals Corporation of America v. Usery, 579 F.2d 536 (9th Cir. 1978); Fry's Tank Service, Inc. and Cities Service Oil Company, 4 OSHC 1515 (1976), *aff'd* 577 F.2d 126 (10th Cir. 1978); and Atlantic Sugar Association, 4 OSHC 1253 (1976).

Extrapolation of standards from one industry to employers in another has generally not been allowed as an evidentiary basis for imputing knowledge.[36]

[ii] Proof of Failure to Maintain Premises Free from Recognized Hazards

Because employers are required only to take reasonable precautionary steps to protect workers from preventable hazards, proof of violation of the duty requires a showing that the hazard was reasonably foreseeable prior to employee exposure.[37] OSHA is not, however, required to prove that a particular chain of events leading to a specific incident was foreseeable. It need only prove that the general hazard was foreseeable.[38]

[iii] Proof of Causation of Harm

It is not necessary for proof of a violation of the general duty clause that it be demonstrated that an accident or harmful exposure has actually occurred, or even that it is likely to occur. A violation is established where it is shown that if an accident or exposure did occur, it is probable that an employee would suffer death or serious physical injury.[39]

[iv] Proof That Employer Could Materially Reduce the Hazard

The actual occurrence of hazardous conduct will not by itself sustain a violation of the general duty clause, even where injury has resulted. OSHA must prove that demonstrably feasible measures would have reduced the likelihood that such an event would have occurred.[40] The government is required to show the precautionary steps the cited employer should have taken to avoid violating the duty, and must demonstrate the feasibility and likely effectiveness of those measures.[41]

---

[36] See H.30, Inc. v. Marshall, 597 F.2d 534 (10th Cir. 1979). See also Usery v. Kennecott Copper Corp., 577 F.2d 1113 (10th Cir. 1978); Brennan v. OSHRC (Republic Creosoting Co.), 501 F.2d 1109 (1974).

[37] Empire Detroit Steel Div., Detroit Steel Co. v. OSHRC, 579 F.2d 378 (6th Cir. 1978); Brown & Root, Inc., 8 OSHC 2140 (1980); Pratt & Whitney Aircraft Div., 8 OHC 1329 (1980); Babcox and Wilcox Company v. OSHRC, 622 F.2d 1160 (7t Cir. 1974).

[38] Id.

[39] Babcox and Wilcox Comany v. OSHRC, 622 F.2d 1160 (3d Cir. 1980).

[40] See Champlin Petroleum Company v. OSHRC, 489 F.2d 637 (5th Cir. 1979).

[41] Titanium Metals Corporation v. Usery, 579 F.2d 536 (9th Cir. 1978).

[4] Serious Violations

The OSH Act enforcement scheme contemplates the issuance of "citations" to violators of the regulatory prohibitions and requirements,[42] and the levy of civil penalties, which vary in severity, depending on whether the violation involved is not serious, serious, or willful or repeated.[43] A "serious" violation is defined by Section 17(k) of the OSH Act as one where "there is a substantial probability that death or serious physical harm could result from a condition which exists or from one or more practices, means, methods, operations or processes which have been adopted or are in use . . . unless the employer did not and could not with the exercise of reasonable diligence know of the presence of the violation."

The OSHA Field Operations Manual provides that citations should be issued for general duty clause violations only if they are "serious." The additional elements required are (1) that there be a "substantial probability" rather than a mere likelihood of death or serious injury, and (2) that the employer knew, or with reasonable diligence could have known, that its safety program failed to take the steps needed to prevent the hazard from occurring.[44] Although the matter is not clear, it is arguable that constructive knowledge of the hazard may be insufficient to satisfy the test for a serious violation.

[5] Defenses

The general duty clause has uniformly withstood constitutional attacks grounded on vagueness and unlawful delegation theories.[45] Individual citations have occasionally been attacked successfully on due process grounds, where the citation was not sufficiently specific to afford the employer fair notice of what conduct was prohibited.[46]

Normal common law defenses, such as contributory negligence or

---

[42] Section 10.

[43] Sections 17(c), (b), and (a). In contrast with some of the other statutes discussed in this treatise, the penalties for violating OSHA requirements are relatively minor. The penalty for a nonserious violation is $100, for a serious violation $1000, and for a willful or repeated violation $10,000.

[44] National Realty and Const. Co. v. OSHRC, 489 F.2d 1257 (D.C. Cir. 1973).

[45] See REA Express, Inc. v. Brennan, 495 F.2d 822 (2d Cir. 1974); Bethlehem Steel Corp. v. OSHRC, 607 F.2d 1069 (1979).

[46] See Babcox and Wilcox Company v. OSHRC, 622 F.2d 1160 (3d Cir. 1980). The specificity requirement for citations is that they "specify the particular steps the employer should have taken . . . and . . . demonstrate the feasibility and likely utility of those measures." National Realty and Const. Co. v. OSHRC, 489 F.2d 1257 (D.C. Cir. 1973).

employee assumption of the risk, are unavailable to employers in OSHA enforcement actions.[47] Nevertheless, evidence of actions that would be evidentiary to such defenses may be introduced in rebuttal to the government's *prima facie* case.

Most defenses are factual in nature. Employers may claim in a given case that a specific standard covered the activity, rendering the general duty clause inapplicable, that insufficient employee exposure occurred to prevent harm, that the employer had no knowledge of the hazard, or that it was not preventable, or not forseeable, that OSHA failed to meet its burden of proof on the feasibility of the method of compliance claimed to have been available, that the employer had no notice of the violation, or that the preventive measures advocated by OSHA would have posed an even greater hazard.[48]

§9.03　National Consensus Standards and Preexisting Federal Standards

Most workplace standards for chemical exposure, and, for that matter, virtually all forms of hazards, are national consensus standards. The OSH Act required OSHA to promulgate, as initial standards, within two years of the act's effective date, and without regard for the requirements of the Administrative Procedure Act (APA), national consensus standards (as defined by Section 3(9)), and any preexisting federal occupational safety and health standards unless the agency concluded that the standard would not improve the level of protection for particular employee groups.[49]

National consensus standards are defined by Section 3(9) as occupational safety and health standards that have been adopted by a "nationally recognized standards-producing organization" under procedures ensuring that interested participants reached "substantial agreement" as to their adoption and were formulated in a way that provided an opportunity for diverse views to be considered. OSHA was required to consult with other federal agencies prior to issuing its list of such standards.

---

[47] REA Express, Inc. v. Brennan, 495 F.2d 822, 825 (2d Cir. 1974).

[48] *See* Brisk Waterproofing Co., 1 OSHC 1263 (1973); Ringland-Johnson, Inc., 4 OSHC 1343, *aff'd*, 551 F.2d 1117 (8th Cir. 1977); Penrod Drilling Co., 4 OSHC 1655 (1976); James E. Roberts Co., 1 OSHC 1684 (1974).

[49] Section 6(a).

There is a large number of national consensus standards, the specifications for which OSHA publishes in a handbook, which is updated from time to time. National consensus standards are deemed occupational safety and health standards, and are accordingly enforceable as such.

§9.04 Occupational Safety and Health Standards for Chemical Exposure

[1] In General

OSHA is required to promulgate, modify, and repeal occupational safety and health standards "by rule."[50] The initiative for standard-setting rulemaking may come from within OSHA or from NIOSH, the Department of Health and Human Services, employer or employee organizations, national standard-setting organizations, state or local governments, or "any interested person."[51]

If information submitted by the initiating entity convinces OSHA that a potential problem needs addressing, an advisory committee may be established whose function it is to recommend what action should be taken.[52] Once an advisory committee is appointed, a regulatory clock begins to tick, and subsquent action is required to be in accordance with the statutory timetable.[53] Notice and comment rulemaking is ordinarily employed,[54] unless an objector filing written objections requests a hearing, in which case a hearing must be held. If the rule replaces an existing national consensus standard, OSHA is required to explain in its Federal Register notice the reasons why the new standard will "better effectuate the purposes of" the OSH Act.[55]

An "occupational safety and health standard" is defined by Section 3(8) of the act as "a standard which requires conditions, or the adoption or use of one or more practices, means, methods, operations or pro-

---

[50] Section 6(b).

[51] Section 6(b)(1).

[52] *Id.*

[53] Sections 6(b)(2), (3), and (4).

[54] Although the statute does not explicitly require OSHA to follow the strictures of the APA, 5 USC §§553 *et seq.*, it has been held to require adherence to the APA implicitly. *See* American Iron and Steel Institute v. Marshall, 647 F.2d 1189 (D.C. Cir. 1980).

[55] Section 6(b)(8).

cesses, reasonably necessary or appropriate to provide safe or healthful employment and places of employment."

The general definition is refined by Section 6(b)(7), which sets forth a list of requirements that must or may be imposed by a standard. These are warnings and emergency treatment instructions, "suitable protective equipment," "control or technological processes," exposure monitoring and measuring, and medical examinations of exposed employees (at the employer's expense).[56]

In addition to the explicit statutory requirements, a number of other requirements have been held to be within OSHA's statutory authority. A "medical removal" provision requiring employers to remove employees from the areas of exposure once a minimum threshold of lead in their blood was detected, and also requiring the employer either to provide such employees with other equivalent employment or to continue to pay them while they were not working, was upheld in *United Steelworkers of America v. Marshall.*[57] OSHA's requirement that employers maintain medical records on exposed employees and provide access to the records by not only the government but also "authorized representatives" of the employees (that is, unions) has also been upheld, subject to certain limitations.[58]

The core component of OSHA standards is the "permissible exposure

------

[56] OSHA may also require medical examinations for research purposes at the request of the Department of Health and Human Services, but in such event the other agency must bear the cost. Section 6(b)(7).

[57] 647 F.2d 1189 (D.C. Cir. 1980) (generally upholding OSHA's lead standard). The court rejected challenges based on assertions that OSHA only had the authority provided in Section 6(b)(7) and on a claim that the standard was inconsistent with Section 4(b)(4) of the act, which provides that nothing in the act "shall be construed to supersede or in any manner affect any workmen's compensation law or to enlarge or diminish or affect in any other manner the common law or statutory rights, duties, or liabilities of employers and employees under any law with respect to injuries, diseases, or death of employees arising out of, or in the course of, employment."

A wage guarantee provision in the cotton dust standard was struck down by the Supreme Court, however, in American Textile Mfgrs. Institute v. Donovan, 452 U.S. 490 (1981), citing OSHA's failure to explain why that particular provision bore any relationship to increased health protection.

[58] *Id.* The court of appeals opined that if such a standard allowed unions, without the employee's permission, to "examine the intimate results of physician examinations— information to which the employee and the government do have rightful access—. . .," it might violate both the Privacy Act and the Constitution and reach beyond the allowances of Section 6(b)(7) and Section 6(c). A limited right to examine only the findings as to lead levels was found to be lawful.

OSHA has a general recordkeeping requirement, 29 CFR §§1910.20, premised not on Section 6(b) but rather on Section 8, which provides OSHA with general rulemaking authority. *See* Louisiana Chemical Ass'n, et al. v. Bingham, 657 F.2d 777 (5th Cir. 1981).

limit" (PEL), the amount of a substance OSHA allows an employee to be exposed to during a defined period of exposure. PELs are ordinarily expressed as time-weighted averages, although for some substances instantaneous maximum exposure levels are also set.

[2] Threshold Criteria for Establishment of Occupational Safety and Health Standards

Section 3(8) limits the issuance of occupational safety and health standards to those that are "reasonably necessary or appropriate to provide safe or healthful employment and places of employment." Until the Supreme Court's decision in *Industrial Union Department, AFL-CIO v. American Petroleum Institute* (hereafter *"API"* or *"benzene* case"),[59] OSHA had interpreted the quoted language as not imposing any substantive constraints on standard setting, other than to require that OSHA standards not be irrational. The Supreme Court concluded, however, that the language establishes a threshold test applicable to all occupational safety and health standards, requiring OSHA to make a threshold determination that the exposure in question "poses a significant health risk in the workplace and that a new standard is "reasonably necessary or appropriate. . . ."[60] The Court arrived at this conclusion by interpreting the statutory language to require a threshold determination that the workplace is "unsafe," and for a workplace to be "unsafe," the Court reasoned, it must threaten the workers with a "significant risk of harm."[61]

The second prong of the threshold test is that the risk identified can be "eliminated or lessened by a change in practices."[62]

The Supreme Court in the *benzene* case did not, however, lay down any hard-and-fast guidance as to just what sort of risk will satisfy the "significant risk" criterion. Essentially, the Court required OSHA to undertake a risk analysis, but neither the Court nor the Congress pro-

---

[59] 448 U.S. 607 (1980).

[60] *Id.*

[61] *Id.* The Court rejected the government's argument that one class of standards, those promulgated to address toxic substances and harmful physical agents under Section 6(b)(5), did not have to meet the threshold test.

[62] *Id.*

vided the agency with the standard against which to measure the acceptability of the risk.[63]

Although OSHA must make a significant risk determination on the record prior to acting, the agency has "no duty to calculate the exact probability of harm,"[64] and is "not required to support its finding that significant risk exists with anything approaching scientific certainty."[65]

With respect to carcinogens, moreover, OSHA may "use conservative assumptions in interpreting data" and will be supported so long as the assumptions are supported "by a body of reputable scientific thought."[66]

Given the broad deference to OSHA's choices under Section 3(8), the agency can doubtless act, where nonthreshold effect substances are concerned, on the basis of very low exposure levels.[67] OSHA may act

---

[63] In the plurality opinion, Justice Stevens stated that that was the agency's function. The opinion went on to state, not very helpfully:

> Some risks are plainly acceptable and others are plainly unacceptable. If, for example, the odds are one in a billion that a person will die from cancer by taking a drink of chlorinated water, the risk clearly could not be considered significant. On the other hand, if the odds are one in a thousand that the regular inhalation of gasoline vapors that are 2% benzene will be fatal, a reasonable person might well consider the risk significant. . . .

Justice Stevens's formulation represents the easy case, and even in the examples given there will be dissenters from the conclusions expressed from within the scientific community.

[64] Id.

[65] Id.; and see Industrial Union, AFL-CIO v. Hodgson, 499 F.2d 476 (1974); Society of the Plastics Industry v. OSHA, 509 F.2d 1301 (2d Cir. 1975), cert. denied, 421 U.S. 992.

[66] Id.; and see American Textile Manufacturers Institute v. Donovan, 452 U.S. 490 (1981) (upholding cotton dust standard based on admittedly flawed economic analysis; extreme deference accorded OSHA judgment).

[67] See generally 29 CFR Part 1990 (OSHA Cancer Policy); and 49 Fed. Reg. 21594 (5-84) (Office of Science & Technology Carcinogen Guidelines). OSHA's post-API case decisionmaking indicates that the agency has taken literally Justice Stevens's statement in the Court's opinion that a "reasonable person might well consider [a risk of 1 in 1000] . . . significant and take appropriate steps to decrease or eliminate it." 448 U.S. at 655. Thus, the Agency has found to be "significant" risks of cancer or other illness estimated by computer modeling to fall into the following ranges: 71 to 620 in 10,000 (50 Fed. Reg. 50462 (12-10-85)—formaldehyde); 44 to 152 in 1000 (50 Fed. Reg. 50538 (12-10-85)); 148 to 125 in 1000 (48 Fed. Reg. 1896 (1-14-83)—airborne inorganic arsenic; upheld in ASARCO, Inc. v. OSHA, 746 F.2d 483 (9th Cir. 1984)); 63 to 109 in 1000 (48 Fed. Reg. 17295 (4-21-83)—ethylene oxide; and 70 to 110 per 1000 (48 Fed. Reg. 45975 (10-7-83)—ethylene dibromide).

With the exception of formaldehyde, all of these risk estimates are well above Justice Stevens's 1 in 1000. If one were to include the toxicological evidence of benign tumor formation in the quantitative risk analysis for formaldehyde, excluded by OSHA (see 50 Fed. Reg. 50463), even that chemical exceeds the 1 in 1000 threshold.

The risk estimates calculated by means of mathematical modeling techniques vary

on the basis of a low probability of harm to a large group of workers, or on the basis of a higher probability of harm to very small groups of workers.

[3] Standards for Toxic Materials and Harmful Physical Agents

Once the threshold determination required by Section 3(8) and the Supreme Court's *benzene* decision have been made, if the hazard involves a "toxic chemical or harmful physical agent," the standard is governed by Section 6(b)(5).[68] That provision requires OSHA to set standards for such substances at levels that ensure, "to the extent feasible, on the basis of the best available evidence, that no employee will suffer material impairment of health or functional capacity even if such employee has regular exposure to the hazard dealt with by such standard for the period of his working life."

Section 6(b)(5)'s basic criterion, thus, is that the hazard be reduced to the limit of feasibility, so far as can be determined on the basis of evidence available at the time. A standard is feasible if it is "capable of being done."[69] OSHA may determine feasibility on the basis of the evidence before it, and if the evidence is not conclusive, the agency has a great deal of latitude to exercise its "expertise" in the face of data gaps.[70]

The requirement of Section 6(b)(5) that the standard be one that "most adequately protects" the employees has been construed to mean the standard that "best" protects them.[71] The requirement that the standard ensure that no employee will suffer "material impairment" is

---

significantly with the assumptions used in the model and its methodology. There are conservative and less conservative models. EPA, for example, calculated risk assessments for formaldehyde using four different models, and the results varied by as much as two orders of magnitude for some occupational exposures. OSHA, in its formaldehyde rulemaking, seems to have relied principally on three- and five-stage multistage models (*see* 50 Fed. Reg. 50460), which lie at about the midpoint between conservativeness and less conservativeness.

[68] The government argued unsuccessfully in the *benzene* case that Section 6(b)(5) was the sole regulatory provision for such hazards, and that no threshold determination need be made. That theory, which would have allowed OSHA automatically to set a very stringent standard solely on the basis of the nature of the substance involved, was expressly rejected by the Supreme Court.

[69] American Textile Manufacturers Institute v. Donovan, 452 U.S. 490 (1981).

[70] *Id.*

[71] United Steelworkers of America, AFL-CIO v. Marshall, 647 F.2d 1189 (D.C. Cir. 1980).

not entirely clear, since the term "material" is capable of a number of different interpretations. It might be construed as simply requiring reduction of the risk to just below the level of "significance," which is the trigger for regulatory action under Section 3(8). It might mean something more than *de minimus* or trivial. Or it may mean physically overt or manifest effects.

The D.C. Circuit in *United Steelworkers v. Marshall* construed the "material" impairment requirement to legitimize a PEL for lead that was designed to protect workers from subclinical effects.[72]

The feasibility requirement, finally, requires an analysis of two separate issues: whether the standard is technologically feasible, and whether it is economically feasible.[73] One thing the statute clearly does *not* permit is a cost-benefit analysis as a prerequisite to issuing a standard.[74]

[a] Technological Feasibility

The OSH Act is "technology forcing."[75] The generally accepted view of the legislative history is that OSHA can impose a standard that only the most technologically advanced plants in an industry have been able to achieve, even if only in some operations some of the time.[76] In addition, OSHA can force industry to develop and implement new technology,[77] but the industry must be given a "reasonable time to develop new technology."[78] OSHA must present "substantial evidence that companies acting vigorously and in good faith can develop the technology."[79]

OSHA's burden of proof on the technology issue is substantially tempered by the deferential nature of judicial review of its technical and scientific judgments. The agency is not required to demonstrate certainty that the standard will be achieved within the timetable provided

---

[72] 647 F.2d 1189 (D.C. Cir. 1980); *see also* AFL-CIO v. Marshall, 617 F.2d 636 (D.C. Cir. 1979), *aff'd sub nom.* American Textile Institute v. Donovan, 452 U.S. 490 (1981) (approving a PEL designed to prevent acute but reversible symptoms of byssinosis).

[73] American Iron and Steel Institute v. OSHA, 577 F.2d 825, 832 (3d Cir. 1978); United Steelworkers of America, AFL-CIO-CLC v. Marshall, 647 F.2d 1189 (D.C. Cir. 1980).

[74] American Textile Manufacturers Institute v. Donovan, 452 U.S. 490 (1981).

[75] AFL-CIO v. Brennan, 530 F.2d 109 (3d Cir. 1975).

[76] American Iron & Steel Institute v. OSHA, 577 F.2d 825 (3d Cir. 1978).

[77] Society of Plastics Industries, Inc. v. OSHA, 509 F.2d 1301 (2d Cir. 1975), *cert. denied sub nom.* Firestone Plastics Co. v. U.S. Dept. of Labor, 421 U.S. 992 (1975).

[78] United Steelworkers v. Marshall, *supra* note 71.

[79] *Id.*

for compliance.[80] Its evidentiary obligation has been described as a requirement that it show "that modern technology has at least conceived some industrial strategies or devices which are likely to be capable of meeting the PEL and which the industries are generally capable of adopting."[81]

Of course, it is always possible that OSHA will guess wrong, and that industry will not develop adequate technology to meet a forward-looking PEL. In such a case, unless OSHA is willing to modify either the PEL or the time period for achieving it, industries will have to attempt to raise the feasibility issue in defense of enforcement actions[82] or in variance requests, to the extent OSHA variances provide any significant relief.[83]

[b] Economic Feasibility

The criterion of economic feasibility under Section 6(b)(5) is often misunderstood. An OSHA standard is not infeasible simply because it is financially burdensome, or even if it threatens survival of some of the companies within an industry.[84] The benchmark of an infeasible standard is if it causes "massive dislocation" to the industry as a whole,[85] or imperils the industry's existence.[86]

More specifically, a standard is economically nonfeasible if it threatens the competitive stability of an industry, or if intraindustry or interindustry discrimination in the standard might wreck existing

---

[80] Society of Plastics Industries, *supra* note 77, 509 F.2d at 1309.

[81] United Steelworkers v. Marshall, *supra* note 71 (relying on the statutory requirement that the standard be based on the "best available evidence": "OSHA cannot let workers suffer while it awaits the Godot of scientific certainty. It can and must make reasonable predictions on the basis of 'credible sources of information,' whether data from existing plants or expert testimony.").

[82] *See* Atlantic & Gulf Stevedores v. OSHRC, 534 F.2d 541, 555 (3d Cir. 1976) (general infeasibility); and Marshall v. West Point Pepperell, Inc., 588 F.2d 979 (5th Cir. 1979) (specific infeasibility).

[83] *See* Section 6(d); and *see* American Iron & Steel Institute v. OSHA, *supra* note 76, 577 F.2d at 835; Society of Plastics Industries, Inc. v. OSHA, *supra* note 77, 509 F. 2d at 1310; *but see* United Steelworkers of America v. Marshall, 647 F. 2d 1189 (D.C. Cir. 1980) (opining that the variance window is very narrow).

[84] Industrial Union Dept., AFL-CIO v. Hodgson, 499 F.2d 467, 478 (D.C. Cir. 1974).

[85] AFL-CIO v. Brennan, 530 F.2d 109, 123 (3d Cir. 1975); United Steelworkers v. Marshall, *supra* note 71.

[86] American Iron & Steel Institute v. OSHA, 577 F.2d 825, 836 (3d Cir. 1978).

stability or lead to undue concentration.[87]

Proof of economic feasibility requires OSHA to provide a "reasonable assessment of the likely range of costs of its standards and the likely effects of those costs on the industry."[88] The courts have given the agency wide latitude in making economic prognostications. It may rely on the industry's estimates, formulate its own opinion after considering and rejecting the industry's estimates, employ its own consultants, or make its own in-house analysis. The only real burden placed upon the agency is that of explication. It must explain why it rejected independent economic analyses, and how it arrived at its own prognostications, from whatever data they might have been derived.[89]

[4] Emergency Temporary Standards

[a] In General

The Occupational Safety and Health Act authorized the Secretary of Labor to issue both permanent standards and emergency temporary standards (ETSs). Permanent standards may be promulgated only by following the subsection 6(b) rulemaking procedures, which are similar to those prescribed by the Administrative Procedure Act.[90] ETSs, however, may be issued[91] without regard to those notice and hearing requirements.

Under subsection 6(c) of the act the Secretary is required to issue an ETS if he determines (1) that employees are exposed to grave danger from exposure to substances as agents determined to be toxic or physically harmful or from new hazards and (2) that such emergency stan-

---

[87] Industrial Union Dept. v. Hodgson, *supra*, 499 F.2d at 478-481.

[88] United Steelworkers of America, AFL-CIO-CLC v. Marshall, 647 F.2d 1189 (D.C. Cir. 1980).

[89] American Textile Manufacturers Institute v. Donovan, 452 U.S. 490 (1981); United Steelworkers of America v. Marshall, 647 F.2d 1189 (D.C. Cir. 1980). Even this burden is not terribly heavy. In the *American Textile* case, OSHA rejected its own consultant's estimate as a gross overestimate of the cost of the standard. It also examined an industry-sponsored study that had addressed a less stringent proposed standard, and concluded that the industry study overestimated the cost of compliance with the standard it addressed, but seized upon the industry study as a reasonable estimate of the cost of the very different standard the agency ultimately adopted. The Supreme Court upheld the standard.

[90] 5 USC §§551 *et seq.*

[91] It has been held that ETSs may be amended in the same manner and under the same criteria that govern their initial issuance. Florida Peach Growers Association, Inc. v. United States Department of Labor, 489 F.2d 120 (5th Cir. 1974).

dard is necessary to protect employees from such danger.[92] The ETS takes effect immediately upon publication in the Federal Register. However, an ETS remains effective for no more than six months, and the Secretary must conduct and complete subsection 6(b) permanent rulemaking procedures within that period. As the legislative history of the OSH Act indicates, emergency standards are to be used in only "limited situations," and the "extraordinary" power to adopt such standards should be delicately exercised and used only as "an unusual response to exceptional circumstances."[93]

[b] The Grave Danger Standard

As the Supreme Court noted in the context of a permanent standard, the determination of whether a sufficient risk of harm exists to justify regulation is a policy consideration that belongs initially to OSHA.[94] Any inquiry into the gravity of danger would require an evaluation of the nature of the consequences of exposure as well as the number of workers likely to suffer the consequences.[95] In determining the necessity for emergency measures to meet a grave danger, it would be appropriate to consider the danger of incurable, permanent, or fatal consequences to workers, as opposed to easily curable and fleeting effects on their health; however, the Secretary certainly need not wait until workers have actually been harmed to issue an ETS.[96] Finally, although OSHA has urged that the harm likely to accrue should be assessed over at least a year, it has been held that the grave danger that

---

[92] Note that before the Secretary may promulgate a permanent standard, he need only determine (1) that there is a significant risk, and (2) that additional regulation is "reasonably necessary or appropriate." Public Citizen Health Research Group v. Auchter, 554 F. Supp. 242, 246n.4 (D.D.C. 1983).

[93] Public Citizen Health Research Group v. Auchter, 702 F.2d 1150 at 1155 (D.C. Cir. 1983). See also Taylor Driving & Salvage v. Department of Labor, 537 F.2d 819, 820-21 (5th Cir. 1976); Florida Peach Growers Association, Inc. v. United States Department of Labor, 489 F.2d 120, 129 (5th Cir. 1974); Dry Color Manufacturers' Association Inc. v. Department of Labor, 486 F.2d 98, 104n.9a (3d Cir. 1973).

[94] Asbestos Information Association/North America v. OSHA, 727 F.2d 415, 425 (5th Cir. 1984). See also Industrial Union Department v. American Petroleum Institute, 448 U.S. 607, 655n.62, 100 S. Ct. 2844, 2871n.62.

[95] Asbestos Information Association/North American v. Occupational Safety and Health Administration, 727 F.2d 415, 424 (5th Cir. 1984).

[96] Florida Peach Growers Association, Inc. v. United States Department of Labor, 489 F.2d 120, 132 (5th Cir. 1974).

the ETS may alleviate should be assessed only during the six-month period that is the life of the standard.[97]

[c] Necessity

Subsection 6(c) of the OSH Act requires, in addition to a grave danger, that an emergency standard be a "necessary" means to protect employees. An inquiry into the necessity of an ETS would include an evaluation of alternative kinds of regulation and also of the proscribed proceedures.[98]

[d] Judicial Review

Petitions for review of an ETS and motions to stay the effective date of an ETS pending judicial review are authorized under subsection 6(f), which provides:

> Any person who may be adversely affected by a standard issued under this section may at any time prior to the sixtieth day after such standard is promulgated file a petition challenging the validity of such standard with the United States court of appeals for the circuit wherein such person resides or has his principal place of business, for a judicial review of such standard. . . . The Filing of such petition shall not, unless otherwise ordered by the court, operate as a stay of the standard. The determinations of the Secretary shall be conclusive if supported by substantial evidence in the record considered as a whole.

The substantial evidence standard of review mandated by subsection 6(f) is anomalous in the context of informal rulemaking and would not apply if review were governed solely by the Administrative Procedure Act.[99] It has been held that in review of informal decisionmaking, and of an ETS in particular, the substantial evidence test basically requires the determination of whether the Secretary carried out his essentially legislative task in a reasonable manner based on the record before him.[100]

The agency's essentially legislative task in deciding whether to issue

---

[97] Asbestos Information Association/North America, 727 F.2d 415, 422 (5th Cir. 1984).

[98] Dry Color Manufacturers' Association, Inc. v. Department of Labor, 486 F.2d 98, 107 (3d Cir. 1973).

[99] See 5 USC §706. See also Associated Industries of New York State, Inc. v. United States Department of Labor, 487 F.2d 342 (2d Cir. 1973) (noting that Congress applied the substantial evidence test as a result of a legislative trade-off).

[100] Florida Peach Growers Association, Inc. v. United States Department of Labor, 489 F.2d 120, 129 (5th Cir. 1974).

a standard, temporary or otherwise, necessarily requires it to make two types of determinations, only one of which is reviewable under the usual substantial evidence test. The agency makes the reviewable decisions primarily by evaluating data and drawing conclusions from those data. A court can review the data in the record and determine whether they substantially support the Secretary's findings. Other determinations, however, involve factual determinations on the frontiers of scientific knowledge, resembling policy determinations more than they do factual ones. Judicial review of those inherently legislative decisions requires deference to the agency that is furthering goals that Congress thought salutory.[101]

In review of whether the agency's action is supported by substantial evidence in the record considered as a whole, it has been held that evidence in support of the determination that an ETS is necessary to alleviate a grave risk during its six-month period must include the effect of enforcing a permanent standard already in effect.[102] In the determination of whether the record supports the conclusion that a grave danger exists, it has been found that evidence based on risk assessment analysis,[103] evidence of toxicity,[104] and evidence of metabolite carcinogenicity in humans based on extrapolation from data gathered in rodent experiments[105] alone do not support a finding of grave danger of exposure to substances determined to be toxic or physically harmful. While evidence of nausea, excessive salivation and perspiration, blurred vision, abdominal cramps, vomiting, diarrhea, headache, fatigue, and vertigo do not support a determination of a grave danger,[106] evidence

---

[101] Asbestos Information Association/North America, 727 F.2d 415, 421-22 (5th Cir. 1984). *See also* Industrial Union Department, AFL-CIO v. Hodgson, 499 F.2d 467 (D.C. Cir. 1974).

[102] Asbestos Information Association/North America v. OSHA, 727 F.2d 415 (5th Cir. 1984).

[103] *Id.*

[104] Florida Peach Growers Association, Inc. v. United States Department of Labor, 489 F.2d 120 (5th Cir. 1974).

[105] Dry Color Manufacturers' Association, Inc. v. Deparatment of Labor, 486 F.2d 98 (3d Cir. 1973) (the court of appeals noted, however, that such extrapolation would carry most weight in cases where it was the chemical substance itself that produced cancer, rather than where the carcinogenic effect of the substance, as in the case before the court, was attributable to a metabolite of that substance).

[106] Florida Peach Growers Association, Inc. v. United States Department of Labor, 489 F.2d 120 (5th Cir. 1974).

of cancer and asbestosis do.[107] Moreover, a report recommending that "any substance which is known conclusively to cause tumors in animals should be considered carcinogenic and therefore a potential cancer hazard for man" constitutes substantial evidence in support of the position that a chemical that causes cancer in rodents presents a grave danger to humans.[108]

In review of agency action, a court will determine not only whether substantial evidence in the record supports OSHA's findings but also whether the agency's statement of reasons mandated by subsection 6(c) for the issuance of the ETS in question is adequate.[109] Subsection 6(c) provides:

> Whenever the Secretary promulgates any standard, . . . he shall include a statement of the reasons for such action, which shall be published in the Federal Register.

To satisfy that subsection, the statement of reasons should indicate (1) "which data in the record is being principally relied on and why that data suffices to show that the substances covered by the standard are harmful and pose a grave danger of exposure to employees"; and (2) "why the procedures prescribed were chosen in light of the recommendations of scientific experts and other governmental bodies, the types of industrial practices with these chemicals, and the alternative kinds of regulations considered by OSHA."[110] Thus, where OSHA offered a statement of reasons consisting of the finding that the listed chemicals were carcinogens and the conclusion that the conditions necessary for the issuance of an ETS were met, it was held that the statement of reasons was insufficient.[111] The court in *Dry Color Manufacturers Association v. Department of Labor* noted that the requirement would have been satisfied by a brief statement that the cited scientific data

---

[107] Asbestos Information Association/North America v. OSHA, 727 F.2d 415 (5th Cir. 1984).

[108] Dry Color Manufacturers' Association, Inc. v. Department of Labor, 486 F.2d 98 (3d Cir. 1973).

[109] Even where there is no statutory requirement for a statement of reasons, the basis for a decision should appear on the record. Dry Color Manufacturers' Association, Inc. v. Department of Labor, 486 F.2d 98 (3d Cir. 1973). *See also* Environmental Defense Fund v. Hardin, 428 F.2d 1093 (D.C. Cir. 1970).

[110] Dry Color Manufacturers' Association, Inc. v. Department of Labor, 486 F.2d 98, 106-07 (3d Cir. 1973).

[111] *Id.* at 106.

indicated that the chemicals listed produced cancer in rodents and supported the conclusion that they were therefore carcinogenic in humans.[112] Where OSHA argued that the issuance of an ETS was justified on the grounds that OSHA feared successful challenge of its permanent standard and an ETS would educate employees, the court found those reasons could hardly justify resort to the extraordinary ETS power.[113]

Additionally, even if an ETS is adequately explained, a court must examine its anticipated benefit in light of its probable economic consequences to the industry regulated. Although a formal cost-benefit analysis is not required of the agency, the costs of an ETS should be reasonable and not outweigh the protection afforded to workers.[114]

Finally, in *Public Citizen Health Research Group v. Auchter,*[115] the court was invited to review OSHA's denial of a petition to issue an ETS. The district court held that OSHA had abused its discretion in denying the petition, and ordered OSHA to promulgate an ETS. The District of Columbia Circuit held that the district court had impermissibly substituted its evaluation for that of OSHA, and overturned the judgment below. The court of appeals found that although there was not adequate evidence in the record to support the determination that a grave danger existed, necessitating an ETS, there was substantial evidence indicating that some workers and their progeny were exposed to a potentially grave danger. The court held that, in light of this evidence, OSHA's delay in instituting permanent rulemaking procedures and its refusal to assign any priority status to that rulemaking constituted agency action "unreasonably delayed" within the meaning of Section 706(1) of the Administrative Procedure Act and acted to compel action pursuant to that action, ordering OSHA to issue a notice of proposed rulemaking within thirty days of the date of the decision.

---

[112] *Id.* at 106-07.

[113] Asbestos Information Association/North America v. OSHA, 727 F.2d 415 (5th Cir. 1984).

[114] Asbestos Information Association/North America v. OSHA, 727 F.2d 415 (5th Cir. 1984). *See also* American Petroleum Institute v. OSHA, 581 F.2d 493 (5th Cir. 1978), *aff'd sub nom.* Industrial Union Department v. American Petroleum Institute, 448 U.S. 607, 100 S. Ct. 2844; Florida Peach Growers Association, Inc. v. United States Department of Labor, 489 F.2d 120 (5th Cir. 1974).

[115] 554 F. Supp. 242 (D.D.C. 1983), *rev'd in part,* 226 U.S. App. D.C. 242, 702 F.2d 1150 (1983).

[5] Disclosure of Hazards to Employees—Requirements

Section 6(b)(7) authorizes OSHA to require notice to employees of the existence and nature of hazardous conditions regulated under the OSH Act to which the employees are exposed. Until 1984, however, OSHA had required notices to be posted only with respect to twenty or so substances for which it had promulgated standards under Section 6(b)(5), having not included a notice and posting requirement for any of the substances for which national consensus standards were adopted (so-called subpart Z standards).[116]

Political pressures on state labor departments to provide requirements that employers apprize their employees of the hazards to which the latter are exposed resulted in the development of such requirements in a number of states under state "little OSHA" programs or other state environmental and public health laws, beginning in the late 1970s.[117]

OSHA promulgated a chemical hazard communication requirement under Section 6(b) and its general rulemaking authority under Section 8(g), applicable to chemicals found in the workplace.[118] OSHA maintained in the rulemaking explanation that the hazard communication regulation would preempt state worker right to know laws, by virtue of Section 18's preemption provisions.[119]

---

116 29 CFR §1910.1000, subpart Z. *See also* West Virginia Manufacturers Ass'n v. West Virginia, 542 F.Supp. 1247 (S.D.W.Va. 1982).

117 *See, e.g.*, W.Va. Code, Section 21-3-18. This statute was upheld against a preemption challenge in West Virginia Manufacturers Ass'n v. West Virginia, 542 F.Supp. 1247 (S.D.W.Va. 1982), but struck down as unconstitutional delegation of power insofar as it provided that the list of substances for which disclosure was required would change automatically with additions and deletions to the subpart Z list by OSHA. On the preemption issue, the court opined that the states could not adopt their own disclosure requirements for substances as to which OSHA had promulgated such requirements.

118 29 CFR §1910.1200, 48 Fed. Reg. 53280. The hazard communication regulation was remanded in minor respects by the Third Circuit, in United Steelworkers of America v. Auchter, 763 F.2d 728 (3d Cir. 1985). The remand had to do with the Agency's definition of trade secrets, access of employees and their representatives to trade secrets, the scope of industries covered by trade secret protection, and access by nurses to trade secret information. OSHA proposed amendments in 1985, which are expected to be promulgated early in 1986. *See* 50 Fed. Reg. 48750 and 48794 (11-27-85) and 50 Fed. Reg. 49410 (12-2-85) (proposed rules).

119 *See* 29 CFR §1910.1200(a)(2), and 48 Fed. Reg. 53280 (11-25-83). The preemptive effect of this regulation was upheld in United Steelworkers of America v. Auchter, 763 F.2d 728 (3d Cir. 1985).

[6] Regulatory Overlap

OSHA, particularly under Section 6(b)(5), has regulatory responsibility over a broad range of chemical substances that are also subject to government regulation by other federal agencies and, in some instances, states, operating under either environmental or public health regulatory statutes. This regulatory overlap has sometimes effectively ousted OSHA from jurisdiction, or has affected the considerations that bear on the feasibility of an OSHA standard.

Some regulatory overlap is accounted for in the OSH Act. Section 4(b)(1) states that the act will not apply "to working conditions of employees with respect to which other federal agencies . . . exercise statutory authority to prescribe or enforce standards or regulations affecting occupational safety and health."[120] The two judicial decisions construing the provision have left unresolved the question of how much of a barrier it is to concurrent jurisdiction.[121] The better view disables OSHA from acting only where the other agency has directly addressed the issue OSHA wishes to address, and in more than a passing or minimal way.[122]

Agencies not having explicit authority over occupational exposure may nevertheless address the same risks the OSH Act encompasses, under regulatory authority and utilizing procedures that are very different from those employed by the OSH Act. For example, ethylene dibromide (EDB) is a chemical for which OSHA had a long-standing national consensus standard covering a number of occupational settings, including pesticide handlers, food handlers, and petroleum industry and chemical industry workers. At the same time OSHA was refusing to adopt an ETS for the chemical, EPA, acting on the same toxicological data base, suspended a number of pesticidal uses for the product, primarily on the basis of occupational exposure, and also took action with respect to consumer exposure, the former the authority of the Federal Insecticide, Fungicide and Rodenticide Act and the latter

---

[120] This provision was apparently included primarily to preserve the jurisdiction of the U.S. Department of Agriculture, whose jurisdiction under the pre-1971 Federal Insecticide, Fungicide and Rodenticide Act extended to all types of pesticide exposure, including occupational exposure, the Atomic Energy Commission, and the Mine Safety and Health Administration, a subdivision of the U.S. Department of the Interior.

[121] *Compare* Organized Migrants in Community Action v. Brennan, 520 F.2d 1161 (D.C. Cir. 1975), *with* Public Citizen Health Research Group v. Auchter, 702 F.2d 1150,1156fn.23 (D.C. Cir. 1983).

[122] Public Citizen Health Research Group v. Auchter, *supra* note 121.

under the pesticide tolerance provisions of the Federal Food, Drug and Cosmetic Act. In addition, a number of states, acting under public health authority, placed even more rigorous restrictions on the chemical.

Other examples are formaldehyde and lead. OSHA has a PEL for formaldehyde, and in 1983 it rejected a citizen petition that sought an ETS that would have severely reduced the PEL. A year later, the Environmental Protection Agency (EPA), acting under Section 4(f) of the Toxic Substances Control Act, proposed to take immediate action eliminating formaldehyde from certain manufacturing processes, based on extrapolated cancer rates for workers in those industries. In the case of lead, EPA's regulatory activity under the Clean Air Act could have had an effect on OSHA's economic feasibility analysis for its own lead standard. If EPA's standard had been adopted a few years before OSHA's, OSHA would have had to factor the industry's regulatory cost of compliance with EPA's standard into its feasibility analysis, even though OSHA's and EPA's standards dealt with very different exposed populations.[123]

Some of the other overlapping statutes contain much broader regulatory authority than the OSH Act; others are more limited. The overall stringency of regulation of worker exposure to chemicals is accordingly somewhat dependent upon the choice and timing of the regulatory authority employed.

§9.05   State Programs

[1]   In General

Section 18(a) of the OSH Act provides that a state may regulate in the area of occupational safety and health on any issue "with respect to which no standard is in effect" under Section 6. State activity over activities "with respect to which a Federal standard has been promulgated" is subject to a prerequisite of OSHA delegation of authority upon approval of the state's "plan," pursuant to Sections 18(b) and (c).[124] Under this scheme federal jurisdiction is ceded only after a period of

---

[123] See dictum in United Steelworkers of America, AFL-CIO-CLC v. Marshall, 647 F.2d 1189 (D.C. Cir. 1980) (Part VI.C).

[124] OSHA breaks the delegation process into two stages: initial approval and final approval. See 29 USC §667.

concurrent jurisdiction, during which the state's program is monitored by OSHA.[125]

A state's plan is approvable if, in OSHA's judgment, the plan satisfies the criteria set forth in Section 18(c). That provision sets forth eight criteria that must be satisfied by the state plan, which is embodied in state statutes and regulations. The state plan must include (1) a single agency that administers the program, (2) provision for the "development and enforcement" of standards for the issues covered[126] that "are or will be at least as effective in providing safe and healthful employment and places of employment . . ." as the federal standards but are applied to products in interstate commerce only to meet "compelling local needs" and do not unduly burden interstate commerce, (3) "at least as effective" rights of inspection and entry, including a prohibition against advance notice of inspections to employers, (4) "satisfactory assurances" that there are adequate enforcement authority, funding, and personnel,[127] (5) regulatory coverage of public employees, and (6) provision for reporting by employers and to the state and the state to OSHA.[128]

State "little OSHA" programs are often enabled by broad enabling statutes that simply authorize the state agency to adopt the federal standards.[129]

[2] Preemption

There are three forms of OSH Act preemption. Section 18(a) prohibits federally unauthorized state regulation of hazard situations as to which a federal standard applies. That provision has been construed narrowly to legitimize state regulations that affect a component of a federally regulated hazard or provide a form of regulation of the hazard

---

[125] 29 CFR §§667(e) and (f).

[126] Section 18 accommodates less than full program assumption. A state may elect to regulate some hazards and not others. This contrasts to the "all or nothing" delegation approach taken under Section 402 of the Clean Water Act and other EPA-administered programs.

[127] Curiously, the only litigated issue on enforcement delegation involved the question of whether this provision required states to provide *better* enforcement capability than the minimal resource levels OSHA had employed. *See* American Federation of Labor v. Marshall, 570 F.2d 1030 (D.C. Cir. 1978). The court concluded that initial approval could be based on federal equivalence but final approval required an independent judgment as to the adequacy of the legal authority and staffing.

[128] Section 18(c)(1)-(8)

[129] *See, e.g.,* Conn. Gen. Stat., Sections 31-367 *et seq.*

not addressed in the OSHA standard.[130]

Section 18(c)(2) contains what is called the "product standard" clause. As one of the enumerated criteria for approval of state programs, this provision requires, among other things, that state OSH standards, "when applicable to products which are distributed or used in interstate commerce, are required by compelling local conditions and do not unduly burden interstate commerce."[131] Just what local conditions are compelling and what burden on commerce is "undue" must first be determined by OSHA, and direct challenges to state standards by private parties will normally not survive a motion to dismiss.[132]

---

[130] West Virginia Manufacturers Ass'n v. West Virginia, 542 F. Supp. 1247 (S.D.W.Va. 1982).

[131] There is some curious legislative history that suggests a narrower construction of this provision than appears from the face of the statute. *See* Subcommittee of Labor of Senate Committee on Labor and Public Welfare, Legislative History of the Occupational Safety and Health Act of 1970 at 500-01, 1401-02.

[132] *See* Florida Citrus Packers v. California, 549 F.Supp. 213 (N.D. Cal. 1982) (attempt by Florida citrus industry to seek injunction against California standard applicable to exposure to ethylene dibromide rejected in the absence of OSHA determination that the standard was either consistent or inconsistent with Section 18(c)(2)).

Appendixes

Chapter 6

Chapter 7

Chapter 8

APPENDIXES

Chapter 9

Appendix 2A   Table of Session Law to U.S. Code Cross-References: Toxic Substances Control Act (TSCA)

TSCA Session Law Number*	Title 15 U.S. Code Number
§2	§2601
§3	§2602
§4	§2603
§5	§2604
§6	§2605
§7	§2606
§8	§2607
§9	§2608
§10	§2609
§11	§2610
§12	§2611
§13	§2612
§14	§2613
§15	§2614
§16	§2615
§17	§2616
§18	§2617
§19	§2618
§20	§2619
§21	§2620
§22	§2621
§23	§2622
§24	§2623
§25	§2624
§26	§2625
§27	§2626
§28	§2627
§29	§2628
§30	§2629

* Toxic Substances Control Act (15 USC §§2601 *et seq.*), Pub. L. 94-469, October 11, 1976, as amended by Pub.L. 97-129, December 29, 1981, and Pub.L. 98-620, November 8, 1984. 90 Stat. 2004.

Appendix 2B   Glossary of TSCA-Related Terms and Acronyms

Acronyms

CAS   Chemical Abstracts Service. CAS maintains a standardized chemical nomenclature format and assigns numerical designations to chemicals for computer coding. TSCA information requests usually specify the CAS Registry Number for a chemical.

IUPAC   International Union of Pure and Applied Chemistry. IUPAC maintains a chemical nomenclature format.

OTS   EPA's Office of Toxic Substances.

OPTS   EPA's Office of Pesticides and Toxic Substances—a sometimes-used reference to the OTS, which falls under the same Assistant Administrator as does the Office of Pesticide Programs (OPP), which administers the Federal Insecticide, Fungicide and Rodenticide Act.

ITC   Interagency Testing Committee.

APA   Administrative Procedures Act, 5 USC §§501 *et seq.*

Definitions from Regulations

Article   A manufactured item that—

(1)   is formed to a specific shape or design during manufacture,

(2)   has end use function(s) dependent in whole or in part upon its shape or design during end use, and

(3)   has either no change of chemical composition during its end use or only those changes of composition that have no commercial purpose separate from that of the article and result from a chemical reaction that occurs upon end use of other chemical substances, mixtures, or articles

except that fluids and particles are not considered articles regardless of shape or design. 40 CFR §704.3(b).

By-product   A chemical substance produced without a separate commercial intent during the manufacture, processing, use, or disposal of another chemical substance(s) or mixture(s). 40 CFR §704.3(c).

Importer   1. Any person who imports any chemical substance or any chemical substance as part of a mixture or article into the customs territory of the United States, including—

(i)   the person primarily liable for the payment of any duties on the merchandise; or

(ii)   an authorized agent acting on his behalf (as defined in 19 CFR §1.11).

2. "Importer" also includes, as appropriate—

(i)   the consignee;

(ii)   the importer of record;

(iii)   the actual owner if an actual owner's declaration and superseding bond has been filed in accordance with 19 CFR 141.20; and

(iv) the transferee if the right to draw merchandise in a bonded warehouse has been transferred in accordance with subpart C of 19 CFR Part 144.

For the purpose of this definition, the customs territory of the United States consists of the fifty states, Puerto Rico, and the District of Columbia. 40 CFR §704.3(f).

Impurity A chemical substance that is unintentionally present with another chemical substance. 40 CFR §704.3(h).

Manufacture To manufacture for commercial purposes. 40 CFR §704.3(i).

Manufacture for commercial purposes **1.** To import, produce, or manufacture with the purpose of obtaining an immediate or eventual commercial advantage for the manufacturer. The term includes, among other things, such "manufacture" of any amount of a chemical substance or mixture—

(i) for commercial distribution, including test marketing; or

(ii) for use by the manufacturer, including use in product research and development or as an intermediate.

2. "Manufacture for commercial purposes" also applies to substances that are produced coincidentally during the manufacture, processing, use, or disposal of another substance or mixture, including both by-products that are separated from that other substance or mixture and impurities that remain in that substance or mixture. Such by-products and impurities may or may not in themselves have commercial value. They are nonetheless produced for the purpose of obtaining a commercial advantage since they are part of the manufacture of a chemical product for a commercial purpose. 40 CFR §704.4(j).

Propose to manufacture or import To make a firm management decision to commit financial resources for the manufacture or import of the specified chemicals. 40 CFR §104.3(p).

Exporter The person who, as the principal party in interest in the export transaction, has the power and responsibility for determining and controlling the sending of the chemical substance or mixture to a destination outside the customs territory of the United States. 40 CFR §707.63(b).

Chemical substance Any organic or inorganic substance of a particular molecular identity, including any combination of such substances occurring in whole or in part as a result of a chemical reaction or occurring in nature, and any chemical element or uncombined radical, except that "chemical substance" does *not* include—

(1) any mixture;

(2) any pesticide that is manufactured, processed, or distributed in commerce for use as a pesticide;

(3) tobacco or any tobacco product (but the exclusion does not extend to derivative products);

(4) any source material, special nuclear material, or by-product material;

(5) any pistol, firearm, revolver, shells, or cartridges; or

(6) any food, food additive, drug, cosmetic, or device that is manufactured, processed, or distributed in commerce for use as a food, food additive, drug, cosmetic, or device.

40 CFR §710.2(h).

Commerce Trade, traffic, transportation, or other commerce that (1) occurs between a place in a state and any place outside of such state or (2) affects trade, traffic, transportation, or commerce between a place in a state and any place outside of such state. 40 CFR §710.2(i).

Distribute in commerce or **Distribution in commerce** With respect to a chemical substance or mixture or article containing such a substance or mixture, to sell or mean to sell, or the sale of, the substance, mixture, or article in commerce; to introduce or deliver for introduction into commerce, or the introduction or delivery for introduction into commerce of, the substance, mixture, or article; or to hold, or the holding of, the substance, mixture, or article after its introduction into commerce. 40 CFR §710.2(j).

Isolated intermediate Any chemical substance that—

(1) is intentionally removed from the equipment in which it is manufactured; and

(2) either is consumed in whole or in part in chemical reaction(s) used for the intentional manufacture of other chemical substance(s) or mixture(s) or is intentionally present for the purpose of altering the rate of such chemical reaction(s).

Note: The "equipment in which it was manufactured" includes the reaction vessel in which the chemical substance was manufactured and other equipment that is strictly ancillary to the reaction vessel, and any other equipment through which the chemical substance may flow during a continuous flow process, but does not include tanks or other vessels in which the chemical substance is stored after its manufacture. 40 CFR §710.2(n).

Mixture Any combination of two or more chemical substances if the combination does not occur in nature and is not, in whole or in part, the result of a chemical reaction, except that "mixture" does include (1) any combination that occurs, in whole or in part, as a result of a chemical reaction if the combination could have been manufactured for commercial purposes without a chemical reaction at the time the chemical substances comprising the combination were combined and if, after the effective date or premanufacture notification requirements, none of the chemical substances comprising the combination is a new chemical substance and (2) hydrates of a chemical substance or hydrated ions formed by association of a chemical substance with water. 40 CFR §710.2(q).

Process The preparation of a chemical substance or mixture, after its manufacture, for distribution in commerce (1) in the same form or physical state as, or in a different form or physical state from, that in which it was received by the person so preparing such substance or mixture or (2) as part of a mixture or article containing the chemical substance or mixture. 40 CFR §710.2(t).

Test marketing The distribution in commerce of no more than a predetermined amount of a chemical substance, mixture, or article containing that chemical substance or mixture, by a manufacturer or processor to no more than a defined number of potential customers to explore market capability in a competitive situation during a predetermined testing period prior to the broader distribution of that chemical substance, mixture, or article in commerce. 40 CFR §710.3(bb).

Import in bulk form To import a chemical substance (other than as part of a mixture or article) in any quantity, in cans, bottles, drums, barrels, packages, tanks, bags, or other containers used for purposes of transportation or containment, if the chemical substance has an end use or commercial purpose separate from the container. 40 CFR §712.3(c).

Co-product A chemical substance produced for a commercial purpose during the manufacture, processing, use, or disposal of another chemical substance(s) or mixture(s). 40 CFR §716.3(b).

Health and safety study or **Study** Any study of any effect of a chemical substance or mixture on health or the environment or on both, including underlying data and epidemiological studies; studies of occupational exposure to a chemical substance or mixture; toxicological, clinical, ecological, and other studies of a chemical substance or mixture; and any test performed under TSCA. 40 CFR §714.3(e). Examples are—

(i) Long- and short-term tests of mutagenicity, carcinogenicity, or teratogenicity; behavioral disorders effects; dermatoxicity; pharmacological effects; mammalian absorption, distribution, metabolism, and excretion; cumulative, additive, and synergistic effects; and acute, subchronic, and chronic effects. 40 CFR §716.3(2)(i).

(ii) Tests for ecological or other environmental effects on invertebrates, fish, or other animals and on plants, including acute toxicity tests, chronic toxicity tests, critical life stage tests, behavioral tests, algal growth tests, seed germination tests, plant growth or damage tests, microbial function tests, bioconcentration or bioaccumulation tests, and model ecosystem (microcosm) studies. 40 CFR §716.3(2)(ii).

(iii) Assessments of human and environmental exposure, including workplace exposure, and assessments of impacts of a particular chemical substance or mixture on the environment, including surveys, tests, and studies of the following: biological, photochemical, and chemical degradation; structure/activity relationships; air, water, and soil transport; biomagnification and bioconcentration; and chemical and physical properties, for example, boiling point, vapor pressure, evaporation rates from soil and water, octanol/water partition coefficient, and water solubility. 40 CFR §716.3(2)(iii).

Intermediate Any chemical substance that is consumed, in whole or in part, in chemical reactions used for the intentional manufacture of another chemical substance(s) or mixture(s) or that is intentionally present for the purpose of altering the rates of such chemical reaction. 40 CFR §720.3(n).

Inventory The list of chemical substances manufactured or processed in the United States that EPA compiled and keeps current under Section 8(b) of the Act. 40 CFR §720.3(o).

Nonisolated intermediate Any intermediate that is not intentionally removed from the equipment in which it is manufactured, including the reaction vessel in which it is manufactured, equipment ancillary to the reaction vessel, and any equipment through which the chemical substance passes during a continuous flow process, but not including tanks or other vessels in which the substance is stored after its manufacture. 40 CFR §720.3(w).

Capacitor A device for accumulating and holding a charge of electricity and consisting of conducting surfaces separated by a dielectric. 40 CFR §761.3(d).

Chemical waste landfill A landfill at which protection against risk of injury to health or the environment from migration of PCBs to land water or the atmosphere from PCBs and PCB items deposited in the landfill is provided by locating, engineering, and operating the landfill as specified in Section 761.75 of 40 CFR §761.3(f).

Marking The marking of PCB items and PCB storage areas and transport vehicles by means of applying a legible mark by painting, fixation of an adhesive label, or any other method that meets the requirements of these regulations. 40 CFR §761.3(p).

PCB Any chemical substance that is limited to the biphenyl molecule and has been chlorinated to varying degrees or any combination of substances that contains such substance. (*See* 40 CFR §761.1(b) for applicable concentrations of PCBs.) 40 CFR §761.3(s).

PCB article Any manufactured article, other than a PCB container, that contains PCBs and whose surface(s) has been in direct contact with PCBs. "PCB article" includes capacitors, transformers, electric motors, pumps, pipes, and any other manufactured item that (1) is formed to a specific shape or design during manufacture, (2) has end use function(s) dependent in whole or in part upon its shape or design during end use, and (3) has either no change of chemical composition during its end use or only those changes of composition that have no commercial purpose separate from that of the PCB article. 40 CFR §761.3(t).

PCB equipment Any manufactured item, other than a PCB container or a PCB article container, that contains a PCB article or other PCB equipment, including microwave ovens, electronic equipment, and fluorescent light ballasts and fixtures. 40 CFR §761.3(w).

Closed manufacturing process A manufacturing process in which PCBs are generated but less than 10 micrograms per cubic meter from any resolvable gas chromatographic peak are contained in any release to air, less than 100 micrograms per liter from any resolvable gas chromatographic peak are contained in any release to water, and less than 2 micrograms per gram from any resolvable gas chromatographic peak are contained in any product or any process waste. 40 CFR §761.3(jj).

Controlled waste manufacturing process A manufacturing process in which PCBs are generated but (1) less than 10 micrograms per cubic meter from any resolvable gas chromatographic peak are contained in any release to air, less than 100 micrograms per liter from any resolvable gas chromatographic peak are contained in any release to water, and less than 2 micrograms per gram from any resolvable gas chromatographic peak are contained in any product and (2) the remainder of PCBs generated are incinerated in a qualified incinerator, landfilled in a landfill approved under the provisions of Section 761.75, or stored for such incineration or landfilling in accordance with the requirements of Section 761.65(b)(1).

Asbestos The asbestiform varieties of chrysotile (serpentine), crocidolite (riebeckite), amosite (cummingtonite-grunerite), anthophyllite, tremolite, and actinolite. 40 CFR §763.63(a).

Appendix 2C Cumulative Removals from TSCA Section 4(e) Priority List, November 1983

Chemical/Group	EPA Responses to Committee Recommendations	
	Federal Register Citation	Publication Date
1. Acetonitrile	47 FR 58020-58023	Dec. 29, 1982
2. Acrylamide	48 FR 725-727	Jan. 6, 1983
3. Alkyl phthalates	46 FR 53775-53777	Oct. 30, 1981
4. Alkyltin compounds	46 FR 5456-5463	Feb. 5, 1982*
5. Antimony metal	48 FR 717-725	Jan. 6, 1983
6. Antimony sulfide	48 FR 717-725	Jan. 6, 1983
7. Antimony trioxide	48 FR 717-725	Jan. 6, 1983
8. Benzidine-based dyes	46 FR 55004-55006	Nov. 5, 1981
9. Benzyl butyl phthalate	46 FR 53775-53777	Oct. 30, 1981
10. Biphenyl	48 FR 23080-23086	May 23, 1983
11. Butyl glycolyl butyl phthalate	46 FR 54487	Nov. 2, 1981
12. Chlorendic acid	47 FR 44878-44879	Oct. 12, 1982
13. Chlorinated naphthalenes	46 FR 54491	Nov. 2, 1981
14. Chlorinated paraffins	47 FR 1017-1019	Jan. 8, 1982
15. Chlorobenzotrifluoride	47 FR 50555-50558	Nov. 8, 1982
16. Chloromethane	45 FR 48524-48564	July 18, 1980
17. 2-Chlorotoluene	47 FR 18172-18175	April 28, 1982
18. Cresols	48 FR 31812-31819	July 11, 1983
19. o-Dianisidine-based dyes	46 FR 55004-55006	Nov. 5, 1981
20. Dichloromethane	46 FR 30300-30320	June 5, 1981
21. Diethylenetriamine	47 FR 18386-18391	April 29, 1982
22. Ethyltoluene	48 FR 23088-23095	May 23, 1983
23. Fluoroalkenes	46 FR 53704-53708	Oct. 30, 1981
24. Formamide	48 FR 23098-23102	May 23, 1983
25. Hexachloro-1,3-butadiene	47 FR 58029-58031	Dec. 29, 1982
26. Hexachlorocyclopentadiene	47 FR 58023-58025	Dec. 29, 1982
27. Hexachloroethane	47 FR 18175-18176	April 28, 1982
28. Isophorone	48 FR 727-730	Jan. 6, 1983
29. Mesityl oxide	48 FR 30700-30706	July 5, 1983
30. 4,4'Methylenedianiline	48 FR 31806-31810	July 11, 1983
31. Methyl ethyl ketone	47 FR 58025-58029	Dec. 29, 1982
32. Methyl isobutyl ketone	47 FR 58025-58029	Dec. 29, 1982
33. Nitrobenzene	46 FR 30300-30320	June 5, 1981
34. Phenylenediamines	47 FR 973-983	Jan. 8, 1982
35. Polychlorinated terphenyls	46 FR 54482-54483	Nov. 2, 1981
36. Pyridine	47 FR 58031-58035	Dec. 29, 1982
37. o-Tolidine-based dyes	46 FR 55004-55006	Nov. 5, 1981
38. Toluene	47 FR 56391-56392	Dec. 16, 1982
39. 1,2,4-Trimethylbenzene	48 FR 23088-23095	May 23, 1983
40. Trimethylbenzenes	48 FR 23088-23095	May 23, 1983
41. 1,1,1-Trichloroethane	46 FR 30300-30320	June 5, 1981
42. Tris(2-chloroethyl)phosphite	47 FR 49466-49467	Nov. 1, 1982
43. Xylenes	47 FR 56392-56394	Dec. 16, 1982

* Removed by the Committee for reconsideration. Seven individual group members were subsequently designated in the 11th ITC Report for priority consideration.

Appendix 2D Index to EPA's Environmental Effects Testing Guidelines and Support Documents

Document	Guideline	Support Document
Daphnid Acute Toxicity Test	EG-1	ES-1
Daphnid Chronic Toxicity Test	EG-2	ES-1
Mysid Shrimp Acute Toxicity Test	EG-3	ES-2
Mysid Shrimp Chronic Toxicity Test	EG-4	ES-2
Oyster Acute Toxicity Test	EG-5	ES-3
Oyster Bioconcentration Test	EG-6	ES-3
Penaeid Shrimp Acute Toxicity Test	EG-7	ES-4
Algal Acute Toxicity Test	EG-8	ES-5
Fish Acute Toxicity Test	EG-9	ES-6
Fish Bioconcentration Test	EG-10	ES-7
Fish Early Life Stage Toxicity Test	EG-11	ES-8
Seed Germination/Root Elongation Toxicity Test	EG-12	ES-9
Early Seedling Growth Toxicity Test	EG-13	ES-10
Plant Uptake and Translocation Test	EG-14	ES-11
Avian Dietary Test	EG-15	ES-12
Bobwhite Reproduction Test	EG-16	ES-13
Mallard Reproduction Test	EG-17	ES-14
Daphnid Chronic Toxicity Test (OECD)	EG-18	
Algal Acute Toxicity Test (OECD)	EG-19	
Fish Acute Toxicity Test (OECD)	EG-20	
Fish Bioconcentration Test (OECD)	EG-12	

Appendix 2E Index to EPA's Chemical Fate Testing Guidelines and Support Documents

Guideline Title	Guideline No.	Support Document No.
Physical and Chemical Properties		
Absorption in Aqueous Solution, ultraviolet/visible spectra	CG-1050	
Boiling Temperature	CG-1100	
Density/Relative Density	CG-1150	
Dissociation Constants in Water	CG-1200	
Henry's Law Constant	CG-1250	
Melting Temperature	CG-1300	
Particle Size Distribution/Fiber Length and Diameter Distributions	CG-1350	
Partition Coefficient (n-Octanol/Water)	CG-1400	CS-1400
pH of Water Solution or Suspension	CG-1450	
Water Solubility	CG-1500	CS-1500
Vapor Pressure	CG-1600	CS-1600
Transport Processes		
Soil Thin-Layer Chromatography	CG-1700	CS-1700
Sediment and Soil Adsorption Isotherm	CG-1710	CS-1710
Transformation Processes		
Biodegradation, Aerobic Aquatic	CG-2000	CS-2000
Biodegradation, Ready	CG-2010	
Biodegradation, Anaerobic	CG-2050	CS-2050
Biodegradation in Soil	CG-2075	
Biodegradation, Sewage Treatment Simulations	CG-2100	
Complex Formation Ability in Water	CG-4000	
Hydrolysis as a Function of pH at 25°C.	CG-5000	CS-5000
Photolysis in Aqueous Solution in Sunlight	CG-6000	CS-6000

Appendix 2F   Index to EPA's Health Effects Testing Guidelines

Guidelines	*Index*
I. General Toxicity Testing	
Acute Exposure	
Dermal Toxicity	HG-Acute-Dermal
Inhalation Toxicity	HG-Acute-Inhal
Oral Toxicity	HG-Acute-Oral
Subchronic Exposure	
Dermal Toxicity	HG-Subchronic-Dermal
Inhalation Toxicity	HG-Subchronic-Inhal
Oral Toxicity	HG-Subchronic-Oral
Chronic Exposure	
Chronic Toxicity	HG-Chronic
Oncogenicity	HG-Chronic-Onco
Combined Chronic	
Toxicity/Oncogenicity	HG-Chronic-Combined
II. Specific Organ/Tissue Toxicity	
Dermal Sensitization	HG-Organ/Tissue-Dermal Sensit
Primary Dermal Irritation	HG-Organ/Tissue-Dermal Irrit
Primary Eye Irritation	HG-Organ/Tissue-Eye Irrit
Reproduction/Fertility Effects	HG-Organ/Tissue-Repro/Fert
Teratogenicity	HG-Organ/Tissue-Terato
III. Mutagenicity	
Gene Mutations	
Salmonella typhimurium	HG-Gene Muta-S. *typhimurium*
Escheria coli WP2 and WP2 *uvrA*	HG-Gene Muta-E. *coli*
Aspergillus nidulans	HG-Gene Muta-A. *nidulans*
Neurospora crassa	HG-Gene Muta-N. *crassa*
Sex Linked Recessive Lethal Test in	
Drosophila melanogaster	HG-Gene Muta-Insects
Somatic Cells in Culture	HG-Gene Muta-Somatic Cells
Mouse Specific-Locus Test	HG-Gene Muta-Mammal
Chromosomal Effects	
In Vitro Mammalian Cytogenetics	HG-Chromo-In vitro
In Vivo Mammalian Bone Marrow	
Cytogenetics Tests Chromosomal	
Analysis	HG-Chromo-Bone Marrow
In Vivo Micronucleus Assay	HG-Chromo-Micronuc
Heritable Translocation Test in	
Drosophila melanogaster	HG-Chromo-Insects
Dominant Lethal Assay	HG-Chromo-Dom Lethal

Rodent Heritable Translocation Assay   HG-Chromo-Herit Translocat

DNA Effects

Differential Growth Inhibition of
Repair Deficient Bacteria:
"Bacterial DNA Damage or
Repair Tests"   HG-DNA-Damage/Repair

Unscheduled DNA Synthesis in
Mammalian Cells in Culture   HG-DNA-Unsched Syn

Mitotic Gene Conversion in
Saccharomyces cerevisiae   HG-DNA-Gene Conversion

In Vitro Sister Chromatid
Exchange Assay   HG-DNA-Sister-Chrom-In vitro

In Vivo Sister Chromatid
Exchange Assay   HG-DNA-Sister-Chrom-In vivo

IV. Neurotoxicity

Neuropathology   HG-Neuro-Path
Support Document   HS-Neuro-Path
Peripheral Nerve Function   HG-Neuro-Peri Nerve
Support Document   HS-Neuro-Peri Nerve
Motor Activity   HG-Neuro-Motor Act
Support Document   HS-Neuro-Motor Act
Acute Delayed Neurotoxicity of
Organophosphorus Substances   HG-Neuro-Acute Delayed
Subchronic Delayed Neurotoxicity
of Organophosphorous Substances   HG-Neuro-Subchronic Delayed

V. Special Studies

Metabolism   HG-Spec Stud-Metab

Appendix 2G Recordkeeping, Reporting, and Inspection Provisions Under TSCA Section 8 (40 CFR Part 717)

§717.15 Recordkeeping requirements.

(a) *Establishment and location of records.* A firm subject to this Part shall establish and maintain records of significant adverse reactions alleged to have been caused by chemical substances or mixtures manufactured or processed by the firm. Such records shall be kept at the firm's headquarters or at any other appropriate location central to the firm's chemical operations.

(b) *Content of records.* The record shall consist of the following:

(1) The original allegation as received.

(2) An abstract of the allegation and other pertinent information as follows:

(i) The name and address of the plant site which received the allegation.

(ii) The date the allegation was received at that site.

(iii) The implicated substance, mixture, article, company process or operation, or site discharge.

(iv) A description of the alleger (e.g., "company employee," "individual consumer," "plant neighbor"). If the allegation involves a health effect, the sex and year of birth of the individual should be recorded, if ascertainable.

(v) A description of the alleged health effect(s). The description must relate how the effect(s) became known and the route of exposure, if explained in the allegation.

(vi) A description of the nature of the alleged environmental effect(s), identifying the affected plant and/or animal species, or contaminated portion of the physical environment.

(3) The results of any self-initiated investigation with respect to an allegation. (EPA does not require persons subject to this Part to investigate allegations received, and no provision of this Part shall be construed to imply that EPA recommends, encourages or requires such investigation.)

(4) Copies of any further required records or reports relating to the allegation. For example, if an employee allegation results in a requirement for the firm to record the case on Occupational Safety and Health Form 101 or appropriate substitute (see 29 CFR Part 1904 for requirements under the Occupational Safety and Health Act of 1970), a copy of that OSHA record must be included in the allegation record.

(c) *File structure.* Records must be retrievable by the alleged cause of the significant adverse reaction, which cause may be one of the following:

(1) A specific chemical identity.

(2) A mixture.

(3) An article.

(4) A company process or operation.

(5) A site emission, effluent or other discharge.

(d) *Retention period.* Records of significant adverse reactions to the health of employees shall be retained for a period of 30 years from the date such reactions were first reported to or known by the person maintaining such records. This provision requires persons subject to this Part to retain for 30 years an employee health related allegation, arising from any employment related exposure, whether or not such allegation was submitted by or on the behalf of that recordkeeper's own employee. Any other record of significant adverse reactions shall be maintained for a period of five years from the date the information contained in the record was first reported to or known by the person maintaining the record.

(e) *Transfer of records.* (1) If a firm ceases to do business, the successor must receive and keep all the records that must be kept under this Part.

(2) If a firm ceases to do business and there is no successor to receive and keep the records for the prescribed period, these records must be transmitted to EPA. See § 717.17(c) for the address to which such records must be sent.

§717.17 Inspection and reporting requirements.

(a) *Inspection.* Firms must make records of allegations available for inspection by any duly designated representative of the Administrator.

(b) *Reporting.* Each person who is required to keep records under this Part must submit copies of those records to the Agency as required by the EPA Administrator or appropriate designee. EPA will notify those responsible for reporting by letter or will announce any such requirements for submitting copies of records by a notice in the Federal Register. Such letter or notice will be signed by the Administrator or appropriate designee, and will specify which records or portion of records must be submitted. The reporting period will be specified by the letter or notice but in no case will such reporting period be less than 45 days from the date of the letter or the effective date of the notice.

(c) *How to report.* When required to report, firms must submit copies of records (preferably by certified mail) to the Document Control Officer, Office of Pesticides and Toxic Substances (TS-793), Environmental Protection Agency, Washington, DC 20460.

Appendix 2H   Reporting Mechanics and Requirements Under TSCA Section 8(e) (43 Fed. Reg. 11110)

1. Examples of Effects Required to Be Reported

(a) *Human health effects*—(1) Any instance of cancer, birth defects, mutagenicity, death, or serious or prolonged incapacitation, including the loss of or inability to use a normal bodily function with a consequent relatively serious impairment of normal activities, if one (or a few) chemical(s) is strongly implicated.

(2) Any pattern of effects or evidence which reasonably supports the conclusion that the chemical substance or mixture can produce cancer, mutation, birth defects or toxic effects resulting in death, or serious or prolonged incapacitation.

(b) *Environmental effects*—(1) Widespread and previously unsuspected distribution in environmental media, as indicated in studies (excluding materials contained within appropriate disposal facilities).

(2) Pronounced bioaccumulation. Measurements and indicators of pronounced bioaccumulation heretofore unknown to the Administrator (including bioaccumulation in fish beyond 5,000 times water concentration in a 30-day exposure or having an n-octanol/water partition coefficient greater than 25,000) should be reported when coupled with potential for widespread exposure and any non-trivial adverse effect.

(3) Any non-trivial adverse effect, heretofore unknown to the Administrator, associated with a chemical known to have bioaccumulated to a pronounced degree or to be widespread in environmental media.

(4) Ecologically significant changes in species' interrelationships; that is, changes in population behavior, growth, survival, etc. that in turn affect other species' behavior, growth, or survival.

Examples include: (i) Excessive stimulation of primary producers (algae, macrophytes) in aquatic ecosystems, e.g., resulting in nutrient enrichment, or eutrophication, of aquatic ecosystems.

(ii) Interference with critical biogeochemical cycles, such as the nitrogen cycle.

(5) Facile transformation or degradation to a chemical having an unacceptable risk as defined above.

(c) *Emergency incidents of environmental contamination*—Any environmental contamination by a chemical substance or mixture to which any of the above adverse effects has been ascribed and which because of the pattern, extent, and amount of contamination (1) seriously threatens humans with cancer, birth defects, mutation, death, or serious or prolonged incapacitation, or (2) seriously threatens non-human organisms with large-scale or ecologically significant population destruction.

2. Types of Information Not Required to Be Reported

Information need not be reported if it:

(a) Has been published by EPA in reports;

(b) Has been submitted in writing to EPA pursuant to mandatory reporting requirements under TSCA or any other authority administered by EPA (including the Federal Insecticide, Fungicide and Rodenticide Act, the Clean Air Act, the Federal Water Pollution Control Act, the Marine Protection, Research, and Sanctuaries Act, the Safe Drinking Water Act, and the Resource Conservation and Recovery Act), provided that the information: (1) Encompasses that required by Part IX (c) through (f); and (2) is from now on submitted within the time constraints set forth in Part IV and identified as a section 8(e) notice in accordance with Part IX(b);

(c) Has been published in the scientific literature and referenced by the following abstract services: (1) Agricola, (2) Biological Abstracts, (3) Chemical Abstracts, (4) Dissertation Abstracts, (5) Index Medicus, (6) National Technical Information Service.

(d) Is corroborative of well-established adverse effects already documented in the scientific literature and referenced as described in (c) above, unless such information concerns emergency incidents of environmental contamination as described in Part V(c), or

(e) Is contained in notification of spills under section 311(b)(5) of the Federal Water Pollution Control Act.

3. How and Where to File Section 8(e) Reports

Notices shall be delivered to the Document Control Officer, Chemical Information Division, Office of Toxic Substances (WH-557), Environmental Protection Agency, 401 M Street SW., Washington, D.C. 20460.

A notice should:

(a) Be sent by certified mail, or in any other way permitting verification of its receipt by the Agency,

(b) State that it is being submitted in accordance with section 8(e),

(c) Contain the job title, name, address, telephone number, and signature of the person reporting and the name and address of the manufacturing, processing, or distributing establishment with which he is associated,

(d) Identify the chemical substance or mixture (including, if known, the CAS Registry Number),

(e) Summarize the adverse effects being reported, describing the nature and the extent of the risk involved, and

(f) Contain the specific source of the information together with a summary and the source of any available supporting technical data.

For emergency incidents of environmental contamination (see Part V(c)), a person shall report the incident to the Administrator by telephone as soon as he has knowledge of the incident (see below for appropriate telephone contacts). The report should contain as much of the information required by instructions (b) through (f) above as possible. A written report, in accordance with instructions (a) through (f) above, is to be submitted within 15 days. Twenty-four hour emergency telephone numbers are:

Region I (Maine, Rhode Island, Connecticut, Vermont, Massachusetts, New Hampshire), 617-223-7265.

Region II (New York, New Jersey, Puerto Rico, Virgin Islands), 201-548-8730.

Region III (Pennsylvania, West Virginia, Virginia, Maryland, Delaware, District of Columbia), 215-597-9898.

Region IV (Kentucky, Tennessee, North Carolina, South Carolina, Georgia, Alabama, Mississippi, Florida), 404-881-4062.

Region V (Wisconsin, Illinois, Indiana, Michigan, Ohio, Minnesota), 312-353-2318.

Region VI (New Mexico, Texas, Oklahoma, Arkansas, Louisiana), 214-749-3840.

Region VII (Nebraska, Iowa, Missouri, Kansas), 816-374-3778.

Region VIII (Colorado, Utah, Wyoming, Montana, North Dakota, South Dakota), 303-837-3880.

Region IX (California, Nevada, Arizona, Hawaii, Guam), 415-556-6254.

Region X (Washington, Oregon, Idaho, Alaska), 206-442-1200.

Appendix 2I   EPA's TSCA Penalty Policy*

TSCA Civil Penalty System

Introduction

The Toxic Substances Control Act (TSCA), passed by Congress and signed into law in 1978, provides for increased regulation of chemical substances and mixtures. The Environmental Protection Agency is charged with carrying out and enforcing the requirements of the Act and any rules promulgated under the Act.

Section 16 of the Act provides for civil and criminal penalties for violations of TSCA or TSCA rules. Civil penalty amounts may range up to $25,000 per violation, with each day that a violation continues constituting a separate violation. Civil penalties are to be administratively imposed, after the person is given a written notice and the opportunity to request a hearing. There is a right to review in the United States Courts of Appeals after the penalty has been imposed by the Administrator.

Section 16 of TSCA requires that a number of factors be considered in assessing a civil penalty, as follows:

> In determining the amount of a civil penalty, the Administrator shall take into account the nature, circumstances, extent, and gravity of the violation or violations and, with respect to the violator, ability to pay, effect on ability to continue to do business, and history of prior such violations, the degree of culpability, and such other matters as justice may require.

The purpose of the general penalty system is to assure that TSCA civil penalties be assessed in a fair, uniform and consistent manner; that the penalties are appropriate for the violation committed; that economic incentives for violating TSCA are eliminated; and that persons will be deterred from committing TSCA violations.

Scope of the Civil Penalty System

The penalty system described in this document provides the general framework for civil penalty assessment under TSCA. It establishes standardized definitions and applications of factors the Act requires the Administrator to consider in assessing a penalty. As regulations are developed, specific penalty guidelines will be developed adopting in detail the application of the general penalty system to the new regulation. These specific guidelines will generally be issued when enforcement strategies are issued for each new regulation.

Note.—This document does not discuss whether assessment of a civil penalty is the correct enforcement response to a given violative condition. Rather, this document focuses on determining what the proper civil penalty should be if a decision has been made that a civil penalty is the proper enforcement remedy to pursue.

---

* 45 Fed. Reg. 59770.

Brief Description of the System

The general civil penalty system is designed to assign penalties for TSCA violations in accordance with the statutory requirements of Section 16. Penalties are determined in two stages: (1) Determination of a "gravity based penalty" (GBP), and (2) adjustments to the gravity based penalty.

To determine the gravity based penalty, the following factors affecting a violation's gravity are considered:

- The "nature" of the violation,
- The "extent" of environmental harm that could result from a given violation, and
- The "circumstances" of the violation.

These factors are incorporated on a matrix which allows determination of the appropriate gravity based penalty.

Once the gravity based penalty has been determined, upward or downward adjustments to the penalty amount are made in consideration of these other factors:

- Culpability,
- History of such violations,
- Ability to pay,
- Ability to continue in business, and
- Such other matters as justice may require.

Civil Penalty System and Its Application

This section describes in detail the general civil penalty system, how specific penalty guidances will be developed and applied, and the reasoning behind the development of the system.

The Penalty Factors

The Act requires the consideration of eight named factors in any penalty assessment, as well as "other factors as justice may require."

The first four factors—nature, circumstances, extent, and gravity—relate to the violation. Under the penalty system these four factors are charted on a matrix which yields the Gravity Based Penalty (GBP). This matrix is a *constant* throughout the penalty system. As will be seen below, however, the specific penalty guidelines will affect into which category along each axis of the matrix the violation will fall.

Once a GBP figure is reached, several adjustment factors are applied:

- An upward or downward adjustment may be made for particularly culpable or non-culpable conduct. An upward adjustment of up to 100% may be made where there is a history of such a violation.
- Two other adjustments (not specifically required by the Act, but authorized under the "as justice may require" language of § 16) are to recover cleanup costs paid by the United States, and to reduce or eliminate any financial or competitive advantage gained by the violator as a result of his failure to follow the Act, or its regulations. Other case-by-case adjust-

ments may also be warranted under the "as justice may require" language.

• The final statutory adjustment factors are the violator's ability to pay and the effect on the violator's ability to continue to do business. For several reasons we have combined the concepts involved in these factors onto one "ability to pay" factor. This factor will often act as a limit on the amount of penalty assessed, even where other factors indicate a higher penalty is warranted.

Calculation of the Gravity Based Penalty

The gravity based penalty (GBP) is found on the following matrix:

Circumstances (probability of damages)	Extent of potential damage		
	A major	B significant	C minor
High range:			
1...	$25,000	$17,000	$5,000
2...	20,000	13,000	3,000
Mid range:			
3...	15,000	10,000	1,500
4...	10,000	6,000	1,000
Low range:			
5...	5,000	3,000	500
6...	2,000	1,300	200

NOTE.—Significant violations are assessed at 60-68% of major violations, while minor violations are assessed at 20% and 15% of major violations for levels 1 and 2, and 10% for levels 3-6.

The GBP incorporates nature, extent, circumstances, and gravity as follows:

1. *Nature.* The "nature" factor, as all factors in the penalty system, is used in accordance with its commonly understood meaning: "The essential character of a thing; quality or qualities that make something what it is; essence" (Webster's New World Dictionary).

In the context of penalty assessment, this factor indicates which specific penalty guideline should be used to determine appropriate matrix levels of "extent" and "circumstances" (of environmental harm surrounding the violation). Thus, the nature (essential character) of a violation is best defined by the set of requirements violated, such as the PCB rule, or the premanufacture notification requirement. Since each TXCA [*sic*] section, rule, or other appropriate group of requirements will have a separate specific penalty guideline that will include criteria for assigning violations to the several levels of "extent" of potential harm, and probability of harm, the specific tailoring of these operational criteria for each section or rule ensures that penalties assessed will reflect the nature of the violation.

Also incorporated in the concept of "nature" is whether the violation is of a *chemical control, control-associated data gathering, or hazard assessment* nature:

Chemical control: Chemical control regulations are aimed at minimizing the risk presented by a chemical substance, by placing constraints on how it is handled. Sections 6, 7, 12, 13 and subsections 5(e), and 5(f) authorize a wide variety of chemical control actions, from labeling requirements to total bans on manufacture. These requirements are variously imposed by rulemaking, administrative order, court injunction, or by the Act itself.

Control-associated data gathering: Control-associated data gathering requirements are the recordkeeping and/or reporting requirements associated with a chemical control regulation. These requirements enable the Agency to evaluate the effectiveness of the regulation, and to monitor compliance.

Hazard assessment: Hazard assessment requirements are used to develop and gather the information necessary to intelligently weigh and assess the risks and benefits presented by particular chemical substances, and to impose chemical control requirements when appropriate. The requirements include those of premanufacture notification under § 5, testing under §4, and reporting and recordkeeping under §8.

As discussed in the next two sections the "nature" of the violation will have a direct effect on the measure used to determine which "extent" and "circumstances" categories are selected on the GBP matrix.

2. *Extent.* "Extent" is used to take into consideration the degree, range, or scope of the violation. The matrix provides three levels for measuring extent:

Level A (Major):

—Potential for "serious" damage to human health or for *major* damage to the environment.

Level B (Significant):

—Potential for *"significant"* amount of damage to human health or the environment.

Level C (Minor):

—Potential for a lesser amount of damage to human health or the environment.

A number of factors affect into which level of "extent" a particular violation fits. The specific application of these factors depends in large degree on the specific penalty system's treatment of a particular violation. For example, the specific penalty system will not only provide guidance for PCBs in general, but also for the type of PCB violation.

Chemical control: For a chemical control violation (e.g., rules for storage and disposal of PCBs), the *quantity* of the regulated substance involved might be the principal basis for categorizing extent. In other words, a violation involving under 10 pounds of a given substance might be Level C, 10 to 100 pounds Level B, and over 100 pounds Level A.[1] In the development of specific guidelines, environmental impact data and other analyses developed in support of the

---

[1] Other criteria, such as number of people exposed or potentially exposed, could have been utilized here, but (1) those factors are difficult and expensive to quantify for individual violations, and (2) these factors are already considered, to some extent, under "circumstances."

chemical control rule making will generally be the basis for determining "extent" levels.

Control-associated data-gathering: For control-associated data gathering regulations, the quantity of regulated substance involved in the recordkeeping will be used as the indicator of the extent of the violation. For example, not reporting the whereabouts of 1,000 pounds of PCBs is more serious than not reporting one pound. In general, the quantity measures used to define the "extent" of such a violation will be the same as those used to define the "extent" categories of the control violation with which it is associated. As with chemical control rules, factors other than quantity may be used when appropriate to indicate the "extent" of potential damage.

Hazard assessment: Hazard assessment data-gathering regulations require a different approach to make an "extent" determination. Unlike chemical control and control-associated data-gathering regulations, the degree of danger or "hazard" presented by the substance in question may not be known. Indeed, this lack of knowledge is the principle [*sic*] reason for the data-gathering. The measure of "extent" of harm will focus on the goals of the given hazard assessment regulation, and the types of harm it is designed to prevent. For example, a §4 test violation will be of Level A extent *if* it "seriously" affects the validity of a test on a substance which is manufactured in large quantities, with lesser violations treated accordingly, whereas manufacturing a chemical without submitting a premanufacture notification form 90 days in advance, could either be treated as (1) always being of Level A or, (2) varying in level of "extent" according to the volume illegally manufactured. Thus, a great number of judgments must be made in the formulation of the specific penalty policy.

3. *Circumstances.* "Circumstances" is used in the penalty policy to reflect on the probability of the assigned level of "extent" of harm actually occurring. In other words, a variety of facts surrounding the violations [*sic*] as it occurred are examined to determine whether the circumstances of the violation are such that there is a *high, medium,* or *low* probability that damage will occur. The matrix provides the following levels for measuring circumstances (probability factors):

Levels 1 and 2 (High): The violation is *likely* to cause damage.
Levels 3 and 4 (Medium): There is a *significant* chance that damage will result from the violation.
Levels 5 and 6 (Low): There is a *small likelihood* that damage will result from the violation.

The probability of harm, as assessed in evaluating circumstances, will always be based on the risk inherent in the violation *as it was committed.* In other words, a violation which presented a high probability of causing harm when it was committed (and/or was allowed to exist) must be classified as a "high probability" violation and *penalized* as such, even if through some fortuity no actual harm resulted in that particular case. Otherwise some who commit dangerous violations would be absolved. Similarly, when harm has actually resulted from a violation, the "circumstances" of the violation should be investigated to calculate what the probabilities were for harm occurring at the time of the violation. The theory is that violators should be penalized for the violative conduct, and the "good" or "bad" luck of whether or not the proscribed conduct *actually* caused harm should *not* be an overriding factor in penalty assessment. However, the responsibility for clean-up attaches without regard to the probability of harm (see Adjustment Factor 3, Government Clean-up Costs). As with "extent," the specific penalty guidelines are an essential tool in characterizing the circumstances of a violation.

Chemical control: With chemical control violations, probability is determined primarily by physical factors which affect the chance of improper exposure to the chemical's effects. For example, certain types of improper storage of PCBs are more likely than others to result in release of PCBs into the environment, and actual dumping of PCBs is virtually certain to do some harm. Criteria for assessing the probability of harm resulting from a violation will whenever possible be based on information developed in support of the chemical control rule.

Data-gathering and hazard assessment: A slightly different approach is taken to evaluate circumstances of data-gathering violations. The effect on the Agency's ability to implement of enforce the Act is the principal circumstance to be considered. Thus, the matrix levels for measuring circumstances (probability) for data-gathering and hazard assessment violations are as follows:

Levels 1 and 2 (High)—Violations which seriously impair the Agency's ability to monitor (data-gathering) or evaluate chemicals (hazard assessment).

Levels 3 and 4 (Medium)—Violations which impair the Agency's ability to monitor or evaluate chemicals in a less than critical way.

Levels 5 and 6 (Low)—Violations that impair the Agency's ability to monitor or evaluate chemicals in a less than important way.

Under these criteria, a violation of a Section 4 test standard (serious enough to make a study totally unreliable) has a higher probability of resulting in harm to the public through its effect on the Agency and would probably be Level 1 or 2, while late submission of a required report might be only a Level 5 or 6 violation.

Whenever possible, the specific penalty system will attempt to classify certain types of violations according to probability of damage. For example, certain types of violations of a disposal rule might always involve a high probability of damage. But other types of violations might involve such a large range of probability of harm that each case would have to be evaluated individually. In the latter case, the specific penalty guideline will include criteria to guide the evaluation of each violation. It is difficult to estimate the probability of harm presented by given situation, particularly in light of the many variables that make up "circumstances." However, "circumstances" can be evaluated for guideline purposes by comparing situations. For example, it is clear that, as a general rule, there is a greater probability of a falsified laboratory test leading to *actual damage,* than to have such damage resulting from minor errors in test report formatting.

The specific guidelines will also address the range of probabilities within each of the six "circumstances" classifications. For some violations, any probability of causing harm of over 10% might be in the "high" range, while other violations might be classified quite differently. One particular factor that may affect probability determinations is the length of time during which the violation presents a threat to health or the environment. Dumping PCBs in an unapproved landfill may not cause harm immediately but may inevitably cause harm as it leaches into nearby groundwater. But where only temporary improper *storage* is intended, and removal is planned, the probability of harm would be decreased accordingly.

4. *Gravity.* "Gravity" refers to the overall seriousness of the violation. As used in this penalty system, "gravity" is a dependent variable, i.e., the evaluation of "nature," "extent," and "circumstances" will yield a dollar figure on the matrix that determines the gravity based penalty.

The Adjustment Factors

The gravity based penalty reflects the seriousness of the violation's threat to health and environment. The Act also requires the Agency to consider certain factors in assessing the violator's conduct: Culpability, history of such violations, ability to pay, and ability to continue in business. In addition, the Act authorizes the Agency some discretion to consider "other factors as justice may require." Under this last authorization, two additional factors are considered and balanced: the cost of the violation to the government, and the benefits received by the violator due to his non-compliance. In order to compute penalty adjustments in a logical fashion, these adjustment factors are considered in the following sequence:

(1) Culpability;
(2) History;
(3) Cost to the government;
(4) Benefits from non-compliance; and
(5) Ability to pay/ability to continue in business.

1. *Culpability.* Since the law only requires the Agency to consider the culpability of the violator as an adjustment factor, the existence of a violation can be established without relying solely on this "blameworthiness" factor. In other words, the Agency may pursue a policy of strict liability in penalizing for a violation, though some allowance must be made based on the extent of the violator's culpability.[2] Under this penalty system, the gravity based penalty may be increased or decreased, or may remain the same depending on the violator's "culpability."

---

[2] There are certain circumstances where an "act of God" or some other circumstance totally out of a company's control may not result in assessment of a violation (no legal liability). For example where PCBs are *properly* stored, and a plane crashes into the storage facility, causing a spill, there will probably be no violation.

The two principal criteria for assessing culpability are (a) the violator's *knowledge* of the particular TSCA requirement, and (b) the degree of the violator's *control* over the violative condition.

(a) *The violator's knowledge:* The lack of knowledge of a particular requirement would not necessarily reduce culpability, since the Agency has no intention of encouraging ignorance of TSCA and its requirements. The test under TSCA will be whether the violator knew or should have known of the relevant TSCA requirement *or* of the general hazardousness of his actions. This latter point will allow the Agency to find a violator fully culpable even if he has no knowledge of a particular regulatory requirement when he does have knowledge that the particular substance he was dealing with was hazardous. For example, lack of knowledge of the PCB rules would not reduce culpability if the violator had knowledge that the dumping of PCBs creates a serious threat to human health. Thus, a reduction in the penalty based on lack of knowledge could only occur where a reasonably prudent and responsible person in the violator's position would not have known that the conduct was hazardous or violative of TSCA. It is anticipated that such situations and attendant reductions will be rare.

(b) *Degree of control over the violation:* There may be situations where the violator may be less than fully responsible for the violation's occurrence. For example, another company may have had some role in creating the violative conditions and thus must also share in the legal responsibility for the resulting consequences. Or an employee whose conduct caused the violation may have been disobeying his employer's instructions. Such situations would probably warrant some reduction in the penalties.

(c) *Initial culpability determination:* For penalty assessment purposes, three levels of culpability have been assigned, as follows:

Level I: The violation is willful, i.e., the violator intentionally committed an act which he knew would be a violation or would be hazardous to human health or the environment.
—Adjust the GBP *Upward* 25%.

Level II: The violator either had sufficient knowledge to recognize the hazard created by his conduct, or significant control over the situation to avoid committing the violation.
—No adjustment to the GBP.

Level III: The violator lacked sufficient knowledge of the potential hazard created by his conduct, and also lacked control over the situation to prevent occurrence of the violation.
—Adjust the GBP *downward* 25%.

It is anticipated that most cases will present Level II culpability. Level I situations, in many instances, could be treated as criminal violations (and often will be so treated). However, the decision to file a criminal action has no effect on civil penalty calculations and is a totally separate issue.

(d) *Attitude of the violator:* In assessing the violator's "attitude," the Agency will look at the following factors: Whether the violator is making "good faith" efforts to comply with the appropriate regulations; the promptness of the violator's corrective actions; and any assistance given to EPA to minimize any harm to the environment caused by the violation.

Since "attitude" is already reflected in Level I culpability, and since it is largely irrelevant to Level III culpability, this adjustment will really only be utilized where "knowledge" and "control" result in a Level II culpability finding. While Level II normally yields no reduction or increase in penalty, the attitude of the violator may justify a penalty adjustment of up to 15% of the GBP in either direction. Objective evidence, such as statements or actions of the violator, should be used to justify such adjustments.

2. *History of prior such violations.* The gravity based penalty matrix is designed to apply to "first offenders." Where a violator has demonstrated a similar history of "such violations," the Act requires the penalty to be adjusted upward. The need for such an upward adjustment derives from the violator's not being sufficiently motivated to comply (deferred from non-complying) by the penalty assessed for the previous violation, either because of economic factors consciously analyzed by the firm, or because of negligence. Another reason for penalizing repeat violators more severely than "first offenders" is the increased enforcement resources that are spent on the same violator.

The Agency's policy is to interpret "prior *such* violations" as referring only to prior violations of *TSCA*, even though it would seem "such" could refer to *any* violations of EPA statutes, or remedial statutes in general (e.g., OSHA, CPSC). However, since Congress did not *explicitly* state it wanted the Agency to go beyond TSCA in determining violation history, the Agency is using this narrower interpretation. The penalty system distinguishes between previous TSCA violations in general, and previous violations of the same set of regulatory requirements.

The following rules apply in evaluating history of prior such violations:

(a) In order to constitute a prior violation, the prior violation must have resulted in a *final order*, either as a result of an uncontested complaint, or as a result of a contested complaint which is finally resolved against the violator. Violations litigated in the Federal courts, under the Act's imminent hazard (§7), specific enforcement and seizure (§17), and criminal (§18(b)) provisions, are part of a violator's "history" for penalty assessment purposes, as are violations for which civil penalties have been previously assessed. However, a notice of non-compliance does *not constitute* a *"prior* such *violation"*, since no violation has formally been found, and no opportunity to contest the notice has been given.

(b) To be considered a "prior such violation", the violation must have occurred within five years of the present violation. This five year period begins when the prior violation becomes a final order. Beyond five years, the prior violative conduct becomes too distant to require compounding of the penalty for the present violation.

(c) Generally, companies with multiple establishments are considered as one when determining history. Thus, if one establishment of a company commits a TSCA violation, it counts as history when another establishment of the same company, anywhere in the country, commits another TSCA violation. However, two companies held by the same parent corporation do not necessarily affect each other's history if they are in substantially different lines of business, and they are substantially independent of one another in their management, and in the functioning of their Boards of Directors. In the case of wholly- or partly-owned subsidiaries, the violation history of a parent corporation shall apply to its subsidiaries, and that of the subsidiaries to the parent.

(d) If the prior such violation is of a different TSCA provision or regulation, the penalty should be upwardly adjusted 25 percent for a first repetition and 50 percent for a second repetition of the violation. If the prior "such" violation is of the same, or closely similar provision or regulation, the penalty should be upwardly adjusted 50 percent for the first repetition and 100 percent for the second repetition.

For these purposes, a prior such violation is the "same or closely related" if it is *similar* to the present violation. Each TSCA rule or regulation is considered a separate entity for "closely related" purposes. Thus the identical provision does *not* have to be violated both times for this higher adjustment to be made. For example, *two separate* unlawful disposals of PCBs may be "closely similar" if the PCBs were unlawfully dumped on the highways in the first instance, and in the second instance, PCBs of over 500 ppm were burned in a facility that did not comply with the PCB incinerator standards.

> The specific guidelines will give some guidance on what violations are "closely similar" to others, and may set up a sliding scale of upward adjustment percentages rather than the 50 percent or 100 percent figures provided here.

3. *Government clean-up costs.* An adjustment factor not specified in the statute, but which the Agency feels "justice * * * require[s]," is reimbursement to the government for funds expended to investigate, clean-up, or otherwise mitigate the effects of a violation.

Generally, the clean-up expense of a violator is to be borne by the violator as a necessary cost of violation in addition to any civil penalty assessed. The government may seek a Federal district court injunction under §§7 or 17 to require the violator to clean-up, but there will almost certainly be situations where the government will have to clean-up the violation to quickly alleviate any hazards created. Where these latter situations happen, the government could probably file a non-statutory suit in Federal district court to recover funds which it expended, but it could even more easily assess these costs, when they are sufficiently low, in an administrative proceeding under §16, particularly where a . . . §16 action is going to be filed anyway.

The major limitation to seeking reimbursement of government investigatory and clean-up costs is the limit of $25,000 for each violation. However, since each day a violation continues constitutes a separate violation for which a $25,000 penalty may be assessed, in many instances clean-up and investigatory costs can be recovered where the violation is a continuing one. However, where a penalty would be in the area of $25,000 for the violation even before government investigatory and clean-up costs are considered, a §16 action would be of little value in recovering these additional costs.

In adjusting the penalty, the government investigatory and clean-up cost should be added to the penalty calculated thus far. Where the total penalty under this method exceeds $25,000, the penalty should be cut back to $25,000. As will be discussed later, this type of situation lends itself to utilization of the continuing violation provisions of §16.

It is important to note that consideration of government investigatory and clean-up costs in the penalty assessment is *not* intended to in any way affect the *right* of the government to *recover investigatory and clean-up costs* in a separate court action. A violator may argue that investigatory and clean-up costs have been abrogated by settlement of the penalty. Thus, if there is a reasonable possibility that the Agency will seek to recover such costs in a separate suit, this factor should *not* be utilized in assessing the §16 penalty. Thus the investigatory and clean-up costs will *not* be included twice in calculating a penalty for a violation.

4. *Gains from noncompliance.* Another adjustment factor which "justice * * * require(s)" is that the violator not profit from its violative acts. TSCA's ability to prevent harm to public health and the environment is severely weakened whenever an economic incentive exists to violate the law. The penalty system attempts to eliminate, or at least reduce, these economic incentives, by adding to the base penalty an estimate of the economic gains obtained by the violator as a result of his noncompliance.

Among such economic gains would be money saved by not investing in new equipment, or by not following more costly operating procedures, or profits gained through the sale of illegal products. Removing such gains not only protects the public by deterring violations, but also prevents violators from gaining unfair competitive advantage over those who are complying with the law. For example, a company which manufactures a new chemical without submitting a premanufacture notice, pursuant to §5, may gain a strong competitive advantage over another company who intends to manufacture the same chemical, but follows the §5 procedure. The violator should be penalized at least to the extent of the economic gains achieved through his noncompliance. Any other result would put a premium on noncompliance.

The specific penalty guidelines should, where possible, indicate the types of economic gains from noncompliance, and include either standard estimates of such gains (e.g., the purchase price of required new equipment or facilities), or a procedure for estimating the gain. In cases where economic gains resulted from the company's failure to make required capital and operation and maintenance expenditures, those gains must be calculated in accordance with the Agency's September 27, 1978, "Technical Support Document" for computing civil penalties under the April 11, 1978, Civil Penalty Policy. The resulting economic savings figure must be reviewed by the Civil Penalty Policy Panel for consistency with that policy. In many instances, the GBP will be sufficiently high without adjustment for this factor. In other situations where there is no economic motive or benefit from noncompliance, or when the cost of cleaning up a violation outweighs any economic benefits received, this adjustment factor need not be applied.

5. *Ability to pay and ability to continue in business.* (a) *Usage of these terms.*

The Act lists "ability to pay" and "ability to continue in business" as two adjustment factors, but for the purposes of the penalty system the distinctions between the two are so narrow and artificial that they are treated as one. In making this determination it was considered that "ability to pay" might be limited (in the extreme sense) to such indicators as the market value of the violator in liquidation, the profits accrued by the firm over a given time period, the net sales or income generated over a given time period, the value of cash and other liquid assets held by the firm, and the value of all liquid assets plus borrowable cash. Essentially, however, a firm can pay up to the point where it can no longer do business.[3] However, it is evident that Congress, by inserting these two factors into the Act, for *most* cases did not intend that TSCA civil penalties present so great a burden as to pose the threat of destroying, or even severely impairing, a firm's business.

Measuring a firm's ability to pay[4] a cash penalty, without ceasing to be operable, can be extremely complex. The focus is on the solvency of the firm. Rather than performing extensive financial analysis of a firm, which would take an unreasonable effort on the part of both the Agency and the firm, it is believed that a year's net income, as determined by a fixed percentage of total sales, will generally yield an amount which the firm can afford to pay. The average ratio of net income to sales level for U.S. manufacturing in the past five years is approximately five percent (*1978 Economic Report of the President*). Since small firms are generally slightly less profitable than average sized firms, and since small firms are the ones most likely to have difficulty paying TSCA penalties, the guideline is reduced to four percent.

Even where the net income is negative, four percent of gross sales should still be used as the "ability to pay" guideline, since companies with high sales will be presumed to have sufficient cash to pay penalties even where there have been net losses.

For purposes of calculating the ability to pay, figures for the current year and the prior three years should be averaged. Four percent of the average sales will serve as the guideline for whether the company has the ability to pay.

(b) *Application of ability to pay.* While it would be possible for an inspector to utilize Dunn and Bradstreet, or to inquire during the course of the inspection to ascertain sales data, the firm should be presumed to have the ability to pay at the time the complaint is issued. This is preferable not only for purposes of administrative convenience, but also because many firms will not have their sales information in Dunn and Bradstreet or similar publications, and because the Act indicates that financial and sales data are only subject to inspection when "the nature and extent of such data are described with reasonable specificity in the written notice (of inspection)," §11(b)(2). This singling out by Congress of these factors indicates that they are not to be routinely asked for in every inspection, and since any alleged violator can raise the issue of ability

---

[3] Technically, a firm would often be able to pay even if imposing a penalty would cause it to file for bankruptcy, since a reorganization might still leave the business in operation.

[4] Henceforth "ability to pay" will be used to include "ability to continue in business".

to pay in his answer to the complaint, both the Agency and the inspected firm will save time and resources by using this approach. Of course, if such information can easily be obtained prior to or during the inspection, there is no harm in doing so.

If the firm raises the issue of inability to pay in its answer, or in the course of settlement discussions, the four percent guideline discussed above should be the model to follow. The firm should be asked to bring appropriate documentation to indicate what their sales have been, such as tax returns, financial statements, etc. If the proposed penalty exceeds four percent of total sales, the penalty may be reduced to an affordable level.

There may be some cases where a firm argues that it cannot afford to pay even though the penalty as adjusted does not exceed four percent of sales. A variety of factors, too complex to discuss here, might require such further adjustment to be made. In complex cases, the agency may need to rely on a management division economist or an accountant to analyze the firm's ability to pay and, on a case-by-case basis, to further reduce the proposed penalty.[5]

6. *Other factors at [sic] justice may require.* While two "other factors" have been incorporated as adjustment factors, other issues might arise, on a case-by-case basis, which should be considered in assessing penalties. Among these factors are:

- *Money spent by the violator in cleaning up or otherwise mitigation [sic] the harm caused by the violation.* Normally there should be no reduction for these costs, since it is part of the cost of violation. However, there may be instances where the cost of penalty, plus cost of cleanup, are excessive for the particular violation, so that some credit for these expenditures should be given.
- *New ownership for "history of violations."* It may be unfair in some cases to burden new ownership with the previous owner's history.

---

[5] The analyst must keep several particular points in mind. First, small firms often report no taxable income, and instead provide a return of their owner/operators through salaries and benefits such as automobiles, medical plans, and so forth. When reconstructing the firm's cash flow, owner/operators should receive as payment for services only that amount which they could obtain for providing similar services in the general labor market. The rest of their compensation should properly be assigned to profit for the company. The second point to keep in mind in examining tax returns is that small, privately-owned plants often have several corporations set up to handle various aspects of the business. If one or more of these corporations is culpable for some part of the TSCA violation, the tax returns for all involved corporations should be examined and a combined cash flow prepared. Once the firm's historical cash flows have been assembled, the analyst must make some assessment of the likely future path of the company. In so doing, the analyst must consider the firm's ability to earn cash from its operations, its ability to liquidate assets to meet penalty amounts (and still remain in business), and its ability to raise additional cash from lenders and its owners. The analyst must judge these factors without expending excessive resources on the analysis. Such a process can be assisted through discussions with individuals knowledgeable in the particular industry, such as local bankers, consultants, and others, if appropriate.

- *National defense.*
- *Foreign policy.*
- *Conflict or ambiguity vis-a-vis other Federal statutes and regulations* (e.g., OSHA, USDA, DOE).
- *Environmentally beneficial expenditure.* Circumstances may arise where a violator will offer to make expenditures for environmentally beneficial purposes above and beyond those required by law, in lieu of paying civil penalties. The Agency, in penalty actions in the U.S. District Courts under the Clean Air and Water Acts, has determined that crediting such expenditures is consistent with the purpose of civil penalty assessment. Although civil penalties under TSCA are administratively assessed, the same rational [*sic*] applies. This adjustment, which constitutes a credit against the actual penalty amount, will normally be discussed only in the course of settlement negotiations. The criteria for acceptable credits are discussed in detail in section VIII of the April 11, 1978 Civil Penalty Policy. Before proposed credit amounts can be incorporated into a settlement, the complainant must assure himself that the penalty (with credit adjustment) is consistent with the April 11, 1978, Civil Penalty Policy, and that the company has not already received credits in another enforcement action for the same environmentally beneficial expenditures. The settlement agreement incorporating such an adjustment should make clear what the actual *penalty* assessment is, after which the terms of the reduction should be spelled out in detail and in a clearly enforceable manner.
- *Significant-minor borderline violations.* Occasionally a violation, while of significant extent, will be so close to the borderline separating minor and significant violations that the penalty may seem disproportionately high. In this situation, additional reduction of up to 25% off the GBP may be applied before the other adjustment factor [*sic*] are considered.

Continuing Violations

Since the Act provides not only that civil penalties may be assessed up to $25,000 for each violation, but that each day a violation continues constitutes a separate violation for which additional penalties may be assessed, there is a potential for very large penalties to be assessed in many situations. In some cases, such large penalties will be appropriate for continuing violations, while for others, such as late inventory reporting, assessing an additional penalty for each day of violation would yield a penalty assessment for greater than the violation merits. The specific penalty guidelines will discuss the types of continuing violations which should be assessed on a per-day basis. This discussion should indicate how criteria such as this [*sic*] will be applied, e.g., which continuing violations should never be penalized on a per-day basis, and which should usually or always be so penalized.

When a penalty is assessed on a per-day basis for a continuing violation, care must be taken to assure that the adjustment factors, "government clean up costs", and "economic benefits from non-compliance" are spread over the entire penalty, since these figures are calculated by looking at the entire violative situation. For example, if a continuing violation lasted four days and generated $40,000 in government clean-up costs, these $40,000 in costs should be added to the daily penalties (although each day would still be limited to a maximum $25,000 penalty).

Continuing violations are distinguished from multiple violations and violations which occur several separate times. These latter violations will generally be separately assessed.

Settlement

This guidance does not prescribe a specific percentage guideline for penalty reductions in the course of settlement. While, as a general rule, penalties may be altered in the course of settlement, there should always be some substantive reason given, which is to be incorporated in any settlement agreement and consent decree and final order for any penalty reduction. Other aspects of settlement are discussed in the context of particular penalty factors.

Designing and Applying a Specific Penalty Guidance

Designing a Specific Penalty Guidance

The specific penalty guidance, which will usually be developed as part of the enforcement strategy for a particular regulation, will provide the detailed information needed to fit particular violations in the overall civil penalty system. Each specific penalty guidance will address:

- To the extent possible, the types of violations that can occur;
- How to evaluate the nature (i.e., whether chemical control; or information gathering) of a violation;
- How to determine and classify the extent of possible harm posed by a given violations [sic];
- Special considerations in using the adjustment factors, particularly including means of estimating government clean-up costs and economic benefits from non-compliance;
- How and when to utilize the concept of multi-day violations;
- Any "other matters as justice may require" which may particularly apply to the given regulation; and
- Anything else necessary to effectuate enforcement of the regulation and the Act's penalty policy.

Applying a Specific Penalty Guidance

This section briefly summarizes the steps necessary to calculate a proposed penalty assessment.

Step 1: Utilizing the specific penalty guidances, determine the nature, extent, and circumstances of the violation.

Step 2: Find the appropriate extent and circumstances levels on the gravity based penalty matrix to determine the gravity based penalty (GBP).

Step 3: Determine the percentage adjustment for culpability, if any.

Step 4: Determine the percentage adjustment for history, if any.

Step 5: Add the adjustment percentages from steps 3 and 4 and apply the GBP. If the amount is in excess of $25,000, reduce the penalty to $25,000.

Step 6: Multiply the step 5 figure by the number of days of violation.

Step 7: Apply government cleanup costs adjustment, if applicable. Add to the step 6 figure.

Step 8: Apply economic gains from non-compliance adjustment, if applicable. Add to the step 6 figure.

Step 9: Make other adjustments "as justice may require."

Step 10: Issue formal complaint proposing the penalty.

Step 11: Discuss settlement any time before a final administrative law judge's decision (unless the complaint is not contested and becomes final as a matter of law). If applicable, determine violator's ability to pay. If appropriate, reduce penalty to amount violator can afford to pay. Penalties may be reduced as a condition of settlement.

Step 12: Issue Final order.

Civil Penalty Assessment Worksheet

Name of Respondent: _____

Address of Respondent: _____

_____

(1) Complaint I.D. Number: _____
(2) Date Complaint Issued: _____
(3) Date Answer Received: _____
(4) Date Default Order Sent: _____
(5) Date Consent Agreement Signed:_____
(6) Date Final Order Sent: _____
(7) Date Remittance Received: _____

    1. Gravity Based Penalty (GBP) from matrix, $____.

    2. Percent increase or decrease for culpability, %____.

    3. Percent increase for violation history, %____.

    4. Add lines 2 and 3, %____.

    5. Multiply GBP by percentage total on line 4, %____.

    6. Add lines 1 and 5 (subtract line 5 from line 1 if negative percentage), $____.

    7. Enter line 6 amount or $25,000, whichever is *less*, $____.

    8. Multiply line 7 by the number of days of violation, $____.

    9. Government clean-up costs, if any, $____.

    10. Economic gains from non-compliance, if appropriate, $____.

    11. Add lines 8 through 10, $____.

    12. Total of other adjustments as justice may require, $____.

    13. If line 12 represents a net *increase* to the penalty add line 12 to line 11, $____,

or

If line 12 represents a net *decrease* to the penalty subtract line 12 from line 1, $____.

Note.—Line 13 should be the proposed penalty for a given violation. This procedure is repeated for each violation.

Appendix 2J   Summaries of Recent Regulatory Activities Under TSCA

Introduction

This appendix gives summaries and references to significant regulatory action up to the early part of 1985. The author is indebted to Sanford Gaines, Esq., an attorney at the Chemical Manufacturers Association, who originally compiled this material.

A.   *Toxicity Testing of Existing Chemicals (Section 4 Actions)*

   1.   *Administrative Actions*

      a.   *Final General Rules*

         • *Test Rule Development and Exemption Procedure*
          49 Fed. Reg. 39774, Oct. 10, 1984

          This rule prescribes who must conduct testing and administrative procedures for development of data in response to test rules. It also describes procedures that persons subject to test rules must follow in order to obtain exemptions or receive reimbursement of test costs.

      b.   *Final Test Rules*

         • *1,1,1-Trichloroethane*
          49 Fed. Reg. 39810, Oct. 10, 1984

          This rule requires manufacturers and processors to test this substance for developmental toxicity effects. Manufacturers and processors are also required to submit test protocols to EPA.

      c.   *Proposed General Rules*

         • *Chemical Information Rule*
          49 Fed. Reg. 45598, Nov. 19, 1984

          EPA proposed to amend the Section 8(a) Preliminary Assessment Information Rule to extend the automatic reporting provision (40 CFR §712) to include those chemicals recommended by the ITC but not designated for action by EPA within twelve months. This would allow rapid collection of information on those chemicals without separate rulemakings. Opportunity is provided for manufacturers to request removal from the list.

         • *Health and Safety Data Reporting*
          49 Fed. Reg. 45602, Nov. 19, 1984

          The proposed changes to the automatic reporting provision

of the Health and Safety Data Reporting Rule under Section 8(d) (40 CFR §716) parallel the proposal under Section 8(a) described above. This will facilitate the reporting of unpublished health and safety studies on chemicals recommended for testing by the ITC but not designated for action by EPA within twelve months.

d. *Proposed Test Rules*

- *Chlorinated Benzenes*
  49 Fed. Reg. 50408, Dec. 28, 1984

  In July 1980, EPA initiated proceedings to require health effects testing of chlorinated benzenes. Three years later, the Agency withdrew all proposed test requirements except for oncogenicity testing of 1,2,4-trichlorobenzene and health effects testing of 1,2,4,5-tetrachlorobenzene. 48 Fed. Reg. 54836, Dec. 7, 1983. EPA now proposes three decisions concerning the proceedings: (1) a final decision to withdraw certain portions of the proposed test rule; (2) in obedience to a recent court decision, a decision not to accept the negotiated testing program submitted by the Chlorobenzene Producers Association; and (3) a decision to conduct final rulemaking on chlorobenzenes health effects testing in a single rule, to be completed by June 1986 under court order.

- *Hexafluoropropylene Oxide*
  48 Fed. Reg. 57686, Dec. 30, 1983

  EPA proposed testing for mutagenicity, oncogenicity, and reproductive effects.

- *Propylene Oxide*
  49 Fed. Reg. 430, Jan. 4, 1984

  EPA proposed testing for teratogenicity.

- *Hydroquinone*
  49 Fed. Reg. 439, Jan. 4, 1984

  EPA proposed tests to evaluate hydroquinone's toxicokinetics and to evaluate its potential nervous system, teratogenic, mutagenic, reproductive, and environmental effects and chemical fate. EPA also proposed two epidemiological studies.

- *Quinone*
  49 Fed. Reg. 456, Jan. 4, 1984

  EPA proposed testing for carcinogenic effects, chemical fate, and environmental effects.

- *1,2-Dichloropropane*
  49 Fed. Reg. 899, Jan. 6, 1984

  EPA proposed neurotoxicity, mutagenicity, teratogenicity, and reproductive effects tests and environmental effects tests for acute and chronic toxicity in aquatic invertebrates and plants.

- *Mono- , Di- , and Tri-Chlorinated Benzene*
  49 Fed. Reg. 1760, Jan. 13, 1984

  EPA proposed certain chemical fate and environmental effects tests.

- *Oleylamine*
  49 Fed. Reg. 45610, Nov. 11, 1984

  EPA proposed testing for developmental toxicity, ninety-day dermal subchronic toxicity, and mutagenicity by means of a tiered scheme with triggers to oncogenicity testing.

e. *Advance Notices of Proposed Rulemaking*

- *Aryl Phosphates*
  48 Fed. Reg. 57452, Dec. 29, 1983

  At the ITC's recommendation, EPA suggested health effects testing for carcinogenicity, mutagenicity, teratogenicity, and neurotoxicity and environmental effects testing.

- *Glycidol and Its Derivatives*
  49 Fed. Reg. 57562, Dec. 30, 1983

  This notice proposed testing for carcinogenic, mutagenic, teratogenic, and other adverse health effects, and also sought public comment on EPA's plan to propose a test rule for this category.

- *Anilene and Chloro- , Bromo- , and/or Nitroanilenes*
  49 Fed. Reg. 108, Jan. 3, 1984

  In response to the ITC's recommendation, this notice initiated rulemaking to require health effects testing for carcinogenicity, mutagenicity, teratogenicity, chronic effects, and environmental effects.

- *Alkyl Epoxides*
  49 Fed. Reg. 449, Jan. 4, 1984

  This notice responded to the ITC's recommendation that alkyl epoxides be tested for mutagenicity, carcinogenicity, teratogenicity, other chronic effects (with emphasis on organ effects and behavioral changes), and environmental fate.

B. *New Chemical Notification and Control (Section 5 Actions)*

   1. *Administrative Actions*

      a. *Final Rules*

- *PMN Exemption for Polymers*
  49 Fed. Reg. 46066, Nov. 21, 1984

  EPA granted a Section 5(h)(4) "exemption" to those persons who manufacture or import (1) polyesters that are made from a specified list of reactants or (2) polymers with a number-average molecular weight greater than 1000 (with some exceptions) because the Agency determined that these substances would not present an unreasonable risk of injury to health or the environment. The "exemption" provides for quick (twenty-one-day) review of an abbreviated PMN.

- *Significant New Use Rule—General*
  49 Fed. Reg. 35011, Sept. 5, 1984

  This rule contains two parts, one of which sets forth general procedures and requirements applicable to all SNURs. These general rules cover such topics as the duty of manufacturers to submit notices to EPA, the duty of manufacturers to notify customers of the SNUR restrictions, and the effective date of rules.

- *Certain Phosphates*
  49 Fed. Reg. 35011, Sept. 5, 1984

  The other part of EPA's first final significant new use rule (SNUR) requires persons to notify EPA at least ninety days before manufacturing, importing, or processing potassium N-N-bis (hydroxyethyl) cocoamine oxide phosphate and potassium N,N-bis (hydroxyethyl) tallowamine oxide phosphate for use in consumer product formulations containing greater than 5 percent by weight of these substances.

- *Derivative of Tetrachloroethylene*
  49 Fed. Reg. 42928, Oct. 25, 1984

  EPA issued this SNUR requiring that (1) persons employed by or under the control of the manufacturer or processor who are involved in and in the immediate area of any operation where dermal contact and/or inhalation of the substance may occur wear impervious gloves and a NIOSH-approved respirator and (2) any container of the substance or formulation of the substance be packaged to prevent leakage and labeled with the statement that the substance should only be handled by persons using NIOSH-approved respirators and impervious gloves.

- *1,2-Benzenediamine, 4-Ethoxy, Sulfate*
  49 Fed. Reg. 43058, Oct. 26, 1984

  EPA designated the manufacture, import, or processing of this chemical substance as a significant new use because the Agency believes that the chemical may possess carcinogenic potential following inhalation or ingestion.

- *Dicarboxylic Acid Monoester*
  49 Fed. Reg. 43061, Oct. 26, 1984

  EPA designated as significant new uses (1) any manufacture in the United States for commercial purposes; (2) failure to require the use of impervious gloves and/or failure to require the use of protective clothing to prevent dermal contact during an operation where dermal contact may occur; and (3) distribution in commerce by any person, including importers, processors, and distributors, without affixing of a warning label to each container of any formulation containing the substance.

- *Substituted Polyglycidyl Benzeneamine*
  49 Fed. Reg. 43649, Oct. 31, 1984

  EPA has designated as significant new uses of this substance (1) use in spray applications; (2) manufacturing or processing without (a) use of impervious gloves, face shields, and protective clothing, (b) informing persons required to wear protective equipment of the health concerns presented by the substance, and (c) placing warning labels on any package containing the substance.

- *Isopropylamine, Distillation Residues, and Ethylamine, Distillation Residues*
  49 Fed. Reg. 46373, Nov. 26, 1984

  EPA issued this SNUR to require persons to notify EPA at least ninety days before manufacturing, importing, or processing the substances for use in metalworking fluids. EPA believes that the substances may react with nitrosating agents in metalworking fluids to form carcinogenic nitrosamines and that use of the contaminated fluids could result in significant human exposure to nitrosamines.

- *Substituted Methylpyridine and Substituted 2-Phenoxypyridine*
  49 Fed. Reg. 50396, Dec. 28, 1984

EPA has designated as significant new uses manufacturing or processing without the use of personal protective equipment for persons in the immediate area of any operation where dermal contact or inhalation may occur.

b. *Immediately Effective Rules—Section 5(f)*

- *Nitrites*
  49 Fed. Reg. 2762, Jan. 23, 1984

  EPA issued this immediately effective proposed rule to prohibit nitrites in metalworking fluids because they may present an unreasonable risk to human health before a final rule can be promulgated under Section 6.

- *Triethanolamine Salt of a Substituted Organic Acid*
  49 Fed. Reg. 24658, June 14, 1984

  EPA issued an immediately effective proposed rule under Section 5(f)(2) because the substance may cause an unreasonable risk to human health before a final rule can be promulgated under Section 6. The rule prohibits the addition of any nitrosating agent to triethanolamine when it could be used in metalworking fluids; and it requires distributors to notify machine shop workers of health hazards through labels on metalworking fluids containing the substance.

c. *Final Orders Under Section 5(e)*

Section 5(e) of TSCA authorizes EPA to restrict or prohibit the manufacture, processing, distribution in commerce, use, or disposal of a PMN substance if the Agency determines that such activities may present an unreasonable risk to human health or the environment.

During 1984 the Office of Toxic Substances not only increased the number of consent orders and unilateral orders under the authority of Section 5(e) (EPA issued sixteen such orders in the first eight months of 1984) but also made the substantive requirements of these orders more detailed and more stringent.

d. *Proposed Rules*

- *Revisions to PMN Rules—Research and Development*
  49 Fed. Reg. 50201, Dec. 27, 1984

  When the final PMN rule was issued in May 1983, the Chemical Manufacturers Association petitioned for a stay and reconsideration of several provisions. In September 1983, EPA agreed to stay four provisions and put the rest of the rule into effect. This latest proposal modifies the four stayed provisions, and clarifies or revises a few other aspects of the rule.

The heart of the proposal contains regulatory definitions of research and development chemicals, which Section 5 of TSCA exempts from PMN requirements. The proposal sets definitions and criteria for determining what constitutes research and development, but allows flexibility in terms of volume manufactured and how the chemical is used. The proposal also contains hazard notification and recordkeeping requirements for research and development chemicals. Other parts of the proposal revise definitions of what chemicals are considered "related" to the PMN chemical, what information is deemed to be in the manufacturer's "possession or control," and what constitutes manufacture solely for export.

- *8-Acetyl-3-Dodecyl 1-7,7,9-9-Tetramethyl-1,3,8-Triaza-Spiro(4,5)Decane-2,4-dione*
  49 Fed. Reg. 1753, Jan. 13, 1984

  EPA proposed to define as new uses any manufacture within the United States, processing the substance without use of certain personal protective equipment, and any distribution without a precautionary label statement affixed to all containers.

- *Methylpyridine and 2-Phenoxypyridine*
  49 Fed. Reg. 4390, Feb. 6, 1984

  EPA proposed that manufacture or processing without use of certain protective equipment be designated a significant new use of both substances and that release into navigable waters from manufacture or processing of methylpyridine be labeled a new use.

- *Alkyl Aryl Phosphate*
  49 Fed. Reg. 36880, Sept. 20, 1984

  EPA proposed to designate as significant new uses (1) manufacturing, importing, or processing without establishing and enforcing a program whereby exposed workers use respirators and wear protective clothing; (2) manufacturing or importing amounts that exceed the terms in the PMN submitter's Section 5(e) consent order; and (3) distribution by any person without affixing of a warning label to each container of the chemical.

- *Certain Chemicals*
  49 Fed. Reg. 38303, Sept. 28, 1984

  EPA proposed this SNUR for four chemical substances (brominated aryl alkyl ether, ethylated amino phenol, amino phenol, and anilino ether), which were the subject of PMNs and a Section 5(e) consent order. The Agency believes that the substances may present an unreasonable risk to human health if they are manufactured or processed without the use of certain personal protective equipment.

- *Hexamethylphosphoramide and Uerthane*
  49 Fed. Reg. 39703, Oct. 10, 1984

  EPA proposed that any manufacture, import, or processing for commercial purposes of these substances be a significant new use requiring ninety-day notice. These chemicals are on the TSCA Inventory but are no longer made in the United States. EPA wants notice of any resumption of production.

- *[(Dinitrophenyl)   Azo]-[2,4-Diamino-5-Methoxybenzene] Derivatives*
  40 Fed. Reg. 42960, Oct. 25, 1984

  EPA proposed that manufacture, import, or processing as a powder or a dry solid be designated as a significant new use of the chemical substance.

- *Disubstituted Diamino Anisols*
  49 Fed. Reg. 47874, Dec. 7, 1984

  EPA believes this substance may be hazardous and that uncontrolled manufacture, processing, import, distribution in commerce, use, or disposal may result in significant human or environmental exposure.

- *Alkyl Glycoether Acrylic Acid Derivative*
  49 Fed. Reg. 49868, Dec. 24, 1984

  EPA proposed to regulate uncontrolled manufacture, processing, import, distribution in commerce, use, and disposal as significant new uses because the substance may present carcinogenic risk to human health following inhalation, ingestion, or dermal contact.

- *Certain Polyamino Chemical Substances*
  49 Fed. Reg. 50209, Dec. 27, 1984

  EPA determined that three polyamino chemical substances may result in significant human exposure and thus proposed that use as or in intumescent coatings (chemical substances that form fire-resistant or fire-retardant coatings when exposed to heat) be designated a significant new use.

- *Benzoic Acid 3, 3-Methylene bis [6-Amino-,Di-2-Propenyl Ester*
  50 Fed. Reg. 127, Jan. 2, 1985

EPA proposed that any use or method of manufacture other than those described in the original PMN be deemed a significant new use. The PMN use and method of manufacture, however, are confidential business information, so any subsequent manufacturer of the same substance will need to file a notice.

C. Regulation of Chemicals in Commerce

1. Administrative Actions

a. Final Rules

- *PCBs—Inadvertent Generation and Other Issues*
  49 Fed. Reg. 28154, 28173, and 28193, July 10, 1984

  This final rule adopts the bulk of the consensus proposal on inadvertent generation of PCBs developed jointly by the Chemical Manufacturers Association, the Environmental Defense Fund, and the Natural Resources Defense Council. Generally speaking, this rule permits manufacture and distribution of products containing up to 50 parts per million of PCBs inadvertently generated during the manufacture of the product. In some situations, lower concentration levels are specified. Environmental releases are also addressed. On the basis of this general rule, EPA denied a number of petitions for exemption from the PCB regulations. EPA also allows use of PCBs in microscopy.

b. Designations of Chemicals for Priority Review Under Section 4(f)

- *1,3 Butadiene*
  49 Fed. Reg. 845, Jan. 5, 1984

  This notice announced initiation of a 180-day review of 1,3-Butadiene as a result of two animal studies that appeared to demonstrate butadiene's potential to cause oncogenic effects. OSHA issued a parallel notice on the same day, 49 Fed. Reg. 844.

- *Formaldehyde*
  49 Fed. Reg. 21898, May 23, 1984

  This notice announced EPA's determination to give formaldehyde priority review under Section 4(f) for two exposure situations: apparel manufacturing and residential housing. This designation completed a reconsideration begun in November 1983 as an outgrowth of litigation challenging EPA's 1982 decision *not* to give priority consideration to formaldehyde.

c. *Proposed Rules*

- *PCBs in Electrical Transformers*
  49 Fed. Reg. 39966, Oct. 11, 1984

  This proposal contains various adjustments and new requirements in EPA's rules for PCBs in transformers to reduce the risk of fire and fire-related releases of PCBs and combustion products.

d. *Advance Notices of Proposed Rulemaking*

- *Glycol Ethers*
  49 Fed. Reg. 2921, Jan. 21, 1984

  EPA announced its consideration of regulation to control risks from the uses of four glycol ethers, primarily in the workplace. Among the controls being considered are total or partial bans on the substances, regulation of concentration levels, and labeling.

- *1,3-Butadiene*
  49 Fed. Reg. 20524, May 15, 1984

  This notice constitutes the initiation of action in response to the designation of butadiene under Section 4(f). EPA particularly desires to gain a better understanding of exposure to butadiene. Because butadiene is used as an ingredient in synthetic rubber and the exposure occurs primarily in the workplace, EPA's proceeding will move forward in tandem with OSHA.

- *Formaldehyde*
  49 Fed. Reg. 21870, May 23, 1984

  EPA issued this notice for Section 6 rulemaking simultaneously with its designation of formaldehyde under Section 4(f). EPA will focus on two exposure situations: apparel manufacturing and residential housing. EPA seeks a better understanding of the toxicokinetics of formaldehyde and the actual levels of exposure in the two situations of greatest interest.

e. *Response to Petition*
   50 Fed. Reg. 4426, January 30, 1985

   On October 22, 1984, the Environmental Defense Fund and the National Wildlife Foundation submitted to EPA a petition under TSCA Section 21 seeking immediate and comprehensive regulation of dioxins and dibenzofurens. EPA decided to grant the petition in part and deny it in part. EPA granted the requests for collecting further information about these compounds under Sections 4 and 8 of TSCA. EPA denied all other requests, specifically including requests for regulation under Section 6 of TSCA. EPA also asserted that requests for action under laws other than TSCA cannot be properly included in a Section 21 petition.

Appendix 3A Table of Session Law to U.S. Code Cross-References: Federal Insecticide, Fungicide and Rodenticide Act (FIFRA)

FIFRA Session Law Number*	Title 7 U.S. Code Number
§2	§136
§3	§136a
§4	§136b
§5	§136c
§6	§136d
§7	§136e
§8	§136f
§9	§136g
§10	§136h
§11	§136i
§12	§136j
§13	§136k
§14	§136l
§15	§136m
§16	§136n
§17	§136o
§18	§136p
§19	§136q
§20	§136r
§21	§136s
§22	§136t
§23	§136u
§24	§136v
§25	§136w
§26	§136w-1
§27	§136w-2
§28	§136w-3
§29	§136w-4
§30	§136x
§31	§136y

* Federal Insecticide, Fungicide and Rodenticide Act (7 USC §§136 *et seq.*), Pub. L. 92-516, 92d Congress, H.R. 10729, October 21, 1972, as amended by Pub.L. 94-140, 94th Congress, H.R. 8841, November 28, 1975, Pub.L. 95-396, 95th Congress, S. 1678, September 30, 1978, and Pub.L. 96-539, 96th Congress, December 17, 1980. 86 Stat. 973-999.

Appendix 5A Table of Session Law to U.S. Code Cross-References: Resource Conservation and Recovery Act (RCRA)

RCRA Session Law Number*	Title 42 U.S. Code Number
§1002	§6901
§1003	§6902
§1004	§6903
§1005	§6904
§1006	§6905
§1007	§6906
§1008	§6907
§2001	§6911
§2002	§6912
§2003	§6913
§2004	§6914
§2005	§6915
§2006	§6916
§3001	§6921
§3002	§6922
§3003	§6923
§3004	§6924
§3005	§6925
§3006	§6926
§3007	§6927
§3008	§6928
§3009	§6929
§3010	§6930
§3011	§6931
§3012	§6933
§3013	§6934
§3014 [11-8-84]	§6932
§3015 [11-8-84]	§6935
§3016 [11-8-84]	§6936
§3017 [11-8-84]	§6937
§3018 [11-8-84]	§6938
§3019 [11-8-84]	§6939
§4001	§6941
§4002	§6942

---

* Resource Conservation and Recovery Act of 1976 (42 USC §§6901 *et seq.*), Pub.L. 94-580, October 21, 1976, as amended by Pub.L. 95-609, November 8, 1978, Pub.L. 96-463, October 15, 1980, Pub.L. 96-482, October 21, 1980, Pub.L. 96-510, December 11, 1980, Pub.L. 97-272, September 30, 1982, Pub.L. 97-375, December 21, 1982, Pub.L. 98-45, July 12, 1983, Pub.L. 98-371, July 18, 1984, Pub.L. 98-616, November 8, 1984. 90 Stat. 95.

Appendix 5B   Part 261 Hazardous Waste Lists and Appendixes

Subpart D—Lists of Hazardous Wastes

§ 261.30 General.

(a) A solid waste is a hazardous waste if it is listed in this subpart, unless it has been excluded from this list under §§ 260.20 and 260.22.

(b) The Administrator will indicate his basis for listing the classes or types of wastes listed in this Subpart by employing one or more of the following Hazard Codes:

Ignitable Waste	(I)
Corrosive Waste	(C)
Reactive Waste	(R)
EP Toxic Waste	(E)
Acute Hazardous Waste	(H)
Toxic Waste	(T)

Appendix VII identifies the constituent which caused the Administrator to list the waste as an EP Toxic Waste (E) or Toxic Waste (T) in §§ 261.31 and 261.32.

(c) Each hazardous waste listed in this subpart is assigned an EPA Hazardous Waste Number which precedes the name of the waste. This number must be used in complying with the notification requirements of Section 3010 of the Act and certain record-keeping and reporting requirements under Parts 262 through 265 and Part 270 of this chapter.

(d) The following hazardous wastes listed in § 261.31 or § 261.32 are subject to the exclusion limits for acutely hazardous wastes established in § 261.5: EPA Hazardous Wastes Nos. FO20, FO21, FO22, FO23, FO26, and FO27.

[45 FR 33119, May 19, 1980, as amended at 48 FR 14294, Apr. 1, 1983; 50 FR 2000, Jan. 14, 1985]

EFFECTIVE DATE NOTE: At 50 FR 2000, Jan. 14, 1985, § 261.30(d) was revised, effective July 15, 1985. For the convenience of the user, the superseded text is set out below:

§ 261.30 General.

*   *   *   *   *

(d) The following hazardous wastes listed in § 261.31 or § 261.32 are subject to the exclusion limits for acutely hazardous wastes established in § 261.F: [Reserved]

§ 261.31 Hazardous wastes from non-specific sources.

The following solid wastes are listed hazardous wastes from non-specific sources unless they are excluded under §§ 260.20 and 260.22 and listed in Appendix IX.

Industry and EPA hazardous waste No.	Hazardous waste	Hazard code
Generic: F001	The following spent halogenated solvents used in degreasing: tetrachloroethylene, trichloroethylene, methylene chloride, 1,1,1-trichloroethane, carbon tetrachloride, and chlorinated fluorocarbons; all spent solvent mixtures/blends used in degreasing containing, before use, a total of ten percent or more (by volume) of one or more of the above halogenated solvents or those solvents listed in F002, F004, and F005; and still bottoms from the recovery of these spent solvents and spent solvent mixtures.	(T)
F002	The following spent halogenated solvents: tetrachloroethylene, methylene chloride, trichloroethylene, 1,1,1-trichloroethane, chlorobenzene, 1,2,2-trichloro-1,2,2-trifluoroethane, ortho-dichlorobenzene, and trichlorofluoromethane; all spent solvent mixtures/blends containing, before use, a total of ten percent or more (by volume) of one or more of the above halogenated solvents or those solvents listed in F001, F004, and, F005; and still bottoms from the recovery of these spent solvents and spent solvent mixtures.	(T)

Industry and EPA hazardous waste No.	Hazardous waste	Hazard code
F003	The following spent non-halogenated solvents: xylene, acetone, ethyl acetate, ethyl benzene, ethyl ether, methyl isobutyl ketone, n-butyl alcohol, cyclohexanone, and methanol; all spent solvent mixtures/blends containing, before use, only the above spent non-halogenated solvents; and all spent solvent mixtures/blends containing, before use, one or more of the above non-halogenated solvents, and, a total of ten percent or more (by volume) of one or more of those solvents listed in F001, F002, F004, and F005; and still bottoms from the recovery of these spent solvents and spent solvent mixtures.	(I)*
F004	The following spent non-halogenated solvents: cresols and cresylic acid, and nitrobenzene; all spent solvent mixtures/blends containing, before use, a total of ten percent or more (by volume) of one or more of the above non-halogenated solvents or those solvents listed in F001, F002, and F005; and still bottoms from the recovery of these spent solvents and spent solvent mixtures.	(T)
F005	The following spent non-halogenated solvents: toluene, methyl ethyl ketone, carbon disulfide, isobutanol, and pyridine; all spent solvent mixtures/blends containing, before use, a total of ten percent or more (by volume) of one or more of the above non-halogenated solvents or those solvents listed in F001, F002, and F004; and still bottoms from the recovery of these spent solvents and spent solvent mixtures.	(T)

*(I,T) should be used to specify mixtures containing ignitable and toxic constituents.

§ 261.32 Hazardous wastes from specific sources.

The following solid wastes are listed hazardous wastes from specific sources unless they are excluded under §§ 260.20 and 260.22 and listed in Appendix IX.

Industry and EPA hazardous waste No.	Hazardous waste	Hazard code
Wood preservation: K001	Bottom sediment sludge from the treatment of wastewaters from wood preserving processes that use creosote and/or pentachlorophenol.	(T)

App. 5B-2

Industry and EPA hazardous waste No.	Hazardous waste	Hazard code
Inorganic pigments:		
K002	Wastewater treatment sludge from the production of chrome yellow and orange pigments.	(T)
K003	Wastewater treatment sludge from the production of molybdate orange pigments	(T)
K004	Wastewater treatment sludge from the production of zinc yellow pigments	(T)
K005	Wastewater treatment sludge from the production of chrome green pigments	(T)
K006	Wastewater treatment sludge from the production of chrome oxide green pigments (anhydrous and hydrated).	(T)
K007	Wastewater treatment sludge from the production of iron blue pigments	(T)
K008	Oven residue from the production of chrome oxide green pigments	(T)
Organic chemicals:		
K009	Distillation bottoms from the production of acetaldehyde from ethylene	(T)
K010	Distillation side cuts from the production of acetaldehyde from ethylene	(T)
K011	Bottom stream from the wastewater stripper in the production of acrylonitrile	(R, T)
K013	Bottom stream from the acetonitrile column in the production of acrylonitrile	(R, T)
K014	Bottoms from the acetonitrile purification column in the production of acrylonitrile	(T)
K015	Still bottoms from the distillation of benzyl chloride	(T)
K016	Heavy ends or distillation residues from the production of carbon tetrachloride	(T)
K017	Heavy ends (still bottoms) from the purification column in the production of epichlorohydrin.	(T)
K018	Heavy ends from the fractionation column in ethyl chloride production	(T)
K019	Heavy ends from the distillation of ethylene dichloride in ethylene dichloride production.	(T)
K020	Heavy ends from the distillation of vinyl chloride in vinyl chloride monomer production.	(T)
K021	Aqueous spent antimony catalyst waste from fluoromethanes production	(T)
K022	Distillation bottom tars from the production of phenol/acetone from cumene	(T)
K023	Distillation light ends from the production of phthalic anhydride from naphthalene	(T)
K024	Distillation bottoms from the production of phthalic anhydride from naphthalene	(T)
K093	Distillation light ends from the production of phthalic anhydride from ortho-xylene	(T)
K094	Distillation bottoms from the production of phthalic anhydride from ortho-xylene	(T)
K025	Distillation bottoms from the production of nitrobenzene by the nitration of benzene	(T)
K026	Stripping still tails from the production of methy ethyl pyridines	(T)
K027	Centrifuge and distillation residues from toluene diisocyanate production	(R, T)
K028	Spent catalyst from the hydrochlorinator reactor in the production of 1,1,1-trichloroethane.	(T)
K029	Waste from the product steam stripper in the production of 1,1,1-trichloroethane	(T)
K095	Distillation bottoms from the production of 1,1,1-trichloroethane	(T)
K096	Heavy ends from the heavy ends column from the production of 1,1,1-trichloroethane.	(T)
K030	Column bottoms or heavy ends from the combined production of trichloroethylene and perchloroethylene.	(T)
K083	Distillation bottoms from aniline production	(T)
K103	Process residues from aniline extraction from the production of aniline	(T)
K104	Combined wastewater streams generated from nitrobenzene/aniline production	(T)
K085	Distillation or fractionation column bottoms from the production of chlorobenzenes	(T)
K105	Separated aqueous stream from the reactor product washing step in the production of chlorobenzenes.	(T)
Inorganic chemicals:		
K071	Brine purification muds from the mercury cell process in chlorine production, where separately prepurified brine is not used.	(T)
K073	Chlorinated hydrocarbon waste from the purification step of the diaphragm cell process using graphite anodes in chlorine production.	(T)
K106	Wastewater treatment sludge from the mercury cell process in chlorine production	(T)
Pesticides:		
K031	By-product salts generated in the production of MSMA and cacodylic acid	(T)
K032	Wastewater treatment sludge from the production of chlordane	(T)
K033	Wastewater and scrub water from the chlorination of cyclopentadiene in the production of chlordane.	(T)
K034	Filter solids from the filtration of hexachlorocyclopentadiene in the production of chlordane.	(T)
K097	Vacuum stripper discharge from the chlordane chlorinator in the production of chlordane.	(T)
K035	Wastewater treatment sludges generated in the production of creosote	(T)
K036	Still bottoms from toluene reclamation distillation in the production of disulfoton	(T)
K037	Wastewater treatment sludges from the production of disulfoton	(T)
K038	Wastewater from the washing and stripping of phorate production	(T)
K039	Filter cake from the filtration of diethylphosphorodithioic acid in the production of phorate.	(T)
K040	Wastewater treatment sludge from the production of phorate	(T)
K041	Wastewater treatment sludge from the production of toxaphene	(T)
K098	Untreated process wastewater from the production of toxaphene	(T)

App. 5B-3

Industry and EPA hazardous waste No.	Hazardous waste	Hazard code
K042	Heavy ends or distillation residues from the distillation of tetrachlorobenzene in the production of 2,4,5-T.	(T)
K043	2,6-Dichlorophenol waste from the production of 2,4-D	(T)
K099	Untreated wastewater from the production of 2,4-D	(T)
Explosives:		
K044	Wastewater treatment sludges from the manufacturing and processing of explosives	(R)
K045	Spent carbon from the treatment of wastewater containing explosives	(R)
K046	Wastewater treatment sludges from the manufacturing, formulation and loading of lead-based initiating compounds.	(T)
K047	Pink/red water from TNT operations	(R)
Petroleum refining:		
K048	Dissolved air flotation (DAF) float from the petroleum refining industry	(T)
K049	Slop oil emulsion solids from the petroleum refining industry	(T)
K050	Heat exchanger bundle cleaning sludge from the petroleum refining industry	(T)
K051	API separator sludge from the petroleum refining industry	(T)
K052	Tank bottoms (leaded) from the petroleum refining industry	(T)
Iron and steel:		
K061	Emission control dust/sludge from the primary production of steel in electric furnaces.	(T)
K062	Spent pickle liquor from steel finishing operations	(C, T)
Secondary lead:		
K069	Emission control dust/sludge from secondary lead smelting	(T)
K100	Waste leaching solution from acid leaching of emission control dust/sludge from secondary lead smelting.	(T)
Veterinary pharmaceuticals:		
K084	Wastewater treatment sludges generated during the production of veterinary pharmaceuticals from arsenic or organo-arsenic compounds.	(T)
K101	Distillation tar residues from the distillation of aniline-based compounds in the production of veterinary pharmaceuticals from arsenic or organo-arsenic compounds.	(T)
K102	Residue from the use of activated carbon for decolorization in the production of veterinary pharmaceuticals from arsenic or organo-arsenic compounds.	(T)
Ink formulation: K086	Solvent washes and sludges, caustic washes and sludges, or water washes and sludges from cleaning tubs and equipment used in the formulation of ink from pigments, driers, soaps, and stabilizers containing chromium and lead.	(T)
Coking:		
K060	Ammonia still lime sludge from coking operations	(T)
K087	Decanter tank tar sludge from coking operations	(T)

[46 FR 4618, Jan. 16, 1981, as amended at 46 FR 27476-27477, May 20, 1981; 49 FR 37070, Sept. 21, 1984]

§ 261.33 Discarded commercial chemical products, off-specification species, container residues, and spill residues thereof.

The following materials or items are hazardous wastes when they are discarded or intended to be discarded as described in § 261.2(a)(2)(i), when they are burned for purposes of energy recovery in lieu of their original intended use, when they are used to produce fuels in lieu of their original intended use, when they are applied to the land in lieu of their original intended use, or when they are contained in products that are applied to the land in lieu of their original intended use.

(a) Any commercial chemical product, or manufacturing chemical intermediate having the generic name listed in paragraph (e) or (f) of this section.

(b) Any off-specification commercial chemical product or manufacturing chemical intermediate which, if it met specifications, would have the generic name listed in paragraph (e) or (f) of this section.

(c) Any container or inner liner removed from a container that has been used to hold any commercial chemical product or manufacturing chemical intermediate having the generic names listed in paragraph (e) of this section, or any container or inner liner removed from a container that has been used to hold any off-specification chemical product and manufacturing chemical intermediate which, if it met specifications, would have the generic name listed in paragraph (e) of this section, unless the container is empty as defined in § 261.7(b)(3) of this chapter.

[*Comment:* Unless the residue is being beneficially used or reused, or legitimately recycled or reclaimed; or being accumulated, stored, transported or treated prior to such use, re-use, recycling or reclamation, EPA considers the residue to be intended for discard, and thus a hazardous waste. An example of a legitimate re-use of the residue would be where the residue remains in the container and the container is used to hold the same commerical chemical product or manufacturing chemical intermediate it previously held. An example of the discard of the residue would be where the drum is sent to a drum reconditioner who reconditions the drum but discards the residue.]

(d) Any residue or contaminated soil, water or other debris resulting from the cleanup of a spill into or on any land or water of any commercial chemical product or manufacturing chemical intermediate having the generic name listed in paragraph (e) or (f) of this section, or any residue or contaminated soil, water or other debris resulting from the cleanup of a spill, into or on any land or water, of any off-specification chemical product and manufacturing chemical intermediate which, if it met specifications, would have the generic name listed in paragraph (e) or (f) of this section.

[*Comment:* The phrase "commercial chemical product or manufacturing chemical intermediate having the generic name listed in . . ." refers to a chemical substance which is manufactured or formulated for commercial or manufacturing use which consists of the commercially pure grade of the chemical, any technical grades of the chemical that are produced or marketed, and all formulations in which the chemical is the sole active ingredient. It does not refer to a material, such as a manufacturing process waste, that contains any of the substances listed in paragraphs (e) or (f). Where a manufacturing process waste is deemed to be a hazardous waste because it contains a substance listed in paragraphs (e) or (f), such waste will be listed in either §§ 261.31 or 261.32 or will be identified as a hazardous waste by the characteristics set forth in Subpart C of this part.]

(e) The commercial chemical products, manufacturing chemical intermediates or off-specification commercial chemical products or manufacturing chemical intermediates referred to in paragraphs (a) through (d) of this section, are identified as acute hazardous wastes (H) and are subject to be the small quantity exclusion defined in § 261.5(e).

[*Comment:* For the convenience of the regulated community the primary hazardous properties of these materials have been indicated by the letters T (Toxicity), and R (Reactivity). Absence of a letter indicates that the compound only is listed for acute toxicity.]

These wastes and their corresponding EPA Hazardous Waste Numbers are:

Hazardous waste No.	Substance
P023	Acetaldehyde, chloro-
P002	Acetamide, N-(aminothioxomethyl)-
P057	Acetamide, 2-fluoro-
P058	Acetic acid, fluoro-, sodium salt
P066	Acetimidic acid, N-[(methylcarbamoyl)oxy]thio-, methyl ester
P001	3-(alpha-Acetonylbenzyl)-4-hydroxycoumarin and salts, when present at concentrations greater than 0.3%
P002	1-Acetyl-2-thiourea
P003	Acrolein
P070	Aldicarb
P004	Aldrin
P005	Allyl alcohol
P006	Aluminum phosphide
P007	5-(Aminomethyl)-3-isoxazolol
P008	4-aAminopyridine
P009	Ammonium picrate (R)
P119	Ammonium vanadate
P010	Arsenic acid
P012	Arsenic (III) oxide
P011	Arsenic (V) oxide
P011	Arsenic pentoxide
P012	Arsenic trioxide
P038	Arsine, diethyl-
P054	Aziridine
P013	Barium cyanide
P024	Benzenamine, 4-chloro-
P077	Benzenamine, 4-nitro-
P028	Benzene, (chloromethyl)-
P042	1,2-Benzenediol, 4-[1-hydroxy-2-(methylamino)ethyl]-
P014	Benzenethiol
P028	Benzyl chloride
P015	Beryllium dust
P016	Bis(chloromethyl) ether
P017	Bromoacetone
P018	Brucine
P021	Calcium cyanide
P123	Camphene, octachloro-
P103	Carbamimidoselenoic acid
P022	Carbon bisulfide
P022	Carbon disulfide
P095	Carbonyl chloride
P033	Chlorine cyanide
P023	Chloroacetaldehyde
P024	p-Chloroaniline
P026	1-(o-Chlorophenyl)thiourea
P027	3-Chloropropionitrile
P029	Copper cyanides

Hazardous waste No.	Substance	Hazardous waste No.	Substance
P030	Cyanides (soluble cyanide salts), not elsewhere specified	P068	Methyl hydrazine
P031	Cyanogen	P064	Methyl isocyanate
P033	Cyanogen chloride	P069	2-Methyllactonitrile
P036	Dichlorophenylarsine	P071	Methyl parathion
P037	Dieldrin	P072	alpha-Naphthylthiourea
P038	Diethylarsine	P073	Nickel carbonyl
P039	O,O-Diethyl S-[2-(ethylthio)ethyl] phosphorodithioate	P074	Nickel cyanide
		P074	Nickel(II) cyanide
		P073	Nickel tetracarbonyl
P041	Diethyl-p-nitrophenyl phosphate	P075	Nicotine and salts
P040	O,O-Diethyl O-pyrazinyl phosphorothioate	P076	Nitric oxide
P043	Diisopropyl fluorophosphate	P077	p-Nitroaniline
P044	Dimethoate	P078	Nitrogen dioxide
P045	3,3-Dimethyl-1-(methylthio)-2-butanone, O-[(methylamino)carbonyl] oxime	P076	Nitrogen(II) oxide
		P078	Nitrogen(IV) oxide
P071	O,O-Dimethyl O-p-nitrophenyl phosphorothioate	P081	Nitroglycerine (R)
		P082	N-Nitrosodimethylamine
P082	Dimethylnitrosamine	P084	N-Nitrosomethylvinylamine
P046	alpha, alpha-Dimethylphenethylamine	P050	5-Norbornene-2,3-dimethanol, 1,4,5,6,7,7-hexachloro, cyclic sulfite
P047	4,6-Dinitro-o-cresol and salts		
P034	4,6-Dinitro-o-cyclohexylphenol	P085	Octamethylpyrophosphoramide
P048	2,4-Dinitrophenol	P087	Osmium oxide
P020	Dinoseb	P087	Osmium tetroxide
P085	Diphosphoramide, octamethyl-	P088	7-Oxabicyclo[2.2.1]heptane-2,3-dicarboxylic acid
P039	Disulfoton		
P049	2,4-Dithiobiuret	P089	Parathion
P109	Dithiopyrophosphoric acid, tetraethyl ester	P034	Phenol, 2-cyclohexyl-4,6-dinitro-
P050	Endosulfan	P048	Phenol, 2,4-dinitro-
P088	Endothall	P047	Phenol, 2,4-dinitro-6-methyl-
P051	Endrin	P020	Phenol, 2,4-dinitro-6-(1-methylpropyl)-
P042	Epinephrine	P009	Phenol, 2,4,6-trinitro-, ammonium salt (R)
P046	Ethanamine, 1,1-dimethyl-2-phenyl-	P036	Phenyl dichloroarsine
P084	Ethenamine, N-methyl-N-nitroso-	P092	Phenylmercuric acetate
P101	Ethyl cyanide	P093	N-Phenylthiourea
P054	Ethylenimine	P094	Phorate
P097	Famphur	P095	Phosgene
P056	Fluorine	P096	Phosphine
P057	Fluoroacetamide	P041	Phosphoric acid, diethyl p-nitrophenyl ester
P058	Fluoroacetic acid, sodium salt	P044	Phosphorodithioic acid, O,O-dimethyl S-[2-(methylamino)-2-oxoethyl]ester
P065	Fulminic acid, mercury(II) salt (R,T)		
P059	Heptachlor	P043	Phosphorofluoric acid, bis(1-methylethyl)-ester
P051	1,2,3,4,10,10-Hexachloro-6,7-epoxy-1,4,4a,5,6,7,8,8a-octahydro-endo,endo-1,4:5,8-dimethanonaphthalene		
		P094	Phosphorothioic acid, O,O-diethyl S-(ethylthio)methyl ester
P037	1,2,3,4,10,10-Hexachloro-6,7-epoxy-1,4,4a,5,6,7,8,8a-octahydro-endo,exo-1,4:5,8-demethanonaphthalene	P089	Phosphorothioci acid, O,O-diethyl O-(p-nitrophenyl) ester
		P040	Phosphorothioic acid, O,O-diethyl O- pyrazinyl ester
P060	1,2,3,4,10,10-Hexachloro-1,4,4a,5,8,8a-hexahydro-1,4:5,8-endo, endo-dimeth- anonaphthalene	P097	Phosphorothioic acid, O,O-dimethyl O-[p-((dimethylamino)-sulfonyl)phenyl]ester
P004	1,2,3,4,10,10-Hexachloro-1,4,4a,5,8,8a-hexahydro-1,4:5,8-endo,exo-dimethanonaphthalene	P110	Plumbane, tetraethyl-
		P098	Potassium cyanide
P060	Hexachlorohexahydro-exo,exo-dimethanonaphthalene	P099	Potassium silver cyanide
P062	Hexaethyl tetraphosphate	P070	Propanal, 2-methyl-2-(methylthio)-, O-[(methylamino)carbonyl]oxime
P116	Hydrazinecarbothioamide		
P068	Hydrazine, methyl-	P101	Propanenitrile
P063	Hydrocyanic acid	P027	Propanenitrile, 3-chloro-
P063	Hydrogen cyanide	P069	Propanenitrile, 2-hydroxy-2-methyl-
P096	Hydrogen phosphide	P081	1,2,3-Propanetriol, trinitrate- (R)
P064	Isocyanic acid, methyl ester	P017	2-Propanone, 1-bromo-
P007	3(2H)-Isoxazolone, 5-(aminomethyl)-	P102	Propargyl alcohol
P092	Mercury, (acetato-O)phenyl-	P003	2-Propenal
P065	Mercury fulminate (R,T)	P005	2-Propen-1-ol
P016	Methane, oxybis(chloro-	P067	1,2-Propylenimine
P112	Methane, tetranitro- (R)	P102	2-Propyn-1-ol
P118	Methanethiol, trichloro-	P008	4-Pyridinamine
P059	4,7-Methano-1H-indene, 1,4,5,6,7,8,8-heptachloro-3a,4,7,7a-tetrahydro-	P075	Pyridine, (S)-3-(1-methyl-2-pyrrolidinyl)-, and salts
		P111	Pyrophosphoric acid, tetraethyl ester
P066	Methomyl	P103	Selenourea
P067	2-Methylaziridine	P104	Silver cyanide
		P105	Sodium azide

App. 5B-6

Hazardous waste No.	Substance
P106	Sodium cyanide
P107	Strontium sulfide
P108	Strychnidin-10-one, and salts
P018	Strychnidin-10-one, 2,3-dimethoxy-
P108	Strychnine and salts
P115	Sulfuric acid, thallium(I) salt
P109	Tetraethyldithiopyrophosphate
P110	Tetraethyl lead
P111	Tetraethylpyrophosphate
P112	Tetranitromethane (R)
P062	Tetraphosphoric acid, hexaethyl ester
P113	Thallic oxide
P113	Thallium(III) oxide
P114	Thallium(I) selenite
P115	Thallium(I) sulfate
P045	Thiofanox
P049	Thioimidodicarbonic diamide
P014	Thiophenol
P116	Thiosemicarbazide
P026	Thiourea, (2-chlorophenyl)-
P072	Thiourea, 1-naphthalenyl-
P093	Thiourea, phenyl-
P123	Toxaphene
P118	Trichloromethanethiol
P119	Vanadic acid, ammonium salt
P120	Vanadium pentoxide
P120	Vanadium(V) oxide
P001	Warfarin, when present at concentrations greater than 0.3%
P121	Zinc cyanide
P122	Zinc phosphide (R,T)
P122	Zinc phosphide, when present at concentrations greater than 10%

(f) The commercial chemical products, manufacturing chemical intermediates, or off-specification commercial chemical products referred to in paragraphs (a) through (d) of this section, are identified as toxic wastes (T) unless otherwise designated and are subject to the small quantity exclusion defined in § 261.5 (a) and (f).

[Comment: For the convenience of the regulated community, the primary hazardous properties of these materials have been indicated by the letters T (Toxicity), R (Reactivity), I (Ignitability) and C (Corrosivity). Absence of a letter indicates that the compound is only listed for toxicity.]

These wastes and their corresponding EPA Hazardous Waste Numbers are:

Hazardous Waste No.	Substance
U001	Acetaldehyde (I)
U034	Acetaldehyde, trichloro-
U187	Acetamide, N-(4-ethoxyphenyl)-
U005	Acetamide, N-9H-fluoren-2-yl-
U112	Acetic acid, ethyl ester (I)
U144	Acetic acid, lead salt
U214	Acetic acid, thallium(I) salt

Hazardous Waste No.	Substance
U002	Acetone (I)
U003	Acetonitrile (I,T)
U248	3-(alpha-Acetonylbenzyl)-4-hydroxycoumarin and salts, when present at concentrations of 0.3% or less
U004	Acetophenone
U005	2-Acetylaminofluorene
U006	Acetyl chloride (C,R,T)
U007	Acrylamide
U008	Acrylic acid (I)
U009	Acrylonitrile
U150	Alanine, 3-[p-bis(2-chloroethyl)amino] phenyl-, L-
U011	Amitrole
U012	Aniline (I,T)
U014	Auramine
U015	Azaserine
U010	Azirino(2′,3′:3,4)pyrrolo(1,2-a)indole-4,7-dione, 6-amino-8-[((aminocarbonyl) oxy)methyl]-1,1a,2,8,8a,8b-hexahydro-8a-methoxy-5-methyl-,
U157	Benz[j]aceanthrylene, 1,2-dihydro-3-methyl-
U016	Benz[c]acridine
U016	3,4-Benzacridine
U017	Benzal chloride
U018	Benz[a]anthracene
U018	1,2-Benzanthracene
U094	1,2-Benzanthracene, 7,12-dimethyl-
U012	Benzenamine (I,T)
U014	Benzenamine, 4,4′-carbonimidoylbis(N,N-dimethyl-
U049	Benzenamine, 4-chloro-2-methyl-
U093	Benzenamine, N,N′-dimethyl-4-phenylazo-
U158	Benzenamine, 4,4′-methylenebis(2-chloro-
U222	Benzenamine, 2-methyl-, hydrochloride
U181	Benzenamine, 2-methyl-5-nitro
U019	Benzene (I,T)
U038	Benzeneacetic acid, 4-chloro-alpha-(4-chlorophenyl)-alpha-hydroxy, ethyl ester
U030	Benzene, 1-bromo-4-phenoxy-
U037	Benzene, chloro-
U190	1,2-Benzenedicarboxylic acid anhydride
U028	1,2-Benzenedicarboxylic acid, [bis(2-ethylhexyl)] ester
U069	1,2-Benzenedicarboxylic acid, dibutyl ester
U088	1,2-Benzenedicarboxylic acid, diethyl ester
U102	1,2-Benzenedicarboxylic acid, dimethyl ester
U107	1,2-Benzenedicarboxylic acid, di-n-octyl ester
U070	Benzene, 1,2-dichloro-
U071	Benzene, 1,3-dichloro-
U072	Benzene, 1,4-dichloro-
U017	Benzene, (dichloromethyl)-
U223	Benzene, 1,3-diisocyanatomethyl- (R,T)
U239	Benzene, dimethyl-(I,T)
U201	1,3-Benzenediol
U127	Benzene, hexachloro-
U056	Benzene, hexahydro- (I)
U188	Benzene, hydroxy-
U220	Benzene, methyl-
U105	Benzene, 1-methyl-1-2,4-dinitro-
U106	Benzene, 1-methyl-2,6-dinitro-
U203	Benzene, 1,2-methylenedioxy-4-allyl-
U141	Benzene, 1,2-methylenedioxy-4-propenyl-
U090	Benzene, 1,2-methylenedioxy-4-propyl-
U055	Benzene, (1-methylethyl)- (I)
U169	Benzene, nitro- (I,T)
U183	Benzene, pentachloro-
U185	Benzene, pentachloro-nitro-
U020	Benzenesulfonic acid chloride (C,R)
U020	Benzenesulfonyl chloride (C,R)
U207	Benzene, 1,2,4,5-tetrachloro-
U023	Benzene, (trichloromethyl)-(C,R,T)

Hazardous Waste No.	Substance
0234	Benzene, 1,3,5-trinitro- (R,T)
U021	Benzidine
U202	1,2-Benzisothiazolin-3-one, 1,1-dioxide
U120	Benzo[j,k]fluorene
U022	Benzo[a]pyrene
U022	3,4-Benzopyrene
U197	p-Benzoquinone
U023	Benzotrichloride (C,R,T)
U050	1,2-Benzphenanthrene
U085	2,2'-Bioxirane (I,T)
U021	(1,1'-Biphenyl)-4,4'-diamine
U073	(1,1'-Biphenyl)-4,4'-diamine, 3,3'-dichloro-
U091	(1,1'-Biphenyl)-4,4'-diamine, 3,3'-dimethoxy-
U095	(1,1'-Biphenyl)-4,4'-diamine, 3,3'-dimethyl-
U024	Bis(2-chloroethoxy) methane
U027	Bis(2-chloroisopropyl) ether
U244	Bis(dimethylthiocarbamoyl) disulfide
U028	Bis(2-ethylhexyl) phthalate
U246	Bromine cyanide
U225	Bromoform
U030	4-Bromophenyl phenyl ether
U128	1,3-Butadiene, 1,1,2,3,4,4-hexachloro-
U172	1-Butanamine, N-butyl-N-nitroso-
U035	Butanoic acid, 4-[Bis(2-chloroethyl)amino] benzene-
U031	1-Butanol (I)
U159	2-Butanone (I,T)
U160	2-Butanone peroxide (R,T)
U053	2-Butenal
U074	2-Butene, 1,4-dichloro- (I,T)
U031	n-Butyl alchohol (I)
U136	Cacodylic acid
U032	Calcium chromate
U238	Carbamic acid, ethyl ester
U178	Carbamic acid, methylnitroso-, ethyl ester
U176	Carbamide, N-ethyl-N-nitroso-
U177	Carbamide, N-methyl-N-nitroso-
U219	Carbamide, thio-
U097	Carbamoyl chloride, dimethyl-
U215	Carbonic acid, dithallium(I) salt
U156	Carbonochloridic acid, methyl ester (I,T)
U033	Carbon oxyfluoride (R,T)
U211	Carbon tetrachloride
U033	Carbonyl fluoride (R,T)
U034	Chloral
U035	Chlorambucil
U036	Chlordane, technical
U026	Chlornaphazine
U037	Chlorobenzene
U039	4-Chloro-m-cresol
U041	1-Chloro-2,3-epoxypropane
U042	2-Chloroethyl vinyl ether
U044	Chloroform
U046	Chloromethyl methyl ether
U047	beta-Chloronaphthalene
U048	o-Chlorophenol
U049	4-Chloro-o-toluidine, hydrochloride
U032	Chromic acid, calcium salt
U050	Chrysene
U051	Creosote
U052	Cresols
U052	Cresylic acid
U053	Crotonaldehyde
U055	Cumene (I)
U246	Cyanogen bromide
U197	1,4-Cyclohexadienedione
U056	Cyclohexane (I)
U057	Cyclohexanone (I)
U130	1,3-Cyclopentadiene, 1,2,3,4,5,5-hexa- chloro-
U058	Cyclophosphamide
U240	2,44-D, salts and esters
U059	Daunomycin

Hazardous Waste No.	Substance
U060	DDD
U061	DDT
U142	Decachlorooctahydro-1,3,4-metheno-2H-cyclobuta[c,d]-pentalen-2-one
U062	Diallate
U133	Diamine (R,T)
U221	Diaminotoluene
U063	Dibenz[a,h]anthracene
U063	1,2:5,6-Dibenzanthracene
U064	1,2:7,8-Dibenzopyrene
U064	Dibenz[a,i]pyrene
U066	1,2-Dibromo-3-chloropropane
U069	Dibutyl phthalate
U062	S-(2,3-Dichloroallyl) di sopropylthiocarbamate
U070	o-Dichloroben ene
U071	m-Dichlorobenzene
U072	p-Dichlorobenzene
U073	3,3'-Dichlorobenzidine
U074	1,4-Dichloro-2-butene (I,T)
U075	Dichlorodifluoromethane
U192	3,5-Dichloro-N-(1,1-dimethyl-2-propynyl) benzamide
U060	Dichloro diphenyl dichloroethane
U061	Dichloro diphenyl trichloroethane
U078	1,1-Dichloroethylene
U079	1,2-Dichloroethylene
U025	Dichloroethyl ether
U081	2,4-Dichlorophenol
U082	2,6-Dichlorophenol
U240	2,4-Dichlorophenoxyacetic acid, salts and esters
U083	1,2-Dichloropropane
U084	1,3-Dichloropropene
U085	1,2:3,4-Diepoxybutane (I,T)
U108	1,4-Diethylene dioxide
U086	N,N-Diethylhydrazine
U087	O,O-Diethyl-S-methyl-dithiophosphate
U088	Diethyl phthalate
U089	Diethylstilbestrol
U148	1,2-Dihydro-3,6-pyradizinedione
U090	Dihydrosafrole
U091	3,3'-Dimethoxybenzidine
U092	Dimethylamine (I)
U093	Dimethylaminoazobenzene
U094	7,12-Dimethylbenz[a]anthracene
U095	3,3'-Dimethylbenzidine
U096	alpha,alpha-Dimethylbenzylhydroperoxide (R)
U097	Dimethylcarbamoyl chloride
U098	1,1-Dimethylhydrazine
U099	1,2-Dimethylhydrazine
U101	2,4-Dimethylphenol
U102	Dimethyl phthalate
U103	Dimethyl sulfate
U105	2,4-Dinitrotoluene
U106	2,6-Dinitrotoluene
U107	Di-n-octyl phthalate
U108	1,4-Dioxane
U109	1,2- Diphenylhydrazine
U110	Dipropylamine (I)
U111	Di-N-propylnitrosamine
U001	Ethanal (I)
U174	Ethanamine, N-ethyl-N-nitroso-
U067	Ethane, 1,2-dibromo-
U076	Ethane, 1,1-dichloro-
U077	Ethane, 1,2-dichloro-
U114	1,2-Ethanediylbiscarbamodithioic acid
U131	Ethane, 1,1,1,2,2,2-hexachloro-
U024	Ethane, 1,1'-[methylenebis(oxy)]bis[2-chloro-
U003	Ethanenitrile (I, T)
U117	Ethane,1,1'-oxybis- (I)
U025	Ethane, 1,1'-oxybis[2-chloro-
U184	Ethane, pentachloro-

Hazardous Waste No.	Substance
U208	Ethane, 1,1,1,2-tetrachloro-
U209	Ethane, 1,1,2,2-tetrachloro-
U218	Ethanethioamide
U247	Ethane, 1,1,1,-trichloro-2,2-bis(p-methoxy-phenyl).
U227	Ethane, 1,1,2-trichloro-
U043	Ethene, chloro-
U042	Ethene, 2-chloroethoxy-
U078	Ethene, 1,1-dichloro-
U079	Ethene, trans-1,2-dichloro-
U210	Ethene, 1,1,2,2-tetrachloro-
U173	Ethanol, 2,2'-(nitrosoimino)bis-
U004	Ethanone, 1-phenyl-
U006	Ethanoyl chloride (C,R,T)
U112	Ethyl acetate (I)
U113	Ethyl acrylate (I)
U238	Ethyl carbamate (urethan)
U038	Ethyl 4,4'-dichlorobenzilate
U114	Ethylenebis(dithiocarbamic acid)
U067	Etylene dibromide
U077	Ethylene dichloride
U115	Ethlene oxide (I,T)
U116	Ethylene thiourea
U117	Ethyl ether (I)
U076	Ethylidene dichloride
U118	Ethylmethacrylate
U119	Ethyl methanesulfonate
U139	Ferric dextran
U120	Fluoranthene
U122	Formaldehyde
U123	Formic acid (C,T)
U124	Furan (I)
U125	2-Furancarboxaldehyde (I)
U147	2,5-Furandione
U213	Furan, tetrahydro- (I)
U125	Furfural (I)
U124	Furfuran (I)
U206	D-Glucopyranose, 2-deoxy-2(3-methyl-3-nitro-soureido)-
U126	Glycidylaldehyde
U163	Guanidine, N-nitroso-N-methyl-N'nitro-
U127	Hexachlorobenzene
U128	Hexachlorobutadiene
U129	Hexachlorocyclohexane (gamma isomer)
U130	Hexachlorocyclopentadiene
U131	Hexachloroethane
U132	Hexachlorophene
U243	Hexachloropropene
U133	Hydrazine (R,T)
U086	Hydrazine, 1,2-diethyl-
U098	Hydrazine, 1,1-dimethyl-
U099	Hydrazine, 1,2-dimethyl-
U109	Hydrazine, 1,2-diphenyl-
U134	Hydrofluoric acid (C,T)
U134	Hydrogen fluoride (C,T)
U135	Hydrogen sulfide
U096	Hydroperoxide, 1-methyl-1-phenylethyl- (R)
U136	Hydroxydimethylarsine oxide
U116	2-Imidazolidinethione
U137	Indeno[1,2,3-cd]pyrene
U139	Iron dextran
U140	Isobutyl alcohol (I,T)
U141	Isosafrole
U142	Kepone
U143	Lasiocarpine
U144	Lead acetate
U145	Lead phosphate
U146	Lead subacetate
U129	Lindane
U147	Maleic anhydride
U148	Maleic hydrazide
U149	Malononitrile

Hazardous Waste No.	Substance
U150	Melphalan
U151	Mercury
U152	Methacrylonitrile (I,T)
U092	Methanamine, N-methyl- (I)
U029	Methane, bromo-
U045	Methane, chloro- (I,T)
U046	Methane, chloromethoxy-
U068	Methane, dibromo-
U080	Methane, dichloro-
U075	Methane, dichlorodifluoro-
U138	Methane, iodo-
U119	Methanesulfonic acid, ethyl ester
U211	Methane, tetrachloro-
U121	Methane, trichlorofluoro-
U153	Methanethiol (I,T)
U225	Methane, tribromo-
U044	Methane, trichloro-
U121	Methane, trichlorofluoro-
U123	Methanoic acid (C,T)
U036	4,7-Methanoindan, 1,2,4,5,6,7,8,8-octa-chloro-3a,4,7,7a-tetrahydro-
U154	Methanol (I)
U155	Methapyrilene
U247	Methoxychlor.
U154	Methyl alcohol (I)
U029	Methyl bromide
U186	1-Methylbutadiene (I)
U045	Methyl chloride (I,T)
U156	Methyl chlorocarbonate (I,T)
U226	Methylchloroform
U157	3-Methylcholanthrene
U158	4,4'-Methylenebis(2-chloroaniline)
U132	2,2'-Methylenebis(3,4,6-trichlorophenol)
U068	Methylene bromide
U080	Methylene chloride
U122	Methylene oxide
U159	Methyl ethyl ketone (I,T)
U160	Methyl ethyl ketone peroxide (R,T)
U138	Methyl iodide
U161	Methyl isobutyl ketone (I)
U162	Methyl methacrylate (I,T)
U163	N-Methyl-N'-nitro-N-nitrosoguanidine
U161	4-Methyl-2-pentanone (I)
U164	Methylthiouracil
U010	Mitomycin C
U059	5,12-Naphthacenedione, (8S-cis)-8-acetyl-10-[(3-amino-2,3,6-trideoxy-alpha-L-lyxo-hexopyranosyl)oxyl]-7,8,9,10-tetrahydro-6,8,11-trihydroxy-1-methoxy-
U165	Naphthalene
U047	Naphthalene, 2-chloro-
U166	1,4-Naphthalenedione
U236	2,7-Naphthalenedisulfonic acid, 3,3'-[(3,3'-di-methyl-(1,1'-biphenyl)-4,4'diyl)]-bis (azo)bis(5-amino-4-hydroxy)-,tetrasodium salt
U166	1,4,Naphthaquinone
U167	1-Naphthylamine
U168	2-Naphthylamine
U167	alpha-Naphthylamine
U168	beta-Naphthylamine
U026	2-Naphthylamine, N,N'-bis(2-chloromethyl)-
U169	Nitrobenzene (I,T)
U170	p-Nitrophenol
U171	2-Nitropropane (I)
U172	N-Nitrosodi-n-butylamine
U173	N-Nitrosodiethanolamine
U174	N-Nitrosodiethylamine
U111	N-Nitroso-N-propylamine
U176	N-Nitroso-N-ethylurea
U177	N-Nitroso-N-methylurea
U178	N-Nitroso-N-methylurethane

Hazardous Waste No.	Substance
U179	N-Nitrosopiperidine
U180	N-Nitrosopyrrolidine
U181	5-Nitro-o-toluidine
U193	1,2-Oxathiolane, 2,2-dioxide
U058	2H-1,3,2-Oxazaphosphorine, 2-[bis(2-chloro-ethyl)amino]tetrahydro-, oxide 2-
U115	Oxirane (I,T)
U041	Oxirane, 2-(chloromethyl)-
U182	Paraldehyde
U183	Pentachlorobenzene
U184	Pentachloroethane
U185	Pentachloronitrobenzene
See F027	Pentachlorophenol
U186	1,3-Pentadiene (I)
U187	Phenacetin
U188	Phenol
U048	Phenol, 2-chloro-
U039	Phenol, 4-chloro-3-methyl-
U081	Phenol, 2,4-dichloro-
U082	Phenol, 2,6-dichloro-
U101	Phenol, 2,4-dimethyl-
U170	Phenol, 4-nitro-
See F027	Phenol, pentachloro-
Do	Phenol, 2,3,4,6-tetrachloro-
Do	Phenol, 2,4,5-trichloro-
Do	Phenol, 2,4,6-trichloro-
U137	1,10-(1,2-phenylene)pyrene
U145	Phosphoric acid, Lead salt
U087	Phosphorodithioic acid, O,O-diethyl-, S-methyl-lester
U189	Phosphorous sulfide (R)
U190	Phthalic anhydride
U191	2-Picoline
U192	Pronamide
U194	1-Propanamine (I,T)
U110	1-Propanamine, N-propyl- (I)
U066	Propane, 1,2-dibromo-3-chloro-
U149	Propanedinitrile
U171	Propane, 2-nitro- (I)
U027	Propane, 2,2'oxybis[2-chloro-
U193	1,3-Propane sultone
U235	1-Propanol, 2,3-dibromo-, phosphate (3:1)
U126	1-Propanol, 2,3-epoxy-
U140	1-Propanol, 2-methyl- (I,T)
U002	2-Propanone (I)
U007	2-Propenamide
U084	Propene, 1,3-dichloro-
U243	1-Propene, 1,1,2,3,3,3-hexachloro-
U009	2-Propenenitrile
U152	2-Propenenitrile, 2-methyl- (I,T)
U008	2-Propenoic acid (I)
U113	2-Propenoic acid, ethyl ester (I)
U118	2-Propenoic acid, 2-methyl-, ethyl ester
U162	2-Propenoic acid, 2-methyl-, methyl ester (I,T)
See F027	Propionic acid, 2-(2,4,5-trichlorophenoxy)-
U194	n-Propylamine (I,T)
U083	Propylene dichloride
U196	Pyridine
U155	Pyridine, 2-[(2-(dimethylamino)-2-thenyla-mino]-
U179	Pyridine, hexahydro-N-nitroso-
U191	Pyridine, 2-methyl-
U164	4(1H)-Pyrimidinone, 2,3-dihydro-6-methyl-2-thioxo-
U180	Pyrrole, tetrahydro-N-nitroso-
U200	Reserpine
U201	Resorcinol
U202	Saccharin and salts
U203	Safrole
U204	Selenious acid
U204	Selenium dioxide
U205	Selenium disulfide (R,T)

Hazardous Waste No.	Substance
U015	L-Serine, diazoacetate (ester)
See F027	Silvex
U089	4,4'-Stilbenediol, alpha,alpha'-diethyl-
U206	Streptozotocin
U135	Sulfur hydride
U103	Sulfuric acid, dimethyl ester
U189	Sulfur phosphide (R)
U205	Sulfur selenide (R,T)
See F027	2,4,5-T
U207	1,2,4,5-Tetrachlorobenzene
U208	1,1,1,2-Tetrachloroethane
U209	1,1,2,2-Tetrachloroethane
U210	Tetrachloroethylene
See F027	2,3,4,6-Tetrachlorophenol
U213	Tetrahydrofuran (I)
U214	Thallium(I) acetate
U215	Thallium(I) carbonate
U216	Thallium(I) chloride
U217	Thallium(I) nitrate
U218	Thioacetamide
U153	Thiomethanol (I,T)
U219	Thiourea
U244	Thiram
U220	Toluene
U221	Toluenediamine
U223	Toluene diisocyanate (R,T)
U222	O-Toluidine hydrochloride
U011	1H-1,2,4-Triazol-3-amine
U226	1,1,1-Trichloroethane
U227	1,1,2-Trichloroethane
U228	Trichloroethene
U228	Trichloroethylene
U121	Trichloromonofluoromethane
See F027	2,4,5-Trichlorophenol
Do	2,4,6-Trichlorophenol
Do	2,4,5-Trichlorophenoxyacetic acid
U234	sym-Trinitrobenzene (R,T)
U182	1,3,5-Trioxane, 2,4,5-trimethyl-
U235	Tris(2,3-dibromopropyl) phosphate
U236	Trypan blue
U237	Uracil, 5[bis(2-chloromethyl)amino]-
U237	Uracil mustard
U043	Vinyl chloride
U248	Warfarin, when present at concentrations of 0.3% or less
U239	Xylene (I)
U200	Yohimban-16-carboxylic acid, 11,17-dimeth-oxy-18-[(3,4,5-trimethoxy-benzoyl)oxy]-, methyl ester
U249	Zinc phosphide, when present at concentra-tions of 10% or less.

[45 FR 78529, 78541, Nov. 25, 1980, as amended at 46 FR 27477, May 20, 1981; 49 FR 19923, May 10, 1984; 49 FR 665, Jan. 4, 1985; 50 FR 2000, Jan. 14, 1985]

EFFECTIVE DATE NOTE: At 50 FR 665, Jan. 4, 1985, § 261.33 introductory text was revised, effective July 5, 1985. At 50 FR 2000, Jan. 14, 1985, the table in paragraph (f) was amended by revising certain hazardous waste numbers, effective July 15, 1985. For the convenience of the user, the superseded introductory text (published at 49 FR 37070, Sept. 21, 1984), and entries in the paragraph (f) table, are set out below:

§ 261.33 Discarded commercial chemical products, off-specification species, container residues and spill residues thereof.

The following materials or items are hazardous wastes if and when they are discarded or intended to be discarded unless they are excluded under §§ 260.20 and 260.22 and listed in Appendix IX.

*   *   *   *   *

(f) * * *

Hazardous waste No.	Substance
* * * * *	
U242	Pentachlorophenol.
* * * *	
U242	Phenol, pentachloro-.
U212	Phenol, 2,3,4,6-tetrachloro-.
U212	Phenol, 2,4,5-trichloro-.
U230	Phenol, 2,4,6-trichloro-.
* * * * *	
U231	Propionic acid, 2-(2,4,5-trichlorophenoxy)-.
* * * *	
U233	Silvex.
* * * *	
U232	2,4,5-T.
* * * *	
U212	2,3,4,6-Tetrachlorophenol.
* * * *	
U230	2,4,5-Trichlorophenol.
U231	2,4,6-Trichlorophenol.
U230	2,4,5-Trichlorophenoxyacetic acid.
* * * * *	

APPENDIX I—REPRESENTATIVE SAMPLING METHODS

The methods and equipment used for sampling waste materials will vary with the form and consistency of the waste materials to be sampled. Samples collected using the sampling protocols listed below, for sampling waste with properties similar to the indicated materials, will be considered by the Agency to be representative of the waste.

Extremely viscous liquid—ASTM Standard D140-70 Crushed or powdered material—ASTM Standard D346-75 Soil or rock-like material—ASTM Standard D420-69 Soil-like material—ASTM Standard D1452-65

Fly Ash-like material—ASTM Standard D2234-76 [ASTM Standards are available from ASTM, 1916 Race St., Philadelphia, PA 19103]

Containerized liquid wastes—"COLIWASA" described in "Test Methods for the Evaluation of Solid Waste, Physical/Chemical Methods," [a] U.S. Environmental Protection Agency, Office of Solid Waste, Washington, D.C. 20460. [Copies may be obtained from Solid Waste Information, U.S. Environmental Protection Agency, 26 W. St. Clair St., Cincinnati, Ohio 45268]

Liquid waste in pits, ponds, lagoons, and similar reservoirs.—"Pond Sampler" described in "Test Methods for the Evaluation of Solid Waste, Physical/Chemical Methods." [a]

This manual also contains additional information on application of these protocols.

APPENDIX II—EP TOXICITY TEST PROCEDURES

A. Extraction Procedure (EP)

1. A representative sample of the waste to be tested (minimum size 100 grams) shall be obtained using the methods specified in Appendix I or any other method capable of yielding a representative sample within the meaning of Part 260. [For detailed guidance on conducting the various aspects of the EP see "Test Methods for the Evaluation of Solid Waste, Physical/Chemical Methods" (incorporated by reference, see § 260.11).]

2. The sample shall be separated into its component liquid and solid phases using the method described in "Separation Procedure" below. If the solid residue [b] obtained using this method totals less than 0.5% of the original weight of the waste, the residue can be discarded and the operator shall treat the liquid phase as the extract and proceed immediately to Step 8.

3. The solid material obtained from the Separation Procedure shall be evaluated for its particle size. If the solid material has a surface area per gram of material equal to, or greater than, 3.1 cm^2 or passes through a 9.5 mm (0.375 inch) standard sieve, the operator shall proceed to Step 4. If the surface area is smaller or the particle size larger than specified above, the solid material shall be prepared for extraction by crushing, cutting or grinding the material so that

---

[a] These methods are also described in "Samplers and Sampling Procedures for Hazardous Waste Streams," EPA 600/2-80-018, January 1980.

[b] The percent solids is determined by drying the filter pad at 80°C until it reaches constant weight and then calculating the percent solids using the following equation:

Percent solids =

$$\frac{(\text{weight of pad} + \text{solid}) - (\text{tare weight of pad})}{\text{initial weight of sample}} \times 100$$

it passes through a 9.5 mm (0.375 inch) sieve or, if the material is in a single piece, by subjecting the material to the "Structural Integrity Procedure" described below.

4. The solid material obtained in Step 3 shall be weighed and placed in an extractor with 16 times its weight of deionized water. Do not allow the material to dry prior to weighing. For purposes of this test, an acceptable extractor is one which will impart sufficient agitation to the mixture to not only prevent stratification of the sample and extraction fluid but also insure that all sample surfaces are continuously brought into contact with well mixed extraction fluid.

5. After the solid material and deionized water are placed in the extractor, the operator shall begin agitation and measure the pH of the solution in the extractor. If the pH is greater than 5.0, the pH of the solution shall be decreased to 5.0 ± 0.2 by adding 0.5 N acetic acid. If the pH is equal to or less than 5.0, no acetic acid should be added. The pH of the solution shall be monitored, as described below, during the course of the extraction and if the pH rises above 5.2, 0.5N acetic acid shall be added to bring the pH down to 5.0 ± 0.2. However, in no event shall the aggregate amount of acid added to the solution exceed 4 ml of acid per gram of solid. The mixture shall be agitated for 24 hours and maintained at 20°-40°C (68°-104°F) during this time. It is recommended that the operator monitor and adjust the pH during the course of the extraction with a device such as the Type 45-A pH Controller manufactured by Chemtrix, Inc., Hillsboro, Oregon 97123 or its equivalent, in conjunction with a metering pump and reservoir of 0.5N acetic acid. If such a system is not available, the following manual procedure shall be employed:

(a) A pH meter shall be calibrated in accordance with the manufacturer's specifications.

(b) The pH of the solution shall be checked and, if necessary, 0.5N acetic acid shall be manually added to the extractor until the pH reaches 5.0 ± 0.2. The pH of the solution shall be adjusted at 15, 30 and 60 minute intervals, moving to the next longer interval if the pH does not have to be adjusted more than 0.5N pH units.

(c) The adjustment procedure shall be continued for at least 6 hours.

(d) If at the end of the 24-hour extraction period, the pH of the solution is not below 5.2 and the maximum amount of acid (4 ml per gram of solids) has not been added, the pH shall be adjusted to 5.0 ± 0.2 and the extraction continued for an additional four hours, during which the pH shall be adjusted at one hour intervals.

6. At the end of the 24 hour extraction period, deionized water shall be added to the extractor in an amount determined by the following equation:

$$V = (20)(W) - 16(W) - A$$

V = ml deionized water to be added

W = weight in grams of solid charged to extractor

A = ml of 0.5N acetic acid added during extraction

7. The material in the extractor shall be separated into its component liquid and solid phases as described under "Separation Procedure."

8. The liquids resulting from Steps 2 and 7 shall be combined. This combined liquid (or the waste itself if it has less than ½ percent solids, as noted in step 2) is the extract and shall be analyzed for the presence of any of the contaminants specified in Table I of § 261.24 using the Analytical Procedures designated below.

Separation Procedure

Equipment: A filter holder, designed for filtration media having a nominal pore size of 0.45 micrometers and capable of applying a 5.3 kg/cm² (75 psi) hydrostatic pressure to the solution being filtered, shall be used. For mixtures containing nonabsorptive solids, where separation can be effected without imposing a 5.3 kg/cm² pressure differential, vacuum filters employing a 0.45 micrometers filter media can be used. (For further guidance on filtration equipment or procedures see "Test Methods for Evaluating Solid Waste, Physical/Chemical Methods" incorporated by reference, see § 260.11). Procedure:[2]

(i) Following manufacturer's directions, the filter unit shall be assembled with a filter bed consisting of a 0.45 micrometer filter membrane. For difficult or slow to filter mixtures a prefilter bed consisting of the following prefilters in increasing pore size (0.65 micrometer membrane, fine glass

---

[2] This procedure is intended to result in separation of the "free" liquid portion of the waste from any solid matter having a particle size >0.45 μm. If the sample will not filter, various other separation techniques can be used to aid in the filtration. As described above, pressure filtration is employed to speed up the filtration process. This does not alter the nature of the separation. If liquid does not separate during filtration, the waste can be centrifuged. If separation occurs during centrifugation, the liquid portion (centrifugate) is filtered through the 0.45 μm filter prior to becoming mixed with the liquid portion of the waste obtained from the initial filtration. Any material that will not pass through the filter after centrifugation is considered a solid and is extracted.

fiber prefilter, and coarse glass fiber prefilter) can be used.

(ii) The waste shall be poured into the filtration unit.

(iii) The reservoir shall be slowly pressurized until liquid begins to flow from the filtrate outlet at which point the pressure in the filter shall be immediately lowered to 10-15 psig. Filtration shall be continued until liquid flow ceases.

(iv) The pressure shall be increased stepwise in 10 psi increments to 75 psig and filtration continued until flow ceases or the pressurizing gas begins to exit from the filtrate outlet.

(v) The filter unit shall be depressurized, the solid material removed and weighed and then transferred to the extraction apparatus, or, in the case of final filtration prior to analysis, discarded. Do not allow the material retained on the filter pad to dry prior to weighing.

(vi) The liquid phase shall be stored at 4°C for subsequent use in Step 8.

B. Structural Integrity Procedure

Equipment: A Structural Integrity Tester having a 3.18 cm (1.25 in.) diameter hammer weighing 0.33 kg (0.73 lbs.) and having a free fall of 15.24 cm (6 in.) shall be used. This device is available from Associated Design and Manufacturing Company, Alexandria, VA 22314, as Part No. 125, or it may be fabricated to meet the specifications shown in Figure 1.

Procedure

1. The sample holder shall be filled with the material to be tested. If the sample of waste is a large monolithic block, a portion shall be cut from the block having the dimensions of a 3.3 cm (1.3 in.) diameter x 7.1 cm (2.8 in.) cylinder. For a fixated waste, samples may be cast in the form of a 3.3 cm (1.3 in.) diameter x 7.1 cm (2.8 in.) cylinder for purposes of conducting this test. In such cases, the waste may be allowed to cure for 30 days prior to further testing.

2. The sample holder shall be placed into the Structural Integrity Tester, then the hammer shall be raised to its maximum height and dropped. This shall be repeated fifteen times.

3. The material shall be removed from the sample holder, weighed, and transferred to the extraction apparatus for extraction.

Analytical Procedures for Analyzing Extract Contaminants

The test methods for analyzing the extract are as follows:

1. For arsenic, barium, cadmium, chromium, lead, mercury, selenium, silver, endrin, lindane, methoxychlor, toxaphene, 2,4-D[2,4-dichlorophenoxyacetic acid] or 2,4,5-TP [2,4,5-trichlorophenoxypropionic acid]: "Test Methods for the Evaluation of Solid Waste, Physical/Chemical Methods" (incorporated by reference, see § 260.11).

2. [Reserved]

For all analyses, the methods of standard addition shall be used for quantification of species concentration.

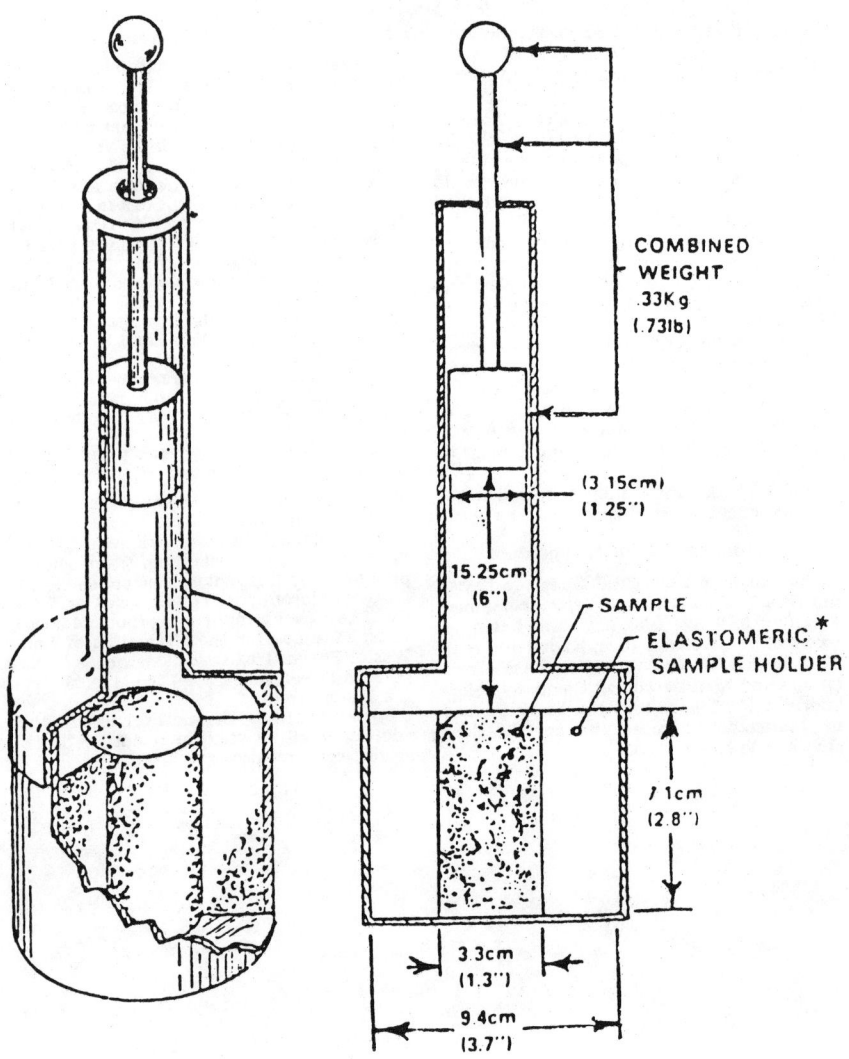

COMBINED
WEIGHT
.33Kg
(.73lb)

(3.15cm)
(1.25")

15.25cm
(6")

SAMPLE

ELASTOMERIC *
SAMPLE HOLDER

7.1cm
(2.8")

3.3cm
(1.3")

9.4cm
(3.7")

*ELASTOMERIC SAMPLE HOLDER FABRICATED OF
MATERIAL FIRM ENOUGH TO SUPPORT THE SAMPLE

Figure 1
COMPACTION TESTER

[45 FR 33119, May 19, 1980, as amended at 46 FR 35247, July 7, 1981]

Appendix III—Chemical Analysis Test Methods

Tables 1, 2, and 3 specify the appropriate analytical procedures, described in "Test Methods for Evaluating Solid Waste, Physical/Chemical Methods," (incorporated by reference, see § 260.11) which shall be used to determine whether a sample contains a given Appendix VII or VIII toxic constituent.

Table 1 identifies each Appendix VII or VIII organic constituent along with the approved measurement method. Table 2 identifies the corresponding methods for inorganic species. Table 3 summarizes the contents of SW-846 and supplies specific section and method numbers for sampling and analysis methods.

Prior to final sampling and analysis method selection the analyst should consult the specific section or method described in SW-846 for additional guidance on which of the approved methods should be employed for a specific sample analysis situation.

Table 1—Analysis Methods for Organic Chemicals Contained in SW-846

Compound	First edition method(s)	Second edition method(s)
Acetonitrile	8.03, 8.24	8030, 8240
Acrolein	8.03, 8.24	8030, 8240
Acrylamide	8.01, 8.24	8015, 8240
Acrylonitrile	8.03, 8.24	8030, 8240
Benzene	8.02, 8.24	8020, 8024
Benz(a)anthracene	8.10, 8.25	8100, 8250, 8310
Benzo(a)pyrene	8.10, 8.25	8100, 8250, 8310
Benzotrichloride	8.12, 8.25	8120, 8250
Benzyl chloride	8.01, 8.12, 8.24, 8.25	8120, 8250
Benzo(b)fluoanthene	8.10, 8.25	8100, 8250, 8310
Bis(2-chloroethoxymethane)	8.01, 8.24	8010, 8240
Bis(2-chloroethyl)ether	8.01, 8.24	8010, 8240
Bis(2-chloroisopropyl)ether	8.01, 8.24	8010, 8240
Carbon disulfide	8.01, 8.24	8015, 8240
Carbon tetrachloride	8.01, 8.24	8010, 8240
Chlordane	8.08, 8.25	8080, 8250
Chlorinated biphenyls	8.08, 8.25	8080, 8250
Chlorinated dibenzo-p-dioxins		8280
Chlorinated dibenzofurans		8280
Chloroacetaldehyde	8.01, 8.24	8010, 8240
Chlorobenzene	8.01, 8.02, 8.24	8020, 8240
Chloroform	8.01, 8.24	8010, 8240
Chloromethane	8.01, 8.24	8010, 8240
2-Chlorophenol	8.04, 8.25	8040, 8250
Chrysene	8.10, 8.25	8100, 8250, 8310
Creosote [1]	8.10, 8.25	8100, 8250
Cresol(s)	8.04, 8.25	8040, 8250
Cresylic Acid(s)	8.04, 8.25	8040, 8250

Table 1—Analysis Methods for Organic Chemicals Contained in SW-846—Continued

Compound	First edition method(s)	Second edition method(s)
Dichlorobenzene(s)	8.01, 8.02, 8.12, 8.25	8010, 8120, 8250
Dichloroethane(s)	8.01, 8.24	8010, 8240
Dichloromethane	8.01, 8.24	8010, 8240
Dichlorophenoxyacetic acid	8.40, 8.25	8150, 8250
Dichloropropanol	8.12, 8.25	8120, 8250
2,4-Dimethylphenol	8.04, 8.25	8040, 8250
Dinitrobenzene	8.09, 8.25	8090, 8250
4,6-Dinitro-o-cresol	8.04, 8.25	8040, 8250
2,4-Dinitrotoluene	8.09, 8.25	8090, 8250
Endrin	8.08, 8.25	8080, 8250
Ethyl ether	8.01, 8.02, 8.24	8015, 8240
Formaldehyde	8.01, 8.24	8015, 8240
Formic acid	8.06, 8.25	8250
Heptachlor	8.06, 8.25	8080, 8250
Hexachlorobenzene	8.12, 8.25	8120, 8250
Hexachlorobutadiene	8.12, 8.25	8120, 8250
Hexachloroethane	8.12, 8.25	8010, 8240
Hexachlorocyclopentadiene	8.12, 8.25	8120, 8250
Lindane	8.08, 8.25	8080, 8250
Maleic anhydride	8.06, 8.25	8250
Methanol	8.01, 8.24	8010, 8240
Methomyl	8.32	8250
Methyl ethyl ketone	8.01, 8.02, 8.24	8015, 8240
Methyl isobutyl ketone	8.01, 8.02, 8.24	8015, 8240
Napthalene	8.10, 8.25	8100, 8250
Napthoquinone	8.06, 8.09, 8.25	8090, 8250
Nitrobenzene	8.09, 8.25	8090, 8250
4-Nitrophenol	8.04, 8.25	8040, 8240
Paraldehyde (trimer of acetaldehyde)	8.01, 8.24	8015, 8240
Pentachlorophenol	8.04, 8.25	8040, 8250
Phenol	8.04, 8.25	8040, 8250
Phorate	8.22	8140
Phosphorodithioic acid esters	8.06, 8.09, 8.22	8140
Phthalic anhydride	8.06, 8.09, 8.25	8090, 8250
2-Picoline	8.06, 8.09, 8.25	8090, 8250
Pyridine	8.06, 8.09, 8.25	8090, 8250
Tetrachlorobenzene(s)	8.12, 8.25	8120, 8250
Tetrachloroethane(s)	8.01, 8.24	8010, 8240
Tetrachloroethene	8.01, 8.24	8010, 8240
Tetrachlorophenol	8.04, 8.24	8040, 8250
Toluene	8.02, 8.24	8020, 8024
Toluenediamine	8.25	8250
Toluene diisocyanate(s)	8.06, 8.25	8250
Toxaphene	8.08, 8.25	8080, 8250
Trichloroethane	8.01, 8.24	8010, 8240
Trichloroethene(s)	8.01, 8.24	8010, 8240
Trichlorofluoromethane	8.01, 8.24	8010, 8240
Trichlorophenol(s)	8.04, 8.25	8040, 8250
2,4,5-Trichlorophenoxy propionic acid	8.40, 8.25	8150, 8250
Trichloropropane	8.01, 8.24	8010, 8240
Vinyl chloride	8.01, 8.24	8010, 8240
Vinylidene chloride	8.01, 8.24	8010, 8240
Xylene	8.02, 8.24	8020, 8240

CHEMICAL REGULATION & HAZARDOUS WASTE

[1] Analyne for phenanthrene and carbazole; if these are present in a ratio between 1.4:1 and 5:1 creosote should be considered present.

TABLE 2—ANALYSIS METHODS FOR INORGANIC CHEMICALS CONTAINED IN SW-846

Compound	First edition method(s)	Second edition method(s)
Antimony	8.50	7040, 7041
Arsenic	8.51	7060, 7061
Barium	8.52	7080, 7081
Cadmium	8.53	7090, 7091
Chromium	8.54	7190, 7191
Chromium: Hexavalent	8.545, 8.546,	7195, 7196,

TABLE 2—ANALYSIS METHODS FOR INORGANIC CHEMICALS CONTAINED IN SW-846—Continued

Compound	First edition method(s)	Second edition method(s)
Lead	8.547 8.56	7197 7420, 7421
Mercury	8.57	7470, 7471
Nickel	8.58	7520, 7521
Selenium	8.59	7740, 7741
Silver	8.60	7760, 7761
Cyanides	8.55	9010
Total Organic Halogen	8.66	9020
Sulfides	8.67	9030

TABLE 3—SAMPLING AND ANALYSIS METHODS CONTAINED IN SW-846

Title	First edition Section No.	First edition Method No.	Second edition Section No.	Second edition Method No.
Sampling of Solid Wastes	1.0		1.0	
Development of Appropriate Sampling Plans	1.0		1.1	
Regulatory and Scientific Objectives	1.0-2		1.1.1	
Fundamental Statistical Concepts	1.0-3		1.1.2	
Basic Statistical Strategies	1.0-7		1.1.3	
Simple Random Sampling			1.1.3.1	
Stratified Random Sampling			1.1.3.2	
Systematic Random Sampling			1.1.3.3	
Special Considerations	1.0-7			
Composite Sampling			1.1.4.1	
Subsampling			1.1.4.2	
Cost and Loss Functions			1.1.4.3	
Implementation of Sampling Plan	1.0-7		1.2	
Selection of Sampling Equipment			1.2.1	
Composite Liquid Waste Sampler	3.2.1		1.2.1.1	
Weighted Bottle	3.2.2		1.2.1.2	
Dipper	3.2.3		1.2.1.3	
Thief	3.2.4		1.2.1.4	
Trier	3.2.5		1.2.1.5	
Auger	3.2.6		1.2.1.6	
Scoop and Shovel	3.2.7		1.2.1.7	
Selection of Sample Containers	3.3		1.2.2	
Processing and Storage of Samples	3.3		1.2.3	
Documentation of Chain of Custody	2.0		1.3	
Sample Labels	2.0-1		1.3.1	
Sample Seals	2.0-3		1.3.2	
Field Log Book	2.0-5		1.3.3	
Chain-of-Custody Record	2.0-6		1.3.4	
Sample Analysis Request Sheet	2.0-9		1.3.5	
Sample Delivery to Laboratory	2.0-10		1.3.6	
Shipping of Samples	2.0-10		1.3.7	
Receipt and Logging of Sample	2.0-12		1.3.8	
Assignment of Sample for Analysis	2.0-13		1.3.9	
Sampling Methodology	3.0		1.4	
Containers	3.2-2		1.4.1	
Tanks	3.2-2		1.4.2	
Waste Piles	3.2-2		1.4.3	
Landfills and Lagoons	3.2-2		1.4.4	
Waste Evaluation Procedures			2.0	
Characteristics of Hazardous Waste			2.1	
Ignitability	4.0		2.1.1	
Pensky-Martens Closed-Cup Method	4.1		2.1.1	1010
Setaflash Closed-Cup Method	4.1		2.1.1	1020
Corrosivity	5.0		2.1.2	
Corrosivity Toward Steel	5.3		2.1.2	1110
Reactivity	6.0		2.1.3	
Extraction Procedure Toxicity	7.0		2.1.4	

App. 5B-16

TABLE 3—SAMPLING AND ANALYSIS METHODS CONTAINED IN SW-846—Continued

Title	First edition		Second edition	
	Section No.	Method No.	Section No.	Method No.
Extraction Procedure Toxicity Test	7.1, 7.2, 7.5			
Method and Structural Integrity Test	7.4		2.1.4	1310
Sample Workup Techniques			4.0	
Inorganic Techniques	8.49		4.1	
Acid Digestion for Flame AAS	ı		4.1	3010
Acid Digestion for Furnace AAS	ı		4.1	3020
Acid Digestion of Oil, Grease, or Wax	8.49-9		4.1	3030
Dissolution Procedure for Oil, Grease or Wax	8.49-8		4.1	
Alkaline Digestion	8.0	8.458	4.1	3060
Organic Techniques	8.0		4.2	
Separatory Funnel Liquid-Liquid Extraction	9.0	9.1	4.2	3510
Continuous Liquid-Liquid Extraction	9.0	9.01	4.2	3520
Acid-Base Cleanup Extraction	8.0	8.84	4.2	3530
Soxhlet Extraction	8.0	8.86	4.2	3540
Sonication Extraction	8.0	8.85	4.2	3550
Sample Introduction Techniques			5.0	
Headspace	8.0	8.82	5.0	5020
Purge-and-Trap	8.0	8.83	5.0	5030
Inorganic Analytical Methods	8.0		7.0	
Antimony, Flame AAS	8.0	8.50	7.0	7470
Antimony, Furnace AAS	8.0	8.50	7.0	7471
Arsenic, Flame AAS	8.0	8.51	7.0	7060
Arsenic, Furnace AAS	8.0	8.51	7.0	7061
Barium, Flame AAS	8.0	8.52	7.0	7080
Barium, Furnace AAS	8.0	8.52	7.0	7081
Cadmium, Flame AAS	8.0	8.53	7.0	7130
Cadmium, Furnace AAS	8.0	8.53	7.0	7131
Chromium, Flame AAS	8.0	8.54	7.0	7090
Chromium, Furnace AAS	8.0	8.54	7.0	7191
Chromium, Hexavalent, Coprecipitation	8.0	8.545	7.0	7195
Chromium, Hexavalent, Colorimetric	8.0	8.546	7.0	7196
Chromium, Hexavalent, Chelation	8.0	8.547	7.0	7197
Lead, Flame AAS	8.0	8.56	7.0	7420
Lead, Furnace AAS	8.0	8.56	7.0	7421
Mercury, Cold Vapor, Liquid	8.0	8.57	7.0	7470
Mercury, Cold Vapor, Solid	8.0	8.57	7.0	7471
Nickel, Flame AAS	8.0	8.58	7.0	7520
Nickel, Furnace AAS	8.0	8.58	7.0	7521
Selenium, Flame AAS	8.0	8.59	7.0	7740
Selenium, Gaseous Hydride AAS	8.0	8.59	7.0	7741
Silver, Flame AAS	8.0	8.60	7.0	7760
Silver, Furnace AAS	8.0	8.60	7.0	7761
Organic Analytical Methods	8.0		8.0	
Gas Chromatographic Methods	8.0		8.1	
Halogenated Volatile Organics	8.0	8.01	8.1	8010
Nonhalogenated Volatile Organics	8.0	8.01	8.1	8015
Aromatic Volatile Organics	8.0	8.02	8.1	8020
Acrolein, Acrylonitrile, Acetonitrile	8.0	8.03	8.1	8030
Phenols	8.0	8.04	8.1	8040
Phthalate Esters	8.0	8.06	8.1	8060
Organochlorine Pesticides and PCBs	8.0	8.08	8.1	8080
Nitroaromatics and Cyclic Ketones	8.0	8.09	8.1	8090
Polynuclear Aromatic Hydrocarbons	8.0	8.10	8.1	8100
Chlorinated Hydrocarbons	8.0	8.12	8.1	8120
Organophosphorus Pesticides	8.0	8.22	8.1	8140
Chlorinated Herbicides	8.0	8.40	8.1	8150
Gas Chromatographic/Mass Spectroscopy Methods (GC/MS)	8.0		8.2	
GC/MS Volatiles	8.0	8.24	8.2	8240
GC/MS Semi-Volatiles, Packed Column	8.0	8.25	8.2	8250
GC/MS Semi-Volatiles, Capillary	8.0	8.27	8.2	8270
Analysis of Chlorinated Dioxins and Dibenzofurans			8.2	8280
High Performance Liquid Chromatographic Methods (HPLC)	8.0		8.3	
Polynuclear Aromatic Hydrocarbons	8.0	8.10	8.3	8310
Miscellaneous Analytical Methods	8.0		9.0	
Cyanide, Total and Amenable to Chlorination	8.0	8.55	9.0	9010
Total Organic Halogen (TOX)	8.0	8.66	9.0	9020
Sulfides	8.0	8.67	9.0	9030
pH Measurement	5.0	5.2	9.0	9040

TABLE 3—SAMPLING AND ANALYSIS METHODS CONTAINED IN SW–846—Continued

Title	First edition		Second edition	
	Section No.	Method No.	Section No.	Method No.
Quality Control/Quality Assurance	10.0		10.1	
Introduction	10.0		10.1	
Program Design	10.0		10.2	
Sampling	10.0		10.3	
Analysis	10.0		10.4	
Data Handling	10.0		10.5	

¹See specific metal.

[48 FR 15257, Apr. 8, 1983, as amended at 50 FR 2000, Jan. 14, 1985]

EFFECTIVE DATE NOTE: At 50 FR 2000, Jan. 14, 1985, Part 261, App. III was amended as follows: In Table 1, the entry for "Chlorinated dibenzodioxins" was removed, and the entries for "Chlorinated dibenzo-p-dioxins," and "Chlorinated dibenzofurans" were added. In Table 3, the entry for "Analysis of Chlorinated Dioxins and Dibenzofurans" was added under "Organic Analytical Methods—Gas Chromatographic/Mass Spectroscopy Methods (GC/MS)" after the entry "GC/MS Semi-Volatiles, Capillary". These amendments are effective July 15, 1985. For the convenience of the user, the superseded entry from Table 1 is set out below:

TABLE 1—ANALYTICAL METHODS FOR ORGANIC CHEMICALS CONTAINED IN SW–846

Compound	First edition method(s)	Second edition method(s)
· · · · ·		
Chlorinated dibenzodioxins	8.08, 8.25	8080, 8250
· · · · ·		

APPENDIX IV—[RESERVED FOR RADIOACTIVE WASTE TEST METHODS]

APPENDIX V—[RESERVED FOR INFECTIOUS WASTE TREATMENT SPECIFICATIONS]

APPENDIX VI—[RESERVED FOR ETIOLOGIC AGENTS]

APPENDIX VII—BASIS FOR LISTING HAZARDOUS WASTE

EPA hazardous waste No.	Hazardous constituents for which listed
F001	Tetrachloroethylene, methylene chloride trichloroethylene, 1,1,1-trichloroethane, carbon tetrachloride, chlorinated fluorocarbons.
F002	Tetrachloroethylene, methylene chloride, trichloroethylene, 1,1,1-trichloroethane, chlorobenzene, 1,1,2-trichloro-1,2,2-trifluoroethane, ortho-dichlorobenzene, trichlorofluoromethane.
F003	N.A.
F004	Cresols and cresylic acid, nitrobenzene.
F005	Toluene, methyl ethyl ketone, carbon disulfide, isobutanol, pyridine.
F006	Cadmium, hexavalent chromium, nickel, cyanide (complexed).
F007	Cyanide (salts).
F008	Cyanide (salts).
F009	Cyanide (salts).
F010	Cyanide (salts).
F011	Cyanide (salts).
F012	Cyanide (complexed).
F019	Hexavalent chromium, cyanide (complexed).
F020	Tetra- and pentachlorodibenzo-p-dioxins; tetra and pentachlorodi-benzofurans; tri- and tetrachlorophenols and their chlorophenoxy derivative acids, esters, ethers, amine and other salts.
F021	Penta- and hexachlorodibenzo-p-dioxins; penta- and hexachlorodibenzofurans; pentachlorophenol and its derivatives.
F022	Tetra-, penta-, and hexachlorodibenzo-p-dioxins; tetra-, penta-, and hexachlorodibenzofurans.
F023	Tetra-, and pentachlorodibenzo-p-dioxins; tetra- and pentachlorodibenzofurans; tri- and tetrachlorophenols and their chlorophenoxy derivative acids, esters, ethers, amine and other salts.

EPA hazardous waste No.	Hazardous constituents for which listed
F024	Chloromethane, dichloromethane, trichloromethane, carbon tetrachloride, chloroethylene, 1,1-dichloroethane, 1,2-dichloroethane, trans-1-2-dichloroethylene, 1,1-dichloroethylene, 1,1,1-trichloroethane, 1,1,2-trichloroethane, trichloroethylene, 1,1,1,2-tetra-chloroethane, 1,1,2,2-tetrachloroethane, tetrachloroethylene, pentachloroethane, hexachloroethane, allyl chloride (3-chloropropene), dichloropropane, dichloropropene, 2-chloro-1,3-butadiene, hexachloro-1,3-butadiene, hexachlorocyclopentadiene, hexachlorocyclohexane, benzene, chlorbenzene, dichlorobenzenes, 1,2,4-trichlorobenzene, tetrachlorobenzene, pentachlorobenzene, hexachlorobenzene, toluene, naphthalene.
F026	Tetra-, penta-, and hexachlorodibenzo-*p*-dioxins; tetra-, penta-, and hexachlorodibenzofurans.
F027	Tetra-, penta-, and hexachlorodibenzo-*p*-dioxins; tetra-, penta-, and hexachlorodibenzofurans; tri-, tetra-, and pentachlorophenols and their chlorophenoxy derivative acids, esters, ethers, amine and other salts.
F028	Tetra-, penta-, and hexachlorodibenzo-*p*-dioxins; tetra-, penta-, and hexachlorodibenzofurans; tri-, tetra-, and pentachlorophenols and their chlorophenoxy derivative acids, esters, ethers, amine and other salts.
K001	Pentachlorophenol, phenol, 2-chlorophenol, p-chloro-m-cresol, 2,4-dimethylphenyl, 2,4-dinitrophenol, trichlorophenols, tetrachlorophenols, 2,4-dinitrophenol, cresosote, chrysene, naphthalene, fluoranthene, benzo(b)fluoranthene, benzo(a)pyrene, indeno(1,2,3-cd)pyrene, benz(a)anthracene, dibenz(a)anthracene, acenaphthalene.
K002	Hexavalent chromium, lead
K003	Hexavalent chromium, lead.
K004	Hexavalent chromium.
K005	Hexavalent chromium, lead.
K006	Hexavalent chromium.
K007	Cyanide (complexed), hexavalent chromium.
K008	Hexavalent chromium.
K009	Chloroform, formaldehyde, methylene chloride, methyl chloride, paraldehyde, formic acid.
K010	Chloroform, formaldehyde, methylene chloride, methyl chloride, paraldehyde, formic acid, chloroacetaldehyde.
K011	Acrylonitrile, acetonitrile, hydrocyanic acid.
K013	Hydrocyanic acid, acrylonitrile, acetonitrile.
K014	Acetonitrile, acrylamide.
K015	Benzyl chloride, chlorobenzene, toluene, benzotrichloride.
K016	Hexachlorobenzene, hexachlorobutadiene, carbon tetrachloride, hexachloroethane, perchloroethylene.
K017	Epichlorohydrin, chloroethers [bis(chloromethyl) ether and bis (2-chloroethyl) ethers], trichloropropane, dichloropropanols.
K018	1,2-dichloroethane, trichloroethylene, hexachlorobutadiene, hexachlorobenzene.
K019	Ethylene dichloride, 1,1,1-trichloroethane, 1,1,2-trichloroethane, tetrachloroethanes (1,1,2,2-tetrachloroethane and 1,1,1,2-tetrachloroethane), trichloroethylene, tetrachloroethylene, carbon tetrachloride, chloroform, vinyl chloride, vinylidene chloride.

EPA hazardous waste No.	Hazardous constituents for which listed
K020	Ethylene dichloride, 1,1,1-trichloroethane, 1,1,2-trichloroethane, tetrachloroethanes (1,1,2,2-tetrachloroethane and 1,1,1,2-tetrachloroethane), trichloroethylene, tetrachloroethylene, carbon tetrachloride, chloroform, vinyl chloride, vinylidene chloride.
K021	Antimony, carbon tetrachloride, chloroform.
K022	Phenol, tars (polycyclic aromatic hydrocarbons).
K023	Phthalic anhydride, maleic anhydride.
K024	Phthalic anhydride, 1,4-naphthoquinone.
K025	Meta-dinitrobenzene, 2,4-dinitrotoluene.
K026	Paraldehyde, pyridines, 2-picoline.
K027	Toluene diisocyanate, toluene-2, 4-diamine.
K028	1,1,1-trichloroethane, vinyl chloride.
K029	1,2-dichloroethane, 1,1,1-trichloroethane, vinyl chloride, vinylidene chloride, chloroform.
K030	Hexachlorobenzene, hexachlorobutadiene, hexachloroethane, 1,1,1,2-tetrachloroethane, 1,1,2,2-tetrachloroethane, ethylene dichloride.
K031	Arsenic.
K032	Hexachlorocyclopentadiene.
K033	Hexachlorocyclopentadiene.
K034	Hexachlorocyclopentadiene.
K035	Creosote, chrysene, naphthalene, fluoranthene benzo(b) fluoranthene, benzo(a)pyrone, indeno(1,2,3-cd) pyrene, benzo(a)anthracene, dibenzo(a)anthracene, acenaphthalene.
K036	Toluene, phosphorodithioic and phosphorothioic acid esters.
K037	Toluene, phosphorodithioic and phosphorothioic acid esters.
K038	Phorate, formaldehyde, phosphorodithioic and phosphorothioic acid esters.
K039	Phosphorodithioic and phosphorothioic acid esters.
K040	Phorate, formaldehyde, phosphorodithioic and phosphorothioic acid esters.
K041	Toxaphene.
K042	Hexachlorobenzene, ortho-dichlorobenzene.
K043	2,4-dichlorophenol, 2,6-dichlorophenol, 2,4,6-trichlorophenol.
K044	N.A.
K045	N.A.
K046	Lead.
K047	N.A.
K048	Hexavalent chromium, lead.
K049	Hexavalent chromium, lead.
K050	Hexavalent chromium.
K051	Hexavalent chromium, lead.
K052	Lead.
K060	Cyanide, napthalene, phenolic compounds, arsenic.
K061	Hexavalent chromium, lead, cadmium.
K062	Hexavalent chromium, lead.
K069	Hexavalent chromium, lead, cadmium.
K071	Mercury.
K073	Chloroform, carbon tetrachloride, hexacholroethane, trichloroethane, tetrachloroethylene, dichloroethylene, 1,1,2,2-tetrachloroethane.
K083	Aniline, diphenylamine, nitrobenzene, phenylenediamine.
K084	Arsenic.
K085	Benzene, dichlorobenzenes, trichlorobenzenes, tetrachlorobenzenes, pentachlorobenzene, hexachlorobenzene, benzyl chloride.
K086	Lead, hexavalent chromium.
K087	Phenol, naphthalene.
K093	Phthalic anhydride, maleic anhydride
K094	Phthalic anhydride.

EPA hazard- ous waste No.	Hazardous constituents for which listed
K095........	1,1,2-trichloroethane, 1,1,1,2-tetrachloroethane, 1,1,2,2-tetrachloroethane.
K096........	1,2-dichloroethane, 1,1,1-trichloroethane, 1,1,2-trichloroethane.
K097........	Chlordane, heptachlor.
K098........	Toxaphene.
K099........	2,4-dichlorophenol, 2,4,6-trichlorophenol.
K100........	Hexavalent chromium, lead, cadmium.
K101........	Arsenic.
K102........	Arsenic.
K103........	Aniline, nitrobenzene, phenylenediamine.
K104........	Aniline, benzene, diphenylamine, nitrobenzene, phenylenediamine.
K105........	Benzene, monochlorobenzene, dichlorobenzenes, 2,4,6-trichlorophenol.
K106........	Mercury.

N.A.—Waste is hazardous because it fails the test for the characteristic of ignitability, corrosivity, or reactivity.

[46 FR 4619, Jan. 16, 1981, as amended at 46 FR 27477, May 20, 1981; 49 FR 5312, Feb. 10, 1984; 50 FR 2000, Jan. 14, 1985]

EFFECTIVE DATE NOTE: At 50 FR 2000, Jan. 14, 1985, Part 261, App. VII was amended by adding the entries for F020 through F023, and F026 through F028, effective July 15, 1985.

APPENDIX VIII—HAZARDOUS CONSTITUENTS

Acetonitrile (Ethanenitrile)
Acetophenone (Ethanone, 1-phenyl)
3-(alpha-Acetonylbenzyl)-4-hydroxycoumarin and salts (Warfarin)
2-Acetylaminofluorene (Acetamide, N-(9H-fluoren-2-yl)-)
Acetyl chloride (Ethanoyl chloride)
1-Acetyl-2-thiourea (Acetamide, N-(aminothioxomethyl)-)
Acrolein (2-Propenal)
Acrylamide (2-Propenamide)
Acrylonitrile (2-Propenenitrile)
Aflatoxins
Aldrin (1,2,3,4,10,10-Hexachloro-1,4,4a,5,8,8a,8b-hexahydro-endo,exo-1,4:5,8-Dimethanonaphthalene)
Allyl alcohol (2-Propen-1-ol)
Aluminum phosphide
4-Aminobiphenyl ([1,1'-Biphenyl]-4-amine)
6-Amino-1,1a,2,8,8a,8b-hexahydro-8-(hydroxymethyl)-8a-methoxy-5-methyl-carbamate azirino[2',3':3,4]pyrrolo[1,2-a]indole-4,7-dione, (ester) (Mitomycin C) (Azirino[2'3':3,4]pyrrolo[1,2-a]indole-4,7-dione, 6-amino-8-[((aminocarbonyl)oxy)methyl]-1,1a,2,8,8a,8b-hexahydro-8amethoxy-5-methy-)
5-(Aminomethyl)-3-isoxazolol (3(2H)-Isoxazolone, 5-(aminomethyl)-) 4-Aminopyridine (4-Pyridinamine)
Amitrole (1H-1,2,4-Triazol-3-amine)

Aniline (Benzenamine)
Antimony and compounds, N.O.S.*
Aramite (Sulfurous acid, 2-chloroethyl-, 2-[4-(1,1-dimethylethyl)phenoxy]-1-methylethyl ester)
Arsenic and compounds, N.O.S.*
Arsenic acid (Orthoarsenic acid)
Arsenic pentoxide (Arsenic (V) oxide)
Arsenic trioxide (Arsenic (III) oxide)
Auramine (Benzenamine, 4,4'-carbonimidoylbis[N,N-Dimethyl-, monohydrochloride)
Azaserine (L-Serine, diazoacetate (ester))
Barium and compounds, N.O.S.*
Barium cyanide
Benz[c]acridine (3,4-Benzacridine)
Benz[a]anthracene (1,2-Benzanthracene)
Benzene (Cyclohexatriene)
Benzenearsonic acid (Arsonic acid, phenyl-)
Benzene, dichloromethyl- (Benzal chloride)
Benzenethiol (Thiophenol)
Benzidine ([[1,1'-Biphenyl]-4,4'diamine)
Benzo[b]fluoranthene (2,3-Benzofluoranthene)
Benzo[j]fluoranthene (7,8-Benzofluoranthene)
Benzo[a]pyrene (3,4-Benzopyrene)
p-Benzoquinone (1,4-Cyclohexadienedione)
Benzotrichloride (Benzene, trichloromethyl-)
Benzyl chloride (Benzene, (chloromethyl)-)
Beryllium and compounds, N.O.S.*
Bis(2-chloroethoxy)methane (Ethane, 1,1'-[methylenebis(oxy)]bis[2-chloro-])
Bis(2-chloroethyl) ether (Ethane, 1,1'-oxybis[2-chloro-])
N,N-Bis(2-chloroethyl)-2-naphthylamine (Chlornaphazine)
Bis(2-chloroisopropyl) ether (Propane, 2,2'-oxybis[2-chloro-])
Bis(chloromethyl) ether (Methane, oxybis[chloro-])
Bis(2-ethylhexyl) phthalate (1,2-Benzenedicarboxylic acid, bis(2-ethylhexyl) ester)
Bromoacetone (2-Propanone, 1-bromo-)
Bromomethane (Methyl bromide)
4-Bromophenyl phenyl ether (Benzene, 1-bromo-4-phenoxy-)
Brucine (Strychnidin-10-one, 2,3-dimethoxy-)
2-Butanone peroxide (Methyl ethyl ketone, peroxide)
Butyl benzyl phthalate (1,2-Benzenedicarboxylic acid, butyl phenylmethyl ester)
2-sec-Butyl-4,6-dinitrophenol (DNBP) (Phenol, 2,4-dinitro-6-(1-methylpropyl)-)
Cadmium and compounds, N.O.S.*
Calcium chromate (Chromic acid, calcium salt)
Calcium cyanide

*The abbreviation N.O.S. (not otherwise specified) signifies those members of the general class not specifically listed by name in this appendix.

Carbon disulfide (Carbon bisulfide)

Carbon oxyfluoride (Carbonyl fluoride)

Chloral (Acetaldehyde, trichloro-)

Chlorambucil (Butanoic acid, 4-[bis(2-chloroethyl)amino]benzene-)

Chlordane (alpha and gamma isomers) (4,7-Methanoindan, 1,2,4,5,6,7,8,8-octachloro-3,4,7,7a-tetrahydro-) (alpha and gamma isomers)

Chlorinated benzenes, N.O.S.*

Chlorinated ethane, N.O.S.*

Chlorinated fluorocarbons, N.O.S.*

Chlorinated naphthalene, N.O.S.*

Chlorinated phenol, N.O.S.*

Chloroacetaldehyde (Acetaldehyde, chloro-)

Chloroalkyl ethers, N.O.S.*

p-Chloroaniline (Benzenamine, 4-chloro-)

Chlorobenzene (Benzene, chloro-)

Chlorobenzilate (Benzeneacetic acid, 4-chloro-alpha-(4-chlorophenyl)-alpha-hydroxy-, ethyl ester)

2-Chloro-1, 3-butadiene (chloroprene)

p-Chloro-m-cresol (Phenol, 4-chloro-3-methyl)

1-Chloro-2,3-epoxypropane (Oxirane, 2-(chloromethyl)-)

2-Chloroethyl vinyl ether (Ethene, (2-chloroethoxy)-)

Chloroform (Methane, trichloro-)

Chloromethane (Methyl chloride)

Chloromethyl methyl ether (Methane, chloromethoxy-)

2-Chloronaphthalene (Naphthalene, beta-chloro-)

2-Chlorophenol (Phenol, o-chloro-)

1-(o-Chlorophenyl)thiourea (Thiourea, (2-chlorophenyl)-)

3-Chloropropene (allyl chloride)

3-Chloropropionitrile (Propanenitrile, 3-chloro-)

Chromium and compounds, N.O.S.*

Chrysene (1,2-Benzphenanthrene)

Citrus red No. 2 (2-Naphthol, 1-[(2,5-dimethoxyphenyl)azo]-)

Coal tars

Copper cyanide

Creosote (Creosote, wood)

Cresols (Cresylic acid) (Phenol, methyl-)

Crotonaldehyde (2-Butenal)

Cyanides (soluble salts and complexes), N.O.S.*

Cyanogen (Ethanedinitrile)

Cyanogen bromide (Bromine cyanide)

Cyanogen chloride (Chlorine cyanide)

Cycasin (beta-D-Glucopyranoside, (methyl-ONN-azoxy)methyl-)

2-Cyclohexyl-4,6-dinitrophenol (Phenol, 2-cyclohexyl-4,6-dinitro-)

Cyclophosphamide (2H-1,3,2,-Oxazaphosphorine, [bis(2-chloroethyl)amino]-tetrahydro-, 2-oxide)

Daunomycin (5,12-Naphthacenedione, (8S-cis)-8-acetyl-10-[(3-amino-2,3,6-trideoxy)-alpha-L-lyxo-hexopyranosyl)oxy]-7,8,9,10-tetrahydro-6,8,11-trihydroxy-1-methoxy-)

DDD (Dichlorodiphenyldichloroethane) (Ethane, 1,1-dichloro-2,2-bis(p-chlorophenyl)-)

DDE (Ethylene, 1,1-dichloro-2,2-bis(4-chlorophenyl)-)

DDT (Dichlorodiphenyltrichloroethane) (Ethane, 1,1,1-trichloro-2,2-bis(p-chlorophenyl)-)

Diallate (S-(2,3-dichloroallyl) diisopropylthiocarbamate)

Dibenz[a,h]acridine (1,2,5,6-Dibenzacridine)

Dibenz[a,j]acridine (1,2,7,8-Dibenzacridine)

Dibenz[a,h]anthracene (1,2,5,6-Dibenzanthracene)

7H-Dibenzo[c,g]carbazole (3,4,5,6-Dibenzcarbazole)

Dibenzo[a,e]pyrene (1,2,4,5-Dibenzpyrene)

Dibenzo[a,h]pyrene (1,2,5,6-Dibenzpyrene)

Dibenzo[a,i]pyrene (1,2,7,8-Dibenzpyrene)

1,2-Dibromo-3-chloropropane (Propane, 1,2-dibromo-3-chloro-)

1,2-Dibromoethane (Ethylene dibromide)

Dibromomethane (Methylene bromide)

Di-n-butyl phthalate (1,2-Benzenedicarboxylic acid, dibutyl ester)

o-Dichlorobenzene (Benzene, 1,2-dichloro-)

m-Dichlorobenzene (Benzene, 1,3-dichloro-)

p-Dichlorobenzene (Benzene, 1,4-dichloro-)

Dichlorobenzene, N.O.S.* (Benzene, dichloro-, N.O.S.*)

3,3'-Dichlorobenzidine ([1,1'-Biphenyl]-4,4'-diamine, 3,3'-dichloro-)

1,4-Dichloro-2-butene (2-Butene, 1,4-dichloro-)

Dichlorodifluoromethane (Methane, dichlorodifluoro-)

1,1-Dichloroethane (Ethylidene dichloride)

1,2-Dichloroethane (Ethylene dichloride)

trans-1,2-Dichloroethene (1,2-Dichloroethylene)

Dichloroethylene, N.O.S.* (Ethene, dichloro-, N.O.S.*)

1,1-Dichloroethylene (Ethene, 1,1-dichloro-)

Dichloromethane (Methylene chloride)

2,4-Dichlorophenol (Phenol, 2,4-dichloro-)

2,6-Dichlorophenol (Phenol, 2,6-dichloro-)

2,4-Dichlorophenoxyacetic acid (2,4-D), salts and esters (Acetic acid, 2,4-dichlorophenoxy-, salts and esters)

Dichlorophenylarsine (Phenyl dichloroarsine)

Dichloropropane, N.O.S.* (Propane, dichloro-, N.O.S.*)

1,2-Dichloropropane (Propylene dichloride)

Dichloropropanol, N.O.S.* (Propanol, dichloro-, N.O.S.*)

Dichloropropene, N.O.S.* (Propene, dichloro-, N.O.S.*)

1,3-Dichloropropene (1-Propene, 1,3-dichloro-)

Dieldrin (1,2,3,4,10.10-hexachloro-6,7-epoxy-1,4,4a,5,6,7,8,8a-octa-hydro-endo,exo-1,4:5,8-Dimethanonaphthalene)

1,2:3,4-Diepoxybutane (2,2'-Bioxirane)

Diethylarsine (Arsine, diethyl-)

N,N-Diethylhydrazine (Hydrazine, 1,2-diethyl)

O,O-Diethyl S-methyl ester of phosphorodithioic acid (Phosphorodithioic acid, O,O-diethyl S-methyl ester

O,O-Diethylphosphoric acid, O-p-nitrophenyl ester (Phosphoric acid, diethyl p-nitrophenyl ester)

Diethyl phthalate (1,2-Benzenedicarboxylic acid, diethyl ester)

O,O-Diethyl O-2-pyrazinyl phosphorothioate (Phosphorothioic acid, O,O-diethyl O-pyrazinyl ester

Diethylstilbesterol (4,4'-Stilbenediol, alpha,alpha-diethyl, bis(dihydrogen phosphate, (E)-)

Dihydrosafrole (Benzene, 1,2-methylenedioxy-4-propyl-)

3,4-Dihydroxy-alpha-(methylamino)methyl benzyl alcohol (1,2-Benzenediol, 4-[1-hydroxy-2-(methylamino)ethyl]-)

Diisopropylfluorophosphate (DFP) (Phosphorofluoridic acid, bis(1-methylethyl) ester)

Dimethoate (Phosphorodithioic acid, O,O-dimethyl S-[2-(methylamino)-2-oxoethyl] ester

3,3'-Dimethoxybenzidine ([1,1'-Biphenyl]-4,4'diamine, 3-3'-dimethoxy-)

p-Dimethylaminoazobenzene (Benzenamine, N,N-dimethyl-4-(phenylazo)-)

7,12-Dimethylbenz[a]anthracene (1,2-Benzanthracene, 7,12-dimethyl-)

3,3'-Dimethylbenzidine ([1,1'-Biphenyl]-4,4'-diamine, 3,3'-dimethyl-)

Dimethylcarbamoyl chloride (Carbamoyl chloride, dimethyl-)

1,1-Dimethylhydrazine (Hydrazine, 1,1-dimethyl-)

1,2-Dimethylhydrazine (Hydrazine, 1,2-dimethyl-)

3,3-Dimethyl-1-(methylthio)-2-butanone, O-[(methylamino) carbonyl]oxime (Thiofanox)

alpha,alpha-Dimethylphenethylamine (Ethanamine, 1,1-dimethyl-2-phenyl-)

2,4-Dimethylphenol (Phenol, 2,4-dimethyl-)

Dimethyl phthalate (1,2-Benzenedicarboxylic acid, dimethyl ester)

Dimethyl sulfate (Sulfuric acid, dimethyl ester)

Dinitrobenzene, N.O.S.* (Benzene, dinitro-, N.O.S.*)

4,6-Dinitro-o-cresol and salts (Phenol, 2,4-dinitro-6-methyl-, and salts)

2,4-Dinitrophenol (Phenol, 2,4-dinitro-)

2,4-Dinitrotoluene (Benzene, 1-methyl-2,4-dinitro-)

2,6-Dinitrotoluene (Benzene, 1-methyl-2,6-dinitro-)

Di-n-octyl phthalate (1,2-Benzenedicarboxylic acid, dioctyl ester)

1,4-Dioxane (1,4-Diethylene oxide)

Diphenylamine (Benzenamine, N-phenyl-)

1,2-Diphenylhydrazine (Hydrazine, 1,2-diphenyl-)

Di-n-propylnitrosamine (N-Nitroso-di-n-propylamine)

Disulfoton (O,O-diethyl S-[2-(ethylthio)ethyl] phosphorodithioate)

2,4-Dithiobiuret (Thioimidodicarbonic diamide)

Endosulfan (5-Norbornene, 2,3-dimethanol, 1,4,5,6,7,7-hexachloro-, cyclic sulfite)

Endrin and metabolites (1,2,3,4,10,10-hexachloro-6,7-epoxy-1,4,4a,5,6,7,8,8a-octahydro-endo,endo-1,4:5,8-dimethanonaphthalene, and metabolites)

Ethyl carbamate (Urethan) (Carbamic acid, ethyl ester)

Ethyl cyanide (propanenitrile)

Ethylenebisdithiocarbamic acid, salts and esters (1,2-Ethanediylbiscarbamodithioic acid, salts and esters

Ethyleneimine (Aziridine)

Ethylene oxide (Oxirane)

Ethylenethiourea (2-Imidazolidinethione)

Ethyl methacrylate (2-Propenoic acid, 2-methyl-, ethyl ester)

Ethyl methanesulfonate (Methanesulfonic acid, ethyl ester)

Fluoranthene (Benzo[j,k]fluorene)

Fluorine

2-Fluoroacetamide (Acetamide, 2-fluoro-)

Fluoroacetic acid, sodium salt (Acetic acid, fluoro-, sodium salt)

Formaldehyde (Methylene oxide)

Formic acid (Methanoic acid)

Glycidylaldehyde (1-Propanol-2,3-epoxy)

Halomethane, N.O.S.*

Heptachlor (4,7-Methano-1H-indene, 1,4,5,6,7,8,8-heptachloro-3a,4,7,7a-tetrahydro-)

Heptachlor epoxide (alpha, beta, and gamma isomers) (4,7-Methano-1H-indene, 1,4,5,6,7,8,8-heptachloro-2,3-epoxy-3a,4,7,7-tetrahydro-, alpha, beta, and gamma isomers)

Hexachlorobenzene (Benzene, hexachloro-)

Hexachlorobutadiene (1,3-Butadiene, 1,1,2,3,4,4-hexachloro-)

Hexachlorocyclohexane (all isomers) (Lindane and isomers)

Hexachlorocyclopentadiene (1,3-Cyclopentadiene, 1,2,3,4,5,5-hexachloro-)

Hexachlorodibenzo-p-dioxins

Hexachlorodibenzofurans

Hexachloroethane (Ethane, 1,1,1,2,2,2-hexachloro-)

1,2,3,4,10,10-Hexachloro-1,4,4a,5,8,8a-hexahydro-1,4:5,8-endo,endo-dimethanonaphthalene (Hexachlorohexahydro-endo,endo-dimethanonaphthalene)

Hexachlorophene (2,2'-Methylenebis(3,4,6-trichlorophenol))

Hexachloropropene (1-Propene, 1,1,2,3,3,3-hexachloro-)

Hexaethyl tetraphosphate (Tetraphosphoric acid, hexaethyl ester)

Hydrazine (Diamine)

Hydrocyanic acid (Hydrogen cyanide)

Hydrofluoric acid (Hydrogen fluoride)

Hydrogen sulfide (Sulfur hydride)

Hydroxydimethylarsine oxide (Cacodylic acid)

Indeno(1,2,3-cd)pyrene (1,10-(1,2-phenylene)pyrene)

Iodomethane (Methyl iodide)

Iron dextran (Ferric dextran)

Isocyanic acid, methyl ester (Methyl isocyanate)

Isobutyl alcohol (1-Propanol, 2-methyl-)

Isosafrole (Benzene, 1,2-methylenedioxy-4-allyl-)

Kepone (Decachlorooctahydro-1,3,4-Methano-2H-cyclobuta[cd]pentalen-2-one)

Lasiocarpine (2-Butenoic acid, 2-methyl-, 7-[(2,3-dihydroxy-2-(1-methoxyethyl)-3-methyl-1-oxobutoxy)methyl]-2,3,5,7a-tetrahydro-1H-pyrrolizin-1-yl ester)

Lead and compounds, N.O.S.*

Lead acetate (Acetic acid, lead salt)

Lead phosphate (Phosphoric acid, lead salt)

Lead subacetate (Lead, bis(acetato-O)tetrahydroxytri-)

Maleic anhydride (2,5-Furandione)

Maleic hydrazide (1,2-Dihydro-3,6-pyridazinedione)

Malononitrile (Propanedinitrile)

Melphalan (Alanine, 3-[p-bis(2-chloroethyl)amino]phenyl-, L-)

Mercury fulminate (Fulminic acid, mercury salt)

Mercury and compounds, N.O.S.*

Methacrylonitrile (2-Propenenitrile, 2-methyl-)

Methanethiol (Thiomethanol)

Methapyrilene (Pyridine, 2-[(2-dimethylamino)ethyl]-2-thenylamino-)

Metholmyl (Acetimidic acid, N-[(methylcarbamoyl)oxy]thio-, methyl ester

Methoxychlor (Ethane, 1,1,1-trichloro-2,2'-bis(p-methoxyphenyl)-)

2-Methylaziridine (1,2-Propylenimine)

3-Methylcholanthrene (Benz[j]aceanthrylene, 1,2-dihydro-3-methyl-)

Methyl chlorocarbonate (Carbonochloridic acid, methyl ester)

4,4'-Methylenebis(2-chloroaniline) (Benzenamine, 4,4'-methylenebis-(2-chloro-)

Methyl ethyl ketone (MEK) (2-Butanone)

Methyl hydrazine (Hydrazine, methyl-)

2-Methyllactonitrile (Propanenitrile, 2-hydroxy-2-methyl-)

Methyl methacrylate (2-Propenoic acid, 2-methyl-, methyl ester)

Methyl methanesulfonate (Methanesulfonic acid, methyl ester)

2-Methyl-2-(methylthio)propionaldehyde-o-(methylcarbonyl) oxime (Propanal, 2-methyl-2-(methylthio)-, O-[(methylamino)carbonyl]oxime)

N-Methyl-N'-nitro-N-nitrosoguanidine (Guanidine, N-nitroso-N-methyl-N'-nitro-)

Methyl parathion (O,O-dimethyl O-(4-nitrophenyl) phosphorothioate)

Methylthiouracil (4-1H-Pyrimidinone, 2,3-dihydro-6-methyl-2-thioxo-)

Mustard gas (Sulfide, bis(2-chloroethyl)-)

Naphthalene

1,4-Naphthoquinone (1,4-Naphthalenedione)

1-Naphthylamine (alpha-Naphthylamine)

2-Naphthylamine (beta-Naphthylamine)

1-Naphthyl-2-thiourea (Thiourea, 1-naphthalenyl-)

Nickel and compounds, N.O.S.*

Nickel carbonyl (Nickel tetracarbonyl)

Nickel cyanide (Nickel (II) cyanide)

Nicotine and salts (Pyridine, (S)-3-(1-methyl-2-pyrrolidinyl)-, and salts)

Nitric oxide (Nitrogen (II) oxide)

p-Nitroaniline (Benzenamine, 4-nitro-)

Nitrobenzine (Benzene, nitro-)

Nitrogen dioxide (Nitrogen (IV) oxide)

Nitrogen mustard and hydrochloride salt (Ethanamine, 2-chloro-, N-(2-chloroethyl)-N-methyl-, and hydrochloride salt)

Nitrogen mustard N-Oxide and hydrochloride salt (Ethanamine, 2-chloro-, N-(2-chloroethyl)-N-methyl-, and hydrochloride salt)

Nitroglycerine (1,2,3-Propanetriol, trinitrate)

4-Nitrophenol (Phenol, 4-nitro-)

4-Nitroquinoline-1-oxide (Quinoline, 4-nitro-1-oxide-)

Nitrosamine, N.O.S.*

N-Nitrosodi-n-butylamine (1-Butanamine, N-butyl-N-nitroso-)

N-Nitrosodiethanolamine (Ethanol, 2,2'-(nitrosoimino)bis-)

N-Nitrosodiethylamine (Ethanamine, N-ethyl-N-nitroso-)

N-Nitrosodimethylamine (Dimethylnitrosamine)

N-Nitroso-N-ethylurea (Carbamide, N-ethyl-N-nitroso-)

N-Nitrosomethylethylamine (Ethanamine, N-methyl-N-nitroso-)

N-Nitroso-N-methylurea (Carbamide, N-methyl-N-nitroso-)

N-Nitroso-N-methylurethane (Carbamic acid, methylnitroso-, ethyl ester)

N-Nitrosomethylvinylamine (Ethenamine, N-methyl-N-nitroso-)

N-Nitrosomorpholine (Morpholine, N-nitroso-)

N-Nitrosonornicotine (Nornicotine, N-nitroso-)

N-Nitrosopiperidine (Pyridine, hexahydro-, N-nitroso-)

Nitrosopyrrolidine (Pyrrole, tetrahydro-, N-nitroso-)

N-Nitrososarcosine (Sarcosine, N-nitroso-)

5-Nitro-o-toluidine (Benzenamine, 2-methyl-5-nitro-)

Octamethylpyrophosphoramide (Diphosphoramide, octamethyl-)

Osmium tetroxide (Osmium (VIII) oxide)

7-Oxabicyclo[2.2.1]heptane-2,3-dicarboxylic acid (Endothal)

Paraldehyde (1,3,5-Trioxane, 2,4,6-trimethyl-)

Parathion (Phosphorothioic acid, O,O-diethyl O-(p-nitrophenyl) ester

Pentachlorobenzene (Benzene, pentachloro-)

Pentachlorodibenzo-p-dioxins

Pentachlorodibenzofurans

Pentachloroethane (Ethane, pentachloro-)

Pentachloronitrobenzene (PCNB) (Benzene, pentachloronitro-)

Pentachlorophenol (Phenol, pentachloro-)

Phenacetin (Acetamide, N-(4-ethoxyphenyl)-)

Phenol (Benzene, hydroxy-)

Phenylenediamine (Benzenediamine)

Phenylmercury acetate (Mercury, acetatophenyl-)

N-Phenylthiourea (Thiourea, phenyl-)

Phosgene (Carbonyl chloride)

Phosphine (Hydrogen phosphide)

Phosphorodithioic acid, O,O-diethyl S-[(ethylthio)methyl] ester (Phorate)

Phosphorothioic acid, O,O-dimethyl O-[p-((dimethylamino)sulfonyl)phenyl] ester (Famphur)

Phthalic acid esters, N.O.S.* (Benzene, 1,2-dicarboxylic acid, esters, N.O.S.*)

Phthalic anhydride (1,2-Benzenedicarboxylic acid anhydride)

2-Picoline (Pyridine, 2-methyl-)

Polychlorinated biphenyl, N.O.S.*

Potassium cyanide

Potassium silver cyanide (Argentate(1-), dicyano-, potassium)

Pronamide (3,5-Dichloro-N-(1,1-dimethyl-2-propynyl)benzamide)

1,3-Propane sultone (1,2-Oxathiolane, 2,2-dioxide)

n-Propylamine (1-Propanamine)

Propylthiouracil (Undecamethylenediamine, N,N'-bis(2-chlorobenzyl)-, dihydrochloride)

2-Propyn-1-ol (Propargyl alcohol)

Pyridine

Reserpine (Yohimban-16-carboxylic acid, 11,17-dimethoxy-18-[(3,4,5-trimethoxybenzoyl)oxy]-, methyl ester)

Resorcinol (1,3-Benzenediol)

Saccharin and salts (1,2-Benzoisothiazolin-3-one, 1,1-dioxide, and salts)

Safrole (Benzene, 1,2-methylenedioxy-4-allyl-)

Selenious acid (Selenium dioxide)

Selenium and compounds, N.O.S.*

Selenium sulfide (Sulfur selenide)

Selenourea (Carbamimidoselenoic acid)

Silver and compounds, N.O.S.*

Silver cyanide

Sodium cyanide

Streptozotocin (D-Glucopyranose, 2-deoxy-2-(3-methyl-3-nitrosoureido)-)

Strontium sulfide

Strychnine and salts (Strychnidin-10-one, and salts)

1,2,4-Tetrachlorobenzene (Benzene, 1,2,4-tetrachloro-)

2,3,7,8-Tetrachlorodibenzo-p-dioxin (TCDD) (Dibenzo-p-dioxin, 2,3,7,8-tetrachloro-)

Tetrachlorodibenzo-p-dioxins

Tetrachlorodibenzofurans

Tetrachloroethane, N.O.S.* (Ethane, tetrachloro-, N.O.S.*)

1,1,1,2-Tetrachlorethane (Ethane, 1,1,1,2-tetrachloro-)

1,1,2,2-Tetrachlorethane (Ethane, 1,1,2,2-tetrachloro-)

Tetrachloroethene (Ethene, 1,1,2,2-tetrachloro-)

Tetrachloromethane (Carbon tetrachloride)

2,3,4,6,-Tetrachlorophenol (Phenol, 2,3,4,6-tetrachloro-)

Tetraethyldithiopyrophosphate (Dithiopyrophosphoric acid, tetraethyl-ester)

Tetraethyl lead (Plumbane, tetraethyl-)

Tetraethylpyrophosphate (Pyrophosphoric acide, tetraethyl ester)

Tetranitromethane (Methane, tetranitro-)

Thallium and compounds, N.O.S.*

Thallic oxide (Thallium (III) oxide)

Thallium (I) acetate (Acetic acid, thallium (I) salt)

Thallium (I) carbonate (Carbonic acid, dithallium (I) salt)

Thallium (I) chloride

Thallium (I) nitrate (Nitric acid, thallium (I) salt)

Thallium selenite

Thallium (I) sulfate (Sulfuric acid, thallium (I) salt)

Thioacetamide (Ethanethioamide)

Thiosemicarbazide (Hydrazinecarbothioamide)

Thiourea (Carbamide thio-)

Thiuram (Bis(dimethylthiocarbamoyl) disulfide)

Toluene (Benzene, methyl-)

Toluenediamine (Diaminotoluene)

o-Toluidine hydrochloride (Benzenamine, 2-methyl-, hydrochloride)

Tolylene diisocyanate (Benzene, 1,3-diisocyanatomethyl-)

Toxaphene (Camphene, octachloro-)

Tribromomethane (Bromoform)

1,2,4-Trichlorobenzene (Benzene, 1,2,4-trichloro-)

1,1,1-Trichloroethane (Methyl chloroform-)

1,1,2-Trichloroethane (Ethane, 1,1,2-trichloro-)

Trichloroethene (Trichloroethylene)

Trichloromethanethiol (Methanethiol, trichloro-)

Trichloromonofluoromethane (Methane, trichlorofluoro-)

2,4,5-Trichlorophenol (Phenol, 2,4,5-trichloro-)

2,4,6-Trichlorophenol (Phenol, 2,4,6-trichloro-)

2,4,5-Trichlorophenoxyacetic acid (2,4,5-T) (Acetic acid, 2,4,5-trichlorophenoxy-)

2,4,5-Trichlorophenoxypropionic acid (2,4,5-TP) (Silvex) (Propionoic acid, 2-(2,4,5-trichlorophenoxy)-)

Trichloropropane, N.O.S.* (Propane, trichloro-, N.O.S.*)

1,2,3-Trichloropropane (Propane, 1,2,3-trichloro-)

O,O,O-Triethyl phosphorothioate (Phosphorothioic acid, O,O,O-triethyl ester)

sym-Trinitrobenzene (Benzene, 1,3,5-trinitro-)

Tris(1-azridinyl) phosphine sulfide (Phosphine sulfide, tris(1-aziridinyl-)

Tris(2,3-dibromopropyl) phosphate (1-Propanol, 2,3-dibromo-, phosphate)

Trypan blue (2,7-Naphthalenedisulfonic acid, 3,3'-[(3,3'-dimethyl(1,1'-biphenyl)-4,4'-diyl)bis(azo)]bis(5-amino-4-hydroxy-, tetrasodium salt)

Uracil mustard (Uracil 5-[bis(2-chloroethyl)amino]-)

Vanadic acid, ammonium salt (ammonium vanadate)

Vanadium pentoxide (Vanadium (V) oxide)

Vinyl chloride (Ethene, chloro-)

Zinc cyanide

Zinc phosphide

[46 FR 27477, May 20, 1981; 46 FR 29708, June 3, 1981, as amended at 49 FR 5312, Feb. 10, 1984; 50 FR 2000, Jan. 14, 1985]

EFFECTIVE DATE NOTE: At 50 FR 2000, Jan. 14, 1985, Part 261, App. VIII was amended by adding the entries for Hexachlorodibenzo-p-dioxins, Hexachlorodibenzofurans, Pentachlorodibenzo-p-dioxins, Pentachlorodibenzofurans, Tetrachlorodibenzo-p-dioxins, and Tetrachlorodibenzofurans, effective July 15, 1985.

APPENDIX IX—WASTES EXCLUDED UNDER §§ 260-20 AND 260.22

TABLE 1—WASTES EXCLUDED FROM NON-SPECIFIC SOURCES

Facility	Address	Waste description
Kay-Fries, Inc...	Stoney Point, NY.	Biological aeration lagoon sludge and filter press sludge generated after September 21, 1984, which contain EPA Hazardous Waste Nos. F003 and F005 as well as that disposed of in a holding lagoon as of September 21, 1984.
Metropolitan Sewer District of Greater Cincinnati.	Cincinnati, OH..	Sluiced bottom ash sludge (approximately 25,000 cubic yards), contained in the North Lagoon, on September 21, 1984, which contains EPA Hazardous Wastes Nos. F001, F002, F003, F004, and F005.

TABLE 2—WASTES EXCLUDED FROM SPECIFIC SOURCES

Facility	Address	Waste description
(Reserved)		

TABLE 3—WASTES EXCLUDED FROM COMMERCIAL CHEMICAL PRODUCTS, OFF-SPECIFICATION SPECIES, CONTAINER RESIDUES, AND SOIL RESIDUES THEREOF

Facility	Address	Waste description
Union Carbide Corp.	Taft, LA............	Contaminated soil (approximately 11,000 cubic yards), which contains acrolein in concentrations of less than 9 ppm.

[49 FR 37070, Sept. 21, 1984]

APPENDIX X—METHOD OF ANALYSIS FOR CHLORINATED DIBENZO-P-DIOXINS AND -DIBENZOFURANS [1, 2, 3, 4]

Method 8280

1. Scope and Application

[1] This method is appropriate for the analysis of tetra-, penta-, and hexachlorinated dibenzo-p-dioxins and -dibenzofurans.

[2] Analytical protocol for determination of TCDDs in phenolic chemical wastes and soil samples obtained from the proximity of chemical dumps. T.O. Tiernan and M. Taylor. Brehm Laboratory, Wright State University, Dayton, OH 45435.

[3] Analytical protocol for determination of chlorinated dibenzo-p-dioxins and chlorinated dibenzofurans in river water. T.O. Tiernan and M. Taylor. Brehm Laboratory, Wright State University, Dayton, OH 45435.

[4] In general, the techniques that should be used to handle these materials are those which are followed for radioactive or infectious laboratory materials. Assistance in evaluating laboratory practices may be obtained from industrial hygienists and persons specializing in safe laboratory practices. Typical infectious waste incinerators are probably not satisfactory devices for disposal of materials highly contaminated with CDDs or CDFs. Safety instructions are outlined in EPA Test Method 613(4.0)

See also: 1) "Program for monitoring potential contamination in the laboratory following the handling and analyses of chlorinated dibenzo-p-dioxins and dibenzofurans" by F. D. Hileman et al., In: Human and En-

Continued

1.1 This method measures the concentration of chlorinated dibenzo-p-dioxins and chlorinated dibenzofurans in chemical wastes including still bottoms, filter aids, sludges, spent carbon, and reactor residues, and in soils.

1.2 The sensitivity of this method is dependent upon the level of interferences.

1.3 This method is recommended for use only by analysts experienced with residue analysis and skilled in mass spectral analytical techniques.

1.4 Because of the extreme toxicity of these compounds, the analyst must take necessary precautions to prevent exposure to himself, or to others, of materials known or believed to contain CDDs or CDFs.

2. *Summary of the Method*

2.1 This method is an analytical extraction cleanup procedure, and capillary column gas chromatograph-low resolution mass spectrometry method, using capillary column GC/MS conditions and internal standard techniques, which allow for the measurement of PCDDs and PCDFs in the extract.

2.2 If interferences are encountered, the method provides selected general purpose cleanup procedures to aid the analyst in their elimination.

3. *Interferences*

3.1 Solvents, reagents, glassware, and other sample processing hardware may yield discrete artifacts and/or elevated baselines causing misinterpretation of gas chromatograms. All of these materials must be demonstrated to be free from interferences under the conditions of the analysis by running method blanks. Specific selection of reagents and purification of solvents by distillation in all-glass systems may be required.

3.2 Interferences co-extracted from the samples will vary considerably from source to source, depending upon the diversity of the industry being sampled. PCDD is often associated with other interfering chlorinated compounds such as PCB's which may be at concentrations several orders of magnitude higher than that of PCDD. While general cleanup techniques are provided as part of this method, unique samples may require additional cleanup approaches to achieve the sensitivity stated in Table 1.

3.3 The other isomers of tetrachlorodibenzo-p-dioxin may interfere with the measurement of 2,3,7,8-TCDD. Capillary column gas chromatography is required to resolve

those isomers that yield virtually identical mass fragmentation patterns.

4. *Apparatus and Materials*

4.1. Sampling equipment for discrete or composite sampling.

4.1.1 Grab sample bottle—amber glass, 1-liter or 1-quart volume. French or Boston Round design is recommended. The container must be washed and solvent rinsed before use to minimize interferences.

4.1.2. Bottle caps—threaded to screw on to the sample bottles. Caps must be lined with Teflon. Solvent washed foil, used with the shiny side towards the sample, may be substituted for the Teflon if sample is not corrosive.

4.1.3. Compositing equipment—automatic or manual composing system. No tygon or rubber tubing may be used, and the system must incorporate glass sample containers for the collection of a minimum of 250 ml. Sample containers must be kept refrigerated after sampling.

4.2 Water bath—heated, with concentric ring cover, capable of temperature control (± 2 °C). The bath should be used in a hood.

4.3 Gas chromatograph/mass spectrometer data system.

4.3.1 Gas chromatograph: An analytical system with a temperature-programmable gas chromatograph and all required accessories including syringes, analytical columns and gases.

4.3.2 Column: SP-2250 coated on a 30 m long $\times$ 0.25 mm I.D. glass column (Supelco No. 2-3714 or equivalent). Glass capillary column conditions: Helium carrier gas at 30 cm/sec linear velocity run splitless. Column temperature is 210 °C.

4.3.3 Mass spectrometer: Capable of scanning from 35 to 450 amu every 1 sec or less, utilizing 70 volts (nominal) electron energy in the electron impact ionization mode and producing a mass spectrum which meets all the criteria in Table 2 when 50 ng of decafluorotriphenyl-phosphine (DFTPP) is injected through the GC inlet. The system must also be capable of selected ion monitoring (SIM) for at least 4 ions simultaneously, with a cycle time of 1 sec or less. Minimum integration time for SIM is 100 ms. Selected ion monitoring is verified by injecting .015 ng of TCDD Cl^{37} to give a minimum signal to noise ratio of 5 to 1 at mass 328.

4.3.4 GC/MS interface: Any GC-to-MS interface that gives acceptable calibration points at 50 ng per injection for each compound of interest and achieves acceptable tuning performance criteria (see Sections 6.1-6.3) may be used. GC-to-MS interfaces constructed of all glass or glass-lined materials are recommended. Glass can be deactivated by silanizing with dichlorodimethylsilane. The interface must be capable of

vironmental Risks of Chlorinated Dioxins and Related Compounds, R.E. Tucker, et al, eds., Plenum Publishing Corp., 1983. 2) Safety procedures outlined in EPA Method 613, Federal Register volume 44, No. 233, December 3, 1979.

transporting at least 10 ng of the components of interest from the GC to the MS.

4.3.5 Data system: A computer system must be interfaced to the mass spectrometer. The system must allow the continuous acquisition and storage on machine-readable media of all mass spectra obtained throughout the duration of the chromatographic program. The computer must have software that can search any GC/MS data file for ions of a specific mass and that can plot such ion abundances versus time or scan number. This type of plot is defined as an Extracted Ion Current Profile (EICP). Software must also be able to integrate the abundance, in any EICP, between specified time or scan number limits.

4.4 Pipettes-Disposable, Pasteur, 150 mm long × 5 mm ID (Fisher Scientific Co., No. 13-678-6A or equivalent).

4.5 Flint glass bottle (Teflon-lined screw cap).

4.6 Reacti-vial (silanized) (Pierce Chemical Co.).

5. Reagents

5.1 Potassium hydroxide-(ACS), 2% in distilled water.

5.2 Sulfuric acid-(ACS), concentrated.

5.3 Methylene chloride, hexane, benzene, petroleum ether, methanol, tetradecane-pesticide quality or equivalent.

5.4 Prepare stock standard solutions of TCDD and ^{37}Cl-TCDD (molecular weight 328) in a glove box. The stock solutions are stored in a glovebox, and checked frequently for signs of degradation or evaporation, especially just prior to the preparation of working standards.

5.5 Alumina-basic, Woelm; 80/200 mesh. Before use activate overnight at 600°C, cool to room temperature in a dessicator.

5.6 Prepurified nitrogen gas

6.0 Calibration

6.1 Before using any cleanup procedure, the analyst must process a series of calibration standards through the procedure to validate elution patterns and the absence of interferences from reagents.

6.2 Prepare GC/MS calibration standards for the internal standard technique that will allow for measurement of relative response factors of at least three CDD/ ^{37}CDD ratios. Thus, for TCDDs, at least three TCDD/^{37}Cl-TCDD and TCDF/^{37}Cl-TCDF must be determined.[5] The ^{37}Cl-

TCDD/F concentration in the standard should be fixed and selected to yield a reproducible response at the most sensitive setting of the mass spectrometer. Response factors for PCDD and HxCDD may be determined by measuring the response of the tetrachloro-labelled compounds relative to that of the unlabelled 1,2,3,4- or 2,3,7,8-TCDD, 1,2,3,4,7-PCDD or 1,2,3,4,7,8-HxCDD, which are commercially available.[6]

6.3 Assemble the necessary GC/MS apparatus and establish operating parameters equivalent to those indicated in Section 11.1 of this method. Calibrate the GC/MS system according to Eichelberger, et al. (1975) by the use of decafluorotriphenyl phosphine (DFTPP). By injecting calibration standards, establish the response factors for CDDs vs. ^{37}Cl-TCDD, and for CDFs vs. ^{37}Cl-TCDF. The detection limit provided in Table 1 should be verified by injecting .015 ng of ^{37}Cl-TCDD which should give a minimum signal to noise ratio of 5 to 1 at mass 328.

7. Quality Control

7.1 Before processing any samples, the analyst should demonstrate through the analysis of a distilled water method blank, that all glassware and reagents are interference-free. Each time a set of samples is extracted, or there is a change in reagents, a method blank should be processed as a safeguard against laboratory contamination.

7.2 Standard quality assurance practices must be used with this method. Field replicates must be collected to measure the precision of the sampling technique. Laboratory replicates must be analyzed to establish the precision of the analysis. Fortified samples must be analyzed to establish the accuracy of the analysis.

8. Sample Collection, Preservation, and Handling

8.1 Grab and composite samples must be collected in glass containers. Conventional sampling practices should be followed, except that the bottle must not be prewashed with sample before collection. Composite samples should be collected in glass containers in accordance with the requirements of the RCRA program. Sampling equipment must be free of tygon and other potential sources of contamination.

8.2 The samples must be iced or refrigerated from the time of collection until ex-

---

[5] ^{37}Cl-labelled 2,3,7,8-TCDD and 2,3,7,8-TCDF are available from K.O.R. Isotopes, and Cambridge Isotopes, Inc., Cambridge, MA. Proper standardization requires the use of a specific labelled isomer for each congener to be determined. However, the only labelled isomers readily available are ^{37}Cl-2,3,7,8-TCDD and ^{37}Cl-2,3,7,8-TCDF. This method therefore uses these isomers as surrogates for the CDDs and CDFs. When

other labelled CDDs and CDFs are available, their use will be required.

[6] This procedure is adopted because standards are not available for most of the CDDs and CDFs, and assumes that all the congeners will show the same response as the unlabelled congener used as a standard. Although this assumption may not be true in all cases, the error will be small.

traction. Chemical preservatives should not be used in the field unless more than 24 hours will elapse before delivery to the laboratory. If an aqueous sample is taken and the sample will not be extracted within 48 hours of collection, the sample should be adjusted to a pH range of 6.0-8.0 with sodium hydroxide or sulfuric acid.

8.3 All samples must be extracted within 7 days and completely analyzed within 30 days of collection.

9. *Extraction and Cleanup Procedures*

9.1 Use an aliquot of 1-10 g sample of the chemical waste or soil to be analyzed. Soils should be dried using a stream of prepurified nitrogen and pulverized in a ball-mill or similar device. Perform this operation in a clear area with proper hood space. Transfer the sample to a tared 125 ml flint glass bottle (Teflon-lined screw cap) and determine the weight of the sample. Add an appropriate quantity of ^{37}Cl-labelled 2,3,7,8-TCDD (adjust the quantity according to the required minimum detectable concentration), which is employed as an internal standard.

9.2 Extraction

9.2.1 Extract chemical waste samples by adding 10 ml methanol, 40 ml petroleum ether, 50 ml doubly distilled water, and then shaking the mixture for 2 minutes. Tars should be completely dissolved in any of the recommended neat solvents. Activated carbon samples must be extracted with benzene using method 3540 in SW-846 (Test Methods for Evaluating Solid Waste—Physical/Chemical Methods, available from G.P.O. Stock #055-022-81001-2). Quantitatively transfer the organic extract or dissolved sample to a clean 250 ml flint glass bottle (Teflon lined screw cap), add 50 ml doubly distilled water and shake for 2 minutes. Discard the aqueous layer and proceed with Step 9.3.

9.2.2 Extract soil samples by adding 40 ml of petroleum ether to the sample, and then shaking for 20 minutes. Quantitatively transfer the organic extract to a clean 250 ml flint glass bottle (Teflon-lined screw cap), add 50 ml doubly distilled water and shake for 2 minutes. Discard the aqueous layer and proceed with Step 9.3.

9.3 Wash the organic layer with 50 ml of 20% aqueous potassium hydroxide by shaking for 10 minutes and then remove and discard the aqueous layer.

9.4 Wash the organic layer with 50 ml of doubly distilled water by shaking for 2 minutes, and discard the aqueous layer.

9.5 Cautiously add 50 ml concentrated sulfuric acid and shake for 10 minutes. Allow the mixture to stand until layers separate (approximately 10 minutes), and remove and discard the acid layer. Repeat acid washing until no color is visible in the acid layer.

9.6 Add 50 ml of doubly distilled water to the organic extract and shake for 2 minutes. Remove and discard the aqueous layer and dry the organic layer by adding 10g of anhydrous sodium sulfate.

9.7 Concentrate the extract to incipient dryness by heating in a 55° C water bath and simultaneously flowing a stream of prepurified nitrogen over the extract. Quantitatively transfer the residue to an alumina microcolumn fabricated as follows:

9.7.1 Cut off the top section of a 10 ml disposable Pyrex pipette at the 4.0 ml mark and insert a plug of silanized glass wool into the tip of the lower portion of the pipette.

9.7.2 Add 2.8g of Woelm basic alumina (previously activated at 600° C overnight and then cooled to room temperature in a desiccator just prior to use).

9.7.3 Transfer sample extract with a small volume of methylene chloride.

9.8 Elute the microcolumn with 10 ml of 3% methylene chloride-in-hexane followed by 15 ml of 20% methylene chloride-in-hexane and discard these effluents. Elute the column with 15 ml of 50% methylene chloride-in-hexane and concentrate this effluent (55° C water bath, stream of prepurified nitrogen) to about 0.3-0.5 ml.

9.9 Quantitatively transfer the residue (using methylene chloride to rinse the container) to a silanized Reacti-Vial (Pierce Chemical Co.). Evaporate, using a stream of prepurified nitrogen, almost to dryness, rinse the walls of the vessel with approximately 0.5 ml methylene chloride, evaporate just to dryness, and tightly cap the vial. Store the vial at 5° C until analysis, at which time the sample is reconstituted by the addition of tridecane.

9.10 Approximately 1 hour before GC-MS (HRGC-LRMS) analysis, dilute the residue in the micro-reaction vessel with an appropriate quantity of tridecane. Gently swirl the tridecane on the lower portion of the vessel to ensure dissolution of the CDDs and CDFs. Analyze a sample by GC/EC to provide insight into the complexity of the problem, and to determine the manner in which the mass spectrometer should be used. Inject an appropriate aliquot of the sample into the GC-MS instrument, using a syringe.

9.11 If, upon preliminary GC-MS analysis, the sample appears to contain interfering substances which obscure the analyses for CDDs and CDFs, high performance liquid chromatographic (HPLC) cleanup of the extract is accomplished, prior to further GC-MS analysis.

10. *HPLC Cleanup Procedure*[7]

---

[7] For cleanup see also method #8320 or #8330, SW-846, Test Methods for Evaluating Solid Waste, Physical/Chemical Methods (1982).

10.1 Place approximately 2 ml of hexane in a 50 ml flint glass sample bottle fitted with a Teflon-lined cap.

10.2 At the appropriate retention time, position sample bottle to collect the required fraction.

10.3 Add 2 ml of 5% (w/v) sodium carbonate to the sample fraction collected and shake for one minute.

10.4 Quantitatively remove the hexane layer (top layer) and transfer to a micro-reaction vessel.

10.5 Concentrate the fraction to dryness and retain for further analysis.

11. *GC/MS Analysis*

11.1 The following column conditions are recommended: Glass capillary column conditions: SP-2250 coated on a 30 m long x 0.25 mm I.D. glass column (Supelco No. 2-3714, or equivalent) with helium carrier gas at 30 cm/sec linear velocity, run splitless. Column temperature is 210°C. Under these conditions the retention time for TCDDs is about 9.5 minutes. Calibrate the system daily with, a minimum, three injections of standard mixtures.

11.2 Calculate response factors for standards relative to ^{37}Cl-TCDD/F (see Section 12).

11.3 Analyze samples with selected ion monitoring of at least two ions from Table 3. Proof of the presence of CDD or CDF exists if the following conditions are met:

11.3.1 The retention time of the peak in the sample must match that in the standard, within the performance specifications of the analytical system.

11.3.2 The ratio of ions must agree within 10% with that of the standard.

11.3.3 The retention time of the peak maximum for the ions of interest must exactly match that of the peak.

11.4 Quantitate the CDD and CDF peaks from the response relative to the ^{37}Cl-TCDD/F internal standards. Recovery of the internal standard should be greater than 50 percent.

11.5 If a response is obtained for the appropriate set of ions, but is outside the expected ratio, a co-eluting impurity may be suspected. In this case, another set of ions characteristic of the CDD/CDF molecules should be analyzed. For TCDD a good choice of ions is m/e 257 and m/e 259. For TCDF a good choice of ions is m/e 241 and 243. These ions are useful in characterizing the molecular structure to TCDD or TCDF. For analysis of TCDD good analytical technique would require using all four ions, m/e 257, 320, 322, and 328, to verify detection and signal to noise ratio of 5 to 1. Suspected impurities such as DDE, DDD, or PCB residues can be confirmed by checking for their major fragments. These materials can be removed by the cleanup columns. Failure to meet criteria should be explained in the report, or the sample reanalyzed.

11.6 If broad background interference restricts the sensitivity of the GC/MS analysis, the analyst should employ cleanup procedures and reanalyze by GC/MS. See section 10.0.

11.7 In those circumstances where these procedures do not yield a definitive conclusion, the use of high resolution mass spectrometry is suggested.

12. *Calculations*

12.1 Determine the concentration of individual compounds according to the formula:

$$\text{Concentration, } \mu g/gm = \frac{A \times A_s}{G \times A_{is} \times R_f}$$

where:

A = μg of internal standard added to the sample [a]

G = gm of sample extracted

A_s = area of characteristic ion of the compound being quantified.

A_{is} = area of characteristic ion of the internal standard

R_f = response factor [b]

Response factors are calculated using data obtained from the analysis of standards according to the formula:

---

[a] The proper amount of standard to be used is determined from the calibration curve (See Section 6.0).

[b] If standards for PCDDs/Fs and HxCDDs/Fs are not available, response factors for ions derived from these congeners are calculated relative to ^{37}Cl-TCDD/F. The analyst may use response factors for 1,2,3,4- or 2.3.7.8-TCDD, 1,2,3,4,7-PeCDD, or 1,2,3,4,7,8-HxCDD for quantitation of TCDDs/Fs, PeCDDs/Fs and HxCDDs/Fs, respectively. Implicit in this requirement is the assumption that the same response is obtained from PCDDs/Fs ccontaining the same numbers of chlorine atoms.

$$Rf \quad \frac{A_s \times C_{is}}{A_{is} \times C_s}$$

where:

C_{is} = concentration of the internal standard
C_c = concentration of the standard compound

12.2 Report results in micrograms per gram without correction for recovery data. When duplicate and spiked samples are analyzed, all data obtained should be reported.

12.3 Accuracy and Precision. No data are available at this time.

TABLE 1—GAS CHROMATOGRAPHY OF TCDD

Column	Retention time (min.)	Detection limit (μg/kg)[1]
Glass capillary	9.5	0.003

[1] Detection limit for liquid samples is 0.003 μg/l. This is calculated from the minimum detectable GC response being

equal to five times the GC background noise assuming a 1 ml effective final volume of the 1 liter sample extract, and a GC injection of 5 microliters. Detection levels apply to both electron capture and GC/MS detection. For further details see 44 FR 69526 (December 3, 1979).

TABLE 2—DFTPP KEY IONS AND ION ABUNDANCE CRITERIA [1]

Mass	Ion abundance criteria
51	30–60% of mass 198.
68	Less than 2% of mass 69.
70	Less than 2% of mass 69.
127	40–60% of mass 198.
197	Less than 1% of mass 198.
198	Base peak, 100% relative abundance.
199	5–9% of mass 198.
275	10–30% of mass 198.
365	Greater than 1% of mass 198.
441	Present but less than mass 443.
442	Greater than 40% of mass 198.
443	17–23% of mass 442.

[1] J. W. Eichelberger, L.E. Harris, and W.L. Budde. 1975. Reference compound to calibrate ion abundance measurement in gas chromatography-mass spectrometry. Analytical Chemistry 47:995.

TABLE 3—LIST OF ACCURATE MASSES MONITORED USING GC SELECTED-ION MONITORING, LOW RESOLUTION, MASS SPECTROMETRY FOR SIMULTANEOUS DETERMINATION OF TETRA-, PENTA-, AND HEXACHLORINATED DIBENZO-*p*-DIOXINS AND DIBENZOFURANS

Class of chlorinated dibenzodioxin or dibenzofuran	Number of chlorine substituents (x)	Monitored m/z for dibenzodioxins $C_{12}H_{8-x}O_2I_x$	Monitored m/z for dibenzofurans $C_{12}H_{8-x}OCl_x$	Approximate theoretical ratio expected on basis of isotopic abundance
Tetra	4	[1] 319.897	[1] 303.902	0.74
		321.894	305.903	1.00
		[2] 327.885	[2] 311.894	
		[3] 256.933		0.21
		[3] 258.930		0.20
Penta	5	[1] 353.858	[1] 337.863	0.57
		355.855	339.860	1.00
Hexa	6	389.816	373.821	1.00
		391.813	375.818	0.87

[1] Molecular ion peak.
[2] Cl₄—labelled standard peaks.
[3] Ions which can be monitored in TCDD analyses for confirmation purposes.

[50 FR 2001, Jan. 14, 1985]

EFFECTIVE DATE NOTE: At 50 FR 2001, Jan. 14, 1985, Part 261, App. X was added, effective July 15, 1985.

Appendix 5C   Notification of Hazardous Waste Activity Form and Instructions (EPA Form 8700-12)

Please print or type with ELITE type (12 characters per inch) in the unshaded areas only

Form Approved. OMB No. 2050-0028. Expires 9-30-88
GSA No. 0246-EPA-OT

United States Environmental Protection Agency
Washington, DC 20460

⊕EPA   Notification of Hazardous Waste Activity

Please refer to the *Instructions for Filing Notification* before completing this form. The information requested here is required by law *(Section 3010 of the Resource Conservation and Recovery Act)*.

For Official Use Only

Comments

C.
C

Installation's EPA ID Number | Approved | Date Received (yr. mo. day)
C.
F | T/A C
1

I. Name of Installation

II. Installation Mailing Address

Street or P.O. Box
C.
3

City or Town | State | ZIP Code
C.
4

III. Location of Installation

Street or Route Number
C.
5

City or Town | State | ZIP Code
C.
6

IV. Installation Contact

Name and Title *(last, first, and job title)* | Phone Number *(area code and number)*
C.
2

V. Ownership

A. Name of Installation's Legal Owner | B. Type of Ownership *(enter code)*
C.
R

VI. Type of Regulated Waste Activity *(Mark 'X' in the appropriate boxes. Refer to instructions.)*

A. Hazardous Waste Activity

- ☐ 1a. Generator
- ☐ 2. Transporter
- ☐ 3. Treater/Storer/Disposer
- ☐ 4. Underground Injection
- ☐ 5. Market or Burn Hazardous Waste Fuel *(enter 'X' and mark appropriate boxes below)*
  - ☐ a. Generator Marketing to Burner
  - ☐ b. Other Marketer
  - ☐ c. Burner

☐ 1b. Less than 1,000 kg/mo.

B. Used Oil Fuel Activities

- ☐ 6. Off-Specification Used Oil Fuel *(enter 'X' and mark appropriate boxes below)*
  - ☐ a. Generator Marketing to Burner
  - ☐ b. Other Marketer
  - ☐ c. Burner
- ☐ 7. Specification Used Oil Fuel Marketer (Or On-Site Burner) Who First Claims the Oil Meets the Specification.

VII. Waste Fuel Burning: Type of Combustion Device *(enter 'X' in all appropriate boxes to indicate type of combustion device(s) in which hazardous waste fuel or off-specification used oil fuel is burned. See instructions for definitions of combustion devices.)*

☐ A. Utility Boiler   ☐ B. Industrial Boiler   ☐ C. Industrial Furnace

VIII. Mode of Transportation *(transporters only — enter 'X' in the appropriate box(es)*

☐ A. Air   ☐ B. Rail   ☐ C. Highway   ☐ D. Water   ☐ E. Other *(specify)*

IX. First or Subsequent Notification

Mark 'X' in the appropriate box to indicate whether this is your installation's first notification of hazardous waste activity or a subsequent notification. If this is not your first notification, enter your installation's EPA ID Number in the space provided below.

☐ A. First Notification   ☐ B. Subsequent Notification *(complete item C)*

C. Installation's EPA ID Number

EPA Form 8700-12 (Rev. 11-85) Previous edition is obsolete.

Continue on reverse

ID — For Official Use Only

| C | | | | | | | | | | | | | T/A | C |
| W | | | | | | | | | | | | | | 1 |

IX. Description of Hazardous Wastes *(continued from front)*

A. Hazardous Wastes from Nonspecific Sources. Enter the four-digit number from 40 *CFR* Part 261.31 for each listed hazardous waste from nonspecific sources your installation handles. Use additional sheets if necessary.

1	2	3	4	5	6
7	8	9	10	11	12

B. Hazardous Wastes from Specific Sources. Enter the four-digit number from 40 *CFR* Part 261.32 for each listed hazardous waste from specific sources your installation handles. Use additional sheets if necessary.

13	14	15	16	17	18
19	20	21	22	23	24
25	26	27	28	29	30

C. Commercial Chemical Product Hazardous Wastes. Enter the four-digit number from 40 *CFR* Part 261.33 for each chemical substance your installation handles which may be a hazardous waste. Use additional sheets if necessary.

31	32	33	34	35	36
37	38	39	40	41	42
43	44	45	46	47	48

D. Listed Infectious Wastes. Enter the four-digit number from 40 *CFR* Part 261.34 for each hazardous waste from hospitals, veterinary hospitals, or medical and research laboratories your installation handles. Use additional sheets if necessary.

49	50	51	52	53	54

E. Characteristics of Nonlisted Hazardous Wastes. Mark 'X' in the boxes corresponding to the characteristics of nonlisted hazardous wastes your installation handles. *(See 40 CFR Parts 261.21 — 261.24)*

☐ 1. Ignitable *(D001)*　　☐ 2. Corrosive *(D002)*　　☐ 3. Reactive *(D003)*　　☐ 4. Toxic *(D000)*

X. Certification

I certify under penalty of law that I have personally examined and am familiar with the information submitted in this and all attached documents, and that based on my inquiry of those individuals immediately responsible for obtaining the information, I believe that the submitted information is true, accurate, and complete. I am aware that there are significant penalties for submitting false information, including the possibility of fine and imprisonment.

Signature	Name and Official Title *(type or print)*	Date Signed

EPA Form 8700-12 (Rev. 11-85) Reverse

BILLING CODE 6560-50-C

IV. Line-by-Line Instructions for Completing EPA Form 8700-12

Type or print in black ink all items except Item XI, "Signature," leaving a blank box between words. When typing, hit the space bar once between characters and three times between words. If you must use additional sheets, indicate clearly the number of the item on the form to which the information on the separate sheet applies.

Items I–III—Name, Mailing Address, and Location of Installation:

Complete Items I–III. Please note that the address you give for Item III, "Location of Installation," must be a physical address, *not a post office box or route number.* If the mailing address and physical facility location are the same, you can print "Same" in box for Item III.

Item IV—Installation Contact:

Enter the name, title, and business telephone number of the person who should be contacted regarding information submitted on this form.

Item V—Ownership:

(A) *Name:* Enter the name of the legal owner(s) of the installation, including the property owner. Use additional sheets if necessary to list more than one owner.
(B) *Type:* Using the codes listed below, indicate the legal status of the owner of the facility:

FF = Federally Owned, Federally Operated
FC = Federally Owned, Operated By A Private Contractor to the Federal Government
FP = Federally Owned, Privately Operated
PF = Privately Owned, Constructed For Use By The Federal Government and Operated By The Federal Government
PL = Privately Owned, Leased And Operated By The Federal Government
PI = Privately Owned, Indian Land
FI = Federally Owned, Indian Land
C = County
D = District
M = Municipal
P = Private
S = State

Item VI—Type of Regulated Waste Activity:

(A) *Hazardous Waste Activity:* Mark the appropriate box(es) to show which hazardous waste activities are going on at this installation.
(1) *Generator:* (a) If you generate a hazardous waste that is identified by characteristic or listed in 40 CFR Part 261, mark an "X" in this box.
(b) In addition, *if you generate less than 1000 kilograms of non-acutely-hazardous waste per calendar month, mark on "X" in this box.*
(2) *Transporter:* If you move hazardous waste by air, rail, highway, or water then mark an "X" in this box. All transporters must complete Item VIII. Transporters do not have to complete Item X of this form, but must sign the certification in Item XI. Refer to Part 263 of the CFR for an explanation of the Federal regulations for hazardous waste transporters.
(3) *Treater/Storer/Disposer:* If you treat, store or dispose of regulated hazardous

waste, then mark an "X" in this box. You are reminded to contact the appropriate addressee listed for your State in Section III(C) of this package to request Part A of the RCRA Permit Application. Refer to Parts 264 and 265 of the CFR for an explanation of the Federal regulations for hazardous waste facility owners/operators.
(4) *Underground Injection:* Persons who generate and/or treat or dispose of hazardous waste must place an "X" in this box if an injection well is located at their installation. An injection well is defined as any hole in the ground, including septic tanks, that is deeper than it is wide and that is used for the subsurface placement of fluids.
(5) *Market or Burn Hazardous Waste Fuel:* If you market or burn hazardous waste fuel, place an "X" in this box. Then mark the appropriate boxes underneath to indicate your specific activity. *If you mark "Burner" you must complete Item VII —"Type of Combustion Device."*
Note.—Generators are required to notify for waste-as-fuel activities only if they market directly to the burner.
"Other Marketer" is defined as any person, other than the generator marketing his hazardous waste, who markets hazardous waste fuel.
(B) *Used Oil Fuel Activities:* Mark an "X" in the appropriate box(es) below to indicate which used oil fuel activities are taking place at this installation.
(6) *Off-Specification Used Oil Fuel:* If you market or burn off-specification used oil, place an "X" in this box. Then mark the appropriate boxes underneath to indicate your specific activity. *If you mark "Burner" you must complete Item VII—Type of Combustion Device."*
Note.—Used oil generators are required to notify only if marketing directly to the burner.
"Other Marketer" is defined as any person, other than a generator marketing his or her used oil, who markets used oil fuel.
(7) Specification Used Oil Fuel: If you are the first to claim that the used oil meets the specification established in 40 CFR Part 266.40(e) and is exempt from further regulation, you must mark an "X" in this box.

Item VII—Waste-Fuel Burning: Type of Combustion Device:

Enter an "X" in all appropriate boxes to indicate type(s) of combustion devices in which hazardous waste fuel or off-specification used oil fuel is burned. (Refer to definition section for complete description of each device.)

Item VIII—Mode of Transportation:

Complete this item only if you are the transporter of hazardous waste. Mark an "X" in each appropriate box to indicate the method(s) of transportation you use.

Item IX—First or Subsequent Notification:

Place an "X" in the appropriate box to indicate whether this is your first or a subsequent notification. If you have filed a previous notification, enter your EPA Identification Number in the boxes provided.
Note.—When the owner of a facility changes, the new owner must notify U.S. EPA

of the change, even if the previous owner already received a U.S. EPA Identification Number. Because the U.S. EPA ID Number is "site-specific," the new owner will keep the existing ID number. If the facility moves to another location, the owner/operator must notify EPA of this change. In this instance a new U.S. EPA Identification Number will be assigned, since the facility has changed locations.

Item X—Description of Hazardous Waste:

(Only persons involved in hazardous waste activity (Item VI(A)) need to complete this item. Transporters requesting a U.S. EPA Identification Number do not need to complete this item, but must sign the "Certification" in Item XI.)
You will need to refer to Title 40 CFR Part 261 (enclosed) in order to complete this section. Part 261 identifies those wastes that EPA defines as hazardous. If you need help completing this section please contact the appropriate addressee for your state as listed in Section III(C) of this package.
Section A.—If you handle hazardous wastes that are listed in the "nonspecific sources" category in Part 261.31, enter the appropriate 4-digit numbers in the boxes provided.
Section B—If you handle hazardous wastes that are listed in the "specific industrial sources" category in Part 261.32, enter the appropriate four-digit numbers in the boxes provided.
Section C—If you handle any of the "commercial chemical products" listed as wastes in Part 261.33, enter the appropriate four-digit numbers in the boxes provided.
Section D—Disregard, since EPA has not yet published infectious waste regulations.
Section E—If you handle hazardous wastes which are not listed in any of the categories above, but do possess a hazardous characteristic, you should describe these wastes by their hazardous characteristic. (An explanation of each characteristic found at Part 261.21–261.24.) Place an "X" in the box next to the characteristic of the wastes that you handle.

Item XI—Certification:

This certification must be signed by the owner, operator, or an authorized representative of your installation. An "authorized representative" is a person responsible for the overall operation of the facility (i.e., a plant manager or superintendent, or a person of equal responsibility). *All notifications must include this certification to be complete.*

V. Definitions

The following definitions are included to help you to understand and complete the Notification Form:
Act or RCRA—means the Solid Waste Disposal Act, as amended by the Resource Conservation and Recovery Act of 1976, as amended by the Hazardous and Solid Waste Amendments of 1984, 42 U.S.C. Section 6901 *et seq.*
Authorized Representative—means the person responsible for the overall operation of the facility or an operational unit (i.e., part of a facility), e.g., the plant manager,

superintendent or person of equivalent responsibility.

Boiler—means an enclosed device using controlled flame combustion and having the following characteristics:

(1) The unit has physical provisions for recovering and exporting energy in the form of steam, heated fluids, or heated gases;

(2) The unit's combustion chamber and primary energy recovery section(s) are of integral design (i.e., they are physically formed into one manufactured or assembled unit);

(3) The unit continuously maintains an energy recovery efficiency of at least 60 percent, calculated in terms of the recovered energy compared with the thermal value of the fuel; and

(4) The unit exports and utilizes at least 75 percent of the recovered energy, calculated on an annual basis (excluding recovered heat used internally in the same unit to, for example, preheat fuel or combustion air or drive fans or feedwater pumps).

Burner—means the owner or operator of a utility boiler, industrial boiler or industrial furnace that burns waste-fuel for energy recovery and that is not regulated as a RCRA hazardous waste incinerator.

Disposal—means the discharge, deposit, injection, dumping, spilling, leaking, or placing of any solid waste or hazardous waste into or on any land or water so that such solid waste or hazardous waste or any constituent thereof may enter the environment or be emitted into the air or discharged into any waters, including ground waters.

Disposal Facility—means a facility or part of a facility at which hazardous waste is intentionally placed into or on any land or water, and at which waste will remain after closure.

EPA Identification (I.D.) Number—means the number assigned by EPA to each generator, transporter, and treatment, storage, or disposal facility.

Facility—means all contiguous land, and structures, other appurtenances, and improvements on the land, used for treating, storing, or disposing of hazardous waste. A facility may consist of several treatment, storage, or disposal operational units (e.g., one or more landfills, surface impoundments, or combinations of them).

Generator—means any person, by site, whose act or process produces hazardous waste identified or listed in Part 261 of this chapter or whose act first causes a hazardous waste to become subject to regulation.

Hazardous Waste—means a hazardous waste as defined in 40 CFR Part 261.

Hazardous Waste Fuel—means hazardous waste and any fuel that contains hazardous waste that is burned for energy recovery in a boiler or industrial furnace that is not subject to regulation as a RCRA hazardous waste incinerator. However, the following hazardous waste fuels are subject to regulation as used oil fuels:

(1) Used oil fuel that is also a hazardous waste solely because it exhibits a characteristic of hazardous waste identified in Subpart C of 40 CFR Part 261, provided it is not mixed with hazardous waste; and

(2) Used oil fuel mixed with hazardous wastes generated by a small quantity generator subject to 40 CFR Part 261.5.

Industrial Boiler—means a boiler located on the site of a facility engaged in a manufacturing process where substances are transformed into new products, by mechanical or chemical processes.

Industrial Furnace—means any of the following enclosed devices that are integral components of manufacturing processes and that use controlled flame combustion to accomplish recovery of materials or energy: cement kilns, lime kilns, aggregate kilns (including asphalt kilns), phosphate kilns, coke ovens, blast furnaces, smelting furnaces, refining furnaces, titanium dioxide chloride process oxidation reactors, and methane reforming furnaces (and other devices as the Administrator may add to this list).

Marketer—means a person who markets hazardous waste fuel or used oil fuel. However, the following marketers are not subject to waste-as-fuel requirements (including notification) under Subparts D and E of 40 CFR Part 266:

(1) Generators and initial transporters (i.e., transporters who receive hazardous waste or used oil directly from generators including initial transporters who operate transfer stations) who do not market directly to persons who burn the fuels; and

(2) Persons who market used oil fuel that meets the specification provided under 40 CFR 266.40(e) and who are not the first to claim the oil meets the specification.

Off-Specification Used Oil Fuel—means used oil fuel that does not meet the specification provided under 40 CFR 266.40(e).

Operator—means the person responsible for the overall operation of a facility.

Owner—means a person who owns a facility or part of a facility, including land owner.

Specification Used Oil Fuel—means used oil fuel that meets the specification provided under 40 CFR 266.40(e).

Storage—means the holding of hazardous waste for a temporary period, at the end of which the hazardous waste is treated, disposed of, or stored elsewhere.

Transportation—means the movement of hazardous waste by air, rail, highway, or water.

Transporter—means a person engaged in the off-site transportation of hazardous waste by air, rail, highway, or water.

Treatment—means any method, technique, or process, including neutralization, designed to change the physical, chemical, or biological character or composition of any hazardous waste so as to neutralize such waste, or so as to recover energy or material resources from the waste, or so as to render such waste nonhazardous, or less hazardous; safer to transport, store or dispose of; or amenable for recovery, amenable for storage, or reduced in volume.

Used Oil—means any oil that has been refined from crude oil, used, and as a result of such use, is contaminated by physical or chemical impurities. Wastes that contain oils that have not been used (e.g., fuel oil storage tank bottom clean-out wastes) are not used oil unless they are mixed with used oil.

Used Oil Fuel—means any used oil burned (or destined to be burned) for energy recovery including any fuel produced from used oil by processing, blending or other treatment, and that does not contain hazardous waste (other than that generated by a small quantity generator and exempt from regulation as hazardous waste under provisions of 40 CFR 261.5). Used oil fuel may itself exhibit a characteristic of hazardous waste and remain subject to regulation as used oil fuel provided it is not mixed with hazardous waste.

Utility Boiler—means a boiler that is used to produce electricity, steam or heated or cooled air for sale.

Waste Fuel—means hazardous waste fuel or off-specification used oil fuel.

[FR Doc. 85–27903 Filed 11–27–85; 8:45 am]

BILLING CODE 6560-50-M

APPENDIX 5D

Appendix 5D Uniform Manifest (EPA Forms 8700-22, 8700-22A) and Instructions (Appendix to 40 CFR Part 262)

Please print or type.

Form Approved. OMB No. 2000-0404. Expires 7-31-86

UNIFORM HAZARDOUS WASTE MANIFEST

1. Generator's US EPA No. — Manifest Document No.

2. Page 1 of

Information in the shaded areas is not required by Federal Law.

GENERATOR

3. Generator's Name and Mailing Address

4. Generator's Phone (   )

A. State Manifest Document No.

B. Generator's ID

5. Transporter 1 (Company Name)

6. US EPA ID Number

C. State Transporter's ID

D. Transporter's Phone

7. Transporter 2 (Company Name)

8. US EPA ID Number

E. State Transporter's ID

F. Transporter's Phone (   )

9. Designated Facility Name and Site Address

10. US EPA ID Number

G. State Facility's ID

H. Facility's Phone (   )

11. US DOT Description (Including Proper Shipping Name, Hazard Class and ID Number)	12. Containers No.	Type	13. Total Quantity	14. Unit Wt/Vol	I. Waste No.
a.					
b.					
c.					
d.					

J. Additional Descriptions for Materials listed Above

a | c

b | d

K. Handling Codes for Wastes Listed Above

a ☐ | c ☐

b ☐ | d ☐

15. Special Handling Instructions and Additional Information

16. **GENERATOR'S CERTIFICATION:** I hereby declare that the contents of this consignment are fully and accurately described above by proper shipping name and are classified, packed, marked and labeled, and are in all respects in proper condition for transport by highway according to applicable international and national government regulations and state laws and regulations.

Unless I am a small quantity generator who has been exempted by statute or regulation from the duty to make a waste minimization certification under Section 3002 (b) of RCRA, I also certify that I have a program in place to reduce volume and toxicity of waste generated to the degree I have determined to be economically practicable and I have selected the method of treatment, storage, or disposal currently available to me which minimizes the present and future threat to human health and the environment.

Printed/Typed Name | Signature | Mo. Day Year

TRANSPORTER

17. Transporter 1 (Acknowledgement of Receipt of Materials)

Printed/Typed Name | Signature | Mo. Day Year

18. Transporter 2 (Acknowledgement or Receipt of Materials)

Printed/Typed Name | Signature | Mo. Day Year

FACILITY

19. Discrepancy Indication Space

20. Facility Owner or Operator: Certification of receipt of hazardous materials covered by this manifest except as noted in Item 19.

Printed/Typed Name | Signature | Mo. Day Year

In case of emergency or spill immediately call the National Response Center (800) 424-8802 and the [state telephone number]

EPA Form 8700-22 (Rev. 4-85) Previous edition is obsolete.

APPENDIX—UNIFORM HAZARDOUS WASTE
MANIFEST AND INSTRUCTIONS (EPA
FORMS 8700-22 AND 8700-22A AND
THEIR INSTRUCTIONS)

U.S. EPA Form 8700-22

Read all instructions before completing this form.

This form has been designed for use on a 12-pitch (elite) typewriter; a firm point pen may also be used—press down hard

Federal regulations require generators and transporters of hazardous waste and owners or operators of hazardous waste treatment, storage, and disposal facilities to use this form (8700-22) and, if necessary, the continuation sheet (Form 8700-22A) for both inter and intrastate transportation.

Federal regulations also require generators and transporters of hazardous waste and owners or operators of hazardous waste treatment, storage and disposal facilities to complete the following information:

* * * * *

GENERATORS

*Item 1. Generator's U.S. EPA ID Number—
Manifest Document Number*

Enter the generator's U.S. EPA twelve digit identification number and the unique five digit number assigned to this Manifest (e.g., 00001) by the generator.

Item 2. Page 1 of ——

Enter the total number of pages used to complete this Manifest, i.e., the first page (EPA Form 8700-22) plus the number of Continuation Sheets (EPA Form 8700-22A), if any.

*Item 3. Generator's Name and Mailing
Address*

Enter the name and mailing address of the generator. The address should be the location that will manage the returned Manifest forms.

Item 4. Generator's Phone Number

Enter a telephone number where an authorized agent of the generator may be reached in the event of an emergency.

Item 5. Transporter 1 Company Name

Enter the company name of the first transporter who will transport the waste.

Item 6. U.S. EPA ID Number

Enter the U.S. EPA twelve digit identification number of the first transporter identified in item 5.

Item 7. Transporter 2 Company Name

If applicable, enter the company name of the second transporter who will transport the waste. If more than two transporters are used to transport the waste, use a Continuation Sheet(s) (EPA Form 8700-22A) and list the transporters in the order they will be transporting the waste.

Item 8. U.S. EPA ID Number

If applicable, enter the U.S. EPA twelve digit identification number of the second transporter identified in item 7.

NOTE: If more than two transporters are used, enter each additional transporter's company name and U.S. EPA twelve digit identification number in items 24-27 on the Continuation Sheet (EPA Form 8700-22A). Each Continuation Sheet has space to record two additional transporters. Every transporter used between the generator and the designated facility must be listed.

Item 9. Designated Facility Name and Site Address

Enter the company name and site address of the facility designated to receive the waste listed on this Manifest. The address must be the site address, which may differ from the company mailing address.

Item 10. U.S. EPA ID Number

Enter the U.S. EPA twelve digit identification number of the designated facility identified in item 9.

Item 11. U.S. DOT Description [Including Proper Shipping Name, Hazard Class, and ID Number (UN/NA)]

Enter the U.S. DOT Proper Shipping Name, Hazard Class, and ID Number (UN/NA) for each waste as identified in 49 CFR 171 through 177.

NOTE: If additional space is needed for waste descriptions, enter these additional descriptions in item 28 on the Continuation Sheet (EPA Form 8700-22A).

Item 12. Containers (No. and Type)

Enter the number of containers for each waste and the appropriate abbreviation from Table I (below) for the type of container.

Table I—Types of Containers

DM = Metal drums, barrels, kegs
DW = Wooden drums, barrels, kegs
DF = Fiberboard or plastic drums, barrels, kegs
TP = Tanks portable
TT = Cargo tanks (tank trucks)
TC = Tank cars
DT = Dump truck
CY = Cylinders
CM = Metal boxes, cartons, cases (including roll-offs)
CW = Wooden boxes, cartons, cases
CF = Fiber or plastic boxes, cartons, cases
BA = Burlap, cloth, paper or plastic bags

Item 13. Total Quantity

Enter the total quantity of waste described on each line.

Item 14. Unit (Wt./Vol.)

Enter the appropriate abbreviation from Table II (below) for the unit of measure.

Table II—Units of Measure

G = Gallons (liquids only)
P = Pounds
T = Tons (2000 lbs)
Y = Cubic yards
L = Liters (liquids only)
K = Kilograms
M = Metric tons (1000 kg)
N = Cubic meters

Item 15. Special Handling Instructions and Additional Information

Generators may use this space to indicate special transportation, treatment, storage, or disposal information or Bill of Lading information. States may not require additional, new, or different information in this space. For international shipments, generators must enter in this space the point of departure (City and State) for those shipments destined for treatment, storage, or disposal outside the jurisdiction of the United States.

Item 16. Generator's Certification

The generator must read, sign (by hand), and date the certification statement. If a mode other than highway is used, the word "highway" should be lined out and the appropriate mode (rail, water, or air) inserted in the space below. If another mode in addition to the highway mode is used, enter the appropriate additional mode (e.g., and rail) in the space below.

NOTE: All of the above information *except* the handwritten signature required in item 16 may be preprinted.

•   •   •   •   •

TRANSPORTERS

Item 17. Transporter 1 Acknowledgement of Receipt of Materials

Enter the name of the person accepting the waste on behalf of the first transporter. That person must acknowledge acceptance of the waste described on the Manifest by signing and entering the date of receipt.

Item 18. Transporter 2 Acknowledgement of Receipt of Materials

Enter, if applicable, the name of the person accepting the waste on behalf of the second transporter. That person must acknowledge acceptance of the waste described on the Manifest by signing and entering the date of receipt.

NOTE: International Shipments—Transporter Responsibilities.

Exports—Transporters must sign and enter the date the waste left the United States in item 15 of Form 8700-22.

Imports—Shipments of hazardous waste regulated by RCRA and transported into the United States from another country must upon entry be accompanied by the U.S. EPA Uniform Hazardous Waste Manifest. Transporters who transport hazardous waste into the United States from another country are responsible for completing the Manifest (40 CFR 263.10(c)(1)).

Owners and Operators of Treatment, Storage, or Disposal Facilities

Item 19. Discrepancy Indication Space

The authorized representative of the designated (or alternate) facility's owner or operator must note in this space any significant discrepancy between the waste described on the Manifest and the waste actually received at the facility

Owners and operators of facilities located in unauthorized States (i.e., the U.S. EPA administers the hazardous waste management program) who cannot resolve significant discrepancies within 15 days of receiving the waste must submit to their Regional Administrator (see list below) a letter with a copy of the Manifest at issue describing the discrepancy and attempts to reconcile it (40 CFR 264.72 and 265.72).

Owners and operators of facilities located in authorized States (i.e., those States that have received authorization from the U.S. EPA to administer the hazardous waste program) should contact their State agency for information on State Discrepancy Report requirements.

EPA Regional Administrators

Regional Administrator, U.S. EPA Region I, J.F. Kennedy Fed. Bldg., Boston, MA 02203

Regional Administrator, U.S. EPA Region II, 26 Federal Plaza, New York, NY 10278

Regional Administrator, U.S. EPA Region III, 6th and Walnut Sts., Philadelphia, PA 19106

Regional Administrator, U.S. EPA Region IV, 345 Courtland St., NE., Atlanta. GA 30365

Regional Administrator, U.S. EPA Region V, 230 S. Dearborn St., Chicago, IL 60604

Regional Administrator, U.S. EPA Region VI, 1201 Elm Street, Dallas, TX 75270

Regional Administrator, U.S. EPA Region VII, 324 East 11th Street, Kansas City, MO 64106

Regional Administrator, U.S. EPA Region VIII, 1860 Lincoln Street, Denver, CO 80295

Regional Administrator, U.S. EPA Region IX, 215 Freemont Street, San Francisco, CA 94105

Regional Administrator, U.S. EPA Region X, 1200 Sixth Avenue, Seattle, WA 98101

Item 20. Facility Owner or Operator: Certification of Receipt of Hazardous Materials Covered by This Manifest Except as Noted in Item 19

Print or type the name of the person accepting the waste on behalf of the owner or operator of the facility. That person must acknowledge acceptance of the waste described on the Manifest by signing and entering the date of receipt.

Items A-K are not required by Federal regulations for intra- or interstate transportation. However, States may require generators and owners or operators of treatment, storage, or disposal facilities to complete some or all of items A-K as part of State manifest reporting requirements. Generators and owners and operators of treatment, storage, or disposal facilities are advised to contact State officials for guidance on completing the shaded areas of the Manifest.

APPENDIX 5D

Form Approved OMB No 2000 0404 Expires 7 31 86

UNIFORM HAZARDOUS WASTE MANIFEST (Continuation Sheet)	21. Generator's US EPA ID No		Manifest Document No	22 Page	Information in the shaded areas is not required by Federal law

23 Generator's Name

L State Manifest Document Number

M State Generator's ID

24 Transporter ____ Company Name	25 US EPA ID Number

N State Transporter's ID

26 Transporter ____ Company Name	27 US EPA ID Number

O Transporter's Phone

P State Transporter's ID

Q. Transporter's Phone

28 US DOT Description (Including Proper Shipping Name, Hazard Class, and ID Number)	29 Containers		30 Total Quantity	31 Unit Wt Vol	R Waste No.
	No.	Type			
a					
b					
c.					
d					
e					
f					
g					
h					
i					

S Additional Descriptions for Materials Listed Above

T Handling Codes for Wastes Listed Above

32 Special Handling Instructions and Additional Information

33 Transporter ____ Acknowledgement of Receipt of Materials

Printed/Typed Name	Signature	Date
		Month Day Year

34 Transporter ____ Acknowledgement of Receipt of Materials

Printed/Typed Name	Signature	Date
		Month Day Year

35 Discrepancy Indication Space

EPA Form 8700-22A (3-84)

INSTRUCTIONS—CONTINUATION SHEET, U.S.
EPA FORM 8700-22A

Read all instructions before completing this form.

This form has been designed for use on a 12-pitch (elite) typewriter; a firm point pen may also be used—press down hard.

This form must be used as a continuation sheet to U.S. EPA Form 8700-22 if:

• More than two transporters are to be used to transport the waste;
• More space is required for the U.S. DOT description and related information in Item 11 of U.S. EPA Form 8700-22.

Federal regulations require generators and transporters of hazardous waste and owners or operators of hazardous waste treatment, storage, or disposal facilities to use the uniform hazardous waste manifest (EPA Form 8700-22) and, if necessary, this continuation sheet (EPA Form 8700-22A) for both inter- and intrastate transportation.

GENERATORS

Item 21. Generator's U.S. EPA ID Number— Manifest Document Number

Enter the generator's U.S. EPA twelve digit identification number and the unique five digit number assigned to this Manifest (e.g., 00001) as it appears in item 1 on the first page of the Manifest.

Item 22. Page ——

Enter the page number of this Continuation Sheet.

Item 23. Generator's Name

Enter the generator's name as it appears in item 3 on the first page of the Manifest.

Item 24. Transporter —— Company Name

If additional transporters are used to transport the waste described on this Manifest, enter the company name of each additional transporter in the order in which they will transport the waste. Enter after the word "Transporter" the order of the transporter. For example, Transporter 3 Company Name. Each Continuation Sheet will record the names of two additional transporters.

Item 25. U.S. EPA ID Number

Enter the U.S. EPA twelve digit identification number of the transporter described in item 24.

Item 26. Transporter —— Company Name

If additional transporters are used to transport the waste described on this Manifest, enter the company name of each additional transporter in the order in which they will transport the waste. Enter after the word "Transporter" the order of the transporter. For example, Transporter 4 Company Name. Each Continuation Sheet will record the names of two additional transporters.

Item 27. U.S. EPA ID Number

Enter the U.S. EPA twelve digit identification number of the transporter described in item 26.

Item 28. U.S. DOT Description Including Proper Shipping Name, Hazardous Class, and ID Number (UN/NA)

Refer to item 11.

Item 29. Containers (No. and Type)

Refer to item 12.

Item 30. Total Quantity

Refer to item 13.

Item 31. Unit (Wt./Vol.)

Refer to item 14.

Item 32. Special Handling Instructions

Generators may use this space to indicate special transportation, treatment, storage, or disposal information or Bill of Lading information. States are *not* authorized to require additional, new, or different information in this space.

* * * * *

TRANSPORTERS

Item 33. Transporter —— Acknowledgement of Receipt of Materials

Enter the same number of the Transporter as identified in item 24. Enter also the name of the person accepting the waste on behalf of the Transporter (Company Name) identified in item 24. That person must acknowledge acceptance of the waste described on the Manifest by signing and entering the date of receipt.

Item 34. Transporter —— Acknowledgement of Receipt of Materials

Enter the same number as identified in item 26. Enter also the name of the person accepting the waste on behalf of the Transporter (Company Name) identified in item 26. That person must acknowledge acceptance of the waste described on the Manifest by signing and entering the date of receipt.

* * * * *

Owners and Operators of Treatment, Storage, or Disposal Facilities

Item 35. Discrepancy Indication Space

Refer to item 19.

Items L-R are not required by Federal regulations for intra- or interstate transportation. However, States may require generators and owners or operators of treatment, storage, or disposal facilities to complete some or all of items L-R as part of State manifest reporting requirements. Generators and owners and operators of treatment, storage, or disposal facilities are advised to contact State officials for guidance on completing the shaded areas of the manifest.

[49 FR 10501, Mar. 20, 1984]

EFFECTIVE DATE NOTE: Part 262, Appendix, becomes effective September 20, 1984.

Appendix 5E EPA Biennial Generator Report Form
(EPA Form 8700-13A)

Do not make entries in shaded areas

OMB#: 2050-0024 Expires: 12-31-86

ENVIRONMENTAL PROTECTION AGENCY

GENERATOR BIENNIAL HAZARDOUS WASTE REPORT FOR 1983

This report is for the calendar year ending December 31, 1983.
Read All Instructions Carefully Before Making Any Entries on Form

I. NON-REGULATED STATUS

Complete this section only if you did not generate regulated
quantities of hazardous waste at any time during the 1983
calendar year. Circle the one code at right that best describes
your status during the entire year (see instructions for
explanation of codes).

1	Non-handler
2	Small Quantity Generator
4	Exempt
5	Beneficial Use
9	Closed

Please print/type with elite type (12 characters per inch)

II. GENERATOR'S EPA I.D. NUMBER

TAC

|F| | | | | | | | | | | | |1|
1 2   13 14 15

This Installation's Non-Regulated Status is Expected to Apply:

☐ For 1983 Only   ☐ Permanently

☐ Other_____

C303 ENTRY (OFFICIAL USE ONLY): ☐

III. NAME OF INSTALLATION

| | | | | | | | | | | | | | | | | | | | | | | | | | | | | | | | | | | | | | |
30   69

IV. INSTALLATION MAILING ADDRESS

|3| | | | | | | | | | | | | | | | | | | | | | | | | | | | | |
15 16   45
Street or P.O. Box

|4| | | | | | | | | | | | | | | | | | | | | | | | |4| | | | | | |
15 16   41 42 47   51
City or Town   State Zip Code

V. LOCATION OF INSTALLATION (if different than section IV above)

|5| | | | | | | | | | | | | | | | | | | | | | | | | | | | |
15 16   45
Street or Route number

|6| | | | | | | | | | | | | | | | | | | | | | | | | | | | |
15 16   41 42 47   51
City or Town   State Zip Code

VI. INSTALLATION CONTACT

|2| | | | | | | | | | | | | | | | | | | | | | | | | | | | |
15 16   45
Name (last and first)

| | | | |—| | | |—| | | | |
46   55
Phone No. (area code & no.)

VII. CERTIFICATION

I certify under penalty of law that I have personally examined and am familiar with the information submitted in this and all attached
documents, and that based on my inquiry of those individuals immediately responsible for obtaining the information, I believe that the
submitted information is true, accurate, and complete. I am aware that there are significant penalties for submitting false information,
including the possibility of fine and imprisonment.

_____

Print Type Name   Title   Signature of Authorized Representative   Date Signed

EPA Form 8700-13A(5-80) (Revised 11-83)

Page 1 of ____

App. 5E-1

Do not make entries in shaded areas

ENVIRONMENTAL PROTECTION AGENCY

Generator Biennial Hazardous Waste Report for 1983 (cont.)

This report is for the calendar year ending December 31, 1983.

Date rec'd: _____ Rec'd by: _____

IX. FACILITY NAME (specify facility to which all wastes on this page were shipped)

VIII. GENERATOR'S EPA I.D. NO.

|G| | | | | | | | | | | | |1|

XI. FACILITY ADDRESS

X. FACILITY'S EPA I.D. NO.

|F| | | | | | | | | | | |

XII. TRANSPORTATION SERVICES USED

XIII. WASTE IDENTIFICATION

Sequence #	Line	A. Description of Waste	B. DOT Hazard Code	C. EPA Hazardous Waste No. (see instructions)	D. Amount of Waste	E. Unit of Measure
	1					
	2					
	3					
	4					
	5					
	6					
	7					
	8					
	9					
	10					
	11					
	12					

XIV. COMMENTS (enter information by section number—see instructions)

Page ____ of ____

App. 5E-2

Appendix 5F EPA's List of State Solid and Hazardous Waste Agencies (as of March 1984) *

Appendix II—State Solid and Hazardous Waste Agencies

Environmental Protection Agency Office of Solid Waste

March 1984

Alabama

Daniel E. Cooper, Chief, Land Disposal Program, Alabama Dept. of Environmental Management, Solid & Hazardous Waste Mgmt. Div., State Capitol, Montgomery, Alabama 36130, CML (205) 832–6728

Alaska

Stan Hungerford, Air & Solid Waste Management, Dept. of Environmental Conservation, Pouch O, Juneau, Alaska 99811, FTS (907) 465–2635, CML (907) 465–2635

American Samoa

Pati Faiai, Executive Secretary, Environmental Quality Commission, American Samoa Government, Pago Pago, American Samoa 96799, Overseas Operator, (Commercial Call 633–4116)

Randy Morris, Deputy Director, Department of Public Works, Pago Pago, American Samoa 96799

Arizona

R. Bruce Scott, Chief, Bureau of Waste Control, Department of Health Services, State Health Bldg., Room 202, 1740 West Adams St., Phoenix, Arizona 85007, CML (602) 255–1170

Arkansas

Vincent Blubaugh, Chief, Solid & Hazardous Waste Mtls. Div., Department of Pollution Control and Ecology, P.O. Box 9583, 8001 National Drive, Little Rock, Arkansas 72219, CML (501) 562–7444

California

Richard Wilcoxon, Acting Chief, Hazardous Waste Management Branch, Department of Health Services, 714 P Street, Sacramento, California 95814, FTS (916) 324–1789, CML (916) 324–1789

Terry Trumbull, Chairperson, State Solid Waste Management Board, 1020—9th St., Suite 300, Sacramento, California 95814. CML (916) 322–3330

Colorado

Kenneth Waesche, Director, Waste Management Division, Colorado Department of Health, 4210 E. 11th Ave., Denver, Colorado 80220, CML (303) 320–8333

Mr. Orville Stoddard, Deputy Director, Waste Management Division, Colorado Department of Health, 4210 East 11th Ave., Denver, Colorado 80220, CML (303) 320–8333

Commonwealth of North Mariana Islands

George Chan, Administrator, Division of Environmental Quality, Department of Public Health and Environmental Services, Commonwealth of the North Mariana Island, Saipan, Mariana Islands 96950, Overseas Operator: 6984, Cable address: GOV. NMI Saipan

Connecticut

Stephen Hitchock, Director, Hazardous Materials Management Unit, Department of Environmental Protection, State Office Building, 165 Capitol Ave., Hartford, Connecticut 06115, CML (203) 566–5712

Michael Cawley, Connecticut Resource Recovery Authority, 179 Allyn St., Suite 603, Professional Building, Hartford, Connecticut 06103, CML (203) 549–6390

---

* 49 Fed. Reg. 26289 (6-27-84).

Delaware

William Razor, Supervisor/Resource Engineer, Solid Waste Management Branch, Department of Natural Resources and Environmental Control, 89 King Highway, P.O. Box 1401, Dover, Delaware 19901, CML (302) 736–4781

District of Columbia

Angelos Tampros, Chief, Department of Environmental Services, Pesticides & Hazardous Materials Div., 5000 Overlook Ave., SW., Washington, DC 20032, CML (202) 767–8422

Florida

Robert W. McVety, Administrator, Solid Waste Section, Department of Environmental Regulations, Twin Towers Office Bldg., Room 421, 2600 Blair Stone Road, Tallahassee, Florida 32301, CML (904) 488–0300

Georgia

Harold Reheis, Chief, Land Protection Branch, Environmental Protection Division, Dept. of Natural Resources, 270 Washington St., S.W., Room 822, Atlanta, Georgia 30334, CML (404) 656–2833

Guam

James Branch, Deputy Administrator, EPA, Government of Guam, P.O. Box 2999, Agana, Guam 96910, Overseas Operator, (Commercial Call 646–8863)

Hawaii

Melvin Koizumi, Deputy Director, Environmental Health Division, Dept. of Health, P.O. Box 3378, Honolulu, Hawaii 96801, California FTS Operator, FTS 8–556–0220, CML (808) 548–4139

Idaho

Robert Olson, Supervisor, Hazardous Materials Bureau, Dept. of Health & Welfare, State House, Boise, Idaho 83720, FTS 554–4064, CML (208) 334–4064

Illinois

Robert Kuykendall, Manager, Division of Land Pollution Control, Environmental Protection Agency, 2200 Churchill Rd., Room A–104, Springfield, Illinois 62706, FTS 8–782–0246, CML (217) 782–0246

William Child, Deputy Manager, Division of Land Pollution Control, Environmental Protection Agency, 2200 Churchill Rd., Room A–104, Springfield, Illinois 62706, CML (217) 782–0245

Indiana

David Lamm, Director, Land Pollution Control Division, State Board of Health, 1330 West Michigan St., Room A–304, Indianapolis, Indiana 46206, CML (317) 633–0194

Iowa

Ronald Kolpa, Hazardous Waste Program Coordinator, Dept. of Water, Air & Waste Mgmt., Henry A. Wallace Bldg., 900 East Grand, Des Moines, Iowa 50319, CML (515) 281–8853

Kansas

Dennis Murphey, Director, Bureau of Environmental Sanitation, Dept. of Health & Environment, Forbes Field, Bldg. 321, Topeka, Kansas 66620, CML (913) 862–9360

Kentucky

Alex Barber, Director, Division of Waste Management, Bureau of Environmental Protection, Dept. of Natural Resources and Environmental Protection, 18 Reilly Road, Frankfort, Kentucky 40601, CML (502) 564–6716

Louisiana

John Koury, Administrator, Solid Waste Management Division, Dept. of Environmental Quality, P.O. Box 44066, Baton Rouge, Louisiana 70804, CML (504) 342–1216

Gerald J. Healy, Jr., Administrator, Hazardous Waste Management Division, Dept. of Environmental Quality, P.O. Box 44066, Baton Rouge, Louisiana 70804, CML (504) 342–1227

Maine

David Boulter, Director, Licensing and Enforcement Division, Bureau of Oil and Haz. Materials, Dept. of Environmental Protection, State House—Station 17, Augusta, Maine 04333, CML (207) 289–2651

Maryland

Bernard Bigham, Waste Management Administration, Dept. of Health & Mental Hygiene, 201 West Preston St., Room 212, Baltimore, Maryland 21201, CML (301) 383–5740

Fred Sachs, Chief, Hazardous Waste Division, Waste Management Administration, Dept. of Health & Mental Hygiene, 201 W. Preston Street, Baltimore, Maryland 21201, CML (303) 383–5743

Ronald Nelson, Director, Waste Management Administration, Office of Environmental Programs, Dept. of Health & Mental Hygiene, 201 W. Preston Street, Baltimore, Maryland 21201, CML (301) 383–3123

Massachusetts

William Cass, Director, Division of Hazardous Waste, Department of Environmental Quality Engineering, One Winter Street, Boston, Massachusetts 02108, CML (617) 292–5589

Michigan

Delbert Rector, Chief, Hazardous Waste Division, Environmental Protection Bureau, Dept. of Natural Resources, Box 30028, Lansing, Michigan 48909, CML (517) 373–7917

Allan Howard, Chief, Office of Hazardous Waste Management, Environmental Services Division, Dept. of Natural Resources, Box 30028, Lansing, Michigan 48909, CML (517) 373–2730

(Hazardous Waste, Liquid), David Dennis, Chief, Oil & Hazardous Materials Contol Section, Water Quality Division, Dept. of Natural Resources, Box 30028, Lansing, Michigan 48909, CML (517) 373–2794

(Hazardous Waste, Toxic or Critical Materials), Delbert Rector, Chief, Environmental Services Division, Dept. of Natural Resources, Box 30028, Lansing, Michigan 48909, CML (517) 737–2730

John L. Hesse, Chief, Chemicals & Health Center, Michigan Dept. of Public Health, Box 30035, Lansing, Michigan 48909, CML (517) 373–8050

Minnesota

Dale L. Wikre, Director, Solid & Hazardous Waste Division, Pollution Control Agency, 1935 West County Rd., R–2, Roseville, Minnesota 55113, CML (612) 296–7333

Mississippi

Jack M. McMillan, Director, Division of Solid & Hazardous Waste Management, Bureau of Pollution Control, Dept. of Natural Resources, P.O. Box 10385, Jackson, Mississippi 39209, CML (601) 961–5171

Missouri

David Bedan, Director, Solid Waste Management Program, Dept. of Natural Resources, State Office Bldg., P.O. Box 1368, Jefferson City, Missouri 65102, CML (314) 751–3241

Montana

Duane L. Robertson, Chief, Solid Waste Management Bureau, Dept. of Health & Environmental Services, Cogswell Bldg. Helena, Montana 59602, FTS 8–587–2821, CML (406) 499–2821

Nebraska

Mike Steffensmeier, Acting Director, Hazardous Waste Section, Dept. of Environmental Control, State House Station, P.O. Box 94877, Lincoln, Nebraska 68509, CML (402) 471–2186

Nevada

Verne Rosse, Waste Management Program Director, Division of Environmental Protection, Dept. of Conservation & Natural Resources, Capitol Complex, Carson City, Nevada 89701, CML (702) 885–4670

New Hampshire

Dr. Brian Strohm, Assistant Director, Division of Public Health Services, Office of Waste Management, Dept. of Health & Welfare, Health & Welfare Bldg., Hazen Drive, Concord, New Hampshire 03301, CML (603) 271–4608

New Jersey

Lino F. Pereira, Director, Solid Waste Administration, Division of Environmental Quality, Dept. of Environmental Protection, 32 E. Hanover Street, CN–027, Trenton, New Jersey 08625, CML (609) 292–9121

New Mexico

Tony Drypolcher, Chief, Ground Water & Hazardous Waste Bureau, Environmental Imrovement Division, N.M. Health & Environment Department, P.O. Box 968, Santa Fe, New Mexico 87504, CML (505) 984–0020 Ext. 272

Ray Sisneros, Program Manager, Hazardous Wastes Section, Ground Water & Hazardous Waste Bureau, N.M. Health & Environment Department, P.O. Box 968, Santa Fe, New Mexico 87504, CML (505) 984–0020 Ext. 275

New York

Norman H. Nosenchuck, Director, Division of Solid Waste, Dept. of Environmental Conservation, 50 Wolf Rd., Room 209, Albany, New York 12233–0001, CML (518) 457–6603

North Carolina

O.W. Strickland, Head, Solid & Hazardous Waste Mgmt. Branch, Environmental Health Section, Dept. of Human Services, P.O. Box 2091, Raleigh, North Carolina 27602, CML (919) 733–2178

North Dakota

Jay Crawford, Director, Division of Environmental Waste Management & Research, Dept. of Health, 1200 Missouri Ave., 3rd floor, Bismark, North Dakota 58505, CML (701) 224–2366

Ohio

Steve White, Chief, Division of Solid and Hazardous Waste, Ohio EPA, P.O. Box 1049, Columbus, Ohio 43216, FTS 8–942–8934, CML (614) 466–8934

Oklahoma

H.A Craves, Chief, Industrial & Solid Waste Service, Oklahoma State Dept. of Health, P.O. Box 53551, 1000 N.E. 10th St., Room 803, Oklahoma City, Oklahoma 73152, CML (403) 271–5338

Oregon

Ernest A. Schmidt, Administrator, Solid Waste Management Division, Dept. of Environmental Quality, P.O. Box 1760, 522 S.W. Fifth Avenue, Portland, Oregon 97207, CML (503) 229–5913

Pennsylvania

Donald A. Lazarchik, Director, Bureau of Solid Waste Management, Dept. of Environmental Resources, Fulton Building—8th floor, P.O. Box 2063, Harrisburg, Pennsylvania 17120, CML (717) 787–9870

Puerto Rico

Luis de la Cruz, Director, Solid, Toxics & Hazardous Waste Program, Environmental Quality Board, Box 11488, Santurce, Puerto Rice 00910–1488, CML (809) 725–0439

Rhode Island

John S. Quinn, Jr., Chief, Solid Waste Management Program, Dept. of Environmental Management, 204 Cannon Bldg., 75 Davis Street, Providence, Rhode Island 02908, CML (401) 277–2797

South Carolina

Robert E. Malpass, Chief, Bureau of Solid & Hazardous Waste Management, S.C. Dept. of Health & Environmental Control, J. Marion Simms Bldg., 2600 Bull Street, Columbia, South Carolina 29201, CML (803) 785–5681

South Dakota

Joel C. Smith, Administrator, Office of Air Quality & Solid Waste, Dept. of Water & Natural Resources, Joe Foss Bldg., Pierre, South Dakota 57501, CML (605) 773–3329

Tennessee

Tom Tiesler, Director, Division of Solid Waste Mgmt., Bureau of Environmental Services, Dept. of Public Health, 150 9th Ave., North, Nashville, Tennessee 37203, FTS 8–853–3424, CML (615) 741–3424

Texas

Jack C. Carmichael, Chief, Bureau of Solid Waste Management, Texas Dept. of Health, 1100 West 49th Street, T–602, Austin, Texas 78756, CML (512) 458–7271

Dr. Harry Pruett, Director, Permits Division, Texas Dept. of Water

Resources, 1700 North Congress, Room 237–1, P.O. Box 13987 Capitol Station, Austin, Texas 78711, CML (512) 475–2041

Utah

Dale Parker, Director, Bureau of Solid and Hazardous Waste Management Division, P.O. Box 2500, 150 West North Temple, Salt Lake City, Utah 84110, CML (801) 533–4145

Vermont

Richard A. Valentinetti, Director, Air & Solid Waste Programs, Agency of Environmental Conservation, State Office Bldg., Montpelier, Vermont 05602, FTS 8–832–3395, CML (802) 832–3395

Virgin Islands

Robert V. Eepoel, Director, Hazardous Waste Program, Division of Natural Resources, Dept. of Conservation & Cultural Affairs, P.O. Box 4340, Charlotte Amalie, St. Thomas, Virgin Islands 00801, D.C. Overseas Operator 472–6620, CML (809) 774–6420

Virginia

Willian F. Gilley, Director, Division of Solid & Hazardous Waste Management, Virginia Dept. of Health, Madison Bldg, 109 Governor Street, Richmond, Virginia 23219, FTS 8–225–2667, CML (804) 786–5271

Washington

Earl Tower, Supervisor, Solid Waste Mgmt. Division, Dept. of Ecology, Olympia, Washington 98504, CML (206) 459–6317

West Virginia

John Northeimer, Branch Head, Division of Water Resources, Dept. of Natural Resources, 1201 Greenbrier Street, East Charleston, West Virginia 25311, FTS 8–885–5935, CML (304) 384–5935

Wisconsin

Paul Didier, Director, Bureau of Solid Waste Mgmt, Dept. of Natural Resources, P.O. Box 7921, Madison, Wisconsin 53707, FTS 8–(608) 266–1327, CML (608) 266–1327

Wyoming

Charles Porter, Supervisor, Solid Waste Mgmt. Program, State of Wyoming, Dept. of Environmental Quality, Equality State Bank Bldg., 401 West 19th Street, Cheyenne, Wyoming 82002, CML (307) 777–7752

Appendix 5G   Applicability of Part 264, Part 265, Part 266, and Part 270 Requirements to Classes of Facilities*

Facility Class

Requirements	Storage Facilities	Treatment Facilities						Disposal Facilities		
		Thermal	Land	Waste-water	Tot. Enc.	Elem. Neut.	Other	Ocean†	UI‡	Other (landfills, SIs, incin, WPs, LT)
264.11 I.D.	x	x	x	x			x	x		x
264.12 Notice	x	x	x				x			x
264.13 WA	x	x	x				x			x
264.14 Sec	x	x	x				x			x

*The following abbreviations are used: AccP—accident prevention program; Ch P&BT—chemical, physical, and biological treatment facilities; CloFR—closure financial responsibility; Cntain—container regulations; Elem. Neut.—elemental neutralization treatment facilities; Emerg—emergency planning; GW pro—groundwater protection requirements; Incin—incinerators; IP—inspection program; iw I & IV—Class I and Class IV injection wells; LT—land treatment facilities; Manif—manifest requirements; non gov—nongovernmental; Other siting—other siting requirements, such as groundwater, etc.; Pers—personnel training program; Postclo—postclosure; PostcloFR—postclosure financial responsibility; Prep—preparedness; Sec—security requirements; SIs—surface impoundments; Substan clo—substantive closure requirements; ThermT—thermal treatment facilities; Tot. Enc.—totally enclosed storage units; UI—underground injection; WA—waste analysis; WPs—waste piles

†See MPRSA requirements.

‡See SDWA requirements.

Appendix 5G Applicability of Part 264, Part 265, Part 266, and Part 270 Requirements to Classes of Facilities —Cont.

		Facility Class								
		Treatment Facilities						Disposal Facilities		
Requirements	Storage Facilities	Thermal	Land	Waste-water	Tot. Enc.	Elem. Neut.	Other	Ocean†	UI‡	Other (landfills, SIs, incin, WPs, LT)
264.15 IP	x	x	x				x			x
264.16 Pers	x	x	x				x			x
264.17 AccP	x	x	x				x			x
264.18a Seismic	x	x	x				x			x
Other siting	x (not incin)	x	x				tanks			SIs, landfills, incin, LT
264.30 Prep	x	x	x				x			x
264.50 Emerg	x	x	x				x			x
264.70 Manif	x	x	x	some			x	some		x

Appendix 5G Applicability of Part 264, Part 265, Part 266, and Part 270 Requirements to Classes of Facilities —Cont.

Facility Class

| Requirements | Treatment Facilities | | | | | | | Disposal Facilities | | |
	Storage Facilities	Thermal	Land	Waste-water	Tot. Enc.	Elem. Neut.	Other	Ocean†	UI‡	Other (landfills, SIs, incin, WPs, LT)
264.90 GW pro	WPs, SIs		WPs, SIs				tanks			all but incin
264.111 Substan clo	x	x	x				x		iw I & IV	x
264.117 Postclo	WPS, SIs		WPs, SIs						iw I & IV	x
264.142 CloFR	non	non	non				non		non	non
264.144 PostcloFR	gov	gov	gov				gov		gov	gov
264.170 Cntain	x		WPs, SIs						gov	non
264.190 Tanks	x	x					x			gov
264.220 SIs	x		x				x			SIs

Appendix 5G Applicability of Part 264, Part 265, Part 266, and Part 270 Requirements to Classes of Facilities —Cont.

Facility Class

Requirements	Storage Facilities	Treatment Facilities						Disposal Facilities		
		Thermal	*Land*	*Waste-water*	*Tot. Enc.*	*Elem. Neut.*	*Other*	*Ocean†*	*UI‡*	*Other (landfills, SIs, incin, WPs, LT)*
264.250 WPs	x		x				x			
264.270 Land Treatment			x							
264.300 Landfills										landfills
264.340 Incin		x								incin
265.370 ThermT		x								
265.400 Chp & BT		-					x			

Appendix 5G Applicability of Part 264, Part 265, Part 266, and Part 270 Requirements to Classes of Facilities —Cont.

| | | | | Facility Class | | | | | | |
| | Storage Facilities | Treatment Facilities | | | | | | Disposal Facilities | | |
Requirements		Thermal	Land	Waste-water	Tot. Enc.	Elem. Neut.	Other	Ocean†	UI‡	Other (landfills, SIs, incin, WPs, LT) industrial & nonindustrial boilers & marketers
Part 266 Chemfuel & used oil										x
Part 270 Permit	x	x	x	§			x	‖	#	x

§Permitted under Clean Water Act—permit by rule.
‖Permitted under MPRSA—permit by rule.
#Permitted under SDWA—permit by rule.

Appendix 5H   Technical Appendixes to Part 264

APPENDIX I—RECORDKEEPING INSTRUCTIONS

The recordkeeping provisions of § 264.73 specify that an owner or operator must keep a written operating record at his facility. This appendix provides additional instructions for keeping *portions* of the operating record. See § 264.73(b) for additional record-keeping requirements.

The following information must be record-ed, as it becomes available, and maintained in the operating record until closure of the facility in the following manner:

Records of each hazardous waste received, treated, stored, or disposed of at the facility which include the following:

(1) A description by its common name and the EPA Hazardous Waste Number(s) from Part 261 of this Chapter which apply to the waste. The waste description also must include the waste's physical form, i.e., liquid, sludge, solid, or contained gas. If the waste is not listed in Part 261, Subpart D, of this Chapter, the description also must include the process that produced it (for example, solid filter cake from production of ----, EPA Hazardous Waste Number W051).

Each hazardous waste listed in Part 261, Subpart D, of this Chapter, and each haz-ardous waste characteristic defined in Part 261, Subpart C, of this Chapter, has a four-digit EPA Hazardous Waste Number as-signed to it. This number must be used for recordkeeping and reporting purposes. Where a hazardous waste contains more than one listed hazardous waste, or where more than one hazardous waste characteris-tic applies to the waste, the waste descrip-tion must include all applicable EPA Haz-ardous Waste Numbers.

(2) The estimated or manifest-reported weight, or volume and density, where appli-cable, in one of the units of measure speci-fied in Table 1;

(3) The method(s) (by handling code(s) as specified in Table 2) and date(s) of treat-ment, storage, or disposal.

TABLE 1

Unit of measure	Symbol[1]	Density
Pounds	P	
Short tons (2000 lbs)	T	
Gallons (U.S.)	G	P/G
Cubic yards	Y	T/Y
Kilograms	K	
Tonnes (1000 kg)	M	K/L
Liters	L	M/C
Cubic meters	C	

[1] Single digit symbols are used here for data processing purposes.

TABLE 2—HANDLING CODES FOR TREATMENT, STORAGE, AND DISPOSAL METHODS

Enter the handling code(s) listed below that most closely represents the technique(s) used at the facility to treat, store, or dispose of each quantity of hazardous waste received.

1. Storage
   - S01 Container (barrel, drum, etc.)
   - S02 Tank
   - S03 Waste pile
   - S04 Surface impoundment
   - S05 Other (specify)
2. Treatment
   (a) Thermal Treatment
   - T06 Liquid injection incinerator
   - T07 Rotary kiln incinerator
   - T08 Fluidized bed incinerator
   - T09 Multiple hearth incinerator
   - T10 Infrared furnace incinerator
   - T11 Molten salt destructor
   - T12 Pyrolysis
   - T13 Wet Air oxidation
   - T14 Calcination
   - T15 Microwave discharge
   - T16 Cement kiln
   - T17 Lime kiln
   - T18 Other (specify)
   (b) Chemical Treatment
   - T19 Absorption mound
   - T20 Absorption field
   - T21 Chemical fixation
   - T22 Chemical oxidation
   - T23 Chemical precipitation
   - T24 Chemical reduction
   - T25 Chlorination
   - T26 Chlorinolysis
   - T27 Cyanide destruction
   - T28 Degradation
   - T29 Detoxification
   - T30 Ion exchange
   - T31 Neutralization
   - T32 Ozonation
   - T33 Photolysis
   - T34 Other (specify)
   (c) Physical Treatment
   (1) Separation of components
   - T35 Centrifugation
   - T36 Clarification
   - T37 Coagulation
   - T38 Decanting
   - T39 Encapsulation
   - T40 Filtration
   - T41 Flocculation
   - T42 Flotation
   - T43 Foaming
   - T44 Sedimentation
   - T45 Thickening
   - T46 Ultrafiltration
   - T47 Other (specify)
   (2) Removal of Specific Components
   - T48 Absorption-molecular sieve
   - T49 Activated carbon
   - T50 Blending
   - T51 Catalysis
   - T52 Crystallization
   - T53 Dialysis
   - T54 Distillation
   - T55 Electrodialysis
   - T56 Electrolysis
   - T57 Evaporation
   - T58 High gradient magnetic separation
   - T59 Leaching
   - T60 Liquid ion exchange
   - T61 Liquid-liquid extraction
   - T62 Reverse osmosis
   - T63 Solvent recovery
   - T64 Stripping
   - T65 Sand filter
   - T66 Other (specify)
   (d) Biological Treatment
   - T67 Activated sludge
   - T68 Aerobic lagoon
   - T69 Aerobic tank
   - T70 Anaerobic lagoon
   - T71 Composting
   - T72 Septic tank

T73 Spray irrigation
T74 Thickening filter
T75 Tricking filter
T76 Waste stabilization pond
T77 Other (specify)
T78-79 [Reserved]

3. Disposal
D80 Underground injection
D81 Landfill
D82 Land treatment
D83 Ocean disposal
D84 Surface impoundment (to be closed as a landfill)
D85 Other (specify)

APPENDIX II—III [RESERVED]

APPENDIX IV—COCHRAN'S APPROXIMATION TO THE BEHRENS-FISHER STUDENTS' T-TEST

Using all the available background data (n_b readings), calculate the background mean (X_B) and background variance (s_B^2). For the single monitoring well under investigation (n_m reading), calculate the monitoring mean (X_m) and monitoring variance (s_m^2).

For any set of data ($x_1, x_2 \ldots x_n$) the mean is calculated by:

$$\overline{X} = \frac{X_1 + X_2 \ldots + X_n}{n}$$

and the variance is calculated by:

$$s^2 = \frac{(X_1 - \overline{X})^2 + (X_2 - \overline{X})^2 \ldots + (X_n - \overline{X})^2}{n-1}$$

where "n" denotes the number of observations in the set of data.

The t-test uses these data summary measures to calculate a t-statistic (t^*) and a comparison t-statistic (t_c). The t^* value is compared to the t_c value and a conclusion reached as to whether there has been a statistically significant change in any indicator parameter.

The t-statistic for all parameters except pH and similar monitoring parameters is:

$$t^* = \frac{X_m - \overline{X}_B}{\sqrt{\dfrac{S_m^2}{n_m} + \dfrac{S_B^2}{n_B}}}$$

If the value of this t-statistic is negative then there is no significant difference between the monitoring data and background data. It should be noted that significantly small negative values may be indicative of a failure of the assumption made for test validity or errors have been made in collecting the background data.

The t-statistic (t_c), against which t^* will be compared, necessitates finding t_B and t_m from standard (one-tailed) tables where,

t_B = t-tables with ($n_B - 1$) degrees of freedom, at the 0.05 level of significance.

t_m = t-tables with ($n_m - 1$) degrees of freedom, at the 0.05 level of significance.

Finally, the special weightings W_B and W_m are defined as:

$$W_B = \frac{S_B^2}{n_B} \quad \text{and} \quad W_m = \frac{S_m^2}{n_m}$$

and so the comparison t-statistic is:

$$t_c = \frac{W_B t_B + W_m t_m}{W_B + W_m}$$

The t-statistic (t^*) is now compared with the comparison t-statistic (t_c) using the following decision-rule:

If t^* *is equal to or larger than* t_c, then conclude that there most likely *has been a significant increase* in this specific parameter.

If t^* *is less than* t_c, then conclude that most likely *there has not been a change* in this specific parameter.

—The t-statistic for testing pH and similar monitoring parameters is constructed in the same manner as previously described except the negative sign (if any) is discarded and the caveat concerning the negative value is ignored. The standard (two-tailed) tables are used in the construction t_c for pH and similar monitoring parameters.

If t^* is equal to or larger than t_c, then conclude that there most likely *has been a significant increase* (if the initial t^* had been negative, this would imply a significant decrease). If t^* is less than t_c, then conclude that there most likely has been no change.

A further discussion of the test may be found in *Statistical Methods* (6th Edition, Section 4.14) by G. W. Snedecor and W. G. Cochran, or *Principles and Procedures of Statistics* (1st Edition, Section 5.8) by R. G. D. Steel and J. H. Torrie.

STANDARD T-TABLES 0.05 LEVEL OF SIGNIFICANCE

Degrees of freedom	t-values (one-tail)	t-values (two-tail)
1	6.314	12.706
2	2.920	4.303
3	2.353	3.182
4	2.132	2.776
5	2.015	2.571
6	1.943	2.447
7	1.895	2.365
8	1.860	2.306
9	1.833	2.262
10	1.812	2.228
11	1.796	2.201
12	1.782	2.179
13	1.771	2.160
14	1.761	2.145
15	1.753	2.131
16	1.746	2.120
17	1.740	2.110
18	1.734	2.101
19	1.729	2.093
20	1.725	2.086
21	1.721	2.080
22	1.717	2.074
23	1.714	2.069
24	1.711	2.064
25	1.708	2.060
30	1.697	2.042
40	1.684	2.021

Adopted from Table III of *"Statistical Tables for Biological, Agricultural, and Medical Research"* (1947, R. A. Fisher and F. Yates).

[47 FR 32367, July 26, 1982]

APPENDIX V—EXAMPLES OF POTENTIALLY INCOMPATIBLE WASTE

Many hazardous wastes, when mixed with other waste or materials at a hazardous waste facility, can produce effects which are harmful to human health and the environment, such as (1) heat or pressure, (2) fire or explosion, (3) violent reaction, (4) toxic dusts, mists, fumes, or gases, or (5) flammable fumes or gases.

Below are examples of potentially incompatible wastes, waste components, and materials, along with the harmful consequences which result from mixing materials in one group with materials in another group. The list is intended as a guide to owners or operators of treatment, storage, and disposal facilities, and to enforcement and permit granting officials, to indicate the need for special precautions when managing these potentially incompatible waste materials or components.

This list is not intended to be exhaustive. An owner or operator must, as the regulations require, adequately analyze his wastes so that he can avoid creating uncontrolled substances or reactions of the type listed below, whether they are listed below or not.

It is possible for potentially incompatible wastes to be mixed in a way that precludes a reaction (e.g., adding acid to water rather than water to acid) or that neutralizes them (e.g., a strong acid mixed with a strong base), or that controls substances produced (e.g., by generating flammable gases in a closed tank equipped so that ignition cannot occur, and burning the gases in an incinerator).

In the lists below, the mixing of a Group A material with a Group B material may have the potential consequence as noted.

GROUP 1-A

Acetylene sludge
Alkaline caustic liquids
Alkaline cleaner
Alkaline corrosive liquids
Alkaline corrosive battery fluid
Caustic wastewater
Lime sludge and other corrosive alkalies
Lime wastewater
Lime and water
Spent caustic

GROUP 1-B

Acid sludge
Acid and water
Battery acid
Chemical cleaners
Electrolyte, acid
Etching acid liquid or solvent
Pickling liquor and other corrosive acids
Spent acid
Spent mixed acid
Spent sulfuric acid

Potential consequences: Heat generation; violent reaction.

GROUP 2-A

Aluminum
Beryllium
Calcium
Lithium
Magnesium
Potassium
Sodium
Zinc powder
Other reactive metals and metal hydrides

GROUP 2-B

Any waste in Group 1-A or 1-B

Potential consequences: Fire or explosion; generation of flammable hydrogen gas.

GROUP 3-A

Alcohols
Water

GROUP 3-B

Any concentrated waste in Groups 1-A or 1-B

Calcium
Lithium
Metal hydrides
Potassium
SO_2Cl_2, $SOCl_2$, PCl_3, CH_3SiCl_3
Other water-reactive waste
Potential consequences: Fire, explosion, or heat generation; generation of flammable or toxic gases.

GROUP 4-A

Alcohols
Aldehydes
Halogenated hydrocarbons
Nitrated hydrocarbons
Unsaturated hydrocarbons
Other reactive organic compounds and solvents

GROUP 4-B

Concentrated Group 1-A or 1-B wastes
Group 2-A wastes
Potential consequences: Fire, explosion, or violent reaction.

GROUP 5-A

Spent cyanide and sulfide solutions

GROUP 5-B

Group 1-B wastes
Potential consequences: Generation of toxic hydrogen cyanide or hydrogen sulfide gas.

GROUP 6-A

Chlorates
Chlorine
Chlorites
Chromic acid
Hypochlorites
Nitrates
Nitric acid, fuming
Perchlorates
Permanganates
Peroxides
Other strong oxidizers

GROUP 6-B

Acetic acid and other organic acids
Concentrated mineral acids
Group 2-A wastes
Group 4-A wastes
Other flammable and combustible wastes
Potential consequences: Fire, explosion, or violent reaction.

Source: "Law, Regulations, and Guidelines for Handling of Hazardous Waste." California Department of Health, February 1975.

[46 FR 2872, Jan. 12, 1981]

APPENDIX VI—POLITICAL JURISDICTIONS[1] IN WHICH COMPLIANCE WITH § 264.18(a) MUST BE DEMONSTRATED

ALASKA

Aleutian Islands	Kodiak
Anchorage	Lynn Canal-Icy
Bethel	Straits
Bristol Bay	Palmer-Wasilla-
Cordova-Valdez	Talkeena
Fairbanks-Fort	Seward
Yukon	Sitka
Juneau	Wade Hampton
Kenai-Cook Inlet	Wrangell Petersburg
Ketchikan-Prince of	Yukon-Kuskokwim
Wales	

ARIZONA

Cochise	Greenlee
Graham	Yuma

CALIFORNIA

All

COLORADO

Archuleta	Mineral
Conejos	Rio Grande
Hinsdale	Saguache

HAWAII

Hawaii

IDAHO

Bannock	Franklin
Bear Lake	Fremont
Bingham	Jefferson
Bonneville	Madison
Caribou	Oneida
Cassia	Power
Clark	Teton

MONTANA

Beaverhead	Meagher
Broadwater	Missoula
Cascade	Park
Deer Lodge	Powell
Flathead	Sanders
Gallatin	Silver Bow
Granite	Stillwater
Jefferson	Sweet Grass
Lake	Teton
Lewis and Clark	Wheatland
Madison	

NEVADA

All

[1] These include counties, city-county consolidations, and independent cities. In the case of Alaska, the political jurisdictions are election districts, and, in the case of Hawaii, the political jurisdiction listed is the island of Hawaii.

NEW MEXICO

Bernalillo
Catron
Grant
Hidalgo
Los Alamos
Rio Arriba
Sandoval

Sante Fe
Sierra
Socorro
Taos
Torrance
Valencia

UTAH

Beaver
Box Elder
Cache
Carbon
Davis
Duchesne
Emery
Garfield
Iron
Juab
Millard
Morgan

Piute
Rich
Salt Lake
Sanpete
Sevier
Summit
Tooele
Utah
Wasatch
Washington
Wayne
Weber

WASHINGTON

Chelan
Clallam
Clark
Cowlitz
Douglas
Ferry
Grant
Grays Harbor
Jefferson
King
Kitsap
Kittitas
Lewis

Mason
Okanogan
Pacific
Pierce
San Juan Islands
Skagit
Skamania
Snohomish
Thurston
Wahkiakum
Whatcom
Yakima

WYOMING

Fremont
Lincoln
Park
Sublette

Teton
Uinta
Yellowstone National
Park

[46 FR 57285, Nov. 23, 1981; 47 FR 953, Jan. 8, 1982]

Appendix 5I   EPA Biennial TSD Facility Report Form (EPA Form 8700-13B)

Do not make entries in shaded areas

OMB#: 2050-0024 Expires: 12-31-86

ENVIRONMENTAL PROTECTION AGENCY

FACILITY BIENNIAL HAZARDOUS WASTE REPORT FOR 1983

This report is for the calendar year ending December 31, 1983
Read All Instructions Carefully Before Making Any Entries on Form

I. NON-REGULATED STATUS

See instructions before completing this section.

This facility did not treat, store, or dispose of
regulated quantities of hazardous waste at any
time during 1983. . . . . ☐

Explain your non-regulated status in the space below.

Please print/type with elite type (12 characters per inch)

II. FACILITY EPA I.D. NUMBER

This Facility's Non-Regulated Status is Expected to Apply:

☐ For 1983 Only   ☐ Permanently

☐ Other (explain
in comment section)

C303 ENTRY (OFFICIAL USE ONLY): ☐

III. NAME OF FACILITY

IV. FACILITY MAILING ADDRESS

Street or P.O. Box

City or Town   State   Zip Code

V. LOCATION OF FACILITY (if different than section IV above)

Street or Route number

City or Town   State   Zip Code

VI. FACILITY CONTACT

Name (last and first)

VII. COST ESTIMATES FOR FACILITIES

Phone No. (area code & no.)

$ ⌶⌶⌶ ⌶⌶⌶ ⌶⌶⌶ $ ⌶⌶⌶ . ⌶⌶⌶ . ⌶⌶⌶

A. Cost Estimate for Facility Closure

B. Cost Estimate for Post Closure Monitoring
and Maintenance (disposal facilities only)

VIII. CERTIFICATION

I certify under penalty of law that I have personally examined and am familiar with the information submitted in this and all attached
documents, and that based on my inquiry of those individuals immediately responsible for obtaining the information, I believe that the
submitted information is true, accurate, and complete. I am aware that there are significant penalties for submitting false information,
including the possibility of fine and imprisonment.

Print/Type Name   Title   Signature of Authorized Representative   Date Signed

EPA Form 8700-13B(5-80) (Revised 11-83)

Page 1 of _____

App. 5I-1

CHEMICAL REGULATION & HAZARDOUS WASTE

Do not make entries in shaded areas

ENVIRONMENTAL PROTECTION AGENCY

Facility Biennial Hazardous Waste Report for 1983 (cont.)

This report is for the calendar year ending December 31, 1983.

Date rec'd: _____ Rec'd by: _____

XI. GENERATOR NAME (specify generator from whom all wastes on this page were received)

IX. FACILITY'S EPA I.D. NO.

ON-SITE ☐

|F|_|_|_|_|_|_|_|_|_|_|_|_|1|
1 2   13 14 15

XII. GENERATOR ADDRESS

X. GENERATOR'S EPA I.D. NO.

|G|_|_|_|_|_|_|_|_|_|_|_|_|
16   28

XIII. TOTAL WASTE IN STORAGE ON DECEMBER 31, 1983 (complete this section only once for your facility)

S01 |_|_|_|_|_|_|_|_| |_|_| S02 |_|_|_|_|_|_|_|_| |_|_| S03 |_|_|_|_|_|_|_|_| |_|_|
        AMOUNT OF WASTE   UOM   AMOUNT OF WASTE   UOM   AMOUNT OF WASTE   UOM

S04 |_|_|_|_|_|_|_|_| |_|_| S05 |_|_|_|_|_|_|_|_| |_|_|
        AMOUNT OF WASTE   UOM   AMOUNT OF WASTE   UOM

XIV. WASTE IDENTIFICATION

Sequence #	Line #	A. Description of Waste	B. EPA Hazardous Waste No. (see instructions)	C. Handling Method	D. Amount of Waste	E. Unit of Measure
|_|_|_|_| 29 32	1		33 36 37 40 / 41 44 45 48	49 51	52 60	61
|_|_|_|_|	2					
|_|_|_|_|	3					
|_|_|_|_|	4					
|_|_|_|_|	5					
|_|_|_|_|	6					
|_|_|_|_|	7					
|_|_|_|_|	8					
|_|_|_|_|	9					
|_|_|_|_|	10					
|_|_|_|_|	11					
|_|_|_|_|	12					

XV. COMMENTS (enter information by section number—see instructions)

Page _____ of _____

App. 5I-2

Appendix 5J EPA's Groundwater Concentration Limits for Hazardous Constituents*

TABLE 1—MAXIMUM CONCENTRATION OF CONSTITUENTS FOR GROUND-WATER PROTECTION

Constituent	Maximum concentration [1]
Arsenic	0.05
Barium	1.0
Cadmium	0.01
Chromium	0.05
Lead	0.05
Mercury	0.002
Selenium	0.01
Silver	0.05
Endrin (1,2,3,4,10,10-hexachloro-1,7-epoxy-1,4,4a,5,6,7,8,9a-octahydro-1, 4-endo, endo-5,8-dimethano naphthalene)	0.0002
Lindane (1,2,3,4,5,6-hexachlorocyclohexane, gamma isomer)	0.004
Methoxychlor (1,1,1-Trichloro-2,2-bis (p-methoxyphenylethane)	0.1
Toxaphene ($C_{10}H_{10}Cl_6$, Technical chlorinated camphene, 67–69 percent chlorine)	0.005
2,4-D (2,4-Dichlorophenoxyacetic acid)	0.1
2,4,5-TP Silvex (2,4,5-Trichlorophenoxypropionic acid)	0.01

[1] Milligrams per liter.

* 40 CFR §264.94 Table 1.

Appendix 5K Part 264 Liability Insurance Endorsements and Certificates

§264.151

. . . .

(i) A hazardous waste facility liability endorsement as required in § 264.147 or § 265.147 must be worded as follows, except that instructions in brackets are to be replaced with the relevant information and the brackets deleted:

HAZARDOUS WASTE FACILITY LIABILITY ENDORSEMENT

1. This endorsement certifies that the policy to which the endorsement is attached provides liability insurance covering bodily injury and property damage in connection with the insured's obligation to demonstrate financial responsibility under 40 CFR 264.147 or 265.147. The coverage applies at [list EPA Identification Number, name, and address for each facility] for [insert "sudden accidental occurrences," "nonsudden accidental occurrences," or "sudden and nonsudden accidental occurrences"; if coverage is for multiple facilities and the coverage is different for different facilities, indicate which facilities are insured for sudden accidental occurrences, which are insured for nonsudden accidental occurrences, and which are insured for both]. The limits of liability are [insert the dollar amount of the "each occurrence" and "annual aggregate" limits of the Insurer's liability], exclusive of legal defense costs.

2. The insurance afforded with respect to such occurrences is subject to all of the terms and conditions of the policy; provided, however, that any provisions of the policy inconsistent with subsections (a) through (e) of this Paragraph 2 are hereby amended to conform with subsections (a) through (e):

(a) Bankruptcy or insolvency of the insured shall not relieve the Insurer of its obligations under the policy to which this endorsement is attached.

(b) The Insurer is liable for the payment of amounts within any deductible applicable to the policy, with a right of reimbursement by the insured for any such payment made by the Insurer. This provision does not apply with respect to that amount of any deductible for which coverage is demonstrated as specified in 40 CFR 264.147(f) or 265.147(f).

(c) Whenever requested by a Regional Administrator of the U.S. Environmental Protection Agency (EPA), the Insurer agrees to furnish to the Regional Administrator a signed duplicate original of the policy and all endorsements.

(d) Cancellation of this endorsement, whether by the Insurer or the insured, will be effective only upon written notice and only after the expiration of sixty (60) days after a copy of such written notice is received by the Regional Administrator(s) of the EPA Region(s) in which the facility(ies) is (are) located.

(e) Any other termination of this endorsement will be effective only upon written notice and only after the expiration of thirty (30) days after a copy of such written notice is received by the Regional Administrator(s) of the EPA Region(s) in which the facility(ies) is (are) located.

Attached to and forming part of policy No. ——— issued by [name of Insurer], herein called the Insurer, of [address of Insurer] to [name of insured] of [address] this — day of ———, 19—. The effective date of said policy is — day of ———, 19—.

I hereby certify that the wording of this endorsement is identical to the wording specified in 40 CFR 264.151(i) as such regulation was constituted on the date first above written, and that the Insurer is licensed to transact the business of insurance, or eligible to provide insurance as an excess or surplus lines insurer, in one or more States.

[Signature of Authorized Representative of Insurer]

[Type name]

[Title], Authorized Representive of [name of Insurer]

[Address of Representative]

(j) A certificate of liability insurance as required in § 264.147 or § 265.147 must be worded as follows, except that the instructions in brackets are to be replaced with the relevant information and the brackets deleted:

HAZARDOUS WASTE FACILITY CERTIFICATE OF LIABILITY INSURANCE

1. [Name of Insurer], (the "Insurer"), of [address of Insurer] hereby certifies that it has issued liability insurance covering bodily injury and property damage to [name of insured], (the "insured"), of [address of insured] in connection with the insured's obligation to demonstrate financial responsibility under 40 CFR 264.147 or 265.147. The coverage applies at [list EPA Identification Number, name, and address for each facility] for [insert "sudden accidental occurrences," "nonsudden accidental occurrences," or "sudden and nonsudden accidental occurrences"; if coverage is for multiple facilities and the coverage is different for different facilities, indicate which facilities are insured for sudden accidental occurrences, which are insured for nonsudden accidental occurrences, and which are insured for both]. The limits of liability are [insert the dollar amount of the "each occurrence" and "annual aggregate" limits of the Insurer's liability], exclusive of legal defense costs. The coverage is provided under policy number ———, issued on [date]. The effective date of said policy is [date].

2. The Insurer further certifies tne following with respect to the insurance described in Paragraph 1:

(a) Bankruptcy or insolvency of the insured shall not relieve the Insurer of its obligations under the policy.

(b) The Insurer is liable for the payment of amounts within any deductible applicable to the policy, with a right of reimbursement by the insured for any such payment made by the Insurer. This provision does not apply with respect to that amount of any deductible for which coverage is demonstrated as specified in 40 CFR 264.147(f) or 265.147(f).

(c) Whenever requested by a Regional Administrator of the U.S. Environmental Protection Agency (EPA), the Insurer agrees to furnish to the Regional Administrator a signed duplicate original of the policy and all endorsements.

(d) Cancellation of the insurance, whether by the Insurer or the insured, will be effective only upon written notice and only after the expiration of sixty (60) days after a copy of such written notice is received by the Regional Administrator(s) of the EPA Region(s) in which the facility(ies) is (are) located.

(e) Any other termination of the insurance will be effective only upon written notice and only after the expiration of thirty (30) days after a copy of such written notice is received by the Regional Administrator(s) of the EPA Region(s) in which the facility(ies) is (are) located.

I hereby certify that the wording of this instrument is identical to the wording specified in 40 CFR 264.151(j) as such regulation was constituted on the date first above written, and that the Insurer is licensed to transact the business of insurance, or eligible to provide insurance as an excess or surplus lines insurer, in one or more States.

[Signature of authorized representative of Insurer]

[Type name]

[Title], Authorized Representative of [name of Insurer]

[Address of Representative]

(Approved by the Office of Management and Budget under control number 2000-0445, for paragraphs (g), (i), and (j).)

[47 FR 15059, Apr. 7, 1982, as amended at 47 FR 16556, Apr. 16, 1982; 47 FR 17989, Apr. 27, 1982; 47 FR 19995, May 10, 1982; 47 FR 28627, July 1, 1982]

Appendix 5L Summary of State Hazardous Waste Requirements

KEY

The numbered entries under each state's name correspond to the items presented in this key. For example, the entry numbered I. (2) under "Arizona" indicates Arizona's authorization of its state program and the entry numbered II. (2) indicates Arizona's definition of disposal. The left-hand column of this key shows, where appropriate, the Code of Federal Regulations (CFR) section containing the governing EPA regulation for each definition or item of information. An entry of "SAF" in a state's listing indicates that the state's definition or requirement is the same as the EPA federal standard.

I. State Programs

	I.	(1)	State hazardous waste laws and regulations—citations
		(2)	Authorization of state program
		(3)	Name, address, phone—administering state agency

II. Definitions and General Standards—States

EPA
Regulations:
49 CFR,
Section . . .

261.3	II.	(1)	Definition of hazardous waste
261.3		(2)	Definition of disposal
261.3		(3)	Definition of storage
261.3		(4)	Definition of treatment
261.10		(5)	Criteria for identification and listing of hazardous wastes
260.20		(6)	Rulemaking procedures:
			1) Can citizens initiate rulemaking?
			2) Is public participation required?
			3) Are public hearings required?
		(7)	Where is judicial review obtained?
261.6		(8)	Recyclable materials—standards
		(9)	Additional general standards or requirements

III. Standards Applicable to Generators

	III.	(1)	Identification numbers—Do states have individual numbers?
		(2)	Small generator exemptions
262.2		(3)	Manifests—state requirements
261.3		(4)	Packaging, labeling, marking, and placarding
262.34		(5)	Period of time waste may be accumulated without granting generator status

| 262.40 | (6) | Recordkeeping requirements |
| 262.41 | (7) | Reporting requirements: |

1) Frequency of required reports
2) Does state impose additional requirements?

262.51   (8)   Exceptions

IV. Transporters

263.12	IV.	(1)	Requirements for transfer facilities
263.2		(2)	Manifest requirements
		(3)	Other state requirements

V. Owners and Operators—TSD Facility Requirements

	V.	(1)	Other types of facilities regulated by the state not regulated by EPA
264.12		(2)	Required notice
264.18		(3)	Location standards
264.71		(4)	Manifest standards
264.73		(5)	Operating records
264.75		(6)	Reporting standards
264.92		(7)	Groundwater protection
264.110		(8)	Closure and postclosure requirements
264.140		(9)	Financial requirements
264.147		(10)	Liability
265		(11)	Interim standards
		(12)	Other state requirements

VI. Permitting and Enforcement

270	VI.	(1)	State permit requirements—terminology and forms
		(2)	Public participation for permit issuance—are hearings required?
		(3)	How are disputed permits reviewed?
		(4)	Does hearing request or judicial review automatically stay permit?
		(5)	Permit application fee
270.40		(6)	Are permits transferable?
270.50		(7)	Permit duration
270.60		(8)	Permits by rule—state requirements
270.64		(9)	Permits required for underground injection
270.41		(10)	Revocation and modification of permits:

       1) Does state have to hold hearing before revocation?
       2) Are grounds for modification same as EPA's?

(11) Does state have authority to administer or issue penalties?
(12) Maximum civil penalties imposed
(13) Maximum criminal penalties imposed
       1) Does state have a reckless endangerment provision?

(14) Is there a provision providing extraordinary authority in imminent hazards?
(15) Can citizens bring actions in state courts?
(16) Does state have authority to enter by warrant?
(17) Does state have authority to order TSD owner, operator to undertake sampling and analysis?

ALABAMA

Alabama's hazardous waste management program has been taken over by EPA. Alabama has no authorization to administer a hazardous waste management program.

ALASKA

Alaska has entered into a cooperative agreement with EPA to administer its hazardous waste management program. The Department of Environmental Conservation is the agency in charge of eventually developing a state hazardous waste program.

Hazardous Waste Program
Department of Environmental Conservation
Pouch O
Juneau, Alaska 99811
(907) 465-2666

ARIZONA

I.   (1)   Hazardous Waste Management Act HB2366, 1983 Arizona Revised Statutes, Title 36—Public Health and Safety, Chapter 28
     (2)   Final authorization
     (3)   Department of Health
          Division of Environmental Health Services
          Bureau of Waste Management
          1740 West Adams
          Phoenix, Ariz. 85007
          (602) 255-1160
II.   (1)   SAF
     (2)   SAF
     (3)   SAF
     (4)   SAF
     (5)   Uses different criteria; includes carcinogens
     (6)   1)   No
          2)   No
          3)   No
     (7)   Superior Court in the county where dispute arises, 36-2823
     (8)   SAF
     (9)   SAF
III. (1)   SAF
     (2)   SAF
     (3)   One copy of each manifest must be submitted to Department by generators initiating shipments, R 9-8-1862 E.I.

   (4) SAF

   (5) SAF

   (6) SAF

   (7) 1) Generators must submit annual reports, R9-8-1862

         2) Arizona requires additional reporting, R9-8-1862 D(a)(7)(8)

   (8) SAF

IV. (1) SAF

   (2) Transporters must submit one copy of each manifest within thirty days of end of month to ADHS, R9-8-1863

   (3) SAF

V. (1) SAF

   (2) SAF

   (3) More stringent geologic and hydrologic criteria, 36-2802

   (4) One copy of each manifest must be submitted to ADHS within thirty days after end of month, R9-8-1864F

   (5) SAF

   (6) Quarterly reporting required, additional information required, R9-8-1864E(d)

   (7) SAF

   (8) SAF

   (9) SAF

   (10) SAF

   (11) SAF

   (12) SAF

VI. (1) Additional permit terms, R9-8-1870 B

   (2) Hearings available at request, R9-8-1871 K

   (3) NA

   (4) NA

   (5) $1500 per permit

   (6) SAF

   (7) Ten years

   (8) SAF

   (9) SAF

   (10) 1) Yes

        2) SAF

   (11) Yes

   (12) A.R.S. §§ 36-2823-2825

   (13) A.R.S. §§ 36-2823-2825

        1) No

   (14) No

   (15) No

   (16) Yes

   (17) Yes

ARKANSAS

I.   (1)   Arkansas Hazardous Waste Management Act, Arkansas Stat. Ann., Title 82, Chapter 42
    (2)   Federally authorized, January 1985
    (3)   Solid and Hazardous Waste Division
        Department of Pollution Control and Ecology
        8001 National Drive
        Little Rock, Ark. 72209
        (501) 562-744

II.   (1)   SAF
    (2)   SAF
    (3)   SAF
    (4)   SAF
    (5)   SAF
    (6)   1) No
    (7)   Judicial review governed by 82-4213, 82-4215, 82-4216
    (8)   SAF
    (9)   SAF

III.   (1)   SAF
    (2)   SAF
    (3)   State uses federal uniform manifest
    (4)   SAF
    (5)   SAF
    (6)   SAF
    (7)   1)   Biennial reporting
         2)   SAF
    (8)   SAF

IV.   (1)   SAF
    (2)   SAF
    (3)   Transporters must obtain permits from Arkansas Transportation Commission and Department of Pollution Control and Ecology

V.   (1)   SAF
    (2)   SAF
    (3)   Additional site location criteria, 82-4204(h), §5
    (4)   SAF
    (5)   SAF
    (6)   SAF
    (7)   SAF
    (8)   SAF
    (9)   SAF
    (10) SAF
    (11) SAF
    (12) SAF

VI.   (1)   SAF
    (2)   Hearings are required
    (3)   NA

(4) Yes

(5) Initial application fee $5000; permit renewal fee $5000; annual permit evaluation fee $5000; noncommercial facilities $1000

(6) Yes—with approval of Department

(7) Five years

(8) SAF

(9) SAF

(10) 1) No
2) SAF

(11) Yes

(12) Civil penalties, 82-4213(b)

(13) Misdemeanor, imprisonment one year, fine $10,000/violation
1) No

(14) Yes, 82-4208

(15) Yes, 82-4215(e)

(16) Yes

(17) Yes

CALIFORNIA

I. (1) California Hazardous Waste Control Act, California Health and Safety Code, Division 20, Chapter 6.5

(2) Program reverted to EPA as of January 31, 1986

(3) Department of Health Services
Hazardous Material Management Section
714 P. Street
Sacramento, Cal. 95814
(916) 324-2428

II. (1) SAF

(2) SAF

(3) SAF

(4) SAF

(5) Includes criteria for identifying nonbiodegradable toxic chemical substances, Art. 14-66889; other unique criteria, Art. 11-66699

(6) 1) Yes
2) Yes
3) Available on request

(7) Civil actions shall be brought in county where generation or disposal occurs, or the county where principal office of the defendant is located, or the county in which attorney general has nearest office, Art. 8 25181, 25183

(8) State maintains a technical reference center on hazardous waste disposal recycling practices for public and private use. Other recycling regulations—Art. 7 25170, 25175

(9) SAF

III. (1) California assigns individual identification numbers

    (2) SAF
    (3) SAF
    (4) SAF
    (5) One year, Art. 6 66535
    (6) SAF
    (7) 1) Monthly reports required
         2) SAF
    (8) SAF
IV. (1) SAF
    (2) SAF
    (3) SAF
V.   (1) SAF
    (2) SAF
    (3) Requires buffer zone of 2000 feet around facility, Art.9 25202.5(b)
    (4) SAF
    (5) SAF
    (6) Monthly reports required
    (7) SAF
    (8) SAF
    (9) SAF
    (10) SAF
    (11) SAF
    (12) SAF
VI. (1) State requires permit for extremely hazardous waste disposal, Art. 7,66570; two stages for permit; DOHS permit for TSD; State Water Resources Conservation Board permit to place waste into land
    (2) SAF
    (3) SAF
    (4) No
    (5) $10,000 initial TSD permit fee; reissuance fee of less than $5000; interim status fee of less than $1000, Art. 9 25205.1
    (6) Permits are transferable
    (7) Five years
    (8) SAF
    (9) SAF
    (10) 1) Yes
         2) Different standards for modification, Art. 8 66396
    (11) Yes
    (12) Art. 8, 25189, 25208.9
    (13) Art. 8, 25189.5, 25191, 251191.5, 25195, 25196
         1)   No
    (14) No
    (15) Yes
    (16) Yes
    (17) Yes

COLORADO

I.   (1) Colorado Hazardous Waste Act, Colorado Revised Statutes, Title 25, Article 15; Colorado Waste Facility Siting Rules, Code of Colorado Reg., Title 5, Chapter 1007, Art. 2; Colorado Hazardous Waste Management Regulations, Code of Colorado Regs., Title 5, Chapter 1007, Article 3.
     (2) Final authorization—November 1984
     (3) Department of Health
         Radiation and Hazardous Waste Control Division
         4210 East 11th Avenue
         Denver, Colo. 80220
         (303) 320-8333

II. (1) SAF
     (2) SAF
     (3) SAF
     (4) SAF
     (5) SAF
     (6) 1) Yes
         2) No
         3) Board may, at its discretion, hold an informal public hearing
     (7) District court for the judicial district within which the site or facility may be located
     (8) SAF
     (9) SAF

III. (1) SAF
     (2) SAF
     (3) SAF
     (4) SAF
     (5) SAF—extension may be granted (Permit Rules Title 5)
     (6) SAF
     (7) 1) Annual reports
         2) SAF
     (8) SAF

     (1) SAF
     (2) SAF
     (3) SAF
     (4) SAF
     (5) SAF
     (6) Annual reports required
     (7) SAF
     (8) SAF
     (9) Several different criteria for insurance, bonding
     (10) SAF
     (11) SAF
     (12) SAF

VI. (1) SAF

App. 5L-10

(2) Hearings available if sufficient public interest, Title 5 Chapter 1007, 100.508, 100.507

(3) NA

(4) No

(5) Fees—CCR Title 5, Chapter 1007 100.31-100.34

(6) Permit may be transferred only if it has been modified or revoked under 100.61

(7) Ten years

(8) SAF

(9) CCR Title 5, Chapter 1007 100.23

(10) 1) No
2) SAF

(11) Yes

(12) HW Act. 25-15-309, CRS Title 25, Art. 15—$25,000 per day per violation

(13) 25-15-310 CRS
1) No

(14) No

(15) No

(16) Yes

(17) Yes

CONNECTICUT

I. (1) Connecticut General Statutes, Title 22a Environmental Protection, Chapter 445, Hazardous Waste; Connecticut Hazardous Waste Management Regulations, Regulations of Connecticut State Agencies, Title 25, Chapter 54cc(c)

(2) Program reverted to EPA, January 31, 1986. Reversion expected to be for less than ninety days

(3) Hazardous Waste Management Section
Department of Environmental Protection
122 Washington Street
Hartford, Conn. 06013
(203) 566-5712

II. (1) SAF

(2) SAF

(3) SAF

(4) SAF

(5) Different criteria for identifying hazardous wastes, Connecticut Hazardous Waste Management Regs. Title 25, Chapter 54 cc(c)

(6) 1) Yes
2) No
3) No

(7) Judicial review in appropriate county court

(8) No exemption for reclamation of wastes, (1)(c)(27) Regs.

     (9) Include PCBs in concentrations greater than 50 ppm

III. (1) SAF

     (2) Informational requirements for persons who generate between 100 and 1000 kg per month

     (3) Generators must mail one copy of manifest to commission within three days of shipment

     (4) SAF

     (5) SAF

     (6) SAF

     (7) 1) Annual reports

           2) SAF

     (8) SAF

IV. (1) Hazardous waste transport storage criteria, 25-54 cc (c)-12 Regs.

     (2) State has own version of uniform manifest

     (3) 25-54 cc(c)-12 Regs.

V.   (1) Oil recovery facilities, chemical facilities

     (2) State has more stringent notice regulations

     (3) State has different location criteria and standards

     (4) State has own version of uniform manifest

     (5) SAF

     (6) Annual reports

     (7) SAF

     (8) Postclosure description of use required

     (9) SAF

    (10) SAF

    (11) SAF

    (12) More stringent standards for use of containers

VI. (1) Facilities must obtain certificate of public safety and necessity; other different permit requirements and terminology, 22a-117 CGS

     (2) Hearings are required 22a-119(a) CGS

     (3) Review set forth at 22a-119(f) CGS

     (5) Yes, fee schedule at 22a-118 CGS

     (6) Transferable only upon approval of Commissioner

     (7) Five years for TSD facilities, one year for transporter

     (8) SAF

     (9) Underground injection of hazardous waste is prohibited, 25-54cc(c)-48 Regs.

    (10) 1) No

           2) SAF

    (11) Yes

    (12) 22a-131 CGS

    (13) 22a-131a CGS

           1) No

    (14) Yes

    (15) No

    (16) Yes

    (17) Yes

DELAWARE

I. (1) Delaware Hazardous Waste Management Act, Delaware Code, Title 7, Chapter 63—Hazardous Waste Management
    (2) Final authorization
    (3) Delaware Department of Natural Resources and Environmental Control
        Solid Waste Management Branch
        P. O. Box 1401
        Dover, Del. 19901
        (302) 736-4781

II. (1) SAF
    (2) SAF
    (3) SAF
    (4) SAF
    (5) SAF
    (6) 1) Yes
        2) Yes
        3) Public hearings are mandatory, § 6312
    (7) NA
    (8) SAF
    (9) SAF

III. (1) SAF
    (2) 1000 kg/month
    (3) Generator must send copy of manifest to state where TSD facility is located
    (4) SAF
    (5) SAF
    (6) SAF
    (7) 1) Annual reports
        2) SAF
    (8) SAF

IV. (1) SAF
    (2) State provides own version of manifest
    (3) SAF

V. (1) SAF
    (2) SAF
    (3) Specific location prohibitions, 264-18(c)
    (4) State provides own version of manifest
    (5) SAF
    (6) Annual reports
    (7) TSD facilities required to submit hydrogeologic reports, 264.91
    (8) SAF
    (9) SAF
    (10) Liability determined specifically for each site
    (11) SAF
    (12) SAF

VI. (1) SAF
    (2) Hearings available at request
    (3) Superior Court, Court of Chancery, §6309(c), (f)
    (4) No
    (5) No
    (6) Only if modified or revoked and reissued
    (7) Ten years
    (8) SAF
    (9) Deemed to have a permit, 122.66(b)
    (10) 1) No
         2) SAF
    (11) Yes
    (12) $25,000 per day per violation
    (13) §§ 6309(f)(g)
         1) No
    (14) Yes, §6308
    (15) No
    (16) Yes
    (17) Yes

DISTRICT OF COLUMBIA

I. (1) District of Columbia Code, Title 6, Chapter 5A—Hazardous Waste Management
    (2) Final authorization
    (3) Government of the District of Columbia
       Department of Environmental Services
       Office of Environmental Standards and Compliance
       Bureau of Pesticides and Hazardous Waste Management
       5010 Overlook Avenue, S.W. Suite 114
       Washington, D.C. 20032-5397
       (202) 767-8422

II. (1) SAF
    (2) SAF
    (3) SAF
    (4) SAF
    (5) SAF
    (6) No
    (7) Judiciary—District of Columbia Superior Court
    (8) SAF
    (9) SAF

III. (1) SAF
    (2) SAF
    (3) Uniform federal manifest required
    (4) SAF
    (5) SAF

    (6) SAF
    (7) 1) Annual reports
          2) SAF
    (8) SAF

IV. (1) SAF
    (2) SAF (uniform federal manifest)
    (3) SAF

V. (1) SAF
    (2) SAF
    (3) SAF
    (4) Uniform federal manifest
    (5) SAF
    (6) Annual reports
    (7) SAF
    (8) SAF
    (9) SAF
    (10) SAF
    (11) SAF
    (12) SAF

VI. (1) SAF
    (2) Hearings available at request
    (3) NA
    (4) No
    (5) None
    (6) Upon approval by Department
    (7) Ten years
    (8) SAF
    (9) SAF
    (10) 1) No
          2) SAF
    (11) Yes
    (12) §6-530
    (13) §6-531
          1) No
    (14) No
    (15) Yes, §6-527
    (16) Yes
    (17) Yes

FLORIDA

I. (1) Florida Resource Recovery and Management Act of 1980; Florida Hazardous Waste Rules—Rules of the Florida Department of Environmental Regulation, Chapter 17-30
    (2) Final authorization
    (3) Hazardous Waste Management Program

Department of Environmental Regulation
Tevin Towers Office Building
2600 Blair Store Road
Tallahassee, Fla. 32301
(904) 488-0300

II. (1) SAF
     (2) SAF
     (3) SAF
     (4) SAF
     (5) SAF
     (6) 1) Yes
          2) Yes
          3) Available on request
     (7) Appropriate circuit court
     (8) SAF
     (9) SAF
III. (1) SAF
     (2) SAF
     (3) Uniform federal manifest required
     (4) SAF
     (5) SAF
     (6) SAF
     (7) 1) Annual reports
          2) SAF
     (8) SAF
IV. (1) SAF
     (2) Uniform federal manifest
     (3) SAF
V.   (1) SAF
     (2) SAF
     (3) SAF
     (4) Uniform federal manifest
     (5) SAF
     (6) Annual reports
     (7) Groundwater discharge considerations under §17-4.25 F.A.C. shall be
          incorporated into the facility permits
     (8) SAF
     (9) SAF
     (10) SAF
     (11) SAF
     (12) SAF
VI. (1) SAF
     (2) Hearings available at request
     (3) NA
     (4) No
     (5) Yes, $500 application for modification, $1000 construction permits for
          new facilities

App. 5L-16

(6) Yes, upon Department approval
(7) Five years; three years for temporary operating permit
(8) SAF
(9) SAF
(10) 1) No
2) SAF
(11) Yes
(12) $10,000 per violation
(13) $25,000 per violation
1) No
(14) Yes, §403.726 Florida statutes
(15) No
(16) Yes
(17) Yes

GEORGIA

I. (1) Georgia Hazardous Waste Management Authority Act, Georgia Code, Title 12—Conservation and Natural Resources, Chapter 8, Article 4; Georgia Hazardous Waste Management Act, Code of Georgia, Title 12, Chapter 8, Article 3; Georgia Hazardous Waste Management Rules, Rules and Regulations of the State of Georgia, Title 391, Article 3, Chapter 11.
(2) Final authorization
(3) Industrial and Hazardous Waste Management Program
Environmental Protection Division of Department of Natural Resources
270 Washington Street S.W.
Atlanta, Ga. 30334
(404) 656-2833
II. (1) SAF
(2) SAF
(3) SAF
(4) SAF
(5) SAF
(6) 1) Yes
2) Yes
3) Available on request
(7) Actions shall be commenced in superior court of Fulton County
(8) SAF
(9) SAF
III. (1) SAF
(2) SAF
(3) SAF
(4) SAF
(5) SAF

    (6)   SAF

    (7)   1) Biennial reports

            2) SAF

    (8)   SAF

IV. (1)   SAF

    (2)   Uniform federal manifest

    (3)   Some travel route restrictions

V.   (1)   SAF

    (2)   SAF

    (3)   SAF

    (4)   Uniform federal manifest

    (5)   SAF

    (6)   Biennial reports

    (7)   SAF

    (8)   SAF

    (9)   SAF

    (10) SAF

    (11) SAF

    (12) SAF

VI. (1)   SAF

    (2)   Hearings available if requested by twenty-five persons, Act 12-8-66 (h)

    (3)   Reviewed by Department

    (4)   No

    (5) $100—annual permit fee

    (6)   Transfer must be approved by director

    (7)   Ten years

    (8)   Yes

    (9)   SAF

    (10) 1) Yes

           2) SAF

    (11) Yes

    (12) $25,000 per day, 12-8-81 HWMH

    (13) 12-8-82 HWMH

         1)   No

    (14) Yes, 12-8-75 HWMH

    (15) No

    (16) Yes

    (17) Yes

IDAHO

I.   (1)   Idaho Hazardous Waste Management Act, Idaho Code, Title 39, Chapter 44; Idaho Hazardous Waste Management Regulations, Idaho Department of Health and Welfare, Title 1, Chapter 5—Rules and Regulations for Hazardous Wastes

App. 5L-18

 (2) Cooperative administration with EPA
 (3) Department of Health and Welfare
     Division of Environment
     Statehouse
     Boise, Idaho 83720
     (208) 334-4118

II. (1) SAF
     (2) SAF
     (3) SAF
     (4) SAF
     (5) SAF
     (6) 1) No
     (7) NA
     (8) SAF
     (9) SAF

III. (1) SAF
     (2) SAF
     (3) Federal uniform manifest, no additional requirements
     (4) SAF
     (5) SAF
     (6) SAF
     (7) 1) Quarterly reports required
     (8) SAF

IV. (1) SAF
     (2) Uniform federal manifest
     (3) SAF

V.   (1) SAF
     (2) SAF
     (3) SAF
     (4) Uniform federal manifest
     (5) SAF
     (6) Quarterly reports
     (7) SAF
     (8) SAF
     (9) SAF
     (10) SAF
     (11) SAF
     (12) SAF

VI. (1) SAF
     (2) Any interested person may request a hearing, 01.5301.06 Regs.
     (3) Departmental review
     (4) No
     (5) No
     (6) Upon approval of Department
     (7) Ten years
     (8) SAF
     (9) SAF

(10) 1) Upon timely request by permit holder for a hearing to review the permit suspension or revocation, the director shall conduct a hearing open to the public, 39-4413 Act

(11) Yes

(12) 39-4413 (2), 39-4414 (1) Act

(13) 39-4415 Act
   1)   No

(14) No

(15) No

(16) Yes

(17) Yes

ILLINOIS

I.   (1) Illinois Environmental Protection Act, 1970; Illinois Hazardous Waste Management Regulations, Illinois Administrative Code, Title 35, Subtitle G

   (2) Final authorization

   (3) Division of Land Pollution
   Illinois EPA
   2200 Churchill Road
   Springfield, Ill. 62706
   (217) 782-6762

II. (1) SAF

   (2) SAF

   (3) SAF

   (4) SAF

   (5) SAF

   (6) 1) Any person may initiate rulemaking
      2) Yes
      3) Available at request

   (7) Appropriate county court

   (8) SAF

   (9) Hazardous hospital waste, Ch.9, part IX

III. (1) SAF

   (2) A generator is a small quantity generator if he generates less than 1000 kg per month, except generators of special waste, who must generate less than 100 kg per month, 721.105 rules

   (3) A generator must send one copy of the manifest rules to the agency within two working days, 722.123

   (4) SAF

   (5) SAF

   (6) SAF

   (7) 1) Annual reports
      2) SAF

   (8) SAF

IV. (1) SAF
    (2) State has individualized manifest form and requirements
    (3) Transporters of special waste must have permits
V. (1) SAF
    (2) SAF
    (3) Several state site requirements, 703.184 rules 722 and 725
    (4) State has own manifest forms and requirements
    (5) Operators must keep additional documents, 703.246(c) rules ✓
    (6) Annual reports
    (7) More stringent requirements, 703.185 rules
    (8) SAF
    (9) SAF
    (10) SAF
    (11) SAF
    (12) SAF
VI. (1) Permit information and requirements, 35 Ill. Adm. Code 702, 703, 704, 705
    (2) Hearings available on request
    (3) NA
    (4) No
    (5) No
    (6) Transferable if modified
    (7) Permit duration to be determined on a case-by-case basis, not to exceed ten years, 702.161 rules
    (8) SAF
    (9) SAF
    (10) 1) No
        2) SAF
    (11) Yes
    (12) $10,000/per day violation
    (13) ~~NA~~ < $250,000/day
    (14) No
    (15) No
    (16) Yes
    (17) Yes

INDIANA

I. (1) Indiana Hazardous Waste Act—Indiana Code, Title 13, Environmental Article 7; Indiana Hazardous Waste Management Regulation—Indiana Administrative Code, Title 320, Article 4
    (2) Final authorization
    (3) Hazardous Waste Branch
        Indiana State Board of Health
        1330 W. Michigan Street
        Indianapolis, Ind. 46206

(317) 243-9100

II. (1) SAF
   (2) SAF
   (3) SAF
   (4) SAF
   (5) SAF
   (6) 1) Yes
       2) Yes
       3) Public hearings available on request
   (7) Rule 3, Sec. 7, Ind. Regs.
   (8) SAF
   (9) SAF

III. (1) SAF
   (2) 600 kg per month
   (3) Uniform federal manifest
   (4) SAF
   (5) SAF
   (6) SAF
   (7) 1) Biennial
       2) SAF
   (8) SAF

IV. (1) SAF
   (2) Uniform federal manifest
   (3) SAF

V. (1) SAF
   (2) SAF
   (3) Require environmental assessment of potential impact on air, water, and other natural resources, and also on environmental failure mode assessment, Chapter 8.6, Sec. 5 Act
   (4) Uniform federal manifest
   (5) SAF
   (6) Biennial reports
   (7) SAF
   (8) SAF
   (9) SAF
   (10) SAF
   (11) SAF
   (12) SAF

VI. (1) Require a certificate of environmental compatibility before issuance of a permit
   (2) Hearing must be held in area where facility is to be located
   (3) Chapter 8.6, Sec. 7(c) Act
   (4) No
   (5) User fee of $1.50 per ton
   (6) Yes, Rule 9, Sec. 6 Regs.
   (7) Five years
   (8) SAF

App. 5L-22

(9) Owners and operators of underground injection wells disposing of hazardous waste, if permitted by EPA, are deemed to have state permit, Rule 9.1(c) Regs.

(10) 1) No

2) State has own requirements, Rule 9, Sec. 5 Regs.

(11) Yes

(12) Indiana Code 13-7

(13) Indiana Code 13-7

1) No

(14) No

(15) No

(16) Yes

(17) Yes

IOWA

I. (1) Iowa Hazardous Waste Management Act—Iowa Hazardous Waste Facilities Act Laws of 1981, Chapter 152; Iowa Administrative Code, Division 900, Title X, Chapters 130, 131, Title XI Chapters 140, 141, 150

(2) State program has reverted to EPA for administration

(3) Department of Water, Air and Waste Management
Hazardous Waste Program
Henry A. Wallace Building
Des Moines, Iowa 50319
(515) 281-8915

II. (1) SAF

(2) SAF

(3) SAF

(3) SAF

(4) SAF

(5) SAF

(6) 1) Yes

2) Yes

3) Hearings available on request

(7) Judicial review, 455B.452 Iowa Code Annotated

(8) SAF

(9) SAF

III. (1) SAF

(2) 1000 kg per month

(3) Uniform federal manifest

(4) SAF

(5) SAF

(6) SAF

(7) 1) Biennial reporting

2) SAF

(8) SAF
IV. (1) SAF
   (2) Uniform federal manifest
   (3) SAF
V. (1) SAF
   (2) SAF
   (3) More stringent standards, Ia. Code Ann. Title XVII Ch. 455B,488
   (4) Uniform federal manifest
   (5) SAF
   (6) Biennial reports
   (7) SAF
   (8) SAF
   (9) SAF
  (10) SAF
  (11) SAF
  (12) SAF
VI. (1) Several additional informational requirements, Ia. Admin. Code 150.3 (455B)
   (2) Executive director shall schedule a public hearing if there is opposition in significant public interest in the draft permit, Ia. Haz. Subst. Reqs. 141.13 (15)
   (3) Judicial review, 455B.452
   (4) No
   (5) No
   (6) Permits not transferable unless the permittee and proposed transferee give 120 days' written notice to the Department, Ia. Code 150.10(455)
   (7) Five years
   (8) SAF
   (9) SAF
  (10) 1) No
      2) State has own criteria, 150.11 (455B) Ia. Admin. Code
  (11) Yes
  (12) Proceedings, Ia. Code Ann. Title XVII 455B.454
  (13) Title XVII 455B.454 Ia. Admin. Code
      1) No
  (14) No
  (15) No
  (16) Yes
  (17) Yes

KANSAS

I. (1) Kansas Hazardous Waste Management Act, Kansas Statute, Annotated, Chapter 65, Article 34; Kansas Hazardous Waste Management Regulations—Kansas Administrative Regulation, Title 28, Article 31

      (2) Final authorization
      (3) Department of Health and Environment
           Division of Environment
           Building 740, Ferber Air Force Base
           Topeka, Kan. 66620

II. (1) SAF
    (2) SAF
    (3) SAF
    (4) SAF
    (5) SAF
    (6) 1) Yes
         2) Yes
         3) Available on request
    (7) Action may be commenced in county in which violation occured, 65-3444 Act
    (8) SAF
    (9) SAF

III. (1) SAF
    (2) 50 kg per month generator exclusion until 7/1/86, 25 kg per month after 7/1/86, uncodified laws 1984, Chapter 240
    (3) Uniform federal manifest
    (4) SAF
    (5) SAF
    (6) SAF
    (7) 1) Biennial reports
         2) SAF
    (8) SAF

IV. (1) SAF
    (2) Uniform federal manifest
    (3) Transporters must pay annual fee of $250, must register with the department, and must follow specific routing requirements, 28-31-7 Regs.

V. (1) SAF
    (2) SAF
    (3) SAF
    (4) Uniform federal manifest
    (5) SAF
    (6) Monthly reports, 28-31-11 Regs.
    (7) SAF
    (8) SAF
    (9) SAF
   (10) SAF
   (11) SAF
   (12) SAF

VI. (1) State has several permit requirements, uses own forms and terminology
    (2) Public hearings required, 65-3434 Act

(3) 65-3440 Act
(4) No
(5) Fee of $25,000 with the application, 65-3437 Act
(6) Upon approval of Department
(7) Ten years
(8) SAF
(9) Most reasonable means of disposal required, also alternative technologies must be considered, 65-3437 Act
(10) 1) No
    2) SAF
(11) Yes
(12) $10,000 per violation per day
(13) 65-3441 Act
    1) No
(14) Yes, 65-3443 Act
(15) No
(16) Yes
(17) Yes

KENTUCKY

I. (1) Kentucky Environmental Protection Law—Kentucky Revised Statutes; Kentucky Waste Management Regulations—Kentucky Administrative Regulations, Title 401
  (2) Final authorization
  (3) National Resources and Environmental Protection Cabinet
Division of Waste Management
Fort Boone Plaza, 18 Reilly Road
Frankfort, Ky. 40601
(502) 564-6716
II. (1) SAF
  (2) SAF
  (3) SAF
  (4) SAF
  (5) SAF
  (6) 1) Yes
     2) Public comment required
     3) Hearings held after request of any interested person
  (7) In Franklin Circuit Court
  (8) SAF
  (9) SAF
III. (1) SAF
   (2) 1000 kg per month
   (3) Uniform federal manifest requirements
   (4) SAF
   (6) SAF

App. 5L-26

(7) 1) Annual reports
  2) SAF
(8) SAF

IV. (1) SAF
 (2) Uniform federal manifest
 (3) SAF

V. (1) SAF
 (2) SAF
 (3) Additional siting criteria, 401 KAR 38:030
 (4) Uniform federal manifest
 (5) SAF
 (6) Annual reports
 (7) More stringent groundwater standards, 401 KAR 34:060
 (8) SAF
 (9) SAF
 (10) SAF
 (11) SAF
 (12) SAF

VI. (1) Additional permit terms and requirements, including requirement of certificate of public safety, 401 KAR 38:080, 224.036 sect. 4
 (2) Public hearings held if significant degree of public interest is shown, 401 KAR 38:050 Sec. 9
 (3) Appeals taken to Franklin Circuit Court within thirty days of decision
 (4) No
 (5) Fee schedule, 401 KAR 39:050
 (6) Only if permit has been modified or reissued
 (7) Ten years
 (8) 401 KAR 38:060 Sec. 1
 (9) SAF
 (10) 1) No
   2) SAF
 (11) Yes
 (12) KRS 224.994
 (13) KRS 224.994
   1) No
 (14) No
 (15) No
 (16) Yes
 (17) Yes

LOUISIANA

I. (1) Louisiana Hazardous Waste Control Law, Louisiana Revised Statutes, Title 30, Chapter 2; Louisiana Hazardous Waste Management Plan—Louisiana Department of Natural Resources, Rules and Regulation
 (2) Final authorization

    (3) Department of Environmental Quality
           Office of Solid and Hazardous Waste
           P.O. Box 44369
           Baton Rouge, La. 70804
           (504) 342-1227

II. (1) SAF
    (2) SAF
    (3) SAF
    (4) SAF
    (5) State has unique means of identification of hazardous wastes
    (6) 1) Any person may petition the Administrator
         2) Public participation and comments required
         3) Hearing may be held at discretion of administrator
    (7) Review according to provisions of Administrative Procedure Act (R.S. 49:951) or any other applicable provisions of law
    (8) SAF
    (9) SAF

III. (1) State identification number required
    (2) Small quantity exclusion for waste generated by person who generates and disposes small quantities that pose minimum threat to the environment, Chapter 11.3 (d)(1)
    (3) State requires additional manifest information
    (4) State has more stringent marking criteria
    (5) SAF
    (6) SAF
    (7) 1) Annual reporting
         2) SAF
    (8) Special exemption for wastewater listed in Section 24.1

IV. (1) SAF
    (2) State has several manifest requirements
    (3) State imposes marking requirements

V. (1) SAF
    (2) SAF
    (3) SAF
    (4) State requires quarterly submission of manifests
    (5) SAF
    (6) Annual reports
    (7) SAF
    (8) SAF
    (9) State has separate financial requirements
    (10) SAF
    (11) SAF
    (12) SAF

VI. (1) State requires greater specificity, and has own form
    (2) Public hearings available on request
    (3) Permits reviewed under LRS 49:91
    (4) No

    (5) Yes, $2,500 plus site analysis fee
    (6) Only with approval of the Administering Authority
    (7) Ten years
    (8) SAF
    (9) La. Hazardous Waste Law §1145
    (10) 1) No
          2) More stringent modification standards
    (11) Yes
    (12) La. Hazardous Waste Law §1137
    (13) La. Hazardous Waste Law §1137
    (14) No
    (15) No
    (16) Yes
    (17) Yes

MAINE

I.   (1) Maine Hazardous Waste Septage Act, Maine Revised Statutes, Title 38, Chapter 13; Maine Hazardous Waste Management Rules—Maine Department of Environmental Protection, Rules for Hazardous Waste Management, Chapters 800-857

     (2) Program reverted back to EPA as of January 31, 1986

     (3) Department of Environmental Protection
          Ray Building
          Augusta Mental Health Institute Complex
          Hospital Street
          Augusta, Me. 04330
          (207) 289-2651

II. (1) SAF
     (2) SAF
     (3) SAF
     (4) SAF
     (5) SAF
     (6) 1) Yes
         2) Yes
         3) Available at request
     (7) NA
     (8) License required for reuse or recycling
     (9) SAF

III. (1) SAF
     (2) 200 kg/month small generation exclusion, 38 M.R.S.A. U1301
     (3) State has manifest form and requirements
     (4) SAF
     (5) SAF
     (6) Generator must keep copies of all records and test results for ten years, Rules Chapter 851 9.

(7) 1) Annual reports
    2) SAF

(8) SAF

IV. (1) SAF

(2) State has own manifest forms

(3) Transporters must be licensed by state

V. (1) SAF

(2) SAF

(3) Different requirements, Chapter 854 7 Rules

(4) State has own manifest form

(5) SAF

(6) Annual reports

(7) SAF

(8) SAF

(9) Additional financial requirements, Chapter 854 6 (14)

(10) SAF

(11) SAF

(12) SAF

VI. (1) SAF

(2) Public hearings are required

(3) NA

(4) No

(5) Disposal facilities—$10,000; commercial treatment facilities—$7000; on-site treatment facilities—$4000; other facilities—$2500

(6) Licenses are not transferable without prior approval of the board

(7) Five years

(8) Also grant permit by rule to transfer facilities and incinerators, Chapter 856, 11 Rules

(9) SAF

(10) 1) No
     2) SAF

(11) Yes

(12) § 349 Subsection 2, § 1306-C.5 MRS

(13) § 349 Subsection 3, § 1306 MRS
     1) No

(14) No

(15) No

(16) Yes

(17) Yes

MARYLAND

I. (1) Maryland Hazardous Waste Facility Siting Law, Maryland Natural Resource Code, Title 3, Subtitle 7; Maryland Hazardous Waste Regulations, Code of Maryland Regulations, Title 10, Subtitle 51; Maryland

Hazardous Waste Facility Siting Rules, Code of Maryland Regulations, Title 14

(2) Final authorization
(3) Department of Natural Resources
Environmental Services Division
Tawes State Office Building
Annapolis, Md. 21401

II. (1) SAF
(2) SAF
(3) SAF
(4) SAF
(5) SAF
(6) 1) Yes
2) Yes
3) Secretary, at his discretion, may hold an informal public hearing, Regs. 10.51.01
(7) Appropriate circuit court
(8) SAF
(9) SAF

III. (1) SAF
(2) SAF
(3) State provides own manifest form
(4) SAF
(5) SAF
(6) SAF
(7) 1) Annual reports
2) Additional requirements, 10.51.03.06C
(8) SAF

IV. (1) SAF
(2) A certificate from the state is required ⁷.
(3) SAF

V.   (1) SAF
(2) SAF
(3) SAF
(4) Operator must send manifest copy of the manifest to the Department within ten days after receipt of the waste, 10.51.05.05
(5) SAF
(6) Annual reports
(7) SAF
(8) Public comment and participation required, 10.51.05.07 C (4)
(9) SAF
(10) SAF

VI. (1) Additional permit terms, own form
(2) Public hearings required
(3) Appeals made to circuit court of the jurisdiction of the proposed site, 30712 Siting Law
(4) No

(5) Yes, $50
(6) Only if modified or revoked and reissued
(7) Three years
(8) SAF
(9) Persons may not dispose of hazardous waste by underground injection, 10.51.05.18 Rules
(10) 1) No
    2) SAF
(11) Yes
(12) Natural Resources Article Sections 8-1413.2, 8-1414
(13) Natural Resources Article Section 8-1501
    1) No
(14) No
(15) No
(16) Yes
(17) Yes

MASSACHUSETTS

I. (1) Massachusetts Hazardous Waste Laws—Mass. General Laws, Chapter 21C; Massachusetts General Regulations for Transportation and Storage of Hazardous Waste, Code of Mass. Regulations, Title 315, Chapter 2; Massachusetts Hazardous Waste Facility Regulations, Code of Mass. Regulations, Title 990, Chapters 1-16; Massachusetts Hazardous Waste Management Rule, CMR, Title 310, Chapter 30
   (2) Final authorization
   (3) Office of Environmental Affairs
Department of Environmental Quality
1 Winter Street
Boston, Mass. 02108
II. (1) SAF
   (2) SAF
   (3) The actual or intended containment of hazardous waste on a temporary basis, for a period not exceeding nine months
   (4) SAF
   (5) SAF
   (6) 1) Yes
      2) Yes
      3) Available on request
   (7) Superior court
   (8) SAF
   (9) Radioactive waste, waste oil, solvents, and chlorinated oil
III. (1) SAF
   (2) SAF
   (3) State has own manifest, seven copies required
   (4) SAF

    (5) SAF

    (6) SAF

    (7) 1) Annual reports

         2) SAF

    (8) SAF

IV. (1) SAF

    (2) State has own manifest form and requirements

    (3) Extensive insurance requirements, state license required

V. (1) SAF

    (2) SAF

    (3) Mass. Facility Siting Regs. 5.04

    (4) One copy must be sent to generator and state within fourteen days

    (5) SAF

    (6) Monthly reports

    (7) Extensive requirements, 310 CMR 30.660, Mass. Waste Rules 30.661

    (8) SAF

    (9) SAF

    (10) SAF

    (11) Additional requirements, Mass. Rules 30.099

    (12) SAF

VI. (1) State uses own terminology and from 30.800 Rules

    (2) Required public hearings

    (3) Superior Court

    (4) No

    (5) $50

    (6) No

    (7) Five years

    (8) SAF

    (9) SAF

    (10) 1) Yes

         2) Mass. Rules, 30.851

    (11) Yes

    (12) $25,000 per violation

    (13) $25,000 fine, five years' imprisonment

         1) No

    (14) Yes, 30.020 Rules

    (15) No

    (16) Yes

    (17) Yes

MICHIGAN

I. (1) Michigan Environmental Response Act, Michigan Compiled Laws Annotated, Chapter 299; Michigan Hazardous Waste Management Rules—Michigan Administrative Code Rules 299.6101-299.7305

    (2) No authorization—EPA administers programs

    (3) Department of Natural Resources
         Hazardous Waste Division
         P. O. Box 30038
         Lansing, Mich. 48909
         (517) 373-2730

II. (1) SAF
    (2) SAF
    (3) SAF
    (4) SAF
    (5) Additional EP toxicity criteria, Rule 317
    (6) 1) Yes
         2) Yes
         3) Available on request
    (7) NA
    (8) All material sold for a net gain and recycled is exempt
    (9) Include infectious waste and seven severely toxic wastes, Rule 371

III. (1) Separate numbers used, Rule 299.6205
    (2) SAF
    (3) Uniform federal manifest
    (4) SAF
    (5) SAF
    (6) SAF
    (7) 1) Biennial reports
         2) SAF
    (8) SAF

IV. (1) No short-term storage for hazardous waste haulers
    (2) Uniform manifest
    (3) Transporters must be licensed, vehicles may be inspected, R 299.6804

V. (1) SAF
    (2) SAF
    (3) SAF
    (4) Uniform manifest
    (5) SAF
    (6) Monthly reports must be submitted, additional information required
    (7) SAF
    (8) Additional requirements, R 299.6411
    (9) SAF
    (10) SAF
    (11) SAF
    (12) SAF

VI. (1) State has own terminology, facilities must be licensed
    (2) Public participation and public hearing required
    (3) Reviewed through Department
    (4) No
    (5) $500
    (6) Transferable, R 299.6507
    (7) Five years

   (8) SAF
   (9) SAF
  (10) 1) No
        2) SAF
  (11) Yes
  (12) $25,000 per violation per day
  (13) Misdemeanor, $25,000 per violation per day or one year's imprisonment
        1)   Yes, 299.548(3) Act
  (14) Yes
  (15) Persons having an interest that may be affected may intervene, 299.548(11) Act
  (16) Yes
  (17) Yes

MINNESOTA

I.   (1)   Minnesota Hazardous Waste Regulations, Minn. Rules, Chapter 7045; Minnesota Hazardous Waste Priority Assessment Criteria, Minn. Rules, Chapter 7044; Minnesota Hazardous Waste Facility Rules, Minn. Code of Agency Rules; Minnesota Permit Rules for Hazardous Waste Processing Facilities, Minn. Rules, Chapter 9200
      (2)   Final authorization
      (3)   Division of Solid and Hazardous Waste
          Minnesota Pollution Control Agency
          1935 West County Road B2
          Roseville, Minn. 55113
          (612) 296-7373
II.   (1)   SAF
      (2)   SAF
      (3)   SAF
      (4)   SAF
      (5)   SAF
      (6)   1) Yes
           2) Yes
           3) Available on request
      (7)   NA
      (8)   SAF
      (9)   Additional wastes listed, including mixtures, 6 MCAR 4.9128
III. (1)   SAF
      (2)   SAF
      (3)   Uniform federal manifest
      (4)   SAF
      (5)   SAF
      (6)   SAF
      (7)   1) Annual reporting

      2) SAF
- (8) SAF

IV. (1) SAF
- (2) Uniform federal manifest
- (3) SAF

V. (1) SAF
- (2) SAF
- (3) Additional siting criteria, including wetlands and shorelands, 6 MCAR 4.9288
- (4) Uniform federal manifest
- (5) SAF
- (6) Annual reports
- (7) Special groundwater monitoring requirement, 6 MCAR 7045.0484
- (8) SAF
- (9) SAF
- (10) SAF
- (11) SAF
- (12) SAF

VI. (1) Additional information required, 6 MCAR 7001.0530
- (2) Public comment required, hearings available on request
- (3) Petition to the Department
- (4) No
- (5) Facility fees, 6 MCAR 4.9702
- (6) No
- (7) Five years
- (8) Yes
- (9) SAF
- (10) 1) No
  - 2) SAF
- (11) Yes
- (12) $10,000 per violation
- (13) $10,000 per violation
  - 1) No
- (14) No
- (15) No
- (16) Yes
- (17) Yes

MISSISSIPPI

I. (1) Mississippi Hazardous Waste Regulations
- (2) Final authorization
- (3) Division of Solid Waste Management
  Bureau of Pollution Control
  Department of Natural Resources
  P. O. Box 10385

Jackson, Miss. 39209
(601) 961-5171

II.   (1)   SAF
      (2)   SAF
      (3)   SAF
      (4)   SAF
      (5)   SAF
      (6)   1)   Yes
            2)   Yes
            3)   Available on request
      (7)   Appropriate circuit court
      (8)   SAF
      (9)   SAF
III.   (1)   SAF
      (2)   1000 kg/month
      (3)   Uniform federal manifest
      (4)   SAF
      (5)   SAF
      (6)   SAF
      (7)   1)   Biennial Reports
            2)   SAF
      (8)   SAF
IV.   (1)   SAF
      (2)   Uniform federal manifest
      (3)   SAF
V.   (1)   SAF
      (2)   SAF
      (3)   Buffer zones required, other more stringent location standards, including stringent geological requirements, Part 264 Subpart B
      (4)   Uniform federal manifest
      (5)   SAF
      (6)   Biennial reports
      (7)   SAF
      (8)   SAF
      (9)   Detailed financial information required, Part 270.20
      (10) SAF
      (11) SAF
      (12) SAF
VI.   (1)   Perpetual care plans must be submitted with permit, 270.20
      (2)   Hearings available on request
      (3)   NA
      (4)   No
      (5)   No
      (6)   Upon revocation or modification
      (7)   Five years
      (8)   SAF
      (9)   SAF

(10) 1) No
     2) SAF
(11) Yes
(12) Miss. Code § 17-17-29
(13) Miss. Code § 17-17-29
     1) No
(14) No
(15) No
(16) Yes
(17) Yes

MISSOURI

I.   (1) Missouri Hazardous Waste Management Law, Missouri Revised Statutes, Chapter 260, § 350
     (2) Final authorization
     (3) Department of Natural Resources
         P. O. Box 1368
         2010 Mississippi Blvd.
         Jefferson City, Mo. 65102
         (314) 751-3241
II. (1) SAF
     (2) SAF
     (3) SAF
     (4) Unique definition, 260.360
     (5) SAF
     (6) 1) Yes
         2) Yes
         3) Hearings may be held
     (7) Review set forth in Chapter 536, Revised Statutes of Missouri
     (8) SAF
     (9) Waste oil and other wastes not regulated by EPA listed as hazardous waste, 4.010(6)H
III. (1) State has own identification number system
     (2) SAF
     (3) State has own manifest requirements
     (4) SAF
     (5) SAF
     (6) SAF
     (7) 1) Annual reports
         2) SAF
     (8) SAF
IV. (1) SAF
     (2) State has individual manifest requirements
     (3) Transporters must be licensed by Department and must maintain daily log, 6.010

V.　(1)　SAF
　　(2)　SAF
　　(3)　SAF
　　(4)　State has own manifest requirements
　　(5)　Stringent recordkeeping provisions, 7.011(6)(B)
　　(6)　Monthly reports
　　(7)　Extensive monitoring requirements, 7.011(10)
　　(8)　SAF
　　(9)　SAF
　　(10) SAF
　　(11) SAF
　　(12) SAF
VI.　(1)　State has additional permit requirements, 7.011(2)(E)
　　(2)　Public hearings available on request
　　(3)　Review under Chapter 536 Revised Statutes of Missouri
　　(4)　No
　　(5)　$1000 for disposal facilities; $500 for all other facilities
　　(6)　No
　　(7)　Transporters, one year; TSD facilities, permits issued for life of facility or ten years
　　(8)　SAF
　　(9)　SAF
　　(10) 1)　No
　　　　 2)　SAF
　　(11) Yes
　　(12) 260.425 Act
　　(13) 260.425 Act
　　　　 1)　No
　　(14) Imminent hazard actions to be taken, 260.420
　　(15) No
　　(16) Yes
　　(17) Yes

MONTANA

I.　(1)　Montana Hazardous Waste Act, Montana Code Annotated, Title 75, Chapter 10; Montana Hazardous Waste Management Regulation, Montana Administrative Code, Title 16, Chapter 44
　　(2)　Final authorization
　　(3)　Department of Health and Environmental Service
　　　　Cogswell Building
　　　　Helena, Mont. 59601
　　　　(406) 444-2821
II.　(1)　SAF
　　(2)　SAF
　　(3)　SAF

    (4) SAF
    (5) SAF
    (6) 1) Yes
          2) Yes
          3) Available on request
    (7) All proceedings shall be brought in county where facility is located
    (8) SAF
    (9) SAF
III. (1) SAF
    (2) 1000 kg/month
    (3) Uniform federal manifest
    (4) SAF
    (5) SAF
    (6) SAF
    (7) 1) Biennial reports
          2) SAF
    (8) SAF
IV. (1) SAF
    (2) Uniform federal manifest
    (3) SAF
V.   (1) SAF
    (2) SAF
    (3) SAF
    (4) Uniform federal manifest
    (5) SAF
    (6) Biennial reports
    (7) SAF
    (8) SAF
    (9) SAF
   (10) SAF
   (11) SAF
   (12) SAF
VI. (1) SAF
    (2) Public comment required, hearings available on request
    (3) Appeals brought to Department
    (4) No
    (5) Fee schedule, 16.44.125
    (6) Only if modified or revoked and reissued
    (7) Ten years
    (8) SAF
    (9) SAF
   (10) 1) No
         2) SAF
   (11) Yes
   (12) $10,000 per violation per day, 75-10-417
   (13) $10,000 per violation, six months' imprisonment, 75-10-418
         1) No

(14) Imminent hazard provisions, 75-10-415
(15) No
(16) Yes
(17) Yes

NEBRASKA

I. (1) Nebraska Hazardous Waste Rule, Title 128
    (2) Final authorization
    (3) Hazardous Waste Management Section
        Department of Environmental Control
        Box 94877, Statehouse Station
        Lincoln, Neb. 68509
        (402) 471-4217
II. (1) SAF
    (2) SAF
    (3) SAF
    (4) SAF
    (5) SAF
    (6) 1) Yes
        2) Yes
        3) Available on request
    (7) NA
    (8) SAF
    (9) SAF
III. (1) SAF
    (2) 1000 kg/month
    (3) Uniform federal manifest
    (4) SAF
    (5) SAF
    (6) SAF
    (7) 1) Annual reports
        2) SAF
    (8) SAF
IV. (1) SAF
    (2) Uniform federal manifest
    (3) SAF
V. (1) SAF
    (2) SAF
    (3) SAF
    (4) Uniform federal manifest
    (5) SAF
    (6) Annual reports
    (7) SAF
    (8) SAF
    (9) SAF

    (10) SAF
    (11) SAF
    (12) SAF
VI. (1) SAF
    (2) Public comment required, hearings at discretion of Director
    (3) Review by Department
    (4) No
    (5) No
    (6) Not transferable to any person except in case of TSD facility after notice to director, 010.01
    (7) Five years
    (8) SAF
    (9) SAF
    (10) 1) No
         2) SAF
    (11) Yes
    (12) $10,000 per violation
    (13) $10,000 per violation, imprisonment
         1) No
    (14) Yes, 007.02
    (15) No
    (16) Yes
    (17) Yes

NEVADA

I. (1) Nevada Hazardous Waste Disposal Law, Nevada Revised Statutes, Title 40, Chapter 444; Nevada Hazardous Waste Management Regulations, Nevada Administrative Code, Chapter 444
    (2) Final authorization
    (3) Division of Environmental Protection
        Department of Conservation and National Resources
        201 S. Full Street
        Capitol Complex
        Carson City, Nev. 89716
        (702) 885-4670
II. (1) SAF
    (2) SAF
    (3) SAF
    (4) SAF
    (5) SAF
    (6) 1) Yes
        2) Yes
        3) Available on request
    (7) County court where violation occurred
    (8) SAF

    (9) SAF
III. (1) SAF
    (2) SAF
    (3) Federal manifest
    (4) SAF
    (5) SAF
    (6) SAF
    (7) 1) Annual reports
        2) SAF
    (8) SAF
IV. (1) SAF
    (2) Federal manifest
    (3) SAF
V. (1) SAF
    (2) SAF
    (3) SAF
    (4) SAF
    (5) SAF
    (6) Annual reports
    (7) SAF
    (8) SAF
    (9) SAF
    (10) SAF
    (11) SAF
    (12) SAF
VI. (1) SAF
    (2) Hearings available upon request
    (3) NA
    (4) No
    (5) No
    (6) Upon modification, revocation and reissuance
    (7) Five years
    (8) SAF
    (9) SAF
    (10) 1) No
        2) SAF
    (11) Yes
    (12) $10,000 per violation per day
    (13) $25,000 per violation per day, one year's imprisonment, 444.778
        1)   No
    (14) No
    (15) No
    (16) Yes
    (17) Yes

NEW HAMPSHIRE

I. (1) New Hampshire Hazardous Waste Laws, N.H. Revised Statues, Chapters 147-A, 147-B, 147-C; New Hampshire Rules
   (2) Final authorization
   (3) Department of Health and Welfare
   Bureau of Solid Waste Management
   Hagen Drive
   Concord, N. H. 03301
   (603) 271-4664

II. (1) SAF
   (2) SAF
   (3) SAF
   (4) SAF
   (5) Includes specifications for multiple extraction procedures
   (6) 1) Yes
      2) Yes
      3) Mandatory hearings
   (7) Administrative and judicial remedies authorized under RSA 147:512
   (8) SAF
   (9) SAF

III. (1) SAF
   (2) 100 kg/month exclusion
   (3) Eight copies of manifest required; state has individualized form
   (4) SAF
   (5) SAF
   (6) Records must be retained for seven years
   (7) 1) Annual reports
      2) State bureau provides forms
   (8) SAF

IV. (1) SAF
   (2) State has additional manifest requirements
   (3) Transporters must have state permit

V. (1) SAF
   (2) SAF
   (3) Site regulation, 1905.08(g)
   (4) State requires more information
   (5) Records must be retained seven years
   (6) Annual reports
   (7) SAF
   (8) SAF
   (9) SAF
   (10) SAF
   (11) SAF
   (12) Towns may levy fees on facilities located within them, .007 & 1 Kg 147-D:2

VI. (1) State has own permit requirements, 1905.09

(2) Public comment required, hearings on request
(3) Administrative remedies, RSA 147:512
(4) No
(5) $5000—operators; $100—transporters; $3000—generators
(6) Not unless authorized by state bureau
(7) Five years
(8) State permits by rule, 1905.09(6)(H)
(9) SAF
(10) 1) No
     2) SAF
(11) Yes
(12) $50,000 per day per violation
(13) Class B felony, imprisonment, $50,000 per day per violation
     1) Yes
(14) Yes, 147-A:13, 1905.09(d)(5) Rules
(15) No
(16) Yes
(17) Yes

NEW JERSEY

I. (1) New Jersey Hazardous Waste Facilities Siting Act, N.J. Statutes Annotated, Title 13, Chapter 1E; New Jersey Solid and Hazardous Waste Management Regulation
    (2) Final authorization
    (3) Division of Waste Management
        Department of Environmental Protection
        CN 028
        Trenton, N.J. 08625
        (609) 292-8341
II. (1) Definition includes biologically infectious and radioactive waste along with waste oil
    (2) SAF
    (3) SAF
    (4) SAF
    (5) Unique criteria, 7:26 8:6
    (6) 1) Yes
        2) Yes
        3) Available on request
    (7) Governed by N.J. Admin. Pro. Act., NJSA 52:14B-1
    (8) SAF
    (9) Recycling materials are not exempt, other than on-site recycling
III.(1) SAF
    (2) 100 kg/month exclusion
    (3) State uses federal form, requires additional information; generator required to send copies to DEP by the next day

(4) SAF
(5) SAF
(6) SAF
(7) 1) Annual reports
    2) SAF
(8) SAF
IV. (1) SAF
(2) State requires form
(3) Additional responsibilities; required licensing, training, and disclosure statements, 7:26-7.5
V. (1) SAF
(2) SAF
(3) SAF
(4) State has manifest requirements
(5) SAF
(6) Annual reports
(7) SAF
(8) SAF
(9) Additional financial requirements, 7:26-9.10
(10) Liability requirements, 7:26-9.13
(11) SAF
(12) SAF
VI. (1) State has own terms and requirements; Environmental and Health Impact Statement required, 7:26-12:9
(2) Hearings required, 7:26-12:12
(3) Under N.J. Administrative Procedure Act 52:14B-1
(4) No
(5) No
(6) Permits transferable directly to new owner or operator
(7) Five years
(8) SAF
(9) SAF
(10) 1) No
     2) SAF
(11) Yes
(12) Civil penalties, N.J.S.A. 13:1 E
(13) N.J.S.St. 58:10A-1
     1) No
(14) Yes
(15) No
(16) Yes
(17) Yes

NEW MEXICO

I. (1) New Mexico Hazardous Waste Regulations

App. 5L-46

  (2) Final authorization
  (3) Hazardous Waste Unit
    Environmental Improvement Division
    P. O. Box 968
    Sante Fe, N.M. 87503
    (505) 984-0020

II. (1) Hazardous waste definition is substantially different
  (2) SAF
  (3) SAF
  (4) SAF
  (5) SAF
  (6) 1) Yes
     2) Yes
     3) Available on request
  (7) 303E, hearing procedures
  (8) SAF
  (9) SAF

III. (1) SAF
  (2) 1000 kg/month
  (3) Uniform federal manifest
  (4) SAF
  (5) SAF
  (6) SAF
  (7) 1) Biennial reports
     2) SAF
  (8) SAF

IV. (1) SAF
  (2) Uniform federal manifest
  (3) SAF

V. (1) SAF
  (2) SAF
  (3) SAF
  (4) Uniform manifest
  (5) More stringent recordkeeping requirements, 203C.2 & Appendix A (?)
  (6) Biennial reports
  (7) SAF
  (8) SAF
  (9) SAF
  (10) SAF
  (11) Qualifying criteria, 302C
  (12) SAF

VI. (1) Federal permit terminology, own permit form
  (2) Hearings available at request of affected individuals
  (3) Procedures, 303E
  (4) No
  (5) No
  (6) If modified and reissued under 30

(7) One year or more
(8) SAF
(9) SAF
(10) 1) No
     2) SAF
(11) Yes
(12) $10,000 per day per violation
(13) $25,000 per day per violation
(14) No
(15) No
(16) Yes
(17) Yes

NEW YORK

I. (1) New York General Hazardous Waste System Regulations, N.Y. Compilation of Rules and Regulations, Title 6, Chapter 370; New York Rules for Siting Industrial Hazardous Waste Facilities, Title 6, Chapter 361; New York Final Standards for Owners and Operation of Hazardous Waste TSD facilities, Title 6, Chapter 373-2

   (2) Application for final approval; program has temporarily reverted back to EPA; expect final authorization May 1, 1986

   (3) Division of Solid Waste
Department of Environmental Conservation
50 Wolf Road
Albany, N.Y. 12233
(518) 457-6603

II. (1) SAF
   (2) SAF
   (3) SAF
   (4) SAF
   (5) SAF
   (6) 1) Yes
     2) Yes
     3) Available on request
   (7) Article 71 ECL
   (8) Not exempt from regulation
   (9) Includes several PCB categories

III. (1) SAF
   (2) 100 kg/month
   (3) Generator required to send one copy to state within five days
   (4) SAF
   (5) Generators that store waste in sufficient quantities for less than ninety days must have a permit
   (6) SAF
   (7) 1) Annual reports

        2) More information required

   (8) SAF

IV. (1) Transfer facilities must have a state permit

   (2) State version of manifest required

   (3) Transporters must have state permit

V. (1) Facilities that TSD PCBs, generators that store waste on site for less than ninety days, wastewater treatment facilities that discharge to a POTW

   (2) SAF

   (3) Additional siting criteria, 361.7 Siting Rules

   (4) TSD facility must send copy of manifest to state within two days of receipt

   (5) SAF

   (6) Annual reports

   (7) More stringent requirements, 373-2.6

   (8) SAF

   (9) SAF

   (10) $4.5 million per occurrence, $9 million aggregate

   (11) More stringent interim regulations, N.Y. Interim State Standards for Hazardous Waste Facilities, Title 6, Chapter 373

   (12) SAF

VI. (1) State has own permit requirements, Facility Permitting Requirements, Title 6, Chapter 373-1

   (2) Adjudicating public hearing required by facilities siting board

   (3) N.Y. Administrative Procedure Act

   (4) No

   (5) No

   (6) Upon modification

   (7) Five years

   (8) SAF

   (9) SAF

   (10) 1) No

         2) Yes

   (11) Yes

   (12) Article 71 Environmental Conservation Law, Article 27, Title 9.11.13

   (13) Article 71 Environmental Conservation Law, Article 27, Title 9.11.13

        1)   Yes

   (14) Imminent hazard provisions

   (15) No

   (16) Yes

   (17) Yes

NORTH CAROLINA

I. (1) North Carolina Solid and Hazardous Waste Management Act, General Statutes of North Carolina, Chapter 130H, Article 9; North Carolina

Hazardous Waste Management Regulations; North Carolina Administrative Code, Title 10, Subchapter 10F

- (2) Final authorization
- (3) Department of Human Resources
  Division of Health Services
  P. O. Box 2091
  Cooper Memorial Building
  225 North McDowell Street
  Raleigh, N. C. 27602
  (919) 733-2178

II.
- (1) SAF
- (2) SAF
- (3) SAF
- (4) SAF
- (5) SAF
- (6) 1) Yes, .0028 Regs.
  2) Yes
  3) Available upon request
- (7) Review provided for in Article 4 of Chapter 150A of the General Statutes
- (8) SAF
- (9) SAF

III.
- (1) SAF
- (2) 1000 kg/month
- (3) State has own manifest requirements
- (4) SAF
- (5) SAF
- (6) SAF
- (7) 1) Annual
  2) SAF
- (8) SAF

IV.
- (1) SAF
- (2) State laws individualized manifest
- (3) SAF

V.
- (1) SAF
- (2) SAF
- (3) Buffer zones required, additional location requirements
- (4) State manifest
- (5) SAF
- (6) Annual reports
- (7) SAF
- (8) SAF
- (9) SAF
- (10) SAF
- (11) SAF
- (12) More stringent landfill requirements

VI.
- (1) SAF

App. 5L-50

(2) Hearings available upon request

(3) Review provided for by Article 4 of Chapter 150A of the General Statutes

(4) No

(5) None

(6) SAF

(7) Ten years

(8) SAF

(9) SAF

(10) 1) No
2) SAF

(11) Yes

(12) $10,000 per violation

(13) $10,000 per violation
1) No

(14) Yes, Sec. 130A-303 Act

(15) No

(16) Yes

(17) Yes

NORTH DAKOTA

I. (1) North Dakota Hazardous Waste Management Act, N.D. Code Title 23, Chapter 20.3; North Dakota Hazardous Waste Management Regulations, N.D. Admin. Code, Title 33, Article 33-24

(2) Final authorization

(3) Department of Health
Environmental Control Service
1200 Missouri Avenue
Bismark, N.D. 58505
(701) 224-2366

II. (1) SAF

(2) SAF

(3) SAF

(4) SAF

(5) SAF

(6) 1) Yes
2) Yes
3) Available on request

(7) NA

(8) SAF

(9) SAF

III. (1) SAF

(2) 1000 kg/month

(3) Federal uniform manifest

(4) SAF

(5) SAF

(6) SAF

(7) 1) Annual

    2) SAF

(8) SAF

IV. (1) SAF

(2) Uniform Federal manifest

(3) SAF

V. (1) SAF

(2) SAF

(3) SAF

(4) Federal manifest

(5) SAF

(6) Annual reports

(7) SAF

(8) SAF

(9) SAF

(10) SAF

(11) SAF

(12) SAF

VI. (1) Application requires additional information

(2) Hearings available on request

(3) NA

(4) No

(5) Department may assess reasonable fees for permit application, 33-24-00-21 Regs.

(6) After notice to Department

(7) Five years

(8) SAF

(9) SAF

(10) 1) No

    2) SAF

(11) Yes

(12) $25,000 per day per violation

(13) $25,000 per day per violation, one year's imprisonment

    1) Manifest extreme indifference to human life, $50,000 and two years' imprisonment

(14) Yes, 23-20.3-08

(15) Yes, person with an interest adversely affected

(16) Yes

(17) Yes

OHIO

I. (1) Ohio Solid and Hazardous Waste Disposal Law, Ohio Revised Code,

Title 37, Chapter 34; Ohio Hazardous Waste Management Regulations, Ohio Admin. Code, Title 3745, Chapters 50-69

  (2) No authorization as of January 31, 1986—program reverted back to EPA

  (3) Division of Solid and Hazardous Waste Management
Ohio EPA
361 E. Broad Street
Columbus, Ohio 43215
(614) 466-7220

II. (1) SAF
    (2) SAF
    (3) SAF
    (4) SAF
    (5) SAF
    (6) 1) Yes
         2) Yes
         3) Available on request
    (7) Court of common and pleas in the county in which the alleged violation occurred
    (8) SAF
    (9) SAF

III. (1) SAF
    (2) 1000 kg/month
    (3) Federal manifest
    (4) SAF
    (5) SAF
    (6) SAF
    (7) 1) Annual reports
         2) SAF
    (8) SAF

IV. (1) SAF
    (2) Federal manifest
    (3) Transporters must be registered with state if they originate or dispose in Ohio

V. (1) SAF
    (2) SAF
    (3) Facilities shall not be located within 2000 feet of any residence, school, hospital, or prison
    (4) Federal manifest
    (5) SAF
    (6) Annual reports
    (7) SAF
    (8) SAF
    (9) SAF
  (10) SAF
  (11) SAF
  (12) SAF

VI. (1) Additional permit requirements
    (2) Public hearings required
    (3) Court of Appeals, Franklin County. Court shall affirm order of board if it is supported by reliable, probative, and substantial evidence
    (4) No
    (5) Fees, 3734.06
    (6) Only if permit has been modified or reissued
    (7) Five years
    (8) SAF
    (9) Underground injection application, 3745-69-30
    (10) 1) Yes
         2) SAF
    (11) Yes
    (12) $10,000 per day per violation
    (13) $25,000 per day per violation
         1) Reckless violators are guilty of a felony and subject to a fine of $25,000 and imprisonment of four years
    (14) Director may issue emergency orders
    (15) Persons aggrieved or adversely affected by violation
    (16) Yes
    (17) Yes

OKLAHOMA

I. (1) Oklahoma Industrial Waste Management Regulations, Oklahoma Department of Health, Rules and Regs. for Industrial Waste Management
    (2) Final authorization
    (3) Industrial Waste Division
    State Department of Health
    P. O. Box 53551
    Oklahoma City, Okla. 73152
    (405) 271-5338
II. (1) Oklahoma uses "controlled industrial waste" instead of "hazardous waste"; defined as "waste materials and byproducts either solid or liquid, which are to be discarded by the generator; and which are toxic to human, animal or aquatic life . . ."
    (2) SAF
    (3) SAF
    (4) SAF
    (5) SAF
    (6) 1) Yes
         2) Yes
         3) Available on request
    (7) Courts of competent jurisdiction
    (8) Recycling requirements, Chapter 5

    (9) SAF

III. (1) A disposal plan number is issued to each disposal company
    (2) 1000 kg/month
    (3) State has individual manifest
    (4) SAF
    (5) SAF
    (6) Additional recordkeeping requirements, 1.3.1.1
    (7) 1) Quarterly reports
         2) SAF
    (8) SAF

IV. (1) SAF
    (2) State manifest required
    (3) Transporters must be registered with the Department of Health

V. (1) SAF
    (2) SAF
    (3) Site must be capable of retaining total precipitation and runoff generated by a 24-hour, 100-year flood, plus a minimum freeboard of 2 feet; buffer zone also required, 7.2.2
    (4) State manifest
    (5) SAF
    (6) Monthly report
    (7) SAF
    (8) SAF
    (9) SAF
    (10) SAF
    (11) SAF
    (12) Federal regulations incorporated by reference with the exception of 40 CFR § 265.1(C)(4), 265.14, 265.71, 265.272

VI. (1) State uses EPA form
    (2) Hearings available at request
    (3) NA
    (4) No
    (5) No Yes
    (6) Permits not transferable
    (7) Five years
    (8) SAF
    (9) Subject to standards governing permits for other facilities, regulated under Hazardous Waste Rules, Appendix 7-E
    (10) 1) No
         2) SAF
    (11) Yes
    (12) At discretion of court of competent jurisdiction
    (13) Imprisonment allowable at discretion of courts of competent jurisdiction
         1) No
    (14) Commissioner may take such action as is deemed necessary, Chapter 6

(15) No
(16) Yes
(17) Yes

OREGON

I. (1) Oregon Solid and Hazardous Waste Control Law, Oregon Revised Statutes, Chapter 459; Oregon Hazardous Waste Management Regulations, Oregon Administrative Rules, Chapter 340

   (2) Final authorization

   (3) Department of Environmental Quality
Solid Waste Division
1234 S.W. Morrison
Portland, Or. 97205
(503) 378-6689

II. (1) State uses expanded definition of hazardous waste, specifically includes pesticides and herbicides, 340-101-003

   (2) SAF

   (3) SAF

   (4) SAF

   (5) SAF

   (6) 1) Yes
      2) Yes
      3) Hearings available on request

   (7) Subject to review under ORS 183.310

   (8) SAF

   (9) SAF

III. (1) SAF

   (2) 2000 lbs/month

   (3) Uniform federal manifest

   (4) SAF

   (5) SAF

   (6) SAF

   (7) 1) Quarterly reports
      2) Requires certification, 340-102-041

   (8) SAF

IV. (1) SAF

   (2) Uniform manifest

   (3) Transporters regulated by DEQ, Chapter 340-103

V. (1) SAF

   (2) SAF

   (3) SAF

   (4) Uniform federal manifest

   (5) SAF

   (6) Quarterly reports required

   (7) SAF

    (8)   All wastes must be removed on closure

    (9)   SAF

    (10) SAF

    (11) SAF

    (12) SAF

VI.   (1)   SAF

    (2)   Hearings required in areas of proposed sites

    (3)   Subject to review under ORS 183.310

    (4)   No

    (5)   Filing fee of $50; application processing fee varying between $25-$5000 with each application

    (6)   Permits are nontransferable

    (7)   Ten years

    (8)   SAF

    (9)   SAF

    (10) 1) No

           2) Different requirements, 340-105-D41

    (11) Yes

    (12) $10,000 per day per violation

    (13) $25,000 per day per violation

    (14) No

    (15) No

    (16) Yes

    (17) Yes

PENNSYLVANIA

I.   (1)   Pennsylvania Solid Waste Regulations, Penn. Code, Title 25, Chapter 75

    (2)   Final authorization

    (3)   Division of Hazardous Waste Management
Department of Environmental Resources
P.O. Box 2043
Harrisburg, Pa.
(717) 787-7381

II.   (1)   SAF

    (2)   SAF

    (3)   SAF

    (4)   SAF

    (5)   SAF

    (6)   No

    (7)   NA

    (8)   SAF

    (9)   SAF

III. (1)   SAF

    (2)   1000 kg/month

(3) State has individual manifest requirements, 75.262(e)
(4) State requires additional labeling
(5) SAF
(6) Generator must retain copies of manifest for twenty years
(7) 1) Quarterly reports
    2) SAF
(8) SAF

IV. (1) SAF
   (2) State provides manifest forms
   (3) Extensive safety requirements, 75.263 (b); transporter must be licensed by state

V. (1) SAF
  (2) SAF
  (3) SAF
  (4) State manifest requirements
  (5) SAF
  (6) Quarterly reports
  (7) SAF
  (8) SAF
  (9) SAF
  (10) SAF
  (11) Interim requirements, 75.265
  (12) SAF

VI. (1) State has own terminology and forms
   (2) Hearings available on request
   (3) NA
   (4) No
   (5) No
   (6) Upon revocation or modification and reissuance
   (7) Five years
   (8) SAF
   (9) SAF
   (10) 1) No
      2) SAF
   (11) Yes
   (12) Penn. Solid Waste Management Act 6018.605.
   (13) Penn. Solid Waste Management Act 6018.606.
      1) 6018.606 (g)
   (14) Yes
   (15) No
   (16) Yes
   (17) Yes

RHODE ISLAND

I. (1) Rhode Island Hazardous Waste Management Act, Rhode Island General Law Title 23, Chapter 19.1; Rhode Island Management Facility Act, Title 23, Chapter 19.1; Rhode Island Hazardous Waste Rules and Regulations

    (2) Final authorization

    (3) Department of Environment Management
Division of Land Resources
83 Park Street
Providence, R.I. 02903

II. (1) SAF

    (2) SAF

    (3) SAF

    (4) SAF

    (5) Seventeen types of hazardous wastes, wastes classified by degree of hazard, 3.54 - 3.70

    (6) 1) Yes
         2) Require public comment and notice
         3) No hearings

    (7) NA

    (8) Generators must petition for exemption for recycling materials

    (9) State lists extremely hazardous wastes—carcinogens, teratogens, suspect human carcinogens

III. (1) SAF

    (2) No small generator exclusion

    (3) State has manifest requirements

    (4) State has labeling requirements

    (5) SAF

    (6) SAF

    (7) SAF

    (8) SAF

IV. (1) SAF

    (2) State manifest required

    (3) Transporters must have state permits

V. (1) SAF

    (2) SAF

    (3) SAF

    (4) Copy of manifest must be sent to state

    (5) SAF

    (6) Annual reports

    (7) SAF

    (8) SAF

    (9) SAF

    (10) SAF

    (11) SAF

    (12) SAF

VI. (1) SAF
 (2) Public hearings not available
 (3) Court of competent jurisdiction
 (4) No
 (5) $100 per vehicle, $1000 per facility
 (6) Upon approval of Department
 (7) Transporters—one year; TSD facilities—ten years
 (8) SAF
 (9) SAF
 (10) 1) No
   2) SAF
 (11) Yes
 (12) $10,000 per violation
 (13) Knowing endangerment is a felony punishable by a fine of $10,000 and five years' imprisonment, 19.1-18
   1) 19.1-18
 (14) No
 (15) No
 (16) Yes
 (17) Yes

SOUTH CAROLINA

I. (1) South Carolina Hazardous Waste Management Regulations, Rules of South Carolina Department of Health and Environmental Control, Regulation R.61-79.124
 (2) Final authorization
 (3) Bureau of Solid and Hazardous Waste Management
   Department of Health and Environmental Control
   2600 Bull Street
   Columbia, S.C. 29201
   (803) 758-5681

II. (1) SAF
 (2) SAF
 (3) SAF
 (4) SAF
 (5) SAF
 (6) 1) Yes
   2) No public participation required
   3) No hearings
 (7) Actions may be brought in state court of competent jurisdiction
 (8) SAF
 (9) Waste oil and waste batteries are regulated; Appendix 9 lists other wastes considered hazardous

III. (1) SAF
 (2) 100 kg per month

(3) Copy of manifest must be sent to state
(4) SAF
(5) SAF
(6) SAF
(7) 1) Quarterly reports
     2) SAF
(8) SAF
IV. (1) SAF
(2) Manifest copy must be sent to state
(3) Transporters must obtain permit from state, submit quarterly report
V. (1) SAF
(2) SAF
(3) SAF
(4) Copy of manifest must be sent to state
(5) SAF
(6) Quarterly reports
(7) SAF
(8) SAF
(9) SAF
(10) SAF
(11) SAF
(12) Fees—$5/ton, $1/ton for excess of 50 tons
VI. (1) State permit program has separate regulations and technical require-
         ments, § 270
(2) Any person may request a public hearings
(3) NA
(4) No
(5) No
(6) Permit may not be transferred to new owners or operators; Depart-
     ment may transfer permits
(7) Five years for facilities, three years for transporters
(8) SAF
(9) Special waste permits required for UIC wells
(10) 1) No
     2) Permits may be modified, revoked, and reissued at either the
         request of an interested person or upon the Department's initia-
         tive
(11) Yes
(12) South Carolina laws of 1976 § 44-56-50
(13) South Carolina laws of 1976 § 44-56-50
     1) No
(14) Imminent hazard action, 264.4
(15) No
(16) Yes
(17) Yes

SOUTH DAKOTA

I.   (1) South Dakota Hazardous Waste Management Act, S.D. Laws Title 34-A, Chapter 11; South Dakota Hazardous Waste Management Regulations, Admin. Rules of S.D. Title 74
    (2) Final authorization
    (3) Office of Air Quality and Solid Wastes
Department of Water and Natural Resources
Joe Foss Building Rm. 217
Pierre, S.D. 57501
(605) 773-3153

II. (1) SAF
    (2) SAF
    (3) SAF
    (4) SAF
    (5) SAF
    (6) SAF
      1) Yes
      2) Yes
      3) Available on request
    (7) SAF
    (8) SAF
    (9) SAF

III. (1) SAF
    (2) 1000 kg/month
    (3) Uniform federal manifest
    (4) SAF
    (5) SAF
    (6) SAF
    (7) 1) Biennial report
        2) SAF
    (8) SAF

IV. (1) SAF
    (2) Federal manifest
    (3) SAF

V. (1) SAF
    (2) SAF
    (3) SAF
    (4) SAF
    (5) SAF
    (6) Biennial reports
    (7) SAF
    (8) SAF
    (9) SAF
    (10) SAF
    (11) SAF
    (12) SAF

VI. (1) SAF
    (2) Hearings on request
    (3) NA
    (4) No
    (5) No
    (6) Upon Department approval
    (7) Five years
    (8) SAF
    (9) SAF
    (10) 1) No
        2) SAF
    (11) Yes
    (12) $10,000 per violation per day
    13) Class 4 felony
        1) No
    (14) No
    (15) No
    (16) Yes
    (17) Yes

TENNESSEE

I. (1) Tennessee Hazardous Waste Management Act, Tennessee Code, Title 68, Chapter 46; Tennessee Commercial Hazardous Waste Facility Rules, Rules of the Department of Health and Environment, Division of Solid Waste Management, Chapter 1200-1-14
    (2) Final authorization
    (3) Division of Solid Waste Management
        Bureau of Environmental Health Science
        Tennessee Department of Public Health
        301 7th Ave., North
        Nashville, Tenn. 37219
II. (1) SAF
    (2) SAF
    (3) SAF
    (4) SAF
    (5) SAF
    (6) 1) Yes
        2) Public comment required
        3) Hearings at discretion of Commissioner
    (7) State court of competent jurisdiction
    (8) SAF
    (9) SAF
III. (1) SAF
    (2) 1000 kg/month
    (3) Uniform federal manifest

(4) SAF
(5) SAF
(6) SAF
(7) 1) Annual reports
    2) SAF
(8) SAF
IV. (1) SAF
(2) Uniform federal manifest
(3) Transporters must have a permit; certain explosives are forbidden from being transported, 173.51; extensive recordkeeping requirements, 1200-1-11-.04 Rules
V. (1) SAF
(2) SAF
(3) State prohibits sites on wetlands or endangered species habitats
(4) Uniform manifest
(5) Records must be maintained until closing of facility
(6) Annual reports
(7) Monitoring wells must be inspected and approved by state geologist
(8) SAF
(9) SAF
(10) SAF
(11) SAF
(12) SAF
VI. (1) Permit requirements, 1200-1-14.02 Rules; permits must be approved by county
(2) Hearings available on request
(3) Chancery Court of Davidson County—court may grant injunctions or restraining orders; no trial by jury
(4) No
(5) Transporters—$100; on-site TSD facility—$1500 for storage; TSD facility—$2500 for disposal
(6) May be transferred if modified or revoked and reissued.
(7) One year between reviews
(8) SAF
(9) SAF
(10) 1) Hearing may be requested within thirty days after notice is received
    2) SAF
(11) SAF
(12) $10,000 per day per violation
(13) Misdemeanor—fine $10,000, one year's imprisonment; knowing violations are a felony—fine $50,000, two years' imprisonment
    1) No
(14) Emergency procedures allowed
(15) No
(16) Yes
(17) Yes

TEXAS

I. (1) Texas Hazardous Waste Management Regulations, Texas Admin. Code, Title 25, Chapter 325; Texas Industrial Waste Management Regulation, Texas Admin. Code, Title 31, Chapter 335
    (2) Final authorization
    (3) Industrial Solid Waste Section
    Texas Department of Natural Resources
    P.O. Box 13087
    Capital Station
    Austin, Tex. 78711
    (512) 475-2041

II. (1) Defines hazardous industrial waste—any industrial solid waste indentified by §3001 of RCRA
    (2) SAF
    (3) SAF
    (4) SAF
    (5) State includes solid industrial waste and hazardous waste
    (6) 1) Yes
        2) Yes
        3) Available on request
    (7) County where dispute occurs, or Travis County
    (8) SAF
    (9) SAF

III. (1) Texas Municipal Waste Code numbers are required.
    (2) 1000 kg/month
    (3) State manifests—require state waste load identification number, also require shipping tickets, 335.10
    (4) SAF
    (5) SAF
    (6) SAF +Monthly
    (7) 1) Annual
        2) Texas shipping ticket required
    (8) SAF

IV. (1) SAF
    (2) Texas manifest
    (3) SAF

V. (1) SAF
    (2) SAF
    (3) Unsuitable site characteristic, 335, 504
    (4) Shipping tickets required
    (5) SAF
    (6) Monthly reports
    (7) SAF
    (8) SAF
    (9) SAF
    (10) SAF

(11) SAF
(12) SAF
VI. (1) State requires additional information, 325.350
  (2) Public hearings required
  (3) NA
  (4) No
  (5) No
  (6) Application must be made to Department
  (7) Five years
  (8) SAF
  (9) SAF
  (10) SAF
  (11) Yes
  (12) $25,000 per day per violation
  (13) Fine $25,000, one year's imprisonment
     1) Extreme indifference—fine $250,000, five years' imprisonment
  (14) No
  (15) No
  (16) Yes
  (17) Yes

UTAH

I. (1) Utah Solid and Hazardous Waste Act, Utah Code Annotated, Title 26, Chapter 14; Utah Hazardous Waste Facility Management Act, Utah Code Annotated, Title 26, Chapter 131; Utah Hazardous Waste Regulations
  (2) Final authorization
  (3) Bureau of Solid and Hazardous Waste
    Department of Health
    P.O. Box 45500
    Salt Lake City, Utah 84145
    (801) 533-4145
II. (1) SAF
  (2) SAF
  (3) SAF
  (4) SAF
  (5) SAF
  (6) 1) Yes
    2) Public comment required
    3) Hearings required
  (7) County where violation occurred, district court
  (8) SAF
  (9) SAF
III. (1) SAF
  (2) 1000 kg/month

      (3)   Uniform manifest
      (4)   SAF
      (5)   SAF
      (6)   SAF
      (7)   1) Biennial reports
              2) SAF
      (8)   SAF

IV. (1)   SAF
      (2)   Federal manifest
      (3)   SAF

V.   (1)   SAF
      (2)   SAF
      (3)   Location and siting standards in Hazardous Waste Facility Siting Act, Utah Code Annotated, Title 26, Chapter 149.
      (4)   SAF
      (5)   SAF
      (6)   Biennial reports
      (7)   SAF
      (8)   SAF
      (9)   SAF
     (10) SAF
     (11) SAF
     (12) SAF

VI. (1)   Permits designated as "plan"—requirements, 13.31
      (2)   Any person may request a hearing
      (3)   NA
      (4)   No
      (5)   No
      (6)   Only if plan approval has been modified or revoked and reissued.
      (7)   Ten years
      (8)   SAF
      (9)   Permit by rule
     (10) 1) No
             2) SAF
     (11) Yes
     (12) $10,000 per day per violation
     (13) Knowing violation—Class A misdemeanor, $15,000 per day
             1) Yes
     (14) Director may take reasonable action to abate the threat, 26-14-19
     (15) No
     (16) Yes
     (17) Yes

VERMONT

I.   (1) Vermont Solid Waste Management Law, Vermont Statutes Annotated, Title 10, Chapter 154

     (2) Final authorization

     (3) Materials Management Program
Agency of Environmental Conservation
State Office Building
Montpelier, Vt. 05602
(802) 828-3395

II. (1) SAF

     (2) SAF

     (3) SAF

     (4) SAF

     (5) SAF

     (6) 1) Yes
2) Yes
3) Public hearings required

     (7) Circuit court of competent jurisdiction

     (8) SAF

     (9) Additional waste included—hospital wastes, paint, petroleum, PCBs, waste oil, 6-602(2)9

III. (1) SAF

     (2) 1000 kg/month

     (3) Vermont supplies manifest

     (4) SAF

     (5) SAF

     (6) SAF

     (7) 1) Annual reports
2) SAF

     (8) SAF

IV. (1) SAF

     (2) Vermont supplies manifest

     (3) Transporters must be certified by State Transportation Agency

V. (1) SAF

     (2) SAF

     (3) SAF

     (4) SAF

     (5) SAF

     (6) Annual reporting

     (7) SAF

     (8) SAF

     (9) SAF

     (10) SAF

     (11) SAF

     (12) SAF

VI. (1) SAF

(2) Public comment required, public hearings must be held
(3) NA
(4) No
(5) $10
(6) Upon approval of Agency
(7) Five years
(8) SAF
(9) SAF
(10) 1) Hearings may be held within thirty days after revocation
    2) SAF
(11) Yes
(12) 10 V.S.A. Section 6612 or 3 V.S.A. Section 2822
(13) 10 V.S.A. Section 6612 or 3 V.S.A. Section 2822
    1) No
(14) Imminent substantial hazard actions, 6-705
(15) No
(16) Yes
(17) Yes

VIRGINIA

I. (1) Virginia Solid and Hazardous Waste Management Law, Code of Virginia, Title 32.1, Chapter 6, Article 3; Virginia Hazardous Waste Management Regulations
    (2) Final authorization, 1984
    (3) Division of Solid and Hazardous Waste Management
        Department of Health
        101 N. 14th Street
        Richmond, Va. 23219
        (804) 225-2667
II. (1) SAF
    (2) SAF
    (3) SAF
    (4) SAF
    (5) SAF
    (6) 1) Yes, 3.12.02 A
        2) No
        3) No
    (7) Attorney General shall have authority to enforce in the appropriate circuit court
    (8) Recycling activities are subject to notification requirements
    (9) SAF
III. (1) SAF
    (2) 1000 kg/month
    (3) Uniform federal manifest form and terms

(4) Packaging, labeling, and marking must be done in accordance with Virginia Regulations Governing Transport of Hazardous Materials

(5) SAF

(6) SAF

(7) 1) Annual reporting
2) Additional reporting requirements, Appendix 10.2 Regs.

(8) SAF

IV. (1) SAF

(2) state has individualized manifest requirements

(3) Transporters must have a state permit; additional transporter requirements, 7.00 Regs.

V. (1) SAF

(2) SAF

(3) Impact analysis required, Siting Act §10-186.11

(4) SAF

(5) SAF

(6) SAF

(7) SAF

(8) SAF

(9) SAF

(10) SAF

(11) SAF

(12) SAF

VI. (1) SAF

(2) All permits will be subject of public hearings, 1.06.02 Regs.

(3) In accordance with Administrative Process Act, in manner of rules of Supreme Court of Virginia.

(4) No

(5) Permit fee regulations, 12.00 Regs.

(6) Only after notice to Commissioner, 11.10.12(c) Regs.

(7) Ten years

(8) SAF

(9) Disposal of hazardous waste by underground injection is specifically prohibited, 11.01.03 Regs.

(10) 1) No
2) SAF

(11) Yes

(12) $10,000 per violation per day, 1.07.04 Regs

(13) Felony—one year's imprisonment; $10,000 per violation per day
1) No

(14) No

(15) No

(16) Yes

(17) Yes

WASHINGTON

I.   (1) Washington Hazardous Waste Disposal Act, Revised Code Washington, Title 70, Chapter 105; Washington Dangerous Waste Regulations, Washington Administrative Code, 173 Chapter 303
     (2) Final authorization
     (3) Hazardous Waste Section
          Department of Ecology
          Mail Stop PV-11
          Olympia, Wash. 98504
          (206) 459-6305

II. (1) Defines extremely hazardous wastes and dangerous wastes
     (2) SAF
     (3) SAF
     (4) SAF
     (5) State's criteria for waste designation, WAC 173-303-070; waste designated as either extremely hazardous or dangerous; toxicity, persistence, and carcinogenicity are used to identify hazardous waste
     (6) 1) Any person may initiate rulemaking, WAC 173-303-0702
          2) Public comment is required
          3) Public hearings available on request
     (7) Appropriate county court
     (8) SAF
     (9) SAF

III. (1) Generators must have both an EPA and a state identification number
     (2) Several quantity generators exemptions dependent upon waste classification, WAC-173-303-070(8)
     (3) Uniform federal manifest used
     (4) SAF
     (5) Accumulation without sufficient use, reuse, or recycling, WAC-173-303-121
     (6) SAF
     (7) 1) Annual reports
          2) SAF
     (8) SAF

IV. (1) SAF
     (2) SAF
     (3) SAF

V.   (1) SAF
     (2) SAF
     (3) Additional siting standards, requirements of buffer zones, WAC-173-303-420
     (4) SAF
     (5) SAF
     (6) Annual reporting
     (7) SAF
     (8) SAF

(9) SAF
(10) SAF
(11) SAF
(12) SAF
VI. (1) Demonstration of safety required before permit issued
(2) Public participation required; hearings available on request
(3) Appeal to department
(4) No
(5) Washington Hazardous Waste Fee Regulations, Title 173, Chapter 305 WAC-173-305-040
(6) No
(7) Ten years
(8) SAF
(9) SAF
(10) 1) No
    2) SAF
(11) Yes
(12) $10,000 per violation per day
(13) Gross misdemeanor—$10,000 per violation, one year's imprisonment
(14) Yes, Imminent Substantial Endangerment WAC-173-303-280(2)
(15) No
(16) Yes
(17) Yes

WEST VIRGINIA

I. (1) West Virginia Hazardous Waste Management Act, West Virginia Code, Chapter 20, Art. 5E, Chapter 114; West Virginia Hazardous Waste Regulation, Chapter 20-5E
(2) State program has temporarily reverted back to the EPA; final authorization expected May 1986
(3) Department of Natural Resources Hazardous Waste Section
1800 Washington Street East
Charleston, West Va. 25305
II. (1) SAF
(2) SAF
(3) SAF
(4) SAF
(5) SAF
(6) 1) Yes
    2) Public comment required
    3) Hearings available on request
(7) Procedures set forth in Section 7, Article 20, Chapter 16 of West Virginia Code.
(8) SAF
(9) SAF

III. (1) SAF
    (2) 1000 kg/month—subject to notification and recordkeeping requirements
    (3) Uniform federal manifest
    (4) SAF
    (5) SAF
    (6) SAF
    (7) (1) Annual reports—use EPA forms
    (8) SAF
IV. (1) SAF
    (2) Uniform federal manifest
    (3) SAF
V. (1) SAF
    (2) SAF
    (3) More stringent location standards, 11.05.01(1)
    (4) SAF
    (5) SAF
    (6) Annual reports
    (7) Rely on Water Resources Board groundwater protection standards, 8.13 Regs.
    (8) SAF
    (9) SAF
    (10) SAF
    (11) SAF
    (12) New land facilities must have double liners, 8.13 Regs.
VI. (1) SAF
    (2) Any interested person may request a hearing
    (3) Appeal to Water Resources Board, hearing in Charleston, Kanawha County
    (4) No
    (5) Application fees, 11.02.08 Regs.—fees determined by schedule
    (6) Only if permit has been modified or revoked and reissued
    (7) Ten years
    (8) SAF
    (9) SAF
    (10) 1) No
        2) SAF
    (11) Yes
    (12) $25,000 per day per violation
    (13) $50,000 per day per violation, two years' imprisonment
        1) Yes—felony, $250,000 per violation, four years' imprisonment
    (14) Yes, §20-5E-17 Act
    (15) Yes, citizens' suits, §20-5E-18 Act
    (16) Yes
    (17) Yes

WISCONSIN

I. (1) Wisconsin Environmental Protection Law, Wisconsin Statutes Annotated, Title XV, Chapter 144; Wisconsin Hazardous Waste Management Rules, Wisconsin Administrative Code, Chapter 181; Wisconsin Hazardous Waste Management Act, Wisconsin Statutes Annotated, Title XV, Chapter 144

    (3) Hazardous Waste Section
Bureau of Solid Waste Management
Department of Natural Resources
P.O. Box 7921
Madison, Wis. 53707
(608) 266-0833

II. (1) SAF
    (2) SAF
    (3) SAF
    (4) SAF
    (5) SAF
    (6) 1) Yes
       2) Yes
       3) Available on request
    (7) Actions must be commenced in circuit court for the county in which the violation occurred
    (8) Federal exemption not applicable
    (9) Generator must pay groundwater fee of 10 cents per ton, 144.441; restrictions on disposal of 2,4,5 T and Silvex

III. (1) SAF
    (2) 100kg/mo
    (3) Wisconsin has own form and requirements, NR 181.34
    (4) SAF
    (5) SAF
    (6) SAF
    (7) 1) Annual reports
       2) SAF
    (8) SAF

IV. (1) SAF
    (2) Transporters are subject to manifest requirements of NR 181.34
    (3) Transporters must be licensed by state

V. (1) SAF
    (2) SAF
    (3) Affected municipalities may participate in siting process; EIS required
    (4) State has TSD manifest requirements
    (5) SAF
    (6) Quarterly reports required
    (7) SAF
    (8) SAF

    (9) Provides unique financial responsibility mechanisms, NR 181.142(10)

    (10) SAF

    (11) SAF

    (12) Owners and operators must pay tonnage fee of 15 cents per ton

VI. (1) Several different requirements, including submission of feasibility report, NR 181.51

    (2) Hearings available on request

    (3) Review governed by Ch. 227.15-227.21

    (4) No

    (5) Fee schedule, Table IX NR 181.55

    (6) Upon modification or revocation and reissuance

    (7) Two years

    (8) SAF

    (9) Underground injection of hazardous waste is prohibited

    (10) 1) No

         2) SAF

    (11) Yes

    (12) $25,000 per day per violation

    (13) $25,000 per violation, one year's imprisonment

         1) No

    (14) No

    (15) No

    (16) Yes

    (17) Yes

WYOMING

Wyoming has not adopted any legislation authorizing the state to operate a hazardous waste management program. The EPA is currently administering the program in the state.

Appendix 6A Table of Session Law to U.S. Code Cross-References: Comprehensive Environmental Response, Compensation and Liability Act (CERCLA)

CERCLA Session Law Number (Selected)*	Title 42 U.S. Code Number
§101	§9601
§102	§9602
§103	§9603
§104	§9604
§105	§9605
§106	§9606
§107	§9607
§108	§9608
§109	§9609
§110	§9610
§111	§9611
§112	§9612
§113	§9613
§114	§9614
§115	§9615
§116	§9616
§117	§9617
§118	§9618
§119	§9619
§120	§9620
§121	§9621
§122	§9622
§123	§9623
§124	§9624
§125	§9625
§221	§9631
§222	§9632
§223	§9633
§232	§9641
§301	§9651
§302	§9652
§303	§9653
§304	§9654
§305	§9655

---

* Comprehensive Environmental Response, Compensation and Liability Act of 1980 (42 USC §§9601 *et seq.*), Pub.L. 96-510, H.R. 7020, December 11, 1980, as amended by Pub.L. 98-80, August 28, 1983, and affected by Pub.L. 97-272, September 30, 1982, by Pub.L. 98-371, July 18, 1984; and Pub.L. 99-499, October 17, 1986. 94 Stat. 2767.

Appendix 6B Requirements and Guidelines for Spill Prevention Control and Countermeasure (SPCC) Plans*

§ 112.3 Requirements for preparation and implementation of Spill Prevention Control and Countermeasure Plans.

(a) Owners or operators of onshore and offshore facilities in operation on or before the effective date of this part that have discharged or, due to their location, could reasonably be expected to discharge oil in harmful quantities, as defined in 40 CFR Part 110, into or upon the navigable waters of the United States or adjoining shorelines, shall prepare a Spill Prevention Control and Countermeasure Plan (hereinafter "SPCC Plan"), in writing and in accordance with § 112.7. Except as provided for in paragraph (f) of this section, such SPCC Plan shall be prepared within six months after the effective date of this part and shall be fully implemented as soon as possible, but not later than one year after the effective date of this part.

(b) Owners or operators of onshore and offshore facilities that become operational after the effective date of this part, and that have discharged or could reasonably be expected to discharge oil in harmful quantities, as defined in 40 CFR Part 110, into or upon the navigable waters of the United States or adjoining shorelines, shall prepare an SPCC Plan in accordance with § 112.7. Except as provided for in paragraph (f) of this section, such SPCC Plan shall be prepared within six months after the date such facility begins operations and shall be fully implemented as soon as possible, but not later than one year after such facility begins operations.

(c) Owners or operators of onshore and offshore mobile or portable facilities, such as onshore drilling or workover rigs, barge mounted offshore drilling or workover rigs, and portable fueling facilities shall prepare and implement an SPCC Plan as required by paragraphs (a), (b) and (d) of this section. The owners or operators of such facility need not prepare a new SPCC Plan each time the facility is moved to a new site. The SPCC Plan may be a general plan, prepared in accordance with § 112.7, using good engineering practice. When the mobile or portable facility is moved, it must be located and installed using the spill prevention practices outlined in the SPCC Plan for the facility. No mobile or portable facility subject to this regulation shall operate unless the SPCC Plan has been implemented. The SPCC Plan shall only apply while the facility is in a fixed (non-transportation) operating mode.

(d) No SPCC Plan shall be effective to satisfy the requirements of this part unless it has been reviewed by a Registered Professional Engineer and certified to by such Professional Engineer. By means of this certification the engineer, having examined the facility and being familiar with the provisions of this part, shall attest that the SPCC Plan has been prepared in accordance with good engineering practices. Such certification shall in no way relieve the owner or operator of an onshore or offshore facility of his duty to prepare and fully implement such Plan in accordance with § 112.7, as required by paragraphs (a), (b) and (c) of this section.

---

* 40 CFR §§112.3, 112.7.

(e) Owners or operators of a facility for which an SPCC Plan is required pursuant to paragraph (a), (b) or (c) of this section shall maintain a complete copy of the Plan at such facility if the facility is normally attended at least 8 hours per day, or at the nearest field office if the facility is not so attended, and shall make such Plan available to the Regional Administrator for on-site review during normal working hours.

(f) Extensions of time.

(1) The Regional Administrator may authorize an extension of time for the preparation and full implementation of an SPCC Plan beyond the time permitted for the preparation and implementation of an SPCC Plan pursuant to paragraph (a), (b) or (c) of this section where he finds that the owner or operator of a facility subject to paragraphs (a), (b) or (c) of this section cannot fully comply with the requirements of this part as a result of either nonavailability of qualified personnel, or delays in construction or equipment delivery beyond the control and without the fault of such owner or operator or their respective agents or employees.

(2) Any owner or operator seeking an extension of time pursuant to paragraph (f)(1) of this section may submit a letter of request to the Regional Administrator. Such letter shall include:

(i) A complete copy of the SPCC Plan, if completed;

(ii) A full explanation of the cause for any such delay and the specific aspects of the SPCC Plan affected by the delay;

(iii) A full discussion of actions being taken or contemplated to minimize or mitigate such delay;

(iv) A proposed time schedule for the implementation of any corrective actions being taken or contemplated, including interim dates for completion of tests or studies, installation and operation of any necessary equipment or other preventive measures.

In addition, such owner or operator may present additional oral or written statements in support of his letter of request.

(3) The submission of a letter of request for extension of time pursuant to paragraph (f)(2) of this section shall in no way relieve the owner or operator from his obligation to comply with the requirements of § 112.3 (a), (b) or (c). Where an extension of time is authorized by the Regional Administrator for particular equipment or other specific aspects of the SPCC Plan, such extension shall in no way affect the owner's or operator's obligation to comply with the requirements of § 112.3 (a), (b) or (c) with respect to other equipment or other specific aspects of the SPCC Plan for which an extension of time has not been expressly authorized.

[38 FR 34165, Dec. 11, 1973, as amended at 41 FR 12657, Mar. 26, 1976]

§ 112.7 Guidelines for the preparation and implementation of a Spill Prevention Control and Countermeasure Plan.

The SPCC Plan shall be a carefully thought-out plan, prepared in accordance with good engineering practices, and which has the full approval of management at a level with authority to commit the necessary resources. If the plan calls for additional facilities or procedures, methods, or equipment not yet fully operational, these items should be discussed in separate paragraphs, and the details of installation and operational start-up should be explained separately. The complete SPCC Plan shall follow the sequence outlined below, and include a discussion of the facility's conformance with the appropriate guidelines listed:

(a) A facility which has experienced one or more spill events within twelve months prior to the effective date of this part should include a written description of each such spill, corrective action taken and plans for preventing recurrence.

(b) Where experience indicates a reasonable potential for equipment failure (such as tank overflow, rupture, or leakage), the plan should include a prediction of the direction, rate of flow, and total quantity of oil which could be discharged from the facility as a result of each major type of failure.

(c) Appropriate containment and/or diversionary structures or equipment to prevent discharged oil from reaching a navigable water course should be provided. One of the following preventive systems or its equivalent should be used as a minimum:

(1) Onshore facilities:
(i) Dikes, berms or retaining walls sufficiently impervious to contain spilled oil;
(ii) Curbing;
(iii) Culverting, gutters or other drainage systems;
(iv) Weirs, booms or other barriers;
(v) Spill diversion ponds;
(vi) Retention ponds;
(vii) Sorbent materials.
(2) Offshore facilities:
(i) Curbing, drip pans;
(ii) Sumps and collection systems.
(d) When it is determined that the installation of structures or equipment listed in § 112.7(c) to prevent discharged oil from reaching the navigable waters is not practicable from any onshore or offshore facility, the owner or operator should clearly demonstrate such impracticability and provide the following:

(1) A strong oil spill contingency plan following the provision of 40 CFR Part 109.

(2) A written commitment of manpower, equipment and materials required to expeditiously control and remove any harmful quantity of oil discharged.

(e) In addition to the minimal prevention standards listed under § 112.7(c), sections of the Plan should include a complete discussion of conformance with the following applicable guidelines, other effective spill prevention and containment procedures (or, if more stringent, with State rules, regulations and guidelines):

(1) *Facility drainage (onshore); (excluding production facilities).* (i) Drainage from diked storage areas should be restrained by valves or other positive means to prevent a spill or other excessive leakage of oil into the drainage system or inplant effluent treatment system, except where plan systems are designed to handle such leakage. Diked areas may be emptied by pumps or ejectors; however, these should be manually activated and the condition of the accumulation should be examined before starting to be sure no oil will be discharged into the water.

(ii) Flapper-type drain valves should not be used to drain diked areas. Valves used for the drainage of diked areas should, as far as practical, be of manual, open-and-closed design. When plant drainage drains directly into water courses and not into wastewater treatment plants, retained storm water should be inspected as provided in paragraphs (e)(2)(iii) (B), (C) and (D) before drainage.

(iii) Plant drainage systems from undiked areas should, if possible, flow into ponds, lagoons or catchment basins, designed to retain oil or return it to the facility. Catchment basins should not be located in areas subject to periodic flooding.

(iv) If plant drainage is not engineered as above, the final discharge of all in-plant ditches should be equipped with a diversion system that could, in the event of an uncontrolled spill, return the oil to the plant.

(v) Where drainage waters are treated in more than one treatment unit, natural hydraulic flow should be used. If pump transfer is needed, two "lift" pumps should be provided, and at least one of the pumps should be permanently installed when such treatment is continuous. In any event, whatever techniques are used facility drainage systems should be adequately engineered to prevent oil from reaching navigable waters in the event of equipment failure or human error at the facility.

(2) *Bulk storage tanks (onshore); (excluding production facilities).* (i) No tank should be used for the storage of oil unless its material and construction are compatible with the material stored and conditions of storage such as pressure and temperature, etc.

(ii) All bulk storage tank installations should be constructed so that a secondary means of containment is provided for the entire contents of the largest single tank plus sufficient freeboard to allow for precipitation. Diked areas should be sufficiently impervious to contain spilled oil. Dikes, containment curbs, and pits are commonly employed for this purpose, but they may not always be appropriate. An alternative system could consist of a complete drainage trench enclosure arranged so that a spill could terminate and be safely confined in an in-plant catchment basin or holding pond.

(iii) Drainage of rainwater from the diked area into a storm drain or an effluent discharge that empties into an open water course, lake, or pond, and bypassing the in-plant treatment system may be acceptable if:

(A) The bypass valve is normally sealed closed.

(B) Inspection of the run-off rain water ensures compliance with applicable water quality standards and will not cause a harmful discharge as defined in 40 CFR Part 110.

(C) The bypass valve is opened, and resealed following drainage under responsible supervision.

(D) Adequate records are kept of such events.

(iv) Buried metallic storage tanks represent a potential for undetected spills. A new buried installation should be protected from corrosion by coatings, cathodic protection or other effective methods compatible with local soil conditions. Such buried tanks should at least be subjected to regular pressure testing.

(v) Partially buried metallic tanks for the storage of oil should be avoided, unless the buried section of the shell is adequately coated, since partial burial in damp earth can cause rapid corrosion of metallic surfaces, especially at the earth/air interface.

(vi) Aboveground tanks should be subject to periodic integrity testing, taking into account tank design (floating roof, etc.) and using such techniques as hydrostatic testing, visual inspection or a system of non-destructive shell thickness testing. Comparison records should be kept where appropriate, and tank supports and foundations should be included in these inspections. In addition, the outside of the tank should frequently be observed by operating personnel for signs of deterioration, leaks which might cause a spill, or accumulation of oil inside diked areas.

(vii) To control leakage through defective internal heating coils, the following factors should be considered and applied, as appropriate.

(A) The steam return or exhaust lines from internal heating coils which discharge into an open water course should be monitored for contamination, or passed through a settling tank, skimmer, or other separation or retention system.

(B) The feasibility of installing an external heating system should also be considered.

(viii) New and old tank installations should, as far as practical, be fail-safe engineered or updated into a fail-safe engineered installation to avoid spills. Consideration should be given to providing one or more of the following devices:

(A) High liquid level alarms with an audible or visual signal at a constantly manned operation or surveillance station; in smaller plants an audible air vent may suffice.

(B) Considering size and complexity of the facility, high liquid level pump cutoff devices set to stop flow at a predetermined tank content level.

(C) Direct audible or code signal communication between the tank gauger and the pumping station.

(D) A fast response system for determining the liquid level of each bulk storage tank such as digital computers, telepulse, or direct vision gauges or their equivalent.

(E) Liquid level sensing devices should be regularly tested to insure proper operation.

(ix) Plant effluents which are discharged into navigable waters should have disposal facilities observed frequently enough to detect possible system upsets that could cause an oil spill event.

(x) Visible oil leaks which result in a loss of oil from tank seams, gaskets, rivets and bolts sufficiently large to cause the accumulation of oil in diked areas should be promptly corrected.

(xi) Mobile or portable oil storage tanks (onshore) should be positioned or located so as to prevent spilled oil from reaching navigable waters. A secondary means of containment, such as dikes or catchment basins, should be furnished for the largest single compartment or tank. These facilities should be located where they will not be subject to periodic flooding or washout.

(3) *Facility transfer operations, pumping, and in-plant process (onshore); (excluding production facilities).* (i) Buried piping installations should have a protective wrapping and coating and should be cathodically protected if soil conditions warrant. If a section of buried line is exposed for any reason, it should be carefully examined for deterioration. If corrosion damage is found, additional examination and corrective action should be taken as indicated by the magnitude of the damage. An alternative would be the more frequent use of exposed pipe corridors or galleries.

(ii) When a pipeline is not in service, or in standby service for an extended time the terminal connection at the transfer point should be capped or blank-flanged, and marked as to origin.

(iii) Pipe supports should be properly designed to minimize abrasion and corrosion and allow for expansion and contraction.

(iv) All aboveground valves and pipelines should be subjected to regular examinations by operating personnel at which time the general condition of items, such as flange joints, expansion joints, valve glands and bodies, catch pans, pipeline supports, locking of valves, and metal surfaces should be assessed. In addition, periodic pressure testing may be warranted for piping in areas where facility drainage is such that a failure might lead to a spill event.

(v) Vehicular traffic granted entry into the facility should be warned verbally or by appropriate signs to be sure that the vehicle, because of its size, will not endanger above ground piping.

(4) *Facility tank car and tank truck loading/unloading rack (onshore).* (i) Tank car and tank truck loading/unloading procedures should meet the minimum requirements and regulation established by the Department of Transportation.

(ii) Where rack area drainage does not flow into a catchment basin or treatment facility designed to handle spills, a quick drainage system should be used for tank truck loading and unloading areas. The containment system should be designed to hold at least maximum capacity of any single compartment of a tank car or tank truck loaded or unloaded in the plant.

(iii) An interlocked warning light or physical barrier system, or warning signs, should be provided in loading/unloading areas to prevent vehicular departure before complete disconnect of flexible or fixed transfer lines.

(iv) Prior to filling and departure of any tank car or tank truck, the lowermost drain and all outlets of such vehicles should be closely examined for leakage, and if necessary, tightened, adjusted, or replaced to prevent liquid leakage while in transit.

(5) *Oil production facilities (on-shore)*—(i) *Definition.* An onshore production facility may include all wells, flowlines, separation equipment, storage facilities, gathering lines, and auxiliary non-transportation-related equipment and facilities in a single geographical oil or gas field operated by a single operator.

(ii) *Oil production facility (onshore) drainage.* (A) At tank batteries and central treating stations where an accidental discharge of oil would have a reasonable possibility of reaching navigable waters, the dikes or equivalent required under § 112.7(c)(1) should have drains closed and sealed at all times except when rainwater is being drained. Prior to drainage, the diked area should be inspected as provided in paragraphs (e)(2)(iii) (B), (C), and (D). Accumulated oil on the rainwater should be picked up and returned to storage or disposed of in accordance with approved methods.

(B) Field drainage ditches, road ditches, and oil traps, sumps or skimmers, if such exist, should be inspected at regularly scheduled intervals for accumulation of oil that may have escaped from small leaks. Any such accumulations should be removed.

(iii) *Oil production facility (onshore) bulk storage tanks.* (A) No tank should be used for the storage of oil unless its material and construction are compatible with the material stored and the conditions of storage.

(B) All tank battery and central treating plant installations should be provided with a secondary means of containment for the entire contents of the largest single tank if feasible, or alternate means such as those outlined in § 112.7(c)(1). Drainage from undiked areas should be safely confined in a catchment basin or holding pond.

(C) All tanks containing oil should be visually examined by a competent person for condition and need for maintenance on a scheduled periodic basis. Such examination should include the foundation and supports of tanks that are above the surface of the ground.

(D) New and old tank battery installations should, as far as practical, be fail-safe engineered or updated into a fail-safe engineered installation to prevent spills. Consideration should be given to one or more of the following:

(*1*) Adequate tank capacity to assure that a tank will not overfill should a pumper/gauger be delayed in making his regular rounds.

(*2*) Overflow equalizing lines between tanks so that a full tank can overflow to an adjacent tank.

(*3*) Adequate vacuum protection to prevent tank collapse during a pipeline run.

(*4*) High level sensors to generate and transmit an alarm signal to the computer where facilities are a part of a computer production control system.

(iv) *Facility transfer operations, oil production facility (onshore).* (A) All above ground valves and pipelines should be examined periodically on a scheduled basis for general condition of items such as flange joints, valve glands and bodies, drip pans, pipeline supports, pumping well polish rod stuffing boxes, bleeder and gauge valves.

(B) Salt water (oil field brine) disposal facilities should be exained often, particularly following a sudden change in atmospheric temperature to detect possible system upsets that could cause an oil discharge.

(C) Production facilities should have a program of flowline maintenance to prevent spills from this source. The program should include periodic examinations, corrosion protection, flowline replacement, and adequate records, as appropriate, for the individual facility.

(6) *Oil drilling and workover facilities (onshore).* (i) Mobile drilling or workover equipment should be positioned or located so as to prevent spilled oil from reaching navigable waters.

(ii) Depending on the location, catchment basins or diversion structures may be necessary to intercept and contain spills of fuel, crude oil, or oily drilling fluids.

(iii) Before drilling below any casing string or during workover operations, a blowout prevention (BOP) assembly and well control system should be installed that is capable of controlling any well head pressure that is expected to be encountered while that BOP assembly is on the well. Casing and BOP installations should be in accordance with State regulatory agency requirements.

(7) *Oil drilling, production, or workover facilities (offshore).* (i) Definition: "An oil drilling, production or workover facility (offshore)" may include all drilling or workover equipment, wells, flowlines, gathering lines, platforms, and auxiliary nontransportation-related equipment and facilities in a single geographical oil or gas field operated by a single operator.

(ii) Oil drainage collection equipment should be used to prevent and control small oil spillage around pumps, glands, valves, flanges, expansion joints, hoses, drain lines, separators, treaters, tanks, and allied equipment. Drains on the facility should be controlled and directed toward a central collection sump or equivalent collection system sufficient to prevent discharges of oil into the navigable waters of the United States. Where drains and sumps are not practicable oil contained in collection equipment should be removed as often as necessary to prevent overflow.

(iii) For facilities employing a sump system, sump and drains should be adequately sized and a spare pump or equivalent method should be available to remove liquid from the sump and assure that oil does not escape. A regular scheduled preventive maintenance inspection and testing program should be employed to assure reliable operation of the liquid removal system and pump start-up device. Redundant automatic sump pumps and control devices may be required on some installations.

(iv) In areas where separators and treaters are equipped with dump valves whose predominant mode of failure is in the closed position and pollution risk is high, the facility should be specially equipped to prevent the escape of oil. This could be accomplished by extending the flare line to a diked area if the separator is near shore, equipping it with a high liquid level sensor that will automatically shut-in wells producing to the separator, parallel redundant dump valves, or other feasible alternatives to prevent oil discharges.

(v) Atmospheric storage or surge tanks should be equipped with high liquid level sensing devices or other acceptable alternatives to prevent oil discharges.

(vi) Pressure tanks should be equipped with high and low pressure sensing devices to activate an alarm and/or control the flow or other acceptable alternatives to prevent oil discharges.

(vii) Tanks should be equipped with suitable corrosion protection.

(viii) A written procedure for inspecting and testing pollution prevention equipment and systems should be prepared and maintained at the facility. Such procedures should be included as part of the SPCC Plan.

(ix) Testing and inspection of the pollution prevention equipment and systems at the facility should be conducted by the owner or operator on a scheduled periodic basis commensurate with the complexity, conditions and circumstances of the facility or other appropriate regulations.

(x) Surface and subsurface well shut-in valves and devices in use at the facility should be sufficiently described to determine method of activation or control, e.g., pressure differential, change in fluid or flow conditions, combination of pressure and flow, manual or remote control mechanisms. Detailed records for each well, while not necessarily part of the plan should be kept by the owner or operator.

(xi) Before drilling below any casing string, and during workover operations a blowout preventer (BOP) assembly and well control system should be installed that is capable of controlling any well-head pressure that is expected to be encountered while that BOP assembly is on the well. Casing and BOP installations should be in accordance with State regulatory agency requirements.

(xii) Extraordinary well control measures should be provided should emergency conditions, including fire, loss of control and other abnormal conditions, occur. The degree of control system redundancy should vary with hazard exposure and probable consequences of failure. It is recommended that surface shut-in systems have redundant or "fail close" valving. Subsurface safety valves may not be needed in producing wells that will not flow but should be installed as required by applicable State regulations.

(xiii) In order that there will be no misunderstanding of joint and separate duties and obligations to perform work in a safe and pollution free manner, written instructions should be prepared by the owner or operator for contractors and subcontractors to follow whenever contract activities include servicing a well or systems appurtenant to a well or pressure vessel. Such instructions and procedures should be maintained at the offshore production facility. Under certain circumstances and conditions such contractor activities may require the presence at the facility of an authorized representative of the owner or operator who would intervene when necessary to prevent a spill event.

(xiv) All manifolds (headers) should be equipped with check valves on individual flowlines.

(xv) If the shut-in well pressure is greater than the working pressure of the flowline and manifold valves up to and including the header valves associated with that individual flowline, the flowline should be equipped with a high pressure sensing device and shut-in valve at the wellhead unless provided with a pressure relief system to prevent over pressuring.

(xvi) All pipelines appurtenant to the facility should be protected from corrosion. Methods used, such as protective coatings or cathodic protection, should be discussed.

(xvii) Sub-marine pipelines appurtenant to the facility should be adequately protected against environmental stresses and other activities such as fishing operations.

(xviii) Sub-marine pipelines appurtenant to the facility should be in good operating condition at all times and inspected on a scheduled periodic basis for failures. Such inspections should be documented and maintained at the facility.

(8) *Inspections and records.* Inspections required by this part should be in accordance with written procedures developed for the facility by the owner or operator. These written procedures and a record of the inspections, signed by the appropriate supervisor or inspector, should be made part of the SPCC Plan and maintained for a period of three years.

(9) *Security (excluding oil production facilities).* (i) All plants handling, processing, and storing oil should be fully fenced, and entrance gates should be locked and/or guarded when the plant is not in production or is unattended.

(ii) The master flow and drain valves and any other valves that will permit direct outward flow of the tank's content to the surface should be securely locked in the closed position when in non-operating or non-standby status.

(iii) The starter control on all oil pumps should be locked in the "off" position or located at a site accessible only to authorized personnel when the pumps are in a non-operating or non-standby status.

(iv) The loading/unloading connections of oil pipelines should be securely capped or blank-flanged when not in service or standby service for an extended time. This security practice should also apply to pipelines that are emptied of liquid content either by draining or by inert gas pressure.

(v) Facility lighting should be commensurate with the type and location of the facility. Consideration should be given to: (A) Discovery of spills occurring during hours of darkness, both by operating personnel, if present, and by non-operating personnel (the general public, local police, etc.) and (B) prevention of spills occurring through acts of vandalism.

(10) *Personnel, training and spill prevention procedures.* (i) Owners or operators are responsible for properly instructing their personnel in the operation and maintenance of equipment to prevent the discharges of oil and applicable pollution control laws, rules and regulations.

(ii) Each applicable facility should have a designated person who is accountable for oil spill prevention and who reports to line management.

(iii) Owners or operators should schedule and conduct spill prevention briefings for their operating personnel at intervals frequent enough to assure adequate understanding of the SPCC

Plan for that facility. Such briefings should highlight and describe known spill events or failures, malfunctioning components, and recently developed precautionary measures.

APPENDIX—MEMORANDUM OF UNDERSTANDING BETWEEN THE SECRETARY OF TRANSPORTATION AND THE ADMINISTRATOR OF THE ENVIRONMENTAL PROTECTION AGENCY

SECTION II—DEFINITIONS

The Environmental Protection Agency and the Department of Transportation agree that for the purposes of Executive Order 11548, the term:

(1) "Non-transportation-related onshore and offshore facilities" means:

(A) Fixed onshore and offshore oil well drilling facilities including all equipment and appurtenances related thereto used in drilling operations for exploratory or development wells, but excluding any terminal facility, unit or process integrally associated with the handling or transferring of oil in bulk to or from a vessel.

(B) Mobile onshore and offshore oil well drilling platforms, barges, trucks, or other mobile facilities including all equipment and appurtenances related thereto when such mobile facilities are fixed in position for the purpose of drilling operations for exploratory or development wells, but excluding any terminal facility, unit or process integrally associated with the handling or transferring of oil in bulk to or from a vessel.

(C) Fixed onshore and offshore oil production structures, platforms, derricks, and rigs including all equipment and appurtenances related thereto, as well as completed wells and the wellhead separators, oil separators, and storage facilities used in the production of oil, but excluding any terminal facility, unit or process integrally associated with the handling or transferring of oil in bulk to or from a vessel.

(D) Mobile onshore and offshore oil production facilities including all equipment and appurtenances related thereto as well as completed wells and wellhead equipment, piping from wellheads to oil separators, oil separators, and storage facilities used in the production of oil when such mobile facilities are fixed in position for the purpose of oil production operations, but excluding any terminal facility, unit or process integrally associated with the handling or transferring of oil in bulk to or from a vessel.

(E) Oil refining facilities including all equipment and appurtenances related thereto as well as in-plant processing units, storage units, piping, drainage systems and waste treatment units used in the refining of oil, but excluding any terminal facility, unit or process integrally associated with the handling or transferring of oil in bulk to or from a vessel.

(F) Oil storage facilities including all equipment and appurtenances related thereto as well as fixed bulk plant storage, terminal oil storage facilities, consumer storage, pumps and drainage systems used in the storage of oil, but excluding inline or breakout storage tanks needed for the continuous operation of a pipeline system and any terminal facility, unit or process integrally associated with the handling or transferring of oil in bulk to or from a vessel.

(G) Industrial, commercial, agricultural or public facilities which use and store oil, but excluding any terminal facility, unit or process integrally associated with the handling or transferring of oil in bulk to or from a vessel.

(H) Waste treatment facilities including in-plant pipelines, effluent discharge lines, and storage tanks, but excluding waste treatment facilities located on vessels and terminal storage tanks and appurtenances for the reception of oily ballast water or tank washings from vessels and associated systems used for off-loading vessels.

(I) Loading racks, transfer hoses, loading arms and other equipment which are appurtenant to a nontransportation-related facility or terminal facility and which are used to transfer oil in bulk to or from highway vehicles or railroad cars.

(J) Highway vehicles and railroad cars which are used for the transport of oil exclusively within the confines of a nontransportation-related facility and which are not intended to transport oil in interstate or intrastate commerce.

(K) Pipeline systems which are used for the transport of oil exclusively within the confines of a nontransportation-related facility or terminal facility and which are not intended to transport oil in interstate or intrastate commerce, but excluding pipeline systems used to transfer oil in bulk to or from a vessel.

(2) "Transportation-related onshore and offshore facilities" means:

(A) Onshore and offshore terminal facilities including transfer hoses, loading arms and other equipment and appurtenances used for the purpose of handling or transferring oil in bulk to or from a vessel as well as storage tanks and appurtenances for the reception of oily ballast water or tank washings from vessels, but excluding terminal waste treatment facilities and terminal oil storage facilities.

(B) Transfer hoses, loading arms and other equipment appurtenant to a nontransportation-related facility which is used to transfer oil in bulk to or from a vessel.

(C) Interstate and intrastate onshore and offshore pipeline systems including pumps and appurtenances related thereto as well as in-line or breakout storage tanks needed for the continuous operation of a pipeline system, and pipelines from onshore and offshore oil production facilities, but excluding onshore and offshore piping from wellheads to oil separators and pipelines which are used for the transport of oil exclusively within the confines of a nontransportation-related facility or terminal facility and which are not intended to transport oil in interstate or intrastate commerce or to transfer oil in bulk to or from a vessel.

(D) Highway vehicles and railroad cars which are used for the transport of oil in interstate or intrastate commerce and the equipment and appurtenances related thereto, and equipment used for the fueling of locomotive units, as well as the rights-of-way on which they operate. Excluded are highway vehicles and railroad cars and motive power used exclusively within the confines of a nontransportation-related facility or terminal facility and which are not intended for use in interstate or intrastate commerce.

Appendix 6C   Outline of Contents of Remedial Investigation/Feasibility Study (RI/FS)*

1. *Executive Summary*

2. *Develop a Range of Remedial Alternatives*

    2.1 *Overall Approach*

    2.2 *Identify General Response Actions*

        2.2.1 Identify Site Problems

        2.2.2 Identify General Response Actions

    2.3 *Identify and Screen Technologies*

    2.4 *Develop Alternatives by Combining Technologies*

        2.4.1 Source Control Remedies

        2.4.2 Management of Migration Remedies

    2.5 *Screen Alternatives for Public Health, Environmental, and Cost Factors*

        2.5.1 Environmental and Public Health Screening

        2.5.2 Cost Screening Factors

3. *Conduct a Detailed Technical Evaluation*

    3.1 *Performance*

        3.1.1 Effectiveness

        3.1.2 Useful Life

    3.2 *Reliability*

        3.2.1 Operation and Maintenance Requirements

        3.2.2 Demonstrated Performance

    3.3 *Implementability*

        3.3.1 Constructability

        3.3.2 Time

    3.4 *Safety*

    3.5 *Summary of Technical Feasibility Analysis*

4. *Evaluate Institutional Requirements*

---

* From EPA Guidance on Feasibility Studies Under CERCLA, April 1985.

Appendix 6D Excerpts from EPA Settlement Policy*

. . . .

II. Management Guidelines for Negotiation

As a guideline, the Agency will negotiate only if the initial offer from PRPs constitutes a substantial proportion of the costs of cleanup at the site, or a substantial portion of the needed remedial action. Entering into discussion for less than a substantial proportion of cleanup costs or remedial action needed at the site, would not be an effective use of government resources. No specific numerical threshold for initiating negotiations has been established.

In deciding whether to start negotiations, the Regions should weight the potential resource demands for conducting negotiations against the likelihood of getting 100% of costs or a complete remedy.

Where the Region proposes to negotiate for a partial settlement involving less than the total costs of a cleanup, or a complete remedy, the Region should prepare as part of its Case Negotiations Strategy a dreaft [sic] evaluation of the case using the settlement criteria identified in section IV. The draft should discuss how each of the factors in section IV applies to the site in question, and explain why negotiations for less than all of the cleanup costs, or a partial remedy, are appropriate. A copy of the draft should be forwarded to Headquarters. The Headquarters review will be used to identify major issues of national significance or issues that may involve significant legal precedents.

In certain other categories of cases, it may be appropriate for the Regions to enter into negotiations with PRPs, even though the offers from PRPs do not represent a substantial portion of the costs of cleanup. These categories of cases include:

- administrative settlements of cost recovery actions where total cleanup costs were less than $200,000;
- claims in bankruptcy;
- administrative settlements with *de minimis* contributors of wastes.

Actions subject to this exceptions are administrative settlements of cost recovery cases where all the work at the site has been completed and all costs have been incurred. The figure of $200,000 refers to all of the costs of cleanup. The Agency is preparing more detailed guidance on the appropriate form of such settlement agreements, and the types of conditions that must be included.

Negotiation of claims in bankruptcy may involve both present owners, where the United States may have an administrative costs claim, and other parties such as past owners or generators, where the United States may be an unsecured potential creditor. The Regions should avoid becoming involved in bankruptcy proceedings if there is little likelihood of recovery, and should recognize the risks involved in negotiating without creditor status. It may be

---

* 50 Fed. Reg. 5034 (2-5-85).

appropriate to request DOJ filing of a proof of claim. Further guidance is provided in the Memorandum from Courtney Price entitled "Information Regarding CERCLA Enforcement Against Bankrupt Parties," dated May 24, 1984.

In negotiating with *de minimis* parties, the Regions should limit their efforts to low volume, low toxicity disposers who would not normally make a significant contribution to the costs of cleanup in any case.

In considering settlement offer from *de minimis* contributors, the Region should normally focus on achieving cash settlements. Regions should generally not enter into negotiations for full administrative or judicial settlements with releases, contribution protection, or other protective clauses. Substantial resources should not be invested in negotiations with *de minimis* contributors, in light of the limited costs that may be recovered, the time needed to prepare the necessary legal documents, the need for Headquarters review, potential *res judicata* effects, and other effects that *de minimis* settlements may have on the nature of the case remaining to the Government.

Partial settlements may also be considered in situations where the unwillingness of a relatively small group of parties to settle prevents the development of a proposal for a substantial portion of costs or the remedy. Proposals for settlement in these circumstances should be assessed under the criteria set forth in section IV.

Earlier versions of this policy included a threshold for negotiations, which provided that negotiations should not be commenced unless an offer was made to settle for at least 80% of the costs of cleanup, or of the remedial action. This threshold has been eliminated from the final version of this policy. It must be emphasized that elimination of this threshold does not mean that the Agency is therefore more willing to accept offers for partial settlement. The objective of the Agency is still to obtain complete cleanup by PRPs, or 100% of the costs of cleanup.

III. Release of Information

The Agency will release information concerning the site to PRPs to facilitate discussions for settlement among PRPs. This information will include:

— Identity of notice letter recipients;
— Volume and nature of wastes to the extent identified as sent to the site;
— Ranking by volume of material sent to the site, if available.

In determining the type of information to be released, the Region should consider the possible impacts on any potential litigation. The Regions should take steps to assure protection of confidential and deliverative [*sic*] materials. The Agency will generally not release actual evidentiary material. The Region should state on each released summary that it is preliminary, that it was furnished in the course of compromise negotiations (Fed. Rules of Evidence 408), and that it is not binding on the Federal Government.

This information release should be preceded by and combined with a vigorous program for collecting information from responsible parties. It remains standard practice for the Agency to use the information gathering authorities of RCRA and CERCLA with respect to all PRPs at a site. This information release should generally be conditioned on a reciprocal release of information by PRPs. The information request need not be simultaneous, but EPA should receive the information within a reasonable time.

IV. Settlement Criteria

The objective of negotiations is to collect 100% of cleanup costs or complete cleanup from responsible parties. The Agency recognizes that, in narrowly limited circumstances, exceptions to this goal may be appropriate, and has established criteria for determining where such exceptions are allowed. Although the Agency will consider offers of less than 100% in accordance with this policy, it will do so in light of the Agency's position, reinforced by recent court decisions, that PRP liability is strict, joint and several unless it can be shown by the PRPs that injury at a site is clearly divisible.

Based on a full evaluation of the facts and a comprehensive analysis of all of the listed criteria, the Agency may consider accepting offers of less than 100 percent. Rapid and effective settlement depends on a thorough evaluation, and an aggressive information collection program is necessary to prepare effective evaluations. Proposals for less than total settlement should be assessed using the criteria identified below

1 Volume of Wastes Contributed to Site by Each PRP

Information concerning the volume of wastes contributed to the site by PRPs should be collected, if available, and evaluated in each case. The volume of wastes is not the only criterion to be considered, nor may it be the most important. A small quantity of waste may cost proportionately more to contain or remove than a larger quantity of a different waste. However, the volume of waste may contribute significantly and directly to the distribution of contamination on the surface and subsurface (including groundwater), and to the complexity of removal of the contamination. In addition, if the properties of all wastes at the site are relatively equal, the volume of wastes contributed by the PRPs provides a convenient, easily applied criterion for measuring whether a PRP's settlement offer may be reasonable.

This does not mean, however, that PRPs will be required to pay only their proportionate share based on volume of contribution of wastes to the site. At many sites, there will be wastes for which PRPs cannot be identified. If identified, PRPs may be unable to provide funds for cleanup. Private party funding for cleanup of those wastes would, therefore, not be available if volumetric contribution were the only criteria.

Therefore, to achieve the the Agency's goal of obtaining 100 percent of cleanup or the cost of cleanup, it will be necessary in many cases to require a settlement contribution greater than the percentage of wastes contributed by each PRP to the site. These costs can be obtained through the application of the theory of joint and several liability where the harm is indivisible, and through application of these criteria in evaluating settlement proposals.

2. Nature of the Wastes Contributed

The human, animal and environmental toxicity of the hazardous substances contributed by the PRPs, its mobility, persistence and other properties are important factors to consider. As noted above, a small amount of wastes, or a highly mobile waste, may cost more to clean up, dispose, or treat than less toxic or relatively immobile wastes. In addition, any disproportionate adverse effects on the environment by the presence of wastes contributed by those PRPs should be considered.

If a waste contributed by one or more of the parties offering a settlement disproportionately increases the costs of cleanup at the site, it may be appropriate for parties contributing such waste to bear a larger percentage of cleanup costs than would be the case by using solely a volumetric basis.

3. Strength of Evidence Tracing the Wastes at the Site to the Settling Parties

The quality and quantity of the Government's evidence connecting PRPs to the wastes at the site obviously affects the settlement value of the Government's case. The Government must show, by a preponderance of the evidence, that the PRP's are connected with the wastes in one or more of the ways provided in Section 107 of CERCLA. Therefore, if the Government's evidence against a particular PRP is weak, we should weigh that weakness in evaluating a settlement offer from that PRP.

On the other hand, where indivisible harm is shown to exist, under the theory of joint and several liability the Government is in a position to collect 100% of the cost of cleanup from all parties who have contributed to a site. Therefore, where the quality and quantity of the Government's evidence appears to be strong for establishing the PRP's liability, the Government should rely on the strength of its evidence and not decrease the settlement value of its case. Discharging such PRPs from liability in a partial settlement without obtaining a substantial contribution may leave the Government with non-settling parties whose involvement at the site may be more tenuous.

In any evaluation of a settlement offer, the Agency should weigh the amount of information exchange that has occurred before the settlement offer. The more the Government knows about the evidence it has to connect the settling parties to the site, the better this evaluation will be. The information collection provisions of RCRA and/or CERCLA should be used to develop evidence prior to preparation of the evaluation.

4. Ability of the Settling Parties To Pay

Ability to pay is not a defense to an action by the Government. Nevertheless, the evaluation of a settlement proposal should discuss the financial condition of that party, and the practical results of pursuing a party for more than the Government can hope to actually recover. In cost recovery actions it will be difficult to negotiate a settlement for more than a party's assets. The Region should also consider allowing the party to reimburse the Fund in reasonable installments over a period of time, if the party is unable to pay in a lump sum, and installment payments would benefit the Government. A structured settlement providing for payments over time should be at a payment level that takes into account the party's cash flow. An excessive amount could force a party into bankruptcy, which will of course make collection very difficult. See the memorandum dated August 26, 1983, entitled "Cost Recovery Actions under Section 107 of CERCLA" for additional guidance on this subject.

5. Litigative Risks in Proceeding to Trial

Litigative risks which might be encountered at trial and which should weigh in consideration of any settlement offer include traditional factors such as:

a. Admissibility of the Government's evidence

If necessary Government evidence is unlikely to be admitted in a trial because of procedural or substantive problems in the acquisition or creation of the evidence, this infirmity should be considered as reducing the Government's chance of success and, therefore, reducing the amount the Government should expect to receive in a settlement.

b. Adequacy of the Government's evidence

Certain aspects of this point have already been discussed above. However, it deserves mention again because the Government's case depends on substantial quantities of sampling, analytical and other technical data and expert testimony. If the evidence in support of the Government's case is incomplete or based upon controversial science, or if the Government's evidence is otherwise unlikely to withstand the scrutiny of a trial, the amount that the Government might expect to receive in a settlement will be reduced.

c. Availability of defenses

In the unlikely event that one or more of the settling parties appears to have a defense to the Government's action under section 107(b) of CERCLA, the Government should expect to receive less in a settlement from that PRP. Availability of one or more defenses to one PRP which are not common to all PRPs in the case should not, however, lower the expectation of what an entire offering group should pay.

6. Public Interest Considerations

The purpose of site cleanup is to protect public health and the environment. Therefore, in analyzing a settlement proposal the timing of the cleanup and the ability of the Government to clean up the site should be considered. For example, if the State cannot fund its portion of a Fund-financed cleanup, a private-party cleanup proposal may be given more favorable consideration than one received in a case where the State can fund its portion of cleanup costs, if necessary.

Public interest considerations also include the availability of Federal funds for necessary cleanup, and whether privately financed action can begin more quickly than Federally-financed activity. Public interest concerns may be used to justify a settlement of less than 100% only when there is a demonstrated need for a quick remedy to protect public health or the environment.

7. Precedential Value

In some cases, the factual situation may be conducive to establishing a favorable precedent for future Government actions. For example, strong case law can be developed in cases of first impression. In addition, settlements in such cases tend to become precedents in themselves, and are examined extensively by PRPs in other cases. Settlement of such cases should always be on terms most favorable to the Government. Where PRPs will not settle on such terms, and the quality and quantity of evidence is strong, it may be in the overall interest of the Government to try the case.

8. *Value of Obtaining a Present Sum Certain*

If money can be obtained now and turned over to the Fund, where it can earn interest until the time it is spent to clean up a site, the net present value of obtaining the sum offered in settlement now can be computed against the possibility of obtaining a larger sum in the future. This calculation may show that the net present value of the sum offered in settlement is, in reality, higher than the amount the Government can expect to obtain at trial. EPA has developed an economic model to assess these and other related economic factors. More information on this model can be obtained from the Director, Office of Waste Programs Envorcement.

9. *Inequities and Aggravating Factors*

All analyses of settlement proposals should flag for the decision makers any apparent inequities to the settling parties inherent in the Government's case, and apparent inequities to others if the settlement proposal is accepted, and any aggravating factors. However, it must be understood that the statute operates on the underlying principle of strict liability, and that equitable matters are not defenses.

10. *Nature of the Case that Remains After Settlement*

All settlement evaluations should address the nature of the case that remains if the settlement is accepted. For example, if there are no financially viable parties left to proceed against for the balance of the cleanup after the settlement, the settlement offer should constitute everything the Government expects to obtain at that site. The questions are: What does the Government gain by settling this portion of the case? Does the settlement or its terms harm the remaining portion of the case? Will the Government have to expend the same amount of resources to try the remaining portion of the case? If so, why should the settlement offer be accepted?

This analysis is extremely important and should come at the conclusion of the evaluation.

V. Partial Cleanups

On occasion, PRPs may offer to perform or pay for one phase of a site cleanup (such as a surface removal action) but not commit to any other phase of the cleanup (such as ground water treatment). In some circumstances, it may be appropriate to enter into settlements for such partial cleanups, rather than to resolve all issues in one settlement. For example, in some cases it is necessary to conduct initial phases of site cleanup in order to gather sufficient data to evaluate the need for and type of work to be done on subsequent phases. In such cases, offers from PRPs to conduct or pay for less than all phases of site cleanup should be evaluated in the same manner and by the same criteria as set forth above. Settlements performed at the site. This provision does not cover preparation of an RI/FS, which is covered by a separate guidance document: Lee Thomas and Courtney Price's "Participation of Potentially Responsible Parties in RI/FS Development" (March 20, 1984).

VI. Contribution Protection

Contribution among responsible parties is based on the principle that a jointly and severally liable party who has paid all or a portion of a judgment or settlement may be entitled to reimbursement from other jointly or severally liable parties. When the Agency reaches a partial settlement with some parties, it will frequently pursue an enforcement action against non-settling responsible parties to recover the remaining costs of cleanup. If such an action is undertaken, there is a possibility that those non-settlors would in turn sue settling parties. If this action by nonsettling parties is successful, then the settling parties would end up paying a larger share of cleanup costs than was determined in the Agency's settlement. This is obviously a disincentive to settlement.

Contribution protection in a consent decree can prevent this outcome. In a contribution protection clause, the United States would agree to reduce its judgment against the non-settling parties, to the extent necessary to extinguish the settling party's liability to the nonsettling third party.

The Agency recognizes the value of contribution protection in limited situations in order to provide some measure of finality to settlements. Fundamentally, we believe that settling parties are protected from contribution actions as a matter of law, based on the Uniform Contribution Among Tortfeasors Act. That Act provides that, where settlements are entered into in "good faith", the settlors are discharged from "all liability for contribution to any other joint tortfeasors." To the extent that this law is adopted as the Federal rule of decision, there will be no need for specific clauses in consent agreements to provide contribution protection.

There has not yet been any ruling on the issue. Thus, the Agency may still be asked to provide contribution protection in the form of offsets and reductions in judgment. In determining whether explicit contribution protection clauses are appropriate, the Region should consider the following factors:

- Explicit contribution protection clauses are generally not appropriate unless liability can be clearly allocated, so that the risk of reapportionment by a judge in any future action would be minimal.
- Inclusion should depend on case-by-case consideration of the law which is likely to be applied.
- The Agency will be more willing to consider contribution protection in settlements that provide substantially all the costs of cleanup.

If a proposed settlement includes a contribution protection clause, the Region should prepare a detailed justification indicating why this clause is essential to attaining an adequate settlement. The justification should include an assessment of the prospects of litigation regarding the clause. Any proposed settlement that contains a contribution protection clause with a potential ambiguity will be returned for further negotiation.

Any subsequent claims by settling parties against non-settlors must be subordinated to Agency claims against these non-settling parties. In no event will the Agency agree to defend on behalf of a settlor, or to provide direct indemnification. The Government will not enter into any form of contribution protection agreement that could require the Government to pay money to anyone.

If litigation is commenced by non-settlors against settlors, and the Agency became involved in such litigation, the Government would argue to the court that in adjusting equities among responsible parties, positive consideration should be given to those who came forward voluntarily and were a part of a group of settling PRPs.

VII. Releases from Liability

Potentially responsible parties who offer to wholly or partially clean up a site or pay the costs of cleanup normally wish to negotiate a release from liability or a covenant not to sue as a part of the consideration for that cleanup or payment. Such releases are appropriate in some circumstances. The need for finality in settlements must be balanced against the need to insure that PRPs remain responsible for recurring endangerments and unknown conditions.

The Agency recognizes the current state of scientific uncertainty concerning the impacts of hazardous substances, our ability to detect them, and the effectiveness of remedies at hazardous waste sites. It is possible that remedial measures will prove inadequate and lead to imminent and substantial endangerments, because of unknown conditions or because of failures in design, construction or effectiveness of the remedy.

Although the Agency approves all remedial actions for sites on the National Priorities List, releases from liability will not automatically be granted merely because the Agency has approved the remedy. The willingness of the Agency to give expansive releases from liability is directly related to the confidence that Agency has that the remedy will ultimately prove effective and reliable. In general, the Regions will have the flexibility to negotiate releases that are relatively expansive or relatively stringent, depending on the degree of confidence that the Agency has in the remedy.

Releases or covenants must also include certain reopeners which preserve the right of the Government to seek additional cleanup action and recover additional costs from responsible parties in a number of circumstances. They are also subject to a variety of other limitations. These reopener clauses and limitations are described below.

In addition, the the Agency can address future problems at a site by enforcement of the decree or order, rather than by action under a particular reopener clause. Settlements will normally specify a particular type of remedial action to be undertaken. That remedial action will normally be selected to achieve a certain specified level of protection of public health and the environment. When settlements are incorporated into consent decrees or orders, the decrees or orders should wherever possible include performance standards that set out these specified levels of protection. Thus, the Agency will retain its ability to assure cleanup by taking action to enforce these decrees or orders when remedies fail to meet the specified standards.

It is not possible to specify a precise hierarchy of preferred remedies. The degree of confidence in a particular remedy must be determined on an individual basis, taking site-specific conditions into account. In general, however, the more effective and reliable the remedy, the more likely it is that the Agency can negotiate a more expansive release. For example, if a consent decree or order commits a private party to meeting and/or continuing to attain health based performance standards, there can be great certainty on the part of the Agency that an adequate level of public health protection will be met and maintained, as long as the terms of the agreement are met. In this type of case, it may be appropriate to negotiate a more expansive release than, for example, cases involving remedies that are solely technology-based.

Expansive releases may be more appropriate where the private party remedy is a demonstrated effective alternative to land disposal, such as incineration. Such releases are possible whether the hazardous material is transported offsite for treatment, or the treatment takes place on site. In either instance, the use of treatment can result in greater certainty that future problems will not occur.

Other remedies may be less appropriate for expansive releases, particularly if the consent order or agreement does not include performance standards. It may be appropriate in such circumstances to negotiate releases that become effective several years after completion of the remedial action, so that the effectiveness and reliability of the technology can be clearly demonstrated. The Agency anticipates that responsible parties may be able to achieve a greater degree of certainty in settlements when the state of scientific understanding concerning these technical issues has advanced.

Regardless of the relative expansiveness or stringency of the release in other respects, at a minimum settlement documents must include reopeners allowing the Government to modify terms and conditions of the agreement for the following types of circumstances:

- Where previously unknown or undetected conditions that arise or are discovered at the site after the time of the agreement may present an imminent and substantial endangerment to public health, welfare of [sic] the environment;
- Where the Agency receives additional information, which was not available at the time of the agreement, concerning the scientific determinations on which the settlement was premised (for example, health effects associated with levels of exposure, toxicity of hazardous substances, and the appropriateness of the remedial technologies for conditions at the site) and this additional information indicates that site conditions may present an imminent and substantial endangerment to the public health or welfare or the environment.

In addition, release clauses must not preclude the Government from recovering costs incurred in responding to the type of imminent and substantial endangerments identified above.

In extraordinary circumstances, it may be clear after application of the settlement criteria set out in section IV that it is in the public interest to agree to a more limited or more expansive release not subject to the conditions outlined above. Concurrence of the Assistant Administrators for OSWER and OECM (and the Assistant Attorney General when the release is given on behalf of the United States) must be obtained before the Government's negotiating team is authorized to negotiate regarding such a release or covenant.

The extent of releases should be the same, whether the private parties conduct the cleanup themselves or pay for Federal Government cleanup. When responsible parties pay for Federal Government cleanup, the release will ordinarily not become effective until cleanup is completed and the actual costs of the cleanup are ascertained. Responsible parties will thereby bear the risk of uncertainties arising during execution of the cleanup. In limited circumstances, the release may become effective upon payment for Federal Government cleanup, if the payment includes a carefully calculated premium or other financial instrument that adequately insures the Federal Government against these uncertainties. Finally, the Agency may be more willing to settle for less than the total costs of cleanup when it is not precluded by a release clause from eventually recovering any additional costs that might ultimately be incurred at a site.

Release clauses are also subject to the following limitations:

- A release or covenant may be given only to the PRP providing the consideration for the release.
- The release or covenant must not cover any claims other than those involved in the case.
- The release must not address any criminal matter.
- Releases for partial cleanups that do not extend to the entire site must be limited to the work actually completed.
- Federal claims for natural resource damages should not be released without the approval of Federal trustees.
- Responsible parties must release any related claims against the United States, including the Hazardous Substances Response Fund.
- Where the cleanup is to be performed by the PRPs, the release or covenant should normally become effective only upon the completion of the cleanup (or phase of cleanup) in a manner satisfactory to EPA.
- Release clauses should be drafted as covenants not to sue, rather than releases from liability, where this form may be necessary to protect the legal rights of the Federal Government.

A release or covenant not to sue terminates or seriously impairs the Government's rights of action against PRPs. Therefore, the document should be carefully worded so that the intent of the parties and extent of the matters covered by the release or covenant are clearly stated. Any proposed settlement containing a release with a possible ambiguity will be returned for further negotiation.

. . . .

IX. Timing of Negotiations

Under our revised policy on responsible party participation in RI/FS, PRPs have increased opportunities for involvement in the development of the remedial investigations and feasibility studies which the Agency uses to identify the appropriate remedy. In light of the fact that PRPs will have received notice letters and the information identified in section III of this policy, prelitigation negotiations can be conducted in an expeditious fashion.

The Negotiations Decision Document (NDD), which follows completion of the RI/FS, makes the preliminary identification of the appropriate remedy for the site. Prelitigation negotiations between the Government and the PRPs should normally not extend for more than 60 days after approval of the NDD. If significant progress is not made within a reasonable amount of time, the Agency will not hesitate to abandon negotiations and proceed immediately with administrative action or litigation. It should be noted that these steps do not preclude further negotiations.

Extensions can be considered in complex cases where there is no threat of seriously delaying cleanup action. Any extension of this period must be predicated on having a good faith offer from the PRPs which, if successfully negotiated, will save the Government substantial time and resources in attaining the cleanup objectives.

X. Management and Review of Settlement Negotiations

All settlement documents must receive concurrence from OWPE and OECM-Waste, and be approved by the Assistant Administrator of OECM in accordance with delegations. The management guideline discussed in Section II allows the Regions to commence negotiations if responsible parties make an initial offer for a substantial proportion of the cleanup costs. Before commencing negotiations for partial settlements, the Regions should prepare a preliminary draft evaluation of the case using the settlement criteria in section IV of this policy. A copy of this evaluation should be forwarded to Headquarters.

A final detailed evaluation of settlements is required when the Regions request Headquarters approval of these settlements. This written evaluation should be submitted to OECM-Waste and OWPE by the legal and technical personnel on the case. These will normally be the Regional attorney and technical representative.

The evaluation memorandum should indicate whether the settlement is for 100% of the work or cleanup costs. If this figure is less than 100%, the memorandum should include a discussion of the advantages and disadvantages of the proposed settlement as measured by the criteria in section IV. The Agency expects full evaluations of each of the criteria specified in the policy and will return inadequate evaluations.

The Regions are authorized to conclude settlements in certain types of hazardous waste cases on their own, without prior review by Headquarters or

DOJ. Cases selected for this treatment would normally have lower priority for litigation. Categories of cases not subject to Headquarters review include negotiation for cost recovery cases under $200,000 and negotiation of claims filed in bankruptcy. In cost recovery cases, the Regions should pay particular attention to weighing the resources necessary to conduct negotiations and litigation against the amounts that may be recovered, and the prospects for recovery.

Authority to appear and try cases before the Bankruptcy Court would not be delegated to the Regions, but would be retained by the Department of Justice. The Department will file cases where an acceptable negotiated settlement cannot be reached. Copies of settlement documents for such agreements should be provided [to] OWPE and OECM.

Specific details concerning these authorizations will be addressed in delegations that will be forwarded to the Regions under separate cover. Headquarters is conducting an evaluation of the effectiveness of existing delegations, and is assessing the possibility of additional delegations.

Appendix 6E   EPA Forms and Filing Instructions for Preauthorization of Natural Resource Damage Claims Under CERCLA

Appendix A—Application for Preauthorization of Natural Resource Restoration Claim (EPA Form 2075–1)

Form Approved. OMB No. 2050-0043. Approval expires 4-30-88

♻EPA	United States Environmental Protection Agency Washington, DC 20460 **Application for Preauthorization of Natural Resource Restoration Claim**	EPA Docket Number

General Instructions: Complete all items in ink or by typewriter. Where applicable, insert the word "none." Use additional sheets if necessary. Read carefully the specific instructions on the opposite page.

I. Name, Title,,and Address of Trustee/Lead Trustee *(Attach delegation establishing authority to represent all affected trustees.)*

II. Name, Title, and Address of Agent *(if any)* Authorized To Represent Trustee/Lead Trustee

III. Relates to Actual Release of a Hazardous Substance

A. Date/Time *(am/pm)* of Release *(if known)*	B. Date of Discovery of Loss of Natural Resource(s)

C. Location of Release and Injured Natural Resource(s)

D. Description of Release

E. Description of Natural Resource(s)

F. Are Any Potentially Responsible Parties *(PRPs)* Known to You?

☐ Yes *(Attach a list of identified PRPs and describe results of any contacts with them.)*

☐ No *(Describe efforts to identify PRPs)*

IV. Relates to Natural Resource Damage Assessment

A. Provide Date/Briefly Describe the Findings of the Damage Assessment.

B. Briefly Describe the Methodology Used To Assess the Natural Resource Injury.

C. Was Court Action Filed To Recover Assessment Costs?

☐ Yes *(Describe the results and provide case name, case number, jurisdiction of the court, and date of determination.)*

☐ No

EPA Form 2075-1 (10-85)

D. Was a notice of intent to submit a claim for an assessment filed with EPA?

☐ Yes *(Give date.)*

☐ No

E. Was a claim filed against the Fund to recover assessment costs?

☐ Yes *(Give date, describe the results and attach a copy of the Agency's determination.)*

☐ No

V. Relates to Natural Resource Restoration Plan

A. Briefly describe the options considered in developing the restoration plan. *(Attach copy of plan)*

B. Describe in detail the option(s) selected as the basis for the restoration plan.

C. Briefly describe the procedures used to notify the public and to obtain public comments.

D. Was the restoration plan adopted by all trustees and affected Federal agencies?

☐ Yes *(Provide documentation.)*

☐ No *(Explain.)*

VI. Relates to Preauthorization of Restoration

A. Briefly describe the restoration for which you seek preauthorization.

B. Do you propose more than one phase?

☐ Yes *(Describe each phase.)*

☐ No

C. Was a notice of intent to submit a claim for the restoration filed with EPA?

☐ Yes *(Give date.)*   ☐ No

VII. Projected Costs of Restoration		EPA-Approved Costs (EPA Use Only)		
		Phase 1	Phase 2	Phase 3
Restoration	$	$	$	$
Other	$	$	$	$
Total	$	$	$	$

VIII. Is This Proposal Within EPA's Planned Annual Budgetary Appropriation?

☐ Yes   ☐ No

EPA Form 2075-1 (10-85)

IX. Does This Application Revise a Previous Request?	EPA Docket No. of Previous Request
☐ Yes ☐ No	

Certification

I certify that all information contained herein is true to the best of my knowledge. I agree to supply additional information, as requested, in support of this application and access to the site for the purpose of inspection.

Signature of Claimant	Date

Civil Penalty for Presenting Fraudulent Claim	Criminal Penalty for Presenting Fraudulent Claim or Making False Statements
The claimant will forfeit and pay to the United States $2,000, plus double the amount of damages sustained by the United States. *(31 USC 3729 and 3730.)*	The claimant will be charged a maximum fine of not more than $10,000 or be imprisoned for a maximum of 5 years, or both. *(See 62 Stat. 698, 749; 18 USC 287, 1001.)*

EPA Form 2075-1 (10-85)

App. 6E-3

Instructions for Applying for Preauthorization
of Natural Resource Restoration Claim

I. Name any Federal natural resource management agency, principal State, commonwealth, U.S. Trust Territory, or other political entity acting on behalf of all affected trustees. Provide a list *(including name, title, and address)* of all trustees for the injured natural resources and supporting evidence authorizing them to prosecute claims for damages, as defined in 111(b) of CERCLA. If you are the lead trustee, provide this evidence and describe your efforts to identify and coordinate with other trustees.

II. Self-explanatory.

III. A. Provide documentation of the date and time of the release, if known.

B. Provide the date of the initial report first establishing that the injury resulted from the release *(III. A.)* and provide a copy. *(Date of the actual assessment is required in IV. A.)*

C. Provide the name of the city or town and State where the release and the injury occurred. If the location is outside the city's limits, indicate the distance between it and the nearest city or town.

D. Describe in detail all the known facts and circumstances associated with the release of the hazardous substance. Include the name of the substances released *(see "Superfund Notification Requirement and Reportable Quantity Adjustments," 40 CFR Part 302)*, and the type of facility that released the substances *(e.g., any building or structure, pipe or pipeline, well, lagoon, landfill, storage container, motor vehicle)*.

E. Describe in detail the resource(s), its use(s) prior to the release and injury, and its uniqueness or special characteristics. Indicate whether its use and characteristics at the time of the injury were residential, commercial/industrial, agricultural, forestral, recreational, mixed use, etc.

F. List all potentially responsible parties *(PRPs)* known to you. Describe efforts to locate PRPs, date of presentation of your claim, and any reply from the PRPs.

IV. A. Summarize the natural resource impacts, including short- and long-term injury to both media and living organisms. Attach a copy of the damage assessment. Also indicate who approved the assessment, who conducted the assessment, when it was conducted and when it was completed.

B. Does the methodology selected comply with the section 301 damage assessment regula-

tions, or some other reasonable methodology?

C. Self-explanatory.

D. Supply date. EPA recommends that trustees submit a notice of intent to file an assessment claim by means of the annual planning process.

E. Self-explanatory.

V. A. Identify the options considered, e.g., restoration, replacement, rehabilitation, acquisition of the equivalent, or "no action." *(Hereinafter, "restoration" refers to restoring, rehabilitating, replacing, or acquiring the equivalent of injured natural resources.)*

B. Describe the basis for selection of the alternative(s) *(e.g., cost-effectiveness, cost-benefit, total cost, impact on affected ecosystems)*. Attach a copy of the restoration plan. Primary emphasis should be given to the most cost-effective alternative.

C. For example, was there a town meeting, public hearing, etc? How were the public's concerns addressed?

D. Self-explanatory.

VI. A. Provide the timetable for discrete activities, including start and completion dates. Indicate the projected schedule for submission of the claim(s).

B. Trustees may propose claims for operable units *(i.e., phases)* of work. If appropriate, include the timetable for each phase of the planned activities and the projected schedule for submitting each preauthorization request and subsequent claim.

C. Supply date. EPA recommends that trustees submit a notice of intent to file a restoration claim by means of the annual planning process.

VII. Provide an itemization of the estimated costs of restoring the injured natural resources for each category. For the costs projected for actions not identified *(i.e., "Other")*, provide a written statement indicating the nature and extent of said activity. Supply the basis for all estimated costs. If phased claims are requested, provide separate itemization of costs by phase. Explain why the estimated costs and expenses are reasonable, necessary, and cost effective for restoring the injured natural resource(s).

VIII. If EPA notified you that a sufficient level of funding exists to cover your planned restoration, please check "Yes."

IX. Self-explanatory.

EPA Form 2075-1 (10-85)

Appendix B—Claim for CERCLA Natural Resource Action (EPA Form 2075–2)

Form Approved OMB No. 2050-0043. Approval expires 4-30-88

United States Environmental Protection Agency
Washington, DC 20460

♻EPA Claim for CERCLA Natural Resource Action

EPA Docket Number

General Instructions: Complete all items in ink or by typewriter. Where applicable, insert the word "none." Use additional sheets if necessary. Read carefully the specific instructions on the opposite page.

Check as appropriate:

☐ Assessment Claim   ☐ Restoration Claim

I. Name, Title, and Address of Trustee/Lead Trustee

II. Name, Title, and Address of Authorized Agent (if any) to Represent Trustee/Lead Trustee

III. EPA ID Number and Date (For Preauthorized Restoration Claims Only)

IV. Relates to Actual Release of a Hazardous Substance

A. Date/time (am/pm) of release (if known)

B. Date of discovery of loss of natural resource(s)

C. Location of release and injured natural resource(s)

D. Was the claim presented to the responsible party?

☐ No

☐ Yes (Give date and results)

V. Relates to Damage Assessment Claims Only

A. Are claimed costs contained within EPA's annual appropriations?

☐ Yes (Give date)   ☐ No

B. Briefly describe the findings of the damage assessment.

C. Briefly describe the methodology used to assess the natural resource injury.

VI. Relates to Restoration Claims Only

A. Does this claim relate to a previously filed assessment claim?

☐ No

☐ Yes (Give date and number of claim)

B. Indicate date of Agency preauthorization of restoration claim.

EPA Form 2075-2 (10-85)

C. Indicate date of completion of restoration project *(or preauthorized phase).*

D. Detail, if appropriate, how the incident's description and activities as completed have deviated from that given in the approved preauthorization and the reasons for it.

VII. Amount of Damage Assessment Claim *(Attach all documents that support this claim.)*

A. Damage Assessment Costs	$
B. Other Costs *(Specify and justify)*	$
	$
	$
C. Total Costs	$

VIII. Amount of Restoration Claim *(Indicate whether the claim is for total or partial authorized costs. Attach all documents that support this claim.)*

	Preauthorized Costs	Actual Costs
A. Costs for restoration, rehabilitation, replacement, or acquisition of the equivalent	$	$
B. Other Costs *(Specify and justify)*	$	$
	$	$
C. Total Costs	$	$

Check One.

☐ Total authorized costs   ☐ Partial authorized costs

Certification

I certify that the information contained herein is true to the best of my knowledge. I agree to supply additional information, as requested, in support of this claim and access to the site for the purpose of inspection.

Signature of Claimant	Date

Civil Penalty for Presenting Fraudulent Claim	**Criminal Penalty for Presenting Fraudulent Claim or Making False Statements**
The claimant will forfeit and pay to the United States $2,000, plus double the amount of damages sustained by the United States. *(31 USC 3729 and 3730.)*	The claimant will be charged a maximum fine of not more than $10,000 or be imprisoned for a maximum of 5 years, or both. *(See 62 Stat. 698, 749; 18 USC 287, 1001.)*

EPA Form 2075-2 (10-85) Reverse

Instructions for Submitting a Claim for Natural Resource Action

I. Name any Federal natural resource management agency, principal State, commonwealth, U.S. Trust Territory, or other political entity acting on behalf of all affected trustees.

II. Self-explanatory.

III. See the upper right-hand corner of the approved preauthorization form.

IV. A. Provide documentation of the date and time of the release, if known.

B. Provide the date of the initial report first establishing that the injury resulted from the release of a hazardous substance *(IV. A.). (Date of actual damage assessment required in V. B.).*

C. Provide the name of the city or town and State where the release and the injury occurred. If the location is outside the city's limits, indicate the distance between it and the nearest city or town.

D. List all potentially responsible parties *(PRPs)* known to the trustee. Describe efforts to locate PRPs, date of presentation of your claim, and any reply from the PRPs.

V. A. It is recommended that the trustee submit a notice of intent to file an assessment claim by means of the annual planning process. If you have followed this process, give the date of receipt of Federal Government approval. If you check "No," indicate which of these two conditions apply: (1) you submitted a notice of claim as part of the annual planning process, but the assessment was deemed a low priority, or (2) you declined to file a notice of claim.

B. Summarize the natural resource impacts, including short- and long-term injury to both media and living organisms. Attach a copy of the damage assessment. Also indicate who approved the assessment, who conducted the assessment, when it was conducted and when it was completed.

C. Does the methodology selected comply with the Section 301 damage assessment regulations, or some other reasonable methodology? Specify if you are asserting that your assessment is entitled to a rebuttable presumption.

VI. A. If this restoration claim relates to a previously filed assessment claim for the same injury, supply the date on which the claim was filed and the number assigned by EPA. *(Hereinafter, "restoration" refers to restoring, rehabilitating, replacing, or acquiring the equivalent of an injured natural resource).*

B. — C. Self-explanatory.

D. Describe and justify any methods used in taking the natural resource action that deviated from the preauthorized approach. If such deviation required modifying the preauthorized actions or project costs, a request for preauthorization detailing such modifications must be resubmitted and approved. *(See §306.)*

VII. Document that all actions conducted by employees were more economical than using contractors and that all contractors were selected through maximum competition.

A. Submit proof of all aspects of the claimed costs associated with ascertaining actual injury to natural resources.

B. Submit proof of all aspects of the claimed costs associated with actions not identified in "A" above.

VIII. Document that all actions conducted by employees were more economical than using contractors and that all contractors were selected through maximum competition.

A. Supply preauthorized costs and actual costs. Submit proof of all aspects of the claimed costs associated with restoration of injured natural resources and a written statement indicating the nature and extent of such activity.

B. Supply preauthorized costs and actual costs. Submit proof of all aspects of the claimed costs associated with actions not identified in "A" above.

If EPA approved a phased approach authorizing partial reimbursement, check "partial authorized costs"; if EPA approved total reimbursement, check "total authorized costs."

EPA Form 2075-2 (10-85)

[FR Doc. 85–29507 Filed 12–12–85; 8:45 am]
BILLING CODE 6560-50-C

Appendix 6F Reportable Quantities Under CERCLA—EPA's Original Reportable Quantities and Adjustments to Reportable Quantities

Part I: EPA's Original Reportable Quantities (40 CFR Part 302)*

PART 302—DESIGNATION, REPORTABLE QUANTITIES, AND NOTIFICATION

Sec.
302.1 Applicability.
302.2 Abbreviations.
302.3 Definitions.
302.4 Designation of hazardous substances.
302.5 Determination of reportable quantities.
302.6 Notification requirements.
302.7 Penalties.

AUTHORITY: Sec. 102 of the Comprehensive Environmental Response, Compensation, and Liability Act of 1980, 42 U.S.C. 9602; secs. 311 and 501(a) of the Federal Water Pollution Control Act, 33 U.S.C. 1321 and 1361.

SOURCE: 50 FR 13474, Apr. 4, 1985, unless otherwise noted.

§ 302.1 Applicability.

This regulation designates under section 102(a) of the Comprehensive Environmental Response, Compensation, and Liability Act of 1980 ("the Act") those substances in the statutes referred to in section 101(14) of the Act, identifies reportable quantities

---

* See pp. App. 6F-78 et seq., infra, for EPA's subsequent adjustments to these quantities.

for these substances, and sets forth the notification requirements for releases of these substances. This regulation also sets forth reportable quantities for hazardous substances designated under section 311(b)(2)(A) of the Clean Water Act.

§ 302.2 Abbreviations.

CASRN =Chemical Abstracts Service Registry Number
RCRA=Resource Conservation and Recovery Act of 1976, as amended
lb=pound
kg=kilogram
RQ=reportable quantity

§ 302.3 Definitions.

As used in this part, all terms shall have the meaning set forth below:

"The Act", "CERCLA", or "Superfund" means the Comprehensive Environmental Response, Compensation, and Liability Act of 1980 (Pub. L. 96–510);

"Administrator" means the Administrator of the United States Environmental Protection Agency ("EPA");

"Consumer product" shall have the meaning stated in 15 U.S.C. 2052;

"Environment" means (1) the navigable waters, the waters of the contiguous zone, and the ocean waters of which the natural resources are under the exclusive management authority of the United States under the Fishery Conservation and Management Act of 1976, and (2) any other surface water, ground water, drinking water supply, land surface or subsurface strata, or ambient air within the United States or under the jurisdiction of the United States;

"Facility" means (1) any building, structure, installation, equipment, pipe or pipeline (including any pipe into a sewer or publicly owned treatment works), well, pit, pond, lagoon, impoundment, ditch, landfill, storage container, motor vehicle, rolling stock, or aircraft, or (2) any site or area where a hazardous substance has been deposited, stored, disposed of, or placed, or otherwise come to be located; but does not include any consumer product in consumer use or any vessel;

"Hazardous substance" means any substance designated pursuant to 40 CFR Part 302;

"Hazardous waste" shall have the meaning provided in 40 CFR 261.3;

"Navigable waters" or "navigable waters of the United States means waters of the United States, including the territorial seas;

"Offshore facility" means any facility of any kind located in, on, or under, any of the navigable waters of the United States, and any facility of any kind which is subject to the jurisdiction of the United States and is located in, on, or under any other waters, other than a vessel or a public vessel;

"Onshore facility" means any facility (including, but not limited to, motor vehicles and rolling stock) of any kind located in, on, or under, any land or non-navigable waters within the United States;

"Person" means an individual, firm, corporation, association, partnership, consortium, joint venture, commercial entity, United States Government, State, municipality, commission, political subdivision of a State, or any interstate body;

"Release" means any spilling, leaking, pumping, pouring, emitting, emptying, discharging, injecting, escaping, leaching, dumping, or disposing into the environment, but excludes (1) any release which results in exposure to persons solely within a workplace, with respect to a claim which such persons may assert against the employer of such persons, (2) emissions from the engine exhaust of a motor vehicle, rolling stock, aircraft, vessel, or pipeline pumping station engine, (3) release of source, byproduct, or special nuclear material from a nuclear incident, as those terms are defined in the Atomic Energy Act of 1954, if such release is subject to requirements with respect to financial protection established by the Nuclear Regulatory Commission under section 170 of such Act, or for the purposes of section 104 of the Comprehensive Environmental Response, Compensation, and Liability Act or any other response action, any release of source, byproduct, or special nuclear material from any processing site designated under section 102(a)(1) or 302(a) of the Uranium Mill Tailings Radiation Control Act of 1978, and (4) the normal application of fertilizer;

"Reportable quantity" means that quantity, as set forth in this part, the release of which requires notification pursuant to this part;

"United States" include the several States of the United States, the District of Columbia, the Commonwealth of Puerto Rico, Guam, American Samoa, the United States Virgin Islands, the Commonwealth of the Northern Marianas, and any other territory or possession over which the United States has jurisdiction; and

"Vessel" means every description of watercraft or other artificial contrivance used, or capable of being used, as a means of transportation on water.

§ 302.4 Designation of hazardous substances.

(a) *Listed hazardous substances.* The elements and compounds and hazardous wastes appearing in Table 302.4 are designated as hazardous substances under section 102(a) of the Act.

(b) *Unlisted hazardous substances.* A solid waste, as defined in 40 CFR 261.2, which is not excluded from regulation as a hazardous waste under 40 CFR 261.4(b), is a hazardous substance under section 101(14) of the Act if it exhibits any of the characteristics identified in 40 CFR 261.20 through 261.24.

NOTE: The numbers under the column headed "CASRN" are the Chemical Abstracts Service Registry Numbers for each hazardous substance. Other names by which each hazardous substance is identified in other statutes and their implementing regulations are provided in the "Regulatory Synonyms" column. The "Statutory RQ" column lists the RQs for hazardous substances established by section 102 of CERCLA. The "Statutory Code" column indicates the statutory source for designating each substance as a CERCLA hazardous substance: "1" indicates that the statutory source is section 311(b)(4) of the Clean Water Act, "2" indicates that the source is section 307(a) of the Clean Water Act, "3" indicates that the source is section 112 of the Clean Air Act, and "4" indicates that the source is RCRA section 3001. The "RCRA Waste Number" column provides the waste identification numbers assigned to various substances by RCRA regulations. The column headed "Category" lists the code letters "X," "A," "B," "C," and "D," which are associated with reportable quantities of 1, 10, 100, 1000, and 5000 pounds, respectively. The "Pounds (kg)" column provides the reportable quantity for each hazardous substance in pounds and kilograms.

TABLE 302.4—LIST OF HAZARDOUS SUBSTANCES AND REPORTABLE QUANTITIES

[See footnotes at end of Table 302.4]

Hazardous Substance	CASRN	Regulatory Synonyms	Statutory			Final RQ	
			RQ	Code†	RCRA Waste Number	Category	Pounds(Kg)
Acenaphthene..............	83329	....	1*	2	....	X	1## (0.454)
Acenaphthylene	208968	....	1*	2	....	X	1## (0.454)
Acetaldehyde	75070	Ethanal................	1000	1,4	U001	C	1000 (454)
Acetaldehyde, chloro-.......	107200	Chloroacetaldehyde..........	1*	4	P023	C	1000 (454)
Acetaldehyde, trichloro-....	75876	Chloral................	1*	4	U034	X	1#(0.454)
Acetamide, N-(aminothioxomethyl)-.	591082	1-Acetyl-2-thiourea	1*	4	P002	C	1000 (454)
Acetamide, N-(4-ethoxyphenyl)-.	62442	Phenacetin..................	1*	4	U187	X	1# (0.454)
Acetamide, N-9H-fluoren-2-yl-.	53963	2-Acetylaminofluorene	1*	4	U005	X	1# (0.454)
Acetamide, 2-fluoro-..........	640197	Fluoroacetamide	1*	4	P057	B	100(45.4)
Acetic acid.......................	64197	....	1000	1	....	D	5000 (2270)

TABLE 302.4—LIST OF HAZARDOUS SUBSTANCES AND REPORTABLE QUANTITIES—
Continued

[See footnotes at end of Table 302.4]

Hazardous Substance	CASRN	Regulatory Synonyms	Statutory			Final RQ	
			RQ	Code†	RCRA Waste Number	Catego-ry	Pounds(Kg)
Acetic acid, ethyl ester	141786	Ethyl acetate	1°	4	U112	D	5000 (2270)
Acetic acid, fluoro-, sodium salt.	62748	Fluoroacetic acid, sodium salt.	1°	4	P058	A	10 (4.54)
Acetic acid, lead salt........	301042	Lead acetate	5000	1,4	U144	D	5000# (2270)
Acetic acid, thallium(I) salt.	563688	Thallium(I) acetate.............	1°	4	U214	X	1## (0.454)
Acetic anhydride................	108247		1000	1	....	D	5000 (2270)
Acetimidic acid,N-[(methylcarbamoyl) oxy]thio-, methyl ester.	16752775	Methomyl	1°	4	P066	B	100 (45.4)
Acetone................	67641	2-Propanone...............	1°	4	U002	D	5000 (2270)
Acetone cyanohydrin	75865	2-Methyllactonitrile............. Propanenitrile, 2-hydroxy-2-methyl-	10	1,4	P069	A	10 (4.54)
Acetonitrile................	75058	Ethanenitrile	1°	4	U003	D	5000 (2270)
3-(alpha-Acetonylbenzyl)- 4-hydroxycoumarin and salts.	81812	Warfarin	1°	4	P001	B	100 (45.4)
Acetophenone................	98862	Ethanone, 1-phenyl-........	1°	4	U004	D	5000 (2270)
2-Acetylaminofluorene	53963	Acetamide, N-9H-fluoren-2-yl-.	1°	4	U005	X	1# (0.454)
Acetyl bromide..................	506967		5000	1	....	D	5000 (2270)
Acetyl chloride................	75365	Ethanoyl chloride...............	5000	1,4	U006	D	5000 (2270)
1-Acetyl-2-thiourea	591082	Acetamide, N-(aminothioxomethyl)-.	1°	4	P002	C	1000 (454)
Acrolein................	107028	2-Propenal	1	1,2,4	P003	X	1 (0.454)
Acrylamide................	79061	2-Propenamide.................	1°	4	U007	D	5000 (2270)
Acrylic acid................	79107	2-Propenoic acid...............	1°	4	U008	D	5000 (2270)
Acrylonitrile................	107131	2-Propenenitrile................	100	1,2,4	U009	B	100# (45.4)
Adipic acid................	124049		5000	1	....	D	5000 (2270)
Alanine, 3-[p-bis(2-chloroethyl)amino] phenyl-,L-.	148823	Melphalan......................	1°	4	U150	X	1# (0.454)
Aldicarb................	116063	Propanal, 2-methyl-2-(methylthio)-, O-[(methylamino) carbonyl]oxime.	1°	4	P070	X	1 (0.454)

APPENDIX 6F

TABLE 302.4—LIST OF HAZARDOUS SUBSTANCES AND REPORTABLE QUANTITIES—Continued

[See footnotes at end of Table 302.4]

Hazardous Substance	CASRN	Regulatory Synonyms	Statutory RQ	Statutory Code†	Statutory RCRA Waste Number	Final RQ Category	Final RQ Pounds(Kg)
Aldrin	309002	1,2,3,4,10-10-Hexachloro-1,4,4a,5,8,8a-hexahydro- 1,4:5,8-endo, exo-dimethanonaphthalene.	1	1,2,4	P004	X	1# (0.454)
Allyl alcohol	107186	2-Propen-1-ol	100	1,4	P005	B	100 (45.4)
Allyl chloride	107051		1000	1		C	1000 (454)
Aluminum phosphide	20859738		1*	4	P006	B	100 (45.4)
Aluminum sulfate	10043013		5000	1		D	5000 (2270)
5-(Aminomethyl)-3-isoxazolol.	2763964	3(2H)-Isoxazolone, 5-(aminomethyl)-.	1*	4	P007	C	1000 (454)
4-Aminopyridine	504245	4-Pyridinamine	1*	4	P008	C	1000 (454)
Amitrole	61825	1H-1,2,4-Triazol-3-amine	1*	4	U011	X	1# (0.454)
Ammonia	7664417		100	1		B	100## (45.4)
Ammonium acetate	631618		5000	1		D	5000 (2270)
Ammonium benzoate	1863634		5000	1		D	5000 (2270)
Ammonium bicarbonate	1066337		5000	1		D	5000 (2270)
Ammonium bichromate	7789095		1000	1		C	1000# (454)
Ammonium bifluoride	1341497		5000	1		D	5000## (2270)
Ammonium bisulfite	10192300		5000	1		D	5000 (2270)
Ammonium carbamate	1111780		5000	1		D	5000 (2270)
Ammonium carbonate	506876		5000	1		D	5000 (2270)
Ammonium chloride	12125029		5000	1		D	5000 (2270)
Ammonium chromate	7788989		1000	1		C	1000# (454)
Ammonium citrate, dibasic.	3012655		5000	1		D	5000 (2270)
Ammonium fluoborate	13826830		5000	1		D	5000 (2270)
Ammonium fluoride	12125018		5000	1		B	100 (45.4)
Ammonium hydroxide	1336216		1000	1		C	1000 (454)
Ammonium oxalate	6009707 5972736 14258492		5000	1		D	5000 (2270)
Ammonium picrate	131748	Phenol, 2,4,6-trinitro-, ammonium salt.	1*	4	P009	A	10 (4.54)
Ammonium silicofluoride	16919190		1000	1		C	1000 (454)
Ammonium sulfamate	7773060		5000	1		D	5000 (2270)

TABLE 302.4—LIST OF HAZARDOUS SUBSTANCES AND REPORTABLE QUANTITIES—
Continued

[See footnotes at end of Table 302.4]

Hazardous Substance	CASRN	Regulatory Synonyms	Statutory			Final RQ	
			RQ	Code†	RCRA Waste Number	Category	Pounds(Kg)
Ammonium sulfide............	12135761	....	5000	1	....	B	100 (45.4)
Ammonium sulfite.............	10196040	....	5000	1	....	D	5000 (2270)
Ammonium tartrate...........	14307438 3164292	....	5000	1	....	D	5000 (2270)
Ammonium thiocyanate	1762954	....	5000	1	....	D	5000 (2270)
Ammonium thiosulfate	7783188	....	5000	1	....	D	5000 (2270)
Ammonium vanadate	7803556	Vanadic acid, ammonium salt.	1*	4	P119	C	1000 (454)
Amyl acetate .... iso- sec- tert-	628637 123922 626380 625161	....	1000	1	....	D	5000 (2270)
Aniline	62533	Benzenamine	1000	1,4	U012	D	5000 (2270)
Anthracene........................	120127	....	1*	2	....	X	1## (0.454)
Antimony ††.......................	7440360	....	1*	2	....	X	1## (0.454)
ANTIMONY AND COMPOUNDS.	....	....	1*	2	....	....	**
Antimony pentachloride....	7647189	....	1000	1	....	C	1000 (454)
Antimony potassium tartrate.	28300745	....	1000	1	....	B	100 (45.4)
Antimony tribromide	7789619	....	1000	1	....	C	1000 (454)
Antimony trichloride...........	10025919	....	1000	1	....	C	1000(454)
Antimony trifluoride...........	7783564	....	1000	1	....	C	1000 (454)
Antimony trioxide..............	1309644	....	5000	1	....	C	1000 (454)
Aroclor 1016......................	12674112	Polychlorinated Biphenyls (PCBs).	10	1,2	....	A	10# (4.54)
Aroclor 1221......................	11104282	Polychlorinated Biphenyls (PCBs).	10	1,2	....	A	10# (4.54)
Aroclor 1232......................	11141165	Polychlorinated Biphenyls (PCBs).	10	1,2	....	A	10# (4.54)
Aroclor 1242......................	53469219	PolychlorinatedBiphenyls (PCBs).	10	1,2	....	A	10# (4.54)
Aroclor 1248......................	12672296	Polychlorinated Biphenyls (PCBs).	10	1,2	....	A	10# (4.54)
Aroclor 1254......................	11097691	Polychlorinated Biphenyls (PCBs).	10	1,2	....	A	10# (4.54)
Aroclor 1260......................	11096825	Polychlorinated Biphenyls (PCBs).	10	1,2	....	A	10# (4.54)
Arsenic ††	7440382	....	1*	2,3	....	X	1#(0.454)

TABLE 302.4—LIST OF HAZARDOUS SUBSTANCES AND REPORTABLE QUANTITIES—Continued

[See footnotes at end of Table 302.4]

Hazardous Substance	CASRN	Regulatory Synonyms	Statutory			Final RQ	
			RQ	Code†	RCRA Waste Number	Category	Pounds(Kg)
Arsenic acid..................	1327522 7778394		1*	4	P010	X	1# (0.454)
ARSENIC AND COMPOUNDS.	....		1*	2	....	....	**
Arsenic disulfide..............	1303328		5000	1	....	D	5000# (2270)
Arsenic(III) oxide..............	1327533	Arsenic trioxide	5000	1,4	P012	D	5000# (2270)
Arsenic(V) oxide...............	1303282	Arsenic pentoxide.............	5000	1,4	P011	D	5000#(2270)
Arsenic pentoxide.............	1303282	Arsenic(V) oxide................	5000	1,4	P011	D	5000# (2270)
Arsenic trichloride.............	7784341		5000	1	....	D	5000# (2270)
Arsenic trioxide	1327533	Arsenic(III) oxide...............	5000	1,4	P012	D	5000# (2270)
Arsenic trisulfide	1303339		5000	1	....	D	5000# (2270)
Arsine, diethyl-	692422	Diethylarsine....................	1*	4	P038	X	1# (0.454)
Asbestos †††	1332214		1*	2,3	....	X	1# (0.454)
Auramine.....................	492808	Benzenamine, 4,4'-carbonimidoylbis(N,N-dimethyl-.	1*	4	U014	X	1# (0.454)
Azaserine....................	115026	L-Serine, diazoacetate (ester).	1*	4	U015	X	1# (0.454)
Aziridine	151564	Ethylenimine....................	1*	4	P054	X	1# (0.454)
Azirino(2',3':3,4)pyrrolo (1,2-a)indole-4,7-dione,6-amino-8-[((aminocarbonyl)oxy) methyl]-1,1a,2,8,8a,8b-hexahydro-8a-methoxy-5-methyl-.	50077	Mitomycin C....................	1*	4	U010	X	1# (0.454)
Barium cyanide	542621	....	10	1,4	P013	A	10 (4.54)
Benz[j]aceanthrylene, 1,2-dihydro-3-methyl-.	56495	3-Methylcholanthrene........	1*	4	U157	X	1# (0.454)
Benz[c]acridine...............	225514	3,4-Benzacridine	1*	4	U016	X	1# (0.454)
3,4-Benzacridine	225514	Benz[c]acridine.................	1*	4	U016	X	1# (0.454)
Benzal chloride	98873	Benzene, dichloromethyl-.	1*	4	U017	D	5000 (2270)
Benz[a]anthracene..........	56553	1,2-Benzanthracene .... Benzo[a]anthracene	1*	2,4	U018	X	1# (0.454)
1,2-Benzanthracene	56553	Benz[a]anthracene............. Benzo[a]anthracene	1*	2,4	U018	X	1# (0.454)
1,2-Benzanthracene, 7,12-dimethyl-.	57976	7,12-Dimethylbenz[a] anthracene.	1*	4	U094	X	1# (0.454)

TABLE 302.4—LIST OF HAZARDOUS SUBSTANCES AND REPORTABLE QUANTITIES—
Continued

[See footnotes at end of Table 302.4]

Hazardous Substance	CASRN	Regulatory Synonyms	Statutory			Final RQ	
			RQ	Code†	RCRA Waste Number	Category	Pounds(Kg)
Benzenamine	62533	Aniline	1000	1,4	U012	D	5000 (2270)
Benzenamine, 4,4'-carbonimidoylbis(N,N-dimethyl-.	492808	Auramine..............	1*	4	U014	X	1# (0.454)
Benzenamine, 4-chloro-....	106478	p-Chloroaniline	1*	4	P024	C	1000 (454)
Benzenamine, 4-chloro-2-methyl-,hydrochloride.	3165933	4-Chloro-o-toluidine, hydrochloride.	1*	4	U049	X	1# (0.454)
Benzenamine, N,N-dimethyl-4-phenylazo-.	60117	Dimethylaminoazobenzene.	1*	4	U093	X	1# (0.454)
Benzenamine, 4,4'-methylenebis(2-chloro-.	101144	4,4'-Methylenebis(2-chloroaniline).	1*	4	U158	X	1# (0.454)
Benzenamine, 2-methyl-, hydrochloride.	636215	o-Toluidine hydrochloride.	1*	4	U222	X	1# (0.454)
Benzenamine, 2-methyl-5-nitro-.	99558	5-Nitro-o-toluidine	1*	4	U181	X	1# (0.454)
Benzenamine, 4-nitro-.......	100016	p-Nitroaniline	1*	4	P077	D	5000 (2270)
Benzene..............	71432		1000	1,2,3,4	U019	C	1000# (454)
Benzene, 1-bromo-4-phenoxy-.	101553	4-Bromophenyl phenyl ether.	1*	2,4	U030	B	100 (45.4)
Benzene, chloro-	108907	Chlorobenzene..............	100	1,2,4	U037	B	100 (45.4)
Benzene, chloromethyl-....	100447	Benzyl chloride	100	1,4	P028	B	100# (45.4)
Benzene, 1,2-dichloro-......	95501	1,2-Dichlorobenzene .... o-Dichlorobenzene	100	1,2,4	U070	B	100 (45.4)
Benzene, 1,3-dichloro-......	541731	1,3-Dichlorobenzene .... m-Dichlorobenzene	1*	2,4	U071	B	100 (45.4)
Benzene, 1,4-dichloro-......	106467	1,4-Dichlorobenzene .... p-Dichlorobenzene	100	1,2,4	U072	B	100 (45.4)
Benzene, dichloromethyl-.	98873	Benzal chloride	1*	4	U017	D	5000 (2270)
Benzene, 2,4-diisocyanatomethyl-.	584849 91087 26471625	Toluene diisocyanate	1*	4	U223	B	100 (45.4)
Benzene, dimethyl.............. m- o- p-	1330207 108383 95476 106423	Xylene .... m- o- p-	1000	1,4	U239	C	1000 (454)
Benzene, hexachloro-........	118741	Hexachlorobenzene...........	1*	2,4	U127	X	1# (0.454)
Benzene, hexahydro-........	110827	Cyclohexane..............	1000	1,4	U056	C	1000 (454)
Benzene, hydroxy-.............	108952	Phenol..............	1000	1,2,4	U188	C	1000## (454)

TABLE 302.4—LIST OF HAZARDOUS SUBSTANCES AND REPORTABLE QUANTITIES— Continued

[See footnotes at end of Table 302.4]

Hazardous Substance	CASRN	Regulatory Synonyms	Statutory			Final RQ	
			RQ	Code†	RCRA Waste Number	Category	Pounds(Kg)
Benzene, methyl-	108883	Toluene	1000	1,2,4	U220	C	1000 (454)
Benzene, 1-methyl-2,4-dinitro-.	121142	2,4-Dinitrotoluene	1000	1,2,4	U105	C	1000# (454)
Benzene, 1-methyl-2,6-dinitro-.	606202	2,6-Dinitrotoluene	1000	1,2,4	U106	C	1000# (454)
Benzene, 1,2-methylenedioxy-4-allyl-.	94597	Safrole	1*	4	U203	X	1# (0.454)
Benzene, 1,2-methylenedioxy-4-propenyl-.	120581	Isosafrole	1*	4	U141	X	1# (0.454)
Benzene, 1,2-methylenedioxy-4-propyl-.	94586	Dihydrosafrole	1*	4	U090	X	1# (0.454)
Benzene, 1-methylethyl-	98828	Cumene	1*	4	U055	D	5000 (2270)
Benzene, nitro-	98953	Nitrobenzene	1000	1,2,4	U169	C	1000 (454)
Benzene, pentachloro-	608935	Pentachlorobenzene	1*	4	U183	X	1## (0.454)
Benzene, pentachloronitro-.	82688	Pentachloronitrobenzene	1*	4	U185	X	1# (0.454)
Benzene, 1,2,4,5-tetrachloro-.	95943	1,2,4,5-Tetrachlorobenzene.	1*	4	U207	D	5000 (2270)
Benzene, trichloromethyl-.	98077	Benzotrichloride	1*	4	U023	X	1# (0.454)
Benzene, 1,3,5-trinitro-	99354	sym-Trinitrobenzene	1*	4	U234	X	1## (0.454)
Benzeneacetic acid, 4-chloro-alpha-(4-chlorophenyl)-alpha-hydroxy-, ethyl ester.	510156	Ethyl 4,4'-dichlorobenzilate.	1*	4	U038	X	1# (0.454)
1,2-Benzenedicarboxylic acid anhydride.	85449	Phthalic anhydride	1*	4	U190	D	5000 (2270)
1,2-Benzenedicarboxylic acid,[bis(2-ethylhexyl)] ester.	117817	Bis(2-ethylhexyl)phthalate.	1*	2,4	U028	X	1# (0.454)
1,2-Benzenedicarboxylic acid,dibutyl ester.	84742	n-Butyl phthalate Dibutyl phthalate Di-n-butyl phthalate	100	1,2,4	U069	A	10 (4.54)
1,2-Benzenedicarboxylic acid,diethyl ester.	84662	Diethyl phthalate	1*	2,4	U088	C	1000 (454)
1,2-Benzenedicarboxylic acid,dimethyl ester.	131113	Dimethyl phthalate	1*	2,4	U102	D	5000 (2270)
1,2-Benzenedicarboxylic acid, di-n-octyl ester.	117840	Di-n-octyl phthalate	1*	2,4	U107	D	5000 (2270)
1,3-Benzenediol	108463	Resorcinol	1000	1,4	U201	D	5000 (2270)

TABLE 302.4—LIST OF HAZARDOUS SUBSTANCES AND REPORTABLE QUANTITIES—
Continued

[See footnotes at end of Table 302.4]

| Hazardous Substance | CASRN | Regulatory Synonyms | Statutory | | | Final RQ | |
			RQ	Code†	RCRA Waste Number	Catego-ry	Pounds(Kg)
1,2-Benzenediol,4-[1-hydroxy-2-(methylamino)ethyl]-.	51434	Epinephrine	1*	4	P042	C	1000 (454)
Benzenesulfonic acid chloride.	98099	Benzenesulfonyl chloride..	1*	4	U020	B	100 (45.4)
Benzenesulfonyl chloride..	98099	Benzenesulfonic acid chloride.	1*	4	U020	B	100 (45.4)
Benzenethiol	108985	Thiophenol	1*	4	P014	B	100 (45.4)
Benzidine	92875	(1,1'-Biphenyl)-4,4'diamine.	1*	2,4	U021	X	1# (0.454)
1,2-Benzisothiazolin-3-one,1,1-dioxide, and salts.	81072	Saccharin and salts	1*	4	U202	X	1# (0.454)
Benzo[a]anthracene	56553	Benz[a]anthracene 1,2-Benzanthracene	1*	2,4	U018	X	1# (0.454)
Benzo[b]fluoranthene	205992		1*	2		X	1# (0.454)
Benzo[k]fluoranthene	207089		1*	2		X	1# (0.454)
Benzo[j,k]fluorene	206440	Fluoranthene	1*	2,4	U120	X	1## (0.454)
Benzoic acid	65850		5000	1		D	5000 (2270)
Benzonitrile	100470		1000	1		D	5000 (2270)
Benzo[ghi]perylene	191242		1*	2		X	1## (0.454)
Benzo[a]pyrene	50328	3,4-Benzopyrene	1*	2,4	U022	X	1# (0.454)
3,4-Benzopyrene	50328	Benzo[a]pyrene	1*	2,4	U022	X	1# (0.454)
p-Benzoquinone	106514	1,4-Cyclohexadienedione..	1*	4	U197	X	1## (0.454)
Benzotrichloride	98077	Benzene, trichloromethyl-.	1*	4	U023	X	1# (0.454)
Benzoyl chloride	98884		1000	1		C	1000 (454)
1,2-Benzphenanthrene	218019	Chrysene	1*	2,4	U050	X	1# (0.454)
Benzyl chloride	100447	Benzene, chloromethyl-	100	1,4	P028	B	100# (45.4)
Beryllium ††	7440417	Beryllium dust	1*	2,3,4	P015	X	1# (0.454)
BERYLLIUM AND COMPOUNDS.			1*	2			**
Beryllium chloride	7787475		5000	1		D	5000# (2270)
Beryllium dust	7440417	Beryllium	1*	2,3,4	P015	X	1# (0.454)
Beryllium fluoride	7787497		5000	1		D	5000# (2270)
Beryllium nitrate	13597994 7787555		5000	1		D	5000# (2270)

TABLE 302.4—LIST OF HAZARDOUS SUBSTANCES AND REPORTABLE QUANTITIES—Continued

[See footnotes at end of Table 302.4]

Hazardous Substance	CASRN	Regulatory Synonyms	Statutory			Final RQ	
			RQ	Code†	RCRA Waste Number	Category	Pounds(Kg)
alpha - BHC	319846		1*	2		X	1# (0.454)
beta - BHC	319857		1*	2		X	1# (0.454)
gamma - BHC	58899	Hexachlorocyclohexane (gamma isomer). Lindane	1	1,2,4	U129	X	1# (0.454)
delta - BHC	319868		1*	2		X	1## (0.454)
2,2'-Bioxirane	1464535	1,2:3,4-Diepoxybutane	1*	4	U085	X	1# (0.454)
(1,1'-Biphenyl)-4,4'diamine.	92875	Benzidine	1*	2,4	U021	X	1# (0.454)
(1,1'-Biphenyl)-4,4' diamine,3,3'dichloro-.	91941	3,3'-Dichlorobenzidine	1*	2,4	U073	X	1# (0.454)
(1,1'-Biphenyl)-4,4' diamine,3,3'dimethoxy-.	119904	3,3'-Dimethoxybenzidine	1*	4	U091	X	1# (0.454)
(1,1'Biphenyl)-4,4'- diamine,3,3'-dimethyl-.	119937	3,3'-Dimethylbenzidine	1*	4	U095	X	1# (0.454)
Bis(2-chloroethoxy) methane.	111911	Ethane, 1,1'-[methylenebis(oxy)] bis(2-chloro-.	1*	2,4	U024	C	1000 (454)
Bis (2-chloroethyl) ether	111444	Dichloroethyl ether Ethane, 1,1'-oxybis[2-chloro-	1*	2,4	U025	X	1# (0.454)
Bis(2-chloroisopropyl) ether.	108601	Propane, 2,2'-oxybis(2-chloro-.	1*	2,4	U027	C	1000 (454)
Bis(chloromethyl) ether	542881	Methane, oxybis(chloro-	1*	4	P016	X	1# (0.454)
Bis (dimethylthiocarba-moyl) disulfide.	137268	Thiram	1*	4	U244	A	10 (4.54)
Bis(2-ethylhexyl)phthalate.	117817	1,2-Benzenedicarboxylic acid, [bis(2-ethylhexyl)] ester.	1*	2,4	U028	X	1# (0.454)
Bromine cyanide	506683	Cyanogen bromide	1*	4	U246	C	1000 (454)
Bromoacetone	598312	2-Propanone, 1-bromo-	1*	4	P017	C	1000 (454)
Bromoform	75252	Methane, tribromo-	1*	2,4	U225	B	100 (45.4)
4-Bromophenyl phenyl ether.	101553	Benzene, 1-bromo-4-phenoxy-.	1*	2,4	U030	B	100 (45.4)
Brucine	357573	Strychnidin-10-one, 2,3-dimethoxy-.	1*	4	P018	B	100 (45.4)
1,3-Butadiene, 1,1,2,3,4,4-hexachloro-.	87683	Hexachlorobutadiene	1*	2,4	U128	X	1# (0.454)
1-Butanamine, N-butyl-N-nitroso-.	924163	N-Nitrosodi-n-butylamine	1*	4	U172	X	1# (0.454)

TABLE 302.4—LIST OF HAZARDOUS SUBSTANCES AND REPORTABLE QUANTITIES—
Continued

[See footnotes at end of Table 302.4]

Hazardous Substance	CASRN	Regulatory Synonyms	Statutory			Final RQ	
			RQ	Code†	RCRA Waste Number	Category	Pounds(Kg)
Butanoic acid, 4-[bis(2-chlorcethyl)amino] benzene-.	305033	Chlorambucil..............	1*	4	U035	X	1# (0.454)
1-Butanol	71363	n-Butyl alcohol	1*	4	U031	D	.5000 (2270)
2-Butanone......................	78933	Methyl ethyl ketone..........	1*	4	U159	D	.5000 (2270)
2-Butanone peroxide........	1338234	Methyl ethyl ketone peroxide.	1*	4	U160	A	10 (4.54)
2-Butenal	123739 4170303	Crotonaidehyde.................	100	1,4	U053	B	100 (45.4)
2-Butene, 1,4-dichloro-.....	764410	1,4-Dichloro-2-butene........	1*	4	U074	X	1 (0.454)
Butyl acetate...................... iso- sec- tert-	123864 110190 105464 540885	....	5000	1	....	D	5000 (2270)
n-Butyl alcohol	71363	1-Butanol	1*	4	U031	D	5000 (2270)
Butylamine.......................... iso- sec- sec- tert-	109739 78819 513495 13952846 75649	....	1000	1	....	C	1000 (454)
Butyl benzyl phthalate.......	85687	....	1*	2	....	B	100 (45.4)
n-Butyl phthalate................	84742	1,2-Benzenedicarboxylic acid,dibutyl ester. Dibutyl phthalate Di-n-butyl phthalate	100	1,2,4	U069	A	10 (4.54)
Butyric acid........................ iso-	107926 79312	....	5000	1	....	D	5000 (2270)
Cacodylic acid....................	75605	Hydroxydimethylarsine oxide.	1*	4	U136	X	1# (0.454)
Cadmium ††	7440439	....	1*	2	....	X	1# (0.454)
Cadmium acetate..............	543908	....	100	1	....	B	100# (45.4)
CADMIUM AND COMPOUNDS.			1*	2	....		**
Cadmium bromide	7789426	....	100	1	....	B	100# (45.4)
Cadmium chloride.............	10108642	....	100	1	....	B	100# (45.4)
Calcium arsenate...............	7778441	....	1000	1	....	C	1000# (454)
Calcium arsenite.............	52740166	....	1000	1	....	C	1000# (454)
Calcium carbide	75207	....	5000	1	....	A	10 (4.54)
Calcium chromate.............	13765190	Chromic acid, calcium salt.	1000	1,4	U032	C	1000# (454)
Calcium cyanide................	592018	....	10	1,4	P021	A	10 (4.54)

TABLE 302.4—LIST OF HAZARDOUS SUBSTANCES AND REPORTABLE QUANTITIES— Continued

[See footnotes at end of Table 302.4]

Hazardous Substance	CASRN	Regulatory Synonyms	Statutory			Final RQ	
			RQ	Code†	RCRA Waste Number	Category	Pounds(Kg)
Calcium dodecylbenzene sulfonate.	26264062	....	1000	1	....	C	1000 (454)
Calcium hypochlorite........	7778543	....	100	1		A	10(4.54)
Camphene, octachloro-	8001352	Toxaphene.....................	1	1,2,4	P123	X	1# (0.454)
Captan................................	133062	....	10	1	....	A	10## (4.54)
Carbamic acid, ethyl ester.	51796	Ethyl carbamate (Urethan).	1*	4	U238	X	1# (0.454)
Carbamic acid, methylnitroso-,ethyl ester.	615532	N-Nitroso-N-methylurethane.	1*	4	U178	X	1# (0.454)
Carbamide, N-ethyl-N-nitroso-.	759739	N-Nitroso-N-ethylurea	1*	4	U176	X	1# (0.454)
Carbamide, N-methyl-N-nitroso-	684935	N-Nitroso-N-methylurea	1*	4	U177	X	1# (0.454)
Carbamide, thio-	62566	Thiourea........................	1*	4	U219	X	1# (0.454)
Carbamimidoselenoic acid.	630104	Selenourea	1*	4	P103	X	1## (0.454)
Carbamoyl chloride, dimethyl-.	79447	Dimethylcarbamoyl chloride.	1*	4	U097	X	1# (0.454)
Carbaryl............................	63252	....	100	1	....	B	100 (45.4)
Carbofuran........................	1563662	....	10	1	....	A	10 (4.54)
Carbon bisulfide....	75150	Carbon disulfide...............	5000	1,4	P022	D	5000## (2270)
Carbon disulfide...............	75150	Carbon bisulfide...............	5000	1,4	P022	D	5000## (2270)
Carbonic acid, dithallium (I) salt.	6533739	Thallium(I) carbonate	1*	4	U215	X	1## (0.454)
Carbonochloridic acid, methyl ester.	79221	Methyl chlorocarbonate	1*	4	U156	C	1000 (454)
Carbon oxyfluoride	353504	Carbonyl fluoride...............	1*	4	U033	C	1000 (454)
Carbon tetrachloride.	56235	Methane, tetrachloro-........	5000	1,2,4	U211	D	5000# (2270)
Carbonyl chloride..............	75445	Phosgene......................	5000	1,4	P095	A	10 (4.54)
Carbonyl fluoride...............	353504	Carbon oxyfluoride	1*	4	U033	C	1000 (454)
Chloral...............................	75876	Acetaldehyde, trichloro-....	1*	4	U034	X	1#(0.454)
Chlorambucil......................	305033	Butanoic acid, 4-[bis(2-chloroethyl)amino]benzene-.	1*	4	U035	X	1# (0.454)
CHLORDANE (TECHNICAL MIXTURE AND METABOLITES).		....	1*	2	....	....	••

TABLE 302.4—LIST OF HAZARDOUS SUBSTANCES AND REPORTABLE QUANTITIES—
Continued

[See footnotes at end of Table 302.4]

Hazardous Substance	CASRN	Regulatory Synonyms	Statutory			Final RQ	
			RQ	Code†	RCRA Waste Number	Category	Pounds(Kg)
Chlordane	57749	Chlordane, technical .... 4,7-Methanoindan, 1,2,4,5,6,7,8,8- octachloro- 3a,4,7,7a- tetrahydro-	1	1,2,4	U036	X	1# (0.454)
Chlordane, technical	57749	Chlordane .... 4,7-Methanoindan, 1,2,4,5,6,7,8,8- octachloro- 3a,4,7,7a- tetrahydro-	1	1,2,4	U036	X	1# (0.454)
CHLORINATED BENZENES.			1*	2			**
CHLORINATED ETHANES.			1*	2			**
CHLORINATED NAPHTHALENE.			1*	2			**
CHLORINATED PHENOLS.			1*	2			**
Chlorine..........................	7782505		10	1		A	10 (4.54)
Chlorine cyanide	506774	Cyanogen chloride............	10	1,4	P033	A	10 (4.54)
Chlornaphazine	494031	2-Naphthylamine, N,N- bis(2-chloroethyl)-.	1*	4	U026	X	1# (0.454)
Chloroacetaldehyde...........	107200	Acetaldehyde, chloro-	1*	4	P023	C	1000 (454)
CHLOROALKYL ETHERS.			1*	2			**
p-Chloroaniline	106478	Benzenamine, 4-chloro-....	1*	4	P024	C	1000 (454)
Chlorobenzene..................	108907	Benzene, chloro-	100	1,2,4	U037	B	100 (45.4)
4-Chloro-m-cresol	59507	p-Chloro-m-cresol .... Phenol, 4-chloro-3- methyl-	1*	2,4	U039	D	5000 (2270)
p-Chloro-m-cresol	59507	4-Chloro-m-cresol .... Phenol, 4-chloro-3- methyl-	1*	2,4	U039	D	5000 (2270)
Chlorodibromomethane.....	124481		1*	2		B	100 (45.4)
1-Chloro-2,3- epoxypropane.	106898	Epichlorohydrin .... Oxirane, 2- (chloromethyl)-	1000	1,4	U041	C	1000# (454)
Chloroethane....................	75003		1*	2		X	1## (0.454)
2-Chloroethyl vinyl ether....	110758	Ethene, 2-chloroethoxy-....	1*	2,4	U042	C	1000 (454)
Chloroform......................	67663	Methane, trichloro-	5000	1,2,4	U044	D	5000# (2270)
Chloromethyl methyl ether.	107302	Methane, chloromethoxy-.	1*	4	U046	X	1# (0.454)

APPENDIX 6F

TABLE 302.4—LIST OF HAZARDOUS SUBSTANCES AND REPORTABLE QUANTITIES—Continued

[See footnotes at end of Table 302.4]

Hazardous Substance	CASRN	Regulatory Synonyms	Statutory			Final RQ	
			RQ	Code†	RCRA Waste Number	Category	Pounds(Kg)
beta-Chloronaphthalene ...	91587	2-Chloronaphthalene......... Naphthalene, 2-chloro-	1*	2,4	U047	D	5000 (2270)
2-Chloronaphthalene........	91587	beta-Chloronaphthalene ... Naphthalene, 2-chloro-	1*	2,4	U047	D	5000 (2270)
2-Chlorophenol..............	95578	o-Chlorophenol .... Phenol, 2-chloro-	1*	2,4	U048	B	100 (45.4)
o-Chlorophenol	95578	2-Chlorophenol............. Phenol, 2-chloro-	1*	2,4	U048	B	100 (45.4)
4-Chlorophenyl phenyl ether.	7005723		1*	2		D	5000 (2270)
1-(o-Chlorophenyl)thiourea.	5344821	Thiourea, (2-chlorophenyl)-.	1*	4	P026	B	100 (45.4)
3-Chloropropionitrile	542767	Propanenitrile, 3-chloro-....	1*	4	P027	C	1000 (454)
Chlorosulfonic acid..........	7790945		1000	1		C	1000 (454)
4-Chloro-o-toluidine, hydrochloride.	3165933	Benzenamine, 4-chloro-2-methyl-,hydrochloride.	1*	4	U049	X	1# (0.454)
Chlorpyrifos	2921882		1	1		X	1 (0.454)
Chromic acetate	1066304		1000	1		C	1000## (454)
Chromic acid................	11115745 7738945		1000	1		C	1000# (454)
Chromic acid, calcium salt.	13765190	Calcium chromate.............	1000	1,4	U032	C	1000# (454)
Chromic sulfate..............	10101538		1000	1		C	1000## (454)
Chromium ††	7440473		1*	2		X	1# (0.454)
CHROMIUM AND COMPOUNDS.			1*	2			**
Chromous chloride	10049055		1000	1		C	1000## (454)
Chrysene....................	218019	1,2-Benzphenanthrene......	1*	2,4	U050	X	1# (0.454)
Cobaltous bromide	7789437		1000	1		C	1000(454)
Cobaltous formate............	544183		1000	1		C	1000 (454)
Cobaltous sulfamate	14017415		1000	1		C	1000 (454)
Coke Oven Emissions......	N.A.		1*	3		X	1# (0.454)
Copper ††	7440508		1*	2		X	1## (0.454)
COPPER AND COMPOUNDS.			1*	2			**
Copper cyanide..............	544923		1*	4	P029	A	10 (4.54)
Coumaphos	56724		10	1		A	10 (4.54)

TABLE 302.4—LIST OF HAZARDOUS SUBSTANCES AND REPORTABLE QUANTITIES—
Continued

[See footnotes at end of Table 302.4]

Hazardous Substance	CASRN	Regulatory Synonyms	Statutory			Final RQ	
			RQ	Codet	RCRA Waste Number	Category	Pounds(Kg)
Creosote	8001589		1°	4	U051	X	1# (0.454)
Cresol(s) m- o- p-	1319773 108394 95487 106445	Cresylic acid	1000	1,4	U052	C	1000## (454)
Cresylic acid m- o- p-	1319773 108394 95487 106445	Cresol(s)	1000	1,4	U052	C	1000## (454)
Crotonaldehyde	123739 4170303	2-Butenal	100	1,4	U053	B	100 (45.4)
Cumene	98828	Benzene, 1-methylethyl-	1°	4	U055	D	5000 (2270)
Cupric acetate	142712		100	1		B	100 (45.4)
Cupric acetoarsenite	12002038		100	1		B	100# (45.4)
Cupric chloride	7447394		10	1		A	10## (4.54)
Cupric nitrate	3251238		100	1		B	100 (45.4)
Cupric oxalate	5893663		100	1		B	100 (45.4)
Cupric sulfate	7758987		10	1		A	10## (4.54)
Cupric sulfate ammoniated.	10380297		100	1		B	100 (45.4)
Cupric tartrate	815827		100	1		B	100## (45.4)
CYANIDES			1°	2			**
Cyanides (soluble cyanide salts), not elsewhere specified.	57125		1°	4	P030	A	10 (4.54)
Cyanogen	460195		1°	4	P031	B	100 (45.4)
Cyanogen bromide	506683	Bromine cyanide	1°	4	U246	C	1000 (454)
Cyanogen chloride	506774	Chlorine cyanide	10	1,4	P033	A	10 (4.54)
1,4-Cyclohexadienedione	106514	p-Benzoquinone	1°	4	U197	X	1## (0.454)
Cyclohexane	110827	Benzene, hexahydro-	1000	1,4	U056	C	1000(454)
Cyclohexanone	108941		1°	4	U057	D	5000 (2270)
1,3-Cyclopentadiene, 1,2,3,4,5,5-hexachloro-.	77474	Hexachlorocyclopentadiene.	1	1,2,4	U130	X	1# (0.454)
Cyclophosphamide	50180	2H-1,3,2-Oxazaphosphorine,2-[bis(2-chloroethyl)amino] tetrahydro-2-oxide.	1°	4	U058	X	1# (0.454)

App. 6F-16

TABLE 302.4—LIST OF HAZARDOUS SUBSTANCES AND REPORTABLE QUANTITIES—
Continued

[See footnotes at end of Table 302.4]

Hazardous Substance	CASRN	Regulatory Synonyms	Statutory			Final RQ	
			RQ	Code†	RCRA Waste Number	Catego-ry	Pounds(Kg)
2,4-D Acid..............	94757	2,4-D, salts and esters ..... 2,4-Dichlorophenoxyacetic acid, salts and esters	100	1,4	U240	B	100 (45.4)
2,4-D Esters	94111 94791 94804 1320189 1928387 1928616 1929733 2971382 25168267 53467111		100	1	....	B	100 (45.4)
2,4-D, salts and esters	94757	2,4-D Acid............. 2,4-Dichlorophenoxyacetic acid, salts and esters	100	1,4	U240	B	100 (45.4)
Daunomycin.............	20830813	5,12-Naphthacenedione, (8S-cis)-8-acetyl-10-[3-amino- 2,3,6-trideoxy- alpha-L-lyxo-hexopyranosyl)oxy]-7,8,9,10-tetrahydro-6,8,11-trihydroxy- 1-methoxy-.	1*	4	U059	X	1# (0.454)
DDD.............	72548	4,4' DDD .... Dichlorodiphenyl dichloroethane TDE	1	1,2,4	U060	X	1# (0.454)
4,4' DDD	72548	DDD............. Dichlorodiphenyl dichloroethane TDE	1	1,2,4	U060	X	1# (0.454)
DDE.............	72559	4,4' DDE	1*	2	....	X	1# (0.454)
4,4' DDE	72559	DDE.............	1*	2	....	X	1# (0.454)
DDT.............	50293	4,4' DDT .... Dichlorodiphenyl trichloroethane	1	1,2,4	U061	X	1# (0.454)
4,4'DDT.............	50293	DDT .... Dichlorodiphenyl trichloroethane	1	1,2,4	U061	X	1# (0.454)
DDT AND METABOLITES.	....	....	1*	2	....	....	**
Decachlorooctahydro-1,3,4-metheno-2H-cyclobuta[c,d]-pentalen-2-one.	143500	Kepone.............	1	1,4	U142	X	1# (0.454)
Diallate	2303164	S-(2,3-Dichloroallyl) diisopropylthiocarba-mate.	1*	4	U062	X	1# (0.454)

TABLE 302.4—LIST OF HAZARDOUS SUBSTANCES AND REPORTABLE QUANTITIES—
Continued

[See footnotes at end of Table 302.4]

Hazardous Substance	CASRN	Regulatory Synonyms	Statutory			Final RQ	
			RQ	Code†	RCRA Waste Number	Category	Pounds(Kg)
Diamine	302012	Hydrazine	1*	4	U133	X	1# (0.454)
Diaminotoluene	95807 25376458 496720 823405	Toluenediamine	1*	4	U221	X	1# (0.454)
Diazinon	5333415		1	1		X	1 (0.454)
Dibenz[a,h]anthracene	53703	1,2:5,6-Dibenzanthracene. Dibenzo[a,h]anthracene	1*	2,4	U063	X	1# (0.454)
1,2:5,6-Dibenzanthracene.	53703	Dibenz[a,h]anthracene. Dibenzo[a,h]anthracene	1*	2,4	U063	X	1# (0.454)
Dibenzo[a,h]anthracene	53703	Dibenz[a,h]anthracene. 1,2:5,6-Dibenzanthracene	1*	2,4	U063	X	1# (0.454)
1,2:7,8-Dibenzopyrene	189559	Dibenz[a,i]pyrene	1*	4	U064	X	1# (0.454)
Dibenz[a,i]pyrene	189559	1,2:7,8-Dibenzopyrene	1*	4	U064	X	1#(0.454)
1,2-Dibromo-3-chloropropane.	96128	Propane, 1,2-dibromo-3-chloro-.	1*	4	U066	X	1# (0.454)
Dibutyl phthalate	84742	1,2-Benzenedicarboxylic acid,dibutyl ester. Di-n-butyl phthalate n-Butyl phthalate	100	1,2,4	U069	A	10 (4.54)
Di-n-butyl phthalate	84742	1,2-Benzenedicarboxylic acid,dibutyl ester. n-Butyl phthalate Dibutyl phthalate	100	1,2,4	U069	A	10 (4.54)
Dicamba	1918009		1000	1		C	1000 (454)
Dichlobenil	1194656		1000	1		B	100 (45.4)
Dichlone	117806		1	1		X	1 (0.454)
S-(2,3-Dichloroallyl) diisopropylthiocarbamate.	2303164	Diallate	1*	4	U062	X	1# (0.454)
3,5-Dichloro-N-(1,1-dimethyl-2-propynyl)benzamide.	23950585	Pronamide	1*	4	U192	D	5000 (2270)
Dichlorobenzene (mixed)	25321226		100	1		B	100 (45.4)
1,2-Dichlorobenzene	95501	Benzene, 1,2-dichloro-. o-Dichlorobenzene	100	1,2,4	U070	B	100 (45.4)
1,3-Dichlorobenzene	541731	Benzene, 1,3-dichloro-. m-Dichlorobenzene	1*	2,4	U071	B	100 (45.4)
1,4-Dichlorobenzene	106467	Benzene, 1,4-dichloro-. p-Dichlorobenzene	100	1,2,4	U072	B	100 (45.4)

TABLE 302.4—LIST OF HAZARDOUS SUBSTANCES AND REPORTABLE QUANTITIES— Continued

[See footnotes at end of Table 302.4]

Hazardous Substance	CASRN	Regulatory Synonyms	Statutory			Final RQ	
			RQ	Code†	RCRA Waste Number	Category	Pounds(Kg)
m-Dichlorobenzene............	541731	Benzene, 1,3-dichloro-...... 1,3-Dichlorobenzene	1*	2,4	U071	B	100 (45.4)
o-Dichlorobenzene............	95501	Benzene, 1,2-dichloro-...... 1,2-Dichlorobenzene	100	1,2,4	U070	B	100 (45.4)
p-Dichlorobenzene............	106467	Benzene, 1,4-dichloro-...... 1,4-Dichlorobenzene	100	1,2,4	U072	B	100 (45.4)
DICHLOROBENZIDINE			1*	2			**
3,3'-Dichlorobenzidine.......	91941	(1,1'-Biphenyl)- 4,4'diamine,3,3'dichloro-	1*	2,4	U073	X	1# (0.454)
Dichlorobromomethane.....	75274		1*	2		D	5000 (2270)
1,4-Dichloro-2-butene.......	764410	2-Butene, 1,4-dichloro-	1*	4	U074	X	1 (0.454)
Dichlorodifluoromethane...	75718	Methane, dichlorodifluoro-.	1*	4	U075	D	5000 (2270)
Dichlorodiphenyl dichloroethane.	72548	DDD................ 4,4' DDD TDE	1	1,2,4	U060	X	1# (0.454)
Dichlorodiphenyl trichloroethane.	50293	DDT................ 4,4'DDT	1	1,2,4	U061	X	1# (0.454)
1,1-Dichloroethane	75343	Ethane, 1,1-dichloro-......... Ethylidene dichloride	1*	2,4	U076	C	1000 (454)
1,2-Dichloroethane	107062	Ethane, 1,2-dichloro-......... Ethylene dichloride	5000	1,2,4	U077	D	5000# (2270)
1,1-Dichloroethyiene.........	75354	Ethene, 1,1-dichloro-......... Vinylidene chloride	5000	1,2,4	U078	D	5000# (2270)
1,2-trans- Dichloroethylene.	156605	Ethene, trans-1,2- dichloro-.	1*	2,4	U079	C	1000 (454)
Dichloroethyl ether	111444	Bis (2-chloroethyl) ether ... Ethane, 1,1'-oxybis(2- chloro-	1*	2,4	U025	X	1# (0.454)
2,4-Dichlorophenol	120832	Phenol, 2,4-dichloro-.........	1*	2,4	U081	B	100 (45.4)
2,6-Dichlorophenol	87650	Phenol, 2,6-dichloro-.........	1*	4	U082	B	100 (45.4)
2,4- Dichlorophenoxyacetic acid, salts and esters.	94757	2,4-D Acid..................... 2,4-D, salts and esters	100	1,4	U240	B	100 (45.4)
Dichlorophenylarsine........	696286	Phenyl dichlroarsine........	1*	4	P036	X	1# (0.454)
Dichloropropane............. 1,1-Dichloropropane 1,3-Dichloropropane	26638197 78999 142289		5000	1		C	1000 (454)
1,2-Dichloropropane..........	78875	Propylene dichloride..........	5000	1,2,4	U083	C	1000 (454)

TABLE 302.4—LIST OF HAZARDOUS SUBSTANCES AND REPORTABLE QUANTITIES—
Continued

[See footnotes at end of Table 302.4]

Hazardous Substance	CASRN	Regulatory Synonyms	Statutory			Final RQ	
			RQ	Code†	RCRA Waste Number	Category	Pounds(Kg)
Dichloropropane - Dichloropropene (mixture).	8003198		5000	1		D	5000## (2270)
Dichloropropene 2,3-Dichloropropene	26952238 78886		5000	1		D	5000## (2270)
1,3-Dichloropropene.........	542756	Propene, 1,3-dichloro-......	5000	1,2,4	U084	D	5000## (2270)
2,2-Dichloropropionic acid.	75990		5000	1		D	5000 (2270)
Dichlorvos...................	62737		10	1		A	10 (4.54)
Dieldrin	60571	1,2,3,4,10,10-Hexachloro-6,7-epoxy-1,4,4a,5,6,7,8,8a-octahydro-endo,exo-1,4:5,8-dimethanonaphthalene.	1	1,2,4	P037	X	1# (0.454)
1,2:3,4-Diepoxybutane......	1464535	2,2'-Bioxirane	1*	4	U085	X	1# (0.454)
Diethylamine..............	109897		1000	1		C	1000## (454)
Diethylarsine.............	692422	Arsine, diethyl-	1*	4	P038	X	1# (0.454)
1,4-Diethylene dioxide......	123911	1,4-Dioxane	1*	4	U108	X	1# (0.454)
N,N'-Diethylhydrazine.......	1615801	Hydrazine, 1,2-diethyl-......	1*	4	U086	X	1# (0.454)
O,O-Diethyl S-[2-(ethylthio)ethyl] phosphorodithioate.	298044	Disulfoton................	1	1,4	P039	X	1 (0.454)
O,O-Diethyl S-methyl dithiophosphate.	3288582	Phosphorodithioic acid, O,O-diethyl S-methylester.	1*	4	U087	D	5000 (2270)
Diethyl-p-nitrophenyl phosphate.	311455	Phosphoric acid,diethyl p-nitrophenyl ester.	1*	4	P041	B	100 (45.4)
Diethyl phthalate..............	84662	1,2-Benzenedicarboxylic acid,diethyl ester.	1*	2,4	U088	C	1000 (454)
O,O-Diethyl O-pyrazinyl phosphorothioate.	297972	Phosphorothioic acid, O,O-diethyl O-pyrazinyl ester.	1*	4	P040	B	100 (45.4)
Diethylstilbestrol..............	56531	4,4'-Stilbenediol, alpha,alpha'-diethyl-.	1*	4	U089	X	1# (0.454)
1,2-Dihydro-3,6-pyridazinedione.	123331	Maleic hydrazide.............	1*	4	U148	D	5000 (2270)
Dihydrosafrole	94586	Benzene, 1,2-methylenedioxy-4-propyl-.	1*	4	U090	X	1# (0.454)
Diisopropyl fluorophosphate.	55914	Phosphorofluoridic acid,bis(1-methylethyl) ester.	1*	4	P043	B	100 (45.4)

App. 6F-20

TABLE 302.4—LIST OF HAZARDOUS SUBSTANCES AND REPORTABLE QUANTITIES—Continued

[See footnotes at end of Table 302.4]

Hazardous Substance	CASRN	Regulatory Synonyms	Statutory			Final RQ	
			RQ	Code†	RCRA Waste Number	Category	Pounds(Kg)
Dimethoate	60515	Phosphorodithioic acid,O,O-dimethyl S-[2(methylamino)- 2-oxoethyl] ester.	1*	4	P044	A	10 (4.54)
3,3'-Dimethoxybenzidine	119904	(1,1'-Biphenyl)-4,4'diamine,3,3' dimethoxy-.	1*	4	U091	X	1# (0.454)
Dimethylamine	124403	Methanamine, N-methyl-	1000	1,4	U092	C	1000## (454)
Dimethylaminoazobenzene.	60117	Benzenamine, N,N-dimethyl-4-phenylazo-.	1*	4	U093	X	1# (0.454)
7,12-Dimethylbenz[a]anthracene.	57976	1,2-Benzanthracene, 7,12-dimethyl-.	1*	4	U094	X	1# (0.454)
3,3'-Dimethylbenzidine	119937	(1,1'Biphenyl)-4,4'-diamine,3,3'-dimethyl-.	1*	4	U095	X	1# (0.454)
alpha,alpha-Dimethylbenzylhydroperoxide.	80159	Hydroperoxide, 1-methyl-1-phenylethyl-.	1*	4	U096	A	10 (4.54)
3,3-Dimethyl-1-(methylthio)-2-butanone, O-[(methylamino) carbonyl] oxime.	39196184	Thiofanox	1*	4	P045	B	100 (45.4)
Dimethylcarbamoyl chloride.	79447	Carbamoyl chloride, dimethyl-.	1*	4	U097	X	1# (0.454)
1,1-Dimethylhydrazine	57147	Hydrazine, 1,1-dimethyl-	1*	4	U098	X	1# (0.454)
1,2-Dimethylhydrazine	540738	Hydrazine, 1,2-dimethyl-	1*	4	U099	X	1# (0.454)
O,O-Dimethyl O-p-nitrophenyl phosphorothioate.	298000	Methyl parathion	100	1,4	P071	B	100## (45.4)
Dimethyinitrosamine	62759	N-Nitrosodimethylamine	1*	2,4	P082	X	1# (0.454)
alpha,alpha-Dimethylphenethylamine.	122098	Ethanamine, 1,1-dimethyl-2-phenyl-.	1*	4	P046	D	5000 (2270)
2,4-Dimethylphenol	105679	Phenol, 2,4-dimethyl-	1*	2,4	U101	B	100 (45.4)
Dimethyl phthalate	131113	1,2-Benzenedicarboxylic acid,dimethyl ester.	1*	2,4	U102	D	5000 (2270)
Dimethyl sulfate	77781	Sulfuric acid, dimethyl ester.	1*	4	U103	X	1# (0.454)
Dinitrobenzene (mixed) m- o- p-	25154545 99650 528290 100254		1000	1		B	100 (45.4)
4,6-Dinitro-o-cresol and salts.	534521	Phenol, 2,4-dinitro-6-methyl-, and salts.	1*	2,4	P047	A	10 (4.54)

TABLE 302.4—LIST OF HAZARDOUS SUBSTANCES AND REPORTABLE QUANTITIES—Continued

[See footnotes at end of Table 302.4]

| Hazardous Substance | CASRN | Regulatory Synonyms | Statutory | | | Final RQ | |
			RQ	Codet	RCRA Waste Number	Category	Pounds(Kg)
4,6-Dinitro-o-cyclohexylphenol.	131895	Phenol, 2-cyclohexyl-4,6-dinitro-.	1*	4	P034	B	100 (45.4)
Dinitrophenol 2,5- 2,6-	25550587 329715 573568		1000	1		A	10 (4.54)
2,4-Dinitrophenol	51285	Phenol, 2,4-dinitro-	1000	1,2,4	P048	A	10 (4.54)
Dinitrotoluene 3,4-Dinitrotoluene	25321146 610399		1000	1,2		C	1000# (454)
2,4-Dinitrotoluene	121142	Benzene, 1-methyl-2,4-dinitro-.	1000	1,2,4	U105	C	1000# (454)
Dinoseb	88857	Phenol, 2,4-dinitro-6-(1-methylpropyl)-.	1*	4	P020	C	1000 (454)
Di-n-octyl phthalate	117840	1,2-Benzenedicarboxylic acid,di-n-octyl ester.	1*	2,4	U107	D	5000 (2270)
1,4-Dioxane	123911	1,4-Diethylene dioxide	1*	4	U108	X	1# (0.454)
DIPHENYLHYDRAZINE			1*	2			**
1,2-Diphenylhydrazine	122667	Hydrazine, 1,2-diphenyl-	1*	2,4	U109	X	1# (0.454)
Diphosphoramide, octamethyl-.	152169	Octamethylpyrophosphoramide.	1*	4	P085	B	100 (45.4)
Dipropylamine	142847	1-Propanamine, N-propyl-.	1*	4	U110	D	5000 (2270)
Di-n-propylnitrosamine	621647	N-Nitrosodi-n-propylamine.	1*	2,4	U111	X	1# (0.454)
Diquat	85007 2764729		1000	1		C	1000 (454)
Disulfoton	298044	O,O-Diethyl S-[2-(ethylthio)ethyl] phosphorodithioate.	1	1,4	P039	X	1 (0.454)
2,4-Dithiobiuret	541537	Thioimidodicarbonic diamide.	1*	4	P049	B	100 (45.4)
Dithiopyrophosphoric acid, tetraethyl ester.	3689245	Tetraethyldithiopyrophosphate.	1*	4	P109	B	100 (45.4)
Diuron	330541		100	1		B	100 (45.4)
Dodecylbenzenesulfonic acid.	27176870		1000	1		C	1000 (454)
Endosulfan	115297	5-Norbornene-2,3-dimethanol,1,4,5,6,7,7-hexachloro, cyclic sulfite.	1	1,2,4	P050	X	1 (0.454)
alpha - Endosulfan	959988		1*	2		X	1 (0.454)
beta - Endosulfan	33213659		1*	2		X	1 (0.454)

TABLE 302.4—LIST OF HAZARDOUS SUBSTANCES AND REPORTABLE QUANTITIES—
Continued

[See footnotes at end of Table 302.4]

Hazardous Substance	CASRN	Regulatory Synonyms	Statutory			Final RQ	
			RQ	Code†	RCRA Waste Number	Category	Pounds(Kg)
ENDOSULFAN AND METABOLITES.			1*	2			**
Endosulfan sulfate............	1031078		1*	2		X	1 (0.454)
Endothall..........................	145733	7-Oxabicyclo[2,2,1] heptane-2,3-dicarboxylic acid.	1*	4	P088	C	1000 (454)
Endrin................................	72208	1,2,3,4,10,10-Hexachloro-6,7-epoxy-1,4,4a,5,6,7,8,8a-octahydro-endo,endo-1,4:5,8-dimethanonaphthalene.	1	1,2,4	P051	X	1 (0.454)
Endrin aldehyde................	7421934		1*	2		X	1 (0.454)
ENDRIN AND METABOLITES.			1*	2			**
Epichlorohydrin	106898	1-Chloro-2,3-epoxypropane. Oxirane, 2-(chloromethyl)-	1000	1,4	U041	C	1000# (454)
Epinephrine	51434	1,2-Benzenediol, 4-[1-hydroxy-2-(methylamino)ethyl]-.	1*	4	P042	C	1000 (454)
Ethanal.............................	75070	Acetaldehyde	1000	1,4	U001	C	1000 (454)
Ethanamine, 1,1-dimethyl-2-phenyl-.	122098	alpha,alpha-Dimethylphenethylamine.	1*	4	P046	D	5000 (2270)
Ethanamine, N-ethyl-N-nitroso-.	55185	N-Nitrosodiethylamine........	1*	4	U174	X	1# (0.454)
Ethane, 1,2-dibromo-.........	106934	Ethylene dibromide............	1000	1,4	U067	C	1000# (454)
Ethane, 1,1-dichloro-.........	75343	1,1-Dichloroethane............ Ethylidene dichloride	1*	2,4	U076	C	1000 (454)
Ethane, 1,2-dichloro-.........	107062	1,2-Dichloroethane............ Ethylene dichloride	5000	1,2,4	U077	D	5000# (2270)
Ethane, 1,1,1,2,2,2-hexachloro-.	67721	Hexachloroethane	1*	2,4	U131	X	1# (0.454)
Ethane, 1,1'-[methylenebis(oxy)] bis(2-chloro-.	111911	Bis(2-chloroethoxy) methane.	1*	2,4	U024	C	1000 (454)
Ethane, 1,1'-oxybis-..........	60297	Ethyl ether	1*	4	U117	B	100 (45.4)
Ethane, 1,1'-oxybis(2-chloro-.	111444	Bis (2-chloroethyl) ether ... Dichloroethyl ether	1*	2,4	U025	X	1# (0.454)
Ethane, pentachloro-.........	76017	Pentachloroethane	1*	4	U184	X	1## (0.454)

TABLE 302.4—LIST OF HAZARDOUS SUBSTANCES AND REPORTABLE QUANTITIES—
Continued

[See footnotes at end of Table 302.4]

| Hazardous Substance | CASRN | Regulatory Synonyms | Statutory | | | Final RQ | |
			RQ	Code†	RCRA Waste Number	Catego-ry	Pounds(Kg)
Ethane, 1,1,1,2-tetrachloro-.	630206	1,1,1,2-Tetrachloroethane.	1*	4	U208	X	1# (0.454)
Ethane, 1,1,2,2-tetrachloro-.	79345	1,1,2,2-Tetrachloroethane.	1*	2,4	U209	X	1# (0.454)
Ethane, 1,1,2-trichloro-	79005	1,1,2-Trichloroethane	1*	2,4	U227	X	1# (0.454)
Ethane, 1,1,1-trichloro-2,2-bis(p-methoxyphenyl)-.	72435	Methoxychlor....................	1	1,4	U247	X	1 (0.454)
1,2-Ethanediylbiscarbamo-dithioic acid.	111546	Ethylenebis (dithiocarbamic acid).	1*	4	U114	D	5000 (2270)
Ethanenitrile	75058	Acetonitrile....................	1*	4	U003	D	5000 (2270)
Ethanethioamide..............	62555	Thioacetamide..................	1*	4	U218	X	1# (0.454)
Ethanol, 2,2'-(nitrosoimino)bis-.	1116547	N-Nitrosodiethanolamine ..	1*	4	U173	X	1# (0.454)
Ethanone, 1-phenyl-..........	98862	Acetophenone..................	1*	4	U004	D	5000 (2270)
Ethanoyl chloride..............	75365	Acetyl chloride	5000	1,4	U006	D	5000 (2270)
Ethenamine, N-methyl-N-nitroso-.	4549400	N-Nitrosomethylvinyla-mine.	1*	4	P084	X	1# (0.454)
Ethene, chloro-	75014	Vinyl chloride..................	1*	2,3,4	U043	X	1# (0.454)
Ethene, 2-chloroethoxy-....	110758	2-Chloroethyl vinyl ether...	1*	2,4	U042	C	1000 (454)
Ethene, 1,1-dichloro-........	75354	1,1-Dichloroethylene.......... Vinylidene chloride	5000	1,2,4	U078	D	5000# (2270)
Ethene, 1,1,2,2-tetrachloro-.	127184	Tetrachloroethylene..........	1*	2,4	U210	X	1# (0.454)
Ethene, trans-1,2-dichloro-.	156605	1,2-trans-Dichloroethylene.	1*	2,4	U079	C	1000 (454)
Ethion............................	563122		10	1	....	A	10## (4.54)
Ethyl acetate	141786	Acetic acid, ethyl ester.....	1*	4	U112	D	5000 (2270)
Ethyl acrylate	140885	2-Propenoic acid, ethyl ester.	1*	4	U113	C	1000 (454)
Ethylbenzene..................	100414		1000	1,2	....	C	1000 (454)
Ethyl carbamate (Urethan).	51796	Carbamic acid, ethyl ester.	1*	4	U238	X	1# (0.454)
Ethyl cyanide..................	107120	Propanenitrile	1*	4	P101	A	10 (4.54)
Ethyl 4,4'-dichlorobenzilate.	510156	Benzeneacetic acid, 4-chloro-alpha-(4-chlorophenyl)- alpha-hydroxy-, ethyl ester.	1*	4	U038	X	1# (0.454)

TABLE 302.4—LIST OF HAZARDOUS SUBSTANCES AND REPORTABLE QUANTITIES—
Continued

[See footnotes at end of Table 302.4]

Hazardous Substance	CASRN	Regulatory Synonyms	Statutory			Final RQ	
			RQ	Code†	RCRA Waste Number	Category	Pounds(Kg)
Ethylene dibromide..........	106934	Ethane, 1,2-dibromo-.........	1000	1,4	U067	C	1000# (454)
Ethylene dichloride..........	107062	1,2-Dichloroethane .... Ethane, 1,2-dichloro-	5000	1,2,4	U077	D	5000# (2270)
Ethylene oxide	75218	Oxirane.............................	1*	4	U115	X	1# (0.454)
Ethylenebis (dithiocarbamic acid).	111546	1,2-Ethanediylbiscarbamodithioic acid.	1*	4	U114	D	5000 (2270)
Ethylenediamine..............	107153	....	1000	1	....	D	5000 (2270)
Ethylenediamine tetraacetic acid (EDTA).	60004	....	5000	1	....	D	5000 (2270)
Ethylenethiourea..............	96457	2-Imidazolidinethione........	1*	4	U116	X	1# (0.454)
Ethylenimine	151564	Aziridine	1*	4	P054	X	1# (0.454)
Ethyl ether......................	60297	Ethane, 1,1'-oxybis-.........	1*	4	U117	B	100 (45.4)
Ethylidene dichloride........	75343	1,1-Dichloroethane .... Ethane, 1,1-dichloro-	1*	2,4	U076	C	1000 (454)
Ethyl methacrylate............	97632	2-Propenoic acid, 2-methyl-, ethyl ester.	1*	4	U118	C	1000 (454)
Ethyl methanesulfonate	62500	Methanesulfonic acid, ethyl ester.	1*	4	U119	X	1# (0.454)
Famphur...........................	52857	Phosphorothioic acid, O,O-dimethyl-O-[p-[(dimethylamino)-sulfonyl]phenyl] ester.	1*	4	P097	C	1000 (454)
Ferric ammonium citrate...	1185575	....	1000	1	....	C	1000 (454)
Ferric ammonium oxalate.	2944674 55488874	....	1000	1	....	C	1000 (454)
Ferric chloride..................	7705080	....	1000	1	....	C	1000 (454)
Ferric dextran..................	9004664	Iron dextran....................	1*	4	U139	X	1## (0.454)
Ferric fluoride..................	7783508	....	100	1	....	B	100 (45.4)
Ferric nitrate....................	10421484	....	1000	1	....	C	1000 (454)
Ferric sulfate	10028225	....	1000	1	....	C	1000 (454)
Ferrous ammonium sulfate.	10045893	....	1000	1	....	C	1000 (454)
Ferrous chloride...............	7758943	....	100	1	....	B	100 (45.4)
Ferrous sulfate.................	7720787 7782630	....	1000	1	....	C	1000 (454)
Fluoroacetic acid, sodium salt.	62748	Acetic acid, fluoro-, sodium salt.	1*	4	P058	A	10 (4.54)

TABLE 302.4—LIST OF HAZARDOUS SUBSTANCES AND REPORTABLE QUANTITIES—Continued

[See footnotes at end of Table 302.4]

Hazardous Substance	CASRN	Regulatory Synonyms	Statutory			Final RQ	
			RQ	Code†	RCRA Waste Number	Category	Pounds(Kg)
Fluoranthene	206440	Benzo[j,k]fluorene	1*	2,4	U120	X	1## (0.454)
Fluorene	86737		1*	2		X	1## (0.454)
Fluorine	7782414		1*	4	P056	A	10 (4.54)
Fluoroacetamide	640197	Acetamide, 2-fluoro-	1*	4	P057	B	100 (45.4)
Formaldehyde	50000	Methylene oxide	1000	1,4	U122	C	1000# (454)
Formic acid	64186	Methanoic acid	5000	1,4	U123	D	5000 (2270)
Fulminic acid, mercury(II)salt.	628864	Mercury fulminate	1*	4	P065	X	1## (0.454)
Fumaric acid	110178		5000	1		D	5000 (2270)
Furan	110009	Furfuran	1*	4	U124	B	100 (45.4)
Furan, tetrahydro-	109999	Tetrahydrofuran	1*	4	U213	C	1000 (454)
2-Furancarboxaldehyde	98011	Furfural	1000	1,4	U125	D	5000 (2270)
2,5-Furandione	108316	Maleic anhydride	5000	1,4	U147	D	5000 (2270)
Furfural	98011	2-Furancarboxaldehyde	1000	1,4	U125	D	5000 (2270)
Furfuran	110009	Furan	1*	4	U124	B	100 (45.4)
D-Glucopyranose, 2-deoxy-2-(3-methyl-3-nitrosoureido)-.	18883664	Streptozotocin	1*	4	U206	X	1# (0.454)
Glycidylaldehyde	765344	1-Propanal, 2,3-epoxy-	1*	4	U126	X	1# (0.454)
Guanidine, N-nitroso-N-methyl-N'-nitro-.	70257	N-Methyl-N'-nitro-N-nitrosoguanidine.	1*	4	U163	X	1# (0.454)
Guthion	86500		1	1		X	1 (0.454)
HALOETHERS			1*	2			••
HALOMETHANES			1*	2			••
Heptachlor	76448	4,7-Methano-1H-indene,1,4,5,6,7,8,8-heptachloro-3a,4,7,7a-tetrahydro-.	1	1,2,4	P059	X	1#(0.454)
HEPTACHLOR AND METABOLITES.			1*	2			••
Heptachlor epoxide	1024573		1*	2		X	1# (0.454)
Hexachlorobenzene	118741	Benzene, hexachloro-	1*	2,4	U127	X	1# (0.454)
Hexachlorobutadiene	87683	1,3-Butadiene, 1,1,2,3,4,4-hexachloro-.	1*	2,4	U128	X	1# (0.454)
HEXACHLOROCYCLO-HEXANE (all isomers).	608731		1*	2			••

TABLE 302.4—LIST OF HAZARDOUS SUBSTANCES AND REPORTABLE QUANTITIES— Continued

[See footnotes at end of Table 302.4]

Hazardous Substance	CASRN	Regulatory Synonyms	Statutory			Final RQ	
			RQ	Code†	RCRA Waste Number	Category	Pounds(Kg)
Hexachlorocyclohexane (gamma isomer).	58899	gamma - BHC .... Lindane	1	1,2,4	U129	X	1# (0.454)
Hexachlorocyclopenta- diene.	77474	1,3-Cyclopentadiene, 1,2,3,4,5,5-hexachloro-.	1	1,2,4	U130	X	1# (0.454)
1,2,3,4,10,10- Hexachloro-6,7-epoxy- 1,4,4a,5,6,7,8,8a- octahydro-endo,endo- 1,4:5,8- dimethanonaphthalene.	72208	Endrin...............................	1	1,2,4	P051	X	1 (0.454)
1,2,3,4,10,10- Hexachloro-6,7-epoxy- 1,4,4a,5,6,7,8,8a- octahydro-endo,exo- 1,4:5,8- dimethanonaphthalene.	60571	Dieldrin.............................	1	1,2,4	P037	X	1# (0.454)
Hexachloroethane	67721	Ethane, 1,1,1,2,2,2- hexachloro-.	1*	2,4	U131	X	1# (0.454)
Hexachlorohexahydro- endo,endo- dimethanonaphthalene.	465736	1,2,3,4,10,10- Hexachloro- 1,4,4a,5,8,8a- hexahydro- 1,4,5,8- endo,endo- dimethanonaphthalene.	1*	4	P060	X	1 (0.454)
1,2,3,4,10,10- Hexachloro- 1,4,4a,5,8,8a- hexahydro- 1,4,5,8- endo,endo- dimethanonaphthalene.	465736	Hexachlorohexahydro- endo,endo- dimethanonaphthalene.	1*	4	P060	X	1 (0.454)
1,2,3,4,10-10- Hexachloro- 1,4,4a,5,8,8a- hexahydro-1,4:5,8- endo, exo- dimethanonaphthalene.	309002	Aldrin.................................	1	1,2,4	P004	X	1# (0.454)
Hexachlorophene..............	70304	2,2'-Methylenebis(3,4,6- trichlorophenol).	1*	4	U132	X	1## (0.454)
Hexachloropropene..........	1888717	1-Propene, 1,1,2,3,3,3- hexachloro-.	1*	4	U243	C	1000 (454)
Hexaethyl tetraphosphate.	757584	Tetraphosphoric acid, hexaethyl ester.	1*	4	P062	B	100 (45.4)
Hydrazine..........................	302012	Diamine	1*	4	U133	X	1# (0.454)
Hydrazine, 1,2-diethyl-......	1615801	N,N'-Diethylhydrazine........	1*	4	U086	X	1# (0.454)
Hydrazine, 1,1-dimethyl- ...	57147	1,1-Dimethylhydrazine.......	1*	4	U098	X	1# (0.454)
Hydrazine, 1,2-dimethyl- ...	540738	1,2-Dimethylhydrazine.......	1*	4	U099	X	1# (0.454)
Hydrazine, 1,2-diphenyl- ...	122667	1,2-Diphenylhydrazine.......	1*	2,4	U109	X	1# (0.454)

TABLE 302.4—LIST OF HAZARDOUS SUBSTANCES AND REPORTABLE QUANTITIES—
Continued

[See footnotes at end of Table 302.4]

Hazardous Substance	CASRN	Regulatory Synonyms	Statutory			Final RQ	
			RQ	Code†	RCRA Waste Number	Category	Pounds(Kg)
Hydrazine, methyl-..........	60344	Methyl hydrazine..............	1*	4	P068	A	10 (4.54)
Hydrazinecarbothioamide .	79196	Thiosemicarbazide............	1*	4	P116	B	100 (45.4)
Hydrochloric acid............	7647010	....	5000	1	....	D	5000 (2270)
Hydrocyanic acid	74908	Hydrogen cyanide..............	10	1,4	P063	A	10 (4.54)
Hydrofluoric acid............	7664393	Hydrogen fluoride	5000	1,4	U134	B	100 (45.4)
Hydrogen cyanide............	74908	Hydrocyanic acid	10	1,4	P063	A	10 (4.54)
Hydrogen fluoride	7664393	Hydrofluoric acid............	5000	1,4	U134	B	100 (45.4)
Hydrogen phosphide	7803512	Phosphine....................	1*	4	P096	B	100 (45.4)
Hydrogen sulfide............	7783064	Hydrosulfuric acid............ Sulfur hydride	100	1,4	U135	B	100## (45.4)
Hydroperoxide, 1-methyl-1-phenylethyl-.	80159	alpha,alpha-Dimethylbenzylhydroperoxide.	1*	4	U096	A	10 (4.54)
Hydrosulfuric acid............	7783064	Hydrogen sulfide.............. Sulfur hydride	100	1,4	U135	B	100## (45.4)
Hydroxydimethylarsine oxide.	75605	Cacodylic acid....................	1*	4	U136	X	1# (0.454)
2-Imidazolidinethione........	96457	Ethylenethiourea.............	1*	4	U116	X	1# (0.454)
Indeno(1,2,3-cd)pyrene.....	193395	1,10-(1,2-Phenylene)pyrene.	1*	2,4	U137	X	1# (0.454)
Iron dextran..................	9004664	Ferric dextran................	1*	4	U139	X	1## (0.454)
Isobutyl alcohol..............	78831	1-Propanol, 2-methyl-........	1*	4	U140	D	5000 (2270)
Isocyanic acid, methyl ester.	624839	Methyl isocyanate..............	1*	4	P064	X	1###(0.454)
Isophorone..................	78591	....	1*	2	....	D	5000 (2270)
Isoprene....................	78795	....	1000	1	....	C	1000## (454)
Isopropanolamine dodecylbenzenesulfonate.	42504461	....	1000	1	....	C	1000 (454)
Isosafrole........................	120581	Benzene, 1,2-methylenedioxy-4-propenyl-.	1*	4	U141	X	1# (0.454)
3(2H)-Isoxazolone, 5-(aminomethyl)-.	2763964	5-(Aminomethyl)-3-isoxazolol.	1*	4	P007	C	1000 (454)
Kelthane....................	115322	....	5000	1	....	A	10 (4.54)
Kepone....................	143500	Decachlorooctahydro-1,3,4-metheno-2H-cyclobuta[c,d]-pentalen-2-one.	1	1,4	U142	X	1# (0.454)

TABLE 302.4—LIST OF HAZARDOUS SUBSTANCES AND REPORTABLE QUANTITIES—Continued

[See footnotes at end of Table 302.4]

Hazardous Substance	CASRN	Regulatory Synonyms	Statutory			Final RQ	
			RQ	Code†	RCRA Waste Number	Catego-ry	Pounds(Kg)
Lasiocarpine	303344		1*	4	U143	X	1# (0.454)
Lead ††	7439921		1*	2		X	1## (0.454)
Lead acetate	301042	Acetic acid, lead salt	5000	1,4	U144	D	5000# (2270)
LEAD AND COMPOUNDS.			1*	2			**
Lead arsenate	7784409 7645252 10102484		5000	1		D	5000# (2270)
Lead chloride	7758954		5000	1		D	5000## (2270)
Lead fluoborate	13814965		5000	1		D	5000## (2270)
Lead fluoride	7783462		1000	1		C	1000## (454)
Lead iodide	10101630		5000	1		D	5000## (2270)
Lead nitrate	10099748		5000	1		D	5000## (2270)
Lead phosphate	7446277	Phosphoric acid, lead salt.	1*	4	U145	X	1# (0.454)
Lead stearate	7428480 1072351 56189094 52652592		5000	1		D	5000## (2270)
Lead subacetate	1335326		1*	4	U146	X	1# (0.454)
Lead sulfate	15739807 7446142		5000	1		D	5000## (2270)
Lead sulfide	1314870		5000	1		D	5000## (2270)
Lead thiocyanate	592870		5000	1		D	5000## (2270)
Lindane	58899	gamma - BHC Hexachlorocyclohexane (gamma isomer)	1	1,2,4	U129	X	1# (0.454)
Lithium chromate	14307358		1000	1		C	1000# (454)
Malathion	121755		10	1		B	100 (45.4)
Maleic acid	110167		5000	1		D	5000 (2270)
Maleic anhydride	108316	2,5-Furandione	5000	1,4	U147	D	5000 (2270)
Maleic hydrazide	123331	1,2-Dihydro-3,6-pyridazinedione.	1*	4	U148	D	5000 (2270)
Malononitrile	109773	Propanedinitrile	1*	4	U149	C	1000 (454)
Melphalan	148823	Alanine, 3-[p-bis(2-chloroethyl)amino] phenyl-,L-.	1*	4	U150	X	1# (0.454)
Mercaptodimethur	2032657		100	1		A	10 (4.54)

TABLE 302.4—LIST OF HAZARDOUS SUBSTANCES AND REPORTABLE QUANTITIES—Continued

[See footnotes at end of Table 302.4]

Hazardous Substance	CASRN	Regulatory Synonyms	Statutory			Final RQ	
			RQ	Code†	RCRA Waste Number	Category	Pounds(Kg)
Mercuric cyanide................	592041	....	1	1	....	X	1 (0.454)
Mercuric nitrate................	10045940	....	10	1	....	A	10## (4.54)
Mercuric sulfate	7783359	....	10	1	....	A	10## (4.54)
Mercuric thiocyanate........	592858	....	10	1	....	A	10## (4.54)
Mercurous nitrate............	10415755 7782867	....	10	1	....	A	10## (4.54)
Mercury..........................	7439976	....	1°	2,3,4	U151	X	1 (0.454)
MERCURY AND COMPOUNDS.	....	....	1°	2	....		**
Mercury, (acetato-O)phenyl-.	62384	Phenylmercuric acetate	1°	4	P092	X	1##(0.454)
Mercury fulminate............	628864	Fulminic acid, mercury(II)salt.	1°	4	P065	X	1## (0.454)
Methacrylonitrile................	126987	2-Propenenitrile, 2-methyl-.	1°	4	U152	C	1000 (454)
Methanamine, N-methyl-...	124403	Dimethylamine................	1000	1,4	U092	C	1000## (454)
Methane, bromo-............	74839	Methyl bromide	1°	2,4	U029	C	1000 (454)
Methane, chloro-............	74873	Methyl chloride................	1°	2,4	U045	X	1## (0.454)
Methane, chloromethoxy-.	107302	Chloromethyl methyl ether.	1°	4	U046	X	1# (0.454)
Methane, dibromo-	74953	Methylene bromide............	1°	4	U068	C	1000 (454)
Methane, dichloro-............	75092	Methylene chloride............	1°	2,4	U080	C	1000 (454)
Methane, dichlorodifluoro-.	75718	Dichlorodifluoromethane...	1°	4	U075	D	5000 (2270)
Methane, iodo-................	74884	Methyl iodide................	1°	4	U138	X	1# (0.454)
Methane, oxybis(chloro- ...	542881	Bis(chloromethyl) ether.....	1°	4	P016	X	1# (0.454)
Methane, tetrachloro-........	56235	Carbon tetrachloride........	5000	1,2,4	U211	D	5000# (2270)
Methane, tetranitro-........	509148	Tetranitromethane	1°	4	P112	A	10 (4.54)
Methane, tribromo-........	75252	Bromoform....................	1°	2,4	U225	B	100 (45.4)
Methane, trichloro-........	67663	Chloroform....................	5000	1,2,4	U044	D	5000# (2270)
Methane, trichlorofluoro-...	75694	Trichloromonofluoro-methane.	1°	4	U121	D	5000 (2270)
Methanesulfonic acid, ethyl ester.	62500	Ethyl methanesulfonate	1°	4	U119	X	1# (0.454)
Methanethiol..................	74931	Methylmercaptan .... Thiomethanol	100	1,4	U153	B	100 (45.4)

TABLE 302.4—LIST OF HAZARDOUS SUBSTANCES AND REPORTABLE QUANTITIES— Continued

[See footnotes at end of Table 302.4]

Hazardous Substance	CASRN	Regulatory Synonyms	Statutory			Final RQ	
			RQ	Code†	RCRA Waste Number	Catego-ry	Pounds(Kg)
Methanesulfenyl chloride, trichloro-.	594423	Trichloromethanesulfenyl chloride.	1*	4	P118	B	100 (45.4)
4,7-Methano-1H-indene,1,4,5,6,7,8,8-heptachloro-3a,4,7,7a-tetrahydro-.	76448	Heptachlor	1	1,2,4	P059	X	1# (0.454)
Methanoic acid	64186	Formic acid	5000	1,4	U123	D	5000 (2270)
4,7-Methanoindan, 1,2,4,5,6,7,8,8-octachloro- 3a,4,7,7a-tetrahydro-.	57749	Chlordane Chlordane, technical	1	1,2,4	U036	X	1# (0.454)
Methanol	67561	Methyl alcohol	1*	4	U154	D	5000 (2270)
Methapyrilene	91805	Pyridine, 2-[(2-(dimethylamino)ethyl)-2-thenylamino]-.	1*	4	U155	D	5000 (2270)
Methomyl	16752775	Acetimidic acid, N-[(methylcarbamoyl)oxy] thio-, methyl ester.	1*	4	P066	B	100 (45.4)
Methoxychlor	72435	Ethane, 1,1,1-trichloro-2,2-bis(p-methoxyphenyl)-.	1	1,4	U247	X	1 (0.454)
Methyl alcohol	67561	Methanol	1*	4	U154	D	5000 (2270)
2-Methylaziridine	75558	1,2-Propylenimine	1*	4	P067	X	1# (0.454)
Methyl bromide	74839	Methane, bromo-	1*	2,4	U029	C	1000 (454)
1-Methylbutadiene	504609	1,3-Pentadiene	1*	4	U186	B	100 (45.4)
Methyl chloride	74873	Methane, chloro-	1*	2,4	U045	X	1## (0.454)
Methyl chlorocarbonate	79221	Carbonochloridic acid, methyl ester.	1*	4	U156	C	1000 (454)
Methyl chloroform	71556	1,1,1-Trichloroethane	1*	2,4	U226	C	1000 (454)
4,4'-Methylenebis(2-chloroaniline).	101144	Benzenamine, 4,4'-methylenebis(2-chloro-.	1*	4	U158	X	1# (0.454)
2,2'-Methylenebis(3,4,6-trichlorophenol).	70304	Hexachlorophene	1*	4	U132	X	1## (0.454)
3-Methylcholanthrene	56495	Benz[j]aceanthrylene, 1,2-dihydro-3-methyl-.	1*	4	U157	X	1# (0.454)
Methylene bromide	74953	Methane, dibromo-	1*	4	U068	C	1000 (454)
Methylene chloride	75092	Methane, dichloro-	1*	2,4	U080	C	1000 (454)
Methylene oxide	50000	Formaldehyde	1000	1,4	U122	C	1000# (454)
Methyl ethyl ketone	78933	2-Butanone	1*	4	U159	D	5000 (2270)
Methyl ethyl ketone peroxide.	1338234	2-Butanone peroxide	1*	4	U160	A	10 (4.54)

TABLE 302.4—LIST OF HAZARDOUS SUBSTANCES AND REPORTABLE QUANTITIES—
Continued

[See footnotes at end of Table 302.4]

Hazardous Substance	CASRN	Regulatory Synonyms	Statutory			Final RQ	
			RQ	Code†	RCRA Waste Number	Category	Pounds(Kg)
Methyl hydrazine...............	60344	Hydrazine, methyl-.............	1*	4	P068	A	10 (4.54)
Methyl iodide......................	74884	Methane, iodo-...................	1*	4	U138	X	1# (0.454)
Methyl isobutyl ketone......	108101	4-Methyl-2-pentanone......	1*	4	U161	D	5000 (2270)
Methyl isocyanate..............	624839	Isocyanic acid, methyl ester.	1*	4	P064	X	1###(0.454)
2-Methyllactonitrile............	75865	Acetone cyanohydrin .... Propanenitrile, 2-hydroxy-2-methyl-	10	1,4	P069	A	10 (4.54)
Methylmercaptan	74931	Methanethiol...................... Thiomethanol	100	1,4	U153	B	100 (45.4)
Methyl methacrylate..........	80626	2-Propenoic acid, 2-methyl-, methyl ester.	5000	1,4	U162	C	1000 (454)
N-Methyl-N'-nitro-N-nitrosoguanidine.	70257	Guanidine, N-nitroso-N-methyl-N'-nitro-.	1*	4	U163	X	1# (0.454)
Methyl parathion...............	298000	O,O-Dimethyl O-p-nitrophenyl phosphorothioate.	100	1,4	P071	B	100## (45.4)
4-Methyl-2-pentanone	108101	Methyl isobutyl ketone......	1*	4	U161	D	5000 (2270)
Methylthiouracil................	56042	4(1H)-Pyrimidinone, 2,3-dihydro-6-methyl-2-thioxo-.	1*	4	U164	X	1# (0.454)
Mevinphos	7786347	....	1	1	....	A	10 (4.54)
Mexacarbate......................	315184	....	1000	1	....	C	1000 (454)
Mitomycin C......................	50077	Azirino(2',3':3,4)pyrrolo(1,2-a)indole-4,7-dione,6-amino-8-[((aminocarbonyl)oxy) methyl]-1,1a,2,8,8a,8b-hexahydro-8a-methoxy- 5-methyl-.	1*	4	U010	X	1# (0.454)
Monoethylamine................	75047	....	1000	1	....	C	1000## (454)
Monomethylamine	74895	....	1000	1	....	B	100 (45.4)
Naled...............................	300765	....	10	1	....	A	10 (4.54)
5,12-Naphthacenedione, (8S-cis)-8-acetyl-10-[3-amino- 2,3,6-trideoxy-alpha-L- lyxo-hexopyranosyl)oxy]-7,8,9,10-tetrahydro-6,8,11-trihydroxy- 1-methoxy-.	20830813	Daunomycin....................	1*	4	U059	X	1# (0.454)
Naphthalene......................	91203	....	5000	1,2,4	U165	B	100 (45.4)

TABLE 302.4—LIST OF HAZARDOUS SUBSTANCES AND REPORTABLE QUANTITIES— Continued

[See footnotes at end of Table 302.4]

Hazardous Substance	CASRN	Regulatory Synonyms	Statutory			Final RQ	
			RQ	Code†	RCRA Waste Number	Category	Pounds(Kg)
Naphthalene, 2-chloro-.....	91587	beta-Chloronaphthalene ... 2-Chloronaphthalene	1*	2,4	U047	D	5000 (2270)
1,4-Naphthalenedione.......	130154	1,4-Naphthoquinone.........	1*	4	U166	D	5000 (2270)
2,7-Naphthalenedisulfonic acid,3,3'-[(3,3'-dimethyl- (l,1'-biphenyl)-4,4'-diyl)-bis(azo)]bis(5-amino-4-hydroxy)-tetrasodium salt.	72571	Trypan blue	1*	4	U236	X	1# (0.454)
Naphthenic acid................	1338245		100	1		B	100 (45.4)
1,4-Naphthoquinone.........	130154	1,4-Naphthalenedione.......	1*	4	U166	D	5000 (2270)
1-Naphthylamine..............	134327	alpha-Naphthylamine........	1*	4	U167	X	1# (0.454)
2-Naphthylamine..............	91598	beta-Naphthylamine	1*	4	U168	X	1# (0.454)
alpha-Naphthylamine........	134327	1-Naphthylamine...............	1*	4	U167	X	1# (0.454)
beta-Naphthylamine	91598	2-Naphthylamine...............	1*	4	U168	X	1# (0.454)
2-Naphthylamine, N,N-bis(2-chloroethyl)-.	494031	Chlornaphazine	1*	4	U026	X	1# (0.454)
alpha-Naphthylthiourea	86884	Thiourea, 1-naphthalenyl-.	1*	4	P072	B	100 (45.4)
Nickel ††	7440020		1*	2		X	1# (0.454)
NICKEL AND COMPOUNDS.			1*	2			**
Nickel ammonium sulfate.	15699180		5000	1		D	5000# (2270)
Nickel carbonyl	13463393	Nickel tetracarbonyl	1*	4	P073	X	1# (0.454)
Nickel chloride	7718549 37211055		5000	1		D	5000# (2270)
Nickel cyanide..................	557197	Nickel(II) cyanide	1*	4	P074	X	1# (0.454)
Nickel(II) cyanide	557197	Nickel cyanide..................	1*	4	P074	X	1# (0.454)
Nickel hydroxide	12054487		1000	1		C	1000# (454)
Nickel nitrate	14216752		5000	1		D	5000# (2270)
Nickel sulfate	7786814		5000	1		D	5000# (2270)
Nickel tetracarbonyl	13463393	Nickel carbonyl	1*	4	P073	X	1# (0.454)
Nicotine and salts.............	54115	Pyridine, (S)-3-(1-methyl-2-pyrrolidinyl)-, and salts.	1*	4	P075	B	100 (45.4)
Nitric acid........................	7697372		1000	1		C	1000 (454)

TABLE 302.4—LIST OF HAZARDOUS SUBSTANCES AND REPORTABLE QUANTITIES—
Continued

[See footnotes at end of Table 302.4]

Hazardous Substance	CASRN	Regulatory Synonyms	Statutory			Final RQ	
			RQ	Code†	RCRA Waste Number	Category	Pounds(Kg)
Nitric oxide...............	10102439	Nitrogen(II) oxide	1*	4	P076	A	10 (4.54)
p-Nitroaniline	100016	Benzenamine, 4-nitro-.......	1*	4	P077	D	5000 (2270)
Nitrobenzene.................	98953	Benzene, nitro-..................	1000	1,2,4	U169	C	1000 (454)
Nitrogen dioxide...............	10102440 10544726	Nitrogen(IV) oxide.............	1000	1,4	P078	A	10 (4.54)
Nitrogen(II) oxide	10102439	Nitric oxide.........................	1*	4	P076	A	10 (4.54)
Nitrogen(IV) oxide.............	10102440 10544726	Nitrogen dioxide.................	1000	1,4	P078	A	10 (4.54)
Nitroglycerine	55630	1,2,3-Propanetriol, trinitrate-.	1*	4	P081	A	10 (4.54)
Nitrophenol (mixed)........... m- o- p-	25154556 554847 88755 100027	2-Nitrophenol 4-Nitrophenol Phenol, 4-nitro-	1000	1	....	B	100 (45.4)
p-Nitrophenol..................	100027	4-Nitrophenol.................... Phenol, 4-nitro-	1000	1,2,4	U170	B	100 (45.4)
2-Nitrophenol..................	88755	o-Nitrophenol....................	1000	1,2	....	B	100 (45.4)
4-Nitrophenol..................	100027	p-Nitrophenol.................... Phenol, 4-nitro-	1000	1,2,4	U170	B	100 (45.4)
NITROPHENOLS.............			1*	2	....		**
2-Nitropropane	79469	Propane, 2-nitro-.................	1*	4	U171	X	1# (0.454)
NITROSAMINES.............			1*	2	....		**
N-Nitrosodi-n-butylamine ..	924163	1-Butanamine, N-butyl-N-nitroso-.	1*	4	U172	X	1# (0.454)
N-Nitrosodiethanolamine ...	1116547	Ethanol, 2,2'-(nitrosoimino)bis-.	1*	4	U173	X	1# (0.454)
N-Nitrosodiethylamine......	55185	Ethanamine, N-ethyl-N-nitroso-.	1*	4	U174	X	1# (0.454)
N-Nitrosodimethylamine....	62759	Dimethylnitrosamine	1*	2,4	P082	X	1# (0.454)
N-Nitrosodiphenylamine....	86306		1*	2	....	B	100 (45.4)
N-Nitrosodi-n-propylamine.	621647	Di-n-propylnitrosamine	1*	2,4	U111	X	1# (0.454)
N-Nitroso-N-ethylurea	759739	Carbamide, N-ethyl-N-nitroso-.	1*	4	U176	X	1# (0.454)
N-Nitroso-N-methylurea	684935	Carbamide, N-methyl-N-nitroso-.	1*	4	U177	X	1# (0.454)
N-Nitroso-N-methylurethane.	615532	Carbamic acid, methylnitroso-,ethyl ester.	1*	4	U178	X	1# (0.454)

TABLE 302.4—LIST OF HAZARDOUS SUBSTANCES AND REPORTABLE QUANTITIES—Continued

[See footnotes at end of Table 302.4]

Hazardous Substance	CASRN	Regulatory Synonyms	Statutory			Final RQ	
			RQ	Code†	RCRA Waste Number	Category	Pounds(Kg)
N-Nitrosomethylvinyla-mine.	4549400	Ethenamine, N-methyl-N-nitroso-.	1*	4	P084	X	1# (0.454)
N-Nitrosopiperidine	100754	Pyridine, hexahydro-N-nitroso-.	1*	4	U179	X	1# (0.454)
N-Nitrosopyrrolidine	930552	Pyrrole, tetrahydro-N-nitroso-.	1*	4	U180	X	1# (0.454)
Nitrotoluene m- o- p-	1321126 99081 88722 99990		1000	1		C	1000 (454)
5-Nitro-o-toluidine	99558	Benzenamine, 2-methyl-5-nitro-.	1*	4	U181	X	1# (0.454)
5-Norbornene-2,3-dimethanol,1,4,5,6,7,7-hexachloro, cyclic sulfite.	115297	Endosulfan	1	1,2,4	P050	X	1 (0.454)
Octamethylpyrophos-phoramide.	152169	Diphosphoramide, octamethyl-.	1*	4	P085	B	100 (45.4)
Osmium oxide	20816120	Osmium tetroxide	1*	4	P087	C	1000 (454)
Osmium tetroxide	20816120	Osmium oxide	1*	4	P087	C	1000 (454)
7-Oxabicyclo[2.2.1]heptane-2,3-dicarboxylic acid.	145733	Endothall	1*	4	P088	C	1000 (454)
1,2-Oxathiolane, 2,2-dioxide.	1120714	1,3-Propane sultone	1*	4	U193	X	1# (0.454)
2H-1,3,2-Oxazaphosphorine,2-[bis(2-chloroethyl)amino]tetrahydro-2-oxide.	50180	Cyclophosphamide	1*	4	U058	X	1# (0.454)
Oxirane	75218	Ethyleneoxide	1*	4	U115	X	1# (0.454)
Oxirane, 2-(chloromethyl)-.	106898	1-Chloro-2,3-epoxypropane. Epichlorohydrin	1000	1,4	U041	C	1000# (454)
Paraformaldehyde	30525894		1000	1		C	1000 (454)
Paraldehyde	123637	1,3,5-Trioxane, 2,4,6-trimethyl-.	1*	4	U182	C	1000 (454)
Parathion	56382	Phosphorothioic acid,O,O-diethyl O-(p-nitrophenyl) ester.	1	1,4	P089	X	1# (0.454)
Pentachlorobenzene	608935	Benzene, pentachloro-	1*	4	U183	X	1## (0.454)
Pentachloroethane	76017	Ethane, pentachloro-	1*	4	U184	X	1## (0.454)

TABLE 302.4—LIST OF HAZARDOUS SUBSTANCES AND REPORTABLE QUANTITIES—
Continued

[See footnotes at end of Table 302.4]

Hazardous Substance	CASRN	Regulatory Synonyms	Statutory			Final RQ	
			RQ	Code†	RCRA Waste Number	Category	Pounds(Kg)
Pentachloronitrobenzene..	82688	Benzene, pentachloronitro-.	1*	4	U185	X	1# (0.454)
Pentachlorophenol............	87865	Phenol, pentachloro-.........	10	1,2,4	U242	A	10# (4.54)
1,3-Pentadiene	504609	1-Methylbutadiene	1*	4	U186	B	100 (45.4)
Phenacetin....................	62442	Acetamide, N-(4-ethoxyphenyl)-.	1*	4	U187	X	1# (0.454)
Phenanthrene................	85018	....	1*	2	....	X	1## (0.454)
Phenol	108952	Benzene, hydroxy-...........	1000	1,2,4	U188	C	1000## (454)
Phenol, 2-chloro-	95578	2-Chlorophenol............ o-Chlorophenol	1*	2,4	U048	B	100 (45.4)
Phenol, 4-chloro-3-methyl-.	59507	4-Chloro-m-cresol .... p-Chloro-m-cresol	1*	2,4	U039	D	5000 (2270)
Phenol, 2-cyclohexyl-4,6-dinitro-.	131895	4,6-Dinitro-o-cyclohexylphenol.	1*	4	P034	B	100 (45.4)
Phenol, 2,4-dichloro-	120832	2,4-Dichlorophenol	1*	2,4	U081	B	100 (45.4)
Phenol, 2,6-dichloro-	87650	2,6-Dichlorophenol	1*	4	U082	B	100 (45.4)
Phenol, 2,4-dimethyl-	105679	2,4-Dimethylphenol............	1*	2,4	U101	B	100 (45.4)
Phenol, 2,4-dinitro-	51285	2,4-Dinitrophenol............	1000	1,2,4	P048	A	10 (4.54)
Phenol, 2,4-dinitro-6-(1-methylpropyl)-.	88857	Dinoseb................	1*	4	P020	C	1000 (454)
Phenol, 2,4-dinitro-6-methyl-, and salts.	534521	4,6-Dinitro-o-cresol and salts.	1*	2,4	P047	A	10 (4.54)
Phenol, 4-nitro-	100027	p-Nitrophenol.................. 4-Nitrophenol	1000	1,2,4	U170	B	100 (45.4)
Phenol, pentachloro-.........	87865	Pentachlorophenol............	10	1,2,4	U242	A	10# (4.54)
Phenol, 2,3,4,6-tetrachloro-.	58902	2,3,4,6-Tetrachlorophenol.	1*	4	U212	A	10 (4.54)
Phenol, 2,4,5-trichloro-......	95954	2,4,5-Trichlorophenol	10	1,4	U230	A	10# (4.54)
Phenol, 2,4,6-trichloro-......	88062	2,4,6-Trichlorophenol	10	1,2,4	U231	A	10# (4.54)
Phenol, 2,4,6-trinitro-, ammonium salt.	131748	Ammonium picrate............	1*	4	P009	A	10 (4.54)
Phenyl dichloroarsine........	696286	Dichlorophenylarsine.........	1*	4	P036	X	1# (0.454)
1,10-(1,2-Phenylene)pyrene.	193395	Indeno(1,2,3-cd)pyrene	1*	2,4	U137	X	1# (0.454)
Phenylmercuric acetate	62384	Mercury, (acetato-O)phenyl-.	1*	4	P092	X	1## (0.454)
N-Phenylthiourea	103855	Thiourea, phenyl-.............	1*	4	P093	B	100 (45.4)

TABLE 302.4—LIST OF HAZARDOUS SUBSTANCES AND REPORTABLE QUANTITIES—
Continued

[See footnotes at end of Table 302.4]

Hazardous Substance	CASRN	Regulatory Synonyms	Statutory			Final RQ	
			RQ	Code†	RCRA Waste Number	Category	Pounds(Kg)
Phorate	298022	Phosphorodithioic acid, O,O-diethyl S-(ethylthio), methyl ester.	1*	4	P094	X	1## (0.454)
Phosgene.............................	75445	Carbonyl chloride..............	5000	1,4	P095	A	10 (4.54)
Phosphine.............................	7803512	Hydrogen phosphide........	1*	4	P096	B	100 (45.4)
Phosphoric acid	7664382		5000	1	....	D	5000 (2270)
Phosphoric acid,diethyl p-nitrophenyl ester.	311455	Diethyl-p-nitrophenyl phosphate.	1*	4	P041	B	100 (45.4)
Phosphoric acid, lead salt.	7446277	Lead phosphate.................	1*	4	U145	X	1# (0.454)
Phosphorodithioic acid, O,O-diethyl S-methylester.	3288582	O,O-Diethyl S-methyl dithiophosphate.	1*	4	U087	D	5000 (2270)
Phosphorodithioic acid, O,O-diethyl S-(ethylthio), methyl ester.	298022	Phorate	1*	4	P094	X	1## (0.454)
Phosphorodithioic acid,O,O-dimethyl S-[2(methylamino)-2-oxoethyl] ester.	60515	Dimethoate	1*	4	P044	A	10 (4.54)
Phosphorofluoridic acid,bis(1-methylethyl) ester.	55914	Diisopropyl fluorophosphate.	1*	4	P043	B	100 (45.4)
Phosphorothioic acid,O,O-diethyl O-(p-nitrophenyl) ester.	56382	Parathion...........................	1	1,4	P089	X	1# (0.454)
Phosphorothioic acid, O,O-diethyl O-pyrazinyl ester.	297972	O,O-Diethyl O-pyrazinyl phosphorothioate.	1*	4	P040	B	100 (45.4)
Phosphorothioic acid, O,O-dimethyl O-[p-[(dimethylamino)-sulfonyl]phenyl] ester.	52857	Famphur...........................	1*	4	P097	C	1000 (454)
Phosphorus	7723140		1	1	....	X	1 (0.454)
Phosphorus oxychloride....	10025873		5000	1	....	C	1000 (454)
Phosphorus pentasulfide ..	1314803	Phosphorus sulfide............ Sulfur phosphide	100	1,4	U189	B	100 (45.4)
Phosphorus sulfide...........	1314803	Phosphorus pentasulfide .. Sulfur phosphide	100	1,4	U189	B	100 (45.4)
Phosphorus trichloride	7719122		5000	1	....	C	1000 (454)
PHTHALATE ESTERS.......			1*	2	....	....	••

(Release #1, 5/87)

TABLE 302.4—LIST OF HAZARDOUS SUBSTANCES AND REPORTABLE QUANTITIES—Continued

[See footnotes at end of Table 302.4]

Hazardous Substance	CASRN	Regulatory Synonyms	Statutory			Final RQ	
			RQ	Code†	RCRA Waste Number	Category	Pounds(Kg)
Phthalic anhydride............	85449	1,2-Benzenedicarboxylic acid anhydride.	1*	4	U190	D	5000 (2270)
2-Picoline........................	109068	Pyridine,2-methyl-.............	1*	4	U191	D	5000 (2270)
Plumbane, tetraethyl-........	78002	Tetraethyl lead.................	100	1,4	P110	B	100## (45.4)
POLYCHLORINATED BIPHENYLS (PCBs).	1336363	Aroclors.................	10	1,2	....	A	10# (4.54)
	12674112	Aroclor 1016					
	11104282	Aroclor 1221					
	11141165	Aroclor 1232					
	53469219	Aroclor 1242					
	12672296	Aroclor 1248					
	11097691	Aroclor 1254					
	11096825	Aroclor 1260					
POLYNUCLEAR AROMATIC HYDROCARBONS.	....	....	1*	2	....	....	••
Potassium arsenate...........	7784410		1000	1		C	1000# (454)
Potassium arsenite............	10124502		1000	1		C	1000# (454)
Potassium bichromate.......	7778509		1000	1		C	1000# (454)
Potassium chromate..........	7789006		1000	1		C	1000# (454)
Potassium cyanide............	151508		10	1,4	P098	A	10 (4.54)
Potassium hydroxide.........	1310583		1000	1		C	1000 (454)
Potassium permanganate.	7722647		100	1		B	100 (45.4)
Potassium silver cyanide ..	506616		1*	4	P099	X	1 (0.454)
Pronamide	23950585	3,5-Dichloro-N-(1,1-dimethyl-2-propynyl)benzamide.	1*	4	U192	D	5000 (2270)
1-Propanal, 2,3-epoxy-......	765344	Glycidylaldehyde................	1*	4	U126	X	1# (0.454)
Propanal, 2-methyl-2-(methylthio)-,O-[(methylamino) carbonyl]oxime.	116063	Aldicarb................................	1*	4	P070	X	1 (0.454)
1-Propanamine...................	107108	n-Propylamine	1*	4	U194	D	5000 (2270)
1-Propanamine, N-propyl-.	142847	Dipropylamine	1*	4	U110	D	5000 (2270)
Propane, 1,2-dibromo-3-chloro-.	96128	1,2-Dibromo-3-chloropropane.	1*	4	U066	X	1# (0.454)
Propane, 2-nitro-...............	79469	2-Nitropropane	1*	4	U171	X	1# (0.454)
Propane, 2,2'-oxybis(2-chloro-.	108601	Bis(2-chloroisopropyl) ether.	1*	2,4	U027	C	1000 (454)

TABLE 302.4—LIST OF HAZARDOUS SUBSTANCES AND REPORTABLE QUANTITIES— Continued

[See footnotes at end of Table 302.4]

Hazardous Substance	CASRN	Regulatory Synonyms	Statutory			Final RQ	
			RQ	Code†	RCRA Waste Number	Catego-ry	Pounds(Kg)
1,3-Propane sultone	1120714	1,2-Oxathiolane, 2,2-dioxide.	1*	4	U193	X	1# (0.454)
Propanedinitrile	109773	Malononitrile	1*	4	U149	C	1000 (4.54)
Propanenitrile	107120	Ethyl cyanide	1*	4	P101	A	10 (4.54)
Propanenitrile, 3-chloro-	542767	3-Chloropropionitrile	1*	4	P027	C	1000 (454)
Propanenitrile, 2-hydroxy-2-methyl-.	75865	Acetone cyanohydrin 2-Methyllactonitrile	10	1,4	P069	A	10 (4.54)
1,2,3-Propanetriol, trinitrate-.	55630	Nitroglycerine	1*	4	P081	A	10 (4.54)
1-Propanol, 2,3-dibromo-, phosphate (3:1).	126727	Tris(2,3-dibromopropyl) phosphate.	1*	4	U235	X	1# (0.454)
1-Propanol, 2-methyl-	78831	Isobutyl alcohol	1*	4	U140	D	5000 (2270)
2-Propanone	67641	Acetone	1*	4	U002	D	5000 (2270)
2-Propanone, 1-bromo-	598312	Bromoacetone	1*	4	P017	C	1000 (454)
Propargite	2312358		10	1		A	10 (4.54)
Propargyl alcohol	107197	2-Propyn-1-ol	1*	4	P102	C	1000 (454)
2-Propenal	107028	Acrolein	1	1,2,4	P003	X	1 (0.454)
2-Propenamide	79061	Acrylamide	1*	4	U007	D	5000 (2270)
Propene, 1,3-dichloro-	542756	1,3-Dichloropropene	5000	1,2,4	U084	D	5000## (2270)
1-Propene, 1,1,2,3,3,3-hexachloro-.	1888717	Hexachloropropene	1*	4	U243	C	1000 (454)
2-Propenenitrile	107131	Acrylonitrile	100	1,2,4	U009	B	100# (45.4)
2-Propenenitrile, 2-methyl-.	126987	Methacrylonitrile	1*	4	U152	C	1000 (454)
2-Propenoic acid	79107	Acrylic acid	1*	4	U008	D	5000 (2270)
2-Propenoic acid, ethyl ester.	140885	Ethyl acrylate	1*	4	U113	C	1000 (454)
2-Propenoic acid, 2-methyl-, ethyl ester.	97632	Ethyl methacrylate	1*	4	U118	C	1000 (454)
2-Propenoic acid, 2-methyl-, methyl ester.	80626	Methyl methacrylate	5000	1,4	U162	C	1000 (454)
2-Propen-1-ol	107186	Allyl alcohol	100	1,4	P005	B	100 (45.4)
Propionic acid	79094		5000	1		D	5000 (2270)
Propionic acid, 2-(2,4,5-trichlorophenoxy)-.	93721	Silvex 2,4,5-TP acid	100	1,4	U233	B	100 (45.4)
Propionic anhydride	123626		5000	1		D	5000 (2270)

TABLE 302.4—LIST OF HAZARDOUS SUBSTANCES AND REPORTABLE QUANTITIES—
Continued

[See footnotes at end of Table 302.4]

Hazardous Substance	CASRN	Regulatory Synonyms	Statutory			Final RQ	
			RQ	Code†	RCRA Waste Number	Category	Pounds(Kg)
n-Propylamine	107108	1-Propanamine	1*	4	U194	D	5000 (2270)
Propylene dichloride	78875	1,2-Dichloropropane	5000	1,2,4	U083	C	1000 (454)
Propylene oxide	75569		5000	1		B	100 (45.4)
1,2-Propylenimine	75558	2-Methylaziridine	1*	4	P067	X	1# (0.454)
2-Propyn-1-ol	107197	Propargyl alcohol	1*	4	P102	C	1000 (454)
Pyrene	129000		1*	2		X	1## (0.454)
Pyrethrins	121299 121211 8003347		1000	1		X	1 (0.454)
4-Pyridinamine	504245	4-Aminopyridine	1*	4	P008	C	1000 (454)
Pyridine	110861		1*	4	U196	X	1## (0.454)
Pyridine, 2-[2-(dimethylamino)ethyl)-2-thenylamino]-.	91805	Methapyrilene	1*	4	U155	D	5000 (2270)
Pyridine, hexahydro-N-nitroso-.	100754	N-Nitrosopiperidine	1*	4	U179	X	1# (0.454)
Pyridine,2-methyl-	109068	2-Picoline	1*	4	U191	D	5000 (2270)
Pyridine, (S)-3-(1-methyl-2-pyrrolidinyl)-, and salts.	54115	Nicotine and salts	1*	4	P075	B	100 (45.4)
4(1H)-Pyrimidinone, 2,3-dihydro-6-methyl-2-thioxo-.	56042	Methylthiouracil	1*	4	U164	X	1# (0.454)
Pyrophosphoric acid, tetraethyl ester.	107493	Tetraethyl pyrophosphate.	100	1,4	P111	B	100## (45.4)
Pyrrole, tetrahydro-N-nitroso-.	930552	N-Nitrosopyrrolidine	1*	4	U180	X	1 § (0.454)
Quinoline	91225		1000	1		D	5000 (2270)
RADIONUCLIDES			1*	3		X	1§ (0.454)
Reserpine	50555	Yohimban-16-carboxylic acid,11,17-dimethoxy-18- [(3,4,5-trimethoxybenzoyl)oxy]-, methyl ester.	1*	4	U200	D	5000 (2270)
Resorcinol	108463	1,3-Benzenediol	1000	1,4	U201	D	5000 (2270)
Saccharin and salts	81072	1,2-Benzisothiazolin-3-one,1,1-dioxide, and salts.	1*	4	U202	X	1# (0.454)
Safrole	94597	Benzene, 1,2-methylenedioxy-4-allyl-.	1*	4	U203	X	1# (0.454)
Selenious acid	7783008		1*	4	U204	X	1## (0.454)

TABLE 302.4—LIST OF HAZARDOUS SUBSTANCES AND REPORTABLE QUANTITIES—Continued

[See footnotes at end of Table 302.4]

| Hazardous Substance | CASRN | Regulatory Synonyms | Statutory | | | Final RQ | |
			RQ	Code†	RCRA Waste Number	Catego-ry	Pounds(Kg)
Selenium ††	7782492		1*	2		X	1## (0.454)
SELENIUM AND COMPOUNDS.			1*	2			**
Selenium dioxide	7446084	Selenium oxide	1000	1,4	U204	C	1000## (454)
Selenium disulfide	7488564	Sulfur selenide	1*	4	U205	X	1# (0.454)
Selenium oxide	7446084	Selenium dioxide	1000	1,4	U204	C	1000## (454)
Selenourea	630104	Carbamimidoselenoic acid.	1*	4	P103	X	1## (0.454)
L-Serine, diazoacetate (ester).	115026	Azaserine	1*	4	U015	X	1# (0.454)
Silver ††	7440224		1*	2		C	1000 (454)
SILVER AND COMPOUNDS.			1*	2			**
Silver cyanide	506649		1*	4	P104	X	1 (0.454)
Silver nitrate	7761888		1	1		X	1 (0.454)
Silvex	93721	Propionic acid, 2-(2,4,5-trichlorophenoxy)-. 2,4,5-TP acid	100	1,4	U233	B	100 (45.4)
Sodium	7440235		1000	1		A	10 (4.54)
Sodium arsenate	7631892		1000	1		C	1000# (454)
Sodium arsenite	7784465		1000	1		C	1000# (454)
Sodium azide	26628228		1*	4	P105	C	1000 (454)
Sodium bichromate	10588019		1000	1		C	1000# (454)
Sodium bifluoride	1333831		5000	1		D	5000## (2270)
Sodium bisulfite	7631905		5000	1		D	5000 (2270)
Sodium chromate	7775113		1000	1		C	1000# (454)
Sodium cyanide	143339		10	1,4	P106	A	10 (4.54)
Sodium dodecylbenzene sulfonate.	25155300		1000	1		C	1000 (454)
Sodium fluoride	7681494		5000	1		C	1000 (454)
Sodium hydrosulfide	16721805		5000	1		D	5000 (2270)
Sodium hydroxide	1310732		1000	1		C	1000 (454)
Sodium hypochlorite	7681529 10022705		100	1		B	100 (45.4)
Sodium methylate	124414		1000	1		C	1000 (454)
Sodium nitrite	7632000		100	1		B	100## (45.4)

TABLE 302.4—LIST OF HAZARDOUS SUBSTANCES AND REPORTABLE QUANTITIES—
Continued

[See footnotes at end of Table 302.4]

Hazardous Substance	CASRN	Regulatory Synonyms	Statutory			Final RQ	
			RQ	Codet	RCRA Waste Number	Category	Pounds(Kg)
Sodium phosphate, dibasic.	7558794	....	5000	1	....	D	5000 (2270)
	10039324						
	10140655						
Sodium phosphate, tribasic.	7601549	....	5000	1	....	D	5000 (2270)
	7785844						
	10101890						
	10361894						
	7758294						
	10124568						
Sodium selenite	10102188	....	1000	1	....	C	1000## (454)
	7782823						
4,4'-Stilbenediol, alpha,alpha'-diethyl-.	56531	Diethylstilbestrol	1*	4	U089	X	1# (0.454)
Streptozotocin	18883664	D-Glucopyranose, 2-deoxy-2-(3-methyl-3-nitrosoureido)-.	1*	4	U206	X	1# (0.454)
Strontium chromate	7789062	....	1000	1	....	C	1000# (454)
Strontium sulfide	1314961	....	1*	4	P107	B	100 (45.4)
Strychnidin-10-one, and salts.	57249	Strychnine and salts	10	1,4	P108	A	10 (4.54)
Strychnidin-10-one, 2,3-dimethoxy-.	357573	Brucine	1*	4	P018	A	10 (4.54)
Strychnine and salts	57249	Strychnidin-10-one, and salts.	10	1,4	P108	A	10 (4.54)
Styrene	100425	....	1000	1	....	C	1000 (454)
Sulfur hydride	7783064	Hydrogen sulfide / Hydrosulfuric acid	100	1,4	U135	B	100## (45.4)
Sulfur monochloride	12771083	....	1000	1	....	C	1000 (454)
Sulfur phosphide	1314803	Phosphorus pentasulfide / Phosphorus sulfide	100	1,4	U189	B	100 (45.4)
Sulfur selenide	7488564	Selenium disulfide	1*	4	U205	X	1# (0.454)
Sulfuric acid	7664939	....	1000	1	....	C	1000 (454)
	8014957						
Sulfuric acid, dimethyl ester.	77781	Dimethyl sulfate	1*	4	U103	X	1# (0.454)
Sulfuric acid, thallium(I) salt.	7446186	Thallium(I) sulfate	1000	1,4	P115	C	1000## (454)
	10031591						
2,4,5-T	93765	2,4,5-T acid / 2,4,5-Trichlorophenoxyacetic acid	100	1,4	U232	C	1000 (454)

TABLE 302.4—LIST OF HAZARDOUS SUBSTANCES AND REPORTABLE QUANTITIES— Continued

[See footnotes at end of Table 302.4]

Hazardous Substance	CASRN	Regulatory Synonyms	Statutory			Final RQ	
			RQ	Code†	RCRA Waste Number	Category	Pounds(Kg)
2,4,5-T acid	93765	2,4,5-T 2,4,5-Trichlorophenoxyacetic acid	100	1,4	U232	C	1000 (454)
2,4,5-T amines	2008460 6369966 6369977 1319728 3813147		100	1		D	5000 (2270)
2,4,5-T esters	93798 2545597 61792072 1928478 25168154		100	1		C	1000 (454)
2,4,5-T salts	13560991		100	1		C	1000 (454)
TDE	72548	DDD 4,4' DDD Dichlorodiphenyl dichloroethane	1	1,2,4	U060	X	1# (0.454)
1,2,4,5-Tetrachlorobenzene.	95943	Benzene, 1,2,4,5-tetrachloro-.	1*	4	U207	D	5000 (2270)
2,3,7,8-Tetrachlorodibenzo-p-dioxin(TCDD).	1746016		1*	2		X	1# (0.454)
1,1,1,2-Tetrachloroethane.	630206	Ethane,1,1,1,2-tetrachloro-.	1*	4	U208	X	1# (0.454)
1,1,2,2-Tetrachloroethane.	79345	Ethane, 1,1,2,2-tetrachloro-.	1*	2,4	U209	X	1# (0.454)
Tetrachloroethylene	127184	Ethene, 1,1,2,2-tetrachloro-.	1*	2,4	U210	X	1# (0.454)
2,3,4,6-Tetrachlorophenol.	58902	Phenol, 2,3,4,6-tetrachloro-.	1*	4	U212	A	10 (4.54)
Tetraethyldithiopyrophosphate.	3689245	Dithiopyrophosphoric acid,tetraethyl ester.	1*	4	P109	B	100 (45.4)
Tetraethyl lead	78002	Plumbane, tetraethyl-	100	1,4	P110	B	100## (45.4)
Tetraethyl pyrophosphate.	107493	Pyrophosphoric acid, tetraethyl ester.	100	1,4	P111	B	100## (45.4)
Tetrahydrofuran	109999	Furan, tetrahydro-	1*	4	U213	C	1000 (454)
Tetranitromethane	509148	Methane, tetranitro-	1*	4	P112	A	10 (4.54)
Tetraphosphoric acid, hexaethyl ester.	757584	Hexaethyl tetraphosphate.	1*	4	P062	B	100 (45.4)
Thallic oxide	1314325	Thallium(III) oxide	1*	4	P113	X	1## (0.454)
Thallium	7440280		1*	2		X	1## (0.454)

TABLE 302.4—LIST OF HAZARDOUS SUBSTANCES AND REPORTABLE QUANTITIES—
Continued

[See footnotes at end of Table 302.4]

Hazardous Substance	CASRN	Regulatory Synonyms	Statutory			Final RQ	
			RQ	Code†	RCRA Waste Number	Category	Pounds(Kg)
THALLIUM AND COMPOUNDS.			1*	2			**
Thallium(I) acetate............	563688	Acetic acid, thallium(I) salt.	1*	4	U214	X	1## (0.454)
Thallium(I) carbonate	6533739	Carbonic acid, dithallium (I) salt.	1*	4	U215	X	1## (0.454)
Thallium(I) chloride............	7791120		1*.	4	U216	X	1## (0.454)
Thallium(I) nitrate..............	10102451		1*	4	U217	X	1## (0.454)
Thallium(III) oxide	1314325	Thallic oxide	1*	4	P113	X	1## (0.454)
Thallium(I) selenide	12039520		1*	4	P114	X	1## (0.454)
Thallium(I) sulfate	7446186 10031591	Sulfuric acid, thallium(I) salt.	1000	1,4	P115	C	1000## (454)
Thioacetamide...................	62555	Ethanethioamide...............	1*	4	U218	X	1# (0.454)
Thiofanox........................	39196184	3,3-Dimethyl-1-(methylthio)-2-butanone,O-[(methylamino)carbonyl] oxime.	1*	4	P045	B	100 (45.4)
Thioimidodicarbonic diamide.	541537	2,4-Dithiobiuret..................	1*	4	P049	B	100 (45.4)
Thiomethanol	74931	Methanethiol......................... Methylmercaptan	100	1,4	U153	B	100 (45.4)
Thiophenol.......................	108985	Benzenethiol..................	1*	4	P014	B	100 (45.4)
Thiosemicarbazide.............	79196	Hydrazinecarbothioamide .	1*	4	P116	B	100 (45.4)
Thiourea..........................	62566	Carbamide, thio-	1*	4	U219	X	1# (0.454)
Thiourea, (2-chlorophenyl)-.	5344821	1-(o-Chlorophenyl)thiourea.	1*	4	P026	B	100 (45.4)
Thiourea, 1-naphthalenyl-.	86884	alpha-Naphthylthiourea	1*	4	P072	B	100 (45.4)
Thiourea, phenyl-.............	103855	N-Phenylthiourea	1*	4	P093	B	100 (45.4)
Thiram.............................	137268	Bis (dimethylthiocarbamoyl) disulfide.	1*	4	U244	A	10 (4.54)
Toluene...........................	108883	Benzene, methyl-...............	1000	1,2,4	U220	C	1000 (454)
Toluenediamine..................	95807 25376458 496720 823405	Diaminotoluene	1*	4	U221	X	1# (0.454)

APPENDIX 6F

TABLE 302.4—LIST OF HAZARDOUS SUBSTANCES AND REPORTABLE QUANTITIES—Continued

[See footnotes at end of Table 302.4]

Hazardous Substance	CASRN	Regulatory Synonyms	Statutory			Final RQ	
			RQ	Code†	RCRA Waste Number	Category	Pounds(Kg)
Toluene diisocyanate........	584849 91087 26471625	Benzene, 2,4-diisocyanatomethyl-.	1*	4	U223	B	100 (45.4)
o-Toluidine hydrochloride.	636215	Benzenamine, 2-methyl-, hydrochloride.	1*	4	U222	X	1# (0.454)
Toxaphene......................	8001352	Camphene, octachloro-....	1	1,2,4	P123	X	1# (0.454)
2,4,5-TP acid..............	93721	Propionic acid, 2-(2,4,5-trichlorophenoxy)-. Silvex	100	1,4	U233	B	100 (45.4)
2,4,5-TP acid esters..........	32534955		100	1		B	100 (45.4)
1H-1,2,4-Triazol-3-amine...	61825	Amitrole.....................	1*	4	U011	X	1# (0.454)
Trichlorfon..................	52686		1000	1		C	1000## (454)
1,2,4-Trichlorobenzene	120821		1*	2		B	100 (45.4)
1,1,1-Trichloroethane	71556	Methyl chloroform............	1*	2,4	U226	C	1000 (454)
1,1,2-Trichloroethane	79005	Ethane, 1,1,2-trichloro-.....	1*	2,4	U227	X	1# (0.454)
Trichloroethene................	79016	Trichloroethylene	1000	1,2,4	U228	C	1000# (454)
Trichloroethylene	79016	Trichloroethene...............	1000	1,2,4	U228	C	1000# (454)
Trichloromethanesulfenyl chloride.	594423	Methanesulfenyl chloride, trichloro-.	1*	4	P118	B	100 (45.4)
Trichloromonofluoro-methane.	75694	Methane, trichlorofluoro-...	1*	4	U121	D	5000 (2270)
Trichlorophenol............. 2,3,4-Trichlorophenol 2,3,5-Trichlorophenol 2,3,6-Trichlorophenol 2,4,5-Trichlorophenol 2,4,6-Trichlorophenol 3,4,5-Trichlorophenol	25167822 15950660 933788 933755 95954 88062 609198	Phenol, 2,4,5-trichloro- Phenol, 2,4,6-trichloro-	10	1		A	10# (4.54)
2,4,5-Trichlorophenol	95954	Phenol, 2,4,5-trichloro-......	10	1,4	U230	A	10# (4.54)
2,4,6-Trichlorophenol	88062	Phenol, 2,4,6-trichloro-......	10	1,2,4	U231	A	10# (4.54)
2,4,5-Trichlorophenoxyacetic acid.	93765	2,4,5-T.................... 2,4,5-T acid	100	1,4	U232	C	1000 (454)
Triethanolamine dodecylbenzenesulfonate.	27323417		1000	1		C	1000 (454)

TABLE 302.4—LIST OF HAZARDOUS SUBSTANCES AND REPORTABLE QUANTITIES—
Continued

[See footnotes at end of Table 302.4]

Hazardous Substance	CASRN	Regulatory Synonyms	Statutory			Final RQ	
			RQ	Code†	RCRA Waste Number	Category	Pounds(Kg)
Triethylamine......................	121448	....	5000	1	....	D	5000 (2270)
Trimethylamine....................	75503	....	1000	1	....	C	1000## (454)
sym-Trinitrobenzene...........	99354	Benzene, 1,3,5-trinitro-.....	1*	4	U234	X	1## (0.454)
1,3,5-Trioxane, 2,4,6-trimethyl-.	123637	Paraldehyde......................	1*	4	U182	C	1000 (454)
Tris(2,3-dibromopropyl) phosphate.	126727	1-Propanol, 2,3-dibromo-, phosphate (3:1).	1*	4	U235	X	1# (0.454)
Trypan blue	72571	2,7-Naphthalenedisulfonic acid,3,3'-[(3,3'-dimethyl- (l,1'-biphenyl)-4,4'-diyl)-bis(azo)]bis(5-amino-4- hydroxy)-tetrasodium salt.	1*	4	U236	X	1# (0.454)
Unlisted Hazardous Wastes.	....	....	1*	4	....		
Characteristic of Ignitability.	....	....	1*	4	D001	B	100 (45.4)
Characteristic of Corrosivity.	....	....	1*	4	D002	B	100 (45.4)
Characteristic of Reactivity.	....	....	1*	4	D003	B	100 (45.4)
Characteristic of EP Toxicity.	....	....	1*	4			
Arsenic...........			1*	4	D004	X	1# (0.454)
Barium			1*	4	D005	C	1000 (454)
Cadmium			1*	4	D006	X	1# (0.454)
Chromium.........			1*	4	D007	X	1# (0.454)
Lead...............			1*	4	D008	X	1## (0.454)
Mercury...........			1*	4	D009	X	1 (0.454)
Selenium			1*	4	D010	X	1## (0.454)
Silver...............			1*	4	D011	X	1 (0.454)
Endrin			1	1,4	D012	X	1 (0.454)
Lindane............			1	1,4	D013	X	1# (0.454)
Methoxychlor ...			1	1,4	D014	X	1 (0.454)
Toxaphene.......			1	1,4	D015	X	1# (0.454)
2,4-D...............			100	1,4	D016	B	100 (45.4)
2,4,5-TP.........			100	1,4	D017	B	100 (45.4)

APPENDIX 6F

TABLE 302.4—LIST OF HAZARDOUS SUBSTANCES AND REPORTABLE QUANTITIES— Continued

[See footnotes at end of Table 302.4]

Hazardous Substance	CASRN	Regulatory Synonyms	Statutory			Final RQ	
			RQ	Code†	RCRA Waste Number	Category	Pounds(Kg)
Uracil, 5-[bis(2-chloroethyl)amino]-.	66751	Uracil mustard..........	1*	4	U237	X	1# (0.454)
Uracil mustard..............	66751	Uracil, 5-[bis(2-chloroethyl)amino]-.	1*	4	U237	X	1# (0.454)
Uranyl acetate..............	541093		5000	1	....	D	5000## (2270)
Uranyl nitrate..............	10102064 36478769		5000	1	....	D	5000## (2270)
Vanadic acid, ammonium salt.	7803556	Ammonium vanadate	1*	4	P119	C	1000 (454)
Vanadium(V) oxide	1314621	Vanadium pentoxide..........	1000	1,4	P120	C	1000## (454)
Vanadium pentoxide........	1314621	Vanadium(V) oxide	1000	1,4	P120	C	1000## (454)
Vanadyl sulfate	27774136		1000	1	....	C	1000## (454)
Vinyl acetate..............	108054		1000	1	....	D	5000 (2270)
Vinyl chloride..............	75014	Ethene, chloro-	1*	2,3,4	U043	X	1# (0.454)
Vinylidene chloride	75354	1,1-Dichloroethylene.......... Ethene, 1,1-dichloro-	5000	1,2,4	U078	D	5000# (2270)
Warfarin	81812	3-(alpha-Acetonylbenzyl)-4-hydroxycoumarin and salts.	1*	4	P001	B	100 (45.4)
Xylene (mixed) .... m- o- p-	1330207 108383 95476 106423	Benzene,dimethyl .... m- o- p-	1000	1,4	U239	C	1000 (454)
Xylenol	1300716		1000	1	....	C	1000 (454)
Yohimban-16-carboxylic acid,11,17-dimethoxy-18-[(3,4,5-trimethoxybenzoyl)oxy]-, methylester.	50555	Reserpine	1*	4	U200	D	5000 (2270)
Zinc ††.............	7440666		1*	2	....	X	1## (0.454)
ZINC AND COMPOUNDS.	....		1*	2	....	......	**
Zinc acetate	557346		1000	1	....	C	1000## (454)
Zinc ammonium chloride ..	52628258 14639975 14639986		5000	1	....	D	5000## (2270)
Zinc borate.............	1332076		1000	1	....	C	1000## (454)
Zinc bromide	7699458		5000	1	....	D	5000## (2270)
Zinc carbonate.............	3486359		1000	1	....	C	1000## (454)
Zinc chloride.............	7646857		5000	1	....	D	5000## (2270)

TABLE 302.4—LIST OF HAZARDOUS SUBSTANCES AND REPORTABLE QUANTITIES—
Continued

[See footnotes at end of Table 302.4]

| Hazardous Substance | CASRN | Regulatory Synonyms | Statutory | | | Final RQ | |
			RQ	Codet	RCRA Waste Number	Category	Pounds(Kg)
Zinc cyanide	557211		10	1,4	P121	A	10## (4.54)
Zinc fluoride	7783495		1000	1		C	1000## (454)
Zinc formate	557415		1000	1		C	1000## (454)
Zinc hydrosulfite	7779864		1000	1		C	1000## (454)
Zinc nitrate	7779886		5000	1		D	5000## (2270)
Zinc phenolsulfonate	127822		5000	1		D	5000## (2270)
Zinc phosphide	1314847		1000	1,4	P122	C	1000## (454)
Zinc silicofluoride	16871719		5000	1		D	5000##(2270)
Zinc sulfate	7733020		1000	1		C	1000## (454)
Zirconium nitrate	13746899		5000	1		D	5000 (2270)
Zirconium potassium fluoride.	16923958		5000	1		C	1000 (454)
Zirconium sulfate	14644612		5000	1		D	5000 (2270)
Zirconium tetrachloride	10026116		5000	1		D	5000 (2270)
F001			1*	4	F001	X	1# (0.454)
The following spent halogenated solvents used in degreasing and sludges from the recovery of these solvents in degreasing operations:							
(a) Tetrachloro-ethylene.	127184					X	1# (0.454)
(b) Trichloroethylene	79016					C	1000# (454)
(c) Methylene chloride.	75092					C	1000 (454)
(d) 1,1,1-Trichloroethane.	71556					C	1000 (454)
(e) Carbon tetrachloride.	56235					D	5000# (2270)
(f) Chlorinated fluorocarbons.	(N.A.)					D	5000 (2270)
F002			1*	4	F002	X	1# (0.454)
The following spent halogenated solvents and the still bottoms from the recovery of these solvents:							
(a) Tetrachloro-ethylene.	127184					X	1# (0.454)
(b) Methylene Chloride.	75092					C	1000 (454)
(c) Trichloroethylene.	79016					C	1000# (454)
(d) 1,1,1-Trichloroethane.	71556					C	1000 (454)
(e) Chlorobenzene	108907					B	100 (45.4)

TABLE 302.4—LIST OF HAZARDOUS SUBSTANCES AND REPORTABLE QUANTITIES—
Continued

[See footnotes at end of Table 302.4]

Hazardous Substance	CASRN	Regulatory Synonyms	Statutory			Final RQ	
			RQ	Code†	RCRA Waste Number	Category	Pounds(Kg)
(f) 1,1,2-Trichloro-1,2,2-trifluoroethane.	76131					D	5000 (2270)
(g) o-Dichlorobenzene.	106467					B	100 (45.4)
(h) Trichlorofluoro-methane.	75694					D	5000 (2270)
F003			1*	4	F003	B	100 (45.4)
The following spent non-halogenated solvents and the still bottoms from the recovery of these solvents:							
(a) Xylene................	1330207					C	1000 (454)
(b) Acetone...............	67641					D	5000 (2270)
(c) Ethyl acetate.........	141786					D	5000 (2270)
(d) Ethylbenzene.........	100414					C	1000 (454)
(e) Ethyl ether	60297					B	100 (45.4)
(f) Methyl isobutyl ketone.	108101					D	5000 (2270)
(g) n-Butyl alcohol......	71363					D	5000 (2270)
(h) Cyclohexanone.....	108941					D	5000 (2270)
(i) Methanol..............	67561					D	5000 (2270)
F004			1*	4	F004	X	1## (0.454)
The following spent non-halogenated solvents and the still bottoms from the recovery of these solvents:							
(a) Cresols/Cresylic acid.	1319773					C	1000# (454)
(b) Nitrobenzene	98953					C	1000 (454)
F005			1*	4	F005	X	1## (0.454)
The following spent non-halogenated solvents and the still bottoms from the recovery of these solvents:							
(a) Toluene	108883					C	1000 (454)
(b) Methyl ethyl ketone.	78933					D	5000 (2270)
(c) Carbon disulfide ...	75150					D	5000# (2270)
(d) Isobutanol	78831					D	5000 (2270)
(e) Pyridine..............	110861					X	1## (0.454)

TABLE 302.4—LIST OF HAZARDOUS SUBSTANCES AND REPORTABLE QUANTITIES—
Continued

[See footnotes at end of Table 302.4]

Hazardous Substance	CASRN	Regulatory Synonyms	Statutory			Final RQ	
			RQ	Code†	RCRA Waste Number	Category	Pounds(Kg)
F006 .... Wastewater treatment sludges from electroplating operations except from the following processes: (1) Sulfuric acid anodizing of aluminum; (2) tin plating on carbon steel; (3) zinc plating (segregated basis) on carbon steel; (4) aluminum or zinc-aluminum plating on carbon steel; (5) cleaning/stripping associated with tin, zinc and aluminum plating on carbon steel; and (6) chemical etching and milling of aluminum			1*	4	F006	X	1# (0.454)
F007 .... Spent cyanide plating bath solutions from electroplating operations (except for precious metals electroplating spent cyanide plating bath solutions)			1*	4	F007	A	10 (4.54)
F008 .... Plating bath sludges from the bottom of plating baths from electroplating operations where cyanides are used in the process (except for precious metals electroplating plating bath sludges)			1*	4	F008	A	10 (4.54)

TABLE 302.4—LIST OF HAZARDOUS SUBSTANCES AND REPORTABLE QUANTITIES—
Continued

[See footnotes at end of Table 302.4]

Hazardous Substance	CASRN	Regulatory Synonyms	Statutory			Final RQ	
			RQ	Codet	RCRA Waste Number	Category	Pounds(Kg)
F009 .... Spent stripping and cleaning bath solutions from electroplating operations where cyanides are used in the process (except for precious metals electroplating spent stripping and cleaning bath solutions)			1*	4	F009	A	10 (4.54)
F010 .... Quenching bath sludge from oil baths from metal heat treating operations where cyanides are used in the process (except for precious metals heat-treating quenching bath sludges)			1*	4	F010	A	10 (4.54)
F011 .... Spent cyanide solutions from salt bath pot cleaning from metal heat treating operations (except for precious metals heat treating spent cyanide solutions from salt bath pot cleaning)			1*	4	F011	A	10 (4.54)
F012 .... Quenching wastewater treatment sludges from metal heat treating operations where cyanides are used in the process (except for precious metals heat treating quenching wastewater teatment sludges)			1*	4	F012	A	10 (4.54)
F019 .... Wastewater treatment sludges from the chemical conversion coating of aluminum			1*	4	F019	X	1# (0.454)

TABLE 302.4—LIST OF HAZARDOUS SUBSTANCES AND REPORTABLE QUANTITIES—
Continued

[See footnotes at end of Table 302.4]

Hazardous Substance	CASRN	Regulatory Synonyms	Statutory			Final RQ	
			RQ	Code†	RCRA Waste Number	Category	Pounds(Kg)
F024 .... Wastes, including but not limited to distillation residues, heavy ends, tars, and reactor cleanout wastes, from the production of chlorinated aliphatic hydrocarbons,having carbon content from one to five, utilizing free radical catalyzed processes. (This listing does not include light ends, spent filters and filter aids, spent dessicants(sic), wastewater, wastewater treatment sludges, spent catalysts,and wastes listed in § 261.32.)			1*	4	F024	X	1# (0.454)
K001 .... Bottom sediment sludge from the treatment of wastewaters from wood preserving processes that use creosote and/or pentachlorophenol			1*	4	K001	X	1# (0.454)
K002 .... Wastewater treatment sludge from the production of chrome yellow and orange pigments			1*	4	K002	X	1# (0.454)
K003 .... Wastewater treatment sludge from the production of molybdate orange pigments			1*	4	K003	X	1# (0.454)
K004 .... Wastewater treatment sludge from the production of zinc yellow pigments			1*	4	K004	X	1# (0.454)

APPENDIX 6F

TABLE 302.4—LIST OF HAZARDOUS SUBSTANCES AND REPORTABLE QUANTITIES—
Continued

[See footnotes at end of Table 302.4]

Hazardous Substance	CASRN	Regulatory Synonyms	Statutory			Final RQ	
			RQ	Code†	RCRA Waste Number	Category	Pounds(Kg)
K005................................ Wastewater treatment sludge from the production of chrome green pigments			1*	4	K005	X	1# (0.454)
K006................................ Wastewater treatment sludge from the production of chrome oxide green pigments (anhydrous and hydrated)			1*	4	K006	X	1# (0.454)
K007................................ Wastewater treatment sludge from the production of iron blue pigments			1*	4	K007	X	1# (0.454)
K008................................ Oven residue from the production of chrome oxide green pigments			1*	4	K008	X	1# (0.454)
K009................................ Distillation bottoms from the production of acetaldehyde from ethylene			1*	4	K009	X	1# (0.454)
K010................................ Distillation side cuts from the production of acetaldehyde from ethylene			1*	4	K010	X	1# (0.454)
K011................................ Bottom stream from the wastewater stripper in the production of acrylonitrile			1*	4	K011	X	1# (0.454)
K013................................ Bottom stream from the acetonitrile column in the production of acrylonitrile			1*	4	K013	X	1# (0.454)
K014................................ Bottoms from the acetonitrile purification column in the production of acrylonitrile			1*	4	K014	D	5000 (2270)

TABLE 302.4—LIST OF HAZARDOUS SUBSTANCES AND REPORTABLE QUANTITIES—
Continued

[See footnotes at end of Table 302.4]

Hazardous Substance	CASRN	Regulatory Synonyms	Statutory			Final RQ	
			RQ	Code†	RCRA Waste Number	Category	Pounds(Kg)
K015............. Still bottoms from thedistillation of benzyl chloride			1*	4	K015	X	1# (0.454)
K016............. Heavy ends or distillation residues from the productionof carbon tetrachloride			1*	4	K016	X	1# (0.454)
K017............. Heavy ends (still bottoms) from the purification column in the production of epichlorohydrin			1*	4	K017	X	1# (0.454)
K018............. Heavy ends from the fractionation column in ethyl chloride production			1*	4	K018	X	1# (0.454)
K019............. Heavy ends from the distillation of ethylene dichloride in ethylene dichloride production			1*	4	K019	X	1# (0.454)
K020............. Heavy ends from the distillation of vinyl chloride in vinyl chloride monomer production			1*	4	K020	X	1# (0.454)
K021............. Aqueous spent antimony catalyst waste from fluoromethanes production			1*	4	K021	X	1# (0.454)
K022............. Distillation bottom tars from the production of phenol/acetone from cumene			1*	4	K022	X	1# (0.454)
K023............. Distillation light ends from the production of phthalic anhydride from naphthalene			1*	4	K023	D	5000 (2270)

TABLE 302.4—LIST OF HAZARDOUS SUBSTANCES AND REPORTABLE QUANTITIES—
Continued

[See footnotes at end of Table 302.4]

Hazardous Substance	CASRN	Regulatory Synonyms	Statutory			Final RQ	
			RQ	Code†	RCRA Waste Number	Category	Pounds(Kg)
K024 .ˑ Distillation bottoms from the production of phthalic anhydride from naphthalene			1*	4	K024	D	5000 (2270)
K025 Distillation bottoms from the production of nitrobenzene by the nitration of benzene			1*	4	K025	X	1# (0.454)
K026 Stripping still tails from the production of methyl ethyl pyridines			1*	4	K026	X	1## (0.454)
K027 Centrifuge and distillation residues from toluene diisocyanate production			1*	4	K027	X	1# (0.454)
K028 Spent catalyst from the hydrochlorinator reactor in the production of 1,1,1-trichloroethane			1*	4	K028	X	1# (0.454)
K029 Waste from the product steam stripper in the production of 1,1,1-trichloroethane			1*	4	K029	X	1# (0.454)
K030 Column bottoms or heavy ends from the combined production of trichloroethylene and perchloroethylene			1*	4	K030	X	1# (0.454)
K031 By-product salts generated in the production of MSMA and cacodylic acid			1*	4	K031	X	1# (0.454)
K032 Wastewater treatment sludge from the production of chlordane			1*	4	K032	X	1# (0.454)

TABLE 302.4—LIST OF HAZARDOUS SUBSTANCES AND REPORTABLE QUANTITIES—Continued

[See footnotes at end of Table 302.4]

Hazardous Substance	CASRN	Regulatory Synonyms	Statutory			Final RQ	
			RQ	Code†	RCRA Waste Number	Category	Pounds(Kg)
K033.............. Wastewater and scrub water from the chlorination of cyclopentadiene in the production of chlordane			1*	4	K033	X	1# (0.454)
K034.............. Filter solids from the filtration of hexachlorocyclopen-tadiene in the production of chlordane			1*	4	K034	X	1# (0.454)
K035.............. Wastewater treatment sludges generated in the production of creosote			1*	4	K035	X	1# (0.454)
K036.............. Still bottoms from toluene reclamation distillation in the production of disulfoton			1*	4	K036	X	1 (0.454)
K037.............. Wastewater treatment sludges from the production of disulfoton			1*	4	K037	X	1 (0.454)
K038.............. Wastewater from the washing and stripping of phorate production			1*	4	K038	X	1# (0.454)
K039.............. Filter cake from the filtration of diethylphosphoro-dithioic acid in the production of phorate			1*	4	K039	X	1## (0.454)
K040.............. Wastewater treatment sludge from the production of phorate			1*	4	K040	X	1# (0.454)
K041.............. Wastewater treatment sludge from the production of toxaphene			1*	4	K041	X	1# (0.454)

App. 6F-56

TABLE 302.4—LIST OF HAZARDOUS SUBSTANCES AND REPORTABLE QUANTITIES—Continued

[See footnotes at end of Table 302.4]

Hazardous Substance	CASRN	Regulatory Synonyms	Statutory			Final RQ	
			RQ	Code†	RCRA Waste Number	Category	Pounds(Kg)
K042............ Heavy ends or distillation residues from the distillation of tetrachlorobenzene in the production of 2,4,5-T			1*	4	K042	X	1# (0.454)
K043............ 2,6-Dichlorophenol waste from the production of 2,4-D			1*	4	K043	X	1# (0.454)
K044............ Wastewater treatment sludges from the manufacturing and processing of explosives			1*	4	K044	A	10 (4.54)
K045............ Spent carbon from the treatment of wastewater containing explosives			1*	4	K045	A	10 (4.54)
K046............ Wastewater treatment sludges from the manufacturing, formulation and loading of lead-based initiating compounds			1*	4	K046	X	1## (0.454)
K047............ Pink/red water from TNT operations			1*	4	K047	A	10 (4.54)
K048............ Dissolved air flotation (DAF) float from the petroleum refining industry			1*	4	K048	X	1# (0.454)
K049............ Slop oil emulsion solids from the petroleum refining industry			1*	4	K049	X	1# (0.454)
K050............ Heat exchanger bundle cleaning sludge from the petroleum refining industry			1*	4	K050	X	1# (0.454)

TABLE 302.4—LIST OF HAZARDOUS SUBSTANCES AND REPORTABLE QUANTITIES—Continued

[See footnotes at end of Table 302.4]

Hazardous Substance	CASRN	Regulatory Synonyms	Statutory			Final RQ	
			RQ	Code†	RCRA Waste Number	Catego-ry	Pounds(Kg)
K051............ API separator sludge from the petroleum refining industry			1*	4	K051	X	1# (0.454)
K052............ Tank bottoms (leaded) from the petroleum refining industry			1*	4	K052	X	1## (0.454)
K060............ Ammonia still lime sludge from coking operations			1*	4	K060	X	1# (0.454)
K061............ Emission control dust/ sludge from the primary production of steel in electric furnaces			1*	4	K061	X	1# (0.454)
K062............ Spent pickle liquor from steel finishing operations			1*	4	K062	X	1# (0.454)
K069............ Emission control dust/ sludge from secondary lead smelting			1*	4	K069	X	1# (0.454)
K071............ Brine purification muds from the mercury cell process in chlorine production, where separately prepurified brine is not used			1*	4	K071	X	1 (0.454)
K073............ Chlorinated hydrocarbon waste from the purification step of the diaphragm cell process using graphite anodes in chlorine production			1*	4	K073	X	1# (0.454)
K083............ Distillation bottoms from aniline extraction			1*	4	K083	B	100 (45.4)

TABLE 302.4—LIST OF HAZARDOUS SUBSTANCES AND REPORTABLE QUANTITIES—
Continued

[See footnotes at end of Table 302.4]

Hazardous Substance	CASRN	Regulatory Synonyms	Statutory			Final RQ	
			RQ	Code†	RCRA Waste Number	Category	Pounds(Kg)
K084............................. Wastewater treatment sludges generated during the production of veterinary pharmaceuticals from arsenic or organo-arsenic compounds			1*	4	K084	X	1# (0.454)
K085............................. Distillation or fractionation column bottoms from the production of chlorobenzenes			1*	4	K085	X	1# (0.454)
K086............................. Solvent washes and sludges, caustic washes and sludges, or water washes and sludges from cleaning tubs and equipment used in the formulation of ink from pigments, driers, soaps, and stabilizers containing chromium and lead			1*	4	K086	X	1# (0.454)
K087............................. Decanter tank tar sludge from coking operations			1*	4	K087	X	1## (0.454)
K093............................. Distillation light ends from the production of phthalic anhydride from ortho-xylene			1*	4	K093	D	5000 (2270)
K094............................. Distillation bottoms from the production of phthalic anhydride from ortho-xylene			1*	4	K094	D	5000 (2270)
K095............................. Distillation bottoms from the production of 1,1,1-trichloroethane			1*	4	K095	X	1# (0.454)

TABLE 302.4—LIST OF HAZARDOUS SUBSTANCES AND REPORTABLE QUANTITIES—Continued

[See footnotes at end of Table 302.4]

Hazardous Substance	CASRN	Regulatory Synonyms	Statutory			Final RQ	
			RQ	Code†	RCRA Waste Number	Category	Pounds(Kg)
K096................................ Heavy ends from the heavy ends column from the production of 1,1,1-trichloroethane			1*	4	K096	X	1# (0.454)
K097................................ Vacuum stripper discharge from the chlordane chlorinator in the production of chlordane			1*	4	K097	X	1# (0.454)
K098................................ Untreated process wastewater from the production of toxaphene			1*	4	K098	X	1# (0.454)
K099................................ Untreated wastewater from the production of 2,4-D			1*	4	K099	X	1# (0.454)
K100................................ Waste leaching solution from acid leaching of emission control dust/sludge from secondary lead smelting (Components of this waste are identical with those of K069).			1*	4	K100	X	1# (0.454)
K101................................ Distillation tar residues from the distillation of aniline-based compounds in the production of veterinary pharmaceuticals from arsenic or organo-arsenic compounds			1*	4	K101	X	1# (0.454)
K102................................ Residue from the use of activated carbon for decolorization in the production of veterinary pharmaceuticals from arsenic or organo-arsenic compounds			1*	4	K102	X	1# (0.454)

TABLE 302.4—LIST OF HAZARDOUS SUBSTANCES AND REPORTABLE QUANTITIES— Continued

[See footnotes at end of Table 302.4]

Hazardous Substance	CASRN	Regulatory Synonyms	Statutory			Final RQ	
			RQ	Code†	RCRA Waste Number	Category	Pounds(Kg)
K103.............. Process residues from aniline extraction from the production of aniline			1*	4	K103	B	100 (45.4)
K104.............. Combined wastewater streams generated from nitrobenzene/ aniline chlorobenzenes			1*	4	K104	X	1# (0.454)
K105.............. Separated aqueous stream from the reactor product washing step in the production of chlorobenzenes			1*	4	K105	X	1# (0.454)
K106.............. Wastewater treatment sludge from the mercury cell process in chlorine production			1*	4	K106	X	1 (0.454)

† - Indicates the statutory source as defined by 1, 2, 3, or 4 below
1 - Indicates that the statutory source for designation of this hazardous substance under CERCLA is CWA section 311(b)(4)
2 - Indicates that the statutory source for designation of this hazardous substance under CERCLA is CWA section 307(a)
3 - Indicates that the statutory source for designation of this hazardous substance under CERCLA is CAA section 112
4 - Indicates that the statutory source for designation of this hazardous substance under CERCLA is RCRA section 3001
†† - No reporting of releases of this hazardous substance is required if the diameter of the pieces of the solid metal released is equal to or exceeds 100 micrometers (0.004 inches)
††† - The RQ for asbestos is limited to friable forms only
§ - The Agency may adjust the RQ for radionuclides in a future rulemaking; until then the statutory 1-pound RQ applies
1* - Indicates that the 1-pound RQ is a CERCLA statutory RQ
** - Indicates that no RQ is being assigned to the generic or broad class
# - Indicates that the RQ is subject to change when the assessment of potential carcinogenicity and/or chronic toxicity is completed
- Indicates that an adjusted RQ is proposed in a separate NPRM in today's Federal Register [45 FR 13514, Apr. 4, 1985]
- The Agency may adjust the RQ for methyl isocyanate in a future rulemaking; until then the statutory 1-pound RQ applies

APPENDIX A—SEQUENTIAL CAS REGISTRY NUMBER LIST OF CERCLA HAZARDOUS SUBSTANCES

CASRN	Hazardous Substance
50000	Formaldehyde Methylene oxide
50077	Azirino(2',3':3,4)pyrrolo(1,2-a)indole-4,7-dione,6- amino-8- [((aminocarbonyl)oxy)methyl]- 1,1a,2,8,8a,8b-hexahydro-8a-methoxy-5-methyi- Mitomycin C
50180	Cyclophosphamide 2H-1,3,2-Oxazaphosphorine,2-[bis(2- chloroethyl)amino]tetrahydro-2-oxide

APPENDIX A—SEQUENTIAL CAS REGISTRY NUMBER LIST OF CERCLA HAZARDOUS SUBSTANCES—Continued

CASRN	Hazardous Substance
50293	DDT 4,4' DDT Dichlorodiphenyl trichloroethane
50328	Benzo[a]pyrene 3,4-Benzopyrene
50555	Reserpine Yohimban-16-carboxylic acid,11,17-dimethoxy-18- [(3,4,5-trimethoxybenzoyl)oxy]-,methyl ester

CASRN	Hazardous Substance
51285	2,4-Dinitrophenol Phenol, 2,4-dinitro-
51434	1,2-Benzenediol,4-[1-hydroxy-2-(methylamino)ethyl]- Epinephrine
51796	Carbamic acid, ethyl ester Ethyl carbamate (Urethan)
52686	Trichlorfon
52857	Famphur Phosphorothioic acid, O,O-dimethyl-O-[p-[(dimethylamino)-sulfonyl]phenyl] ester
53703	Dibenz[a,h]anthracene 1,2:5,6-Dibenzanthracene Dibenzo[a,h]anthracene
53963	Acetamide, N-9H-fluoren-2-yl- 2-Acetylaminofluorene
54115	Nicotine and salts Pyridine, (S)-3-(1-methyl-2-pyrrolidinyl)-,and salts
55185	Ethanamine, N-ethyl-N-nitroso- N-Nitrosodiethylamine
55630	Nitroglycerine 1,2,3-Propanetriol, trinitrate-
55914	Diisopropyl fluorophosphate Phosphorofluoridic acid,bis(1-methylethyl) ester
56042	Methylthiouracil 4(1H)-Pyrimidinone, 2,3-dihydro-6-methyl-2-thioxo-
56235	Carbon tetrachloride Methane, tetrachloro-
56382	Parathion Phosphorothioic acid,O,O-diethyl O-(p-nitrophenyl)ester
56495	Benz[j]aceanthrylene, 1,2-dihydro-3-methyl- 3-Methylcholanthrene
56531	Diethylstilbestrol 4,4'-Stilbenediol, alpha,alpha'-diethyl-
56553	Benz[a]anthracene 1,2-Benzanthracene Benzo[a]anthracene
56724	Coumaphos
57125	Cyanides (soluble cyanide salts), not elsewherespecified
57147	1,1-Dimethylhydrazine Hydrazine, 1,1-dimethyl-
57249	Strychnidin-10-one, and salts Strychnine and salts

CASRN	Hazardous Substance
57749	Chlordane Chlordane, technical 4,7-Methanoindan, 1,2,4,5,6,7,8,8-octachloro-3a,4,7,7a-tetrahydro-
57976	1,2-Benzanthracene, 7,12-dimethyl- 7,12-Dimethylbenz[a]anthracene
58899	gamma - BHC Hexachlorocyclohexane (gamma isomer) Lindane
58902	Phenol, 2,3,4,6-tetrachloro- 2,3,4,6-Tetrachlorophenol
59507	4-Chloro-m-cresol p-Chloro-m-cresol Phenol, 4-chloro-3-methyl-
60004	Ethylenediamine tetraacetic acid (EDTA)
60117	Benzenamine, N,N-dimethyl-4-phenylazo- Dimethylaminoazobenzene
60297	Ethane, 1,1'-oxybis- Ethyl ether
60344	Hydrazine, methyl- Methyl hydrazine
60515	Dimethoate Phosphorodithioic acid,O,O-dimethyl S-[2(methylamino)-2-oxoethyl] ester
60571	Dieldrin 1,2,3,4,10,10-Hexachloro-6,7-epoxy-1,4,4a,5,6,7,8,8a-octahydro-endo,exo-1,4:5,8-dimethanonaphthalene
61825	Amitrole 1H-1,2,4-Triazol-3-amine
62384	Mercury, (acetato-O)phenyl- Phenylmercuric acetate
62442	Acetamide, N-(4-ethoxyphenyl)- Phenacetin
62500	Ethyl methanesulfonate Methanesulfonic acid, ethyl ester
62533	Aniline Benzenamine
62555	Ethanethioamide Thioacetamide
62566	Carbamide, thio- Thiourea
62737	Dichlorvos
62748	Acetic acid, fluoro-, sodium salt Fluoroacetic acid, sodium salt
62759	Dimethylnitrosamine N-Nitrosodimethylamine

APPENDIX A—SEQUENTIAL CAS REGISTRY NUMBER LIST OF CERCLA HAZARDOUS SUBSTANCES—Continued

CASRN	Hazardous Substance
63252	Carbaryl
64186	Formic acid Methanoic acid
64197	Acetic acid
65850	Benzoic acid
66751	Uracil, 5-[bis(2-chloroethyl)amino]- Uracil mustard
67561	Methanol Methyl alcohol
67641	Acetone 2-Propanone
67663	Chloroform Methane, trichloro-
67721	Ethane, 1,1,1,2,2,2-hexachloro- Hexachloroethane
70257	Guanidine, N-nitroso-N-methyl-N'-nitro- N-Methyl-N'-nitro-N-nitrosoguanidine
70304	Hexachlorophene 2,2'-Methylenebis(3,4,6-trichlorophenol)
71363	1-Butanol n-Butyl alcohol
71432	Benzene
71556	Methyl chloroform 1,1,1-Trichloroethane
72208	Endrin 1,2,3,4,10,10-Hexachloro-6,7-epoxy- 1,4,4a,5,6,7,8,8a-octahydro-endo,endo-1,4:5,8- dimethanonaphthalene
72435	Ethane, 1,1,1-trichloro-2,2-bis(p-methoxyphenyl)- Methoxychlor
72548	DDD 4,4' DDD Dichlorodiphenyl dichloroethane TDE
72559	DDE 4,4' DDE
72571	2,7-Naphthalenedisulfonic acid,3,3'-[(3,3'- dimethyl-(I,1'-biphenyl)-4,4'-diyl)-bis(azo)]bis(5- amino-4-hydroxy)-tetrasodium salt Trypan blue
74839	Methane, bromo- Methyl bromide
74873	Methane, chloro- Methyl chloride
74884	Methane, iodo- Methyl iodide

APPENDIX A—SEQUENTIAL CAS REGISTRY NUMBER LIST OF CERCLA HAZARDOUS SUBSTANCES—Continued

CASRN	Hazardous Substance
74895	Monomethylamine
74908	Hydrocyanic acid Hydrogen cyanide
74931	Methanethiol Methylmercaptan Thiomethanol
74953	Methane, dibromo- Methylene bromide
75003	Chloroethane
75014	Ethene, chloro- Vinyl chloride
75047	Monoethylamine
75058	Acetonitrile Ethanenitrile
75070	Acetaldehyde Ethanal
75092	Methane, dichloro- Methylene chloride
75150	Carbon bisulfide Carbon disulfide
75207	Calcium carbide
75218	Ethylene oxide Oxirane
75252	Bromoform Methane, tribromo-
75274	Dichlorobromomethane
75343	1,1-Dichloroethane Ethane, 1,1-dichloro- Ethylidene dichloride
75354	1,1-Dichloroethylene Ethene, 1,1-dichloro- Vinylidene chloride
75365	Acetyl chloride Ethanoyl chloride
75445	Carbonyl chloride Phosgene
75503	Trimethylamine
75558	2-Methylaziridine 1,2-Propylenimine
75569	Propylene oxide
75605	Cacodylic acid Hydroxydimethylarsine oxide

APPENDIX A—SEQUENTIAL CAS REGISTRY
NUMBER LIST OF CERCLA HAZARDOUS
SUBSTANCES—Continued

CASRN	Hazardous Substance
75649	tert-Butylamine
75694	Methane, trichlorofluoro- Trichloromonofluoromethane
75718	Dichlorodifluoromethane Methane, dichlorodifluoro-
75865	Acetone cyanohydrin 2-Methyllactonitrile Propanenitrile, 2-hydroxy-2-methyl-
75876	Acetaldehyde, trichloro- Chloral
75990	2,2-Dichloropropionic acid
76017	Ethane, pentachloro- Pentachloroethane
76448	Heptachlor 4,7-Methano-1H-indene,1,4,5,6,7,8,8-heptachloro- 3a,4,7,7a-tetrahydro-
77474	1,3-Cyclopentadiene, 1,2,3,4,5,5-hexachloro- Hexachlorocyclopentadiene
77781	Dimethyl sulfate Sulfuric acid, dimethyl ester
78002	Plumbane, tetraethyl- Tetraethyl lead
78591	Isophorone
78795	Isoprene
78819	iso-Butylamine
78831	Isobutyl alcohol 1-Propanol, 2-methyl-
78875	1,2-Dichloropropane Propylene dichloride
78886	2,3-Dichloropropene
78933	2-Butanone Methyl ethyl ketone
78999	1,1-Dichloropropane
79005	Ethane, 1,1,2-trichloro- 1,1,2-Trichloroethane
79016	Trichloroethene Trichloroethylene
79061	Acrylamide 2-Propenamide
79094	Propionic acid
79107	Acrylic acid 2-Propenoic acid

APPENDIX A—SEQUENTIAL CAS REGISTRY
NUMBER LIST OF CERCLA HAZARDOUS
SUBSTANCES—Continued

CASRN	Hazardous Substance
79196	Hydrazinecarbothioamide Thiosemicarbazide
79221	Carbonochloridic acid, methyl ester Methyl chlorocarbonate
79312	iso-Butyric acid
79345	Ethane, 1,1,2,2-tetrachloro- 1,1,2,2-Tetrachloroethane
79447	Carbamoyl chloride, dimethyl- Dimethylcarbamoyl chloride
79469	2-Nitropropane Propane, 2-nitro-
80159	alpha,alpha-Dimethylbenzylhydroperoxide Hydroperoxide, 1-methyl-1-phenylethyl-
80626	Methyl methacrylate 2-Propenoic acid, 2-methyl-, methyl ester
81072	1,2-Benzisothiazolin-3-one,1,1-dioxide, and salts Saccharin and salts
81812	3-(alpha-Acetonylbenzyl)-4-hydroxycoumarin and salts Warfarin
82688	Benzene, pentachloronitro- Pentachloronitrobenzene
83329	Acenaphthene
84662	1,2-Benzenedicarboxylic acid,diethyl ester Diethyl phthalate
84742	1,2-Benzenedicarboxylic acid,dibutyl ester n-Butyl phthalate Dibutyl phthalate Di-n-butyl phthalate
85007	Diquat
85018	Phenanthrene
85449	1,2-Benzenedicarboxylic acid anhydride Phthalic anhydride
85687	Butyl benzyl phthalate
86306	N-Nitrosodiphenylamine
86500	Guthion
86737	Fluorene
86884	alpha-Naphthylthiourea Thiourea, 1-naphthalenyl-
87650	2,6-Dichlorophenol Phenol, 2,6-dichloro-
87683	1,3-Butadiene, 1,1,2,3,4,4-hexachloro- Hexachlorobutadiene

APPENDIX 6F

CASRN	Hazardous Substance
87865	Pentachlorophenol Phenol, pentachloro-
88062	Phenol, 2,4,6-trichloro 2,4,6-Trichlorophenol
88722	o-Nitrotoluene
88755	o-Nitrophenol 2-Nitrophenol
88857	Dinoseb Phenol, 2,4-dinitro-6-(1-methylpropyl)-
91087	Benzene, 2,4-diisocyanatomethyl- Toluene diisocyanate
91203	Naphthalene
91225	Quinoline
91587	beta-Chloronaphthalene 2-Chloronaphthalene Naphthalene, 2-chloro-
91598	2-Naphthylamine beta-Naphthylamine
91805	Methapyrilene Pyridine, 2-[(2-(dimethylamino)ethyl)-2- thenylamino]-
91941	(1,1'-Biphenyl)-4,4'diamine,3,3'dichloro- 3,3'-Dichlorobenzidine
92875	Benzidine (1,1'-Biphenyl)-4,4'diamine
93721	Propionic acid, 2-(2,4,5-trichlorophenoxy)- Silvex 2,4,5-TP acid
93765	2,4,5-T 2,4,5-T acid 2,4,5-Trichlorophenoxyacetic acid
93798	2,4,5-T esters
94111	2,4-D Esters
94586	Benzene, 1,2-methylenedioxy-4-propyl- Dihydrosafrole
94597	Benzene, 1,2-methylenedioxy-4-allyl- Safrole
94757	2,4-D Acid 2,4-D, salts and esters 2,4-Dichlorophenoxyacetic acid, salts and esters
94791	2,4-D Esters
94804	2,4-D Esters
95476	Benzene, o-dimethyl- o-Xylene

CASRN	Hazardous Substance
95487	o-Cresol o-Cresylic acid
95501	Benzene, 1,2-dichloro- 1,2-Dichlorobenzene o-Dichlorobenzene
95578	2-Chlorophenol o-Chlorophenol Phenol, 2-chloro-
95807	Diaminotoluene Toluenediamine
95943	Benzene, 1,2,4,5-tetrachloro- 1,2,4,5-Tetrachlorobenzene
95954	Phenol, 2,4,5-trichloro- 2,4,5-Trichlorophenol
96128	1,2-Dibromo-3-chloropropane Propane, 1,2-dibromo-3-chloro-
96457	Ethylenethiourea 2-Imidazolidinethione
97632	Ethyl methacrylate 2-Propenoic acid, 2-methyl-, ethyl ester
98011	2-Furancarboxaldehyde Furfural
98077	Benzene, trichloromethyl- Benzotrichloride
98099	Benzenesulfonic acid chloride Benzenesulfonyl chloride
98828	Benzene, 1-methylethyl- Cumene
98862	Acetophenone Ethanone, 1-phenyl-
98873	Benzal chloride Benzene, dichloromethyl-
98884	Benzoyl chloride
98953	Benzene, nitro- Nitrobenzene
99081	m-Nitrotoluene
99354	Benzene, 1,3,5-trinitro- sym-Trinitrobenzene
99558	Benzenamine, 2-methyl-5-nitro- 5-Nitro-o-toluidine
99650	m-Dinitrobenzene
99990	p-Nitrotoluene
100016	Benzenamine, 4-nitro- p-Nitroaniline

APPENDIX A—SEQUENTIAL CAS REGISTRY NUMBER LIST OF CERCLA HAZARDOUS SUBSTANCES—Continued

CASRN	Hazardous Substance
100027	p-Nitrophenol 4-Nitrophenol Phenol, 4-nitro-
100254	p-Dinitrobenzene
100414	Ethylbenzene
100425	Styrene
100447	Benzene, chloromethyl- Benzyl chloride
100470	Benzonitrile
100754	N-Nitrosopiperidine Pyridine, hexahydro-N-nitroso-
101144	Benzenamine, 4,4'-methylenebis(2-chloro- 4,4'-Methylenebis(2-chloroaniline)
101553	Benzene, 1-bromo-4-phenoxy- 4-Bromophenyl phenyl ether
103855	N-Phenylthiourea Thiourea, phenyl-
105464	sec-Butyl acetate
105679	2,4-Dimethylphenol Phenol, 2,4-dimethyl-
106423	Benzene, p-dimethyl- p-Xylene
106445	p-Cresol p-Cresylic acid
106467	Benzene, 1,4-dichloro- 1,4-Dichlorobenzene p-Dichlorobenzene
106478	Benzenamine, 4-chloro- p-Chloroaniline
106514	p-Benzoquinone 1,4-Cyclohexadienedione
106898	1-Chloro-2,3-epoxypropane Epichlorohydrin Oxirane, 2-(chloromethyl)-
106934	Ethane, 1,2-dibromo- Ethylene dibromide
107028	Acrolein 2-Propenal
107051	Allyl chloride
107062	1,2-Dichloroethane Ethane, 1,2-dichloro- Ethylene dichloride
107108	1-Propanamine n-Propylamine

APPENDIX A—SEQUENTIAL CAS REGISTRY NUMBER LIST OF CERCLA HAZARDOUS SUBSTANCES—Continued

CASRN	Hazardous Substance
107120	Ethyl cyanide Propanenitrile
107131	Acrylonitrile 2-Propenenitrile
107153	Ethylenediamine
107186	Allyl alcohol 2-Propen-1-ol
107197	Propargyl alcohol 2-Propyn-1-ol
107200	Acetaldehyde, chloro- Chloroacetaldehyde
107302	Chloromethyl methyl ether Methane, chloromethoxy-
107493	Pyrophosphoric acid, tetraethyl ester Tetraethyl pyrophosphate
107926	Butyric acid
108054	Vinyl acetate
108101	Methyl isobutyl ketone 4-Methyl-2-pentanone
108247	Acetic anhydride
108316	2,5-Furandione Maleic anhydride
108383	Benzene, m-dimethyl- m-Xylene
108394	m-Cresol m-Cresylic acid
108463	1,3-Benzenediol Resorcinol
108601	Bis(2-chloroisopropyl) ether Propane, 2,2'-oxybis(2-chloro-
108883	Benzene, methyl- Toluene
108907	Benzene, chloro- Chlorobenzene
108941	Cyclohexanone
108952	Benzene, hydroxy- Phenol
108985	Benzenethiol Thiophenol
109068	2-Picoline Pyridine, 2-methyl-

APPENDIX A—SEQUENTIAL CAS REGISTRY NUMBER LIST OF CERCLA HAZARDOUS SUBSTANCES—Continued

CASRN	Hazardous Substance
109739	Butylamine
109773	Malononitrile Propanedinitrile
109897	Diethylamine
109999	Furan, tetrahydro- Tetrahydrofuran
110009	Furan Furfuran
110167	Maleic acid
110178	Fumaric acid
110190	iso-Butyl acetate
110758	2-Chloroethyl vinyl ether Ethene, 2-chloroethoxy-
110827	Benzene, hexahydro- Cyclohexane
110861	Pyridine
111444	Bis (2-chloroethyl) ether Dichloroethyl ether Ethane, 1,1'-oxybis(2-chloro-
111546	1,2-Ethanediylbiscarbamodithioic acid Ethylenebis(dithiocarbamic acid)
111911	Bis(2-chloroethoxy) methane Ethane, 1,1'-[methylenebis(oxy)]bis(2-chloro-
115026	Azaserine L-Serine, diazoacetate (ester)
115297	Endosulfan 5-Norbornene-2,3-dimethanol,1,4,5,6,7,7- hexachloro,cyclic sulfite
115322	Kelthane
116063	Aldicarb Propanal, 2-methyl-2-(methylthio)-,O- [(methylamino)carbonyl]oxime
117806	Dichlone
117817	1,2-Benzenedicarboxylic acid,[bis(2-ethylhexyl)] ester Bis(2-ethylhexyl)phthalate
117840	1,2-Benzenedicarboxylic acid,di-n-octyl ester Di-n-octyl phthalate
118741	Benzene, hexachloro- Hexachlorobenzene
119904	(1'-Biphenyl)-4,4'diamine,3,3'dimethoxy- 3,3'-Dimethoxybenzidine
119937	(1,1'-Biphenyl)-4,4-diamine,3,3'-dimethyl- 3,3'-Dimethylbenzidine

APPENDIX A—SEQUENTIAL CAS REGISTRY NUMBER LIST OF CERCLA HAZARDOUS SUBSTANCES—Continued

CASRN	Hazardous Substance
120127	Anthracene
120581	Benzene, 1,2-methylenedioxy-4-propenyl- Isosafrole
120821	1,2,4-Trichlorobenzene
120832	2,4-Dichlorophenol Phenol, 2,4-dichloro-
121142	Benzene, 1-methyl-2,4-dinitro- 2,4-Dinitrotoluene
121211	Pyrethrins
121299	Pyrethrins
121448	Triethylamine
121755	Malathion
122098	alpha,alpha-Dimethylphenethylamine Ethanamine, 1,1-dimethyl-2-phenyl-
122667	1,2-Diphenylhydrazine Hydrazine, 1,2-diphenyl-
123331	1,2-Dihydro-3,6-pyridazinedione Maleic hydrazide
123626	Propionic anhydride
123637	Paraldehyde 1,3,5-Trioxane, 2,4,6-trimethyl-
123739	2-Butenal Crotonaldehyde
123864	Butyl acetate
123911	1,4-Diethylene dioxide 1,4-Dioxane
123922	iso-Amyl acetate
124049	Adipic acid
124403	Dimethylamine Methanamine, N-methyl-
124414	Sodium methylate
124481	Chlorodibromomethane
126727	1-Propanol, 2,3-dibromo-, phosphate (3:1) Tris(2,3-dibromopropyl) phosphate
126987	Methacrylonitrile 2-Propenenitrile, 2-methyl-
127184	Ethane, 1,1,2,2-tetrachloro- Tetrachloroethylene

CASRN	Hazardous Substance
127822	Zinc phenolsulfonate
129000	Pyrene
130154	1,4-Naphthalenedione 1,4-Naphthoquinone
131113	1,2-Benzenedicarboxylic acid,dimethyl ester Dimethyl phthalate
131748	Ammonium picrate Phenol, 2,4,6-trinitro-, ammonium salt
131895	4,6-Dinitro-o-cyclohexylphenol Phenol, 2-cyclohexyl-4,6-dinitro-
133062	Captan
134327	1-Naphthylamine alpha-Naphthylamine
137268	Bis(dimethylthiocarbamoyl) disulfide Thiram
140885	Ethyl acrylate 2-Propenoic acid, ethyl ester
141786	Acetic acid, ethyl ester Ethyl acetate
142289	1,3-Dichloropropane
142712	Cupric acetate
142847	Dipropylamine 1-Propanamine, N-propyl-
143339	Sodium cyanide
143500	Decachlorooctahydro-1,3,4-metheno-2H- cyclobuta[c,d]-pentalen-2-one Kepone
145733	Endothall 7-Oxabicyclo[2,2,1]heptane-2,3-dicarboxylic acid
148823	Alanine, 3-[p-bis(2-chloroethyl)amino]phenyl-,L- Melphalan
151508	Potassium cyanide
151564	Aziridine Ethylenimine
152169	Diphosphoramide, octamethyl- Octamethylpyrophosphoramide
156605	1,2-trans-Dichloroethylene Ethene, trans-1,2-dichloro-
189559	1,2:7,8-Dibenzopyrene Dibenz[a,i]pyrene
191242	Benzo[ghi]perylene
193395	Indeno(1,2,3-cd)pyrene 1,10-(1,2-Phenylene)pyrene

CASRN	Hazardous Substance
205992	Benzo[b]fluoranthene
206440	Benzo[j,k]fluorene Fluoranthene
207089	Benzo[k]fluoranthene
208968	Acenaphthylene
218019	1,2-Benzphenanthrene Chrysene
225514	Benz[c]acridine 3,4-Benzacridine
297972	O,O-Diethyl O-pyrazinyl phosphorothioate Phosphorothioic acid, O,O-diethyl, O-pyrazinyl ester
298000	O,O-Dimethyl O-p-nitrophenyl phosphorothioate Methyl parathion
298022	Phorate Phosphorodithioic acid, O,O-diethyl S- (ethylthio),methyl ester
298044	O,O-Diethyl S-[2-(ethylthio)ethyl] phosphorodithioate Disulfoton
300765	Naled
301042	Acetic acid, lead salt Lead acetate
302012	Diamine Hydrazine
303344	Lasiocarpine
305033	Butanoic acid, 4-[bis(2-chloroethyl)amino] benzene- Chlorambucil
309002	Aldrin 1,2,3,4,10,10-Hexachloro-1,4,4a,5,8,8a- hexahydro-1,4:5,8-endo,exo- dimethanonaphthalene
311455	Diethyl-p-nitrophenyl phosphate Phosphoric acid,diethyl,p-nitrophenyl ester

APPENDIX 6F

CASRN	Hazardous Substance
315184	Mexacarbate
319846	alpha - BHC
319857	beta - BHC
319868	delta - BHC
329715	2,5-Dinitrophenol
330541	Diuron
333415	Diazinon
353504	Carbon oxyfluoride Carbonyl fluoride
357573	Brucine Strychnidin-10-one, 2,3-dimethoxy-
460195	Cyanogen
465736	Hexachlorohexahydro-endo,endo- dimethanonaphthalene 1,2,3,4,10,10-Hexachloro-1,4,4a,5,8,8a- hexahydro-1,4:5,8-endo,endo- dimethanonaphthalene
492808	Auramine Benzenamine, 4,4'-carbonimidoylbis (N,N- dimethyl-
494031	Chlornaphazine 2-Naphthylamine, N,N-bis(2-chloroethyl)-
496720	Diaminotoluene Toluenediamine
504245	4-Aminopyridine 4-Pyridinamine
504609	1-Methylbutadiene 1,3-Pentadiene
506616	Potassium silver cyanide
506649	Silver cyanide
506683	Bromine cyanide Cyanogen bromide
506774	Chlorine cyanide Cyanogen chloride
506876	Ammonium carbonate
506967	Acetyl bromide
509148	Methane, tetranitro- Tetranitromethane
510156	Benzeneacetic acid, 4-chloro-alpha-(4- chlorophenyl)-alpha-hydroxy-,ethyl ester Ethyl 4,4'-dichlorobenzilate

APPENDIX A—SEQUENTIAL CAS REGISTRY NUMBER LIST OF CERCLA HAZARDOUS SUBSTANCES—Continued

CASRN	Hazardous Substance
513495	sec-Butylamine
528290	o-Dinitrobenzene
534521	4,6-Dinitro-o-cresol and salts Phenol,2,4-dinitro-6-methyl-, and salts
540738	1,2-Dimethylhydrazine Hydrazine, 1,2-dimethyl-
540885	tert-Butyl acetate
541093	Uranyl acetate
541537	2,4-Dithiobiuret Thioimidodicarbonic diamide
541731	Benzene, 1,3-dichloro- 1,3-Dichlorobenzene m-Dichlorobenzene
542621	Barium cyanide
542756	1,3-Dichloropropene Propene, 1,3-dichloro-
542767	3-Chloropropionitrile Propanenitrile, 3-chloro-
542881	Bis(chloromethyl) ether Methane, oxybis(chloro-
543908	Cadmium acetate
544183	Cobaltous formate
544923	Copper cyanide
554847	m-Nitrophenol
557197	Nickel cyanide Nickel(II) cyanide
557211	Zinc cyanide
557346	Zinc acetate
557415	Zinc formate
563122	Ethion
563688	Acetic acid, thallium(I) salt Thallium(I) acetate
573568	2,6-Dinitrophenol
584849	Benzene, 2,4-diisocyanatomethyl- Toluene diisocyanate
591082	Acetamide, N-(aminothioxomethyl)- 1-Acetyl-2-thiourea

APPENDIX A—SEQUENTIAL CAS REGISTRY
NUMBER LIST OF CERCLA HAZARDOUS
SUBSTANCES—Continued

CASRN	Hazardous Substance
592018	Calcium cyanide
592041	Mercuric cyanide
592858	Mercuric thiocyanate
592870	Lead thiocyanate
594423	Methanesulfenyl chloride, trichloro- Trichloromethanesulfenyl chloride
596312	Bromoacetone 2-Propanone, 1-bromo-
606202	Benzene, 1-methyl-2,6-dinitro- 2,6-Dinitrotoluene
608935	Benzene, pentachloro- Pentachlorobenzene
609198	3,4,5-Trichlorophenol
610399	3,4-Dinitrotoluene
615532	Carbamic acid, methylnitroso-,ethyl ester N-Nitroso-N-methylurethane
621647	Di-n-propylnitrosamine N-Nitrosodi-n-propylamine
624839	Isocyanic acid, methyl ester Methyl isocyanate
625161	tert-Amyl acetate
626380	sec-Amyl acetate
628637	Amyl acetate
628864	Fulminic acid, mercury(II)salt Mercury fulminate
630104	Carbamimidoselenoic acid Selenourea
630206	Ethane, 1,1,1,2-tetrachloro- 1,1,1,2-Tetrachloroethane
631618	Ammonium acetate
636215	Benzenamine, 2-methyl-, hydrochloride o-Toluidine hydrochloride
640197	Acetamide, 2-fluoro- Fluoroacetamide
684935	Carbamide, N-methyl-N-nitroso- N-Nitroso-N-methylurea
692422	Arsine, diethyl- Diethylarsine
696286	Dichlorophenylarsine Phenyl dichloroarsine
757584	Hexaethyl tetraphosphate Tetraphosphoric acid, hexaethyl ester

APPENDIX A—SEQUENTIAL CAS REGISTRY
NUMBER LIST OF CERCLA HAZARDOUS
SUBSTANCES—Continued

CASRN	Hazardous Substance
759739	Carbamide, N-ethyl-N-nitroso- N-Nitroso-N-ethylurea
764410	2-Butene, 1,4-dichloro- 1,4-Dichloro-2-butene
765344	Glycidylaldehyde 1-Propanal, 2,3-epoxy-
815827	Cupric tartrate
823405	Diaminotoluene Toluenediamine
924163	1-Butanamine, N-butyl-N-nitroso- N-Nitrosodi-n-butylamine
930552	N-Nitrosopyrrolidine Pyrrole, tetrahydro-N-nitroso-
933755	2,3,6-Trichlorophenol
933788	2,3,5-Trichlorophenol
959988	alpha - Endosulfan
1024573	Heptachlor epoxide
1031078	Endosulfan sulfate
1066304	Chromic acetate
1066337	Ammonium bicarbonate
1072351	Lead stearate
1111780	Ammonium carbamate
1116547	Ethanol, 2,2'-(nitrosoimino)bis- N-Nitrosodiethanolamine
1120714	1,2-Oxathiolane, 2,2-dioxide 1,3-Propane sultone
1185575	Ferric ammonium citrate
1194656	Dichlobenil
1300716	Xylenol
1303282	Arsenic(V) oxide Arsenic pentoxide
1303328	Arsenic disulfide
1303339	Arsenic trisulfide
1309644	Antimony trioxide
1310583	Potassium hydroxide
1310732	Sodium hydroxide
1314325	Thallic oxide Thallium(III) oxide

APPENDIX 6F

CASRN	Hazardous Substance
1314621	Vanadium(V) oxide Vanadium pentoxide
1314803	Phosphorus pentasulfide Phosphorus sulfide Sulfur phosphide
1314847	Zinc phosphide
1314870	Lead sulfide
1314961	Strontium sulfide
1319728	2,4,5-T amines
1319773	Cresol(s) Cresylic acid
1320189	2,4-D Esters
1321126	Nitrotoluene
1327522	Arsenic acid
1327533	Arsenic(III) oxide Arsenic trioxide
1330207	Benzene, dimethyl- Xylene
1332076	Zinc borate
1332214	Asbestos
1333831	Sodium bifluoride
1335326	Lead subacetate
1336216	Ammonium hydroxide
1336363	POLYCHLORINATED BIPHENYLS (PCBs) Aroclors
1338234	2-Butanone peroxide Methyl ethyl ketone peroxide
1338245	Naphthenic acid
1341497	Ammonium bifluoride
1464535	2,2'-Bioxirane 1,2:3,4-Diepoxybutane
1563662	Carbofuran
1615801	N,N'-Diethylhydrazine Hydrazine, 1,2-diethyl-
1746016	2,3,7,8-Tetrachlorodibenzo-p-dioxin(TCDD)
1762954	Ammonium thiocyanate
1863634	Ammonium benzoate
1888717	Hexachloropropene 1-Propene, 1,1,2,3,3,3-hexachloro-

CASRN	Hazardous Substance
1918009	Dicamba
1928387	2,4-D Esters
1928478	2,4,5-T esters
1928616	2,4-D Esters
1929733	2,4-D Esters
2008460	2,4,5-T amines
2032657	Mercaptodimethur
2303164	Diallate S-(2,3-Dichloroallyl) diisopropylthiocarbamate
2312358	Propargite
2545597	2,4,5-T esters
2763964	5-(Aminomethyl)-3-isoxazolol 3(2H)-Isoxazolone, 5-(aminomethyl)-
2764729	Diquat
2921882	Chlorpyrifos
2944674	Ferric ammonium oxalate
2971382	2,4-D Esters
3012655	Ammonium citrate, dibasic
3164292	Ammonium tartrate
3165933	Benzenamine, 4-chloro-2-methyl-,hydrochloride 4-Chloro-o-toluidine, hydrochloride
3251238	Cupric nitrate
3288582	O,O-Diethyl S-methyl dithiophosphate Phosphorodithioic acid, O,O-diethyl S-methylester
3486359	Zinc carbonate
3689245	Dithiopyrophosphoric acid,tetraethyl ester Tetraethyldithiopyrophosphate
3813147	2,4,5-T amines
4170303	2-Butenal Crotonaldehyde
4549400	Ethenamine, N-methyl-N-nitroso- N-Nitrosomethylvinylamine
5344821	1-(o-Chlorophenyl)thiourea Thiourea, (2-chlorophenyl)-

APPENDIX A—SEQUENTIAL CAS REGISTRY NUMBER LIST OF CERCLA HAZARDOUS SUBSTANCES—Continued

CASRN	Hazardous Substance
5893663	Cupric oxalate
5972736	Ammonium oxalate
6009707	Ammonium oxalate
6369966	2,4,5-T amines
6369977	2,4,5-T amines
6533739	Carbonic acid, dithallium (I) salt Thallium(I) carbonate
7005723	4-Chlorophenyl phenyl ether
7421934	Endrin aldehyde
7428480	Lead stearate
7439921	Lead
7439976	Mercury
7440020	Nickel
7440224	Silver
7440235	Sodium
7440280	Thallium
7440360	Antimony
7440382	Arsenic
7440417	Beryllium Beryllium dust
7440439	Cadmium
7440473	Chromium
7440506	Copper
7440666	Zinc
7446084	Selenium dioxide Selenium oxide
7446142	Lead sulfate
7446186	Sulfuric acid, thallium(I) salt Thallium(I) sulfate
7446277	Lead phosphate Phosphoric acid, lead salt
7447394	Cupric chloride
7488564	Selenium disulfide Sulfur selenide

APPENDIX A—SEQUENTIAL CAS REGISTRY NUMBER LIST OF CERCLA HAZARDOUS SUBSTANCES—Continued

CASRN	Hazardous Substance
7558794	Sodium phosphate, dibasic
7601549	Sodium phosphate, tribasic
7631892	Sodium arsenate
7631905	Sodium bisulfite
7632000	Sodium nitrite
7645252	Lead arsenate
7646857	Zinc chloride
7647010	Hydrochloric acid
7647189	Antimony pentachloride
7664382	Phosphoric acid
7664393	Hydrofluoric acid Hydrogen fluoride
7664417	Ammonia
7664939	Sulfuric acid
7681494	Sodium fluoride
7681529	Sodium hypochlorite
7697372	Nitric acid
7699458	Zinc bromide
7705080	Ferric chloride
7718549	Nickel chloride
7719122	Phosphorus trichloride
7720787	Ferrous sulfate
7722647	Potassium permanganate
7723140	Phosphorus
7733020	Zinc sulfate

APPENDIX 6F

CASRN	Hazardous Substance
7738945	Chromic acid
7758294	Sodium phosphate, tribasic
7758943	Ferrous chloride
7758954	Lead chloride
7758987	Cupric sulfate
7761888	Silver nitrate
7773060	Ammonium sulfamate
7775113	Sodium chromate
7778394	Arsenic acid
7778441	Calcium arsenate
7778509	Potassium bichromate
7778543	Calcium hypochlorite
7779864	Zinc hydrosulfite
7779886	Zinc nitrate
7782414	Fluorine
7782492	Selenium
7782505	Chlorine
7782630	Ferrous sulfate
7782823	Sodium selenite
7782867	Mercurous nitrate
7783008	Selenious acid
7783064	Hydrogen sulfide Hydrosulfuric acid Sulfur hydride
7783188	Ammonium thiosulfate

APPENDIX A—SEQUENTIAL CAS REGISTRY NUMBER LIST OF CERCLA HAZARDOUS SUBSTANCES—Continued

CASRN	Hazardous Substance
7783359	Mercuric sulfate
7783462	Lead fluoride
7783495	Zinc fluoride
7783508	Ferric fluoride
7783564	Antimony trifluoride
7784341	Arsenic trichloride
7784409	Lead arsenate
7784410	Potassium arsenate
7784465	Sodium arsenite
7785844	Sodium phosphate, tribasic
7786347	Mevinphos
7786814	Nickel sulfate
7787475	Beryllium chloride
7787497	Beryllium fluoride
7787555	Beryllium nitrate
7788989	Ammonium chromate
7789006	Potassium chromate
7789062	Strontium chromate
7789095	Ammonium bichromate
7789426	Cadmium bromide
7789437	Cobaltous bromide
7789619	Antimony tribromide
7790945	Chlorosulfonic acid
7791120	Thallium(I) chloride
7803512	Hydrogen phosphide Phosphine
7803556	Ammonium vanadate Vanadic acid, ammonium salt
8001352	Camphene, octachloro- Toxaphene
8001589	Creosote
8003198	Dichloropropane - Dichloropropene (mixture)
8003347	Pyrethrins
8014957	Sulfuric acid
9004664	Ferric dextran Iron dextran

APPENDIX A—SEQUENTIAL CAS REGISTRY
NUMBER LIST OF CERCLA HAZARDOUS
SUBSTANCES—Continued

CASRN	Hazardous Substance
10022705	Sodium hypochlorite
10025873	Phosphorus oxychloride
10025919	Antimony trichloride
10026116	Zirconium tetrachloride
10028225	Ferric sulfate
10031591	Sulfuric acid, thallium(I) salt Thallium(I) sulfate
10039324	Sodium phosphate, dibasic
10043013	Aluminum sulfate
10045893	Ferrous ammonium sulfate
10045940	Mercuric nitrate
10049055	Chromous chloride
10099748	Lead nitrate
10101538	Chromic sulfate
10101630	Lead iodide
10101890	Sodium phosphate, tribasic
10102064	Uranyl nitrate
10102188	Sodium selenite
10102439	Nitric oxide Nitrogen(II) oxide
10102440	Nitrogen dioxide Nitrogen(IV) oxide
10102451	Thallium(I) nitrate
10102484	Lead arsenate
10108642	Cadmium chloride
10124502	Potassium arsenite
10124568	Sodium phosphate, tribasic
10140655	Sodium phosphate, dibasic
10192300	Ammonium bisulfite
10196040	Ammonium sulfite
10361894	Sodium phosphate, tribasic
10380297	Cupric sulfate ammoniated
10415755	Mercurous nitrate
10421484	Ferric nitrate
10544726	Nitrogen dioxide Nitrogen(IV) oxide

APPENDIX A—SEQUENTIAL CAS REGISTRY
NUMBER LIST OF CERCLA HAZARDOUS
SUBSTANCES—Continued

CASRN	Hazardous Substance
10588019	Sodium bichromate
11096825	Aroclor 1260 Polychlorinated Biphenyls (PCBs)
11097691	Aroclor 1254 Polychlorinated Biphenyls (PCBs)
11104282	Aroclor 1221 Polychlorinated Biphenyls (PCBs)
11115745	Chromic acid
11141165	Aroclor 1232 Polychlorinated Biphenyls (PCBs)
12002038	Cupric acetoarsenite
12039520	Thallium(I) selenide
12054487	Nickel hydroxide
12125018	Ammonium fluoride
12125029	Ammonium chloride
12135761	Ammonium sulfide
12672296	Aroclor 1248 Polychlorinated Biphenyls (PCBs)
12674112	Aroclor 1016 Polychlorinated Biphenyls (PCBs)
12771083	Sulfur monochloride
13463393	Nickel carbonyl Nickel tetracarbonyl
13560991	2,4,5-T salts
13597994	Beryllium nitrate
13746899	Zirconium nitrate
13765190	Calcium chromate Chromic acid, calcium salt

APPENDIX 6F

CASRN	Hazardous Substance
13814965	Lead fluoborate
13826630	Ammonium fluoborate
13952846	sec-Butylamine
14017415	Cobaltous sulfamate
14216752	Nickel nitrate
14258492	Ammonium oxalate
14307358	Lithium chromate
14307438	Ammonium tartrate
14639975	Zinc ammonium chloride
14639986	Zinc ammonium chloride
14644612	Zirconium sulfate
15699180	Nickel ammonium sulfate
15739807	Lead sulfate
15950660	2,3,4-Trichlorophenol
16721805	Sodium hydrosulfide
18752775	Acetimidic acid, N-[(methylcarbamoyl)oxy]thio-,methyl ester Methomyl
16871719	Zinc silicofluoride
16919190	Ammonium silicofluoride
16923958	Zirconium potassium fluoride
18883664	D-Glucopyranose, 2-deoxy-2-(3-methyl-3-nitrosoureido)- Streptozotocin
20816120	Osmium oxide Osmium tetroxide
20830813	Daunomycin 5,12-Naphthacenedione. (8S-cis)-8-acetyl-10-[3-amino-2,3,6-trideoxy-alpha-L-lyxo-hexopyranosyl)oxy]-7,8,9,10-tetrahydro-6,8,11-trihydroxy-1-methoxy-
20859738	Aluminum phosphide
23950585	3,5-Dichloro-N-(1,1-dimethyl-2-propynyl)benzamide Pronamide

CASRN	Hazardous Substance
25154545	Dinitrobenzene (mixed)
25154556	Nitrophenol (mixed)
25155300	Sodium dodecylbenzene sulfonate
25167822	Trichlorophenol
25168154	2,4,5-T esters
25168267	2,4-D Esters
25321146	Dinitrotoluene
25321226	Dichlorobenzene (mixed)
25376458	Diaminotoluene Toluenediamine
25550587	Dinitrophenol
26264062	Calcium dodecylbenzene sulfonate
26471625	Benzene, 2,4-diisocyanatomethyl- Toluene diisocyanate
26628228	Sodium azide
26638197	Dichloropropane
26952238	Dichloropropene
27176870	Dodecylbenzenesulfonic acid
27323417	Triethanolamine dodecylbenzene sulfonate
27774136	Vanadyl sulfate
28300745	Antimony potassium tartrate
30525894	Paraformaldehyde
32534955	2,4,5-TP acid esters
33213659	beta - Endosulfan
36478769	Uranyl nitrate
37211055	Nickel chloride
39196184	3,3-Dimethyl-1-(methylthio)-2-butanone,O-[(methylamino)carbonyl] oxime Thiofanox
42504461	Isopropanolamine dodecylbenzene sulfonate
52628258	Zinc ammonium chloride
52652592	Lead stearate
52740166	Calcium arsenite
53467111	2,4-D Esters
53469219	Aroclor 1242 Polychlorinated Biphenyls (PCBs)

APPENDIX A—SEQUENTIAL CAS REGISTRY
NUMBER LIST OF CERCLA HAZARDOUS
SUBSTANCES—Continued

CASRN	Hazardous Substance
55488874	Ferric ammonium oxalate
56189094	Lead stearate
61792072	2,4,5-T esters

§ 302.5 Determination of reportable quantities.

(a) *Listed hazardous substances.* The quantity listed in the column "Final RQ" for each substance in Table 302.4 is the reportable quantity for that substance.

(b) *Unlisted hazardous substances.* Unlisted hazardous substances designated by 40 CFR 302.4(b), which substances are wastes prior to their initial release into the environment, have the reportable quantity of 100 pounds, except for those unlisted hazardous wastes exhibiting the characteristic of extraction procedure (EP) toxicity identified in 40 CFR 261.24. Unlisted hazardous wastes which exhibit EP toxicity have the reportable quantities listed in Table 302.4 for the contaminant on which the characteristic of EP toxicity is based. The reportable quantity applies to the waste itself, not merely to the toxic contaminant. If an unlisted hazardous waste exhibits EP toxicity on the basis of more than one contaminant, the reportable quantity for that waste shall be the lowest of the reportable quantities listed in Table 302.4 for those contaminants. If an unlisted hazardous waste exhibits the characteristic of EP toxicity and one or more of the other characteristics referenced in 40 CFR 302.4(b), the reportable quantity for that waste shall be the lowest of the applicable reportable quantities.

§ 302.6 Notification requirements.

(a) Any person in charge of a vessel or an offshore or an onshore facility shall, as soon as he has knowledge of any release (other than a federally permitted release or application of a pesticide) of a hazardous substance from such vessel or facility in a quan-

tity equal to or exceeding the reportable quantity determined by this part in any 24-hour period, immediately notify the National Response Center ((800) 424-8802; in Washington, D.C. (202) 426-2675).

(b) Releases of mixtures and solutions are subject to these notification requirements only where a component hazardous substance of the mixture or solution is released in a quantity equal to or greater than its reportable quantity.

(c) Notification of the release of an RQ of solid particles of antimony, arsenic, beryllium, cadmium, chromium, copper, lead, nickel, selenium, silver, thallium, or zinc is not required if the mean diameter of the particles released is larger than 100 micrometers (0.004 inches).

(Approved by the Office of Management and Budget under the control number 2115-0137)

§ 302.7 Penalties.

(a) Any person—

(1) In charge of a vessel from which a hazardous substance is released, other than a federally permitted release, into or upon the navigable waters of the United States, adjoining shorelines, or into or upon the waters of the contiguous zone,

(2) In charge of a vessel from which a hazardous substance is released, other than a federally permitted release, which may affect natural resources belonging to, appertaining to, or under the exclusive management authority of the United States (including resources under the Fishery Conservation and Management Act of 1976), and who is otherwise subject to the jurisdiction of the United States at the time of the release, or

(3) In charge of a facility from which a hazardous substance is released, other than a federally permitted release, in a quantity equal to or greater than that reportable quantity determined under this part who fails to notify immediately the National Response Center as soon as he has knowledge of such release shall be subject to all of the sanctions, including criminal penalties, set forth in sec-

tion 103 of the Act with respect to such failure to notify.

(b) Notification received pursuant to this section or information obtained by the exploitation of such notification shall not be used against any such person in any criminal case, except a prosecution for perjury or for giving a false statement.

(c) This section shall not apply to the application of a pesticide product registered under the Federal Insecticide, Fungicide, and Rodenticide Act or to the handling and storage of such a pesticide product by an agricultural producer.

Part II: EPA's Adjustments to Reportable Quantities
(51 Fed. Reg. 34541, September 29, 1986)

PART 302—DESIGNATION, REPORTABLE QUANTITIES, AND NOTIFICATION

1. The authority citation for Part 302 continues to read as follows:

Authority: Sec. 102 of the Comprehensive Environmental Response, Compensation, and Liability Act of 1980, 42 U.S.C. 9602; secs. 311 and 501(a) of the Federal Water Pollution Control Act, 33 U.S.C. 1321 and 1361.

2. Section 302.4 is amended by revising Table 302.4 to read as follows:

§ 302.4   Designation of hazardous substances.

. . . . . .

Table 302.4—List of Hazardous Substances and Reportable Quantities

Note—The numbers under the column headed "CASRN" are the Chemical Abstracts Service Registry Numbers for each hazardous substance. Other names by which each hazardous substance is identified in other statutes and their implementing regulations are provided in the "Regulatory Synonyms"

column. The "Statutory RQ" column lists the RQs for hazardous substances established by section 102 of CERCLA. The "Statutory Code" column indicates the statutory source for designating each substance as a CERCLA hazardous substance: "1" indicates that the statutory source is section 311(b)(4) of the Clean Water Act, "2" indicates that the source is section 307(a) of the Clean Water Act, "3" indicates that the source is section 112 of the Clean Air Act, and "4" indicates that the source is RCRA section 3001. The "RCRA Waste Number" column provides the waste identification numbers assigned to various substances by RCRA regulations. The column headed "Category" lists the code letters "X", "A", "B", "C", and "D", which are associated with reportable quantities of 1, 10, 100, 1000, and 5000 pounds, respectively. The "Pounds (kg)" column provides the reportable quantity for each hazardous substance in pounds and kilograms.

TABLE 302.4 - LIST OF HAZARDOUS SUBSTANCES AND REPORTABLE QUANTITIES

Hazardous Substance	CASRN	Regulatory Synonyms	Statutory RQ	Code †	RCRA Waste Number	Category	Pounds(Kg)
Acenaphthene	83329		1*	2		B	100 (45.4)
Acenaphthylene	208968		1*	2		D	5000 (2270)
Acetic acid, thallium(I) salt	563688	Thallium(I) acetate	1*	4	U214	B	100 (45.4)
2-Amino-1-methyl benzene	95534	o-Toluidine	1*	4	U328	X	1 # (0.454)
4-Amino-1-methyl benzene	106490	p-Toluidine	1*	4	U353	X	1 # (0.454)
Ammonia	7664417		100	1		B	100 (45.4)
Ammonium bifluoride	1341497		5000	1		B	100 (45.4)
Anthracene	120127		1*	2		D	5000 (2270)
Antimony ††	7440360		1*	2		D	5000 (2270)
Benzene, hydroxy-	108952	Phenol	1000	1,2,4	U188	C	1000 (454)
Benzene, pentachloro-	608935	Pentachlorobenzene	1*	4	U183	A	10 (4.54)
Benzene, 1,3,5-trinitro-	99354	sym-Trinitrobenzene	1*	4	U234	A	10 (4.54)
Benzo[j,k]fluorene	206440	Fluoranthene	1*	2,4	U120	B	100 (45.4)
Benzo[ghi]perylene	191242		1*	2		D	5000 (2270)
p-Benzoquinone	106514	1,4-Cyclohexadenedione	1*	4	U197	A	10 (4.54)
delta - BHC	319868		1*	2		X	1 (0.454)
Captan	133062		10	1		A	10 # (4.54)
Carbamimidoselenoic acid	630104	Selenourea	1*	4	P103	C	1000 (454)
Carbon bisulfide	75150	Carbon disulfide	5000	1,4	P022	B	100 (45.4)
Carbon disulfide	75150	Carbon bisulfide	5000	1,4	P022	B	100 (45.4)
Carbonic acid, dithallium(I) salt	6533739	Thallium(I) carbonate	1*	4	U215	B	100 (45.4)
Chloroethane	75003		1*	2		B	100 (45.4)
Chromic acetate	1066304		1000	1		C	1000 (454)
Chromic sulfate	10101538		1000	1		C	1000 (454)
Chromous chloride	10049055		1000	1		C	1000 (454)
Copper ††	7440508		1*	2		D	5000 (2270)
Cresol(s)	1319773	Cresylic acid	1000	1,4	U052	C	1000 # (454)
m-	108394						
o-	95487						

TABLE 302.4 - LIST OF HAZARDOUS SUBSTANCES AND REPORTABLE QUANTITIES—Continued

Hazardous Substance	CASRN	Regulatory Synonyms	Statutory RQ	Code †	RCRA Waste Number	Final RQ Category	Pounds(Kg)
p-	106445						
Cresylic acid	1319773	Cresol(s)	1000	1,4	U052	C	1000 # (454)
m-	108394						
o-	95487						
p-	106445						
Cupric chloride	7447394		10	1		A	10 (4.54)
Cupric sulfate	7758987		10	1		A	10 (4.54)
Cupric tartrate	815827		100	1		B	100 (45.4)
1,4-Cyclohexadienedione	106514	p-Benzoquinone	1*	4	U197	A	10 (4.54)
Dichloropropane - Dichloropropene (mixture)	8003198		5000	1		B	100 # (45.4)
Dichloropropene(s)	26952238		5000	1		B	100 (45.4)
2,3-Dichloropropene (isomer)	78886						
1,3-Dichloropropene	542756	Propene, 1,3-dichloro-	5000	1,2,4	U084	B	100 # (45.4)
Diethylamine	109897		1000	1		B	100 (45.4)
Dimethylamine	124403	Methanamine, N-methyl-	1000	1,4	U092	C	1000 (454)
O,O-Dimethyl O-p-nitrophenyl phosphorothioate	298000	Methyl parathion	100	1,4	P071	B	100 (45.4)
Ethane, pentachloro-	76017	Pentachloroethane	1*	4	U184	X	1 # (0.454)
Ethion	563122		10	1		A	10 (4.54)
2-Ethoxyethanol	110805	Ethylene glycol monoethyl ether	1*	4	U359	X	1 # (0.454)
Ethylene glycol monoethyl ether	110805	2-Ethoxyethanol	1*	4	U359	X	1 # (0.454)
Ferric dextran ***	9004664	Iron dextran ***	1*	4	U139	D	5000 (2270)
Fluoranthene	206440	Benzo(j,k)fluorene	1*	2,4	U120	B	100 (45.4)
Fluorene	86737		1*	2		D	5000 (2270)
Fulminic acid, mercury(II) salt	628864	Mercury fulminate	1*	4	P065	A	10 (4.54)
Hexachlorophene	70304	2,2'-Methylenebis(3,4,6-trichlorophenol)	1*	4	U132	B	100 (45.4)
Hydrogen sulfide	7783064	Hydrosulfuric acid Sulfur hydride	100	1,4	U135	B	100 (45.4)
Hydrosulfuric acid	7783064	Hydrogen sulfide Sulfur hydride	100	1,4	U135	B	100 (45.4)
Iron dextran ***	9004664	Ferric dextran ***	1*	4	U139	D	5000 (2270)
Isoprene	78795		1000	1		B	100 (45.4)
Lead ††	7439921		1*	2		X	1 # (0.454)
Lead chloride	7758954		5000	1		B	100 # (45.4)
Lead fluoborate	13814965		5000	1		B	100 (45.4)
Lead fluoride	7783462		1000	1		B	100 (45.4)
Lead iodide	10101630		5000	1		B	100 (45.4)
Lead nitrate	10099748		5000	1		B	100 # (45.4)
Lead stearate	7428480 1072351 52652592 56189094 15739807		5000	1		D	5000 (2270)
Lead sulfate	7446142		5000	1		B	100 (45.4)
Lead sulfide	1314870		5000	1		D	5000 (2270)
Lead thiocyanate	592870		5000	1		B	100 (45.4)
Mercuric nitrate	10045940		10	1		A	10 (4.54)
Mercuric sulfate	7783359		10	1		A	10 (4.54)
Mercuric thiocyanate	592858		10	1		A	10 (4.54)

TABLE 302.4 - LIST OF HAZARDOUS SUBSTANCES AND REPORTABLE QUANTITIES—Continued

Hazardous Substance	CASRN	Regulatory Synonyms	Statutory			Final RQ	
			RQ	Code †	RCRA Waste Number	Catego-ry	Pounds(Kg)
Mercurous nitrate	10415755		10	1		A	10 (4.54)
Mercury fulminate	628864	Fulminic acid, mercury(II) salt	1*	4	P065	A	10 (4.54)
Mercury, (acetato-O)phenyl-	62384	Phenylmercuric acetate	1*	4	P092	B	100 (45.4)
Methanamine, N-methyl-	124403	Dimethylamine	1000	1,4	U092	C	1000 (454)
Methane, chloro-	74873	Methyl chloride	1*	2,4	U045	X	1# (0.454)
Methyl chloride	74873	Methane, chloro-	1*	2,4	U045	X	1# (0.454)
Methyl parathion	298000	O,O-Dimethyl O-p-nitrophenyl phosphorothioate	100	1,4	P071	B	100 (45.4)
2,2'-Methylenebis(3,4,6-trichlorophenol)	70304	Hexachlorophene	1*	4	U132	B	100 (45.4)
Monoethylamine	75047		1000	1		B	100 (45.4)
Pentachlorobenzene	608935	Benzene, pentachloro-	1*	4	U183	A	10 (4.54)
Pentachloroethane	76017	Ethane, pentachloro-	1*	4	U184	X	1# (0.454)
Phenanthrene	85018		1*	2		D	5000 (2270)
Phenol	108952	Benzene, hydroxy-	1000	1,2,4	U188	C	1000 (454)
Phenylmercuric acetate	62384	Mercury, (acetato-O)phenyl-	1*	4	P092	B	100 (45.4)
Phorate	298022	Phosphorodithioic acid, O,O-diethyl S-(ethylthio) methyl ester	1*	4	P094	A	10 (4.54)
Phosphorodithioic acid, O,O-diethyl S-(ethylthio) methyl ester.	298022	Phorate	1*	4	P094	A	10 (4.54)
Plumbane, tetraethyl-	78002	Tetraethyl lead	100	1,4	P110	A	10# (4.54)
Propene, 1,3-dichloro-	542756	1,3-Dichloropropene	5000	1,2,4	U084	B	100# (45.4)
Pyrene	129000		1*	2		D	5000 (2270)
Pyridine	110861		1*	4	U196	C	1000 (454)
Pyrophosphoric acid, tetraethyl ester	107493	Tetraethyl pyrophosphate	100	1,4	P111	A	10 (4.54)
Selenious acid	7783008		1*	4	U204	A	10 (4.54)
Selenium ††	7782492		1*	2		B	100 (45.4)
Selenium dioxide	7446084	Selenium oxide	1000	1,4	U204	A	10 (4.54)
Selenium oxide	7446084	Selenium dioxide	1000	1,4	U204	A	10 (4.54)
Selenourea	630104	Carbamimidoselenoic acid	1*	4	P103	C	1000 (454)
Sodium bifluoride	1333831		5000	1		B	100 (45.4)
Sodium nitrite	7632000		100	1		B	100 (45.4)
Sodium selenite	10102188		1000	1		B	100 (45.4)
Sulfur hydride	7783064	Hydrogen sulfide Hydrosulfuric acid	100	1,4	U135	B	100 (45.4)
Sulfuric acid, thallium(I) salt	7446186 10031591	Thallium(I) sulfate	1000	1,4	P115	B	100 (45.4)
Tetraethyl lead	78002	Plumbane, tetraethyl-	100	1,4	P110	A	10# (4.54)
Tetraethyl pyrophosphate	107493	Pyrophosphoric acid, tetraethyl ester	100	1,4	P111	A	10 (4.54)
Thallic oxide	1314325	Thallium(III) oxide	1*	4	P113	B	100 (45.4)
Thallium ††	7440280		1*	2		C	1000 (454)
Thallium(I) acetate	563688	Acetic acid, thallium(I) salt	1*	4	U214	B	100 (45.4)
Thallium(I) carbonate	6533739	Carbonic acid, dithallium(I) salt	1*	4	U215	B	100 (45.4)
Thallium(I) chloride	7791120		1*	4	U216	B	100 (45.4)
Thallium(I) nitrate	10102451		1*	4	U217	B	100 (45.4)
Thallium(III) oxide	1314325	Thallic oxide	1*	4	P113	B	100 (45.4)
Thallium(I) selenide	12039520		1*	4	P114	C	1000 (454)

TABLE 302.4 - LIST OF HAZARDOUS SUBSTANCES AND REPORTABLE QUANTITIES—Continued

Hazardous Substance	CASRN	Regulatory Synonyms	Statutory			Final RQ	
			RQ	Code †	RCRA Waste Number	Catego-ry	Pounds(Kg)
Thallium(I) sulfate	7446186 10031591	Sulfuric acid, thallium(I) salt	1000	1,4	P115	B	100 (45.4)
o-Toluidine	95534	2-Amino-1-methyl benzene	1*	4	U328	X	1 # (0.454)
p-Toluidine	106490	4-Amino-1-methyl benzene	1*	4	U353	X	1 # (0.454)
Trichlorfon	52686		1000	1		B	100 (45.4)
Trimethylamine	75503		1000	1		B	100 (45.4)
sym-Trinitrobenzene	99354	Benzene, 1,3,5-trinitro-	1*	4	U234	A	10 (4.54)
Unlisted Hazardous Wastes Characteristic of EP Toxicity	N.A.						
Selenium D010	N.A.		1*	4	D010	A	10 (4.54)
Uranyl acetate ****	541093		5000	1		B	100 (45.4)
Uranyl nitrate ****	10102064		5000	1		B	100 (45.4)
Vanadium(V) oxide	1314621	Vanadium pentoxide	1000	1,4	P120	C	1000 (454)
Vanadium pentoxide	1314621	Vanadium(V) oxide	1000	1,4	P120	C	1000 (454)
Vanadyl sulfate	27774136		1000	1		C	1000 (454)
Zinc ††	7440666		1*	2		C	1000 (454)
Zinc acetate	557346		1000	1		C	1000 (454)
Zinc ammonium chloride	52628258		5000	1		C	1000 (454)
Zinc borate	1332076		1000	1		C	1000 (454)
Zinc bromide	7699458		5000	1		C	1000 (454)
Zinc carbonate	3486359		1000	1		C	1000 (454)
Zinc chloride	7646857		5000	1		C	1000 (454)
Zinc cyanide	557211		10	1,4	P121	A	10 (4.54)
Zinc fluoride	7783495		1000	1		C	1000 (454)
Zinc formate	557415		1000	1		C	1000 (454)
Zinc hydrosulfite	7779864		1000	1		C	1000 (454)
Zinc nitrate	7779886		5000	1		C	1000 (454)
Zinc phenolsulfonate	127822		5000	1		D	5000 (2270)
Zinc phosphide	1314847		1000	1,4	P122	B	100 (45.4)
Zinc silicofluoride	16871719		5000	1		D	5000 (2270)
Zinc sulfate	7733020		1000	1		C	1000 (454)
F004 The following spent non-halogenated solvents and the still bottoms from the recovery of these solvents: (a) Cresols/Cresylic acid (b) Nitrobenzene			1*	4	F004	C	1000 # (454)
F005 The following spent non-halogenated solvents and the still bottoms from the recovery of these solvents: (a) Toluene (b) Methyl ethyl ketone (c) Carbon disulfide (d) Isobutanol (e) Pyridine			1*	4	F005	B	100 (45.4)
F020 Wastes (except wastewater and spent carbon from hydrogen chloride purification) from the production or manufacturing use (as a reactant, chemical intermediate, or component in a formulating process) of tri- or tetrachlorophenol, or of intermediates used to produce their pesticide derivatives. (This listing does not include wastes from the production of hexachlorophene from highly purified 2,4,5-trichlorophenol.)			1*	4	F020	X	1 # (0.454)

TABLE 302.4 - LIST OF HAZARDOUS SUBSTANCES AND REPORTABLE QUANTITIES—Continued

Hazardous Substance	CASRN	Regulatory Synonyms	Statutory			Final RQ	
			RQ	Code †	RCRA Waste Number	Catego-ry	Pounds(Kg)
F021 .... Wastes (except wastewater and spent carbon from hydrogen chloride purification) from the production or manufacturing use (as a reactant, chemical intermediate, or component in a formulating process) of pentachlorophenol, or of intermediates used to produce its derivatives.			1*	4	F021	X	1# (0.454)
F022 .... Wastes (except wastewater and spent carbon from hydrogen chloride purification) from the manufacturing use (as a reactant, chemical intermediate, or component in a formulating process) of tetra-, penta-, or hexachlorobenzenes under alkaline conditions.			1*	4	F022	X	1# (0.454)
F023 .... Wastes (except wastewater and spent carbon from hydrogen chloride purification) from the production of materials on equipment previously used for the production or manufacturing use (as a reactant, chemical intermediate, or component in a formulating process) of tri- and tetrachlorophenols . (This listing does not include wastes from equipment used only for the production or use of hexachlorophene from highly purified 2,4,5- trichlorophenol.)			1*	4	F023	X	1# (0.454)
F026 .... Wastes (except wastewater and spent carbon from hydrogen chloride purification) from the production of materials on equipment previously used for the manufacturing use (as a reactant, chemical intermediate, or component in a formulating process) of tetra-, penta-, or hexachlorobenzene under alkaline conditions.			1*	4	F026	X	1# (0.454)
F027 .... Discarded unused formulations containing tri-, tetra-, or pentachlorophenol or discarded unused formulations containing compounds derived from these chlorophenols. (This listing does not include: formulations containing hexachlorophene synthesized from prepurified 2,4,5-trichlorophenol as the sole component.)			1*	4	F027	X	1# (0.454)
F028 .... Residues resulting from the incineration or thermal treatment of soil contaminated with EPA Hazardous Waste Nos. F020, F021, F022, F023, F026, and F027.			1*	4	F028	X	1# (0.454)
K026 .... Stripping still tails from the production of methyl ethyl pyridines			1*	4	K026	C	1000 (454)
K039 .... Filter cake from the filtration of diethylphosphorodithioic acid in the production of phorate			1*	4	K039	A	10 (4.54)
K046 .... Wastewater treatment sludges from the manufacturing , formulation and loading of lead-based initiating compounds			1*	4	K046	B	100 (45.4)
K052 .... Tank bottoms (leaded) from the petroleum refining industry			1*	4	K052	A	10# (4.54)
K087 .... Decanter tank tar sludge from coking operations			1*	4	K087	B	100 (45.4)
K111 .... Product washwaters from the production of dinitrotoluene via nitration of toluene.			1*	4	K111	X	1# (0.454)
K112 .... Reaction by-product water from the drying column in the production of toluenediamine via hydrogenation of dinitrotoluene.			1*	4	K112	X	1# (0.454)
K113 .... Condensed liquid light ends from the purification of toluenediamine in the production of toluenediamine via hydrogenation of dinitrotoluene.			1*	4	K113	X	1# (0.454)

TABLE 302.4 - LIST OF HAZARDOUS SUBSTANCES AND REPORTABLE QUANTITIES—Continued

Hazardous Substance	CASRN	Regulatory Synonyms	Statutory			Final RQ	
			RQ	Code †	RCRA Waste Number	Category	Pounds(Kg)
K114 .... Vicinals from the purification of toluenediamine in the production of toluenediamine via hydrogenation of dinitrotoluene.			1*	4	K114	X	1 # (0.454)
K115 .... Heavy ends from the purification of toluenediamine in the production of toluenediamine via hydrogenation of dinitrotoluene.			1*	4	K115	X	1 # (0.454)
K116 .... Organic condensate from the solvent recovery column in the production of toluene diisocyanate via phosgenation of toluenediamine.			1*	4	K116	X	1 # (0.454)
K117 .... Wastewater from the reaction vent gas scrubber in the production of ethylene bromide via bromination of ethene.			1*	4	K117	X	1 # (0.454)
K118 .... Spent absorbent solids from purification of ethylene dibromide in the production of ethylene dibromide.			1*	4	K118	X	1 # (0.454)
K136 .... Still bottoms from the purification of ethylene dibromide in the production of ethylene dibromide via bromination of ethene.			1*	4	K136	X	1 # (0.454)

† - indicates the statutory source as defined by 1, 2, 3, or 4 below
†† - no reporting of releases of this hazardous substance is required if the diameter of the pieces of the solid metal released is equal to or exceeds 100 micrometers (0.004 inches)
1 - indicates that the statutory source for designation of this hazardous substance under CERCLA is CWA Section 311(b)(4)
2 - indicates that the statutory source for designation of this hazardous substance under CERCLA is CWA Section 307(a)
3 - indicates that the statutory source for designation of this hazardous substance under CERCLA is CAA Section 112
4 - indicates that the statutory source for designation of this hazardous substance under CERCLA is RCRA Section 3001
1* - indicates that the 1-pound RQ is a CERCLA statutory RQ
*** - Iron dextran was designated as a hazardous substance under CERCLA solely because of its listing as a hazardous waste under Section 3001 of RCRA. The Agency recently proposed to delist iron dextran under RCRA(50 FR 46468-46470, November 8,1985). The Agency has also proposed to delist iron dextran from Table 302.4 of 40 CFR 302.4 and thereby remove its designation as a CERCLA hazardous substance.
**** - Uranyl acetate and uranyl nitrate currently are being evaluated for their radioactive properties. Their RQs may be further adjusted in a future rulemaking adjusting the RQ of radionuclides.
# - indicates that the RQ is subject to change when the assessment of potential carcinogenicity and/or chronic toxicity is completed

APPENDIX A - SEQUENTIAL CAS REGISTRY NUMBER LIST OF CERCLA HAZARDOUS SUBSTANCES

CASRN	Hazardous Substance
52686	Trichlorfon
62384	Mercury, (acetato-O)phenyl- Phenylmercuric acetate
70304	Hexachlorophene 2,2'-Methylenebis(3,4,6-trichlorophenol)
74873	Methane, chloro- Methyl chloride
75003	Chloroethane
75047	Monoethylamine
75150	Carbon bisulfide Carbon disulfide
75503	Trimethylamine
76017	Ethane, pentachloro- Pentachloroethane
78002	Plumbane, tetraethyl- Tetraethyl lead
78795	Isoprene
78886	2,3-Dichloropropene (isomer)

APPENDIX A - SEQUENTIAL CAS REGISTRY NUMBER LIST OF CERCLA HAZARDOUS SUBSTANCES—Continued

CASRN	Hazardous Substance
83329	Acenaphthene
85018	Phenanthrene
86737	Fluorene
95487	o-Cresol o-Cresylic acid
95534	o-Toluidine 2-Amino-1-methyl benzene
99354	Benzene, 1,3,5-trinitro- sym-Trinitrobenzene
106445	p-Cresol p-Cresylic acid
106490	p-Toluidine 4-Amino-1-methyl benzene
106514	p-Benzoquinone 1,4-Cyclohexadienedione
107493	Pyrophosphoric acid, tetraethyl ester Tetraethyl pyrophosphate
108294	m-Cresol m-Cresylic acid

APPENDIX A - SEQUENTIAL CAS REGISTRY NUMBER LIST OF CERCLA HAZARDOUS SUBSTANCES—Continued

CASRN	Hazardous Substance
108952	Benzene, hydroxy- Phenol
109897	Diethylamine
110805	Ethylene glycol monoethyl ether 2-Ethoxyethanol
110861	Pyridine
120127	Anthracene
124403	Dimethylamine Methanamine, N-methyl-
127822	Zinc phenolsulfonate
129000	Pyrene
133062	Captan
191242	Benzo[ghi]perylene
206440	Benzo[j,k]fluorene Fluoranthene
208968	Acenaphthylene
298000	Methyl parathion O,O-Dimethyl O-p-nitrophenyl phosphorothioate

APPENDIX A - SEQUENTIAL CAS REGISTRY NUMBER LIST OF CERCLA HAZARDOUS SUBSTANCES—Continued	

CASRN	Hazardous Substance
298022	Phorate
	Phosphorodithioic acid, O,O-diethyl S-(ethylthio) methyl ester
319868	delta - BHC
541093	Uranyl acetate
542756	Propene, 1,3-dichloro-
	1,3-Dichloropropene
557211	Zinc cyanide
557346	Zinc acetate
557415	Zinc formate
563122	Ethion
563688	Acetic acid, thallium(I) salt
	Thallium(I) acetate
592858	Mercuric thiocyanate
592870	Lead thiocyanate
608935	Benzene, pentachloro-
	Pentachlorobenzene
628864	Fulminic acid, mercury(II) salt
	Mercury fulminate
630104	Carbamimidoselenoic acid
	Selenourea
815827	Cupric tartrate
1066304	Chromic acetate
1072351	Lead stearate
1314325	Thallic oxide
	Thallium(III) oxide
1314621	Vanadium pentoxide
	Vanadium(V) oxide
1314847	Zinc phosphide
1314870	Lead sulfide
1319773	Cresol(s)
	Cresylic acid
1332076	Zinc borate
1333831	Sodium bifluoride
1341497	Ammonium bifluoride
3486359	Zinc carbonate
6533739	Carbonic acid, dithallium(I) salt
	Thallium(I) carbonate
7428480	Lead stearate
7439921	Lead
7440280	Thallium
7440360	Antimony
7440508	Copper
7440666	Zinc
7446084	Selenium dioxide
	Selenium oxide
7446142	Lead sulfate
7446186	Sulfuric acid, thallium(I) salt
	Thallium(I) sulfate

APPENDIX A - SEQUENTIAL CAS REGISTRY NUMBER LIST OF CERCLA HAZARDOUS SUBSTANCES—Continued	

CASRN	Hazardous Substance
7447394	Cupric chloride
7632000	Sodium nitrite
7646857	Zinc chloride
7664417	Ammonia
7699458	Zinc bromide
7733020	Zinc sulfate
7758954	Lead chloride
7758987	Cupric sulfate
7779864	Zinc hydrosulfite
7779886	Zinc nitrate
7782492	Selenium
7783008	Selenious acid
7783064	Hydrogen sulfide
	Hydrosulfuric acid
	Sulfur hydride
7783359	Mercuric sulfate
7783462	Lead fluoride
7783495	Zinc fluoride
7791120	Thallium(I) chloride
8003190	Dichloropropane - Dichloropropene (mixture)
9004664	Ferric dextran
	Iron dextran
10031591	Sulfuric acid, thallium(I) salt
	Thallium(I) sulfate
10045940	Mercuric nitrate
10049055	Chromous chloride
10099748	Lead nitrate
10101538	Chromic sulfate
10101630	Lead iodide
10102064	Uranyl nitrate
10102188	Sodium selenite
10102451	Thallium(I) nitrate
10415755	Mercurous nitrate
12039520	Thallium(I) selenide
13814965	Lead fluoborate
15739807	Lead sulfate
16871719	Zinc silicofluoride
26952238	Dichloropropene(s)
27774136	Vanadyl sulfate
52628258	Zinc ammonium chloride
52652592	Lead stearate
56189094	Lead stearate

3. Section 302.5 is revised to read as follows:

§ 302.5 Determination of reportable quantities.

(a) *Listed hazardous substances.* The quantity listed in the column "Final RQ" for each substance in Table 302.4 is the reportable quantity for that substance.

(b) *Unlisted hazardous substances.* Unlisted hazardous substances designated by 40 CFR 302.4(b) have the reportable quantity of 100 pounds, except for those unlisted hazardous wastes which exhibit extraction procedure (EP) toxicity identified in 40 CFR 261.24. Unlisted hazardous wastes which exhibit EP toxicity have the reportable quantities listed in Table 302.4 for the contaminant on which the characteristic of EP toxicity is based. The reportable quantity applies to the waste itself, not merely to the toxic contaminant. If an unlisted hazardous waste exhibits EP toxicity on the basis of more than one contaminant, the reportable quantity for that waste shall be the lowest of the reportable quantities listed in Table 302.4 for those contaminants. If an unlisted hazardous waste exhibits the characteristic of EP toxicity and one or more of the other characteristics referenced in 40 CFR 302.4(b), the reportable quantity for that waste shall be the lowest of the applicable reportable quantities.

40 CFR Part 117 is amended as follows:

PART 117—DETERMINATION OF REPORTABLE QUANTITIES FOR HAZARDOUS SUBSTANCES

4. The authority citation for Part 117 continues to read as follows:

Authority: Secs 311 and 501(a), Federal Water Pollution Control Act (33 U.S.C. 1251 et seq.), and Executive Order 11735.

5. Section 117.3 is amended by revising Table 117.3 to read as follows:

§ 117.3 Determination of reportable quantities.

* * * * *

Table 117.3—Reportable Quantities of Hazardous Substances

Note—The first number under the column headed "RQ" is the reportable quantity in pounds. The number in parentheses is the metric equivalent in kilograms. For convenience, the table contains a column headed "Category" which lists the code letters "X", "A", "B", "C", and "D" associated with reportable quantities 1, 10, 100, 1000, and 5000 pounds, respectively.

TABLE 117.3 - REPORTABLE QUANTITIES OF HAZARDOUS SUBSTANCES

NOTE: The first number under the column headed "RQ" is the reportable quantity in pounds. The number in parentheses is the metric equivalent in kilograms. For convenience, the table contains a column headed "Category" which lists the code letters "X", "A", "B", "C", and "D" associated with reportable quantities of 1, 10, 100, 1000 and 5000 pounds respectively.

Material	Category	RQ in pounds (Kilograms)
Acetaldehyde	C	1,000 (454)
Acetic acid	D	5,000 (2,270)
Acetic anhydride	D	5,000 (2,270)
Acetone cyanohydrin	A	10 (4.54)
Acetyl bromide	D	5,000 (2,270)
Acetyl chloride	D	5,000 (2,270)
Acrolein	X	1 (0.454)
Acrylonitrile	B	100 (45.4)
Adipic acid	D	5,000 (2,270)
Aldrin	X	1 (0.454)
Allyl alcohol	B	100 (45.4)
Allyl chloride	C	1,000 (454)
Aluminum sulfate	D	5,000 (2,270)
Ammonia	B	100 (45.4)
Ammonium acetate	D	5,000 (2,270)
Ammonium benzoate	D	5,000 (2,270)
Ammonium bicarbonate	D	5,000 (2,270)
Ammonium bichromate	C	1,000 (454)
Ammonium bifluoride	B	100 (45.4)
Ammonium bisulfite	D	5,000 (2,270)
Ammonium carbamate	D	5,000 (2,270)
Ammonium carbonate	D	5,000 (2,270)
Ammonium chloride	D	5,000 (2,270)
Ammonium chromate	C	1,000 (454)
Ammonium citrate	D	5,000 (2,270)
Ammonium fluoborate	D	5,000 (2,270)
Ammonium fluoride	B	100 (45.4)
Ammonium hydroxide	C	1,000 (454)
Ammonium oxalate	D	5,000 (2,270)
Ammonium silicofluoride	C	1,000 (454)
Ammonium sulfamate	D	5,000 (2,270)
Ammonium sulfide	B	100 (45.4)
Ammonium sulfite	D	5,000 (2,270)
Ammonium tartrate	D	5,000 (2,270)
Ammonium thiocyanate	D	5,000 (2,270)
Ammonium thiosulfate	D	5,000 (2,270)
Amyl acetate	D	5,000 (2,270)
Aniline	D	5,000 (2,270)
Antimony pentachloride	C	1,000 (454)
Antimony potassium tartrate	B	100 (45.4)
Antimony tribromide	C	1,000 (454)
Antimony trichloride	C	1,000 (454)
Antimony trifluoride	C	1,000 (454)
Antimony trioxide	C	1,000 (454)
Arsenic disulfide	D	5,000 (2,270)
Arsenic pentoxide	D	5,000 (2,270)
Arsenic trichloride	D	5,000 (2,270)
Arsenic trioxide	D	5,000 (2,270)
Arsenic trisulfide	D	5,000 (2,270)
Barium cyanide	A	10 (4.54)
Benzene	C	1,000 (454)
Benzoic acid	D	5,000 (2,270)
Benzonitrile	D	5,000 (2,270)
Benzoyl chloride	C	1,000 (454)
Benzyl chloride	B	100 (45.4)
Beryllium chloride	D	5,000 (2,270)
Beryllium fluoride	D	5,000 (2,270)
Beryllium nitrate	D	5,000 (2,270)
Butyl acetate	D	5,000 (2,270)
Butylamine	C	1,000 (454)
n-Butyl phthalate	A	10 (4.54)
Butyric acid	D	5,000 (2,270)
Cadmium acetate	B	100 (45.4)
Cadmium bromide	B	100 (45.4)
Cadmium chloride	B	100 (45.4)
Calcium arsenate	C	1,000 (454)
Calcium arsenite	C	1,000 (454)
Calcium carbide	A	10 (4.54)
Calcium chromate	C	1,000 (454)
Calcium cyanide	A	10 (4.54)
Calcium dodecylbenzenesulfonate.	C	1,000 (454)
Calcium hypochlorite	A	10 (4.54)
Captan	A	10 (4.54)
Carbaryl	B	100 (45.4)
Carbofuran	A	10 (4.54)
Carbon disulfide	B	100 (45.4)
Carbon tetrachloride	D	5,000 (2,270)
Chlordane	X	1 (0.454)
Chlorine	A	10 (4.54)
Chlorobenzene	B	100 (45.4)
Chloroform	D	5,000 (2,270)
Chlorosulfonic acid	C	1,000 (454)

TABLE 117.3 - REPORTABLE QUANTITIES OF HAZARDOUS SUBSTANCES—Continued

NOTE: The first number under the column headed "RQ" is the reportable quantity in pounds. The number in parentheses is the metric equivalent in kilograms. For convenience, the table contains a column headed "Category" which lists the code letters "X", "A", "B", "C", and "D" associated with reportable quantities of 1, 10, 100, 1000 and 5000 pounds respectively.

Material	Category	RQ in pounds (Kilograms)
Chlorpyrifos	X	1 (0.454)
Chromic acetate	C	1,000 (454)
Chromic acid	C	1,000 (454)
Chromic sulfate	C	1,000 (454)
Chromous chloride	C	1,000 (454)
Cobaltous bromide	C	1,000 (454)
Cobaltous formate	C	1,000 (454)
Cobaltous sulfamate	C	1,000 (454)
Coumaphos	A	10 (4.54)
Cresol	C	1,000 (454)
Crotonaldehyde	B	100 (45.4)
Cupric acetate	B	100 (45.4)
Cupric acetoarsenite	B	100 (45.4)
Cupric chloride	A	10 (4.54)
Cupric nitrate	B	100 (45.4)
Cupric oxalate	B	100 (45.4)
Cupric sulfate	A	10 (4.54)
Cupric sulfate ammoniated	B	100 (45.4)
Cupric tartrate	B	100 (45.4)
Cyanogen chloride	A	10 (4.54)
Cyclohexane	C	1,000 (454)
2,4-D Acid	B	100 (45.4)
2,4-D Esters	B	100 (45.4)
DDT	X	1 (0.454)
Diazinon	X	1 (0.454)
Dicamba	C	1,000 (454)
Dichlobenil	B	100 (45.4)
Dichlone	X	1 (0.454)
Dichlorobenzene	B	100 (45.4)
Dichloropropane	C	1,000 (454)
Dichloropropene	B	100 (45.4)
Dichloropropene-	B	100 (45.4)
Dichloropropane Mixture.		
2,2-Dichloropropionic acid	D	5,000 (2,270)
Dichlorvos	A	10 (4.54)
Dieldrin	X	1 (0.454)
Diethylamine	B	100 (45.4)
Dimethylamine	C	1,000 (454)
Dinitrobenzene	B	100 (45.4)
Dinitrophenol	A	10 (4.54)
Dinitrotoluene	C	1,000 (454)
Diquat	C	1,000 (454)
Disulfoton	X	1 (0.454)
Diuron	B	100 (45.4)
Dodecylbenzenesulfonic acid	C	1,000 (454)
Endosulfan	X	1 (0.454)
Endrin	X	1 (0.454)
Epichlorohydrin	C	1,000 (454)
Ethion	A	10 (4.54)
Ethylbenzene	C	1,000 (454)
Ethylenediamine	D	5,000 (2,270)
Ethylene dibromide	C	1,000 (454)
Ethylene dichloride	D	5,000 (2,270)
EDTA	D	5,000 (2,270)
Ferric ammonium citrate	C	1,000 (454)
Ferric ammonium oxalate	C	1,000 (454)
Ferric chloride	C	1,000 (454)
Ferric fluoride	B	100 (45.4)
Ferric nitrate	C	1,000 (454)
Ferric sulfate	C	1,000 (454)
Ferrous ammonium sulfate	C	1,000 (454)
Ferrous chloride	B	100 (45.4)
Ferrous sulfate	C	1,000 (454)
Formaldehyde	C	1,000 (454)
Formic acid	D	5,000 (2,270)
Fumaric acid	D	5,000 (2,270)
Furfural	D	5,000 (2,270)
Guthion	X	1 (0.454)
Heptachlor	X	1 (0.454)
Hexachlorocyclopentadiene	X	1 (0.454)
Hydrochloric acid	D	5,000 (2,270)
Hydrofluoric acid	B	100 (45.4)
Hydrogen cyanide	A	10 (4.54)
Hydrogen sulfide	B	100 (45.4)
Isoprene	B	100 (45.4)
Isopropanolamine	C	1,000 (454)
dodecylbenzenesulfonate.		
Kelthane	A	10 (4.54)
Kepone	X	1 (0.454)
Lead acetate	D	5,000 (2,270)
Lead arsenate	D	5,000 (2,270)
Lead chloride	B	100 (45.4)
Lead fluoborate	B	100 (45.4)

TABLE 117.3 - REPORTABLE QUANTITIES OF HAZARDOUS SUBSTANCES—Continued

NOTE: The first number under the column headed "RQ" is the reportable quantity in pounds. The number in parentheses is the metric equivalent in kilograms. For convenience, the table contains a column headed "Category" which lists the code letters "X", "A", "B", "C", and "D" associated with reportable quantities of 1, 10, 100, 1000 and 5000 pounds respectively.

Material	Category	RQ in pounds (Kilograms)
Lead fluoride	B	100 (45.4)
Lead iodide	B	100 (45.4)
Lead nitrate	B	100 (45.4)
Lead stearate	D	5,000 (2,270)
Lead sulfate	B	100 (45.4)
Lead sulfide	D	5,000 (2,270)
Lead thiocyanate	B	100 (45.4)
Lindane	X	1 (0.454)
Lithium chromate	C	1,000 (454)
Malathion	B	100 (45.4)
Maleic acid	D	5,000 (2,270)
Maleic anhydride	D	5,000 (2,270)
Mercaptodimethur	A	10 (4.54)
Mercuric cyanide	X	1 (0.454)
Mercuric nitrate	A	10 (4.54)
Mercuric sulfate	A	10 (4.54)
Mercuric thiocyanate	A	10 (4.54)
Mercurous nitrate	A	10 (4.54)
Methoxychlor	X	1 (0.454)
Methyl mercaptan	B	100 (45.4)
Methyl methacrylate	C	1,000 (454)
Methyl parathion	B	100 (45.4)
Mevinphos	A	10 (4.54)
Mexacarbate	C	1,000 (454)
Monoethylamine	B	100 (45.4)
Monomethylamine	B	100 (45.4)
Naled	A	10 (4.54)
Naphthalene	B	100 (45.4)
Naphthenic acid	B	100 (45.4)
Nickel ammonium sulfate	D	5,000 (2,270)
Nickel chloride	D	5,000 (2,270)
Nickel hydroxide	C	1,000 (454)
Nickel nitrate	D	5,000 (2,270)
Nickel sulfate	D	5,000 (2,270)
Nitric acid	C	1,000 (454)
Nitrobenzene	C	1,000 (454)
Nitrogen dioxide	A	10 (4.54)
Nitrophenol	B	100 (45.4)
Nitrotoluene	C	1,000 (454)
Paraformaldehyde	C	1,000 (454)
Parathion	X	1 (0.454)
Pentachlorophenol	A	10 (4.54)
Phenol	C	1,000 (454)
Phosgene	A	10 (4.54)
Phosphoric acid	D	5,000 (2,270)
Phosphorus	X	1 (0.454)
Phosphorus oxychloride	C	1,000 (454)
Phosphorus pentasulfide	B	100 (45.4)
Phosphorus trichloride	C	1,000 (454)
Polychlorinated biphenyls	A	10 (4.54)
Potassium arsenate	C	1,000 (454)
Potassium arsenite	C	1,000 (454)
Potassium bichromate	C	1,000 (454)
Potassium chromate	C	1,000 (454)
Potassium cyanide	A	10 (4.54)
Potassium hydroxide	C	1,000 (454)
Potassium permanganate	B	100 (45.4)
Propargite	A	10 (4.54)
Propionic acid	D	5,000 (2,270)
Propionic anhydride	D	5,000 (2,270)
Propylene oxide	B	100 (45.4)
Pyrethrins	X	1 (0.454)
Quinoline	D	5,000 (2,270)
Resorcinol	D	5,000 (2,270)
Selenium oxide	A	10 (4.54)
Silver nitrate	X	1 (0.454)
Sodium	A	10 (4.54)
Sodium arsenate	C	1,000 (454)
Sodium arsenite	C	1,000 (454)
Sodium bichromate	C	1,000 (454)
Sodium bifluoride	B	100 (45.4)
Sodium bisulfite	D	5,000 (2,270)
Sodium chromate	C	1,000 (454)
Sodium cyanide	A	10 (4.54)
Sodium dodecylbenzenesulfonate.	C	1,000 (454)
Sodium fluoride	C	1,000 (454)
Sodium hydrosulfide	D	5,000 (2,270)
Sodium hydroxide	C	1,000 (454)
Sodium hypochlorite	B	100 (45.4)
Sodium methylate	C	1,000 (454)
Sodium nitrite	B	100 (45.4)
Sodium phosphate, dibasic	D	5,000 (2,270)

TABLE 117.3 - REPORTABLE QUANTITIES OF HAZARDOUS SUBSTANCES—Continued

NOTE: The first number under the column headed "RQ" is the reportable quantity in pounds. The number in parentheses is the metric equivalent in kilograms. For convenience, the table contains a column headed "Category" which lists the code letters "X", "A", "B", "C", and "D" associated with reportable quantities of 1, 10, 100, 1000 and 5000 pounds respectively.

Material	Category	RQ in pounds (Kilograms)
Sodium phosphate, tribasic	D	5,000 (2,270)
Sodium selenite	B	100 (45.4)
Strontium chromate	C	1,000 (454)
Strychnine	A	10 (4.54)
Styrene	C	1,000 (454)
Sulfuric acid	C	1,000 (454)
Sulfur monochloride	C	1,000 (454)
2,4,5-T acid	C	1,000 (454)
2,4,5-T amines	D	5,000 (2,270)
2,4,5-T esters	C	1,000 (454)
2,4,5-T salts	C	1,000 (454)
TDE	X	1 (0.454)
2,4,5-TP acid	B	100 (45.4)
2,4,5-TP acid esters	B	100 (45.4)
Tetraethyl lead	A	10 (4.54)
Tetraethyl pyrophosphate	A	10 (4.54)
Thallium sulfate	B	100 (45.4)
Toluene	C	1,000 (454)
Toxaphene	X	1 (0.454)
Trichlorfon	B	100 (45.4)

TABLE 117.3 - REPORTABLE QUANTITIES OF HAZARDOUS SUBSTANCES—Continued

NOTE: The first number under the column headed "RQ" is the reportable quantity in pounds. The number in parentheses is the metric equivalent in kilograms. For convenience, the table contains a column headed "Category" which lists the code letters "X", "A", "B", "C", and "D" associated with reportable quantities of 1, 10, 100, 1000 and 5000 pounds respectively.

Material	Category	RQ in pounds (Kilograms)
Trichloroethylene	C	1,000 (454)
Trichlorophenol	A	10 (4.54)
Triethanolamine	C	1,000 (454)
dodecylbenzenesulfonate.		
Triethylamine	D	5,000 (2,270)
Trimethylamine	B	100 (45.4)
Uranyl acetate	B	100 (45.4)
Uranyl nitrate	B	100 (45.4)
Vanadium pentoxide	C	1,000 (454)
Vanadyl sulfate	C	1,000 (454)
Vinyl acetate	D	5,000 (2,270)
Vinylidene chloride	D	5,000 (2,270)
Xylene	C	1,000 (454)
Xylenol	C	1,000 (454)
Zinc acetate	C	1,000 (454)
Zinc ammonium chloride	C	1,000 (454)
Zinc borate	C	1,000 (454)
Zinc bromide	C	1,000 (454)
Zinc carbonate	C	1,000 (454)
Zinc chloride	C	1,000 (454)

TABLE 117.3 - REPORTABLE QUANTITIES OF HAZARDOUS SUBSTANCES—Continued

NOTE: The first number under the column headed "RQ" is the reportable quantity in pounds. The number in parentheses is the metric equivalent in kilograms. For convenience, the table contains a column headed "Category" which lists the code letters "X", "A", "B", "C", and "D" associated with reportable quantities of 1, 10, 100, 1000 and 5000 pounds respectively.

Material	Category	RQ in pounds (Kilograms)
Zinc cyanide	A	10 (4.54)
Zinc fluoride	C	1,000 (454)
Zinc formate	C	1,000 (454)
Zinc hydrosulfite	C	1,000 (454)
Zinc nitrate	C	1,000 (454)
Zinc phenolsulfonate	D	5,000 (2,270)
Zinc phosphide	B	100 (45.4)
Zinc silicofluoride	D	5,000 (2,270)
Zinc sulfate	C	1,000 (454)
Zirconium nitrate	D	5,000 (2,270)
Zirconium potassium fluoride	C	1,000 (454)
Zirconium sulfate	D	5,000 (2,270)
Zirconium tetrachloride	D	5,000 (2,270)

[FR Doc. 86–19709 Filed 9–26–86; 8:45 am]

BILLING CODE 6560–50–M

Appendix 6G Interim Final Reportable Quantities Under Title III of SARA

PART 300—NATIONAL OIL AND HAZARDOUS SUBSTANCES POLLUTION CONTINGENCY PLAN

Subpart I—Emergency Planning and Community Right to Know

Sec.
300.91 Purpose.
300.92 Definitions.
300.93 Emergency planning.
300.94 Emergency release notification.
300.95 Penalties.

3. Following Subpart H in Part 300, a new Subpart I is added as follows:

Subpart I—Emergency Planning and Community Right to Know

§ 300.91 Purpose.

This regulation establishes the list of extremely hazardous substances, threshold planning quantities, and facility notification responsibilities necessary for the development and implementation of State and local emergency response plans.

§ 300.92 Definitions.

Terms not specifically defined in this section have the same meaning as in Subpart A of this part.

Act means the Superfund Amendments and Reauthorization Act of 1986.

CERCLA Hazardous Substance means a substance listed in Table 302.4 of 40 CFR Part 302.

Commission means the State of emergency response commission (or, for the purpose of emergency planning, the Governor if there is no commission) for the State in which the facility is located.

Environment includes water, air, and land and the interrelationship which exists among and between water, air, and land and all living things.

Extremely hazardous substance means a substance listed in Appendix D of this part.

Facility means all buildings, equipment, structures, and other stationary items which are located on a single site or on contiguous or adjacent sites and which are owned or operated by the same person (or by any person which controls, is controlled by, or under common control with, such person). For purposes of emergency release notification, the term includes motor vehicles, rolling stock, and aircraft.

Hazardous Chemical means any hazardous chemical as defined under § 1910.1200(c) of Title 29 of the Code of Federal Regulations, except that such term does not include the following substances:

(1) Any food, food additive, color additive, drug, or cosmetic regulated by the Food and Drug Administration.

(2) Any substance present as a solid in any manufactured item to the extent exposure to the substance does not occur under normal conditions of use.

(3) Any substance to the extent it is used for personal, family, or household purposes, or is present in the same form and concentration as a product packaged for distribution and use by the general public.

(4) Any substance to the extent it is used in a research laboratory or a hospital or other medical facility under the direct supervision of a technically qualified individual.

(5) Any substance to the extent it is used in routine agricultural operations or is a fertilizer held for sale by a retailer to the ultimate customer.

Person means any individual, trust, firm, joint stock company, corporation (including a government corporation), partnership, association, State, municipality, commission, political subdivision of a State, or interstate body.

Release means any spilling, leaking, pumping, pouring, emitting, emptying, discharging, injecting, escaping, leaching, dumping, or disposing into the environment (including the abandonment or discarding of barrels, containers, and other closed receptacles) of any hazardous chemical, extremely hazardous substance, or CERCLA hazardous substance.

Reportable quantity means, for any CERCLA hazardous substance, the reportable quantity established in Table 302.4 of 40 CFR Part 302, for such substance; for any other substance, the reportable quantity is one pound.

Threshold planning quantity means for a substance listed in Appendix D, the quantity listed in the column "threshold planning quantity" for that substance.

§ 300.93 Emergency planning.

(a) *Applicability.* The requirements of this section apply to any facility at which there is present an amount of any extremely hazardous substance in excess of its threshold planning quantity, or designated, after public notice and opportunity for comment, by the Commission or the Governor for the State in which the facility is located.

(b) *Emergency Planning Notification.* The owner or operator of a facility subject to this section shall provide notification to the commission that it is a facility subject to the emergency planning requirements of this subpart. Such notification shall be provided: (1) On or before May 17, 1987 or (2) within sixty days after a facility first becomes subject to the requirements of this section, whichever is later.

(c) *Facility Emergency Coordinator.* The owner or operator of a facility subject to this Section shall designate a facility representative who will participate in the local emergency planning process as a facility emergency response coordinator. The owner or operator shall notify the local emergency planning committee (or the Governor if there is no committee) of the facility representative on or before September 17, 1987 or 30 days after establishment of a local emergency planning committee, whichever is earlier.

(d) *Provision of Information.* (1) The owner or operator of a facility subject to this section shall inform the local emergency planning committee of any changes occurring at the facility which may be relevant to emergency planning.

(2) Upon request of the local emergency planning committee, the owner or operator of a facility subject to this section shall promptly provide to

the committee any information necessary for development or implementation of the local emergency plan.

(Approved by the Office of Management and Budget under the control Number 2050-0046)

§ 300.94 Emergency release notification.

(a) *Applicability.* The requirements of this Section apply to any facility: (1) At which a hazardous chemical is produced, used, or stored and (2) at which there is release of a reportable quantity of any extremely hazardous substance or CERCLA hazardous substance which results in exposure to persons outside of the boundaries of the facility. This Section does not apply to any such release which is a federally permitted release.

(b) *Notice Requirements.* (1) The owner or operator of a facility subject to this Section shall immediately notify the local emergency coordinator for the local emergency planning committee of any area likely to be affected by the release and the State emergency planning commission of any State likely to be affected by the release. If there is no local emergency planning committee or State emergency planning commission, notification shall be provided under this section to relevant local or state emergency response personnel.

(2) The notice required under this Section shall include the following to the extent known at the time of notice and so long as no delay in notice or emergency response results:

(i) The chemical name or identity of any substance involved in the release.

(ii) An indication of whether the substance is on the list referred to in section 302(a).

(iii) An estimate of the quantity of any such substance that was released into the environment.

(iv) The time and duration of the release.

(v) The medium or media into which the release occurred.

(vi) Any known or anticipated acute or chronic health risks associated with the emergency and, where appropriate, advice regarding medical attention necessary for exposed individuals.

(vii) Proper precautions to take as a result of the release, including evacuation (unless such information is readily available to the community emergency coordinator pursuant to the emergency plan).

(viii) The name and telephone number of the person or persons to be contacted for further information.

(3) As soon as practicable after a release which requires notice under (b)(1) of this section, such owner or operator shall provide a written follow-up emergency notice (or notices, as more information becomes available) setting forth and updating the information required under paragraph (b)(2) of this section, and including additional information with respect to—

(i) Actions taken to respond to and contain the release,

(ii) Any known or anticipated acute or chronic health risks associated with release, and,

(iii) Where appropriate, advice regarding medical attention necessary for exposed individuals.

(4) Exceptions. (i) In lieu of the notices specified in paragraphs (b) (2) and (3) of this section, any owner or operator of a facility subject to this section from which there is a release of a CERCLA hazardous substance which is not an extremely hazardous substance and has a statutory reportable quantity may provide the same notice required under CERCLA section 103(a) to the local emergency planning committee.

(ii) In lieu of the notices specified in paragraphs (b) (2) and (3) of this section, any owner or operator of a facility subject to this section from which there is a release during transportation or storage incident to transportation, may provide notice by dialing 911 or, in the absence of a 911 emergency telephone number, calling the operator.

(Approved by the Office of Management and Budget under the control number 2050-0046)

§ 300.95 Penalties.

(a) *Civil Penalties.* Any person who fails to comply with the requirements of § 300.94 shall be subject to civil penalties of up to $25,000 for each violation in accordance with section 325(b)(1) of the Act.

(b) *Civil Penalties for Continuing Violations.* Any person who fails to comply with the requirements of § 300.94 shall be subject to civil penalties of up to $25,000 for each day during which the violation continues, in accordance with section 325(b)(2) of the Act. In the case of a second or subsequent violation, any such person may be subject to civil penalties of up to $75,000 for each day the violation continues, in accordance with section 325(b)(2) of the Act.

(c) *Criminal Penalties.* Any person knowingly and willfully fails to provide notice in accordance with § 300.94 shall, upon conviction, be fined not more than $25,000 or imprisoned for not more than two (2) years, or both (or, in the case of a second or subsequent conviction, shall be fined not more than $50,000 or imprisoned for not more than five (5) years, or both, in accordance with 325(b)(4) of the Act.

3. Following Appendix C of Part 300 new Appendix D and Appendix E are added as follows:

APPENDIX D.—LIST OF EXTREMELY HAZARDOUS SUBSTANCES, THRESHOLD PLANNING QUANTITIES, AND REPORTABLE QUANTITIES

[Alphabetical Order]

Chemical name	CAS No.	Ambient physical state	Threshold planning quantity (pounds)	Reportable quantity (pounds)
Acetone cyanohydrin	75-86-5	Liquid	1,000	10
Acetone thiosemicarbazide	1752-30-3	Solid	1,000	ª 1
Acrolein	107-02-8	Liquid	500	1
Acrylamide	79-06-1	Solid	1,000	5,000
Acrylonitrile	107-13-1	Liquid	10,000	ª 100
Acrylyl chloride	814-68-6	Liquid	500	ª 1
Adiponitrile	111-69-3	Liquid	1,000	ª 1
Aldicarb	116-06-3	Solid	ª 100	1
Aldrin	309-00-2	Solid	500	ª 1
Allyl alcohol	107-18-6	Liquid	1,000	100
Allylamine	107-11-9	Liquid	500	ª 1
Aluminum phosphide	20859-73-8	Solid	ª 500	100
Aminopterin	54-62-6	Solid	500	ª 1
Amiton	78-53-5	Liquid	500	ª 1
Ammonia	3734-97-2	Solid	100	ª 1
Ammonia	7664-41-7	Gas	500	100
Ammonium chloroplatinate	ª 16919-58-7	Solid	10,000	ª 1
Amphetamine	300-62-9	Liquid	1,000	ª 1
Aniline	62-53-3	Liquid	1,000	5,000

APPENDIX 6G

APPENDIX D.—LIST OF EXTREMELY HAZARDOUS SUBSTANCES, THRESHOLD PLANNING QUANTITIES, AND REPORTABLE QUANTITIES—Continued

[Alphabetical Order]

Chemical name	CAS No.	Ambient physical state	Threshold planning quantity (pounds)	Reportable quantity (pounds)
Aniline, 2,4,6-trimethyl-	88-05-1	Liquid	500	[1] 1
Antimony pentafluoride	7783-70-2	Liquid	500	[1] 1
Antimycin A	1397-94-0	Solid	[4] 1,000	[1] 1
Antu	86-68-4	Solid	500	100
Arsenic pentoxide	1303-28-2	Solid	100	[2] 5,000
Arsenous oxide	1327-53-3	Solid	500	[2] 5,000
Arsenous trichloride	7784-34-1	Liquid	500	[2] 5,000
Arsine	7784-42-1	Gas	100	[1] 1
Azinphos-ethyl	2642-71-9	Solid	100	[1] 1
Azinphos-methyl	86-50-0	Solid	10,000	1
Bacitracin	[5] 1405-87-4(a)	Solid	10,000	[1] 1
Benzal chloride	98-87-3	Liquid	500	5,000
Benzenamine, 3-(trifluoromethyl)-	98-16-8	Liquid	500	[1] 1
Benzene, 1-(chloromethyl)-4-Nitro-	100-14-1	Solid	500	[1] 1
Benzenearsonic acid	98-05-5	Solid	2	[1] 1
Benzenesulfonyl chloride	[5] 98-09-9	Liquid	10,000	100
Benzotrichloride	98-07-7	Liquid	100	[2] 1
Benzyl chloride	100-44-7	Liquid	500	[2] 100
Benzyl cyanide	140-29-4	Liquid	1,000	[1] 1
Bicyclo[2.2.1]heptane-2-carbonitrile, 5-chloro-6-(((methylamino)Carbonyl)oxy)im...	15271-41-7	Solid	500	[1] 1
Bis(chloromethyl) ketone	534-07-6	Solid	2	[1] 1
Bitoscanate	4044-65-9	Solid	500	[1] 1
Boron trichloride	10294-34-5	Liquid	500	[1] 1
Boron trifluoride	7637-07-2	Gas	500	[1] 1
Boron trifluoride compound with methyl ether (1:1)	353-42-4	Liquid	1,000	[1] 1
Bromadiolone	28772-56-7	Solid	100	[1] 1
Bromine	7726-95-6	Liquid	500	[1] 1
Butadiene	[5] 106-99-0	Gas	10,000	[1] 1
Butyl isovalerate	[5] 109-19-3	Liquid	10,000	[1] 1
Butyl vinyl ether	[5] 111-34-2	Liquid	10,000	[1] 1
C.I. basic green 1	[5] 633-03-4	Solid	10,000	[1] 1
Cadmium oxide	1306-19-0	Solid	100	[1] 1
Cadmium stearate	2223-93-0	Solid	[2] 1,000	[1] 1
Calcium arsenate	7778-44-1	Solid	500	[2] 1,000
Camphechlor	8001-35-2	Solid	500	[4] 1
Cantharidin	56-25-7	Solid	100	[1] 1
Carbachol chloride	51-83-2	Solid	500	[1] 1
Carbamic acid, methyl-, O-(((2,4-Dimethyl-1, 3-Dithiolan-2-yl)Methylene)Amino)-	26419-73-8	Solid	100	[1] 1
Carbofuran	1563-66-2	Solid	2	10
Carbon disulfide	75-15-0	Liquid	10,000	100
Carbophenothion	786-19-6	Liquid	500	[1] 1
Carvone	[5] 2244-16-8	Liquid	10,000	[1] 1
Chlordane	57-74-9	Liquid	1,000	[1] 1
Chlorfenvinfos	470-90-6	Liquid	500	[1] 1
Chlorine	7782-50-5	Gas	100	10
Chlormephos	24934-91-6	Liquid	500	[1] 1
Chlormequat chloride	999-81-5	Solid	1,000	[1] 1
Chloroacetaldehyde	[5] 107-20-0	Liquid	1,000	1,000
Chloroacetic acid	79-11-8	Solid	100	[1] 1
Chloroethanol	107-07-3	Liquid	500	[1] 1
Chloroethyl chloroformate	627-11-2	Liquid	1,000	[1] 1
Chloroform	67-66-3	Liquid	10,000	[2] 5,000
Chloromethyl ether	542-88-1	Liquid	100	[2] 1
Chloromethyl methyl ether	107-30-2	Liquid	[3] 100	[2] 1
Chlorophacinone	3691-35-8	Solid	100	[1] 1
Chloroxuron	1982-47-4	Solid	500	[1] 1
Chlorthiophos	21923-23-9	Liquid	1,000	[1] 1
Chromic chloride	10025-73-7	Solid	2	[1] 1
Cobalt	[5] 7440-48-4	Solid	10,000	[1] 1
Cobalt carbonyl	10210-68-1	Solid	100	[1] 1
Cobalt, ((2,2'-(1,2-ethanediylbis (nitrilomethylidyne))bis(6-fluorophenolato))(2)-	62207-76-5	Solid	100	[1] 1
Colchicine	64-86-8	Solid	100	[1] 1
Coumafuryl	[5] 117-52-2	Solid	10,000	[1] 1
Coumaphos	56-72-4	Solid	100	10
Coumatetralyl	5836-29-3	Solid	500	[1] 1
Cresol, o-	95-48-7	Solid	1,000	[2] 1,000
Crimidine	535-89-7	Solid	100	[1] 1
Crotonaldehyde	4170-30-3	Liquid	1,000	100
Crotonaldehyde, (E)-	123-73-9	Liquid	1,000	100
Cyanogen bromide	506-68-3	Solid	500	1,000
Cyanogen iodide	506-78-5	Solid	1,000	[1] 1
Cyanophos	2636-26-2	Liquid	1,000	[1] 1
Cyanuric fluoride	675-14-9	Liquid	100	[1] 1
Cyclohexmide	66-81-9	Solid	100	[1] 1
Cyclohexylamine	108-91-8	Liquid	10,000	[1] 1
Cyclopentane	[5] 287-92-3	Liquid	10,000	[1] 1
Decaborane (14)	17702-41-9	Solid	500	[1] 1
Demeton	8065-48-3	Liquid	500	[1] 1
Demeton-s-methyl	919-86-8	Liquid	500	[1] 1
Dialifos	10311-84-9	Solid	100	[1] 1
Diborane	19287-45-7	Gas	100	[1] 1
Dibutyl phthalate	[5] 84-74-2	Liquid	10,000	10
Dichlorobenzalkonium chloride	[5] 8023-53-8	Solid	10,000	[1] 1
Dichloroethyl ether	111-44-4	Liquid	10,000	[1] 1
Dichloromethylphenylsilane	149-74-6	Liquid	1,000	[1] 1
Dichlorvos	62-73-7	Liquid	1,000	10
Dicrotophos	141-66-2	Liquid	100	[1] 1
Dieporybutane	1464-53-5	Liquid	500	[1] 1
Diethyl chlorophosphate	814-49-3	Liquid	1,000	[1] 1

APPENDIX D.—LIST OF EXTREMELY HAZARDOUS SUBSTANCES, THRESHOLD PLANNING QUANTITIES, AND REPORTABLE QUANTITIES—Continued

[Alphabetical Order]

Chemical name	CAS No.	Ambient physical state	Threshold planning quantity (pounds)	Reportable quantity (pounds)
Diethyl-p-phenylenediamine	*93–05–0	Liquid	10,000	*1
Diethylcarbamazine citrate	1642–54–2	Solid	100	*1
Digitoxin	71–63–6	Solid	*100	*1
Diglycidyl ether	2238–07–5	Liquid	1,000	*1
Digoxin	20830–75–5	Solid	100	*1
Dimefox	115–26–4	Liquid	500	*1
Dimethoate	60–51–5	Solid	500	10
Dimethyl phosphorochloridothioate	2524–03–0	Liquid	500	*1
Dimethyl phthalate	*131–11–3	Liquid	10,000	5,000
Dimethyl sulfate	77–78–1	Liquid	500	*1
Dimethyl sulfide	75–18–3	Liquid	100	1
Dimethyl-p-phenylenediamine	99–98–9	Solid	2	*1
Dimethyldichlorosilane	75–78–5	Liquid	10,000	*1
Dimethylhydrazine	57–14–7	Liquid	1,000	*1
Dimetilan	644–64–4	Solid	500	*1
Dinitrocresol	534–52–1	Solid	2	10
Dinoseb	88–85–7	Solid	100	1,000
Dinoterb	1420–07–1	Solid	500	*1
Dioctyl phthalate	*117–84–0	Liquid	10,000	5,000
Dioxathion	78–34–2	Liquid	500	*1
Dioxolane	*646–06–0	Liquid	10,000	*1
Diphacinone	82–66–6	Solid	2	100
Diphosphoramide, octamethyl-	152–16–9	Liquid	100	100
Disulfoton	298–04–4	Liquid	500	*1
Dithiazanine iodide	514–73–8	Solid	500	*1
Dithiobiuret	541–53–7	Solid	100	100
Emetine, dihydrochloride	316–42–7	Solid	1,000	*1
Endosulfan	115–29–7	Solid	2	1
Endothion	2778–04–3	Solid	500	*1
Endrin	72–20–8	Solid	500	1
Epichlorohydrin	106–89–8	Liquid	1,000	*1,000
EPN	2104–64–5	Solid	100	*1
Ergocalciferol	50–14–6	Solid	*1,000	*1
Ergotamine tartrate	379–79–3	Solid	500	*1
Ethanesulfonyl chloride, 2-chloro-	1622–32–8	Liquid	500	*1
Ethanol, 1,2-dichloro-, acetate	10140–87–1	Liquid	1,000	*1
Ethion	563–12–2	Liquid	1,000	10
Ethoprophos	13194–48–4	Liquid	1,000	*1
Ethyl thiocyanate	542–90–5	Liquid	10,000	*1
Ethylbis(2-chloroethyl)amine	538–07–8	Liquid	10,000	*1
Ethylene fluorohydrin	371–62–0	Liquid	*2	*1
Ethylene oxide	75–21–8	Gas	1,000	*1
Ethylenediamine	107–15–3	Liquid	10,000	5,000
Ethyleneimine	151–56–4	Liquid	500	*1
Ethylmercuric phosphate	*2235–25–8	Solid	10,000	*1
Fenamiphos	22224–92–6	Solid	2	*1
Fenitrothion	122–14–5	Liquid	500	*1
Fensulfothion	115–90–2	Liquid	1,000	*1
Fluenetil	4301–50–2	Solid	100	*1
Fluorine	7782–41–4	Gas	100	10
Fluoroacetamide	640–19–7	Solid	*2	100
Fluoroacetic acid	144–49–0	Solid	2	*1
Fluoroacetyl chloride	359–06–8	Liquid	*2	*1
Fluorouracil	51–21–8	Solid	500	*1
Fonofos	944–22–9	Liquid	500	*1
Formaldehyde	50–00–0	Gas	500	*1,000
Formaldehyde cyanohydrin	107–16–4	Liquid	10,000	*1
Formetanate	23422–53–9	Solid	100	*1
Formothion	2540–82–1	Liquid	100	*1
Formparanate	17702–57–7	Solid	100	*1
Fosthietan	21548–32–3	Liquid	500	*1
Fuberdazole	3878–19–1	Solid	100	*1
Furan	110–00–9	Liquid	500	100
Gallium trichloride	13450–90–3	Solid	500	*1
Hexachlorocyclopentadiene	77–47–4	Liquid	500	*1
Hexachloronaphthalene	*1335–87–1	Solid	10,000	*1
Hexamethylenediamine, N,N'-dibutyl-	4835–11–4	Liquid	500	*1
Hydrazine	302–01–2	Liquid	1,000	*1
Hydrocyanic acid	74–90–8	Gas	100	10
Hydrogen chloride	7647–01–0	Gas	500	5,000
Hydrogen fluoride	7664–39–3	Gas	100	100
Hydrogen peroxide (concentration greater than 52%)	7722–84–1	Liquid	1,000	*1
Hydrogen selenide	7783–07–5	Gas	2	*1
Hydrogen sulfide	7783–06–4	Gas	500	100
Hydroquinone	123–31–9	Solid	500	*1
Indomethacin	*53–86–1	Solid	10,000	*1
Indium tetrachloride	*10025–97–5	Solid	10,000	*1
Iron, Pentacarbonyl-	*13463–40–6	Liquid	100	*1
Isobenzan	297–78–9	Solid	100	*1
Isobutyronitrile	78–82–0	Liquid	10,000	*1
Isocyanic acid, 3,4-dichlorophenyl ester	102–36–3	Solid	500	*1
Isodrin	465–73–6	Solid	100	1
Isofluorphate	55–91–4	Liquid	*100	100
Isophorone diisocyanate	4098–71–9	Solid	*100	*1
Isopropyl chloroformate	108–23–6	Liquid	1,000	*1
Isopropyl formate	625–55–8	Liquid	500	*1
Isopropylmethylpyrazolyl dimethylcarbamate	119–38–0	Liquid	500	*1
Lactonitrile	78–97–7	Liquid	1,000	*1
Leptophos	21609–90–5	Solid	500	*1

APPENDIX D.—LIST OF EXTREMELY HAZARDOUS SUBSTANCES, THRESHOLD PLANNING QUANTITIES, AND REPORTABLE QUANTITIES—Continued

[Alphabetical Order]

Chemical name	CAS No.	Ambient physical state	Threshold planning quantity (pounds)	Reportable quantity (pounds)
Lewisite	541-25-3	Liquid	10	10
Lindane	58-89-9	Solid	1,000	1
Lithium hydride	7580-67-8	Solid	100	1
Malononitrile	109-77-3	Solid	500	1,000
Manganese, tricarbonyl methylcyclopentadienyl	12108-13-3	Liquid	100	1
Mechlorethamine	51-75-2	Liquid	10	1
Mephosfolan	950-10-7	Liquid	500	1
Mercuric acetate	1600-27-7	Solid	500	1
Mercuric chloride	7487-94-7	Solid	500	1
Mercuric oxide	21908-53-2	Solid	500	1
Mesitylene	108-67-8	Liquid	10,000	1
Methacrolein diacetate	10476-95-6	Liquid	1,000	1
Methacrylic anhydride	760-93-0	Liquid	500	1
Methacrylonitrile	126-98-7	Liquid	500	1,000
Methacryloyl chloride	920-46-7	Liquid	100	1
Methacryloyloxyethyl isocyanate	30674-80-7	Liquid	100	1
Methamidophos	10265-92-6	Solid	100	1
Methanesulfonyl fluoride	558-25-8	Liquid	1,000	1
Methidathion	950-37-8	Solid	500	1
Methiocarb	2032-65-7	Solid	500	10
Methomyl	16752-77-5	Solid	500	100
Methoxyethylmercuric acetate	151-38-2	Solid	500	1
Methyl 2-chloroacrylate	80-63-7	Liquid	500	1
Methyl bromide	74-83-9	Gas	1,000	1,000
Methyl chloroformate	79-22-1	Liquid	500	1,000
Methyl disulfide	624-92-0	Liquid	100	1
Methyl isocyanate	624-83-9	Liquid	500	1
Methyl isothiocyanate	556-61-6	Solid	500	1
Methyl mercaptan	74-93-1	Gas	500	100
Methyl phenkapton	3735-23-7	Liquid	500	1
Methyl phosphonic dichloride	676-97-1	Liquid	100	1
Methyl thiocyanate	556-64-9	Liquid	10,000	1
Methyl vinyl ketone	78-94-4	Liquid	10	1
Methylhydrazine	60-34-4	Liquid	500	10
Methylmercuric dicyanamide	502-39-6	Solid	500	1
Methyltrichlorosilane	75-79-6	Liquid	500	1
Metolcarb	1129-41-5	Solid	100	1
Mevinphos	7786-34-7	Liquid	500	10
Mexacarbate	315-18-4	Solid	500	1,000
Mitomycin C	50-07-7	Solid	500	1
Monocrotophos	6923-22-4	Solid	10	1
Muscimol	2763-96-4	Solid	500	1,000
Mustard gas	505-60-2	Liquid	500	1
Nickel	7440-02-0	Solid	1,000	1
Nickel carbonyl	13463-39-3	Liquid	1	10
Nicotine	54-11-5	Solid	100	1
Nicotine sulfate	65-30-5	Solid	100	100
Nitric acid	7697-37-2	Liquid	1,000	1,000
Nitric oxide	10102-43-9	Gas	100	10
Nitrobenzene	98-95-3	Liquid	10,000	1,000
Nitrocyclohexane	1122-60-7	Solid	500	1
Nitrogen dioxide	10102-44-0	Gas	100	10
Nitrosodimethylamine	62-75-9	Liquid	1,000	1
Norbormide	991-42-4	Solid	100	1
Organorhodium complex (PMN-82-147)	0	Solid	10	1
Orotic acid	65-86-1	Solid	10,000	1
Osmium tetroxide	20816-12-0	Solid	10,000	1,000
Ouabain	630-60-4	Solid	100	1
Oxamyl	23135-22-0	Solid	100	1
Oxetane, 3,3-bis(chloromethyl)-	78-71-7	Liquid	500	1
Oxydisulfoton	2497-07-6	Liquid	500	1
Ozone	10028-15-6	Gas	100	1
Paraquat	1910-42-5	Solid	10	1
Paraquat methosulfate	2074-50-2	Liquid	10	1
Parathion	56-38-2	Liquid	100	10
Parathion-methyl	298-00-0	Solid	100	100
Paris green	12002-03-8	Solid	500	1
Pentaborane	19624-22-7	Solid	500	1
Pentachloroethane	76-01-7	Liquid	10,000	1
Pentachlorophenol	87-86-5	Solid	10,000	10
Pentadecylamine	2570-26-5	Liquid	500	1
Peracetic acid	79-21-0	Liquid	500	1
Perchloromethylmercaptan	594-42-3	Liquid	500	100
Phenol	108-95-2	Solid	500	1,000
Phenol, 2,2'-thiobis[4,6-dichloro-	97-18-7	Solid	100	1
Phenol, 2,2'-thiobis[4-chloro-6-methyl-	4418-66-0	Solid	100	1
Phenol, 3-(1-methylethyl)-, methylcarbamate	64-00-6	Solid	500	1
Phenoxarsine, 10,10'-oxydi-	58-36-6	Solid	500	1
Phenyl dichloroarsine	696-28-6	Liquid	1,000	1
Phenylhydrazine hydrochloride	59-88-1	Solid	1,000	1
Phenylmercury acetate	62-38-4	Solid	500	100
Phenylsilatrane	2097-19-0	Solid	500	1
Phenylthiourea	103-85-5	Solid	100	100
Phorate	298-02-2	Liquid	10	10
Phosacetim	4104-14-7	Solid	100	1
Phosfolan	947-02-4	Solid	100	1
Phosgene	75-44-5	Gas	10	10
Phosmet	732-11-6	Solid	10	10
Phosphamidon	13171-21-6	Liquid	100	1

APPENDIX D.—LIST OF EXTREMELY HAZARDOUS SUBSTANCES, THRESHOLD PLANNING QUANTITIES, AND REPORTABLE QUANTITIES—Continued

[Alphabetical Order]

Chemical name	CAS No.	Ambient physical state	Threshold planning quantity (pounds)	Reportable quantity (pounds)
Phosphine	7803-51-2	Gas	500	100
Phosphonothioic acid, methyl-, O-ethyl O-(4-(methylthio)phenyl) ester	2703-13-1	Liquid	500	' 1
Phosphonothioic acid, methyl-, S-(2-(bis(1-methylethyl)amino)ethyl) O-ethyl ester	50782-69-9	Liquid	100	' 1
Phosphonothioic acid, methyl-,O-(4-nitrophenyl) O-phenyl ester	2665-30-7	Liquid	500	' 1
Phosphonic acid, dimethyl 4-(methylthio) phenyl ester	3254-63-5	Liquid	500	' 1
Phosphorous trichloride	7719-12-2	Liquid	1,000	1,000
Phosphorous	7723-14-0	Solid	' 500	1
Phosphorus	10025-87-3	Liquid	500	1,000
Phosphorus oxychloride	10026-13-8	Solid	' 500	' 1
Phosphorus pentachloride	1314-56-3	Solid	' 2	' 1
Phosphorus pentoxide	' 84-80-0	Liquid	10,000	' 1
Phylloquinone	57-47-6	Solid	100	' 1
Physostigmine	57-64-7	Solid	100	' 1
Physostigmine, salicylate (1:1)	124-87-8	Solid	500	' 1
Picrotoxin	110-89-4	Liquid	1,000	' 1
Piperidine	5281-13-0	Solid	100	' 1
Piprotal	23505-41-1	Liquid	1,000	' 1
Pirimifos-ethyl	' 10025-65-7	Solid	10,000	' 1
Platinous chloride	' 13454-96-1	Solid	10,000	' 1
Platinum tetrachloride	10124-50-2	Solid	500	' 1,000
Potassium arsenite	151-50-8	Solid	' 100	1
Potassium cyanide	506-61-6	Solid	' 500	1
Potassium silver cyanide	2631-37-0	Solid	1,000	' 1
Fromecarb	106-96-7	Liquid	2	' 1
Propargyl bromide	57-57-8	Liquid	500	' 1
Propioacetone, beta-	107-12-0	Liquid	500	10
Propionitrile	542-76-7	Liquid	1,000	1,000
Propionitrile, 3-chloro-	109-61-5	Liquid	500	' 1
Propyl chloroformate	' 1331-17-5	Liquid	10,000	' 1
Propylene glycol, allyl ether	75-56-9	Liquid	10,000	100
Propylene oxide	75-55-8	Liquid	10,000	' 1
Propyleneimine	2275-18-5	Solid	100	' 1
Prothoate	' 95-63-6	Liquid	10,000	' 1
Pseudocumene	129-00-0	Solid	' 1,000	5,000
Pyrene	140-76-1	Liquid	500	' 1
Pyridine, 2-methyl-5-vinyl-	504-24-5	Solid	100	1,000
Pyridine, 4-amino-	1124-33-0	Solid	500	' 1
Pyridine, 4-nitro-, 1-oxide	53558-25-1	Solid	1,000	' 1
Pyrimidi	' 10049-07-7	Solid	10,000	' 1
Rhodium trichloride	14167-18-1	Solid	500	' 1
Salcomine	107-44-8	Liquid	' 2	' 1
Sarin	7791-23-3	Liquid	500	' 1
Selenium oxychloride	7738-00-8	Solid	1,000	10
Selenous acid	563-41-7	Solid	1,000	' 1
Semicarbazide hydrochloride	3037-72-7	Liquid	500	' 1
Silane, (4-aminobutyl)diethoxymethyl-	' 126-56-3	Solid	10,000	' 1
Sodium anthraquinone-1-sulfonate	7631-89-2	Solid	100	' 1,000
Sodium arsenate	7784-46-5	Solid	500	' 1,000
Sodium arsenite	26628-22-8	Solid	' ' 100	1,000
Sodium azide (Na(N3))	124-65-2	Solid	100	10
Sodium cacodylate	143-33-9	Solid	' 100	10
Sodium cyanide (Na(CN))	62-74-8	Solid	2	10
Sodium fluoroacetate	131-52-2	Solid	100	' 1
Sodium pentachlorophenate	13410-01-0	Solid	100	' 1
Sodium selenate	10102-18-8	Solid	500	100
Sodium selenite	10102-20-2	Solid	500	' 1
Sodium tellurite	57-24-9	Solid	100	10
Strychnine	60-41-3	Solid	100	' 1
Strychnine, sulfate	3689-24-5	Liquid	500	100
Sulfotep	3569-57-1	Liquid	500	' 1
Sulfoxide, 3-chloropropyl octyl	7446-09-5	Gas	500	' 1
Sulfur dioxide	7783-60-0	Gas	100	' 1
Sulfur tetrafluoride	7446-11-9	Solid	' 100	' 1
Sulfur trioxide	7664-93-9	Liquid	1,000	1,000
Sulfuric acid	77-81-6	Liquid	' 2	' 1
Tabun	13494-80-9	Solid	500	' 1
Tellurium	7783-80-4	Gas	2	10
Tellurium hexafluoride	107-49-3	Liquid	100	10
Tepp	13071-79-9	Solid	500	' 1
Terbufos	78-00-2	Liquid	' 100	' 10
Tetraethyllead	597-64-8	Liquid	' 100	' 1
Tetraethyltin	75-74-1	Liquid	' 100	' 1
Tetramethyl lead	509-14-8	Liquid	500	10
Tetranitromethane	' 1314-32-5	Liquid	10,000	100
Thallic oxide	10031-59-1	Solid	100	100
Thallium sulfate	6533-73-9	Solid	' 100	100
Thallous carbonate	7791-12-0	Solid	' 100	100
Thallous chloride	2757-18-8	Solid	' 100	100
Thallous malonate	7446-18-6	Solid	100	100
Thallous sulfate	2231-57-4	Solid	1,000	100
Thiocarbazide	' 21564-17-0	Solid	10,000	' 1
Thiocyanic acid, 2-(benzothazolylthio)methyl ester	39196-18-4	Solid	100	100
Thiofanox	' 640-15-3	Liquid	10,000	' 1
Thiometon	297-97-2	Liquid	500	100
Thionazin	108-98-5	Liquid	500	100
Thiophenol	79-19-6	Solid	100	100
Thiosemicarbazide	5344-82-1	Liquid	100	100
Thiourea, (2-chlorophenyl)-	614-78-8	Solid	500	' 1
Thiourea, (2-methylphenyl)-	7550-45-0	Liquid	100	' 1
Titanium tetrachloride				

Appendix D.—List of Extremely Hazardous Substances, Threshold Planning Quantities, and Reportable Quantities—Continued

[Alphabetical Order]

Chemical name	CAS No.	Ambient physical state	Threshold planning quantity (pounds)	Reportable quantity (pounds)
Toluene 2,4-diisocyanate	548-84-9	Liquid	500	100
Toluene 2,6-diisocyanate	91-08-7	Liquid	100	100
Trans-1,4-dichlorobutene	110-57-6	Liquid	500	[1] 1
Triamiphos	1031-47-6	Solid	500	[1] 1
Triazofos	24017-47-8	Liquid	500	[1] 1
Trichloro(chloromethyl)silane	1558-25-4	Liquid	100	[1] 1
Trichloro(dichlorophenyl)silane	27137-85-5	Liquid	500	[1] 1
Trichloroacetyl chloride	76-02-8	Liquid	500	[1] 1
Trichloroethylsilane	115-21-9	Liquid	500	[1] 1
Trichloronate	327-98-0	Liquid	10,000	[1] 1
Trichlorophenylsilane	98-13-5	Liquid	1,000	[1] 1
Trichlorophon	[5] 52-68-6	Solid	2	[1] 1
Triethoxysilane	998-30-1	Liquid	10,000	100
Trimethylchlorosilane	75-77-4	Liquid	500	[1] 1
Trimethylolpropane phosphite	824-11-3	Solid	1,000	[1] 1
Trimethyltin chloride	1066-45-1	Solid	500	[1] 1
Triphenyltin chloride	639-58-7	Solid	500	[1] 1
Tris(2-chloroethyl)amine	555-77-1	Liquid	1,000	[1] 1
Valinomycin	2001-95-8	Solid	1,000	[1] 1
Vanadium pentoxide	1314-62-1	Solid	[3] [1] 100	[1] 1
Vinyl acetate monomer	108-05-4	Liquid	[1] 100	1,000
Vinylnorbornene	[5] 3048-64-4	Liquid	1,000	5,000
Warfarin	81-81-2	Solid	10,000	[1] 1
Warfarin sodium	129-06-6	Solid	500	100
Xylylene dichloride	28347-13-9	Liquid	1,000	[1] 1
Zinc phosphide	1314-84-7	Solid	[1] 500	100
Zinc, dichloro(4,4-dimethyl-5-((((methylamino)carbonyl)oxy)imino)pentanenitrile)-	58270-08-9	Solid	100	[1] 1

[1] Statutory reportable quantity for purposes of emergency notification under SARA section 304(a)(2).
[2] Indicates that the reportable quantity is subject to change when the assessment of potential carcinogenicity and/or chronic toxicity is completed.
[3] The calculated threshold quantity changed after technical review as described in the text.
[4] This material is a reactive solid. The threshold planning quantity will not become 10,000 pounds for the non-powder form.
[5] This chemical is proposed for deletion from list. Threshold planning quantity is in the interim assigned to the category of lowest concern, 10,000 pounds.
[6] The statutory one-pound reportable quantity for methyl isocyanate under CERCLA section 102(b) may be adjusted in a future rulemaking action.

Appendix E.—List of Extremely Hazardous Substances, Threshold Planning Quantities, and Reportable Quantities

[CAS Order]

CAS No.	Chemical name	Ambient physical state	Threshold planning quantity (pounds)	Reportable quantity (pounds)
0	Organorhodium complex (PMN-82-147)	Solid	2	[1] 1
50-00-0	Formaldehyde	Gas	500	[2] 1,000
50-07-7	Mitomycin C	Solid	500	[2] 1
50-14-6	Ergocalciferol	Solid	1,000	[1] 1
51-21-8	Fluorouracil	Solid	[3] 1,000	[1] 1
51-75-2	Mechlorethamine	Solid	500	[1] 1
51-83-2	Carbachol chloride	Liquid	[2] 2	[1] 1
52-68-6 [5]	Trichlorophon	Solid	500	[1] 1
53-86-1 [5]	Indomethacin	Solid	10,000	100
54-11-5	Nicotine	Solid	10,000	[1] 1
54-62-6	Aminopterin	Liquid	[3] 100	100
55-91-4	Isofluorphate	Solid	500	[1] 1
56-25-7	Canthandin	Liquid	[3] 100	100
56-38-2	Parathion	Solid	100	[1] 1
56-72-4	Coumaphos	Liquid	[3] 100	[2] 1
57-14-7	Dimethylhydrazine	Solid	100	10
57-24-9	Strychnine	Liquid	1,000	[2] 1
57-47-6	Physostigmine	Solid	[3] 100	10
57-57-8	Propiolactone, beta-	Liquid	500	[1] 1
57-64-7	Physostigmine, salicylate (1:1)	Solid	100	[1] 1
57-74-9	Chlordane	Solid	100	[1] 1
58-36-6	Phenoxarsine, 10, 10'-oxydi-	Liquid	1,000	[2] 1
58-89-9	Lindane	Solid	500	[1] 1
59-88-1	Phenylhydrazine hydrochloride	Solid	1,000	[2] 1
60-34-4	Methylhydrazine	Solid	1,000	[1] 1
60-41-3	Strychnine, sulfate	Liquid	500	10
60-51-5	Dimethoate	Solid	100	[1] 1
62-38-4	Phenylmercury acetate	Solid	500	10
62-53-3	Aniline	Solid	500	100
62-73-7	Dichlorvos	Liquid	1,000	5,000
62-74-8	Sodium fluoroacetate	Solid	1,000	10
62-75-9	Nitrosodimethylamine	Liquid	2	10
64-00-6	Phenol, 3-(1-methylethyl)-, methylcarbamate	Solid	500	[2] 1
64-86-8	Colchicine	Solid	500	[1] 1
65-30-5	Nicotine sulfate	Solid	100	[1] 1
65-86-1 [5]	Orotic acid	Solid	10,000	[1] 1
66-81-9	Cycloheximide	Solid	100	[1] 1
67-66-3	Chloroform	Liquid	10,000	[2] 5,000
71-63-6	Digitoxin	Solid	[3] 100	[1] 1
72-20-8	Endrin	Solid	500	1
74-83-9	Methyl bromide	Gas	1,000	1,000
74-90-8	Hydrocyanic acid	Gas	100	10
74-93-1	Methyl mercaptan	Gas	500	100
75-15-0	Carbon disulfide	Liquid	10,000	100
75-18-3	Dimethyl sulfide	Liquid	100	[1] 1

APPENDIX E.—LIST OF EXTREMELY HAZARDOUS SUBSTANCES, THRESHOLD PLANNING QUANTITIES, AND REPORTABLE QUANTITIES—Continued

[CAS Order]

CAS No.	Chemical name	Ambient physical state	Threshold planning quantity (pounds)	Reportable quantity (pounds)
75-21-8	Ethylene oxide	Gas	1,000	ª 1
75-44-5	Phosgene	Gas	2	10
75-55-8	Propyleneimine	Liquid	10,000	ª 1
75-56-9	Propylene oxide	Liquid	ª 100	100
75-74-1	Tetramethyl lead	Liquid	1,000	ª 1
75-77-4	Trimethylchlorosilane	Liquid	10,000	ª 1
75-78-5	Dimethyldichlorosilane	Liquid	10,000	ª 1
75-79-6	Methyltrichlorosilane	Liquid	1,000	10
75-86-5	Acetone cyanohydrin	Liquid	10,000	ª 1
76-01-7 ª	Pentachloroethane	Liquid	500	ª 1
76-02-8	Trichloroacetyl chloride	Liquid	500	ª 1
77-47-4	Hexachlorocyclopentadiene	Liquid	500	ª 1
77-78-1	Dimethyl sulfate	Liquid	ª 2	ª 1
77-81-6	Tabun	Liquid	ª 100	ª 10
78-00-2	Tetraethyllead	Liquid	500	ª 1
78-34-2	Dioxathion	Liquid	500	ª 1
78-53-5	Amiton	Liquid	500	ª 1
78-71-7	Oxetane, 3,3-bis(chloromethyl)-	Liquid	10,000	ª 1
78-82-0	Isobutyronitrile	Liquid	2	ª 1
78-94-4	Methyl vinyl ketone	Liquid	1,000	ª 1
78-97-7	Lactonitrile	Solid	1,000	5,000
79-06-1	Acrylamide	Solid	100	ª 1
79-11-8	Chloroacetic acid	Solid	100	100
79-19-6	Thiosemicarbazide	Solid	500	ª 1
79-21-0	Peracetic acid	Liquid	10,000	1,000
79-22-1	Methyl Chloroformate	Liquid	500	ª 1
80-63-7	Methyl 2-chloroacrylate	Solid	500	100
81-81-2	Warfarin	Solid	2	ª 1
82-66-6	Diphacinone	Liquid	10,000	10
84-74-2 ª	Dibutyl phthalate	Liquid	10,000	ª 1
84-80-0 ª	Phylloquinone	Liquid	2	1
86-50-0	Azinphos-methyl	Solid	500	100
86-88-4	Antu	Solid	10,000	ª 10
87-86-5 ª	Pentachlorophenol	Solid	500	ª 1
88-05-1	Aniline, 2,4,6-trimethyl-	Liquid	100	1,000
88-85-7	Dinoseb	Solid	100	100
91-08-7	Toluene 2,6-diisocyanate	Liquid	10,000	ª 1
93-05-0 ª	Diethyl-p-phenylenediamine	Solid	1,000	ª 1,000
95-48-7	Cresol, o-	Liquid	10,000	ª 1
95-63-6 ª	Pseudocumene	Solid	100	ª 1
97-18-7	Phenol, 2,2'-thiobis(4,6-dichloro-	Solid	2	ª 1
98-05-5	Benzenearsonic acid	Solid	100	ª 1
98-07-7	Benzotrichloride	Liquid	10,000	100
98-09-9 ª	Benzenesulfonyl chloride	Liquid	2	ª 1
98-13-5	Trichlorophenylsilane	Liquid	500	ª 1
98-16-8	Benzenamine, 3-(trifluoromethyl)-	Liquid	500	5,000
98-87-3	Benzal chloride	Liquid	10,000	1,000
98-95-3	Nitrobenzene	Solid	2	ª 1
99-98-9	Dimethyl-p-phenylenediamine	Solid	500	ª 1
100-14-1	Benzene, 1-(chloromethyl)-4-nitro-	Solid	500	ª 100
100-44-7	Benzyl Chloride	Liquid	500	100
102-36-3	Isocyanic acid, 3,4-dichlorophenyl ester	Solid	100	100
103-85-5	Phenylthiourea	Solid	1,000	ª 1,000
106-89-8	Epichlorohydrin	Liquid	2	ª 1
106-96-7	Propargyl bromide	Liquid	10,000	ª 1
106-99-0 ª	Butadiene	Gas	500	ª 1
107-02-8	Acrolein	Liquid	500	ª 1
107-07-3	Chloroethanol	Liquid	500	ª 1
107-11-9	Allylamine	Liquid	500	10
107-12-0	Propionitrile	Liquid	10,000	ª 100
107-13-1	Acrylonitrile	Liquid	10,000	5,000
107-15-3	Ethylenediamine	Liquid	10,000	ª 1
107-16-4	Formaldehyde cyanohydrin	Liquid	1,000	100
107-18-6	Allyl alcohol	Liquid	10,000	1,000
107-20-0 ª	Chloroacetaldehyde	Liquid	ª 100	ª 1
107-30-2	Chloromethyl methyl ether	Liquid	ª 2	ª 1
107-44-8	Sarin	Liquid	ª 100	10
107-49-3	Tepp	Liquid	1,000	5,000
108-05-4	Vinyl acetate monomer	Liquid	1,000	ª 1
108-23-6	Isopropyl chloroformate	Liquid	1,000	ª 1
108-67-8 ª	Mesitylene	Liquid	10,000	ª 1
108-91-8	Cyclohexylamine	Solid	500	1,000
108-95-2	Phenol	Solid	500	100
108-98-5	Thiophenol	Liquid	10,000	ª 1
109-19-3 ª	Butyl isovalerate	Liquid	500	ª 1
109-61-5	Propyl chloroformate	Solid	500	1,000
109-77-3	Malononitrile	Liquid	500	ª 1
110-00-9	Furan	Liquid	500	ª 1
110-57-6	Trans-1,4-dichlorobutene	Liquid	1,000	ª 1
110-89-4	Piperidine	Liquid	10,000	ª 1
111-34-2 ª	Butyl vinyl ether	Liquid	10,000	ª 1
111-44-4	Dichloroethyl ether	Liquid	10,000	ª 1
111-69-3	Adiponitrile	Liquid	10,000	ª 1
115-21-9	Trichloroethylsilane	Liquid	500	ª 1
115-26-4	Dimefox	Solid	2	ª 1
115-29-7	Endosulfan	Liquid	1,000	ª 1
115-90-2	Fensulfothion	Solid	ª 100	1
116-06-3	Aldicarb			

APPENDIX E.—LIST OF EXTREMELY HAZARDOUS SUBSTANCES, THRESHOLD PLANNING QUANTITIES, AND REPORTABLE QUANTITIES—Continued

[CAS Order]

CAS No.	Chemical name	Ambient physical state	Threshold planning quantity (pounds)	Reportable quantity (pounds)
117-52-2 *	Coumafuryl	Solid	10,000	[1] 1
117-84-0 *	Dioctyl phthalate	Liquid	10,000	5,000
119-38-0	Isopropylmethylpyrazolyl dimethylcarbamate	Liquid	500	[1] 1
122-14-5	Fenitrothion	Liquid	500	[1] 1
123-31-9	Hydroquinone	Solid	500	[1] 1
123-73-9	Crotonaldehyde, (E)-	Liquid	1,000	100
124-65-2	Sodium cacodylate	Solid	100	[1] 1
124-87-8	Picrotoxin	Solid	500	[1] 1
126-98-7	Methacrylonitrile	Liquid	500	[1] 1
128-56-3 *	Sodium anthraquinone-1-sulfonate	Solid	10,000	1,000
129-00-0	Pyrene	Solid	10,000	[1] 1
129-06-6	Warfarin sodium	Solid	[3] 1,000	5,000
131-11-3 *	Dimethyl phthalate	Solid	10,000	[1] 1
131-52-2	Sodium pentachlorophenate	Liquid	10,000	5,000
140-29-4	Benzyl cyanide	Solid	100	[1] 1
140-76-1	Pyridine, 2-methyl-5-vinyl-	Liquid	1,000	[1] 1
141-66-2	Dicrotophos	Liquid	500	[1] 1
143-33-9	Sodium cyanide (Na(CN))	Solid	100	10
144-49-0	Fluoroacetic acid	Solid	[3] 100	10
149-74-6	Dichloromethylphenylsilane	Solid	2	[1] 1
151-38-2	Methoxyethylmercuric acetate	Liquid	1,000	[1] 1
151-50-8	Potassium cyanide	Solid	500	[1] 1
151-56-4	Ethyleneimine	Liquid	[3] 100	10
152-16-9	Diphosphoramide, octamethyl-	Solid	500	[1] 1
207-92-3 *	Cyclopentane	Liquid	100	100
297-78-9	Isobenzan	Liquid	10,000	[1] 1
297-97-2	Thionazin	Solid	100	[1] 1
298-00-0	Parathion-methyl	Liquid	500	100
298-02-2	Phorate	Solid	[3] 100	100
298-04-4	Disulfoton	Liquid	500	1
300-62-9	Amphetamine	Liquid	500	[1] 1
302-01-2	Hydrazine	Liquid	1,000	[1] 1
309-00-2	Aldrin	Solid	500	[2] 1
315-18-4	Mexacarbate	Solid	500	[2] 1
316-42-7	Emetine, dihydrochloride	Solid	1,000	1,000
327-98-0	Trichloronate	Liquid	500	[1] 1
353-42-4	Boron trifluoride compound with methyl ether (1:1)	Liquid	1,000	[1] 1
359-06-8	Fluoroacetyl chloride	Liquid	[3] 2	[1] 1
371-62-0	Ethylene fluorohydrin	Liquid	[3] 2	[1] 1
379-79-3	Ergotamine tartrate	Solid	500	[1] 1
465-73-6	Isodrin	Solid	100	[1] 1
470-90-6	Chlorfenvinfos	Liquid	500	[1] 1
502-39-6	Methylmercuric dicyanamide	Solid	500	[1] 1
504-24-5	Pyridine, 4-amino-	Solid	500	[1] 1
505-60-2	Mustard gas	Liquid	100	1,000
506-61-6	Potassium silver cyanide	Solid	[3] 500	[1] 1
506-68-3	Cyanogen bromide	Solid	500	1,000
506-78-5	Cyanogen iodide	Solid	1,000	[1] 1
509-14-8	Tetranitromethane	Liquid	500	10
514-73-8	Dithiazanine iodide	Solid	500	[1] 1
534-07-6	Bis (chloromethyl) ketone	Solid	2	[1] 1
534-52-1	Dinitrocresol	Solid	2	10
535-89-7	Crimidine	Solid	100	[1] 1
538-07-8	Ethylbis (2-chloroethyl) amine	Liquid	10,000	[1] 1
541-25-3	Lewisite	Liquid	10,000	[1] 1
541-53-7	Dithiobiuret	Solid	100	100
542-76-7	Propionitrile, 3-chloro-	Liquid	1,000	1,000
542-88-1	Chloromethyl ether	Liquid	1,000	[2] 1
542-90-5	Ethyl thiocyanate	Liquid	10,000	[1] 1
555-77-1	Tris (2-chloroethyl) amine	Liquid	1,000	[1] 1
556-61-6	Methyl isothiocyanate	Solid	[3] 500	[1] 1
556-64-9	Methyl thiocyanate	Liquid	10,000	[1] 1
558-25-8	Methanesulfonyl fluoride	Liquid	1,000	[1] 1
563-12-2	Ethion	Liquid	1,000	10
563-41-7	Semicarbazide hydrochloride	Solid	1,000	[1] 1
584-84-9	Toluene 2, 4-desocyanate	Solid	500	100
594-42-3	Perchloromethylmercaptan	Liquid	500	100
597-64-8	Tetraethyltin	Liquid	100	[1] 1
614-78-8	Thiourea, (2-methylphenyl)-	Solid	[3] 100	[1] 1
624-83-9	Methyl isocyanate	Liquid	500	[1] 1
624-92-0	Methyl disulfide	Liquid	100	[1] 1
625-55-8	Isopropyl formate	Liquid	500	[1] 1
627-11-2	Chloroethyl chloroformate	Liquid	1,000	[1] 1
630-60-4	Ouabain	Solid	[3] 100	[1] 1
633-03-4 *	C.I. basic green 1	Solid	10,000	[1] 1
639-58-7	Triphenyltin chloride	Solid	500	[1] 1
640-15-3 *	Thiometon	Liquid	10,000	[1] 1
640-19-7	Fluoroacetamide	Solid	[3] 2	100
644-64-4	Dimetilan	Solid	500	[1] 1
646-06-0 *	Dioxane	Liquid	10,000	[1] 1
675-14-9	Cyanuric fluoride	Liquid	100	[1] 1
676-97-1	Methyl phosphonic dichloride	Solid	[3] 100	[1] 1
696-28-6	Phenyl dichloroarsine	Liquid	1,000	[1] 1
732-11-6	Phosmet	Solid	2	[1] 1
760-93-0	Methacrylic anhydride	Liquid	500	[1] 1
786-19-6	Carbophenothion	Liquid	500	[1] 1
814-49-3	Diethyl chlorophosphate	Liquid	1,000	[1] 1
814-68-6	Acrylyl chloride	Liquid	500	[1] 1

APPENDIX E.—LIST OF EXTREMELY HAZARDOUS SUBSTANCES, THRESHOLD PLANNING QUANTITIES, AND REPORTABLE QUANTITIES—Continued

[CAS Order]

CAS No.	Chemical name	Ambient physical state	Threshold planning quantity (pounds)	Reportable quantity (pounds)
824–11–3	Trimethylolpropane phosphite	Solid	500	¹ 1
919–86–8	Demeton-S-methyl	Liquid	500	¹ 1
920–46–7	Methacryloyl chloride	Liquid	100	¹ 1
944–22–9	Fonofos	Solid	500	¹ 1
947–02–4	Phosfolan	Solid	100	¹ 1
950–10–7	Mephosfolan	Liquid	500	¹ 1
950–37–8	Methidathion	Solid	500	¹ 1
991–42–4	Norbormide	Solid	100	¹ 1
998–30–1	Triethoxysilane	Liquid	500	¹ 1
999–81–5	Chlormequat chloride	Solid	1,000	¹ 1
1031–47–6	Triamiphos	Solid	500	¹ 1
1066–45–1	Trimethyltin chloride	Solid	500	¹ 1
1122–60–7	Nitrocyclohexane	Liquid	500	¹ 1
1124–33–0	Pyridine, 4-nitro-, 1-oxide	Solid	500	¹ 1
1129–41–5	Metolcarb	Solid	100	¹ 1
1303–28–2	Arsenic pentoxide	Solid	100	⁵ 5,000
1306–19–0	Cadmium oxide	Solid	100	¹ 1
1314–32–5 *	Thallic oxide	Solid	10,000	100
1314–56–3	Phosphorus pentoxide	Solid	² 2	¹ 1
1314–62–1	Vanadium pentoxide	Solid	⁵ 100	1,000
1314–84–7	Zinc phosphide	Solid	⁵ 500	100
1327–53–3	Arsenous oxide	Solid	500	⁵ 5000
1331–17–5 *	Propylene glycol, allyl ether	Liquid	10,000	¹ 1
1335–87–1 *	Hexachloronaphthalene	Solid	10,000	¹ 1
1397–94–0 *	Antimycin A	Solid	¹ 1,000	¹ 1
1405–87–4 *	Bacitracin	Solid	1,000	¹ 1
1420–07–1	Dinoterb	Solid	500	¹ 1
1464–53–5	Diepoxybutane	Liquid	500	¹ 1
1558–25–4	Trichloro(chloromethyl)silane	Liquid	100	¹ 1
1563–66–2	Carbofuran	Solid	2	10
1600–27–7	Mercuric acetate	Solid	500	¹ 1
1622–32–8	Ethanesulfonyl chloride, 2-chloro-	Liquid	500	¹ 1
1642–54–2	Diethylcarbamazine citrate	Solid	100	¹ 1
1752–30–3	Acetone thiosemicarbazide	Solid	1,000	¹ 1
1910–42–5	Paraquat	Solid	2	¹ 1
1982–47–4	Chloroxuron	Solid	500	¹ 1
2001–95–8	Valinomycin	Solid	¹ 1,000	10
2032–65–7	Methiocarb	Solid	500	10
2074–50–2	Paraquat methosulfate	Solid	2	¹ 1
2097–19–0	Phenylsilatrane	Solid	500	¹ 1
2104–64–5	EPN	Solid	100	¹ 1
2223–93–0	Cadmium stearate	Solid	1,000	¹ 1
2231–57–4	Thiocarbazide	Solid	1,000	¹ 1
2235–25–8 *	Ethylmercuric phosphate	Solid	10,000	¹ 1
2238–07–5	Diglycidyl ether	Liquid	1,000	¹ 1
2244–16–8 *	Carvone	Liquid	10,000	¹ 1
2275–18–5	Porthoate	Liquid	100	¹ 1
2497–07–6	Oxydisulfoton	Solid	1,000	¹ 1
2524–03–0	Dimethyl phosphorochloridothioate	Liquid	500	¹ 1
2540–82–1	Formothion	Liquid	100	¹ 1
2570–26–5	Pentadecylamine	Liquid	100	¹ 1
2631–37–0	Promecarb	Solid	1,000	¹ 1
2636–26–2	Cyanophos	Solid	1,000	¹ 1
2642–71–9	Azinphos-ethyl	Liquid	100	¹ 1
2665–30–7	Phosphonothioic acid, methyl-0-(4-nitrophenyl) 0-phenyl ester	Liquid	500	¹ 1
2703–13–1	Phosphonothioic acid, methyl-,0-ethyl 0-(4-(methylthio)phenyl) ester	Liquid	⁵ 100	¹ 1
2757–18–8	Thallous malonate	Solid	500	1,000
2763–96–4	Muscimol	Solid	500	¹ 1
2778–04–3	Endothion	Solid	500	¹ 1
3037–72–7	Silane, (4-aminobutyl)diethoxymethyl-	Liquid	1,000	¹ 1
3048–64–4 *	Vinylnorbornene	Liquid	10,000	¹ 1
3254–63–5	Phosphoric acid, dimethyl 4-(methylthio)phenyl ester	Liquid	500	¹ 1
3569–57–1	Sulfoxide, 3-chloropropyl octyl	Liquid	500	100
3689–24–5	Sulfotep	Liquid	500	¹ 1
3691–35–8	Chlorophacinone	Solid	100	¹ 1
3734–97–2	Amiton oxalate	Solid	100	¹ 1
3735–23–7	Methyl phenkapton	Liquid	500	¹ 1
3878–19–1	Fuberidazole	Solid	100	¹ 1
4044–65–9	Bitoscanate	Solid	500	¹ 1
4098–71–9	Isophorone diisocyanate	Solid	⁵ 100	¹ 1
4104–14–7	Phosacetim	Solid	100	100
4170–30–3	Crotonaldehyde	Liquid	1,000	¹ 1
4301–50–2	Fluenetil	Solid	100	¹ 1
4418–66–0	Phenol, 2,2'-thiobis[4-chloro-6-methyl-	Solid	100	¹ 1
4835–11–4	Hexamethylenediamine, N,N'-dibutyl-	Liquid	500	100
5281–13–0	Piprotal	Solid	100	¹ 1
5344–82–1	Thiourea, (2-chlorophenyl)-	Solid	100	100
5836–29–3	Coumatetralyl	Solid	⁵ 100	100
6533–73–9	Thallous carbonate	Solid	2	¹ 1
6923–22–4	Monocrotophos	Solid	10,000	¹ 1
7440–02–0 *	Nickel	Solid	10,000	¹ 1
7440–48–4 *	Cobalt	Solid	500	¹ 1
7446–09–5	Sulfur dioxide	Gas	⁵ 100	¹ 1
7446–11–9	Sulfur trioxide	Solid	100	100
7446–18–6	Thallous sulfate	Solid	100	¹ 1
7487–94–7	Mercuric chloride	Solid	500	¹ 1
7550–45–0	Titanium tetrachloride	Liquid	⁵ 100	¹ 1
7580–67–8	Lithium hydride	Solid	100	¹ 1

APPENDIX 6G

[CAS Order]

CAS No.	Chemical name	Ambient physical state	Threshold planning quantity (pounds)	Reportable quantity (pounds)
7631-89-2	Sodium arsenate	Solid	1,000	1,000 (d)
7637-07-2	Boron trifluoride	Gas	500	1 1
7647-01-0	Hydrogen chloride	Gas	500	5,000
7664-39-3	Hydrogen fluoride	Gas	100	100
7664-41-7	Ammonia	Gas	500	100
7664-93-9	Sulfuric acid	Liquid	1,000	1,000
7697-37-2	Nitric acid	Liquid	1,000	1,000
7719-12-2	Phosphorous trichloride	Liquid	1,000	1,000
7722-84-1	Hydrogen peroxide (concentration greater than 25%)	Liquid	1,000	1 1
7723-14-0	Phoshorus	Solid	1,000	1 1
7726-95-6	Bromine	Liquid	ª 500	1 1
7778-44-1	Calcium arsenate	Solid	500	1 1
7782-41-4	Fluorine	Gas	500	² 1,000
7782-50-5	Chlorine	Gas	100	10
7783-00-8	Selenous acid	Solid	1,000	10
7783-06-4	Hydrogen sulfide	Gas	500	100
7783-07-5	Hydrogen selende	Gas	2	1 1
7783-60-0	Sulfur tetrafluoride	Gas	100	1 1
7783-70-2	Antimony pentafluoride	Liquid	500	1 1
7783-80-4	Tellurium nexafluoride	Gas	2	1 1
7784-34-1	Arsenous trichloride	Liquid	500	ª 5,000
7784-42-1	Arsine	Gas	100	1 1
7784-46-5	Sodium arsenite	Solid	500	² 1,000
7786-34-7	Mevinphos	Liquid	ª 100	100
7791-12-0	Thallous chloride	Solid	100	10
7791-23-3	Selenium Oxychloride	Liquid	500	1 1
7803-51-2	Phosphine	Gas	500	100
8001-35-2	Camphechlor	Solid	500	2 1
8023-53-8 ª	Dichlorobenzalkonium chloride	Solid	10,000	1 1
8065-48-3	Demeton	Liquid	500	1 1
10025-65-7 ª	Platinous chloride	Solid	10,000	1 1
10025-73-7	Chromic chloride	Solid	2	1 1
10025-87-3	Phosphorus oxychloride	Liquid	500	1,000
10025-97-5 ª	Indium tetrachloride	Solid	10,000	1 1
10026-13-8	Phosphorus pentachloride	Solid	ª 500	1 1
10028-15-6	Ozone	Gas	100	1 1
10031-59-1	Thallium sulfate	Solid	100	100
10049-07-7 ª	Rhodium trichloride	Solid	10,000	1 1
10102-18-8	Sodium selenite	Solid	500	100
10102-20-2	Sodium tellurite	Solid	500	1 1
10102-43-9	Nitric oxide	Gas	ª 100	10
10102-44-0	Nitrogen dioxide	Gas	100	10
10124-50-2	Potassium arsenite	Solid	500	² 1,000
10140-87-1	Ethanol, 1,2-dichloro-, acetate	Liquid	1,000	1 1
10210-68-1	Cobalt carbonyl	Solid	100	1 1
10265-92-6	Methamidophos	Solid	100	1 1
10294-34-5	Boron trichloride	Gas	500	1 1
10311-84-9	Dialifos	Solid	100	1 1
10416-95-6	Methacrolein diacetate	Liquid	1,000	1 1
12002-03-8	Paris green	Solid	500	ª 100
12108-13-3	Manganese, tricarbonyl methylcyclopentadienyl-	Liquid	10,000	1 1
13071-79-9	Terbufos	Liquid	500	1 1
13171-21-6	Phosphamdon	Liquid	100	1 1
13194-48-4	Ethoprophos	Liquid	1,000	1 1
13410-01-0	Sodium selenate	Solid	100	1 1
13450-90-3	Gallium trichloride	Solid	500	1 1
13454-96-1 ª	Platinum tetrachloride	Solid	10,000	1 1
13463-39-3	Nickel carbonyl	Liquid	ª Any	1 1
13463-40-6	Iron, pentacarbonyl-	Liquid	100	1 1
13494-80-9	Tellurium	Solid	500	1 1
14167-18-1	Salcomine	Solid	500	1 1
15271-41-7	Bicyclo[2.2.1]heptane-2-carbonitrile, 5-chloro-6-(((methylamino)carbonyl)oxyim	Solid	500	100
16752-77-5	Methomyl	Solid	1,000	10,000
18883-66-4 ª	Ammonium chloroplatinate	Solid	10,000	1 1
17702-41-9	Decaborane(14)	Solid	500	1 1
17702-57-7	Formpararate	Solid	100	1 1
19287-45-7	Diborane	Gas	100	500
19624-22-7	Pentaborane	Gas	500	1 1
20816-12-0 ª	Osmium tetroxide	Liquid	10,000	1,000
20850-75-5	Digoxin	Solid	100	1 1
20859-73-8	Aluminum phosphide	Solid	ª 500	100
21548-32-3	Fosthietan	Liquid	500	1 1
21564-17-0	Thiocyanic acid, 2-(benzothiazolylthio)methyl ester	Liquid	10,000	1 1
21609-90-5	Leptophos	Solid	500	1 1
21908-53-2	Mercuric oxide	Solid	500	1 1
21923-23-9	Chlorthiophos	Liquid	1,000	1 1
22224-92-6	Fenamiphos	Solid	2	1 1
23135-22-0	Oxamyl	Solid	100	1 1
23422-53-9	Formetanate	Solid	500	1 1
24017-47-8	Triazofos	Liquid	1,000	1 1
24934-91-6	Chlormephos	Liquid	500	1 1
26419-73-8	Carbamic acid, methyl-, O-(((2,4-dimethyl-1,3-dithiolan-2-yl)methylene)amino)-	Solid	100	1 1
26628-22-8	Sodium azide (Na(N₃))	Solid	ª ª 100	1,000
27137-85-5	Trichloro(dichlorophenyl)silane	Liquid	500	1 1
28772-13-9	Xylylene dichloride	Solid	100	1 1
28772-56-7	Bromadiolone	Solid	100	1 1
30674-80-7	Methacryloyloxyethyl isocyanate	Liquid	500	1 1

APPENDIX E.—LIST OF EXTREMELY HAZARDOUS SUBSTANCES, THRESHOLD PLANNING QUANTITIES, AND REPORTABLE QUANTITIES—Continued

[CAS Order]

CAS No.	Chemical name	Ambient physical state	Threshold planning quantity (pounds)	Reportable quantity (pounds)
39196-18-4	Thiofanox	Solid	100	100
50782-69-9	Phosphonothioic acid, methyl-, S-(2-(bis(1-methylethyl)amino)ethyl) O-ethyl ester	Liquid	100	¹ 1
53558-25-1	Pyriminil	Solid	1,000	¹ 1
58270-08-9	Zinc, dichloro(4,4-dimethyl-5(((methylamino) carbonyl)oxy)imino)pentanenitrile)	Solid	100	¹ 1
62207-76-5	Cobalt, ((2,2'-(1,2-ethanediylbis (nitrilomethylidyne))bis(6-fluorophenolato))(2)	Solid	100	¹ 1

¹ Statutory reportable quantity for purposes of emergency notification under SARA section 304(a)(2).
² Indicates that the reportable quantity is subject to change when the assessment of potential carcinogenicity and/or chronic toxicity is completed.
³ The calculated threshold quantity changed after technical review as described in the text.
⁴ This chemical is proposed for deletion from list. Threshold planning quantity is in the interim assigned to the category of lowest concern, 10,000 pounds.
⁵ This material is a reactive solid. The threshold planning quantity will not become 10,000 pounds for the non-powder form.
⁶ The statutory one-pound reportable quantity for methyl isocyanate under CERCLA section 102(b) may be adjusted in a future rulemaking action.

[FR Doc. 86-25959 Filed 11-14-86; 8:45 am]
BILLING CODE 6560-50-M

Appendix 6H   Senate Committee List of Toxic Chemicals Subject to Section 313 of the Emergency Planning and Community Right-to-Know Act of 1986*

The following toxic chemicals are subject to annual reporting of releases into the environment under section 313 of the Emergency Planning and Community Right to Know Act of 1986. This list may be revised from time to time by the Administrator of the Environmental Protection Agency consistent with the provisions of that Act.

Chemical abstract service [CAS] number	Chemical name	Chemical abstract service [CAS] number	Chemical name
50–00–0	Formaldehyde	75–01–4	Vinyl chloride (monomer)
51–28–5	2,4-Dinitrophenol	75–05–8	Acetonitrile
51–75–2	Nitrogen mustard	75–07–0	Acetaldehyde
51–79–6	Urethane (Ethyl carbamate) (monomer)	75–09–2	Dichloromethane
52–68–6	Trichlorfon	75–15–0	Carbon disulfide
53–96–3	2-Acetylaminofluorene	75–21–8	Ethylene oxide
55–18–5	N-Nitrosodiethylamine	75–25–2	Bromoform (Tribromomethane)
55–21–0	Benzamide	75–27–4	Dichlorobromomethane
55–63–0	Nitroglycerin	75–35–4	Vinylidene chloride
56–23–5	Carbon tetrachloride	75–44–5	Phosgene
56–38–2	Parathion	75–55–8	Propyleneimine
57–12–5	Cyanide compounds	75–56–9	Propylene oxide
57–14–7	1,1-Dimethyl hydrazine	75–65–0	tert-Butyl alcohol
57–57–8	beta-Propiolactone	76–13–1	Chlorinated fluorocarbon (Freon 113; 1,1,2-
57–74–9	Chlordane		Trichloro-1,2,2-trifluoroethane)
58–89–9	Lindane	76–44–8	Heptachlor
59–89–2	N-Nitrosomorpholine	77–47–4	Hexachlorocyclopentadiene
60–09–3	4-Aminoazobenzene	77–78–1	Dimethyl sulfate
60–11–7	4-Dimethylaminoazobenzene	78–84–2	Isobutyraldehyde
60–34–4	Methyl hydrazine	78–87–5	1,2-Dichloropropane
60–35–5	Acetamide	78–92–2	sec-Butyl alcohol
62–53–3	Aniline	78–93–3	Methyl ethyl ketone
62–55–5	Thioacetamide	79–00–5	1,1,2-Trichloroethane
62–56–6	Thiourea	79–01–6	Trichloroethylene
62–73–7	Dichlorvos	79–06–1	Acrylamide
62–75–9	N-Nitrosodimethylamine	79–10–7	Acrylic acid
63–25–2	Carbaryl	79–11–8	Chloroacetic acid
64–67–5	Diethyl sulfate	79–21–0	Peracetic acid
67–56–1	Methanol	79–34–5	1,1,2,2-Tetrachloroethane
67–63–0	Isopropyl alcohol (manufacturing-strong acid process)	79–44–7	Dimethylcarbamyl chloride
		79–46–9	2-Nitropropane
67–64–1	Acetone	80–05–7	4,4-Isopropylidenediphenol
67–66–3	Chloroform	80–15–9	Cumene hydroperoxide
67–72–1	Hexachloroethane	80–62–6	Methyl methacrylate
68–76–8	Triaziquone	81–07–2	Saccharin (manufacturing)
71–36–3	n-Butyl alcohol	81–88–9	C.I. Food Red 15
71–43–2	Benzene	82–28–0	1-Amino-2-methylanthraquinone
71–55–6	1,1,1-Trichloroethane (Methyl chloroform)	82–68–8	Quintozene (Pentachloronitrobenzene)
72–43–5	Methoxychlor	84–66–2	Diethyl phthalate
74–83–9	Bromomethane (Methyl bromide)	84–74–2	Dibutyl phthalate
74–85–1	Ethylene	85–44–9	Phthalic anhydride
74–87–3	Chloromethane (Methyl chloride)	85–68–7	Butyl benzyl phthalate
74–88–4	Methyl iodide	86–30–6	N-Nitrosodiphenylamine
74–90–8	Hydrogen cyanide	87–62–7	2,6-Xylidine
74–95–3	Methylene bromide	87–68–3	Hexachloro-1,3-butadiene
75–00–3	Chloroethane (Ethyl chloride)	87–86–5	Pentachlorophenol (PCP)

*Staff of Senate Comm. on Environment and Public Works, 99th Cong., 2d Sess., List of Toxic Chemicals Subject to the Provisions of Section 313 of the Emergency Planning and Community Right to Know Act of 1986 (Comm. Print 1986).

Chemical abstract service [CAS] number	Chemical name	Chemical abstract service [CAS] number	Chemical name
88-06-2	2,4,6-Trichlorophenol	107-21-1	Ethylene glycol
88-75-5	2-Nitrophenol	107-30-2	Chloromethyl methyl ether
88-89-1	Picric acid	108-05-4	Vinyl acetate
90-04-0	o-Anisidine	108-10-1	Methyl isobutyl ketone
90-43-7	2-Phenylphenol	108-31-6	Maleic anhydride
90-94-8	Michler's keytone	108-38-3	m-Xylene
91-08-7	Toluene-2,6-diisocyanate	108-39-4	m-Cresol
91-20-3	Naphthalene	108-60-1	Bis(2-chloro-1-methylethyl) ether
91-22-5	Quinoline	108-78-1	Melamine
91-59-8	beta-Naphthylamine	108-88-3	Toluene
91-94-1	3,3'-Dichlorobenzidine	108-90-7	Chlorobenzene
92-52-4	Biphenyl	108-95-2	Phenol
92-67-1	4-Aminobiphenyl	109-86-4	2-Methoxyethanol
92-87-5	Benzidine	110-80-5	2-Ethoxyethanol
92-93-3	4-Nitrobiphenyl	110-82-7	Cyclohexane
94-36-0	Benzoyl peroxide	110-86-1	Pyridine
94-59-7	Safrole	111-42-2	Diethanolamine
94-75-7	2,4-D	111-44-4	Bis (2-chlororethyl) ether
95-47-6	o-Xylene	114-26-2	Propoxur
95-48-7	o-Cresol	115-07-1	Propylene (Propene)
95-50-1	1,2-Dichlorobenzene	115-32-2	Dicofol
95-53-4	o-Toluidine	117-79-3	2-Aminoanthraquinone
95-63-6	1,2,4-Trimethyl benzene	117-81-7	Di(2-ethylhexyl) phthalate [DEHP]
95-80-7	2,4-Diaminotoluene	117-84-0	n-Dioctylphthalate
95-95-4	2,4,5-Trichlorophenol	118-74-1	Hexachlorobenzene
96-09-3	Styrene oxide	119-90-4	3,3'-Dinethoxybenzidine
96-12-8	1,2-Dibromo-3-chloropropane (DBCP)	119-93-7	3,3'-Dimethylbenzidine (o-Tolidine)
96-33-3	Methyl acrylate	120-12-7	Anthracene
96-45-7	Ethylene thiourea	120-71-8	p-Cresidine
97-56-3	C.I. Solvent Yellow 3	120-80-9	Catechol
98-07-7	Benzoic trichloride (Benzotrichloride)	120-82-1	1,2,4-Trichlorobenzene
98-82-8	Cumene	120-83-2	2,4-Dichlorophenol
98-87-3	Benzal chloride	121-14-2	2,4-Dinitrotoluene
98-88-4	Benzoyl chloride	121-69-7	N,N-Dimethylaniline
98-95-3	Nitrobenzene	122-66-7	1,2-Diphenyl hydrazine (Hydrazobenzene)
99-59-2	5-Nitro-o-anisidine	123-31-9	Hydroquinone
100-02-7	4-Nitrophenol	123-38-6	Propionaldehyde
100-21-0	Terephthalic acid	123-72-8	Butyraldehyde
100-41-4	Ethyl benzene	123-91-1	1,4-Dioxane
100-42-5	Styrene (monomer)	126-72-7	Tris(2,3-dibromopropyl) phosphate
100-44-7	Benzyl chloride	126-99-8	Chloroprene
100-75-4	N-Nitrosopiperidine	127-18-4	Tetrachloroethylene (Perchloroethylene)
101-14-4	4,4'-Methylene bis(2-chloroaniline) (MOCA)	128-66-5	C.I. Vat Yellow 4
101-61-1	4,4'-Methylene bis(N,N-dimethyl) benzenamine	131-11-3	Dimethyl phthalate
101-68-8	Methylene bis(phenylisocyanate) (MBI)	132-64-9	Dibenzofuran
101-77-9	4,4-Methylene dianiline	133-06-2	Captan
101-80-4	4,4'-Diaminodiphenyl ether	133-90-4	Chloramben
103-23-1	Bis(2-ethylhexyl) adipate	134-29-2	o-Anisidine hydrochloride
104-94-9	p-Anisidine	134-32-7	alpha-Naphthylamine
105-67-9	2,4-Dimethylphenol	135-20-6	Cupferron
106-42-3	p-Xylene	139-13-9	Nitrilotriacetic acid
106-44-5	p-Cresol	139-65-1	4,4'-Thiodianiline
106-46-7	1,4-Dichlorobenzene	140-88-5	Ethyl acrylate
106-50-3	p-Phenylenediamine	141-32-2	Butyl acrylate
106-51-4	Quinone	151-56-4	Ethyleneimine (Aziridine)
106-88-7	1,2-Butylene oxide	156-10-5	p-Nitrosodiphenylamine
106-89-8	Epichlorohydrin	156-62-7	Calcium cyanamide
106-93-4	1,2-Dibromoethane (Ethylene dibromide)	302-01-2	Hydrazine
106-99-0	1,3-Butadiene	309-00-2	Aldrin
107-02-8	Acrolein	334-88-3	Diazomethane
107-05-1	Allyl chloride	463-58-1	Carbonyl sulfide
107-06-2	1,2-Dichloroethane (Ethylene dichloride)	492-80-8	Auramine
107-13-1	Acrylonitrile	505-60-2	Mustard gas

Chemical abstract service [CAS] number	Chemical name	Chemical abstract service [CAS] number	Chemical name
510-15-6	Chlorobenzilate	7440-22-4	Silver and compounds
532-27-4	2-Chloroacetophenone	7440-28-0	Thallium and compounds
534-52-1	4,6-Dinitro-o-cresol	7440-36-0	Antimony and compounds
540-59-0	1,2-Dichloroethylene	7440-38-2	Arsenic and compounds
541-41-3	Ethyl chloroformate	7440-39-3	Barium and compounds
541-73-1	1,3-Dichlorobenzene	7440-41-7	Beryllium and compounds
542-75-6	1,3-Dichloropropylene	7440-43-9	Cadmium and compounds
542-88-1	Bis(chloromethyl) ether	7440-47-3	Chromium and compounds
569-64-2	C.I. Basic Acid Green 4	7440-48-4	Cobalt and compounds
584-84-9	Toluene-2,4-diisocyanate	7440-50-8	Copper and compounds
593-60-2	Vinyl bromide	7440-62-2	Vanadium (fume or dust)
606-20-2	2,6-Dinitrotoluene	7440-66-6	Zinc (fume and dust) and compounds
615-05-4	2,4-Diaminoanisole	7550-45-0	Titanium tetrachloride
621-64-7	N-Nitrosodi-n-propylamine	7647-01-0	Hydrochloric acid
624-83-9	Methyl isocyanate	7664-38-2	Phosphoric acid
636-21-5	o-Toluidine hydrochloride	7664-39-3	Hydrogen fluoride
680-31-9	Hexamethylphosphoramide	7664-41-7	Ammonia
684-93-5	N-Nitroso-N-methylurea	7664-93-9	Sulfuric acid
759-73-9	N-Nitroso-N-ethylurea	7697-37-2	Nitric acid
842-07-9	C.I. Solvent Yellow 14	7723-14-0	Phosphorus (yellow or white)
924-16-3	N-Nitrosodi-n-butylamine	7757-82-6	Sodium sulfate (solution)
961-11-5	Tetrachlorvinphos	7782-49-2	Selenium and compounds
989-38-8	C.I. Basic Red 1	7782-50-5	Chlorine
1120-71-4	Propane sultone	7783-20-2	Ammonium sulfate (solution)
1163-19-5	Decabromodiphenyl oxide	8001-35-2	Toxaphene
1310-73-2	Sodium hydroxide (solution)	10034-93-2	Hydrazine sulfate
1313-27-5	Molybdenum trioxide	10049-04-4	Chlorine dioxide
1314-20-1	Thorium dioxide	12122-67-7	Zineb
1319-77-3	Cresol (mixed isomers)	12427-38-2	Maneb
1330-20-7	Xylene (mixed isomers)	13463-67-7	Titanium dioxide
1332-21-4	Asbestos (friable)	16071-86-6	Direct Brown 95
1335-87-1	Hexachloronaphthalene	16543-55-8	N-Nitrosonornicotine
1336-36-3	Polychlorinated biphenyls (PCBs)	20816-12-0	Osmium tetroxide
1344-28-1	Aluminum oxide	25321-22-6	Dichlorobenzene (mixed isomers)
1464-53-5	Diepoxybutane	25376-45-8	Diaminotoluene (mixed isomers)
1582-09-8	Trifluralin	39156-41-7	2,4-Diaminoanisole sulfate
1634-04-4	Methyl tert-butyl ether		Antimony Compounds
1836-75-5	Nitrofen		Arsenic Compounds
1897-45-6	Chlorothalonil		Barium Compounds
1937-37-7	Direct Black 38		Beryllium Compounds
2164-17-2	Fluometuron		Cadmium Compounds
2234-13-1	Octachloronaphthalene		Chlorophenols
2303-16-4	Diallate		Chromium Compounds
2602-46-2	Direct Blue 6		Cobalt Compounds
2650-18-2	C.I. Acid Blue 9, diammonium salt		Copper Compounds
2832-40-8	C.I. Disperse Yellow 3		Cyanide Compounds
3118-97-6	C.I. Solvent Orange 7		Glycol Ethers
3761-53-3	Cl. Food Red 5		Lead Compounds
3844-45-9	C.I. Acid Blue 9, disodium salt		Manganese Compounds
4549-40-0	N-Nitrosomethylvinylamine		Mercury Compounds
4680-78-8	C.I. Acid Green 3		Nickel Compounds
6484-52-2	Ammonium nitrate (solution)		Polybrominated Biphenyls (PBBs)
7429-90-5	Aluminum (fume or dust)		Selenium Compounds
7439-92-1	Lead and compounds		Silver Compounds
7439-96-5	Manganese and compounds		Thallium Compounds
7439-97-6	Mercury and compounds		Zinc Compounds
7440-02-0	Nickel and compounds		

Appendix 6I   Joint Defense and Dispute Resolution Agreement for a Superfund Site

Purpose of form. The following form is designed for use in connection with a superfund site at which a preliminary allocation or an EPA Nonbinding Allocation of Responsibility (NBAR) has been made, which is based on insufficient evidence for a final allocation, and where the parties desire to enter into a consent decree or administrative settlement with EPA and commence site remediation prior to developing a final allocation.

The form agreement contains joint defense and contribution provisions, a system for resolving allocation disputes, a mechanism for interim funding of both remedial action and the costs of administering the organized settling group, and a number of housekeeping provisions common to superfund settlements.

This is a "complex" form of settlement agreement, which is obviously not necessary for all sites. Simpler agreements, which omit one or more of the features of the complex agreement, can be fashioned from its language, however. For example, if sufficient evidence exists for determination of a defensible allocation formula prior to the date settlement with the government is imminent, the provisions relating to development of an allocation formula and the diapute resolution provisions may be omitted.

Trust agreements and small quantity buyouts. The form does not include a sample trust agreement or specific terms for small quantity buyouts. Trust agreements vary in their terms from bank to bank (ordinarily banks have been used as trustees for superfund settlements). Banks will usually proffer a form trust agreement, the terms of which, principally the costs and fees, and whether the accounts will bear interest, are negotiated.

Small quantity buyouts are very site dependent. The issues facing major participants are at what level of contribution (volumetric or combined volumetric/hazardous characteristic) to offer buyouts, what multiplier over the allocated share to apply to buyout candidates (do they pay only their share, or twice their share or three times their share?), and the form of release provided.

TABLE OF CONTENTS

AGREEMENT

This Agreement (the "Agreement") is made as of the effective date stated herein between and among the companies listed on Attachment A whose authorized representatives have executed this Agreement (hereinafter the "Parties").

WHEREAS, in order to decrease the potential for protracted litigation as concerns each Party's fair share of funding past and future costs and expenses incurred or to be incurred because of work at and around real estate located at [location of site], where [site name] conducted business (hereinafter the "Site"), the Parties prefer to submit this issue for resolution as provided in this Agreement;

WHEREAS, the undertakings of this Agreement will require substantial sums of monies, which should rightfully come from all persons who may be liable therefor but which may come only from the Parties;

WHEREAS, it is necessary to establish a framework for the fair and equitable sharing of administrative costs among the Parties in implementing this Agreement initially and finally and to investigate, preserve, document and pursue claims against those who do not participate in this Agreement; and

WHEREAS, the Parties desire to express their agreement by these presents,

NOW THEREFORE, and upon the mutual and several covenants herein contained, the agreement to make specified payments hereunder and the waiver of claims set forth herein, and for other good and valuable consideration, the Parties hereto hereby agree as follows:

I. DEFINITIONS

1.1 "Adjudicator"—the person, firm, company or other entity selected to conduct the final review in accordance with Article XI.

1.2 "Administrative Expense Obligations"—the obligations of the Parties to fund the costs of implementing this Sharing Agreement, which shall include the costs of Common Counsel, the investigation, and/or the adjudication process, all as described herein.

1.3 "Allocation"—the product of the Volumetric Determination of a Party.

1.4 [Definition of Site or Facility]

1.5 "[Site or Facility Name] Site Trust Fund"—a trust fund to be funded by the Parties pursuant to this Agreement at the (Name of Bank) for the purposes set forth in this Agreement.

1.6 "Coalition"—the Parties to this Agreement when acting as a group pursuant to this Agreement. In the event that a Party has elected not to participate as a member of the group for limited purposes only, then such Party shall not be a part of the Coalition with respect to such purpose.

1.7 "Common Counsel"—that attorney retained for the purposes set forth in Section 4.7.

1.8 "Consent Decree"—any Consent Decree, Administrative Consent Order, Settlement Agreement, or similar document approved by the Vote of the Parties and executed by one or more of the Parties, in settlement of claims relating to the Site with the United States Environmental Protection Agency ("USEPA") and/or the State of _____ ("State").

1.9 "Cost Sharing Obligations"—the obligations of the Parties to fund any and all expenses required under any past or future judicial or administrative Consent Decrees with the EPA relating to the Site.

1.10 "EPA"—United States Environmental Protection Agency.

1.11 "Final Allocation"—the Allocation which becomes binding upon a Party pursuant to this Agreement.

1.12 "Final Assessment Percentage" (FAP)—the FAP of each Party shall be the quotient, expressed as a percentage, of the Final Allocation of that Party divided by the total of the Final Allocations of all Parties.

1.13 "Groundwater"—water in a saturated zone or stratum beneath the surface of land or water.

1.14 "Interim Assessment Percentage"—the share, calculated pursuant to Paragraphs 7.3 and 8.1 and expressed as a percentage, of Cost Sharing Obligations which each Party is initially obligated to pay to the Trust Fund until its FAP is calculated.

1.15 "Investigator"—the person, firm, company or other entity selected to conduct the investigation as specified in Article IX.

1.16 "Material"—anything that contains a hazardous substance, pollutant, or contaminant.

1.17 "Obligations"—Cost Sharing Obligations and Administrative Expense Obligations as defined herein.

1.18 "Party"—as determined from time to time, any signatory to this Agreement, including any Person admitted to the Agreement pursuant to Article XV, but not including an entity who has withdrawn or is in default.

1.19 "Person"—any natural person or entity, whether a corporation, partnership, government or subdivision, agency or department thereof, or other organization.

1.20 "Potentially Responsible Party" or "PRP"—any Person who is or may be a "potentially responsible party" within the meaning of Section 107 of CERCLA.

1.21 "Total Final Allocation Percentage" or "TFAP"—The TFAP of each Person shall be the quotient, expressed as a percentage, of the Final Allocation for that Party or Allocation of other Persons as determined by Phase II of the Investigator's report divided by the total of the Final Allocations of all Parties and other Persons.

1.22 "Volumetric Determination"—the volume of Material generated by a Party which was transported to and disposed of at or deposited onto or into the Site.

1.23 "Vote"—a majority vote with each Party present casting one vote, unless otherwise specified.

II. PURPOSE OF AGREEMENT

2.1 *Generally.* It is the intent of the Parties to negotiate a Consent Decree which incorporates and authorizes the implementation of the remedial measures identified and approved in the EPA's Record of Decision issued on [date].

[Note: The Parties may wish to insert here other descriptive material, including any negotiated modifications to the ROD, or provisions anticipating unforeseen cost increases and specifying the conditions under which the parties are bound to contribute toward such increases.]

2.2 *Cost Sharing.* It is the intention of the Parties to secure equitable participation of all PRPs for the costs of carrying out the Consent Decree whether or not Parties to this Agreement, and to provide for fair and equitable apportionment of all Cost Sharing Obligations and Administrative Expense Obligations in accordance with the methods and procedures set forth herein.

2.3 *Parties' Cooperation.* The Parties shall cooperate with one another to effectuate the purposes of this Agreement, including providing timely and accurate information as required under this Agreement, and shall make timely payments as required by this Agreement.

III. ORGANIZATION

3.1 *Committees.* In order to carry out the purposes of this Agreement, the Parties hereby establish two committees, the Steering Committee and the Technical Committee.

3.2 *Authority to Decide.* The Coalition shall act by and through the Steering Committee in accordance with Article IV, except that the Parties reserve to themselves the right at any time and from time to time to directly authorize action to be undertaken pursuant to this Agreement in accordance with the voting requirements set forth in this Agreement.

3.3 *Meetings.* The Parties may authorize or direct actions under this Agreement only at meetings duly held and called for such purpose, which meetings may be called by the Chair of the Steering Committee, by any three or more members of the Steering Committee, or by notice signed by at least one third of the Parties to this Agreement.

3.4 *Majority Rule.* Any matter under this Agreement which may be referred to a meeting of the Coalition; shall be decided by a Vote at the meeting.

3.5 *Notice of Meetings.* Written notice of the time, place and agenda for any meeting of the Parties shall be given to each Party entitled to vote at such meeting at least five (5) days and not more than thirty (30) days before the date of such meeting either personally or by mail or by other means of written communication, charges prepaid, at the addresses appearing on Attachment A or at such other address provided by the Party pursuant to Paragraph 33.3.

3.6 *Quorum.* The presence in person or by proxy of fifty percent (50%) of the Parties to this Agreement shall constitute a Quorum for the transaction of business.

IV. POWERS AND DUTIES OF STEERING COMMITTEE AND COMMON COUNSEL

4.1 *Generally.* For the specific purposes set forth in this Agreement and except as otherwise specified herein or as directed by Vote at a duly held meeting of the Parties, the Parties agree to act through and be bound by decisions of the Steering Committee. The Steering Committee shall be composed of Parties. Each Party which serves on the Steering Committee shall designate one person to serve as its designee on the Steering Committee; that designee may specify an alternate to serve in his or her absence. Other persons associated with Parties may attend meetings of the Steering Committee without a vote. The Steering Committee shall be authorized to act by a Vote of its members. The Steering Committee shall give at least five (5) days' advance notice of its meetings to its members.

4.2 *Membership.* The initial members of the Steering Committee shall be those Parties listed on Attachment D. Membership on the Steering Committee shall be open to any Party which expresses a willingness to and does make its representative reasonably available to participate actively in the functions of the Steering Committee. Failure to participate in three consecutive meetings, failure to perform the reasonable duties of the Committee, or a material breach of this agreement by a Party shall be grounds for removal of a Party's representative from the Steering Committee. Removal shall only take effect by a Vote of the Steering Committee at a duly called and constituted meeting of the Committee. Members shall not be liable for any act or omission as a member of the Steering Committee. The Parties shall indemnify and hold harmless, including costs of defense, any member from claims based solely on any act or omission performed as a member of the Steering Committee.

4.3 *Enumerated Powers of the Steering Committee.* Subject to the specific provisions of this Agreement, the Steering Committee is empowered to select and contract with contractors and consultants to perform the work required under any Consent Decree; to select and contract with the Investigator, the Common Counsel, and the Adjudicator; to establish the cost and fee basis for contractors, consultants, Investigator, Adjudicator, and Common Counsel; to determine, and cause to be paid into the [Trust Fund], sums needed to pay the Administrative Expense Obligations and Cost Sharing Obligations; to prepare necessary budgets; to select a trustee and/or trustees for the [Trust Fund]; to negotiate with EPA and other governmental authorities with respect to matters arising out of the Site; to direct Common Counsel; to collect or to waive in appropriate cases the late joining fees specified in Paragraph 15.2; to enforce the terms hereof; and to conduct any other activity which is necessary and proper to carry out the purposes of this Agreement.

4.4 *Budgets.*

a. Administrative Expense Obligations: The Coalition shall approve and adopt by Vote the budget of anticipated Administrative Expense Obligations proposed by the Steering Committee. The Steering Committee cannot exceed any budget item by twenty-five percent (25%) or the total budget by ten percent (10%) without Coalition approval. The Steering Committee is obligated to notify the Parties when it first anticipates that the total budget is to be exceeded by more than ten percent (10%) and obtain approval by Vote to exceed the budget at a meeting of the Coalition.

b. Cost Sharing Obligations: The Steering Committee shall prepare a budget covering the activities necessary to carry out the terms of the Consent Decree, shall revise the budget from time to time to provide for additional costs incurred and shall provide periodic accounting.

4.5 *Reports to the Parties to Call for Meetings.* The Steering Committee shall report in writing its decisions, actions, and recommendations to the Parties to keep them reasonably informed of matters covered by this Agreement.

4.6 *Compensation of Steering Committee.* The members of the Steering Committee shall serve without compensation.

4.7 *Common Counsel.* The Steering Committee may retain Common Counsel, who shall be approved by Vote of the Coalition, for any or all of the following purposes:

a. To provide advice and legal research to the Steering Committee.

b. To take legal action as directed by the Steering Committee to protect and preserve the common interests of the Coalition.

4.8 *Right of Separate Counsel.* Subject to Article XIV, notwithstanding that Common Counsel may be retained with respect to any matter, each Party reserves the right to select and retain its own counsel to represent it on any matter and to advise Common Counsel that such Party is not to be represented by or through Common Counsel with respect to any such matter. Any Party may exercise this right by providing written notice to the Steering Committee that it does not consent to have Common Counsel represent its interests in one or more matters. Any Party exercising this right and retaining separate counsel shall not be obligated to pay that portion of the Administrative Expense Obligation which arises from costs of Common Counsel for such matter, and, likewise, shall not benefit with respect to such matter.

V. POWERS AND DUTIES OF THE TECHNICAL COMMITTEE

5.1 *Generally.* The Technical Committee shall be composed of Parties. Each Party which serves on the Technical Committee shall, consistent with Paragraph 5.2, designate one person to serve as its designee on the Technical

Committee; that designee may specify an alternate to serve in his or her absence. Other persons associated with Parties may attend meetings of the Technical Committee without a vote. The Technical Committee shall be authorized to act by a Vote of its members. The Technical Committee shall give at least five (5) days' advance notice of its meetings to its members.

5.2 *Membership.* The Technical Committee shall consist of volunteers from the Coalition, who shall supply technically qualified representatives prepared to participate actively on the Technical Committee. Failure to participate in three consecutive meetings, failure to perform the reasonable duties of the Technical Committee, or a material breach of this Agreement by a Party shall be grounds for removal of a Party's representative from the Technical Committee. Removal shall only take effect by a Vote of the Technical Committee at a duly called and constituted meeting of the Committee.

5.3 *Powers of the Technical Committee.* The Technical Committee shall be empowered to recommend consultants to the Steering Committee and the fee basis for such consultants; to act as liaison between the Steering Committee and the consultants in technical matters; and to make such recommendations on technical matters to the Steering Committee or Common Counsel as may from time to time be appropriate.

5.4 *Compensation of Technical Committee.* The members of the Technical Committee shall serve without compensation.

VI. DEALINGS WITH THE EPA

6.1 *Negotiation of the Consent Decree.* Promptly after the effective date of this Agreement the Steering Committee shall enter into negotiations with the EPA regarding the form and substance of a Consent Decree. After the Steering Committee has obtained what it believes to be the best terms and conditions possible from the EPA, it shall promptly call a meeting of the Parties for its approval or rejection of the Consent Decree.

6.2 *Effect of Party Approval; Signing of Consent Decree.* Upon the affirmative Vote of the Parties whose Interim Assessment Percentages or Final Assessment Percentages, whichever is in effect, total at least _____ percent (__%), the costs of implementing the Consent Decree shall become Cost Sharing Obligations of the Parties, whether or not all Parties become signatories to the Consent Decree.

6.3 *Effect of EPA Adversary Litigation and Judgment.* If in the absence of a Consent Decree, or otherwise, the EPA or the State of Connecticut initiates litigation against some or all of the Parties, the Coalition shall undertake the defense of that litigation as an Administrative Expense Obligation. If judgment is entered against some or all of the Parties in such litigation, the terms and conditions of that judgment shall become Cost Sharing Obligations of the Parties to the extent such terms and conditions apply to any Parties. Nothing herein shall be construed to cause the several liability of any Person not a Party to become a Cost Sharing Obligation or impair the rights of the Coalition to seek contribution from other Persons.

VII. PAYMENTS TO THE TRUST FUND

7.1 *Commitment to Pay Administrative Expense Obligations and Cost Sharing Obligations.* Each Party shall pay to the Trust Fund its share of the Administrative Expense Obligations and Cost Sharing Obligations in accordance with the provisions of this Agreement.

7.2 *Periodic Payments.* Interim assessments to collect funds to pay the Administrative Expense Obligations and Cost Sharing Obligations shall occur at periodic intervals as called for by the Steering Committee, which shall call for funds only as required to meet current obligations.

7.3 *Interim Assessments.* Until the FAPs are determined, the percentage of each interim assessment which each Party is obligated to pay to the Fund shall be paid and borne as follows:

a. Administrative Expense Obligations shall be borne by the Parties in tiers pursuant to Attachment B, and paid in accordance with Paragraph 7.2.

b. Cost Sharing Obligations shall be borne as determined under Paragraph 8.1 and paid in accordance with Paragraph 7.2.

7.4 *Trust Fund.* Each Party shall execute a Trust Agreement in form approved by the Steering Committee. The Trust Fund shall be operated in accordance with the Trust Agreement. The Trustee shall be the representative of the Trust Fund for all purposes. If any money is in the Trust Fund at the time of its dissolution, said money shall be distributed among the Parties according to the FAP of each party.

VIII. PAYMENTS; CALCULATION OF ASSESSMENTS

8.1 *Calculation of Interim Assessment Percentages.* The Interim Assessment Percentage of each Party for Cost Sharing Obligations shall be the quotient, expressed as a percentage, of the volume assigned to that Party on Attachment C divided by the total of the volumes assigned on Attachment C to all Parties. Such percentage shall be used for the calculation of payments only until the FAPs are determined, at which time the Interim Assessment Percentages shall be of no further effect. The Interim Assessment Percentages shall be recalculated upon any event, such as the addition, withdrawal or default of a Party, which would necessitate the calculation of them to change prior to the determination of the FAPs.

8.2 The FAPs shall be recalculated upon any event, such as the addition, withdrawal or default of a Party, which would necessitate the calculation of them to change.

8.3 *Readjustment of Past Payments Upon Calculation of FAPs.* After the determination of FAPs, all past assessments shall be recalculated in accordance with the FAPS to determine the amount each Party has been overassessed or underassessed. If a Party has been overassessed, and has paid such assessments, the Steering Committee shall make appropriate arrangements to refund to such Party the full amount of its overpayment plus interest upon such overpayment computed from the date of payment at eight percent (8%). If a Party has been underassessed, the Steering Committee shall issue a supplemental assessment to that Party for the amount so underassessed plus interest on such amount computed from the date of the original underassessment at eight percent (8%).

8.4 *Due Dates.* Each Party shall pay each assessment of the Steering Committee within thirty (30) days of the date thereof, by check payable to the Trust Fund.

8.5 *Binding Effect of Final Allocations.* FAPs and Final Allocations shall be binding on all Parties, as among the Parties, and may be entered in court as a final judgment and shall bar any relitigation of any issue involved in the calculation of the FAPs.

IX. INVESTIGATOR

9.1 *Selection of Investigator.* Promptly after the execution of this Agreement, the Steering Committee shall compile a list of not more than three candidates to serve as Investigator. Each candidate for Investigator will be provided a copy of Attachment E, attached hereto and incorporated herein by reference, and invited to make a short presentation to the Steering Committee to explain his or her qualifications and experience, staff capabilities, and other facts relevant to the selection of the Investigator. Each Investigator candidate shall be specifically required to provide an estimate of the costs associated with the Investigation, as outlined on Attachment E, and the time period required to complete the Investigation.

9.2 *Duties and Obligations of Investigator.* The Investigator shall undertake the responsibilities and duties as set forth in Attachment E, which requires both a Phase I and Phase II investigation and allocation report. It is the intent of the Parties that the Phase I report, the Consensus specified in Article X following the Phase I report, or the Final Review specified in Article XI following the Phase I report, shall result in the FAPs and Final Allocations as among the Parties hereto. The Phase II report is intended to provide a basis of allocation for Persons subsequently desirous of becoming Parties hereto pursuant to Article XV and to form a basis upon which the Parties may proceed in seeking contribution from Persons not Parties to this Agreement. The Phase II report shall in no way affect the allocation of Obligations as among the Parties except to the extent that the FAPs may be modified consistent with Paragraph 8.2 as a result of addition of new Parties under Article XV, or other events necessitating recalculation of the FAPs.

9.3 *Parties' Obligations in Investigations.* Each Party will comply fully with all requirements for submittal of information to the Investigator required or authorized pursuant to the terms and provisions of Attachment E, including the requirement for submittal of affidavits and other sworn statements, and shall make its employees available to be interviewed by the Investigator upon the Investigator's reasonable request. Each Party shall use its best efforts to assist in obtaining information from non-Parties, where relevant to the issues to be considered under this Agreement; provided, however, that "best efforts" shall not be construed to require any Party to commence or pursue litigation against non-Parties. Any and all costs incurred as a direct result of the failure of any

Party to comply with obligations hereunder in a timely fashion shall be assessed directly against and paid by said Party, and shall not be included as Cost Sharing Obligations or Administrative Expense Obligations. Each Party shall be fully bound by all provisions in Attachment E which impose restrictions, obligations, or duties on the Parties.

9.4 *Investigator's Consultants.* The Investigator may engage consultants to assist in the Investigation. All consultants shall disclose all past and present relationships with Parties and other PRPs and shall be retained only upon the approval, by Vote, of the Steering Committee. In no event shall the retention of consultants increase the amount budgeted for the Investigation without the express consent and approval, by Vote, in writing, of the Steering Committee.

X. OPPORTUNITY FOR FORMATION OF CONSENSUS

10.1 *Consensus Period.* During the thirty-day period after the Investigator issues the Phase I report, the Parties shall make a good faith attempt to achieve consensus on the allocation of Cost Sharing Obligations and Administrative Expense Obligations among the Parties.

10.2 *Extension of Consensus Period.* Upon Vote of the Parties, an additional period of time, not to exceed sixty days, may be designated for further negotiations pursuant to Paragraph 10.1 above.

10.3 *Reconsideration of Investigator's Report.* During the thirty-day time period referred to in Paragraph 10.1 above, any Party may submit a written proposal to the Steering Committee for reconsideration by the Investigator of all or any portion of the Report. Such request for reconsideration shall specify the following:

a. Those portions of the report which the Party believes require reconsideration.

b. The basis for the reconsideration (e.g., failure of the Investigator to consider evidence and arguments properly submitted, abuse of discretion, clearly erroneous conclusions, etc.).

The Steering Committee, by Vote, shall either reject or approve the request. If the request is approved, the request shall be forwarded to the Investigator, along with any and all arguments advanced in support or opposition by any Party. The Investigator shall reconsider its prior decisions in light of all approved reconsideration requests, and shall issue a revised report or a reaffirmation of the original report, as provided in Paragraph D.2.g of Attachment E.

10.4 *Consensus on Final Allocation.* At the end of the thirty-day period under Paragraph 10.1, as extended pursuant to Paragraph 10.2, if all Parties are in agreement as to the allocation, a written agreement to this effect will be signed by all Parties, and the allocation shall become the Final Allocation.

10.5 *Effect of Disputed Allocation.* If, at the end of the thirty-day period under Paragraph 10.1, as extended pursuant to Paragraph 10.2, a Party disputes its allocation or the allocation of any other Party under the Investigator's report, that Party will submit its dispute to the Final Review process described in Article XI below. Those Parties which do not dispute the allocation may, at their option, participate in the Final Review process, but will not be required to do so. However, all Parties, whether participating in the Final Review process or not, will be bound by the Adjudicator's decision.

XI. FINAL REVIEW

11.1 *Agreement to Final Review; Selection of Adjudicator.* Any disputes among the Parties regarding the Investigator's Allocations contained in its Phase I Report shall be resolved by binding final review, conducted pursuant to the authority of this Agreement. At the time of the signing of this Agreement the Steering Committee will initiate a search for a potential Adjudicator of allocation disputes by requesting the names, qualifications and charges of at least five persons from the Center for Public Resources as potential Adjudicators. Each such potential Adjudicator must be experienced in environmental matters, and must be prepared to hear and resolve all allocation disputes among the Parties submitted under this Article. As soon as reasonably practical, the Steering Committee will notify all parties of the names, qualifications, charges and relationships of the potential Adjudicators. Any Party may, within seven (7) days of the date of that Notice, submit comments regarding the selection of an Adjudicator to the Steering Committee. The Steering Committee shall not be bound by such comments, but shall take them into account together with other submitted information, and shall select, by Vote, an Adjudicator.

11.2 *Submission of Objections.* Not later than thirty (30) days after the submission of the Investigator's Phase I Report, pursuant to Paragraph 10.3, to the Steering Committee, or after the end of the consensus period under Article X whichever is later, any Party may submit to the Adjudicator written objections to the Investigator's Allocation with regard to any Party or Parties. Any allocation to which there is no timely submitted objection shall be final and binding upon all Parties. No Party shall be permitted to participate in any way in the final review of an Allocation unless that Party has submitted a timely filed objection under this section or a timely filed reply under Paragraph 11.4. Upon receipt of an objection, the Adjudicator shall inform the Steering Committee, and the Investigator's Report will be submitted to the Adjudicator, together with all evidence and documents in the Investigator's possession, custody or control including any documents submitted to the Investigator by any Party. Such evidence shall constitute the exclusive evidentiary record to which the Adjudicator may look.

11.3 *Form of Objections.* Objections shall contain an explanation of why an Allocation should be changed, and shall contain specific references to the evidentiary record before the Investigator. The Adjudicator shall not be required to examine the evidentiary record for materials other than those to which its attention is directed, and it shall be the burden of the contesting Parties to point out specific evidence which they assert to support their positions. An objecting Party may, but need not, attach an appendix containing copies of the evidence to which it refers, but in any case no evidence which was not in the Investigator's possession, custody or control may be referred to by an objecting Party. Any Party submitting an objection shall simultaneously serve copies, together with any attachments or appendices, by certified mail upon that Party to whose specific Allocation it objects and upon the Steering Committee and serve copies without attachments and appendices by regular mail upon all other Parties.

11.4 *Replies.* Any Party to whose allocation objection has been made may, not later than fifteen (15) days after the date of receipt of such objection, submit to the Adjudicator a written statement in support of its allocation. Where a Party has submitted a timely objection under Paragraph 10.2 to its own Allocation, any other Party may, not later than fifteen (15) days of the date of receipt of such objection, submit to the Adjudicator a written statement in support of the Allocation. As in the case of objections, the Adjudicator shall not be required to examine the evidentiary record for materials other than those to which its attention is directed. No evidence which was not in the Investigator's possession, custody or control may be referred to in any such statement. Any Party submitting such a statement shall simultaneously serve a copy, together with any attachments or appendices, by certified mail upon the Party which originally raised the objection, and serve copies without attachments and appendices by regular mail upon all other Parties. The absence of a reply statement by a Party will not be deemed an admission, concession or waiver upon any issue other than a waiver of the right to participate in the Final Review Process.

11.5 *Oral Hearing.* Any objecting or replying Party may, not later than the time it submits its written objection or reply, request an oral hearing. Any Party whose Allocation is objected to, whether or not it submits a written statement in support of its Allocation, may request an oral hearing not later than fifteen (15) days of the date of its receipt of the objection, which request shall be deemed a reply for purposes of participation in the Final Review process. Upon receipt of such a request, timely filed, or upon its own request, the Adjudicator shall schedule an oral hearing as soon thereafter as its schedule reasonably permits. The purpose of such a hearing is to permit the Parties to informally explain their positions and respond to questions of the Adjudicator, and not to raise issues not previously raised by timely filed objections or replies. The Parties may, however, direct the Adjudicator during oral argument to new or additional portions of the existing evidentiary record in support of their positions. In the absence of a written request submitted to the Adjudicator prior to a scheduled hearing, the oral argument of a Party shall be limited to one hour. The Adjudicator may, upon receipt of such a request and in its sole discretion, extend the time for oral argument. A Party may, at its own expense, arrange for a transcription by certified court stenographer of the argument made at such hearing.

11.6 *Issues Before the Adjudicator.* The Adjudicator is to determine, after consideration of the record and oral hearing, if any, as to each contested allocation, whether the determination of the Investigator is arbitrary and capricious.

11.7 *Evidentiary Considerations and Presumptions.* The Adjudicator shall consider all of those parts of the evidentiary record transmitted from the Investigator to which his attention has been directed in the course of the final review proceedings, and may examine any other evidence transmitted from the Investigator and other parts of the Investigator's Report. Where there is some evidence of the existence of a material fact but the evidence is incomplete to support a precise determination, the Adjudicator may and should use common sense and good judgment to extrapolate from such evidence to make the determinations required. The Adjudicator may rely upon evidence not admissible in a court of law, such as hearsay and documents which lack precise authentication, giving them such credence and weight as they merit. The Adjudicator may consider whether a Party delivered material to a transporter who used the Site for disposal, but if that transporter also used other sites for disposal during the same time period, the mere fact of delivery to that transporter is insufficient, in and of itself, to support a determination that the material was deposited at the Site.

11.8 *Decision; Binding Effect.* Not later than sixty (60) days after the hearing or receipt of timely submitted objections or reply statements, whichever is later, the Adjudicator will issue its decision in writing, setting forth its determinations under Paragraph 11.6, together with the reasons for each such determination. Each determination shall be final and binding upon all Parties to this Agreement.

11.9 *Fees and Expenses.* The Adjudicator shall submit a bill to the Steering Committee which apportions its fees and expenses among the various contested allocations in accordance with the actual time and expenses associated with each, and is allocated according to the following formula: If an originally objecting Party has totally prevailed before the Adjudicator with regard to its position, the fees and expenses associated with that contested Allocation shall be an Administrative Expense Obligation, and shall not be charged solely to the prevailing Party. If an originally objecting Party has totally failed to prevail before the Adjudicator with regard to its position, the fees and expenses associated with that contested Allocation shall be charged to such Party. If an originally objecting Party has partially prevailed before the Adjudicator with regard to its position, the fees and expenses associated with that contested Allocation shall be divided as the Adjudicator sees fit between an Administrative Expense Obligation, and a charge to such partially prevailing Party. In any case the Steering Committee shall pay such bill and shall assess any charges to the Party in accordance with said formula. If there are fees and expenses of the Adjudicator not associated with specified allocation contests, those fees and expenses will be Administrative Expense Obligations of the Coalition.

XII. ENFORCEMENT AND USE OF FINAL ASSESSMENT PERCENTAGES

12.1 Judgment may be entered for the Parties' shares of Cost Sharing Obligations and Administrative Expense Obligations based upon the FAPs including any interest owed to a party for any previous overpayment, in any Court having jurisdiction thereof.

12.2 *Choice of Forum.* In event that this Agreement or the FAPs must be enforced judicially or a contribution action is to be commenced after the TFAP, such proceeding shall take place in the State of _____. If any non-Parties are not subject to the jurisdiction of the United States District Court for the District of _____, claims may be pursued against them in other appropriate jurisdictions.

12.3 *Contribution Action.* Subject to the provisions of Paragraph 4.8, TFAPs and the information developed by the Investigator will be used as the basis for a contribution action by the Parties against any or all non-Parties, and, without any waiver of available claims or causes of action for default under this Agreement, as a basis for an action against any Parties which fail to make payments as required by this Agreement. If there is federal jurisdiction, any such proceeding shall be commenced in the United States District Court for the District of _____.

12.4 *Governmental Assistance.* The TFAPs may be used to request and encourage the EPA and other governmental authorities to take appropriate action to ensure that there is an equitable sharing by all PRPs of the responsibility and costs for remedying conditions at the Site.

12.5 *Limited Application.* No allocation or assessment under this agreement shall be binding as to any matter or cost which is outside the scope of this Agreement.

XIII. FINAL ASSESSMENTS

13.1 *Computation of Final Assessments.* Within twenty-one (21) days after the determination of the FAP, the Steering Committee will send a statement to each Party setting forth:

a. The total Cost Sharing Obligations and Administrative Expense Obligations incurred by the Coalition as of the effective date of the FAP multiplied by the FAP for said party.

b. Interest on any amounts of the Administrative Expense Obligations and the Cost Sharing Obligations assessed to date which resulted from said Party either having failed to pay or being now underpaid. Interest is to be computed for each underpayment of an assessment from the date the assessment was due to be paid at an annual percentage rate of eight percent (8%).

c. The parties' shares, if any, of the costs of the Adjudicator as determined pursuant to Paragraph 11.9.

d. To the extent that any party contributed funds for any Cost Sharing Obligation or Administrative Expense Obligation interim assessment, such party shall receive a credit or refund for such payments, including interest for any overpayment of an assessment from the date such assessment was paid. Interest on any overpayment is to be computed from the date of payment to the date of the FAP at an annual rate of eight percent (8%).

XIV. PURSUIT OF CONTRIBUTION AND OTHER CLAIMS

14.1 *Common Counsel.* Common Counsel shall pursue contribution claims against non-Parties and claims against defaulting Parties as directed by the Steering Committee, after approval by Vote of the Coalition.

14.2 *Assignment of Claims.* Any Party which does not wish to be a named plaintiff in a contribution action shall give written notice to the Steering Committee. The giving of such notice shall constitute an assignment of its claim against the defendant(s) named in the action to the Coalition.

14.3 *Resolution of Claims.* The Steering Committee shall direct Common Counsel in regard to claims and may decide by Vote to compromise such claims on behalf of the Parties' Coalition.

14.4 *Proceeds.* The proceeds of any claims shall be distributed to the Parties according to the FAP.

14.5 *Individual Actions.* In the event the Steering Committee declines to recommend, or the Coalition declines to pursue, an action in contribution against any non-Party, any Party may bring such an action against any such non-Party in that Party's name and for its own account.

XV. ADDING PARTIES TO THE AGREEMENT

15.1 *Additions Permitted.* Upon approval of the Steering Committee, a Person may be added to this Agreement as a Party, not less than thirty (30) days before the Investigator's Report, Phase I, is due to be submitted. After thirty (30) days before the Investigator's Report, Phase I, has been submitted, no Person will be added as a Party until the TFAP has been issued. After the TFAP has been issued, a Person may be added as a Party.

15.2 *Payments Required.* Prior to the Investigator's Report's being submitted, no new Person shall be added as a Party until such Person has paid to the Trust Fund its share of the Administrative Expense Obligations and Cost Sharing Obligations plus interest for unpaid interim assessments. Interest is to be computed at eight percent (8%) per annum. As a condition and at the time of being added as a Party after the TFAP, a Party must pay its obligations as computed under Paragraph 13.1. In addition, each added Party who was given an opportunity to be an initial Party to this agreement and refused must pay a late joining fee of _____ percent (__%) of such amounts (including interest thereon), unless the added Party joins after the TFAP, in which case the late joining fee shall be _____ percent (__%) of such amounts (including interest thereon), and must meet any other terms and conditions which the Steering Committee may impose. For purposes of this paragraph, initial Parties shall mean those Parties who executed this Agreement.

15.3 *Credits to Other Parties.* To the extent that newly added Parties make payments to the Trust Fund, the Trustee will issue credits or refunds to the other Parties in proportion to, and at the time of, the determination of their Final Assessments.

XVI. BUY-OUTS

16.1 *Buy-outs Permitted.* Any Person may offer a lump sum of money to the Coalition and request that in exchange for this sum, the Parties will agree not to pursue that Person for contribution for Cost Sharing Obligations and Administrative Expense Obligations. If a reason for such an offer is inability to pay the prescribed assessments, the Person making the Buy-out offer must present to the Steering Committee affidavits of its responsible officers or principals, along with certified financial and insurance information, establishing its inability to pay, which information will be kept confidential. Included in the material to be supplied to the Steering Committee shall be copies of all insurance policies issued to the Person during the relevant time period and an agreement to assign to the Parties any rights thereunder.

16.2 *Action on Buy-Out Offers.* The Steering Committee will screen and recommend to the Coalition a response to any Buy-out offer, which shall be accepted or rejected by the Coalition. Acceptance of any such offer will be conditioned on the offering Party's assignment to the Coalition of all claims it may have for contribution.

16.3 *Discovery Response Required.* Any Person requesting a Buy-out must respond fully to the Investigator's discovery requests.

XVII. WAIVER OF CLAIMS AMONG THE PARTIES

17.1 *Waiver.* Subject to Paragraphs 14.2 and 17.2 of this Agreement, each Party hereby waives any and all claims relating to contribution or indemnification against each Party who complies with this Agreement.

17.2 *Reservation of Other Claims.* Nothing in this Agreement shall or is intended to constitute a waiver of any claims for contribution or indemnity that may exist between Parties arising out of their dealings with each other, their contractual relationship, or any other legal relationship between them, such as (but not by way of limitation) the relationship of transporter to generator, or of successor to predecessor.

XVIII. CONFLICT OF INTEREST

18.1 *Waiver of Conflict of Interest.* The Parties agree that each will not claim or assert during the period this Agreement is in effect that Common Counsel has a conflict of interest in representing the Coalition or the Parties in authorized litigation arising solely out of the work under or out of this Agreement on the ground that certain interests among the Parties may be inconsistent. Each Party agrees that if it defaults under this Agreement or its representation by Common Counsel terminates for any reason, it will raise no objection to the continued representation by Common Counsel for the Coalition or all or any of the other Parties in any authorized litigation arising in connection with this Agreement.

18.2 *Disclosure.* Any candidate for the position of Common Counsel, Investigator or Adjudicator shall be required to disclose to the Steering Committee any past or present relationships with any Party or other entity which has been identified as a Potentially Responsible Party.

XIX. ARBITRATION

19.1 *Arbitration of Disputes Concerning the Meaning of This Agreement.* Any dispute between and among the Parties as to the interpretation of this Agreement, except those matters assigned to the Investigator under Article IX and Adjudicator under Article XI, may be submitted in writing to the Steering Committee for its interpretation of the Agreement with regard to the issue in dispute. The Steering Committee, upon receipt of such a written notice, shall promptly review the matter and issue a written decision stating its interpretation of the Agreement with regard to the issue in dispute. Any Party which disagrees with that interpretation may submit the issue to arbitration by providing written notice of such submission to the Steering Committee within thirty (30) days of the date of its receipt of the Steering Committee's decision. The Party and the Steering Committee shall attempt to agree upon a qualified person to serve as Arbitrator. If no Arbitrator is chosen within thirty (30) days of the date of the notice of submission, the Party and the Steering Committee shall each select a qualified person, and the two persons selected shall select a qualified and neutral third person to serve as Arbitrator.

The Arbitrator shall promptly review the issue as submitted to the Steering Committee and the decision of the Steering Committee, and shall hear oral argument by a representative of the Steering Committee and a representative of the Party which submitted the issue to arbitration. Within thirty (30) days after hearing oral argument, the Arbitrator shall issue a decision in writing. The decision of the Arbitrator shall be final and binding upon the Party and the Coalition, and shall be enforceable in any court having jurisdiction.

XX. CONFIDENTIALITY AND USE

20.1 *Generally.* In the disclosure or transmission to one another, to the Investigator or to the Adjudicator of any information pursuant to this Agreement, any and all employees, representatives and agents of Parties to whom such information is disclosed or made accessible shall keep such information confidential, shall not use it for any purpose unrelated to this Agreement, and shall execute written agreements to this effect. Such information shall be strictly supervised by Common Counsel, or counsel to each Party as the case may be, as to the exclusive uses to which information can be put, so as to preserve and protect such information from further disclosure.

20.2 *Confidential Business Information.* It is recognized that some of the information the Parties are required to submit to the Investigator, or may have already submitted to the EPA, are considered by such Parties as confidential business information. Any information received by the Investigator and claimed by a Party to be confidential business information shall not, notwithstanding anything to the contrary herein, be disclosed to any Party or other Person by the Investigator or the Adjudicator. The Investigator and, if appropriate, the Adjudicator, shall indicate in the final report, or other written communication, the existence of any such claim of confidentiality and the extent to which any information claimed as confidential was relevant to the conclusions reached. In the event any Party objects, pursuant to Paragraphs 10.3 and 11.2, to any allocation which was determined by the Investigator and significantly affected by consideration of such confidential information, the Party claiming confidentiality shall be immediately so notified and may:

a. agree to disclosure of such information;

b. agree to disclosure of a summary of such information which, in the opinion of the Investigator or Adjudicator, as the case may be, fairly provides the other Parties with the information relied upon by the Investigator or Adjudicator; or

c. maintain its claim of confidentiality.

If the Party maintains its claim of confidentiality, the Investigator or Adjudicator shall sustain the objection to the extent the Allocation was based on said confidential information. For purposes of this paragraph, if the information claimed to be confidential is relevant only to the extent that it is used to determine whether the Party's waste is Material, and, the Investigator or Adjudicator determines such waste to be Material, the information shall not be considered to have significantly affected the determination of the Investigator or Adjudicator.

XXI. DEFAULT

21.1 In the event any Party fails to pay any portion of any assessed Obligation pursuant to this Agreement, the unpaid balance of the defaulting Party's share shall be borne by the other Parties (without waiving any rights such Parties may have against the defaulting Party or its successors or assigns) in the same proportion as the other Parties would have been obligated to pay if the defaulting Party had not been a signatory of this Agreement.

XXII. IN-HOUSE RESOURCES

22.1 To the extent any Party provides in-house resources, whether by way of legal, technical or management expertise, such resources shall be provided free of cost, except that the Steering Committee may authorize reimbursement of reasonable expenses.

XXIII. INTEREST

23.1 Any funds held by the Trustee for purposes of this Agreement shall be invested in appropriate accounts.

XXIV. DENIAL OF LIABILITY

24.1 The Parties deny liability or fault for any and all of the facts, legal contentions, and occurrences alleged to date, or anticipated to be alleged, in any Consent Decree or Order by way of finding, conclusion or otherwise. Nothing in this Agreement shall constitute or be used as evidence of any admission of any law or fact by any Party as among themselves or by any other Person not a Party hereto.

24.2 No part of this Agreement shall constitute or be interpreted or construed as an admission by any of the parties of any liability to any Person under any federal, state, or local law or as an admission that any Party is in violation of or has ever violated any laws, rules or regulations.

XXV. RIGHTS AS TO THIRD PARTIES

25.1 Except as otherwise provided herein, nothing contained in this Agreement shall prevent the assertion of any right, claim, interest, or cause of action of any Party with respect to Persons not Parties to this Agreement, including without limitation, claims for contribution and indemnity against Persons not Parties to this Agreement.

XXVI. INSURANCE CARRIER NOTIFICATION

26.1 Each Party represents that it has given notice to its insurance carriers of its intention to enter into this Agreement, if such was required.

XXVII. SUCCESSORS AND ASSIGNS

27.1 This Agreement shall be binding upon the successors and assigns of the Parties. Each Party shall give notice to the Steering Committee at least thirty (30) days in advance of any assignment of its obligations under this Agreement to a successor or any sale of substantially all or all the assets or the common shares of the Party.

XXVIII. EFFECTIVE DATE, BINDING EFFECT AND COUNTERPART SIGNATURES

28.1 *Counterparts.* This Agreement may be signed in counterparts and shall be binding between and among each signatory Party without regard to the number of other persons who may later elect to become Parties.

28.2 *Effective Date.* This Agreement shall become effective upon the execution of this Agreement by Persons representing _____ percent (__%) by volume of materials according to the [insert reference to NBAR or other preliminary allocation] volumetric allocation. In the event that this Agreement is not executed by such Persons, it shall be considered null and void and of no legal effect.

XXIX. MODIFICATIONS

29.1 *Modifications by the Parties.* This Agreement may only be modified by a unanimous vote of the Parties.

29.2 *Savings Provisions.* If any provision of this Agreement is deemed invalid or unenforceable, the court having jurisdiction shall have the power to modify such provision so that it will be valid and enforceable, and in any case, the balance of this Agreement shall remain in full force and effect.

29.3 *Severability of Clauses.* Any clause in this Agreement which may be prohibited under applicable state or federal laws shall be deemed ineffective in those jurisdictions where prohibited.

APPENDIX 6I

XXX. NON-ATTORNEYS

30.1 To the extent otherwise permitted by law, Parties need not be represented by attorneys at law in proceedings with the Investigator, or the Adjudicator.

XXXI. ENTIRE AGREEMENT

31.1 This Agreement and the Trust Agreement establishing the Trust Fund constitute the entire understanding of the Parties with respect to this subject matter and replace prior agreements or understandings, if any, among the Parties.

XXXII. ADVICE OF COUNSEL

32.1 *Agreement Reviewed by Counsel.* No Party, or representative or counsel for any Party, has acted as counsel for any party not expressly engaged by such Party with respect to such Party's entering into this Agreement, and each Party represents that it has had adequate opportunity to seek and obtain any appropriate legal advice necessary prior to entering into this Agreement.

32.2 *Steering Committee.* No Party's representative serving on the Steering Committee shall act or be deemed to act as legal counsel to any other Party, unless expressly engaged by such Party for such purpose, and no attorney/client relationship is intended to be created between representatives on the Steering Committee and the Parties.

XXXIII. NOTICE

33.1 *To Coalition.* Notice to the Coalition shall be accomplished by ordinary mail delivery (or such other expedited delivery as is comparable to or better than ordinary mail delivery) to the agent designated by the Steering Committee to receive notice.

33.2 *To Steering Committee.* Notice to the Steering Committee shall be accomplished in like fashion and sent to: [insert name and address of chair, clerk, common counsel, etc., to whom notices will be sent].

33.3 *To Parties.* Notice to any Party shall be accomplished in like fashion and sent to the respective addresses listed on Attachment A, unless a Party has provided written notice to the Steering Committee of an address change, which shall then be the designated address of the Party.

IN WITNESS THEREOF, the Parties thereto, which may be by and through their appointed counsel, enter into this Agreement. Each person signing this Agreement represents and warrants that he or she has been duly authorized to enter into this Agreement by the company on whose behalf it is indicated that the person is signing and that prior to signing, he or she has read the Agreement, understands its provisions and consents to its provisions on behalf of the Party he or she represents.

Date of Execution:

_____
Name of Party

_____ 19__

By: _____
Title

ATTACHMENT A

This document would contain the names, addresses and telephone and telecopier numbers of the signatories.

ATTACHMENT B

This document would contain the initial tiering of the parties, for the purpose of making administrative expense assessments. Administrative expenses may, of course, be assessed in the same manner as are remedial costs. This form contemplates a different mechanism for funding administrative and remedial costs, with separate accounts and assessment criteria.

ATTACHMENT C

This form would contain the interim assessment percentages for cost-sharing purposes. It might be EPA's NBAR, if that is used, or some other preliminary ranking. There should be two columns, one which assigns percentages ranking *all* known PRPs, and a second which includes post-signature adjusted percentages that reflects upward revision of settling parties' percentages reflecting non-settlers, bankrupts, and the like, which will not be players.

ATTACHMENT D

This document would list the names, addresses, and telephone numbers of all Steering Committee members.

ATTACHMENT E

This document would spell out in detail the duties of an investigator retained to develop an allocation for the site. Each site will have its own historical characteristics, and thus the text of this attachment will vary from site to site. It could be drafted to perform the function of a bid proposal document.

Appendix 7A   Table of Session Law to U.S. Code Cross-References: Clean Air Act (CAA), Clean Water Act (CWA), and Safe Drinking Water Act (SDWA)

CAA Session Law Number* (Selected)	Title 42 U.S. Code Number
§107	§7407
§108	§7408
§109	§7409
§110	§7410
§111	§7411
§112	§7412
§113	§7413
§114	§7414
Part C [§§160-169A]	§§7470-7491
Part D [§§172-178]	§§7502-7508
§301	§7601
§302	§7602
§303	§7603
§304	§7604
§307	§7607
§309	§7609

* The Clean Air Act (42 USC §§7401 *et seq.*), Pub.L. 88-206 (1963), as amended by the Motor Vehicle Air Pollution Control Act—Pub.L. 89-272, October 20, 1965, the Clean Air Act Amendments of 1966—Pub.L. 89-675, October 15, 1966, the Air Quality Act of 1967—Pub.L. 90-148, November 21, 1967, the Clean Air Amendments of 1970—Pub.L. 91-604, December 31, 1970, the Comprehensive Health Manpower Training Act of 1971—Pub.L. 92-157, November 18, 1971, the Energy Supply and Environmental Coordination Act of 1974—Pub.L. 93-319, June 22, 1974, Clean Air Act Amendments of 1977—Pub.L. 95-95, August 7, 1977, Safe Drinking Water Act of 1977—Pub. L. 95-190, November 16, 1977, Pub.L. 96-300, July 2, 1980, Pub.L. 97-23, July 17, 1981, and Pub.L. 98-45, July 12, 1983. 91 Stat. 685.

CWA Session Law Number* (Selected)	Title 33 U.S. Code Number
§301	§1311
§302	§1312
§303	§1313
§304	§1314
§305	§1315
§306	§1316
§307	§1317
§308	§1318
§309	§1319
§311	§1321
§401	§1341
§402	§1342
§403	§1343
§502	§1362
§504	§1364
§505	§1365
§509	§1369

---

* Federal Water Pollution Control Act (commonly referred to as the Clean Water Act) (33 USC §§1251 *et seq.*), Pub.L. 92-500, as amended by Pub.L. 93-207, December 28, 1973, and Pub.L. 93-243, January 2, 1974, Pub.L. 93-592, January 2, 1975, Pub.L. 94-238, March 23, 1976, Pub.L. 94-273, April 21, 1976, Pub.L. 94-558, October 19, 1976, Pub.L. 95-217, December 28, 1977, Pub.L. 95-576, November 2, 1978, Pub.L. 96-148, December 16, 1979, Pub.L. 96-478, Pub.L. 96-483, October 21, 1980, Pub.L. 96-561, December 22, 1980, Pub.L. 97-35, August 13, 1981, Pub.L. 96-510, December 11, 1981, Pub.L. 97-117, December 29, 1981, Pub.L. 97-164, April 2, 1982, affected by Pub.L. 97-216, July 18, 1982, and Pub.L. 97-272, September 30, 1982, amended by Pub.L. 97-440, January 8, 1983, and affected by Pub.L. 98-45, July 12, 1983, Pub.L. 98-371, July 19, 1984, Pub.L. 93-396, August 22, 1984, and Pub.L. 99-88, August 15, 1985. 86 Stat. 816.

SDWA

Session Law Number* (Selected)	Title 42 U.S. Code Number
§1401	§300f
§1411	§300g
§1412	§300g-1
§1413	§300g-2
§1414	§300g-3
§1415	§300g-4
§1416	§300g-5
§1417	§300g-6
§1421	§300h
§1422	§300h-1
§1423	§300h-2
§1424	§300h-3
§1425	§300h-4
§1426	§300h-5
§1427	§300h-6
§1428	§300h-7
§1431	§300i
§1432	§300i-1
§1441	§300j
§1442	§300j-1
§1443	§300j-2
§1444	§300j-3
§1445	§300j-4
§1446	§300j-5
§1447	§300j-6
§1448	§300j-7
§1449	§300j-8
§1450	§300j-10
§1451	§300j-11

---

* Safe Drinking Water Act (42 USC §§300f *et seq.*), Pub.L. 93-523, December 16, 1974, as amended by Pub.L. 94-317, June 23, 1976, Pub.L. 94-484, October 12, 1976, Pub.L. 95-190, November 16, 1977, Pub.L. 96-63, September 6, 1979, Pub.L. 96-502, December 5, 1980, Pub.L. 98-620, November 11, 1984, and Pub.L. 99-339, June 19, 1986. 88 Stat 1660.

Appendix 7B List of CFR Parts and Sections Containing Toxic Effluent Limitations (Excluding Metals)*

I. Special Limitations for Nonconventional Pollutants in General—Effluent Limitation Guidelines and Standards (Part 401 *et seq.*)

§401.15	List of 65 Toxic Pollutants for Priority Action
§413	Electroplating
§420.10	Coke Plants
§420.100	Iron & Steel Cold Forming Subcategory
§421.20	Primary Aluminum Smelting
§423.17	Steam Elec. Power Gen.—Cooling Tower Blowdown
§430	Pulp, Paper & Paperboard
§440.32	Uranium, Radium & Vanadium Mining
§455	Pesticide Manufacturing
§465	Coil Coating
§467	Aluminum Forming
§468	Copper Forming
§469	Electrical & Electronic Components

II. Toxic Effluent Standards

§129.100	Aldrin/Dieldrin
§129.101	DDT, DDD, & DDE
§129.102	Endrin
§129.103	Toxaphene
§129.104	Benzidine
§129.105	Polychlorinated biphenyls

III. Pretreatment Standards

Part 403 App. B   List of 65 Toxics

Note: Categorical pretreatment standards are published along with the general effluent guidelines and standards.

---

* All sections 40 CFR.

Appendix 7C   Underground Injection Control Permit Application

Form **4** UIC	⬥EPA	UNITED STATES ENVIRONMENTAL PROTECTION AGENCY **UNDERGROUND INJECTION CONTROL PERMIT APPLICATION** *(Collected under the authority of the Safe Drinking Water Act, Sections 1421, 1422, 40 CFR 144)*	I. EPA ID NUMBER U	T/A	C

READ ATTACHED INSTRUCTIONS BEFORE STARTING
FOR OFFICIAL USE ONLY

Application approved mo day year	Date Received mo day year	Permit/Well Number	Comments

II. FACILITY NAME AND ADDRESS

Facility Name

Street Address

City	State	ZIP Code

III. OWNER/OPERATOR AND ADDRESS

Owner/Operator Name

Street Address

City	State	ZIP Code

IV. OWNERSHIP STATUS *(Mark 'x')*

☐ A. Federal   ☐ B. State   ☐ C. Private

☐ D. Public   ☐ E. Other *(Explain)*

V. SIC CODES

VI. WELL STATUS *(Mark 'x')*

☐ A. Operating   Date Started mo day year   ☐ B. Modification/Conversion   ☐ C. Proposed

VII. TYPE OF PERMIT REQUESTED *(Mark 'x' and specify if required)*

☐ A. Individual ☐ B. Area	Number of Existing wells	Number of Proposed wells	Name(s) of field(s) or project(s)

VIII. CLASS AND TYPE OF WELL *(see reverse)*

A. Class(es) *(enter code(s))*	B. Type(s) *(enter code(s))*	C. If class is "other" or type is code 'x,' explain	D. Number of wells per type (if area permit)

IX. LOCATION OF WELL(S) OR APPROXIMATE CENTER OF FIELD OR PROJECT

A. Latitude			B. Longitude			Township and Range							**X. INDIAN LANDS** *(Mark 'x')*
Deg	Min	Sec	Deg	Min	Sec	Twsp	Range	Sec	¼ Sec	Feet from	Line	Feet from	Line ☐ Yes ☐ No

XI. ATTACHMENTS

(Complete the following questions on a separate sheet(s) and number accordingly; see instructions)

FOR CLASSES I, II, III (and other classes) complete and submit on separate sheet(s) Attachments A — U (pp 2-6) as appropriate. Attach maps where required. List attachments by letter which are applicable and are included with your application:

XII. CERTIFICATION

I certify under the penalty of law that I have personally examined and am familiar with the information submitted in this document and all attachments and that, based on my inquiry of those individuals immediately responsible for obtaining the information, I believe that the information is true, accurate, and complete. I am aware that there are significant penalties for submitting false information, including the possibility of fine and imprisonment. (Ref. 40 CFR 144.32)

A. Name and Title *(Type or Print)*	B. Phone No. *(Area Code and No.)*
C. Signature	D. Date Signed

EPA Form 7520-6 (2-84)

Well Class and Type Codes

Class I	Wells used to inject waste below the deepest underground source of drinking water.
Type "I"	Nonhazardous industrial disposal well
"M"	Nonhazardous municipal disposal well
"W"	Hazardous waste disposal well injecting below USDWs
"X"	Other Class I wells (not included in Type "I," "M," or "W")
Class II	Oil and gas production and storage related injection wells.
Type "D"	Produced fluid disposal well
"R"	Enhanced recovery well
"H"	Hydrocarbon storage well (excluding natural gas)
"X"	Other Class II wells (not included in Type "D," "R," or "H")
Class III	Special process injection wells.
Type "G"	Solution mining well
"S"	Sulfur mining well by Frasch process
"U"	Uranium mining well (excluding solution mining of conventional mines)
"X"	Other Class III wells (not included in Type "G," "S," or "U")
Other Classes	Wells not included in classes above.
	Class V wells which may be permitted under §144.12
	Wells not currently classified as Class I, II, III, or V.

Attachments to Permit Application

Class	Attachments
I new well	A, B, C, D, F, H — S, U
existing	A, B, C, D, F, H — U
II new well	A, B, C, E, G, H, M, Q, R; optional — I, J, K, O, P, U
existing	A, E, G, H, M, Q, R — U; optional — J, K, O, P, Q
III new well	A, B, C, D, F, H, I, J, K, M — S, U
existing	A, B, C, D, F, H, J, K, M — U
Other Classes	To be specified by the permitting authority

EPA Form 7520-6 (2-84)   page 2 of 5

App. 7C-2

INSTRUCTIONS — Form 4 — Underground Injection Control (UIC) Permit Application

Form 4 must be completed by all owners or operators of Class I, II, and III injection wells and others who may be directed to apply for a UIC permit by the Director.

I. EPA I.D. NUMBER — Fill in your EPA Identification Number. If you do not have a number, leave blank.

II. FACILITY NAME AND ADDRESS — Name of well, well field or company and address.

III. OWNER/OPERATOR NAME AND ADDRESS — Name and address of owner/operator of well or well field.

IV. OWNERSHIP STATUS — Mark the appropriate box to indicate the type of ownership.

V. SIC CODES — List at least one and no more than four Standard Industrial Classification (SIC) Codes that best describe the nature of the business in order of priority.

VI. WELL STATUS — Mark Box A if the well(s) were operating as injection wells on the effective date of the UIC Program for the State. Mark Box B if the well(s) existed on the effective date of the UIC Program for the State but were not utilized for injection. Box C should be marked if the application is for an underground injection project not constructed or not completed by the effective date of the UIC Program for the State.

VII. TYPE OF PERMIT — Mark "Individual" or "Area" to indicate the type of permit desired. Note that area permits are at the discretion of the Director and that wells covered by an area permit must be at one site, under the control of one person and do not inject hazardous waste. If an area permit is requested the number of wells to be included in the permit must be specified and the wells described and identified by location. If the area has a commonly used name, such as the "Jay Field," submit the name in the space provided. In the case of a project or field which crosses State lines, it may be possible to consider an area permit if EPA has jurisdiction in both States. Each such case will be considered individually, if the owner/operator elects to seek an area permit.

VIII. CLASS AND TYPE OF WELL — Enter in these two positions the Class and type of injection well for which a permit is requested. Use the most pertinent code selected from the list on the reverse side of Form 4. When selecting type X please explain in the space provided.

IX. LOCATION OF WELL — Enter the latitude and longitude of the existing or proposed well expressed in degrees, minutes, and seconds or the location by township, and range, and section, as required by 40 CFR 146. If an area permit is being requested, give the latitude and longitude of the approximate center of the area.

X. INDIAN LANDS — Place an "X" in the box if any part of the facility is located on Indian lands.

XI. ATTACHMENTS — Note that information requirements vary depending on the injection well class and status. Attachments for Class I, II, and III are described on pages 4 and 5 of this document and listed by Class on page 2. Place EPA ID number in the upper right hand corner of each page.

XII. CERTIFICATION — All permit applications (except Class II) must be signed by a responsible corporate officer for a corporation, by a general partner for a partnership, by the proprietor of a sole proprietorship, and by a principal executive or ranking elected official for a public agency. For Class II, the person described above should sign, or a representative duly authorized in writing.

EPA Form 7520-6 (2-84)

INSTRUCTIONS — Attachments to Form 4

Attachments to be submitted with permit application for Class I, II, III and other wells.

A. **AREA OF REVIEW METHODS** — Give the methods and, if appropriate, the calculations used to determine the size of the area of review (fixed radius or equation). The area of review shall be a fixed radius of ¼ mile from the well bore unless the use of an equation is approved in advance by the Director.

B. **MAPS OF WELLS / AREA AND AREA OF REVIEW** — Submit a topographic map, extending one mile beyond the property boundaries, showing the injection well(s) or project area for which a permit is sought and the applicable area of review. The map must show all intake and discharge structures and all hazardous waste, treatment, storage, or disposal facilities. If the application is for an area permit, the map should show the distribution manifold (if applicable) applying injection fluid to all wells in the area, including all system monitoring points. Within the area of review, the map must show the following:

Class I

The number, or name, and location of all producing wells, injection wells, abandoned wells, dry holes, surface bodies of water, springs, mines (surface and subsurface), quarries, and other pertinent surface features, including residences and roads, and faults, if known or suspected. In addition, the map must identify those wells, springs, other surface water bodies, and drinking water wells located with one quarter mile of the facility property boundary. Only information of public record is required to be included on this map;

Class II

In addition to requirements for Class I, include pertinent information known to the applicant. This requirement does not apply to existing Class II wells;

Class III

In addition to requirements for Class I, include public water systems and pertinent information known to the applicant.

C. **CORRECTIVE ACTION PLAN AND WELL DATA** — Submit a tabulation of data reasonably available from public records or otherwise known to the applicant on all wells within the area of review, including those on the map required in B, which penetrate the proposed injection zone. Such data shall include the following:

Class I

A description of each well's type, construction, date drilled, location, depth, record of plugging and/or completion, and any additional information the Director may require. In the case of new injection wells, include the corrective action proposed to be taken by the applicant under 40 CFR 144.55.

Class II

In addition to requirements for Class I, in the case of Class II wells operating over the fracture pressure of the injection formation, all known wells within the area of review which penetrate formations affected by the increase in pressure. This requirement does not apply to existing Class II wells.

Class III

In addition to requirements for Class I, the corrective action proposed under 40 CFR 144.55 for all Class III wells.

D. **MAPS AND CROSS SECTIONS OF USDWs** — Submit maps and cross sections indicating the vertical limits of all underground indicating the vertical limits of all underground sources of drinking water within the area of review (both vertical and lateral limits for Class I), their position relative to the injection formation and the direction of water movement, where known, in every underground source of drinking water which may be affected by the proposed injection. (Does not apply to Class II wells.)

E. **NAME AND DEPTH OF USDWs (CLASS II)** — For Class II wells, submit geologic name, and depth to bottom of all underground sources of drinking water which may be affected by the injection.

F. **MAPS AND CROSS SECTIONS OF GEOLOGIC STRUCTURE OF AREA** — Submit maps and cross sections detailing the geologic structure of the local area (including the lithology of injection and confining intervals) and generalized maps and cross sections illustrating the regional geologic setting. (Does not apply to Class II wells.)

G. **GEOLOGICAL DATA ON INJECTION AND CONFINING ZONES (CLASS II)** — For Class II wells, submit appropriate geological data on the injection zone and confining zones including lithologic description, geological name, thickness, depth and fracture pressure.

H. OPERATING DATA — Submit the following proposed operating data for each well (including all those to be covered by area permits):(1) average and maximum daily rate and volume of the fluids to be injected; (2) average and maximum injection pressure; (3) nature of annulus fluid; (4) for Class I wells, source and analysis of the chemical, physical, radiological and biological characteristics, including density and corrosiveness, of injection fluids; (5) for Class II wells, source and analysis of the physical and chemical characteristics of the injection fluid; (6) for Class III wells, a qualitative analysis and ranges in concentrations of all constituents of injected fluids. If the information is proprietary, maximum concentrations only may be submitted, but all records must be retained.

I. FORMATION TESTING PROGRAM — Describe the proposed formation testing program. For Class I wells the program must be designed to obtain data on fluid pressure, temperature, fracture pressure, other physical, chemical, and radiological characteristics of the injection matrix and physical and chemical characteristics of the formation fluids.

For Class II wells the testing program must be designed to obtain data on fluid pressure, estimated fracture pressure, physical and chemical characteristics of the injection zone. (Does not apply to existing Class II wells or projects.)

For Class III wells the program must be designed to obtain data on fluid pressure, fracture pressure, and physical and chemical characteristics of the formation fluids if the formation is naturally water bearing. Only fracture pressure is required if the formation is not water bearing. (Does not apply to existing Class III wells or projects.)

J. STIMULATION PROGRAM — Outline any proposed stimulation program.

K. INJECTION PROCEDURES — Describe the proposed injection procedures including pump, surge, tank, etc.

L. CONSTRUCTION PROCEDURES — Discuss the construction procedures (according to §146.12 for Class I, §146.22 for Class II, and §146.32 for Class III) to be utilized. This should include details of the casing and cementing program, logging procedures, deviation checks, and the drilling, testing and coring programs, and proposed annulus fluid. (Request and submission of justifying data must be made to use an alternative to a packer for Class I.)

M. CONSTRUCTION DETAILS — Submit schematic or other appropriate drawings of the surface and subsurface construction details of the well.

N. CHANGES IN INJECTED FLUID — Discuss expected changes in pressure, native fluid displacement, and direction of movement of injected fluid. (Class III wells only.)

O. PLANS FOR WELL FAILURES — Outline contingency plans (proposed plans, if any, for Class II) to cope with all shut-ins or well failures, so as to prevent migration of fluids into any USDW.

P. MONITORING PROGRAM — Discuss the planned monitoring program. This should be thorough, including maps showing the number and location of monitoring wells as appropriate and a discussion of monitoring devices, sampling frequency, and parameters measured. If a manifold monitoring program is utilized, pursuant to §146.23(b)(5), describe the program and compare it to individual well monitoring.

Q. PLUGGING AND ABANDONMENT PLAN — Submit a plan for plugging and abandonment of the well including: (1) describe the type, number, and placement (including the elevation of the top and bottom) of plugs to be used; (2) describe the type, grade, and quantity of cement to be used; and (3) describe the method to be used to place plugs, including the method used to place the well in a state of static equilibrium prior to placement of the plugs. Also for a Class III well that underlies or is in an exempted aquifer, demonstrate adequate protection of USDWs. Submit this information on EPA Form 7520-14, Plugging and Abandonment Plan.

R. NECESSARY RESOURCES — Submit evidence such as a surety bond or financial statement to verify that the resources necessary to close, plug or abandon the well are available.

S. AQUIFER EXEMPTIONS — If an aquifer exemption is requested, submit data necessary to demonstrate that the aquifer meets the following criteria: (1) does not serve as a source of drinking water; (2) cannot now and will not in the future serve as a source of drinking water; and (3) the TDS content of the ground water is more than 3,000 and less than 10,000 mg/l and is not reasonably expected to supply a public water system. Data to demonstrate that the aquifer is expected to be mineral or hydrocarbon producing, such as general description of the mining zone, analysis of the amenability of the mining zone to the proposed method, and time table for proposed development must also be included. For additional information on aquifer exemptions, see 40 CFR 144.7 and 146.04.

T. EXISTING EPA PERMITS — List program and permit number of any existing EPA permits, for example, NPDES, PSD, RCRA, etc.

U. DESCRIPTION OF BUSINESS — Give a brief description of the nature of the business.

EPA Form 7520-6 (2-84)

Appendix 7D List of Chemicals from S. Rep. No. 99-575 That EPA Is Required to Evaluate for MCL Goals and Primary Safe Drinking Water Regulations

Volative Organic Chemicals

Trichloroethylene
Tetrachloroethylene
Carbon tetrachloride
1,1,1-Trichloroethane
1,2-Dichloroethane
Vinyl chloride
Methylene chloride

Benzene
Chlorobenzene
Dichlorobenzene(s)
Trichlorobenzene(s)
1,1-Dichloroethylene
trans-1,2-Dichloroethylene
cis-1,2-Dichloroethylene

Microbiology and Turbidity

Total coliforms
Turbidity
Giardia lamblia

Viruses
Standard plate count
Legionella

Inorganics

Arsenic
Barium
Cadmium
Chromium
Lead
Mercury
Nitrate
Selenium
Silver
Fluoride
Aluminum
Antimony

Molybdenum
Asbestos
Sulfate
Copper
Vanadium
Sodium
Nickel
Zinc
Thallium
Beryllium
Cyanide

Organics

Endrin
Lindane
Methoxychlor
Toxaphene
2,4-D
2,4,5-TP
Aldicarb
Chlordane
Dalapon
Diquat
Endothall

1,1,2-Trichloroethane
Vydate
Simazine
PAH's
PCB's
Atrazine
Phthalates
Acrylamide
Dibromochloropropane (DBCP)
1,2-Dichloropropane
Pentachlorophenol

Glyphosate
Carbofuran
Alachlor
Epichlorohydrin
Toluene
Adipates
2,3,7,8-TCDD (Dioxin)

Pichloram
Dinoseb
Ethylene dibromide
Dibromomethane
Xylene
Hexachlorocyclopentadiene

Radionuclides

Radium 226 and 228
Beta particle and photon
    radioactivity

Uranium
Gross alpha particle activity
Radon

Appendix 8A: Table of Session Law to U.S. Code Cross-References: Federal Food, Drug and Cosmetic Act (FFDCA)

FFDCA Session Law Number* (Selected)†	Title 21 U.S. Code Number
§201	§321
§301	§331
§302	§332
§303	§333
§304	§334
§305	§335
§306	§336
§307	§337
§401	§341
§402	§342
§403	§343
§404	§344
§405	§345
§406	§346
§408	§346a
§409	§348

---

* Federal Food, Drug and Cosmetic Act (21 USC §§301 *et seq.*), June 25, 1938, c. 675, as amended by 1940 Reorg. Plan No. IV, June 30, 1940, 5 F.R. 2422, 54 Stat. 1237, 1953 Reorg. Plan No. 1, Apr. 11, 1953, 18 F.R. 2053, 67 Stat. 631, July 22, 1954, c. 559, 68 Stat. 511, Sept. 6, 1958, Pub.L. 85-929, July 12, 1960, Pub.L. 86-618, Oct. 10, 1962, Pub.L. 87-781, July 15, 1965, Pub.L. 89-74, July 13, 1968, Pub.L. 90-399, Oct. 24, 1968, Pub.L. 90-639, Oct. 27, 1970, Pub.L. 91-513, Aug. 16, 1972, Pub.L. 92-387, May 28, 1976, Pub.L. 94-295, Sept. 26, 1980, Pub.L. 96-359. 52 Stat. 1041.

† Includes only provisions discussed in Chapter 8, *supra.*

Appendix 9A Table of Session Law to U.S. Code Cross-References: Occupational Safety and Health Act (OSH Act)

OSH Act Session Law Number*	Title 29 U.S. Code Number
§2	§651
§3	§652
§4	§653
§5	§654
§6	§655
§7	§656
§8	§657
§9	§658
§10	§659
§11	§660
§12	§661
§13	§662
§14	§663
§15	§664
§16	§665
§17	§666
§18	§667
§19	§668
§20	§669
§21	§670
§22	§671
§23	§672
§24	§673
§25	§674
§26	§675
§27	§676

* Occupational Safety and Health Act of 1970 (29 USC §§ 651 *et seq.*), Pub.L. 91-596, S. 2193, December 29, 1970 (eff. April 28, 1971), as amended by Pub.L. 93-237, January 2, 1974. 84 Stat. 1590.

Table of Cases

References are to sections

References are to sections

National Audubon Society v. Todhunter, 3.04, n205

National League of Cities v. Usery, 6.06, n339

National Lime Ass'n v. EPA, 7.02, n25

National Nutritional Foods Ass'n v. Kennedy, 8.02, n60

National Organization for the Reform of Marijuana Laws v. United States Drug Enforcement Administration, 3.04, n201

National Realty & Constr. Co. v. OSHRC, 9.02, nn19, 20, 21, 22, 23, 24, 26, 27, 28, 29, 44, 45

National Standard Insurance Co. v. Continental Insurance Co., 5.06, n476

National Wildlife Federation v. Ruckelshaus, 7.04, n104

Natural Resources Defense Council, Inc. v. Costle, 2.02, n7; 2.07, n204

Natural Resources Defense Council, Inc. v. EPA, 2.02, n10; 3.03, n82

Natural Resources Defense Council v. Ruckelshaus, 2.07, n204

Natural Resources Defense Council v. Train (1976), 6.06, n323; 7.03, n49

Natural Resources Defense Council v. Train (1974), 5.02, n100

New York, State of v. Shore Realty Corp., 6.07, nn432, 442, 444, 463, 465, 468, 470

Nicolet, Inc. v. Eichler, Regional Administrator, 6.05, n255

Neal v. Darby, 5.08, n646.1

New Jersey, State of v. Ruckelshaus, 6.06, nn360, 360.1; 6.08, n487

New York, City of v. United States, 6.02, n36

New York, State of v. Auchter, 9.04, n119

New York, State of v. General Electric Co., 6.06, n271; 6.07, nn412, 433, 458, 468

New York, State of v. Gorsuch, 7.02, n31

O

Ohio v. Kovacs, 6.03, nn184, 187; 6.09, nn516, 518, 519

Ohio v. Rohm and Haas Co., 6.09, n528

O'Leary v. Moyer's Landfill, Inc., 6.07, n461

O'Neill v. City of New York, 5.10, nn787, 788; 6.03, n186; 6.09 n521; see also In re Quanta Resources

Order Pursuant to Section 3013(d) RCRA, In re, 5.09, n663

Oregon Environmental Council v. Kunzman, 3.03, n106.3; 3.04, n201; 3.07, n311

Organized Migrants in Community Action v. Brennan, 9.04, n121

Oswego Barge Corp., In re, 6.10, n556

Ottenheimer v. Whitaker, 5.10, nn788, 790

Outboard Marine Corp. v. Costle, 2.08, n271

Outboard Marine Corp. v. Illinois, 2.08, n271

Outboard Marine Corp. v. Thomas, 6.06, nn311, 350.2, 350.3

P

Pacific Gas and Electric Co. v. State Energy Resources Conservation and Dev. Comm'n, 2.09, n281

Pacific Legal Foundation v. State Energy Resources Conservation and Dev. Comm'n, 2.09, n281

Painesville, City of v. EPA, 7.02, n21

Parklane Hosiery Co. v. Shore, 6.07, n427

PBI-Gordon Corp. v. Thomas, 3.03, n98

References are to sections

References are to sections

Index

References are to sections

A

Accidents
Notice of, under TSCA, 2.03[3][e]
Additives
Food, *see* **Food**
Administrative penalties
Under FIFRA, 3.07[3][c]
Under TSCA, 2.07[2][c]
Affirmative obligation
In oil spills, 6.02[7]
Cleanup of spill, 6.02[7][c]
Duty to report spills, 6.02[7][a]
Spill Prevention Control and
Countermeasure (SPCC)
plans, 6.02[7][b]
Agricultural commodities
Residue tolerances of pesticides
on, under FIFRA, 3.03[4]
Certificate of usefulness,
3.03[4][b]
In general, 3.03[4][a]
Temporary tolerance, 3.03[4][d]
Tolerance or exemption,
3.03[4][c]
Agricultural wastes, 5.02[2][d][v][D]
Air emissions, hazardous, 7.02
Hazardous emission standards,
7.02[4]
Applicability, 7.02[4][a]
Section 112 regulatory
authority, 7.02[4][b]
New source performance
standards, 7.02[3]
Overview of Clean Air Act,
7.02[1]

Air emissions, hazardous—*Cont.*
Regulation of pollutants under
Sections 108, 109, and 110,
7.02[2]
Lead, 7.02[2][b]
Particulates and volatile organic
compounds, 7.02[2][a]
Air transport
Manifest requirements for, by
transporters of hazardous
waste, 5.04[5][b]
Application requirements
For TSD facility permits, 5.07[3]
Information requirements,
5.07[3][c]
RCRA-based requirements,
5.07[3][a]
Requirements of other laws,
5.07[3][b]
Applicators and dealers
Pesticide, under FIFRA, 3.02[2][d]
Arbitration
Under CERCLA, 6.08[4][c]
Asbestos
Report on, under TSCA, 2.06[1]
Authority, *see specific matter*

B

Bankruptcy
Under CERCLA, 6.09[3]
Imminent hazard actions under
RCRA and remedies in
cases of, 6.03[2][d][iii]
RCRA provisions on hazardous
waste and, 5.10[8]

References are to sections

INDEX

References are to sections

References are to sections